FOUNDATIONS OF DYNAMIC ECONOMIC ANALYSIS

Optimal Control Theory and Applications

Foundations of Dynamic Economic Analysis presents a modern and thorough exposition of the fundamental mathematical formalism used to study continuous time dynamic economic processes and to interpret dynamic economic behavior, namely, optimal control theory. The style of presentation, with its continual emphasis on the economic interpretation of mathematics and models, distinguishes it from several other excellent texts on the subject. This approach is aided dramatically by introducing the dynamic envelope theorem and the method of comparative dynamics early in the exposition. Accordingly, motivated and economically revealing proofs of the transversality conditions come about by use of the dynamic envelope theorem. Furthermore, such sequencing of the material naturally leads to the development of the primal-dual method of comparative dynamics and dynamic duality theory, two modern approaches used to tease out the empirical content of optimal control models. The stylistic approach ultimately draws attention to the empirical richness of optimal control theory, a feature missing in virtually all other textbooks of this type.

Michael R. Caputo is Professor of Economics in the College of Business Administration, University of Central Florida, in Orlando. He was awarded his Ph.D. in economics from the University of Washington, where he received the Henry C. Beuchel memorial award for distinguished undergraduate teaching by the Department of Economics in 1986. Professor Caputo then taught in the Department of Agriculture and Resource Economics at the University of California, Davis, from 1987 to 2003. In 1998, he was inducted into the volume *Who's Who Among America's Teachers*. Professor Caputo's research has appeared in numerous peer-reviewed journals, including *Review of Economic Studies*, *Journal of Economic Theory*, *International Economic Review*, *Review of Economics and Statistics*, *Journal of Economic Dynamics and Control*, *Journal of Mathematical Economics*, *Journal of Optimization Theory and Applications*, *Journal of Economics*, and *American Journal of Agricultural Economics*.

Foundations of Dynamic Economic Analysis

Optimal Control Theory and Applications

MICHAEL R. CAPUTO
University of Central Florida

CAMBRIDGE
UNIVERSITY PRESS

CAMBRIDGE
UNIVERSITY PRESS

University Printing House, Cambridge CB2 8BS, United Kingdom

One Liberty Plaza, 20th Floor, New York, NY 10006, USA

477 Williamstown Road, Port Melbourne, VIC 3207, Australia

314-321, 3rd Floor, Plot 3, Splendor Forum, Jasola District Centre, New Delhi - 110025, India

79 Anson Road, #06-04/06, Singapore 079906

Cambridge University Press is part of the University of Cambridge.

It furthers the University's mission by disseminating knowledge in the pursuit of education, learning and research at the highest international levels of excellence.

www.cambridge.org
Information on this title: www.cambridge.org/9780521603683

First published 2005

A catalogue record for this publication is available from the British Library

Library of Congress Cataloging in Publication data
Caputo, Michael Ralph.
Foundations of dynamic economic analysis : optimal control theory and applications / Michael R. Caputo.
p. cm.
Includes bibliographical references and index.
ISBN 0-521-84272-7 – ISBN 0-521-60368-4 (pbk)
1. Economics–Mathematical models. 2. Control theory. 3. Mathematical optimization.
I. Title.
HB135.C27 2005
333′01′515642 – dc22 2004046568

ISBN 978-0-521-84272-3 Hardback
ISBN 978-0-521-60368-3 Paperback

Contents

Foreword

I've been basking in Michael Caputo's reflected glory since he was my graduate student in the 1980s, and I am pleased to do it again with the publication of this book. Michael is carrying on the tradition of exploring mathematical models not for their elegance or descriptive qualities, but for the refutable implications they generate. It was Paul Samuelson, who, in 1947, in his *Foundations of Economic Analysis*, first articulated the methodology that equilibrium conditions themselves were typically unobservable and sterile, and that meaningful theorems in economics consisted of statements that restricted the direction of change of decision variables when the data or parameters of a system changed in an observable way. In the traditional comparative statics models, such as those I analyzed in *The Structure of Economics*, refutable propositions emerged from a maximization hypothesis in a static framework. However, there has never been until now, a treatise that extended Samuelson's methodology to dynamic models, where decisions today affect the entire time path of events in the future.

Michael Caputo's contribution here and elsewhere has been to keep resource and other economists focused on this central issue of scientific methodology so that we can see the scientific usefulness of dynamic models: what refutable implications do they generate? If some initial stock or other parameter in a dynamic resource model, say, increases, under what circumstances can we make a definitive statement about the way the path or terminal conditions of the state and control variables respond? Here at last we have a systematic treatment of this class of problems that comprise positive or scientific economic analysis of dynamic models.

Professor Eugene Silberberg
Department of Economics,
University of Washington

Preface

Forward-looking individuals recognize that decisions made today affect those to be made in the future, at least in part, by expanding or contracting the set of admissible choices, that is, by lowering or raising the cost of a future choice. Such intertemporal linkages reside at the core of all dynamic processes in economics. Consequently, mathematical methods that account for such intertemporal linkages are fundamental, in principle, to all economic decisions. This book presents an introductory but thorough exposition of the fundamental mathematical formalism used to study continuous time dynamic economic processes and to interpret dynamic economic behavior, namely, optimal control theory and its ancillary techniques.

The style of presentation distinguishes the book from several other excellent texts on the subject. First of all, there is a continual emphasis on the economic interpretation of the mathematics and the models, aided dramatically by way of the method of comparative dynamics, from both a primal and dual point of view. In my twelve years of teaching the course upon which the book is based, I have found that this approach permits the students to garner a deeper conceptual understanding of intertemporal economic models. One of the keys to a deeper conceptual understanding, I believe, is the introduction of the dynamic envelope theorem relatively early in the presentation of optimal control theory. This strategy paves the way for many of the succeeding chapters of the book to be built around this vital theorem, and not only complements the aforementioned emphasis on economic interpretation and conceptualization, but also leads to motivated proofs of the transversality conditions, an area long on technicalities and short on intuition. Furthermore, this sequencing of the material naturally leads to the development of the primal-dual method of comparative dynamics and dynamic duality theory, two modern approaches used to tease out the empirical content of optimal control models. In sum, the stylistic approach ultimately draws attention to the empirical richness of optimal control theory, something missing in virtually all other such textbooks.

Several other novel features of the book are worth mentioning. For one, each chapter contains numerous fully worked examples, a feature of the book on which students have always commented positively. Moreover, the inclusion of several examples in each chapter is typically the best way for newcomers to the fold to learn the material, for as is well known, learning characteristically occurs gradually, by conquering the specific before the general. The examples range from the simple mathematical variety designed to demonstrate how a particular theorem is applied to solve a control problem, to more sophisticated ones, in which a nontrivial economic problem is motivated, set up, solved either explicitly or qualitatively, and then usually scrutinized for its comparative dynamics properties. In a similar vein, the comparative dynamics methods are applied to seminal economic models rather than just simple mathematical problems, adding further to the development of the students' conceptual understanding of intertemporal economic theory. In addition, every chapter ends with a vast array of mental exercises. These range from routine and purely mathematical problems designed as a check on one's basic understanding of the material (many of which have been culled from the cited references), to proofs of theorems given in a chapter, to more complicated and detailed economic problems designed as a much deeper check on one's understanding and as an extension of the development given in the text (all of which originated in my teaching of the subject matter). There are even exercises that explore the consequences of some of the technical assumptions made in the text, for those interested in such matters.

The essential mathematics prerequisites are a standard introductory calculus sequence that includes vector calculus, a basic course in linear algebra, and an introductory course in ordinary differential equations. In other words, the archetypal two-year mathematics sequence that is taken by engineering, physics, and mathematics majors, and expected of all incoming Ph.D. students in economics, is the fundamental mathematics prerequisite. As far as training in economics is concerned, one Ph.D. level course in microeconomic theory focusing on the neoclassical theory of the consumer and the firm and their comparative static properties is essential. This is because oftentimes motivation for an intertemporal economic concept is built upon its counterpart from static microeconomic theory. The best microeconomic theory text in this regard is Silberberg's *The Structure of Economics*, as my book's focus and style is akin to his in that it is long on explanation, economic interpretation, and the development of the empirically relevant features of economic models. In fact, I have more or less used Silberberg's *The Structure of Economics* as the scaffolding for this book.

The textbook is aimed at first-year and second-year Ph.D. students in economics, agricultural and resource economics, operations research, and management science who wish a thorough but elementary treatment and economic interpretation of continuous time dynamic optimization methods and their use in economics and allied areas. More generally, the target audience I had in mind when writing the book comprises the *users* of optimal control theory, not seasoned veterans of dynamic optimization methods or individuals who are interested in developing further theorems in this area. In accord with this vision, I have adopted basic assumptions that are consistent with this audience and with the use of optimal control techniques in professional journals. Consequently, the latter two categories of individuals may find the book long on motivation, explanation, and economic interpretation, and thus may desire a book that is more direct and terse. To them, I say go get any of the mathematics texts on the subject. Nonetheless, the statements of the definitions and theorems are comparatively rigorous by modern mathematical standards because I have taken them from mathematics texts. They are not, however, stated at the highest level of generality because of the aforementioned audience I have in mind. The prior two claims also apply to the proofs of the theorems, except in a few instances in which the proofs are altogether omitted, as in the case of generalized necessary conditions.

Based on my experiences teaching from earlier drafts of the book, there is more than enough material contained in it for a four-unit quarter-length course (10 weeks) or a three-unit semester-length course (15 weeks) in optimal control theory with economics applications. In fact, if one wishes to probe all the subjects thoroughly, it would take a year to cover them all. Nonetheless, one could easily pick and choose chapters based on one's preferences and intended course, as the book provides a good deal of flexibility. In the four-unit quarter-length course that I taught at University of California, Davis, to Ph.D. students in the Department of Agricultural and Resource Economics and the Department of Economics, I'd typically cover Chapters 1–5, 9, 10, 12, 13, 14, and one or two of Chapters 15, 16, and 17. I would assign long weekly problem sets, usually consisting of a half dozen or so exercises, as I have found that this is the best way for the students to internalize the material. The students who complete the course then characteristically take a three-unit quarter-length course in natural resource economics the following quarter, which applies the methods the students just learned. Chapters 7, 8, 11, 18, 19, and 20 are then covered in an advanced topics course in economic dynamics.

Several of my teachers and colleagues have been influential in my development as an economist and thus of this book. In chronological order, they are Randy Nelson, who first piqued my serious interest in microeconomic theory when I took intermediate price theory from him in the fall of 1981; Jim Mulligan, who, as my first mentor, regularly handed out sagacious advice and set high standards for himself, all of which still resonate with me today; Gene Silberberg, who took me to the next level by way of his first-quarter Ph.D. microeconomic theory course and who asked me a single, probing question about my research interests as a third-year Ph.D. student that has largely defined my research career; and finally Quirino Paris, who challenged and stimulated me to think deeply and more importantly, symmetrically, about economic questions. To each and every one of them, I give my heartfelt thanks and appreciation. There is no doubt that they all are responsible, in part, for the researcher and person I am today. All of my former students at UC Davis who provided me with feedback on the previous drafts of the book also deserve thanks. Specifically, I'd like to single out Lone Gronbæk, Jim Murphy, and Neill Norman for truly outstanding effort in this regard. In addition, Scott Parris, my editor at Cambridge University Press, deserves a big thank you for helping to shape the book and improve its quality. Finally, I wish to thank the four reviewers of the text, namely, Gerhard Sorger of the University of Vienna; L. Joe Moffitt of the University of Massachusetts, Amherst; Subal Kumbhakar of SUNY Binghamton; and one who wished to remain anonymous, for their thoughtful and constructive comments. Gerhard Sorger deserves special mention, as he provided me with literally hundreds of minor comments and corrections, and dozens of deep and probing observations, essentially all of which made it into the text. All of these individuals, indubitably, helped improve the final product.

ONE

Essential Elements of Continuous Time Dynamic Optimization

In order to motivate the following introductory material on dynamic optimization problems, it will be advantageous to draw heavily on your knowledge of static optimization theory. To that end, we begin by recalling the definition of the prototype unconstrained static optimization problem, namely,

$$\phi(\boldsymbol{\alpha}) \stackrel{\text{def}}{=} \max_{\mathbf{x}\in\Re^N} f(\mathbf{x};\boldsymbol{\alpha}), \tag{1}$$

where $\mathbf{x} \in \Re^N$ is a vector of *decision* or *choice variables*, $\boldsymbol{\alpha} \in \Re^A$ is a vector of *parameters*, $f(\cdot)$ is the twice continuously differentiable *objective function*, that is, $f(\cdot) \in C^{(2)}$, and $\phi(\cdot)$ is the *indirect* or *maximized objective function*. This is terminology you should be more or less familiar with from prior courses.

Because we will deal repeatedly with vectors and matrices as well as the derivatives of scalar- and vector-valued functions in this book, we pause momentarily to establish three notational conventions that we shall adhere to throughout. First, all vectors are treated as column vectors. To denote a row vector, we therefore employ the transpose operator, denoted by the symbol $'$. Thus $\mathbf{x} \in \Re^N$ is taken to be an N-element column vector, whereas $\mathbf{x}'$ is an N-element row vector. Note also that vectors appear in **boldface** type.

Second, if $\mathbf{g}(\cdot) : \Re^N \to \Re^M$ is a $C^{(1)}$ vector-valued function, thereby implying that $\mathbf{g}(\cdot) \stackrel{\text{def}}{=} (g^1(\cdot), g^2(\cdot), \ldots, g^M(\cdot))'$, then at any $\mathbf{x} \in \Re^N$, we define the $M \times N$ Jacobian matrix of $\mathbf{g}(\cdot)$ by

$$\underbrace{\mathbf{g}_{\mathbf{x}}(\mathbf{x})}_{M\times N} \stackrel{\text{def}}{=} \begin{bmatrix} g^1_{x_1}(\mathbf{x}) & g^1_{x_2}(\mathbf{x}) & \cdots & g^1_{x_N}(\mathbf{x}) \\ g^2_{x_1}(\mathbf{x}) & g^2_{x_2}(\mathbf{x}) & \cdots & g^2_{x_N}(\mathbf{x}) \\ \vdots & \vdots & \ddots & \vdots \\ g^M_{x_1}(\mathbf{x}) & g^M_{x_2}(\mathbf{x}) & \cdots & g^M_{x_N}(\mathbf{x}) \end{bmatrix}, \tag{2}$$

where $g^m_{x_n}(\mathbf{x})$ is the partial derivative of $g^m(\cdot)$ with respect to x_n evaluated at the point $(\mathbf{x})$. It is also the element in the mth row and nth column of $\mathbf{g}_{\mathbf{x}}(\mathbf{x})$. This definition implies that if $M = 1$, so that $g(\cdot) : \Re^N \to \Re$ is now a scalar-valued function, then

$g_{\mathbf{x}}(\mathbf{x}) = (g_{x_1}(\mathbf{x}), g_{x_2}(\mathbf{x}), \ldots, g_{x_N}(\mathbf{x}))$ is a row vector, or equivalently, a $1 \times N$ matrix. This means that the derivative of a scalar-valued function with respect to a column vector is a row vector. As an extension of this notation, if we now assume that $\mathbf{g}(\cdot) : \Re^{N+A} \to \Re^M$ is a $C^{(1)}$ function whose arguments are the vectors $\mathbf{x} \in \Re^N$ and $\boldsymbol{\alpha} \in \Re^A$, then $\mathbf{g}_{\mathbf{x}}(\mathbf{x}; \boldsymbol{\alpha})$ is the $M \times N$ Jacobian matrix given in Eq. (2), whereas $\mathbf{g}_{\boldsymbol{\alpha}}(\mathbf{x}; \boldsymbol{\alpha})$ is an $M \times A$ Jacobian matrix defined similarly.

Third, if $g(\cdot) : \Re^{N+A} \to \Re$ is a $C^{(2)}$ scalar-valued function whose arguments are the vectors $\mathbf{x} \in \Re^N$ and $\boldsymbol{\alpha} \in \Re^A$, then there are four Hessian matrices that can be defined based on $g(\cdot)$ because of the two different sets of variables that it depends on, scilicet,

$$\underbrace{g_{\mathbf{xx}}(\mathbf{x}; \boldsymbol{\alpha})}_{N \times N} \stackrel{\text{def}}{=} \begin{bmatrix} g_{x_1x_1}(\mathbf{x}; \boldsymbol{\alpha}) & g_{x_1x_2}(\mathbf{x}; \boldsymbol{\alpha}) & \cdots & g_{x_1x_N}(\mathbf{x}; \boldsymbol{\alpha}) \\ g_{x_2x_1}(\mathbf{x}; \boldsymbol{\alpha}) & g_{x_2x_2}(\mathbf{x}; \boldsymbol{\alpha}) & \cdots & g_{x_2x_N}(\mathbf{x}; \boldsymbol{\alpha}) \\ \vdots & \vdots & \ddots & \vdots \\ g_{x_Nx_1}(\mathbf{x}; \boldsymbol{\alpha}) & g_{x_Nx_2}(\mathbf{x}; \boldsymbol{\alpha}) & \cdots & g_{x_Nx_N}(\mathbf{x}; \boldsymbol{\alpha}) \end{bmatrix},$$

$$\underbrace{g_{\mathbf{x}\boldsymbol{\alpha}}(\mathbf{x}; \boldsymbol{\alpha})}_{N \times A} \stackrel{\text{def}}{=} \begin{bmatrix} g_{x_1\alpha_1}(\mathbf{x}; \boldsymbol{\alpha}) & g_{x_1\alpha_2}(\mathbf{x}; \boldsymbol{\alpha}) & \cdots & g_{x_1\alpha_A}(\mathbf{x}; \boldsymbol{\alpha}) \\ g_{x_2\alpha_1}(\mathbf{x}; \boldsymbol{\alpha}) & g_{x_2\alpha_2}(\mathbf{x}; \boldsymbol{\alpha}) & \cdots & g_{x_2\alpha_A}(\mathbf{x}; \boldsymbol{\alpha}) \\ \vdots & \vdots & \ddots & \vdots \\ g_{x_N\alpha_1}(\mathbf{x}; \boldsymbol{\alpha}) & g_{x_N\alpha_2}(\mathbf{x}; \boldsymbol{\alpha}) & \cdots & g_{x_N\alpha_A}(\mathbf{x}; \boldsymbol{\alpha}) \end{bmatrix},$$

$$\underbrace{g_{\boldsymbol{\alpha\alpha}}(\mathbf{x}; \boldsymbol{\alpha})}_{A \times A} \stackrel{\text{def}}{=} \begin{bmatrix} g_{\alpha_1\alpha_1}(\mathbf{x}; \boldsymbol{\alpha}) & g_{\alpha_1\alpha_2}(\mathbf{x}; \boldsymbol{\alpha}) & \cdots & g_{\alpha_1\alpha_A}(\mathbf{x}; \boldsymbol{\alpha}) \\ g_{\alpha_2\alpha_1}(\mathbf{x}; \boldsymbol{\alpha}) & g_{\alpha_2\alpha_2}(\mathbf{x}; \boldsymbol{\alpha}) & \cdots & g_{\alpha_2\alpha_A}(\mathbf{x}; \boldsymbol{\alpha}) \\ \vdots & \vdots & \ddots & \vdots \\ g_{\alpha_A\alpha_1}(\mathbf{x}; \boldsymbol{\alpha}) & g_{\alpha_A\alpha_2}(\mathbf{x}; \boldsymbol{\alpha}) & \cdots & g_{\alpha_A\alpha_A}(\mathbf{x}; \boldsymbol{\alpha}) \end{bmatrix},$$

and the $A \times N$ matrix $g_{\boldsymbol{\alpha}\mathbf{x}}(\mathbf{x}; \boldsymbol{\alpha})$, the computation of which we leave for a mental exercise. We remark in passing that there is a matrix version of the invariance of the second-order partial derivatives to the order of differentiation, and this too is left for a mental exercise.

With the notational matters settled, let's now return to the unconstrained static optimization problem defined in Eq. (1). Assume that an optimal solution exists to problem (1), say $\mathbf{x} = \mathbf{x}^*(\boldsymbol{\alpha})$. Typically, we would find the solution by simultaneously solving the first-order necessary conditions (FONCs) of problem (1), which are given by

$$f_{\mathbf{x}}(\mathbf{x}; \boldsymbol{\alpha}) = \mathbf{0}_N'$$

in vector notation, where $\mathbf{0}_N$ is the null (column) vector in $\Re^N$, or by

$$f_{x_n}(\mathbf{x}; \boldsymbol{\alpha}) = 0, \quad n = 1, 2, \ldots, N$$

in index notation. Unless the objective function $f(\cdot)$ happened to be of a particularly simple functional form, an explicit solution for $\mathbf{x} = \mathbf{x}^*(\boldsymbol{\alpha})$ is more often than not rare. If, however, we assume that the second-order sufficient condition (SOSC) holds at $\mathbf{x} = \mathbf{x}^*(\boldsymbol{\alpha})$, that is,

$$\mathbf{h}' f_{\mathbf{xx}}(\mathbf{x}^*(\boldsymbol{\alpha}); \boldsymbol{\alpha})\mathbf{h} < 0 \,\forall\, \mathbf{h} \in \Re^N, \quad \mathbf{h} \neq \mathbf{0}_N,$$

or

$$\sum_{i=1}^{N}\sum_{j=1}^{N} f_{x_i x_j}(\mathbf{x}^*(\boldsymbol{\alpha}); \boldsymbol{\alpha}) h_i h_j < 0, \quad \text{not all } h_i = 0,$$

then we can apply the implicit function theorem to the FONCs to solve for the optimal choice vector $\mathbf{x} = \mathbf{x}^*(\boldsymbol{\alpha})$ *in principle*. To see why this is so, recall that the Jacobian matrix of the FONCs is given by the $N \times N$ matrix $f_{\mathbf{xx}}(\mathbf{x}; \boldsymbol{\alpha})$, which is identical to the Hessian matrix of the objective function. Moreover, the SOSC implies that the Hessian determinant of the FONCs is nonvanishing at the optimal solution, that is, that $|f_{\mathbf{xx}}(\mathbf{x}; \boldsymbol{\alpha})| \neq 0$ when evaluated at $\mathbf{x} = \mathbf{x}^*(\boldsymbol{\alpha})$. Because this is equivalent to the nonvanishing of the Jacobian determinant of the FONCs, the implicit function theorem may be applied to the FONCs to solve, in principle, for the optimal choice vector $\mathbf{x} = \mathbf{x}^*(\boldsymbol{\alpha})$. Again, this line of reasoning should be familiar to you from prior courses in microeconomic theory.

In light of the dynamic problems that will occupy us in this book, the most important aspect of the above discussion concerning problem (1) is that for a given value of the parameters, say, $\boldsymbol{\alpha} = \boldsymbol{\alpha}^\circ$, we typically solve for a particular value for each of the decision or choice variables, say, $x_n^\circ = x_n^*(\boldsymbol{\alpha}^\circ)$, $n = 1, 2, \ldots, N$. We do this by solving a set of algebraic equations, that is to say, the FONCs. If the parameter vector is different, say, $\boldsymbol{\alpha} = \boldsymbol{\alpha}^1$, then usually a different value of the choice variables is implied, say, $x_n^1 = x_n^*(\boldsymbol{\alpha}^1)$, $n = 1, 2, \ldots, N$. By their very nature, therefore, static optimization problems ask the decision maker to pick out a particular value of the decision variables given the parameters of the problem. For $A = N = 1$, Figure 1.1 depicts this situation graphically.

To add an economic spin to all of this, recall the prototype profit-maximizing model of the price-taking firm:

$$\pi^*(p, w_1, w_2) \stackrel{\text{def}}{=} \max_{x_1, x_2}\{pF(x_1, x_2) - w_1 x_1 - w_2 x_2\},$$

where $F(\cdot)$ is the twice continuously differentiable production function, x_1 and x_2 are the decision variables representing the inputs of the firm, w_1 and w_2 are the market prices of the inputs, p is the output price, and $\pi^*(\cdot)$ is the indirect profit function. Given a particular set of prices, say, $(p, w_1, w_2) = (p^\circ, w_1^\circ, w_2^\circ)$, the firm seeks to determine the values of the inputs that maximize its profit, say, $x_n^\circ = x_n^*(p^\circ, w_1^\circ, w_2^\circ)$, $n = 1, 2$. If such optimal values exist, then they are found, in principle, by simultaneously solving the FONCs, given by

$$p^\circ F_{x_1}(x_1, x_2) - w_1^\circ = 0,$$

$$p^\circ F_{x_2}(x_1, x_2) - w_2^\circ = 0.$$

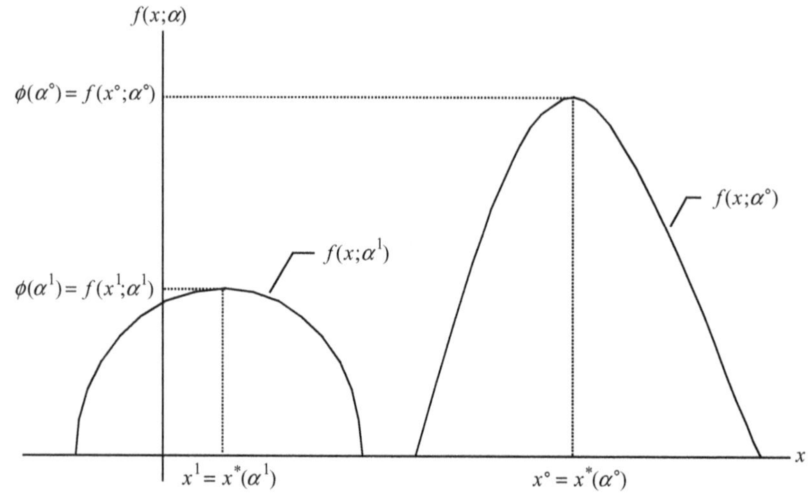

Figure 1.1

Note that these are *algebraic equations* that in general must be solved simultaneously for the optimal values of the inputs. To repeat, the most important point to take away from this discussion is that the choice of the optimal input combination is made just one time: there is no planning for the future, nor are there future decisions to be made in this problem. This is exactly as the static framework of the problem dictates.

In contrast, given the parameters of a dynamic optimization problem, its solution is a *sequence* of optimal decisions in discrete time, or a *time path* or *curve* of optimal decisions in continuous time, over the relevant *planning period* or *planning horizon*, not just one partic

rent from that in static problems. Because

the solution to a continuous time dynamic optimization problem is a time path or curve, it appears to be reasonable and even natural for the objective function to place a value on the decision variables at each point in time of the planning horizon and to add up the resulting values over the relevant planning period, akin to what is done when one computes the present value of some stream of net benefits that are received over time.

To better motivate the form of the objective function in dynamic problems, consider Figure 1.2. Here three typical time paths of a function $x(\cdot)$, or curves $x(t)$ associated with the function $x(\cdot)$, are displayed along with the resulting value of the objective function associated with each time path $J[x(\cdot)]$, the latter of which we refer to as a *path value*. We have denoted the independent variable by the letter t and refer to it as time, as this is the natural interpretation of the independent variable in intertemporal problems in economics. Notice that all time paths or curves begin

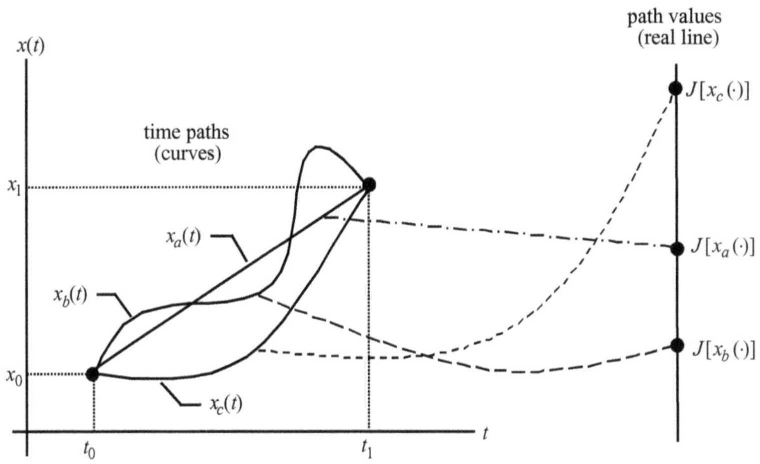

Figure 1.2

at time $t = t_0$ at the point $x = x_0$ and end at time $t = t_1$ at the point $x = x_1$, all four of which are given or fixed, thereby requiring that the paths being compared begin and end at the same position and time. The typical problem in dynamic optimization seeks to find a time path or curve $x(t)$, or equivalently a function $x(\cdot)$, that, say, maximizes the objective function $J[\cdot]$. Thus to each time path or curve $x_i(t), i = a, b, c$, or function $x_i(\cdot), i = a, b, c$, there is a corresponding value of the objective function $J[x_i(\cdot)], i = a, b, c$.

The relationship between paths $x(t)$ or functions $x(\cdot)$ and the resulting value $J[x(\cdot)]$ is quite different from that encountered in typical lower division mathematics courses. It represents a mapping from paths or curves to real numbers, or equivalently, from functions to real numbers, and therefore is not a mapping from real numbers to real numbers as in the case of functions. Such a mapping from paths or curves to path values, or from functions to real numbers, is what Figure 1.2 depicts and is called a *functional*. The general notation we shall employ for such a mapping from functions to real numbers is $J[x(\cdot)]$, which has been employed above. This notation emphasizes that the functional $J[\cdot]$ depends on the *function* $x(\cdot)$, or equivalently, on the *entire curve* $x(t)$. Moreover, it highlights the fact that it is a change in the position of the entire path or curve $x(t)$, that is, the *variation* in the path or curve $x(t)$, rather than the change in t, that results in a change in the path value or functional $J[\cdot]$. Thus, a dynamic optimization problem in continuous time seeks to find a path or curve $x(t)$, or equivalently, a function $x(\cdot)$, that optimizes an objective functional $J[\cdot]$.

Next we consider in more detail the form of an archetype objective functional $J[\cdot]$. Because the optimal solution to a continuous time dynamic optimization problem is a path or curve $x(t)$, as noted above, associated with the path is its slope $\dot{x}(t) \overset{\text{def}}{=} dx(t)/dt$ at each point in time t in the planning horizon, assuming, of course, that the path $x(t)$ is smooth enough so that $\dot{x}(t)$ is defined. Suppose, moreover, that there exists a function, say, $F(\cdot)$, that assigns or imputes a value to the path and its associated derivative at each point in time in the planning horizon, the latter represented by the closed interval $[t_0, t_1]$, $0 < t_0 < t_1$. The imputed value of the path at each point in the planning horizon, therefore, depends on the moment of time t the decision is made and the value of the decision or choice variable at that time $x(t)$, as well as on the slope at that time $\dot{x}(t)$. Hence we have $F(t, x(t), \dot{x}(t))$ as the value of the function that imputes a value to the path $x(t)$ with slope $\dot{x}(t)$ at time t. Because the path $x(t)$ must necessarily travel through an interval of time, namely, the planning horizon, its total value as represented by the functional $J[x(\cdot)]$ is given by the "sum" of all the imputed values $F(t, x(t), \dot{x}(t))$ for each t in the planning horizon $[t_0, t_1]$. Moreover, because we are operating in continuous time, the appropriate notion of summation is represented by a definite integral over the closed interval $[t_0, t_1]$. Thus, the value of the functional we wish to optimize is given by

$$J[x(\cdot)] \stackrel{\text{def}}{=} \int_{t_0}^{t_1} F(t, x(t), \dot{x}(t))\, dt. \tag{3}$$

In economics, $J[x(\cdot)]$ often represents the present value of net benefits from pursuing the policy $x(t)$, with instantaneous net benefits given by $F(t, x(t), \dot{x}(t))$. In general, one calls $x(t)$ the state of the system, or value of the state variable, at time t, and $\dot{x}(t)$ the rate of change of the system, or velocity, at time t. Typically, the *explicit* appearance of t as an argument of $F(\cdot)$ is a result of discounting in economic problems. Equation (3) represents the prototype form of the objective functional for *calculus of variations* problems, which are but one class of continuous time dynamic optimization problems. More general objective functionals will be introduced shortly, when we commence with the study of optimal control theory. But for now, the present discussion and motivation are sufficient, for the idea of a mapping from paths or curves to the real line and the form of the objective functional is what one must come away with.

Before moving on to some additional motivational material, a few remarks about the form of the objective functional in Eq. (3) are warranted. First, the functional $J[\cdot]$ is *not*, in general, the area under the curve $x(t)$ between the points $t = t_0$ and $t = t_1$, the latter of which is represented by the integral $\int_{t_0}^{t_1} x(t)dt$. Thus, in optimizing $J[\cdot]$, we are *not* making decisions to optimize the area under the curve $x(t)$. Rather, we are picking paths $x(t)$ such that the "sum" of the values imputed to the path $x(t)$ and its derivative $\dot{x}(t)$ at each point in time in the planning horizon is optimized. Second, the form of $J[\cdot]$ given in Eq. (3) is not the most general form of the objective functional for calculus of variations problems, but it is the most common or canonical in economic theory, as examples to be introduced latter will confirm. In motivating the form of $J[\cdot]$, for example, there is no particular reason why $F(\cdot)$ would not, in general, depend on the second or higher derivatives of $x(t)$. What dictates which derivatives of the path $x(t)$ that are relevant to the form of $J[\cdot]$

is the particular economic phenomena under study, and as we will shortly see, most of the problems of relevance to economists dictate the presence of $\dot{x}(t)$ in $F(\cdot)$, but rarely higher derivatives.

The question you may now be wrestling with is: How does one know when to construct a dynamic model, as opposed to a static model, to study the economic events under investigation? The answer is most easily explained and motivated within the context of a simple example. Imagine an individual on an isolated island on which fresh water is available in an unlimited supply, and for which essentially no effort is required to collect the water. You may picture a brook or stream of fresh water passing next to the individual's hut. The only source of food is fish, which does require the expenditure of effort on the part of this individual. Clearly this individual can survive on this island, and the problem that this person faces is how much fish to catch each day for consumption.

Initially, let's assume that the harvested fish are impossible to store for any length of time, either because of the extreme heat of the environment or because of the lack of materials necessary to build a suitable storage facility. As this individual gets up on any day, the decision to be made is how much fish to catch *for this day only*, as storage has been ruled out. Any fish caught beyond the amount to be consumed that day simply rots and is wasted. Because fishing is costly to the individual, the catch on any day will not exceed the individual's consumption per day. Notice that the decision of how much fish to catch this day is independent of fish caught on previous days or fish expected to be caught on future days, as the lack of storage prevents any carryover of the fish. This lack of storage breaks any link between past decisions and the present decision, and any link between the present decision and future decisions. In other words, the absence of any durable asset or the inability of this person to store any of the asset (fish) renders current choices or actions independent of those made in the past, or those to be made in the future. For example, even if this person caught twice as many fish as could be consumed in a day, this would not relieve the individual of fishing the following day because the fish simply spoil, leaving zero edible fish for tomorrow. Thus the decision of how much fish to catch on any day is dependent only on the circumstances or environmental conditions of that day. As the reader may have guessed, this is exactly what dictates the decision problem faced by this individual as simply a sequence of static choice problems, each day's decision being independent of past and future decisions, and identical to that to be made on any other day, save for differing environmental conditions.

The reader may wonder why this situation is not a dynamic optimization problem since a sequence of optimal decisions must be made through time. It is not the sequence of decisions or the introduction of time per se that defines a dynamic choice problem but the link between past, present, and future decisions that makes a problem dynamic. In the scenario above, the lack of storage breaks this link, reducing the problem to a sequence of independent static optimization problems. So to have a dynamic optimization problem, *there must be some systematic link between past, present, and future decisions.*

Now let's assume that fish caught on any day in excess of that day's consumption can be stored. Because we are concerned here about the structure of a problem that makes it dynamic, the actual period of time in which the fish can be stored or preserved is not important; the fact that fish caught on one day can be stored for future consumption is the important idea. Just as in the previous scenario, when this individual wakes up on any given day, a decision about how much fish to catch that day must be made. What is different, however, is that a stock of fish may exist in storage from the previous day's catch, and this stock must be taken into account in today's harvesting decision. Thus, the assumption of storage (or a durable good) provides a direct link between past decisions and the current decision, a link that was absent when storage was ruled out. Likewise, the decision to catch fish (or not) today impacts the amount of fish in storage for future consumption, and therefore impacts future decisions about catching fish. Storage provides a link between current decisions and future decisions as well. It is exactly this intertemporal linking of decisions that makes this second scenario a dynamic choice problem: decisions made in the past affect the current choice, which, in turn, affects future choices.

Although it may appear that in this simple example, there is only one variable, scilicet, fish, there are actually two: catching fish and fish in storage. The storage of fish is not a variable that is controlled directly by the individual; it responds to the amount caught, amount eaten, and time elapsed between catches. In macroeconomic terminology, the amount of fish in storage is a stock variable, or a state variable in the language of optimal control theory; that is, it is defined at a point in time, not over a period or length of time. The act of fishing, on the other hand, is defined over a period of time (a flow variable) and is directly under the control of the individual. In the language of optimal control theory, the catch rate of the fish is the control variable.

With the essence of a continuous time dynamic optimization problem now conveyed, let's turn to the motivation and basic mathematical setup of an optimal control problem. We therefore elect to proceed directly to optimal control theory rather than first formally introducing the calculus of variations and *then* optimal control theory.

Optimal control theory is based on a new way of viewing and formulating calculus of variations problems, and thus enables one to see them in a different light. In particular, optimal control theory often brings the economic intuition and content of a continuous time dynamic optimization problem to the surface more readily than does the calculus of variations, thereby enhancing one's economic understanding of the problem. It is this change of vista that makes optimal control theory a powerful tool for solving dynamic economic problems, for the calculus of variations can solve all problems that can be solved with optimal control theory, though not necessarily as easily, in which case both theories yield equivalent results. In fact, some textbooks, such as Hadley and Kemp (1971), develop the calculus of variations in its full generality and then use the results to prove those in optimal control theory.

The focus in optimal control theory is on some system. In economic problems, this may be the economy, an individual, or a firm. As is usual in intertemporal problems, we are interested in optimizing, in some specified sense, the behavior of the system through time. It is assumed that the manner in which the system changes through time can be described by specifying the time behavior of certain variables, say $\mathbf{x}(t) \in \Re^N$, called *state variables*, where t is the independent variable that we will almost always refer to as time. In general, the vector-valued function $\mathbf{x}(\cdot) : \Re \to \Re^N$ is assumed to be a *piecewise smooth* function of time with not more than a finite number of corners. This means that the component functions $x_n(\cdot)$, $n = 1, 2, \ldots, N$, are continuous but that the derivative functions $\dot{x}_n(\cdot)$, $n = 1, 2, \ldots, N$, are *piecewise continuous* in the sense that $\dot{x}_n(\cdot)$ has at most a finite number of discontinuities on each finite interval with finite jumps (i.e., one-sided limits) at each point of discontinuity. In economic problems, a capital stock, a stock of money or any asset for that matter (e.g., wealth), a stock of fish, the amount of some mineral in the ground, the stock of water in an aquifer, the number of chairs in a classroom, or even the distribution function of a random variable may represent a state variable. Generally, the state variables are defined at a given point in time, as the aforementioned examples indicate. This is why state variables are often referred to as stocks by economists.

Before pressing on, it is prudent at this juncture to pause momentarily and give a precise definition of a piecewise continuous function and a piecewise smooth function, for such functions will be encountered with some regularity in optimal control theory. To that end, we have the following definition.

Definition 1.1: A function $\phi(\cdot)$ is said to be *piecewise continuous* on an interval $\alpha \le t \le \beta$ if the interval can be partitioned by a finite number of points $\alpha = t_0 < t_1 < \cdots < t_K = \beta$ so that

1. $\phi(\cdot)$ is continuous on each open subinterval $t_{k-1} < t < t_k, k = 1, 2, \ldots, K$, and
2. $\phi(\cdot)$ approaches a finite limit as the end points of each subinterval are approached from within the subinterval.

In other words, a function $\phi(\cdot)$ is piecewise continuous on an interval $\alpha \le t \le \beta$ if it is continuous there except for a finite number of jump discontinuities. An example of a piecewise continuous function is shown in Figure 1.3. Given this definition, it is now a relatively simple matter to define a piecewise smooth function.

Definition 1.2: A function $\Phi(\cdot)$ is said to be *piecewise smooth* on an interval $\alpha \le t \le \beta$ if its derivative function $\dot{\Phi}(\cdot)$ is piecewise continuous on the interval $\alpha \le t \le \beta$.

This definition therefore implies that the derivative of a piecewise smooth function is piecewise continuous, and that the integral of a piecewise continuous function is piecewise smooth.

It is also assumed that there exists another class of variables known as *control variables*, say $\mathbf{u}(t) \in \Re^M$, where $M \neq N$ in general. The control variables may undergo jump changes and are therefore only restricted to be *piecewise continuous* in general, that is, the function $\mathbf{u}(\cdot) : \Re \to \Re^M$ is assumed to be a *piecewise continuous*

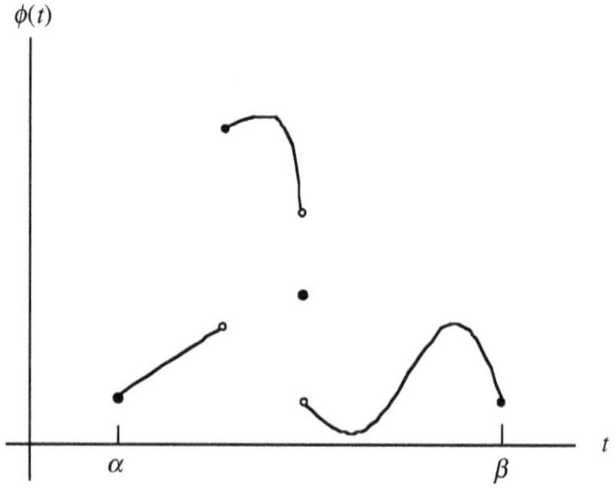

Figure 1.3

function of time. In economic problems, control variables are usually represented by flow variables that are typically defined over an interval of time. Archetypal control variables in economic problems include the investment rate in an asset, the consumption rate of a good, and the harvest rate of a resource. Control variables are those variables that the decision maker has explicit control of in the optimal control problem, as the name implies. Control variables are thus the analogues of the choice or decision variables in static optimization theory. The control variables will not, in general, be allowed to take on arbitrary values. Generally, it is assumed that for each t in the planning horizon, the control variables are restricted to vary in a fixed and prespecified set $U \subseteq \Re^M$, called the *control set* or *control region*. It is typically required that $\mathbf{u}(t) \in U$ for the entire planning horizon. The control set U may be any fixed set in $\Re^M$, say, an open or closed set, but is not restricted in any special way. Of particular importance is the case in which U is a closed set in $\Re^M$. In this case, the control variables are allowed to take values at the boundary of the control set, a situation that the classical calculus of variations cannot handle so easily. In typical economic problems, the control set may be represented by nonnegativity restrictions on the control variables or by fixed inequality constraints that bound the control variables. Finally, it is assumed that every variable of interest can be classified as a state variable or a control variable.

In view of the restrictions placed on the two classes of variables, we may think of the control variables as governing not the values of the state variables, but their rate of change. More specifically, it will be assumed that the dependence of the state variables on the control variables can be described by a first-order differential equation system, namely,

$$\dot{\mathbf{x}}(t) = \mathbf{g}(t, \mathbf{x}(t), \mathbf{u}(t))$$

in vector notation, or

$$\dot{x}_n(t) = g^n(t, \mathbf{x}(t), \mathbf{u}(t)), \quad n = 1, 2, \ldots, N$$

in index notation, known as the *state equation*. The *transition functions* $g^n(\cdot)$, $n = 1, 2, \ldots, N$, are given functions that describe the dynamics of the system. In general, the rate of change of each state variable depends on all of the state variables, all of the control variables, various economic and technical parameters, and explicitly on time t, though the specific problem under consideration will dictate the exact form of the state equation and the variables appearing in it. The explicit dependence of the transition functions on t allows for the evolution of the state variables to depend on important exogenous factors, such as technological progress. Furthermore, suppose that the state of the system is known at time t_0, so that $\mathbf{x}(t_0) = \mathbf{x}_0$, where $\mathbf{x}_0 \in \Re^N$ is a given vector. If the time path of the control variables is specified by a certain control function, say, $\mathbf{u}(\cdot)$, defined for $t \geq t_0$, and we substitute it into the state equation, we obtain a system of N first-order ordinary differential equations for the N unknown functions $x_n(\cdot)$, $n = 1, 2, \ldots, N$. Because the initial value $\mathbf{x}_0 \in \Re^N$ of the state variable is given, the state equation will have a unique solution $\mathbf{x}(t)$ under rather mild assumptions, given by the fundamental existence and uniqueness theorem for ordinary differential equations. This solution is represented geometrically by a curve in $\Re^N$. Because this solution is essentially a response to the control function $\mathbf{u}(\cdot)$, it would be appropriate to denote it by $\mathbf{x}_{\mathbf{u}}(t)$, but we will drop the subscript $\mathbf{u}$ as is customarily done. Clearly, we could have selected another control function, and a corresponding time path of the state variable would be generated. Thus, in general, for each control function selected, there corresponds a path for the state variables that represents the solution to the state equation and initial condition. As a result of this observation, it follows that the control and state variables are essentially paired, in that once a control function is specified, the corresponding time path of the state variables is completely determined via the state equation.

To complete our statement of an optimal control problem, we must define a measure of the effectiveness of a control. Such a measure is provided by the functional

$$J[\mathbf{x}(\cdot), \mathbf{u}(\cdot)] \stackrel{\text{def}}{=} \int_{t_0}^{t_1} f(t, \mathbf{x}(t), \mathbf{u}(t))\, dt,$$

where the closed interval $[t_0, t_1]$ is called the *planning horizon*, t_0 is the *initial date* of the planning horizon, and t_1 is the *terminal date* of the planning horizon. The integrand function $f(\cdot)$ depends, in general, on all of the state variables, all of the control variables, various economic and technical parameters, and explicitly on time t, though as in the case of the state equation, the specific problem under consideration will dictate the exact form of the integrand function and the variables appearing in it. In economic problems, the integrand function typically represents the net benefits at each instant of time t in the planning horizon resulting from the control $\mathbf{u}(t)$ and its corresponding state $\mathbf{x}(t)$. In most economic problems, the explicit appearance of t in the integrand function is a result of the process of discounting the future net benefits using the function $t \mapsto e^{-rt}$, where $r > 0$ is the discount rate. Note, in passing, that t is a *dummy variable of integration* in the objective functional, and as such, we are free to replace it with another symbol that suits our purpose, say, s or τ, without affecting the optimal control problem. We will in fact do so in later chapters.

The archetypal optimal control problem can now be stated as follows: select a control function $\mathbf{u}(\cdot)$ such that $\mathbf{u}(t) \in U \; \forall \, t \in [t_0, t_1]$, so that when the state vector $\mathbf{x}(t)$ is determined from the state equation $\dot{\mathbf{x}}(t) = \mathbf{g}(t, \mathbf{x}(t), \mathbf{u}(t))$ and an initial condition $\mathbf{x}(t_0) = \mathbf{x}_0$ is given, the functional $J[\mathbf{x}(\cdot), \mathbf{u}(\cdot)]$ is maximized. Such a control function is called *an optimal control*, and the associated path $\mathbf{x}(t)$ is called *an optimal path*. That is, the problem is to find a control *function* $\mathbf{u}(\cdot)$ that solves the following problem:

$$\max_{\mathbf{u}(\cdot), \mathbf{x}_1} J[\mathbf{x}(\cdot), \mathbf{u}(\cdot)] \overset{\text{def}}{=} \int_{t_0}^{t_1} f(t, \mathbf{x}(t), \mathbf{u}(t))\, dt$$

$$\text{s.t.} \quad \dot{\mathbf{x}}(t) = \mathbf{g}(t, \mathbf{x}(t), \mathbf{u}(t)), \tag{4}$$

$$\mathbf{x}(t_0) = \mathbf{x}_0, \;\; \mathbf{x}(t_1) = \mathbf{x}_1, \;\; \mathbf{u}(t) \in U,$$

where $\mathbf{x}_0$ is the *initial value* of the state vector and is taken as given in Eq. (4), whereas $\mathbf{x}_1$ is the *terminal value* of the state vector, which, as the notation of Eq. (4) should convey, is a choice variable rather than being fixed (or given or predetermined) like $\mathbf{x}_0$. The initial value of the state variable is normally thought to be "inherited" from the past actions of the decision maker and is thus not subject to choice. Notice that the control variables influence the value of the objective functional $J[\mathbf{x}(\cdot), \mathbf{u}(\cdot)]$ both directly through their own values and indirectly through their impact on the evolution of the state variables through the state equation. Though in general all of the state and control variables enter the integrand function $f(\cdot)$ and the transition function $\mathbf{g}(\cdot)$, as noted above, it is perfectly acceptable for $f(\cdot)$ and $\mathbf{g}(\cdot)$ to be a function of only some of the state variables or some of the control variables. As remarked above, the economic problem under investigation will dictate the form of $f(\cdot)$ and $\mathbf{g}(\cdot)$. It is important to note, however, that at least one control variable must appear in at least one state equation; otherwise the state equation could not be controlled by the choices of the decision maker, who has explicit command of only the control variables. It is not necessary for at least one control variable to appear in every state equation, however. To see this, consider an example where $M = 1$ and $N = 2$, and where the state equations take the form $\dot{x}_1(t) = u(t)$ and $\dot{x}_2(t) = x_1(t)$. In this instance, the decision maker directly influences $x_1(t)$ and thus indirectly influences $x_2(t)$, even though the control variable does not appear in the second state equation. In other words, the definition of an optimal control problem requires that the decision maker can influence the evolution of the state of the system, which dictates that at least one control variable appear in at least one state equation. Also notice that the highest derivative appearing in the problem formulation is the first derivative of the state variable, and it appears only as the left-hand side of the state equation. No derivatives of the control variables appear in the formulation of the optimal control problem. This does not result in any loss of generality, for one can always redefine the variables so that an optimal control problem takes on the prototype form given in Eq. (4). This is analogous to converting, say, a second-order differential equation into a system of two first-order differential equations. It is important to emphasize that because an optimal control problem may have several state variables and several control variables in general, each state variable would evolve according to a differential equation. Moreover, the number of control variables may be greater than, less than, or equal to the number of state variables.

Thus far, we have omitted a statement of the fundamental continuity restrictions to be placed on the integrand function $f(\cdot)$ and the transition function $\mathbf{g}(\cdot)$. The minimum assumptions that we shall impose on the aforementioned functions are as follows:

(A.1) $f(\cdot) \in C^{(0)}$ with respect to the $1 + N + M$ variables $(t, \mathbf{x}, \mathbf{u})$.
(A.2) $g^{\ell}(\cdot) \in C^{(0)}$ with respect to the $1 + N + M$ variables $(t, \mathbf{x}, \mathbf{u})$ for $\ell = 1, 2, \ldots, N$.
(A.3) $\partial f(\cdot)/\partial x_n \in C^{(0)}$ with respect to the $1 + N + M$ variables $(t, \mathbf{x}, \mathbf{u})$ for $n = 1, 2, \ldots, N$.
(A.4) $\partial g^{\ell}(\cdot)/\partial x_n \in C^{(0)}$ with respect to the $1 + N + M$ variables $(t, \mathbf{x}, \mathbf{u})$ for $\ell, n = 1, 2, \ldots, N$.

We will maintain at least these four assumptions throughout the remainder of the book. Notice that differentiability of the integrand function $f(\cdot)$ and the transition function $\mathbf{g}(\cdot)$ with respect to the control variables is not required. Although this is true in general, we will often impose stronger continuity assumptions on the functions, especially in the beginning of our development of the theory, and often for pedagogical reasons. Such instances will be noted in the ensuing chapters.

A prototypical calculus of variations problem is of the form

$$\max_{\mathbf{x}(\cdot), \mathbf{x}_1} J[\mathbf{x}(\cdot)] \stackrel{\text{def}}{=} \int_{t_0}^{t_1} F(t, \mathbf{x}(t), \dot{\mathbf{x}}(t))\, dt \qquad (5)$$
$$\text{s.t.} \quad \mathbf{x}(t_0) = \mathbf{x}_0, \ \ \mathbf{x}(t_1) = \mathbf{x}_1.$$

Note that the terminal value of the state vector is a decision variable in this formulation, as is signified by the appearance of $\mathbf{x}_1$ under the max operator. This calculus of variations problem can be transformed into the prototypical optimal control problem by defining the control variable as $\mathbf{u}(t) \stackrel{\text{def}}{=} \dot{\mathbf{x}}(t)$, so that Eq. (5) becomes

$$\max_{\mathbf{u}(\cdot),\mathbf{x}_1} J[\mathbf{x}(\cdot),\mathbf{u}(\cdot)] \stackrel{\text{def}}{=} \int_{t_0}^{t_1} F(t,\mathbf{x}(t),\mathbf{u}(t))\,dt$$

$$\text{s.t.} \quad \dot{\mathbf{x}}(t) = \mathbf{u}(t), \tag{6}$$

$$\mathbf{x}(t_0) = \mathbf{x}_0,\ \mathbf{x}(t_1) = \mathbf{x}_1.$$

Hence the state vector is $\mathbf{x}(t)$, $\dot{\mathbf{x}}(t) = \mathbf{u}(t)$ is the state equation, and $\mathbf{u}(t)$ is the control vector. Because there are no constraints on the control variables in Eq. (6), the control set U is the entire real N-dimensional space, that is, $U = \Re^N$.

With some of the essentials of optimal control problems now in place, we can turn to the presentation of some canonical continuous time dynamic optimization problems in economics. In particular, we intend to provide a rather detailed formulation and discussion of four dynamic optimization problems, all of which will be solved and generalized in later chapters.

Example 1.1 (Fish Farming): Let's imagine that the sole owner of a fish farm with well-defined property rights (an aquaculture environment) wants to determine the optimal rate at which to harvest and sell the fish through time. Remember that what makes a particular problem a dynamic one is that past, present, and future choices are linked in some manner, not that we have some dimension of time in the problem per se. The assumption of sole ownership with well-defined property rights allows us to avoid the problems associated with common ownership, such as in the case of ocean fishing. The problems associated with such circumstances are not properly handled through this first model.

First, let's consider the production function associated with harvesting. Clearly, the amount of fish that can be harvested, say, h, depends on the stock of fish in the body of water (e.g., a lake), which we denote by x. As the stock of fish grows, ceteris paribus, more fish can be harvested, but as is typical with production functions, this process is subject to a declining marginal product. In addition, the harvest rate is dependent on the quantity of variable inputs used. In the fisheries literature, it is commonplace to assume that all such variable inputs can be combined into one homogeneous index called effort, which we denote by e. An increase in effort, ceteris paribus, leads to a bigger catch, but this input is subject to a declining marginal product as well. Overall, diminishing returns to scale are prevalent for the $C^{(2)}$ production function $f(\cdot)$ (which is not to be confused with the integrand function in the above exposition). These assumptions can be stated mathematically as

$$h = f(x,e),\ f_x(x,e) > 0,\ f_e(x,e) > 0,\ f_{ex}(x,e) > 0,$$

$$f_{xx}(x,e) < 0,\ f_{ee}(x,e) < 0,\ f_{xx}(x,e)f_{ee}(x,e) - [f_{ex}(x,e)]^2 > 0.$$

Notice that $f_{ex}(x, e) > 0$ is also assumed, which says that the marginal product of effort is larger the more fish there are in the lake. This effect and $f_x(x, e) > 0$ are known as the prototypical stock effect in resource harvesting problems.

The cost function $C(\cdot)$ dual to the production function $f(\cdot)$ is defined in the archetypal manner by

$$C(x, h; w) \stackrel{\text{def}}{=} \min_e \{w \cdot e \text{ s.t. } h = f(x, e)\}, \tag{7}$$

where $w > 0$ is defined as the time-independent (i.e., constant over time) per-unit cost of effort. The cost function $C(\cdot)$ is called a *minimum restricted cost function*, the adjective *restricted* being employed because the stock of fish, x, is treated as fixed in the static optimization problem (7). It is left for the reader, as a mental exercise, to show that the following properties (and more) hold for the minimum restricted cost function $C(\cdot)$:

$$C_x(x, h; w) < 0,\ C_h(x, h; w) > 0,\ C_{hx}(x, h; w) < 0,$$

$$C_{xx}(x, h; w) > 0,\ C_{hh}(x, h; w) > 0,$$

$$C_{xx}(x, h; w)C_{hh}(x, h; w) - [C_{hx}(x, h; w)]^2 > 0,$$

$$C_w(x, h; w) > 0,\ C_{ww}(x, h; w) \equiv 0.$$

The proof of these results is an application of the implicit function theorem because problem (7) has but one decision variable and one constraint.

The owner of the fish farm is assumed to be a price taker in both the output and input markets. The market price of the harvested fish is $p > 0$ and is time independent. The owner is interested in maximizing the present discounted value of profits over the planning horizon of T years. Here we are taking time to be a continuous variable. Profit per period is the integrand function and is given by the expression $\pi(x(t), h(t); p, w) \stackrel{\text{def}}{=} ph(t) - C(x(t), h(t); w)$. Moreover, profit flow is discounted at the constant rate $r > 0$. Because we are in continuous time, the usual summation and discounting of per-period profits associated with discrete time is replaced with integration and continuous discounting over the planning horizon of T years. Thus, the objective functional is given by

$$J[x(\cdot), h(\cdot)] \stackrel{\text{def}}{=} \int_0^T [ph(t) - C(x(t), h(t); w)]\, e^{-rt}\, dt.$$

The problem statement is not complete, however, as the growth of the fish population and the effects of harvesting on it must be taken into account. Because $x(t)$ is the stock (or number) of fish at a point in time, $\dot{x}(t) \stackrel{\text{def}}{=} \frac{d}{dt}x(t)$ is the stock's rate of growth or decline. The growth rate of the fish stock obviously depends on the stock of fish in the lake, say, $\dot{x}(t) = F(x(t))$, where $F(x(t))$ is the stock's natural growth rate in the absence of harvesting. One common functional form for $F(\cdot)$ is the logistic, given by $F(x; \gamma, K) \stackrel{\text{def}}{=} \gamma x[1 - xK^{-1}]$. So far, this formulation of the rate of change of the fish stock ignores the effects of harvesting. Harvesting simply reduces the stock's growth rate by the number of fish harvested over a period of time. Thus, the stock's net growth becomes $\dot{x}(t) = F(x(t)) - h(t)$. This is a simplifying assumption because the stock's natural growth rate $F(x(t))$ may be influenced by the age of the species harvested. The natural growth function $F(\cdot)$ is concave, is twice continuously differentiable, and has a unique maximum at $x = x_{MSY}$, the maximum sustainable yield level of the fish stock. The stock x_{MSY} is therefore the solution to $F'(x) = 0$. Moreover, the natural growth function is increasing in the fish stock for $x < x_{MSY}$ and is decreasing in the fish stock for $x > x_{MSY}$. In addition, the individual owner begins the operations at time $t = 0$ with a fixed number of fry, say, $x(0) = x_0 > 0$, but may choose the stock of fish to terminate with, say x_T, when the given terminal period T of the planning horizon arrives.

Armed with this information, the optimal control problem the manager must solve to maximize the present discounted value of profits is

$$\max_{h(\cdot),x_T} J[x(\cdot), h(\cdot)] \stackrel{\text{def}}{=} \int_0^T [ph(t) - C(x(t), h(t); w)]\, e^{-rt}\, dt$$

$$\text{s.t.} \quad \dot{x}(t) = F(x(t)) - h(t), \tag{8}$$

$$x(0) = x_0, \;\; x(T) = x_T.$$

The solution (if it exists) to problem (8) yields the optimal time paths of the harvest rate and fish stock over the owner's planning horizon. Denote these solutions by $h^*(t; \boldsymbol{\beta})$ and $x^*(t; \boldsymbol{\beta})$, respectively, where $\boldsymbol{\beta} \stackrel{\text{def}}{=} (p, w, r, x_0, T) \in \Re^5_{++}$. Notice that the solutions depend not only on the parameters of the problem, as do the solutions to static optimization problems, but they also depend on the independent variable time. It is important to note that it is the differential equation that makes problem (8) a dynamic optimization problem because the decision to harvest today leaves fewer fish in the future to reproduce, thus impacting future stock levels and future harvesting decisions. The same is true regarding how past harvesting decisions affect the current harvesting decision.

In the next example, we formulate an intertemporal model of a profit-maximizing firm that uses capital and labor to produce its output and faces costs of adjusting its capital stock.

Example 1.2 (Adjustment Cost Model): This example presents a typical price-taking (in both input and output markets), capital-accumulating model of the firm, known as the *adjustment cost model of the firm.* For simplicity, assume there are two inputs to the production process, one variable input that we will call labor (L), purchased at the constant unit price of $w > 0$, and the other, a quasi-fixed input that we will call the capital stock (K), which incurs a constant per-unit maintenance cost of $c > 0$. The $C^{(2)}$ production function of this firm, say, $f(\cdot)$, depends on L and K

in the prototypical manner. In addition, the firm invests in the capital stock at the rate I and pays the constant price of $g > 0$ per unit purchased. The price of the good produced by the firm is also constant and given by $p > 0$. The firm discounts its cash flow at the rate $r > 0$. The installation of capital is costly to the firm in that it uses up resources to install the equipment and get it ready for productive uses, resources that would have otherwise been used to produce the final good. Such adjustment costs, denoted by $C(I)$, are assumed to have the following archetypal properties, to wit, $\operatorname{sign}(C'(I)) = \operatorname{sign}(I)$, $C(0) = C'(0) = 0$, and $C''(I) > 0$. The cash flow per period for this firm is therefore given by

$$\begin{aligned}&\pi(K(t), I(t), L(t); c, p, g, w)\\ &\quad\stackrel{\text{def}}{=} pf(K(t), L(t)) - wL(t) - cK(t) - gI(t) - C(I(t)).\end{aligned}$$

Capital depreciates at a rate $\delta > 0$ proportional to its existing stock. The rate of change of the capital stock, scilicet, $\dot{K}(t) \stackrel{\text{def}}{=} \frac{d}{dt}K(t)$, depends on the rate at which new investment goods are purchased, $I(t)$, and the rate at which the existing capital depreciates, $\delta K(t)$. Thus the net rate of change in the capital stock is given by the ordinary differential equation $\dot{K}(t) = I(t) - \delta K(t)$. Finally, this firm expects to operate its business for a period of T years, which it takes as given, and begins its operations at time $t = 0$ with an initial stock of capital $K(0) = K_0 > 0$, and ends its operations with a terminal stock of capital $K(T) = K_T > 0$. Notice that in this example, in contrast to Example 1.1 and the prototypical form of the optimal control problem given in Eq. (4), the terminal value of the state variable is fixed rather than chosen by the decision maker.

The optimal control problem the manager must solve in order to determine the optimal time paths of the capital stock, labor input, and investment rate throughout the firm's operating life is therefore given by

$$\begin{aligned}&\max_{I(\cdot),L(\cdot)} J[K(\cdot), I(\cdot), L(\cdot)]\\ &\quad\stackrel{\text{def}}{=} \int_0^T [pf(K(t), L(t)) - wL(t) - cK(t) - gI(t) - C(I(t))]e^{-rt}\,dt\\ &\qquad\qquad \text{s.t. } \dot{K}(t) = I(t) - \delta K(t),\\ &\qquad\qquad K(0) = K_0,\; K(T) = K_T.\end{aligned} \tag{9}$$

The solution to the optimal control problem (9) is denoted by $K^*(t; \alpha)$, $I^*(t; \alpha)$, and $L^*(t; \alpha)$, where $\alpha \stackrel{\text{def}}{=} (\delta, c, g, p, r, w, K_0, T, K_T) \in \Re^9_{++}$ are the parameters of the problem, and gives the optimal time paths for the capital stock, investment rate, and labor input, respectively. As in Example 1.1, it is the state equation of problem (9) that makes it dynamic. To see this, simply note that the state equation implies that the optimal investment rate depends on the existing stock of capital, which itself is a result of investment decisions in prior periods. Additionally, the rate at which capital depreciates depends on the existing capital stock. In sum then, the current decision of how much investment to undertake depends on the current capital stock, which itself is dependent on previous investment decisions, thus providing the link between current and past decisions that typifies dynamic problems.

Notice that in Examples 1.1 and 1.2, we made explicit the dependence of the optimal solutions on the parameters of the control problem. This a practice we shall generally adhere to and one that is in accord with your experience with static optimization theory. Moreover, it is a necessary prerequisite if one is to do any qualitative analysis of an optimal control model. Such qualitative analysis, known as *comparative dynamics* in dynamic optimization problems, often, but not always, seeks to answer the following question: What is the effect of, say, an increase in the price of the finished good on the time path of the investment rate of the firm? In other words, what is the sign of $\partial I^*(t;\alpha)/\partial p$ for all t in the planning horizon? A comparative dynamics investigation thus may seek to determine how a parameter change influences the decision variables at every point in the planning horizon. Recall that comparative statics is performed in a timeless world, so once the sign of a comparative statics expression is determined (or not), the result continues to hold for all time periods. In contrast, a comparative dynamics analysis may show, for example, that $\partial I^*(t;\alpha)/\partial p$ is initially positive, then turns negative for some time, only to go to zero as the terminal period approaches. For this reason, it can be more difficult to derive unequivocal or refutable results from a comparative dynamics analysis than from a comparative statics analysis. This does not mean, however, that refutable results do not exist in comparative dynamics. Quite the contrary, in fact, as we shall see in many of the later chapters.

For our next example, we present an intertemporal version of the prototype utility maximization problem.

Example 1.3 (Intertemporal Utility Maximization): Consider an individual who wants to choose her consumption rate $c(t)$ at each moment in time t so as to maximize her discounted stream of utility over her known lifetime of length $T > 0$ years. The instantaneous utility function of consumption $U(\cdot)$ is assumed to have positive but declining marginal utility of consumption, that is, $U'(c) > 0$ and $U''(c) < 0$. She discounts her future utility of consumption at the rate $r > 0$ and derives income at any given moment from an exogenously determined and time-invariant wage $w > 0$ and interest earnings of $ik(t)$ on her capital asset $k(t)$, where $i > 0$ is the constant rate of interest earned on the capital asset. One may think of the capital asset as a savings account or a money market fund. The individual may borrow capital, implying that $k(t) < 0$, as well as lend capital, implying that $k(t) > 0$, at the interest rate $i > 0$. Because $k(t)$ is the stock of her capital asset at time t, $\dot{k}(t)$ is, by definition of the derivative, the rate of change of the stock of her asset at time t. Therefore, when $\dot{k}(t) > 0$, she is purchasing or buying the capital asset, whereas $\dot{k}(t) < 0$ means she is selling the capital asset. The price at which capital is traded is normalized at unity. Her income in each period thus consists of interest earnings from her capital asset $ik(t)$ and wage income $w > 0$, whereas expenditures in each period consist of consumption expenditures $c(t)$ and investment expenditures $\dot{k}(t)$. Her budget constraint requires that in each period $t \in [0, T]$, income equals expenditures, thereby implying that her instantaneous budget constraint is given by $w + ik(t) = c(t) + \dot{k}(t)$. She begins her consumption planning with a given amount of the capital asset, say, $k(0) = k_0 > 0$, and ends up with a given amount at the time of her death, say, $k(T) = k_T > 0$. The assumptions that she knows the date of her death and that she must end up with a given amount of the asset at the time of her death are artificial and will be relaxed in the course of our development of the theory of optimal control. The planning problem she must solve is therefore given by

$$\max_{c(\cdot)} J[k(\cdot), c(\cdot)] \stackrel{\text{def}}{=} \int_0^T e^{-rt} U(c(t))\, dt$$

$$\text{s.t.} \quad \dot{k}(t) = w + ik(t) - c(t),$$

$$k(0) = k_0, \; k(T) = k_T.$$

That is, she must choose a consumption *function* $c(\cdot)$ so as to maximize her discounted lifetime utility over her known lifetime, given an initial and terminal stock of the capital asset. An important feature of this intertemporal utility maximization problem is that the independent variable time enters the integrand in an *explicit* fashion via the discount factor only. In other words, t enters the integrand explicitly only through the discount term e^{-rt}. This is typical of most problems in economics and is a property shared by the previous two examples as well.

We finish this introductory chapter by developing one more dynamic economic model to further reinforce some of the points made earlier. This economic model will be a workhorse for us, as you will see. In contrast to the three previous examples, we will develop an explicit functional form for the integrand, thereby allowing us to solve it for an explicit solution.

Example 1.4 (Optimal Inventory Accumulation): A firm has received an order for $x_T > 0$ units of product to be delivered at time $T > 0$. It seeks a production schedule or plan for filling this order by the specified delivery date at minimum cost. Let $x(t)$ denote the inventory accumulated by time $t \in [0, T]$. Because the firm does not have any of the good in its inventory when the order is first placed at $t = 0$, we have $x(0) = 0$ as the initial condition. By the delivery date $t = T$, however, the contract calls for delivery of $x_T > 0$ units, so the firm is required by the contract to have $x_T > 0$ units in its inventory at time $t = T$ in order to meet its obligation; hence $x(T) = x_T$ is the terminal condition. The inventory level $x(t)$ at any moment $t \in [0, T]$ is the cumulated past production; hence the rate of change of the inventory, namely, $\dot{x}(t)$, is the production rate. More formally, the relationship between the inventory level $x(t)$ and production rate $\dot{x}(t)$ at any time $t \in [0, T]$ is given by $x(t) \overset{\text{def}}{=} \int_0^t \dot{x}(s)ds$. The cost of producing the good consists of two components, a unit production cost that rises linearly with the production rate, and a unit holding cost of inventory per unit time that is assumed to be constant. Define $c_2 > 0$ as the unit cost of holding inventory and $c_1\dot{x}(t)$ as the unit cost of production, where $c_1 > 0$. Hence total cost at any date $t \in [0, T]$ is defined as

$$TC(t) \overset{\text{def}}{=} c_1\dot{x}(t) \cdot \dot{x}(t) + c_2 x(t) = c_1[\dot{x}(t)]^2 + c_2 x(t).$$

The firm's objective is to determine a production rate path $\dot{x}(t)$ and therefore an inventory accumulation path $x(t)$, so as to minimize its total costs over the planning period $[0, T]$. The firm, therefore, seeks to solve the following calculus of variations problem:

$$\min_{x(\cdot)} J[x(\cdot)] \overset{\text{def}}{=} \int_0^T \left[c_1[\dot{x}(t)]^2 + c_2 x(t)\right] dt$$

$$\text{s.t.} \quad x(0) = 0, \ x(T) = x_T.$$

Observe that the production rate is not constrained to be nonnegative in this version of the problem. We will address this complication later, when we have the tools to handle it. Also notice that only the first-order derivative of $x(\cdot)$ appears in the integrand, consistent with an earlier observation that the first-order derivative is the highest that typically appears in economic applications of the calculus of variations. Finally, take note of the fact that the integrand does not depend explicitly on the independent variable time, that is, t does not enter the integrand $F(t, x(t), \dot{x}(t)) \overset{\text{def}}{=} c_1[\dot{x}(t)]^2 + c_2 x(t)$ independently of the functions $x(\cdot)$ and $\dot{x}(\cdot)$. Since t does not appear explicitly in the integrand, this calculus of variations problem is called *autonomous*.

To convert this calculus of variations problem into an optimal control problem, all we are required to do is to select a control variable. This is straightforward, for we have emphasized all along that $\dot{x}(t)$ is the production rate, a flow variable, so it is the natural choice for the control variable. More formally, define $u(t) \overset{\text{def}}{=} \dot{x}(t)$ as the control variable. This differential equation thus becomes our state equation in the optimal control formulation of the problem. But remember that no derivatives of the state variable (or control variable for that matter) appear in the integrand of the objective functional of an optimal control problem; hence we must replace $\dot{x}(t)$ in the objective functional with the control variable $u(t)$. Doing just that allows us to rewrite the calculus of variations form of the inventory accumulation problem as an equivalent optimal control problem, namely,

$$\min_{u(\cdot)} J[x(\cdot), u(\cdot)] \stackrel{\text{def}}{=} \int_0^T \left[c_1[u(t)]^2 + c_2 x(t)\right] dt$$

$$\text{s.t.} \quad \dot{x}(t) = u(t),$$

$$x(0) = 0, \;\; x(T) = x_T.$$

This is a problem that will aid us greatly in our understanding of optimal control theory.

Now that we have seen the essential distinction between static and dynamic optimization problems, the generic form of the objective functional for continuous time dynamic optimization problems, and several economic models that fall naturally in the realm of continuous time dynamic optimization, the next chapter will develop the necessary conditions that will be the centerpiece of much of the ensuing analysis. In particular, the ensuing chapter presents the necessary conditions for the simplest optimal control problem, which consists of a single state variable, a single control variable, and a free terminal value of the state variable. We will offer a simple and motivated proof of the necessary conditions under stronger assumptions on the integrand function $f(\cdot)$, the transition function $\mathbf{g}(\cdot)$, and the state and control variables than those given in this chapter.

MENTAL EXERCISES

1.1 Let $g(\cdot) : \Re^{N+A} \to \Re$ be a $C^{(2)}$ scalar-valued function whose arguments are the vectors $\mathbf{x} \in \Re^N$ and $\boldsymbol{\alpha} \in \Re^A$.
   (a) Compute the $A \times N$ matrix $g_{\boldsymbol{\alpha}\mathbf{x}}(\mathbf{x}; \boldsymbol{\alpha})$.
   (b) Prove that $g_{\mathbf{x}\boldsymbol{\alpha}}(\mathbf{x}; \boldsymbol{\alpha}) = g_{\boldsymbol{\alpha}\mathbf{x}}(\mathbf{x}; \boldsymbol{\alpha})'$. This is the matrix version of the invariance of the second-order partial derivatives to the order of differentiation.

1.2 Assume that the production function $f(\cdot) \in C^{(2)}$ has the properties

$$f_x(x, e) > 0, \;\; f_e(x, e) > 0, \;\; f_{ex}(x, e) > 0,$$

$$f_{xx}(x, e) < 0, \;\; f_{ee}(x, e) < 0, \;\; f_{xx}(x, e) f_{ee}(x, e) - [f_{ex}(x, e)]^2 > 0.$$

Prove that the minimum restricted cost function $C(\cdot)$ defined by

$$C(x, h; w) \stackrel{\text{def}}{=} \min_e \{w \cdot e \text{ s.t. } h = f(x, e)\}$$

has the following properties

$$C_x(x, h; w) < 0, \;\; C_h(x, h; w) > 0, \;\; C_{hx}(x, h; w) < 0, \;\; C_{xx}(x, h; w) > 0,$$

$$C_{hh}(x, h; w) > 0,$$

$$C_{xx}(x, h; w)C_{hh}(x, h; w) - [C_{hx}(x, h; w)]^2 > 0,$$

$$C_w(x, h; w) > 0, \; C_{ww}(x, h; w) \equiv 0.$$

1.3 Draw a graph of a piecewise smooth function that is consistent with Figure 1.1 being a graph of its piecewise continuous derivative function.

FURTHER READING

There are several textbook treatments of optimal control theory that are suitable for students of economics, depending on your mathematical preparation and that intangible quality that often goes by the moniker *mathematical maturity*. The Chiang (1992) textbook covers both the calculus of variations and optimal control theory and is written at the level of his mathematical economics textbook, which is essentially the prerequisite. That is to say, it is an introductory exposition of the material emphasizing intuition and conceptual understanding over mathematical rigor. The next step up in mathematical rigor are the books by Kamien and Schwartz (1981, 1991 2nd Ed.) and Léonard and Van Long (1992). The former is a classic in economics but is showing its age somewhat, even considering the revision more than a decade ago. It is a self-contained, tightly written book aimed at graduate students and practitioners of the subjects of the calculus of variations and optimal control. The Léonard and Van Long (1992) book is well written and more modern in its approach, as it eschews the calculus of variations and proceeds directly to optimal control theory (after a brief chapter on ordinary differential equations). The Hadley and Kemp (1971) book is a step up in mathematical rigor and prerequisites from the last two. It is very well written but a bit dated, however, in that it develops the calculus of variations in its full generality and then uses those theorems to prove their counterparts in optimal control. This makes for a rather long stint before one gets to the modern theory of optimal control. The Seierstad and Sydsæter (1987) book is a nearly exhaustive and well-written account of the theorems in optimal control theory. It is definitely not written as an introductory exposition of optimal control, unless you have a solid mathematical background and a high level of mathematical maturity. It is an outstanding reference book. The Leitmann (1981) and Troutman (1996, 2nd Ed.) books are mathematics texts, with the former using engineering applications and the latter the same plus applications from physics, to demonstrate the methods. Both are accessible by any student of economics who has had courses in linear algebra, advanced calculus, and ordinary differential equations.

REFERENCES

Chiang, A.C. (1992), *Elements of Dynamic Optimization* (New York: McGraw-Hill, Inc.).

Hadley, G. and Kemp, M.C. (1971), *Variational Methods in Economics* (Amsterdam: North-Holland Publishing Co.).

Kamien, M.I. and Schwartz, N.L. (1981; 1991, 2nd Ed.), *Dynamic Optimization: The Calculus of Variations and Optimal Control in Economics and Management* (New York: Elsevier Science Publishing Co., Inc.).

Leitmann, G. (1981), *The Calculus of Variations and Optimal Control* (New York: Plenum Press).

Léonard, D. and Van Long, N. (1992), *Optimal Control Theory and Static Optimization in Economics* (New York: Cambridge University Press).

Seierstad, A. and Sydsæter, K. (1987), *Optimal Control Theory with Economic Applications* (New York: Elsevier Science Publishing Co., Inc.).

Troutman, J.L. (1996, 2nd Ed.), *Variational Calculus and Optimal Control: Optimization with Elementary Convexity* (New York: Springer-Verlag Inc.).

TWO

Necessary Conditions for a Simplified Control Problem

The goal of this chapter is to derive the necessary conditions that an optimal solution *path* or solution *curve* must obey, or equivalently, that an optimal *function* must obey, for the simplest problem in optimal control theory. The necessary conditions to be derived below are known collectively as the Pontryagin necessary conditions. They are the dynamic analogue of the FONCs in unconstrained optimization problems, the latter of which you will recall require that all the first-order partial derivatives of the objective function vanish at the optimal solution.

The simplest problem in optimal control requires that the planning horizon and initial value of the state variable be fixed. The terminal value of the state variable, however, is freely chosen, that is, it is a decision variable. To simplify matters even further in this chapter, we also assume that $M = 1$ and $N = 1$, thereby implying that we are dealing with a single control variable and a single state variable. Given these assumptions, the optimal control problem we will be analyzing in this chapter is given by

$$\max_{u(\cdot),x_1} J[x(\cdot), u(\cdot)] \stackrel{\text{def}}{=} \int_{t_0}^{t_1} f(t, x(t), u(t))\, dt$$

$$\text{s.t.} \quad \dot{x}(t) = g(t, x(t), u(t)), \tag{1}$$

$$u(t) \in U, \; x(t_0) = x_0, \; x(t_1) = x_1,$$

where $U \subset \Re$ is a fixed control set that does not depend on the state or control variables. Recall, for example, that U may be a nonnegativity constraint on the control variable or a fixed upper bound on the control variable, among other constraints. Take note of the fact that the terminal value of the state variable is a decision variable, just as the notation of problem (1) conveys.

In order to make the ensuing proofs and presentation as clear as possible, and to avoid getting caught up in somewhat tangential mathematical details (for our purposes), we adopt an overly strong set of assumptions. The adopted assumptions, however, have the distinct advantage of allowing us to derive the necessary conditions for problem (1) from the so-called variational point of view. Therefore, to this end, we adopt the following assumptions in addition to the basic ones given in Chapter 1:

(A.1) $f(\cdot) \in C^{(1)}$ and $g(\cdot) \in C^{(1)}$ over an open set.
(A.2) $\exists$ a $C^{(0)}$ optimal control function $v(\cdot)$ defined on $[t_0, t_1]$ that solves problem (1), along with its $C^{(1)}$ associated state function $z(\cdot)$.
(A.3) $v(t) \in \operatorname{int} U \; \forall \, t \in [t_0, t_1]$.

It is important to observe that the assumed $C^{(1)}$ nature of $f(\cdot)$ and $g(\cdot)$ can be weakened. At this point in the development of optimal control theory, however, we will require these stronger assumptions because of the variational-based proof of the necessary conditions that we shall adopt. More generally, all we really need to assume is that $f(\cdot)$ and $g(\cdot)$ are $C^{(0)}$ and that $f_x(\cdot)$ and $g_x(\cdot)$ are likewise $C^{(0)}$, as noted in Chapter 1. The assumed continuity of the optimal control function $v(\cdot)$ and the assumed $C^{(1)}$ nature of the corresponding state function $z(\cdot)$ are similarly overly strong. For now, the strong assumptions are fine given our pedagogical inclination, but we will certainly relax them later to show the full power and reach of optimal control theory. Assumption (A.3) asserts that the optimal control path lies in the *interior* of the control set for the entire planning horizon. This assumption therefore means that the constraints on the control variable are not binding in an optimal plan and can henceforth be ignored for our present development of the necessary conditions. More formally, assumption (A.3) implies that for each $t \in [t_0, t_1]$, $v(t) \in U$ and $B(v(t); \delta) \stackrel{\text{def}}{=} \{u(\cdot) : |u(t) - v(t)| < \delta\} \in U$ for some $\delta > 0$, that is, for each period of the planning horizon, the value of the optimal control belongs to the control set and is the center of an open ball that is contained in the control set for some positive radius defining the open ball. Finally, the assumption that $f(\cdot) \in C^{(1)}$ and $g(\cdot) \in C^{(1)}$ over an *open set* in (A.1) eliminates the need to consider one-sided derivatives in the foregoing analysis seeing as an open set consists only of interior points by its very definition.

Rather than denote the optimal pair of curves by, say, $(x^*(t), u^*(t))$, or the optimal pair of functions by $(x^*(\cdot), u^*(\cdot))$, we prefer to use the notation $(z(t), v(t))$ and $(z(\cdot), v(\cdot))$ for the optimal pair of curves and functions, respectively. As we will see, this has the advantage of reducing notational clutter as we proceed to more general optimal control problems. Proceeding as we would in static optimization theory, we now turn to the definition of admissibility for an optimal control problem (1).

Definition 2.1: If $u(\cdot) \in C^{(0)}$ and $u(t) \in \operatorname{int} U \; \forall \, t \in [t_0, t_1]$, and $x(\cdot) \in C^{(1)} \; \forall \, t \in [t_0, t_1]$ is the corresponding state function that satisfies $\dot{x}(t) = g(t, x(t), u(t))$ and $x(t_0) = x_0$, then $(x(t), u(t))$ is called an *admissible pair*.

Recall that once we specify the path of the control variable $u(t) \; \forall \, t \in [t_0, t_1]$, the path of the state variable is completely determined by the solution of the state equation and initial condition. This follows from the fact that if we substitute a given control path $u(t)$ into the state equation, we can in principle integrate the state equation and use the initial condition to solve for the corresponding path of the state variable. Said differently, the state variable path is completely determined once the solution for the control variable is found. It is natural, therefore, to think of the state and control variables as coming in *pairs*, so we will use this term repeatedly throughout the text. Moreover, we may speak of finding the control function because a corresponding state function is implied. Given that the selection of the control determines the state, it determines the value of the functional $J[\cdot]$ as well.

The domain of the objective functional $J[\cdot]$ is taken to be the set of all admissible function pairs $(x(\cdot), u(\cdot))$. Now recall that $f(\cdot) \in C^{(1)}$ by assumption (A.1), and $u(\cdot) \in C^{(0)}\,\forall\, t \in [t_0, t_1]$ and $x(\cdot) \in C^{(1)}\,\forall\, t \in [t_0, t_1]$ by the definition of admissibility. Therefore, if a specific admissible function pair $(x(\cdot), u(\cdot))$ is substituted in $f(\cdot)$, then when we consider $f(\cdot)$ as a function of the single independent variable t, it must be $C^{(0)}$. Because the definite integral of a $C^{(0)}$ function exists by a fundamental theorem of integral calculus (see, e.g., Taylor and Mann, Chapter 18, Theorem III), the integral (or functional) $J[x(\cdot), u(\cdot)]$ exists. That is, $J[x(\cdot), u(\cdot)]$ is a finite value that depends on the admissible function pair $(x(\cdot), u(\cdot))$. In other words, the objective functional $J[\cdot]$ exists for all admissible function pairs $(x(\cdot), u(\cdot))$. The fundamental problem of optimal control, therefore, is that of finding an admissible function pair $(x(\cdot), u(\cdot))$ that extremizes the functional $J[\cdot]$.

In order to derive the necessary conditions in as simple and straightforward a manner as is possible, we take a *local* view of the situation. The reasoning behind this strategy is as follows. We know that if a function yields a global maximum to the objective functional $J[\cdot]$, it also yields a local maximum. Consequently, a condition that is necessary for a local maximum is also necessary for a lobal maximum. Thus, by deriving the necessary conditions for a local maximum, we simultaneously derive the necessary conditions for a global maximum. Moreover, seeing as an admissible pair $(z(\cdot), v(\cdot))$ that maximizes $J[\cdot]$ also minimizes $-J[\cdot]$, we need only consider optimal control problems in which a maximum is sought when deriving necessary conditions. As a consequence of these observations, we intend to construct an entire family of control curves that are close to, or live in a neighborhood of, the optimal control curve $v(t)$, with the property that for a particular value of some parameter, we can recover the optimal control curve $v(t)$ from the said family. Such a family of comparison curves is known as a weak variation of the optimal control function $v(\cdot)$.

To this end, we therefore consider a one-parameter family of *comparison* or *varied control curves*, that is, *weak variations* of the optimal control curve $v(t)$, defined by

$$u(t;\varepsilon) \stackrel{\text{def}}{=} v(t) + \varepsilon\eta(t), \tag{2}$$

where $v(\cdot) \in C^{(0)}$ and $v(t) \in \operatorname{int} U\ \forall\, t \in [t_0, t_1]$ is the optimal control by assumptions (A.2) and (A.3), respectively, $\eta(\cdot) \in C^{(0)}$ is an *arbitrary* fixed function, and ε is a

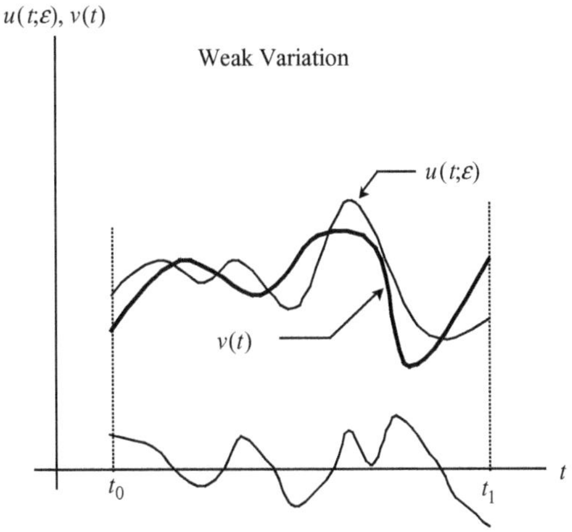

Figure 2.1

parameter. A typical graph of a weak variation of the optimal control curve $v(t)$ is given in Figure 2.1. Recall that because $v(\cdot) \in C^{(0)}$ and $u(\cdot;\varepsilon) \in C^{(0)}$, the two curves displayed in Figure 2.1 may have kinks in them, but not jumps or breaks. It is important to emphasize that in Eq. (2) the *entire* optimal path $v(t)$ has undergone a variation by the term $\varepsilon\eta(t)$, rather than just a particular value of (or point on) the optimal path. Note that this observation also holds in Figure 2.1, for the entire curve $v(t)$ has been altered to produce the neighboring curve $u(t;\varepsilon)$, entirely consistent with the construction in Eq. (2). In other words, the neighboring curve $u(t;\varepsilon)$ in Figure 2.1 was *not* produced from the curve $v(t)$ by changing only a few isolated points of it. This is directly related to the idea behind a functional introduced in Chapter 1, namely, that a functional is a map from curves to the real line. Hence, in considering how a functional varies, we must vary the *entire curve* or *function* and not just a particular point on the curve or a particular value of the function.

The idea behind the above definition of a weak variation of an optimal control curve is rather simple. In particular, given that the optimal control function $v(\cdot)$ is known to exist, we can construct an entire family of functions that have values close to those of the optimal control function by multiplying an arbitrary perturbing function $\eta(\cdot) \in C^{(0)}$ by a sufficiently small scalar ε, and then adding the resulting product $\varepsilon\eta(\cdot)$ to $v(\cdot)$. The smallness of ε ensures that the value of the product $\varepsilon\eta(t)$ is sufficiently small too. To see this, simply observe that because $\eta(\cdot) \in C^{(0)}\ \forall\, t \in [t_0, t_1]$, $\eta(t)$ is bounded due to a basic property of continuous functions defined on closed and bounded sets (see, e.g., Taylor and Mann, Chapter 17, Theorem III). In other words, because the arbitrary function $\eta(\cdot) \in C^{(0)}\ \forall\, t \in [t_0, t_1]$, there exists a number β such that $|\eta(t)| \leq \beta$ for all $t \in [t_0, t_1]$. Consequently, there exists a sufficiently small value of ε, say, $|\varepsilon| < \varepsilon_0$, such that the product $\varepsilon\eta(t)$ is sufficiently small too. Moreover, such an $\varepsilon_0 > 0$ can be found for every arbitrary perturbing function $\eta(\cdot) \in C^{(0)}$. As a result of these observations, it follows that the comparison control curves $u(t;\varepsilon)$ defined in Eq. (2) can be made to lie arbitrarily close to the optimal control curve $v(t)$

for all $t \in [t_0, t_1]$, a fact you are asked to verify in a mental exercise. What's more, because the optimal control curve $v(t) \in \text{int } U \, \forall t \in [t_0, t_1]$ by assumption (A.3), it follows that $u(t; \varepsilon) \in \text{int } U \, \forall t \in [t_0, t_1]$ as well, another fact left for a mental exercise. Note that no restrictions are placed on the value of the function $\eta(\cdot)$ at $t = t_0$ or $t = t_1$ in view of the fact that the control path is not required to meet any initial or terminal boundary conditions, unlike the state variable path.

Let us now examine what the above construction of a weak variation of the optimal control curve $v(t)$ implies for the resulting state variable time path. To begin, define $x(t; \varepsilon)$ as the time path of the state variable that results from substituting the comparison control time path $u(t; \varepsilon) \stackrel{\text{def}}{=} v(t) + \varepsilon\eta(t)$ into the state equation $\dot{x}(t) = g(t, x(t), u(t; \varepsilon))$, and integrating it using the initial condition $x(t_0) = x_0$. That is, $x(t; \varepsilon)$ is the comparison curve of the state variable that is the companion to, or paired with, $u(t; \varepsilon) \stackrel{\text{def}}{=} v(t) + \varepsilon\eta(t)$. By their very construction, therefore, it follows that $(x(t; \varepsilon), u(t; \varepsilon))$ is an admissible pair of curves for all $|\varepsilon| < \varepsilon_0$, or equivalently, $(x(\cdot; \varepsilon), u(\cdot; \varepsilon))$ is an admissible pair of functions for all $|\varepsilon| < \varepsilon_0$. In line with assumption (A.2), we now assume that $x(\cdot) \in C^{(1)}$ in both of its arguments, where ε enters parametrically. Finally, note that given a general functional form for the transition function $g(\cdot)$, it is, in general, impossible to get an explicit solution for the comparison curves $x(t; \varepsilon)$ of the state variable.

Next, observe that by definition (or construction), $u(t; 0) = v(t)$ is the optimal path of the control variable, and thus $x(t; 0) = z(t)$ is the corresponding optimal path of the state variable. It is important to emphasize that admissibility requires that *all* comparison paths of the state variable satisfy the initial condition $x(t_0) = x_0$. In other words, we have the following identity for the initial value of the comparison paths of the state variable:

$$x(t_0; \varepsilon) \equiv x_0. \tag{3}$$

This identity must hold for all $|\varepsilon| < \varepsilon_0$ in order for the comparison curves $x(t; \varepsilon)$ of the state variable to be admissible. We will return to this identity in due course.

Now *fix* the functions $\eta(\cdot) \in C^{(0)}$, $z(\cdot) \in C^{(1)}$, and $v(\cdot) \in C^{(0)}$ for all $t \in [t_0, t_1]$, and then evaluate the objective functional $J[\cdot]$ along the comparison functions $u(\cdot; \varepsilon) \stackrel{\text{def}}{=} v(\cdot) + \varepsilon\eta(\cdot)$ and $x(\cdot; \varepsilon)$. This implies that $J[\cdot]$ is a *function* of the parameter ε rather than a functional, for we have fixed the functions in its domain, and therefore the only thing left to vary is the parameter ε. Hence, we can define the function $\Phi(\cdot)$ of the single parameter ε by

$$\Phi(\varepsilon) \stackrel{\text{def}}{=} \int_{t_0}^{t_1} f(t, x(t; \varepsilon), u(t; \varepsilon))\, dt. \tag{4}$$

Recalling that $(x(t; 0), u(t; 0)) = (z(t), v(t))$ is the optimal pair by construction, it follows that $\Phi(0) = J[z(\cdot), v(\cdot)]$, which is the maximum value of the objective functional $J[\cdot]$ by assumption (A.2). Thus, by construction, $\Phi(\varepsilon) \le \Phi(0)$ for all $|\varepsilon| < \varepsilon_0$, thereby implying that the function $\Phi(\cdot)$ of one real variable ε has a relative maximum at $\varepsilon = 0$ by construction. It is important to remember, however, that the optimal and comparison paths of the state and control variables must obey the state equation in order for them to be admissible. Consequently, the optimal value of ε, videlicet, $\varepsilon = 0$, cannot be chosen without taking into account how the state equation impinges on it. For that reason, in finding the necessary conditions that a solution to problem (1) must obey, we follow a procedure reminiscent of solving constrained optimization problems by way of the method of Lagrange multipliers.

More formally, because $(x(t;\varepsilon), u(t;\varepsilon))$ is an admissible pair for all sufficiently small ε by construction, it must satisfy the state equation as an identity, that is,

$$g(t, x(t;\varepsilon), u(t;\varepsilon)) - \dot{x}(t;\varepsilon) \equiv 0 \; \forall t \in [t_0, t_1], \tag{5}$$

and for all $|\varepsilon| < \varepsilon_0$. Seeing as Eq. (5) is identically zero for all $t \in [t_0, t_1]$, we may multiply it by some as of yet unknown *function* $\lambda(\cdot) \in C^{(1)} \; \forall t \in [t_0, t_1]$, and the resulting expression will still be identically equal to zero for all $t \in [t_0, t_1]$. It is worthwhile to emphasize that because Eq. (5) is a constraint that holds for each $t \in [t_0, t_1]$, we must multiply it by a function of t rather than a single multiplier value as it is not a single constraint in the ordinary sense. Doing just that and then integrating the resulting expression over the closed interval $[t_0, t_1]$ gives

$$\int_{t_0}^{t_1} \lambda(t)[g(t, x(t;\varepsilon), u(t;\varepsilon)) - \dot{x}(t;\varepsilon)]\, dt \equiv 0 \; \forall t \in [t_0, t_1]. \tag{6}$$

Observe that Eq. (6) is identically zero for each $t \in [t_0, t_1]$ and for all $|\varepsilon| < \varepsilon_0$ because the integrand is identically zero for each $t \in [t_0, t_1]$ and for all $|\varepsilon| < \varepsilon_0$ by Eq. (5). The function $\lambda(\cdot)$ is called the *costate* or *adjoint function*. Given that the left-hand side of Eq. (6) is identically zero, we are permitted to add it to $\Phi(\varepsilon)$ in Eq. (4) without affecting the latter's value. We then use the fact that the sum of integrals is the integral of the sum, provided the integrands are continuous, which they are here under our assumptions. The result of these two operations is a new form for $\Phi(\varepsilon)$, namely,

$$\Phi(\varepsilon) \stackrel{\text{def}}{=} \int_{t_0}^{t_1} [f(t, x(t;\varepsilon), u(t;\varepsilon)) + \lambda(t)[g(t, x(t;\varepsilon), u(t;\varepsilon)) - \dot{x}(t;\varepsilon)]]\, dt, \tag{7}$$

which incorporates the state equation into the analysis. We are now in a position to proceed with the derivation of the necessary conditions.

To commence with the said derivation, we integrate the term

$$\int_{t_0}^{t_1} \lambda(t)\dot{x}(t;\varepsilon)\, dt$$

by parts. This is the expression to integrate by parts, for any term in the integrand that has been differentiated with respect to the independent variable is a prime candidate for an integration by parts operation. Thus,

$$\text{let:} \quad \left. \begin{array}{ll} p = \lambda(t) & dq = \dot{x}(t;\varepsilon)\,dt \\ dp = \dot{\lambda}(t)\,dt & q = x(t;\varepsilon) \end{array} \right\} \Rightarrow$$

$$\int_{t_0}^{t_1} \lambda(t)\dot{x}(t;\varepsilon)\,dt = \lambda(t_1)x(t_1;\varepsilon) - \lambda(t_0)x(t_0;\varepsilon) - \int_{t_0}^{t_1} \dot{\lambda}(t)x(t;\varepsilon)\,dt. \quad (8)$$

By substituting Eq. (8) into Eq. (7), we can write $\Phi(\varepsilon)$ in the following convenient form:

$$\begin{aligned} \Phi(\varepsilon) \overset{\text{def}}{=} & \int_{t_0}^{t_1} [f(t, x(t;\varepsilon), u(t;\varepsilon)) + \lambda(t)g(t, x(t;\varepsilon), u(t;\varepsilon)) + \dot{\lambda}(t)x(t;\varepsilon)]\,dt \\ & - \lambda(t_1)x(t_1;\varepsilon) + \lambda(t_0)x(t_0;\varepsilon). \end{aligned} \quad (9)$$

Because $\Phi(\varepsilon)$ attains its maximum value at $\varepsilon = 0$ by construction, as noted above, we know from static optimization theory that a necessary condition that the optimal value of ε must obey is $\Phi'(\varepsilon)|_{\varepsilon=0} = 0$ in view of the fact that we have already accounted for the effects of the state equation on the choice of ε. Hence, differentiating $\Phi(\varepsilon)$ using Leibniz's rule (Theorem A.2.1 in the appendix to this chapter), evaluating the resulting derivative at $\varepsilon = 0$, and then collecting terms, the necessary condition $\Phi'(0) \overset{\text{def}}{=} \Phi'(\varepsilon)|_{\varepsilon=0} = 0$ takes the form

$$\begin{aligned} \Phi'(0) = & \int_{t_0}^{t_1} [f_x(t, z(t), v(t)) + \lambda(t)g_x(t, z(t), v(t)) + \dot{\lambda}(t)]\, x_\varepsilon(t;0)\,dt \\ & + \int_{t_0}^{t_1} [f_u(t, z(t), v(t)) + \lambda(t)g_u(t, z(t), v(t))]\eta(t)\,dt \\ & -\lambda(t_1)x_\varepsilon(t_1;0) + \lambda(t_0)x_\varepsilon(t_0;0) = 0, \end{aligned} \quad (10)$$

where we have used $(x(t;0), u(t;0)) = (z(t), v(t))$ and $u_\varepsilon(t;0) = \eta(t)$ to simplify the resulting expression. This is the equation we want to work with in order to determine the necessary conditions of optimal control problem (1).

The first thing to notice about Eq. (10) is that the last term is identically zero due to the fixed initial condition $x(t_0;\varepsilon) \equiv x_0$, as given in Eq. (3). Recall that this identity must hold for all admissible state paths. Noting that x_0 is given (or fixed) and is therefore independent of ε, we can differentiate the identity $x(t_0;\varepsilon) \equiv x_0$ with respect to ε and evaluate the resulting derivative at $\varepsilon = 0$ to get $x_\varepsilon(t_0;0) \equiv 0$. This proves that the last term in Eq. (10) vanishes identically, as claimed. Using this result, we may rewrite Eq. (10) as

$$\Phi'(0) = \int_{t_0}^{t_1} [f_x(t, z(t), v(t)) + \lambda(t) g_x(t, z(t), v(t)) + \dot{\lambda}(t)]\, x_\varepsilon(t; 0)\, dt$$
$$+ \int_{t_0}^{t_1} [f_u(t, z(t), v(t)) + \lambda(t) g_u(t, z(t), v(t))]\, \eta(t)\, dt - \lambda(t_1) x_\varepsilon(t_1; 0) = 0, \tag{11}$$

which is the form with which we will henceforth use.

Now recall that the perturbing function $\eta(\cdot) \in C^{(0)}$ was held fixed in the above development, *but was otherwise arbitrary*. Moreover, the function $x(\cdot; \varepsilon)$ and the value $x_\varepsilon(t_1; 0)$ are arbitrary too, for the curve $u(t; \varepsilon)$ depends on the arbitrarily chosen function $\eta(\cdot)$ and thus so does the curve $x(t; \varepsilon)$, as it is the companion to $u(t; \varepsilon)$. Given these two observations, the only way to guarantee that Eq. (11) holds for *any* continuous function $\eta(\cdot)$ is for the coefficients of the two arbitrary functions $\eta(\cdot)$ and $x_\varepsilon(\cdot; 0)$ to vanish for all $t \in [t_0, t_1]$ and for the coefficient of the arbitrary value $x_\varepsilon(t_1; 0)$ to vanish at $t = t_t$. This fact therefore implies that the time path of the costate variable $\lambda(t)$ satisfies the ensuing linear ordinary differential equation and terminal boundary condition

$$\dot{\lambda}(t) = -[f_x(t, z(t), v(t)) + \lambda(t) g_x(t, z(t), v(t))], \ \lambda(t_1) = 0, \tag{12}$$

and that the following stationary condition holds:

$$f_u(t, z(t), v(t)) + \lambda(t) g_u(t, z(t), v(t)) = 0 \ \forall\, t \in [t_0, t_1]. \tag{13}$$

Remember that $z(\cdot)$ and $v(\cdot)$ are *given* functions of t, namely, the optimal ones in problem (1). Also recall that we required that the state equation and initial condition be satisfied in the course of the above development, for they were required to hold by the definition of admissibility. Hence, we have proven the following basic theorem.

Theorem 2.1 (Necessary Conditions): *Suppose $v(\cdot) \in C^{(0)}$ and $v(t) \in \text{int}U\ \forall\, t \in [t_0, t_1]$, and let $z(\cdot) \in C^{(1)}\ \forall\, t \in [t_0, t_1]$ be the corresponding state function that satisfies the state equation $\dot{x}(t) = g(t, x(t), u(t))$ and initial condition $x(t_0) = x_0$, so that $(z(t), v(t))$ is an admissible pair. Then if $(z(t), v(t))$ yields the absolute (or global) maximum of $J[x(\cdot), u(\cdot)]$ when $x(t_1) = x_1$ is a decision variable, it is necessary that there exist a function $\lambda(\cdot) \in C^{(1)}\ \forall\, t \in [t_0, t_1]$ such that*

$$f_u(t, z(t), v(t)) + \lambda(t) g_u(t, z(t), v(t)) = 0 \ \forall\, t \in [t_0, t_1], \tag{14}$$

$$\dot{\lambda}(t) = -[f_x(t, z(t), v(t)) + \lambda(t) g_x(t, z(t), v(t))], \ \lambda(t_1) = 0, \tag{15}$$

$$\dot{z}(t) = g(t, z(t), v(t)), \ z(t_0) = x_0. \tag{16}$$

Equation (14) may be called the *simplified Maximum Principle*, the adjective simplified arising from our assumption that $v(t) \in \text{int } U \ \forall t \in [t_0, t_1]$. The pair of differential equations (15) and (16) are frequently called the *canonical equations*. Individually, Eq. (15) is referred to as the *costate equation*, whereas Eq. (16) is called the *state equation*. The free terminal boundary condition $\lambda(t_1) = 0$ is often called a *transversality condition*.

Recall that in constrained static optimization problems, the necessary and sufficient conditions are best stated and remembered by introducing an auxiliary function known as the Lagrangian. We can employ a similar function for optimal control problems, called the *Hamiltonian* $H(\cdot)$. It is defined as

$$H(t, x, u, \lambda) \stackrel{\text{def}}{=} f(t, x, u) + \lambda g(t, x, u), \tag{17}$$

from which it follows that

$$\frac{\partial H}{\partial u}(t, x, u, \lambda) = f_u(t, x, u) + \lambda g_u(t, x, u),$$

$$\frac{\partial H}{\partial x}(t, x, u, \lambda) = f_x(t, x, u) + \lambda g_x(t, x, u),$$

$$\frac{\partial H}{\partial \lambda}(t, x, u, \lambda) = g(t, x, u).$$

Given these results, we can restate Theorem 2.1 in the following form, which is far easier to remember and use.

Theorem 2.2 (Necessary Conditions): *Suppose* $v(\cdot) \in C^{(0)}$ *and* $v(t) \in \text{int} U \ \forall t \in [t_0, t_1]$, *and let* $z(\cdot) \in C^{(1)} \ \forall t \in [t_0, t_1]$ *be the corresponding state function that satisfies the state equation* $\dot{x}(t) = g(t, x(t), u(t))$ *and initial condition* $x(t_0) = x_0$, *so that* $(z(t), v(t))$ *is an admissible pair. Define the Hamiltonian as* $H(t, x, u, \lambda) \stackrel{def}{=} f(t, x, u) + \lambda g(t, x, u)$. *Then if* $(z(t), v(t))$ *yields the absolute (or global) maximum of* $J[x(\cdot), u(\cdot)]$ *when* $x(t_1) = x_1$ *is a decision variable, it is necessary that there exist a function* $\lambda(\cdot) \in C^{(1)} \ \forall t \in [t_0, t_1]$ *such that*

$$H_u(t, z(t), v(t), \lambda(t)) = 0 \ \forall t \in [t_0, t_1], \tag{18}$$

$$\dot{\lambda}(t) = -H_x(t, z(t), v(t), \lambda(t)), \ \ \lambda(t_1) = 0, \tag{19}$$

$$\dot{z}(t) = H_\lambda(t, z(t), v(t), \lambda(t)), \ \ z(t_0) = x_0. \tag{20}$$

The form of the necessary conditions given in Theorem 2.2 is that which you should remember. Moreover, it is important to understand the notation employed in the necessary condition $H_u(t, z(t), v(t), \lambda(t)) = 0 \ \forall t \in [t_0, t_1]$. It means that the Hamiltonian function $H(\cdot)$ is first partially differentiated with respect to the control variable, and *then* evaluated along the optimal solution path. That is, more explicitly,

$$H_u(t, z(t), v(t), \lambda(t)) = \left. \frac{\partial H}{\partial u}(t, x, u, \lambda) \right|_{(z(t), v(t), \lambda(t))} = 0 \ \forall t \in [t_0, t_1].$$

Notice that by formulating the necessary conditions in terms of the Hamiltonian, it becomes clear that the condition $\partial H/\partial u = 0$ means that for each $t \in [t_0, t_1]$, we choose the control variable so that the Hamiltonian function is stationary for given values of the state and costate variables. In fact, as we will show in Chapter 4, when we present the necessary conditions for a more general class of control problems, the control variable will be chosen so as to maximize the Hamiltonian at each $t \in [t_0, t_1]$ for given values of the state and costate variables.

In principle, the optimal control problem can be solved in the following way to arrive at the paths of the optimal solution triplet $(z(t), v(t), \lambda(t))$, assuming, of course, that such an optimal solution exists. First, notice that we have three equations in Theorem 2.2 in which to solve for the three unknown paths $(z(t), v(t), \lambda(t))$, so in principle, we have the correct number of equations. Moreover, the solution of the canonical equations yields two constants of integration, which can be determined from the initial condition and transversality condition.

Next, notice that the necessary condition $\partial H/\partial u = 0$ is just like a first-order necessary condition from static optimization theory. Written in full it is

$$\frac{\partial H}{\partial u}(t, x, u, \lambda) = 0. \tag{21}$$

Hence if $H_{uu} \neq 0$ along the optimal path for all $t \in [t_0, t_1]$, then by the implicit function theorem we can in principle solve Eq. (21) for u in terms of (t, x, λ), say, $u = \hat{u}(t, x, \lambda)$. Then we can substitute $u = \hat{u}(t, x, \lambda)$ into the canonical differential equations to get

$$\dot{x} = H_\lambda(t, x, \hat{u}(t, x, \lambda), \lambda), \ x(t_0) = x_0, \tag{22}$$

$$\dot{\lambda} = -H_x(t, x, \hat{u}(t, x, \lambda), \lambda), \ \lambda(t_1) = 0. \tag{23}$$

Notice that the control variable u no longer appears in Eqs. (22) and (23) since we have used the implicit function theorem to solve $\partial H/\partial u = 0$ for u in terms of (t, x, λ). Hence, the canonical differential equations (22) and (23) depend only on (t, x, λ). They form a two-point boundary value problem because the state variable is fixed at the initial date of the planning horizon and the costate variable is fixed at zero at the terminal date. Solution of the canonical differential equations along with the boundary conditions yields the optimal solution path for the state and costate variables, scilicet, $(z(t), \lambda(t))$. Substituting these optimal paths into $u = \hat{u}(t, x, \lambda)$ yields the optimal path of the control variable, namely, $v(t) \stackrel{\text{def}}{=} \hat{u}(t, z(t), \lambda(t))$. The optimal path of the control variable $v(t)$ is termed the *open-loop* solution because the control variable is expressed as a function of the independent variable t (and the problem's parameters) but not the value of the state variable at time t.

It is beneficial at this juncture to introduce the economic interpretation of the costate variable $\lambda(t)$. To this end, let's interpret the state variable $x(t)$ as the capital stock of a firm at time t. The objective of the firm is the maximization of its present discounted value of profit, that is, its wealth. Such a wealth-maximizing firm implicitly places a monetary value on the capital stock it owns, and thus similarly places a monetary value on increments to its capital stock at each date of its planning horizon. The costate variable $\lambda(t)$ is precisely the value to the firm of an additional unit of the capital stock. That is, $\lambda(t)$ is the firm's *internal* valuation of another unit of capital. In other words, $\lambda(t)$ measures the increase in the firm's wealth if it had one more unit of capital on hand at time t. Thus $\lambda(t)$ is the most the firm would pay for another unit of capital at time t. In economics, such internal incremental valuations go by the name of *shadow price, shadow value*, or *marginal value*. We may therefore interpret $\lambda(t)$ as the shadow value of the firm's capital stock at time t. Formal justification for this economic interpretation will have to wait for Chapter 9, but we will see some mathematical justification for it in Chapters 3 and 4.

Let's now examine two simple mathematical examples to get some practice at solving the necessary conditions of Theorem 2.2 under our set of simplifying assumptions. After this, we will solve an optimal control problem of some importance in dynamic economic theory, to wit, the adjustment cost model of the firm, and then investigate some of its qualitative properties.

Example 2.1: Consider the optimal control problem

$$\max_{u(\cdot),x_1} J[x(\cdot),u(\cdot)] \stackrel{\text{def}}{=} \int_0^1 \left[-x(t) - \frac{1}{2}\alpha[u(t)]^2\right] dt$$

$$\text{s.t.} \quad \dot{x}(t) = u(t),$$

$$x(0) = x_0, \; x(1) = x_1,$$

where $\alpha > 0$ is a parameter. The Hamiltonian is defined as $H(t,x,u,\lambda;\alpha) \stackrel{\text{def}}{=} -x - \frac{1}{2}\alpha u^2 + \lambda u$. By Theorem 2.2, the necessary conditions are

$$H_u(t,x,u,\lambda;\alpha) = -\alpha u + \lambda = 0,$$

$$\dot{\lambda} = -H_x(t,x,u,\lambda;\alpha) = 1, \; \lambda(1) = 0,$$

$$\dot{x} = H_\lambda(t,x,u,\lambda;\alpha) = u, \; x(0) = x_0.$$

Solving the necessary condition $H_u(t,x,u,\lambda;\alpha) = -\alpha u + \lambda = 0$, we get $u = \alpha^{-1}\lambda$. Substituting this into the canonical differential equations gives

$$\dot{\lambda} = 1, \; \lambda(1) = 0,$$

$$\dot{x} = \alpha^{-1}\lambda, \; x(0) = x_0.$$

Notice that we have followed the recipe given earlier for solving the necessary conditions of optimal control problems.

Now integrate the costate equation $\dot{\lambda} = 1$ to get the general solution $\lambda(t) = t + c_1$, where c_1 is an arbitrary constant of integration. Using the transversality condition $\lambda(1) = 0$ implies that $c_1 = -1$, so the specific solution of the costate equation is $\lambda(t) = t - 1$. Substituting this into the state equation yields $\dot{x} = \alpha^{-1}(t-1)$, and a routine integration results in the general solution $x(t) = (2\alpha)^{-1}t^2 - \alpha^{-1}t + c_2$, where c_2 is another constant of integration. Using the initial condition $x(0) = x_0$ implies that $c_2 = x_0$, so the specific solution of the state equation is $z(t;\alpha, x_0) = (2\alpha)^{-1}t^2 - \alpha^{-1}t + x_0$. Finally, substitute $\lambda(t) = t - 1$ into $u = \alpha^{-1}\lambda$ to find the corresponding path of the control variable, namely, $v(t;\alpha) = \alpha^{-1}(t-1)$. Hence the solution to the necessary conditions is given by

$$\begin{aligned} v(t;\alpha) &= \alpha^{-1}(t-1), \\ z(t;\alpha, x_0) &= (2\alpha)^{-1}t^2 - \alpha^{-1}t + x_0, \\ \lambda(t) &= t - 1. \end{aligned}$$

Notice the paths for the state and control variables depend on the parameters α and x_0, just like solutions to static optimization problems. Hence, we could differentiate $v(\cdot)$ and $z(\cdot)$ with respect to α to compute the comparative dynamics of the problem. We will delay such considerations until Example 2.3, however, when a meaningful economic problem is developed and solved.

Example 2.2: Consider the control problem

$$\max_{u(\cdot), x_1} J[x(\cdot), u(\cdot)] \overset{\text{def}}{=} \int_0^1 \left[\alpha t u(t) - \frac{1}{2}[u(t)]^2\right] dt$$

$$\begin{aligned} \text{s.t.} \quad & \dot{x}(t) = u(t) - x(t), \\ & x(0) = x_0, \ x(1) = x_1. \end{aligned}$$

The Hamiltonian is given by $H(t, x, u, \lambda; \alpha) \overset{\text{def}}{=} \alpha t u - \frac{1}{2}u^2 + \lambda[u - x]$, so the necessary conditions from Theorem 2.2 are given by

$$\begin{aligned} H_u(t, x, u, \lambda; \alpha) &= \alpha t - u + \lambda = 0, \\ \dot{\lambda} = -H_x(t, x, u, \lambda; \alpha) &= \lambda, \ \lambda(1) = 0, \\ \dot{x} = H_\lambda(t, x, u, \lambda; \alpha) &= u - x, \ x(0) = x_0. \end{aligned}$$

From $H_u = 0$, we have $u = \alpha t + \lambda$. Separate the variables in the costate equation to get $\frac{d\lambda}{\lambda} = dt$, which readily integrates to $\ln \lambda = t + c_1$, where c_1 is a constant of integration. This general solution can be rewritten as $\lambda(t) = k_1 e^t$, where $k_1 \overset{\text{def}}{=} e^{c_1}$. The transversality condition $\lambda(1) = 0$ implies that $k_1 = 0$. Hence the specific solution of the costate equation is $\lambda(t) = 0 \; \forall \, t \in [0, 1]$. This, in turn, implies that $v(t;\alpha) = \alpha t$ is the path of the control variable. Using $v(t;\alpha) = \alpha t$ in the state equation gives $\dot{x} = \alpha t - x$, or $\dot{x} + x = \alpha t$. The integrating factor for this ordinary differential equation is given by

$$\mu(t) \stackrel{\text{def}}{=} \exp\left[\int^t ds\right] = e^t.$$

Hence, upon multiplying $\dot{x} + x = \alpha t$ on both sides by e^t we have $\dot{x}e^t + xe^t = \frac{d}{dt}[xe^t] = \alpha te^t$. Integrating both sides gives $xe^t = \alpha \int te^t dt + k_2$, where k_2 is a constant of integration. Now perform an integration-by-parts exercise on this by letting $p = t$, so that $dp = dt$, and letting $dq = e^t\, dt$, so that $q = e^t$, thereby yielding

$$\int te^t dt = te^t - \int e^t dt = e^t[t-1].$$

Thus the general solution of the state equation is $x(t) = \alpha[t-1] + k_2 e^{-t}$. Using the initial condition $x(0) = x_0$ implies that $k_2 = \alpha + x_0$. The specific solution to the state equation is therefore given by $z(t; \alpha, x_0) = \alpha[t-1] + [\alpha + x_0]\, e^{-t}$. In sum, the solution to the necessary conditions is

$$v(t; \alpha) = \alpha t,$$

$$z(t; \alpha, x_0) = \alpha[t-1] + [\alpha + x_0]\, e^{-t},$$

$$\lambda(t) = 0\ \forall\, t \in [0, 1],$$

which depends on the parameters α and x_0, just like the solution of the necessary conditions in Example 2.1.

In closing out this example, it is worthwhile to pause and emphasize a somewhat unexpected feature of the solution of the necessary conditions. In particular, take note of the fact that the time path of the control variable that solves the necessary conditions, to wit, $v(t; \alpha) = \alpha t$, is *identical* to the value of the control variable that maximizes the integrand function at each t. In effect, this means that the above control problem is not really a dynamic optimization problem. Moreover, the state equation has no effect on the solution for the control variable. This is consistent with the discussion in Chapter 1, in which we emphasized that it was the state equation, and the appearance of the control variable in it, that made for a dynamic optimization problem. In this example, however, the control variable does appear in the state equation, so that is not the source of this atypical result. Two features are responsible for the peculiarity: (i) the integrand function is independent of the state variable, and (ii) the terminal value of the state variable is a decision variable. In Chapter 3, we will see in general why this is so.

Now that we have seen how to use Theorem 2.2 to find solution candidates, let's now use it to examine an intertemporal economic model of the firm and, more importantly, demonstrate how qualitative information about the model may be uncovered. This example and the manner in which it is solved and analyzed are therefore more in accord with how economists use optimal control theory in order to reach economic insights about a particular behavioral model.

Example 2.3: In this example, we examine a simplified version of the adjustment cost model of the capital accumulating firm that we introduced in Example 1.2. Moreover, by making some functional form assumptions, we will be able to explicitly calculate the solution to the necessary conditions. To that end, let the single output-producing firm have a linear production function, say, $f(K) \stackrel{\text{def}}{=} K$, where the capital stock at time t, $K(t)$, is measured in units such that one unit of capital produces one unit of output. The output is sold at the constant price $p > 0$, and holding (or maintenance) costs per unit of the capital stock are constant and given by $w > 0$, where it is assumed that $p - w > 0$. The cost of buying and installing new purchases of the capital stock are given by the cost of adjustment function $C(\cdot)$, with values $C(I) \stackrel{\text{def}}{=} \frac{1}{2}cI^2$, where $I(t)$ is the gross investment rate at time t and $c > 0$ is a cost of adjustment parameter. Assume that depreciation is nonexistent, so that $I(t)$ can then also be interpreted as the net investment rate at time t. For the purpose of obtaining a simpler solution of the necessary conditions, assume that the firm does *not* discount its flow of profit. The firm begins its operation at time $t = 0$ with the given capital stock $K_0 > 0$, but has the freedom to choose its terminal capital stock $K_T > 0$ at the end of its given planning horizon $T > 0$. The firm must have a nonnegative stock of capital on hand at all times, which implies the constraint $K(t) \geq 0 \; \forall \, t \in [0, T]$, but it may buy or sell the capital stock, thereby implying that $I(t)$ may be positive, zero, or negative in each period of the planning horizon. The firm is asserted to solve the following optimal control problem:

$$\max_{I(\cdot), k_T} J[K(\cdot), I(\cdot)] \stackrel{\text{def}}{=} \int_0^T \left[pK(t) - wK(t) - \frac{1}{2}c[I(t)]^2 \right] dt$$

$$\text{s.t.} \quad \dot{K}(t) = I(t),\, K(0) = K_0,\, K(T) = K_T.$$

Notice that we have ignored that constraint $K(t) \geq 0 \; \forall \, t \in [0, T]$ in the problem statement. We will show that this is justified by proving that a solution of the necessary conditions will have $K(t) > 0 \; \forall \, t \in [0, T]$.

Defining the Hamiltonian as $H(K, I, \lambda) \stackrel{\text{def}}{=} [p - w]K - \frac{1}{2}cI^2 + \lambda I$, Theorem 2.2 yields the ensuing necessary conditions:

$$H_I(K, I, \lambda) = -cI + \lambda = 0, \tag{24}$$

$$\dot{\lambda} = -H_K(K, I, \lambda) = w - p, \; \lambda(T) = 0, \tag{25}$$

$$\dot{K} = H_\lambda(K, I, \lambda) = I, \; K(0) = K_0. \tag{26}$$

Before solving the necessary conditions, let's see what qualitative information can be gleaned from them. First, observe that because $[p - w] > 0$ by assumption $\dot{\lambda}(t) < 0 \; \forall \, t \in [0, T]$ from Eq. (25). Second, because $\lambda(T) = 0$, it in addition follows that $\lambda(t) > 0 \; \forall \, t \in [0, T)$. Third, in view of the fact that $I(t) = c^{-1}\lambda(t)$ from Eq. (24), $c > 0$ by assumption, and $\lambda(t) > 0 \; \forall \, t \in [0, T)$, it follows that $I(t) > 0 \; \forall \, t \in [0, T)$. Fourth, as $I(t) = c^{-1}\lambda(t)$ and $\lambda(T) = 0$, we have that $I(T) = 0$. Fifth, given that $\dot{K}(t) = I(t)$ and $K(0) = K_0 > 0$ from Eq. (26), and that $I(t) > 0 \; \forall \, t \in [0, T)$ and

$I(T) = 0$, it follows that $\dot{K}(t) > 0 \; \forall \, t \in [0, T)$, $\dot{K}(T) = 0$ and that $K(t) > 0 \; \forall \, t \in [0, T]$, the latter demonstrating that the nonnegativity restriction on the capital stock is not binding in an optimal plan (assuming that one exists). In words, we have shown that (i) the shadow value of the capital stock is positive throughout the planning horizon and zero only at the terminal date, (ii) the shadow value of the capital stock is decreasing throughout the planning horizon, (iii) the investment rate is positive throughout the planning horizon and zero only at the terminal date, and (iv) the capital stock is positive throughout the planning horizon. Observe that the above results demonstrate the equivalence of the transversality condition $\lambda(T) = 0$ and the investment rate $I(T) = 0$. This equivalence is intuitive, for once the firm enters the last period of the planning horizon, there is no more future. Thus by purchasing capital goods in the last period, the firm would only incur costs of adjustment, but no benefits (increased future output) from doing so. Finally, note that all of these qualitative conclusions were derived without actually solving the necessary conditions. Let's now turn to the explicit solution of the necessary conditions.

Integrating the costate equation, we get the general solution $\lambda(t) = [w - p]t + a_1$, where a_1 is a constant of integration. The transversality condition $\lambda(T) = 0$ implies that $a_1 = [p - w]T > 0$, given that $[p - w] > 0$. The specific solution to the costate equation is therefore given by the expression $\lambda(t; p, w, T) = [p - w][T - t] \geq 0 \; \forall \, t \in [0, T]$. Because $I(t) = c^{-1}\lambda(t)$ from Eq. (24), the time path of the investment rate is given by $I^*(t; c, p, w, T) = c^{-1}[p - w][T - t] \geq 0 \; \forall \, t \in [0, T]$. Using this expression, the state equation becomes $\dot{K} = c^{-1}[p - w][T - t]$, which upon integration yields the general solution $K(t) = c^{-1}[p - w][T - (t/2)]t + a_2$, where a_2 is another constant of integration. Using the initial condition $K(0) = K_0$ gives $a_2 = K_0$ as the value of the constant of integration. The specific solution for the time path of the capital stock is therefore given by $K^*(t; c, p, w, K_0, T) = c^{-1}[p - w][T - (t/2)]t + K_0$. Recalling that the production function is given by $f(K) \stackrel{\text{def}}{=} K$, we may also interpret $K^*(t; c, p, w, K_0, T)$ equivalently as the time path of output of the firm. In passing, note that because the triplet $(K^*(t; c, p, w, K_0, T), I^*(t; c, p, w, T), \lambda(t; p, w, T))$ is the *only* solution of the necessary conditions, we know that *if* an optimal solution exists to the adjustment cost model, then this triplet is the unique optimal solution.

In the prototypical models of the competitive firm, such as cost minimization and profit maximization, the demand and supply functions are positively homogeneous of degree zero in the prices. The same is true of the investment demand function $I^*(\cdot)$ in the above adjustment cost model. To see this, simply observe that for any $\theta \in \Re_{++}$, we have that

$$\begin{aligned} I^*(t; \theta c, \theta p, \theta w, T) &= \frac{[\theta p - \theta w]}{\theta c}[T - t] = \frac{\theta[p - w]}{\theta c}[T - t] \\ &= \frac{[p - w]}{c}[T - t] = I^*(t; c, p, w, T), \end{aligned}$$

which is the definition of positive homogeneity of degree zero in (c, p, w). This asserts that if the output price, holding cost per unit of capital, and adjustment costs all rise proportionally, then there is no change in the investment rate of the firm. A mental exercise asks you to examine some other homogeneity properties present in the model. Let's now turn to some comparative dynamics calculations.

Because we have explicit solutions for the time paths of the capital stock (or equivalently, output), the investment rate, and the shadow value of the capital stock, one method of conducting a comparative dynamics analysis is to differentiate these explicit solutions with respect to the parameter of interest. By way of example, let's consider the effects of an increase in the output price p. Differentiating the triplet $(K^*(t; c, p, w, K_0, T), I^*(t; c, p, w, T), \lambda(t; p, w, T))$ with respect to p yields

$$\frac{\partial K^*}{\partial p}(t; c, p, w, K_0, T) = c^{-1}[T - (t/2)]t \begin{cases} = 0 \text{ at } t = 0 \\ > 0 \; \forall t \in (0, T], \end{cases} \tag{27}$$

$$\frac{\partial I^*}{\partial p}(t; c, p, w, T) = c^{-1}[T - t] \begin{cases} > 0 \; \forall t \in [0, T) \\ = 0 \text{ at } t = T, \end{cases} \tag{28}$$

$$\frac{\partial \lambda}{\partial p}(t; p, w, T) = [T - t] \begin{cases} > 0 \; \forall t \in [0, T) \\ = 0 \text{ at } t = T. \end{cases} \tag{29}$$

Equation (28) shows that an increase in the output price drives up the investment rate of the firm in every period but the last. This is not unexpected, for the capital stock of the firm is the only input to production, and Eq. (27) shows that the firm produces more of its now more valuable output. Hence the only way to achieve this end is for the firm to invest more in its only input. Finally, in view of the fact that product produced by the firm is now more valuable in the market, the firm values its capital input more highly too, just as Eq. (29) shows. We elect to end the discussion here and relegate the remaining comparative dynamics calculations and interpretations to a mental exercise.

The final theorem in this chapter is an important generalization of Theorem 2.2. Moreover, the generalization is a natural one from an economic point of view. To see this, you may have noticed that in the control problem (1) studied so far, there was no value placed on the state variable remaining at the terminal time; that is, the benefit associated with a positive stock of capital at the terminal date was zero. In other words, even though we let the decision maker optimally select the terminal amount of the state variable, we assumed that the salvage or scrap value of the state variable remaining at the terminal date was zero. In most economic situations, the capital remaining after the firm has shut down still has some value in the market. Hence, we now relax that rather simple-minded situation and consider the following *scrap value* or *salvage value* optimal control problem:

$$\max_{u(\cdot),x_1} J_S[x(\cdot), u(\cdot)] \stackrel{\text{def}}{=} \int_{t_0}^{t_1} f(t, x(t), u(t))\, dt + S(x_1)$$

$$\text{s.t.} \quad \dot{x}(t) = g(t, x(t), u(t)), \tag{30}$$

$$x(t_0) = x_0, \ x(t_1) = x_1.$$

In order to proceed, we must impose the following additional assumption on problem (30):

(A.4) $S(\cdot) \in C^{(1)}$ over an open convex set.

The proof of the following theorem is relegated to the mental exercises, as it is a straightforward extension of the proof of Theorem 2.1.

Theorem 2.3 (Necessary Conditions, Salvage Value): *Suppose that* $v(\cdot) \in C^{(0)}$ *and that* $v(t) \in \text{int}\, U\ \forall\, t \in [t_0, t_1]$, *and let* $z(\cdot) \in C^{(1)}\ \forall\, t \in [t_0, t_1]$ *be the corresponding state function that satisfies the state equation* $\dot{x}(t) = g(t, x(t), u(t))$ *and initial condition* $x(t_0) = x_0$, *so that* $(z(t), v(t))$ *is an admissible pair. Then if* $(z(t), v(t))$ *yields the absolute (or global) maximum of* $J_S[x(\cdot), u(\cdot)]$ *when* $x(t_1) = x_1$ *is a decision variable, it is necessary that there exist a function* $\lambda(\cdot) \in C^{(1)}\ \forall\, t \in [t_0, t_1]$ *such that*

$$H_u(t, z(t), v(t), \lambda(t)) = 0\ \forall\, t \in [t_0, t_1], \tag{31}$$

$$\dot{\lambda}(t) = -H_x(t, z(t), v(t), \lambda(t)), \ \lambda(t_1) = S'(z(t_1)), \tag{32}$$

$$\dot{z}(t) = H_\lambda(t, z(t), v(t), \lambda(t)), \ z(t_0) = x_0. \tag{33}$$

In the last example of this chapter, we employ Theorem 2.3 to solve a variant of the inventory accumulation problem introduced in Example 1.4. Moreover, we will conduct a relatively comprehensive comparative dynamics analysis of the problem, without which the economic intuition and insight provided by the model would be less than what one would get from interpretation of the necessary conditions alone.

Example 2.4: Let's revisit the inventory accumulation problem originally stated in Example 1.4, but with a slight twist on it. Specifically, now contemplate the case in which the firm in question can decide on the terminal amount of the good held in inventory, that is, $x(T) = x_T$ is now a decision variable. Moreover, the firm can sell its accumulated inventory $x(T) = x_T$ at the terminal date T in one chunk to a retail firm at a price of $p > 0$, thereby generating revenue of px_T dollars. The firm still incurs production and inventory holding costs as before, but now seeks a production schedule to maximize its profit from the production and sale of the good produced.

That is, the firm now solves the following salvage value control problem:

$$\max_{u(\cdot),x_T} J_S[x(\cdot), u(\cdot)] \stackrel{\text{def}}{=} px_T - \int_0^T \left[c_1[u(t)]^2 + c_2 x(t)\right] dt$$

$$\text{s.t.} \quad \dot{x}(t) = u(t), \; x(0) = 0, \; x(T) = x_T,$$

where all terms are as defined earlier. Notice that in this version of the problem, the revenue received by the firm comes only at the terminal date when all the inventory is sold, whereas production and storage costs are incurred continuously throughout the planning horizon as the good is produced and stored. Assume that $p > c_2 T$, an assumption that we will return to in the course of solving this problem.

Define the Hamiltonian for this salvage value control problem as

$$H(x, u, \lambda; c_1, c_2) \stackrel{\text{def}}{=} -c_1 u^2 - c_2 x + \lambda u,$$

where λ is the costate variable. We will prove in Chapter 9 that λ at time t has the economic interpretation of the marginal or shadow value of the state variable at time t. Hence we may interpret $\lambda(t)$ as the shadow value of a unit of the good in inventory at time t, given that the state variable $x(t)$ is the stock of the good in inventory at time t. Note that the Hamiltonian is defined *excluding* the salvage value term.

According to Theorem 2.3, the necessary conditions are given by

$$H_u = -2c_1 u + \lambda = 0,$$

$$\dot{\lambda} = -H_x = c_2, \lambda(T) = p,$$

$$\dot{x} = H_\lambda = u, \; x(0) = 0.$$

Seeing as the necessary condition $H_u = 0$ defines the production rate in terms of the shadow value of the stock, that is, $u = \lambda/(2c_1)$, and the state equation defines the rate of change of the stock in terms of the production rate, that is, $\dot{x} = u$, the key to solving the necessary conditions is to therefore solve the costate equation.

Before we begin solving the necessary conditions, observe that because $\dot{\lambda} = c_2 > 0$ and $\lambda(T) = p > 0$, the shadow value of the inventory increases over the planning horizon until it equals the market price of the good at the terminal date, at which time the stock of inventory is sold. This is intuitive, for an additional unit of inventory at the initial date must incur larger storage costs than an additional unit of inventory produced at a later date, so we would expect the shadow value of the inventory to rise over time. Furthermore, at the terminal date, an additional unit of inventory does not have to be held and so incurs no storage cost, and thus is valued at the market price.

To solve the costate equation $\dot{\lambda} = c_2$, separate the variables to get $d\lambda = c_2\, dt$, and then integrate to get the general solution $\lambda = a_1 + c_2 t$, where a_1 is a constant of integration. Next, use the transversality condition $\lambda(T) = p$ to find that $a_1 = p - c_2 T > 0$, the inequality resulting from the assumption that $p > c_2 T$. The specific solution to the costate equation is therefore given by $\lambda(t; c_2, p, T) = p + c_2[t - T]$.

In view of the fact that $\lambda(0; c_2, p, T) = p - c_2T > 0$, we conclude, in addition to what we did in the previous paragraph, that the shadow value of the inventory is positive throughout the planning horizon. Moreover, notice that it is the presence of the inventory holding costs that causes the divergence between the shadow value of the inventory and the market price of the good. In other words, if the good was costless to store, then the shadow value of the inventory would be equal to the market price of the good throughout the planning horizon.

The solution of the necessary conditions for the production rate is found by substituting $\lambda(t; c_2, p, T) = p + c_2[t - T]$ into $u = \lambda/(2c_1)$, thereby yielding $v(t; \beta) = [p + c_2[t - T]]/(2c_1)$, where $\beta \stackrel{\text{def}}{=} (c_1, c_2, p, T)$ is the parameter vector for the problem. Since $v(0; \beta) = [p - c_2T]/(2c_1) > 0$ and $\dot{v}(t; \beta) = c_2/(2c_1) > 0$, the production rate is positive throughout the planning horizon and increasing over time. This latter feature is a result of the storage cost of the inventory, that is, $c_2 > 0$ rather than $c_2 = 0$. In other words, the positive cost associated with inventory storage biases the firm's production plan to produce the good at a higher rate in the latter part of the planning horizon because such goods will incur lower storage costs than those produced earlier in the planning horizon.

The time path of the inventory stock that solves the necessary conditions is found by substituting $v(t; \beta) = [p + c_2[t - T]]/(2c_1)$ in the state equation, separating the variables and integrating, thus giving $x = t[2p + c_2[t - 2T]]/(4c_1) + a_2$ as the general solution, where a_2 is a constant of integration. The initial condition $x(0) = 0$ implies that $a_2 = 0$. Thus the specific solution for the inventory stock is $z(t; \beta) = t[2p + c_2[t - 2T]]/(4c_1)$. In passing, note that the assumption $p > c_2T$ is sufficient to conclude that for all $t \in [0, T]$, the shadow value of the inventory is positive and the production rate is positive, and thus a positive amount of the good will be produced and sold by the firm. The assumption $p > c_2T$ means that the market price of the good is greater than the storage cost of a unit of the good produced in the initial period of the planning horizon.

To finish up this example, let's do a simple comparative dynamics exercise and provide an economic interpretation of the results, focusing on the time path of the production rate $v(t; \beta) = [p + c_2[t - T]]/(2c_1)$, the shadow value of the inventory $\lambda(t; c_2, p, T) = p + c_2[t - T]$, and the amount of the good sold $z(T; \beta) = T[2p - c_2T]/(4c_1)$ (given that this is a decision variable in the current version of the model). Differentiating these solutions with respect to, say, c_2, gives

$$\frac{\partial v(t; \beta)}{\partial c_2} = \frac{t - T}{2c_1} \begin{cases} < 0 \ \forall\, t \in [0, T), \\ = 0 \ \text{ at } \ t = T, \end{cases} \tag{34}$$

$$\frac{\partial \lambda(t; c_2, p, T)}{\partial c_2} = [t - T] \begin{cases} < 0 \ \forall\, t \in [0, T), \\ = 0 \ \text{ at } \ t = T, \end{cases} \tag{35}$$

$$\frac{\partial z(T; \beta)}{\partial c_2} = \frac{-T^2}{4c_1} < 0. \tag{36}$$

Equation (36) shows that the higher inventory holding costs result in lower total production of the good. By Eq. (36), the firm accomplishes this by producing the good at a slower rate in all the periods in the planning horizon except the last. Equation (35) shows that the shadow value of the inventory is lower as a result of the increase in the inventory holding costs. This was to be expected, given that an additional unit of the good in inventory now costs the firm more to hold and is thus less valuable to the firm.

These comparative dynamics results turn out to contrast sharply with those of the simple version of the inventory accumulation model developed in Example 1.4, as we will see in Chapter 4. For example, in the simple model, an increase in holding costs does not affect total production of the good because it is fixed by assumption. Rather, it results in the production rate being lower in the first half of the planning horizon and higher in the second half of the planning horizon, with the net effect leaving total production unchanged. The remaining comparative dynamics of this model and their economic interpretation are left for the mental exercises.

In closing out this chapter, it is worthwhile to stress a few important aspects of the results developed herein. First, remember that Theorems 2.2 and 2.3 give a set of *necessary conditions* for a pair of curves $(z(t), v(t))$ to yield a maximum (or minimum) of the functional $J[\cdot]$ or $J_s[\cdot]$. Therefore, just because a pair of curves satisfies the necessary conditions of Theorems 2.2 and 2.3, we cannot, at this juncture, be sure that the pair actually solves the optimal control problem under consideration. In particular, we *cannot* conclude that the solutions of the necessary conditions of Examples 2.1–2.4 solve the posed optimal control problem. That is the nature of necessary conditions in optimization problems. Once we have studied sufficient conditions in the next chapter, however, we will be able to conclude that the solutions of the necessary conditions of Examples 2.1–2.4 are in fact the unique solutions to the posed optimal control problems. In attempting to find a solution to an optimal control problem, one therefore searches for solutions of the necessary conditions, for an optimal solution must satisfy them. In other words, if a function does not satisfy the necessary conditions, then it cannot be the solution to the optimal control problem under consideration.

Typically, a central issue in economics when employing optimal control theory is this: "Given an objective functional $J[\cdot]$, find an admissible pair of functions $(z(\cdot), v(\cdot))$ such that $J[z(\cdot), v(\cdot)] \geq J[x(\cdot), u(\cdot)]$ for all admissible function pairs $(x(\cdot), u(\cdot))$." As a result, we can employ Theorem 2.2 (or its numerous generalizations) to obtain candidate functions. *If a maximizing pair of functions exists* and the hypotheses of Theorem 2.2 are met, then a maximizing pair of functions is among the solutions to the necessary conditions of Theorem 2.2. To verify that a particular admissible pair is indeed maximizing, one may proceed in two ways:

(i) Find *all* pairs of functions that are solutions of the necessary conditions. Prove the existence of a maximizing pair of functions that are admissible and show that all the hypotheses of Theorem 2.2 are met. Compare the values of $J[\cdot]$ for all solution pairs of the necessary conditions.

(ii) Employ *sufficient* conditions for a maximizing pair of functions to verify that a particular solution pair of the necessary conditions is maximizing.

In any case, the usual first step is to utilize Theorem 2.2 to deduce solutions to the necessary conditions.

APPENDIX

In the appendix, we present, but do not prove, a theorem that shows how to differentiate a function that is defined by an integral when the integrand function and its domain are bounded. This theorem will be used repeatedly throughout our development of the necessary conditions of optimal control theory, as well as in developing the dynamic counterpart of the envelope theorem. It often, but not always, goes by the name of Leibniz's rule. See Protter and Morrey (1991, Theorem 11.3) for a proof of the theorem.

Theorem A.2.1 (Leibniz's Rule): *Let $f(\cdot)$ be a function with domain a rectangle given by $R \stackrel{\text{def}}{=} \{(t, y) : a \leq y \leq b, c \leq t \leq d\} \subset \Re^2$, and with a range in $\Re$. Suppose that $f(\cdot)$ and $f_y(\cdot)$ are continuous on R and that the functions $h_0(\cdot)$ and $h_1(\cdot)$ both have a continuous first derivative on the interval $I \stackrel{\text{def}}{=} \{y : a \leq y \leq b\} \subset \Re$ with range on $J \stackrel{\text{def}}{=} \{t : c \leq t \leq d\} \subset \Re$. If the function $\phi(\cdot) : I \to \Re$ is defined by*

$$\phi(y) \stackrel{\text{def}}{=} \int_{h_0(y)}^{h_1(y)} f(t, y)\, dt,$$

then its derivative is given by

$$\phi'(y) = f(h_1(y), y)h_1'(y) - f(h_0(y), y)h_0'(y) + \int_{h_0(y)}^{h_1(y)} f_y(t, y)\, dt.$$

We will demonstrate Theorem A.2.1 with some examples.

Example A.2.1: Consider the function $\phi(\cdot)$ defined by the integral

$$\phi(y) \stackrel{\text{def}}{=} \int_0^1 \frac{\sin yt}{1+t}\, dt.$$

Thus $f(t, y) \overset{\text{def}}{=} \frac{\sin yt}{1+t}$ in this case. Because $f(\cdot)$ and $f_y(\cdot) = \frac{t \cos yt}{1+t}$ are continuous for $t \in [0, 1]$ and $y \in \Re$, we can apply Theorem A.2.1 to get

$$\phi'(y) = \int_0^1 \frac{t \cos yt}{1+t}\, dt.$$

Notice that we do not have to compute the integral to find the value of the derivative, as this is one of the benefits of Leibniz's rule.

Example A.2.2: Given the function $F(\cdot)$ defined by

$$F(x, y) \overset{\text{def}}{=} \int_y^{\ln x} \frac{\sin xt}{t(1+y)}\, dt,$$

let's find $F_x(x, y)$. In order to find this partial derivative using Leibniz's rule, we simply treat the variable y as fixed and apply Theorem A.2.1. Doing just that, we get

$$F_x(x, y) = \left[\frac{\sin(x \ln x)}{\ln x(1+y)}\right] \frac{1}{x} + \int_y^{\ln x} \frac{\cos xt}{(1+y)}\, dt$$

as the result we are after.

MENTAL EXERCISES

2.1 Let $\phi(x) \overset{\text{def}}{=} \int_0^1 [(1+t)^{-1} \sin xt]\, dt$. Find $\phi'(x)$.

2.2 Let $\phi(x) \overset{\text{def}}{=} \int_1^2 e^{-t}(1+xt)^{-1}\, dt$. Find $\phi'(x)$.

2.3 Let $\phi(q) \overset{\text{def}}{=} \int_1^{q^2} \cos(t^2)\, dt$. Find $\phi'(q)$.

2.4 Let $\phi(y) \overset{\text{def}}{=} \int_{y^2}^{y} \sin(yt)\, dt$. Find $\phi'(y)$.

2.5 Let $\phi(x) \overset{\text{def}}{=} \int_{\cos x}^{1+x^2} e^{-t}(1+xt)^{-1}\, dt$. Find $\phi'(x)$.

2.6 Let $\phi(y) \overset{\text{def}}{=} \int_{y^2}^{y} t^{-1} \sin(yt)\, dt$. Find $\phi'(y)$.

2.7 Let $\phi(x) \overset{\text{def}}{=} \int_{x^m}^{x^n} (x+t)^{-1}\, dt$. Find $\phi'(x)$.

2.8 Let $F(x, y) \overset{\text{def}}{=} \int_y^{x^2} t^{-1} e^{xt}\, dt$. Find $F_x(x, y)$ and $F_y(x, y)$.

2.9 Let $F(x, y) \overset{\text{def}}{=} \int_{x^2+y^2}^{x^2-y^2} (t^2 + 2x^2 - y^2)\, dt$. Find $F_x(x, y)$ and $F_y(x, y)$.

2.10 Let $F(x, y) \overset{\text{def}}{=} \int_{h_0(x,y)}^{h_1(x,y)} f(t, x, y)\, dt$. Find $F_x(x, y)$ and $F_y(x, y)$.

2.11 Suppose that the equation $\int_{h_0(y)}^{h_1(x)} f(t, x, y)\, dt = 0$, which is a relation between x and y, actually defines y as a function of x. If we write $y = \phi(x)$ for this function, find the derivative $\phi'(x)$.

2.12 In the discussion contained in the appendix concerning the differentiation of functions defined by definite integrals, no mention was made of the derivative with respect to the variable of integration t. Is that a justifiable omission? Why or why not?

2.13 Prove that the comparison control curves $u(t;\varepsilon)$ defined in Eq. (2) can be made to lie arbitrarily close to the optimal control curve $v(t)$ for all $t \in [t_0, t_1]$. More formally, prove that there exists a value $\varepsilon_0(\delta)$ such that for all $|\varepsilon| < \varepsilon_0(\delta)$, $u(t;\varepsilon) \in B(v(t);\delta)\ \forall\, t \in [t_0, t_1]$. Make sure you also find the value $\varepsilon_0(\delta)$.

2.14 Prove that if $v(t) \in \operatorname{int} U\ \forall\, t \in [t_0, t_1]$, then $u(t;\varepsilon) \in \operatorname{int} U\ \forall\, t \in [t_0, t_1]$, where the comparison control curves $u(t;\varepsilon)$ are defined in Eq. (2).

2.15 Consider the optimal control problem

$$\max_{u(\cdot),x_1} J[x(\cdot), u(\cdot)] \stackrel{\text{def}}{=} \int_0^1 [x(t) + u(t)]\,dt$$

$$\text{s.t.} \quad \dot{x}(t) = 1 - [u(t)]^2,\ x(0) = 1,\ x(1) = x_1.$$

(a) Write down the necessary conditions for this problem.
(b) Find the paths for the state, control, and costate variables that satisfy the necessary conditions.

2.16 Find the solution of the necessary conditions for the control problem

$$\min_{u(\cdot),x_T} J[x(\cdot), u(\cdot)] \stackrel{\text{def}}{=} \int_0^T [[x(t)]^2 + ax(t) + bu(t) + c[u(t)]^2]\,dt$$

$$\text{s.t.} \quad \dot{x}(t) = u(t),\ x(0) = x_0,\ x(T) = x_T,$$

where $c > 0$ holds, but no restrictions are placed on a or b.

2.17 Find the solution of the necessary conditions for the control problem

$$\max_{u(\cdot),x_5} J[x(\cdot), u(\cdot)] \stackrel{\text{def}}{=} \int_1^5 [u(t)x(t) - [x(t)]^2 - [u(t)]^2]\,dt$$

$$\text{s.t.} \quad \dot{x}(t) = x(t) + u(t),\ x(1) = 2,\ x(5) = x_5.$$

2.18 Find the solution of the necessary conditions for the control problem

$$\min_{u(\cdot),x_1} J[x(\cdot), u(\cdot)] \stackrel{\text{def}}{=} \int_0^1 [u(t)]^2\,dt$$

$$\text{s.t.} \quad \dot{x}(t) = x(t) + u(t),\ x(0) = 1,\ x(1) = x_1.$$

2.19 Find the solution of the necessary conditions for the control problem

$$\max_{u(\cdot),x_2} J[x(\cdot), u(\cdot)] \stackrel{\text{def}}{=} \int_0^2 [x(t) - [u(t)]^2]\, dt$$

$$\text{s.t.} \quad \dot{x}(t) = u(t), \; x(0) = 0, \; x(1) = x_2.$$

2.20 Find the solution of the necessary conditions for the control problem

$$\max_{u(\cdot),x_1} J[x(\cdot), u(\cdot)] \stackrel{\text{def}}{=} \int_0^1 -\frac{1}{2} [[x(t)]^2 + [u(t)]^2]\, dt$$

$$\text{s.t.} \quad \dot{x}(t) = u(t) - x(t), \; x(0) = 1, \; x(1) = x_1.$$

2.21 Find the solution of the necessary conditions for the control problem

$$\min_{u(\cdot),x_1} J[x(\cdot), u(\cdot)] \stackrel{\text{def}}{=} \int_0^1 [[x(t)]^2 + [u(t)]^2]\, dt$$

$$\text{s.t.} \quad \dot{x}(t) = u(t), \; x(0) = 1, x(1) = x_1.$$

2.22 Find the solution of the necessary conditions for the control problem

$$\min_{u(\cdot),x_1} J[x(\cdot), u(\cdot)] \stackrel{\text{def}}{=} \int_0^1 [tu(t) + [u(t)]^2]\, dt$$

$$\text{s.t.} \quad \dot{x}(t) = u(t), \; x(0) = 1, \; x(1) = x_1.$$

2.23 Find the solution of the necessary conditions for the control problem

$$\min_{u(\cdot),x_2} J[x(\cdot), u(\cdot)] \stackrel{\text{def}}{=} \int_0^2 [t^2 + [u(t)]^2]\, dt$$

$$\text{s.t.} \quad \dot{x}(t) = u(t), \; x(0) = 4, \; x(1) = x_2.$$

2.24 Consider the following variant of the intertemporal utility maximization problem introduced in Example 1.3:

$$\max_{c(\cdot),k_T} J[k(\cdot), c(\cdot)] \stackrel{\text{def}}{=} \int_0^T e^{-rt} U(c(t))\, dt$$

$$\text{s.t.} \quad \dot{k}(t) = w + ik(t) - c(t), \; k(0) = k_0, \; k(T) = k_T.$$

Note that unlike Example 1.3, the terminal capital stock is freely chosen in this version of the problem. Also recall that $U(\cdot) \in C^{(1)}$, $U'(c) > 0$, and $U''(c) < 0$ are assumed to hold.

(a) Write down all the necessary conditions.

(b) Show that no solution to the problem exists.

(c) Can you provide an economic explanation for this nonexistence result?
(d) Determine two different ways to avoid the nonexistence result.

2.25 This mental exercise continues the qualitative investigation of the adjustment cost model of the firm started in Example 2.3.
(a) Prove that for all $\theta \in \Re_{++}$, $K^*(t;\theta c,\theta p,\theta w,K_0,T)=K^*(t;c,p,w,K_0,T)$. Provide an economic interpretation of this result.
(b) Prove that for all $\theta \in \Re_{++}$, $K^*(t;c,\theta p,\theta w,\theta K_0,T)=\theta K^*(t;c,p,w,K_0,T)$. Provide an economic interpretation of this result.
(c) Prove that for all $\theta \in \Re_{++}$, $\lambda(t;\theta p,\theta w,T)=\theta\lambda(t;p,w,T)$. Provide an economic interpretation of this result.
(d) Derive the comparative dynamics for the parameter c. Provide an economic interpretation of the results.
(e) Derive the comparative dynamics for the parameter w. Provide an economic interpretation of the results.
(f) Derive the comparative dynamics for the parameter K_0. Provide an economic interpretation of the results.
(g) Derive the comparative dynamics for the parameter T. Provide an economic interpretation of the results.
(h) Show and explain why

$$\frac{d}{dT}\dot{K}^*(T;\beta)=\ddot{K}^*(T;\beta)+\frac{\partial}{\partial T}\dot{K}^*(T;\beta)\equiv 0,$$

where $\beta \overset{\text{def}}{=} (c,p,w,K_0,T)$. Provide an economic interpretation of this comparative dynamics result.

2.26 Derive the necessary conditions obeyed by an optimal solution $(z(t),v(t))$ of the optimal control problem

$$\max_{u(\cdot),x_0,x_1} J[x(\cdot),u(\cdot)] \overset{\text{def}}{=} \int_{t_0}^{t_1} f(t,x(t),u(t))\,dt$$

$$\text{s.t. } \dot{x}(t)=g(t,x(t),u(t)),\ x(t_0)=x_0,\ x(t_1)=x_1,$$

under assumptions (A.1), (A.2), and (A.3).

2.27 Consider the optimal control problem

$$\max_{u(\cdot),x_0,x_1} J[x(\cdot),u(\cdot)] \overset{\text{def}}{=} \int_{t_0}^{t_1} f(t,x(t),u(t))\,dt$$

$$\text{s.t. } \dot{x}(t)=g(t,x(t),u(t)),\ x(t_0)=x_0,\ x(t_1)=x_1.$$

(a) Write down all the necessary conditions.

(b) Prove that

$$\int_{t_0}^{t_1} H_x(t, z(t), v(t))\, dt = 0,$$

where $H(\cdot)$ is the Hamiltonian and $(z(t), v(t))$ is a solution of the necessary conditions.

(c) Provide an interpretation of this result.

2.28 Find the solution of the necessary conditions for the control problem

$$\min_{u(\cdot), x_0, x_1} J[x(\cdot), u(\cdot)] \stackrel{\text{def}}{=} \int_0^1 \left[\frac{1}{2}[u(t)]^2 + x(t)u(t) + x(t)\right] dt$$

$$\text{s.t.} \quad \dot{x}(t) = u(t), \; x(0) = x_0, \; x(1) = x_1.$$

2.29 Prove Theorem 2.3.

2.30 Find the solution of the necessary conditions for the optimal control problem

$$\min_{u(\cdot), x_1} J[x(\cdot), u(\cdot)] \stackrel{\text{def}}{=} \int_0^1 [u(t)]^2\, dt + [x_1]^2$$

$$\text{s.t.} \quad \dot{x}(t) = x(t) + u(t), \; x(0) = 1, \; x(1) = x_1.$$

2.31 Consider the optimal control problem

$$\max_{u(\cdot), x_1} J[x(\cdot), u(\cdot)] \stackrel{\text{def}}{=} \int_{t_0}^{t_1} f(t, x(t), u(t))\, dt$$

$$\text{s.t.} \quad \dot{x}(t) = g(t, x(t), u(t)), \; x(t_0) = x_0, \; x(t_1) = x_1.$$

Let $(z(t), v(t))$ be the optimal pair of curves, and let $\lambda(t)$ be the corresponding time path of the costate variable. Define the Hamiltonian as

$$H(t, x, u, \lambda) \stackrel{\text{def}}{=} f(t, x, u) + \lambda g(t, x, u).$$

(a) Prove that

$$\frac{d}{dt} H(t, z(t), v(t), \lambda(t)) = \frac{\partial}{\partial t} H(t, z(t), v(t), \lambda(t)).$$

(b) Prove that if the optimal control problem is autonomous, that is, the independent variable t doesn't enter $f(\cdot)$ or $g(\cdot)$ explicitly, i.e., $f_t(t, x, u) = g_t(t, x, u) \equiv 0$, then $H(\cdot)$ is constant along the optimal path.

(c) An autonomous calculus of variations problem is defined as

$$\max_{x(\cdot), x_1} J[x(\cdot)] \stackrel{\text{def}}{=} \int_{t_0}^{t_1} F(x(t), \dot{x}(t))\, dt$$

$$\text{s.t.} \quad x(t_0) = x_0, \; x(t_1) = x_1.$$

It can be shown that the Euler equation for this autonomous calculus of variations problem may be written as

$$F(x, \dot{x}) - \dot{x} F_{\dot{x}}(x, \dot{x}) = \text{constant}.$$

Show that $F(x, \dot{x}) - \dot{x} F_{\dot{x}}(x, \dot{x}) = \text{constant}$ if and only if $H(t, x, u, \lambda) =$ constant. Note that you are to rewrite the above autonomous calculus of variations problem as an optimal control problem in order to demonstrate this equivalence.

2.32 Derive and interpret the comparative dynamics corresponding to the parameters (c_1, p, T) for Example 2.4.

2.33 **True, False, Explain:** If you found two different solutions to the necessary conditions, then you would have two different solutions of the optimal control problem.

2.34 **True, False, Explain:** An admissible pair $(x(t), u(t))$ that does not satisfy the necessary conditions is not a solution of a given optimal control problem.

2.35 **True, False, Explain:** If $(x_1(t), u_1(t))$ and $(x_2(t), u_2(t))$ are the only two admissible pairs and $J[x_1(\cdot), u_1(\cdot)] > J[x_2(\cdot), u_2(\cdot)]$, then the pair $(x_1(t), u_1(t))$ would be the solution of the optimal control problem under consideration.

2.36 Let the pair of curves $(z(t), v(t))$ be the optimal solution to

$$\max_{u(\cdot)} J[x(\cdot), u(\cdot)] \stackrel{\text{def}}{=} \int_{t_0}^{t_1} f(t, x(t), u(t))\, dt$$

$$\text{s.t.} \quad \dot{x}(t) = g(t, x(t), u(t)), \; x(t_0) = x_0, \; x(t_1) = x_1.$$

Now select a point $\tau \in (t_0, t_1)$, and let $x_\tau = z(\tau)$. The fact that both end points are fixed in this control problem and that we have not examined the necessary conditions for such a class of control problems is irrelevant in answering this question.

(a) Prove that the pair of curves $(z(t), v(t))$ is the optimal solution to

$$\max_{u(\cdot)} J[x(\cdot), u(\cdot)] \stackrel{\text{def}}{=} \int_{t_0}^{\tau} f(t, x(t), u(t))\, dt$$

$$\text{s.t.} \quad \dot{x}(t) = g(t, x(t), u(t)), \; x(t_0) = x_0, \; x(\tau) = x_\tau.$$

(b) Explain in words what you have just proved.

2.37 Prove that if the pair of curves $(z(t), v(t))$ is the optimal solution to

$$\max_{u(\cdot), x_1} J[x(\cdot), u(\cdot)] \stackrel{\text{def}}{=} \int_{t_0}^{t_1} f(t, x(t), u(t))\, dt$$

$$\text{s.t.} \quad \dot{x}(t) = g(t, x(t), u(t)), \; x(t_0) = x_0, \; x(t_1) = x_1,$$

then the pair of curves $(z(t), v(t))$ is also the optimal solution to

$$\max_{u(\cdot),x_1} \hat{J}[x(\cdot), u(\cdot)] \stackrel{\text{def}}{=} \int_{t_0}^{t_1} [f(t, x(t), u(t)) + F(t)]\, dt$$

$$\text{s.t.} \quad \dot{x}(t) = g(t, x(t), u(t)), \;\; x(t_0) = x_0, \;\; x(t_1) = x_1.$$

Explain your steps and reasoning clearly.

FURTHER READING

The advanced calculus text by Taylor and Mann (1983, 3rd Ed.) is both a highly readable treatment of the material and an outstanding reference. Their insight into some of the subtleties of advanced calculus is without peer. The real analysis book by Protter and Morrey (1991, 2nd Ed.) is also highly recommended, for much the same reasons. The gentlest introduction to the theorems of this chapter may be found in Chiang (1992). This book, for all intents and purposes, is pitched at the advanced undergraduate level, requiring only Chiang's (1984, 3rd Ed.) *Fundamental Methods of Mathematical Economics* as a mathematical prerequisite. The Kamien and Schwartz (1991, 2nd Ed.) text, on the other hand, is pitched at a higher level, arguably the same level as the exposition of the chapter proper, albeit with rather terse development of the material.

REFERENCES

Chiang, A.C. (1984, 3rd Ed.), *Fundamental Methods of Mathematical Economics* (New York: McGraw-Hill, Inc.).

Chiang, A.C. (1992), *Elements of Dynamic Optimization* (New York: McGraw-Hill, Inc.).

Kamien, M.I. and Schwartz, N.L. (1991, 2nd Ed.), *Dynamic Optimization: The Calculus of Variations and Optimal Control in Economics and Management* (New York: Elsevier Science Publishing Co., Inc.).

Protter, M.H. and Morrey, C.B. (1991, 2nd Ed.), *A First Course in Real Analysis* (New York: Springer-Verlag, Inc.).

Taylor, A.E. and Mann, W.R. (1983, 3rd Ed.), *Advanced Calculus* (New York: John Wiley and Sons, Inc.).

THREE

Concavity and Sufficiency in Optimal Control Problems

In unconstrained static optimization problems, we know that if the objective function is a $C^{(1)}$ concave function of the decision variables, then the solution of the FONCs is the solution of the optimization problem under consideration. That is, the FONCs are both necessary *and* sufficient conditions for optimality if the objective function is a $C^{(1)}$ concave function of the decision variables. The goal of this chapter is to demonstrate that essentially an analogous result holds for optimal control problems. More precisely, we seek to derive an economically useful set of conditions under which a solution of the necessary conditions of Theorems 2.2 or 2.3 is a solution of the posed optimal control problem. We will also prove a more general sufficiency theorem due to Arrow.

To begin, recall that the optimal control problem under consideration is given by

$$\max_{u(\cdot),x_1} J[x(\cdot),u(\cdot)] \stackrel{\text{def}}{=} \int_{t_0}^{t_1} f(t,x(t),u(t))\,dt$$

$$\text{s.t.}\quad \dot{x}(t) = g(t,x(t),u(t)), \tag{1}$$

$$x(t_0) = x_0,\ \ x(t_1) = x_1,$$

with the Hamiltonian defined by $H(t,x,u,\lambda) \stackrel{\text{def}}{=} f(t,x,u) + \lambda g(t,x,u)$. The necessary conditions are given by Theorem 2.2 and read

$$H_u(t,x,u,\lambda) = f_u(t,x,u) + \lambda g_u(t,x,u) = 0,$$

$$\dot{\lambda} = -H_x(t,x,u,\lambda) = -f_x(t,x,u) - \lambda g_x(t,x,u),\ \ \lambda(t_1) = 0,$$

$$\dot{x} = H_\lambda(t,x,u,\lambda) = g(t,x,u),\ \ x(t_0) = x_0.$$

Given these preliminaries, we now state and prove the following sufficiency theorem for the optimal control problem (1).

Theorem 3.1 (Mangasarian Sufficient Conditions): *Let $(z(t), v(t))$ be an admissible pair for problem (1). Suppose that $(z(t), v(t))$ satisfy the necessary conditions of Theorem 2.2 for problem (1) with costate variable $\lambda(t)$, and let $H(t, x, u, \lambda) \stackrel{\text{def}}{=} f(t, x, u) + \lambda g(t, x, u)$ be the value of the Hamiltonian function. If $H(\cdot)$ is a concave function of $(x, u)\,\forall\, t \in [t_0, t_1]$ over an open convex set containing all the admissible values of $(x(\cdot), u(\cdot))$ when the costate variable is $\lambda(t)$, then $v(t)$ is an optimal control and $(z(t), v(t))$ yields the global maximum of $J[\cdot]$. If $H(\cdot)$ is a strictly concave function under the same conditions, then $(z(t), v(t))$ yields the unique global maximum of $J[\cdot]$.*

Proof: Let $(x(t), u(t))$ be an admissible pair of curves. By hypothesis, $H(\cdot)$ is concave in $(x, u)\,\forall\, t \in [t_0, t_1]$. Moreover, because $f(\cdot)$ and $g(\cdot)$ are $C^{(1)}$ functions by assumption, so is $H(\cdot)$. Therefore, by Theorem 21.3 in Simon and Blume (1994), we have that

$$H(t, x(t), u(t), \lambda(t)) \leq H(t, z(t), v(t), \lambda(t)) + H_x(t, z(t), v(t), \lambda(t))[x(t) - z(t)] + H_u(t, z(t), v(t), \lambda(t))[u(t) - v(t)]. \tag{2}$$

Now recall that $(z(t), v(t))$ satisfy the necessary conditions of Theorem 2.2 by hypothesis; hence $H_u(t, z(t), v(t), \lambda(t)) \equiv 0\,\forall\, t \in [t_0, t_1]$. This implies that the last term on the right-hand side of Eq. (2) is identically zero. Moreover, the inequality in Eq. (2) holds for all $t \in [t_0, t_1]$, so we can integrate it over $[t_0, t_1]$ and the inequality is preserved. Doing just that yields

$$\int_{t_0}^{t_1} H(t, x(t), u(t), \lambda(t))\,dt \leq \int_{t_0}^{t_1} [H(t, z(t), v(t), \lambda(t)) + H_x(t, z(t), v(t), \lambda(t))[x(t) - z(t)]]\,dt. \tag{3}$$

Now use the costate equation $\dot{\lambda}(t) \equiv -H_x(t, z(t), v(t), \lambda(t))$, the definition of the Hamiltonian function $H(t, x, u, \lambda) \stackrel{\text{def}}{=} f(t, x, u) + \lambda g(t, x, u)$ evaluated along the curves $(z(t), v(t))$ and $(x(t), u(t))$, and the definition of functional $J[x(\cdot), u(\cdot)] \stackrel{\text{def}}{=} \int_{t_0}^{t_1} f(t, x(t), u(t))\,dt$ evaluated along the curves $(z(t), v(t))$ and $(x(t), u(t))$, to rewrite Eq. (3) in the form

$$J[x(\cdot), u(\cdot)] \leq J[z(\cdot), v(\cdot)] + \int_{t_0}^{t_1} [\lambda(t)[g(t, z(t), v(t)) - g(t, x(t), u(t))] - \dot{\lambda}(t)[x(t) - z(t)]]\,dt. \tag{4}$$

Next, define $h(t) \stackrel{\text{def}}{=} x(t) - z(t)$ and integrate the term $\int_{t_0}^{t_1} \dot{\lambda}(t)h(t)\,dt$ of Eq. (4) by parts to get

$$\int_{t_0}^{t_1} \dot{\lambda}(t)h(t)\,dt = \lambda(t_1)h(t_1) - \lambda(t_0)h(t_0) - \int_{t_0}^{t_1} \lambda(t)\dot{h}(t)\,dt. \tag{5}$$

Because $x(t)$ satisfies the state equation and initial condition by virtue of it being admissible, as does $z(t)$ by virtue of it being a solution of the necessary conditions, it therefore follows that $h(t_0) \stackrel{\text{def}}{=} x(t_0) - z(t_0) = x_0 - x_0 \equiv 0$. Moreover, $\lambda(t_1) = 0$ by the necessary transversality condition. Hence, using Eq. (5) and these two results in Eq. (4) yields

$$J[x(\cdot), u(\cdot)] \le J[z(\cdot), v(\cdot)] + \int_{t_0}^{t_1} \lambda(t)[[g(t, z(t), v(t)) - \dot{z}(t)]$$
$$+[\dot{x}(t) - g(t, x(t), u(t))]]\,dt. \tag{6}$$

Because the curves $(x(t), u(t))$ are admissible, they must satisfy the state equation identically, that is, $\dot{x}(t) \equiv g(t, x(t), u(t))$. Similarly, seeing as the curves $(z(t), v(t))$ are a solution of the necessary conditions, they must satisfy the state equation identically too, that is, $\dot{z}(t) \equiv g(t, z(t), v(t))$. Thus the integrand of Eq. (6) is identically zero, thereby implying that $J[x(\cdot), u(\cdot)] \le J[z(\cdot), v(\cdot)]$. If $H(\cdot)$ is strictly concave in $(x, u)\,\forall\, t \in [t_0, t_1]$, then the inequality in Eq. (2) becomes strict if either $x(t) \ne z(t)$ or $u(t) \ne v(t)$ for some $t \in [t_0, t_1]$. Continuity would then imply that there exists an interval over that $x(t) \ne z(t)$ or $u(t) \ne v(t)$ held. Carrying the strict inequality through the proof leads to the conclusion that $J[x(\cdot), u(\cdot)] < J[z(\cdot), v(\cdot)]$. This argument thus shows that any admissible pair $(x(t), u(t))$ that is not identically equal to $(z(t), v(t))$ is nonoptimal. Q.E.D.

Now the question becomes: Under what conditions is the Hamiltonian $H(\cdot)$ a concave function of $(x, u)\,\forall\, t \in [t_0, t_1]$? The following theorem, which you are asked to prove in the mental exercises, provides some necessary technical input for applying Theorem 3.1 in many optimal control problems in economics.

Theorem 3.2: *A nonnegative linear combination of concave functions is also a concave function. That is, if* $f^i(\cdot) : \mathrm{X} \to \Re$, $i = 1, 2, \ldots, m$, *are concave functions on a convex subset* $\mathrm{X} \subset \Re^n$, *then* $f(\mathbf{x}) \stackrel{\text{def}}{=} \sum_{i=1}^{m} \alpha_i f^i(\mathbf{x})$, *where* $\alpha_i \in \Re_+$, $i = 1, 2, \ldots, m$, *is also a concave function on* $\mathrm{X} \subset \Re^n$.

To see what Theorem 3.2 implies for Theorem 3.1, first recall the definition of the Hamiltonian, namely, $H(t, x, u, \lambda) \stackrel{\text{def}}{=} f(t, x, u) + \lambda g(t, x, u)$. Therefore, if $f(\cdot)$ and $g(\cdot)$ are concave functions of $(x, u)\,\forall\, t \in [t_0, t_1]$, and if $\lambda(t) \ge 0\,\forall\, t \in [t_0, t_1]$, then $H(\cdot)$ is a concave function of $(x, u)\,\forall\, t \in [t_0, t_1]$ by Theorem 3.2, because the Hamiltonian is a nonnegative linear combination of concave functions in this instance. Similarly, if $f(\cdot)$ is concave in $(x, u)\,\forall t \in [t_0, t_1]$, $g(\cdot)$ is convex in $(x, u)\,\forall t \in [t_0, t_1]$, and $\lambda(t) \leq 0\,\forall t \in [t_0, t_1]$, then $H(\cdot)$ is concave in $(x, u)\,\forall t \in [t_0, t_1]$. To see this, first define $\mu(t) \stackrel{\text{def}}{=} -\lambda(t) \geq 0$. This definition allows us to rewrite the Hamiltonian in the form $H(t, x, u, \lambda) \stackrel{\text{def}}{=} f(t, x, u) + \lambda g(t, x, u) = f(t, x, u) + \mu[-1 \cdot g(t, x, u)]$. Given that $g(\cdot)$ is convex in $(x, u)\,\forall t \in [t_0, t_1]$, $-g(\cdot)$ is concave in $(x, u)\,\forall t \in [t_0, t_1]$ by definition. Moreover, because $\mu(t) \geq 0\,\forall t \in [t_0, t_1]$, $H(\cdot)$ is concave in $(x, u)\,\forall t \in [t_0, t_1]$ by Theorem 3.2 in view of the fact that it is a nonnegative linear combination of concave functions. Thus, in either case, $H(\cdot)$ is concave in $(x, u)\,\forall t \in [t_0, t_1]$, and therefore by Theorem 3.1, a solution of the necessary conditions of Theorem 2.2 is a solution to the optimal control problem (1).

Finally, if $g(\cdot)$ is linear in $(x, u)\,\forall t \in [t_0, t_1]$, then $\lambda(t)$ may be of any sign and $H(\cdot)$ will be concave in $(x, u)\,\forall t \in [t_0, t_1]$ if $f(\cdot)$ is concave in $(x, u)\,\forall t \in [t_0, t_1]$. This should be clear because if $g(\cdot)$ is linear in $(x, u)\,\forall t \in [t_0, t_1]$, then it is *both* concave and convex in $(x, u)\,\forall t \in [t_0, t_1]$, and therefore $\lambda(t)g(\cdot)$ is both concave and convex in $(x, u)\,\forall t \in [t_0, t_1]$ regardless of the sign of $\lambda(t)$. Hence, if $g(\cdot)$ is linear in $(x, u)\,\forall t \in [t_0, t_1]$ and $f(\cdot)$ is concave in $(x, u)\,\forall t \in [t_0, t_1]$, then $H(\cdot)$ is concave in $(x, u)\,\forall t \in [t_0, t_1]$ as it is a nonnegative linear combination of concave functions. In this instance, we may also conclude that a solution of the necessary conditions of Theorem 2.2 is a solution to the optimal control problem (1) by Theorem 3.1. In the mental exercises, you are asked to provide a different proof for the concavity of $H(\cdot)$, in this case using Theorem 21.5 of Simon and Blume (1994), which states that a function is concave in certain variables if and only if its Hessian matrix with respect to the said variables is negative semidefinite. We summarize our results of this and the preceding paragraph in the following corollary.

Corollary 3.1: *For problem (1), if $f(\cdot)$ is concave in $(x, u)\,\forall t \in [t_0, t_1]$, and any one of the following three additional conditions hold:*

(i) $g(\cdot)$ is concave in $(x, u)\,\forall t \in [t_0, t_1]$ and $\lambda(t) \geq 0\,\forall t \in [t_0, t_1]$, or
(ii) $g(\cdot)$ is convex in $(x, u)\,\forall t \in [t_0, t_1]$ and $\lambda(t) \leq 0\,\forall t \in [t_0, t_1]$, or
(iii) $g(\cdot)$ is linear in $(x, u)\,\forall t \in [t_0, t_1]$,

then $H(\cdot)$ is concave in $(x, u)\,\forall t \in [t_0, t_1]$ and the solution to the necessary conditions of Theorem 2.2 is a solution to the optimal control problem (1).

One point that may cross your mind as you read Corollary 3.1 is that we must know the sign of the costate variable over the entire planning horizon to use it, unless, of course, the transition function $g(\cdot)$ is linear in $(x, u)\,\forall t \in [t_0, t_1]$, a case that is fairly common but certainly not universal in economic problems. It would be nice, therefore, if a simple sufficient condition could be found that would guarantee the uniform sign of the costate variable over the planning horizon. The following lemma provides such a simple sufficient condition. The proof is a technical one, but it introduces a clever way to get an economic interpretation of the costate variable and demonstrate the forward-looking nature of it, and so is included in the text.

Lemma 3.1: *Let $(z(t), v(t))$ be the optimal solution to problem (1), with corresponding costate variable $\lambda(t)$.*

(i) If $f_x(t, z(t), v(t)) > 0 \,\forall\, t \in [t_0, t_1]$, then $\lambda(t) > 0 \,\forall\, t \in [t_0, t_1)$;
(ii) If $f_x(t, z(t), v(t)) < 0 \,\forall\, t \in [t_0, t_1]$, then $\lambda(t) < 0 \,\forall\, t \in [t_0, t_1)$;
(iii) If $f_x(t, z(t), v(t)) = 0 \,\forall\, t \in [t_0, t_1]$, then $\lambda(t) = 0 \,\forall\, t \in [t_0, t_1]$.

Proof: The proof is not hard but involves a clever twist in solving the costate equation. Moreover, the twist imparts intuition to the economic interpretation of the costate variable. To begin, recall the costate equation and transversality condition evaluated along the optimal solution, and write out the individual functions rather than just the Hamiltonian, that is,

$$\dot{\lambda}(t) = -f_x(t, z(t), v(t)) - \lambda(t) g_x(t, z(t), v(t)),\ \lambda(t_1) = 0.$$

Defining $f_x^*(t) \stackrel{\text{def}}{=} f_x(t, z(t), v(t))$ and $g_x^*(t) \stackrel{\text{def}}{=} g_x(t, z(t), v(t))$, the costate equation can be rewritten more compactly as $\dot{\lambda} + g_x^*(t)\lambda = -f_x^*(t)$. The integrating factor for this first-order linear ordinary differential equation is found in the standard manner, scilicet, $\omega(t) \stackrel{\text{def}}{=} \exp[\int_{t_0}^{t} g_x^*(s)ds]$, where s is a dummy variable of integration. Note that the integrating factor is positive by definition. Next, multiply the costate equation $\dot{\lambda} + g_x^*(t)\lambda = -f_x^*(t)$ through by the integrating factor $\omega(t)$ to get

$$\omega(t)\dot{\lambda} + \omega(t) g_x^*(t)\lambda = -\omega(t) f_x^*(t). \tag{7}$$

Because $\dot{\omega}(t) = g_x^*(t)\omega(t)$ by Leibniz's rule, the left-hand side of Eq. (7) can be rewritten as $\omega(t)\dot{\lambda} + \omega(t) g_x^*(t)\lambda = \frac{d}{dt}[\omega(t)\lambda]$, thereby permitting Eq. (7) to be rewritten as

$$\frac{d}{dt}[\omega(t)\lambda] = -\omega(t) f_x^*(t). \tag{8}$$

Integrating both sides of Eq. (8) with respect to t yields the general solution of the costate equation, namely,

$$\lambda(t) = -[\omega(t)]^{-1} \int_{t_0}^{t} \omega(\tau) f_x^*(\tau)\, d\tau + [\omega(t)]^{-1} c_1, \tag{9}$$

where c_1 is a constant of integration and τ is another dummy variable of integration. That this is a general solution can be verified by differentiating it with respect to t using Leibniz's rule. The specific (or definite) solution can be found by applying the transversality condition to determine the value of c_1. In the mental exercises, you are asked to show that the resulting definite solution is identical to that derived below.

We thus stop the present derivation so that we can proceed with the aforementioned clever solution method.

The clever idea in solving the differential equation (8) is to integrate it *forward* from date t, that is, from $t < t_1$ to t_1, rather than backward from date t as we did above, that is, from t_0 to $t > t_0$. Moreover, when integrating Eq. (8) forward from $t < t_1$ to t_1 we must insert a minus sign on the right-hand side to reflect the fact that the index t now occurs as a lower limit of integration rather than as the upper limit of integration, just as Leibniz's rule dictates. To be consistent with this approach to solving the costate equation, we therefore define a new integrating factor by the formula $\varpi(t) \stackrel{\text{def}}{=} \exp[-\int_t^{t_1} g_x^*(s)\,ds]$. This integrating factor is also positive by definition, and an application of Leibniz's rule shows it satisfies the differential equation $\dot{\varpi}(t) = g_x^*(t)\varpi(t)$, in accord with the previous integrating factor.

Proceeding as above, we multiply the costate equation $\dot{\lambda} + g_x^*(t)\lambda = -f_x^*(t)$ through by the integrating factor $\varpi(t)$ to get

$$\varpi(t)\dot{\lambda} + \varpi(t)g_x^*(t)\lambda = -\varpi(t)f_x^*(t). \tag{10}$$

In view of the fact that $\dot{\varpi}(t) = g_x^*(t)\varpi(t)$, as noted above, the left-hand side of Eq. (10) can be rewritten as $\varpi(t)\dot{\lambda} + \varpi(t)g_x^*(t)\lambda = \frac{d}{dt}[\varpi(t)\lambda]$, thereby permitting Eq. (10) to be rewritten as

$$\frac{d}{dt}[\varpi(t)\lambda] = -\varpi(t)f_x^*(t). \tag{11}$$

Integrating Eq. (11) from $t < t_1$ to t_1 therefore yields the general solution

$$\lambda(t) = [\varpi(t)]^{-1}\int_t^{t_1} \varpi(\tau)f_x^*(\tau)d\tau + [\varpi(t)]^{-1}c_2, \tag{12}$$

where c_2 is a constant of integration that is different from c_1, a fact that you will verify in the aforementioned mental exercise. That this is a general solution can be verified by differentiating it with respect to t using Leibniz's rule. Now apply the transversality condition $\lambda(t_1) = 0$ to Eq. (12) to find the value of the constant of integration c_2:

$$\lambda(t_1) = [\varpi(t_1)]^{-1}\int_{t_1}^{t_1} \varpi(\tau)f_x^*(\tau)\,d\tau + [\varpi(t_1)]^{-1}c_2 = [\varpi(t_1)]^{-1}c_2 = 0 \Leftrightarrow c_2 = 0,$$

because $\varpi(t_1) \stackrel{\text{def}}{=} \exp[-\int_{t_1}^{t_1} g_x(s, z(s), v(s))\,ds] = 1$. The specific solution to the costate equation is thus

$$\lambda(t) = [\varpi(t)]^{-1}\int_t^{t_1} \varpi(\tau)f_x(\tau, z(\tau), v(\tau))\,d\tau. \tag{13}$$

Inspection of Eq. (13) and the three parts of the lemma completes the proof. Q.E.D.

The economic interpretation of Lemma 3.1 is straightforward. Take, for example, part (i), and interpret $f(t, x, u)$ as the net benefit associated with the capital stock x and control u at time t. Part (i) asserts that if the marginal net benefit of the capital stock is positive in an optimal plan, then the shadow value of the capital stock is likewise positive in an optimal plan, that is, the capital stock has a positive marginal value to the decision maker in an optimal plan. Part (ii) has an analogous interpretation and thus need not be explicitly discussed.

Part (iii) asserts that if the marginal net benefit of the capital stock is zero in an optimal plan, then the shadow value of the capital stock is similarly zero in an optimal plan, that is, the capital stock has no marginal value to the decision maker in an optimal plan. This result sheds light on Example 2.2, in which we concluded that the posed optimal control problem was not really a dynamic optimization problem. In Example 2.2, recall that the integrand function is independent of the state variable, thereby implying that $f_x(t, x, u) \equiv 0$. By Lemma 3.1(iii), this implies that $\lambda(t) = 0 \,\forall\, t \in [t_0, t_1]$ in an optimal plan. But with $\lambda(t) = 0 \,\forall\, t \in [t_0, t_1]$, the Hamiltonian $H(\cdot)$ is identical to the integrand function $f(\cdot)$, which implies that the value of the control variable that satisfies $H_u(t, x, u, \lambda) = 0$ is identically equal to the value of the control variable that satisfies $f_u(t, x, u) = 0$. This, then, is the reason that Example 2.2 is not really a dynamic optimization problem. In other words, with $\lambda(t) = 0 \,\forall\, t \in [t_0, t_1]$, the state equation is essentially eliminated as a factor in determining the solution of the control problem. But it is precisely the state equation that makes the optimal control problem a dynamic problem, a feature we discussed in Chapter 1, as you may recall. Hence, with $\lambda(t) = 0 \,\forall\, t \in [t_0, t_1]$, the state equation is irrelevant and the optimal control problem essentially reduces to a static optimization problem.

In each of the three cases in Lemma 3.1, you may have noticed that the sign of the derivative $g_x(t, z(t), v(t))$ plays absolutely no role in determining the sign of $\lambda(t)$. This may appear strange at first glance. Inspection of the costate equation in the form $\dot{\lambda} + g_x^*(t)\lambda = -f_x^*(t)$, however, shows that the role of $g_x(t, z(t), v(t))$ is to dictate the rate of growth of the shadow value of the stock, not its level or value.

As remarked at the beginning of the proof of Lemma 3.1, the solution for the costate variable points to a nice economic interpretation of it. To tease out the economic interpretation, let's again interpret $f(t, x, u)$ as the net benefit associated with the capital stock x and control u at time t. Because the integrating factor for the forward integration solution of the costate equation is $\varpi(t) \overset{\text{def}}{=} \exp[-\int_t^{t_1} g_x^*(s)\, ds]$, we have that

$$\frac{\varpi(\tau)}{\varpi(t)} = \frac{\exp\left[-\int_\tau^{t_1} g_x^*(s)\, ds\right]}{\exp\left[-\int_t^{t_1} g_x^*(s)\, ds\right]} = \exp\left[-\int_\tau^{t_1} g_x^*(s)\, ds\right] \exp\left[\int_t^{t_1} g_x^*(s)\, ds\right]$$

$$= \exp\left[\int_t^{t_1} g_x^*(s)\, ds - \int_\tau^{t_1} g_x^*(s)\, ds\right] = \exp\left[\int_t^{\tau} g_x^*(s)\, ds\right],$$

as $\tau \geq t$. Given the exponential nature of the ratio $\varpi(\tau)/\varpi(t)$, we may therefore interpret it as a *time-varying* discount factor. Using this observation, we can rewrite Eq. (13) as

$$\lambda(t) = \int_t^{t_1} \frac{\varpi(\tau)}{\varpi(t)} f_x(\tau, z(\tau), v(\tau))\, d\tau.$$

This form of the solution is easy to impart an economic interpretation to in light of the above development. In particular, the costate variable at time t, namely, $\lambda(t)$, may be interpreted as the discounted value of the net marginal benefits of the capital stock x from the present moment t until the terminal period t_1, in an optimal plan. This thus reinforces our earlier assertion that $\lambda(t)$ is the shadow value of the capital stock at time t.

Another aspect of Eq. (13) deserves to be reinforced, to wit, the *forward-looking* nature of the solution. That is, the optimal value of the costate variable at time t reflects the discounted value of the net marginal benefits of the capital stock x from the present moment t until the terminal period t_1. It is in this sense that the costate variable "looks ahead" to determine its optimal value. This is another reason why when $\lambda(t) = 0\, \forall\, t \in [t_0, t_1]$, the optimal control problem is essentially a static optimization problem.

Finally, observe that the conditions of Lemma 3.1 are straightforward and relatively easy to check. For example, in many optimal control problems in economics, the signs of the partial derivatives of the functions $f(\cdot)$ and $g(\cdot)$ are specified by the researcher as part of the problem statement. This means that the sign of $f_x(t, z(t), v(t))$ is known without ever solving the optimal control problem under consideration, and thus so is the sign $\lambda(t)$ by Lemma 3.1. We now return to our general discussion of sufficient conditions for problem (1).

Theorem 3.1 is due to Mangasarian and is straightforward (if at times tedious) to check in many optimal control problems in economics. Some dynamic economic models may not satisfy the strong concavity restrictions it requires, however. A generalization of Theorem 3.1 due to Arrow applies to a larger class of problems, but in practice, it can be more difficult to check than Mangasarian's theorem. Before we state and prove the Arrow sufficiency theorem, we need to define a new function and restate Theorem 2.2, the necessary conditions for problem (1), using this newly defined function. To this end, we have the following definition:

Definition 3.1: For the control problem (1), the *maximized Hamiltonian* $M(\cdot)$ is defined as

$$M(t, x, \lambda) \stackrel{\text{def}}{=} \max_u H(t, x, u, \lambda), \tag{14}$$

where $H(t, x, u, \lambda) \stackrel{\text{def}}{=} f(t, x, u) + \lambda g(t, x, u)$ is the Hamiltonian for problem (1).

Seeing as no constraints are placed on the control variable u in problem (1), a necessary condition that must be obeyed by the control that solves the maximization problem in Eq. (14) is the familiar vanishing derivative condition, namely, $H_u(t, x, u, \lambda) = f_u(t, x, u) + \lambda g_u(t, x, u) = 0$, which must hold for every $t \in [t_0, t_1]$. Now if $H_{uu}(t, x, u, \lambda) \neq 0$ along the optimal path, then by the implicit function theorem, we can in principle solve $H_u(t, x, u, \lambda) = 0$ for u in terms of (t, x, λ), say, $u = \hat{u}(t, x, \lambda)$. That is, the necessary condition $H_u(t, x, u, \lambda) = 0$ implicitly defines u in terms of (t, x, λ). We acknowledge that this is the maximizing value of the control variable by using the notation $\hat{u}(t, x, \lambda) \stackrel{\text{def}}{=} \arg\max_u H(t, x, u, \lambda)$. Substituting $u = \hat{u}(t, x, \lambda)$ into the Hamiltonian $H(\cdot)$ yields the value of the maximized Hamiltonian $M(\cdot)$, that is to say

$$M(t, x, \lambda) \equiv H(t, x, \hat{u}(t, x, \lambda), \lambda) = f(t, x, \hat{u}(t, x, \lambda)) + \lambda g(t, x, \hat{u}(t, x, \lambda)). \tag{15}$$

Equation (15) demonstrates how one would go about constructing the maximized Hamiltonian in practice. Given Definition 3.1, we are now in a position to restate Theorem 2.2 in terms of the maximized Hamiltonian $M(\cdot)$.

Theorem 3.3 (Necessary Conditions): *Suppose $v(\cdot) \in C^{(0)}$ and $v(t) \in \operatorname{int} U \; \forall t \in [t_0, t_1]$, and let $z(\cdot) \in C^{(1)} \; \forall t \in [t_0, t_1]$ be the corresponding state function that satisfies the state equation $\dot{x}(t) = g(t, x(t), u(t))$ and initial condition $x(t_0) = x_0$, so that $(z(t), v(t))$ is an admissible pair. Then if $(z(t), v(t))$ yields the global maximum of $J[\cdot]$ when $x(t_1) = x_1$ is a decision variable, then it is necessary that there exists a function $\lambda(\cdot) \in C^{(1)} \; \forall t \in [t_0, t_1]$ such that*

$$H_u(t, z(t), v(t), \lambda(t)) = 0 \; \forall t \in [t_0, t_1],$$

$$\dot{\lambda}(t) = -M_x(t, z(t), \lambda(t)), \;\; \lambda(t_1) = 0,$$

$$\dot{z}(t) = M_\lambda(t, z(t), \lambda(t)), \;\; z(t_0) = x_0,$$

where $M(t, x, \lambda) \stackrel{\text{def}}{=} \max_u H(t, x, u, \lambda)$ is the maximized Hamiltonian for problem (1) and $v(t) \stackrel{\text{def}}{=} \hat{u}(t, z(t), \lambda(t))$.

Theorem 3.3 is equivalent to Theorem 2.2, so the two may be used interchangeably. The proof of their equivalence is short and relatively simple because it makes use of the envelope theorem, and so is left for the mental exercises. The sufficiency counterpart to Theorem 3.3 can now be stated. You are asked to complete the proof of it in the mental exercises.

Theorem 3.4 (Arrow Sufficiency Theorem): *Let $(z(t), v(t))$ be an admissible pair for problem (1). Suppose that $(z(t), v(t))$ satisfy the necessary conditions of Theorem 3.3 for problem (1) with costate variable $\lambda(t)$, and let*

$M(t, x, \lambda) \overset{\text{def}}{=} \max_u H(t, x, u, \lambda)$ *be the value of the maximized Hamiltonian function. If* $M(\cdot)$ *is a concave function of* x *for all* $t \in [t_0, t_1]$ *over an open convex set containing all the admissible values of* $x(\cdot)$ *when the costate variable is* $\lambda(t)$*, then the pair* $(z(t), v(t))$ *yields the global maximum of* $J[\cdot]$*. If* $M(\cdot)$ *is a strictly concave function under the same conditions, then* $J[z(\cdot), v(\cdot)] > J[x(\cdot), u(\cdot)]$ *and* $z(t)$ *is unique, but* $v(t)$ *is not necessarily unique.*

Proof: Let $(x(t), u(t))$ be an admissible pair, where $u(t) \overset{\text{def}}{=} \hat{u}(t, x(t), \lambda(t))$. You are asked to show that $M(\cdot) \in C^{(1)}$ in x in completing this proof. Because $M(\cdot)$ is concave in x $\forall\, t \in [t_0, t_1]$ given $\lambda(t)$ by hypothesis, it follows from Theorem 21.3 in Simon and Blume (1994) that

$$M(t, x(t), \lambda(t)) \leq M(t, z(t), \lambda(t)) + M_x(t, z(t), \lambda(t))[x(t) - z(t)].$$

Given that this inequality holds $\forall\, t \in [t_0, t_1]$, we can integrate it over $[t_0, t_1]$ and the inequality is preserved, thereby yielding

$$\int_{t_0}^{t_1} M(t, x(t), \lambda(t))\, dt \leq \int_{t_0}^{t_1} [M(t, z(t), \lambda(t)) + M_x(t, z(t), \lambda(t))[x(t) - z(t)]]\, dt.$$

The remainder of the proof is similar to that of Theorem 3.1 and is therefore left for you to complete in a mental exercise. Q.E.D.

The Arrow sufficiency theorem replaces the assumption of concavity of the Hamiltonian $H(\cdot)$ in (x, u) of the Mangasarian theorem, with the assumption that the maximized Hamiltonian $M(\cdot)$ is concave in x. Note, however, that checking the curvature properties of a derived function like $M(\cdot)$ can be more difficult than checking the curvature properties of $H(\cdot)$.

The following theorem demonstrates that the Mangasarian sufficiency theorem is a *special case* of Arrow's sufficiency theorem by establishing that if $H(\cdot)$ is concave in (x, u), then $M(\cdot)$ is concave in x. It is also important to note that even if $H(\cdot)$ is not concave in (x, u), it is still possible that $M(\cdot)$ is concave in x, so that Arrow's theorem applies to a larger class of problems than does Mangasarian's. The ensuing theorem is stated for the vector case in view of the fact that we will make use of that form in a later chapter.

Theorem 3.5: *If* $F(\cdot) : \mathrm{X} \times \mathrm{U} \to \Re$ *is concave over the convex sets* $\mathrm{X} \subset \Re^n$ *and* $\mathrm{U} \subset \Re^m$*, then*

$$\phi(\mathbf{x}) \overset{\text{def}}{=} \max_{\mathbf{u}} F(\mathbf{x}, \mathbf{u})$$

is a concave function of $\mathbf{x}$.

Proof: For given $\mathbf{x}_i$, let $\mathbf{u}_i = \mathbf{u}^*(\mathbf{x}_i) \stackrel{\text{def}}{=} \arg\max_{\mathbf{u}} F(\mathbf{x}_i, \mathbf{u})$, $i = 1, 2$, and let $\alpha \in [0, 1]$. Then we have the following string of equalities and inequalities, which we will explain below:

$$\begin{aligned}
\alpha\phi(\mathbf{x}_1) + (1-\alpha)\phi(\mathbf{x}_2) &\stackrel{\text{def}}{=} \alpha \max_{\mathbf{u}} F(\mathbf{x}_1, \mathbf{u}) + (1-\alpha)\max_{\mathbf{u}} F(\mathbf{x}_2, \mathbf{u}) \\
&= \alpha F(\mathbf{x}_1, \mathbf{u}_1) + (1-\alpha)F(\mathbf{x}_2, \mathbf{u}_2) \\
&\leq F(\alpha\mathbf{x}_1 + (1-\alpha)\mathbf{x}_2, \alpha\mathbf{u}_1 + (1-\alpha)\mathbf{u}_2,) \\
&\leq \max_{\mathbf{u}} F(\alpha\mathbf{x}_1 + (1-\alpha)\mathbf{x}_2, \mathbf{u}) \\
&\stackrel{\text{def}}{=} \phi(\alpha\mathbf{x}_1 + (1-\alpha)\mathbf{x}_2).
\end{aligned}$$

The first two equalities follow from the definitions of $\phi(\cdot)$ and $\mathbf{u}_i = \mathbf{u}^*(\mathbf{x}_i)$, respectively, and by noting that $\phi(\mathbf{x}_i) \equiv F(\mathbf{x}_i, \mathbf{u}^*(\mathbf{x}_i))$, $i = 1, 2$. The first inequality follows from the hypothesis that $F(\cdot)$ is concave $\forall\, (\mathbf{x}, \mathbf{u}) \in X \times U$, that is, we have used the defining property of concavity. The next inequality follows from the definition of a maximum, that is, $\alpha\mathbf{u}_1 + (1-\alpha)\mathbf{u}_2$ is a feasible choice for the given value of $\alpha\mathbf{x}_1 + (1-\alpha)\mathbf{x}_2$, but it is not necessarily the optimal value of $\mathbf{u}$. The last equality follows from the definition of $\phi(\cdot)$. Q.E.D.

Before stating our final sufficiency theorem of the chapter, it will be beneficial to examine five examples so that we can demonstrate how the theorems developed in this chapter are used. We begin with the two purely mathematical problems we first examined in Chapter 2. Next we proceed to a case in which the Mangasarian sufficiency theorem does not hold but the Arrow sufficiency theorem does. Then we present a more general problem with economic content and point out a crucial feature of the sufficiency theorems. Finally, we examine an intertemporal model of a nonrenewable resource–extracting firm.

Example 3.1: Consider the optimal control problem from Example 2.1:

$$\max_{u(\cdot), x_1} J[x(\cdot), u(\cdot)] \stackrel{\text{def}}{=} \int_0^1 \left[-x(t) - \frac{1}{2}\alpha[u(t)]^2\right] dt$$

$$\text{s.t.} \quad \dot{x}(t) = u(t),$$

$$x(0) = x_0,\ x(1) = x_1,$$

where $\alpha > 0$ is a parameter. The Hamiltonian is defined as $H(t, x, u, \lambda; \alpha) \stackrel{\text{def}}{=} -x - \frac{1}{2}\alpha u^2 + \lambda u$.

One way to determine if $H(\cdot)$ is a concave function of (x, u), and thus conclude that a solution to the necessary conditions is a solution of the control problem, is to simply inspect the Hamiltonian to see if it is a concave function of (x, u). This approach is viable when $f(\cdot)$ and $g(\cdot)$ are made up of elementary functions, as in this example. Inspection of the transition function $g(\cdot)$ reveals that it is independent of the state variable and linear in the control variable. Similarly, the integrand function $f(\cdot)$ is jointly concave in the state and control variables. Hence, by Corollary 3.1(iii), a solution of the necessary conditions is also a solution of the optimal control problem.

Alternatively and equivalently, we can determine if $H(\cdot)$ is concave in (x, u) by seeing if the Hessian matrix of the Hamiltonian with respect to (x, u) is negative semidefinite, seeing as a function is concave with respect to a set of variables in its domain if and only if its Hessian matrix with respect to those variables is negative semidefinite by Theorem 21.5 of Simon and Blume (1994). Accordingly, we are led to compute the following three principal minors of the Hessian matrix of $H(\cdot)$ with respect to (x, u):

$$H_{uu} = -\alpha < 0,\ H_{xx} = 0,\ \begin{vmatrix} H_{uu} & H_{ux} \\ H_{xu} & H_{xx} \end{vmatrix} = \begin{vmatrix} -\alpha & 0 \\ 0 & 0 \end{vmatrix} = 0.$$

In view of the fact that all the first-order principal minors are nonpositive and the determinant is nonnegative, Theorem 16.2 of Simon and Blume (1994) implies that $H(\cdot)$ is a concave function of (x, u). Thus, by Theorem 3.1, the solution of the necessary conditions is also a solution of the optimal control problem. Note, however, that because $H(\cdot)$ is linear in x, the Hamiltonian is not strictly concave in the state and control variables. This means that we are not permitted to use Theorem 3.1 to conclude that the solution of the control problem is unique. In spite of this observation, we still may in fact conclude that the solution of the control problem is unique seeing as we found only one solution of the necessary conditions in Example 2.1.

A third way to check the concavity of the Hamiltonian in the state and control variables is to compute the eigenvalues of the Hessian matrix of $H(\cdot)$ with respect to (x, u). Because the Hessian matrix of $H(\cdot)$ with respect to (x, u) is diagonal, the eigenvalues are the diagonal elements themselves by Theorem 23.1 of Simon and Blume (1994). Inspection of the above Hessian matrix reveals that one eigenvalue is negative and the other is zero. By Theorems 23.17 and 21.5 of Simon and Blume (1994), we may again conclude that $H(\cdot)$ is concave in (x, u). Thus, by Theorem 3.1, the solution of the necessary conditions is a solution of the optimal control problem.

Though we know that Arrow's sufficiency theorem will hold (why?), let's verify that explicitly. Because $H_{uu}(t, x, u, \lambda; \alpha) = -\alpha < 0$, the solution $u = \hat{u}(t, x, \lambda; \alpha) \stackrel{\text{def}}{=} \alpha^{-1}\lambda$ of the necessary condition $H_u(t, x, u, \lambda; \alpha) = -\alpha u + \lambda = 0$

is in fact the unique value of the control variable that maximizes the Hamiltonian. Hence the value of the maximized Hamiltonian $M(\cdot)$ is given by

$$\begin{aligned} M(t,x,\lambda;\alpha) &\equiv H(t,x,\hat{u}(t,x,\lambda;\alpha),\lambda;\alpha) \\ &= -x - \frac{1}{2}\alpha(\alpha^{-1}\lambda)^2 + \lambda\alpha^{-1}\lambda \\ &= -x + \frac{1}{2}\alpha^{-1}\lambda^2, \end{aligned}$$

which is linear and thus concave in the state variable. Theorem 3.4 thus implies that the solution of the necessary conditions is a solution of the optimal control problem. In a mental exercise, you are asked to verify that the necessary conditions of Theorem 3.3 for the above control problem are identical to those of Theorem 2.2 given in Example 2.1. Finally, note that the solution for the costate variable $\lambda(t) = t - 1$ is negative $\forall t \in [0, 1)$, just as one would expect based on Lemma 3.1(ii), given that $f_x(t, x, u) = -1 < 0$ in the control problem.

Example 3.2: Consider the optimal control problem from Example 2.2:

$$\max_{u(\cdot),x_1} J[x(\cdot),u(\cdot)] \stackrel{\text{def}}{=} \int_0^1 \left[\alpha t u(t) - \frac{1}{2}[u(t)]^2\right] dt$$

$$\text{s.t.} \quad \dot{x}(t) = u(t) - x(t),$$

$$x(0) = x_0, \; x(1) = x_1.$$

The Hamiltonian is given by $H(t,x,u,\lambda;\alpha) \stackrel{\text{def}}{=} \alpha t u - \frac{1}{2}u^2 + \lambda[u - x]$. Because this example is not that different from Example 3.1, we will be more terse in our exposition, thereby leaving some details to a mental exercise.

The integrand is a concave function of the state and control variables, and the state equation is linear in the state and control variables. As a result, we may again appeal to Corollary 3.1(iii) to conclude that a solution of the necessary conditions is a solution of the control problem. Uniqueness then follows from the same argument we employed in Example 3.1.

By Theorem 3.5, we know that Arrow's sufficiency theorem will hold. Nonetheless, let's verify explicitly that it indeed does for practice. Since $H_{uu}(t,x,u,\lambda;\alpha) = -1 < 0$, the solution $u = \hat{u}(t,x,\lambda;\alpha) \stackrel{\text{def}}{=} \alpha t + \lambda$ of the necessary condition $H_u(t,x,u,\lambda;\alpha) = \alpha t - u + \lambda = 0$ is the unique value of the control variable that maximizes the Hamiltonian. Hence the maximized Hamiltonian is given by

$$\begin{aligned} M(t,x,\lambda;\alpha) &\equiv H(t,x,\hat{u}(t,x,\lambda;\alpha),\lambda;\alpha) \\ &= \alpha t(\alpha t + \lambda) - \frac{1}{2}(\alpha t + \lambda)^2 + \lambda(\alpha t + \lambda - x) \end{aligned}$$

$$= \alpha^2 t^2 + \alpha t\lambda - \frac{1}{2}\alpha^2 t^2 - \alpha t\lambda - \frac{1}{2}\lambda^2 + \alpha t\lambda + \lambda^2 - \lambda x$$

$$= \frac{1}{2}\alpha^2 t^2 + \frac{1}{2}\lambda^2 + \alpha t\lambda - \lambda x,$$

which is linear and thus concave in the state variable. Theorem 3.4 thus implies that a solution of the necessary conditions is a solution of the optimal control problem. In passing, note that the solution for the costate variable, namely $\lambda(t) = 0 \,\forall\, t \in [0, 1]$, is as expected based on Lemma 3.1(iii), seeing as $f_x(t, x, u) \equiv 0$ in this control problem.

In the third example, we encounter a case in which the Mangasarian sufficiency theorem does not hold but the Arrow sufficiency theorem does, thereby reinforcing our earlier conclusion of the more general nature of the latter.

Example 3.3: Now consider the ensuing optimal control problem:

$$\max_{u(\cdot),x_T} J[x(\cdot), u(\cdot)] \stackrel{\text{def}}{=} \int_0^T \left[-\frac{1}{2}[u(t)]^2 - x(t) \right] dt$$

$$\text{s.t.} \quad \dot{x}(t) = [u(t)]^2 x(t),$$

$$x(0) = x_0 > 0, \; x(T) = x_T.$$

First, observe that the integrand is a strictly decreasing function of the state variable, so that by Lemma 3.1(ii), we may conclude that $\lambda(t) < 0 \,\forall\, t \in [0, T)$, and furthermore that $\lambda(T) = 0$ by the necessary transversality condition. Next, notice that because $x(0) = x_0 > 0$, the state equation implies that *all* admissible values of the state variable are positive.

The Hamiltonian for this problem is defined as $H(t, x, u, \lambda) \stackrel{\text{def}}{=} -\frac{1}{2}u^2 - x + \lambda u^2 x$. To determine if $H(\cdot)$ is concave in (x, u), we compute the Hessian matrix of the Hamiltonian with respect to (x, u) and check to see if it is negative semidefinite. This leads to the results

$$H_{uu} = -1 + 2\lambda x < 0, \; H_{xx} = 0,$$

$$\begin{vmatrix} H_{uu} & H_{ux} \\ H_{xu} & H_{xx} \end{vmatrix} = \begin{vmatrix} -1 + 2\lambda x & 2\lambda u \\ 2\lambda u & 0 \end{vmatrix} = -4\lambda^2 u^2 < 0 \,\forall\, u \neq 0.$$

Because the determinant of the Hessian matrix is negative, it is not negative semidefinite, and consequently, $H(\cdot)$ is not concave in (x, u). Thus Theorem 3.1 (Mangasarian's theorem) does not apply. Let's now see if Theorem 3.4 (Arrow's theorem) does.

The necessary condition $H_u(t, x, u, \lambda) = -u + 2\lambda u x = 0$ has the solution $u = \hat{u}(t, x, \lambda) \stackrel{\text{def}}{=} 0$ *or* $2\lambda x = 1$. The latter equation cannot be satisfied by any admissible solution, however, because it implies that λ and x have the same sign, which we know they cannot because all admissible $x(t) > 0\,\forall t \in [0, T]$ and $\lambda(t) \le 0\,\forall t \in [0, T]$, as noted above. We may therefore conclude that $u = \hat{u}(t, x, \lambda) \overset{\text{def}}{=} 0$ is the solution of the necessary condition $H_u(t, x, u, \lambda) = -u + 2\lambda u x = 0$. Given that $H_{uu}(t, x, u, \lambda) = -1 < 0$, the Hamiltonian is a strictly concave function of the control variable. Thus $u = \hat{u}(t, x, \lambda) \overset{\text{def}}{=} 0$ yields the unique global maximum of the Hamiltonian. The maximized Hamiltonian is then given by

$$M(t, x, \lambda) \equiv H(t, x, \hat{u}(t, x, \lambda), \lambda) = -x,$$

which is linear and thus concave in x. Therefore, by Theorem 3.4 (Arrow's theorem), we may conclude that the solution to the necessary conditions, namely, $v(t) = 0$, $z(t) = x_0$, and $\lambda(t) = t - T$, is also a solution to the optimal control problem. In the mental exercises, you are asked to argue directly, that is, without using the sufficiency theorems, that this solution to the necessary conditions is the solution to the control problem.

We now return to the intertemporal utility maximization problem and point out a particular feature of the sufficiency theorems that will put you on alert when you go to apply them in your own work.

Example 3.4: As you may recall, the intertemporal utility maximization problem is given by

$$\max_{c(\cdot), k_T} J[k(\cdot), c(\cdot)] \overset{\text{def}}{=} \int_0^T U(c(t))\, e^{-rt}\, dt$$

$$\text{s.t.}\quad \dot{k}(t) = w + ik(t) - c(t),\ k(0) = k_0,\ k(T) = k_T.$$

The Hamiltonian is defined as $H(t, k, c, \lambda) \overset{\text{def}}{=} U(c)\, e^{-rt} + \lambda[w + ik - c]$. Also recall that we have assumed that $U'(c) > 0$ and $U''(c) < 0$.

First, we check to see if $H(\cdot)$ is concave in (k, c) for a given λ by computing the Hessian matrix of the Hamiltonian with respect to (k, c) and seeing if it is negative semidefinite:

$$H_{cc} = U''(c)\, e^{-rt} < 0,\ H_{kk} \equiv 0,\ H_{cc}H_{kk} - [H_{ck}]^2 = U''(c)\, e^{-rt} \cdot 0 - 0 = 0.$$

These calculations show that $H(\cdot)$ is concave in (k, c) for a given λ, so a solution (if it exists) to the necessary conditions is a solution to the control problem by Mangasarian's theorem (Theorem 3.1).

To check whether Arrow's theorem can be applied to reach the same conclusion, we need the maximized Hamiltonian $M(\cdot)$. Because $H_{cc} = U''(c)\, e^{-rt} < 0$, the solution (if one exists) to the necessary condition $H_c = U'(c)\, e^{-rt} - \lambda = 0$ does indeed maximize the Hamiltonian. Moreover, because $H_{cc} = U''(c)\, e^{-rt} < 0$, the implicit function theorem implies that if the solution to $H_c = U'(c)\, e^{-rt} - \lambda = 0$ exists, one could in principle find it in the form $c = \hat{c}(t, \lambda; r)$. Hence, the maximized Hamiltonian is given by

$$M(t, k, \lambda) \equiv H(t, k, \hat{c}(t, \lambda; r), \lambda) = U(\hat{c}(t, \lambda; r))\, e^{-rt} + \lambda[ik - \hat{c}(t, \lambda; r)].$$

Because $M(\cdot)$ is a linear function of k, it is therefore is a concave function of the capital stock, that is, the state variable. Hence by Arrow's theorem (Theorem 3.4), a solution of the necessary conditions, if one exists, is a solution of the optimal control problem.

Notice that all throughout this example, we have continually said "if a solution exists," because the sufficiency theorems presume the existence of a solution to the necessary conditions. In fact, no solution exists to the necessary conditions for this form of the problem under the stated assumptions. To see this, first observe that the integrand is independent of the capital stock, thereby implying, via Lemma 3.1(iii), that the costate variable is zero throughout the planning horizon. This, in turn, implies that the necessary condition $H_c = U'(c)\, e^{-rt} - \lambda = 0$ reduces to $U'(c)\, e^{-rt} = 0$. Seeing as $e^{-rt} \neq 0$, the necessary condition becomes $U'(c) = 0$, which *does not* have a solution because it was assumed that $U'(c) > 0$. Hence no solution to the necessary conditions exists for the intertemporal utility maximization problem under the stated assumptions. The way out of this situation is to fix the terminal capital stock or add a salvage value term to the problem. The important point to take away from this example is that you must be sure that a solution exists to the necessary conditions to employ the sufficiency theorems.

Let's now examine, in some detail, a classical economic model of the firm first introduced into the economics literature by Hotelling (1931). It will afford us the opportunity to use both the necessary and sufficient conditions developed so far in a model with economic content, as well as give us a taste of how the literature attempts to extract economic information from a dynamic economic model specified in general qualitative terms.

Example 3.5: Consider a firm that wishes to maximize the present discounted value of extracting a known and finite stock of a nonrenewable resource from the ground and selling it over a fixed and finite period of time. Define $x(t)$ as the stock of the nonrenewable resource in the ground at time t, $q(t)$ as the extraction rate of the nonrenewable resource at time t, $x_0 > 0$ as the given initial amount of the nonrenewable resource in the ground at the initial date of the planning horizon $t = 0$, and $T > 0$ as the terminal date of the planning horizon. As a result, the stock of the nonrenewable resource remaining in the ground at time t by definition equals the initial stock less the cumulative amount of it extracted up to time t, that is,

$$x(t) \stackrel{\text{def}}{=} x_0 - \int_0^t q(s)\,ds.$$

By Leibniz's rule, it therefore follows that

$$\dot{x}(t) = -q(t), \ x(0) = x_0.$$

We assume that the firm is free to choose how much of the nonrenewable resource to leave unextracted, that is, in the ground, when the planning horizon comes to a close. In other words, $x(T) = x_T$ is a choice or decision variable for the firm. We also assume that the firm's instantaneous profit function, say $\pi(\cdot) \in C^{(2)}$, depends not only on the rate of extraction $q(t)$, but also on the stock of the nonrenewable resource in the ground $x(t)$, and that $\pi_q(q, x) > 0$ and $\pi_x(q, x) > 0$. The former implies that profit increases with the extraction rate for a given stock, and the latter implies that for a given extraction rate, a larger stock of the nonrenewable resource in the ground is cheaper to extract, thus resulting in higher profit. The latter effect, videlicet, $\pi_x(q, x) > 0$, is called the *stock effect*, and can be motivated by imagining that in order to extract increasing amounts of the nonrenewable resource, the firm must dig deeper and deeper in the ground. This results in higher extraction costs, and thus lower profit, compared with the extraction of the initial units of the stock, which lie closer to the surface. Finally, we assume that the marginal profit of extraction is a decreasing function of the extraction rate, that is, $\pi_{qq}(q, x) < 0$.

The firm is asserted to maximize the present discounted value of profit using the discount rate $r > 0$, subject to the above differential equation governing the movement of the nonrenewable resource over time. Hence the optimal control problem facing the firm is given by

$$\max_{q(\cdot), x_T} \int_0^T \pi(q(t), x(t))\, e^{-rt}\, dt$$

$$\text{s.t.} \quad \dot{x}(t) = -q(t), \ x(0) = x_0, \ x(T) = x_T.$$

To simplify matters at this stage, we assume that both the extraction rate and resource stock are nonnegative through the planning horizon, and that a solution to the necessary conditions exists.

The Hamiltonian for this control problem is given by $H(t, x, q, \lambda) \stackrel{\text{def}}{=} \pi(q, x)e^{-rt} - \lambda q$. By Theorem 2.2, the necessary conditions are thus

$$H_q(t, x, q, \lambda) = \pi_q(q, x)\, e^{-rt} - \lambda = 0, \tag{16}$$

$$\dot{\lambda} = -\pi_x(q, x)\, e^{-rt}, \ \lambda(T) = 0, \tag{17}$$

$$\dot{x}(t) = -q(t), \ x(0) = x_0. \tag{18}$$

As remarked in Chapter 2 and discussed in the context of Lemma 3.1, the costate variable at any time t has the interpretation of the shadow value or price of the state variable at time t. In this model, therefore, $\lambda(t)$ is the *present value* shadow price of the nonrenewable resource stock in the ground at time t. The noun *present value* is employed because the objective functional is the present discounted value of profit. With this in mind, Eq. (16) asserts that in an optimal extraction plan, the firm will equate the present value marginal profit of extraction at time t with the present value shadow price of the nonrenewable resource stock at time t. That is, an optimal extraction rate is one that at every date of the planning horizon leaves the firm indifferent to extracting another unit of the nonrenewable resource stock and increasing the present value of marginal profit by $\pi_q(q(t), x(t))\, e^{-rt}$, and leaving the unit in the ground to extract at a later date, which has the present value of $\lambda(t)$ to the firm.

Because the costate equation in Eq. (17) holds for all $t \in [0, T]$, we may integrate it over the interval $[t, t+\varepsilon]$ for any $t \in [0, T-\varepsilon]$ and it stills holds. Doing just that and using s as the dummy variable of integration yields

$$\int_t^{t+\varepsilon} \dot{\lambda}(s)\, ds = -\int_t^{t+\varepsilon} \pi_x(q(s), x(s))\, e^{-rs}\, ds.$$

Integrating the left-hand side and rearranging the result yields

$$\lambda(t) = \int_t^{t+\varepsilon} \pi_x(q(s), x(s))\, e^{-rs} ds + \lambda(t+\varepsilon).$$

Substituting $\lambda(t) = \pi_q(q(t), x(t))\, e^{-rt}$ from Eq. (16) into the previous equation gives the expression of interest, namely,

$$\pi_q(q(t), x(t))\, e^{-rt} = \int_t^{t+\varepsilon} \pi_x(q(s), x(s))\, e^{-rs} ds + \pi_q(q(t+\varepsilon), x(t+\varepsilon))\, e^{-r(t+\varepsilon)}. \tag{19}$$

This equation asserts that in an optimal extraction plan, the firm is indifferent to extracting "today" and earning the present value marginal profit $\pi_q(q(t), x(t))\, e^{-rt}$, and extracting "tomorrow" and earning the present value marginal profit $\pi_q(q(t+\varepsilon), x(t+\varepsilon))\, e^{-r(t+\varepsilon)}$, *plus* the present value of the sum of the marginal profit earned, that is, costs saved, over the interval $[t, t+\varepsilon]$ because of the higher stock that results from delaying the extraction, to wit, $\int_t^{t+\varepsilon} \pi_x(q(s), x(s))\, e^{-rs} ds$.

Now define $\mu(t) \stackrel{\text{def}}{=} \lambda(t)\, e^{rt}$ as the *current value* shadow price of the nonrenewable resource stock. Differentiating this definition with respect to t yields $\dot{\mu}(t) = r\lambda(t)\, e^{rt} + \dot{\lambda}(t)\, e^{rt}$. Substituting $\dot{\lambda}(t) = -\pi_x(q(t), x(t))\, e^{-rt}$ from Eq. (17) and $\mu(t) \stackrel{\text{def}}{=} \lambda(t)\, e^{rt}$ in $\dot{\mu}(t) = r\lambda(t)\, e^{rt} + \dot{\lambda}(t)\, e^{rt}$ gives $\dot{\mu}(t) = r\mu(t) - \pi_x(q(t), x(t))$, which can be rearranged to read

$$\frac{\dot{\mu}(t)}{\mu(t)} = r - \frac{\pi_x(q(t), x(t))}{\mu(t)} < r. \tag{20}$$

This is the generalized version of *Hotelling's rule*, given that the instantaneous profit of the firm depends on the extraction rate as well as the amount of the nonrenewable resource stock in the ground. Equation (1) shows that in general, the current value shadow price of the nonrenewable resource stock grows at a rate less than the discount rate because $\mu(t) = \pi_q(q(t), x(t)) > 0$ from Eq. (16) and $\pi_x(q, x) > 0$. In fact, if $\pi_x(q, x)/\mu > r$, then the current value shadow price of the nonrenewable resource stock would be decreasing over some interval in the planning horizon. Thus, under the rather mild assumptions we are invoking, the current value shadow price of the nonrenewable resource stock may increase or decrease over the planning horizon, that is, its movement over time is not necessarily monotonic.

We now show that in general, the optimal extraction rate is not necessarily a decreasing function of time when stock effects are present. This is the analogue to the prior conclusion concerning the nonrenewable resource stock. Thus, periods of increasing extraction, declining extraction, or even constant extraction are entirely consistent with the nonrenewable resource–extracting model of the firm in the presence of stock effects. To see this mathematically, first differentiate $\mu(t) = \pi_q(q(t), x(t))$ with respect to t using the chain rule to get the equation $\dot{\mu}(t) = \pi_{qq}(q(t), x(t))\dot{q}(t) + \pi_{qx}(q(t), x(t))\dot{x}(t)$. Next, solve this equation for $\dot{q}(t)$ and substitute the current value version of the costate equation $\dot{\mu}(t) = r\mu(t) - \pi_x(q(t), x(t))$ and the state equation $\dot{x}(t) = -q(t)$ in it to get

$$\dot{q}(t) = \frac{\pi_{qx}(q(t), x(t))q(t) + r\pi_q(q(t), x(t)) - \pi_x(q(t), x(t))}{\pi_{qq}(q(t), x(t))} \gtrless 0. \tag{21}$$

Seeing as $\pi_q(q, x) > 0$ and $\pi_x(q, x) > 0$, it is clear from inspection of Eq. (21) that the optimal extraction rate may be increasing, decreasing, or constant over time, or may display all three characteristics over the planning horizon, regardless of the sign of the cross-partial derivative $\pi_{qx}(q, x)$. Typically, it is assumed that $\pi_{qx}(q, x) > 0$, which means that the marginal profit of extraction is higher when the stock of the asset in the ground is larger, which may be termed the *marginal stock effect*. This is entirely consistent with our prior assumption $\pi_x(q, x) > 0$ reflecting the stock effect.

In the special case in which profit (or equivalently, extraction cost) doesn't depend on the remaining stock in the ground, that is, $\pi_x(q, x) \equiv 0$, the archetype Hotelling rule follows immediately from Eq. (20), namely, $\dot{\mu}(t)/\mu(t) = r$. This implies that the current value shadow price of the nonrenewable resource stock rises at the discount rate. Moreover, in view of the fact that $\pi_x(q, x) \equiv 0$ implies that $\pi_{qx}(q, x) \equiv 0$, Eq. (21) reduces to

$$\dot{q}(t) = \frac{r\pi_q(q(t), x(t))}{\pi_{qq}(q(t), x(t))} < 0,$$

because $\pi_q(q, x) > 0$ and $\pi_{qq}(q, x) < 0$. Thus, in the absence of stock effects, the optimal extraction rate falls over the planning period. This is not an unexpected result, for the effect of positive discounting is to make the firm prefer current profit over future profit, thereby providing the incentive to extract at a higher rate in the beginning of the planning horizon.

For the special case in which the firm doesn't discount future profits at a positive rate, that is, $r \equiv 0$, it follows from Eq. (20) that the current value shadow price of the nonrenewable resource grows at a negative rate given by $\dot{\mu}(t)/\mu(t) = -\pi_x(q(t), x(t))/\mu(t) < 0$ because $\pi_x(q, x) > 0$. Similarly, it follows from Eq. (21) that

$$\dot{q}(t) = \frac{\pi_{qx}(q(t), x(t))q(t) - \pi_x(q(t), x(t))}{\pi_{qq}(q(t), x(t))}. \tag{22}$$

Thus, under the archetype marginal stock effect assumption $\pi_{qx}(q, x) > 0$, the optimal extraction rate may be increasing, decreasing, or constant over the planning horizon, or, more generally, display all three of these characteristics. If, in addition, we assume that $\pi_{qx}(q, x) \equiv 0$ but continue to maintain that $\pi_x(q, x) > 0$, then it follows from Eq. (22) that the optimal extraction rate is increasing over the planning horizon. If we furthermore assume that $\pi_x(q, x) \equiv 0$, then it follows from Eq. (22) that the optimal extraction rate is constant over the planning horizon.

To finish up the examination of the necessary conditions, we now consider the transversality condition associated with the choice of the stock of the nonrenewable resource left in the ground at the terminal time. From Eq. (17), we know that the terminal value of the present value shadow price of the resource stock is zero at the ending date, that is, $\lambda(T) = 0$. Moreover, from Eq. (16), we have that $\pi_q(q(T), x(T))\, e^{-rT} = \lambda(T)$. Seeing as $e^{-rT} \neq 0$, the prior two observations allow us to write the transversality condition associated with the choice of the terminal stock of the nonrenewable resource as

$$\pi_q(q(T), x(T))\, e^{-rT} = 0.$$

In the last period, therefore, with the terminal amount of the nonrenewable resource stock remaining in the ground an unrestricted choice variable, the firm behaves just like a static profit maximizing firm, setting marginal profit equal to zero. But this is surely not surprising, for if the firm is in the last period of its planning horizon, there is no future for which to plan. Thus, all the firm has to consider when making a decision in the last period is the consequences of its decision in that period, just like a static profit maximizing firm.

To finish up the analysis of this model, we seek to determine if the above necessary conditions given in Eqs. (16) through (18) are sufficient. We thus begin by computing the Hessian matrix of the Hamiltonian function with respect to the resource stock and extraction rate, that is,

$$\begin{bmatrix} H_{xx} & H_{xq} \\ H_{qx} & H_{qq} \end{bmatrix} = \begin{bmatrix} \pi_{xx}(q, x)\, e^{-rt} & \pi_{xq}(q, x)\, e^{-rt} \\ \pi_{qx}(q, x)\, e^{-rt} & \pi_{qq}(q, x)\, e^{-rt} \end{bmatrix}.$$

From this we see that concavity of the $H(\cdot)$ in (x, q) is equivalent to concavity of the $\pi(\cdot)$ in (x, q), given that $e^{-rt} > 0$. As a result, by Theorem 3.1, a solution of the necessary conditions given in Eqs. (16) through (18) is a solution of the optimal control problem if $\pi(\cdot)$ is concave in (x, q).

The last theorem of the chapter gives a Mangasarian-type set of sufficient conditions for the following *scrap value* or *salvage value* optimal control problem:

$$\max_{u(\cdot),x_1} J_S[x(\cdot), u(\cdot)] \stackrel{\text{def}}{=} \int_{t_0}^{t_1} f(t, x(t), u(t))\, dt + S(x_1)$$
$$\text{s.t.} \quad \dot{x}(t) = g(t, x(t), u(t)), \tag{23}$$
$$x(t_0) = x_0, \;\; x(t_1) = x_1.$$

The proof of the ensuing theorem follows that of Theorem 3.1 and is therefore left for a mental exercise.

Theorem 3.6 (Mangasarian Sufficient Conditions, Scrap Value): *Let $(z(t), v(t))$ be an admissible pair for problem (23). Suppose, moreover, that the pair $(z(t), v(t))$ satisfies the necessary conditions of Theorem 2.4 for problem (23) with the costate variable $\lambda(t)$, and let $H(t, x, u, \lambda) \stackrel{\text{def}}{=} f(t, x, u) + \lambda g(t, x, u)$ be the Hamiltonian that corresponds to the costate variable $\lambda(t)$. If $H(\cdot)$ is a concave function of $(x, u)\, \forall\, t \in [t_0, t_1]$ over an open convex set containing all the admissible values of $(x(\cdot), u(\cdot))$ and $S(\cdot)$ is a concave function of x over an open convex set containing all the admissible values of $x(\cdot)$, then $v(t)$ is an optimal control and $(z(t), v(t))$ yields the global maximum of $J_S[\cdot]$. If $H(\cdot)$ and $S(\cdot)$ are strictly concave functions under the same conditions, then $(z(t), v(t))$ yields the unique global maximum of $J_S[\cdot]$.*

We finish up this chapter by applying Theorem 3.6 to our modified inventory accumulation problem in Example 2.4.

Example 3.6: Recall the version of the inventory accumulation problem with a salvage value function from Example 2.4:

$$\max_{u(\cdot),x_T} J_S[x(\cdot), u(\cdot)] \stackrel{\text{def}}{=} px(T) - \int_0^T [c_1[u(t)]^2 + c_2 x(t)]\, dt$$
$$\text{s.t.} \quad \dot{x}(t) = u(t), \;\; x(0) = 0, \;\; x(T) = x_T.$$

The Hamiltonian, defined as $H(x, u, \lambda; c_1, c_2) \stackrel{\text{def}}{=} -c_1 u^2 - c_2 x + \lambda u$, is a concave function of $(x, u)\, \forall\, t \in [0, T]$ because its Hessian matrix with respect to (x, u) is negative semidefinite, that is,

$$H_{uu} = -2c_1 < 0,\ H_{xx} = 0,\ \begin{vmatrix} H_{uu} & H_{ux} \\ H_{xu} & H_{xx} \end{vmatrix} = \begin{vmatrix} -2c_1 & 0 \\ 0 & 0 \end{vmatrix} = 0.$$

Given that the salvage function is linear in the state variable, it is concave in it too. Hence by Theorem 3.6, the solution to the necessary conditions given in Example 2.4 is also a solution to the optimal control problem. Uniqueness follows from the observation that there is only one solution of the necessary conditions.

Thus far in our study of optimal control theory, we have limited our attention to problems with one state variable, one control variable, a terminal value of the state variable that is an unrestricted decision variable, and a salvage value function. Moreover, we have developed necessary and sufficient conditions for this class of control problems in which the optimal control is a continuous function of time, and the corresponding state and costate functions are continuously differentiable with respect to time. In the next chapter, we broaden the class of optimal control problems we examine to a considerable degree. Specifically, we extend the theorems of this and the previous chapter by examining optimal control problems with many state and control variables, constraints on the control variables, optimal controls that are piecewise continuous functions of time, and states and costates that are piecewise smooth functions of time. This will permit us to tackle many more dynamic problems of interest to economists, as we will see in the chapters to come.

MENTAL EXERCISES

3.1 For Mental Exercises 2.15–2.19, determine whether the solution of the necessary conditions solves the optimal control problem under consideration. Is the solution unique? Be sure to show your work.

3.2 For Mental Exercises 2.20–2.23, determine whether the solution of the necessary conditions solves the optimal control problem under consideration. Is the solution unique? Be sure to show your work.

3.3 Prove that if the Hamiltonian $H(t, x, u, \lambda) \stackrel{\text{def}}{=} f(t, x, u) + \lambda g(t, x, u)$ for the optimal control problem

$$\max_{u(\cdot),x_1} J[x(\cdot), u(\cdot)] \stackrel{\text{def}}{=} \int_{t_0}^{t_1} f(t, x(t), u(t))\, dt$$

$$\text{s.t.}\quad \dot{x}(t) = g(t, x(t), u(t)),\ x(t_0) = x_0,\ x(t_1) = x_1,$$

is concave in $(x, u)\, \forall t \in [t_0, t_1]$, and the triplet $(z(t), v(t), \lambda(t))$ satisfies the necessary conditions of Theorem 3.2, then $v(t)$ maximizes $H(t, z(t), u, \lambda(t))$ for each $t \in [t_0, t_1]$ with respect to u.

3.4 Prove Theorem 3.2.

3.5 Prove part (iii) of Corollary 3.1 using the fact that a function is concave in a subset of variables if and only if its Hessian matrix with respect to the subset of variables is negative semidefinite.

3.6 With respect to the derivation in Lemma 3.1, show that the specific solution for the costate variable is identical whether you integrate the costate equation backward from t_0 to $t > t_0$ or forward from $t < t_1$ to t_1. Show further that the constant of integration c_1 differs from c_2.

3.7 Prove Theorem 3.3.

3.8 Complete the proof of Theorem 3.4.

3.9 In Example 3.1, show that the necessary conditions of Theorem 3.3 are identical to those of Theorem 2.2 given in Example 2.1.

3.10 In Example 3.2, demonstrate that:
(a) $H(\cdot)$ is concave in (x, u) by showing that the Hessian matrix of $H(\cdot)$ with respect to (x, u) is negative semidefinite.
(b) $H(\cdot)$ is concave in (x, u) by showing that the eigenvalues of the Hessian matrix of $H(\cdot)$ with respect to (x, u) are nonpositive.
(c) The solution of the necessary conditions is the unique solution of the control problem.
(d) The necessary conditions of Theorem 3.3 are identical to those of Theorem 2.2 given in Example 2.2.

3.11 In Example 3.3, demonstrate that:
(a) The solution to the necessary conditions is given by $v(t) = 0$, $z(t) = x_0$, and $\lambda(t) = t - T$.
(b) The solution to the necessary conditions is the solution to the control problem *without* using the sufficiency theorems.

3.12 Prove Theorem 3.6.

3.13 Show that for Mental Exercise 2.30, the solution of the necessary conditions does indeed solve the optimal control problem. Is the solution unique? Show your work.

3.14 State and prove a Mangasarian-type sufficiency theorem for the optimal control problem

$$\max_{u(\cdot),x_0,x_1} J[x(\cdot), u(\cdot)] \stackrel{\text{def}}{=} \int_{t_0}^{t_1} f(t, x(t), u(t))\, dt$$

$$\text{s.t.} \quad \dot{x}(t) = g(t, x(t), u(t)), \; x(t_0) = x_0, \; x(t_1) = x_1.$$

3.15 Show that for Mental Exercise 2.28, the solution of the necessary conditions does indeed solve the optimal control problem. Is the solution unique? Show your work.

3.16 In Example 3.4, show and explain why the integrand is not strictly concave in the state and control variables even though $U''(c) < 0$. Explain carefully how fixing the terminal capital stock or adding a salvage function can get one out of the problem of nonexistence.

3.17 **True, False, Uncertain:** If the Hamiltonian is not a concave function of the state and control variables and the maximized Hamiltonian is not a concave function of the state variable, then one *cannot* determine which of several solutions of the necessary conditions is optimal, assuming that an optimal solution exists.

FURTHER READING

An excellent book, reference and otherwise, for the prerequisite mathematics, is Simon and Blume (1994). If you do not have a copy of this book, then it would most likely behoove you to buy a copy of it as soon as possible. As is clear from the chapter proper, we will rely on many of the theorems developed in that book during the course of our exposition of optimal control theory. A proof of the Arrow sufficiency theorem, under more general conditions than stated here, may be found in Arrow and Kurz (1970). Kamien and Schwartz (1971) offer another proof of Arrow's theorem. Lemma 3.1 is a special case of a more general result established by Léonard (1981). Chiang (1992), Kamien and Schwartz (1991), Léonard and Van Long (1992), and Seierstad and Sydsaeter (1987) contain sufficiency theorems akin to those given in this chapter. As should be obvious, Theorem 3.1 is due to Mangasarian (1966). In the next chapter, we will introduce more general sufficiency theorems than those examined in the present chapter.

REFERENCES

Arrow, K.J. and Kurz, M. (1970), *Public Investment, the Rate of Return, and Optimal Fiscal Policy* (Baltimore: Johns Hopkins University Press).

Chiang, A.C. (1992), *Elements of Dynamic Optimization* (New York: McGraw-Hill, Inc.).

Hotelling, H. (1931), "The Economics of Exhaustible Resources," *Journal of Political Economy*, 39, 137–175.

Kamien, M.I. and Schwartz, N.L. (1971), "Sufficient Conditions in Optimal Control Theory," *Journal of Economic Theory*, 3, 207–214.

Kamien, M.I. and Schwartz, N.L. (1991, 2nd Ed.), *Dynamic Optimization: The Calculus of Variations and Optimal Control in Economics and Management* (New York: Elsevier Science Publishing Co., Inc.).

Léonard, D. (1981), "The Signs of the Costate Variables and Sufficiency Conditions in a Class of Optimal Control Problems," *Economics Letters*, 8, 321–325.

Léonard, D. and Van Long, N. (1992), *Optimal Control Theory and Static Optimization in Economics* (New York: Cambridge University Press).

Mangasarian, O.L. (1966), "Sufficient Conditions for the Optimal Control of Nonlinear Systems," *SIAM Journal on Control*, 4, 139–152.

Seierstad, A. and Sydsæter, K. (1987), *Optimal Control Theory with Economic Applications* (New York: Elsevier Science Publishing Co., Inc.).

Simon, C.P. and Blume, L. (1994), *Mathematics for Economists* (New York: W.W. Norton & Company, Inc.).

FOUR

The Maximum Principle and Economic Interpretations

Until this juncture, our development of the necessary and sufficient conditions of optimal control theory was essentially a reformulation of those from the classical calculus of variations. As a result, the power and reach of optimal control theory have not been fully exposed or exploited. The goal of this chapter, therefore, is to state and prove some necessary and sufficient conditions for a class of control problems that permit the full capability of optimal control theory to be realized. The theorems are not the most general we will encounter, but they do highlight the motivation for the name *Maximum Principle*. Moreover, our proof of the necessary conditions will employ some continuity assumptions that are, strictly speaking, not needed for a rigorous proof, but will nonetheless be employed so as to ease the technical burden and bring in some connections with the principle of optimality and dynamic programming. We will then use the necessary conditions to explicitly solve for the optimal paths of some examples, some of which will be devoid of any economic content so as to emphasize how to arrive at a solution in practice. The reader is encouraged to work through the proof of the necessary and sufficient conditions, as it provides the reader with a better understanding of how they differ from those presented earlier. Note that the theorems are stated and proven for a class of control problems with many state and control variables.

The optimal control problem under consideration is to find a piecewise continuous control vector function $\mathbf{u}(\cdot) \stackrel{\text{def}}{=} (u_1(\cdot), u_2(\cdot), \ldots, u_M(\cdot))$ and its associated piecewise smooth state vector function $\mathbf{x}(\cdot) \stackrel{\text{def}}{=} (x_1(\cdot), x_2(\cdot), \ldots, x_N(\cdot))$, defined on the fixed time interval $[t_0, t_1]$ that will solve the optimal control problem

$$V(t_0, \mathbf{x}_0, t_1, \mathbf{x}_1) \stackrel{\text{def}}{=} \left\{ \max_{\mathbf{u}(\cdot)} J[\mathbf{x}(\cdot), \mathbf{u}(\cdot)] \stackrel{\text{def}}{=} \int_{t_0}^{t_1} f(t, \mathbf{x}(t), \mathbf{u}(t))\, dt \right\}$$

$$\text{s.t.} \quad \dot{\mathbf{x}}(t) = \mathbf{g}(t, \mathbf{x}(t), \mathbf{u}(t)), \tag{1}$$

$$\mathbf{u}(t) \in U \subseteq \Re^M, \;\; \mathbf{x}(t_0) = \mathbf{x}_0, \;\; \mathbf{x}(t_1) = \mathbf{x}_1,$$

where $\mathbf{g}(\cdot) \stackrel{\text{def}}{=} (g^1(\cdot), g^2(\cdot), \ldots, g^N(\cdot))$ and $\dot{\mathbf{x}}(\cdot) \stackrel{\text{def}}{=} (\dot{x}_1(\cdot), \dot{x}_2(\cdot), \ldots, \dot{x}_N(\cdot))$. Notice that the terminal boundary condition $\mathbf{x}(t_1) = \mathbf{x}_1$ specifies that the value of the state variable must be equal to some given (i.e., fixed) value at the terminal date of the planning horizon, seeing as $\mathbf{x}_1$ is not specified to be a decision variable in the problem statement. Thus problem (1) is a *fixed endpoints problem*, unlike that encountered in Chapters 2 and 3, in which $\mathbf{x}(t_1) = \mathbf{x}_1$ was a decision variable. Also recall that the control set U specifies the region in which the values of the control variable must lie, and that it is a fixed subset of $\Re^M$ that is assumed to be *independent of the state variables*. We will relax this assumption in a later chapter.

In typical economic problems, $V(t_0, \mathbf{x}_0, t_1, \mathbf{x}_1)$ represents the maximum present discounted profit of a firm that begins its operations with the capital stock $\mathbf{x}_0$ at time t_0, and ends its operations with the capital stock $\mathbf{x}_1$ at time t_1. Alternatively, $V(t_0, \mathbf{x}_0, t_1, \mathbf{x}_1)$ is the maximum total value of the asset $\mathbf{x}_0$ at time t_0, and thus is the purchase price of the asset $\mathbf{x}_0$ at time t_0, because the maximum present value of the stream of net benefits from holding $\mathbf{x}_0$ at time t_0 and using the optimal plan is $V(t_0, \mathbf{x}_0, t_1, \mathbf{x}_1)$. The function $V(\cdot)$ is called the *optimal value function.*

Because we are allowing for a more general class of control variables than we did earlier, we must amend our definition of an admissible control. To this end, we have the following definition, which should be contrasted with that given earlier in Definition 2.1.

Definition 4.1: We call $(\mathbf{x}(t), \mathbf{u}(t))$ an *admissible pair* if $\mathbf{u}(\cdot)$ is any piecewise continuous control vector function such that $\mathbf{u}(t) \in U \; \forall \, t \in [t_0, t_1]$ and $\mathbf{x}(\cdot)$ is a piecewise smooth state vector function such that $\dot{\mathbf{x}}(t) = \mathbf{g}(t, \mathbf{x}(t), \mathbf{u}(t))$, $\mathbf{x}(t_0) = \mathbf{x}_0$, and $\mathbf{x}(t_1) = \mathbf{x}_1$.

In developing the necessary conditions in Chapter 2, we found it convenient to define a function called the Hamiltonian, and we will find it convenient to do so here too. In the present case there are N state variables and N ordinary differential equations describing their rates of changes with respect to time. Consequently, we associate with each of the differential equations a costate function, say $\lambda_n(\cdot)$, $n = 1, 2, \ldots, N$, and form the Hamiltonian for problem (1), namely,

$$H(t, \mathbf{x}, \mathbf{u}, \boldsymbol{\lambda}) \stackrel{\text{def}}{=} f(t, \mathbf{x}, \mathbf{u}) + \sum_{n=1}^{N} \lambda_n g^n(t, \mathbf{x}, \mathbf{u})$$

$$\stackrel{\text{def}}{=} f(t, \mathbf{x}, \mathbf{u}) + \boldsymbol{\lambda}'\mathbf{g}(t, \mathbf{x}, \mathbf{u}), \tag{2}$$

where $\boldsymbol{\lambda} \stackrel{\text{def}}{=} (\lambda_1, \lambda_2, \ldots, \lambda_N)$ and $\boldsymbol{\lambda}'\mathbf{g}(t, \mathbf{x}, \mathbf{u}) \stackrel{\text{def}}{=} \sum_{n=1}^{N} \lambda_n g^n(t, \mathbf{x}, \mathbf{u})$ is the scalar or inner product of the vectors $\boldsymbol{\lambda}$ and $\mathbf{g}(t, \mathbf{x}, \mathbf{u})$.

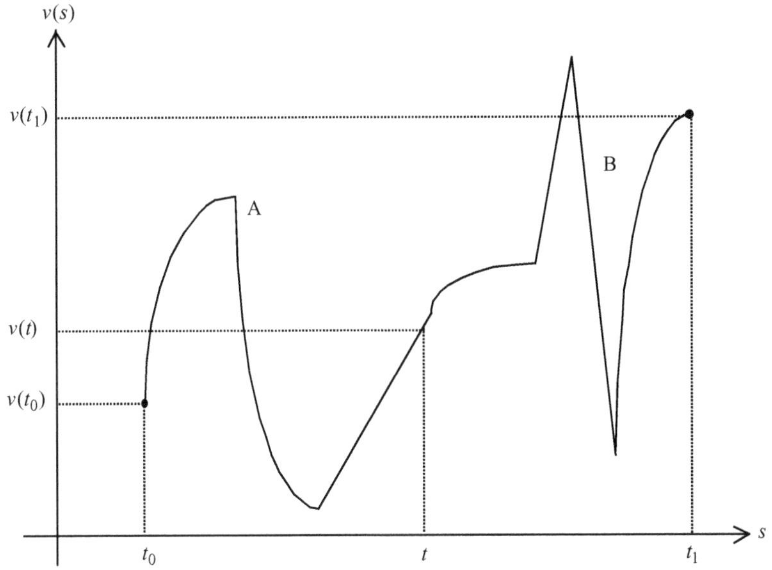

Figure 4.1

The ensuing proof of the necessary conditions for problem (1) will rely on the following three assumptions, in addition to the fundamental ones stated in Chapter 1:

(A.1) Let $S \in \Re^N$ be a nonempty set of points from which one can bring the system to the terminal point $\mathbf{x}_1$ at time t_1 by the use of an optimal control, where $\mathbf{x}_0 \in S$.

(A.2) S is an *open* set.

(A.3) $V(\cdot) \in C^{(2)} \,\forall\, (t, \mathbf{x}) \in (t_0, t_1) \times S$, where $V(\cdot)$ is the optimal value function for problem (1).

Assumption (A.1) means that there exists values of the state vector such that when we take the initial state as one of these values, we can arrive at the given terminal state by the terminal date of the planning horizon using an optimal control. Assumption (A.2) says that the boundary of the set S is not part of S, that is to say, S consists only of interior points. The $C^{(2)}$ nature of the optimal value function in assumption (A.3) is adopted so as to avoid getting caught up in technical details. It will be pointed out during the proof of the necessary conditions where these assumptions are used. The approach we take below to prove the necessary conditions of problem (1) is often referred to as the "dynamic programming proof" of the necessary conditions. As you will shortly see, this method of proof is quite different from the variational proof of the necessary conditions given in Chapter 2.

Before we state and prove the necessary conditions, it is preferable to introduce the key principle behind the foregoing proof, videlicet, the *principle of optimality*. The principle of optimality is illustrated in Figure 4.1 for an optimal control problem

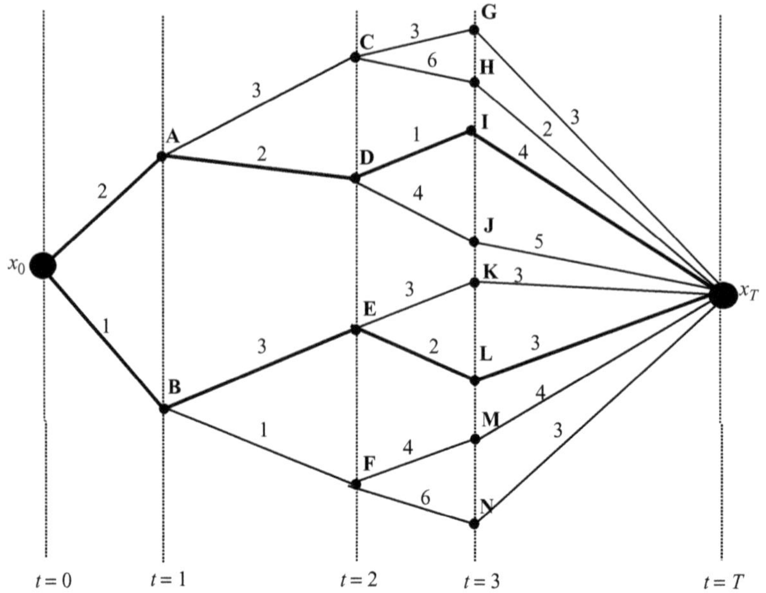

Figure 4.2

with one control variable. Let the curve $v(s)$ be the optimal path of the control variable for the entire planning horizon $[t_0, t_1]$, beginning with stock x_0 at time t_0 and ending with stock x_1 at time t_1. In Figure 4.1, this path is divided into two parts, A and B, with time $s = t$ being the break point in the time horizon. The principle of optimality asserts that trajectory B, defined for the interval $[t, t_1]$, must, in its own right, be the optimal path for this interval given that, at time $s = t$, $t \in (t_0, t_1)$, the initial state is taken as $z(t)$, the terminal state from the interval $[t_0, t]$. Notice that we have not drawn the optimal path of the control variable as a differentiable function of time so as to emphasize the more general character of the optimal control problem we are studying in this chapter relative to that studied in the prior two chapters.

An alternative view of the principle of optimality is given in Figure 4.2, where the problem is to find the least cost path from the initial state x_0 to the terminal state x_T. The numbers along each arc indicate the cost of moving between the adjacent points. First note that the optimal path is *not* unique and is given by the two thick paths. They represent the least cost paths of reaching the terminal state x_T from the given initial state x_0. In this context, the principle of optimality asserts that, roughly speaking, if you chop off the first arc (or any beginning set of arcs) from an optimal sequence of arcs, the remaining abridged sequence of arcs must still be optimal in its own right. In other words, the principle of optimality asserts that any portion of an optimal arc is optimal.

For example, in Figure 4.2, the path x_0ADIx_T is an optimal path from x_0 to x_T. Thus by the principle of optimality, the least cost path from A to x_T must be $ADIx_T$, which is precisely the remaining part of the overall optimal path when taking A as the initial state, as inspection of Figure 4.2 confirms. Conversely, because the path $ADIx_T$ is the least cost path from state A to state x_T, any longer optimal path, say from x_0 to x_T, that passes through A must use the path $ADIx_T$ to reach state x_T. Again, inspection of Figure 4.2 confirms this too. The same results would also hold if we took, say, state D as the initial state, as you should confirm. Likewise, similar results hold if we use the other optimal arc x_0BELx_T, as you should also confirm.

Finally, note that the *myopic* optimal path is given by x_0BFMx_T. This is the path chosen by an individual who looks only at the cost of moving from one state to the next, and chooses the path that minimizes the period-by-period cost of moving from x_0 to x_T. Observe that the total cost along the path x_0BFMx_T is greater than that along paths x_0ADIx_T and x_0BELx_T. This illustrates the general result that a myopic one-stage-at-a-time optimization procedure will *not*, in general, yield the least cost path in a dynamic environment.

The principle of optimality can be proven in a straightforward way by a contrapositive argument. It is important to prove this principle and to follow it carefully because, as noted above, the principle of optimality forms the basis of the ensuing proof of the necessary conditions of optimal control theory.

Theorem 4.1 (The Principle of Optimality): *An optimal policy has the property that whatever the initial state and initial decision are, the remaining decisions must constitute an optimal policy with regard to the state resulting from the first decision.*

Proof: Let $\mathbf{v}(s)$ be the optimal control path $\forall s \in [t_0, t_1]$, beginning at time t_0 in state $\mathbf{x}_0$ and ending at time t_1 in state $\mathbf{x}_1$, and let $\mathbf{z}(s)$ be the corresponding state path. A contrapositive proof will be employed. Assume, therefore, that $\mathbf{v}(s)$ is the optimal control path $\forall s \in [t_0, t]$, $t \in (t_0, t_1)$, beginning at time t_0 in state $\mathbf{x}_0$ and ending at time t with state $\mathbf{z}(t)$. Also assume, contrary to the conclusion of the theorem, that $\mathbf{u}(s) \neq \mathbf{v}(s)$ is the optimal control path $\forall s \in (t, t_1]$, beginning with state $\mathbf{z}(t)$ at time t and ending with state $\mathbf{x}_1$ at time t_1. Then $\mathbf{v}(s)$ could not be the optimal control path $\forall s \in [t_0, t_1]$ because one could use $\mathbf{v}(s) \forall s \in [t_0, t]$ and switch to $\mathbf{u}(s) \forall s \in (t, t_1]$, thereby giving the objective functional a larger value than using $\mathbf{v}(s) \forall s \in [t_0, t_1]$. This contradicts the assumed optimality (the hypothesis) of $\mathbf{v}(s) \forall s \in [t_0, t_1]$, thereby proving the principle of optimality. Q.E.D.

We are now ready to state and prove the necessary conditions for problem (1).

Theorem 4.2 (The Maximum Principle): *Let* $(\mathbf{z}(t), \mathbf{v}(t))$ *be an admissible pair for problem (1). Then if* $(\mathbf{z}(t), \mathbf{v}(t))$ *yields the absolute maximum of* $J[\cdot]$, *it is necessary that there exists a piecewise smooth vector-valued function*

$\boldsymbol{\lambda}(\cdot) \stackrel{\text{def}}{=} (\lambda_1(\cdot), \lambda_2(\cdot), \ldots, \lambda_N(\cdot))$ *such that for all* $t \in [t_0, t_1]$,

$$\mathbf{v}(t) = \arg\max_{\mathbf{u}\in U} H(t, \mathbf{z}(t), \mathbf{u}, \boldsymbol{\lambda}(t)),$$

that is, if

$$M(t, \mathbf{z}(t), \boldsymbol{\lambda}(t)) \stackrel{\text{def}}{=} \max_{\mathbf{u}\in U} H(t, \mathbf{z}(t), \mathbf{u}, \boldsymbol{\lambda}(t)),$$

then

$$M(t, \mathbf{z}(t), \boldsymbol{\lambda}(t)) \equiv H(t, \mathbf{z}(t), \mathbf{v}(t), \boldsymbol{\lambda}(t)),$$

or equivalently,

$$H(t, \mathbf{z}(t), \mathbf{v}(t), \boldsymbol{\lambda}(t)) \geq H(t, \mathbf{z}(t), \mathbf{u}, \boldsymbol{\lambda}(t))\, \forall\, \mathbf{u} \in U.$$

That is, for each $t \in [t_0, t_1]$, $H(\cdot)$ *attains at* $\mathbf{v}(t)$ *its maximum with respect to* $\mathbf{u}$, $\forall\, \mathbf{u} \in U$ *and* $(t, \mathbf{z}(t), \boldsymbol{\lambda}(t))$ *fixed. Furthermore, except for the points of discontinuities of* $\mathbf{v}(t)$,

$$\dot{z}_n(t) = \frac{\partial H}{\partial \lambda_n}(t, \mathbf{z}(t), \mathbf{v}(t), \boldsymbol{\lambda}(t)) = g^n(t, \mathbf{z}(t), \mathbf{v}(t)), \quad n = 1, 2, \ldots, N,$$

$$\dot{\lambda}_n(t) = -\frac{\partial H}{\partial x_n}(t, \mathbf{z}(t), \mathbf{v}(t), \boldsymbol{\lambda}(t)), \quad n = 1, 2, \ldots, N,$$

where the above notation means that the functions are first differentiated with respect to the particular variable and then evaluated at $(t, \mathbf{z}(t), \mathbf{v}(t), \boldsymbol{\lambda}(t))$.

Proof: To begin the proof of the necessary conditions, recall the definition of the optimal value function $V(\cdot)$ from problem (1):

$$V(t_0, \mathbf{x}_0) \stackrel{\text{def}}{=} \max_{\mathbf{u}(\cdot)} \int_{t_0}^{t_1} f(s, \mathbf{x}(s), \mathbf{u}(s))\, ds$$

$$\text{s.t. } \dot{\mathbf{x}}(s) = \mathbf{g}(s, \mathbf{x}(s), \mathbf{u}(s)),\ \mathbf{u}(s) \in U, \mathbf{x}(t_0) = \mathbf{x}_0,\ \mathbf{x}(t_1) = \mathbf{x}_1. \tag{3}$$

Note that we now use s as the dummy variable of integration in light of the fact that we intend to let t denote a particular date in the planning horizon. Because the optimal pair $(\mathbf{z}(\cdot), \mathbf{v}(\cdot))$ is assumed to exist, this definition is equivalent to

$$V(t_0, \mathbf{x}_0) \equiv \int_{t_0}^{t_1} f(s, \mathbf{z}(s), \mathbf{v}(s))\, ds. \tag{4}$$

Given that $(t_0, \mathbf{x}_0, t_1, \mathbf{x}_1)$ are the parameters of problem (1), the optimal value function $V(\cdot)$ depends on all four parameters in general, as well as any other parameter that might appear in problem (1). The notation in Eqs. (3) and (4), namely, $V(t_0, \mathbf{x}_0)$, is adopted to streamline the exposition, for the parameters $(t_1, \mathbf{x}_1)$ play no essential role in what follows.

By the principle of optimality, it follows that Eq. (4) can be written as

$$V(t_0, \mathbf{x}_0) \equiv \int_{t_0}^{t} f(s, \mathbf{z}(s), \mathbf{v}(s))\, ds + V(t, \mathbf{z}(t)), \tag{5}$$

which holds for every $t \in [t_0, t_1]$. From the definitions of $V(\cdot)$ in Eqs. (3) and (4), it should be clear that

$$V(t, \mathbf{z}(t)) \equiv \int_{t}^{t_1} f(s, \mathbf{z}(s), \mathbf{v}(s))\, ds, \tag{6}$$

in which case the correctness of Eq. (5) should now seem more evident given the additive property of integrals with respect to the limits of integration. Equation (6) asserts that $V(t, \mathbf{z}(t))$ is the maximum total value of the asset $\mathbf{z}(t)$ at time t, and thus is the purchase price of the asset $\mathbf{z}(t)$ at time t, because the maximum present value of the stream of net benefits from holding $\mathbf{z}(t)$ at time t and using the optimal plan is $V(t, \mathbf{z}(t))$. Equation (5) thus asserts that the total value of the asset $\mathbf{x}_0$ at time t_0 may be thought of as two separate additive components: (i) the return beginning with stock $\mathbf{x}_0$ at time t_0 and continuing the optimal plan until time t, and (ii) the return beginning with stock $\mathbf{z}(t)$ at time t and continuing on with the optimal plan, where $\mathbf{z}(t)$ is the stock at time t that resulted from the optimal plan in (i). This assertion is, in its essence, the principle of optimality.

Now differentiate Eq. (5) with respect to t using the chain rule and Leibniz's rule to get

$$0 \equiv \frac{d}{dt}\left[\int_{t_0}^{t} f(s, \mathbf{z}(s), \mathbf{v}(s))\, ds + V(t, \mathbf{z}(t))\right],$$

or

$$0 \equiv f(t, \mathbf{z}(t), \mathbf{v}(t)) + V_t(t, \mathbf{z}(t)) + \sum_{n=1}^{N} V_{x_n}(t, \mathbf{z}(t))\dot{z}_n(t), \tag{7}$$

which also holds for every $t \in [t_0, t_1]$. Because $(\mathbf{z}(\cdot), \mathbf{v}(\cdot))$ is the optimal pair in problem (1), it must satisfy the state equation identically, that is, $\dot{\mathbf{z}}(t) \equiv \mathbf{g}(t, \mathbf{z}(t), \mathbf{v}(t))$ for all $t \in [t_0, t_1]$. Substituting $\dot{\mathbf{z}}(t) \equiv \mathbf{g}(t, \mathbf{z}(t), \mathbf{v}(t))$ into Eq. (7) therefore yields

$$V_t(t, \mathbf{z}(t)) + \sum_{n=1}^{N} V_{x_n}(t, \mathbf{z}(t)) g^n(t, \mathbf{z}(t), \mathbf{v}(t)) + f(t, \mathbf{z}(t), \mathbf{v}(t)) \equiv 0\, \forall\, t \in [t_0, t_1]. \tag{8}$$

This is the fundamental partial differential equation obeyed by the optimal value function $V(\cdot)$, known as the *Hamilton-Jacobi-Bellman equation*. The Hamilton-Jacobi-Bellman equation is commonly written in the alternative form $-V_t(t, \mathbf{z}(t)) \equiv f(t, \mathbf{z}(t), \mathbf{v}(t)) + V_{\mathbf{x}}(t, \mathbf{z}(t))\, \mathbf{g}(t, \mathbf{z}(t), \mathbf{v}(t))$. We will return to this fundamental result in later chapters, when we discuss continuous time dynamic programming and intertemporal duality theory. Equation (8) is an important result in this proof. We will return to it shortly.

Now consider the control vector $\varepsilon \in U$, and define the *perturbed control* as

$$\mathbf{u}(s) \overset{\text{def}}{=} \begin{cases} \varepsilon & \forall\, s \in [t_0, t_0 + \Delta t) \\ \mathbf{u}^{\varepsilon}(s) & \forall\, s \in [t_0 + \Delta t, t_1], \end{cases}$$

where $\Delta t > 0$, $\mathbf{u}^{\varepsilon}(s)$ is the time path of the optimal control corresponding to the initial point $(t_0 + \Delta t, \mathbf{x}^{\varepsilon}(t_0 + \Delta t))$, and $\mathbf{x}^{\varepsilon}(s)$ is the time path of the state vector corresponding to the perturbed control path $\mathbf{u}(s)$. By assumption, $\mathbf{v}(\cdot)$ is the optimal control, thereby implying that $\mathbf{u}(\cdot)$ is a *suboptimal control*. As a result, it follows that

$$\begin{aligned} V(t_0, \mathbf{x}_0) &\equiv J[\mathbf{z}(\cdot), \mathbf{v}(\cdot)] \geq J[\mathbf{x}^{\varepsilon}(\cdot), \mathbf{u}(\cdot)] \\ &= \int_{t_0}^{t_0+\Delta t} f(s, \mathbf{x}^{\varepsilon}(s), \varepsilon)\, ds + V(t_0 + \Delta t, \mathbf{x}^{\varepsilon}(t_0 + \Delta t)). \end{aligned} \tag{9}$$

The pair $(\mathbf{x}^{\varepsilon}(\cdot), \mathbf{u}(\cdot))$ must be admissible if we are to compare the value of problem (1) using the controls $\mathbf{u}(\cdot)$ and $\mathbf{v}(\cdot)$. This implies that $\mathbf{x}^{\varepsilon}(t_0) = \mathbf{z}(t_0) = \mathbf{x}_0$ and $\mathbf{x}^{\varepsilon}(t_1) = \mathbf{z}(t_1) = \mathbf{x}_1$. Upon substituting $\mathbf{x}^{\varepsilon}(t_0) = \mathbf{x}_0$ in Eq. (9) and rearranging it, we get

$$V(t_0 + \Delta t, \mathbf{x}^{\varepsilon}(t_0 + \Delta t)) - V(t_0, \mathbf{x}^{\varepsilon}(t_0)) \leq -\int_{t_0}^{t_0+\Delta t} f(s, \mathbf{x}^{\varepsilon}(s), \varepsilon)\, ds. \tag{10}$$

Now divide Eq. (10) by $\Delta t > 0$, and let $\Delta t \to 0$ to get

$$\lim_{\Delta t \to 0} \frac{V(t_0 + \Delta t, \mathbf{x}^{\varepsilon}(t_0 + \Delta t)) - V(t_0, \mathbf{x}^{\varepsilon}(t_0))}{\Delta t} \leq -\lim_{\Delta t \to 0} \frac{\int_{t_0}^{t_0+\Delta t} f(s, \mathbf{x}^{\varepsilon}(s), \varepsilon)\, ds}{\Delta t}. \tag{11}$$

The inequality in Eq. (10) is preserved as $\Delta t \to 0$ because of the assumed differentiability of $V(\cdot)$ from assumption (A.3). Our goal now is to evaluate the limits in Eq. (11) so that it can be put in the form of Eq. (8).

We begin with the left-hand side of Eq. (11). To this end, define the function $G(\cdot)$ by the formula $G(\Delta t) \overset{\text{def}}{=} V(t_0 + \Delta t, \mathbf{x}^{\varepsilon}(t_0 + \Delta t))$, which implies that $G(0) = V(t_0, \mathbf{x}^{\varepsilon}(t_0))$. By the chain rule, we also have that $G'(\Delta t) = V_t(t_0 + \Delta t, \mathbf{x}^{\varepsilon}(t_0 + \Delta t)) + \sum_{n=1}^{N} V_{x_n}(t_0 + \Delta t, \mathbf{x}^{\varepsilon}(t_0 + \Delta t))\ \dot{x}_n^{\varepsilon}(t_0 + \Delta t)$. Using these results and the definition of the derivative, the left-hand side of Eq. (11)

becomes

$$\lim_{\Delta t\to 0}\frac{V(t_0+\Delta t,\mathbf{x}^{\varepsilon}(t_0+\Delta t))-V(t_0,\mathbf{x}^{\varepsilon}(t_0))}{\Delta t}=\lim_{\Delta t\to 0}\frac{G(0+\Delta t)-G(0)}{\Delta t}$$

$$\overset{\text{def}}{=} G'(\Delta t)\big|_{\Delta t=0}=G'(0)=V_t(t_0,\mathbf{x}^{\varepsilon}(t_0))+\sum_{n=1}^{N}V_{x_n}(t_0,\mathbf{x}^{\varepsilon}(t_0))\,\dot{x}_n^{\varepsilon}(t_0). \quad (12)$$

We will return to this result shortly.

To evaluate the right-hand side of Eq. (11), define the function $F(\cdot)$ by the formula

$$F(\Delta t)\overset{\text{def}}{=}\int_{t_0}^{t_0+\Delta t} f(s,\mathbf{x}^{\varepsilon}(s),\varepsilon)\,ds,$$

and then recognize that $F(0)=\int_{t_0}^{t_0} f(s,\mathbf{x}^{\varepsilon}(s),\varepsilon)\,ds=0$ and that $F'(\Delta t)=f(t_0+\Delta t,\mathbf{x}^{\varepsilon}(t_0+\Delta t),\varepsilon)$ by Leibniz's rule. Using these results and the definition of the derivative, the right-hand side of Eq. (11) becomes

$$\begin{aligned}-\lim_{\Delta t\to 0}\frac{\int_{t_0}^{t_0+\Delta t} f(s,\mathbf{x}^{\varepsilon}(s),\varepsilon)\,ds}{\Delta t}&=-\lim_{\Delta t\to 0}\frac{F(\Delta t)}{\Delta t}=-\lim_{\Delta t\to 0}\frac{F(0+\Delta t)-F(0)}{\Delta t}\\&=-\,F'(\Delta t)\big|_{\Delta t=0}\\&=-F'(0)=-f\left(t_0+\Delta t,\mathbf{x}^{\varepsilon}(t_0+\Delta t),\varepsilon\right)\big|_{\Delta t=0}\\&=-f(t_0,\mathbf{x}^{\varepsilon}(t_0),\varepsilon).\end{aligned} \quad (13)$$

Substituting Eqs. (12) and (13) in Eq. (11) gives

$$V_t(t_0,\mathbf{x}_0)+\sum_{n=1}^{N}V_{x_n}(t_0,\mathbf{x}_0)\dot{x}_n^{\varepsilon}(t_0)\le -f(t_0,\mathbf{x}_0,\varepsilon), \quad (14)$$

where $\mathbf{x}^{\varepsilon}(t_0)=\mathbf{x}_0$ was used because the pair $(\mathbf{x}^{\varepsilon}(\cdot),\mathbf{u}(\cdot))$ is admissible by assumption. Recall also that admissibility requires that $\mathbf{x}^{\varepsilon}(\cdot)$ satisfy the state equation; hence $\dot{\mathbf{x}}^{\varepsilon}(t_0)=\mathbf{g}(t_0,\mathbf{x}^{\varepsilon}(t_0),\varepsilon)$. Substituting $\dot{\mathbf{x}}^{\varepsilon}(t_0)=\mathbf{g}(t_0,\mathbf{x}^{\varepsilon}(t_0),\varepsilon)$ into Eq. (14) and again using $\mathbf{x}^{\varepsilon}(t_0)=\mathbf{x}_0$ gives

$$V_t(t_0,\mathbf{x}_0)+\sum_{n=1}^{N}V_{x_n}(t_0,\mathbf{x}_0)g^n(t_0,\mathbf{x}_0,\varepsilon)+f(t_0,\mathbf{x}_0,\varepsilon)\le 0. \quad (15)$$

Now replace the initial point $(t_0,\mathbf{x}_0)$ in Eq. (15) with an *arbitrary point* $(t,\mathbf{x})\in[t_0,t_1]\times S$ to get the inequality

$$V_t(t,\mathbf{x})+\sum_{n=1}^{N}V_{x_n}(t,\mathbf{x})g^n(t,\mathbf{x},\varepsilon)+f(t,\mathbf{x},\varepsilon)\le 0, \quad (16)$$

which is valid $\forall\,\mathbf{x}\in S$, $\forall\,t\in[t_0,t_1]$, and $\forall\,\varepsilon\in U$. This is where assumption (A.1) is used.

By defining the function $\phi(\cdot)$ as

$$\phi(t, \mathbf{x}, \varepsilon) \stackrel{\text{def}}{=} V_t(t, \mathbf{x}) + \sum_{n=1}^{N} V_{x_n}(t, \mathbf{x}) g^n(t, \mathbf{x}, \varepsilon) + f(t, \mathbf{x}, \varepsilon), \tag{17}$$

and then referring to Eq. (8) and Eq. (16), respectively, it should be clear that we have shown that

$$\phi(t, \mathbf{z}(t), \mathbf{v}(t)) \equiv 0 \,\forall\, t \in [t_0, t_1], \tag{18}$$

as well as

$$\phi(t, \mathbf{x}, \varepsilon) \leq 0 \,\forall\, \mathbf{x} \in S,\ \forall t \in [t_0, t_1], \quad \text{and} \quad \forall \varepsilon \in U. \tag{19}$$

The Maximum Principle and the costate equation follow from Eqs. (18) and (19), as we now proceed to demonstrate.

To see how the Maximum Principle follows from Eqs. (18) and (19), first set $\mathbf{x} = \mathbf{z}(t)$ and hold it fixed. Then Eqs. (18) and (19) imply that

$$\phi(t, \mathbf{z}(t), \mathbf{v}(t)) = \max_{\varepsilon \in U} \phi(t, \mathbf{z}(t), \varepsilon). \tag{20}$$

Next, define

$$\lambda_j(t) \stackrel{\text{def}}{=} V_{x_j}(t, \mathbf{z}(t)), \quad j = 1, 2, \ldots, N, \tag{21}$$

$$\lambda_0 \stackrel{\text{def}}{=} 1, \tag{22}$$

$$H(t, \mathbf{x}, \mathbf{u}, \boldsymbol{\lambda}) \stackrel{\text{def}}{=} \lambda_0 f(t, \mathbf{x}, \mathbf{u}) + \boldsymbol{\lambda}' \mathbf{g}(t, \mathbf{x}, \mathbf{u}) = \lambda_0 f(t, \mathbf{x}, \mathbf{u}) + \sum_{n=1}^{N} \lambda_n g^n(t, \mathbf{x}, \mathbf{u}). \tag{23}$$

Upon using Eq. (17), that is, the definition of the function $\phi(\cdot)$, Eq. (20) takes the form

$$V_t(t, \mathbf{z}(t)) + \sum_{n=1}^{N} V_{x_n}(t, \mathbf{z}(t)) g^n(t, \mathbf{z}(t), \mathbf{v}(t)) + f(t, \mathbf{z}(t), \mathbf{v}(t))$$
$$= \max_{\varepsilon \in U} \left\{ V_t(t, \mathbf{z}(t)) + \sum_{n=1}^{N} V_{x_n}(t, \mathbf{z}(t)) g^n(t, \mathbf{z}(t), \varepsilon) + f(t, \mathbf{z}(t), \varepsilon) \right\}.$$

Because $V_t(t, \mathbf{z}(t))$ is independent of ε, it can be canceled from both sides of the above equality. On using the definitions (21), (22), and (23), the above equation becomes

$$H(t, \mathbf{z}(t), \mathbf{v}(t), \boldsymbol{\lambda}(t)) = \max_{\varepsilon \in U} H(t, \mathbf{z}(t), \varepsilon, \boldsymbol{\lambda}(t)),$$

which is the Maximum Principle.

To derive the adjoint or costate equation, set $\varepsilon = \mathbf{v}(t)$ and hold it fixed in Eqs. (18) and (19). Then Eqs. (18) and (19) imply that $\phi(t, \mathbf{x}, \mathbf{v}(t))$ attains its maximum value at $\mathbf{x} = \mathbf{z}(t)$. Because $\mathbf{x} \in S$ and S is an open set by assumption (A.2), the fact that $\phi(t, \mathbf{x}, \mathbf{v}(t))$ attains its maximum value at $\mathbf{x} = \mathbf{z}(t)$ implies the first-order necessary condition

$$\left.\frac{\partial \phi}{\partial x_j}(t, \mathbf{x}, \mathbf{v}(t))\right|_{\mathbf{x}=\mathbf{z}(t)} = 0, \quad j = 1, 2, \ldots, N. \tag{24}$$

Using the definition of $\phi(\cdot)$ in Eq. (17) and carrying out the differentiation in Eq. (24) thus yields

$$\begin{aligned} V_{tx_j}(t, \mathbf{z}(t)) &+ \sum_{n=1}^{N} V_{x_n}(t, \mathbf{z}(t))\, g^n_{x_j}(t, \mathbf{z}(t), \mathbf{v}(t)) \\ &+ \sum_{n=1}^{N} V_{x_n x_j}(t, \mathbf{z}(t))\, g^n(t, \mathbf{z}(t), \mathbf{v}(t)) + f_{x_j}(t, \mathbf{z}(t), \mathbf{v}(t)) = 0, \end{aligned} \tag{25}$$

for $j = 1, 2, \ldots, N$. Note that assumption (A.3), namely, $V(\cdot) \in C^{(2)}\, \forall\, (t, \mathbf{x}) \in (t_0, t_1) \times S$, has been used in deriving Eq. (25). Now differentiate Eq. (21) with respect to t, and use the fact that $\dot{\mathbf{z}}(t) \equiv \mathbf{g}(t, \mathbf{z}(t), \mathbf{v}(t))$ to get

$$\dot{\lambda}_j(t) = V_{x_j t}(t, \mathbf{z}(t)) + \sum_{n=1}^{N} V_{x_j x_n}(t, \mathbf{z}(t))\, g^n(t, \mathbf{z}(t), \mathbf{v}(t)), \quad j = 1, 2, \ldots, N. \tag{26}$$

Using Young's theorem on Eq. (26) and then substituting Eq. (26) into Eq. (25) and rearranging the resulting expression yields

$$\dot{\lambda}_j(t) = -f_{x_j}(t, \mathbf{z}(t), \mathbf{v}(t)) - \sum_{n=1}^{N} V_{x_n}(t, \mathbf{z}(t))\, g^n_{x_j}(t, \mathbf{z}(t), \mathbf{v}(t)), \quad j = 1, 2, \ldots, N. \tag{27}$$

Finally, using the definitions (21), (22), and (23) in Eq. (27) gives

$$\dot{\lambda}_j(t) = -H_{x_j}(t, \mathbf{z}(t), \mathbf{v}(t), \boldsymbol{\lambda}(t)), \quad j = 1, 2, \ldots, N,$$

which is the costate or adjoint equation. This completes the proof of the necessary conditions. The reader should note that given our three assumptions, this proof is rigorous. Q.E.D.

Notice that in the definition of the Hamiltonian in Eq. (23), a *constant* costate variable λ_0 multiplies the integrand $f(t, \mathbf{x}, \mathbf{u})$. This is the correct way to write the Hamiltonian in general. In this case, the necessary conditions would then include the additional requirement that

$$(\lambda_0, \boldsymbol{\lambda}(t)') \neq \mathbf{0}'_{N+1} \; \forall\, t \in [t_0, t_1],$$

where $\mathbf{0}_{N+1}$ is the null (column) vector in $\Re^{N+1}$, and furthermore that

$$\lambda_0 = 0 \quad \text{or} \quad \lambda_0 = 1.$$

In most economic applications of optimal control theory, one can safely set $\lambda_0 = 1$. In essence, assuming that $\lambda_0 = 1$ means that the integrand matters in determining the optimal solution to the control problem. Alternatively, if $\lambda_0 = 0$, then the integrand does not matter for determining the optimal solution to the control problem in that the necessary conditions of Theorem 4.2 do not change if we replace the integrand function $f(\cdot)$ with *any* other function. The case $\lambda_0 = 0$ is thus appropriately referred to as *abnormal*. We will typically assume that $\lambda_0 = 1$ for the remainder of the book, even though, strictly speaking, it is possible for $\lambda_0 = 0$ to hold, as the ensuing example illustrates. The mental exercises present some other control problems for which $\lambda_0 = 0$ in an optimal solution.

Example 4.1: Consider the fixed endpoints optimal control problem

$$\max_{u(\cdot)} J[x(\cdot), u(\cdot)] \stackrel{\text{def}}{=} \int_0^T u(t)\, dt$$

$$\text{s.t.} \quad \dot{x}(t) = [u(t)]^2,$$

$$x(0) = 0, \; x(T) = 0.$$

Notice that the *only* admissible pair for this problem is $(x(t), u(t)) = (0, 0)$ for all $t \in [0, T]$, as inspection of the state equation and boundary conditions will verify. Defining the Hamiltonian by setting $\lambda_0 = 1$ yields $H(t, x, u, \lambda) \stackrel{\text{def}}{=} u + \lambda u^2$. Given that there are no constraints on the control variable, the necessary condition $\max_u H(t, x, u, \lambda)$ of Theorem 4.2 reduces to the familiar condition $H_u(t, x, u, \lambda) = 1 + 2\lambda u = 0$. Note, however, that the only admissible value of the control variable, namely, $u(t) = 0$, is not a solution to this necessary condition. If we instead define the Hamiltonian with a constant costate variable λ_0 attached to the integrand function and assume it is not equal to unity, then we have $\bar{H}(t, x, u, \lambda) \stackrel{\text{def}}{=} \lambda_0 u + \lambda u^2$. The necessary condition then reads $\bar{H}_u(t, x, u, \lambda) = \lambda_0 + 2\lambda u = 0$. If we choose $\lambda_0 = 0$, then $u(t) = 0$ does indeed satisfy this necessary condition.

Let's now provide an economic interpretation to the necessary conditions of Theorem 4.2 and the functions used in their derivation. First, consider a typical costate variable $\lambda_j(t)$, and recall that it is defined in Eq. (21) as $\lambda_j(t) \stackrel{\text{def}}{=} V_{x_j}(t, \mathbf{z}(t))$, $j = 1, 2, \ldots, N$. Also recall that $V(t, \mathbf{z}(t))$ is the *total value* of the stock $\mathbf{z}(t)$ in an optimal plan that begins at time t. This interpretation therefore implies that

$\lambda_j(t) \stackrel{\text{def}}{=} V_{x_j}(t, \mathbf{z}(t))$, $j = 1, 2, \ldots, N$, is the *marginal value* or *shadow value* of the *j*th stock $z_j(t)$ at time t in an optimal plan. That is, $\lambda_j(t)$ is the dollar amount by which the value of the optimal program $V(t, \mathbf{z}(t))$ would increase owing to a marginal increase in the *j*th stock at time t, the initial date of the optimal plan. Note that we will further refine and expand on the economic interpretation of $\boldsymbol{\lambda}(t)$ when we prove the dynamic envelope theorem. For now, this interpretation and intuition will suffice.

Next we turn to an economic interpretation of the Hamiltonian defined in Eq. (2), scilicet, $H(t, \mathbf{x}, \mathbf{u}, \boldsymbol{\lambda}) \stackrel{\text{def}}{=} f(t, \mathbf{x}, \mathbf{u}) + \boldsymbol{\lambda}'\mathbf{g}(t, \mathbf{x}, \mathbf{u})$. The integrand $f(t, \mathbf{x}, \mathbf{u})$ may be thought of as the flow of profits over a short time interval to the value of the objective functional $J[\mathbf{x}(\cdot), \mathbf{u}(\cdot)]$. The state equation $\dot{\mathbf{x}} = \mathbf{g}(t, \mathbf{x}, \mathbf{u})$ represents the flow of investment in the capital stock in physical terms over this time interval, since $\mathbf{x}$ is the capital stock vector and $\dot{\mathbf{x}}$ is the time rate of change of, or investment in, the vector of stocks. Taking the inner product of $\mathbf{g}(t, \mathbf{x}, \mathbf{u})$ with $\boldsymbol{\lambda}$ converts the physical flow $\mathbf{g}(t, \mathbf{x}, \mathbf{u})$ into dollar terms, since $\boldsymbol{\lambda}$ is the marginal value of the capital stock vector at time t. The sum $\boldsymbol{\lambda}'\mathbf{g}(t, \mathbf{x}, \mathbf{u})$ therefore represents the value of the capital accumulated in a short interval of time. Thus the Hamiltonian $H(t, \mathbf{x}, \mathbf{u}, \boldsymbol{\lambda}) \stackrel{\text{def}}{=} f(t, \mathbf{x}, \mathbf{u}) + \boldsymbol{\lambda}'\mathbf{g}(t, \mathbf{x}, \mathbf{u})$ measures the total contribution of the activities that take place in a short interval of time, which includes the immediate effect $f(t, \mathbf{x}, \mathbf{u})$ of profit flow, and the future effect $\boldsymbol{\lambda}'\mathbf{g}(t, \mathbf{x}, \mathbf{u})$ of the value of the capital accumulated. The Maximum Principle, namely, $H(t, \mathbf{z}(t), \mathbf{v}(t), \boldsymbol{\lambda}(t)) \geq H(t, \mathbf{z}(t), \mathbf{u}, \boldsymbol{\lambda}(t))\ \forall\, \mathbf{u} \in U$, thus directs us to maximize the sum of the current and future value flow at each point in time with our choice of the control variable $\mathbf{u}$. That is, it is simply an assertion that for every $t \in [t_0, t_1]$, the value $\mathbf{v}(t)$ of the optimal control vector must maximize the value of the Hamiltonian over all admissible values of the control vector $\mathbf{u}(t) \in U$.

Finally, we come to the adjoint or costate equation $-\dot{\lambda}_j = f_{x_j}(t, \mathbf{x}, \mathbf{u}) + \sum_{n=1}^{N} \lambda_n g^n_{x_j}(t, \mathbf{x}, \mathbf{u})$, $j = 1, 2, \ldots, N$. Because λ_j is the shadow value of the *j*th stock, $\dot{\lambda}_j$ may be thought of as the rate at which the shadow value of the *j*th stock is changing or appreciating through time. Thus, $-\dot{\lambda}_j$ is the rate at which the marginal value of the *j*th stock is depreciating through time. The costate equation therefore asserts that along the optimal path, the decrease in the marginal value of the *j*th capital stock at any point in time is the sum of *j*th capital stock's marginal contribution to profit, videlicet, $f_{x_j}(t, \mathbf{x}, \mathbf{u})$, and its marginal contribution to the enhancement of the value of all the capital stocks, to wit, $\sum_{n=1}^{N} \lambda_n g^n_{x_j}(t, \mathbf{x}, \mathbf{u})$.

With the economic interpretation of Theorem 4.2 now complete, let's consider a corollary to Theorem 4.2 that applies to a large class of optimal control problems that is often encountered in economic theory. Consider, therefore, a situation in which $\mathbf{v}(t) \in \text{int}\, U\ \forall\, t \in [t_0, t_1]$, that is, the optimal solution for the control variables (assuming one exists) is in the interior of the control region for the entire planning horizon. Equivalently, assume that the constraints on the control variables are not binding on the optimal control for the entire planning horizon. Alternatively, one could more strongly assume that $U = \Re^M$, thereby implying that there are no constraints on the control variables. Under either of these two assumptions, the Maximum Principle of Theorem 4.2, namely, $H(t, \mathbf{z}(t), \mathbf{v}(t), \boldsymbol{\lambda}(t)) \geq H(t, \mathbf{z}(t), \mathbf{u}, \boldsymbol{\lambda}(t)) \, \forall \, \mathbf{u} \in U$, implies the first-order necessary condition

$$H_{\mathbf{u}}(t, \mathbf{z}(t), \mathbf{v}(t), \boldsymbol{\lambda}(t))' = \mathbf{0}_M \, \forall \, t \in [t_0, t_1],$$

as well as the second-order necessary condition

$$\mathbf{h}' H_{\mathbf{uu}}(t, \mathbf{z}(t), \mathbf{v}(t), \boldsymbol{\lambda}(t))\mathbf{h} \leq 0 \, \forall \, t \in [t_0, t_1] \quad \text{and} \quad \forall \, \mathbf{h} \in \Re^M,$$

assuming, of course, that $H(\cdot) \in C^{(2)}$ in $\mathbf{u}$. The proof of these necessary conditions follows immediately from the first-order necessary and second-order necessary conditions from static optimization theory, since (i) we are choosing $\mathbf{u} \in U$ at each $t \in [t_0, t_1]$ to maximize $H(\cdot)$, and (ii) the constraints are either not binding on the optimal control or simply do not exist under the above two scenarios. We have therefore proven the following economically important corollary to Theorem 4.2.

Corollary 4.2 (Simplified Maximum Principle): *Let* $(\mathbf{z}(t), \mathbf{v}(t))$ *be an admissible pair for problem (1). Then if* $\mathbf{v}(t) \in \text{int}\, U \; \forall t \in [t_0, t_1]$, $(\mathbf{z}(t), \mathbf{v}(t))$ *yields the absolute maximum of* $J[\cdot]$, *and* $H(\cdot) \in C^{(1)}$ *in* $\mathbf{u}$, *it is necessary that there exists a piecewise smooth vector-valued function* $\boldsymbol{\lambda}(\cdot) \overset{\text{def}}{=} (\lambda_1(\cdot), \lambda_2(\cdot), \ldots, \lambda_N(\cdot))$ *such that for all* $t \in [t_0, t_1]$,

$$H_{u_m}(t, \mathbf{z}(t), \mathbf{v}(t), \boldsymbol{\lambda}(t)) = 0, \quad m = 1, 2, \ldots, M,$$

and

$$\sum_{\ell=1}^{M} \sum_{m=1}^{M} H_{u_\ell u_m}(t, \mathbf{z}(t), \mathbf{v}(t), \boldsymbol{\lambda}(t)) h_\ell h_m \leq 0 \, \forall \, \mathbf{h} \in \Re^M.$$

Furthermore, except for the points of discontinuities of $\mathbf{v}(t)$,

$$\dot{z}_n(t) = \frac{\partial H}{\partial \lambda_n}(t, \mathbf{z}(t), \mathbf{v}(t), \boldsymbol{\lambda}(t)) = g^n(t, \mathbf{z}(t), \mathbf{v}(t)), \quad n = 1, 2, \ldots, N,$$

$$\dot{\lambda}_n(t) = -\frac{\partial H}{\partial x_n}(t, \mathbf{z}(t), \mathbf{v}(t), \boldsymbol{\lambda}(t)), \quad n = 1, 2, \ldots, N.$$

We now pause to illustrate how to use Corollary 4.2 with a simple mathematical example.

Example 4.2: Consider the optimal control problem

$$\max_{u(\cdot)} \int_0^1 \left[-x(t) - \frac{1}{2}\alpha[u(t)]^2 \right] dt$$

$$\text{s.t.} \quad \dot{x}(t) = u(t), \; x(0) = x_0, \; x(1) = x_1,$$

where $\alpha > 0$ is a parameter. Define the Hamiltonian as $H(x, u, \lambda) \overset{\text{def}}{=} -x - \frac{1}{2}\alpha u^2 + \lambda u$. Given that there are no constraints on the control variable, the necessary conditions are given by Corollary 4.2; hence

$$H_u(x, u, \lambda) = -\alpha u + \lambda = 0, \; H_{uu}(x, u, \lambda) = -\alpha \leq 0.$$

Because $\alpha > 0$, it follows that $H_{uu}(x, u, \lambda) = -\alpha < 0$. Solving $H_u(x, u, \lambda) = -\alpha u + \lambda = 0$ for the control variable gives $u = \alpha^{-1}\lambda$. The other necessary conditions are thus

$$\dot{x} = H_\lambda(x, u, \lambda) = u, \;\; x(0) = x_0, \;\; x(1) = x_1,$$
$$\dot{\lambda} = -H_x(x, u, \lambda) = 1.$$

Substituting $u = \alpha^{-1}\lambda$ into these differential equations yields

$$\dot{x} = \alpha^{-1}\lambda, \;\; x(0) = x_0, \;\; x(1) = x_1,$$
$$\dot{\lambda} = 1.$$

Separating the variables in $\dot{\lambda} = 1$ and integrating gives the general solution $\lambda(t) = t + c_1$, where c_1 is a constant of integration. Substituting $\lambda(t) = t + c_1$ into $\dot{x} = \alpha^{-1}\lambda$ gives $\dot{x} = \alpha^{-1}[t + c_1]$, and separating the variables and integrating yields the general solution $x(t) = \frac{1}{2}\alpha^{-1}t^2 + \alpha^{-1}c_1 t + c_2$, where c_2 is another constant of integration. The constants of integration c_1 and c_2 are determined by using the initial and terminal conditions $x(0) = x_0$ and $x(1) = x_1$:

$$x(0) = x_0 \Rightarrow c_2 = x_0,$$
$$x(1) = x_1 \Rightarrow c_1 = \alpha[x_1 - x_0] - \frac{1}{2}.$$

These constants of integration are then substituted into the general solution for the state and costate variables found above to get the specific solutions

$$z(t; \alpha, x_0, x_1) = \frac{1}{2}\alpha^{-1}t^2 + \left[x_1 - x_0 - \frac{1}{2}\alpha^{-1}\right] t + x_0,$$

$$\lambda(t; \alpha, x_0, x_1) = t + \alpha[x_1 - x_0] - \frac{1}{2}.$$

Finally, substitute $\lambda(t; \alpha, x_0, x_1) = t + \alpha[x_1 - x_0] - \frac{1}{2}$ into $u = \alpha^{-1}\lambda$ to find the path of the control variable that satisfies the necessary conditions:

$$v(t; \alpha, x_0, x_1) = \alpha^{-1}\left[t - \frac{1}{2}\right] + x_1 - x_0.$$

Notice that the solution to the necessary conditions depends explicitly on the parameters (α, x_0, x_1) of the control problem. The above solution to the necessary conditions should be compared to that of Example 2.1, since the control problems are identical in the two examples, save for a fixed terminal state in the present example.

The ensuing example has a closed and bounded (i.e., compact) control region. As a result, we must use Theorem 4.2 in order to derive the correct necessary conditions. Moreover, the optimal control problem is linear in the control variable and thus must be handled differently if one is to solve the necessary conditions.

Example 4.3: Consider the following optimal control problem:

$$\max_{u(\cdot),x_1} J[x(\cdot), u(\cdot)] \stackrel{\text{def}}{=} \int_0^1 x(t)\,dt$$

$$\text{s.t.} \quad \dot{x}(t) = x(t) + u(t), \;\; x(0) = 0, \;\; x(1) = x_1,$$

$$u(t) \in U \stackrel{\text{def}}{=} \{u(\cdot) : -1 \leq u(t) \leq 1\}.$$

Here we have an explicit representation of the control set U, a *closed interval* on the real line. The fact that U is a closed set (i.e., it includes its boundary as part of the set) is important, for this means the optimal value of the control may be at the boundary, and thus the derivative form of the Maximum Principle, namely, $H_u(t, x, u, \lambda) = 0$, is not in general valid. Hence, by Theorem 4.2, the necessary condition is to choose u to maximize the Hamiltonian subject to $u \in U$.

The Hamiltonian is defined as $H(x, u, \lambda) \stackrel{\text{def}}{=} x + \lambda[x + u] = x[1 + \lambda] + \lambda u$. The optimal path of the costate variable must necessarily satisfy $\dot{\lambda} = -H_x(x, u, \lambda) = -1 - \lambda$ and $\lambda(1) = 0$, the latter of which results from the fact that x_1 is a decision variable. The integrating factor for this linear ordinary differential equation with constant coefficients is $\mu(t) \stackrel{\text{def}}{=} \exp[\int^t ds] = e^t$, so upon multiplying both sides of $\dot{\lambda} + \lambda = -1$ by e^t, it follows that the resulting differential equation is equivalent to $\frac{d}{dt}[\lambda e^t] = -e^t$. Upon integrating, we find that $\lambda(t) = ce^{-t} - 1$, where c is a constant of integration. The free boundary condition $\lambda(1) = 0$ implies that $c = e$. Thus the specific solution to the costate equation is $\lambda(t) = e^{1-t} - 1$, so the costate path is fully determined. Finally, because $\dot{\lambda}(t) = -e^{1-t} < 0\,\forall\, t \in [0, 1]$ and $\lambda(1) = 0$, we conclude that $\lambda(t) > 0\,\forall\, t \in [0, 1)$. This fact is important in what follows.

Now let's examine the Hamiltonian $H(x, u, \lambda) \stackrel{\text{def}}{=} x[1 + \lambda] + \lambda u$. Seeing as the term λu in the Hamiltonian is the only one that depends on u, maximizing the Hamiltonian with respect to u subject to $u \in [-1, 1]$ is equivalent to maximizing λu with respect to u subject to $u \in [-1, 1]$. Because $\lambda(t) > 0\,\forall\, t \in [0, 1)$, the maximum of λu (and thus $H(x, u, \lambda)$) with respect to u subject to $u \in [-1, 1]$ is attained at $u = v(t) = 1$. From the transversality condition $\lambda(1) = 0$, it follows that the Hamiltonian is independent of the control variable at $t = 1$, thereby implying that maximizing $H(\cdot)$ with respect to u subject to $u \in [-1, 1]$ does not determine the value of the control at $t = 1$. As a result, the choice of the control at $t = 1$ is arbitrary. We therefore set $v(1) = 1$ so that the control function $v(\cdot)$ is continuous on $[-1, 1]$. In sum, the control that maximizes the Hamiltonian is $v(t) = 1\,\forall t \in [0, 1]$.

Given this control, the state variable must satisfy the differential equation $\dot{x} - x = 1$ and the initial condition $x(0) = 0$. The integrating factor of this linear first-order differential equation is $\gamma(t) \stackrel{\text{def}}{=} \exp[-\int^t ds] = e^{-t}$, so that upon multiplying both sides of $\dot{x} - x = 1$ by e^{-t}, it follows that the resulting differential equation is equivalent to $\frac{d}{dt}[xe^{-t}] = e^{-t}$. Upon integrating, we have the general solution $x(t) = ke^t - 1$, where k is a constant of integration. The initial condition $x(0) = 0$ implies that $k = 1$; hence $z(t) = e^t - 1$ is the specific solution of the state equation. Note also that the value of the objective functional is

$$J[z(\cdot), v(\cdot)] = \int_0^1 [e^t - 1]\,dt = [e^t - t]\Big|_{t=0}^{t=1} = e - 2 > 0.$$

Because we don't have as of yet any sufficiency theorems for this class of control problems, we will have to wait to conclude that our solution of the necessary conditions actually is the solution of the optimal control problem.

It is natural at this juncture to complement the necessary conditions of Theorem 4.2 with a set of sufficient conditions that also apply directly to optimal control problem (1). The proof of the following sufficient conditions differs from our earlier proof of sufficient conditions in Chapter 3, however, because now we have to be careful to properly account for the presence of the control region U in our analysis, just as we did in the proof of Theorem 4.2. We begin, therefore, with a preliminary technical result that is of value in the proof of the sufficiency theorem.

Lemma 4.1: *Let $F(\cdot) : A \to \Re$, where $A \subseteq \Re^N$, and let $F(\cdot) \in C^{(1)}$ on A. Also, let $S \in$ int A be a convex set and $\bar{\mathbf{x}} \in S$.*

(i) $F(\bar{\mathbf{x}}) \geq F(\mathbf{x})\,\forall\,\mathbf{x} \in S \Rightarrow F_{\mathbf{x}}(\bar{\mathbf{x}})\,[\mathbf{x} - \bar{\mathbf{x}}] \leq 0\,\forall\,\mathbf{x} \in S$.
(ii) If $F(\cdot)$ is concave $\forall\,\mathbf{x} \in S$, then

$$F_{\mathbf{x}}(\bar{\mathbf{x}})\,[\mathbf{x} - \bar{\mathbf{x}}] \leq 0\,\forall\,\mathbf{x} \in S \Rightarrow F(\bar{\mathbf{x}}) \geq F(\mathbf{x})\,\forall\,\mathbf{x} \in S.$$

Proof: To prove part (i), first define $G(\alpha) \stackrel{\text{def}}{=} F(\bar{\mathbf{x}}) - F(\alpha\mathbf{x} + (1 - \alpha)\bar{\mathbf{x}})$ for $\alpha \in [0, 1]$. Given that S is a convex set, $\alpha\mathbf{x} + (1 - \alpha)\bar{\mathbf{x}} \in S\,\forall\,\mathbf{x} \in S$ and $\alpha \in [0, 1]$. Thus $F(\bar{\mathbf{x}}) \geq F(\mathbf{x})\,\forall\,\mathbf{x} \in S$ is equivalent to the statement $G(\alpha) \stackrel{\text{def}}{=} F(\bar{\mathbf{x}}) - F(\alpha\mathbf{x} + (1 - \alpha)\bar{\mathbf{x}}) \geq 0$ for $\alpha \in [0, 1]$. Because $G(\alpha) \geq 0$ for all $\alpha \in [0, 1]$ and $G(0) = F(\bar{\mathbf{x}}) - F(\bar{\mathbf{x}}) = 0$, it follows that $G'(0) \geq 0$ must hold; hence

$$G'(0) = -F_{\mathbf{x}}(\bar{\mathbf{x}})\,[\mathbf{x} - \bar{\mathbf{x}}] \geq 0.$$

Multiplying through by minus unity completes the proof of part (i).

To prove part (ii), first note that by Theorem 21.3 of Simon and Blume (1994), we have the familiar inequality fundamental to concave functions, namely,

$$F(\mathbf{x}) \leq F(\bar{\mathbf{x}}) + F_{\mathbf{x}}(\bar{\mathbf{x}})\,[\mathbf{x} - \bar{\mathbf{x}}]\,\forall\,\mathbf{x} \in S.$$

Because $F_{\mathbf{x}}(\bar{\mathbf{x}})\,[\mathbf{x} - \bar{\mathbf{x}}] \leq 0\,\forall\,\mathbf{x} \in S$ by hypothesis, the above inequality immediately gives the desired conclusion, to wit, $F(\bar{\mathbf{x}}) \geq F(\mathbf{x})\,\forall\,\mathbf{x} \in S$. Q.E.D.

With Lemma 4.1 in hand, we may proceed to prove the ensuing sufficiency theorem for the class of control problems we have been considering in this chapter.

Theorem 4.3 (Mangasarian Sufficient Conditions): *Let* $(\mathbf{z}(t), \mathbf{v}(t))$ *be an admissible pair for problem (1). Assume that* U *is a convex set and that* $\partial f(\cdot)/\partial\mathbf{u}$ *and* $\partial\mathbf{g}(\cdot)/\partial\mathbf{u}$ *exist and are continuous, in addition to our basic assumptions on* $f(\cdot)$ *and* $\mathbf{g}(\cdot)$. *Suppose that* $(\mathbf{z}(t), \mathbf{v}(t))$ *satisfies the necessary conditions of Theorem 4.2 for problem (1) with costate vector* $\boldsymbol{\lambda}(t)$, *and let* $H(t, \mathbf{x}, \mathbf{u}, \boldsymbol{\lambda}) \stackrel{\text{def}}{=} f(t, \mathbf{x}, \mathbf{u}) + \boldsymbol{\lambda}'\mathbf{g}(t, \mathbf{x}, \mathbf{u})$ *be the value of the Hamiltonian function. If* $H(\cdot)$ *is a concave function of* $(\mathbf{x}, \mathbf{u})\,\forall\,t \in [t_0, t_1]$ *over an open convex set containing all the admissible values of* $(\mathbf{x}(\cdot), \mathbf{u}(\cdot))$ *when the costate vector is* $\boldsymbol{\lambda}(t)$, *then* $\mathbf{v}(t)$ *is an optimal control and* $(\mathbf{z}(t), \mathbf{v}(t))$ *yields the global maximum of* $J[\cdot]$. *If* $H(\cdot)$ *is a strictly concave function under the same conditions, then* $(\mathbf{z}(t), \mathbf{v}(t))$ *yields the unique global maximum of* $J[\cdot]$.

Proof: Let $(\mathbf{x}(t), \mathbf{u}(t))$ be any admissible pair. By hypothesis, $H(\cdot)$ is a $C^{(1)}$ concave function of $(\mathbf{x}, \mathbf{u})\,\forall\,t \in [t_0, t_1]$. It therefore follows from Theorem 21.3 of Simon and Blume (1994) that

$$\begin{aligned} H(t, \mathbf{x}(t), \mathbf{u}(t), \boldsymbol{\lambda}(t)) &\leq H(t, \mathbf{z}(t), \mathbf{v}(t), \boldsymbol{\lambda}(t)) + H_{\mathbf{x}}(t, \mathbf{z}(t), \mathbf{v}(t), \boldsymbol{\lambda}(t))\,[\mathbf{x}(t) - \mathbf{z}(t)] \\ &\quad + H_{\mathbf{u}}(t, \mathbf{z}(t), \mathbf{v}(t), \boldsymbol{\lambda}(t))\,[\mathbf{u}(t) - \mathbf{v}(t)], \end{aligned} \tag{28}$$

for every $t \in [t_0, t_1]$. Integrating both sides of the above inequality over the interval $[t_0, t_1]$ and using the definitions of $H(\cdot)$ and $J[\cdot]$ yields

$$\begin{aligned} J[\mathbf{x}(\cdot), \mathbf{u}(\cdot)] \leq J[\mathbf{z}(\cdot), \mathbf{v}(\cdot)] &+ \int_{t_0}^{t_1} \boldsymbol{\lambda}(t)'[\mathbf{g}(t, \mathbf{z}(t), \mathbf{v}(t)) - \mathbf{g}(t, \mathbf{x}(t), \mathbf{u}(t))]\,dt \\ &+ \int_{t_0}^{t_1} H_{\mathbf{x}}(t, \mathbf{z}(t), \mathbf{v}(t), \boldsymbol{\lambda}(t))\,[\mathbf{x}(t) - \mathbf{z}(t)]\,dt \\ &+ \int_{t_0}^{t_1} H_{\mathbf{u}}(t, \mathbf{z}(t), \mathbf{v}(t), \boldsymbol{\lambda}(t))\,[\mathbf{u}(t) - \mathbf{v}(t)]\,dt. \end{aligned} \tag{29}$$

By admissibility, $\dot{\mathbf{z}}(t) \equiv \mathbf{g}(t, \mathbf{z}(t), \mathbf{v}(t))$ and $\dot{\mathbf{x}}(t) \equiv \mathbf{g}(t, \mathbf{x}(t), \mathbf{u}(t))$ for every $t \in [t_0, t_1]$, whereas Theorem 4.2 implies that $\dot{\boldsymbol{\lambda}}(t)' \equiv -H_{\mathbf{x}}(t, \mathbf{z}(t), \mathbf{v}(t), \boldsymbol{\lambda}(t))$ for every $t \in [t_0, t_1]$. Substituting these three results in Eq. (29) gives

$$J[\mathbf{x}(\cdot), \mathbf{u}(\cdot)] \leq J[\mathbf{z}(\cdot), \mathbf{v}(\cdot)] + \int_{t_0}^{t_1} [\boldsymbol{\lambda}(t)'[\dot{\mathbf{z}}(t) - \dot{\mathbf{x}}(t)] + \dot{\boldsymbol{\lambda}}(t)'[\mathbf{z}(t) - \mathbf{x}(t)]]\, dt + \int_{t_0}^{t_1} H_{\mathbf{u}}(t, \mathbf{z}(t), \mathbf{v}(t), \boldsymbol{\lambda}(t))\, [\mathbf{u}(t) - \mathbf{v}(t)]\, dt. \tag{30}$$

Because $H(\cdot)$ is concave in $(\mathbf{x}, \mathbf{u})\, \forall\, t \in [t_0, t_1]$, it is also concave in $\mathbf{u}$ alone for each $t \in [t_0, t_1]$. Thus, by Lemma 4.1, we have that

$$H_{\mathbf{u}}(t, \mathbf{z}(t), \mathbf{v}(t), \boldsymbol{\lambda}(t))\, [\mathbf{u}(t) - \mathbf{v}(t)] \leq 0\, \forall\, \mathbf{u} \in U$$
$$\Leftrightarrow H(t, \mathbf{z}(t), \mathbf{v}(t), \boldsymbol{\lambda}(t)) \geq H(t, \mathbf{z}(t), \mathbf{u}, \boldsymbol{\lambda}(t))\, \forall\, \mathbf{u} \in U.$$

Using this fact in Eq. (30) permits the conclusion

$$J[\mathbf{x}(\cdot), \mathbf{u}(\cdot)] \leq J[\mathbf{z}(\cdot), \mathbf{v}(\cdot)] + \int_{t_0}^{t_1} [\boldsymbol{\lambda}(t)'[\dot{\mathbf{z}}(t) - \dot{\mathbf{x}}(t)] + \dot{\boldsymbol{\lambda}}(t)'[\mathbf{z}(t) - \mathbf{x}(t)]]\, dt. \tag{31}$$

To wrap up the proof, simply note that

$$\begin{aligned} \frac{d}{dt}[\boldsymbol{\lambda}(t)'[\mathbf{z}(t) - \mathbf{x}(t)]] &= \boldsymbol{\lambda}(t)'[\dot{\mathbf{z}}(t) - \dot{\mathbf{x}}(t)] + [\mathbf{z}(t) - \mathbf{x}(t)]'\dot{\boldsymbol{\lambda}}(t) \\ &= \boldsymbol{\lambda}(t)'[\dot{\mathbf{z}}(t) - \dot{\mathbf{x}}(t)] + \dot{\boldsymbol{\lambda}}(t)'[\mathbf{z}(t) - \mathbf{x}(t)], \end{aligned}$$

and substitute this result into Eq. (31) to get

$$\begin{aligned} J[\mathbf{x}(\cdot), \mathbf{u}(\cdot)] &\leq J[\mathbf{z}(\cdot), \mathbf{v}(\cdot)] + \int_{t_0}^{t_1} \frac{d}{dt}[\boldsymbol{\lambda}(t)'[\mathbf{z}(t) - \mathbf{x}(t)]]\, dt \\ &= J[\mathbf{z}(\cdot), \mathbf{v}(\cdot)] + \boldsymbol{\lambda}(t)'\,[\mathbf{z}(t) - \mathbf{x}(t)]\Big|_{t=t_0}^{t=t_1} \\ &= J[\mathbf{z}(\cdot), \mathbf{v}(\cdot)], \end{aligned}$$

since by admissibility, we have $\mathbf{x}(t_0) = \mathbf{x}_0$, $\mathbf{z}(t_0) = \mathbf{x}_0$, $\mathbf{x}(t_1) = \mathbf{x}_1$, and $\mathbf{z}(t_1) = \mathbf{x}_1$. We have thus shown that $J[\mathbf{x}(\cdot), \mathbf{u}(\cdot)] \leq J[\mathbf{z}(\cdot), \mathbf{v}(\cdot)]$ for all admissible functions $(\mathbf{x}(\cdot), \mathbf{u}(\cdot))$, just as we wished to. If $H(\cdot)$ is strictly concave in $(\mathbf{x}, \mathbf{u})\, \forall\, t \in [t_0, t_1]$, then the inequality in Eq. (28) becomes strict if either $\mathbf{x}(t) \neq \mathbf{z}(t)$ or $\mathbf{u}(t) \neq \mathbf{v}(t)$ for some $t \in [t_0, t_1]$. Then $J[\mathbf{x}(\cdot), \mathbf{u}(\cdot)] < J[\mathbf{z}(\cdot), \mathbf{v}(\cdot)]$ follows. This shows that any admissible pair of functions $(\mathbf{x}(\cdot), \mathbf{u}(\cdot))$ that are not identically equal to $(\mathbf{z}(\cdot), \mathbf{v}(\cdot))$ are suboptimal. Q.E.D.

Let's pause briefly so we can see this theorem in action.

Example 4.4: We begin by examining Example 4.2. Recall that this control problem does not have any constraints on the control variable, that is, $U = \Re$, a convex set. Also recall that

$$z(t; \alpha, x_0, x_1) = \frac{1}{2}\alpha^{-1}t^2 + \left[x_1 - x_0 - \frac{1}{2}\alpha^{-1}\right]t + x_0,$$

$$v(t; \alpha, x_0, x_1) = \alpha^{-1}\left[t - \frac{1}{2}\right] + x_1 - x_0,$$

$$\lambda(t; \alpha, x_0, x_1) = t + \alpha[x_1 - x_0] - \frac{1}{2}$$

is the *only* solution of the necessary conditions. We will now show that the Hamiltonian for this control problem, scilicet, $H(x, u, \lambda) \stackrel{\text{def}}{=} -x - \frac{1}{2}\alpha u^2 + \lambda u$, is a concave function of (x, u) for all $t \in [0, 1]$. To check concavity, we compute the Hessian matrix of $H(\cdot)$:

$$\begin{bmatrix} H_{uu} & H_{ux} \\ H_{xu} & H_{xx} \end{bmatrix} = \begin{bmatrix} -\alpha & 0 \\ 0 & 0 \end{bmatrix}.$$

Because the eigenvalues are $-\alpha < 0$ and 0, the Hessian matrix is negative semidefinite and therefore $H(\cdot)$ is concave in (x, u) for all $t \in [0, 1]$. Thus the above triplet is the unique solution to the posed control problem. Note that since $H(\cdot)$ is a polynomial, the continuity conditions of Theorem 4.3 are satisfied.

Now turn to Example 4.3. In this example, the control region $U = [-1, 1]$ is a closed and bounded convex set. Given that the Hamiltonian $H(x, u, \lambda) \stackrel{\text{def}}{=} x + \lambda[x + u]$ is linear in (x, u), it is concave in (x, u) for all $t \in [0, 1]$. The continuity conditions of Theorem 4.3 are satisfied because of the aforementioned linearity. Seeing as $v(t) = 1$, $z(t) = e^t - 1$, and $\lambda(t) = e^{1-t} - 1$ satisfy all the necessary conditions of Theorem 4.2 and are unique except at $t = 1$ when any admissible value of the control variable is optimal, Theorem 4.3 implies that this triplet is indeed the unique solution of the control problem.

With the mechanics of Theorems 4.2 and 4.3 in place, let's now analyze the inventory accumulation problem presented in Example 1.4 using these theorems. If your memory of this optimal control model is a bit fuzzy, you should return to Example 1.4 right now and refresh it.

Example 4.5: Referring to Example 1.4, the optimal control problem that is to be solved to determine the optimal inventory accumulation policy is given by

$$\min_{u(\cdot)} J[x(\cdot), u(\cdot)] \stackrel{\text{def}}{=} \int_0^T \left[c_1[u(t)]^2 + c_2 x(t)\right] dt$$

$$\text{s.t.} \quad \dot{x}(t) = u(t),$$

$$x(0) = 0, \ x(T) = x_T,$$

where $x(t)$ is the stock of inventory at time t, $u(t)$ is the production rate at time t, and $x_T > 0$ is the contracted (and thus fixed) amount of the good that must be delivered by the terminal date of the planning horizon $T > 0$. Recall that $c_1 > 0$ is a constant that shifts the average and marginal cost of production and $c_2 > 0$ is the constant unit cost of holding inventory. The fundamental economic trade-off in this control problem is between the cost of producing the good and the cost of storing it. For example, if the firm's manager produces a relatively large quantity of the good early in the planning horizon, then those goods must be held in inventory for a relatively long period of time, thereby driving up the inventory holding cost. On the other hand, if the manager waited until later in the planning horizon to produce a large quantity of the good, then inventory cost would be relatively low but production cost would be relatively high because of the "rush" at the end of the planning period to produce the contracted amount $x_T > 0$. The optimal production plan balances these two costs. Note that the production rate is not constrained to be nonnegative in the above statement of the control problem. We thus assume that it is not binding in the optimal plan. Later in this example, we will reexamine this assumption. Furthermore, after we introduce two additional theorems on necessary and sufficient conditions, we will explicitly account for the nonnegativity constraint on the production rate and examine how it affects the optimal solution.

The Hamiltonian for the control problem is defined as $H(x, u, \lambda) \stackrel{\text{def}}{=} c_1 u^2 + c_2 x + \lambda u$, where λ is the shadow *cost* of the inventory, for we are dealing with a cost minimization problem. Because we have assumed that the nonnegativity constraint on the production rate is not binding, the necessary conditions are given by Corollary 4.2, and therefore read

$$H_u(x, u, \lambda) = 2c_1 u + \lambda = 0, \tag{32}$$

$$H_{uu}(x, u, \lambda) = 2c_1 \geq 0, \tag{33}$$

$$\dot{\lambda} = -H_x(x, u, \lambda) = -c_2, \tag{34}$$

$$\dot{x} = H_\lambda(x, u, \lambda) = u, \ x(0) = 0, \ x(T) = x_T. \tag{35}$$

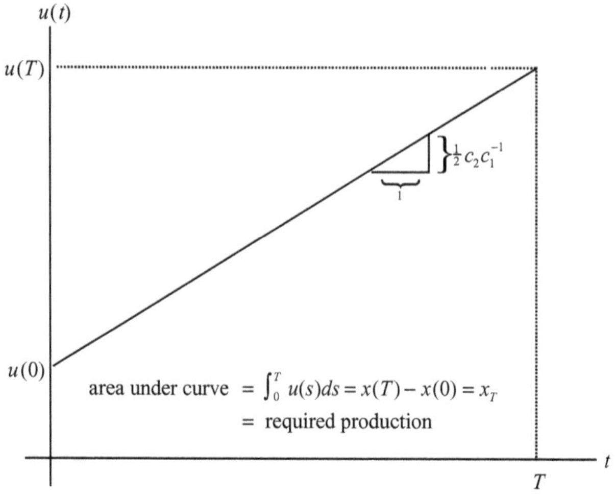

Figure 4.3

Because $c_2 > 0$, it follows that Eq. (33) is satisfied with a strict inequality, that is to say, $H_{uu}(x, u, \lambda) = 2c_1 > 0$ (remember that we are dealing with a minimization problem here).

Without even solving the necessary conditions, we can glean some economic information about the pattern of production. To see this, first solve Eq. (32) for the production rate to get $u = -\lambda/(2c_1)$, and then differentiate this expression with respect to t and use Eq. (34) to arrive at $\dot{u} = c_2/(2c_1) > 0$. This shows that the production rate rises over the planning horizon. Thus the firm produces the fewest units of the good per unit of time at the beginning of the planning horizon, and the most units of the good per unit of time at the end of the planning horizon. Figure 4.3 displays this qualitative conclusion graphically. Note that the slope of the curve in Figure 4.3 is given by the right-hand side of $\dot{u} = c_2/(2c_1)$, which is a positive constant.

Examination of Eq. (34) similarly reveals qualitative information. In particular, we see that the shadow cost of inventory falls over the planning horizon. This is not at all surprising, for an additional unit of stock received at the beginning of the planning period must be held in inventory longer (and is thus more costly) than one received near the end of the planning horizon. The declining shadow cost of the stock is essentially dual to the rising production rate, for one can interpret the former as driving the latter, or the latter as driving the former. Also noteworthy is the fact that because we assumed that the nonnegativity constraint on the production rate is not binding, the shadow cost of inventory is *negative*. That this is true can be seen from Eq. (32), or equivalently, from $u = -\lambda/(2c_1)$. This observation means that one more unit of stock in inventory lowers the total cost of production, which is not at all surprising seeing as one more unit of the good in inventory implies that one less unit of the good must be produced in order to reach the terminal stock of x_T.

Let's now solve the necessary conditions. Separating the variables and integrating the costate equation (34) gives the general solution $\lambda(t) = k_1 - c_2 t$, where k_1 is a constant of integration. Substituting this expression in Eq. (32) yields $u = (c_2 t - k_1)/(2c_1)$, which when substituted in the state equation (35), produces $\dot{x} = (c_2 t - k_1)/(2c_1)$. Separating the variables and integrating the state equation gives the general solution for the inventory stock $x(t) = \frac{1}{4} c_2 c_1^{-1} t^2 - \frac{1}{2} c_1^{-1} k_1 t + k_2$, where k_2 is another constant of integration. Now use the two boundary conditions to find the two constants of integration:

$$x(0) = 0 \Rightarrow k_2 = 0,$$

$$x(T) = x_T \Rightarrow k_1 = \frac{1}{2} c_2 T - 2c_1 x_T T^{-1}.$$

Next substitute the values of k_1 and k_2 into the general solution for the inventory stock to find the specific or definite solution that satisfies the boundary conditions:

$$z(t; c_1, c_2, T, x_T) = \frac{1}{4} c_2 c_1^{-1} t[t - T] + x_T T^{-1} t. \tag{36}$$

The corresponding production rate may be found by using $u = (c_2 t - k_1)/(2c_1)$ or differentiating Eq. (26) with respect to t, since $\dot{x} = u$:

$$v(t; c_1, c_2, T, x_T) = \frac{1}{4} c_2 c_1^{-1} [2t - T] + x_T T^{-1}. \tag{37}$$

Finally, the time path of the shadow cost of the inventory stock is found by substituting the value of k_1 in $\lambda(t) = k_1 - c_2 t$ to arrive at

$$\lambda(t; c_1, c_2, T, x_T) = \frac{1}{2} c_2 [T - 2t] - 2c_1 x_T T^{-1}. \tag{38}$$

It is important to emphasize that the solution to the necessary conditions depends explicitly on the parameters $\boldsymbol{\alpha} \stackrel{\text{def}}{=} (c_1, c_2, T, x_T)$ of the inventory accumulation problem, just as the solution to a static optimization problem does. Unlike the solution to a static optimization problem, however, the solution to the necessary conditions in general depends on the independent variable time as well, thus indicating that even if the parameters are constant over the planning horizon, the inventory level and the production rate will in general vary over the planning period.

Before studying the comparative dynamics properties of the above solution, let's confirm that it is in fact the solution to the posed optimal control problem. Because we are dealing with a minimization problem and we have assumed that the nonnegativity constraint on the production rate is not binding, all we have to do is verify that the Hamiltonian is a convex function of the state and control variables. Inspection of the optimal control problem shows that the integrand function is convex in (x, u) and the transition function is linear in (x, u); hence by the analogue of Theorem 3.2 for convex functions, we may conclude that the Hamiltonian is a convex function of (x, u). As a result, by the analogue of Theorem 4.3 for minimization problems, we know that the above solution to the necessary conditions is a solution of the optimal control problem. Actually, we can claim a bit more. In view of the fact that the above solution of the necessary conditions is the only one, it is therefore the unique solution of the control problem. Recall, however, that this conclusion is true only if $v(t;\boldsymbol{\alpha}) \geq 0 \, \forall \, t \in [0, T]$.

Turning to the comparative dynamics, observe that because we have an explicit solution to the inventory accumulation problem, we may proceed to differentiate it with respect to the parameters of interest to conduct the comparative dynamics analysis. Let's therefore proceed to uncover and economically interpret some of the comparative dynamics properties of the unique solution, leaving the rest of them for a mental exercises.

The production rate $v(t;\boldsymbol{\alpha})$ and the shadow cost of the inventory stock $\lambda(t;\boldsymbol{\alpha})$ are the more interesting economic variables, so we will focus our attention on them rather than on the inventory stock. To begin the comparative dynamics analysis, partially differentiate the production rate given in Eq. (37), and the shadow cost of the inventory given in Eq. (38), with respect to the unit cost of holding inventory c_2 to find that

$$\frac{\partial v}{\partial c_2}(t;\boldsymbol{\alpha}) = \frac{1}{4} c_1^{-1}[2t - T] \begin{cases} < 0 \, \forall \, t \in [0, \frac{1}{2}T) \\ = 0 \text{ for } t = \frac{1}{2}T \\ > 0 \, \forall \, t \in (\frac{1}{2}T, T] \end{cases}, \tag{39}$$

$$\frac{\partial \lambda}{\partial c_2}(t;\boldsymbol{\alpha}) = \frac{1}{2}[T - 2t] \begin{cases} > 0 \, \forall \, t \in [0, \frac{1}{2}T) \\ = 0 \text{ for } t = \frac{1}{2}T \\ < 0 \, \forall \, t \in (\frac{1}{2}T, T] \end{cases}. \tag{40}$$

The first thing to notice about Eqs. (39) and (40) is that unlike a comparative statics result, a comparative dynamics result can change sign with the passage of time. The economic interpretation of Eq. (39) is straightforward and makes economic sense. Because inventory is now more costly to hold, the production rate is decreased in the first half of the planning horizon so that less inventory accumulates in this period. Because the firm must still have $x_T > 0$ units in inventory at the terminal time $t = T$, and T is fixed (i.e., the planning horizon is fixed), the production rate must increase in the second half of the planning horizon in order to make up for the lower production rate in the first half of the planning horizon. In this way, fewer units are held in inventory for a longer period of time, thereby partially offsetting the higher cost of holding inventory. Figure 4.4 depicts the effect of the increase in the inventory holding cost on the production rate. Notice that the production rate path pivots counterclockwise about the point $t = \frac{1}{2}T$ as a result of the higher inventory holding costs. Observe, however, that because the firm is required to always produce the same number of units of the good over the same period of time, the area under each time path, which is the required production, is the same in each case. In other words, the area between the two curves in Figure 4.4 must be the same, implying that Area 1 equals Area 2.

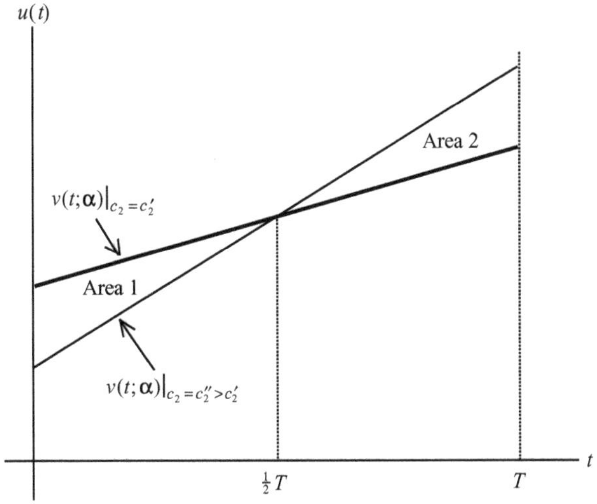

Figure 4.4

The effect of the increase in inventory holding costs on the shadow cost of inventory, given in Eq. (40), also has a straightforward economic interpretation. In this case, we see that an increase in the cost of holding inventory increases the shadow cost of inventory in the first half of the planning horizon and decreases it in the second half, just the opposite of its effect on the production rate. The economic explanation for this feature is essentially the same as that behind the declining value of the shadow cost of inventory over the planning horizon, namely, an additional unit of stock received at the beginning of the planning period must be held in inventory longer (and is thus more costly) than one received near the end of the planning horizon.

Now let's reexamine our assumption that the nonnegativity constraint on the production rate is not binding. We begin by checking to see if in fact the production rate $v(t;\alpha)$ satisfies the constraint $u(t) \geq 0 \,\forall\, t \in [0, T]$. Given that $\dot{v}(t;\alpha) = \frac{1}{2}c_2c_1^{-1} > 0$, the production rate $v(t;\alpha)$ is an increasing function of time. Therefore, if the production rate at the initial date of the planning period is nonnegative, then the production rate is nonnegative throughout the planning period because it is a strictly increasing function of time. Conversely, if the production rate is nonnegative throughout the planning horizon, then it is surely nonnegative at the initial date of the planning period. Stated more formally, we've shown that $v(0;\alpha) \geq 0$ if and only if $v(t;\alpha) \geq 0 \,\forall\, t \in [0, T]$. Therefore, the nonnegativity constraint $u(t) \geq 0$ will be satisfied for all $t \in [0, T]$ if and only if $v(0;\alpha) = x_T T^{-1} - \frac{1}{4}c_2c_1^{-1}T \geq 0$, or equivalently, if and only if

$$x_T \geq \frac{1}{4}c_2c_1^{-1}T^2. \tag{41}$$

Thus the pair of curves $(z(t;\alpha), v(t;\alpha))$ is the solution of the inventory accumulation problem if and only if Eq. (41) holds. The economic interpretation of the inequality in Eq. (41) is that the total production x_T is large relative to the delivery date T, and the unit storage cost c_2 is sufficiently small relative to the unit production cost coefficient c_1, if and only if the production rate is nonnegative throughout the planning period. If Eq. (41) does not hold, then the start of production is postponed in the optimal plan. We will investigate this situation in the subsequent example, in which we will explicitly take the nonnegativity constraint into account.

Recall that Theorem 4.2 was developed under the assumption that U is a *fixed* set, that is, U is *not* a function of the state variables or time. We will treat the case in which U is a function of the state variables in a later chapter. It turns out, however, that Theorem 4.2 actually covers the case in which U is a function of t, say, $U(t)$, provided a constraint qualification (to be detailed below) is satisfied. Let's endeavor to see why this is so.

At one level, it is easy to see why Theorem 4.2 applies when $U(t)$ is the control region: nothing in the proof of Theorem 4.2 depended on the fact that the control region U was independent of t. In actual applications of optimal control theory to economic problems, however, the set $U(t)$ is almost always defined by a system of inequality constraints, that is,

$$U(t) \stackrel{\text{def}}{=} \{\mathbf{u}(\cdot) : h^k(t, \mathbf{u}(t)) \geq 0, \quad k = 1, 2, \ldots, K\}. \tag{42}$$

For instance, in Example 4.3, we had that $u(t) \in U \stackrel{\text{def}}{=} \{u(t) : -1 \leq u(t) \leq 1\}$. This constraint can be rewritten to conform to Eq. (42) as follows:

$$h^1(t, u(t)) \stackrel{\text{def}}{=} u(t) + 1 \geq 0,$$

$$h^2(t, u(t)) \stackrel{\text{def}}{=} 1 - u(t) \geq 0.$$

For our purposes, therefore, there is no loss in generality in defining the control region by a system of inequality constraints. We will thus do so for the remainder of the textbook when constraints are considered. Because of this convention, we must therefore introduce a constraint qualification on the constraint functions $h^k(\cdot)$, $k = 1, 2, \ldots, K$, just as is done when studying static optimization problems with constraints.

The optimal control problem for which we now seek to develop necessary and sufficient conditions can be stated as follows:

$$\max_{\mathbf{u}(\cdot)} J[\mathbf{x}(\cdot), \mathbf{u}(\cdot)] \stackrel{\text{def}}{=} \int_{t_0}^{t_1} f(t, \mathbf{x}(t), \mathbf{u}(t))\, dt$$

$$\text{s.t.} \quad \dot{\mathbf{x}}(t) = \mathbf{g}(t, \mathbf{x}(t), \mathbf{u}(t)), \ \mathbf{x}(t_0) = \mathbf{x}_0, \ \mathbf{x}(t_1) = \mathbf{x}_1, \tag{43}$$

$$\mathbf{h}(t, \mathbf{u}(t)) \geq \mathbf{0}_K,$$

where $\mathbf{u}(\cdot) \stackrel{\text{def}}{=} (u_1(\cdot), u_2(\cdot), \ldots, u_M(\cdot))$, $\mathbf{g}(\cdot) \stackrel{\text{def}}{=} (g^1(\cdot), g^2(\cdot), \ldots, g^N(\cdot))$, $\dot{\mathbf{x}}(\cdot) \stackrel{\text{def}}{=} (\dot{x}_1(\cdot), \dot{x}_2(\cdot), \ldots, \dot{x}_N(\cdot))$, $\mathbf{h}(\cdot) \stackrel{\text{def}}{=} (h^1(\cdot), h^2(\cdot), \ldots, h^K(\cdot))$, and $\mathbf{0}_K$ is the K-element null vector in $\Re^K$. It is important to observe that the vector of constraints $\mathbf{h}(t, \mathbf{u}(t)) \geq \mathbf{0}_K$ in problem (43) is equivalent to the requirement $\mathbf{u}(t) \in U(t) \stackrel{\text{def}}{=} \{\mathbf{u}(\cdot) : h^k(t, \mathbf{u}(t)) \geq 0,\ k = 1, 2, \ldots, K\}$ from Eq. (42). Before stating the theorems, we first introduce a definition that is a prerequisite for the constraint qualification we shall adopt.

Definition 4.2: Let X be a set. Then card(X), the *cardinal number* of X, is the number of elements in X.

For finite sets, the only type that we will employ when using Definition 4.2, this is an elementary and straightforward concept. As usual, we let $(\mathbf{z}(\cdot), \mathbf{v}(\cdot))$ be an optimal pair of functions for problem (43). We may now state the constraint qualification of interest to us.

Rank Constraint Qualification: Define $\iota(t, \mathbf{v}(t)) \stackrel{\text{def}}{=} \{k : h^k(t, \mathbf{v}(t)) = 0,\ k = 1, 2, \ldots, K\}$ as the index set of the binding constraints along the optimal path. For all $t \in [t_0, t_1]$, if $\iota(t, \mathbf{v}(t)) \neq \emptyset$, that is, $\iota(t, \mathbf{v}(t))$ is nonempty, then the card$(\iota(t, \mathbf{v}(t))) \times M$ Jacobian matrix

$$\left[\frac{\partial h^k}{\partial u_m}(t, \mathbf{v}(t))\right]_{\substack{k \in \iota(t,\, \mathbf{v}(t)) \\ m=1,\, 2,\, \ldots,\, M}} \tag{44}$$

has a rank equal to card$(\iota(t, \mathbf{v}(t)))$. That is, the rank of the above Jacobian matrix is equal to the number of its rows.

For example, if k' of the inequality constraints bind at a given point t in the planning horizon, $0 < k' < K$, then the above Jacobian matrix will be of order $k' \times M$ and the constraint qualification will be satisfied if the rank of the Jacobian equals k'. This rank condition on the Jacobian has two important consequences. First, it implies that at least one control variable must be present in each of the binding constraints. To see this, assume that the constraint qualification holds but that one of the k' binding constraints, say, the first (without loss of generality), does not have any control variables in it. In this case, the first row of the above Jacobian would be identically zero, thereby implying that the rows of the Jacobian are linearly dependent. This, in turn, implies that the Jacobian is of rank less than k', thus violating the constraint qualification. Second, the constraint qualification implies that the number of binding constraints k' cannot be greater than the number of control variables M. To see this, assume that the constraint qualification holds but that $k' > M$. Then there are more rows (k') in the Jacobian than there are columns (M). But the rank of a matrix cannot exceed the minimum of the number of its rows or columns. This, in turn, implies that the rank of the Jacobian is $\min(k', M) = M$, which is less than k', thereby violating the constraint qualification.

With the constraint qualification now dealt with, we can turn to the necessary conditions for problem (43). For ease of exposition, we first remind the reader of the definition of the Hamiltonian:

$$H(t, \mathbf{x}, \mathbf{u}, \boldsymbol{\lambda}) \stackrel{\text{def}}{=} f(t, \mathbf{x}, \mathbf{u}) + \boldsymbol{\lambda}'\mathbf{g}(t, \mathbf{x}, \mathbf{u}) = f(t, \mathbf{x}, \mathbf{u}) + \sum_{n=1}^{N} \lambda_n g^n(t, \mathbf{x}, \mathbf{u}).$$

We should also note that in addition to the standard assumptions on the functions $f(\cdot)$ and $\mathbf{g}(\cdot)$ given in Chapter 1, we now make the following *additional* ones:

(A.1) $\partial f(\cdot)/\partial u_m \in C^{(0)}$ with respect to the $1 + N + M$ variables $(t, \mathbf{x}, \mathbf{u})$ for $m = 1, 2, \ldots, M$.
(A.2) $\partial g^n(\cdot)/\partial u_m \in C^{(0)}$ with respect to the $1 + N + M$ variables $(t, \mathbf{x}, \mathbf{u})$ for $m = 1, 2, \ldots, M$ and $n = 1, 2, \ldots, N$.
(A.3) $h^k(\cdot) \in C^{(0)}$ with respect to the $1 + M$ variables $(t, \mathbf{u})$ for $k = 1, 2, \ldots, K$.
(A.4) $\partial h^k(\cdot)/\partial u_m \in C^{(0)}$ with respect to the $1 + M$ variables $(t, \mathbf{u})$ for $k = 1, 2, \ldots, K$ and $m = 1, 2, \ldots, M$.

We may now state the necessary conditions pertaining to problem (43).

Theorem 4.4 (Necessary Conditions, Inequality Constraints): *Let* $(\mathbf{z}(t), \mathbf{v}(t))$ *be an admissible pair for problem* (43)*, and assume that the rank constraint qualification is satisfied. Then if* $(\mathbf{z}(t), \mathbf{v}(t))$ *yields the absolute maximum of* $J[\cdot]$*, it is necessary that there exist a piecewise smooth vector-valued function* $\boldsymbol{\lambda}(\cdot) \stackrel{\text{def}}{=} (\lambda_1(\cdot), \lambda_2(\cdot), \ldots, \lambda_N(\cdot))$ *and a piecewise continuous vector-valued Lagrange multiplier function* $\boldsymbol{\mu}(\cdot) \stackrel{\text{def}}{=} (\mu_1(\cdot), \mu_2(\cdot), \ldots, \mu_K(\cdot))$*, such that for all* $t \in [t_0, t_1]$*,*

$$\mathbf{v}(t) = \arg\max_{\mathbf{u}}\{H(t, \mathbf{z}(t), \mathbf{u}, \boldsymbol{\lambda}(t)) \text{ s.t. } \mathbf{h}(t, \mathbf{u}(t)) \geq \mathbf{0}_K\};$$

that is, if

$$M(t, \mathbf{z}(t), \boldsymbol{\lambda}(t)) \stackrel{\text{def}}{=} \max_{\mathbf{u}}\{H(t, \mathbf{z}(t), \mathbf{u}, \boldsymbol{\lambda}(t)) \text{ s.t. } \mathbf{h}(t, \mathbf{u}(t)) \geq \mathbf{0}_K\},$$

then

$$M(t, \mathbf{z}(t), \boldsymbol{\lambda}(t)) \equiv H(t, \mathbf{z}(t), \mathbf{v}(t), \boldsymbol{\lambda}(t)),$$

or equivalently

$$H(t, \mathbf{z}(t), \mathbf{v}(t), \boldsymbol{\lambda}(t)) \geq H(t, \mathbf{z}(t), \mathbf{u}, \boldsymbol{\lambda}(t)) \forall\, \mathbf{u} \in U(t),$$

where $U(t) \stackrel{\text{def}}{=} \{\mathbf{u}(\cdot) : h^k(t, \mathbf{u}(t)) \geq 0,\ k = 1, 2, \ldots, K\}$*. Because the rank constraint qualification is assumed to hold, the above necessary condition implies that*

$$\frac{\partial L}{\partial u_m}(t, \mathbf{z}(t), \mathbf{v}(t), \boldsymbol{\lambda}(t), \boldsymbol{\mu}(t)) = 0, \quad m = 1, 2, \ldots, M,$$

$$\frac{\partial L}{\partial \mu_k}(t, \mathbf{z}(t), \mathbf{v}(t), \boldsymbol{\lambda}(t), \boldsymbol{\mu}(t)) \geq 0,$$

$$\mu_k(t) \geq 0,\ \mu_k(t)\frac{\partial L}{\partial \mu_k}(t, \mathbf{z}(t), \mathbf{v}(t), \boldsymbol{\lambda}(t), \boldsymbol{\mu}(t)) = 0, \quad k = 1, 2, \ldots, K,$$

where

$$L(t, \mathbf{x}, \mathbf{u}, \boldsymbol{\lambda}, \boldsymbol{\mu}) \stackrel{\text{def}}{=} H(t, \mathbf{x}, \mathbf{u}, \boldsymbol{\lambda}) + \boldsymbol{\mu}'\mathbf{h}(t, \mathbf{u})$$
$$= f(t, \mathbf{x}, \mathbf{u}) + \sum_{n=1}^{N} \lambda_n g^n(t, \mathbf{x}, \mathbf{u}) + \sum_{k=1}^{K} \mu_k h^k(t, \mathbf{u})$$

is the Lagrangian function. Furthermore, except for the points of discontinuities of $\mathbf{v}(t)$,

$$\dot{z}_n(t) = \frac{\partial H}{\partial \lambda_n}(t, \mathbf{z}(t), \mathbf{v}(t), \boldsymbol{\lambda}(t)) = g^n(t, \mathbf{z}(t), \mathbf{v}(t)), \quad n = 1, 2, \ldots, N,$$

$$\dot{\lambda}_n(t) = -\frac{\partial H}{\partial x_n}(t, \mathbf{z}(t), \mathbf{v}(t), \boldsymbol{\lambda}(t)), \quad n = 1, 2, \ldots, N,$$

where the above notation means that the functions are first differentiated with respect to the particular variable and then evaluated at $(t, \mathbf{z}(t), \mathbf{v}(t), \boldsymbol{\lambda}(t), \boldsymbol{\mu}(t))$.

The proof of this theorem is a straightforward consequence of Theorem 4.2 and the Karush-Kuhn-Tucker theorem, stated as Theorem 18.4 in Simon and Blume (1994). It is therefore left for a mental exercise. Before stating a corresponding sufficiency theorem, we note several important consequences of Theorem 4.4. First, in general, the Lagrange multiplier function $\boldsymbol{\mu}(\cdot) \stackrel{\text{def}}{=} (\mu_1(\cdot), \mu_2(\cdot), \ldots, \mu_K(\cdot))$ is piecewise continuous on $[t_0, t_1]$. It turns out, however, that $\boldsymbol{\mu}(\cdot)$ is continuous whenever the optimal control function $\mathbf{v}(\cdot)$ is continuous. Thus the discontinuities in the Lagrange multipliers can only occur at points where the optimal control is discontinuous. Second, the Lagrangian function evaluated along the optimal solution is a continuous function of t, that is, $L(t, \mathbf{z}(t), \mathbf{v}(t), \boldsymbol{\lambda}(t), \boldsymbol{\mu}(t))$ is a continuous function of t. Third, the *total derivative* of $L(t, \mathbf{z}(t), \mathbf{v}(t), \boldsymbol{\lambda}(t), \boldsymbol{\mu}(t))$ with respect to t, scilicet,

$$\dot{L}(t, \mathbf{z}(t), \mathbf{v}(t), \boldsymbol{\lambda}(t), \boldsymbol{\mu}(t)) \stackrel{\text{def}}{=} \frac{d}{dt}L(t, \mathbf{z}(t), \mathbf{v}(t), \boldsymbol{\lambda}(t), \boldsymbol{\mu}(t)),$$

is equal to the *partial derivative* of $L(t, \mathbf{z}(t), \mathbf{v}(t), \boldsymbol{\lambda}(t), \boldsymbol{\mu}(t))$ with respect to t, namely,

$$L_t(t, \mathbf{z}(t), \mathbf{v}(t), \boldsymbol{\lambda}(t), \boldsymbol{\mu}(t)) \stackrel{\text{def}}{=} \frac{\partial}{\partial t}L(t, \mathbf{z}(t), \mathbf{v}(t), \boldsymbol{\lambda}(t), \boldsymbol{\mu}(t)),$$

at all continuity points of the optimal control function $\mathbf{v}(\cdot)$, assuming that $f(\cdot)$, $\mathbf{g}(\cdot)$, and $\mathbf{h}(\cdot)$ are $C^{(1)}$ functions of $(t, \mathbf{x}, \mathbf{u})$. Other results similar to those derived in Mental Exercise 2.31 also hold, as you will discover in a mental exercise in this chapter.

It is also worthwhile at this juncture to provide a rather thorough set of remarks on the role that the rank constraint qualification plays in solving an optimal control problem. Following Seierstad and Sydsæter (1987, pp. 278–279), the crucial observation is that the set of candidates for optimality are contained in the *union* of the following two sets:

$$A \stackrel{\text{def}}{=} \{\text{admissible pairs satisfying the necessary conditions}\},$$

$$B \stackrel{\text{def}}{=} \{\text{admissible pairs that fail to satisfy the rank constraint qualification}\}.$$

In other words, the set $A \cup B$ contains all the candidates for optimality. Because we have the identity $A \cup B \equiv B \cup (A - B)$, a valid two-step approach for obtaining all of the candidates for optimality is as follows:

(i) First find all the admissible pairs that fail to satisfy the rank constraint qualification for some $t \in [t_0, t_1]$.
(ii) Then find all the admissible pairs that satisfy the necessary conditions *and* the rank constraint qualification.

This is the approach applied in the book to find the candidates for optimality, and it is also the procedure recommended because it is often the most successful. Note, however, that the identity $A \cup B \equiv A \cup (B - A)$ is equally valid and suggests a different two-step procedure for obtaining all of the candidates for optimality, to wit:

(i′) First find all the admissible pairs that satisfy the necessary conditions, *disregarding* the rank constraint qualification.
(ii′) Then find all the admissible pairs that fail to satisfy the rank constraint, *excluding* those obtained in (i′).

Remember that either two-step procedure will yield all the candidates for optimality.

The following sufficiency theorem is not the most general known, but it will suffice for our present purposes. Its proof is similar to that of Theorem 4.3 and so is left for a mental exercise. It is a Mangasarian-type sufficiency result.

Theorem 4.5 (Sufficient Conditions, Inequality Constraints): *Let* $(\mathbf{z}(t), \mathbf{v}(t))$ *be an admissible pair for problem (43). Suppose that* $(\mathbf{z}(t), \mathbf{v}(t))$ *satisfies the necessary conditions of Theorem 4.4 for problem (43) with costate vector* $\boldsymbol{\lambda}(t)$ *and the Lagrange multiplier vector* $\boldsymbol{\mu}(t)$*, and let* $L(t, \mathbf{x}, \mathbf{u}, \boldsymbol{\lambda}, \boldsymbol{\mu}) \stackrel{\text{def}}{=} f(t, \mathbf{x}, \mathbf{u}) + \boldsymbol{\lambda}'\mathbf{g}(t, \mathbf{x}, \mathbf{u}) + \boldsymbol{\mu}'\mathbf{h}(t, \mathbf{u})$ *be the value of the Lagrangian function. If* $L(\cdot)$ *is a concave function of* $(\mathbf{x}, \mathbf{u})\, \forall\, t \in [t_0, t_1]$ *over an open convex set containing all the admissible values of* $(\mathbf{x}(\cdot), \mathbf{u}(\cdot))$ *when the costate vector is* $\boldsymbol{\lambda}(t)$ *and the Lagrange multiplier vector is* $\boldsymbol{\mu}(t)$*, then* $\mathbf{v}(t)$ *is an optimal control and* $(\mathbf{z}(t), \mathbf{v}(t))$ *yields the global maximum of* $J[\cdot]$*. If* $L(\cdot)$ *is a strictly concave function under the same conditions, then* $(\mathbf{z}(t), \mathbf{v}(t))$ *yields the unique global maximum of* $J[\cdot]$.

A very important observation about this sufficiency theorem is that the rank constraint qualification is *not* required, in sharp contrast to the necessary conditions of

Theorem 4.4. It is also noteworthy that this theorem may be strengthened to give an Arrow-type sufficiency result. We will pursue this in a later chapter, however, when we study a more general class of optimal control problems. Let's now demonstrate Theorems 4.4 and 4.5 by returning to the inventory accumulation problem of Example 4.5, but this time, we explicitly take into account the nonnegativity restriction on the production rate.

Example 4.6: Recall the inventory accumulation problem from Example 4.5:

$$\max_{u(\cdot)} J[x(\cdot), u(\cdot)] \stackrel{\text{def}}{=} \int_0^T -\left[c_1[u(t)]^2 + c_2 x(t)\right] dt$$

$$\text{s.t.} \quad \dot{x}(t) = u(t), \; x(0) = 0, \; x(T) = x_T,$$

$$h(t, u(t)) \stackrel{\text{def}}{=} u(t) \geq 0.$$

Notice that in this instance, we have multiplied the objective functional by minus unity in order to convert it into a maximization problem, the form required by Theorems 4.4 and 4.5. Recall that in Example 4.5, we showed that the production rate constraint $u(t) \geq 0 \, \forall \, t \in [0, T]$ is satisfied if and only if $x_T \geq \frac{1}{4} c_2 c_1^{-1} T^2$ [recall Eq. (41)]. In the present situation, let's therefore assume that $x_T < \frac{1}{4} c_2 c_1^{-1} T^2$, so that the nonnegativity constraint on the production rate will be binding for some period of time in the planning horizon. This is clearly the only case in which the nonnegativity constraint is interesting.

To solve this version of the problem, we begin by defining the Hamiltonian and Lagrangian functions:

$$H(x, u, \lambda) \stackrel{\text{def}}{=} -c_1 u^2 - c_2 x + \lambda u,$$

$$L(x, u, \lambda, \mu) \stackrel{\text{def}}{=} -c_1 u^2 - c_2 x + \lambda u + \mu u.$$

Because $h_u(t, u) = 1$, the rank constraint qualification is satisfied. Thus by Theorem 4.4, the necessary conditions are

$$L_u(x, u, \lambda, \mu) = -2c_1 u + \lambda + \mu = 0, \tag{45}$$

$$L_\mu(x, u, \lambda, \mu) = u \geq 0, \; \mu \geq 0, \; \mu u = 0, \tag{46}$$

$$\dot{\lambda} = -H_x(x, u, \lambda) = c_2, \tag{47}$$

$$\dot{x} = H_\lambda(x, u, \lambda) = u, \; x(0) = 0, \; x(T) = x_T. \tag{48}$$

The Hessian matrix of the Lagrangian function is given by

$$\begin{bmatrix} L_{uu}(x, u, \lambda, \mu) & L_{ux}(x, u, \lambda, \mu) \\ L_{xu}(x, u, \lambda, \mu) & L_{xx}(x, u, \lambda, \mu) \end{bmatrix} = \begin{bmatrix} -2c_1 & 0 \\ 0 & 0 \end{bmatrix},$$

which has eigenvalues $-2c_1 < 0$ and zero. Thus the Hessian matrix of the Lagrangian function is negative semidefinite, which, as you know by now, is equivalent to the concavity of $L(\cdot)$ in (x, u). By Theorem 4.5, therefore, any solution of the necessary conditions is a solution of the optimal control problem. Note, however, that because $L(\cdot)$ is not strictly concave in (x, u), we cannot appeal to Theorem 4.5 to claim uniqueness.

Given that we have assumed that $x_T < \frac{1}{4}c_2c_1^{-1}T^2$, we know that the length of the planning horizon T is long relative to the amount of the product required to be produced x_T. Moreover, we also know that inventory is costly to hold, that is, $c_2 > 0$. In light of these two observations, a reasonable hypothesis as to the structure of the solution for the production rate is that there is an initial period of the planning horizon, say, $0 \leq t \leq s$, $s \in (0, T)$, in which the production rate is zero, that is, $u(t) = 0$ for all $t \in [0, s]$, after which the production rate is positive, that is, $u(t) > 0$ for all $t \in (s, T]$. The time after which the production rate turns positive, namely, $s \in (0, T)$, is called the *switching time*. It is an endogenous variable, determined by the condition that the cumulative amount produced by the end of the planning horizon equals the amount required by the contract. We thus seek a solution of the necessary conditions with these characteristics. Such a solution will be the solution of the control problem because of the aforementioned concavity of $L(\cdot)$ in (x, u).

To begin, first solve Eq. (45) for the control variable to get

$$u = \frac{\lambda + \mu}{2c_1}. \tag{49}$$

Our conjecture is that $u(t) = 0$ for all $t \in [0, s]$, $s \in (0, T)$. Clearly, this is equivalent to $\lambda(t) + \mu(t) = 0$ for all $t \in [0, s]$. Seeing as $\dot{\lambda} = c_2 > 0$ by Eq. (47) (the costate equation), $\lambda(t) \neq 0$ for all $t \in [0, T]$, with the possible exception of an instant. This implies that the Lagrange multiplier $\mu(t) \neq 0$ for all $t \in [0, s]$, with the possible exception of an instant, since $\lambda(t) + \mu(t) = 0$ for all $t \in [0, s]$. Integrating $\dot{\lambda} = c_2 > 0$ yields $\lambda(t) = c_2t + a_1$ for all $t \in [0, T]$, where a_1 is a constant of integration. Because $\lambda(t) + \mu(t) = 0$ for all $t \in [0, s]$, $\mu(t) = -c_2t - a_1$ for all $t \in [0, s]$. To find the value of the constant of integration, recall our conjecture that $u(t) > 0$ for all $t \in (s, T]$, which implies, by way of Eq. (46), that $\mu(t) = 0$ for all $t \in (s, T]$. Because the control function is a continuous (but not a differentiable) function of t under our hypothesis, the Lagrange multiplier function is too, confirming a remark made after Theorem 4.4. We thus use the fact that $\mu(\cdot)$ is continuous at $t = s$ to get $\mu(s) = -c_2s - a_1 = 0$, or $a_1 = -c_2s$. Using this value of the constant of integration yields the specific solution for the costate variable and Lagrange multiplier:

$$\lambda(t; s, c_2) = c_2[t - s] \, \forall t \in [0, T], \tag{50}$$

$$\mu(t; s, c_2) = \begin{cases} c_2[s - t] & \forall t \in [0, s], \\ 0 & \forall t \in (s, T]. \end{cases} \tag{51}$$

Note that on the closed interval $[0, s]$, $\lambda(t; s, c_2)$ and $\mu(t; s, c_2)$ are only equal to zero at $t = s$, an instant, just as claimed above. Substituting Eqs. (50) and (51) into Eq. (49) yields our specific solution for the production rate:

$$v(t; s, c_1, c_2) = \begin{cases} 0 & \forall t \in [0, s], \\ \dfrac{c_2[t - s]}{2c_1} & \forall t \in (s, T]. \end{cases} \tag{52}$$

Observe that $\mu(\cdot)$ and $v(\cdot)$ are continuous functions of t, just as asserted above. More precisely, $\mu(\cdot)$ and $v(\cdot)$ are piecewise smooth functions of t.

To finish up the solution, we must find the time path of the stock of inventory and the switching time s. Using Eq. (52), the state equation $\dot{x} = u$ becomes

$$\dot{x} = \begin{cases} 0 & \forall t \in [0, s], \\ \dfrac{c_2[t - s]}{2c_1} & \forall t \in (s, T]. \end{cases}$$

Integrating this differential equation separately over each time interval yields the general solution

$$x(t) = \begin{cases} a_2 & \forall t \in [0, s], \\ \dfrac{c_2 t^2}{4c_1} - \dfrac{c_2 s t}{2c_1} + a_3 & \forall t \in (s, T], \end{cases} \tag{53}$$

where a_2 and a_3 are constants of integration. Using the initial condition $x(0) = 0$ gives $a_2 = 0$. Because $x(\cdot)$ is a continuous function of t by Theorem 4.4, we can solve for a_3 by equating both portions of the solution in Eq. (53) at $t = s$ using $a_2 = 0$. This yields the equation

$$\frac{c_2 s^2}{4c_1} - \frac{c_2 s^2}{2c_1} + a_3 = 0,$$

which, when solved for a_3, gives

$$a_3 = \frac{c_2 s^2}{4c_1}. \tag{54}$$

Substituting Eq. (54) into Eq. (53) yields the specific solution of the state equation

$$z(t; s, c_1, c_2) = \begin{cases} 0 & \forall t \in [0, s], \\ \dfrac{c_2}{4c_1}[t - s]^2 & \forall t \in (s, T]. \end{cases} \tag{55}$$

As expected, $z(\cdot)$ is a piecewise smooth function of t.

Finally, we seek to determine the switching time s. Because the only unused boundary condition is the terminal one, namely, $x(T) = x_T$, it can be used to determine s. Using this boundary condition in Eq. (55) gives $\frac{c_2}{4c_1}[T - s]^2 = x_T$, which yields

$$s = T - 2\sqrt{\frac{c_1 x_T}{c_2}} \tag{56}$$

as the solution for the switching time, as you are asked to show in a mental exercise. In sum, Eqs. (50), (51), (52), (53), and (56) represent the unique solution to the problem, since they are the only solution to the necessary and sufficient conditions.

An interesting feature of the solution for the switching time is that the length of the subinterval in which production occurs, videlicet,

$$T - s = 2\sqrt{\frac{c_1 x_T}{c_2}},$$

is identical to the length of the planning horizon the firm would choose if T was a decision variable, as we will see in Chapter 8. This observation means that the length of the subinterval in which production occurs is unaffected by how distant the terminal period T is, as long as our original assumption on the length of the planning horizon holds, to wit, $x_T < \frac{1}{4}c_2 c_1^{-1} T^2$. This, in turn, implies that the production rate in the interval $[s, T]$ in also unaffected by an increase in T. As can be seen from Eq. (56), $\partial s/\partial T = 1$; thus an increase in T lengthens the initial period when no production occurs, but leaves the length of the period in which positive production occurs unchanged, thereby implying that the positive production rate in the interval $[s, T]$ is unaffected too. We leave the remaining comparative dynamics results for a mental exercise.

In the next chapter, we take up the study of optimal control problems that often exhibit piecewise continuous optimal control functions. In order to solve such problems, we often must approach them somewhat differently because the differential calculus has a more limited role in the characterization of the optimal control. To convince you that this generality is not simply of mathematical interest, we will present and solve three economic problems that exhibit piecewise continuous optimal control functions.

MENTAL EXERCISES

4.1 Consider the fixed endpoints optimal control problem

$$\min_{u(\cdot)} J[x(\cdot), u(\cdot)] \stackrel{\text{def}}{=} \int_0^1 [u(t)]^2 \, dt$$

$$\text{s.t.} \quad \dot{x}(t) = x(t) + u(t), \; x(0) = 1, \; x(1) = 0.$$

(a) Find the solution to the necessary conditions.
(b) Prove that the solution found in (a) solves the optimal control problem.

4.2 Consider the fixed endpoints optimal control problem

$$\max_{u(\cdot)} J[x(\cdot), u(\cdot)] \stackrel{\text{def}}{=} \int_0^1 [\alpha t u(t) - \frac{1}{2}[u(t)]^2]\, dt$$

$$\text{s.t.} \quad \dot{x}(t) = u(t) - x(t),\; x(0) = x_0,\; x(1) = 0.$$

(a) Find the solution to the necessary conditions.
(b) Prove that the solution found in (a) solves the optimal control problem.

4.3 The following questions pertain to Example 4.3.
(a) Show that $u_1(t) = \sin t$ is an admissible control.
(b) Show that $u_2(t) = \frac{1}{2}$ is an admissible control.
(c) Compute $J[x_1(\cdot), u_1(\cdot)]$ and $J[x_2(\cdot), u_2(\cdot)]$.
(d) Compare $J[x_1(\cdot), u_1(\cdot)]$ and $J[x_2(\cdot), u_2(\cdot)]$ with the value of $J[\cdot]$ computed in the example.

4.4 Consider the optimal control problem

$$\max_{u(\cdot), x_1} J[x(\cdot), u(\cdot)] \stackrel{\text{def}}{=} \int_0^1 [x(t) + u(t)]\, dt$$

$$\text{s.t.} \quad \dot{x}(t) = -x(t) + u(t) + t,\; x(0) = 1,\; x(1) = x_1,$$

$$u(t) \in U \stackrel{\text{def}}{=} \{u(\cdot) : 0 \leq u(t) \leq 1\}.$$

(a) Write down all the necessary conditions for this problem.
(b) Find the unique solution of the costate equation.
(c) Find the decision rule governing the optimal control, and find $v(t)$.
(d) Determine the associated path of the state variable $z(t)$.
(e) Prove that the solution to the necessary conditions is the optimal solution of the control problem.
(f) Solve the control problem directly, that is, without the aid of the Maximum Principle. **Hint:** Solve the state equation.

4.5 Consider the fixed endpoints optimal control problem

$$\max_{u(\cdot)} J[x(\cdot), u(\cdot)] \stackrel{\text{def}}{=} \int_0^1 u(t)\, dt$$

$$\text{s.t.} \quad \dot{x}(t) = x(t) + [u(t)]^2,\; x(0) = 1,\; x(1) = \alpha,$$

where α is some parameter.
(a) Show that there is no solution to the optimal control problem if $\alpha \leq 1$.
(b) Would your answer to part (a) change if "max" were replaced by "min"? Why or why not?

4.6 Consider the optimal control problem

$$\max_{u(\cdot)} \int_0^1 u(t)\,dt$$

$$\text{s.t.} \quad \dot{x}(t) = [u(t) - (u(t))^2]^2, \; x(0) = 0, \; x(1) = 0,$$

$$u(t) \in [0, 2].$$

Prove that $v(t) = 1 \,\forall\, t \in [0, 1]$ is the optimal control and satisfies the Maximum Principle only for $\lambda_0 = 0$.

4.7 Consider the two state variable optimal control problem

$$\max_{u(\cdot), x_1} \int_0^1 \left[t - \frac{1}{2}\right] u(t)\,dt$$

$$\text{s.t.} \quad \dot{x}(t) = u(t), \; x(0) = 0, \; x(1) = x_1,$$

$$\dot{y}(t) = [x(t) - tu(t)]^2, \; y(0) = 0, \; y(1) = 0.$$

Prove that any constant control is optimal and satisfies the Maximum Principle only for $\lambda_0 = 0$. **Hint:** Note that $x(t) - tu(t) \equiv 0 \Rightarrow \dot{x}(t) - t\dot{u}(t) - u(t) \equiv -t\dot{u}(t) \equiv 0$.

4.8 Consider the two control variable optimal control problem

$$\max_{u_1(\cdot), u_2(\cdot)} \int_0^1 [u_1(t) - 2u_2(t)]\,dt$$

$$\text{s.t.} \quad \dot{x}(t) = [u_1(t) - u_2(t)]^2, \; x(0) = 0, \; x(1) = 0,$$

$$u_1(t) \in [-1, 1], \; u_2(t) \in [-1, 1].$$

Prove that $v_1(t) = 1 \,\forall\, t \in [0, 1]$ and $v_2(t) = 1 \,\forall\, t \in [0, 1]$ are optimal and satisfy the Maximum Principle only for $\lambda_0 = 0$.

4.9 Find necessary conditions for a solution of the fixed endpoints optimal control problem with a bounded control variable, namely,

$$\max_{u(\cdot)} \int_{t_0}^{t_1} f(t, x(t), u(t))\,dt$$

$$\text{s.t.} \quad \dot{x}(t) = g(t, x(t), u(t)), \; x(t_0) = x_0, \; x(t_1) = x_1,$$

$$a(t) \le u(t) \le b(t).$$

4.10 Consider the optimal control problem

$$\max_{u(\cdot),x_2} J[x(\cdot),u(\cdot)] \stackrel{\text{def}}{=} \int_0^2 [2x(t) - 3u(t) - [u(t)]^2]\,dt$$

$$\text{s.t.} \quad \dot{x}(t) = x(t) + u(t),\ x(0) = 4,\ x(2) = x_2,$$

$$u(t) \in U \stackrel{\text{def}}{=} \{u(\cdot) : 0 \le u(t) \le 2\}.$$

Note that this problem is probably best tackled *after* Example 5.1 is understood.

(a) Find the solution to the necessary conditions.

(b) Prove that the solution found in (a) solves the optimal control problem.

4.11 Consider the optimal control problem

$$\max_{u(\cdot),x_4} J[x(\cdot),u(\cdot)] \stackrel{\text{def}}{=} \int_0^4 3x(t)\,dt$$

$$\text{s.t.} \quad \dot{x}(t) = x(t) + u(t),\ x(0) = 5,\ x(4) = x_4,$$

$$u(t) \in U \stackrel{\text{def}}{=} \{u(\cdot) : 0 \le u(t) \le 2\}.$$

(a) Find the solution to the necessary conditions.

(b) Prove that the solution found in (a) solves the optimal control problem.

4.12 Prove Theorem 4.4.

4.13 Consider the optimal control problem (43):

$$\max_{\mathbf{u}(\cdot)} J[\mathbf{x}(\cdot),\mathbf{u}(\cdot)] \stackrel{\text{def}}{=} \int_{t_0}^{t_1} f(t,\mathbf{x}(t),\mathbf{u}(t))\,dt$$

$$\text{s.t.} \quad \dot{\mathbf{x}}(t) = \mathbf{g}(t,\mathbf{x}(t),\mathbf{u}(t)),\ \mathbf{x}(t_0) = \mathbf{x}_0,\ \mathbf{x}(t_1) = \mathbf{x}_1,$$

$$\mathbf{h}(t,\mathbf{u}(t)) \ge \mathbf{0}_K.$$

Let $(\mathbf{z}(t),\mathbf{v}(t))$ be the optimal pair, $\boldsymbol{\lambda}(t)$ the corresponding time path of the costate vector, and $\boldsymbol{\mu}(t)$ the time path of the corresponding Lagrange multiplier vector. Define the Hamiltonian as

$$H(t,\mathbf{x},\mathbf{u},\boldsymbol{\lambda}) \stackrel{\text{def}}{=} f(t,\mathbf{x},\mathbf{u}) + \boldsymbol{\lambda}'\mathbf{g}(t,\mathbf{x},\mathbf{u}) = f(t,\mathbf{x},\mathbf{u}) + \sum_{n=1}^{N} \lambda_n g^n(t,\mathbf{x},\mathbf{u})$$

and the Lagrangian as

$$\begin{aligned} L(t,\mathbf{x},\mathbf{u},\boldsymbol{\lambda},\boldsymbol{\mu}) &\stackrel{\text{def}}{=} H(t,\mathbf{x},\mathbf{u},\boldsymbol{\lambda}) + \boldsymbol{\mu}'\mathbf{h}(t,\mathbf{u}) \\ &= f(t,\mathbf{x},\mathbf{u}) + \sum_{n=1}^{N} \lambda_n g^n(t,\mathbf{x},\mathbf{u}) + \sum_{k=1}^{K} \mu_k h^k(t,\mathbf{u}). \end{aligned}$$

Assume that $f(\cdot) \in C^{(1)}$, $\mathbf{g}(\cdot) \in C^{(1)}$, and $\mathbf{h}(\cdot) \in C^{(1)}$ in $(t, \mathbf{x}, \mathbf{u})$.

(a) Prove that

$$\frac{d}{dt} L(t, \mathbf{z}(t), \mathbf{v}(t), \boldsymbol{\lambda}(t), \boldsymbol{\mu}(t)) = \frac{\partial}{\partial t} L(t, \mathbf{z}(t), \mathbf{v}(t), \boldsymbol{\lambda}(t), \boldsymbol{\mu}(t)).$$

(b) Prove that if the optimal control problem is autonomous, that is, the independent variable t doesn't enter the functions $f(\cdot)$, $\mathbf{g}(\cdot)$, or $\mathbf{h}(\cdot)$ explicitly, that is, $f_t(t, \mathbf{x}, \mathbf{u}) \equiv 0$, $\mathbf{g}_t(t, \mathbf{x}, \mathbf{u}) \equiv \mathbf{0}_N$, and $\mathbf{h}_t(t, \mathbf{u}) \equiv \mathbf{0}_K$, then $L(\cdot)$ is constant along the optimal path.

(c) Prove that

$$\frac{d}{dt} H(t, \mathbf{z}(t), \mathbf{v}(t), \boldsymbol{\lambda}(t)) = \frac{\partial}{\partial t} H(t, \mathbf{z}(t), \mathbf{v}(t), \boldsymbol{\lambda}(t)).$$

Note that this result is *not* the same as that in Mental Exercise 2.31.

(d) Prove that if the optimal control problem is autonomous, then $H(\cdot)$ is constant along the optimal path too.

4.14 Prove Theorem 4.5.

4.15 This mental exercise asks you to compute and economically interpret the remaining comparative dynamics of the optimal inventory accumulation problem in Example 4.5.

(a) Derive the comparative dynamics result for an increase in total required production x_T on the production rate and the shadow cost of inventory. Provide an economic interpretation.

(b) Derive the comparative dynamics result for an increase in the unit cost of production coefficient c_1 on the production rate and the shadow cost of inventory. Provide an economic interpretation.

(c) Derive the comparative dynamics result for an increase in the length of the production run T on the production rate and the shadow cost of inventory. Provide an economic interpretation.

4.16 With reference to Example 4.6, the inventory accumulation problem with a nonnegativity constraint on the production rate:

(a) Explain why $s \in (0, T)$ must hold.

(b) Provide an economic interpretation of $\lambda(s; s, c_2) = 0$.

(c) Derive Eq. (56) for the switching time and explain your steps fully and carefully.

(d) Derive the comparative dynamics for the switching time and production rate for an increase in c_1. Provide an economic interpretation.

(e) Derive the comparative dynamics for the switching time and production rate for an increase in c_2. Provide an economic interpretation.

(f) Derive the comparative dynamics for the switching time and production rate for an increase in x_T. Provide an economic interpretation.

4.17 Consider the optimal control problem

$$\min_{u(\cdot)} J[x(\cdot), u(\cdot)] \stackrel{\text{def}}{=} \int_0^1 [tu(t) + [u(t)]^2]\, dt$$

$$\text{s.t.} \quad \dot{x}(t) = u(t),\ x(0) = x_0,\ x(1) = x_1.$$

(a) Find the solution of the necessary conditions, and denote the solution triplet by $(z(t; x_0, x_1), v(t; x_0, x_1), \lambda(t; x_0, x_1))$.
(b) Prove that the solution found in part (a) is the unique solution of the optimal control problem.
(c) Define the optimal value function by

$$V(x_0, x_1) \stackrel{\text{def}}{=} \int_0^1 \left[tv(t; x_0, x_1) + [v(t; x_0, x_1)]^2\right] dt.$$

The optimal value function is thus the value of the objective functional $J[x(\cdot), u(\cdot)]$ evaluated along the solution curve. Find an explicit expression for $V(x_0, x_1)$.
(d) Compute $\frac{\partial}{\partial x_0} V(x_0, x_1)$ and $\frac{\partial}{\partial x_1} V(x_0, x_1)$.
(e) Show that

$$\frac{\partial}{\partial x_0} V(x_0, x_1) = \lambda(0; x_0, x_1)$$

and

$$\frac{\partial}{\partial x_1} V(x_0, x_1) = -\lambda(1; x_0, x_1).$$

This is a special case of the *dynamic envelope theorem*, which will be covered in a general fashion in Chapter 9. Note also that the first result is equivalent to the definition given in Eq. (21).

4.18 Consider a simple generalization of the optimal inventory accumulation problem in Example 4.5. Assume now that the firm discounts its costs at the rate $r > 0$, but the problem is otherwise unchanged. Thus the firm is asserted to solve

$$\min_{u(\cdot)} J[x(\cdot), u(\cdot)] \stackrel{\text{def}}{=} \int_0^T \left[c_1[u(t)]^2 + c_2 x(t)\right] e^{-rt}\, dt$$

$$\text{s.t.} \quad \dot{x}(t) = u(t),\ x(0) = 0,\ x(T) = x_T.$$

Assume that the nonnegativity constraint $u(t) \geq 0\, \forall\, t \in [0, T]$ is *not* binding. This assumption will be addressed later in this question.

(a) Derive the necessary conditions. Show that

$$2e^{-rt}c_1u(t) + \int_t^{t+\varepsilon} e^{-rs}c_2\,ds = 2e^{-r[t+\varepsilon]}c_1u(t+\varepsilon)$$

along an optimal path, where $\varepsilon > 0$ is sufficiently small. Provide an economic interpretation of this integral equation.

(b) Find the solution of the necessary conditions, and denote the solution triplet by $(z(t;\gamma), v(t;\gamma), \lambda(t;\gamma))$, where $\gamma \overset{\text{def}}{=} (c_1, c_2, r, T, x_T)$.

(c) Prove that the solution of the necessary conditions is the unique solution of the optimal control problem.

(d) Show that $\dot{v}(t;\gamma) > 0$ holds in the optimal plan. Provide an economic interpretation of this result.

(e) Derive a necessary and sufficient condition for the nonnegativity constraint $u(t) \geq 0\,\forall\, t \in [0, T]$ to be nonbinding in an optimal production plan.

(f) Show that $\partial\lambda(t;\gamma)/\partial x_T < 0\,\forall\, t \in [0, T]$ and $\partial\dot{z}(t;\gamma)/\partial x_T > 0\,\forall\, t \in [0, T]$. Provide an economic interpretation of these comparative dynamics results. Note that there are no simple refutable comparative dynamics results for the shadow cost of the inventory or the production rate for the remaining parameters, in sharp contrast to the basic inventory accumulation model studied in Example 4.5 and in Mental Exercise 4.15, which had the discount rate set equal to zero.

4.19 Consider another generalization of the optimal inventory accumulation problem in Example 4.5, in which now the production cost function is given by $g(\cdot)$ and is assumed to have the following properties:

$$g(\cdot) \in C^{(2)},\ g(0) = 0,\ g'(u) \geq 0, \quad \text{and} \quad g''(u) > 0 \ \text{for}\ u \geq 0.$$

Thus production costs are a nondecreasing, strongly convex function of the production rate. Also assume that costs are discounted at the rate $r > 0$. Under these assumptions, the optimal inventory accumulation problem is given by

$$\min_{u(\cdot)} J[x(\cdot), u(\cdot)] \overset{\text{def}}{=} \int_0^T e^{-rt}\,[g(u(t)) + c_2x]\,dt$$

$$\text{s.t.}\quad \dot{x}(t) = u(t),\ x(0) = 0,\ x(T) = x_T.$$

(a) Derive the necessary conditions.

(b) Show that $\dot{u}(t) > 0$ holds in an optimal plan. Provide an economic interpretation of this result.

(c) Show that

$$e^{-rt}g'(u(t)) + \int_t^{t+\varepsilon} e^{-rs}c_2\,ds = e^{-r[t+\varepsilon]}g'(u(t+\varepsilon))$$

in an optimal plan, where $\varepsilon > 0$ is sufficiently small. Provide an economic interpretation of this integral equation.

(d) Now set the discount rate to zero, that is, set $r \equiv 0$, and derive the necessary conditions.

(e) Show that for a given $u(t)$, $\dot{u}(t)$ is larger for $r > 0$ than for $r \equiv 0$. Explain, in economic terms, why this makes sense. Draw a graph in tu-space to show your reasoning geometrically.

(f) For the $r > 0$ and $r \equiv 0$ cases, show that for a given $u(t)$, $\dot{u}(t)$ increases with an increase in the per-unit holding cost of the inventory c_2. Explain, in economic terms, why this makes sense. Draw a graph in tu-space to show your reasoning geometrically.

4.20 Recall the intertemporal utility maximization problem developed in Example 1.3:

$$\max_{c(\cdot)} J[k(\cdot), c(\cdot)] \stackrel{\text{def}}{=} \int_0^T e^{-rt} U(c(t))\, dt$$

$$\text{s.t.} \quad \dot{k}(t) = w + ik(t) - c(t), \ k(0) = k_0, \ k(T) = k_T.$$

Please refer back to Example 1.3 for the economic interpretation of the model and its variables and parameters if your memory of it is vague. Also recall that $U(\cdot) \in C^{(2)}$ and that $U'(c) > 0$ and $U''(c) < 0$.

(a) Derive the necessary conditions and provide an economic interpretation of the Maximum Principle equation.

(b) Prove that a solution of the necessary conditions, assuming that one exists, is a solution of the intertemporal utility maximization problem.

(c) Prove that

$$e^{-rt} U'(c(t)) = i \int_t^{t+\varepsilon} e^{-rs} U'(c(s))\, ds + e^{-r(t+\varepsilon)} U'(c(t+\varepsilon))$$

along an optimal path, where $\varepsilon > 0$ is sufficiently small. Provide an economic interpretation of this integral equation.

(d) Prove that

$$\dot{c} = \left[\frac{-U'(c)}{U''(c)}\right] [i - r]$$

along an optimal path. Provide an economic interpretation.

In order to tease out some more qualitative results and come up with a closed form solution of the problem, assume that $U(c) \stackrel{\text{def}}{=} \ln c$, $k_T = 0$, and $w = 0$.

(e) Derive the unique solution of the control problem under the above simplifying assumptions. Denote it by $(k^*(t; \boldsymbol{\beta}), c^*(t; \boldsymbol{\beta}), \lambda(t; \boldsymbol{\beta}))$, where $\boldsymbol{\beta} \stackrel{\text{def}}{=} (i, r, k_0, T)$.

(f) Obtain the comparative dynamics of the optimal triplet with respect to i, and provide an economic interpretation.
(g) Obtain the comparative dynamics of the optimal triplet with respect to r, and provide an economic interpretation.
(h) Obtain the comparative dynamics of the optimal triplet with respect to k_0, and provide an economic interpretation.
(i) Obtain the comparative dynamics of the optimal triplet with respect to T, and provide an economic interpretation.

4.21 Suppose that at time $t = 0$ (the present), a mine contains an amount $x_0 > 0$ of a nonrenewable resource stock, say, for example, coal. The profit flow that results from extracting and selling the resource at the rate $q(t)$ is given by $\pi(q) \stackrel{\text{def}}{=} \ln q$. The firm lives over the closed interval $[0, T]$ and discounts its profit at the rate $r > 0$. Moreover, the firm is required to extract all the asset by time $t = T$, implying that cumulative extraction over the planning horizon $[0, T]$ must equal the initial size of the deposit $x_0 > 0$. Stated in mathematical terms, this constraint is given by

$$\int_0^T q(s)\,ds = x_0.$$

The firm is asserted to maximize its present discounted value of profit. The optimal control problem can therefore be posed as

$$\max_{q(\cdot)} \int_0^T \pi(q(t))e^{-rt}\,dt$$

$$\text{s.t.} \quad \int_0^T q(t)\,dt = x_0.$$

Unfortunately, at this juncture, we are not able to solve this *isoperimetric* control problem. We will have to wait until Chapter 7 to solve it in this form. We can, however, transform it to a form readily solvable by our current methods. To this end, define $x(t)$ as the cumulative amount of the asset extracted by time t, that is,

$$x(t) \stackrel{\text{def}}{=} \int_0^t q(s)\,ds.$$

Applying Leibniz's rule to this definition and using the integral constraint on the extraction rate yields the associated differential equation and boundary conditions, namely,

$$\dot{x}(t) = q(t),\ x(0) = 0,\ x(T) = x_0.$$

Hence, the equivalent optimal control problem in a form we can handle via the theorems developed so far is given by

$$\max_{q(\cdot)} J[x(\cdot), q(\cdot)] \stackrel{\text{def}}{=} \int_0^T [\ln q(t)]\, e^{-rt}\, dt$$

$$\text{s.t.} \quad \dot{x}(t) = q(t), \; x(0) = 0, \; x(T) = x_0.$$

(a) Derive the solution of the necessary conditions and denote the resulting triplet by $(x^*(t; r, x_0, T), q^*(t; r, x_0, T), \lambda(t; r, x_0, T))$.

(b) Prove that the solution of the necessary conditions is the unique solution of the control problem.

(c) Compute the comparative dynamics of an increase in the initial stock on the present value shadow price of the stock and the extraction rate. That is, derive

$$\frac{\partial \lambda}{\partial x_0}(t; r, x_0, T) \text{ and } \frac{\partial q^*}{\partial x_0}(t; r, x_0, T).$$

Explain, in economic jargon, your results.

(d) Compute the comparative dynamics of an increase in the discount rate on the present value shadow price of the stock and the extraction rate. Because you will not be able to sign this result $\forall\, t \in [0, T]$, evaluate your comparative dynamics results at $t = 0$ and $t = T$. Explain, in economic jargon, your results. **Hint:** Recall that the Taylor series representation for e^y about the point $y = 0$ is given by $e^y = \sum_{k=0}^{+\infty} \frac{y^k}{k!}$.

(e) Compute the comparative dynamics of an increase in the planning horizon on the cumulative stock of the resource and the extraction rate. Explain, in economic jargon, your results.

Now let the profit flow be a general $C^{(2)}$ function of the extraction rate, say, $\pi(q)$, with $\pi'(q) > 0$ and $\pi''(q) < 0$ for $q \geq 0$. Answer the remaining three parts of the exercise based on the general profit function.

(f) Prove that the present value of marginal profit is constant over the entire horizon.

(g) Prove that marginal profit grows exponentially at the discount rate r.

(h) Prove that the optimal extraction rate declines through time.

4.22 Consider the so-called simplest problem in the calculus of variations, defined by

$$\max_{x(\cdot)} J[x(\cdot)] \stackrel{\text{def}}{=} \int_{t_0}^{t_1} f(t, x(t), \dot{x}(t))\, dt$$

$$\text{s.t.} \quad x(t_0) = x_0, \; x(t_1) = x_1.$$

Observe that there are no constraints in the problem and that both of the endpoints are fixed. Assume that $f(\cdot) \in C^{(2)}$ over an open set and that admissible functions are $C^{(2)}$. It is well known that a necessary condition obeyed by the optimizing curve $z(t)$ is given by the differential equation

$$\frac{d}{dt} f_{\dot{x}}(t, x(t), \dot{x}(t)) = f_x(t, x(t), \dot{x}(t)),$$

known as the *Euler equation*. This question asks you to prove that the necessary conditions of the optimal control problem corresponding to the simplest problem in the calculus of variations are equivalent to the Euler equation. One benefit of answering this question is that it provides some background material for Chapter 7.

(a) Transform the above calculus of variations problem into an equivalent optimal control problem by letting $\dot{x}(t) \stackrel{\text{def}}{=} u(t)$ be the state equation.

(b) Write down the necessary conditions for the optimal control problem in (a).

(c) Show that if $(z(\cdot), v(\cdot)) = (z(\cdot), \dot{z}(\cdot))$ is a solution of the necessary conditions of the optimal control problem in (a), then it is also a solution of the Euler equation.

(d) Show that if $(z(\cdot), \dot{z}(\cdot))$ is a solution of the Euler equation, then it is also a solution of the necessary conditions of the optimal control problem in (a). **Hint:** Define the variable $\lambda(t) \stackrel{\text{def}}{=} -f_{\dot{x}}(t, z(t), \dot{z}(t))$.

FURTHER READING

The original statement of the principle of optimality is contained in Bellman (1957). Bellman and Dreyfus (1962) is another useful reference on the principle. Both of these books still provide readable and informative introductions to dynamic programming. Our use of the principle of optimality in this chapter was very specific to the purpose at hand, namely, to prove the necessary conditions for a rather general optimal control problem. As we will see in later chapters, the principle of optimality will lead to the derivation of a useful partial differential equation called the Hamilton-Jacobi-Bellman equation. This equation will become the centerpiece of our foray into intertemporal duality theory. Chiang (1992), Léonard and Van Long (1992), and Kamien and Schwartz (1991) all provide at least some discussion of the principle of optimality and dynamic programming, with the latter providing a bit more than the first two.

REFERENCES

Bellman, R. (1957), *Dynamic Programming* (Princeton, N.J.: Princeton University Press).

Bellman, R. and Dreyfus, S. (1962), *Applied Dynamic Programming* (Princeton, N.J.: Princeton University Press).

Chiang, A.C. (1992), *Elements of Dynamic Optimization* (New York: McGraw-Hill, Inc.).

Kamien, M.I. and Schwartz, N.L. (1991, 2nd Ed.), *Dynamic Optimization: The Calculus of Variations and Optimal Control in Economics and Management* (New York: Elsevier Science Publishing Co., Inc.).

Léonard, D. and Van Long, N. (1992), *Optimal Control Theory and Static Optimization in Economics* (New York: Cambridge University Press).

Seierstad, A. and Sydsæter, K. (1987), *Optimal Control Theory with Economic Applications* (New York: Elsevier Science Publishing Co., Inc.).

Simon, C.P. and Blume, L. (1994), *Mathematics for Economists* (New York: W.W. Norton & Company, Inc.).

FIVE

Linear Optimal Control Problems

We now turn to the examination of optimal control problems that are linear in the control variables. A prominent feature of this class of problems is that the optimal control often turns out to be a piecewise continuous function of time. Recall that in Chapter 4, we defined an admissible pair of curves $(\mathbf{x}(t), \mathbf{u}(t))$ by allowing the control vector to be a piecewise continuous function of time and the state vector to be a piecewise smooth function of time. Though we allowed for this possibility in the theorems of Chapter 4, we did not solve or confront an optimal control problem whose solution exhibited these properties. You may recall, however, that in Example 4.6, where we solved the ubiquitous inventory accumulation problem subject to a nonnegativity constraint on the production rate, the optimal production rate was a continuous but not a differentiable function of time, that is, it was a piecewise smooth function of time. There are two reasons why the optimal production rate turned out to be a piecewise smooth function of time, namely, (i) the nonnegativity constraint on the production rate and (ii) the assumption of a "long" production period. One important lesson from this example, therefore, is that once an inequality constraint is imposed on the control variable, the differentiability of an optimal control function with respect to time may not hold.

Several of the optimal controls examined in this chapter are even less smooth with respect to time than the optimal production rate of Example 4.6. Generally speaking, the structural feature of an optimal control problem that is primarily responsible for this feature is its linearity in the control variables. In such linear control problems, the optimal control often, but not always, turns out to be at one boundary of the control region for some finite period of time and then it "bangs" into the other end of the control region for the remainder of the time. Optimal controls with such a characteristic are known as *bang-bang controls*. Such jump discontinuities are not just mathematical curiosities, for we will show that bang-bang controls arise quite naturally in linear optimal control problems with nontrivial economic content. It is important to note, however, that linearity in the control variable is not sufficient for a bang-bang control to be optimal. This observation follows from Example 4.3, for that problem was linear in the control variable but the optimal control turned out to be a continuous function of time (a constant in this example).

So as to avoid giving the (false) impression that all linear optimal control problems yield a bang-bang optimal control, we present an example in which the coefficient on the control variable in the Hamiltonian vanishes for a finite interval of time. In such instances, the optimal control is found in an atypical way from the necessary conditions and is referred to as a *singular control*. Accordingly, the corresponding solution of the linear control problem is known as the *singular solution*. As we shall demonstrate, the basic behavior of a singular control is essentially the opposite of a bang-bang control.

In view of the fact that there is little in the way of general theorems for dealing with the special nature of linear control problems, we take the tact of demonstrating the way to approach them via four examples. We pause after the third example, however, and make some general remarks that set the stage for the final example in which a singular control is optimal. The first example is purely mathematical and so prepares the way for the next three economic examples. This way, one can get the technicalities of the approach down first, and then hone one's skills and build economic intuition on the latter examples.

Example 5.1: Consider the following linear optimal control problem:

$$\max_{u(\cdot),x_2} \int_0^2 [2x(t) - 3u(t)]\,dt$$

$$\text{s.t.} \quad \dot{x}(t) = x(t) + u(t), \ x(0) = 4, \ x(2) = x_2,$$

$$u(t) \in U \stackrel{\text{def}}{=} \{u(\cdot) : 0 \le u(t) \le 2\}.$$

Because we have a closed and bounded, that is, compact, control set U, we use the general set of necessary conditions to solve the control problem, that is to say, Theorem 4.2. First, define the Hamiltonian as $H(x, u, \lambda) \stackrel{\text{def}}{=} 2x - 3u + \lambda[x + u] = [2 + \lambda]x + [\lambda - 3]u$. Noting that the terminal value of the state variable is to be optimally chosen, the necessary conditions are

$$\max_{u\in[0,2]} H(x, u, \lambda) \stackrel{\text{def}}{=} [2 + \lambda]x + [\lambda - 3]u,$$

$$\dot{\lambda} = -H_x(x, u, \lambda) = -2 - \lambda, \ \lambda(2) = 0,$$

$$\dot{x} = H_\lambda(x, u, \lambda) = x + u, \ x(0) = 4.$$

Rewriting the costate equation as $\dot{\lambda} + \lambda = -2$, the integrating factor is seen to be e^t. Upon multiplying the costate equation through by e^t, we have that $\frac{d}{dt}[\lambda e^t] = -2e^t$. Integrating this equation yields $\lambda(t) = ce^{-t} - 2$ as the general solution, where c is a constant of integration. Applying the transversality condition $\lambda(2) = 0$ to the general solution gives $c = 2e^2$, so the specific path for the costate variable is given by

$$\lambda(t) = 2[e^{2-t} - 1].$$

Since $\dot{\lambda}(t) = -2e^{2-t} < 0 \, \forall \, t \in [0, 2]$ and $\lambda(2) = 0$, it follows that $\lambda(t) > 0 \, \forall \, t \in [0, 2)$.

Inspection of the Hamiltonian reveals that it is linear in the control variable u. Moreover, because the control set U is closed, setting $\partial H/\partial u = 0$ is not in general the correct necessary condition for this problem. Given that $H(\cdot)$ is linear in u, if the coefficient on u is positive, that is, $[\lambda - 3] > 0$, then in order to maximize $H(\cdot)$ with respect to u, we must choose u to be as large as possible, subject to, of course, u being in the control set U, which in our case amounts to setting $u = 2$. Likewise, if the coefficient on u is negative, that is, $[\lambda - 3] < 0$, then we choose u to be as small as possible subject to being in the control set, which amounts to setting $u = 0$. If $\lambda - 3 = 0$ at an instant or over an interval, then the choice of the control variable will not affect the value of the Hamiltonian. As a result, we are permitted to choose any admissible value of the control variable. In summary, we have shown that the optimal control must satisfy

$$v(t) = \begin{cases} 2 & \text{if } \lambda(t) > 3 \\ \in [0, 2] & \text{if } \lambda(t) = 3 \\ 0 & \text{if } \lambda(t) < 3. \end{cases} \tag{1}$$

This is, in effect, a *decision rule* for the choice of the optimal control variable, for it dictates the optimal value of the control variable at each date of the planning horizon conditional on the value of the costate variable.

The decision rule in Eq. (1) shows that in order to pin down the exact nature of the time path of the control variable, we must first determine some specific properties of the costate variable. To that end, recall that $\dot{\lambda}(t) = -2e^{2-t} < 0 \, \forall \, t \in [0, 2]$, so that if $\lambda(t) = 3$, it occurs only for an instant. Also note that $\lambda(0) = 2[e^2 - 1] \approx 12.778 > 3$ and $\lambda(2) = 0$. Thus $\lambda(t)$ is greater than three for some initial period of time and then it falls to values less than three but greater than or equal to zero for the remaining period of time. Because $\dot{\lambda}(t) < 0 \, \forall \, t \in [0, 2]$, there exists a unique value of t, say, $t = \tau$, such that $\lambda(\tau) = 3$. In other words, the equation $\lambda(\tau) = 3$ implicitly defines the *switching time* τ for when the control jumps from its maximum value of two to its minimum value of zero. Hence $\lambda(\tau) = 2[e^{2-\tau} - 1] = 3$ can be solved for τ to yield $\tau = 2 - \ln \frac{5}{2} \approx 1.096$. Using this information, we see that the time path of the control variable, that is, its *open-loop* form, that satisfies the necessary conditions can be precisely specified as

$$v(t) = \begin{cases} 2 \, \forall \, t \in \left[0, 2 - \ln \frac{5}{2}\right] \\ 0 \, \forall \, t \in \left(2 - \ln \frac{5}{2}, 2\right]. \end{cases}$$

Because $\lambda(t) = 3$ only for the instant $t = \tau$, the control variable fails to enter the Hamiltonian only at this instant too. Hence any admissible choice of the control variable is optimal at $t = \tau$. Notice that we chose $v(\tau) = 2$ so that the control variable is continuous over the closed interval $[0, 2 - \ln \frac{5}{2}]$. We thus have our first instance in which the control variable is a piecewise continuous function of time, that is to say, we have a bang-bang control. Note that this has occurred in an optimal control problem that is linear in the control variable.

To finish up determining the solution of the necessary conditions, we solve for the time path of the state variable. Given that the control is a piecewise continuous function of time, we solve the state equation separately for each interval in which the control variable is a continuous function of time. Thus the differential equation we intend to solve is given by

$$\dot{x} = \begin{cases} x + 2 \; \forall t \in \left[0, 2 - \ln \frac{5}{2}\right] \\ x \qquad \forall t \in \left(2 - \ln \frac{5}{2}, 2\right]. \end{cases}$$

The integrating factor for either state equation is e^{-t}, as you should readily discern by now. The general solution, which you should also verify, is given by

$$z(t) = \begin{cases} z_1(t) = c_1 e^t - 2, \; t \in \left[0, 2 - \ln \frac{5}{2}\right] \\ z_2(t) = c_2 e^t, \qquad t \in \left(2 - \ln \frac{5}{2}, 2\right], \end{cases}$$

where c_1 and c_2 are constants of integration. Because $x(0) = 4$ is the initial condition, it can be applied to $z_1(t)$, since this solution encompasses the initial time. Applying the initial condition $x(0) = 4$ to $z_1(t)$ yields $c_1 = 6$. The definite solution of the state equation for the first time interval is therefore

$$z_1(t) = 6e^t - 2, \; t \in \left[0, 2 - \ln \frac{5}{2}\right].$$

Notice that we do not have a terminal requirement for the state variable, as $x(2) = x_2$ is a choice variable in the problem. It therefore appears we can't definitize the constant of integration c_2 from the second time interval. Recall, however, that the state variable path is required to be a continuous function of t by the very definition of admissibility. To ensure such continuity at the switching time $t = \tau$, we equate the solution of the state variable from the first time interval at $t = \tau$, namely, $z_1(\tau)$, to the solution for the state variable from the second time interval at $t = \tau$, namely, $z_2(\tau)$. That is, we set $z_1(\tau) = z_2(\tau)$, thereby yielding $6e^\tau - 2 = c_2 e^\tau$, and solve it for c_2 to get $c_2 = 6 - 2e^{-\tau} = 6 - 2e^{-[2-\ln \frac{5}{2}]} \approx 5.324$. Thus the specific solution to the state equation is

$$z(t) = \begin{cases} z_1(t) = 6e^t - 2, \qquad t \in \left[0, 2 - \ln \frac{5}{2}\right] \\ z_2(t) = \left[6 - 2e^{-[2-\ln \frac{5}{2}]}\right] e^t, \; t \in \left(2 - \ln \frac{5}{2}, 2\right]. \end{cases}$$

Note that although the state variable is a continuous function of t, its time derivative is only a piecewise continuous function of t because of the piecewise continuity of the control variable with respect to t.

In order to wrap up this example, we now demonstrate that the solution to the necessary conditions is in fact an optimal solution to the optimal control problem. First, observe that the control set U is convex. Next, take note of the fact that the partial derivative of the integrand function $f(t, x, u) \stackrel{\text{def}}{=} 2x - 3u$ and transition function $g(t, x, u) \stackrel{\text{def}}{=} x + u$ with respect to u are continuous, as is required by Theorem 4.3. Hence, in order to prove that the above solution of the necessary conditions is a solution of the control problem, we are required to show that the Hamiltonian is a concave function of (x, u). This is simple, however, for $H(\cdot)$ is linear in (x, u) and hence concave in (x, u).

Let us now turn to the first economic problem that exhibits a piecewise continuous control function as its optimal solution. It is a simple model of optimal savings for an economy.

Example 5.2: Imagine a central planner who wants to choose a savings rate $s(t) \in [0, 1]$ for an economy so as to maximize its aggregate utility of consumption over a finite period of time, say, $[0, T]$, where $T > 1$. Let $k(t)$ be the economy's capital stock at time t, and let the production function be linear in the capital stock, say, $y(t) = f(k(t)) \stackrel{\text{def}}{=} k(t)$. Consumption is the fraction of output not saved, that is, $c(t) = [1 - s(t)]k(t)$. Assuming no depreciation, the investment rate $\dot{k}(t)$ is equal to the fraction of output saved, namely, $\dot{k}(t) = s(t)k(t)$. If the instantaneous utility function $U(\cdot)$ is linear in consumption, say, $U(c(t)) \stackrel{\text{def}}{=} c(t)$, then the optimal control problem to be solved by the central planner is given by

$$\max_{s(\cdot), k_T} \int_0^T [1 - s(t)]k(t)\,dt$$

$$\text{s.t. } \dot{k}(t) = s(t)k(t),\ k(0) = k_0,\ k(T) = k_T,$$

$$s(t) \in U \stackrel{\text{def}}{=} \{s(\cdot) : 0 \leq s(t) \leq 1\},\ k(t) \geq 0,$$

where $k_0 > 0$ is the economy's initial stock of capital.

One new feature of the problem is the *explicit* appearance of the nonnegativity constraint on the stock of capital, that is, a state constraint. Inasmuch as we do not have theorems to handle state constraints, we will deal with it directly by showing that it is automatically satisfied for the control problem and can thus be ignored. To begin, note that the integrating factor for the state equation $\dot{k} - s(t)k = 0$ is $\mu(t) \stackrel{\text{def}}{=} \exp[-\int^t s(\tau)d\tau]$. After multiplying the state equation through by $\mu(t)$, the differential equation to be solved is given by $\frac{d}{dt}[\mu(t)k] = 0$. Integrating and rearranging yields $k(t) = c_1 \exp[\int_0^t s(\tau)\,d\tau]$, where c_1 is a constant of integration and where we have taken the lower value of the limit of integration to be zero, without loss of generality. Using the initial condition $k(0) = k_0$ yields $c_1 = k_0$. Hence the specific solution of the state equation for any admissible time path of the savings rate is given by $k(t; k_0) = k_0 \exp[\int_0^t s(\tau)\, d\tau]$. Because $k_0 > 0$ and the function $\exp(\cdot)$ takes on only positive values, it follows that all admissible values of the capital stock are positive. Thus the nonnegativity constraint on the capital stock never binds, as was to be shown.

The Hamiltonian for the problem is defined as $H(k, s, \lambda) \stackrel{\text{def}}{=} k + [\lambda - 1]sk$, where λ is the costate variable and has the economic interpretation of the shadow value or marginal value of the capital stock. By Theorem 4.2, the necessary condition for the choice of the savings rate is

$$\max_{s\in[0,1]} H(k, s, \lambda) \stackrel{\text{def}}{=} k + [\lambda - 1]\, sk.$$

Insofar as $k(t) > 0\, \forall\, t \in [0, T]$, as demonstrated above, this immediately yields the decision rule that the optimal savings rate must obey:

$$s(t) = \begin{cases} 1 & \text{if } \lambda(t) > 1 \\ \in [0, 1] & \text{if } \lambda(t) = 1 \\ 0 & \text{if } \lambda(t) < 1. \end{cases} \tag{2}$$

Because $U(c) \stackrel{\text{def}}{=} c$, $U'(c) = 1$, so the decision rule asserts that if the marginal value of the capital stock is greater than the marginal utility of consuming it, then the planner should save all the output for future consumption, which is intuitive. Similarly, if the marginal value of the capital stock is less than the marginal utility of consuming it, then the planner should not save any of the output, thereby implying that the economy should consume it all.

The next step is to determine some basic properties of the shadow value of the capital stock because Eq. (2) shows that once it is determined, so too is the optimal savings rate. To that end, the costate equation and transversality condition are given by

$$\dot{\lambda} = -H_k(k, s, \lambda) = -1 - [\lambda - 1]s, \ \ \lambda(T) = 0. \tag{3}$$

Using the decision rule in Eq. (2), we see that if $\lambda(t) > 1$, then $s(t) = 1$, thereby implying that $\dot{\lambda}(t) < 0$ from Eq. (3). Similarly, if $\lambda(t) = 1$, then $s(t) = [0, 1]$, and Eq. (3) again implies that $\dot{\lambda}(t) < 0$. Finally, if $\lambda(t) < 1$, then $s(t) = 0$, again implying from Eq. (3) that $\dot{\lambda}(t) < 0$. Thus, we have shown that $\dot{\lambda}(t) < 0\, \forall\, t \in [0, T]$. Bringing together this fact with the transversality condition $\lambda(T) = 0$ yields the intuitive conclusion that $\lambda(t) > 0\, \forall\, t \in [0, T)$. That is, the shadow value of the capital stock is declining over the entire planning horizon and its value is positive in all periods except the last.

Looking at the decision rule in Eq. (2), we see that the key to determining the exact behavior of the optimal savings rate is determining how large the shadow value of capital is relative to the marginal utility of consuming the capital, the latter being unity, as you may recall. We will show in this paragraph and the next that the qualitative behavior of the shadow value of the capital stock is given by

$$\lambda(t) \begin{cases} > 1 \ \forall\, t \in [0, t^*) \\ = 1 \text{ for } t = t^* \\ < 1 \ \forall\, t \in (t^*, T], \end{cases} \tag{4}$$

where $t^* \in [0, T]$ is the switching time. In order to do so, we employ a proof by contradiction. To that end, we assume that $\lambda(t) \leq 1 \, \forall\, t \in [0, T]$. Using the decision rule in Eq. (2) and setting $s(t) = 0$ when $\lambda(t) = 1$ (which can occur only at $t = 0$ because $\dot{\lambda}(t) < 0 \, \forall\, t \in [0, T]$) implies that the costate equation reduces to $\dot{\lambda} = -1$, which readily integrates to $\lambda(t) = c_2 - t$, where c_2 is a constant of integration. Using the transversality condition $\lambda(T) = 0$ yields $c_2 = T$, thereby implying that the specific solution to the costate equation is $\lambda(t; T) = T - t$. Recalling that $T > 1$, we see that $\lambda(0; T) = T > 1$, thereby contradicting our initial assumption that $\lambda(t) \leq 1 \, \forall\, t \in [0, T]$. We may therefore conclude that $\lambda(t) \leq 1 \, \forall\, t \in [0, T]$ is *not* the solution to the costate equation and transversality condition. Combining this fact with the previous result that $\dot{\lambda}(t) < 0 \, \forall\, t \in [0, T]$ and the transversality condition $\lambda(T) = 0$ implies that (i) there exists a unique switching time t^* at which $\lambda(t^*) = 1$, (ii) $\lambda(t) > 1 \, \forall\, t \in [0, t^*)$, and (iii) $\lambda(t) \in [0, 1) \, \forall\, t \in (t^*, T]$. This establishes the veracity of Eq. (4).

To determine the exact value of the switching time t^*, we have to solve the equation $\lambda(t^*) = 1$ for t^*. In order to do so, we must first solve the costate equation. Using the decision rule (2) and Eq. (4), the costate equation (3) takes the form

$$\dot{\lambda} = \begin{cases} -\lambda \ \forall\, t \in [0, t^*) \\ -1 \ \forall\, t \in [t^*, T], \end{cases}$$

where we have chosen to set $s(t^*) = 1$, as we are free to do. Integrating this differential equation yields the general solution

$$\lambda(t) = \begin{cases} \lambda_1(t) = a_1 e^{-t} \ \ \forall\, t \in [0, t^*) \\ \lambda_2(t) = a_2 - t \ \forall\, t \in [t^*, T], \end{cases}$$

where a_1 and a_2 are constants of integration. The transversality condition $\lambda(T) = 0$ can be applied to the solution for the interval $[t^*, T]$, to wit, $\lambda_2(t)$, and implies that $a_2 = T$. Using this result and the fact that $\lambda(t^*) = \lambda_2(t^*) = 1$ gives $T - t^* = 1$, or $t^* = T - 1 > 0$. To find the constant of integration a_1, recall the requirement from Theorem 4.2 that the costate function is a piecewise smooth and hence continuous function of t. This means that $\lambda_1(t^*) = 1 = \lambda_2(t^*)$ must hold, which gives $\lambda_1(t^*) = a_1 e^{-t^*} = 1$ or $a_1 = e^{t^*} = e^{T-1}$. Hence the specific solution of the costate equation is

$$\lambda(t; T) = \begin{cases} \lambda_1(t; T) = e^{T-t-1} \ \forall\, t \in [0, T-1) \\ \lambda_2(t; T) = T - t \ \ \forall\, t \in [T-1, T]. \end{cases} \tag{5}$$

Notice that at $t = T - 1$, the derivatives of each portion of the solution with respect to t are equal to minus unity. That is, $\dot{\lambda}_1(T-1;T) = -1 = \dot{\lambda}_2(T-1;T)$, thereby demonstrating that $\lambda(\cdot)$ is $C^{(1)}$ with respect to t, which is more smoothness, in general, than Theorem 4.2 imposes on the costate variables.

Using the information in Eq. (4) or Eq. (5), the decision rule (2) governing the savings rate can be restated as

$$s^*(t) = \begin{cases} 1 \, \forall t \in [0, T-1) \\ 0 \, \forall t \in [T-1, \mathrm{T}]. \end{cases}$$

This control asserts that the central planner prescribes the maximum savings rate for the economy up until just before the switching time $t^* = T - 1$, and then immediately changes to the maximum consumption rate from the switching date until the end of the planning horizon. That is, all the output produced by the economy is initially saved. Once the switching date is reached, however, none of the output is saved. Instead, output should be consumed at the maximum possible rate from the switching date until the horizon comes to a close. We leave the solution of the state equation for a mental exercise.

The next example concerns the optimal rate at which to clean up a stock of hazardous waste. An extension of it appears in the mental exercises of a later chapter.

Example 5.3: A spill of a toxic substance has occurred at time $t = 0$ (the present) in the known amount of $x(0) = x_0 > 0$, where $x(t)$ is the stock of the toxic substance left in the environment at time t. The federal government has contracted with your company to reduce the size of the toxic waste from its initial size of x_0 to x_T by the time $t = T > 0$, where, of course, $x_0 > x_T$, so that the waste stock is smaller at $t = T$ than at $t = 0$. As head economist of the company, you are charged with determining the cleanup rate $u(t)$ that minimizes the present discounted cost of cleaning up the fixed amount $x_0 - x_T$ of the toxic substance over the fixed horizon $[0, T]$. The cleanup technology is linear in the cleanup rate, say $cu(t)$, where $c > 0$. The cleanup rate is bounded below by zero and above by a fixed finite rate $\bar{u} > 0$, where $\bar{u} > [x_0 - x_T]/T$. Given that $x(t)$ is defined as the toxic stock left in the environment at time t, it follows that

$$x(t) \stackrel{\text{def}}{=} x_0 - \int_0^t u(s)\,ds.$$

Hence, by Leibniz's rule,

$$\dot{x}(t) = -u(t),$$

$$x(0) = x_0, \; x(T) = x_T$$

are the state equation and boundary conditions for the problem. The complete statement of the optimal control problem is given by

$$C(\beta) \stackrel{\text{def}}{=} \min_{u(\cdot)} \int_0^T cu(t)e^{-rt}\, dt$$

$$\text{s.t.} \quad \dot{x}(t) = -u(t), \; x(0) = x_0, \; x(T) = x_T,$$

$$u(t) \in U \stackrel{\text{def}}{=} \{u(\cdot) : 0 \leq u(t) \leq \bar{u}, \bar{u} > [x_0 - x_T]/T\},$$

where $r > 0$ is the discount rate and $\beta \stackrel{\text{def}}{=} (c, r, \bar{u}, x_0, T, x_T)$. Note that in contrast to the first two examples in this chapter, this is a fixed endpoints optimal control problem.

Let's begin the analysis of this model by providing an economic interpretation of the inequality $\bar{u} > [x_0 - x_T]/T$. The first thing to notice about it is that $\bar{u} > [x_0 - x_T]/T$ if and only if $\bar{u}T > [x_0 - x_T]$. The latter expression is easily interpreted. It asserts that if the firm cleans up at the maximum rate for the entire time planning horizon, then it would clean up more waste than is required by the federal government contract. Recalling that the firm is required to clean up the amount $x_0 - x_T$ (because of fixed endpoints) by time T, we reach an important conclusion, namely, that cleaning up at the maximum rate for the entire period is not admissible, and therefore not optimal; that is, $u(t) = \bar{u}\; \forall\, t \in [0, T]$ is not an admissible control and therefore not an optimal control.

The Hamiltonian for this problem is defined as $H(t, x, u, \lambda) \stackrel{\text{def}}{=} cue^{-rt} - \lambda u = [ce^{-rt} - \lambda]u$. According to Theorem 4.2, the necessary conditions are

$$\min_{u \in [0, \bar{u}]} H(t, x, u, \lambda) \stackrel{\text{def}}{=} [ce^{-rt} - \lambda]u, \tag{6}$$

$$\dot{\lambda} = -H_x(t, x, u, \lambda) = 0, \tag{7}$$

$$\dot{x} = H_\lambda(t, x, u, \lambda) = -u, \; x(0) = x_0, \; x(T) = x_T, \tag{8}$$

where λ is the *present value* shadow cost of a unit of the toxic waste at any time $t \in [0, T]$. The adjective *present value* is necessary because of the presence of the discount factor e^{-rt} in the integrand. In addition, λ is a shadow cost (rather than a shadow value) in view of the fact that the objective functional of the firm is the present discounted value of cleanup costs. Because of the fixed endpoint $x(T) = x_T$, a larger initial stock of toxic waste requires more cleanup. Moreover, cleaning up is a costly activity. Hence the present value shadow cost of a unit of toxic waste at any time $t \in [0, T]$ must be positive in an optimal plan.

The decision rule governing the optimal choice of the cleanup rate follows from inspection of Eq. (6), and is given by

$$u(t) = \begin{cases} 0 & \text{if } ce^{-rt} > \lambda \\ \in [0, \bar{u}] & \text{if } ce^{-rt} = \lambda \\ \bar{u} & \text{if } ce^{-rt} < \lambda. \end{cases} \tag{9}$$

The economic interpretation of the decision rule is straightforward. It asserts that if the present value marginal cost of cleaning up is greater than the present value shadow cost of the toxic stock, then no cleanup should take place. Likewise, if the present value marginal cost of cleaning up is less than the present value shadow cost of the toxic stock, then cleanup should take place at the maximum rate. As is typical in linear control problems, we must determine the behavior of the costate variable before the solution of the control variable is fully determined.

Before finding the solution of the costate equation, let's rule out another solution for the cleanup rate as being optimal. To that end, note that if $u(t) = 0\,\forall\, t \in [0, T]$, then $\dot{x} = 0\,\forall\, t \in [0, T]$ from the state equation (8). Using the initial condition $x(0) = x_0$ yields $x(t; x_0) = x_0\,\forall\, t \in [0, T]$ as the specific solution of the state equation. This solution, however, violates the terminal boundary requirement, scilicet, $x(T) = x_T$, since $x_0 > x_T$. Hence $u(t) = 0\,\forall\, t \in [0, T]$ is not an admissible control and therefore not an optimal control.

From Eq. (7), we see that $\dot{\lambda} = 0$, so that the general solution is $\lambda(t) = \bar{\lambda}$, where $\bar{\lambda}$ is a constant. Because the control problem has both endpoints fixed, it appears that we have no way of determining the value of the constant $\bar{\lambda}$ and hence the present value shadow cost of the toxic waste. This is not true, as we shall see shortly. What is more important at this juncture is that we can determine the optimal cleanup rate fully from the decision rule (9), and as we will now show, this does not require exact knowledge of $\bar{\lambda}$. To demonstrate this, observe that if $\bar{\lambda} < ce^{-rt}\,\forall\, t \in [0, T]$, then $u(t) = 0\,\forall\, t \in [0, T]$ from Eq. (9). But as we demonstrated above, $u(t) = 0\,\forall\, t \in [0, T]$ is not admissible; hence $\bar{\lambda} < ce^{-rt}\,\forall\, t \in [0, T]$ *cannot* hold. Similarly, if $\bar{\lambda} > ce^{-rt}\,\forall\, t \in [0, T]$, then $u(t) = \bar{u}\,\forall\, t \in [0, T]$ from Eq. (9). But $u(t) = \bar{u}\,\forall\, t \in [0, T]$ is not admissible, as shown above; therefore $\bar{\lambda} > ce^{-rt}\,\forall\, t \in [0, T]$ *cannot* hold either. Because $\lambda(t) = \bar{\lambda}$ is constant and $\frac{d}{dt}[ce^{-rt}] = -rce^{-rt} < 0$, when combined with the above two results, these latter two imply that (i) $\bar{\lambda} < ce^{-rt}$ for some finite period of time at the beginning of the planning horizon, (ii) $\bar{\lambda} = ce^{-rt}$ only for an instant, say, at $t = \tau$, the switching time, and (iii) $\bar{\lambda} > ce^{-rt}$ for some finite period of time at the end of the planning horizon. This means that our decision rule (9) now takes the form

$$v(t; \beta) = \begin{cases} 0\,\forall\, t \in [0, \tau] \\ \bar{u}\,\forall\, t \in (\tau, \mathrm{T}], \end{cases} \tag{10}$$

thereby implying that the optimal cleanup policy is bang-bang, with no cleanup in the first time interval and the maximum rate of cleanup in the second.

Given the decision rule in Eq. (10), the state equation (8) takes the form

$$\dot{x} = \begin{cases} 0 & \forall t \in [0, \tau] \\ -\bar{u} & \forall t \in (\tau, \mathrm{T}]. \end{cases}$$

Integrating each portion of the differential equation, and using the initial condition $x(0) = x_0$ for the first and the terminal condition $x(T) = x_T$ for the second, yields

$$z(t; \boldsymbol{\beta}) = \begin{cases} x_0 & \forall t \in [0, \tau] \\ x_T + \bar{u}[T - t] & \forall t \in (\tau, \mathrm{T}] \end{cases} \tag{11}$$

as the time path of the toxic waste stock.

We still have yet to determine the value of $\bar{\lambda}$ and the switching time τ. The value of τ can be determined from the continuity of the state function $z(\cdot)$ with respect to t. Just as we did in the two previous examples, we equate the values of the two portions of the state variable solution at the switching time to get the equation $x_0 = x_T + \bar{u}[T - \tau]$, and then solve it for the switching time to find that

$$\tau = \tau^*(\boldsymbol{\beta}) \stackrel{\text{def}}{=} T - [x_0 - x_T]/\bar{u}. \tag{12}$$

As a check on the plausibility of this value, we want to ensure that $\tau^*(\boldsymbol{\beta}) \in (0, T)$, so that the switch between no cleanup and maximum cleanup actually takes place within the planning period. That $\tau^*(\boldsymbol{\beta}) \in (0, T)$ follows from our assumption $\bar{u} > [x_0 - x_T]/T$. To see this, simply rearrange it to read $T - [x_0 - x_T]/\bar{u} > 0$ and compare it to the value of the switching time given in Eq. (12).

Next, we solve for the present value shadow cost of the toxic waste by recalling that $\lambda(t) = \bar{\lambda}$, with $\bar{\lambda}$ a constant, and that $\bar{\lambda} = ce^{-rt}$ at $t = \tau^*(\boldsymbol{\beta})$, the switching time. These observations yield the constant value of the present value shadow cost of the toxic waste, to wit,

$$\lambda(t; \boldsymbol{\beta}) = ce^{-r[T - [x_0 - x_T]/\bar{u}]}, \tag{13}$$

which is positive, as argued after Eq. (8).

It is an easy matter to show that the solution of the necessary conditions given in Eqs. (10) through (13) solves the optimal control problem. As in Example 5.1, we observe that the control set U is convex, and that the partial derivatives with respect to u of the integrand function $f(\cdot)$ with values $f(t, x, u) \stackrel{\text{def}}{=} cue^{-rt}$, and transition function $g(\cdot)$ with values $g(t, x, u) \stackrel{\text{def}}{=} -u$, are continuous, as is required by Theorem 4.3. Because the Hamiltonian $H(t, x, u, \lambda) \stackrel{\text{def}}{=} cue^{-rt} - \lambda u$ is independent of x and linear in u, it is concave in (x, u); hence by Theorem 4.3, the solution of the necessary conditions given in Eqs. (10) through (13) is a solution of the optimal control problem. Moreover, seeing as the solution given in Eqs. (10) through (13) is the only solution of the necessary conditions, save for the fact that at the switching time the control variable can take on any admissible value, this solution is the unique solution of the control problem.

With the unique optimal solution now in hand, we turn to the construction of the optimal value function $C(\cdot)$, the firm's minimum present discounted value cleanup cost function. By definition, the value of $C(\cdot)$ is given by

$$C(\beta) \stackrel{\text{def}}{=} \int_0^T cv(t;\bar{u})\,e^{-rt}\,dt = \int_{\tau^*(\beta)}^T c\bar{u}e^{-rt}\,dt = \frac{c\bar{u}}{r}\,[e^{-r[T-[x_0-x_T]/\bar{u}]} - e^{-rt}] > 0, \tag{14}$$

where we have used Eqs. (10) and (12). Differentiating Eq. (14) with respect to x_0 yields

$$\frac{\partial C(\beta)}{\partial x_0} = ce^{-r[T-[x_0-x_T]/\bar{u}]} = \lambda(t;\beta), \tag{15}$$

thereby confirming how the costate variable was defined in the proof of the maximum principle by way of dynamic programming in Chapter 4.

In closing out this example, let's consider a few comparative dynamics properties of the solution, and leave the remainder for a mental exercise. One interesting comparative dynamics result is that the solution of the problem is virtually unaffected by the instantaneous marginal cost of cleanup c. As inspection of Eqs. (10) through (14) will confirm, an increase in c raises the present value shadow cost of the toxic waste and the minimum present discounted value of cleanup costs, but leaves all other variables unaffected. Thus, even though the instantaneous marginal cost of cleanup is higher, neither the switching time nor the cleanup rate are affected, a curious result at first glance. How can it be that an increase in the instantaneous marginal cost of cleanup does not affect the optimal cleanup rate? Inspection of the statement of the optimal control problem reveals why. Because c is a positive time invariant constant, it can be factored out of the integrand, thereby demonstrating that it has no effect on the optimal solution for the cleanup rate, switching time, or the stock of toxic waste. Seeing as c affects the optimal value function, however, it must also affect the present value shadow cost of the toxic waste stock.

For the next comparative dynamics exercise, let's investigate the effect of an increase in the maximum cleanup rate $\bar{u}$ on the optimal control problem. One may think of an increase in $\bar{u}$ as resulting from an improvement in the cleanup technology. Differentiating Eqs. (10) through (14) with respect to $\bar{u}$ yields

$$\frac{\partial v(t;\beta)}{\partial \bar{u}} = \begin{cases} 0\,\forall\, t \in [0, \tau^*(\beta)] \\ 1\,\forall\, t \in (\tau^*(\beta), T], \end{cases}$$

$$\frac{\partial z(t;\beta)}{\partial \bar{u}} = \begin{cases} 0 & \forall\, t \in [0, \tau^*(\beta)] \\ [T-t] & \forall\, t \in (\tau^*(\beta), T], \end{cases}$$

$$\frac{\partial \tau^*(\beta)}{\partial \bar{u}} = \frac{[x_0 - x_T]}{\bar{u}^2} > 0,$$

$$\frac{\partial \lambda(t;\boldsymbol{\beta})}{\partial \bar{u}} = -rce^{-r[T-[x_0-x_T]/\bar{u}]}\frac{[x_0 - x_T]}{\bar{u}^2} < 0,$$

$$\frac{\partial C(\boldsymbol{\beta})}{\partial \bar{u}} = -\frac{c}{\bar{u}}e^{-r[T-[x_0-x_T]/\bar{u}]}[x_0 - x_T] + \frac{c}{r}[e^{-r[T-[x_0-x_T]/\bar{u}]} - e^{-rt}] \gtrless 0.$$

This set of comparative dynamics results has an interesting economic interpretation. For example, an increase in the maximum cleanup rate permits the switching time to be delayed, that is, the switching time is pushed closer to the end of the planning horizon. This is not an unexpected occurrence in view of the fact that more waste can be cleaned up in a given period of time. In other words, the length of the period in which the firm cleans up is reduced when the maximum rate it can clean up is increased. The shorter period in which the cleanup takes place translates into a lower present value shadow cost of waste and an increase in the amount of waste in each period but the last in the cleanup period. The effect of the increase in the maximum cleanup rate on the firm's present discounted cleanup costs, however, is ambiguous. Two opposing factors are at work in this case, namely, (i) costs increase, ceteris paribus, because the maximum rate of cleanup is higher and cleaning up is a costly activity, and (ii) costs decrease, ceteris paribus, because the period in which cleanup takes place is shorter.

To finish up this example, let's consider the effects of an increase in the initial stock of the toxic waste. We thus differentiate Eqs. (10) through (14) with respect to x_0 to get

$$\frac{\partial v(t;\boldsymbol{\beta})}{\partial x_0} = 0\,\forall\, t \in [0, T],$$

$$\frac{\partial z(t;\boldsymbol{\beta})}{\partial x_0} = \begin{cases} 1\,\forall\, t \in [0, \tau^*(\boldsymbol{\beta})] \\ 0\,\forall\, t \in (\tau^*(\boldsymbol{\beta}), T], \end{cases}$$

$$\frac{\partial \tau^*(\boldsymbol{\beta})}{\partial x_0} = -\frac{1}{\bar{u}} < 0,$$

$$\frac{\partial^2 C(\boldsymbol{\beta})}{\partial x_0^2} = \frac{\partial \lambda(t;\boldsymbol{\beta})}{\partial x_0} = ce^{-r[T-[x_0-x_T]/\bar{u}]}\frac{r}{\bar{u}} > 0,$$

$$\frac{\partial C(\boldsymbol{\beta})}{\partial x_0} = ce^{-r[T-[x_0-x_T]/\bar{u}]} > 0,$$

where we used Eq. (15) in the next to last equation. These comparative dynamics results demonstrate that an increase in the initial stock of the toxic waste leaves the cleanup rate unaffected but increases the period in which the cleanup take place, that is, the switching time occurs earlier in the planning horizon. It is this latter effect that enables the firm to bring the larger initial stock down to its required level by the end of the planning horizon without increasing its rate of cleanup. This larger initial waste stock drives up both the firm's present value cost of cleanup and its present value shadow cost of the stock. Finally, observe that the last two equations show that the firm's value function $C(\cdot)$ is a strictly increasing and strictly convex function of the initial stock of toxic waste. We leave the remaining comparative dynamics results for a mental exercise.

Having fully worked three examples, we now pause to make a few general observations about linear optimal control problems. In doing so, we also pave the way for the final example in which a singular control is optimal. To begin, let us first write down a sufficiently general class of linear optimal control problems, to wit,

$$\max_{u(\cdot)} \int_{t_0}^{t_1} [f^1(t,x(t)) + f^2(t,x(t))\,u(t)]\,dt$$

$$\text{s.t.} \quad \dot{x}(t) = g^1(t,x(t)) + g^2(t,x(t))\,u(t), \;\; x(t_0) = x_0, \;\; x(t_1) = x_1, \tag{16}$$

$$u(t) \in U \stackrel{\text{def}}{=} \{u(\cdot) : \underline{u} \le u(t) \le \bar{u},\, \underline{u} < \bar{u}\}.$$

We assume that the integrand and transition functions are $C^{(1)}$ in what follows, and, as usual, let $(z(\cdot), v(\cdot))$ be the optimal pair of solution functions for problem (16) with corresponding costate function $\lambda(\cdot)$. Note that we could have alternatively taken the terminal value of the state variable to be a decision variable, seeing as this change has no essential bearing on the ensuing discussion.

The Hamiltonian for problem (16) is defined as

$$\begin{aligned} H(t,x,u,\lambda) &\stackrel{\text{def}}{=} f^1(t,x) + f^2(t,x)u + \lambda[g^1(t,x) + g^2(t,x)u] \\ &= f^1(t,x) + \lambda g^1(t,x) + [f^2(t,x) + \lambda g^2(t,x)]u, \end{aligned}$$

where λ is the costate variable. If we define $\sigma(\cdot)$ by the formula $\sigma(t,x,\lambda) \stackrel{\text{def}}{=} f^2(t,x) + \lambda g^2(t,x)$, then the Hamiltonian may be rewritten as

$$H(t,x,u,\lambda) \stackrel{\text{def}}{=} f^1(t,x) + \lambda g^1(t,x) + \sigma(t,x,\lambda)\,u. \tag{17}$$

The function $\sigma(\cdot)$ is known as the *switching function*. By Theorem 4.2, the necessary condition for the selection of the optimal control is $\max_{u\in U} H(t,x,u,\lambda)$, which, upon using Eq. (17), is seen to be equivalent to the decision rule

$$u(t) = \begin{cases} \underline{u} & \text{if } \sigma(t,x,\lambda) < 0 \\ \in [\underline{u}, \bar{u}] & \text{if } \sigma(t,x,\lambda) = 0 \\ \bar{u} & \text{if } \sigma(t,x,\lambda) > 0. \end{cases} \tag{18}$$

In view of the fact that the sign of $\sigma(\cdot)$ completely determines the value of the optimal control as well as its switch, if any, from its upper and lower bounds, the designation "switching function" is an apt label for $\sigma(\cdot)$.

Now recall that in Examples 5.1 through 5.3, the Hamiltonian was a linear function of the control variable, but that the coefficient on the control variable, that is, the value of the switching function, was equal to zero only for an instant. This latter conclusion was a result of the fact that $\sigma(\cdot)$ was a monotonically decreasing function of time in each example, as you will be asked to verify in a mental exercise. Consequently, in each of these examples, we were led to the conclusion that the optimal control was of the bang-bang variety. Not one of these examples exhibited a switching function that vanished for a subinterval of the planning horizon of positive length along the optimal solution. That is to say, Examples 5.1 through 5.3 did not possess the property that $\sigma(t, x, \lambda) \equiv 0 \, \forall \, t \in (t_a, t_b) \subset [t_0, t_1]$ along the optimal path. If in fact $\sigma(t, x, \lambda) \equiv 0 \, \forall \, t \in (t_a, t_b)$ along the optimal solution, then the Hamiltonian becomes independent of the control variable, and accordingly, the maximum principle does not determine the value of the optimal control by way of the typical route. Nonetheless, it is possible to manipulate the other necessary conditions to determine the value of the optimal control in such instances.

Definition 5.1: When $\sigma(t, x, \lambda) = 0$ for an interval of time, the resulting optimal solution triplet of functions, say, $(x^s(\cdot), v^s(\cdot), \lambda^s(\cdot))$, is said to be the *singular solution.*

Let's now proceed to demonstrate how, in principle, the singular solution can be determined. In view of the fact that $\sigma(t, z^s(t), \lambda^s(t)) \equiv 0 \, \forall \, t \in (t_a, t_b)$ by Definition 5.1, it follows that $\frac{d}{dt}\sigma(t, z^s(t), \lambda^s(t)) \equiv 0 \, \forall \, t \in (t_a, t_b)$ as well. Consequently, by the chain rule

$$\begin{aligned} \frac{d}{dt}\sigma(t, z^s(t), \lambda^s(t)) = {} & f_t^2(t, z^s(t)) + \lambda^s(t) g_t^2(t, z^s(t)) \\ & + \left[f_x^2(t, z^s(t)) + \lambda^s(t) g_x^2(t, z^s(t))\right] \dot{z}^s(t) \\ & + g^2(t, z^s(t)) \dot{\lambda}^s(t) \equiv 0 \end{aligned}$$

for all $t \in (t_a, t_b)$. Upon using $\sigma(t, z^s(t), \lambda^s(t)) \equiv 0 \, \forall \, t \in (t_a, t_b)$ and the remaining necessary conditions from Theorem 4.2, and furthermore assuming that $g^2(t, z^s(t)) \neq 0 \, \forall \, t \in (t_a, t_b)$, it can be demonstrated that the above differential equation is equivalent to

$$\begin{aligned} & \left[f_t^2(t, z^s(t)) - \frac{f^2(t, z^s(t))}{g^2(t, z^s(t))} g_t^2(t, z^s(t))\right] \\ & \quad + \left[f_x^2(t, z^s(t)) - \frac{f^2(t, z^s(t))}{g^2(t, z^s(t))} g_x^2(t, z^s(t))\right] g^1(t, z^s(t)) \\ & \quad - \left[f_x^1(t, z^s(t)) - \frac{f^2(t, z^s(t))}{g^2(t, z^s(t))} g_x^1(t, z^s(t))\right] g^2(t, z^s(t)) \equiv 0. \qquad (19) \end{aligned}$$

You are asked to confirm the veracity of Eq. (19) in a mental exercise. Said differently, the singular time path of the state variable $z^s(t)$ is the solution to

$$\left[f_t^2(t,x) - \frac{f^2(t,x)}{g^2(t,x)} g_t^2(t,x)\right] + \left[f_x^2(t,x) - \frac{f^2(t,x)}{g^2(t,x)} g_x^2(t,x)\right] g^1(t,x)$$
$$- \left[f_x^1(t,x) - \frac{f^2(t,x)}{g^2(t,x)} g_x^1(t,x)\right] g^2(t,x) = 0. \tag{20}$$

Using $\sigma(t, z^s(t), \lambda^s(t)) \equiv 0 \, \forall \, t \in (t_a, t_b)$, the corresponding singular time path of the costate $\lambda^s(t)$ is therefore given by

$$\lambda^s(t) = -\frac{f^2(t, z^s(t))}{g^2(t, z^s(t))}. \tag{21}$$

Finally, using the state equation, the singular time path of the optimal control $v^s(t)$ is found as

$$v^s(t) = \frac{\dot{z}^s(t) - g^1(t, z^s(t))}{g^2(t, z^s(t))}. \tag{22}$$

Observe that Eqs. (20) through (22) reveal the importance of the assumption $g^2(t, z^s(t)) \neq 0 \, \forall \, t \in (t_a, t_b)$, along the singular solution. Moreover, note that over the interval (t_a, t_b), the optimal triplet of time paths $(z(t), v(t), \lambda(t))$ *is* the singular triplet of time paths $(z^s(t), v^s(t), \lambda^s(t))$.

The necessary conditions of Theorem 4.2 imply that, in general, an optimal control in linear control problems is a combination of bang-bang and singular controls. In Examples 5.1 through 5.3, however, the optimal controls were simply bang-bang. This was not only because of the simple mathematical structure of the problems studied but also because of the introduction of ad hoc assumptions on the parameters. For instance, in Example 5.2, the parameter restriction $T > 1$ was decisive in yielding the conclusion that the optimal control was of the bang-bang type, whereas in Example 5.3, the inequality restriction $\bar{u} > [x_0 - x_T]/T$ was responsible for the optimality of the bang-bang cleanup policy. You are asked to verify these assertions in two mental exercises. In the next (and final) example of the chapter, we study a control problem with economic content in which the optimal control is a combination of bang-bang and singular controls.

Example 5.4: As described and set up in Example 1.1, the optimal control problem faced by a fish farmer can be stated as

$$\max_{h(\cdot), x_T} J[x(\cdot), h(\cdot)] \stackrel{\text{def}}{=} \int_0^T [p - c(x(t); w)]\, h(t)\, e^{-rt}\, dt$$
$$\text{s.t.} \quad \dot{x}(t) = F(x(t)) - h(t),\ x(0) = x_0,\ x(T) = x_T, \tag{23}$$
$$h(t) \in U \stackrel{\text{def}}{=} \{h(\cdot) : 0 \leq h(t) \leq \bar{h}\}.$$

Observe that we have simplified the problem statement compared with that in Example 1.1. In particular, the cost function $C(\cdot)$ now takes the form $C(x, h; w) \stackrel{\text{def}}{=} c(x; w)h$. Consequently, Eq. (23) is a linear optimal control problem. Also notice that since the harvest rate appears linearly in problem (23), lower and upper bounds have been placed on it. The upper bound $\bar{h}$ is the maximum possible rate of harvest by the fish farmer, typically dictated by the technology used, whereas the lower bound rules out a negative rate of harvest. As $C_x(x, h; w) < 0$ and $C_{xx}(x, h; w) > 0$ for all $h > 0$, and because $C_x(x, h; w) = c_x(x; w)h$, it follows that $c_x(x; w) < 0$ and $c_{xx}(x; w) > 0$.

To begin the analysis, first define the Hamiltonian as

$$\begin{aligned} H(t, x, h, \lambda) &\stackrel{\text{def}}{=} [p - c(x; w)]he^{-rt} + \lambda[F(x) - h] \\ &= [[p - c(x; w)]\, e^{-rt} - \lambda]\, h + \lambda F(x), \end{aligned}$$

where λ is the present value shadow price of the fish stock, the adjective *present value* necessitated by the discount factor in the integrand. Defining

$$\sigma(t, x, \lambda) \stackrel{\text{def}}{=} [p - c(x; w)]\, e^{-rt} - \lambda \tag{24}$$

as the value of the switching function $\sigma(\cdot)$, the necessary condition $\max_{h \in U} H(t, x, h, \lambda)$ can be written in an equivalent form, videlicet,

$$h(t) = \begin{cases} 0 & \text{if } \sigma(t, x, \lambda) < 0 \\ \in [0, \bar{h}] & \text{if } \sigma(t, x, \lambda) = 0 \\ \bar{h} & \text{if } \sigma(t, x, \lambda) > 0, \end{cases} \tag{25}$$

which is a decision rule for selecting the optimal harvest rate. The remaining necessary conditions are given by

$$\dot{\lambda} = -H_x(t, x, h, \lambda) = c_x(x; w)\, he^{-rt} - \lambda F'(x),\ \lambda(T) = 0, \tag{26}$$

$$\dot{x} = H_\lambda(t, x, h, \lambda) = F(x) - h,\ x(0) = x_0. \tag{27}$$

Let $(x^*(t; \boldsymbol{\beta}), h^*(t; \boldsymbol{\beta}))$ be the optimal pair of time paths of the fish stock and harvest rate and $\lambda(t; \boldsymbol{\beta})$ be the corresponding time path of the present value shadow price of the fish stock, where $\boldsymbol{\beta} \stackrel{\text{def}}{=} (x_0, T, \bar{h}, p, r, w)$.

To center the discussion on the singular solution, we assume that $x^*(t; \boldsymbol{\beta}) > 0\, \forall\, t \in [t_0, t_1]$ and that $h^*(t; \boldsymbol{\beta}) > 0$ for at least some interval of time in the planning horizon. The first of these assumptions eliminates from consideration the issue of complete eradication of the farmer's fish stock, whereas the second is recognition of the fact that if it is indeed profitable for the farmer to be in business, then some harvest is optimal. By Lemma 3.1, or more precisely, Eq. (13) given in the proof of Lemma 3.1, and the assumption that $h^*(t; \boldsymbol{\beta}) > 0$ for at least some interval of time in the planning horizon, it follows that $\lambda(t; \boldsymbol{\beta}) > 0\, \forall\, t \in [0, T)$. We will make use of this result a little later in the example.

In line with our current interest in singular solutions, we assume that there exists an open interval of time in the planning horizon such that the value of the switching function identically vanishes along the optimal path, that is, a singular solution is optimal for some open interval in the planning horizon. More formally, we assume that $\sigma(t, x, \lambda) \equiv 0 \, \forall \, t \in (t_a, t_b) \subset [t_0, t_1]$, or equivalently by Eq. (24), that $\lambda \equiv [p - c(x; w)]e^{-rt} \, \forall \, t \in (t_a, t_b)$ along the optimal path. The latter equation has a straightforward economic interpretation. If the present value shadow price of the stock of fish is equal to the present value marginal (or average) profit of harvest, then the optimal fishing rate is the singular fishing rate. Said differently, if the maximum the fish farmer would pay at time $t = 0$ for another fish in her pond at time t is exactly equal to the time $t = 0$ value of profit from harvesting the incremental fish at time t, then the singular harvest rate is optimal. We now turn to the determination of the singular harvest rate.

Because $\lambda \equiv [p - c(x; w)]e^{-rt} \, \forall \, t \in (t_a, t_b)$ along the optimal path, we may differentiate it with respect to t and use the chain rule to arrive at

$$\dot{\lambda} = -r[p - c(x; w)]e^{-rt} - c_x(x; w)\dot{x}e^{-rt}. \tag{28}$$

Equating Eq. (26) to Eq. (28) and making use of Eq. (27) and $\lambda \equiv [p - c(x; w)]e^{-rt} \, \forall \, t \in (t_a, t_b)$ gives

$$[p - c(x; w)][r - F'(x)] = -c_x(x; w)F(x), \tag{29}$$

which is the equation defining the singular solution of the stock of fish, say, $x^s(p, r, w) > 0$, which we assume to be unique. Notice that because Eq. (29) is independent of t, so too is the singular fish stock $x^s(p, r, w)$, as is clear from the notation employed. In other words, although the singular solution for the stock of fish does not vary over time, it does change as the output price, input price, or discount rate changes.

In view of the fact that the stock of fish does not change with t along the singular solution, the singular harvest rate must equal the growth rate of the fish stock. More formally, as $\dot{x}^s(p, r, w) \equiv 0$, the state equation implies that the singular harvest rate is given by

$$h^s(p, r, w) = F(x^s(p, r, w)) > 0. \tag{30}$$

Equation (30) shows that the singular harvest rate is time invariant but does indeed vary with the output price, input price, or discount rate, just like the singular value of the fish stock.

Because $\lambda \equiv [p - c(x; w)]e^{-rt} \, \forall \, t \in (t_a, t_b)$ along the singular solution, the singular time path of the present value shadow price of the fish stock is thus

$$\lambda^s(t; p, r, w) = [p - c(x^s(p, r, w); w)]e^{-rt} > 0. \tag{31}$$

In contrast to the fish stock and harvest rate, the present value shadow price of the fish stock varies with t. This is plainly obvious because t appears explicitly on the right-hand side of Eq. (31). In fact, as $\dot{\lambda}^s(t; p, r, w)/\lambda^s(t; p, r, w) = -r < 0$, the rate of change of the present value shadow price of the fish stock is the negative of the interest rate along the singular solution, and therefore declines along it.

Seeing as the transversality condition $\lambda(T) = 0$ necessarily holds along the optimal path, the singular path cannot be the optimal path at $t = T$. To see this, note that Eq. (31) shows that $\lambda^s(t; p, r, w) \to 0$ as $t \to +\infty$. Hence, for any finite value of t, $\lambda^s(t; p, r, w) > 0$ along the singular path and thus cannot meet the necessary transversality condition $\lambda(T) = 0$. Put differently, this logic demonstrates that $t_b < T$ and therefore that the fish farmer must leave the singular path before $t = T$ in order to meet the transversality condition $\lambda(T) = 0$. Continuing along this line of reasoning, as long as $x_0 \neq x^s(p, r, w)$, x_0 cannot be a solution of Eq. (29) because $x^s(p, r, w) > 0$ is assumed to be unique. This implies that the singular solution is not the optimal solution at $t = 0$ either, that is, $t_a > 0$. Hence, we have shown that there exist two intervals, namely, $[0, t_a]$ and $[t_b, T]$, for which the singular solution is not optimal. With that settled, let's now investigate the nature of the optimal solution when it doesn't coincide with the singular solution.

To that end, consider the interval $[0, t_a]$ first and assume that $x_0 > x^s(p, r, w)$. Given that $\sigma(t, x, \lambda) = 0$ along the singular solution, $x_0 > x^s(p, r, w)$, and $c_x(x; w) < 0$, it follows from Eq. (24) that $\sigma(t, x, \lambda) \overset{\text{def}}{=} [p - c(x; w)]e^{-rt} - \lambda > 0$ when evaluated at $x = x_0$. As a result, by Eq. (25), we may conclude that $h^*(t; \boldsymbol{\beta}) = \bar{h}\, \forall\, t \in [0, t_a]$. A mental exercise asks you to conduct the analysis under the assumption $x_0 < x^s(p, r, w)$.

Next, turn to the interval $[t_b, T]$. In this case, we know that $h^*(t; \boldsymbol{\beta}) = 0$ is admissible but results in zero profit, as examination of the integrand of the objective functional confirms. Consequently, if $\sigma(t, x, \lambda) < 0$, then $h^*(t; \boldsymbol{\beta}) = 0$ is implied by the decision rule given in Eq. (25), resulting in zero profit for the fish farmer. On the other hand, if $\sigma(t, x, \lambda) > 0$, then $h^*(t; \boldsymbol{\beta}) = \bar{h}$ is implied by Eq. (25). Moreover, by Eq. (24) $\sigma(t, x, \lambda) > 0 \Leftrightarrow [p - c(x; w)]e^{-rt} > \lambda$. This, in turn, implies that the fish farmer's profit is positive when $h^*(t; \boldsymbol{\beta}) = \bar{h}$, for we have previously established that $\lambda(t; \boldsymbol{\beta}) > 0\, \forall\, t \in [0, T)$. Our conclusion, therefore, is that $h^*(t; \boldsymbol{\beta}) = \bar{h}\, \forall\, t \in [t_b, T]$.

Summing up, we have established that the optimal harvest rate is given by a combination of bang-bang and singular controls, videlicet,

$$h^*(t; \boldsymbol{\beta}) = \begin{cases} \bar{h} & \forall\, t \in [0, t_a] \\ h^s(p, r, w) & \forall\, t \in (t_a, t_b) \\ \bar{h} & \forall\, t \in [t_b, T]. \end{cases} \tag{32}$$

It is important to point out that just as with the optimal harvest rate, one cannot determine an explicit solution for the fish stock, its present value shadow price, or the switching times, for the functional forms of the unit cost function $c(\cdot)$ and the growth function of the fish $F(\cdot)$ have not been specified. Nonetheless, at this point, the determination of the full solution for the fish stock, its present value shadow price, and the switching times t_a and t_b, is analogous to that given in the prior three examples, and so is left for a mental exercise. We wrap up the analysis of the fish farming control problem with a brief examination of the comparative dynamic properties of the singular solution.

Because $x^s(p, r, w) > 0$ is the solution of Eq. (29), we may substitute $x^s(p, r, w)$ back into Eq. (29) and get the identity

$$\begin{aligned}&[p - c(x^s(p, r, w); w)]\,[r - F'(x^s(p, r, w))] \\ &\quad + [c_x(x^s(p, r, w); w) F(x^s(p, r, w))] \equiv 0.\end{aligned} \tag{33}$$

The comparative dynamics of the singular solution of the fish stock follow from differentiating identity (33) with respect to the parameters (p, r, w) using the chain rule. For example, differentiating identity (33) with respect to the output price p gives

$$\begin{aligned}&-[p - c(x^s(p, r, w); w)]\, F''(x^s(p, r, w))\frac{\partial x^s}{\partial p} \\ &\quad + [r - F'(x^s(p, r, w))]\left[1 - c_x(x^s(p, r, w); w)\frac{\partial x^s}{\partial p}\right] \\ &\quad + c_x(x^s(p, r, w); w) F'(x^s(p, r, w))\frac{\partial x^s}{\partial p} \\ &\quad + F(x^s(p, r, w)) c_{xx}(x^s(p, r, w); w)\frac{\partial x^s}{\partial p} \equiv 0.\end{aligned}$$

A bit of algebra then yields

$$\begin{aligned}&\frac{\partial x^s}{\partial p}(p, r, w) \\ &\equiv \frac{F'(x) - r}{F'(x)c_x(x; w) + F(x)c_{xx}(x; w) + [c(x; w) - p]\, F''(x) + [F'(x) - r]\, c_x(x; w)},\end{aligned} \tag{34}$$

which, of course, is evaluated at $x = x^s(p, r, w)$. Note that because we have used the implicit function theorem to derive Eq. (34), we had to assume that the denominator of Eq. (34) is nonzero when evaluated at $x = x^s(p, r, w)$.

In an attempt to sign Eq. (34), we know from Example 1.1 that $F''(x) \leq 0$. Moreover, $F(x^s(p, r, w)) > 0$ by Eq. (30), whereas $p - c(x^s(p, r, w), w) > 0$ by Eq. (31). Finally, by identity (33) and the assumptions made in this example, it follows that $r - F'(x^s(p, r, w)) > 0$, a result you should verify before pressing on. We therefore know that the sign of the numerator of Eq. (34) is negative and all terms in the denominator except the first are nonnegative. Thus, under the assumptions adopted herein, we cannot unambiguously sign the effect of an increase in the output price on the singular stock of fish. Notice that this ambiguity arises because we do not know the sign of $F'(x^s(p, r, w))$ or its precise magnitude, for all we know is that $F'(x^s(p, r, w)) < r$. If, however, we assume that $F'(x^s(p, r, w)) \leq [r/2]$, then the denominator of Eq. (34) is positive and so $\partial x^s(p, r, w)/\partial p < 0$ follows. In this case, we reach the more or less intuitive conclusion that an increase in the price of the harvested fish results in a decline in the singular stock of fish.

In contrast, even under the additional assumption $F'(x^s(p, r, w)) \le [r/2]$, we are not able to sign the effect of an increase in the output price on the singular harvest rate. To verify this claim, differentiate Eq. (30) with respect to p to get

$$\frac{\partial h^s}{\partial p}(p, r, w) = F'(x^s(p, r, w))\frac{\partial x^s}{\partial p}(p, r, w). \tag{35}$$

Because we do not know the sign of $F'(x^s(p, r, w))$, the harvest rate of fish may increase or decrease as the market price of fish increases, thus leading to the possibility of a backward-bending supply curve for the fish along the singular path. Likewise, differentiating Eq. (31) with respect to p and using Eq. (34), we find that

$$\begin{aligned}\frac{\partial \lambda^s}{\partial p}(t; p, r, w) &= \left[1 - c_x(x^s(p, r, w); w)\frac{\partial x^s}{\partial p}(t; p, r, w)\right] e^{-rt}\\ &= \left[\frac{F'(x)c_x(x; w) + F(x)c_{xx}(x; w) + [c(x; w) - p]\, F''(x)}{F'(x)c_x(x; w) + F(x)c_{xx}(x; w) + [c(x; w) - p]\, F''(x) + [F'(x) - r]\, c_x(x; w)}\right] e^{-rt},\end{aligned} \tag{36}$$

evaluated at $x = x^s(p, r, w)$. Consequently, we cannot unambiguously determine the effect of an increase in the market price of fish on the present value shadow price of the fish stock either. Yet, if we adopt the even stronger assumption $F'(x^s(p, r, w)) \le 0$, then Eqs. (34) through (36) imply that $\partial x^s(p, r, w)/\partial p < 0$, $\partial h^s(p, r, w)/\partial p > 0$, and $\partial \lambda^s(t; p, r, w)/\partial p > 0$, respectively. In other words, if the singular stock of fish is greater than or equal to the maximum sustainable fish stock, then an increase in the market price of the fish results in an increase in the singular harvest rate, and consequently, a lower singular stock of fish. In turn, the fish farmer then places a higher present value shadow price on the smaller stock. We leave the remaining comparative dynamics calculations and interpretations for a mental exercise and thus end the example at this juncture.

The first three optimal control problems examined in this chapter were linear in the control variable and had piecewise continuous optimal control functions with respect to t. Such evidence suggests that linearity of the control problem in the control variable is sufficient for the optimal control to be a piecewise continuous function of t. This conclusion, however, is incorrect. As noted in the opening remarks of the chapter, linearity of an optimal control problem in the control variable is not sufficient for a bang-bang control to be optimal. Example 4.3 and its solution refute that claim, as does Example 5.4, in which a combination of bang-bang and singular controls was optimal.

In each of the examples in this chapter, there was also inequality constraints or bounds on the control variable. Hence an important lesson to be taken from these examples is this: whenever an optimal control problem is linear in the control variables and thus has bounds placed on them, one should be aware that the resulting optimal control function may be a piecewise continuous function of t, that is, a bang-bang control may be optimal. In addition, Example 4.6 alerts one to the fact that even if the control problem is nonlinear in the control variable but is subject to an inequality constraint (e.g., nonnegativity), the optimal control may turn out to be only a continuous function of t.

We close with a few remarks on the method we used to solve the control problems of this chapter. Recall that in each example, we solved for the optimal control by using the Maximum Principle directly, that is to say, we examined the necessary condition $\max_{\mathbf{u}\in U} H(t, \mathbf{x}, \mathbf{u}, \boldsymbol{\lambda})$ and determined the equivalent decision rule that the optimal control had to satisfy. In view of the fact that $\max_{\mathbf{u}\in U} H(t, \mathbf{x}, \mathbf{u}, \boldsymbol{\lambda})$ is a constrained static optimization problem, Theorem 4.4 asserts that rather than use the Maximum Principle directly, we may instead form the Lagrangian function associated with the constrained optimization problem $\max_{\mathbf{u}\in U} H(t, \mathbf{x}, \mathbf{u}, \boldsymbol{\lambda})$, and then use the Lagrange or Kuhn-Tucker necessary conditions to determine the optimal control. This method, of course, introduces into the analysis Lagrange multipliers that must be determined. Nonetheless, either approach, when properly executed, yields identical answers. Several mental exercises will ask you to reanalyze three of the examples using this alternative solution procedure and confirm the veracity of Theorem 4.4.

MENTAL EXERCISES

5.1 In Example 5.1, $\lambda(t)$ is a decreasing function of time, that is, $\dot{\lambda}(t) < 0\,\forall\, t \in [0, 2]$, and thus attains the value of three at only the switching time $t = \tau \approx 1.096$. What would happen *if* it turned out that $\lambda(t) = 3\,\forall\, t \in [0, 2]$?

5.2 For Example 5.2, determine the specific solution of the state equation.

5.3 Return to Example 5.3, and for the solution given in Eqs. (10) through (14):
  (a) Derive the comparative dynamics for the discount rate r and provide an economic interpretation of them.
  (b) Derive the comparative dynamics for the final time T and provide an economic interpretation of them.
  (c) Derive the comparative dynamics for the terminal stock x_T and provide an economic interpretation of them.

5.4 Consider the linear optimal control problem

$$\min_{u(\cdot),x_2} \int_0^2 [2x(t) - 3u(t)]\,dt$$

$$\text{s.t.}\quad \dot{x}(t) = x(t) + u(t),\ x(0) = 4,\ x(2) = x_2,$$

$$u(t) \in U \overset{\text{def}}{=} \{u(\cdot) : 0 \le u(t) \le 2\}.$$

(a) Find the solution to the necessary conditions.
(b) Show that the solution in part (a) solves the problem.

5.5 Consider the optimal control problem

$$\min_{u(\cdot)} \int_0^2 [x(t) - 1]^2 \, dt$$

$$\text{s.t.} \quad \dot{x}(t) = u(t), \; x(0) = 0, \; x(2) = 1,$$

$$u(t) \in U \stackrel{\text{def}}{=} \{u(\cdot) : 0 \leq u(t) \leq 1\}.$$

(a) Find the solution to the necessary conditions.
(b) Show that the solution in part (a) solves the problem.

5.6 *Optimal Consumption of a Stock of Wine by a Wine Snob*. You are told by your physician that you have $T > 0$ years to live at time $t = 0$, the present, and you know this to be true. Over the course of your life, you have been an avid collector of wine for the purpose of consuming it rather than using it as an investment. Given the news from your physician, you would like to develop a consumption plan that maximizes the utility of consumption of your stock of wine over your remaining lifetime. At present, you have $w(0) = w_0 > 0$ bottles of wine in your cellar, and because you cannot take the wine with you when you die, you've decided that you will consume it all by the time you die hence $w(T) = 0$. The instantaneous utility that you derive from the consumption of wine and stock of wine is given by

$$U(c, w; \alpha_1, \alpha_2) \stackrel{\text{def}}{=} \alpha_1 c + \alpha_2 w,$$

where $\alpha_1 > 0$ and $\alpha_2 > 0$ are the marginal utilities of consumption and wine capital, respectively. This set of preferences implies that you not only get utility from the consumption of wine, but also from the mere presence of the stock of wine in your cellar, that is, you like to *brag* about the quantity and quality of wine in your cellar, and get enjoyment from that. The stock of wine in your cellar at any moment $t \in [0, T]$ is given by the archetype depletion equation in integral form

$$w(t) = w_0 - \int_0^t c(s) \, ds,$$

so that by Leibniz's rule, $\dot{w}(t) = -c(t)$, $w(0) = w_0$, and $w(T) = 0$ are the state equation and boundary conditions for the optimal control problem that you will solve in order to determine your optimal time path of wine consumption. Because your preferences are linear in the consumption rate, one must place a lower and upper bound on your consumption rate, say, $0 \leq c(t) \leq \bar{c}$, where $\bar{c} > w_0/T$. Note that you do *not* discount your instantaneous utility, that is, your discount rate is zero. Defining the vector of time independent parameters as $\boldsymbol{\beta} \stackrel{\text{def}}{=} (\alpha_1, \alpha_2, \bar{c}, w_0, T) \in \Re^5_{++}$, the optimal control problem that defines the optimal consumption rate of your stock of wine is therefore given by

$$V(\boldsymbol{\beta}) \stackrel{\text{def}}{=} \max_{c(\cdot)} \int_0^T [\alpha_1 c(t) + \alpha_2 w(t)]\, dt$$

$$\text{s.t.} \quad \dot{w}(t) = -c(t),\ w(0) = w_0,\ w(T) = 0,$$

$$c(t) \in U \stackrel{\text{def}}{=} \{c(\cdot) : 0 \leq c(t) \leq \bar{c}, \bar{c} > w_0 T^{-1}\}.$$

(a) Provide an economic interpretation of the inequality $\bar{c} > w_0/T$.

(b) Write down the Hamiltonian for this optimal control problem, letting λ be the costate variable. What is the economic interpretation of λ? Is it positive or negative? How do you know?

(c) Assuming that an optimal solution to the control problem exists, find the decision rule governing the selection of the optimal rate of wine consumption.

(d) Prove that $c(t) = 0\, \forall\, t \in [0, T]$ is *not* an admissible solution. Explain why it therefore cannot be an optimal solution.

(e) Prove that $c(t) = \bar{c}\, \forall\, t \in [0, T]$ is *not* an admissible solution. Explain why it therefore cannot be an optimal solution.

(f) Find the general solution for $\lambda(t)$, letting a_1 be the constant of integration. Prove that $\lambda(t) < \alpha_1\, \forall\, t \in [0, T]$ and $\lambda(t) > \alpha_1\, \forall\, t \in [0, T]$ cannot hold for $\lambda(t)$ in an optimal program.

(g) What, therefore, is the nature of the solution for the optimal consumption rate?

(h) Show that

$$c^*(t; \bar{c}) = \begin{cases} 0\, \forall\, t \in [0, \tau], \\ \bar{c}\, \forall\, t \in (\tau, T], \end{cases}$$

$$w^*(t; \bar{c}, w_0, T) = \begin{cases} w_0 & \forall\, t \in [0, \tau], \\ \bar{c}[T - t]\, & \forall\, t \in (\tau, T], \end{cases}$$

$$\lambda(t; \alpha_1, \alpha_2, \bar{c}, w_0, T) = \alpha_1 + \alpha_2 \left[T - \frac{w_0}{\bar{c}} - t \right],$$

where

$$\tau = \tau^*(\bar{c}, w_0, T) = T - \frac{w_0}{\bar{c}} > 0$$

is the switching time, is a solution to the necessary conditions.

(i) Provide an economic interpretation of the solution to the necessary conditions. It the solution consistent with the person being a wine snob? How so?

(j) Prove that the solution of the necessary conditions solves the control problem.

(k) Derive the comparative dynamics for the optimal time paths of the consumption rate and shadow value of the wine stock, as well as the switching time, for the parameters $\beta \stackrel{\text{def}}{=} (\alpha_1, \alpha_2, \bar{c}, w_0, T) \in \Re^5_{++}$, and provide an economic interpretation of them.

5.7 *Optimal Inventory Accumulation in a Linear World.* We return to our inventory accumulation problem for this question. Now, however, we add two twists to the prototype problem, scilicet, (i) the firm is asserted to maximize the profits from the sale of the good, and (ii) the costs of production are assumed to be linear in the production rate $u(t)$. The optimal control problem corresponding to this modified inventory accumulation problem is therefore given by

$$\max_{u(\cdot),x_T} \left\{ p x_T - \int_0^T [c_1 u(t) + c_2 x(t)]\, dt \right\}$$

$$\text{s.t.} \quad \dot{x}(t) = u(t),\ x(0) = 0,\ x(T) = x_T,$$

$$u(t) \in U \stackrel{\text{def}}{=} \{u(\cdot) : 0 \le u(t) \le \bar{u}\,\forall\, t \in [0, T]\},$$

where $p > 0$ is the market price of the good produced by the firm, $\bar{u} > 0$ is the maximum production rate the firm can achieve given its capital stock, and all the other variables and parameters have their standard (and by now well-known) interpretation. Recall that all the parameters are positive. Furthermore, assume that $p < c_2 T + c_1$ and $p > c_1$.

(a) Provide an economic interpretation of the inequalities $p < c_2 T + c_1$ and $p > c_1$.

(b) Define the Hamiltonian H with costate variable λ, and derive the decision rule for determining the optimal production rate. In defining the Hamiltonian, include the minus sign as part of the integrand so that you are solving a maximization problem.

(c) Solve the costate equation for its specific solution and show that $\dot{\lambda}(t) > 0$.

(d) Show that the production plan

$$v(t; \bar{u}) = \begin{cases} 0\,\forall\, t \in [0, s) \\ \bar{u}\,\forall\, t \in [s, T], \end{cases}$$

is a solution to the necessary conditions, where $s = T - (p - c_1)/c_2 > 0$ is the switching time.

(e) Find the time path of the state variable that solves the necessary conditions.

(f) Is the solution to the necessary conditions a solution to the control problem? Please answer the following five questions for the optimal time paths of the control and costate variables, as well as the optimal switching time.

(g) Derive the comparative dynamics for an increase in the marginal storage cost and provide an economic interpretation.
(h) Derive the comparative dynamics for an increase in the marginal cost of production and provide an economic interpretation.
(i) Derive the comparative dynamics for an increase in the output price and provide an economic interpretation.
(j) Derive the comparative dynamics for an increase in the terminal time and provide an economic interpretation.
(k) Derive the comparative dynamics for an increase in the maximum production rate and provide an economic interpretation.

5.8 Resolve Example 5.1 by using a Lagrangian function and the Kuhn-Tucker necessary conditions of Theorem 4.4.

5.9 Resolve Example 5.2 by using a Lagrangian function and the Kuhn-Tucker necessary conditions of Theorem 4.4.

5.10 Resolve Example 5.3 by using a Lagrangian function and the Kuhn-Tucker necessary conditions of Theorem 4.4.

5.11 Establish the veracity of Eq. (19).

5.12 Solve Example 5.2 under the assumption that $T \leq 1$. Show that the resulting optimal savings rate lies on the boundary of the control set for the entire planning horizon. Provide an economic interpretation of this solution and clearly explain why it occurs.

5.13 Solve Example 5.3 under the assumption that $\bar{u} \leq [x_0 - x_T]/T$. To highlight the importance of this assumption, you are asked to proceed in two stages.
(a) Show that if $\bar{u} = [x_0 - x_T]/T$, then the resulting optimal cleanup rate lies at the boundary of the control set for the entire planning horizon. Provide an economic interpretation of this solution and clearly explain why it occurs.
(b) Now assume that $\bar{u} < [x_0 - x_T]/T$. Explain carefully and fully the technical problem you run into.

5.14 Prove that the switching function $\sigma(\cdot)$ is a monotonically decreasing function of time in Examples 5.1 through 5.3.

5.15 Show that equating Eq. (26) to Eq. (28) and using $\lambda \equiv [p - c(x; w)]e^{-rt}\, \forall\, t \in (t_a, t_b)$ and Eq. (27) yields Eq. (29). Also verify Eq. (29) by applying Eq. (20) directly to the fish farming control problem given in Example 5.4.

5.16 Determine the optimal harvest rate for Example 5.4 over the interval $[0, t_a]$ under the assumption $x_0 < x^s(p, r, w)$. Show your work.

5.17 Write down and, of course, show your work for the complete solution to Example 5.4, the fish farming problem, under the assumptions adopted in the example. Recall that just as with the optimal harvest rate given by Eq. (32), one cannot determine an explicit solution for the fish stock, its present value shadow price, or the switching times, as the functional forms of the unit cost function and the growth function of the fish have not been specified. The answers for the fish stock and its present value shadow price should take a form akin to Eq. (32), whereas the solution for each switching time, t_a and t_b, should be stated as the solution to an implicit equation.

5.18 Complete the comparative dynamics analysis of the singular solution of Example 5.4 under the assumption $F'(x^s(p, r, w)) \leq 0$.
  (a) Derive the comparative dynamics of the singular solution for an increase in the discount rate. Provide an economic interpretation.
  (b) Derive the comparative dynamics of the singular solution for an increase in the wage rate. Provide an economic interpretation.

FURTHER READING

All the referenced textbooks contain at least some discussion of piecewise continuous and bang-bang controls. In addition, they all present the material in much the same way that it has been presented here, that is, by way of examples. Kamien and Schwartz (1991) devote a section to the topic, whereas Léonard and Van Long (1992) allocate an entire chapter to control problems with discontinuous controls. There do not appear to be many published papers in the economics literature that study models that are linear in the control variable and lead to a bang-bang solution for the control. This is not that surprising in view of the fact that the assumption of linearity is quite strong. For example, if the integrand is linear in the control variable, then one is assuming that the marginal product or marginal cost of the control is constant with respect to the control (but it could still vary with time). Discussions of singular controls may be found in Kamien and Schwartz (1991) and Clark (1976).

REFERENCES

Clark, C.W. (1976), *Mathematical Bioeconomics: The Optimal Management of Renewable Resources* (New York: John Wiley & Sons, Inc.).

Kamien, M.I. and Schwartz, N.L. (1991, 2nd Ed.), *Dynamic Optimization: The Calculus of Variations and Optimal Control in Economics and Management* (New York: Elsevier Science Publishing Co., Inc.).

Léonard, D. and Van Long, N. (1992), *Optimal Control Theory and Static Optimization in Economics* (New York: Cambridge University Press).

SIX

Necessary and Sufficient Conditions for a General Class of Control Problems

Until this point, our development of the necessary and sufficient conditions of optimal control theory did not allow for constraints that depended on the control variables *and* the state variables. The goal of this chapter is to state two theorems giving necessary conditions for a class of control problems that contain such constraints, which we refer to as *mixed constraints* because of the presence of the state and control variables in them, as well as to prove two theorems giving sufficient conditions pertaining to this class of problems. We will use the necessary conditions to explicitly solve for the optimal paths of a version of the capital accumulating model of the firm without adjustment costs and irreversible investment. The theorems presented here are the most general we shall present and use in the book.

The problem under consideration in this chapter is to find a piecewise continuous control vector function $\mathbf{u}(\cdot) \stackrel{\text{def}}{=} (u_1(\cdot), u_2(\cdot), \ldots, u_M(\cdot))$ and its associated piecewise smooth state vector function $\mathbf{x}(\cdot) \stackrel{\text{def}}{=} (x_1(\cdot), x_2(\cdot), \ldots, x_N(\cdot))$, defined on the fixed time interval $[t_0, t_1]$ that will solve the ensuing constrained fixed endpoints optimal control problem:

$$\max_{\mathbf{u}(\cdot)} J[\mathbf{x}(\cdot), \mathbf{u}(\cdot)] \stackrel{\text{def}}{=} \int_{t_0}^{t_1} f(t, \mathbf{x}(t), \mathbf{u}(t))\, dt$$

$$\text{s.t.} \quad \dot{\mathbf{x}}(t) = \mathbf{g}(t, \mathbf{x}(t), \mathbf{u}(t)), \;\; \mathbf{x}(t_0) = \mathbf{x}_0, \;\; \mathbf{x}(t_1) = \mathbf{x}_1, \tag{1}$$

$$h^k(t, \mathbf{x}(t), \mathbf{u}(t)) \geq 0, \quad k = 1, 2, \ldots, K',$$

$$h^k(t, \mathbf{x}(t), \mathbf{u}(t)) = 0, \quad k = K'+1, K'+2, \ldots, K,$$

where $\mathbf{g}(\cdot) \stackrel{\text{def}}{=} (g^1(\cdot), g^2(\cdot), \ldots, g^N(\cdot))$, $\dot{\mathbf{x}}(\cdot) \stackrel{\text{def}}{=} (\dot{x}_1(\cdot), \dot{x}_2(\cdot), \ldots, \dot{x}_N(\cdot))$, and $\mathbf{h}(\cdot) \stackrel{\text{def}}{=} (h^1(\cdot), h^2(\cdot), \ldots, h^K(\cdot))$. It is important to observe that the K constraints in problem (1) are equivalent to the requirement that $\mathbf{u}(t) \in U(t, \mathbf{x}(t))$, where the control set

$U(t, \mathbf{x}(t))$ is now more generally defined as

$$U(t, \mathbf{x}(t)) \stackrel{\text{def}}{=} \{\mathbf{u}(\cdot) : h^k(t, \mathbf{x}(t), \mathbf{u}(t)) \geq 0, \quad k = 1, \ldots, K',$$
$$h^k(t, \mathbf{x}(t), \mathbf{u}(t)) = 0, \quad k = K' + 1, \ldots, K\}. \tag{2}$$

Notice that in Eq. (2) we have used notation for the control set (or region) that makes explicit its dependence on the state variables. To simplify notation and make it less cumbersome, we will often use the set inclusion $\mathbf{u}(t) \in U(t, \mathbf{x}(t))$ to signify the values of the control functions that satisfy the system of K' inequality constraints and $K - K'$ equality constraints in problem (1). In passing, note that we will consider the various transversality conditions that arise for perturbations of problem (1) four chapters hence, *after* we establish the dynamic envelope theorem.

Because we are studying a more general class of optimal control problems than we did earlier, we must amend our definition of an admissible pair. To this end, we have the following definition, which should be contrasted with that given earlier in Definitions 2.1 and 4.1.

Definition 6.1: We call $(\mathbf{x}(t), \mathbf{u}(t))$ an *admissible pair* if $\mathbf{u}(\cdot)$ is any piecewise continuous control vector function such that $\mathbf{u}(t) \in U(t, \mathbf{x}(t)) \forall t \in [t_0, t_1]$ and $\mathbf{x}(\cdot)$ is a piecewise smooth state vector function such that $\dot{\mathbf{x}}(t) = \mathbf{g}(t, \mathbf{x}(t), \mathbf{u}(t))$, $\mathbf{x}(t_0) = \mathbf{x}_0$, and $\mathbf{x}(t_1) = \mathbf{x}_1$.

As remarked in Chapter 4 when we dealt with inequality constraints of the simpler form $h^k(t, \mathbf{u}(t)) \geq 0$, $k = 1, 2, \ldots, K$, there is essentially no loss in generality in defining the control region by a system of inequality and equality constraints, for as a practical matter, the control set is almost always specified in such a manner. Accordingly, we must therefore introduce a constraint qualification on the constraint functions $h^k(\cdot)$, $k = 1, 2, \ldots, K$, just as we did in Chapter 4. Before doing so, first recall that by Definition 4.2, if X is a set, then card(X), the cardinal number of X, is the number of elements in X. We are now in a position to state the constraint qualification of interest to us.

Rank Constraint Qualification: Define $\iota(t, \mathbf{z}(t), \mathbf{v}(t)) \stackrel{\text{def}}{=} \{k : h^k(t, \mathbf{z}(t), \mathbf{v}(t)) = 0,$ $k = 1, 2, \ldots, K\}$ as the index set of the binding constraints along the optimal path. For every $t \in [t_0, t_1]$, if $\iota(t, \mathbf{z}(t), \mathbf{v}(t)) \neq \emptyset$, that is, $\iota(t, \mathbf{z}(t), \mathbf{v}(t))$ is nonempty, then the card$(\iota(t, \mathbf{z}(t), \mathbf{v}(t))) \times M$ Jacobian matrix

$$\left[\frac{\partial h^k}{\partial u_m}(t, \mathbf{z}(t), \mathbf{v}(t))\right]_{\substack{k \in \iota(t, \mathbf{z}(t), \mathbf{v}(t)) \\ m=1, 2, \ldots, M}} \tag{3}$$

has a rank equal to card$(\iota(t, \mathbf{z}(t), \mathbf{v}(t)))$. That is, the rank of the above Jacobian matrix is equal to the number of its rows, the maximum rank it can have.

For example, if k_B of the constraints bind at a given point t in the planning horizon, where we note that $k_B \geq K - K'$ because there are $K - K'$ equality constraints in problem (1), then $\text{card}(\iota(t, \mathbf{z}(t), \mathbf{v}(t))) = k_B$. Hence the above Jacobian matrix will be of order $k_B \times M$ and the constraint qualification will be satisfied if the rank of the Jacobian equals k_B. This rank condition on the Jacobian has two important consequences, both of which were noted in Chapter 4. First, it implies that at least one control variable must be present in each of the binding constraints. To see this, assume that the constraint qualification holds but that one of the k_B binding constraints, say, the first (without loss of generality), does not have any control variables in it. In this case, the first row of the Jacobian matrix would be identically zero, thereby implying that the rows of the Jacobian are linearly dependent. This, in turn, implies that the Jacobian is of rank less than k_B, thus violating the constraint qualification. Second, the constraint qualification implies that the number of binding constraints k_B cannot be greater than the number of control variables M. To see this, assume that the constraint qualification holds but that $k_B > M$. Then there are more rows (k_B) in the Jacobian than there are columns (M). But the rank of a matrix cannot exceed the minimum of the number of its rows or columns. This, in turn, implies that the rank of the Jacobian is $\min(k_B, M) = M$, which is less than k_B, thereby violating the constraint qualification. Note, however, that the constraint qualification permits the number of constraints (K) to exceed the number of control variables (M) in view of the fact that some of the inequality constraints may not bind.

In developing the necessary conditions in Chapters 2 and 4, we found it convenient to define a function called the Hamiltonian, and we will similarly find it convenient to do so here. In the present case, there are N state variables and N ordinary differential equations describing their rates of changes with respect to time. Consequently, we associate with each of the differential equations a costate function $\lambda_n(\cdot)$, $n = 1, 2, \ldots, N$, and define the Hamiltonian for problem (1) by

$$\begin{aligned} H(t, \mathbf{x}, \mathbf{u}, \boldsymbol{\lambda}) &\overset{\text{def}}{=} f(t, \mathbf{x}, \mathbf{u}) + \sum_{n=1}^{N} \lambda_n g^n(t, \mathbf{x}, \mathbf{u}) \\ &\overset{\text{def}}{=} f(t, \mathbf{x}, \mathbf{u}) + \boldsymbol{\lambda}' \mathbf{g}(t, \mathbf{x}, \mathbf{u}), \end{aligned} \tag{4}$$

where $\boldsymbol{\lambda} \overset{\text{def}}{=} (\lambda_1, \lambda_2, \ldots, \lambda_N)$ and $\boldsymbol{\lambda}'\mathbf{g}(t, \mathbf{x}, \mathbf{u}) \overset{\text{def}}{=} \sum_{n=1}^{N} \lambda_n g^n(t, \mathbf{x}, \mathbf{u})$ is the scalar or inner product of the vectors $\boldsymbol{\lambda}$ and $\mathbf{g}(t, \mathbf{x}, \mathbf{u})$. As you may recall from Theorem 4.2, the Maximum Principle requires that the optimal control vector maximize the Hamiltonian subject to the constraints that the control variables lie in the control set. Given that the control set is defined by a system of inequality and equality constraints in problem (1), the Maximum Principle dictates that a nonlinear programming problem be solved, to wit, $\max_{\mathbf{u} \in U(t,\mathbf{x})} H(t, \mathbf{x}, \mathbf{u}, \boldsymbol{\lambda})$, in order to find the optimal control vector, something that can be done, in principle, with Theorem 18.5 of Simon and Blume (1994), that is, the Karush-Kuhn-Tucker theorem. This is the same conclusion we arrived at in Chapter 4. Moreover, this observation connotes that a Lagrangian function be formed in order to solve the constrained optimization problem $\max_{\mathbf{u} \in U(t,\mathbf{x})} H(t, \mathbf{x}, \mathbf{u}, \boldsymbol{\lambda})$. To this end, let us define the Lagrangian function $L(\cdot)$

corresponding to the nonlinear programming problem $\max_{\mathbf{u}\in U(t,\mathbf{x})} H(t, \mathbf{x}, \mathbf{u}, \boldsymbol{\lambda})$ dictated by the Maximum Principle, by associating with each constraint function $h^k(\cdot)$ a Lagrange multiplier function $\mu_k(\cdot)$, $k = 1, 2, \ldots, K$, to get

$$\begin{aligned} L(t, \mathbf{x}, \mathbf{u}, \boldsymbol{\lambda}, \boldsymbol{\mu}) &\stackrel{\text{def}}{=} f(t, \mathbf{x}, \mathbf{u}) + \sum_{n=1}^{N} \lambda_n g^n(t, \mathbf{x}, \mathbf{u}) + \sum_{k=1}^{K} \mu_k h^k(t, \mathbf{x}, \mathbf{u}) \\ &\stackrel{\text{def}}{=} f(t, \mathbf{x}, \mathbf{u}) + \boldsymbol{\lambda}'\mathbf{g}(t, \mathbf{x}, \mathbf{u}) + \boldsymbol{\mu}'\mathbf{h}(t, \mathbf{x}, \mathbf{u}) \\ &\stackrel{\text{def}}{=} H(t, \mathbf{x}, \mathbf{u}, \boldsymbol{\lambda}) + \boldsymbol{\mu}'\mathbf{h}(t, \mathbf{x}, \mathbf{u}), \end{aligned} \tag{5}$$

where $\boldsymbol{\mu} \stackrel{\text{def}}{=} (\mu_1, \mu_2, \ldots, \mu_K)$. Note that it is precisely because we have defined the control set in terms of a system of inequality and equality constraints in problem (1) that we are led to such a formulation. With the constraint qualification now dealt with, we may turn to the necessary conditions for problem (1).

In addition to the standard assumptions on the functions $f(\cdot)$ and $\mathbf{g}(\cdot)$ given in Chapter 1, we now make the following *additional* ones:

(A.1) $\partial f(\cdot)/\partial u_m \in C^{(0)}$ with respect to the $1 + N + M$ variables $(t, \mathbf{x}, \mathbf{u})$, for $m = 1, 2, \ldots, M$.
(A.2) $\partial g^n(\cdot)/\partial u_m \in C^{(0)}$ with respect to the $1 + N + M$ variables $(t, \mathbf{x}, \mathbf{u})$ for $m = 1, 2, \ldots, M$ and $n = 1, 2, \ldots, N$.
(A.3) $h^k(\cdot) \in C^{(0)}$ with respect to the $1 + N + M$ variables $(t, \mathbf{x}, \mathbf{u})$ for $k = 1, 2, \ldots, K$.
(A.4) $\partial h^k(\cdot)/\partial x_n \in C^{(0)}$ with respect to the $1 + N + M$ variables $(t, \mathbf{x}, \mathbf{u})$ for $k = 1, 2, \ldots, K$ and $n = 1, 2, \ldots, N$.
(A.5) $\partial h^k(\cdot)/\partial u_m \in C^{(0)}$ with respect to the $1 + N + M$ variables $(t, \mathbf{x}, \mathbf{u})$ for $k = 1, 2, \ldots, K$ and $m = 1, 2, \ldots, M$.

We may now state the necessary conditions pertaining to problem (1).

Theorem 6.1 (Necessary Conditions, Mixed Constraints): *Let $(\mathbf{z}(t), \mathbf{v}(t))$ be an admissible pair for problem (1), and assume that the rank constraint qualification is satisfied. Then if $(\mathbf{z}(t), \mathbf{v}(t))$ yields the absolute maximum of $J[\cdot]$, it is necessary that there exist a piecewise smooth vector-valued function $\boldsymbol{\lambda}(\cdot) \stackrel{\text{def}}{=} (\lambda_1(\cdot), \lambda_2(\cdot), \ldots, \lambda_N(\cdot))$ and a piecewise continuous vector-valued Lagrange multiplier function $\boldsymbol{\mu}(\cdot) \stackrel{\text{def}}{=} (\mu_1(\cdot), \mu_2(\cdot), \ldots, \mu_K(\cdot))$, such that for all $t \in [t_0, t_1]$,*

$$\mathbf{v}(t) = \arg\max_{\mathbf{u}} \{H(t, \mathbf{z}(t), \mathbf{u}, \boldsymbol{\lambda}(t)) \text{ s.t. } \mathbf{u} \in U(t, \mathbf{z}(t))\},$$

that is, if

$$M(t, \mathbf{z}(t), \boldsymbol{\lambda}(t)) \stackrel{\text{def}}{=} \max_{\mathbf{u}} \{H(t, \mathbf{z}(t), \mathbf{u}, \boldsymbol{\lambda}(t)) \text{ s.t. } \mathbf{u} \in U(t, \mathbf{z}(t))\},$$

then

$$M(t, \mathbf{z}(t), \boldsymbol{\lambda}(t)) \equiv H(t, \mathbf{z}(t), \mathbf{v}(t), \boldsymbol{\lambda}(t)),$$

or equivalently

$$H(t, \mathbf{z}(t), \mathbf{v}(t), \boldsymbol{\lambda}(t)) \geq H(t, \mathbf{z}(t), \mathbf{u}, \boldsymbol{\lambda}(t)) \,\forall\, \mathbf{u} \in U(t, \mathbf{z}(t)),$$

where

$$U(t, \mathbf{x}(t)) \stackrel{\text{def}}{=} \{\mathbf{u}(\cdot) : h^k(t, \mathbf{x}(t), \mathbf{u}(t)) \geq 0, \quad k = 1, \ldots, K',$$
$$h^k(t, \mathbf{x}(t), \mathbf{u}(t)) = 0, \quad k = K' + 1, \ldots, K\}$$

is the control set. Because the rank constraint qualification is assumed to hold, the above necessary condition implies that

$$\frac{\partial L}{\partial u_m}(t, \mathbf{z}(t), \mathbf{v}(t), \boldsymbol{\lambda}(t), \boldsymbol{\mu}(t)) = 0, \quad m = 1, 2, \ldots, M,$$

$$\frac{\partial L}{\partial \mu_k}(t, \mathbf{z}(t), \mathbf{v}(t), \boldsymbol{\lambda}(t), \boldsymbol{\mu}(t)) \geq 0, \ \mu_k(t) \geq 0,$$

$$\mu_k(t)\frac{\partial L}{\partial \mu_k}(t, \mathbf{z}(t), \mathbf{v}(t), \boldsymbol{\lambda}(t), \boldsymbol{\mu}(t)) = 0, \quad k = 1, 2, \ldots, K',$$

$$\frac{\partial L}{\partial u_k}(t, \mathbf{z}(t), \mathbf{v}(t), \boldsymbol{\lambda}(t), \boldsymbol{\mu}(t)) = 0, \quad k = K' + 1, K' + 2, \ldots, K,$$

where

$$L(t, \mathbf{x}, \mathbf{u}, \boldsymbol{\lambda}, \boldsymbol{\mu}) \stackrel{\text{def}}{=} H(t, \mathbf{x}, \mathbf{u}, \boldsymbol{\lambda}) + \boldsymbol{\mu}'\mathbf{h}(t, \mathbf{x}, \mathbf{u})$$
$$= f(t, \mathbf{x}, \mathbf{u}) + \sum_{n=1}^{N} \lambda_n g^n(t, \mathbf{x}, \mathbf{u}) + \sum_{k=1}^{K} \mu_k h^k(t, \mathbf{x}, \mathbf{u})$$

is the Lagrangian function. Furthermore, except for the points of discontinuities of $\mathbf{v}(t)$,

$$\dot{z}_n(t) = \frac{\partial L}{\partial \lambda_n}(t, \mathbf{z}(t), \mathbf{v}(t), \boldsymbol{\lambda}(t), \boldsymbol{\mu}(t)) = g^n(t, \mathbf{z}(t), \mathbf{v}(t)), \quad n = 1, 2, \ldots, N,$$

$$\dot{\lambda}_n(t) = -\frac{\partial L}{\partial x_n}(t, \mathbf{z}(t), \mathbf{v}(t), \boldsymbol{\lambda}(t), \boldsymbol{\mu}(t)), \quad n = 1, 2, \ldots, N,$$

where the above notation means that the functions are first differentiated with respect to the particular variable and then evaluated at $(t, \mathbf{z}(t), \mathbf{v}(t), \boldsymbol{\lambda}(t), \boldsymbol{\mu}(t))$.

Let us remark on several important consequences of Theorem 6.1, all of which are analogous to those noted for Theorem 4.4. First, in general, the Lagrange multiplier function $\boldsymbol{\mu}(\cdot) \stackrel{\text{def}}{=} (\mu_1(\cdot), \mu_2(\cdot), \ldots, \mu_K(\cdot))$ is piecewise continuous on $[t_0, t_1]$. It turns out, however, that $\boldsymbol{\mu}(\cdot)$ is continuous whenever the optimal control function $\mathbf{v}(\cdot)$ is continuous. Thus the discontinuities in the Lagrange multipliers can only occur at points where the optimal control is discontinuous. One implication of Theorem 6.1 is that the Lagrangian function evaluated along the optimal solution is a continuous function of t, that is, $L(t, \mathbf{z}(t), \mathbf{v}(t), \boldsymbol{\lambda}(t), \boldsymbol{\mu}(t))$ is a continuous function of t. Another implication, identical in flavor to that derived in Mental Exercises 2.31 and 4.13 for simpler control problems, is that the *total derivative* of $L(t, \mathbf{z}(t), \mathbf{v}(t), \boldsymbol{\lambda}(t), \boldsymbol{\mu}(t))$ with respect to t, scilicet,

$$\dot{L}(t, \mathbf{z}(t), \mathbf{v}(t), \boldsymbol{\lambda}(t), \boldsymbol{\mu}(t)) \stackrel{\text{def}}{=} \frac{d}{dt} L(t, \mathbf{z}(t), \mathbf{v}(t), \boldsymbol{\lambda}(t), \boldsymbol{\mu}(t)),$$

is equal to the *partial derivative* of $L(t, \mathbf{z}(t), \mathbf{v}(t), \boldsymbol{\lambda}(t), \boldsymbol{\mu}(t))$ with respect to t, namely,

$$L_t(t, \mathbf{z}(t), \mathbf{v}(t), \boldsymbol{\lambda}(t), \boldsymbol{\mu}(t)) \stackrel{\text{def}}{=} \frac{\partial}{\partial t} L(t, \mathbf{z}(t), \mathbf{v}(t), \boldsymbol{\lambda}(t), \boldsymbol{\mu}(t)),$$

at all continuity points of the optimal control function $\mathbf{v}(\cdot)$, and assuming that $f(\cdot)$, $\mathbf{g}(\cdot)$, and $\mathbf{h}(\cdot)$ are $C^{(1)}$ functions of $(t, \mathbf{x}, \mathbf{u})$. Other results similar to those derived in Mental Exercises 2.31 and 4.13 also hold, as you will discover in a mental exercise. Finally, we should note that the necessary conditions involving inequalities are complementary slackness conditions exactly analogous to those encountered in linear and nonlinear programming.

Let us now indicate that the necessary conditions of Theorem 6.1 contain enough conditions to determine candidates for optimality. It should be clear from the method of Lagrange and the Karush-Kuhn-Tucker theorem that the necessary conditions

$$\frac{\partial L}{\partial u_m}(t, \mathbf{x}, \mathbf{u}, \boldsymbol{\lambda}, \boldsymbol{\mu}) = 0, \quad m = 1, 2, \ldots, M,$$

$$\frac{\partial L}{\partial \mu_k}(t, \mathbf{x}, \mathbf{u}, \boldsymbol{\lambda}, \boldsymbol{\mu}) \geq 0,\ \mu_k \geq 0,\ \mu_k \frac{\partial L}{\partial \mu_k}(t, \mathbf{x}, \mathbf{u}, \boldsymbol{\lambda}, \boldsymbol{\mu}) = 0, \quad k = 1, 2, \ldots, K',$$

$$\frac{\partial L}{\partial \mu_k}(t, \mathbf{x}, \mathbf{u}, \boldsymbol{\lambda}, \boldsymbol{\mu}) = 0, \quad k = K'+1, K'+2, \ldots, K,$$

in principle determine the control variables and the Lagrange multipliers as functions of time, the state variables, the costate variables, and any parameters of the problem, say, $\mathbf{u} = \hat{\mathbf{u}}(t, \mathbf{x}, \boldsymbol{\lambda})$ and $\boldsymbol{\mu} = \hat{\boldsymbol{\mu}}(t, \mathbf{x}, \boldsymbol{\lambda})$. Substituting these solutions into the canonical equations then gives the system of differential equations

$$\dot{x}_n = \frac{\partial L}{\partial \lambda_n}(t, \mathbf{x}, \hat{\mathbf{u}}(t, \mathbf{x}, \boldsymbol{\lambda}), \boldsymbol{\lambda}, \hat{\boldsymbol{\mu}}(t, \mathbf{x}, \boldsymbol{\lambda})) = g^n(t, \mathbf{x}, \hat{\mathbf{u}}(t, \mathbf{x}, \boldsymbol{\lambda})), \quad n = 1, 2, \ldots, N,$$

$$\dot{\lambda}_n = -\frac{\partial L}{\partial x_n}(t, \mathbf{x}, \hat{\mathbf{u}}(t, \mathbf{x}, \boldsymbol{\lambda}), \boldsymbol{\lambda}, \hat{\boldsymbol{\mu}}(t, \mathbf{x}, \boldsymbol{\lambda})), \quad n = 1, 2, \ldots, N.$$

The solution of this system gives rise to $2N$ constants of integration, which can in principle be determined by using the $2N$ boundary conditions $\mathbf{x}(t_0) = \mathbf{x}_0$ and $\mathbf{x}(t_1) = \mathbf{x}_1$, thereby yielding the solution $(\mathbf{z}(t; t_0, \mathbf{x}_0, t_1, \mathbf{x}_1), \boldsymbol{\lambda}(t; t_0, \mathbf{x}_0, t_1, \mathbf{x}_1))$. This solution can then be substituted back into $\hat{\mathbf{u}}(t, \mathbf{x}, \boldsymbol{\lambda})$ and $\hat{\boldsymbol{\mu}}(t, \mathbf{x}, \boldsymbol{\lambda})$ to determine their optimal solution, say,

$$\mathbf{v}(t; t_0, \mathbf{x}_0, t_1, \mathbf{x}_1) \stackrel{\text{def}}{=} \hat{\mathbf{u}}(t, \mathbf{z}(t; t_0, \mathbf{x}_0, t_1, \mathbf{x}_1), \boldsymbol{\lambda}(t; t_0, \mathbf{x}_0, t_1, \mathbf{x}_1)),$$

$$\boldsymbol{\mu}(t; t_0, \mathbf{x}_0, t_1, \mathbf{x}_1) \stackrel{\text{def}}{=} \hat{\boldsymbol{\mu}}(t, \mathbf{z}(t; t_0, \mathbf{x}_0, t_1, \mathbf{x}_1), \boldsymbol{\lambda}(t; t_0, \mathbf{x}_0, t_1, \mathbf{x}_1)).$$

Thus, in principle, Theorem 6.1 contains enough conditions to find the optimal solution of problem (1), as was to be demonstrated. In passing, recall that in Chapter 4, a rather thorough set of remarks concerning the role that the rank constraint qualification plays in solving an optimal control problem was presented. It is advisable to revisit those remarks at this time if one's memory of them is a bit vague.

Let's now pause and consider an example of a capital accumulating model of the firm that has a bounded investment rate and irreversibility, and solve it with Theorem 6.1.

Example 6.1: This example examines the dynamic behavior of a price-taking capital accumulating firm, but unlike earlier investigations of it, the firm does *not* face any adjustment costs and investment is irreversible. The firm produces a single output y with the production function $f(\cdot)$ with values $f(K(t)) \stackrel{\text{def}}{=} K(t)$, where $K(t)$ is the capital stock of the firm at time t, and is the only input into the production of the good. The good is sold in a competitive market at the constant price $p > 0$. The firm may purchase the capital good at the rate $I(t)$ at the competitive and constant price $c > 0$. For simplicity, we assume that the firm does not discount its profit flow, which is given by $\pi(K(t), I(t); c, p) \stackrel{\text{def}}{=} pK(t) - cI(t)$. Also, for simplicity, we assume that capital does not depreciate, so that the capital stock accumulates according to the differential equation $\dot{K}(t) = I(t)$. The initial capital stock $K(0) = K_0 > 0$ is given, as is the planning horizon $[0, T]$, but the terminal stock of capital $K(T) = K_T$ is chosen by the firm. The irreversibility of the investment rate is captured by a nonnegativity constraint on it, that is, $I(t) \geq 0$. We also assume that the firm cannot borrow to finance its purchases of the capital stock, thereby implying that all investment expenditures must come from the revenue generated from the sale of the good produced. As a result, another constraint on the firm's behavior is the nonnegativity of its profit flow at each date in the planning horizon, that is, $pK(t) - cI(t) \geq 0$. Putting all of this information together, the control problem to be solved by the firm in order to determine its optimal investment rate is

$$\max_{I(\cdot), K_T} \int_0^T [pK(t) - cI(t)]\, dt$$

$$\text{s.t.} \quad \dot{K}(t) = I(t), \ K(0) = K_0, \ K(T) = K_T,$$

$$h^1(t, K(t), I(t)) \stackrel{\text{def}}{=} I(t) \geq 0,$$

$$h^2(t, K(t), I(t)) \stackrel{\text{def}}{=} pK(t) - cI(t) \geq 0.$$

Because the problem is linear in the investment rate, we anticipate that the solution could be piecewise continuous in t. Finally, we assume that $pT > c$. This asserts that total revenue generated from one unit of capital over the entire planning horizon exceeds the cost of purchasing it. As one might expect, without this assumption, the firm would not find investment profitable and thus would essentially cease to operate. To simplify notation, let us define $\beta \stackrel{\text{def}}{=} (c, p, K_0, T)$ as the parameter vector.

Define the Hamiltonian as $H(K, I, \lambda; c, p) \stackrel{\text{def}}{=} pK - cI + \lambda I$ and the Lagrangian as

$$L(K, I, \lambda, \mu_1, \mu_2; c, p) \stackrel{\text{def}}{=} H(K, I, \lambda; c, p) + \mu_1 I + \mu_2[pK - cI].$$

The necessary conditions as dictated by Theorem 6.1 are

$$L_I(K, I, \lambda, \mu_1, \mu_2; c, p) = -c + \lambda + \mu_1 - c\mu_2 = 0, \tag{6}$$

$$L_{\mu_1}(K, I, \lambda, \mu_1, \mu_2; c, p) = I \geq 0,\ \mu_1 \geq 0,\ \mu_1 L_{\mu_1}(K, I, \lambda, \mu_1, \mu_2; c, p) = 0, \tag{7}$$

$$L_{\mu_2}(K, I, \lambda, \mu_1, \mu_2; c, p) = pK - cI \geq 0,\ \mu_2 \geq 0,$$

$$\mu_2 L_{\mu_2}(K, I, \lambda, \mu_1, \mu_2; c, p) = 0, \tag{8}$$

$$\dot{\lambda} = -L_K(K, I, \lambda, \mu_1, \mu_2; c, p) = -p - p\mu_2,\ \lambda(T) = 0, \tag{9}$$

$$\dot{K} = L_\lambda(K, I, \lambda, \mu_1, \mu_2; c, p) = I,\ K(0) = K_0. \tag{10}$$

Note that because K_T is a decision variable, we have employed the terminal transversality condition $\lambda(T) = 0$. Before trying to solve the control problem, let's first establish two preliminary results that will be of value in solving it.

First, seeing as $\mu_2 \geq 0$ from Eq. (8) and $p > 0$ by assumption, inspection of Eq. (9) shows that $\dot{\lambda}(t) < 0\, \forall\, t \in [0, T]$. Moreover, because $\lambda(T) = 0$ from Eq. (9), the prior conclusion implies that $\lambda(t) > 0\, \forall\, t \in [0, T)$. Second, all admissible values of the capital stock are positive for the entire planning period, that is, $K(t) > 0\, \forall\, t \in [0, T]$. This follows from the facts that $K(0) = K_0 > 0$, $I(t) \geq 0\, \forall\, t \in [0, T]$, and $\dot{K} = I$. You are asked to provide a more formal proof of this result in a mental exercise.

We can now show that the rank constraint qualification is satisfied for all admissible pairs. To do so, we first establish that, at most, only one of the two constraints can bind at any time $t \in [0, T]$ for all admissible pairs. If the first constraint $h^1(t, K(t), I(t)) \stackrel{\text{def}}{=} I(t) \geq 0$ binds at time $\bar{t} \in [0, T]$, then $I(\bar{t}) = 0$. But if $I(\bar{t}) = 0$, then $h^2(\bar{t}, K(\bar{t}), I(\bar{t})) \stackrel{\text{def}}{=} pK(\bar{t}) - cI(\bar{t}) = pK(\bar{t}) > 0$ because $K(t) > 0\, \forall\, t \in [0, T]$; hence the second constraint isn't binding when the first one is. By the same token, if the second constraint $h^2(t, K(t), I(t)) \stackrel{\text{def}}{=} pK(t) - cI(t) \geq 0$ binds at some time $\tilde{t} \in [0, T]$, then $I(\tilde{t}) = pc^{-1}K(\tilde{t}) > 0$ because $K(t) > 0\, \forall\, t \in [0, T]$. This therefore implies that $h^1(\tilde{t}, K(\tilde{t}), I(\tilde{t})) \stackrel{\text{def}}{=} I(\tilde{t}) > 0$; thus the first constraint isn't binding when the second one is. As a result, at most one constraint binds at any time $t \in [0, T]$, just as we intended to show. Consequently, the index set $\iota(t, K(t), I(t)) \stackrel{\text{def}}{=} \{k : h^k(t, K(t), I(t)) = 0,\ k = 1, 2\}$ contains at most one element for all admissible function pairs $(K(\cdot), I(\cdot))$, that is to say, $\text{card}(\iota(t, K(t), I(t))) \leq 1$ for all admissible function pairs $(K(\cdot), I(\cdot))$.

Now if the first constraint binds, then $\text{card}(\iota(t, K(t), I(t))) = 1$ and the relevant Jacobian matrix is given by

$$\left[\frac{\partial h^k}{\partial u_m}(t, \mathbf{x}(t), \mathbf{u}(t))\right]_{\substack{k\in\iota(t, \mathbf{x}(t), \mathbf{u}(t)) \\ m=1, 2, \ldots, M}} = \frac{\partial h^1}{\partial I}(t, K(t), I(t)) = 1,$$

which has rank one for all admissible values of the capital stock and investment rate. Similarly, if instead the second constraint binds, then $\text{card}(\iota(t, K(t), I(t))) = 1$ and the relevant Jacobian matrix is

$$\left[\frac{\partial h^k}{\partial u_m}(t, \mathbf{x}(t), \mathbf{u}(t))\right]_{\substack{k\in\iota(t, \mathbf{x}(t), \mathbf{u}(t)) \\ m=1, 2, \ldots, M}} = \frac{\partial h^2}{\partial I}(t, K(t), I(t)) = -c,$$

which also has rank one for all admissible values of the capital stock and investment rate. We may conclude, therefore, that the rank constraint qualification is satisfied for all admissible values of the capital stock and investment rate because the rank of the relevant Jacobian matrix is equal to $\text{card}(\iota(t, K(t), I(t)))$ for all admissible values of the capital stock and investment rate, just as claimed.

Let's now establish that an interior solution, that is, one in which *neither* of the constraints are binding, can only occur for an instant, if at all. In other words, we will show that an interior solution cannot hold for an interval of time. To that end, assume that an interior solution exists for a finite interval of time. This implies, via Eqs. (7) and (8), that $\mu_1 = 0$ and $\mu_2 = 0$. In turn, Eq. (6) reduces to $\lambda(t) = c$, a positive constant. This, however, cannot hold for an interval of time because $\dot{\lambda}(t) < 0 \, \forall \, t \in [0, T]$, as noted above. Thus $\lambda(t) = c$ can only hold for an instant, if at all. Consequently, an interior solution of the problem, if one exists, can only occur for an instant of time.

Let's now make a conjecture about the form (or structure) of the solution to the necessary conditions (6) through (10), and then seek to verify that it solves them. To come up with a plausible conjecture, first recall that we showed an interior solution for the investment rate can only hold for an instant. Hence, we conjecture that the solution for the investment rate is of the bang-bang flavor. Next, inspection of the objective functional yields the conclusion that a larger capital stock, ceteris paribus, furnishes higher profit flow and hence wealth. With all else the same, therefore, the firm would seemingly like to build up its capital stock as fast as possible inasmuch as this would appear to generate the greatest wealth. These observations lead to the following conjecture about the investment rate:

$$I(t) = \begin{cases} pc^{-1}K(t) \; \forall \, t \in [0, s] \\ 0 \qquad\qquad \forall \, t \in (s, T], \end{cases} \tag{11}$$

where $s \in (0, T)$ is the switching time, which is to be determined.

To begin verification of the conjecture in Eq. (11), we assume that $\mu_2(t) > 0 \, \forall \, t \in [0, s]$. From Eq. (8), specifically $\mu_2 L_{\mu_2}(K, I, \lambda, \mu_1, \mu_2; c, p) = \mu_2[pK - cI] = 0$, it follows that $I = pc^{-1}K$, which is the first part of the conjecture about the investment rate given in Eq. (11). Because $K(t) > 0 \, \forall \, t \in [0, T]$, as noted above, $I = pc^{-1}K > 0$ too, which implies by way of Eq. (7) that $\mu_1(t) = 0 \, \forall \, t \in [0, s]$. Using $I = pc^{-1}K$, the state equation (10) becomes $\dot{K} = pc^{-1}K$. Integrating the state equation using the integrating factor $\exp[-pc^{-1}t]$ and the initial condition $K(0) = K_0$ produces $K_1^*(t; \boldsymbol{\beta}) = K_0 e^{pc^{-1}t} > 0$ as the specific solution for the capital stock, where the subscript 1 indicates that this solution corresponds to the first or initial time interval $[0, s]$. Substituting $K_1^*(t; \boldsymbol{\beta}) = K_0 e^{pc^{-1}t}$ into $I = pc^{-1}K$ yields the specific solution for the investment rate, namely, $I_1^*(t; \boldsymbol{\beta}) = pc^{-1}K_0 e^{pc^{-1}t} > 0$. To determine the shadow value of the capital stock, substitute $\mu_1(t) = 0 \, \forall \, t \in [0, s]$ into Eq. (6) to find that $1 + \mu_2 = \lambda c^{-1}$. Substituting this result into the costate equation (9) gives $\dot{\lambda} = -pc^{-1}\lambda$, which in light of the solution of the state equation integrates to $\lambda_1(t; \boldsymbol{\beta}) = \bar{\lambda} e^{-pc^{-1}t}$, where $\bar{\lambda}$ is a constant of integration and (again) the subscript 1 indicates that this solution corresponds to the time interval $[0, s]$. Finally, substituting $\lambda_1(t; \boldsymbol{\beta}) = \bar{\lambda} e^{-pc^{-1}t}$ into $1 + \mu_2 = \lambda c^{-1}$ yields the time path of the second Lagrange multiplier $\mu_2(t; \boldsymbol{\beta}) = c^{-1}\bar{\lambda} e^{-pc^{-1}t} - 1$. This completes the determination of the solution of the necessary conditions for the time interval $[0, s]$. Note, however, that we have not yet determined the constant $\bar{\lambda}$ or the switching time s.

To determine the solution for the second or latter time interval $(s, T]$, we assume that $\mu_1(t) > 0 \, \forall \, t \in (s, T]$. Using this assumption and the fact that $\mu_1 I = 0$ from Eq. (7) implies that $I_2^*(t; \boldsymbol{\beta}) = 0 \, \forall \, t \in (s, T]$, where the subscript 2 indicates that this solution corresponds to the second time interval $(s, T]$. This conclusion verifies the second part of the conjecture about the investment rate given in Eq. (11). This solution implies that the state equation (10) takes the form $\dot{K} = 0$, which has a constant solution, say, $K_2^*(t; \boldsymbol{\beta}) = \bar{K}$, where $\bar{K}$ is a constant of integration to be determined. Because $K(t) > 0 \, \forall \, t \in [0, T]$ and $I_2^*(t; \boldsymbol{\beta}) = 0 \, \forall \, t \in (s, T]$, we have $\mu_2 pK = 0$ from Eq. (8), which implies that $\mu_2(t) = 0 \, \forall \, t \in (s, T]$. This, in turn, implies that the costate equation (9) reduces to $\dot{\lambda} = -p$. Integrating this differential equation with the aid of the transversality condition $\lambda(T) = 0$ gives $\lambda_2(t; \boldsymbol{\beta}) = p[T - t]$ as the specific solution. Finally, because $\mu_2(t) = 0 \, \forall \, t \in (s, T]$ the necessary condition (6) reduces to $-c + \lambda + \mu_1 = 0$, thereby yielding $\mu_1(t; \boldsymbol{\beta}) = c - p[T - t]$ as the solution for the first Lagrange multiplier. This completes the determination of the solution of the necessary conditions for the second time interval $(s, T]$. Note, however, that we have not yet determined the constant $\bar{K}$.

To complete the verification of the conjecture, we must determine the two constants of integration $\bar{K}$ and $\bar{\lambda}$, as well as the switching time s. Let's begin with the switching time s. To that end, recall that an interior solution holds only for an instant. Given that the conjectured solution (11) is bang-bang, the only time at which an interior solution holds is at the switching time s, precisely when the investment rate jumps from its upper bound to its lower bound. Thus at time $t = s$, an interior solution is equivalent to $\mu_1(s) = \mu_2(s) = 0$ by Eqs. (7) and (8). Using this observation in Eq. (6) implies that $\lambda_2(s; \boldsymbol{\beta}) = p[T - s] = c$, which when solved for the switching time s gives $s = s^*(\boldsymbol{\beta}) \stackrel{\text{def}}{=} T - cp^{-1}$. Note that the assumption $pT > c$ implies, and is implied by, a switching time in the open interval $(0, T)$. In other words, the assumption $pT > c$ is necessary and sufficient for a bang-bang solution to the control problem. To find the value of $\bar{\lambda}$, remember that Theorem 6.1 asserts that the costate function is a piecewise smooth and thus continuous function of t. This means that at $t = s$, the value of the costate variable from the interval $[0, s]$ must equal the value of the costate variable from the interval $(s, T]$. That is, $\lambda_1(s; \boldsymbol{\beta}) = \lambda_2(s; \boldsymbol{\beta})$, or $\bar{\lambda}e^{-pc^{-1}s} = p[T - s]$. Substituting $s = s^*(\boldsymbol{\beta}) \stackrel{\text{def}}{=} T - cp^{-1}$ in the latter equation and solving for $\bar{\lambda}$ gives $\bar{\lambda} = ce^{pc^{-1}T-1}$. Finally, because the state function is piecewise smooth and hence continuous by the definition of admissibility, we similarly have that $K_1^*(s; \boldsymbol{\beta}) = K_2^*(s; \boldsymbol{\beta})$, or $\bar{K} = K_0 e^{pc^{-1}s}$. Substituting $s = s^*(\boldsymbol{\beta}) \stackrel{\text{def}}{=} T - cp^{-1}$ in the latter equation yields $\bar{K} = K_0 e^{pc^{-1}T-1}$.

Having determined all the constants of integration and the switching time, we restate our solution of the necessary conditions for ease of reference:

$$K^*(t; \boldsymbol{\beta}) = \begin{cases} K_0 e^{pc^{-1}t} & \forall\, t \in [0, s] \\ K_0 e^{pc^{-1}T-1} & \forall\, t \in (s, T], \end{cases} \tag{12}$$

$$I^*(t; \boldsymbol{\beta}) = \begin{cases} pc^{-1} K_0 e^{pc^{-1}t} & \forall\, t \in [0, s] \\ 0 & \forall\, t \in (s, T], \end{cases} \tag{13}$$

$$\lambda(t; \boldsymbol{\beta}) = \begin{cases} ce^{pc^{-1}[T-t]-1} & \forall\, t \in [0, s] \\ p[T - t] & \forall\, t \in (s, T], \end{cases} \tag{14}$$

$$\mu_1(t; \boldsymbol{\beta}) = \begin{cases} 0 & \forall\, t \in [0, s] \\ c - p[T - t] & \forall\, t \in (s, T], \end{cases} \tag{15}$$

$$\mu_2(t; \boldsymbol{\beta}) = \begin{cases} e^{pc^{-1}[T-t]-1} - 1 & \forall\, t \in [0, s] \\ 0 & \forall\, t \in (s, T], \end{cases} \tag{16}$$

where $s = s^*(\boldsymbol{\beta}) \stackrel{\text{def}}{=} T - cp^{-1}$ is the switching time. Observe that the solutions for the Lagrange multipliers are continuous functions of t, even though Theorem 6.1 permits them to be but piecewise continuous functions of t. We leave formal verification of this fact for a mental exercise.

To close out this example, we derive and then discuss the comparative dynamics of an increase in the output price p. Differentiating Eqs. (12) through (14) yields

$$\frac{\partial K^*(t; \boldsymbol{\beta})}{\partial p} = \begin{cases} c^{-1} t K_0 e^{pc^{-1}t} > 0 & \forall\, t \in [0, s] \\ c^{-1} T K_0 e^{pc^{-1}T-1} > 0 & \forall\, t \in (s, T], \end{cases} \tag{17}$$

$$\frac{\partial I^*(t;\beta)}{\partial p} = \begin{cases} c^{-1}K_0 e^{pc^{-1}t}[1 + pc^{-1}t] > 0 & \forall t \in [0, s] \\ 0 & \forall t \in (s, T], \end{cases} \tag{18}$$

$$\frac{\partial \lambda(t;\beta)}{\partial p} = \begin{cases} [T - t]e^{pc^{-1}[T-t]-1} > 0 & \forall t \in [0, s] \\ [T - t] \geq 0 & \forall t \in (s, T]. \end{cases} \tag{19}$$

These computations show that an increase in the price of the firm's product results in the investment rate, capital stock, and shadow value of the capital stock being higher throughout the planning horizon. The higher capital stock is a result of the higher maximum rate of investment in the interval $[0, s]$ and the lengthening of that interval implied by the delay in the switching time, that is, $\partial s^*(\beta)/\partial p = cp^{-2} > 0$. Given that the final good has gone up in value, so too has the shadow value of the capital stock, since capital is the only input used to produce the good.

In wrapping up this example, observe that the comparative dynamics at time $t = s^*(\beta)$ are a little bit more complicated. The reason is that there are two effects resulting from an increase in the output price, namely, the *explicit* or *direct effect* given by Eqs. (17) through (19), and an *indirect effect* given by the chain rule. For example, for the capital stock, the indirect effect is given by

$$\dot{K}^*(s^*(\beta);\beta)\frac{\partial s^*(\beta)}{\partial p} = \left[pc^{-1}K_0 e^{pc^{-1}s^*(\beta)}\right]cp^{-2} > 0.$$

In other words, the *total effect* of an increase in the output price on the capital stock at time $t = s^*(\beta)$ is given by the chain rule as

$$\frac{\partial K^*(s^*(\beta);\beta)}{\partial p} + \dot{K}^*(s^*(\beta);\beta)\frac{\partial s^*(\beta)}{\partial p} = c^{-1}s^*(\beta)K_0 e^{pc^{-1}s^*(\beta)}$$
$$+ \left[pc^{-1}K_0 e^{pc^{-1}s^*(\beta)}\right]cp^{-2} > 0.$$

We leave the remaining comparative dynamics for a mental exercise.

Let's now state and prove a generalization of the Mangasarian sufficiency theorem we have seen in simpler forms in earlier chapters.

Theorem 6.2 (Mangasarian Sufficient Conditions, Mixed Constraints): *Let* $(\mathbf{z}(t), \mathbf{v}(t))$ *be an admissible pair for problem (1). Suppose that* $(\mathbf{z}(t), \mathbf{v}(t))$ *satisfies the necessary conditions of Theorem 6.1 for problem (1) with costate vector* $\boldsymbol{\lambda}(t)$ *and Lagrange multiplier vector* $\boldsymbol{\mu}(t)$*, and let* $L(t, \mathbf{x}, \mathbf{u}, \boldsymbol{\lambda}, \boldsymbol{\mu}) \stackrel{\text{def}}{=} f(t, \mathbf{x}, \mathbf{u}) + \boldsymbol{\lambda}'\mathbf{g}(t, \mathbf{x}, \mathbf{u}) + \boldsymbol{\mu}'\mathbf{h}(t, \mathbf{x}, \mathbf{u})$ *be the value of the Lagrangian function. If* $L(\cdot)$ *is a concave function of* $(\mathbf{x}, \mathbf{u})\ \forall t \in [t_0, t_1]$ *over an open convex set containing all the admissible values of* $(\mathbf{x}(\cdot), \mathbf{u}(\cdot))$ *when the costate vector is* $\boldsymbol{\lambda}(t)$ *and Lagrange multiplier vector is* $\boldsymbol{\mu}(t)$*, then* $\mathbf{v}(t)$ *is an optimal control and* $(\mathbf{z}(t), \mathbf{v}(t))$ *yields the global maximum of* $J[\cdot]$*. If* $L(\cdot)$ *is a strictly concave function under the same conditions, then* $(\mathbf{z}(t), \mathbf{v}(t))$ *yields the unique global maximum of* $J[\cdot]$.

Proof: Let $(\mathbf{x}(t), \mathbf{u}(t))$ be any admissible pair. By hypothesis, $L(\cdot)$ is a $C^{(1)}$ concave function of $(\mathbf{x}, \mathbf{u})\,\forall\, t \in [t_0, t_1]$. It therefore follows from Theorem 21.3 in Simon and Blume (1994) that

$$\begin{aligned} L(t, \mathbf{x}(t), \mathbf{u}(t), \boldsymbol{\lambda}(t), \boldsymbol{\mu}(t)) &\leq L(t, \mathbf{z}(t), \mathbf{v}(t), \boldsymbol{\lambda}(t), \boldsymbol{\mu}(t)) \\ &\quad + L_{\mathbf{x}}(t, \mathbf{z}(t), \mathbf{v}(t), \boldsymbol{\lambda}(t), \boldsymbol{\mu}(t))\,[\mathbf{x}(t) - \mathbf{z}(t)] \\ &\quad + L_{\mathbf{u}}(t, \mathbf{z}(t), \mathbf{v}(t), \boldsymbol{\lambda}(t), \boldsymbol{\mu}(t))\,[\mathbf{u}(t) - \mathbf{v}(t)], \end{aligned} \tag{20}$$

for every $t \in [t_0, t_1]$. Using the fact that $L_{\mathbf{u}}(t, \mathbf{z}(t), \mathbf{v}(t), \boldsymbol{\lambda}(t), \boldsymbol{\mu}(t)) \equiv \mathbf{0}'_M$ by Theorem 6.1, and then integrating both sides of the resulting reduced inequality over the interval $[t_0, t_1]$ using the definitions of $L(\cdot)$ and $J[\cdot]$, yields

$$\begin{aligned} J[\mathbf{x}(\cdot), \mathbf{u}(\cdot)] \leq J[\mathbf{z}(\cdot), \mathbf{v}(\cdot)] &+ \int_{t_0}^{t_1} \boldsymbol{\lambda}(t)'\,[\mathbf{g}(t, \mathbf{z}(t), \mathbf{v}(t)) - \mathbf{g}(t, \mathbf{x}(t), \mathbf{u}(t))]\,dt \\ &+ \int_{t_0}^{t_1} \boldsymbol{\mu}(t)'\,[\mathbf{h}(t, \mathbf{z}(t), \mathbf{v}(t)) - \mathbf{h}(t, \mathbf{x}(t), \mathbf{u}(t))]\,dt \\ &+ \int_{t_0}^{t_1} L_{\mathbf{x}}(t, \mathbf{z}(t), \mathbf{v}(t), \boldsymbol{\lambda}(t), \boldsymbol{\mu}(t))\,[\mathbf{x}(t) - \mathbf{z}(t)]\,dt. \end{aligned} \tag{21}$$

By admissibility, $\dot{\mathbf{z}}(t) \equiv \mathbf{g}(t, \mathbf{z}(t), \mathbf{v}(t))$ and $\dot{\mathbf{x}}(t) \equiv \mathbf{g}(t, \mathbf{x}(t), \mathbf{u}(t))$ for every $t \in [t_0, t_1]$, whereas Theorem 6.1 implies that $\dot{\boldsymbol{\lambda}}(t)' \equiv -L_{\mathbf{x}}(t, \mathbf{z}(t), \mathbf{v}(t), \boldsymbol{\lambda}(t), \boldsymbol{\mu}(t))$ for every $t \in [t_0, t_1]$. Substituting these three results in Eq. (21) gives

$$\begin{aligned} J[\mathbf{x}(\cdot), \mathbf{u}(\cdot)] \leq J[\mathbf{z}(\cdot), \mathbf{v}(\cdot)] &+ \int_{t_0}^{t_1} [\boldsymbol{\lambda}(t)'[\dot{\mathbf{z}}(t) - \dot{\mathbf{x}}(t)] + \dot{\boldsymbol{\lambda}}(t)'[\mathbf{z}(t) - \mathbf{x}(t)]]\,dt \\ &+ \int_{t_0}^{t_1} \boldsymbol{\mu}(t)'\,[\mathbf{h}(t, \mathbf{z}(t), \mathbf{v}(t)) - \mathbf{h}(t, \mathbf{x}(t), \mathbf{u}(t))]\,dt. \end{aligned} \tag{22}$$

Moreover, Theorem 6.1 also implies that (i) $\mu_k(t)h^k(t, \mathbf{z}(t), \mathbf{v}(t)) \equiv 0$ for $k = 1, 2, \ldots, K$ because $\mu_k(t)h^k(t, \mathbf{z}(t), \mathbf{v}(t)) \equiv 0$ for $k = 1, 2, \ldots, K'$ and $h^k(t, \mathbf{z}(t), \mathbf{v}(t)) \equiv 0$ for $k = K'+1, K'+2, \ldots, K$, (ii) $\mu_k(t)h^k(t, \mathbf{x}(t), \mathbf{u}(t)) \geq 0$ for $k = 1, 2, \ldots, K'$ by virtue of $\mu_k(t) \geq 0$ and $h^k(t, \mathbf{x}(t), \mathbf{u}(t)) \geq 0$ for $k = 1, 2, \ldots, K'$, and (iii) $\mu_k(t)h^k(t, \mathbf{x}(t), \mathbf{u}(t)) \equiv 0$ for $k = K'+1, K'+2, \ldots, K$ on account of $h^k(t, \mathbf{x}(t), \mathbf{u}(t)) \equiv 0$ for $k = K'+1, K'+2, \ldots, K$. These three implications of

Theorem 6.1 therefore imply that

$$\int_{t_0}^{t_1} \boldsymbol{\mu}(t)' \left[\mathbf{h}(t, \mathbf{z}(t), \mathbf{v}(t)) - \mathbf{h}(t, \mathbf{x}(t), \mathbf{u}(t))\right] dt \leq 0. \tag{23}$$

Using the inequality in Eq. (23) permits Eq. (22) to be rewritten in the reduced form

$$J[\mathbf{x}(\cdot), \mathbf{u}(\cdot)] \leq J[\mathbf{z}(\cdot), \mathbf{v}(\cdot)] + \int_{t_0}^{t_1} [\boldsymbol{\lambda}(t)'[\dot{\mathbf{z}}(t) - \dot{\mathbf{x}}(t)] + \dot{\boldsymbol{\lambda}}(t)'[\mathbf{z}(t) - \mathbf{x}(t)]]\, dt. \tag{24}$$

To wrap up the proof, simply note that

$$\begin{aligned}\frac{d}{dt}[\boldsymbol{\lambda}(t)'[\mathbf{z}(t) - \mathbf{x}(t)]] &= \boldsymbol{\lambda}(t)'\,[\dot{\mathbf{z}}(t) - \dot{\mathbf{x}}(t)] + [\mathbf{z}(t) - \mathbf{x}(t)]'\,\dot{\boldsymbol{\lambda}}(t)\\ &= \boldsymbol{\lambda}(t)'\,[\dot{\mathbf{z}}(t) - \dot{\mathbf{x}}(t)] + \dot{\boldsymbol{\lambda}}(t)'[\mathbf{z}(t) - \mathbf{x}(t)],\end{aligned}$$

and substitute this result into Eq. (24) to get

$$\begin{aligned}J[\mathbf{x}(\cdot), \mathbf{u}(\cdot)] &\leq J[\mathbf{z}(\cdot), \mathbf{v}(\cdot)] + \int_{t_0}^{t_1} \frac{d}{dt}[\boldsymbol{\lambda}(t)'[\mathbf{z}(t) - \mathbf{x}(t)]]\, dt\\ &= J[\mathbf{z}(\cdot), \mathbf{v}(\cdot)] + \boldsymbol{\lambda}(t)'\,[\mathbf{z}(t) - \mathbf{x}(t)]\Big|_{t=t_0}^{t=t_1}\\ &= J[\mathbf{z}(\cdot), \mathbf{v}(\cdot)],\end{aligned}$$

because by admissibility, we have $\mathbf{x}(t_0) = \mathbf{x}_0$, $\mathbf{z}(t_0) = \mathbf{x}_0$, $\mathbf{x}(t_1) = \mathbf{x}_1$, and $\mathbf{z}(t_1) = \mathbf{x}_1$. We have thus shown that $J[\mathbf{x}(\cdot), \mathbf{u}(\cdot)] \leq J[\mathbf{z}(\cdot), \mathbf{v}(\cdot)]$ for all admissible functions $(\mathbf{x}(\cdot), \mathbf{u}(\cdot))$, just as we wished to. If $L(\cdot)$ is a strictly concave function of $(\mathbf{x}, \mathbf{u})\,\forall\, t \in [t_0, t_1]$, then the inequality in Eq. (20) becomes strict if either $\mathbf{x}(t) \neq \mathbf{z}(t)$ or $\mathbf{u}(t) \neq \mathbf{v}(t)$ for some $t \in [t_0, t_1]$. Then $J[\mathbf{x}(\cdot), \mathbf{u}(\cdot)] < J[\mathbf{z}(\cdot), \mathbf{v}(\cdot)]$ follows. This shows that any admissible pair of functions $(\mathbf{x}(\cdot), \mathbf{u}(\cdot))$ that are not identically equal to $(\mathbf{z}(\cdot), \mathbf{v}(\cdot))$ are suboptimal. Q.E.D.

An important feature of this sufficiency theorem is that the rank constraint qualification is *not* required, in sharp contrast to the necessary conditions of Theorem 6.1. It is also noteworthy that this theorem can be strengthened to give an Arrow-type sufficiency result. We will pursue this very shortly.

The ensuing lemma gives sufficient conditions for the Lagrangian of problem (1) to be a concave function of $(\mathbf{x}, \mathbf{u})\,\forall\, t \in [t_0, t_1]$. Its proof is left for a mental exercise.

Lemma 6.1: *The Lagrangian function $L(\cdot)$ defined by*

$$L(t, \mathbf{x}, \mathbf{u}, \boldsymbol{\lambda}, \boldsymbol{\mu}) \stackrel{\text{def}}{=} f(t, \mathbf{x}, \mathbf{u}) + \boldsymbol{\lambda}'\mathbf{g}(t, \mathbf{x}, \mathbf{u}) + \boldsymbol{\mu}'\mathbf{h}(t, \mathbf{x}, \mathbf{u})$$

for problem (1) is a concave function of $(\mathbf{x}, \mathbf{u})\,\forall\, t \in [t_0, t_1]$ *if the following conditions hold:*

(i) $f(\cdot)$ *is concave in* $(\mathbf{x}, \mathbf{u})\,\forall\, t \in [t_0, t_1]$,
(ii) $\lambda_n g^n(\cdot), n = 1, 2, \ldots, N$, *is concave in* $(\mathbf{x}, \mathbf{u})\,\forall\, t \in [t_0, t_1]$,
(iii) $\mu_k h^k(\cdot), k = 1, 2, \ldots, K'$, *is concave in* $(\mathbf{x}, \mathbf{u})\,\forall\, t \in [t_0, t_1]$,
(iv) $\mu_k h^k(\cdot), k = K' + 1, K' + 2, \ldots, K$, *is concave in* $(\mathbf{x}, \mathbf{u})\,\forall\, t \in [t_0, t_1]$.

A few remarks on the lemma are in order. First, it should be clear that condition (ii) holds if $g^n(\cdot)$ is concave in $(\mathbf{x}, \mathbf{u})\,\forall\, t \in [t_0, t_1]$ and $\lambda_n(t) \geq 0, n = 1, 2, \ldots, N$, or if $g^n(\cdot)$ is convex in $(\mathbf{x}, \mathbf{u})\,\forall\, t \in [t_0, t_1]$ and $\lambda_n(t) \leq 0, n = 1, 2, \ldots, N$. Second, no such remark is required for condition (iii) because $\mu_k(t) \geq 0$ for $k = 1, 2, \ldots, K'$. Third, condition (iv) holds if $h^k(\cdot)$ is concave in $(\mathbf{x}, \mathbf{u})\,\forall\, t \in [t_0, t_1]$ and $\mu_k(t) \geq 0$, $k = K' + 1, K' + 2, \ldots, K$, or if $h^k(\cdot)$ is convex in $(\mathbf{x}, \mathbf{u})\,\forall\, t \in [t_0, t_1]$ and $\mu_k(t) \leq 0, k = K' + 1, K' + 2, \ldots, K$.

Let's pause briefly so that we can see Theorem 6.2 in action. Specifically, we will use it to determine if the solution of the necessary conditions in Example 6.1 is a solution to the posed control problem.

Example 6.2: Recall that the Lagrangian for the control problem of Example 6.1 is given by

$$L(K, I, \lambda, \mu_1, \mu_2; c, p) \stackrel{\text{def}}{=} pK - cI + \lambda I + \mu_1 I + \mu_2[pK - cI].$$

The Hessian matrix of the Lagrangian with respect to the capital stock and investment rate is

$$\begin{bmatrix} L_{II} & L_{IK} \\ L_{KI} & L_{KK} \end{bmatrix} = \begin{bmatrix} 0 & 0 \\ 0 & 0 \end{bmatrix},$$

which is negative semidefinite. Hence $L(\cdot)$ is a concave function of (K, I) for all $t \in [0, T]$. Thus the solution of the necessary conditions is a solution of the posed control problem. The same conclusion is also arrived at by simply observing that $L(\cdot)$ is a linear and thus a concave function of (K, I) for all $t \in [0, T]$. Note also that because $L(\cdot)$ is a linear function of (K, I), assumptions (A.1) through (A.5) are satisfied.

Just as we did in Chapter 3, we now provide an alternative and equivalent statement of the necessary conditions of Theorem 6.1 in terms of the maximized Hamiltonian. This permits us to introduce a generalized version of the Arrow-type sufficiency theorem alluded to above. First, we introduce the definition of the maximized Hamiltonian for the general control problem under consideration in this chapter.

Definition 6.2: For the control problem (1), the *maximized Hamiltonian* $M(\cdot)$ is defined as

$$M(t, \mathbf{x}, \boldsymbol{\lambda}) \stackrel{\text{def}}{=} \max_{\mathbf{u}}\{H(t, \mathbf{x}, \mathbf{u}, \boldsymbol{\lambda}) \text{ s.t. } u \in U(t, \mathbf{x})\}, \tag{25}$$

where $U(t, \mathbf{x}) \stackrel{\text{def}}{=} \{\mathbf{u} : h^k(t, \mathbf{x}, \mathbf{u}) \geq 0,\ k = 1, \ldots, K', h^k(t, \mathbf{x}, \mathbf{u}) = 0,\ k = K' + 1, \ldots, K\}$ is the control set and $H(t, \mathbf{x}, \mathbf{u}, \boldsymbol{\lambda}) \stackrel{\text{def}}{=} f(t, \mathbf{x}, \mathbf{u}) + \boldsymbol{\lambda}'\mathbf{g}(t, \mathbf{x}, \mathbf{u})$ is the Hamiltonian.

Given that problem (25) is a static constrained optimization problem, the necessary conditions implied by the existence of a maximizing control are a subset of those from Theorem 6.1, to wit,

$$\frac{\partial L}{\partial u_m}(t, \mathbf{x}, \mathbf{u}, \boldsymbol{\lambda}, \boldsymbol{\mu}) = 0, \quad m = 1, 2, \ldots, M,$$

$$\frac{\partial L}{\partial \mu_k}(t, \mathbf{x}, \mathbf{u}, \boldsymbol{\lambda}, \boldsymbol{\mu}) \geq 0,\ \mu_k \geq 0,\ \mu_k \frac{\partial L}{\partial \mu_k}(t, \mathbf{x}, \mathbf{u}, \boldsymbol{\lambda}, \boldsymbol{\mu}) = 0, \quad k = 1, 2, \ldots, K',$$

$$\frac{\partial L}{\partial \mu_k}(t, \mathbf{x}, \mathbf{u}, \boldsymbol{\lambda}, \boldsymbol{\mu}) = 0, \quad k = K' + 1, K' + 2, \ldots, K,$$

where $L(t, \mathbf{x}, \mathbf{u}, \boldsymbol{\lambda}, \boldsymbol{\mu}) \stackrel{\text{def}}{=} f(t, \mathbf{x}, \mathbf{u}) + \boldsymbol{\lambda}'\mathbf{g}(t, \mathbf{x}, \mathbf{u}) + \boldsymbol{\mu}'\mathbf{h}(t, \mathbf{x}, \mathbf{u})$ is the Lagrangian for problem (25) and $\boldsymbol{\mu} \in \Re^K$ is the vector of Lagrange multipliers for the mixed constraints. As remarked earlier, these, in principle, define $\mathbf{u}$ and $\boldsymbol{\mu}$ as functions of time, the state variables, the costate variables, and any parameters of the problem, say, $\mathbf{u} = \hat{\mathbf{u}}(t, \mathbf{x}, \boldsymbol{\lambda})$ and $\boldsymbol{\mu} = \hat{\boldsymbol{\mu}}(t, \mathbf{x}, \boldsymbol{\lambda})$. We acknowledge that $\mathbf{u} = \hat{\mathbf{u}}(t, \mathbf{x}, \boldsymbol{\lambda})$ is the maximizing value of the control variable by using the notation

$$\hat{\mathbf{u}}(t, \mathbf{x}, \boldsymbol{\lambda}) \stackrel{\text{def}}{=} \arg\max_{\mathbf{u}} \{H(t, \mathbf{x}, \mathbf{u}, \boldsymbol{\lambda}) \text{ s.t. } u \in U(t, \mathbf{x})\}.$$

Substituting $\mathbf{u} = \hat{\mathbf{u}}(t, \mathbf{x}, \boldsymbol{\lambda})$ into the Hamiltonian $H(\cdot)$ yields the value of the maximized Hamiltonian $M(\cdot)$, that is,

$$M(t, \mathbf{x}, \boldsymbol{\lambda}) \equiv H(t, \mathbf{x}, \hat{\mathbf{u}}(t, \mathbf{x}, \boldsymbol{\lambda}), \boldsymbol{\lambda}) = f(t, \mathbf{x}, \hat{\mathbf{u}}(t, \mathbf{x}, \boldsymbol{\lambda})) + \boldsymbol{\lambda}' \ \mathbf{g}(t, \mathbf{x}, \hat{\mathbf{u}}(t, \mathbf{x}, \boldsymbol{\lambda})). \tag{26}$$

Equation (26) demonstrates how one would go about constructing the maximized Hamiltonian in practice. Given Definition 6.2, we are now in a position to restate Theorem 6.1 in terms of the maximized Hamiltonian $M(\cdot)$.

Theorem 6.3 (Necessary Conditions, Mixed Constraints): *Let $(\mathbf{z}(t), \mathbf{v}(t))$ be an admissible pair for problem (1), and assume that the rank constraint qualification is satisfied. Then if $(\mathbf{z}(t), \mathbf{v}(t))$ yields the absolute maximum of $J[\cdot]$, it is necessary that there exist a piecewise smooth vector-valued function $\boldsymbol{\lambda}(\cdot) \stackrel{\text{def}}{=} (\lambda_1(\cdot), \lambda_2(\cdot), \ldots, \lambda_N(\cdot))$ and a piecewise continuous vector-valued Lagrange* *multiplier function* $\boldsymbol{\mu}(\cdot) \overset{\text{def}}{=} (\mu_1(\cdot), \mu_2(\cdot), \ldots, \mu_K(\cdot))$, *such that for all* $t \in [t_0, t_1]$,

$$\mathbf{v}(t) = \arg\max_{\mathbf{u}} \{H(t, \mathbf{z}(t), \mathbf{u}, \boldsymbol{\lambda}(t)) \ s.t.\ \mathbf{u} \in U(t, \mathbf{z}(t))\},$$

that is, if

$$M(t, \mathbf{z}(t), \boldsymbol{\lambda}(t)) \overset{\text{def}}{=} \max_{\mathbf{u}} \{H(t, \mathbf{z}(t), \mathbf{u}, \boldsymbol{\lambda}(t)) \ s.t.\ \mathbf{u} \in U(t, \mathbf{z}(t))\},$$

then

$$M(t, \mathbf{z}(t), \boldsymbol{\lambda}(t)) \equiv H(t, \mathbf{z}(t), \mathbf{v}(t), \boldsymbol{\lambda}(t)),$$

or equivalently

$$H(t, \mathbf{z}(t), \mathbf{v}(t), \boldsymbol{\lambda}(t)) \geq H(t, \mathbf{z}(t), \mathbf{u}, \boldsymbol{\lambda}(t)) \, \forall \, \mathbf{u} \in U(t, \mathbf{z}(t)),$$

where

$$U(t, \mathbf{x}(t)) \overset{\text{def}}{=} \{\mathbf{u}(\cdot) : h^k(t, \mathbf{x}(t)\mathbf{u}(t)) \geq 0,\ k = 1, \ldots, K',\ h^k(t, \mathbf{x}(t), \mathbf{u}(t)) = 0,$$
$$k = K' + 1, \ldots, K\}$$

is the control set and $\mathbf{v}(t) \overset{\text{def}}{=} \hat{\mathbf{u}}(t, \mathbf{z}(t), \boldsymbol{\lambda}(t))$. *Because the rank constraint qualification is assumed to hold, the above necessary condition implies that*

$$\frac{\partial L}{\partial u_m}(t, \mathbf{z}(t), \mathbf{v}(t), \boldsymbol{\lambda}(t), \boldsymbol{\mu}(t)) = 0, \quad m = 1, 2, \ldots, M,$$

$$\frac{\partial L}{\partial \mu_k}(t, \mathbf{z}(t), \mathbf{v}(t), \boldsymbol{\lambda}(t), \boldsymbol{\mu}(t)) \geq 0,\ \mu_k(t) \geq 0,$$

$$\mu_k(t)\frac{\partial L}{\partial \mu_k}(t, \mathbf{z}(t), \mathbf{v}(t), \boldsymbol{\lambda}(t), \boldsymbol{\mu}(t)) = 0, \quad k = 1, 2, \ldots, K',$$

$$\frac{\partial L}{\partial \mu_k}(t, \mathbf{z}(t), \mathbf{v}(t), \boldsymbol{\lambda}(t), \boldsymbol{\mu}(t)) = 0, \quad k = K' + 1, K' + 2, \ldots, K,$$

where

$$\begin{aligned} L(t, \mathbf{x}, \mathbf{u}, \boldsymbol{\lambda}, \boldsymbol{\mu}) &\overset{\text{def}}{=} H(t, \mathbf{x}, \mathbf{u}, \boldsymbol{\lambda}) + \boldsymbol{\mu}'\mathbf{h}(t, \mathbf{x}, \mathbf{u}) \\ &= f(t, \mathbf{x}, \mathbf{u}) + \sum_{n=1}^{N} \lambda_n g^n(t, \mathbf{x}, \mathbf{u}) + \sum_{k=1}^{K} \mu_k h^k(t, \mathbf{x}, \mathbf{u}) \end{aligned}$$

is the Lagrangian function. Furthermore, except for the points of discontinuities of $\mathbf{v}(t)$,

$$\dot{z}_n(t) = \frac{\partial M}{\partial \lambda_n}(t, \mathbf{z}(t), \boldsymbol{\lambda}(t)) = g^n(t, \mathbf{z}(t), \mathbf{v}(t)), \quad n = 1, 2, \ldots, N,$$

$$\dot{\lambda}_n(t) = -\frac{\partial M}{\partial x_n}(t, \mathbf{z}(t), \boldsymbol{\lambda}(t)), \quad n = 1, 2, \ldots, N,$$

where the above notation means that the functions are first differentiated with respect to the particular variable and then evaluated at $(t, \mathbf{z}(t), \boldsymbol{\lambda}(t))$.

Notice that the real difference between Theorems 6.1 and 6.3 lies in the statement of the canonical equations. That the two versions are equivalent is a simple matter to demonstrate via the envelope theorem and is therefore left for a mental exercise. Given Theorem 6.3, we can now state the Arrow-type sufficiency theorem. The proof follows that of Theorem 6.2 and so is left for a mental exercise too.

Theorem 6.4 (Arrow Sufficiency Theorem, Mixed Constraints): *Let* $(\mathbf{z}(t), \mathbf{v}(t))$ *be an admissible pair for problem (1). Suppose that* $(\mathbf{z}(t), \mathbf{v}(t))$ *satisfy the necessary conditions of Theorem 6.3 for problem (1) with costate vector* $\boldsymbol{\lambda}(t)$ *and Lagrange multiplier vector* $\boldsymbol{\mu}(t)$*, and let* $M(t, \mathbf{x}, \boldsymbol{\lambda}) \stackrel{\text{def}}{=} \max_{\mathbf{u}}\{H(t, \mathbf{x}, \mathbf{u}, \boldsymbol{\lambda})$ *s.t.* $\mathbf{u} \in U(t, \mathbf{x})\}$ *be the value of the maximized Hamiltonian function. If* $M(\cdot)$ *is a concave function of* $\mathbf{x}\, \forall\, t \in [t_0, t_1]$ *over an open convex set containing all the admissible values of* $\mathbf{x}(\cdot)$ *when the costate vector is* $\boldsymbol{\lambda}(t)$*, then* $\mathbf{v}(t)$ *is an optimal control and* $(\mathbf{z}(t), \mathbf{v}(t))$ *yields the global maximum of* $J[\cdot]$*. If* $M(\cdot)$ *is a strictly concave function of* $\mathbf{x}\, \forall\, t \in [t_0, t_1]$ *under the same conditions, then* $(\mathbf{z}(t), \mathbf{v}(t))$ *yields the unique global maximum of* $J[\cdot]$ *and* $\mathbf{z}(t)$ *is unique, but* $\mathbf{v}(t)$ *is not necessarily unique.*

The Arrow sufficiency theorem replaces the assumption of concavity of the Lagrangian $L(\cdot)$ in $(\mathbf{x}, \mathbf{u})$ from the Mangasarian theorem, with the assumption that the maximized Hamiltonian $M(\cdot)$ is concave in $\mathbf{x}$. Note, however, that checking the curvature properties of a derived function such as $M(\cdot)$ can be more difficult than checking the curvature properties of $L(\cdot)$. By Theorem 3.5, we know that Mangasarian's sufficiency theorem is a *special case* of Arrow's sufficiency theorem. This means that even if $L(\cdot)$ is not concave in $(\mathbf{x}, \mathbf{u})$ it is still possible that $M(\cdot)$ is concave in $\mathbf{x}$, so that Arrow's theorem applies to a larger class of problems.

In Chapter 9, we take up the study of the envelope theorem for optimal control problems. This will (i) permit us to achieve a thorough and complete economic interpretation of the costate vector, (ii) pave the way for the introduction of the primal-dual method of comparative dynamics, and (iii) establish, with relative ease, the numerous transversality conditions that are an integral part of the necessary conditions when the planning horizon and endpoints are decision variables.

Before doing so, however, the next two chapters introduce a class of control problems, scilicet, isoperimetric problems, that are an important class of optimal control problems in several fields of economics. These two chapters may be skipped on a first reading, without loss of continuity.

MENTAL EXERCISES

6.1 In Example 6.1, prove that
   (a) admissible $K(t) > 0\, \forall\, t \in [0, T]$, and
   (b) the Lagrange multipliers are continuous functions of t.

6.2 Derive and economically interpret the comparative dynamics of an increase in c and T in Example 6.1. Do not concern yourself with the Lagrange multipliers.

6.3 Prove Lemma 6.1.

6.4 Prove that Theorem 6.3 is equivalent to Theorem 6.1.

6.5 Prove Theorem 6.4.

6.6 Consider the optimal control problem

$$\min_{u(\cdot),x_T} \int_0^T [x(t) + u(t)]\, dt$$

$$\text{s.t.} \quad \dot{x}(t) = -u(t), \ x(0) = 1, \ x(T) = x_T,$$

$$h^1(t, x(t), u(t)) \stackrel{\text{def}}{=} u(t) \geq 0,$$

$$h^2(t, x(t), u(t)) \stackrel{\text{def}}{=} x(t) - u(t) \geq 0,$$

where $T > 1$.

(a) Show that all admissible solutions satisfy $x(t) > 0 \, \forall\, t \in [0, T]$.
(b) Show that the rank constraint qualification is satisfied for all admissible pairs.
(c) Find a solution to the necessary conditions.
(d) Is the solution of the necessary conditions a solution of the control problem? Show your work and explain.

6.7 Consider the optimal control problem

$$\max_{u(\cdot),x_T} \int_0^T [x(t) - u(t)]dt$$

$$\text{s.t.} \quad \dot{x}(t) = u(t), x(0) = x_0, x(T) = x_T,$$

$$h^1(t, x(t), u(t)) \stackrel{\text{def}}{=} u(t) \geq 0,$$

$$h^2(t, x(t), u(t)) \stackrel{\text{def}}{=} x(t) - u(t) \geq 0.$$

(a) Show that all admissible solutions satisfy $x(t) > 0 \, \forall\, t \in [0, T]$.
(b) Show that the rank constraint qualification is satisfied for all admissible pairs.
(c) Find a solution to the necessary conditions.
(d) Is the solution of the necessary conditions a solution of the control problem? Show your work and explain.

6.8 Show that the *isoperimetric* optimal control problem

$$\max_{\mathbf{u}(\cdot)} J[\mathbf{x}(\cdot), \mathbf{u}(\cdot)] \stackrel{\text{def}}{=} \int_{t_0}^{t_1} f(t, \mathbf{x}(t), \mathbf{u}(t))\, dt$$

$$\text{s.t.} \quad \dot{\mathbf{x}}(t) = \mathbf{g}(t, \mathbf{x}(t), \mathbf{u}(t)), \ \mathbf{x}(t_0) = \mathbf{x}_0, \ \mathbf{x}(t_1) = \mathbf{x}_1,$$

$$\int_{t_0}^{t_1} G^k(t, \mathbf{x}(t), \mathbf{u}(t))\, dt = \gamma_k, \quad k = 1, 2, \ldots, K,$$

can be rewritten as an equivalent mixed constraint optimal control problem. **Hint:** Define a new vector of state variables.

6.9 Solve the optimal control problem

$$\max_{u(\cdot), x_{1/2}} \int_a^{1/2} [-(u(t))^2 - x(t)]\, dt$$

$$\text{s.t.} \quad \dot{x}(t) = -u(t), \ x(a) = 7/4, \ x(1/2) = x_{1/2},$$

$$h^1(t, x(t), u(t)) \stackrel{\text{def}}{=} x(t) - u(t) \geq 0,$$

where $a = -1 - \ln 3$.

6.10 Solve the optimal control problem

$$\max_{u_1(\cdot), u_2(\cdot), x_1} \int_0^1 [u_2(t) - x(t)]\, dt$$

$$\text{s.t.} \quad \dot{x}(t) = u_1(t), \ x(0) = 1/8, \ x(1) = x_1,$$

$$h^1(t, x(t), u_1(t), u_2(t)) \stackrel{\text{def}}{=} u_1(t) \geq 0,$$

$$h^2(t, x(t), u_1(t), u_2(t)) \stackrel{\text{def}}{=} 1 - u_1(t) \geq 0,$$

$$h^3(t, x(t), u_1(t), u_2(t)) \stackrel{\text{def}}{=} x(t) - (u_2(t))^2 \geq 0.$$

Note that there are two control variables and one state variable in this problem.

6.11 Consider the optimal control problem

$$\max_{\mathbf{u}(\cdot)} J[\mathbf{x}(\cdot), \mathbf{u}(\cdot)] \stackrel{\text{def}}{=} \int_{t_0}^{t_1} f(t, \mathbf{x}(t), \mathbf{u}(t))\, dt$$

$$\text{s.t.} \quad \dot{\mathbf{x}}(t) = \mathbf{g}(t, \mathbf{x}(t), \mathbf{u}(t)), \ \mathbf{x}(t_0) = \mathbf{x}_0, \ \mathbf{x}(t_1) = \mathbf{x}_1,$$

$$h^k(t, \mathbf{x}(t), \mathbf{u}(t)) \geq 0, \quad k = 1, 2, \ldots, K',$$

$$h^k(t, \mathbf{x}(t), \mathbf{u}(t)) = 0, \quad k = K' + 1, K' + 2, \ldots, K.$$

Let $(\mathbf{z}(t), \mathbf{v}(t))$ be the optimal pair, $\boldsymbol{\lambda}(t)$ the corresponding value of the costate vector, and $\boldsymbol{\mu}(t)$ the corresponding value of the Lagrange multiplier vector. Define the Hamiltonian as

$$H(t, \mathbf{x}, \mathbf{u}, \boldsymbol{\lambda}) \stackrel{\text{def}}{=} f(t, \mathbf{x}, \mathbf{u}) + \boldsymbol{\lambda}'\mathbf{g}(t, \mathbf{x}, \mathbf{u}) = f(t, \mathbf{x}, \mathbf{u}) + \sum_{n=1}^{N} \lambda_n g^n(t, \mathbf{x}, \mathbf{u}),$$

and the Lagrangian as

$$L(t, \mathbf{x}, \mathbf{u}, \boldsymbol{\lambda}, \boldsymbol{\mu}) \stackrel{\text{def}}{=} H(t, \mathbf{x}, \mathbf{u}, \boldsymbol{\lambda}) + \boldsymbol{\mu}'\mathbf{h}(t, \mathbf{u})$$

$$= f(t, \mathbf{x}, \mathbf{u}) + \sum_{n=1}^{N} \lambda_n g^n(t, \mathbf{x}, \mathbf{u}) + \sum_{k=1}^{K} \mu_k h^k(t, \mathbf{x}, \mathbf{u}).$$

Assume that $f(\cdot) \in C^{(1)}$, $\mathbf{g}(\cdot) \in C^{(1)}$, and $\mathbf{h}(\cdot) \in C^{(1)}$ in $(t, \mathbf{x}, \mathbf{u})$.

(a) Prove that

$$\frac{d}{dt} L(t, \mathbf{z}(t), \mathbf{v}(t), \boldsymbol{\lambda}(t), \boldsymbol{\mu}(t)) = \frac{\partial}{\partial t} L(t, \mathbf{z}(t), \mathbf{v}(t), \boldsymbol{\lambda}(t), \boldsymbol{\mu}(t)).$$

(b) Prove that if the optimal control problem is autonomous, that is, the independent variable t doesn't enter the functions $f(\cdot)$, $\mathbf{g}(\cdot)$, or $\mathbf{h}(\cdot)$ explicitly, that is, $f_t(t, \mathbf{x}, \mathbf{u}) \equiv 0$, $\mathbf{g}_t(t, \mathbf{x}, \mathbf{u}) \equiv \mathbf{0}_N$, and $\mathbf{h}_t(t, \mathbf{u}) \equiv \mathbf{0}_K$, then $L(\cdot)$ is constant along the optimal path.

(c) Prove that

$$\frac{d}{dt} H(t, \mathbf{z}(t), \mathbf{v}(t), \boldsymbol{\lambda}(t)) = \frac{\partial}{\partial t} H(t, \mathbf{z}(t), \mathbf{v}(t), \boldsymbol{\lambda}(t)).$$

Note that this result is *not* the same as that in Mental Exercise 2.31.

(d) Prove that if the optimal control problem is autonomous, then $H(\cdot)$ is constant along the optimal path too.

6.12 *Rational Procrastination.* Here's a typical situation faced by students at universities all across the world. A research paper is assigned by the professor of a class the first day of the term, say, $t = 0$, and is due at the end of the term, say, $T > 0$ hours later. At University of California, Davis, this would mean that the research paper is due in $24 \times 7 \times 10 = 1{,}680$ hours, or 10 weeks, from the present. The total effort required by the typical student to complete the paper is known to be $\varepsilon \in (0, T)$ hours. Define $e(t) \in [0, 1]$ as the proportion of each hour that the student devotes to working on the paper (i.e., research effort), and define $\ell(t) \in [0, 1]$ as the proportion of each hour that the student devotes to leisure activities. It is assumed that the student will complete the term paper by the required date, thereby implying the isoperimetric constraint

$$\int_0^T e(t)dt = \varepsilon.$$

Because each hour is made up entirely of leisure time and research effort, we also have the equality constraint that $e(t) + \ell(t) = 1$ for all $t \in [0, T]$. The instantaneous preferences of the typical student are defined over leisure time, a good, and denoted by $U(\ell)$, where $U(\cdot) \in C^{(2)}$, $U'(\ell) > 0$, and $U''(\ell) < 0$ for all $\ell(t) \in (0, 1)$. We assume that $e(t) \in (0, 1)$ and $\ell(t) \in (0, 1)$ for all $t \in [0, T]$ in an optimal plan, thereby ruling out these constraints from binding. These two assumptions will simplify the analysis considerably. The student is asserted to maximize the present discounted value of utility over the term, subject to completing the research paper. Hence the optimal control problem faced by the typical student can be stated as

$$V(\beta) \stackrel{\text{def}}{=} \max_{e(\cdot),\ell(\cdot)} \int_0^T U(\ell(t))\, e^{-rt}\, dt$$

$$\text{s.t.} \quad \int_0^T e(t) dt = \varepsilon,$$

$$e(t) + \ell(t) = 1,$$

where $r > 0$ is the student's intertemporal rate of time preference and $\beta \stackrel{\text{def}}{=} (\varepsilon, r, T) \in \Re^3_{++}$. Assume that the pair of curves $(e^*(t;\beta), \ell^*(t;\beta))$ is a solution to the necessary conditions of the optimal control problem, with corresponding costate variable $\lambda(t;\beta)$ and Lagrange multiplier $\mu(t;\beta)$. Note that the above optimal control problem is *not* in standard form because the state equation is absent.

(a) Convert the above *isoperimetric* optimal control problem to one in standard form by defining an appropriate state variable, say, $x(t)$, and calling it cumulative effort. Also include the optimal value function in your problem statement. Please do not substitute the equality constraint $e(t) + \ell(t) = 1$ out of the problem.

(b) Write the constraint $e(t) + \ell(t) = 1$ as $1 - e - \ell$ in forming the Lagrangian function, and then derive the necessary conditions for this problem.

(c) Prove that the triplet $(x^*(t;\beta), e^*(t;\beta), \ell^*(t;\beta))$ is a solution of the optimal control problem in standard form.

(d) Prove that $\lambda(t;\beta) = \mu(t;\beta)\,\forall\, t \in [0, T]$ and that $\lambda(t;\beta) > 0\,\forall\, t \in [0, T]$. Provide an economic interpretation of these two results. Does the latter result make sense? Explain.

(e) Prove that $\dot{\ell}^*(t;\beta) < 0\,\forall\, t \in [0, T]$ and $\dot{e}^*(t;\beta) > 0\,\forall\, t \in [0, T]$. Provide an economic interpretation. Is this the rational procrastination result alluded to in the problem? Why or why not?

6.13 *Fattening up the Fish on the Farm.* You are the sole owner of a fish farm and wish to minimize the present discounted value of the fish feeding costs over the fixed planning horizon $[0, T]$. Let $w(t)$ be the weight of the stock of fish at time t, $w(0) = w_0 > 0$ be the fixed initial weight of the fish stock when the fattening plan begins, and $w(T) = w_T > 0$ be the required (and fixed) terminal weight of the fish stock when the fattening operation comes to a close. Assume that $w_T > w_0$, so that the terminal weight of the fish stock is larger than its initial weight. Thus, given the initial weight of the fish stock of $w(0) = w_0 > 0$, you want to minimize the present discounted value of the feeding costs of the stock so as to bring the fish up to the required weight $w(T) = w_T > 0$ over the period $[0, T]$. Let $u(t)$ be the feeding rate of the stock of fish at time t and $r > 0$ be the discount rate that you use in discounting all future cash flows. The instantaneous feeding cost function is given by $C(u) \overset{\text{def}}{=} \frac{1}{2}u^2$. The rate of change in the weight of the fish stock is proportional to the feeding rate; hence the differential equation governing the weight dynamics is $\dot{w} = \alpha^{-1}u$, where $\alpha > 0$ is the inverse of the marginal product of the feeding rate. For notational clarity, define $\boldsymbol{\beta} \overset{\text{def}}{=} (\alpha, r, w_0, T, w_T)$ as the parameter vector of the problem.

(a) Set up this problem as an optimal control problem, and define the optimal value function mathematically, say, $C^*(\cdot)$. Provide an economic interpretation of the optimal value function.

(b) Derive the solution of the necessary conditions, say, $(w^*(t; \boldsymbol{\beta}), u^*(t; \boldsymbol{\beta}))$, and let $\lambda(t; \boldsymbol{\beta})$ be the corresponding time path of the costate variable.

(c) Prove that the pair $(w^*(t; \boldsymbol{\beta}), u^*(t; \boldsymbol{\beta}))$ is the solution to the control problem. Is it the unique solution? Clearly explain your reasoning.

(d) Prove that

$$\frac{\partial u^*}{\partial \alpha}(t; \boldsymbol{\beta}) > 0 \, \forall \, t \in [0, T] \text{ and } \frac{\partial w^*}{\partial \alpha}(t; \boldsymbol{\beta}) \equiv 0 \, \forall \, t \in [0, T].$$

Provide an *economic* (not literal) interpretation of this comparative dynamics result.

(e) Prove that

$$\left.\frac{\partial u^*}{\partial r}(t; \boldsymbol{\beta})\right|_{t=0} < 0 \text{ and } \left.\frac{\partial u^*}{\partial r}(t; \boldsymbol{\beta})\right|_{t=T} > 0.$$

Provide an economic interpretation.

(f) Prove that

$$\frac{\partial u^*}{\partial w_T}(t; \boldsymbol{\beta}) > 0 \, \forall \, t \in [0, T].$$

Provide an economic interpretation.

(g) Derive an explicit expression for the optimal value function $C^*(\cdot)$. Now consider another stage to the optimization problem. In this stage, you are to choose the terminal weight of the fish stock w_T so as to maximize the present discounted value of profit that results from selling the fish at the market-determined price of $p > 0$ per unit of weight.

(h) Set up this new optimization problem for finding the optimal value of w_T.

(i) Solve the first-order necessary condition of this optimization problem for $w_T = W(\boldsymbol{\gamma})$, where $\boldsymbol{\gamma} \overset{\text{def}}{=} (\alpha, p, r, w_0, T)$. Show that $W(\boldsymbol{\gamma}) > w_0$.

(j) Prove that the solution $w_T = W(\boldsymbol{\gamma})$ to the first-order necessary condition is the unique solution to the optimization problem.

(k) Prove that $\partial W(\boldsymbol{\gamma})/\partial p > 0$ and provide an economic interpretation.

(l) Prove that $\partial W(\boldsymbol{\gamma})/\partial \alpha > 0$ and provide an economic interpretation.

(m) Define the optimal feeding rate evaluated at the optimal terminal weight by $u^{**}(t; \boldsymbol{\gamma}) \overset{\text{def}}{=} u^*(t; w_0, T, W(\boldsymbol{\gamma}), \alpha, r)$. Derive an explicit formula for

$u^{**}(t;\gamma)$. Prove that

$$\frac{\partial u^{**}}{\partial p}(t;\gamma) > 0\,\forall t \in [0, T]$$

by differentiating the explicit formula for $u^{**}(t;\gamma)$ as well as by using the above definition. Provide an economic interpretation.

(n) Prove that

$$\frac{\partial u^{**}}{\partial \alpha}(t;\gamma) < 0\,\forall t \in [0, T].$$

Provide an economic interpretation. Moreover, contrast this result with the one obtained in part (d). You should reconsider the definition in part (m) for a sound answer.

FURTHER READING

Readers looking for a discussion of necessary and sufficient conditions for optimal control problems with pure state constraints, that is, constraints that depend only on the state variable and possibly t, are encouraged to consult Kamien and Schwartz (1991), Léonard and Van Long (1992), Seierstad and Sydsæter (1977), and, of course, the textbook by Seierstad and Sydsæter (1987). Optimal control problems with pure state constraints introduce several nontrivial complications, and as such, are best studied *after* one has internalized the necessary and sufficient conditions used in this book. The survey article by Hartl, Sethi, and Vickson (1995) is a comprehensive piece that presents existence, necessary, and sufficient conditions for optimal control problems with state constraints. A straightforward existence theorem is given in Steinberg and Stalford (1973). Tomiyama (1985) and Tomiyama and Rossana (1989) derive necessary conditions for two-stage optimal control problems.

REFERENCES

Hartl, R.F., Sethi, S.P., and Vickson, R.G. (1995), "A Survey of the Maximum Principles for Optimal Control Problems with State Constraints," *SIAM Review*, 37, 181–218.

Kamien, M.I. and Schwartz, N.L. (1991, 2nd Ed.), *Dynamic Optimization: The Calculus of Variations and Optimal Control in Economics and Management* (New York: Elsevier Science Publishing Co., Inc.).

Léonard, D. and Van Long, N. (1992), *Optimal Control Theory and Static Optimization in Economics* (New York: Cambridge University Press).

Seierstad, A. and Sydsæter, K. (1977), "Sufficient Conditions in Optimal Control Theory," *International Economic Review*, 18, 367–391.

Seierstad, A. and Sydsæter, K. (1987), *Optimal Control Theory with Economic Applications* (New York: Elsevier Science Publishing Co., Inc.).

Simon, C.P. and Blume, L. (1994), *Mathematics for Economists* (New York: W.W. Norton & Company, Inc.).

Steinberg, A.M. and Stalford, H.L. (1973), "On Existence of Optimal Controls," *Journal of Optimization Theory and Applications*, 11, 266–273.

Tomiyama, K. (1985), "Two-Stage Optimal Control Problems and Optimality Conditions," *Journal of Economic Dynamics and Control*, 9, 317–337.

Tomiyama, K. and Rossana, R.J. (1989), "Two-Stage Optimal Control Problems with an Explicit Switch Point Dependence: Optimality Criteria and an Example of Delivery Lags and Investment," *Journal of Economic Dynamics and Control*, 13, 319–337.

SEVEN

Necessary and Sufficient Conditions for Isoperimetric Problems

Mathematically, isoperimetric problems are a class of optimal control problems that involve finding an extremum of one integral, subject to another integral having a prescribed value. One such economic problem of this class was presented in Example 3.5 and Mental Exercise 4.21, videlicet, the nonrenewable resource–extracting model of the firm. In each instance, we transformed the given isoperimetric problem into an optimal control problem in standard form so that the control problem could be solved with the theorems developed to that point. The goal of this chapter is to develop theorems, both necessary and sufficient, that will help us solve isoperimetric problems directly.

An important reason for studying this class of control problems is that they provide a unified view of principal-agent problems as well as a general method for their solution. We demonstrate this in Example 7.3 for the optimal contracting problem when the effort (or action) of the agent is observable by the principal. A byproduct of solving the principal-agent problem via this method is that the independent variable t, which we have heretofore always referred to as time, is now the realized value of the random variable profit. As remarked at the end of Chapter 6, one may safely skip this chapter and the next on a first read without loss of continuity. If, however, one wishes to read the chapter, it is recommended that Mental Exercise 4.22 be worked at this juncture, as it introduces basic ideas and concepts for what follows.

A general form of isoperimetric problems is given by

$$V(\beta) \stackrel{\text{def}}{=} \max_{\mathbf{x}(\cdot)} \left\{ J[\mathbf{x}(\cdot)] \stackrel{\text{def}}{=} \int_{t_0}^{t_1} F(t, \mathbf{x}(t), \dot{\mathbf{x}}(t))\, dt \right\}$$

$$\text{s.t.} \quad K[\mathbf{x}(\cdot)] \stackrel{\text{def}}{=} \int_{t_0}^{t_1} G(t, \mathbf{x}(t), \; \dot{\mathbf{x}}(t))\, dt = c, \tag{1}$$

$$\mathbf{x}(t_0) = \mathbf{x}_0, \; \mathbf{x}(t_1) = \mathbf{x}_1,$$

where $c \in \Re$ is a given parameter that we treat as fixed, just like the endpoints $(t_0, \mathbf{x}_0, t_1, \mathbf{x}_1)$; $\beta \stackrel{\text{def}}{=} (c, t_0, \mathbf{x}_0, t_1, \mathbf{x}_1)$ is the parameter vector; and $\mathbf{x}(\cdot) \stackrel{\text{def}}{=} (x_1(\cdot), x_2(\cdot), \ldots, x_N(\cdot))$. The defining feature of isoperimetric problems is the presence of an integral constraint on the curve $\mathbf{x}(t)$, its slope $\dot{\mathbf{x}}(t)$, or either one singly. As such, the value of the function $\mathbf{x}(\cdot)$ and/or the value of the slope function $\dot{\mathbf{x}}(\cdot)$ are *not* restricted at each point in the planning horizon; only the integral of some function of these functions is constrained. Such integral constraints are therefore less constraining than constraints that restrict the value of the function $\mathbf{x}(\cdot)$ and/or the value of the slope function $\dot{\mathbf{x}}(\cdot)$ at each $t \in [t_0, t_1]$. Hence it is perfectly sound for an isoperimetric problem with only one decision function to have any finite number of integral constraints.

As you will recall from Chapter 4, the function $V(\cdot)$ is called the *optimal value function*. It represents the maximum value of the objective functional $J[\cdot]$ conditional on the parameters $\beta \stackrel{\text{def}}{=} (c, t_0, \mathbf{x}_0, t_1, \mathbf{x}_1)$ of the isoperimetric problem (1). The optimal value function is the dynamic analogue of the indirect objective function in static optimization theory. In static microeconomic theory, for example, analogous functions would be the firm's profit function, the firm's cost function, the consumer's expenditure function, or the consumer's indirect utility function. We refer to problem (1) as the *primal* isoperimetric problem, as it is the original form of the problem.

Because the isoperimetric problem (1) differs from the prototype optimal control problem we have been dealing with up until this juncture, we must modify our definition of admissibility. To this end, we have the following definition.

Definition 7.1: Any $C^{(2)}$ function $\mathbf{x}(\cdot)$ on $[t_0, t_1]$, such that $\mathbf{x}(t_0) = \mathbf{x}_0$, $\mathbf{x}(t_1) = \mathbf{x}_1$, and $\int_{t_0}^{t_1} G(t, \mathbf{x}(t), \dot{\mathbf{x}}(t))\, dt = c$, will be called an *admissible function* for the isoperimetric problem (1).

As before, admissibility requires that the candidate functions be sufficiently smooth and satisfy the fixed endpoints of the problem. In addition, admissibility now requires that the candidate functions satisfy the integral constraint of the isoperimetric problem (1). This is a natural extension of our earlier definition of admissibility to isoperimetric problems.

The following assumptions are imposed on the primal isoperimetric problem (1) so as to guarantee that the ensuing analysis is free of tangential mathematical details:

(I.1) $F(\cdot) \in C^{(2)}$ and $G(\cdot) \in C^{(2)}$ on their domains.
(I.2) $\exists$ an optimal solution function $\mathbf{z}(\cdot)$, where $\mathbf{z}(\cdot) \in C^{(2)}\, \forall\, t \in [t_0, t_1]$.
(I.3) The set of admissible curves $\mathbf{x}(t)$ is *not* an empty set.

If assumption (I.3) is not satisfied, then we have no problem, for then there are no curves from which to choose the optimum. In general, we shall assume that there are infinitely many admissible curves $\mathbf{x}(t)$.

Given the basic mathematical structure of the isoperimetric problem (1) and the assumptions imposed on it, we have the following theorem delineating its necessary conditions. The theorem is stated for $\mathbf{x}(t) \in \Re^N$ but proven for the case $N = 1$ for ease of exposition.

Theorem 7.1 (Necessary Conditions): *Let $\mathbf{z}(\cdot)$ be an admissible function that yields an interior maximum of the isoperimetric problem (1) but is not an extremal function for the constraining functional $K[\cdot]$. Then there exists a constant ψ, such that if*

$$\tilde{F}(t, \mathbf{x}, \dot{\mathbf{x}}, \psi) \stackrel{\text{def}}{=} F(t, \mathbf{x}, \dot{\mathbf{x}}) - \psi G(t, \mathbf{x}, \dot{\mathbf{x}}),$$

then it is necessary that the curve $\mathbf{z}(t)$ satisfy the system of augmented Euler equations,

$$\tilde{F}_{x_n}(t, \mathbf{x}, \dot{\mathbf{x}}, \psi) = \frac{d}{dt}\tilde{F}_{\dot{x}_n}(t, \mathbf{x}, \dot{\mathbf{x}}, \psi), \quad n = 1, 2, \ldots, N.$$

In other words, the curve $\mathbf{z}(t)$ must satisfy the necessary conditions for an unconstrained maximum when the integrand function is $\tilde{F}(\cdot)$ not $F(\cdot)$.

Proof: Suppose $z(\cdot)$ is an admissible function that solves problem (1). Let $\eta_1(\cdot)$ and $\eta_2(\cdot)$ be two independent functions of class $C^{(2)}\ \forall\, t \in [t_0, t_1]$ that are arbitrary save for satisfying

$$\eta_1(t_0) = \eta_1(t_1) = 0 \quad \text{and} \quad \eta_2(t_0) = \eta_2(t_1) = 0. \tag{2}$$

Now consider the varied curve given by

$$x(t; \varepsilon_1, \varepsilon_2) \stackrel{\text{def}}{=} z(t) + \varepsilon_1\eta_1(t) + \varepsilon_2\eta_2(t), \tag{3}$$

which is defined for sufficiently small ε_1 and ε_2. Assuming that the varied curve $x(t; \varepsilon_1, \varepsilon_2)$ defined in Eq. (3) is admissible, we have that

$$\varphi(\varepsilon_1, \varepsilon_2) \stackrel{\text{def}}{=} \int_{t_0}^{t_1} G(t, x(t; \varepsilon_1, \varepsilon_2),\ \dot{x}(t; \varepsilon_1, \varepsilon_2))\, dt - c = 0, \tag{4}$$

where $\dot{x}(t; \varepsilon_1, \varepsilon_2) \stackrel{\text{def}}{=} \dot{z}(t) + \varepsilon_1\dot{\eta}_1(t) + \varepsilon_2\dot{\eta}_2(t)$. Observe that Eq. (4) is equivalent to some functional relationship between ε_1 and ε_2, as we will establish below. Because the curve $z(t)$ is the optimal solution to problem (1) by assumption (I.2), it satisfies the integral constraint identically. Moreover, because $x(t; 0, 0) = z(t)$ from Eq. (3), it follows from Eq. (4) and the assumed optimality of the curve $x(t; 0, 0) = z(t)$ that $\varphi(0, 0) = 0$. Differentiating $\varphi(\varepsilon_1, \varepsilon_2)$ defined in Eq. (4) with respect to ε_2 using Leibniz's rule, evaluating the resulting derivative at $(\varepsilon_1, \varepsilon_2) = (0, 0)$, and then using the definition of the varied curve given in Eq. (3) yields

$$\frac{\partial \varphi}{\partial \varepsilon_2}(0,0) = \int_{t_0}^{t_1} [G_x(t, z(t), \dot{z}(t))\eta_2(t) + G_{\dot{x}}(t, z(t), \dot{z}(t))\dot{\eta}_2(t)]\, dt.$$

Given that the curve $z(t)$ is not an extremal for the constraining functional $K[\cdot]$ by assumption, it follows that the function $\eta_2(\cdot)$ can be chosen such that

$$\frac{\partial \varphi}{\partial \varepsilon_2}(0,0) = \int_{t_0}^{t_1} [G_x(t, z(t), \ \dot{z}(t))\eta_2(t) + G_{\dot{x}}(t, z(t), \ \dot{z}(t))\dot{\eta}_2(t)]\, dt \neq 0. \quad (5)$$

This is precisely what it means for the curve $z(t)$ to not be an extremal for the constraining functional $K[\cdot]$, for if $z(t)$ was an extremal, the derivative in Eq. (5) would vanish. Now note that $\varphi(\cdot) \in C^{(2)}$ in some neighborhood of $(\varepsilon_1, \varepsilon_2) = (0, 0)$ by assumption (I.1) and the fact that $\eta_i(\cdot) \in C^{(2)}$, $i = 1, 2$. Because Eq. (5) holds, the implicit function theorem implies that Eq. (4) defines ε_2 as a function of ε_1 in some neighborhood of $(\varepsilon_1, \varepsilon_2) = (0, 0)$, as asserted above. This is because Eq. (5) is the nonvanishing Jacobian of Eq. (4) evaluated at the solution to Eq. (4), which is required for use of the implicit function theorem. For sufficiently small ε_1 and ε_2, therefore, we may regard Eq. (3) as defining a one-parameter family of curves, just as we did for varied curves in proving the necessary conditions of free endpoint optimal control problems in Chapter 2. Thus Eq. (3) defines admissible curves for the isoperimetric problem (1).

Given that the curve $z(t)$ solves problem (1) by assumption (I.2), the function $\Phi(\cdot)$, with values given by

$$\Phi(\varepsilon_1, \varepsilon_2) \stackrel{\text{def}}{=} \int_{t_0}^{t_1} F(t, x(t; \varepsilon_1, \varepsilon_2), \dot{x}(t; \varepsilon_1, \varepsilon_2))\, dt, \quad (6)$$

has a constrained maximum at $(\varepsilon_1, \varepsilon_2) = (0, 0)$ subject to $\varphi(\varepsilon_1, \varepsilon_2) = 0$, since $x(t; 0, 0) = z(t)$ by Eq. (3). Thus the optimal values of ε_1 and ε_2, namely, 0 and 0, are the solution to the following static constrained optimization problem:

$$\max_{\varepsilon_1, \varepsilon_2} \{\Phi(\varepsilon_1, \varepsilon_2) \text{ s.t. } \varphi(\varepsilon_1, \varepsilon_2) = 0\}. \quad (7)$$

Because Eq. (5) is the nondegenerate constraint qualification for problem (7), it can be solved by the method of Lagrange. Forming the Lagrangian function

$$L(\varepsilon_1, \varepsilon_2, \psi) \stackrel{\text{def}}{=} \Phi(\varepsilon_1, \varepsilon_2) - \psi \varphi(\varepsilon_1, \varepsilon_2)$$

and differentiating with respect to ε_1, ε_2, and ψ gives the first-order necessary conditions, which hold at $(\varepsilon_1, \varepsilon_2) = (0, 0)$ by construction. The first two of these necessary conditions are given by

$$\frac{\partial L}{\partial \varepsilon_i}(\varepsilon_1, \varepsilon_2, \psi) = \frac{\partial \Phi}{\partial \varepsilon_i}(\varepsilon_1, \varepsilon_2) - \psi \frac{\partial \varphi}{\partial \varepsilon_i}(\varepsilon_1, \varepsilon_2) = 0, \quad i = 1, 2. \tag{8}$$

A straightforward rearrangement of Eq. (8) yields the familiar tangency conditions of constrained optimization theory, to wit,

$$\frac{\partial \Phi(0,0)/\partial \varepsilon_1}{\partial \varphi(0,0)/\partial \varepsilon_1} = \frac{\partial \Phi(0,0)/\partial \varepsilon_2}{\partial \varphi(0,0)/\partial \varepsilon_2} = \psi. \tag{9}$$

Equation (9) can be rewritten as

$$\frac{\int_{t_0}^{t_1} [F_x(t)\eta_1(t) + F_{\dot{x}}(t)\dot{\eta}_1(t)]\,dt}{\int_{t_0}^{t_1} [G_x(t)\eta_1(t) + G_{\dot{x}}(t)\dot{\eta}_1(t)]\,dt} = \frac{\int_{t_0}^{t_1} [F_x(t)\eta_2(t) + F_{\dot{x}}(t)\dot{\eta}_2(t)]\,dt}{\int_{t_0}^{t_1} [G_x(t)\eta_2(t) + G_{\dot{x}}(t)\dot{\eta}_2(t)]\,dt} = \psi, \tag{10}$$

upon using Eqs. (3), (4), and (6), as you are asked to verify in a mental exercise. Note that the derivatives of the functions $F(\cdot)$ and $G(\cdot)$ are evaluated along the optimal path $z(t)$ because Eq. (9) is evaluated at $(\varepsilon_1, \varepsilon_2) = (0, 0)$, the optimal solution to problem (7). Given that Eq. (10) holds for arbitrary choices of $\eta_1(\cdot)$ and $\eta_2(\cdot)$, ψ is constant. More explicitly, because the variable t is integrated out of Eq. (10), ψ is not a function of t and is therefore constant, as was to be proven.

A simple rearrangement of Eq. (10) yields

$$\int_{t_0}^{t_1} [[F_x(t, z(t), \dot{z}(t)) - \psi G_x(t, z(t), \dot{z}(t))]\eta_i(t)$$
$$+ [F_{\dot{x}}(t, z(t), \dot{z}(t)) - \psi G_{\dot{x}}(t, z(t), \dot{z}(t))]\dot{\eta}_i(t)]\,dt = 0, \tag{11}$$

for $i = 1, 2$. Defining $\tilde{F}(t, x, \dot{x}, \psi) \overset{\text{def}}{=} F(t, x, \dot{x}) - \psi G(t, x, \dot{x})$ and integrating Eq. (11) by parts in the usual manner using Eq. (2) gives

$$\int_{t_0}^{t_1} \left[\tilde{F}_x(t, z(t), \dot{z}(t), \psi) - \frac{d}{dt}[\tilde{F}_{\dot{x}}(t, z(t), \dot{z}(t), \psi)]\right] \eta_i(t)\,dt = 0, \quad i = 1, 2, \tag{12}$$

which you are also asked to verify in a mental exercise. To complete the proof, we must show that the term $\tilde{F}_x(t, z(t), \dot{z}(t), \psi) - \frac{d}{dt}[\tilde{F}_{\dot{x}}(t, z(t), \dot{z}(t), \psi)] \equiv 0$ for all $t \in [t_0, t_1]$ in Eq. (12).

We will use a contrapositive proof to establish this result. This is achieved by assuming that $\tilde{F}_x(t, z(t), \dot{z}(t), \psi) - \frac{d}{dt}[\tilde{F}_{\dot{x}}(t, z(t), \dot{z}(t), \psi)] \not\equiv 0$ and then showing that this assumption violates Eq. (12). Suppose, therefore, that $\tilde{F}_x(t, z(t), \dot{z}(t), \psi) - \frac{d}{dt}[\tilde{F}_{\dot{x}}(t, z(t), \dot{z}(t), \psi)] \not\equiv 0$ at some point $\bar{t} \in [t_0, t_1]$, say, $\tilde{F}_x(t, z(t), \dot{z}(t), \psi) - \frac{d}{dt}[\tilde{F}_{\dot{x}}(t, z(t), \dot{z}(t), \psi)] > 0$ without loss of generality. Then because $\tilde{F}_x(t, z(t), \dot{z}(t), \psi) - \frac{d}{dt}[\tilde{F}_{\dot{x}}(t, z(t), \dot{z}(t), \psi)]$ is a continuous function of t by assumption (I.1), $\tilde{F}_x(t, z(t), \dot{z}(t), \psi) - \frac{d}{dt}[\tilde{F}_{\dot{x}}(t, z(t), \dot{z}(t), \psi)] > 0$ in some interval $[a, b]$, with $a < b$, $\bar{t} \in [a, b]$, and $[a, b] \subset [t_0, t_1]$. Now select $\eta_i(\cdot) \in C^{(2)}$ such that $\eta_i(t) > 0\, \forall\, t \in (a, b)$ and $\eta_i(t) = 0$ for $t \notin (a, b)$, $i = 1, 2$. See Figure 7.1 for

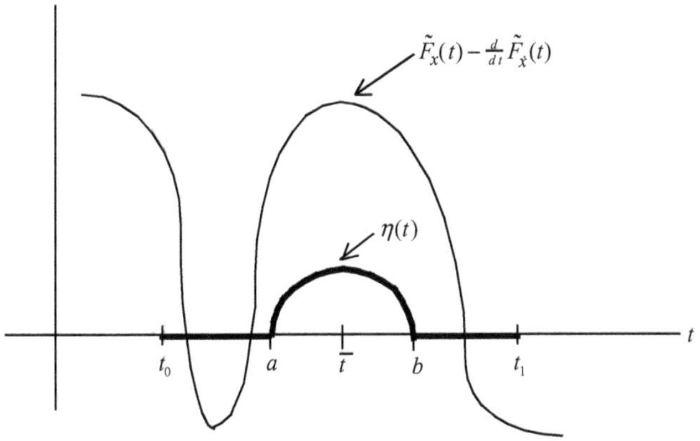

Figure 7.1

the geometry of these restrictions. Under these conditions, it follows that

$$\int_{t_0}^{t_1} \left[\tilde{F}_x(t, z(t), \dot{z}(t), \psi) - \frac{d}{dt} [\tilde{F}_{\dot{x}}(t, z(t), \dot{z}(t), \psi)] \right] \eta_i(t)\, dt$$

$$= \int_a^b \left[\tilde{F}_x(t, z(t), \dot{z}(t), \psi) - \frac{d}{dt} [\tilde{F}_{\dot{x}}(t, z(t), \dot{z}(t), \psi)] \right] \eta_i(t)\, dt > 0,$$

$i = 1, 2$, which contradicts Eq. (12), thereby completing the proof. Q.E.D.

Theorem 7.1 essentially asserts that the curve $\mathbf{z}(t)$ that solves the isoperimetric problem (1) is an extremal for the functional

$$\int_{t_0}^{t_1} \tilde{F}(t, \mathbf{x}(t), \dot{\mathbf{x}}(t), \psi)\, dt \overset{\text{def}}{=} \int_{t_0}^{t_1} [F(t, \mathbf{x}(t), \dot{\mathbf{x}}(t)) - \psi G(t, \mathbf{x}(t), \dot{\mathbf{x}}(t))]\, dt.$$

The two constants of integration that result from integrating the augmented Euler equation, and the constant multiplier ψ, are found using the two boundary conditions and the integral constraint.

Before turning to an example to demonstrate the application of Theorem 7.1, an important property of isoperimetric problems will be established. To this end, consider the following *reciprocal*, or *transposed*, or *mirrored* isoperimetric problem:

$$W(\boldsymbol{\theta}) \overset{\text{def}}{=} \min_{\mathbf{x}(\cdot)} \left\{ K[\mathbf{x}(\cdot)] \overset{\text{def}}{=} \int_{t_0}^{t_1} G(t, \mathbf{x}(t), \dot{\mathbf{x}}(t))\, dt \right\}$$

$$\text{s.t.} \quad J[\mathbf{x}(\cdot)] \overset{\text{def}}{=} \int_{t_0}^{t_1} F(t, \mathbf{x}(t), \dot{\mathbf{x}}(t))\, dt = b, \tag{13}$$

$$\mathbf{x}(t_0) = \mathbf{x}_0,\ \mathbf{x}(t_1) = \mathbf{x}_1,$$

where $\boldsymbol{\theta} \stackrel{\text{def}}{=} (b, t_0, \mathbf{x}_0, t_1, \mathbf{x}_1)$ is the parameter vector and $W(\cdot)$ is the optimal value function for the reciprocal isoperimetric problem (13). The reciprocal problem is simply a rearrangement of the primal isoperimetric problem (1) whereby the objective functional and the integral constraint are interchanged and the objective of maximization is replaced with the objective of minimization. We note that it is *incorrect* to refer to isoperimetric problem (13) as the dual of isoperimetric problem (1) in view of the fact that the decision functions are identical in problems (1) and (13), and thus are members of the same function space. Strictly speaking, the prototype definition of a dual problem is one whose solution lies in a vector space that is different from, or dual to, that of the primal problem, as in, for example, dual pairs of linear programming problems. This definition of *dual* clearly does not hold for isoperimetric problems (1) and (13).

The ensuing theorem and a significant extension of it play an important role in performing a relatively complete comparative dynamics characterization of the nonrenewable resource–extracting model of the firm, as will be seen in Chapter 8.

Theorem 7.2: *Let $b = J[\mathbf{z}(\cdot)]$, or equivalently, let $b = V(\boldsymbol{\beta})$, in the reciprocal isoperimetric problem (13). If the curve $\mathbf{z}(t)$ is a solution to problem (1), then the curve $\mathbf{z}(t)$ is an extremal for problem (13). Moreover, if the corresponding multiplier in problem (1) is ψ, then ψ^{-1} is the corresponding multiplier in problem (13).*

Proof: First observe that $F(t, \mathbf{x}, \dot{\mathbf{x}}) - \psi G(t, \mathbf{x}, \dot{\mathbf{x}}) \equiv -\psi[G(t, \mathbf{x}, \dot{\mathbf{x}}) - \psi^{-1} F(t, \mathbf{x}, \dot{\mathbf{x}})]$, which immediately yields the conclusion regarding the multipliers because $F(t, \mathbf{x}, \dot{\mathbf{x}}) - \psi G(t, \mathbf{x}, \dot{\mathbf{x}})$ is the augmented integrand for problem (1) and $G(t, \mathbf{x}, \dot{\mathbf{x}}) - \psi^{-1} F(t, \mathbf{x}, \dot{\mathbf{x}})$ is the augmented integrand for problem (13). Thus the augmented integrands of isoperimetric problems (1) and (13) differ from each other by a constant, namely, $-\psi$. Next, observe that if the curve $\mathbf{z}(t)$ satisfies the system of augmented Euler equations

$$F_{x_n}(t, \mathbf{x}, \dot{\mathbf{x}}) - \psi G_{x_n}(t, \mathbf{x}, \dot{\mathbf{x}}) = \frac{d}{dt}[F_{\dot{x}_n}(t, \mathbf{x}, \dot{\mathbf{x}}) - \psi G_{\dot{x}_n}(t, \mathbf{x}, \dot{\mathbf{x}})], \quad n = 1, 2, \ldots, N,$$

then it surely satisfies the system of augmented Euler equations

$$G_{x_n}(t, \mathbf{x}, \dot{\mathbf{x}}) - \psi^{-1} F_{x_n}(t, \mathbf{x}, \dot{\mathbf{x}}) = \frac{d}{dt}\left[G_{\dot{x}_n}(t, \mathbf{x}, \dot{\mathbf{x}}) - \psi^{-1} F_{\dot{x}_n}(t, \mathbf{x}, \dot{\mathbf{x}})\right], \quad n = 1, 2, \ldots, N,$$

for the latter is simply the former multiplied by the constant $-\psi^{-1}$. To complete the proof, we must show that the curve $\mathbf{z}(t)$ is admissible in problem (13). Because the endpoints in the pair of problems (1) and (13) are identical, all that is left to demonstrate is that the curve $\mathbf{z}(t)$ satisfies the integral constraint in problem (13).

When $b = V(\boldsymbol{\beta})$, the integral constraint in problem (13) is

$$J[\mathbf{x}(\cdot)] \stackrel{\text{def}}{=} \int_{t_0}^{t_1} F(t, \mathbf{x}(t), \dot{\mathbf{x}}(t))\, dt = V(\boldsymbol{\beta}).$$

By the definition of the optimal value function $V(\cdot)$ in problem (1), the curve $\mathbf{z}(t)$ obviously satisfies this integral condition seeing as it is a solution to problem (1). Q.E.D.

Notice that Theorem 7.1 smacks of the reciprocal nature of the pair of static consumer problems, utility maximization and expenditure minimization. Because we have not imposed much structure on the isoperimetric problem in this chapter, we cannot claim that the solution of the primal maximization isoperimetric problem (1) is also a solution of the reciprocal minimization isoperimetric problem (13), and vice versa, as we can for the aforementioned static consumer problems. This conclusion will have to wait for the next chapter. Similarly, we cannot claim at this juncture that the solution of the augmented Euler equation is the solution of the isoperimetric problem, since the augmented Euler equation is but a necessary condition for optimality. This conclusion will have to wait until the end of this chapter, when a sufficiency theorem is introduced.

Let's now demonstrate how to use Theorems 7.1 and 7.2 in the context of a relatively simple example devoid of economic content.

Example 7.1: Consider the following simple *primal* isoperimetric problem:

$$\min_{x(\cdot)} J[x(\cdot)] \stackrel{\text{def}}{=} \int_0^1 [\dot{x}(t)]^2\, dt$$

$$\text{s.t.} \quad K[x(\cdot)] \stackrel{\text{def}}{=} \int_0^1 x(t)\, dt = c,$$

$$x(0) = 0,\ x(1) = 0,$$

where $c > 0$ is the given parameter of the problem. We begin by defining the augmented integrand by $\tilde{F}(t, x, \dot{x}, \psi) \stackrel{\text{def}}{=} F(t, x, \dot{x}) - \psi G(t, x, \dot{x}) = \dot{x}^2 - \psi x$, where ψ is the constant multiplier from the primal problem, and then computing

$$\tilde{F}_x(t, x, \dot{x}, \psi) = -\psi,\ \ \tilde{F}_{\dot{x}}(t, x, \dot{x}, \psi) = 2\dot{x},\ \ \frac{d}{dt}\tilde{F}_{\dot{x}}(t, x, \dot{x}, \psi) = 2\ddot{x}.$$

The augmented Euler equation $\tilde{F}_x(t, x, \dot{x}, \psi) - \frac{d}{dt}\tilde{F}_{\dot{x}}(t, x, \dot{x}, \psi) = 0$ is therefore given by $\ddot{x} = -\frac{1}{2}\psi$. Separating the variables and integrating twice gives the general solution to the augmented Euler equation, to wit, $x(t) = -\frac{1}{4}\psi t^2 + c_1 t + c_2$, where

(c_1, c_2) are the constants of integration. Using the boundary conditions yields

$$x(0) = 0 \Rightarrow c_2 = 0,$$
$$x(1) = 0 \Rightarrow c_1 = \frac{1}{4}\psi.$$

Plugging these two results into the general solution of the augmented Euler equation gives $x(t) = -\frac{1}{4}\psi t^2 + \frac{1}{4}\psi t = \frac{1}{4}\psi[t - t^2]$, and then using this in the integral constraint yields

$$\int_0^1 x(t)\,dt = \frac{1}{4}\psi \int_0^1 [t - t^2]\,dt = \left[\frac{1}{8}\psi t^2 - \frac{1}{12}\psi t^3\right]\Bigg|_{t=0}^{t=1}$$
$$= \psi\left[\frac{1}{8} - \frac{1}{12}\right] = \frac{1}{24}\psi = c.$$

It thus follows that $\psi = 24c$ and $c_1 = 6c$. Plugging the solutions for (c_1, c_2, ψ) into the general solution of the augmented Euler equation yields the definite solution, its rate of change, and the multiplier:

$$z_1(t; c) = -6ct^2 + 6ct, \ \dot{z}_1(t; c) = -12ct + 6c, \ \psi = 24c. \tag{14}$$

We will present a sufficiency theorem at the end of this chapter that will allow us to conclude that the curve $z_1(t; c)$ is the unique solution of the primal isoperimetric problem.

To finish up this part of the example, plug $\dot{z}_1(t; c) = -12ct + 6c$ in the objective functional $J[\cdot]$ to find its optimal value:

$$V(c) \stackrel{\text{def}}{=} J[z_1(\cdot)] = \int_0^1 [\dot{z}_1(t; c)]^2\,dt = \int_0^1 [-12ct + 6c]^2\,dt$$
$$= \int_0^1 [144c^2t^2 - 144c^2t + 36c^2]\,dt$$
$$= \left[\frac{144}{3}c^2t^3 - 72c^2t^2 + 36c^2t\right]\Bigg|_{t=0}^{t=1} = 12c^2.$$

Recall that the function $V(\cdot)$ is the *optimal value function* and gives the optimal value of the objective functional conditional on the parameters of the variational problem.

Now let's solve the *reciprocal* isoperimetric problem

$$\max_{x(\cdot)} K[x(\cdot)] \stackrel{\text{def}}{=} \int_0^1 x(t)\,dt$$

$$\text{s.t.} \quad J[x(\cdot)] \stackrel{\text{def}}{=} \int_0^1 [\dot{x}(t)]^2\, dt = V(c) = 12c^2,$$

$$x(0) = 0,\ x(1) = 0.$$

Notice that the integral constraint has been forced to have a value equal to that of the optimal value function from the primal isoperimetric problem, exactly as is required by Theorem 7.2. The augmented integrand function $\hat{F}(\cdot)$ for the reciprocal problem has values defined by $\hat{F}(t, x, \dot{x}, \theta) \stackrel{\text{def}}{=} G(t, x, \dot{x}) - \theta F(t, x, \dot{x}) = x - \theta\dot{x}^2$, where θ is the constant multiplier for the reciprocal problem. Differentiating $\hat{F}(t, x, \dot{x}, \theta) \stackrel{\text{def}}{=} x - \theta\dot{x}^2$ gives

$$\hat{F}_x(t, x, \dot{x}, \theta) = 1,\ \hat{F}_{\dot{x}}(t, x, \dot{x}, \theta) = -2\theta\dot{x},\ \frac{d}{dt}\hat{F}_{\dot{x}}(t, x, \dot{x}, \theta) = -2\theta\ddot{x},$$

and hence the augmented Euler equation is given by $\ddot{x} = -\frac{1}{2}\theta^{-1}$. Separating the variables and integrating twice yields the general solution $x(t) = -\frac{1}{4}\theta^{-1}t^2 + k_1 t + k_2$, where (k_1, k_2) are the constants of integration. The three unknowns (k_1, k_2, θ) are found with the help of the two boundary conditions and the integral constraint. Using the boundary conditions gives

$$x(0) = 0 \Rightarrow k_2 = 0,$$

$$x(1) = 0 \Rightarrow k_1 = \frac{1}{4}\theta^{-1}.$$

Substituting $k_2 = 0$ and $k_1 = \frac{1}{4}\theta^{-1}$ into the general solution of the augmented Euler equation gives $x(t) = -\frac{1}{4}\theta^{-1}t^2 + \frac{1}{4}\mu^{-1}t = \frac{1}{4}\theta^{-1}[t - t^2]$, and then using this in the integral constraint yields

$$\int_0^1 [\dot{x}(t)]^2\, dt = \frac{1}{16}\theta^{-2} \int_0^1 [1 - 2t]^2\, dt = \frac{1}{16}\theta^{-2} \int_0^1 [1 - 4t + 4t^2] dt$$

$$= \frac{1}{16}\theta^{-2}\left[t - 2t^2 + \frac{4}{3}t^3\right]\Bigg|_{t=0}^{t=1} = \frac{1}{16}\theta^{-2}\left[1 - 2 + \frac{4}{3}\right]$$

$$= \frac{1}{48}\theta^{-2} = V(c) = 12c^2.$$

Clearly, there are two solutions for θ to the above equation. Because $\theta^{-2} = 12(48)c^2 = 12^2 2^2 c^2$, this implies that $\theta^{-1} = \pm 24c$ and thus $k_1 = \pm 6c$. As a result, the definite solution to the augmented Euler equation of the reciprocal isoperimetric problem is given by *either* of the following two curves and associated multipliers:

$$z_2(t; c) = -6ct^2 + 6ct,\ \dot{z}_2(t; c) = -12ct + 6c,\ \theta = \frac{1}{24c}, \tag{15}$$

$$z_3(t;c) = 6ct^2 - 6ct,\ \dot{z}_3(t;c) = 12ct - 6c,\ \theta = -\frac{1}{24c}. \tag{16}$$

Note that the solution to the augmented Euler equation is not unique, because we have found two solutions. Such nonuniqueness is *not* inconsistent with Theorem 7.2, however, for all Theorem 7.2 asserts is that the solution of the primal isoperimetric problem is an extremal for the reciprocal isoperimetric problem when $b = V(c)$. That this is true in this example can be seen by inspecting Eqs. (14) and (15), which reveals that $z_1(t;c) \equiv z_2(t;c)\, \forall\, t \in [0, 1]$. Theorem 7.2 also asserts that the corresponding multiplier for the primal isoperimetric problem is the reciprocal of a corresponding multiplier in the reciprocal isoperimetric problem when $b = V(c)$. That this is also true in this example can be seen by inspecting Eqs. (14) and (15) again. It is also important to note that Theorem 7.2 does *not* assert that the extremal for the primal isoperimetric problem is the only extremal for the reciprocal isoperimetric problem.

Now substitute the curve $z_2(t;c) = -6ct^2 + 6ct$ in the objective functional $K[\cdot]$ of the reciprocal isoperimetric problem to find its optimal value:

$$\begin{aligned} K[z_2(\cdot)] &= \int_0^1 z_2(t;c)\,dt = \int_0^1 [-6ct^2 + 6ct]\,dt \\ &= [-2ct^3 + 3ct^2]\Big|_{t=0}^{t=1} = -2c + 3c = c > 0. \end{aligned} \tag{17}$$

A similar substitution using the curve $z_3(t;c) = 6ct^2 - 6ct$ yields

$$\begin{aligned} K[z_3(\cdot)] &= \int_0^1 z_3(t)\,dt = \int_0^1 [6ct^2 - 6ct]\,dt \\ &= [2ct^3 - 3ct^2]\Big|_{t=0}^{t=1} = 2c - 3c = -c < 0. \end{aligned} \tag{18}$$

Inspection of Eqs. (17) and (18) shows that the curve $z_2(t;c) = -6ct^2 + 6ct$ yields the *maximum* of the reciprocal isoperimetric problem (which is how it is stated), whereas the curve $z_3(t;c) = 6ct^2 - 6ct$ yields the *minimum* of the reciprocal isoperimetric problem. We will also verify these conclusions in Example 7.3, after we develop a sufficiency theorem.

Another interesting feature of this example can be uncovered by recalling the definition of the optimal value function for the reciprocal isoperimetric problem, namely, $W(b) \stackrel{\text{def}}{=} K[z_2(\cdot)]$, where b is the value of the integral constraint in the reciprocal isoperimetric problem. Equation (17) shows that optimal value function for the maximizing reciprocal isoperimetric problem is the inverse of the optimal value function for the primal isoperimetric problem when $b = V(c)$. To see this, simply observe that $W(V(c)) \stackrel{\text{def}}{=} K[z_2(\cdot)]|_{b=V(c)}$ and that $K[z_2(\cdot)]|_{b=V(c)} = c$ from Eq. (17). These two results imply that $W(V(c)) = c$, or that $W(\cdot) = V^{-1}(\cdot)$. Hence the optimal value functions for the *stated* reciprocal pair of isoperimetric problems are inverses of one another. This inverse relationship between the optimal value functions is in fact true more generally, and not at all an artifact of the simple mathematical structure of this example, as we will see in the next chapter.

The next chapter will explore in more detail, and at a higher level of generality, the qualitative relationships between reciprocal pairs of isoperimetric problems that Theorem 7.2 and Example 7.1 have exposed. In the process of doing so, we will also rather exhaustively study the comparative dynamics properties of the nonrenewable resource–extracting model of the firm.

It is appropriate at this point to turn to an economic interpretation of the multiplier ψ in Theorems 7.1 and 7.2. The analysis that follows smacks of the classical envelope theorem of static microeconomic theory. It is therefore wise to take mental notes on the similarities and differences between the ensuing derivation and the more familiar static envelope theorem, for the envelope theorem plays just as important a role in uncovering the qualitative properties of dynamic optimization problems as it does in static optimization problems.

To begin the analysis, define the *optimal value function* as

$$V(\boldsymbol{\beta}) \stackrel{\text{def}}{=} \max_{\mathbf{x}(\cdot)} \int_{t_0}^{t_1} F(t, \mathbf{x}(t), \dot{\mathbf{x}}(t); \boldsymbol{\alpha})\, dt$$

$$\text{s.t.} \int_{t_0}^{t_1} G(t, \mathbf{x}(t), \dot{\mathbf{x}}(t); \boldsymbol{\alpha})\, dt = c,\ \mathbf{x}(t_0) = \mathbf{x}_0,\ \mathbf{x}(t_1) = \mathbf{x}_1, \tag{19}$$

The solution curve to this problem, which is assumed to exist, is denoted by $\mathbf{z}(t; \boldsymbol{\beta})$, where $\psi^*(\boldsymbol{\beta})$ is the value of the corresponding multiplier and $\boldsymbol{\beta} \stackrel{\text{def}}{=} (\boldsymbol{\alpha}, c, t_0, x_0, t_1, x_1)$ is the vector of parameters of the isoperimetric problem (19). Note that problem (19) is almost identical to problem (1), the difference being that now the functions $F(\cdot)$ and $G(\cdot)$ depend on the parameter vector $\boldsymbol{\alpha} \in \Re^A$.

Observe that the optimal value function $V(\cdot)$ is defined in a manner that is perfectly analogous to the way the indirect objective function of static optimization theory is defined. In other words, the optimal value function is the intertemporal analogue of the indirect objective function. Moreover, the optimal value function $V(\cdot)$ can also be defined *constructively* as

$$V(\boldsymbol{\beta}) \equiv \int_{t_0}^{t_1} F(t, \mathbf{z}(t; \boldsymbol{\beta}),\ \dot{\mathbf{z}}(t; \boldsymbol{\beta}); \boldsymbol{\alpha})\, dt. \tag{20}$$

Note that this constructive way of defining the optimal value function $V(\cdot)$ is completely analogous to the constructive definition of the indirect objective function. By a constructive definition, we mean literally how one would go about finding or constructing the optimal value function $V(\cdot)$ in practice if one had an explicit formula for the optimal path $\mathbf{z}(t; \boldsymbol{\beta})$, its time derivative $\dot{\mathbf{z}}(t; \boldsymbol{\beta})$, and the integrand function $F(\cdot)$.

To get an economic interpretation of the multiplier $\psi^*(\boldsymbol{\beta})$, first recall that by assumption (I.1), $F(\cdot) \in C^{(2)}$ and $G(\cdot) \in C^{(2)}$ on their domains, and that $z(\cdot) \in C^{(2)}$ by assumption (I.2). This means that the partial derivative $\partial V(\boldsymbol{\beta})/\partial c$ exists and can be computed from Eq. (20) by differentiating under the integral sign by way of Leibniz's rule. Doing just that using the heretofore established vector notation yields

$$\frac{\partial V}{\partial c}(\boldsymbol{\beta}) \equiv \int_{t_0}^{t_1} \left[\underbrace{F_{\mathbf{x}}(t, \mathbf{z}(t;\boldsymbol{\beta}), \dot{\mathbf{z}}(t;\boldsymbol{\beta}); \boldsymbol{\alpha})}_{1\times N} \underbrace{\frac{\partial \mathbf{z}}{\partial c}(t;\boldsymbol{\beta})}_{N\times 1} + \underbrace{F_{\dot{\mathbf{x}}}(t, \mathbf{z}(t;\boldsymbol{\beta}), \dot{\mathbf{z}}(t;\boldsymbol{\beta}); \boldsymbol{\alpha})}_{N\times 1} \underbrace{\frac{\partial \dot{\mathbf{z}}}{\partial c}(t;\boldsymbol{\beta})}_{N\times 1} \right] dt. \tag{21}$$

Because the curve $\mathbf{z}(t;\boldsymbol{\beta})$ is the optimal solution to isoperimetric problem (19) it must therefore satisfy the integral constraint, the initial condition, and the terminal condition *identically*. Upon differentiating these three identities with respect to c, we have

$$c - \int_{t_0}^{t_1} G(t, z(t;\boldsymbol{\beta}),\ \dot{z}(t;\boldsymbol{\beta}); \boldsymbol{\alpha})\, dt \equiv 0 \Rightarrow$$

$$1 - \int_{t_0}^{t_1} \left[\underbrace{G_{\mathbf{x}}(t, \mathbf{z}(t;\boldsymbol{\beta}), \dot{\mathbf{z}}(t;\boldsymbol{\beta}); \boldsymbol{\alpha})}_{1\times N} \underbrace{\frac{\partial \mathbf{z}}{\partial c}(t;\boldsymbol{\beta})}_{N\times 1} + \underbrace{G_{\dot{\mathbf{x}}}(t, \mathbf{z}(t;\boldsymbol{\beta}), \dot{\mathbf{z}}(t;\boldsymbol{\beta}); \boldsymbol{\alpha})}_{1\times N} \underbrace{\frac{\partial \dot{\mathbf{z}}}{\partial c}(t;\boldsymbol{\beta})}_{N\times 1} \right] dt \equiv 0, \tag{22}$$

$$\mathbf{z}(t_0;\boldsymbol{\beta}) \equiv \mathbf{x}_0 \Rightarrow \frac{\partial \mathbf{z}}{\partial c}(t_0;\boldsymbol{\beta}) \equiv \mathbf{0}_N, \tag{23}$$

$$\mathbf{z}(t_1;\boldsymbol{\beta}) \equiv \mathbf{x}_1 \Rightarrow \frac{\partial \mathbf{z}}{\partial c}(t_1;\boldsymbol{\beta}) \equiv \mathbf{0}_N. \tag{24}$$

Now multiply Eq. (22) by $\psi^*(\boldsymbol{\beta})$, the multiplier's solution to problem (19), and add the result to Eq. (21) to get

$$\frac{\partial V}{\partial c}(\boldsymbol{\beta}) \equiv \int_{t_0}^{t_1} \left[\tilde{F}_{\mathbf{x}}(t, \mathbf{z}(t;\boldsymbol{\beta}), \dot{\mathbf{z}}(t;\boldsymbol{\beta}), \psi^*(\boldsymbol{\beta}); \boldsymbol{\alpha}) \frac{\partial \mathbf{z}}{\partial c}(t;\boldsymbol{\beta}) + \tilde{F}_{\dot{\mathbf{x}}}(t, \mathbf{z}(t;\boldsymbol{\beta}), \dot{\mathbf{z}}(t;\boldsymbol{\beta}), \psi^*(\boldsymbol{\beta}); \boldsymbol{\alpha}) \frac{\partial \dot{\mathbf{z}}}{\partial c}(t;\boldsymbol{\beta}) \right] dt + \psi^*(\boldsymbol{\beta}), \tag{25}$$

where $\tilde{F}(t, \mathbf{x}, \dot{\mathbf{x}}, \psi; \boldsymbol{\alpha}) \stackrel{\text{def}}{=} F(t, \mathbf{x}, \dot{\mathbf{x}}; \boldsymbol{\alpha}) - \psi G(t, \mathbf{x}, \dot{\mathbf{x}}; \boldsymbol{\alpha})$ is the augmented integrand function defined previously. Note that the step taken in going from Eq. (21) to Eq. (25) is perfectly valid, for all we have done is simply add a term that is *identically zero* to Eq. (21) to arrive at Eq. (25).

Next, integrate the second term of the integrand of Eq. (25) by parts to get

$$\left.\begin{array}{ll} \mathbf{p}' = \tilde{F}_{\dot{\mathbf{x}}}(t, \mathbf{z}(t;\boldsymbol{\beta}), \dot{\mathbf{z}}(t;\boldsymbol{\beta}), \psi^*(\boldsymbol{\beta}); \boldsymbol{\alpha}), & \mathbf{dq} = \dfrac{\partial \dot{\mathbf{z}}}{\partial c}(t;\boldsymbol{\beta})\,dt = \dfrac{d}{dt}\left[\dfrac{\partial \mathbf{z}}{\partial c}(t;\boldsymbol{\beta})\right]dt \\ \mathbf{dp}' = \dfrac{d}{dt}\tilde{F}_{\dot{\mathbf{x}}}(t, \mathbf{z}(t;\boldsymbol{\beta}), \dot{\mathbf{z}}(t;\boldsymbol{\beta}), \psi^*(\boldsymbol{\beta}); \boldsymbol{\alpha})\,dt, & \mathbf{q} = \dfrac{\partial \mathbf{z}}{\partial c}(t;\boldsymbol{\beta}) \end{array}\right\} \Rightarrow$$

$$\int_{t_0}^{t_1}\left[\tilde{F}_{\dot{\mathbf{x}}}(t, \mathbf{z}(t;\boldsymbol{\beta}), \dot{\mathbf{z}}(t;\boldsymbol{\beta}), \psi^*(\boldsymbol{\beta}); \boldsymbol{\alpha})\frac{\partial \dot{\mathbf{z}}}{\partial c}(t;\boldsymbol{\beta})\right]dt$$
$$= \tilde{F}_{\dot{\mathbf{x}}}(t, \mathbf{z}(t;\boldsymbol{\beta}), \dot{\mathbf{z}}(t;\boldsymbol{\beta}), \psi^*(\boldsymbol{\beta}); \boldsymbol{\alpha})\frac{\partial \mathbf{z}}{\partial c}(t;\boldsymbol{\beta})\Big|_{t=t_0}^{t=t_1}$$
$$- \int_{t_0}^{t_1}\left[\frac{d}{dt}\tilde{F}_{\dot{\mathbf{x}}}(t, \mathbf{z}(t;\boldsymbol{\beta}), \dot{\mathbf{z}}(t;\boldsymbol{\beta}), \psi^*(\boldsymbol{\beta}); \boldsymbol{\alpha})\right]\frac{\partial \mathbf{z}}{\partial c}(t;\boldsymbol{\beta})\,dt. \tag{26}$$

Because $\partial \mathbf{z}(t_0;\boldsymbol{\beta})/\partial c \equiv \mathbf{0}_N$ from Eq. (23) and $\partial \mathbf{z}(t_1;\boldsymbol{\beta})/\partial c \equiv \mathbf{0}_N$ from Eq. (24), Eq. (26) reduces to

$$\int_{t_0}^{t_1}\left[\tilde{F}_{\dot{\mathbf{x}}}(t, \mathbf{z}(t;\boldsymbol{\beta}), \dot{\mathbf{z}}(t;\boldsymbol{\beta}), \psi^*(\boldsymbol{\beta}); \boldsymbol{\alpha})\frac{\partial \dot{\mathbf{z}}}{\partial c}(t;\boldsymbol{\beta})\right]dt$$
$$= - \int_{t_0}^{t_1}\left[\frac{d}{dt}\tilde{F}_{\dot{\mathbf{x}}}(t, \mathbf{z}(t;\boldsymbol{\beta}), \dot{\mathbf{z}}(t;\boldsymbol{\beta}), \psi^*(\boldsymbol{\beta}); \boldsymbol{\alpha})\right]\frac{\partial \mathbf{z}}{\partial c}(t;\boldsymbol{\beta})\,dt. \tag{27}$$

Substituting Eq. (27) into Eq. (25) gives the penultimate expression we are after, to wit,

$$\frac{\partial V}{\partial c}(\boldsymbol{\beta}) \equiv \int_{t_0}^{t_1}\Bigg[\tilde{F}_{\mathbf{x}}(t, \mathbf{z}(t;\boldsymbol{\beta}), \dot{\mathbf{z}}(t;\boldsymbol{\beta}), \psi^*(\boldsymbol{\beta}); \boldsymbol{\alpha})$$
$$- \frac{d}{dt}\tilde{F}_{\dot{\mathbf{x}}}(t, \mathbf{z}(t;\boldsymbol{\beta}), \dot{\mathbf{z}}(t;\boldsymbol{\beta}), \psi^*(\boldsymbol{\beta}); \boldsymbol{\alpha})\Bigg]\frac{\partial \mathbf{z}}{\partial c}(t;\boldsymbol{\beta})\,dt + \psi^*(\boldsymbol{\beta}). \tag{28}$$

Because the curve $\mathbf{z}(t;\boldsymbol{\beta})$ is the solution to isoperimetric problem (19) and $\psi^*(\boldsymbol{\beta})$ is the corresponding value of the multiplier, $\tilde{F}_{\mathbf{x}}(t, \mathbf{z}(t;\boldsymbol{\beta}), \dot{\mathbf{z}}(t;\boldsymbol{\beta}), \psi^*(\boldsymbol{\beta}); \boldsymbol{\alpha}) -$

$\frac{d}{dt}\tilde{F}_{\dot{\mathbf{x}}}(t, \mathbf{z}(t;\boldsymbol{\beta}), \dot{\mathbf{z}}(t;\boldsymbol{\beta}), \psi^*(\boldsymbol{\beta});\boldsymbol{\alpha}) \equiv \mathbf{0}'_N$ by Theorem 7.1. Using this result, Eq. (28) simplifies to

$$\frac{\partial V}{\partial c}(\boldsymbol{\beta}) \equiv \psi^*(\boldsymbol{\beta}), \tag{29}$$

which is what we wished to show.

The economic interpretation of $\psi^*(\boldsymbol{\beta})$ comes from looking at the left-hand side of Eq. (29), since it is identically equal to $\psi^*(\boldsymbol{\beta})$. Equation (29) thus asserts that $\psi^*(\boldsymbol{\beta})$ measures the rate of change in the optimal value function when the integral constraint parameter c changes. Thus $\lambda^*(\boldsymbol{\beta})$ has the interpretation of the *marginal value* or *shadow price* of the parameter c.

In sum, we have proven part (ii) of the following important theorem, a dynamic envelope theorem, the remaining parts of which you are asked to prove in the mental exercises.

Theorem 7.3 (Dynamic Envelope Theorem): *For the isoperimetric problem (19), with assumptions (I.1), (I.2), and (I.3) holding, the following dynamic envelope results hold for the optimal value function $V(\cdot)$:*

$$\begin{aligned}
&(i)\ V_{\alpha_i}(\boldsymbol{\beta}) \equiv \int_{t_0}^{t_1} \tilde{F}_{\alpha_i}(t, \mathbf{z}(t;\boldsymbol{\beta}), \dot{\mathbf{z}}(t;\boldsymbol{\beta}), \psi^*(\boldsymbol{\beta});\boldsymbol{\alpha})\,dt, \quad i = 1, 2, \ldots, A,\\
&(ii)\ V_c(\boldsymbol{\beta}) \equiv \psi^*(\boldsymbol{\beta}),\\
&(iii)\ V_{t_0}(\boldsymbol{\beta}) \equiv -\tilde{F}(t_0, \mathbf{x}_0, \dot{\mathbf{z}}(t_0;\boldsymbol{\beta}), \psi^*(\boldsymbol{\beta});\boldsymbol{\alpha})\\
&\qquad\qquad + \tilde{F}_{\dot{\mathbf{x}}}(t_0, \mathbf{x}_0, \dot{\mathbf{z}}(t_0;\boldsymbol{\beta}), \psi^*(\boldsymbol{\beta});\boldsymbol{\alpha})\,\dot{\mathbf{z}}(t_0;\boldsymbol{\beta}),\\
&(iv)\ V_{\mathbf{x}_0}(\boldsymbol{\beta}) \equiv -\tilde{F}_{\dot{\mathbf{x}}}(t_0, \mathbf{x}_0, \dot{\mathbf{z}}(t_0;\boldsymbol{\beta}), \psi^*(\boldsymbol{\beta});\boldsymbol{\alpha}),\\
&(v)\ V_{t_1}(\boldsymbol{\beta}) \equiv \tilde{F}(t_1, \mathbf{x}_1, \dot{\mathbf{z}}(t_1;\boldsymbol{\beta}), \psi^*(\boldsymbol{\beta});\boldsymbol{\alpha}) - \tilde{F}_{\dot{\mathbf{x}}}(t_1, \mathbf{x}_1, \dot{\mathbf{z}}(t_1;\boldsymbol{\beta}), \psi^*(\boldsymbol{\beta});\boldsymbol{\alpha})\,\dot{\mathbf{z}}(t_1;\boldsymbol{\beta}),\\
&(vi)\ V_{\mathbf{x}_1}(\boldsymbol{\beta}) \equiv \tilde{F}_{\dot{\mathbf{x}}}(t_1, \mathbf{x}_1, \dot{\mathbf{z}}(t_1;\boldsymbol{\beta}), \psi^*(\boldsymbol{\beta});\boldsymbol{\alpha}),
\end{aligned}$$

where $\tilde{F}(t, \mathbf{x}, \dot{\mathbf{x}}, \psi;\boldsymbol{\alpha}) \overset{\text{def}}{=} F(t, \mathbf{x}, \dot{\mathbf{x}};\boldsymbol{\alpha}) - \psi G(t, \mathbf{x}, \dot{\mathbf{x}};\boldsymbol{\alpha})$ is the augmented integrand function.

Let's now consider an economic example in order to drive home some of the points just made, namely, the Hotelling model of the nonrenewable resource–extracting firm.

Example 7.2: An owner of a piece of land knows that it has $x_0 > 0$ units of some nonrenewable asset, such as oil, in the ground. The owner wants to determine the extraction path $q(t)$ over a fixed planning period $[0, T]$ that will maximize the present discounted value of profit associated with extracting and selling the asset. Let $\pi(q(t))$ be the instantaneous profit from extracting and selling the nonrenewable resource at rate $q(t)$, which is discounted at rate $r > 0$. Assume that $\pi(\cdot) \in C^{(2)}$ on its domain and that $\pi'(q) > 0$ and $\pi''(q) < 0$. The owner has decided that all of the resource will be extracted by the end of the planning period, implying that cumulative extraction must equal the initial stock. Putting all this information together, we can formally state the isoperimetric problem corresponding to this scenario as

$$\Pi(r, x_0, T) \stackrel{\text{def}}{=} \left\{ \max_{q(\cdot)} J[q(\cdot)] \stackrel{\text{def}}{=} \int_0^T \pi(q(t))\, e^{-rt}\, dt \right\}$$

$$\text{s.t.} \quad K[q(\cdot)] \stackrel{\text{def}}{=} \int_0^T q(t)\, dt = x_0.$$

Note that this formulation is identical to that in Mental Exercise 4.21.

The augmented integrand for this problem is defined as $\tilde{F}(t, q, \psi) \stackrel{\text{def}}{=} \pi(q)e^{-rt} - \psi q$, where by Theorem 7.3, ψ can be interpreted as the present value shadow price of the unextracted resource, the adjective *present value* arising from the presence of the discount factor in the integrand. The partial derivatives of the augmented integrand function are therefore given by $\tilde{F}_q(t, q, \psi) = \pi'(q)e^{-rt} - \psi$ and $\tilde{F}_{\dot{q}}(t, q, \psi) \equiv 0$, thereby implying that the augmented Euler equation takes the form

$$\tilde{F}_q(t, q, \psi) = \pi'(q)\, e^{-rt} - \psi = 0, \tag{30}$$

where ψ is a constant by Theorem 7.1.

Equation (30) says that the optimal extraction rate is such that the present value of marginal profit, to wit, $\pi'(q)e^{-rt}$, is constant over the planning period and equal to the multiplier ψ, the present value shadow price of the unextracted resource. Alternatively, Eq. (30) can be rearranged as $\pi'(q) = \lambda e^{rt}$, implying that marginal profit grows at the discount rate $r > 0$. Because Eq. (30) holds identically in t for all $t \in [0, T]$ along the optimal path, it is valid to differentiate it with respect to t. Doing so and recalling that ψ is a constant gives $\pi''(q)\dot{q}e^{-rt} - r\pi'(q)\, e^{-rt} = 0$. Multiplying this differential equation through by e^{rt}, recognizing that $\frac{d}{dt}\pi'(q) = \pi''(q)\dot{q}$, and then rearranging it gives

$$\frac{\frac{d}{dt}[\pi'(q)]}{\pi'(q)} = \frac{\pi''(q)\dot{q}}{\pi'(q)} = r > 0. \tag{31}$$

Equation (31) is known as *Hotelling's rule*. It asserts that the optimal extraction rate equates the relative rate of change of the marginal profit from extracting and selling a unit of the nonrenewable resource, with the rate at which an alternative asset would grow if it was placed in an interest-bearing account earning interest at the rate $r > 0$.

Solving Hotelling's rule (31) for $\dot{q}$ and recalling that $\pi'(q) > 0$ and $\pi''(q) < 0$ by assumption gives

$$\dot{q} = \frac{\pi'(q)}{\pi''(q)} r < 0. \tag{32}$$

Equation (32) shows that the optimal extraction rate of the nonrenewable resource is declining over the planning horizon $[0, T]$. This implies that the extraction rate

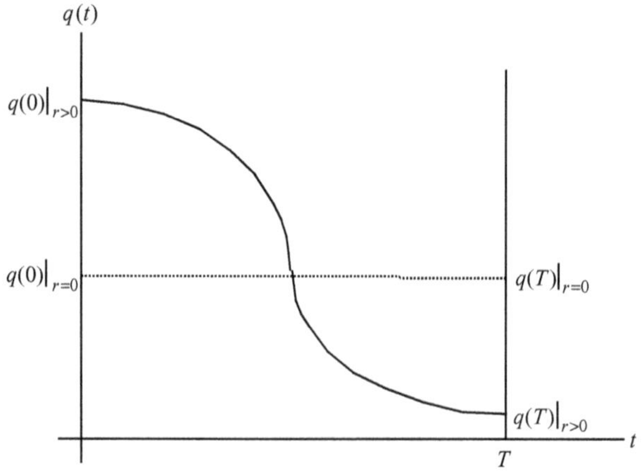

Figure 7.2

is the largest at the initial date of the planning horizon and smallest at the terminal date of the planning horizon. Equation (32) also shows that if $r = 0$, then $\dot{q} = 0$, implying that the extraction rate is constant over the planning horizon if the firm does not discount its future flow of profits. We can therefore conclude from these two observations that the discount rate has the effect of shifting the extraction profile toward the present, a typical impatience result. In fact, since the planning horizon is fixed and the owner is required to extract all the resource from the ground, it follows that the initial extraction rate when $r > 0$ must exceed the extraction rate when $r = 0$, because otherwise, the owner would never extract all of the asset when $r > 0$. Moreover, as the terminal date of the planning horizon approaches, the extraction rate with $r > 0$ must be less than the extraction rate with $r = 0$. Finally, the area under the extraction path when $r > 0$ is identical to the area under the extraction path when $r = 0$ because of the integral constraint that requires the owner to extract all of the asset from the ground over the fixed planning horizon, that is, because of the fact that $\int_0^T q(t)\,dt = x_0$ and T and x_0 are fixed parameters. See Figure 7.2 for the geometry behind these qualitative conclusions.

Let's finish up this example by providing a more motivated and careful economic interpretation of the optimal value of the constant multiplier $\psi^*(r, x_0, T)$ using Theorem 7.3. To begin, recall that the optimal value function $\Pi(\cdot)$ in this model is the maximum present discounted value of profit from extracting and selling the resource stock, and that the equivalent of the parameter c in Theorem 7.3 is the initial size of the nonrenewable resource deposit x_0. By Theorem 7.3, we have that $\partial\Pi(r, x_0, T)/\partial x_0 = \psi^*(r, x_0, T)$. Thus $\psi^*(r, x_0, T)$ is the *present value shadow price* of the initial stock of the resource, since it is the amount by which the present discounted profits of the firm increase when the initial size of the resource deposit increases. In other words, $\psi^*(r, x_0, T)$ is the maximum amount the owner of the firm would pay for a small increase in the initial size of the nonrenewable resource deposit, since $\psi^*(r, x_0, T)$ is precisely the amount by which the present discounted value of profits would rise because of the increase in the initial resource deposit. We can therefore think of $\psi^*(r, x_0, T)$ as the present value of one more unit of the resource stock to the owner of the firm, and in deciding upon whether to purchase one more unit of the stock *in situ*, the owner would compare the value of the stock to her, as given by $\psi^*(r, x_0, T)$, to the market price of the resource stock.

In the third example, we investigate the principal-agent problem with hidden actions. We will make use of the necessary conditions in Theorem 7.1 as well as the dynamic envelope results of Theorem 7.3 to solve the problem and deduce its comparative statics properties.

Example 7.3: Suppose that the owner of a firm, the *principal*, desires to hire a manager, the *agent*, for a one-time project. (It is this sort of conceptualization that has resulted in the appellation *principal-agent* for the resulting optimal control problem.) The profitability of the project is given by the random variable $\tilde{\pi}$ and is determined, in part, by the actions of, or choices made by, the manager. Let π be the project's observed (or realized) profit and $e \in E$ be the manager's effort on the project, where $E \subset \Re$ is the set of possible effort levels of the manager. It is assumed that the profit of the project is influenced by the effort of the manager, though not fully determined by it. Consequently, it is assumed that profit may take on any value in the closed interval $[\underline{\pi}, \bar{\pi}]$, and that $\tilde{\pi}$ is stochastically related to $e \in E$ by way of the conditional probability density function $(\pi, e) \mapsto f(\pi \mid e)$, where $f(\pi \mid e) > 0$ and $f(\cdot) \in C^{(2)}$ for all $e \in E$ and $\pi \in [\underline{\pi}, \bar{\pi}]$. Therefore, any potential realization of $\tilde{\pi}$ may arise following any given effort choice $e \in E$ by the manager.

The manager is an expected utility maximizer with a $C^{(2)}$ von Neumann–Morgenstern utility function $u(\cdot)$, with values $u(w, e)$, where w is the wage received by the manager. It is assumed that $u_w(w, e) > 0$, $u_{ww}(w, e) < 0$, and $u_e(w, e) < 0$ for all (w, e). In other words, the manager prefers more income to less, is strictly risk averse over income lotteries, and prefers lower effort. The owner receives the project's profit less the wage payment to the manager, and is assumed to be risk neutral, thereby implying that his objective is the maximization of expected net profit.

Let's examine the so-called optimal contracting problem when the manager's effort is observable to the owner. A contract in this context specifies not only the manager's effort $e \in E$, but also the manager's wage payment as a function of observed (or realized) profit, say, $w(\pi)$. Assuming that a competitive market for managers exists, the owner must therefore provide the manager with an expected utility of at least $\bar{u}$, the manager's reservation utility, if the manager is to accept the owner's contract offer. Note that if the manager rejects the owner's contract offer, then the owner receives a payoff of zero. We henceforth assume that the owner finds it worthwhile to make the manager an offer that he will accept.

Putting all this information together, we see that the optimal contract for the owner solves the ensuing isoperimetric problem:

$$V^*(\underline{\pi}, \bar{\pi}, \bar{u}) \stackrel{\text{def}}{=} \max_{e \in E, w(\cdot)} \left\{ \int_{\underline{\pi}}^{\bar{\pi}} [\pi - w(\pi)] f(\pi \mid e)\, d\pi \ \text{ s.t. } \int_{\underline{\pi}}^{\bar{\pi}} u(w(\pi), e) f(\pi \mid e)\, d\pi \geq \bar{u} \right\}. \tag{33}$$

At this juncture, it is best to pause and make three rather important remarks about problem (33). First, notice that the independent variable is the realized (or observed) profit of the project. This stands in sharp contrast to every other optimal control problem encountered in the book, where the independent variable has been (or will be) time. Nonetheless, this in no way discredits the optimal contracting problem (33) from being solved by the theorems developed herewith. What is important, therefore, is that problem (33) seeks to determine a *function* of the independent variable; the nature of the independent variable itself, however, is unimportant. Second, problem (33) is a special case of the general isoperimetric problem given in Eq. (1). To see this, simply observe that the choice function in problem (33) is scalar valued, whereas in problem (1), it is vector valued, and that in problem (33), the derivative function $\dot{w}(\cdot)$ is absent. Moreover, it is precisely because problem (33) does not involve the derivative function $\dot{w}(\cdot)$ that no initial and/or terminal conditions on $w(\cdot)$ need to be specified. Third, the isoperimetric constraint always binds at a solution of problem (33). To verify this, note that if it does not bind at a solution $w(\pi)$ for the wage profile, then there exists a lower wage schedule, say, $w(\pi) - \varepsilon$ for sufficiently small $\varepsilon > 0$, such that the manager would still accept the wage schedule $w(\pi) - \varepsilon$, that is, for which, the isoperimetric constraint still does not bind, and that also results in higher expected profit for the owner. This contradicts the optimality of the wage schedule $w(\pi)$ and thus establishes the claim. Henceforth we will write the isoperimetric constraint as an equality constraint.

Rather than tackle problem (33) directly, it is advantageous to solve it in two stages. In the first stage, we fix e at an arbitrary value in the set E, and then seek to determine the best wage function $w(\cdot)$ that the owner should offer the manager. Given this optimal wage function, the second-stage problem determines the optimal choice of the manager's effort e.

The first-stage isoperimetric problem is therefore given by

$$V(e, \underline{\pi}, \bar{\pi}, \bar{u}) \stackrel{\text{def}}{=} \max_{w(\cdot)} \left\{ \int_{\underline{\pi}}^{\bar{\pi}} [\pi - w(\pi)] f(\pi \mid e)\, d\pi \ \text{ s.t. } \int_{\underline{\pi}}^{\bar{\pi}} u(w(\pi), e) f(\pi \mid e)\, d\pi = \bar{u} \right\}. \tag{34}$$

Notice that the optimal value functions in problems (33) and (34) differ, as they should, in view of the fact that problem (34) holds effort fixed whereas problem (33) does not. The augmented integrand of problem (34) is given by $\tilde{F}(\pi, w, \psi; e) \stackrel{\text{def}}{=} [\pi - w]f(\pi \mid e) - \psi u(w, e) f(\pi \mid e)$. By Theorem 7.1, it is necessary that a solution of problem (34) satisfy the Euler equation based on the augmented integrand function, videlicet, $\tilde{F}_w(\pi, w, \psi; e) = \frac{d}{dt}\tilde{F}_{\dot{w}}(\pi, w, \psi; e)$. Because $\tilde{F}_{\dot{w}}(\pi, w, \psi; e) \equiv 0$, the Euler equation reduces to $\tilde{F}_w(\pi, w, \psi; e) = -f(\pi \mid e) - \psi u_w(w, e) f(\pi \mid e) = 0$. Moreover, because $f(\pi \mid e) > 0$ for all $e \in E$ and $\pi \in [\underline{\pi}, \bar{\pi}]$, the augmented Euler equation simplifies to

$$-1 - \psi u_w(w, e) = 0. \tag{35}$$

Furthermore, the multiplier ψ is a constant, that is to say, it is not a function of the independent variable π, by Theorem 7.1. Seeing as e is a given value of effort, these two conclusions therefore imply that the optimal wage function, which necessarily satisfies Eq. (35), is not a function of π either. In other words, the optimal wage contract that the owner offers the manager is independent of the realized profit on the project. This conclusion is a risk-sharing result in that the risk-neutral owner fully insures the risk-averse manager against any income risk by making the manager's wage independent of the profit of the project on which the manager is contracted to work.

Seeing as $u(\cdot) \in C^{(2)}$ and $u_{ww}(w, e) < 0$ for all (w, e), the implicit function theorem implies that Eq. (35) may be solved, in principle, for the wage rate as a locally $C^{(1)}$ function of the effort of the manager and the multiplier, that is,

$$w = \hat{w}(e, \psi). \tag{36}$$

It is important to understand that the solution in Eq. (36) is not the optimal wage rate of the manager, for the corresponding value of the multiplier has yet to be determined. Nonetheless, it is still worthwhile to investigate the comparative statics properties of the function $\hat{w}(\cdot)$. Before doing so, it is prudent to first provide an economic interpretation of the multiplier.

To this end, we begin by recalling Theorem 7.3 part (ii), a dynamic envelope theorem, which when applied to problem (34) gives the effect of a change in the reservation utility of the manager on the owner's maximum expected profit (conditional on effort). Specifically, applying Theorem 7.3 part (ii) to problem (34) gives

$$\frac{\partial V}{\partial \bar{u}}(e, \underline{\pi}, \bar{\pi}, \bar{u}) \equiv \psi^*(e, \underline{\pi}, \bar{\pi}, \bar{u}) < 0, \tag{37}$$

where $\psi^*(e, \underline{\pi}, \bar{\pi}, \bar{u})$ is the yet-to-be-determined optimal value of the multiplier. The sign of $\psi^*(e, \underline{\pi}, \bar{\pi}, \bar{u})$ follows from Eq. (35) and the assumption that $u_w(w, e) > 0$ for all (w, e). Given that $\psi^*(e, \underline{\pi}, \bar{\pi}, \bar{u}) < 0$, Eq. (37) therefore permits us to interpret $\psi^*(e, \underline{\pi}, \bar{\pi}, \bar{u})$ as the marginal cost of the manager's reservation utility. The fact that $\partial V(e, \underline{\pi}, \bar{\pi}, \bar{u})/\partial \bar{u} < 0$ is intuitive, because for a given effort, an improvement in the manager's outside opportunities means that the owner must now compensate the manager with a higher wage if the owner wishes to get the manager to accept the contract. This increase in the wage offered to the manager raises the costs of the project and thus reduces the owner's profit on the project.

Returning to the qualitative properties of the solution $w = \hat{w}(e, \psi)$ of Eq. (35), we find, by way of the implicit function theorem, that

$$\frac{\partial \hat{w}}{\partial e}(e, \psi) \equiv -\frac{u_{we}(\hat{w}(e, \psi), e)}{u_{ww}(\hat{w}(e, \psi), e)} \gtrless 0, \tag{38}$$

$$\frac{\partial \hat{w}}{\partial \psi}(e, \psi) \equiv -\frac{u_{w}(\hat{w}(e, \psi), e)}{\psi u_{ww}(\hat{w}(e, \psi), e)} < 0, \tag{39}$$

because $u_w(w, e) > 0$ and $u_{ww}(w, e) < 0$ for all (w, e) and $\psi < 0$, whereas no assumption was made regarding the sign of $u_{we}(w, e)$. Equation (38) asserts that the wage offered the manager may rise or fall with an increase in the manager's effort, holding constant the marginal cost of the manager's reservation utility. This may seem like an odd result, but it is wise to remember that $w = \hat{w}(e, \psi)$ is *not* the optimal wage, so it is best to reserve judgment about the ambiguity in the sign of Eq. (38). Equation (39), on the other hand, has a definite and intuitive sign. In particular, because $\psi < 0$, it shows that a fall in the marginal cost of the manager's reservation utility reduces the wage offered to the manager. This is intuitive in that as the outside opportunities of the manager decrease, the owner can offer the manager a lower wage and still get the manager to accept the contract.

To determine the optimal value of the marginal cost of the manager's reservation utility, we make use of the remaining necessary condition, to wit, the isoperimetric constraint. Substituting $w = \hat{w}(e, \psi)$ in the isoperimetric constraint thus yields

$$\int_{\underline{\pi}}^{\bar{\pi}} u(\hat{w}(e, \psi), e) f(\pi \mid e)\, d\pi = \bar{u}.$$

But in view of the fact that $w = \hat{w}(e, \psi)$ is independent of π, so is $u(\hat{w}(e, \psi), e)$. Consequently, $u(\hat{w}(e, \psi), e)$ may be factored out in front of the integral, which gives

$$u(\hat{w}(e, \psi), e) \int_{\underline{\pi}}^{\bar{\pi}} f(\pi \mid e)\, d\pi = \bar{u}.$$

Recalling that $f(\pi \mid e)$ is the value of the conditional probability density function, it must, by definition, integrate to unity over the interval $[\underline{\pi}, \bar{\pi}]$. As a result, the above equation reduces to

$$u(\hat{w}(e, \psi), e) = \bar{u}. \tag{40}$$

The Jacobian of Eq. (40) with respect to ψ is given by

$$u_w(\hat{w}(e, \psi), e)\frac{\partial \hat{w}}{\partial \psi}(e, \psi) < 0,$$

the sign of which follows from the assumption that $u_w(w, e) > 0$ for all (w, e) and Eq. (39). Consequently, the implicit function theorem implies that Eq. (40) implicitly determines ψ as a locally $C^{(1)}$ function $(e, \bar{u})$, say,

$$\psi = \psi^*(e, \bar{u}). \tag{41}$$

Equation (41) thus expresses the optimal value of the marginal cost of the manager's reservation utility as a function of the manager's effort and his reservation utility, but not the endpoints $\underline{\pi}$ and $\bar{\pi}$, as we had initially indicated in Eq. (37).

Differentiating the identity $u(\hat{w}(e, \psi^*(e, \bar{u})), e) \equiv \bar{u}$ with respect to e and $\bar{u}$ gives the qualitative properties of the function $\psi^*(\cdot)$, videlicet,

$$\frac{\partial \psi^*}{\partial e}(e, \bar{u}) \equiv -\frac{u_w(\hat{w}(e, \psi^*(e, \bar{u})), e)\frac{\partial \hat{w}}{\partial e}(e, \psi^*(e, \bar{u})) + u_e(\hat{w}(e, \psi^*(e, \bar{u})), e)}{u_w(\hat{w}(e, \psi^*(e, \bar{u})), e)\frac{\partial \hat{w}}{\partial \psi}(e, \psi^*(e, \bar{u}))} \gtreqless 0, \tag{42}$$

$$\frac{\partial \psi^*}{\partial \bar{u}}(e, \bar{u}) \equiv \frac{1}{u_w(\hat{w}(e, \psi^*(e, \bar{u})), e)\frac{\partial \hat{w}}{\partial \psi}(e, \psi^*(e, \bar{u}))} < 0. \tag{43}$$

Equation (43) asserts that the marginal cost of the manager's reservation utility is a strictly decreasing function of the manager's reservation utility. Moreover, by Eqs. (37) and (43), it follows that

$$\frac{\partial^2 V}{\partial \bar{u}^2}(e, \underline{\pi}, \bar{\pi}, \bar{u}) \equiv \frac{\partial \psi^*}{\partial \bar{u}}(e, \bar{u}) < 0,$$

thereby implying that the owner's expected profit is a strictly decreasing and strictly concave function of the manager's reservation utility.

Now turn to the determination of the optimal wage rate of the manager, say $w^*(e, \bar{u})$, conditional on his effort. In particular, substituting $\psi = \psi^*(e, \bar{u})$ into $w = \hat{w}(e, \psi)$ gives $w^*(e, \bar{u})$, that is, the optimal conditional wage rate of the manager is given by the identity

$$w^*(e, \bar{u}) \equiv \hat{w}(e, \psi^*(e, \bar{u})). \tag{44}$$

Differentiating Eq. (44) with respect to e and $\bar{u}$ using the chain rule, and making use of Eqs. (39) and (42) through (44) yields

$$\begin{aligned}\frac{\partial w^*}{\partial e}(e, \bar{u}) &\equiv \frac{\partial \hat{w}}{\partial e}(e, \psi^*(e, \bar{u})) + \frac{\partial \hat{w}}{\partial \psi}(e, \psi^*(e, \bar{u}))\frac{\partial \psi^*}{\partial e}(e, \bar{u}) \\ &= \frac{\partial \hat{w}}{\partial e}(e, \psi^*(e, \bar{u})) - \frac{\partial \hat{w}}{\partial \psi}(e, \psi^*(e, \bar{u})) \\ &\quad \times \left[\frac{u_w(w^*(e, \bar{u}), e)\frac{\partial \hat{w}}{\partial e}(e, \psi^*(e, \bar{u})) + u_e(w^*(e, \bar{u}), e)}{u_w(w^*(e, \bar{u}), e)\frac{\partial \hat{w}}{\partial \psi}(e, \psi^*(e, \bar{u}))}\right]\end{aligned} \tag{45}$$

$$= -\frac{u_e(w^*(e,\bar{u}),e)}{u_w(w^*(e,\bar{u}),e)} > 0,$$

$$\frac{\partial w^*}{\partial \bar{u}}(e,\bar{u}) \equiv \frac{\partial \hat{w}}{\partial \psi}(e,\psi^*(e,\bar{u}))\frac{\partial \psi^*}{\partial \bar{u}}(e,\bar{u}) > 0. \tag{46}$$

Equation (45) shows that an increase in the effort exerted by the manager will be met with a higher conditional wage by the owner, the intuitive result that was lacking in Eq. (38). Equation (46) also yields the intuitive conclusion that the conditional wage rate of the manager increases with an increase in the manager's reservation utility, that is, with his outside opportunities. This completes the examination of the first stage of the optimal contracting problem.

The second stage of the optimal contracting problem seeks to determine the choice of the managers effort, which, as you should recall, was held fixed at an arbitrary value $e \in E$ throughout stage one. In view of the fact that we have broken the optimal contracting problem given in Eq. (33) into two stages, the optimal value function $V^*(\cdot)$ of problem (33) is defined as the maximum value of the optimal value function $V(\cdot)$ found by solving the first-stage problem (34) with respect to the manager's effort, to wit,

$$V^*(\underline{\pi},\bar{\pi},\bar{u}) \stackrel{\text{def}}{=} \max_{e \in E} V(e,\underline{\pi},\bar{\pi},\bar{u}). \tag{47}$$

Assuming that $e = e^*(\underline{\pi},\bar{\pi},\bar{u})$ is a solution to optimization problem (47), the first-order necessary condition this solution must satisfy is therefore $\partial V(e,\underline{\pi},\bar{\pi},\bar{u})/\partial e = 0$. Remembering that $\tilde{F}(\pi,w,\psi;e) \stackrel{\text{def}}{=} [\pi - w]f(\pi \mid e) - \psi u(w,e) f(\pi \mid e)$, Theorem 7.3 part (i) implies that the first-order necessary condition $\partial V(e,\underline{\pi},\bar{\pi},\bar{u})/\partial e = 0$ takes the form

$$\frac{\partial V}{\partial e}(e,\underline{\pi},\bar{\pi},\bar{u}) = \int_{\underline{\pi}}^{\bar{\pi}} \frac{\partial \tilde{F}}{\partial e}(\pi,w,\psi;e)\Bigg|_{\substack{w=w^*(e,\bar{u})\\ \psi=\psi^*(e,\bar{u})}} d\pi$$

$$= \int_{\underline{\pi}}^{\bar{\pi}} [[\pi - w^*(e,\bar{u})]f_e(\pi \mid e) - \psi^*(e,\bar{u})[u(w^*(e,\bar{u}),e)f_e(\pi \mid e)$$

$$+ u_e(w^*(e,\bar{u}),e)f(\pi \mid e)]]\,d\pi = 0.$$

Given that $f(\cdot)$ is a probability density function, it satisfies

$$\int_{\underline{\pi}}^{\bar{\pi}} f(\pi \mid e)\,d\pi = 1 \tag{48}$$

for all $e \in E$, and thus is an identity in e. In view of this conclusion, we may differentiate Eq. (48) with respect to e to get

$$\int_{\underline{\pi}}^{\bar{\pi}} f_e(\pi \mid e)\, d\pi = 0. \tag{49}$$

Substituting Eqs. (48) and (49) into the above first-order necessary condition, and using the fact that $w^*(e, \bar{u})$ and $\psi^*(e, \bar{u})$ are independent π, we arrive at

$$\frac{\partial V}{\partial e}(e, \underline{\pi}, \bar{\pi}, \bar{u}) = \int_{\underline{\pi}}^{\bar{\pi}} \pi f_e(\pi \mid e)\, d\pi - \psi^*(e, \bar{u}) u_e(w^*(e, \bar{u}), e) = 0. \tag{50}$$

Rearranging Eq. (50) yields a simpler form to interpret, scilicet,

$$\int_{\underline{\pi}}^{\bar{\pi}} \pi f_e(\pi \mid e)\, d\pi = \psi^*(e, \bar{u}) u_e(w^*(e, \bar{u}), e). \tag{51}$$

The left-hand side of Eq. (51) is the expected marginal gross profit of the manager's effort, whereas the right-hand side is the product of the marginal cost of the manager's reservation utility and his marginal disutility of effort. Thus the optimal choice of the manager's effort by the owner obeys an intuitive marginal condition, namely, that the expected marginal gross profit of managerial effort equals the marginal cost of managerial effort.

The next step in the analysis is the determination of the qualitative properties of optimal managerial effort, $e = e^*(\underline{\pi}, \bar{\pi}, \bar{u})$. To this end, assume that the second-order sufficient condition holds at the solution to problem (47), that is, $V_{ee}(e^*(\underline{\pi}, \bar{\pi}, \bar{u}), \underline{\pi}, \bar{\pi}, \bar{u}) < 0$. Then substituting $e = e^*(\underline{\pi}, \bar{\pi}, \bar{u})$ in Eq. (50) and differentiating with respect to $(\underline{\pi}, \bar{\pi}, \bar{u})$, using both the chain rule and Leibniz's rule gives

$$\frac{\partial e^*}{\partial \underline{\pi}}(\underline{\pi}, \bar{\pi}, \bar{u}) \equiv \frac{\underline{\pi} f_e(\underline{\pi} \mid e^*(\underline{\pi}, \bar{\pi}, \bar{u}))}{V_{ee}(e^*(\underline{\pi}, \bar{\pi}, \bar{u}), \underline{\pi}, \bar{\pi}, \bar{u})} \gtrless 0, \tag{52}$$

$$\frac{\partial e^*}{\partial \bar{\pi}}(\underline{\pi}, \bar{\pi}, \bar{u}) \equiv \frac{-\bar{\pi} f_e(\bar{\pi} \mid e^*(\underline{\pi}, \bar{\pi}, \bar{u}))}{V_{ee}(e^*(\underline{\pi}, \bar{\pi}, \bar{u}), \underline{\pi}, \bar{\pi}, \bar{u})} \gtrless 0, \tag{53}$$

$$\frac{\partial e^*}{\partial \bar{u}}(\underline{\pi}, \bar{\pi}, \bar{u}) \equiv \frac{\psi^*(e, \bar{u}) u_{ew}(w^*(e, \bar{u}), e) \frac{\partial w^*}{\partial \bar{u}}(e, \bar{u}) + u_e(w^*(e, \bar{u}), e) \frac{\partial \psi^*}{\partial \bar{u}}(e, \bar{u})}{V_{ee}(e^*(\underline{\pi}, \bar{\pi}, \bar{u}), \underline{\pi}, \bar{\pi}, \bar{u})} \gtrless 0. \tag{54}$$

Without further assumptions on the principal-agent problem (33), none of these expressions can be signed, in general. It is certainly plausible that $\underline{\pi} < 0$ and $\bar{\pi} > 0$, since one would expect that negative and positive realizations of gross profit are possible on the project. Under these two conditions, the sign of the expressions in Eqs. (52) and (53) is the same as the sign of the terms $f_e(\underline{\pi} \mid e^*(\underline{\pi}, \bar{\pi}, \bar{u}))$ and $f_e(\bar{\pi} \mid e^*(\underline{\pi}, \bar{\pi}, \bar{u}))$, respectively. Equation (54), on the other hand, can be signed with the aid of the assumption $u_{we}(w, e) \equiv 0$ for all $e \in E$ and w, an assumption that is maintained in much of the literature related to the principal-agent problem. In this case, it follows from Eq. (43) and the aforementioned assumption that $u_e(w, e) < 0$ for all (w, e), that $\partial e^*(\underline{\pi}, \bar{\pi}, \bar{u})/\partial \bar{u} < 0$. Thus, under the standard assumptions made in the literature, an increase in the manager's reservation utility results in a decrease in his effort. In other words, with better outside opportunities for the manager, the owner must offer a contract that requires less effort on the part of the manager if the owner is to get the manager to accept the contract.

The final phase of the analysis is the determination of the *unconditional* optimal wage of the manager, unconditional in the sense that the optimal effort, rather than an arbitrarily given effort, is used to compute it. The unconditional optimal wage rate, say, $w^{**}(\underline{\pi}, \bar{\pi}, \bar{u})$, is thus given by an identity akin to Eq. (44), namely,

$$w^{**}(\underline{\pi}, \bar{\pi}, \bar{u}) \equiv w^*(e^*(\underline{\pi}, \bar{\pi}, \bar{u}), \bar{u}). \tag{55}$$

We terminate our analysis of the principal-agent problem at this juncture and thus relegate the qualitative analysis of identity (55) to a mental exercise.

To close out this chapter, we present a sufficiency theorem for the primal isoperimetric problem (1). It is an obvious extension of earlier sufficiency theorems for optimal control problems, and as such, its proof is left for a mental exercise.

Theorem 7.4 (Sufficient Conditions): *Let $\mathbf{z}(\cdot)$ be an admissible function and ψ be the corresponding value of the multiplier that satisfies the system of augmented Euler equations*

$$\tilde{F}_{x_n}(t, \mathbf{z}(t), \dot{\mathbf{z}}(t), \psi) - \frac{d}{dt}\tilde{F}_{\dot{x}_n}(t, \mathbf{z}(t), \dot{\mathbf{z}}(t), \psi) \equiv 0, \quad n = 1, 2, \ldots, N,$$

where $\tilde{F}(t, \mathbf{x}, \dot{\mathbf{x}}, \psi) \overset{\text{def}}{=} F(t, \mathbf{x}, \dot{\mathbf{x}}) - \psi G(t, \mathbf{x}, \dot{\mathbf{x}})$. Suppose that $\tilde{F}(\cdot) \in C^{(2)}$ is a concave function of $(\mathbf{x}, \dot{\mathbf{x}})\, \forall\, t \in [t_0, t_1]$ over an open convex set containing all the admissible values of $(\mathbf{x}(\cdot), \dot{\mathbf{x}}(\cdot))$ for the above value of ψ, then $J[\mathbf{z}(\cdot)] \geq J[\mathbf{x}(\cdot)]$ for all admissible functions $\mathbf{x}(\cdot)$. That is, the function $\mathbf{z}(\cdot)$ provides the global maximum to $J[\cdot]$ over the space of admissible functions. Furthermore, if $\tilde{F}(\cdot) \in C^{(2)}$ is a strictly concave function under the same conditions, then $J[\mathbf{z}(\cdot)] > J[\mathbf{x}(\cdot)]$ for all admissible functions $\mathbf{x}(\cdot)$, and the function $\mathbf{z}(\cdot)$ is unique.

For an application of this theorem, we return to Example 7.1.

Example 7.4: Recall the primal isoperimetric problem from Example 7.1:

$$\min_{x(\cdot)} J[x(\cdot)] \stackrel{\text{def}}{=} \int_0^1 [\dot{x}(t)]^2 \, dt$$

$$\text{s.t.} \quad K[x(\cdot)] \stackrel{\text{def}}{=} \int_0^1 x(t) dt = c,$$

$$x(0) = 0, \; x(1) = 0,$$

where $c > 0$ is a parameter. Also recall that the augmented integrand function $\tilde{F}(\cdot)$ has values given by $\tilde{F}(t, x, \dot{x}, \psi) \stackrel{\text{def}}{=} F(t, x, \dot{x}) - \psi G(t, x, \dot{x}) = \dot{x}^2 - \psi x$. Now set $\psi = 24c > 0$ and then compute

$$\tilde{F}_{xx}(t, x, \dot{x}, 24c) = 0, \; \tilde{F}_{\dot{x}\dot{x}}(t, x, \dot{x}, 24c) = 2 > 0, \; \tilde{F}_{x\dot{x}}(t, x, \dot{x}, 24c) = 0,$$

$$\tilde{F}_{xx}(t, x, \dot{x}, 24c) \cdot \tilde{F}_{\dot{x}\dot{x}}(t, x, \dot{x}, 24c) - [\tilde{F}_{x\dot{x}}(t, x, \dot{x}, 24c)]^2 = 0.$$

Thus the Hessian matrix of $\tilde{F}(\cdot)$ with respect to $(x, \dot{x})$ is positive semidefinite for all $t \in [0, 1]$ given $\psi = 24c > 0$, which is equivalent to the convexity of the function $\tilde{F}(\cdot)$ by Theorem 21.5 of Simon and Blume (1994). Hence, by Theorem 7.4, the solution curve $z_1(t; c) = -6ct^2 + 6ct$ to the augmented Euler equation of this isoperimetric problem does in fact solve the problem. Moreover, the solution is unique because it is the *only* solution to the augmented Euler equation.

Turning to the reciprocal isoperimetric problem, we have

$$\max_{x(\cdot)} K[x(\cdot)] \stackrel{\text{def}}{=} \int_0^1 x(t) \, dt$$

$$\text{s.t.} \quad J[x(\cdot)] \stackrel{\text{def}}{=} \int_0^1 [\dot{x}(t)]^2 \, dt = V(c) = 12c^2,$$

$$x(0) = 0, \; x(1) = 0.$$

Recall that the augmented integrand for the reciprocal problem is $\hat{F}(t, x, \dot{x}, \theta) \stackrel{\text{def}}{=} x - \theta \dot{x}^2$, and so

$$\hat{F}_{xx}(t, x, \dot{x}, \theta) = 0, \; \hat{F}_{\dot{x}\dot{x}}(t, x, \dot{x}, \theta) = -2\theta, \; \hat{F}_{x\dot{x}}(t, x, \dot{x}, \theta) = 0,$$

$$\hat{F}_{xx}(t, x, \dot{x}, \theta) \cdot \hat{F}_{\dot{x}\dot{x}}(t, x, \dot{x}, \theta) - [\hat{F}_{x\dot{x}}(t, x, \dot{x}, \theta)]^2 = 0.$$

Thus for $\theta = \frac{1}{24c} > 0$, the Hessian matrix of $\hat{F}(\cdot)$ with respect to $(x, \dot{x})$ is negative semidefinite for all $t \in [0, 1]$, which is equivalent to the concavity of the function $\hat{F}(\cdot)$ in $(x, \dot{x})$. Hence, by Theorem 7.4, the solution curve $z_2(t; c) = -6ct^2 + 6ct$ to the augmented Euler equation of the reciprocal isoperimetric problem, which corresponds to the multiplier $\theta = \frac{1}{24c} > 0$, yields the global maximum of the reciprocal isoperimetric problem. In contrast, for $\theta = -\frac{1}{24c} < 0$, the Hessian matrix of $\hat{F}(\cdot)$ with respect to $(x, \dot{x})$ is positive semidefinite for all $t \in [0, 1]$, which is equivalent to the convexity of the function $\hat{F}(\cdot)$ in $(x, \dot{x})$. Hence, by Theorem 7.4, the solution curve $z_3(t; c) = 6ct^2 - 6ct$ to the augmented Euler equation of the reciprocal isoperimetric problem, which corresponds to the multiplier $\theta = -\frac{1}{24c} < 0$, yields the global minimum of the reciprocal isoperimetric problem. These are the same conclusions we reached in Example 7.1 by direct computation of the optimal value function for the curves $z_2(t; c) = -6ct^2 + 6ct$ and $z_3(t; c) = 6ct^2 - 6ct$. Furthermore, note that $z_2(t; c) = -6ct^2 + 6ct$ is the unique curve that yields the global maximum in the reciprocal problem, whereas $z_3(t; c) = 6ct^2 - 6ct$ is the unique curve that yields the global minimum in the reciprocal problem.

The next chapter develops further results for reciprocal pairs of isoperimetric problems that are of economic importance. We demonstrate the power and reach of the general theorems by conducting a rather exhaustive comparative dynamics analysis of a general form of the nonrenewable resource–extracting model of the firm.

MENTAL EXERCISES

7.1 Consider the isoperimetric problem

$$\min_{x(\cdot)} J[x(\cdot)] \stackrel{\text{def}}{=} \int_0^1 [\dot{x}(t)]^2 \, dt$$

$$\text{s.t.} \quad K[x(\cdot)] \stackrel{\text{def}}{=} \int_0^1 [x(t)]^2 dt = 2, \ x(0) = 0, \ x(1) = 0.$$

(a) Show that if the multiplier for the integral constraint is zero, that is, $\psi = 0$, then the curve $z(t) \equiv 0 \, \forall \, t \in [0, 1]$ is the only solution of the augmented Euler equation satisfying the boundary conditions.

(b) Show, however, that the curve $z(t) \equiv 0 \, \forall \, t \in [0, 1]$ is not admissible and thus not optimal.

(c) Show that if $\psi < 0$, then the curve $z(t) \equiv 0 \, \forall \, t \in [0, 1]$ is the only solution of the Euler equation satisfying the boundary conditions. By part (b), this solution is not admissible or optimal.

(d) We now know that the curve $z(t) \equiv 0 \, \forall \, t \in [0, 1]$ is not admissible or optimal. Show that if $\psi > 0$, then the optimal value of ψ is $\psi^* = n^2\pi^2$,

$n = 1, 2, \ldots,$ and the optimal path is given by

$$z(t) = \pm \left[\frac{2}{\int_0^1 [\sin n\pi t]^2 \, dt} \right]^{\frac{1}{2}} \sin n\pi t.$$

7.2 Consider the isoperimetric problem

$$\min_{x(\cdot)} J[x(\cdot)] \stackrel{\text{def}}{=} \int_0^T e^{-rt} x(t)\, dt$$

$$\text{s.t.} \quad K[x(\cdot)] \stackrel{\text{def}}{=} \int_0^T [x(t)]^{\frac{1}{2}}\, dt = c.$$

(a) Find the extremal using Theorem 7.1.
(b) Find the extremal by eliminating the isoperimetric constraint. You must come up with a transformation that allows you to do this.
(c) Why aren't there any boundary conditions for this isoperimetric problem?
(d) Prove that the extremal solves the isoperimetric problem and is unique.

7.3 Consider the isoperimetric problem

$$\min_{x(\cdot)} J[x(\cdot)] \stackrel{\text{def}}{=} \int_0^b [1 + [x(t)]^2]^{\frac{1}{2}}\, dt$$

$$\text{s.t.} \quad K[x(\cdot)] \stackrel{\text{def}}{=} \int_0^b x(t)\, dt = c,$$

where $b > 0$ and $c > 0$ are given parameters.
(a) Find an extremal for the isoperimetric problem.
(b) Does the extremal solve the problem? Show your work.
(c) Is the extremal unique? Explain clearly.

7.4 Consider the isoperimetric problem

$$\max_{x(\cdot)} J[x(\cdot)] \stackrel{\text{def}}{=} \int_0^1 [2x(t) - [x(t)]^2]\, dt$$

$$\text{s.t.} \quad K[x(\cdot)] \stackrel{\text{def}}{=} \int_0^1 tx(t)\, dt = 1.$$

(a) Find an extremal for the isoperimetric problem.
(b) Does the extremal solve the problem? Show your work.
(c) Is the extremal unique? Explain.

7.5 Find the extremals for the functional

$$\min_{x(\cdot)} J[x(\cdot)] \overset{\text{def}}{=} \int_1^2 [t^2 + [\dot{x}(t)]^2]dt$$

$$\text{s.t.} \quad K[x(\cdot)] \overset{\text{def}}{=} \int_1^2 [x(t)]^2 \, dt = 5, \; x(1) = 0, \; x(2) = 0.$$

7.6 Find the extremals for the functional

$$\min_{x(\cdot)} J[x(\cdot)] \overset{\text{def}}{=} \int_0^1 tx(t) \, dt$$

$$\text{s.t.} \quad K[x(\cdot)] \overset{\text{def}}{=} \int_0^1 [\dot{x}(t)]^2 \, dt = 1, \; x(0) = 0, \; x(1) = 0.$$

7.7 Recall the archetype nonrenewable resource–extracting model of the firm in isoperimetric form, given in Example 7.2:

$$\Pi(r, x_0, T) \overset{\text{def}}{=} \max_{q(\cdot)} \int_0^T \pi(q(t)) e^{-rt} \, dt$$

$$\text{s.t.} \quad K[q(\cdot)] \overset{\text{def}}{=} \int_0^T q(t) \, dt = x_0,$$

where $q(t)$ is the extraction rate of the nonrenewable resource, $r > 0$ is the discount rate, $\pi(q(t))$ is the profit flow from extracting at the rate $q(t)$, and $x_0 > 0$ is the initial stock of the nonrenewable resource. Assume that $\pi(\cdot) \in C^{(2)}, \pi'(q) > 0$, and $\pi''(q) < 0$. This question asks you to derive results you've already shown in Mental Exercise 4.21, but this time by solving the problem using Theorems 7.1 and 7.4. You will also extend the previous qualitative properties of the model to account for the results of this chapter, particularly Theorem 7.3. Let $\pi(q) \overset{\text{def}}{=} \ln q$ be the profit flow for this problem.

(a) Find explicit formulas for the optimal extraction rate, say, $q^*(t; r, x_0, T)$, and the value of the multiplier, say, $\psi^*(r, x_0, T)$. Prove that $q^*(t; r, x_0, T)$ is the unique optimal solution.

(b) Find an explicit formula for the optimal value function $\Pi(r, x_0, T)$. You may *not* leave $\Pi(r, x_0, T)$ expressed as an integral.

(c) Compute the partial derivative $\partial \Pi(r, x_0, T)/\partial x_0$ and show that Theorem 7.3 holds in this model. Provide an economic interpretation of this dynamic envelope result.

(d) Compute the comparative dynamics $\partial q^*(t; r, x_0, T)/\partial x_0$ and $\partial \psi^*(r, x_0, T)/\partial x_0$. Can you sign these? Provide an economic explanation of the results.
(e) Compute the comparative dynamics $\partial q^*(t; r, x_0, T)/\partial T$ and $\partial \psi^*(r, x_0, T)/\partial T$. Can you sign these? Provide an economic explanation of the results.
(f) Compute the comparative dynamics $\partial q^*(t; r, x_0, T)/\partial r$ and $\partial \psi^*(r, x_0, T)/\partial r$. Can you sign these? Provide an economic explanation of the results that can be signed.
(g) Consider $\partial q^*(0; r, x_0, T)/\partial r$, the so-called impact effect of the parameter change. Can you sign this? Provide an economic explanation of the result.

7.8 Imagine a research and development (R&D) project in which there are decreasing returns to spending money faster. That is, the more rapidly the money is spent, the less it contributes to total effective effort. For example, more rapid spending may be used for overtime payments, for less productive factors, or for greater use of parallel rather than sequential effort. Let $s(t)$ denote the rate of spending on R&D in dollars at time t, and let $e(t)$ denote the effort rate on R&D at time t. The link between spending and effort alluded to above is given by the production function $e(t) = [s(t)]^{\frac{1}{2}}$, which exhibits a positive but declining marginal product of spending (as the story above asserted). The cumulative effort required to complete the project by the given time $T > 0$ is $A > 0$. It is therefore required that the cumulative effort expended on the R&D project equal the total effort required to complete the project; hence

$$\int_0^T e(t)\,dt = A.$$

The firm is asserted to minimize the present discounted development cost of completing the R&D project. Formally, the isoperimetric problem is given by

$$C(A, r, T) \stackrel{\text{def}}{=} \min_{s(\cdot)} \int_0^T e^{-rt} s(t)\,dt$$

$$\text{s.t.} \quad \int_0^T [s(t)]^{\frac{1}{2}}\,dt = A,$$

where $r > 0$ is the discount rate, and the production function $e(t) = [s(t)]^{\frac{1}{2}}$ has been used to substitute into the integral constraint.
(a) Find the general solution of the augmented Euler equation.
(b) What do you notice unusual about the augmented Euler equation? Is this related to the fact that there are no boundary conditions for the isoperimetric problem?

(c) Find the specific solution to the augmented Euler equation and denote it by $s^*(t; A, r, T)$. Find the corresponding value of the constant multiplier and designate it by $\psi^*(A, r, T)$. Also determine the optimal path of effort and denote it by $e^*(t; A, r, T)$.

(d) Prove that the solution you found in part (c) does indeed solve the isoperimetric problem.

(e) What is the economic interpretation of $\psi^*(A, r, T)$? What theorem did you invoke to get this interpretation?

(f) Find the comparative dynamics $\partial e^*(t; A, r, T)/\partial A$ and $\partial \psi^*(A, r, T)/\partial A$. Provide an economic interpretation of these results.

(g) Find the comparative dynamics $\partial e^*(t; A, r, T)/\partial T$ and $\partial \psi^*(A, r, T)/\partial T$. Provide an economic interpretation of these results.

(h) Find the comparative dynamics $\partial e^*(t; A, r, T)/\partial r$ and $\partial \lambda^*(A, r, T)/\partial r$. Show that $\partial \psi^*(A, r, T)/\partial r < 0$ and provide an economic interpretation.

(i) Show that $\partial e^*(0; A, r, T)/\partial r < 0$. What does this tell you about the effect of the interest rate increase?

7.9 Verify that Eq. (10) follows from Eq. (9) by using Eqs. (3), (4), and (6).

7.10 Verify that Eq. (12) follows from Eq. (11) by integrating Eq. (11) by parts and using Eq. (2).

7.11 Prove part (i) of Theorem 7.3. Provide an economic interpretation of it.

7.12 Prove part (iii) of Theorem 7.3. Provide an economic interpretation of it. You may want to wait until after you have read Chapter 9 to do this proof.

7.13 Prove part (iv) of Theorem 7.3. Provide an economic interpretation of it.

7.14 Prove part (v) of Theorem 7.3. Provide an economic interpretation of it. You may want to wait until after you have read Chapter 9 to do this proof.

7.15 Prove part (vi) of Theorem 7.3. Provide an economic interpretation of it.

7.16 Prove that a solution to the necessary conditions of Example 7.2 is a solution of the isoperimetric problem.

7.17 Prove Theorem 7.4.

7.18 Consider an individual whose consumption rate at time t is given by $c(t)$, and whose *instantaneous* utility function is given by $u(c(t)) \stackrel{\text{def}}{=} \ln c(t)$. Let $\rho > 0$ be the individual's subjective rate of time preference, and let $r > 0$ be the market interest rate, the latter being the rate at which cash flows are discounted. The constant price of the single composite consumption good is $p > 0$, whereas $w > 0$ is the individual's present discounted value of wealth. The consumer lives over the fixed and finite interval $[0, T]$, $T > 0$, and is asserted to maximize the present discounted value of utility by choosing a consumption function $c(\cdot)$ subject to an intertemporal budget constraint that requires the equality of the present discounted value of expenditures with the present discounted value of wealth. Formally, the problem is given by the isoperimetric problem

$$V(\beta)$$

$$\overset{\text{def}}{=} \max_{c(\cdot)} \left\{ U[c(\cdot)] \overset{\text{def}}{=} \int_0^T \ln c(t)\, e^{-\rho t}\, dt \text{ s.t. } E[c(\cdot)] \overset{\text{def}}{=} \int_0^T pc(t)\, e^{-rt}\, dt = w \right\},$$

where $\beta \overset{\text{def}}{=} (p, \rho, r, w, T)$ is the constant parameter vector. Note that this version of the intertemporal utility maximization problem has a lifetime budget constraint, whereas that in Example 1.3 has a budget constraint that must hold for each date in the planning horizon.

(a) Derive the necessary conditions for this variational problem and solve them for the extremal, say, $c^*(t; \beta)$, as well as the associated conjugate variable (or multiplier), say, $\psi^*(\beta)$.

(b) Prove that the extremal you found in part (a) is the solution to the isoperimetric problem. Is it the unique solution? Explain why or why not.

(c) Prove that $\operatorname{sign}[\dot{c}^*(t; \beta)] = \operatorname{sign}[r - \rho]$. Provide an economic interpretation.

(d) Derive the optimal value function $V(\cdot)$. Do not leave $V(\cdot)$ expressed as an integral. Provide an economic interpretation of $V(\cdot)$.

(e) Confirm that Theorem 7.3 holds for this problem and that $V(\cdot)$ is a strictly concave function of w. Provide an economic interpretation of the strict concavity of $V(\cdot)$.

(f) Prove that $\partial c^*(t; \beta)/\partial w > 0\, \forall\, t \in [0, T]$ and provide an economic interpretation.

(g) Prove that $\partial c^*(t; \beta)/\partial r \geq 0\, \forall\, t \in [0, T]$ and provide an economic interpretation.

(h) Prove that $\partial c^*(t; \beta)/\partial p < 0\, \forall\, t \in [0, T]$ and provide an economic interpretation.

7.19 This question asks you to consider some comparative *statics* of the nonrenewable resource–extracting model of the firm in a two-period discrete time framework. Consider, therefore, a firm that "lives" for two periods: period 1, the present, and period 2, the future. Let $s > 0$ be the stock of a nonrenewable resource (say, gold) that is buried under the ground and that the firm has ownership rights to. The extraction of the nonrenewable resource is costly, and such costs may be summarized by the minimum cost function $C(\cdot) \in C^{(2)}$, which is a function of the rate of resource extraction in each period, namely, $q_i i = 1, 2$. Hence $C(q_i)$, $i = 1, 2$, are the costs incurred in each period to extract the resource. The firm is a price taker in the output market, facing prices $p_i > 0$, $i = 1, 2$, for the asset extracted in each period. The firm is asserted to maximize the present discounted value of the profit received from extracting and selling the nonrenewable resource, subject to the requirement that it extract the entire stock of the resource in the two periods in which it lives. The discount rate $r > 0$ is used by the firm in discounting future profit.

(a) Set up the profit maximization problem faced by the firm, including the definition of the indirect (or maximized) objective function. Denote the indirect objective function by $\pi(\cdot)$.

(b) Derive the first-order necessary conditions for this problem and provide an economic interpretation. How would you *in principle* find the optimal extraction rate in each period, say, $q_i = q_i^*(p_1, p_2, r, s)$, $i = 1, 2$, and the optimal value of the Lagrange multiplier, say, $\lambda = \lambda^*(p_1, p_2, r, s)$?

(c) *Prove* that

$$\frac{\partial \pi}{\partial s}(p_1, p_2, r, s) \equiv \lambda^*(p_1, p_2, r, s),$$

and provide an economic interpretation of the result.

(d) Derive the second-order sufficient condition in the form of a determinant condition rather than as a quadratic form. Is increasing marginal cost of extraction implied by the second-order sufficient condition?

(e) Find the comparative statics

$$\frac{\partial q_1^*}{\partial p_2}, \frac{\partial q_2^*}{\partial p_2}, \quad \text{and} \quad \frac{\partial \lambda^*}{\partial p_2},$$

and provide an economic interpretation.

(f) Find the comparative statics

$$\frac{\partial q_1^*}{\partial r}, \frac{\partial q_2^*}{\partial r}, \quad \text{and} \quad \frac{\partial \lambda^*}{\partial r},$$

and provide an economic interpretation.

7.20 *Rational Procrastination.* Here's a typical situation faced by students at universities all across the world. A research paper is assigned by the professor of a class the first day of the term, say, $t = 0$, and is due at the end of the term, say $T > 0$ hours later. At University of California, Davis, this would mean that the research paper is due in $24 \times 7 \times 10 = 1{,}680$ hours, or 10 weeks, from the present. The total effort required by the typical student to complete the paper is known to be $\varepsilon \in (0, T)$ hours. Define $e(t) \in [0, 1]$ as the proportion of each hour that the student devotes to working on the paper (i.e., research effort), and define $\ell(t) \in [0, 1]$ as the proportion of each hour that the student devotes to leisure activities. It is assumed that the student will complete the term paper by the required date, thereby implying the isoperimetric constraint

$$\int_0^T e(t)\,dt = \varepsilon.$$

Given that each hour is made up entirely of leisure time and research effort, we also have the equality constraint that $e(t) + \ell(t) = 1$ for all $t \in [0, T]$. The instantaneous preferences of the typical student are defined over leisure time, a good, and denoted by $U(\ell)$, where $U(\cdot) \in C^{(2)}$, $U'(\ell) > 0$, and $U''(\ell) < 0$ for all $\ell(t) \in (0, 1)$. We assume that $e(t) \in (0, 1)$ and $\ell(t) \in (0, 1)$ for all $t \in [0, T]$ in an optimal plan, thereby ruling out these constraints from binding. These two assumptions will simplify the analysis considerably. The student is asserted to maximize the present discounted value of utility over the term, subject to completing the research paper. Hence the constrained isoperimetric problem faced by the typical student can be stated as

$$V(\beta) \stackrel{\text{def}}{=} \max_{e(\cdot), \ell(\cdot)} \int_0^T U(\ell(t))\, e^{-rt}\, dt$$

$$\text{s.t.} \quad \int_0^T e(t)\, dt = \varepsilon,$$

$$e(t) + \ell(t) = 1,$$

where $r > 0$ is the student's intertemporal rate of time preference and $\beta \stackrel{\text{def}}{=} (\varepsilon, r, T) \in \Re^3_{++}$. Assume that the pair of curves $(e^*(t; \beta), \ell^*(t; \beta))$ is a solution to the necessary conditions of the constrained isoperimetric problem, with corresponding multiplier for the integral constraint $\psi(\beta)$.

(a) Convert the above constrained isoperimetric problem into an unconstrained isoperimetric problem by using the equality constraint $e(t) + \ell(t) = 1$ to eliminate $e(t)$ from the problem.

(b) Derive the necessary conditions for the unconstrained isoperimetric problem.

(c) Prove that $(\ell^*(t; \beta), \psi(\beta))$ is a solution of the unconstrained isoperimetric problem.

(d) Prove that $\psi(\beta) < 0$. Provide an economic interpretation of this result. Does it make sense? Explain.

(e) Prove that $\dot{\ell}^*(t; \beta) < 0\, \forall\, t \in [0, T]$ and $\dot{e}^*(t; \beta) > 0\, \forall\, t \in [0, T]$. Provide an economic interpretation. Is this the rational procrastination result alluded to in the problem? Why or why not?

7.21 *Maximum Entropy and Isoperimetric Problems.* Using a set of four axioms about information, it can be shown if $p \in (0, 1)$ is the probability of an event E occurring, then $h(p) \stackrel{\text{def}}{=} \ln \frac{1}{p} = -\ln p$ is the information contained in the observation that the event E actually occurred. For example, if I attach a low probability to the event that it will rain today, say, $p = 0.01$, then the amount of information transmitted by the message that it has in fact rained today is relatively large, namely, $h(0.01) \stackrel{\text{def}}{=} \ln \frac{1}{0.01} = -\ln 0.01 \approx 4.60517$, since I essentially didn't think it was going to rain today. On the other hand, if I

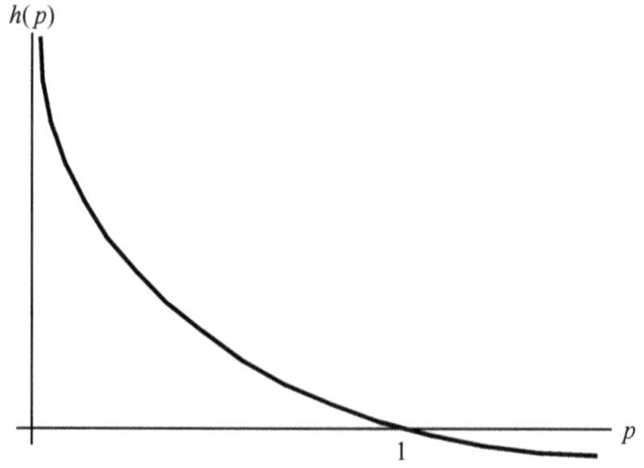

Figure 7.3

attach a high probability that it will rain today, say, $p = 0.99$, then the amount of information transmitted by the message that it has in fact rained today is relatively small, namely, $h(0.99) \overset{\text{def}}{=} \ln \frac{1}{0.99} = -\ln 0.99 \approx 0.0100503$, since I was almost certain that it was going to rain anyway. A graph of the function $h(\cdot)$ appears in Figure 7.3. The classical maximum entropy problem is to find a probability density function $p(\cdot)$ that maximizes the expected value of the information contained in a continuum of messages received from the events. It can be formulated as the following isoperimetric problem:

$$\max_{p(\cdot)} J[p(\cdot)] \overset{\text{def}}{=} -\int_{t_0}^{t_1} p(t) \ln p(t)\, dt$$

$$\text{s.t.} \quad \int_{t_0}^{t_1} p(t)\, dt = 1.$$

(a) Prove that the uniform probability density function yields the unique global optimum of the maximum entropy problem.

(b) Can you provide an intuitive explanation for this result?

7.22 *Minimum Cross-Entropy and Isoperimetric Problems.* The classical maximum entropy problem is to find a probability density function $p(\cdot)$ that maximizes the expected value of the information contained in a continuum of messages received from the events. This was the problem studied in the previous mental exercise. In many situations, however, the researcher may have nonsample or presample information about the probability density function $p(\cdot)$ in the form of a prior probability density function, say, $q(\cdot)$. In other words, the researcher may have an initial hypothesis that $q(\cdot)$ is a plausible probability density function. When such prior knowledge exists, the researcher will often wish to incorporate it into the maximum entropy formalism. This situation is handled via the principle of minimum cross-entropy. This principle implies that one should choose an estimate of the probability density function $p(\cdot)$ that can be discriminated from $q(\cdot)$ with a minimum difference. The principle of minimum cross-entropy thus leads to the following isoperimetric problem:

$$\min_{p(\cdot)} J[p(\cdot)]$$

$$\overset{\text{def}}{=} \left[\int_{t_0}^{t_1} p(t) \ln\left(\frac{p(t)}{q(t)}\right) dt = \int_{t_0}^{t_1} p(t) \ln p(t)\, dt - \int_{t_0}^{t_1} p(t) \ln q(t)\, dt \right]$$

$$\text{s.t.} \quad \int_{t_0}^{t_1} p(t)\, dt = 1.$$

Recall that because $q(\cdot)$ is a probability density function, it must satisfy $\int_{t_0}^{t_1} q(t)\, dt = 1$.

(a) Find the unique global optimum of the minimum cross-entropy problem.

(b) Interpret your result.

7.23 Differentiate the identity in Eq. (55) with respect to $\bar{u}$. Can you sign the resulting comparative statics expression for the unconditional optimal wage? Explain. Provide an economic interpretation of the Slutsky-like equation you just derived.

FURTHER READING

Clegg (1967) and Kamien and Schwartz (1991) contain complementary discussions of isooperimetric problems. Many intertemporal problems in economics naturally result in the formulation of an isoperimetric problem. Besides the seminal paper on the nonrenewable resource–extracting model of the firm by Hotelling (1931), other examples include the project planning model of Cullingford and Prideaux (1973), numerous R&D models by Kamien and Schwartz (1971, 1974a, 1974b, 1978), continuous–time formulations of maximum entropy problems as in Golan, Judge, and Miller (1996), and models of procrastination by Fischer (2001). An excellent place to commence further study of isoperimetric formulations of principal-agent problems is the Mas-Colell, Whinston, and Green (1995) textbook. More advanced work along this line includes Schättler and Sung (1993), Müller (1998), and Theilen (2003).

REFERENCES

Clegg, J.C. (1967), *Calculus of Variations* (New York: Interscience).

Cullingford, G. and Prideaux, J.D.C.A. (1973), "A Variational Study of Optimal Resource Profiles," *Management Science*, 19, 1067–1081.

Fischer, C. (2001), "Read This Paper Later: Procrastination with Time-Consistent Preferences," *Journal of Economic Behavior and Organization*, 46, 249–269.

Golan, A., Judge, G., and Miller, D. (1996), *Maximum Entropy Econometrics* (New York: John Wiley & Sons).

Hotelling, H. (1931), "The Economics of Exhaustible Resources," *Journal of Political Economy*, 39, 137–175.

Kamien, M.I. and Schwartz, N.L. (1971), "Expenditure Patterns for Risky R&D Projects," *Journal of Applied Probability*, 8, 60–73.

Kamien, M.I. and Schwartz, N.L. (1974a), "Risky R&D with Rivalry," *Annals of Economic and Social Measurement*, 3, 267–277.

Kamien, M.I. and Schwartz, N.L. (1974b), "Patent Life and R&D Rivalry," *American Economic Review*, 64, 183–187.

Kamien, M.I. and Schwartz, N.L. (1978), "Self-Financing of an R&D Project," *American Economic Review*, 68, 252–261.

Kamien, M.I. and Schwartz, N.L. (1991, 2nd Ed.), *Dynamic Optimization: The Calculus of Variations and Optimal Control in Economics and Management* (New York: Elsevier Science Publishing Co., Inc.).

Mas-Colell, A., Whinston, M.D., and Green, J.R. (1995), *Microeconomic Theory* (Oxford: Oxford University Press).

Müller, H.M. (1998), "The First-Best Sharing Rule in the Continuous-Time Principal Agent Problem with Exponential Utility," *Journal of Economic Theory*, 79, 276–280.

Schättler, H. and Sung, J. (1993), "The First-Order Approach to the Continuous-Time Principal-Agent Problem with Exponential Utility," *Journal of Economic Theory*, 61, 331–371.

Simon, C.P. and Blume, L. (1994), *Mathematics for Economists* (New York: W.W. Norton & Company, Inc.).

Theilen, B. (2003), "Simultaneous Moral Hazard and Adverse Selection with Risk Averse Agents," *Economics Letters*, 79, 283–289.

EIGHT

Economic Characterization of Reciprocal Isoperimetric Problems

Microeconomic theorists have learned to take advantage of the symmetry afforded by reciprocal pairs of static optimization problems. Recall that the adjective *reciprocal* signifies that the second (or reciprocal) optimization problem reverses the roles of the original (or primal) problem's objective function and constraint function, and substitutes the minimization hypothesis for the maximization hypothesis. The classical economic example of this occurs in the archetype pair of reciprocal (but not dual) consumer problems: utility maximization and expenditure minimization.

A powerful advantage in working with reciprocal pairs of optimization problems is that one has a choice of which problem to analyze in order to extract the economic information, for the information in one problem can always be used to extract the information in the other. For example, in the modern proof of the negative semidefiniteness of the Slutsky matrix one first establishes the negative semidefiniteness of the substitution matrix, which comprises the first partial derivatives of the Hicksian demand functions with respect to the prices, by invoking the concavity of the expenditure function and the envelope theorem. Then one uses this result along with the Slutsky equation to establish the negative semidefiniteness of the Slutsky matrix. Thus the modern proof of the negative semidefiniteness of the Slutsky matrix works off the reciprocal expenditure minimization problem rather than the primal utility maximization problem, even though the theorem to be proven pertains to the utility maximization problem's solution. This avenue of proof is easier and more economically intuitive, which accounts for its prevalence in textbook expositions of the theory of the consumer. Therefore, when working with reciprocal pairs of optimization problems, the choice of which problem to analyze often comes down to determining which problem yields the results of interest with the greatest clarity and most appealing economic intuition.

We showed in Theorem 7.2 that under certain conditions, the solution of the primal isoperimetric problem is an extremal of the reciprocal isoperimetric problem, and that the associated multipliers are reciprocals of one another. We extend the results of Theorem 7.2 in this chapter by developing a fundamental set of identities linking the *optimal* solution functions and optimal value functions of a reciprocal pair of isoperimetric problems. In addition, we elucidate the qualitative relationships between the optimal solution functions and optimal value functions for such a class of problems, and apply the results so obtained to the nonrenewable resource–extracting model of the firm. Those interested in pursuing the technical matters more deeply are referred to Caputo (1998, 1999), where the proofs of the ensuing theorems can be found.

Under consideration in this chapter is a general pair of reciprocal isoperimetric problems, the functions and parameters of which will be discussed below when the assumptions are laid out. In particular, for $\mathbf{x}(t) \overset{\text{def}}{=} (x_1(t), x_2(t), \ldots, x_N(t))$, consider the *primal* maximization problem

$$F^M(\varepsilon, \beta) \overset{\text{def}}{=} \max_{\mathbf{x}(\cdot)} \left\{ \int_0^T F(t, \mathbf{x}(t), \dot{\mathbf{x}}(t); \alpha)\, dt \text{ s.t. } \int_0^T G(t, \mathbf{x}(t), \dot{\mathbf{x}}(t); \alpha)\, dt = \beta, \right.$$

$$\left. \mathbf{x}(0) = \mathbf{x}_0, \mathbf{x}(T) = \mathbf{x}_T \right\}, \tag{P}$$

where $F^M(\cdot)$ is the *optimal value function* and $\mathbf{x}^M(\cdot)$ is its associated *optimal solution function*, defined as

$$\mathbf{x}^M(t; \varepsilon, \beta) \overset{\text{def}}{=} \arg\max_{\mathbf{x}(\cdot)} \left\{ \int_0^T F(t, \mathbf{x}(t), \dot{\mathbf{x}}(t); \alpha)\, dt \text{ s.t. } \int_0^T G(t, \mathbf{x}(t), \dot{\mathbf{x}}(t); \alpha)\, dt = \beta, \right.$$

$$\left. \mathbf{x}(0) = \mathbf{x}_0, \mathbf{x}(T) = \mathbf{x}_T \right\}. \tag{1}$$

Furthermore, also consider the *reciprocal* minimization problem

$$G^m(\varepsilon, \gamma) \overset{\text{def}}{=} \min_{\mathbf{x}(\cdot)} \left\{ \int_0^T G(t, \mathbf{x}(t), \dot{\mathbf{x}}(t); \alpha)\, dt \text{ s.t. } \int_0^T F(t, \mathbf{x}(t), \dot{\mathbf{x}}(t); \alpha)\, dt = \gamma, \right.$$

$$\left. \mathbf{x}(0) = \mathbf{x}_0, \mathbf{x}(T) = \mathbf{x}_T \right\}, \tag{R}$$

where $G^m(\cdot)$ is the optimal value function and $\mathbf{x}^m(\cdot)$ is its associated optimal solution function, defined as

$$\mathbf{x}^m(t; \varepsilon, \gamma) \overset{\text{def}}{=} \arg\min_{\mathbf{x}(\cdot)} \left\{ \int_0^T G(t, \mathbf{x}(t), \dot{\mathbf{x}}(t); \alpha)\, dt \text{ s.t. } \int_0^T F(t, \mathbf{x}(t), \dot{\mathbf{x}}(t); \alpha)\, dt = \gamma, \right.$$

$$\left. \mathbf{x}(0) = \mathbf{x}_0, \mathbf{x}(T) = \mathbf{x}_T \right\}. \tag{2}$$

Note that the reciprocal of the reciprocal problem (R) is the primal problem (P).

The ensuing assumptions are imposed on the isoperimetric problems (P) and (R), and are discussed subsequently. They are sufficient for the following analysis to hold, but are not necessarily the weakest possible.

(A.1) $F(\cdot) : \Re \times X \times \dot{X} \times A \to \Re$, $F(\cdot) \in C^{(2)}$ on its domain, $G(\cdot) : \Re \times X \times \dot{X} \times A \to \Re$, and $G(\cdot) \in C^{(2)}$ on its domain, where $X \subset \Re^N$ and $\dot{X} \subset \Re^N$ are convex and open sets, and $A \subset \Re^L$ is an open set.
(A.2) For each $t \in [0, T]$ and each $\alpha \in A$, $F(\cdot)$ is a concave function of $(\mathbf{x}, \dot{\mathbf{x}})$, $\forall\, (\mathbf{x}, \dot{\mathbf{x}}) \in X \times \dot{X}$, and $G(\cdot)$ is a convex function of $(\mathbf{x}, \dot{\mathbf{x}})$, $\forall\, (\mathbf{x}, \dot{\mathbf{x}}) \in X \times \dot{X}$.
(A.3) There exists a unique admissible solution to the augmented Euler equation of problem (P) denoted by $\mathbf{x}^M(t; \varepsilon, \beta)$, along with the multiplier or conjugate variable $\psi^M(\varepsilon, \beta) > 0$, when the time-independent parameters

$$(\varepsilon, \beta) \stackrel{\text{def}}{=} (\alpha, \mathbf{x}_0, T, \mathbf{x}_T, \beta) = (\varepsilon^\circ, \beta^\circ)$$

$$\stackrel{\text{def}}{=} (\alpha^\circ, \mathbf{x}_0^\circ, T^\circ, \mathbf{x}_T^\circ, \beta^\circ) \in A \times X \times \Re \times X \times \Re,$$

where $(\varepsilon^\circ, \beta^\circ)$ is a given value of the parameter vector (ε, β).
(A.4) There exists a unique admissible solution to the augmented Euler equation of problem (R) denoted by $\mathbf{x}^m(t; \varepsilon, \gamma)$, along with the multiplier or conjugate variable $\psi^m(\varepsilon, \gamma) > 0$, when the time-independent parameters

$$(\varepsilon, \gamma) \stackrel{\text{def}}{=} (\alpha, \mathbf{x}_0, T, \mathbf{x}_T, \gamma) = (\varepsilon^\circ, \gamma^\circ)$$

$$\stackrel{\text{def}}{=} (\alpha^\circ, \mathbf{x}_0^\circ, T^\circ, \mathbf{x}_T^\circ, \gamma^\circ) \in A \times X \times \Re \times X \times \Re,$$

where $(\varepsilon^\circ, \gamma^\circ)$ is a given value of the parameter vector (ε, γ).
(A.5) The augmented integrand function for problem (P) has a nonzero Hessian determinant with respect to $\dot{\mathbf{x}}(t)$ when evaluated at $(\mathbf{x}^M(t; \varepsilon^\circ, \beta^\circ), \psi^M(\varepsilon^\circ, \beta^\circ))$.
(A.6) The augmented integrand function for problem (R) has a nonzero Hessian determinant with respect to $\dot{\mathbf{x}}(t)$ when evaluated at $(\mathbf{x}^m(t; \varepsilon^\circ, \gamma^\circ), \psi^m(\varepsilon^\circ, \gamma^\circ))$.

Assumption (A.1) imposes our standard $C^{(2)}$ assumption on the functions $F(\cdot)$ and $G(\cdot)$. In addition, the domains X and $\dot{X}$ are required to be convex because of the postulated concavity of $F(\cdot)$ and convexity of $G(\cdot)$ in $(\mathbf{x}, \dot{\mathbf{x}})$ from assumption (A.2). Assumptions (A.3) and (A.4) assert the existence of a unique admissible solution to the augmented Euler equation of isoperimetric problems (P) and (R) for a given value of the time-independent parameter vector of each problem, respectively. By Theorem 7.4, the concavity of $F(\cdot)$ and the convexity of $G(\cdot)$ in $(\mathbf{x}, \dot{\mathbf{x}})$ from assumption (A.2), along with the assumption that the multipliers are positive from assumptions (A.3) and (A.4), imply that the curve $\mathbf{x}^M(t; \varepsilon^\circ, \beta^\circ)$ is the unique solution to problem (P) and that the curve $\mathbf{x}^m(t; \varepsilon^\circ, \gamma^\circ)$ is the unique solution to problem (R). Assumptions (A.5) and (A.6) are technical assumptions that permit us to further conclude that the curves $\mathbf{x}^M(t; \varepsilon, \beta)$ and $\mathbf{x}^m(t; \varepsilon, \gamma)$ are the optimal solutions to problems (P) and (R) for all values of (ε, β) and (ε, γ) in an open neighborhood of $(\varepsilon^\circ, \beta^\circ)$ and $(\varepsilon^\circ, \gamma^\circ)$, respectively. The parameter vector α typically represents a vector of market prices and the discount rate that the economic agent in question faces, whereas the parameter β, the isoperimetric constraint parameter for (P), may represent a given amount of some resource by which the economic agent is constrained. The parameter vector ε is defined so as to keep the notation as palatable as possible, but it excludes the isoperimetric constraint parameters (β, γ) because they play a different role in the qualitative analysis than the parameters defined in ε. Finally, we remark that the solution functions $(\mathbf{x}^M(\cdot), \dot{\mathbf{x}}^M(\cdot), \psi^M(\cdot), \mathbf{x}^m(\cdot), \dot{\mathbf{x}}^m(\cdot), \psi^m(\cdot))$ are locally $C^{(1)}$ and that the optimal value functions $F^M(\cdot)$ and $G^m(\cdot)$ are locally $C^{(2)}$.

As noted above, assumptions (A.1) through (A.6) are not the most general sufficient conditions under which the following results will hold. As a result, remarks will be offered after the proof of Theorem 8.1 as to which assumptions may be relaxed and which are crucial for its conclusions. That being said, it is still true that when the focus is on the qualitative properties of a model, as it is here, these assumptions are often (but not always) maintained either implicitly or explicitly in dynamic optimization problems in economics. Given these assumptions, we now state the main result of this chapter, linking the optimal solution functions and optimal value functions of the reciprocal pair of isoperimetric problems (P) and (R).

Theorem 8.1 (Reciprocal Identities): *Under assumptions (A.1) through (A.6), the following identities link the values of the optimal solution functions and optimal value functions of the reciprocal pair of isoperimetric problems (P) and (R):*

$$(\mathbf{x}^M(t;\varepsilon,\beta), \dot{\mathbf{x}}^M(t;\varepsilon,\beta)) \equiv (\mathbf{x}^m(t;\varepsilon,F^M(\varepsilon,\beta)), \dot{\mathbf{x}}^m(t;\varepsilon,F^M(\varepsilon,\beta)))$$

$$\forall\,(t,\varepsilon,\beta) \in [0,T^\circ] \times B((\varepsilon^\circ,\beta^\circ);\delta_P), \tag{a}$$

$$G^m(\varepsilon, F^M(\varepsilon,\beta)) \equiv \beta\,\forall\,(\varepsilon,\beta) \in B((\varepsilon^\circ,\beta^\circ);\delta_P), \tag{b}$$

$$(\mathbf{x}^m(t;\varepsilon,\gamma), \dot{\mathbf{x}}^m(t;\varepsilon,\gamma)) \equiv (\mathbf{x}^M(t;\varepsilon,G^m(\varepsilon,\gamma)), \dot{\mathbf{x}}^M(t;\varepsilon,G^m(\varepsilon,\gamma)))$$

$$\forall\,(t,\varepsilon,\gamma) \in [0,T^\circ] \times B((\varepsilon^\circ,\gamma^\circ);\delta_R), \tag{c}$$

$$F^M(\varepsilon, G^m(\varepsilon,\gamma)) \equiv \gamma\ \forall\,(\varepsilon,\gamma) \in B((\varepsilon^\circ,\gamma^\circ);\delta_R). \tag{d}$$

The interpretation of Theorem 8.1 is important and therefore deserves comment. Part (a) asserts that the value of the function and its time derivative that solves the primal problem (P) is identically equal to the value of the function and its time derivative that solves the reciprocal problem (R) when the value of the isoperimetric constraint in problem (R) is set equal to the maximum value of the functional, that is, the optimal value function, in problem (P). Symmetrically, part (c) asserts that the value of the function and its time derivative that solves the reciprocal problem (R) is identically equal to the value of the function and its time derivative that solves the primal problem (P), when the value of the isoperimetric constraint in problem (P) is set equal to the optimal value function in problem (R). Parts (b) and (d) show that for ε fixed, the optimal value functions are inverses of one another with respect to the isoperimetric constraint parameters β and γ, respectively. Theorem 8.1, therefore, is the generalized intertemporal equivalent of the identities linking the Marshallian and Hicksian demand functions, and the identities linking the indirect utility and expenditure functions, of the archetype utility maximization and expenditure minimization problems of consumer theory.

As noted earlier, Theorem 8.1 holds under more general conditions than those stated in assumptions (A.1) through (A.6). For example, the differentiability assumption in (A.1) can be weakened, without necessarily invalidating Theorem 8.1. Uniqueness of the solutions, however, is needed in the proof of parts (a) and (c) of Theorem 8.1. Parts (b) and (d) of Theorem 8.1, on the other hand, will hold under more general conditions than parts (a) and (c). For instance, the presence of multiple solutions to problems (P) and (R) would not affect parts (b) and (d), but it would invalidate parts (a) and (c) as stated.

By making explicit use of the differentiability of the optimal value functions and optimal solution functions and invoking the chain rule, the following corollary, whose proof is relegated to the mental exercises, links the derivatives of the aforementioned functions. Please observe that in the statement of the corollary, we have selectively noted the dimensionality of the vectors and matrices for clarity.

Corollary 8.1 (Derivative Decomposition): *Under assumptions (A.1) through (A.6), the following derivative decompositions hold for the reciprocal pair of isoperimetric problems (P) and (R):*

$$\underbrace{\frac{\partial \mathbf{x}^M}{\partial \varepsilon}(t;\varepsilon,\beta)}_{N\times(L+2N+1)} \equiv \underbrace{\frac{\partial \mathbf{x}^m}{\partial \varepsilon}(t;\varepsilon,F^M(\varepsilon,\beta))}_{N\times(L+2N+1)} + \underbrace{\frac{\partial \mathbf{x}^m}{\partial \gamma}(t;\varepsilon,F^M(\varepsilon,\beta))}_{N\times 1}\underbrace{\frac{\partial F^M}{\partial \varepsilon}(\varepsilon,\beta)}_{1\times(L+2N+1)}, \tag{a}$$

$$\frac{\partial \dot{\mathbf{x}}^M}{\partial \varepsilon}(t;\varepsilon,\beta) \equiv \frac{\partial \dot{\mathbf{x}}^m}{\partial \varepsilon}(t;\varepsilon,F^M(\varepsilon,\beta)) + \frac{\partial \dot{\mathbf{x}}^m}{\partial \gamma}(t;\varepsilon,F^M(\varepsilon,\beta))\frac{\partial F^M}{\partial \varepsilon}(\varepsilon,\beta),$$

$$\underbrace{\frac{\partial \mathbf{x}^M}{\partial \beta}(t;\varepsilon,\beta)}_{N\times 1} \equiv \underbrace{\frac{\partial \mathbf{x}^m}{\partial \gamma}(t;\varepsilon,F^M(\varepsilon,\beta))}_{N\times 1}\underbrace{\frac{\partial F^M}{\partial \beta}(\varepsilon,\beta)}_{1\times 1},$$

$$\frac{\partial \dot{\mathbf{x}}^M}{\partial \beta}(t;\varepsilon,\beta) \equiv \frac{\partial \dot{\mathbf{x}}^m}{\partial \gamma}(t;\varepsilon,F^M(\varepsilon,\beta))\frac{\partial F^M}{\partial \beta}(\varepsilon,\beta)$$

hold $\forall\,(t,\varepsilon,\beta) \in [0,T^\circ] \times B((\varepsilon^\circ,\beta^\circ);\delta_P)$, and

$$\underbrace{\frac{\partial G^m}{\partial \varepsilon}(\varepsilon,F^M(\varepsilon,\beta))}_{1\times(L+2N+1)} + \underbrace{\frac{\partial G^m}{\partial \gamma}(\varepsilon,F^M(\varepsilon,\beta))}_{1\times 1}\underbrace{\frac{\partial F^M}{\partial \varepsilon}(\varepsilon,\beta)}_{1\times(L+2N+1)} \equiv \mathbf{0}'_{L+2N+1}, \tag{b}$$

$$\underbrace{\frac{\partial G^m}{\partial \gamma}(\varepsilon,F^M(\varepsilon,\beta))}_{1\times 1}\underbrace{\frac{\partial F^M}{\partial \beta}(\varepsilon,\beta)}_{1\times 1} \equiv 1$$

hold $\forall (\varepsilon, \beta) \in B((\varepsilon^{\circ}, \beta^{\circ}); \delta_P)$, and

$$\frac{\partial \mathbf{x}^m}{\partial \varepsilon}(t; \varepsilon, \gamma) \equiv \frac{\partial \mathbf{x}^M}{\partial \varepsilon}(t; \varepsilon, G^m(\varepsilon, \gamma)) + \frac{\partial \mathbf{x}^M}{\partial \beta}(t; \varepsilon, G^m(\varepsilon, \gamma)) \frac{\partial G^m}{\partial \varepsilon}(\varepsilon, \gamma), \quad \text{(c)}$$

$$\frac{\partial \dot{\mathbf{x}}^m}{\partial \varepsilon}(t; \varepsilon, \gamma) \equiv \frac{\partial \dot{\mathbf{x}}^M}{\partial \varepsilon}(t; \varepsilon, G^m(\varepsilon, \gamma)) + \frac{\partial \dot{\mathbf{x}}^M}{\partial \beta}(t; \varepsilon, G^m(\varepsilon, \gamma)) \frac{\partial G^m}{\partial \varepsilon}(\varepsilon, \gamma),$$

$$\frac{\partial \mathbf{x}^m}{\partial \gamma}(t; \varepsilon, \gamma) \equiv \frac{\partial \mathbf{x}^M}{\partial \beta}(t; \varepsilon, G^m(\varepsilon, \gamma)) \frac{\partial G^m}{\partial \gamma}(\varepsilon, \gamma),$$

$$\frac{\partial \dot{\mathbf{x}}^m}{\partial \gamma}(t; \varepsilon, \gamma) \equiv \frac{\partial \dot{\mathbf{x}}^M}{\partial \beta}(t; \varepsilon, G^m(\varepsilon, \gamma)) \frac{\partial G^m}{\partial \gamma}(\varepsilon, \gamma),$$

hold $\forall (t, \varepsilon, \gamma) \in [0, T^{\circ}] \times B((\varepsilon^{\circ}, \gamma^{\circ}); \delta_R)$, and

$$\frac{\partial F^M}{\partial \varepsilon}(\varepsilon, G^m(\varepsilon, \gamma)) + \frac{\partial F^M}{\partial \beta}(\varepsilon, G^m(\varepsilon, \gamma)) \frac{\partial G^m}{\partial \varepsilon}(\varepsilon, \gamma) \equiv \mathbf{0}, \quad \text{(d)}$$

$$\frac{\partial F^M}{\partial \beta}(\varepsilon, G^m(\varepsilon, \gamma)) \frac{\partial G^m}{\partial \gamma}(\varepsilon, \gamma) \equiv 1,$$

hold $\forall (\varepsilon, \gamma) \in B((\varepsilon^{\circ}, \gamma^{\circ}); \delta_R)$.

The first two identities in parts (a) and (c) of Corollary 8.1 are the reciprocal pair of generalized Slutsky-like decompositions for the "prices" of the reciprocal pair of isoperimetric problems (P) and (R), and the last two identities of (a) and (c) are the generalized Slutsky-like decompositions for "income" and "utility level." Similarly, the first identities of parts (b) and (d) are the generalized Roy-like identities, whereas the second identities of parts (b) and (d) demonstrate the reciprocal nature of the conjugate variables for the isoperimetric constraints. To see the latter assertion, simply note that by assumptions (A.3) and (A.4) and Theorem 7.3, $\partial F^M(\varepsilon, \beta)/\partial \beta \equiv \psi^M(\varepsilon, \beta) > 0$ and $\partial G^m(\varepsilon, \gamma)/\partial \gamma \equiv \psi^m(\varepsilon, \gamma) > 0$ are the constant conjugate variables for problems (P) and (R), respectively. This reciprocal relationship between the conjugate variables of problems (P) and (R) should not be too surprising at this juncture of the chapter, since it was noted above that parts (b) and (d) of Theorem 8.1 show that the optimal value functions $F^M(\cdot)$ and $G^m(\cdot)$ are inverses of one another with respect to the isoperimetric constraint parameters (β, γ). Rather than dwell any further on the interpretation of the generic results of Theorem 8.1 and Corollary 8.1, a more complete and intuitive economic interpretation of them is given in the context of the competitive nonrenewable resource–extracting model of the firm, which we now proceed to analyze. In passing, note that not all of the identities in Corollary 8.1 are independent of one another, as you are asked to verify in a mental exercise.

To begin, let $q(t)$ be the extraction rate of the nonrenewable resource at time t and let $p > 0$ be the constant market price of the extracted product, that is, the output price. Define the minimum cost of extracting the resource at the rate $q(t)$ at the constant input price of $w > 0$ by

$$C(q; w) \stackrel{\text{def}}{=} \min_{v}\{w \cdot v \text{ s.t. } q = f(v)\},$$

where $f(\cdot) \in C^{(2)}$ is the production function with the standard properties $f'(v) > 0$ and $f''(v) < 0$, and $v > 0$ is the variable input used to extract the nonrenewable resource. In a mental exercise, you are asked to prove that these assumptions imply that $C_q(q; w) > 0$, $C_{qq}(q; w) > 0$, $C_w(q; w) > 0$, and $C_{qw}(q; w) > 0$. The firm has a fixed planning horizon of $T > 0$ years and a discount rate of $r > 0$. The initial stock of the resource is $s > 0$, and the firm is assumed to extract all of it by the close of the planning horizon.

The primal isoperimetric problem asserts that the firm chooses an extraction function $q(\cdot)$ to maximize the present discounted value of profit over the planning horizon, such that cumulative extraction equals the initial stock:

$$\Pi(\varepsilon, s) \stackrel{\text{def}}{=} \max_{q(\cdot)} \left\{ \int_0^T [pq(t) - C(q(t); w)]\, e^{-rt}\, dt \text{ s.t. } \int_0^T q(t)\, dt = s \right\}, \tag{3}$$

where $\Pi(\varepsilon, s)$ is the maximum present discounted value of profit that can be earned from complete extraction of the initial resource stock s at prices (p, w), discount rate r, and planning horizon T; $q^M(t; \varepsilon, s)$ is the optimal extraction path; $\psi^M(\varepsilon, s)$ is the corresponding shadow value of the initial resource stock, that is, the optimal value of the primal conjugate variable; and $\varepsilon \stackrel{\text{def}}{=} (p, r, w, T)$. The reciprocal problem asserts that the firm chooses an extraction function $q(\cdot)$ to minimize the cumulative amount of the resource extracted over the planning horizon, subject to producing a present discounted value of profit equal to a predetermined level $\pi > 0$:

$$Q(\varepsilon, \pi) \stackrel{\text{def}}{=} \min_{q(\cdot)} \left\{ \int_0^T q(t)\, dt \text{ s.t. } \int_0^T [pq(t) - C(q(t); w)]\, e^{-rt}\, dt = \pi \right\}, \tag{4}$$

where $Q(\varepsilon, \pi)$ is the minimum cumulative extraction that will yield the present discounted value of profit π at prices (p, w), discount rate r, and planning horizon T; $q^m(t; \varepsilon, \pi)$ is the optimal extraction path; and $\psi^m(\varepsilon, s)$ is the corresponding marginal change in cumulative extraction due to an increase in the required present value of profit, that is, the optimal value of the reciprocal conjugate variable.

Applying Theorem 8.1 to the reciprocal isoperimetric problems (3) and (4) yields their fundamental identities:

$$q^M(t; \varepsilon, s) \equiv q^m(t; \varepsilon, \Pi(\varepsilon, s)), \tag{5}$$

$$Q(\varepsilon, \Pi(\varepsilon, s)) \equiv s, \tag{6}$$

$$q^m(t; \varepsilon, \pi) \equiv q^M(t; \varepsilon, Q(\varepsilon, \pi)), \tag{7}$$

$$\Pi(\varepsilon, Q(\varepsilon, \pi)) \equiv \pi. \tag{8}$$

Equation (5) asserts that at the given prices (p, w), discount rate r, planning horizon T, and initial stock size s, the extraction rate that maximizes the present discounted value of profit subject to complete extraction of the initial resource stock is exactly the same extraction rate that minimizes the cumulative amount of the resource extracted subject to earning a present discounted value of profit that is equal to the maximum attainable at prices (p, w), discount rate r, horizon length T, and initial stock size s. Reciprocally, Eq. (7) asserts that at the given prices (p, w), discount rate r, planning horizon T, and required present discounted value of profit π, the extraction rate that minimizes the cumulative amount of the resource extracted subject to earning a given present discounted value of profit is exactly the same extraction rate that maximizes the present discounted value of profit subject to complete extraction of an initial resource stock that is equal to the minimum cumulative amount of the resource one would extract at prices (p, w), discount rate r, planning horizon T, and required present discounted value of profit π. Equation (6) asserts that given the prices (p, w), discount rate r, and planning horizon T, the minimum cumulative extraction required to reach the maximum present discounted value of profit obtainable at prices (p, w), discount rate r, planning horizon T, and initial stock s is identically the initial stock s. Symmetrically, identity (8) asserts that at the given prices (p, w), discount rate r, and planning horizon T, the maximum present discounted value of profit obtainable when the initial stock size is the minimum cumulative extraction that can be achieved at prices (p, w), discount rate r, planning horizon T, and present discounted value of profit π is exactly the present discounted value of profit π. That is, for fixed ε, identities (6) and (8) show that the optimal value functions $\Pi(\cdot)$ and $Q(\cdot)$ are inverses of one another with respect to s and π, respectively.

Though the economic interpretation of the identities (5) through (8) is important, the relationship between the derivatives of the functions in Eqs. (5) through (8) and their economic interpretation is even more so. Using Corollary 8.1, or simply differentiating the identities in Eqs. (5) through (8) with respect to, say, (p, s, π), the chain rule gives

$$\frac{\partial q^M}{\partial p}(t; \varepsilon, s) \equiv \frac{\partial q^m}{\partial p}(t; \varepsilon, \Pi(\varepsilon, s)) + \frac{\partial q^m}{\partial \pi}(t; \varepsilon, \Pi(\varepsilon, s))\frac{\partial \Pi}{\partial p}(\varepsilon, s), \tag{9}$$

$$\frac{\partial q^M}{\partial s}(t; \varepsilon, s) \equiv \frac{\partial q^m}{\partial \pi}(t; \varepsilon, \Pi(\varepsilon, s))\frac{\partial \Pi}{\partial s}(\varepsilon, s), \tag{10}$$

$$\frac{\partial Q}{\partial p}(\varepsilon, \Pi(\varepsilon, s)) + \frac{\partial Q}{\partial \pi}(\varepsilon, \Pi(\varepsilon, s))\frac{\partial \Pi}{\partial p}(\varepsilon, s) \equiv 0, \tag{11}$$

$$\frac{\partial Q}{\partial \pi}(\varepsilon, \Pi(\varepsilon, s))\frac{\partial \Pi}{\partial s}(\varepsilon, s) \equiv 1, \tag{12}$$

$$\frac{\partial q^m}{\partial p}(t; \varepsilon, \pi) \equiv \frac{\partial q^M}{\partial p}(t; \varepsilon, Q(\varepsilon, \pi)) + \frac{\partial q^M}{\partial s}(t; \varepsilon, Q(\varepsilon, \pi))\frac{\partial Q}{\partial p}(\varepsilon, \pi), \tag{13}$$

$$\frac{\partial q^m}{\partial \pi}(t; \varepsilon, \pi) \equiv \frac{\partial q^M}{\partial s}(t; \varepsilon, Q(\varepsilon, \pi))\frac{\partial Q}{\partial \pi}(\varepsilon, \pi), \tag{14}$$

$$\frac{\partial \Pi}{\partial p}(\varepsilon, Q(\varepsilon, \pi)) + \frac{\partial \Pi}{\partial s}(\varepsilon, Q(\varepsilon, \pi))\frac{\partial Q}{\partial p}(\varepsilon, \pi) \equiv 0, \tag{15}$$

$$\frac{\partial \Pi}{\partial s}(\varepsilon, Q(\varepsilon, \pi))\frac{\partial Q}{\partial \pi}(\varepsilon, \pi) \equiv 1. \tag{16}$$

The remaining derivative decompositions for the parameters (r, w, T) are similar and are thus left for a mental exercise. The identities (5) through (8) and (9) through (16) are heretofore undiscovered for this intertemporal model.

Equations (9) and (13) are the reciprocal pair of Slutsky-like decompositions for the output price in the nonrenewable resource–extracting model of the firm. In particular, Eq. (9) asserts that the slope of the present value profit maximizing supply function is composed of two parts: (i) $\partial q^m/\partial p$, the effect of a price change on supply holding constant the present value of profit as well as all other parameters except the market price of the extracted good, that is, the slope of the supply function from the reciprocal problem (4); and (ii) $(\partial q^m/\partial \pi)(\partial \Pi/\partial p)$, the effect the price change has on the maximum present value of profit when it adjusts optimally, and the concomitant effect the change in the present value of profit has on supply. The first effect could be called the *iso-wealth* effect, because, by the definition of the partial derivative, it explicitly holds the present value of profit (i.e., wealth) constant when the output price changes. The second term could be called the *wealth* effect, seeing as it measures the effect the price change has on supply by optimally varying the present discounted value of profit.

Similarly, Eq. (13) asserts that the slope of the cumulative extraction–minimizing supply function consists of two parts: (i) an *iso-stock* effect $\partial q^M/\partial p$, which measures the effect of a price change on supply holding constant the initial stock of the resource as well as all other parameters except the market price of the extracted good, that is, the slope of the supply function from the primal problem (3), and (ii) a *stock* effect $(\partial q^M/\partial s)(\partial Q/\partial p)$, which measures the effect of a price change on minimum cumulative extraction when it adjusts optimally, and the concomitant effect the change in cumulative extraction has on supply. The economic interpretation of Eqs. (10) and (14) is similar to that just given and is therefore left for a mental exercise.

The identities (11) and (15) are the Roy-like identities for the nonrenewable resource–extracting model of the firm. To see this, simply note that by Theorem 7.3, it follows that $\partial \Pi(\varepsilon, s)/\partial p \equiv \int_0^T q^M(t; \varepsilon, s)e^{-rt}\,dt$, so that a rearrangement of Eq. (11) yields

$$\int_0^T q^M(t; \varepsilon, s)e^{-rt}\,dt \equiv \frac{-\frac{\partial Q}{\partial p}(\varepsilon, \Pi(\varepsilon, s))}{\frac{\partial Q}{\partial \pi}(\varepsilon, \Pi(\varepsilon, s))}.$$

One can also arrive at the identical formula by first evaluating Eq. (15) at $\pi = \Pi(\varepsilon, s)$ and using Eq. (6), then using $\partial\Pi(\varepsilon, s)/\partial p \equiv \int_0^T q^M(t; \varepsilon, s)e^{-rt}\,dt$, and finally substituting out $\partial\Pi(\varepsilon, s)/\partial s$ using Eq. (12), as you are asked to verify in a mental exercise. Notice that in this model, the Roy-like identity forces one's attention on the cumulative discounted supply function.

By Theorem 7.3, $\partial\Pi(\varepsilon, s)/\partial s \equiv \psi^M(\varepsilon, s)$ and $\partial Q(\varepsilon, \pi)/\partial\pi \equiv \psi^m(\varepsilon, \pi)$, so Eqs. (12) and (16) demonstrate the reciprocal nature of the time-independent conjugate variables for problems (3) and (4), a result that should now appear intuitive given the earlier observation that $\Pi(\cdot)$ and $Q(\cdot)$ are inverse functions of one another with respect to the isoperimetric constraint parameters (π, s). In other words, at the optimum, the shadow value of the initial stock, $\psi^M(\varepsilon, s)$, is the reciprocal of the marginal change in cumulative extraction due to an increase in the required present value of profit, $\psi^m(\varepsilon, \pi)$, when $s = Q(\varepsilon, \pi)$ or $\pi = \Pi(\varepsilon, s)$.

The above derivative decompositions can yield further insight into the reciprocal pair of isoperimetric problems (3) and (4) upon exploring the comparative dynamics properties of *one* of the problems. Only one of the problems needs to be examined for comparative dynamics results, for the identities in Eqs. (9) through (16) yield the comparative dynamics of the reciprocal problem. Problem (3) is investigated here because it is the primal problem and thus the more common formulation. It is important to point out that the comparative dynamics method used below is quite general, the only limitation being that $\dot{q}$ can't explicitly appear in the problem. Moreover, the method permits the derivation of the comparative dynamics properties of the problem *without* the aid of a phase portrait or specific functional forms.

By Theorem 7.1, the necessary conditions for problem (3) are found by defining the augmented integrand, $\tilde{F}(t, q, \psi; p, r, w) \stackrel{\text{def}}{=} [pq - C(q; w)]\, e^{-rt} - \psi q$, and applying the Euler equation to $\tilde{F}(\cdot)$. Since $\partial\tilde{F}/\partial\dot{q} \equiv 0$, this yields the *algebraic* equation

$$\frac{\partial\tilde{F}}{\partial q} = [p - C_q(q; w)]\, e^{-rt} - \psi = 0. \tag{17}$$

It should be clear that $\psi > 0$, because if $\psi < 0$, then $p < C_q(q; w)$ from Eq. (17), in which case the firm would lose money on every unit of the resource extracted and hence go out of business. Also note that when $\psi = 0$, the firm acts as a static profit maximizer setting $p = C_q(q; w)$. This case is uninteresting, however, because the isoperimetric problem (3) is no longer dynamic when $\psi = 0$ holds. Finally, note that because $\psi > 0$, $\tilde{F}(\cdot)$ is a concave function of $(q, \dot{q})$ for all $t \in [0, T]$ by assumption (A.2). Therefore, by Theorem 7.4, an admissible solution of the augmented Euler equation (17) is a globally optimal solution to the isoperimetric problem (3).

Given that $C(\cdot) \in C^{(2)}$ and $C_{qq}(q; w) > 0$, the Jacobian of Eq. (17) with respect to q is negative everywhere, that is, $\tilde{F}_{qq}(t, q, \psi; p, r, w) = -C_{qq}(q; w)e^{-rt} < 0$. Hence, by the implicit function theorem, Eq. (17) can be solved in principle for the extraction rate as a $C^{(1)}$ function of $(t; \psi, p, r, w)$:

$$q = \hat{q}(t; \psi, p, r, w). \tag{18}$$

The function $\hat{q}(\cdot)$ gives the extraction rate that satisfies the augmented Euler equation *conditional* on the conjugate variable ψ, the shadow value of the initial stock, which is a constant by Theorem 7.1. Thus the function $\hat{q}(\cdot)$ is *not* necessarily admissible as we have yet to verify that it satisfies the integral constraint of problem (3). Therefore, in order to find the *optimal* extraction rate, namely, $q^M(t; \varepsilon, s)$, the value of the constant multiplier ψ must be found so as to make $\hat{q}(\cdot)$ an *admissible* solution of the augmented Euler equation. Before doing so, however, it is instructive to examine the qualitative properties of the function $\hat{q}(\cdot)$ first.

Using the implicit function theorem on Eq. (17) yields the qualitative properties of the function $\hat{q}(\cdot)$:

$$\frac{\partial \hat{q}}{\partial t} \equiv \frac{-r[p - C_q(q; w)]}{C_{qq}(q; w)} < 0, \tag{19}$$

$$\frac{\partial \hat{q}}{\partial \psi} \equiv \frac{-1}{C_{qq}(q; w)e^{-rt}} < 0, \tag{20}$$

$$\frac{\partial \hat{q}}{\partial p} \equiv \frac{1}{C_{qq}(q; w)} > 0, \tag{21}$$

$$\frac{\partial \hat{q}}{\partial r} \equiv \frac{-t\,[p - C_q(q; w)]}{C_{qq}(q; w)} \leq 0, \tag{22}$$

$$\frac{\partial \hat{q}}{\partial w} \equiv \frac{-C_{qw}(q; w)}{C_{qq}(q; w)} < 0 \quad (\because C_{qw}(q; w) > 0), \tag{23}$$

where all the functions in Eqs. (19) through (23) are evaluated at $q = \hat{q}(t; \psi, p, r, w)$. Equation (19) says that the extraction rate declines over the planning horizon, holding constant the shadow value of the initial stock. The qualitative result in Eq. (26) asserts that an increase in the shadow value of the initial stock, ceteris paribus, lowers the extraction rate, which is intuitive, because one would like to leave more of the resource "in the ground" if its shadow value in the unextracted state is higher. Equations (21) and (23) assert, respectively, that holding the shadow value of the initial stock constant, the extraction rate rises with an increase in the output price and a decrease in the input price. These qualitative results are also intuitive, because if the extracted resource is worth more in the market or it is cheaper to extract, then it is sensible for the firm to extract the resource at a faster rate in order to maximize its present discounted value of profit. The comparative dynamics result in Eq. (22) appears counterintuitive, in that normally an increase in the discount rate is thought to increase the extraction rate early in the planning horizon and decrease it later.

Remember, however, that ψ is held fixed in Eqs. (21), (22), and (23), so none of these comparative dynamics results measure the change in the *optimal* extraction rate due to a change in the parameter, for the optimal value of ψ must be determined, and it will be a function of all the parameters except for t.

To find the optimal value of ψ, substitute the extraction rate $q = \hat{q}(t; \psi, p, r, w)$, the solution to the augmented Euler equation (17), into the isoperimetric constraint of problem (3):

$$\int_0^T \hat{q}(t; \psi, p, r, w)\, dt = s. \tag{24}$$

By Eq. (20), the Jacobian of Eq. (24) with respect to ψ is negative, that is,

$$\frac{\partial}{\partial \psi} \int_0^T \hat{q}(t; \psi, p, r, w)\, dt = \int_0^T \frac{\partial \hat{q}}{\partial \psi}(t; \psi, p, r, w)\, dt < 0.$$

Thus, by the implicit function theorem, we can in principle solve Eq. (24) for the shadow value of the initial stock as a $C^{(1)}$ function of the parameters (ε, s):

$$\psi = \psi^M(\varepsilon, s). \tag{25}$$

Recall that Theorem 7.1 asserts that the optimal value of ψ given in Eq. (25) is constant. This is evident by Eq. (24), since t is the dummy variable of integration and is thus integrated out of Eq. (24) when solving for ψ. This fact is also reflected in the notation of Eq. (25) by observing that $\psi^M(\cdot)$ is independent of t.

Applying the implicit function theorem to Eq. (24) yields the comparative dynamics of the shadow value of the initial stock:

$$\frac{\partial \psi^M}{\partial p} \equiv \frac{-\int_0^T \frac{\partial \hat{q}}{\partial p}(t; \psi, p, r, w)\, dt}{\int_0^T \frac{\partial \hat{q}}{\partial \lambda}(t; \psi, p, r, w)\, dt} \in (0, 1), \tag{26}$$

$$\frac{\partial \psi^M}{\partial r} \equiv \frac{-\int_0^T \frac{\partial \hat{q}}{\partial r}(t; \psi, p, r, w)\, dt}{\int_0^T \frac{\partial \hat{q}}{\partial \lambda}(t; \psi, p, r, w)\, dt} < 0, \tag{27}$$

$$\frac{\partial \psi^M}{\partial w} \equiv \frac{-\int_0^T \frac{\partial \hat{q}}{\partial w}(t; \psi, p, r, w)\, dt}{\int_0^T \frac{\partial \hat{q}}{\partial \lambda}(t; \psi, p, r, w)\, dt} < 0, \tag{28}$$

$$\frac{\partial \psi^M}{\partial s} \equiv \frac{1}{\int_0^T \frac{\partial \hat{q}}{\partial \lambda}(t; \psi, p, r, w)\, dt} < 0, \tag{29}$$

$$\frac{\partial \psi^M}{\partial T} \equiv \frac{-\hat{q}(T; \psi, p, r, w)}{\int_0^T \frac{\partial \hat{q}}{\partial \lambda}(t; \psi, p, r, w)\, dt} \geq 0, \tag{30}$$

where the functions in Eqs. (26) through (30) are evaluated at $\psi = \psi^M(\varepsilon, s)$ and the *quantitative* result in Eq. (26) follows from Eqs. (20) and (21). The comparative dynamics given in Eqs. (26) through (30) are the expected economic intuitions. For example, Eq. (26) asserts that an increase in the output price drives up the shadow value of the initial stock, but not by as much as the output price rose, because if the market now values the extracted product more, the rational firm recognizes this *and* the fact that it is costly to extract the resource, and thus places only a fractionally higher shadow value on the unextracted product. In other words, if the extracted good is worth more, then so is its unextracted form, but only fractionally, since the former is derived at a cost from the latter. If the firm becomes more impatient, implying an increase in the discount rate, then Eq. (27) shows that the shadow value of the initial stock falls because the present discounted value of the asset itself is lower too. If the input price rises, then the firm's marginal cost of extraction rises. The firm thus places a lower shadow value on the initial stock in view of the fact that the net profit on each unit extracted is lower, which is the intuition behind Eq. (28). Equation (29) asserts that the shadow value of the initial stock is lower the larger the initial stock of the resource, that is, with a larger initial stock available, the firm values each additional unit less. Alternatively, $\psi^M(\cdot)$ is the firm's inverse demand function for the initial stock of the resource; hence Eq. (29) is simply an assertion that the law of demand holds for the initial resource stock in inverse demand form. Recalling that $\partial\Pi(\varepsilon, s)/\partial s \equiv \psi^M(\varepsilon, s) > 0$, another interpretation of Eq. (29) is that the optimal value function $\Pi(\cdot)$ is strictly concave in the initial resource stock. Finally, if the extraction rate is zero (positive) in the terminal period of the planning horizon, then Eq. (30) shows that the firm places the same (a higher) shadow value on the initial resource stock when the length of the planning horizon increases. This is intuitive because if the firm is not extracting in the last period of the planning horizon, then it has already extracted all of the stock available before the terminal date, and hence there is no additional value to the firm in having more time available to extract the same amount of the stock.

With the shadow value of the initial stock now determined, the optimal extraction rate can be found by substituting Eq. (25) into Eq. (18), thus *defining* the optimal extraction rate:

$$q^M(t; \varepsilon, s) \stackrel{\text{def}}{=} \hat{q}(t; \psi^M(\varepsilon, s), p, r, w). \tag{31}$$

The comparative dynamics of the optimal extraction rate follow from differentiating Eq. (31) with respect to the parameter of interest using the chain rule:

$$\frac{\partial q^M}{\partial t}(t; \varepsilon, s) = \frac{\partial \hat{q}}{\partial t}(t; \psi^M(\varepsilon, s), p, r, w) < 0 \,\forall t \in [0, T], \tag{32}$$

$$\frac{\partial q^M}{\partial p}(t; \varepsilon, s) = \frac{\partial \hat{q}}{\partial \psi}(t; \psi^M(\varepsilon, s), p, r, w)\frac{\partial \psi^M}{\partial p}(\varepsilon, s) + \frac{\partial \hat{q}}{\partial p}(t; \psi^M(\varepsilon, s), p, r, w), \tag{33}$$

$$\frac{\partial q^M}{\partial r}(t;\varepsilon,s) = \frac{\partial \hat{q}}{\partial \psi}(t;\psi^M(\varepsilon,s),p,r,w)\frac{\partial \psi^M}{\partial r}(\varepsilon,s) + \frac{\partial \hat{q}}{\partial r}(t;\psi^M(\varepsilon,s),p,r,w), \tag{34}$$

$$\frac{\partial q^M}{\partial w}(t;\varepsilon,s) = \frac{\partial \hat{q}}{\partial \psi}(t;\psi^M(\varepsilon,s),p,r,w)\frac{\partial \psi^M}{\partial w}(\varepsilon,s) + \frac{\partial \hat{q}}{\partial w}(t;\psi^M(\varepsilon,s),p,r,w), \tag{35}$$

$$\frac{\partial q^M}{\partial s}(t;\varepsilon,s) = \frac{\partial \hat{q}}{\partial \psi}(t;\psi^M(\varepsilon,s),p,r,w)\frac{\partial \psi^M}{\partial s}(\varepsilon,s) > 0\,\forall\, t \in [0,T], \tag{36}$$

$$\frac{\partial q^M}{\partial T}(t;\varepsilon,s) = \frac{\partial \hat{q}}{\partial \psi}(t;\psi^M(\varepsilon,s),p,r,w)\frac{\partial \psi^M}{\partial T}(\varepsilon,s) \leq 0\,\forall\, t \in [0,T]. \tag{37}$$

The sign of Eq. (32) follows from Eq. (19), whereas the signs in Eqs. (36) and (37) follow from Eqs. (20), (29), and (30). Equation (32) is the well-known result that the optimal extraction rate falls over the planning period, and the equality exhibited between $\partial q^M/\partial t$ and $\partial \hat{q}/\partial t$ is a result of the fact that $\psi^M(\cdot)$ is independent of t.

In general, Eqs. (33), (34), and (35) cannot be signed $\forall\, t \in [0,T]$, but this is not surprising. To see why, recall that $q^M(t;\varepsilon,s)$ satisfies the isoperimetric constraint identically; hence

$$\int_0^T q^M(t;\varepsilon,s)\,dt \equiv s.$$

Differentiating this identity with respect to, say, p, yields

$$\frac{\partial}{\partial p}\int_0^T q^M(t;\varepsilon,s)\,dt = \int_0^T \frac{\partial q^M}{\partial p}(t;\varepsilon,s)\,dt \equiv 0 \tag{38}$$

and says that the effect of an output price increase on cumulative extraction is zero, since cumulative extraction must equal the given initial stock, the latter of which is unaffected by the output price increase. Therefore, if $\partial q^M/\partial p$ is positive for some period of time, it must be negative over some other period of time for Eq. (38) to hold. Hence a uniform sign for $\partial q^M/\partial p$ for all $t \in [0,T]$ is precluded by Eq. (38), that is, by the fixed initial stock and the integral constraint that all of the resource be extracted. Note, however, that upon evaluating Eq. (33) at $t = 0$, using Eqs. (20) and (21) to deduce that $\partial \hat{q}(0;\psi,p,r,w)/\partial \psi = -\,\partial \hat{q}(0;\psi,p,r,w)/\partial p < 0$, and then recalling Eq. (26), it follows that Eq. (33) can be written as

$$\frac{\partial q^M}{\partial p}(0;\varepsilon,s) = \frac{\partial \hat{q}}{\partial p}(0;\psi^M(\varepsilon,s),p,r,w)\left[1 - \frac{\partial \psi^M}{\partial p}(\varepsilon,s)\right] > 0. \tag{39}$$

Thus, at the initial date of the planning horizon, an increase in the output price results in an increase in the extraction rate. By continuity of $\partial q^M(\cdot)/\partial p$ in t, $\partial q^M(t;\varepsilon,s)/\partial p > 0$ holds for some finite interval of time near the initial date. It therefore follows from this observation and Eqs. (32) and (38) that $\partial q^M(t;\varepsilon,s)/\partial p < 0$ holds for some finite interval of time near the end of the planning horizon. You are asked to prove this latter result in a mental exercise following the steps and logic used to deduce Eq. (39). In sum, the firm would like to extract more of the resource because it is now worth more in the market. But seeing as the initial stock of the resource is fixed and the extraction rate declines over the planning period, the only way the firm can take advantage of the price increase is by rearranging its extraction profile so that more of the resource is extracted early in the planning horizon and less is extracted later. A similar analysis may be done for Eq. (34), as you are asked to verify in a mental exercise.

Equation (36) asserts that an increase in the initial resource stock increases the optimal extraction rate at each date of the planning horizon. This is judicious, for a larger initial stock necessitates a higher extraction rate given that the planning horizon is unchanged. Equation (37) asserts that if the firm is extracting the resource in the last period of the planning horizon and the length of the planning horizon increases so that it now has more time to extract the same amount of the resource, then it will do so at a slower rate. Moreover, if the firm is not extracting in the last period of the planning horizon, implying that it has already extracted all of the stock available before the terminal date, then an increase in the length of the planning horizon would have no effect on its optimal extraction plan.

Given that the comparative dynamics properties of the primal problem (3) have been deduced, all one has to do now is exploit the identities in Eqs. (9) through (16) to uncover the comparative dynamics properties of the reciprocal problem (4). For example, by Eqs. (13) and (14), it follows that

$$\frac{\partial q^m}{\partial p}(t;\varepsilon,\pi) \equiv \frac{\partial q^M}{\partial p}(t;\varepsilon,Q(\varepsilon,\pi)) + \frac{\partial q^M}{\partial s}(t;\varepsilon,Q(\varepsilon,\pi))\frac{\partial Q}{\partial p}(\varepsilon,\pi), \tag{40}$$

$$\frac{\partial q^m}{\partial \pi}(t;\varepsilon,\pi) \equiv \frac{\partial q^M}{\partial s}(t;\varepsilon,Q(\varepsilon,\pi))\frac{\partial Q}{\partial \pi}(\varepsilon,\pi) > 0\,\forall\, t \in [0,T]. \tag{41}$$

Recalling that $\partial Q(\varepsilon,\pi)/\partial\pi \equiv \psi^m(\varepsilon,\pi) > 0$ by Theorem 7.3 and that $\partial q^M(t;\varepsilon,s)/\partial s > 0$ for all $t \in [0,T]$ by Eq. (36), Eq. (41) asserts that an increase in the required wealth target for the cumulative extraction–minimizing firm will lead to an increase in its extraction rate at every date of the planning horizon, thereby resulting in higher cumulative extraction. That is, given that the firm must now produce a higher level of wealth from the same initial stock of the resource, it must extract a larger amount of the stock over its planning horizon, and in order to do so, it must extract the stock at a faster rate in every period because its planning horizon is unchanged.

Equation (40), on the other hand, has an ambiguous sign even at $t = 0$, but can be manipulated so that an economically intuitive necessary and sufficient condition for signing it emerges. First, evaluate Eqs. (36) and (40) at $t = 0$, and then evaluate Eqs. (36) and (39) at $s = Q(\varepsilon, \pi)$. Next, substitute Eqs. (36) and (39) into Eq. (40) to get

$$\frac{\partial q^m}{\partial p}(0; \varepsilon, \pi) = \frac{\partial \hat{q}}{\partial p}(0; \psi^M(\varepsilon, Q(\varepsilon, \pi)), p, r, w)\left[1 - \frac{\partial \psi^M}{\partial p}(\varepsilon, Q(\varepsilon, \pi))\right]$$
$$+ \frac{\partial \hat{q}}{\partial \psi}(0; \psi^M(\varepsilon, Q(\varepsilon, \pi)), p, r, w)\frac{\partial \psi^M}{\partial s}(\varepsilon, Q(\varepsilon, \pi))\frac{\partial Q}{\partial p}(\varepsilon, \pi). \tag{42}$$

Finally, recall that Eqs. (20) and (21) imply that $\partial \hat{q}(0; \psi, p, r, w)/\partial \psi = -\partial \hat{q}(0; \psi, p, r, w)/\partial p$, thereby implying that Eq. (42) reduces to

$$\frac{\partial q^m}{\partial p}(0; \varepsilon, \pi) = \frac{\partial \hat{q}}{\partial p}(0; \psi^M(\varepsilon, Q(\varepsilon, \pi)), p, r, w)$$
$$\times \left[1 - \frac{\partial \psi^M}{\partial p}(\varepsilon, Q(\varepsilon, \pi)) - \frac{\partial \psi^M}{\partial s}(\varepsilon, Q(\varepsilon, \pi))\frac{\partial Q}{\partial p}(\varepsilon, \pi)\right]. \tag{43}$$

This is the expression sought. Because $\partial \hat{q}/\partial p > 0$ from Eq. (21), $\partial q^m(0; \varepsilon, \pi)/\partial p > 0$ if and only if the bracketed expression in Eq. (43) is positive.

To impart some economic intuition to the bracketed expression in Eq. (43), define the *compensated* shadow value of the initial stock by

$$\psi^c(\varepsilon, \pi) \stackrel{\text{def}}{=} \psi^M(\varepsilon, Q(\varepsilon, \pi)). \tag{44}$$

Thus $\psi^c(\varepsilon, \pi)$ is the shadow value of the initial stock along a level curve of the present value of profit, that is, wealth, constraint. Differentiating Eq. (44) with respect to the output price yields a Slutsky-like equation for the shadow value of the initial stock, namely,

$$\frac{\partial \psi^c}{\partial p}(\varepsilon, \pi) = \frac{\partial \psi^M}{\partial p}(\varepsilon, Q(\varepsilon, \pi)) + \frac{\partial \psi^M}{\partial s}(\varepsilon, Q(\varepsilon, \pi))\frac{\partial Q}{\partial p}(\varepsilon, \pi). \tag{45}$$

It follows from Theorem 7.3 that $\partial Q(\varepsilon, \pi)/\partial p \equiv -\int_0^T \psi^m(\varepsilon, \pi) q^m(t; \varepsilon, \pi) e^{-rt} dt < 0$, implying that minimum cumulative extraction falls with an increase in the output price. This is an intuitive conclusion, because a higher output price allows the firm to reach its target level of wealth by extracting less of the resource over its given planning horizon. Using the above dynamic envelope result and Eqs. (26) and (29), it follows that $\partial \psi^c(\varepsilon, \pi)/\partial p > 0$, but it may be greater than or less than unity. Finally, substituting Eqs. (44) and (45) into Eq. (43) yields the economically more revealing version of Eq. (43), to wit,

$$\frac{\partial q^m}{\partial p}(0; \varepsilon, \pi) = \frac{\partial \hat{q}}{\partial p}(0; \psi^c(\varepsilon, \pi), p, r, w)\left[1 - \frac{\partial \psi^c}{\partial p}(\varepsilon, \pi)\right]. \tag{46}$$

Equation (46) shows that the cumulative extraction–minimizing supply response at the initial date of the planning horizon is positive if and only if the effect of an output price increase on the compensated shadow value of the initial stock lies inside the unit interval, that is, $\partial q^m(0; \varepsilon, \pi)/\partial p > 0 \Leftrightarrow \partial \psi^c(\varepsilon, \pi)/\partial p \in (0, 1)$. In passing, note the wonderful symmetry in the comparative dynamics of the output price at the initial date exhibited by Eqs. (39) and (46).

It is important to note that we could have derived the comparative dynamics properties of the reciprocal problem (4) first, and then used the identities in Eqs. (9) and (10) to uncover the comparative dynamics properties of the primal problem (3). More generally, whether one wants to derive the comparative dynamics of the primal problem (P) first, as was done here, and then use Theorem 8.1 and Corollary 8.1 to derive the qualitative properties of the reciprocal problem (R), or derive the comparative dynamics properties of the reciprocal problem (R) first, and then use Theorem 8.1 and Corollary 8.1 to derive the qualitative properties of the primal problem (P), is simply a matter of choice. The qualitative information extracted is identical regardless of the route taken. That is the beauty, in fact, of dealing with reciprocal pairs of isoperimetric problems. Though the qualitative comparative dynamics properties of the reciprocal problem can be obtained from the primal problem through the use of Corollary 8.1, and vice versa, it may well turn out that deriving the comparative dynamics properties of the primal problem may be easier by first deriving the comparative dynamics properties of the reciprocal problem, and then invoking Corollary 8.1 to recover those of the primal problem, as it is with a reciprocal pair of intertemporal consumer problems. In fact, the application of Theorem 8.1 and Corollary 8.1 may yield new qualitative insights into economic problems that have been extensively analyzed by other methods, as has been demonstrated here with the nonrenewable resource–extracting model of the firm.

In the ensuing chapter, we return to our study of optimal control theory. In particular, we develop the continuous-time intertemporal generalization of the prototype envelope theorem, to wit, the dynamic envelope theorem. This important theorem permits us to achieve a deeper economic understanding of an optimal control problem. Furthermore, in Chapter 10, we use the dynamic envelope theorem to achieve simple and intuitive proofs of a general set of transversality conditions that are ubiquitous in dynamic economic problems.

MENTAL EXERCISES

8.1 In this question, we return to the R&D problem you analyzed in Mental Exercise 7.8. Recall that the R&D project is subject to diminishing marginal productivity of research expenditures. In other words, defining $e(t)$ as the effort rate expended on R&D at time t, the relationship between the effort rate expended on the project at time t and the spending rate $s(t)$ at time t

is given by

$$e(t) = f(s(t); \alpha),$$

where $f(\cdot) \in C^{(2)}$, $f_s(s;\alpha) > 0$, $f_{ss}(s;\alpha) < 0$, $f_\alpha(s;\alpha) > 0$, and $f_{s\alpha}(s;\alpha) > 0$. An increase in the parameter α therefore represents an increase in the total and marginal product of R&D expenditures. Because $f_s(s;\alpha) > 0$ and $f_{ss}(s;\alpha) < 0$, higher R&D expenditures lead to higher effort, but at a decreasing rate, as asserted above. The cumulative or total effort required to complete the R&D project by the predetermined time $T > 0$ is given by $A > 0$. It is assumed that cumulative effort expended on the R&D project equals the total effort required to complete the R&D project; hence

$$\int_0^T f(s(t); \alpha)\, dt = A.$$

The objective for the firm is to minimize the present discounted cost of completing the R&D project by time T, where $r > 0$ is the discount rate. More formally, the firm is asserted to solve the isoperimetric problem

$$C(\alpha, A, r, T) \stackrel{\text{def}}{=} \min_{s(\cdot)} \left\{ \int_0^T e^{-rt} s(t) dt \text{ s.t. } \int_0^T f(s(t); \alpha)\, dt = A \right\}.$$

(a) Solve, in principle, the augmented Euler equation for its general solution, say, $s = \hat{s}(t; \alpha, r, \psi)$, using a theorem you deem appropriate.
(b) Find $\partial\hat{s}(t; \alpha, r, \psi)/\partial\alpha$ and provide an economic interpretation.
(c) Find $\partial\hat{s}(t; \alpha, r, \psi)/\partial r$ and provide an economic interpretation.
(d) Find $\partial\hat{s}(t; \alpha, r, \psi)/\partial\psi$ and provide an economic interpretation.
(e) Using an appropriate theorem, solve, in principle, for the optimal value of the conjugate variable, say, $\psi = \psi^*(\alpha, A, r, T)$. What is the economic interpretation of $\psi = \psi^*(\alpha, A, r, T)$?
(f) Find $\partial\psi^*(\alpha, A, r, T)/\partial\alpha$ and provide an economic interpretation.
(g) Find $\partial\psi^*(\alpha, A, r, T)/\partial r$ and provide an economic interpretation.
(h) Now write down an identity linking $\hat{s}(t; \alpha, r, \psi)$ to the optimal spending rate, say, $s^*(t; \alpha, A, r, T)$, using the information at hand.
(i) Prove that $\partial s^*(t; \alpha, A, r, T)/\partial\alpha$ can be broken up into the sum of two Slutsky-like terms. Provide an economic interpretation of the result. Can you sign it? Why or why not?
(j) Show that at this level of generality, $\partial s^*(t; \alpha, A, r, T)/\partial r$ cannot be signed. Show, however, that $\partial s^*(0; \alpha, A, r, T)/\partial r < 0$. Provide an economic interpretation of this result.

8.2 Prove Corollary 8.1.

8.3 Prove that not all of the identities in Corollary 8.1 are independent of one another.

8.4 Prove that

$$C(q;w) \stackrel{\text{def}}{=} \min_{v} \{w \cdot v \text{ s.t. } q = f(v)\}$$

satisfies $C_q(q;w) > 0$, $C_{qq}(q;w) > 0$, $C_w(q;w) > 0$, and $C_{qw}(q;w) > 0$.

8.5 Derive the derivative decompositions for the nonrenewable resource–extracting model of the firm for the parameters (r, w, T) analogous to those in Eqs. (9) through (16).

8.6 Provide an economic interpretation of Eqs. (10) and (14).

8.7 Show that one can also arrive at the formula

$$\int_0^T q^M(t;\varepsilon,s)\,e^{-rt}\,dt \equiv \frac{-\frac{\partial Q}{\partial p}(\varepsilon,\Pi(\varepsilon,s))}{\frac{\partial Q}{\partial \pi}(\varepsilon,\Pi(\varepsilon,s))}$$

via Eq. (15), as noted in the text.

8.8 Prove that $\partial q^M(t;\varepsilon,s)/\partial p < 0$ holds for some finite interval of time near the end of the planning horizon following the steps and logic used to deduce Eq. (39).

8.9 Using Eq. (34), prove that

$$\frac{\partial q^M}{\partial r}(0;\varepsilon,s) = \frac{\partial \hat{q}}{\partial \psi}(0;\psi^M(\varepsilon,s),p,r,w)\frac{\partial \psi^M}{\partial r}(\varepsilon,s) > 0,$$

and provide an economic interpretation of the result comparable to Eq. (39).

FURTHER READING

As remarked in the third paragraph of the chapter, the references for the results contained herewith are Caputo (1998, 1999). The paper by Caputo (1994) examines the intertemporal Slutsky matrix for an isoperimetric consumer problem and demonstrates an assertion made in the next to last paragraph in the chapter, videlicet, that it may be easier to derive the comparative dynamics properties of the primal problem by first deriving the comparative dynamics properties of the reciprocal problem. Further pertinent references for this chapter are those noted in Chapter 7. Of related interest are the papers by Newman (1982), Weber (1998), and Caputo (2000, 2001). These papers deal with reciprocal constrained optimization problems of the static variety and their associated comparative statics properties. Hotelling (1931) is the source for the nonrenewable resource–extracting model of the firm.

REFERENCES

Caputo, M.R. (1994), "The Slutsky Matrix and Homogeneity in Intertemporal Consumer Theory," *Journal of Economics*, 60, 255–279.

Caputo, M.R. (1998), "Economic Characterization of Reciprocal Isoperimetric Control Problems," *Journal of Optimization Theory and Applications*, 98, 325–350.

Caputo, M.R. (1999), "Economic Characterization of Reciprocal Isoperimetric Control Problems Revisited," *Journal of Optimization Theory and Applications*, 101, 723–730.

Caputo, M.R. (2000), "Lagrangian Transposition Identities and Reciprocal Pairs of Constrained Optimization Problems," *Economics Letters*, 66, 265–273.

Caputo, M.R. (2001), "Further Results on Lagrange Multipliers with Several Binding Constraints," *Economics Letters*, 70, 335–340.

Hotelling, H. (1931), "The Economics of Exhaustible Resources," *Journal of Political Economy*, 39, 137–175.

Newman, P. (1982), "Mirrored Pairs of Optimization Problems," *Economica*, 49, 109–119.

Weber, C.E. (1998), "A Note on Lagrange Multipliers with Several Binding Constraints," *Economics Letters*, 59, 71–75.

NINE

The Dynamic Envelope Theorem and Economic Interpretations

One objective of this chapter is to prove the intertemporal equivalent of the prototype envelope theorem, namely, the *dynamic envelope theorem*, for a general class of fixed endpoint optimal control problems. The second objective is to use this important theorem to impart a deeper economic interpretation to the Hamiltonian and costate variables than we were heretofore able to. In the next chapter, we will use the dynamic envelope theorem to provide simple and motivated proofs of the transversality conditions corresponding to various endpoint conditions in optimal control problems. If your understanding of the prototype envelope theorem is less than ideal, then it would be best to pause at this juncture and deepen your understanding of it before tackling the ensuing material.

To begin, we proceed with the *literal* definition of the optimal value function $V(\cdot)$ for the following fixed endpoints optimal control problem:

$$V(\boldsymbol{\beta}) \stackrel{\text{def}}{=} \max_{\mathbf{u}(\cdot)} \int_{t_0}^{t_1} f(t, \mathbf{x}(t), \mathbf{u}(t); \boldsymbol{\alpha})\, dt$$
$$\text{s.t.} \quad \dot{\mathbf{x}}(t) = \mathbf{g}(t, \mathbf{x}(t), \mathbf{u}(t); \boldsymbol{\alpha}),\ \mathbf{x}(t_0) = \mathbf{x}_0,\ \mathbf{x}(t_1) = \mathbf{x}_1, \tag{OC}$$

where $\mathbf{x}(t) \stackrel{\text{def}}{=} (x_1(t), x_2(t), \ldots, x_N(t)) \in \Re^N$ is the state vector, $\mathbf{u}(t) \stackrel{\text{def}}{=} (u_1(t), u_2(t), \ldots, u_M(t)) \in \Re^M$ is the control vector, $\boldsymbol{\alpha} \stackrel{\text{def}}{=} (\alpha_1, \alpha_2, \ldots, \alpha_A) \in \Re^A$ is a vector of time-independent parameters that affect both the state equation and the integrand, $\mathbf{g}(\cdot) \stackrel{\text{def}}{=} (g^1(\cdot), g^2(\cdot), \ldots, g^N(\cdot))$ is the transition function, and $\boldsymbol{\beta} \stackrel{\text{def}}{=} (\boldsymbol{\alpha}, t_0, \mathbf{x}_0, t_1, \mathbf{x}_1) \in \Re^{2+2N+A}$ is the vector of parameters of the problem. Assuming that an optimal pair of curves $(\mathbf{z}(t; \boldsymbol{\beta}), \mathbf{v}(t; \boldsymbol{\beta}))$ exists to problem (OC) for all $\boldsymbol{\beta} \in B(\boldsymbol{\beta}^\circ; \delta)$, where $B(\boldsymbol{\beta}^\circ; \delta)$ is an open $2 + 2N + A$ – ball centered at the given value of the parameter $\boldsymbol{\beta}^\circ \in \Re^{2+2N+A}$ of radius $\delta > 0$, we can also define the optimal value function $V(\cdot)$ of problem (OC) *constructively* as

$$V(\boldsymbol{\beta}) \equiv \int_{t_0}^{t_1} f(t, \mathbf{z}(t; \boldsymbol{\beta}), \mathbf{v}(t; \boldsymbol{\beta}); \boldsymbol{\alpha})\, dt. \tag{1}$$

Notice that Eq. (1) is exactly how one would go about constructing (or deriving) the optimal value function in practice if one were able to perform all the mathematical operations explicitly. That is, Eq. (1) shows how one would construct $V(\cdot)$ if one could explicitly find the optimal solution $(\mathbf{z}(t;\boldsymbol{\beta}), \mathbf{v}(t;\boldsymbol{\beta}))$ to the control problem, assuming it exists, and then substitute it into the objective functional and integrate over the planning horizon.

Because of the introduction of the parameter vector $\boldsymbol{\alpha}$, and the importance of it in the dynamic envelope theorem, we must modify our basic assumptions on the integrand function and transition functions to take this feature into account. Consequently, we now impose the ensuing assumptions on the functions $f(\cdot)$ and $\mathbf{g}(\cdot)$ throughout the remainder of this chapter:

(A.1) $f(\cdot) \in C^{(1)}$ with respect to the $1+N+M$ variables $(t, \mathbf{x}, \mathbf{u})$ and the A parameters $\boldsymbol{\alpha}$.

(A.2) $\mathbf{g}(\cdot) \in C^{(1)}$ with respect to the $1+N+M$ variables $(t, \mathbf{x}, \mathbf{u})$ and the A parameters $\boldsymbol{\alpha}$.

Given these preliminaries, we are now in a position to prove the following dynamic envelope theorem for the fixed endpoint class of optimal control problems defined by problem (OC).

Theorem 9.1 (Dynamic Envelope Theorem): *Let $(\mathbf{z}(t;\boldsymbol{\beta}), \mathbf{v}(t;\boldsymbol{\beta}))$ be the optimal pair for problem (OC), and let $\boldsymbol{\lambda}(t;\boldsymbol{\beta})$ be the corresponding time path of the costate vector. Define the Hamiltonian as $H(t, \mathbf{x}, \mathbf{u}, \boldsymbol{\lambda}; \boldsymbol{\alpha}) \stackrel{\text{def}}{=} f(t, \mathbf{x}, \mathbf{u}; \boldsymbol{\alpha}) + \sum_{\ell=1}^{N} \lambda_\ell g^\ell(t, \mathbf{x}, \mathbf{u}; \boldsymbol{\alpha})$. If $\mathbf{z}(\cdot) \in C^{(1)}$ and $\mathbf{v}(\cdot) \in C^{(1)}$ in $(t;\boldsymbol{\beta})\,\forall\,(t;\boldsymbol{\beta}) \in [t_0^\circ, t_1^\circ] \times B(\boldsymbol{\beta}^\circ;\delta)$, then $V(\cdot) \in C^{(1)}\,\forall\,\boldsymbol{\beta} \in B(\boldsymbol{\beta}^\circ;\delta)$, and furthermore, $\forall\,\boldsymbol{\beta} \in B(\boldsymbol{\beta}^\circ;\delta)$:*

$$V_{\alpha_i}(\boldsymbol{\beta}) \stackrel{\text{def}}{=} \frac{\partial V(\boldsymbol{\beta})}{\partial \alpha_i} \equiv \int_{t_0}^{t_1} H_{\alpha_i}(t, \mathbf{z}(t;\boldsymbol{\beta}), \mathbf{v}(t;\boldsymbol{\beta}), \boldsymbol{\lambda}(t;\boldsymbol{\beta}); \boldsymbol{\alpha})\, dt, \quad i = 1, 2, \ldots, A, \tag{i}$$

$$V_{t_0}(\boldsymbol{\beta}) \equiv -H(t_0, \mathbf{x}_0, \mathbf{v}(t_0;\boldsymbol{\beta}), \boldsymbol{\lambda}(t_0;\boldsymbol{\beta}); \boldsymbol{\alpha}), \tag{ii}$$

$$V_{x_{0j}}(\boldsymbol{\beta}) \equiv \lambda_j(t_0;\boldsymbol{\beta}), \quad j = 1, 2, \ldots, N, \tag{iii}$$

$$V_{t_1}(\boldsymbol{\beta}) \equiv H(t_1, \mathbf{x}_1, \mathbf{v}(t_1;\boldsymbol{\beta}), \boldsymbol{\lambda}(t_1;\boldsymbol{\beta}); \boldsymbol{\alpha}), \tag{iv}$$

$$V_{x_{1j}}(\boldsymbol{\beta}) \equiv -\lambda_j(t_1;\boldsymbol{\beta}), \quad j = 1, 2, \ldots, N. \tag{v}$$

Proof: We will prove parts (i) and (ii) and leave the rest for the mental exercises. In the proof of part (i), we employ index notation, whereas in the proof of part (ii), we employ vector notation. We employ both types of notation, since the literature uses both.

(i) Differentiate the optimal value function $V(\cdot)$ as defined constructively in Eq. (1) with respect to α_i, and use the chain rule and Leibniz's rule to get

$$V_{\alpha_i}(\boldsymbol{\beta}) \equiv \int_{t_0}^{t_1} \left[\sum_{n=1}^{N} f_{x_n}(t, \mathbf{z}(t;\boldsymbol{\beta}), \mathbf{v}(t;\boldsymbol{\beta}); \boldsymbol{\alpha}) \frac{\partial z_n}{\partial \alpha_i}(t;\boldsymbol{\beta}) + \sum_{m=1}^{M} f_{u_m}(t, \mathbf{z}(t;\boldsymbol{\beta}), \right.$$

$$\left. \mathbf{v}(t;\boldsymbol{\beta}); \boldsymbol{\alpha}) \frac{\partial v_m}{\partial \alpha_i}(t;\boldsymbol{\beta}) + f_{\alpha_i}(t, \mathbf{z}(t;\boldsymbol{\beta}), \mathbf{v}(t;\boldsymbol{\beta}); \boldsymbol{\alpha}) \right] dt, \tag{2}$$

for $i = 1, 2, \ldots, A$. To simplify the notation, define $f_{x_n}^*(t) \overset{\text{def}}{=} f_{x_n}(t, \mathbf{z}(t;\boldsymbol{\beta}), \mathbf{v}(t;\boldsymbol{\beta}); \boldsymbol{\alpha})$, $n = 1, 2, \ldots, N$, and likewise for the other partial derivatives. Because $(\mathbf{z}(t;\boldsymbol{\beta}), \mathbf{v}(t;\boldsymbol{\beta}))$ is an optimal pair, it must satisfy the state equation and boundary conditions identically $\forall\, \boldsymbol{\beta} \in B(\boldsymbol{\beta}^\circ;\delta)$ and $\forall\, t \in [t_0, t_1]$, thereby implying the identities

$$g^\ell(t, \mathbf{z}(t;\boldsymbol{\beta}), \mathbf{v}(t;\boldsymbol{\beta}); \boldsymbol{\alpha}) - \dot{z}_\ell(t;\boldsymbol{\beta}) \equiv 0, \quad \ell = 1, 2, \ldots, N,$$

$$z_\ell(t_0;\boldsymbol{\beta}) \equiv x_{0\ell},\ z_\ell(t_1;\boldsymbol{\beta}) \equiv x_{1\ell}, \quad \ell = 1, 2, \ldots, N.$$

Differentiate these three identities with respect to α_i to arrive at

$$\sum_{n=1}^{N} g_{x_n}^\ell(t, \mathbf{z}(t;\boldsymbol{\beta}), \mathbf{v}(t;\boldsymbol{\beta}); \boldsymbol{\alpha}) \frac{\partial z_n}{\partial \alpha_i}(t;\boldsymbol{\beta}) + \sum_{m=1}^{M} g_{u_m}^\ell(t, \mathbf{z}(t;\boldsymbol{\beta}), \mathbf{v}(t;\boldsymbol{\beta}); \boldsymbol{\alpha}) \frac{\partial v_m}{\partial \alpha_i}(t;\boldsymbol{\beta})$$

$$+ g_{\alpha_i}^\ell(t, \mathbf{z}(t;\boldsymbol{\beta}), \mathbf{v}(t;\boldsymbol{\beta}); \boldsymbol{\alpha}) - \frac{\partial \dot{z}_\ell}{\partial \alpha_i}(t;\boldsymbol{\beta}) \equiv 0, \quad \ell = 1, 2, \ldots, N, \tag{3}$$

$$\frac{\partial z_\ell}{\partial \alpha_i}(t_0;\boldsymbol{\beta}) \equiv 0,\ \frac{\partial z_\ell}{\partial \alpha_i}(t_1;\boldsymbol{\beta}) \equiv 0, \quad \ell = 1, 2, \ldots, N. \tag{4}$$

As we did above, define $g_{u_m}^{\ell *}(t) \overset{\text{def}}{=} g_{u_m}^\ell(t, \mathbf{z}(t;\boldsymbol{\beta}), \mathbf{v}(t;\boldsymbol{\beta}); \boldsymbol{\alpha})$, $m = 1, 2, \ldots, M$, $\ell = 1, 2, \ldots, N$, and similarly for the other partial derivatives. Now multiply the ℓth identity in Eq. (3) by its corresponding costate variable $\lambda_\ell(t;\boldsymbol{\beta})$ and sum the resulting expression over ℓ, from $\ell = 1$ to $\ell = N$. Because the N identities in Eq. (3) are identically zero $\forall\, \boldsymbol{\beta} \in B(\boldsymbol{\beta}^\circ;\delta)$ and $\forall\, t \in [t_0, t_1]$, they are clearly still zero $\forall\, \boldsymbol{\beta} \in B(\boldsymbol{\beta}^\circ;\delta)$ and $\forall\, t \in [t_0, t_1]$ when multiplied by $\lambda_\ell(t;\boldsymbol{\beta})$ and summed over ℓ. Moreover, when the resulting sum is integrated over $[t_0, t_1]$, it is still identically zero and therefore may be added to Eq. (2) without changing the latter's value, thereby yielding

$$V_{\alpha_i}(\boldsymbol{\beta}) \equiv \int_{t_0}^{t_1} \left[\sum_{n=1}^{N} \left[f_{x_n}^*(t) + \sum_{\ell=1}^{N} \lambda_\ell(t;\boldsymbol{\beta}) g_{x_n}^{\ell *}(t) \right] \frac{\partial z_n}{\partial \alpha_i}(t;\boldsymbol{\beta}) \right.$$

$$+ \sum_{m=1}^{M} \left[f_{u_m}^*(t) + \sum_{\ell=1}^{N} \lambda_\ell(t;\boldsymbol{\beta}) g_{u_m}^{\ell *}(t) \right] \frac{\partial v_m}{\partial \alpha_i}(t;\boldsymbol{\beta})$$

$$\left. + \left[f_{\alpha_i}^*(t) + \sum_{\ell=1}^{N} \lambda_\ell(t;\boldsymbol{\beta}) g_{\alpha_i}^{\ell *}(t) \right] - \sum_{\ell=1}^{N} \lambda_\ell(t;\boldsymbol{\beta}) \frac{\partial \dot{z}_\ell}{\partial \alpha_i}(t;\boldsymbol{\beta}) \right] dt. \tag{5}$$

Now define the partial derivatives of the Hamiltonian along the optimal path by

$$H^*_{x_n}(t) \stackrel{\text{def}}{=} f^*_{x_n}(t) + \sum_{\ell=1}^{N} \lambda_\ell(t;\beta) g^{\ell *}_{x_n}(t), \quad n = 1, 2 \ldots, N,$$

$$H^*_{u_m}(t) \stackrel{\text{def}}{=} f^*_{u_m}(t) + \sum_{\ell=1}^{N} \lambda_\ell(t;\beta) g^{\ell *}_{u_m}(t), \quad m = 1, 2 \ldots, M,$$

$$H^*_{\alpha_i}(t) \stackrel{\text{def}}{=} f^*_{\alpha_i}(t) + \sum_{\ell=1}^{N} \lambda_\ell(t;\beta) g^{\ell *}_{\alpha_i}(t), \quad i = 1, 2 \ldots, A.$$

These definitions allow Eq. (5) to be rewritten more cleanly as

$$V_{\alpha_i}(\beta) \equiv \int_{t_0}^{t_1} \Bigg[\sum_{n=1}^{N} H^*_{x_n}(t) \frac{\partial z_n}{\partial \alpha_i}(t;\beta) + \sum_{m=1}^{M} H^*_{u_m}(t) \frac{\partial v_m}{\partial \alpha_i}(t;\beta) + H^*_{\alpha_i}(t)$$
$$- \sum_{\ell=1}^{N} \lambda_\ell(t;\beta) \frac{\partial \dot{z}_\ell}{\partial \alpha_i}(t;\beta) \Bigg] dt. \tag{6}$$

Upon letting

$$p_\ell = \lambda_\ell(t;\beta), \qquad dq_\ell = \frac{\partial \dot{z}_\ell}{\partial \alpha_i}(t;\beta)\, dt = \frac{d}{dt}\left[\frac{\partial z_\ell}{\partial \alpha_i}(t;\beta)\right] dt,$$
$$dp_\ell = \dot{\lambda}_\ell(t;\beta)\, dt, \qquad q_\ell = \frac{\partial z_\ell}{\partial \alpha_i}(t;\beta),$$

$\ell = 1, 2, \ldots, N$, we can integrate each term in the last sum of Eq. (6) by parts, thus yielding

$$-\int_{t_0}^{t_1} \sum_{\ell=1}^{N} \lambda_\ell(t;\beta) \frac{\partial \dot{z}_\ell}{\partial \alpha_i}(t;\beta)\, dt = -\sum_{\ell=1}^{N} \lambda_\ell(t;\beta) \frac{\partial z_\ell}{\partial \alpha_i}(t;\beta) \Bigg|_{t=t_0}^{t=t_1}$$
$$+ \int_{t_0}^{t_1} \sum_{\ell=1}^{N} \dot{\lambda}_\ell(t;\beta) \frac{\partial z_\ell}{\partial \alpha_i}(t;\beta)\, dt = \int_{t_0}^{t_1} \sum_{\ell=1}^{N} \dot{\lambda}_\ell(t;\beta) \frac{\partial z_\ell}{\partial \alpha_i}(t;\beta)\, dt, \tag{7}$$

where we have used Eq. (4) to simplify Eq. (7). Substituting Eq. (7) into Eq. (6) yields

$$V_{\alpha_i}(\beta)$$
$$\equiv \int_{t_0}^{t_1} \left[\sum_{n=1}^{N} [H^*_{x_n}(t) + \dot{\lambda}_n(t;\beta)] \frac{\partial z_n}{\partial \alpha_i}(t;\beta) + \sum_{m=1}^{M} H^*_{u_m}(t) \frac{\partial v_m}{\partial \alpha_i}(t;\beta) + H^*_{\alpha_i}(t) \right] dt.$$
$$\tag{8}$$

Note that in arriving at the final form of Eq. (8), the dummy index of summation ℓ from Eq. (7) was replaced by the dummy index of summation n, which is legitimate in view of the fact that they are both dummy indices and range over identical values. Because $(\mathbf{z}(t;\boldsymbol{\beta}), \mathbf{v}(t;\boldsymbol{\beta}))$ is the optimal pair for problem (OC) and $\boldsymbol{\lambda}(t;\boldsymbol{\beta})$ is the corresponding time path of the costate vector, it follows from Corollary 4.2 that $H^*_{x_n}(t) + \dot{\lambda}_n(t;\boldsymbol{\beta}) \equiv 0, n = 1, 2, \ldots, N$, and that $H^*_{u_m}(t) \equiv 0, m = 1, 2, \ldots, M$, for all $t \in [t_0, t_1]$; hence Eq. (8) simplifies to

$$V_{\alpha_i}(\boldsymbol{\beta}) \equiv \int_{t_0}^{t_1} H^*_{\alpha_i}(t)\,dt \stackrel{\text{def}}{=} \int_{t_0}^{t_1} H_{\alpha_i}(t, \mathbf{z}(t;\boldsymbol{\beta}), \mathbf{v}(t;\boldsymbol{\beta}), \boldsymbol{\lambda}(t;\boldsymbol{\beta}); \boldsymbol{\alpha})\,dt,\ i = 1, 2, \ldots, A,$$

which is what we set out to demonstrate. Q.E.D.

(ii) We employ vector notation and avoid integration by parts in this proof. To begin, differentiate the optimal value function $V(\cdot)$ defined constructively in Eq. (1) with respect to t_0, using the chain rule and Leibniz's rule to get

$$V_{t_0}(\boldsymbol{\beta}) \equiv -f(t_0, \mathbf{z}(t_0;\boldsymbol{\beta}), \mathbf{v}(t_0;\boldsymbol{\beta}); \boldsymbol{\alpha})$$
$$+ \int_{t_0}^{t_1} \left[\underbrace{f_{\mathbf{x}}(t, \mathbf{z}(t;\boldsymbol{\beta}), \mathbf{v}(t;\boldsymbol{\beta}); \boldsymbol{\alpha})}_{1\times N} \underbrace{\frac{\partial \mathbf{z}}{\partial t_0}(t;\boldsymbol{\beta})}_{N\times 1} + \underbrace{f_{\mathbf{u}}(t, \mathbf{z}(t;\boldsymbol{\beta}), \mathbf{v}(t;\boldsymbol{\beta}); \boldsymbol{\alpha})}_{1\times M} \underbrace{\frac{\partial \mathbf{v}}{\partial t_0}(t;\boldsymbol{\beta})}_{M\times 1} \right] dt. \tag{9}$$

As we did above, simplify the notation by defining $f^*_{\mathbf{x}}(t) \stackrel{\text{def}}{=} f_{\mathbf{x}}(t, \mathbf{z}(t;\boldsymbol{\beta}), \mathbf{v}(t;\boldsymbol{\beta}); \boldsymbol{\alpha})$ and likewise for the other vector derivatives. Because $(\mathbf{z}(t;\boldsymbol{\beta}), \mathbf{v}(t;\boldsymbol{\beta}))$ is an optimal pair, it must satisfy the state equation and boundary conditions identically $\forall\, \boldsymbol{\beta} \in B(\boldsymbol{\beta}^\circ;\delta)$ and $\forall\, t \in [t_0, t_1]$; hence we have the following identities:

$$\mathbf{g}(t, \mathbf{z}(t;\boldsymbol{\beta}), \mathbf{v}(t;\boldsymbol{\beta}); \boldsymbol{\alpha}) - \dot{\mathbf{z}}(t;\boldsymbol{\beta}) \equiv \mathbf{0}_N,$$

$$\mathbf{z}(t_0;\boldsymbol{\beta}) \equiv \mathbf{x}_0,\ \mathbf{z}(t_1;\boldsymbol{\beta}) \equiv \mathbf{x}_1.$$

Differentiating these identities with respect to t_0 yields

$$\underbrace{\mathbf{g}_{\mathbf{x}}(t, \mathbf{z}(t;\boldsymbol{\beta}), \mathbf{v}(t;\boldsymbol{\beta}); \boldsymbol{\alpha})}_{N\times N} \underbrace{\frac{\partial \mathbf{z}}{\partial t_0}(t;\boldsymbol{\beta})}_{N\times 1}$$
$$+ \underbrace{\mathbf{g}_{\mathbf{u}}(t, \mathbf{z}(t;\boldsymbol{\beta}), \mathbf{v}(t;\boldsymbol{\beta}); \boldsymbol{\alpha})}_{N\times M} \underbrace{\frac{\partial \mathbf{v}}{\partial t_0}(t;\boldsymbol{\beta})}_{M\times 1} - \underbrace{\frac{\partial \dot{\mathbf{z}}}{\partial t_0}(t;\boldsymbol{\beta})}_{N\times 1} \equiv \mathbf{0}_N, \tag{10}$$

$$\underbrace{\dot{\mathbf{z}}(t_0;\boldsymbol{\beta})}_{N\times 1} + \underbrace{\frac{\partial \mathbf{z}}{\partial t_0}(t_0;\boldsymbol{\beta})}_{N\times 1} \equiv \mathbf{0}_N,\quad \underbrace{\frac{\partial \mathbf{z}}{\partial t_0}(t_1;\boldsymbol{\beta})}_{N\times 1} \equiv \mathbf{0}_N. \tag{11}$$

Note that because t_0 appears as the value of the time argument and as a parameter in the vector $\boldsymbol{\beta}$, we get the sum of two vectors in the first expression of Eq. (11) upon differentiating the identity $\mathbf{z}(t_0;\boldsymbol{\beta}) \equiv \mathbf{x}_0$ with respect to t_0. Again, define $\mathbf{g}_{\mathbf{x}}^*(t) \stackrel{\text{def}}{=} \mathbf{g}_{\mathbf{x}}(t,\mathbf{z}(t;\boldsymbol{\beta}),\mathbf{v}(t;\boldsymbol{\beta});\boldsymbol{\alpha})$ and likewise for the other Jacobian matrix in Eq. (10). Now premultiply the identity in Eq. (10) by its corresponding costate vector $\boldsymbol{\lambda}(t;\boldsymbol{\beta})'$. Because the vector identity in Eq. (10) is identically zero $\forall\, \boldsymbol{\beta} \in B(\boldsymbol{\beta}^\circ;\delta)$ and $\forall\, t \in [t_0,t_1]$, it is still zero $\forall\, \boldsymbol{\beta} \in B(\boldsymbol{\beta}^\circ;\delta)$ and $\forall\, t \in [t_0,t_1]$ when it is premultiplied by $\boldsymbol{\lambda}(t;\boldsymbol{\beta})'$. Moreover, when the resulting scalar is integrated over $[t_0,t_1]$, it is still identically zero and therefore may be added to Eq. (9) without changing the latter's value, thereby yielding

$$V_{t_0}(\boldsymbol{\beta}) \equiv -\, f(t_0,\mathbf{z}(t_0;\boldsymbol{\beta}),\mathbf{v}(t_0;\boldsymbol{\beta});\boldsymbol{\alpha}) + \int_{t_0}^{t_1} \Bigg[\Bigg[\underbrace{f_{\mathbf{x}}^*(t)}_{1\times N} + \underbrace{\boldsymbol{\lambda}(t;\boldsymbol{\beta})'}_{1\times N}\, \underbrace{\mathbf{g}_{\mathbf{x}}^*(t)}_{N\times N} \Bigg] \underbrace{\frac{\partial \mathbf{z}}{\partial t_0}(t;\boldsymbol{\beta})}_{N\times 1}$$

$$+ \Bigg[\underbrace{f_{\mathbf{u}}^*(t)}_{1\times M} + \underbrace{\boldsymbol{\lambda}(t;\boldsymbol{\beta})'}_{1\times N}\, \underbrace{\mathbf{g}_{\mathbf{u}}^*(t)}_{N\times M} \Bigg] \underbrace{\frac{\partial \mathbf{v}}{\partial t_0}(t;\boldsymbol{\beta})}_{M\times 1} - \underbrace{\boldsymbol{\lambda}(t;\boldsymbol{\beta})'}_{1\times N}\, \underbrace{\frac{\partial \dot{\mathbf{z}}}{\partial t_0}(t;\boldsymbol{\beta})}_{N\times 1} \Bigg]\, dt. \tag{12}$$

To ease the notational burden, define the gradient vectors of the Hamiltonian along the optimal path by

$$\underbrace{H_{\mathbf{x}}^*(t)}_{1\times N} \stackrel{\text{def}}{=} \underbrace{f_{\mathbf{x}}^*(t)}_{1\times N} + \underbrace{\boldsymbol{\lambda}(t;\boldsymbol{\beta})'}_{1\times N}\, \underbrace{\mathbf{g}_{\mathbf{x}}^*(t)}_{N\times N},$$

$$\underbrace{H_{\mathbf{u}}^*(t)}_{1\times M} \stackrel{\text{def}}{=} \underbrace{f_{\mathbf{u}}^*(t)}_{1\times M} + \underbrace{\boldsymbol{\lambda}(t;\boldsymbol{\beta})'}_{1\times N}\, \underbrace{\mathbf{g}_{\mathbf{u}}^*(t)}_{N\times M}.$$

These definitions permit Eq. (12) to be rewritten more cleanly as

$$V_{t_0}(\boldsymbol{\beta}) \equiv -f(t_0,\mathbf{z}(t_0;\boldsymbol{\beta}),\mathbf{v}(t_0;\boldsymbol{\beta});\boldsymbol{\alpha})$$

$$+ \int_{t_0}^{t_1} \Bigg[\underbrace{H_{\mathbf{x}}^*(t)}_{1\times N}\, \underbrace{\frac{\partial \mathbf{z}}{\partial t_0}(t;\boldsymbol{\beta})}_{N\times 1} + \underbrace{H_{\mathbf{u}}^*(t)}_{1\times M}\, \underbrace{\frac{\partial \mathbf{v}}{\partial t_0}(t;\boldsymbol{\beta})}_{M\times 1} - \underbrace{\boldsymbol{\lambda}(t;\boldsymbol{\beta})'}_{1\times N}\, \underbrace{\frac{\partial \dot{\mathbf{z}}}{\partial t_0}(t;\boldsymbol{\beta})}_{N\times 1} \Bigg]\, dt. \tag{13}$$

Given that $H_{\mathbf{u}}^*(t) \equiv \mathbf{0}_M'$ and $\dot{\boldsymbol{\lambda}}(t;\boldsymbol{\beta})' \equiv -H_{\mathbf{x}}^*(t) \forall\, t \in [t_0,t_1]$ by Corollary 4.2,

Eq. (13) reduces to

$$V_{t_0}(\beta) \equiv - f(t_0, \mathbf{z}(t_0; \beta), \mathbf{v}(t_0; \beta); \alpha) - \int_{t_0}^{t_1} \left[\underbrace{\dot{\boldsymbol{\lambda}}(t; \beta)'}_{1\times N} \underbrace{\frac{\partial \mathbf{z}}{\partial t_0}(t; \beta)}_{N\times 1} + \underbrace{\boldsymbol{\lambda}(t; \beta)'}_{1\times N} \underbrace{\frac{\partial \dot{\mathbf{z}}}{\partial t_0}(t; \beta)}_{N\times 1} \right] dt. \tag{14}$$

Now observe that

$$\frac{d}{dt}\left[\underbrace{\boldsymbol{\lambda}(t; \beta)'}_{1\times N} \underbrace{\frac{\partial \mathbf{z}}{\partial t_0}(t; \beta)}_{N\times 1} \right] = \underbrace{\dot{\boldsymbol{\lambda}}(t; \beta)'}_{1\times N} \underbrace{\frac{\partial \mathbf{z}}{\partial t_0}(t; \beta)}_{N\times 1} + \underbrace{\boldsymbol{\lambda}(t; \beta)'}_{1\times N} \underbrace{\frac{\partial \dot{\mathbf{z}}}{\partial t_0}(t; \beta)}_{N\times 1}$$

by the product rule of differentiation. Substituting this result and Eq. (11) into Eq. (14) yields

$$\begin{aligned} V_{t_0}(\beta) &\equiv -f(t_0, \mathbf{z}(t_0; \beta), \mathbf{v}(t_0; \beta); \alpha) - \int_{t_0}^{t_1} \frac{d}{dt}\left[\underbrace{\boldsymbol{\lambda}(t; \beta)'}_{1\times N} \underbrace{\frac{\partial \mathbf{z}}{\partial t_0}(t; \beta)}_{N\times 1} \right] dt \\ &= -f(t_0, \mathbf{z}(t_0; \beta), \mathbf{v}(t_0; \beta); \alpha) - \left[\underbrace{\boldsymbol{\lambda}(t; \beta)'}_{1\times N} \underbrace{\frac{\partial \mathbf{z}}{\partial t_0}(t; \beta)}_{N\times 1} \right]_{t=t_0}^{t=t_1} \\ &= -f(t_0, \mathbf{z}(t_0; \beta), \mathbf{v}(t_0; \beta); \alpha) - \boldsymbol{\lambda}(t_0; \beta)'\dot{\mathbf{z}}(t_0; \beta). \end{aligned} \tag{15}$$

Because $\dot{\mathbf{z}}(t_0; \beta) \equiv \mathbf{g}(t_0, \mathbf{z}(t_0; \beta), \mathbf{v}(t_0; \beta); \alpha)$ and $\mathbf{z}(t_0, \beta) \equiv \mathbf{x}_0$ by the admissibility of the optimal pair, Eq. (15) reduces to

$$V_{t_0}(\beta) \equiv -H(t_0, \mathbf{x}_0, \mathbf{v}(t_0; \beta), \boldsymbol{\lambda}(t_0; \beta); \alpha)$$

upon using the definition of the Hamiltonian. Q.E.D.

Before presenting an example to demonstrate how to use Theorem 9.1 to bring out the economic content of an optimal control problem, let's lay out the recipe for applying part (i) of it to a particular optimal control problem, as well as provide an economic interpretation of all its results. For the interpretations below, we assume that the optimal value function can be interpreted as the maximum present discounted profit of a capital accumulating firm. Naturally, if the optimal value function has a different interpretation dictated by the economic content of the control problem under consideration, then the ensuing economic interpretations will be slightly altered. Nonetheless, any economic interpretation will exhibit the same flavor, as future examples and mental exercises will demonstrate.

Part (i): To *apply* this part of the theorem to an optimal control problem, one complies with the following four-step recipe:

(a) Define the Hamiltonian for the control problem under consideration.
(b) Differentiate the Hamiltonian *directly* with respect to the parameter of interest; that is, differentiate the Hamiltonian with respect to the parameter of interest *prior to* substituting in the optimal paths of the state, costate, and control variables.
(c) Substitute the optimal paths of the state, costate, and control variables into the derivative of the Hamiltonian from step (b).
(d) Integrate the result in step (c) over the planning horizon.

This part of the dynamic envelope theorem asserts that the effect of an increase in a time-independent parameter that enters the integrand and state equations on the optimal value function is equivalent to the impact that the parameter has explicitly (or directly) on the Hamiltonian evaluated along the optimal solution paths and integrated over the planning horizon. It should be clear that this part of the dynamic envelope theorem smacks of the classical static envelope theorem, even as far as the "recipe" is concerned, save for the fact that the effect of the parameter change is integrated over a planning horizon. Also note that this dynamic envelope result will recover the dynamic supply and demand functions in the spirit of Shepherd's lemma and Hotelling's lemma, albeit in altered forms, as we will demonstrate.

Part (ii): This part asserts that the effect of an increase in the initial date of the planning horizon on the optimal value function is equal to the negative of the value of the Hamiltonian evaluated at the optimal solution at the initial date of the planning horizon. In other words, an increase in t_0 is like starting the plan a "little later." Assuming that the value of the Hamiltonian is positive at the initial date in the optimal plan, this envelope result shows the effect of a later starting date is to decrease the present discounted value of profits. This means that the value of the Hamiltonian at the initial date is the shadow value of time for the firm, since it tells the firm the maximum amount its present discounted value of profits would increase if it starts the optimizing plan a little sooner. Note that, in general, the value of the Hamiltonian could just as well be negative at the initial date of the planning horizon, as it depends on the economic problem under consideration.

Part (iii): This envelope result asserts that the effect of an increase in the initial value of the jth state variable (or jth stock) on the optimal value function is equal to the value of the corresponding costate variable at the initial date, namely, $\lambda_j(t_0; \beta)$. Given that we are assuming the optimal value function can be interpreted as the maximum present discounted profit of a firm, $\lambda_j(t_0; \beta)$ measures the most a firm would pay for another unit of the jth state variable at the initial date, since $\lambda_j(t_0; \beta)$ gives the change in the maximum present discounted profit of a firm at the initial date due to a marginal increase in the jth initial stock. Hence $\lambda_j(t_0; \beta)$ has the economic interpretation of an *imputed* or *shadow* price of the jth state variable at the initial date in an optimal plan. Intuitively, one expects $\lambda_j(t_0; \beta)$ to be positive if the jth stock is a good, such as the stock of productive capital or the stock of some valuable asset in general, whereas one expects $\lambda_j(t_0; \boldsymbol{\beta})$ to be negative if the jth stock is a bad, such as the stock of waste or pollution.

Part (iv): This is the analogue of part (ii). Here we find that the effect of an increase in the terminal date of the planning horizon on the optimal value function is equal to the value of the Hamiltonian evaluated at the optimal solution at the terminal date of the planning horizon. Analogous to part (ii), an increase in t_1 is like terminating the plan a "little later." Assuming that the value of the Hamiltonian is positive at the terminal date in the optimal plan, the effect of a later ending date results in an increase in the firm's present discounted profit. That is, by finishing the plan a little later, the firm would gain the instantaneous cash flow at the terminal date. As a result, we may interpret the value of the Hamiltonian at the terminal date as the shadow value of time for the firm.

Part (v): This is the analogue of part (iii). In this case, we find that the effect of an increase in the value of the jth state variable at the terminal date on the optimal value function is equal to the negative of the corresponding costate variable at the terminal date, namely, $-\lambda_j(t_1; \boldsymbol{\beta})$. Given that we are assuming the optimal value function can be interpreted as the maximum present discounted profit of a firm, $-\lambda_j(t_1; \boldsymbol{\beta})$ measures the additional cost incurred by the firm in reaching the higher terminal stock requirement if the stock is a good. If, however, the stock is a bad, say pollution, then $-\lambda_j(t_1; \boldsymbol{\beta})$ measures the increase in profits that results from having to clean up less because of the higher stock of pollution permitted at the terminal date.

Let's now hone our understanding of the dynamic envelope theorem by applying it to the capital accumulating model of the firm facing costs of adjustment. We will then examine in some detail the technical issue of the differentiability of the optimal value function.

Example 9.1: Consider the following intertemporal model of a firm:

$$V(\boldsymbol{\beta}) \stackrel{\text{def}}{=} \max_{I(\cdot)} \int_0^T [pf(K(t), I(t)) - cK(t) - gI(t)]\, e^{-rt}\, dt$$

$$\text{s.t.} \quad \dot{K}(t) = I(t) - \delta K(t),\ K(0) = K_0,\ K(T) = K_T.$$

The economic interpretation of this model, known as the *adjustment cost model of the firm*, is similar to the static profit maximizing price-taking model of the firm, as we noted in Example 1.2 when a version of it was first introduced. The function $f(\cdot) : \Re_+^2 \to \Re_+$ is the $C^{(2)}$ *generalized* production function of the firm, for it depends not only on the capital stock of the firm $K(t)$ at any time $t \in [0, T]$, but also on the gross rate of change of the capital stock, or the gross investment rate $I(t)$ at any time $t \in [0, T]$. It is assumed that $f_K(K, I) > 0$, $\text{sign}[f_I(K, I)] = -\text{sign}[I]$, and $f(\cdot)$ is concave in $(K, I)\ \forall\, t \in [0, T]$. In a mental exercise, you are asked to show that the assumption of concavity implies that a solution of the necessary conditions is

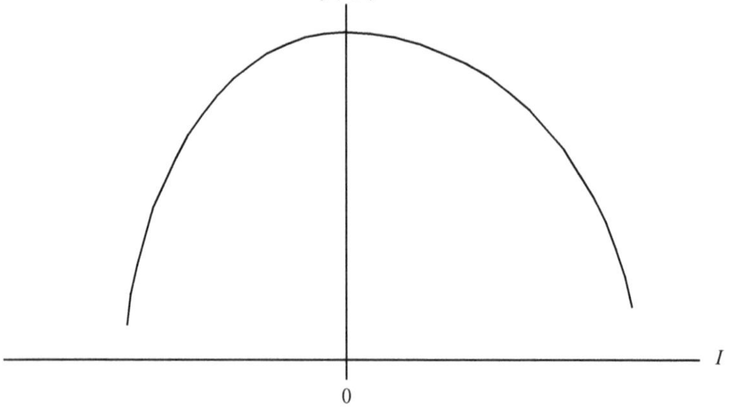

Figure 9.1

a solution of the adjustment cost problem. Note that the assumption $\text{sign}[f_I(K, I)] = -\text{sign}[I]$ is equivalent to the requirement that $f_I(K, I) \gtrless 0$ as $-I \gtrless 0$ and asserts that output decreases as investment ($I > 0$) *or* disinvestment ($I < 0$) in the capital stock takes place. The intuition behind the negative effect of investment on the output of the firm is that when capital is purchased, it must be installed for it to become a productive asset. The process of installation, however, takes resources away from production, thereby resulting in the fall in output. Similarly, when disinvestment takes place, the process of uninstalling the capital also takes resources away from production, thereby resulting in the decrease in output as well. See Figure 9.1 for the geometry of this characterization.

The single good the firm produces via its production function is sold at the constant price of $p > 0$, $c > 0$ is the constant holding cost per unit of the capital stock, and $g > 0$ is the constant price paid per unit of investment or disinvestment in the capital stock. The firm discounts its cash flow at the constant rate $r > 0$, begins its planning with a given capital stock $K_0 > 0$, and terminates its planning with the required capital stock $K_T > 0$. We assume that the natural nonnegativity constraint on the capital stock $K(t) \geq 0$ is not binding for all $t \in [0, T]$. We do not, however, assume that $I(t) \geq 0$ for all $t \in [0, T]$. In other words, we permit the firm to disinvestment; that is, $I(t) \leq 0$ is permitted. Note that $\dot{K}(t)$ is net investment, since depreciation, assumed proportional to the existing stock of capital with depreciation rate $\delta > 0$, is subtracted from gross investment $I(t)$ to arrive at $\dot{K}(t)$. Finally, define $\boldsymbol{\beta} \stackrel{\text{def}}{=} (c, g, p, r, \delta, K_0, T, K_T)$ as the vector of time-independent parameters and let $(K^*(t; \boldsymbol{\beta}), I^*(t; \boldsymbol{\beta}))$ denote the optimal pair, with $\lambda(t; \boldsymbol{\beta})$ being the corresponding time path of the costate variable.

First, consider the output price as the parameter of interest, and apply the four-step recipe after Theorem 9.1 to derive the pertinent dynamic envelope result:

$$H(t, K, I, \lambda; c, g, p, r, \delta) \stackrel{\text{def}}{=} [pf(K, I) - cK - gI]\, e^{-rt} + \lambda[I - \delta K],$$

$$\frac{\partial H}{\partial p} = f(K, I)e^{-rt},$$

$$\left.\frac{\partial H}{\partial p}\right|_{\substack{\text{optimal}\\ \text{path}}} = f(K^*(t;\boldsymbol{\beta}), I^*(t;\boldsymbol{\beta}))\, e^{-rt} \stackrel{\text{def}}{=} y^*(t;\boldsymbol{\beta})\, e^{-rt},$$

$$\frac{\partial V(\boldsymbol{\beta})}{\partial p} = \int_0^T \left.\frac{\partial H}{\partial p}\right|_{\substack{\text{optimal}\\ \text{path}}} dt = \int_0^T y^*(t;\boldsymbol{\beta})\, e^{-rt}\, dt > 0.$$

Note that the definition $y^*(t;\boldsymbol{\beta}) \stackrel{\text{def}}{=} f(K^*(t;\boldsymbol{\beta}), I^*(t;\boldsymbol{\beta}))$ of the instantaneous supply function was used in the above dynamic envelope derivation. The same recipe may be applied to the parameters (c, g, r, δ), but these are left for a mental exercise because they are of the same ilk as p. Given the above economic interpretation of the adjustment cost model, the optimal value function $V(\cdot)$ represents the maximum present discounted value of profit for the firm. Hence the dynamic envelope result $\partial V(\boldsymbol{\beta})/\partial p > 0$ means that an increase in the output price of the firm will increase its maximum present discounted value of profit, not a surprising result. That is, if the output of the firm is more highly valued in the market, then the maximum present value of profit the firm can earn is correspondingly higher. Moreover, note that the dynamic envelope result $\partial V(\boldsymbol{\beta})/\partial p$ recovers the *cumulative discounted supply function* for the adjustment cost firm. That is, the dynamic envelope result $\partial V(\boldsymbol{\beta})/\partial p$ recovers the amount of the good produced by the firm over its planning horizon rather than at a single date in its planning horizon, appropriately discounted. To put this result in perspective, recall that in the competitive model of the static profit maximizing firm, the partial derivative of the indirect profit function with respect to the output price recovers, via the static envelope theorem, the firm's profit maximizing supply function (this result often goes under the heading of Hotelling's lemma). Finally, we note that the recovery of the cumulative discounted supply function by the dynamic envelope theorem is not a complete surprise. This is because the output price is constant, so that an increase in it represents a uniformly higher price for the entire planning horizon, and not just simply a higher price in a given time period.

The dynamic envelope results for the parameters (K_0, K_T, T) are given by

$$\frac{\partial V(\boldsymbol{\beta})}{\partial K_0} = \lambda(0;\boldsymbol{\beta}) \gtrless 0,$$

$$\frac{\partial V(\boldsymbol{\beta})}{\partial K_T} = -\lambda(T;\boldsymbol{\beta}) \gtrless 0,$$

$$\begin{aligned}\frac{\partial V(\boldsymbol{\beta})}{\partial T} &= H(T, K^*(T;\boldsymbol{\beta}), I^*(T;\boldsymbol{\beta}), \lambda(T;\boldsymbol{\beta}); c, g, p, r, \delta)\\ &= \pi^*(T;\boldsymbol{\beta})\, e^{-rT} + \lambda(T;\boldsymbol{\beta})[I^*(T;\boldsymbol{\beta}) - \delta K^*(T;\boldsymbol{\beta})] \gtrless 0,\end{aligned}$$

where $\pi^*(t;\boldsymbol{\beta}) \stackrel{\text{def}}{=} py^*(t;\boldsymbol{\beta}) - cK^*(t;\boldsymbol{\beta}) - gI^*(t;\boldsymbol{\beta})$ is the optimal instantaneous profit flow of the firm. The dynamic envelope result $\partial V(\boldsymbol{\beta})/\partial K_0 = \lambda(0;\boldsymbol{\beta})$ reinforces our earlier interpretation that $\lambda(0;\boldsymbol{\beta})$ is the shadow value of a unit of the capital stock at the beginning of the planning horizon. In the above adjustment cost model, however, investment *or* disinvestment can take place, so it is not necessarily true that $\lambda(0;\boldsymbol{\beta}) > 0$. To see this formally, first compute the necessary condition

$$H_I(t, K, I, \lambda; c, g, p, r, \delta) = [pf_I(K, I) - g]\,e^{-rt} + \lambda = 0.$$

At $t = 0$ along the optimal path, this equation reduces to $\lambda^*(0;\boldsymbol{\beta}) = g - pf_I(K_0, I^*(0;\boldsymbol{\beta})) \gtrless 0$ because $f_I(K, I) \gtrless 0$ as $-I \gtrless 0$, as remarked above. Thus, if $I^*(0;\boldsymbol{\beta}) \geq 0$, then $f_I(K_0, I^*(0;\boldsymbol{\beta})) \leq 0$, and as a result, we may conclude that $\lambda(0;\boldsymbol{\beta}) > 0$. In this case, therefore, $\lambda(0;\boldsymbol{\beta})$ is the maximum amount the firm would pay for an additional unit of capital at the start of the planning horizon, since $\lambda(0;\boldsymbol{\beta})$ measures the amount by which its maximum present discounted value of profit would increase if it had the additional unit of capital at the beginning of its planning horizon and employed it optimally. If $I^*(0;\boldsymbol{\beta}) < 0$, however, then $f_I(K_0, I^*(0;\boldsymbol{\beta})) > 0$ and the sign of $\lambda(0;\boldsymbol{\beta})$ cannot be determined without knowing the magnitudes of $g > 0$ and $f_I(K_0, I^*(0;\boldsymbol{\beta})) > 0$. Thus, in this instance, it is possible that $\lambda(0;\boldsymbol{\beta}) < 0$. This all makes economic sense, for if the firm prefers to disinvest at $t = 0$, then it deems the initial capital stock to be too large. Hence, an increase in the initial capital stock would lower the firm's present discounted value of profit because it would have to rid itself of more capital, a costly endeavor. Essentially, the reciprocal economic interpretation applies to the dynamic envelope result $\partial V(\boldsymbol{\beta})/\partial K_T = -\lambda(T;\boldsymbol{\beta})$, and so is left for a mental exercise.

The third dynamic envelope result $\partial V(\boldsymbol{\beta})/\partial T = H(T, K^*(T;\boldsymbol{\beta}), I^*(T;\boldsymbol{\beta}), \lambda(T;\boldsymbol{\beta}); c, g, p, r, \delta)$ asserts that the value of the Hamiltonian evaluated at the optimal solution and the terminal date is the marginal value (or marginal cost, if negative) to the firm of extending the planning horizon. In other words, if $\partial V(\boldsymbol{\beta})/\partial T > 0$, then the shadow value of extending the planning horizon is positive and the firm would pay up to the amount $H(T, K^*(T;\boldsymbol{\beta}), I^*(T;\boldsymbol{\beta}), \lambda(T;\boldsymbol{\beta}); c, g, p, r, \delta)$ to have the planning horizon extended, since its present discounted value of profits would increase by the amount $H(T, K^*(T;\boldsymbol{\beta}), I^*(T;\boldsymbol{\beta}), \lambda(T;\boldsymbol{\beta}); c, g, p, r, \delta)$ by such an extension. The Hamiltonian evaluated at the optimal solution and the terminal date therefore has the interpretation of the shadow value of time to the firm.

In proving the dynamic envelope theorem, that is, Theorem 9.1, we assumed that $\mathbf{z}(\cdot)$ and $\mathbf{v}(\cdot)$ were locally $C^{(1)}$ functions of $(t;\boldsymbol{\beta})\,\forall\,(t;\boldsymbol{\beta}) \in [t_0^\circ, t_1^\circ] \times B(\boldsymbol{\beta}^\circ;\delta)$, which in turn implied that the optimal value function $V(\cdot)$ was a locally $C^{(1)}$ function of the parameters $\boldsymbol{\beta} \stackrel{\text{def}}{=} (\boldsymbol{\alpha}, t_0, \mathbf{x}_0, t_1, \mathbf{x}_1)$. Though these assumptions on $\mathbf{z}(\cdot)$ and $\mathbf{v}(\cdot)$ may appear to be innocuous from an economic point of view, they are certainly not from a purely mathematical one. For example, even seemingly "simple" optimal control problems may violate these assumptions and thus result in an optimal value function that is not differentiable everywhere, though it usually is at least locally. Let's turn to an example of just such a case.

Example 9.2: Consider the following optimal control problem:

$$V(x_0) \stackrel{\text{def}}{=} \max_{u(\cdot),x_1} \int_0^1 x(t)u(t)\,dt$$

$$\text{s.t.} \quad \dot{x}(t) = 0,\ x(0) = x_0,\ x(1) = x_1,$$

$$0 \le u(t) \le 1.$$

The Hamiltonian is given by $H(x, u, \lambda) \stackrel{\text{def}}{=} xu$, since $g(t, x, u) \equiv 0$. Because $\dot{x}(t) = 0$ and x_1 is a decision variable, all admissible paths of the state variable are given by $z(t; x_0) = x_0$. Therefore, if $x_0 > 0$, then the maximum of $H(x, u, \lambda) \stackrel{\text{def}}{=} xu$ with respect to u occurs at $v(t; x_0) = 1$, whereas if $x_0 < 0$, then the maximum of $H(x, u, \lambda) \stackrel{\text{def}}{=} xu$ with respect to u occurs at $v(t; x_0) = 0$. Finally, observe that if $x_0 = 0$, then the objective functional is identically zero and any admissible value of the control variable is optimal. Putting these three cases together, we may conclude that

$$V(x_0) = \begin{cases} x_0 & \forall x_0 \ge 0, \\ 0 & \forall x_0 < 0, \end{cases} \quad \text{and} \quad v(t; x_0) = \begin{cases} 1 & \forall x_0 \ge 0, \\ 0 & \forall x_0 < 0. \end{cases}$$

It therefore follows that $\lim_{x_0 \to 0^+} V'(x_0) = 1$ while $\lim_{x_0 \to 0^-} V'(x_0) = 0$. Because these limits are not equal, it follows from the definition of differentiability that $V(\cdot)$ is not differentiable at the point $x_0 = 0$. Thus $V(\cdot)$ is not differentiable for all $x_0 \in \Re$, but it *is* differentiable in any neighborhood of $x_0 \ne 0$ not containing the origin. Similarly, because $\lim_{x_0 \to 0^+} v(t; x_0) = 1$ while $\lim_{x_0 \to 0^-} v(t; x_0) = 0$, $v(\cdot)$ is not continuous with respect to x_0 for all $x_0 \in \Re$, but it *is* continuous with respect to x_0 in any neighborhood of $x_0 \ne 0$ not containing the origin. Note that local differentiability is all that is generally required in many applications of optimal control theory to economics. This is because one can often argue that local differentiability of $v(\cdot)$ or $V(\cdot)$ is all that is required for a qualitative characterization of an economic model, just as it typically is when one studies the comparative statics properties of static economic models.

Let's now return to our optimal control problem (OC). Recall that by part (iii) of Theorem 9.1, the dynamic envelope theorem, the effect of an increase in the jth initial value of the state variable on the optimal value function is given by

$$V_{x_{0j}}(\boldsymbol{\beta}) \equiv \lambda_j(t_0; \boldsymbol{\beta}), \quad j = 1, 2, \ldots, N.$$

From this envelope result, we can legitimately interpret $\lambda_j(t_0; \boldsymbol{\beta})$ as the shadow value of the jth state variable in an optimal program at time t_0, the initial time. By part (iii) of Theorem 9.1, we also know that such an interpretation is valid at the terminal time t_1. Given this valid economic interpretation of $\lambda_j(t_0; \boldsymbol{\beta})$ and $\lambda_j(t_1; \boldsymbol{\beta})$, we would like to extend it so that $\lambda_j(t; \boldsymbol{\beta})$ can be *legitimately* interpreted as the shadow value of the jth state variable in an optimal program at any time $t \in (t_0, t_1)$

for problem (OC). It is important that you understand that Theorem 9.1, parts (i) and (iii), do not permit that interpretation of $\lambda_j(t;\boldsymbol{\beta})$ for all $t \in (t_0, t_1)$, for problem (OC).

In view of this intention, let $s \in (t_0, t_1)$ be a fixed but arbitrary initial or starting date of the following *truncation* of the original optimal control problem (OC):

$$V(\boldsymbol{\gamma}) \stackrel{\text{def}}{=} \max_{\mathbf{u}(\cdot)} \int_s^{t_1} f(t, \mathbf{x}(t), \mathbf{u}(t); \boldsymbol{\alpha})\, dt$$

$$\text{s.t.} \quad \dot{\mathbf{x}}(t) = \mathbf{g}(t, \mathbf{x}(t), \mathbf{u}(t); \boldsymbol{\alpha}),\ \mathbf{x}(s) = \mathbf{x}_s,\ \mathbf{x}(t_1) = \mathbf{x}_1, \tag{OC$'$}$$

where $\boldsymbol{\gamma} \stackrel{\text{def}}{=} (\boldsymbol{\alpha}, s, \mathbf{x}_s, t_1, \mathbf{x}_1)$ is the time-independent parameter vector of problem (OC$'$). Problem (OC$'$) is a family of optimal control problems embedded within the control problem (OC), parameterized by the starting date $s \in (t_0, t_1)$ and initial value of the state vector $\mathbf{x}_s$. Assume that an optimal pair exists to problem (OC$'$) and denote it by $(\mathbf{z}(t;\boldsymbol{\gamma}), \mathbf{v}(t;\boldsymbol{\gamma}))$, and let $\boldsymbol{\lambda}(t;\boldsymbol{\gamma})$ be the corresponding time path of the costate vector. Notice that the optimal value functions in problems (OC) and (OC$'$), as well as the solution functions and corresponding costate vector function, are denoted with the same symbols. That this is the case follows immediately from the observation that the integrand and transition functions are identical in problems (OC) and (OC$'$) as is the terminal value of the state vector, whereas all that differ are the initial date and initial value of the state vector. That is, problems (OC) and (OC$'$) are structurally identical. What this means is that the values of the optimal solution functions and corresponding costate vector function may differ, but not their functional forms. This will be seen in Example 9.3 below. With this in mind, we are now in a position to prove the following fundamental theorem.

Theorem 9.2 (The Principle of Optimality): *Let* $(\mathbf{z}(t;\boldsymbol{\beta}), \mathbf{v}(t;\boldsymbol{\beta}))$ *be the optimal pair for problem* (OC) *with corresponding costate vector time path* $\boldsymbol{\lambda}(t;\boldsymbol{\beta})$*, and let* $(\mathbf{z}(t;\boldsymbol{\gamma}), \mathbf{v}(t;\boldsymbol{\gamma}))$ *be the optimal pair for problem* (OC$'$) *with corresponding costate vector time path* $\boldsymbol{\lambda}(t;\boldsymbol{\gamma})$*. Suppose that* $s \in (t_0, t_1)$ *is a fixed but arbitrary starting date for problem* (OC$'$)*. If* $\mathbf{x}_s = \mathbf{z}(s;\boldsymbol{\beta})$*, then the optimal pair for problem* (OC$'$) *is* $(\mathbf{z}(t;\boldsymbol{\beta}), \mathbf{v}(t;\boldsymbol{\beta}))$ *with corresponding costate vector time path* $\boldsymbol{\lambda}(t;\boldsymbol{\beta})$ *for all* $t \in [s, t_1]$*, namely, the same optimal pair and corresponding costate vector for problem* (OC) *for the interval* $[s, t_1]$*. That is, if* $\mathbf{x}_s = \mathbf{z}(s;\boldsymbol{\beta})$*, then for all* $t \in [s, t_1]$*, we have the identities*

$$\mathbf{z}(t;\boldsymbol{\beta}) \equiv \mathbf{z}(t;\boldsymbol{\alpha}, s, \mathbf{z}(s;\boldsymbol{\beta}), t_1, \mathbf{x}_1),$$

$$\mathbf{v}(t;\boldsymbol{\beta}) \equiv \mathbf{v}(t;\boldsymbol{\alpha}, s, \mathbf{z}(s;\boldsymbol{\beta}), t_1, \mathbf{x}_1),$$

$$\boldsymbol{\lambda}(t;\boldsymbol{\beta}) \equiv \boldsymbol{\lambda}(t;\boldsymbol{\alpha}, s, \mathbf{z}(s;\boldsymbol{\beta}), t_1, \mathbf{x}_1).$$

Proof: We use a proof by contraposition to establish the first two identities. Suppose that $(\mathbf{z}(t;\boldsymbol{\beta}), \mathbf{v}(t;\boldsymbol{\beta}))$ is *not* the optimal pair for problem (OC′); in other words, the optimal pair $(\mathbf{z}(t;\boldsymbol{\alpha}, s, \mathbf{z}(s;\boldsymbol{\beta}), t_1, \mathbf{x}_1), \mathbf{v}(t;\boldsymbol{\alpha}, s,\mathbf{z}(s;\boldsymbol{\beta}), t_1, \mathbf{x}_1))$ for problem (OC′) is not identically equal to the optimal pair $(\mathbf{z}(t;\boldsymbol{\beta}), \mathbf{v}(t;\boldsymbol{\beta}))$ for problem (OC) for all $t \in [s, t_1]$. This implies that the objective functional of problem (OC) could be improved upon by following the pair $(\mathbf{z}(t;\boldsymbol{\beta}), \mathbf{v}(t;\boldsymbol{\beta}))$ from $t = t_0$ until $t = s$, and then switching to the pair $(\mathbf{z}(t;\boldsymbol{\alpha}, s, \mathbf{z}(s;\boldsymbol{\beta}), t_1, \mathbf{x}_1), \mathbf{v}(t;\boldsymbol{\alpha}, s, \mathbf{z}(s;\boldsymbol{\beta}), t_1, \mathbf{x}_1))$ from $t = s$ until $t = t_1$, rather than following the pair $(\mathbf{z}(t;\boldsymbol{\beta}), \mathbf{v}(t;\boldsymbol{\beta}))$ for all $t \in [t_0, t_1]$. But this contradicts the assumed optimality of the pair $(\mathbf{z}(t;\boldsymbol{\beta}), \mathbf{v}(t;\boldsymbol{\beta}))$ for problem (OC), thereby establishing the first two identities.

To prove the third identity, we proceed as follows. By the two identities just established, the values of the optimal value functions for problems (OC) and (OC′) are identical over the truncated horizon $[s, t_1]$, and thus so too are their derivatives with respect to the initial value of the state vector, assuming that such derivatives exist. By part (iii) of the dynamic envelope theorem and the fact that the initial time s of the problem (OC′) is a fixed but arbitrary element of the interval (t_0, t_1), the third identity then follows. Q.E.D.

The interpretation of Theorem 9.2 is straightforward and important, for what follows hinges on a sound understanding of it. The principle of optimality, as given above, asserts that if you break up an optimal control problem into two parts, a "beginning" interval over which to plan and an "ending" interval over which to plan, the break point being any value of time in the original planning horizon, then the plan that is optimal over the entire planning horizon is also optimal over the truncated ending planning horizon, provided you begin the ending planning interval with the value of the state vector that occurred at the end of the beginning planning interval. More simply, the principle of optimality asserts that any portion of an optimal path is optimal, which is pretty obvious when stated in this simple form. Recall that we proved the principle of optimality in Chapter 4 when we provided a rigorous proof of the Maximum Principle. This would be an excellent time to return to that statement and proof.

Let's now show that the dynamic envelope theorem and principle of optimality, that is, Theorems 9.1 and 9.2, do not permit us to interpret the costate vector in the manner we wish. To begin, apply part (iii) of the dynamic envelope theorem to the truncated control problem (OC′) to obtain the result

$$V_{x_{sj}}(\boldsymbol{\gamma}) \equiv \lambda_j(s;\boldsymbol{\gamma}), \quad j = 1, 2, \ldots, N. \tag{16}$$

This envelope result means that we are justified in interpreting $\lambda_j(s;\boldsymbol{\gamma})$ as the shadow value of the jth state variable at time s, the initial date of the truncated control problem (OC′). However, because the starting date s for the truncated control problem (OC′) is arbitrary, save for the fact that $s \in (t_0, t_1)$, we are therefore permitted on the basis of this observation and Eq. (16) to interpret $\lambda_j(s;\boldsymbol{\gamma})$ as the shadow value of the jth state variable at any starting time $s \in (t_0, t_1)$ of the corresponding truncated control problem. In other words, the interpretation based on the principle of optimality and the dynamic envelope theorem shows that $\lambda_j(s; \boldsymbol{\gamma})$ is the marginal contribution of $x_{sj} = z_j(s; \boldsymbol{\beta})$ to the value $V(\boldsymbol{\gamma})$, which is the maximum value of the objective functional over the truncated horizon $[s, t_1]$, where $s \in (t_0, t_1)$. It is important to realize, however, that these two theorems *do not* establish the claim that $\lambda_j(s; \boldsymbol{\beta})$ is the marginal contribution of $x_{sj} = z_j(s; \boldsymbol{\beta})$ to the value of $V(\boldsymbol{\beta})$, which is the maximum value of the objective functional over the entire horizon $[t_0, t_1]$. The difficulty of establishing this intended interpretation of the costate vector is that we cannot prove that the derivative of $V(\boldsymbol{\beta})$ with respect to $x_{sj} = z_j(s; \boldsymbol{\beta})$ equals $\lambda_j(s; \boldsymbol{\beta})$ because $x_{sj} = z_j(s; \boldsymbol{\beta})$ is not an exogenous parameter, but rather it is indirectly and optimally chosen via the state equation in solving the optimal control problem (OC). Hence, we must alter our approach to establishing the above economic interpretation of the costate vector in such a way as to formalize the notion that at some time $s \in (t_0, t_1)$, a small amount of the jth state variable is suddenly added to the existing value of the jth state variable. In passing, note that the dynamic envelope result in Eq. (16) is exactly how we *defined* the costate variable in our rigorous proof of the Maximum Principle in Chapter 4.

Before moving on to a rigorously justified economic interpretation of the costate vector, let's pause and consider the following simple mathematical example to demonstrate the principle of optimality explicitly in an optimal control setting.

Example 9.3: Consider the simple control problem

$$V(t_0, x_0, t_1, x_1) \stackrel{\text{def}}{=} \min_{u(\cdot)} \int_{t_0}^{t_1} \frac{1}{2}[u(t)]^2 \, dt$$

$$\text{s.t.} \quad \dot{x}(t) = u(t), x(t_0) = x_0, x(t_1) = x_1.$$

The Hamiltonian is given by $H(x, u, \lambda) \stackrel{\text{def}}{=} \frac{1}{2}u^2 + \lambda u$. Because $H(\cdot)$ is convex in (x, u), Theorem 4.3 asserts that the following equations are both necessary and sufficient to determine the global minimum to the optimal control problem:

$$H_u(x, u, \lambda) = u + \lambda = 0,$$

$$\dot{x} = H_\lambda(x, u, \lambda) = u, x(t_0) = x_0, x(t_1) = x_1,$$

$$\dot{\lambda} = -H_x(x, u, \lambda) = 0.$$

Because $\dot{\lambda} = 0$, the costate variable is a constant, say, $\lambda(t) = c_1$. The necessary condition $H_u = 0$ gives $u(t) = -\lambda(t)$, and when combined with the prior observation, it implies that $u(t) = -c_1$. The state equation therefore becomes $\dot{x} = -c_1$, which, when integrated, yields the general solution $x(t) = c_2 - c_1 t$, where c_2 is another constant of integration. Using the boundary conditions in the general solution of the state equation gives the ensuing system of linear equations to be solved for the constants of integration:

$$x(t_0) = c_2 - c_1 t_0 = x_0,$$
$$x(t_1) = c_2 - c_1 t_1 = x_1.$$

Applying Cramer's rule to this system of linear equations yields

$$c_1 = \frac{x_0 - x_1}{t_1 - t_0},$$
$$c_1 = \frac{t_1 x_0 - t_0 x_1}{t_1 - t_0},$$

as the constants of integration. Plugging the values of the constants of integration into the general solutions for the state, control, and costate variables yields the specific solution to the control problem, namely,

$$\begin{aligned} z(t; t_0, x_0, t_1, x_1) &= \left[\frac{t_1 x_0 - t_0 x_1}{t_1 - t_0}\right] - \left[\frac{x_0 - x_1}{t_1 - t_0}\right] t, \\ v(t; t_0, x_0, t_1, x_1) &= \frac{x_1 - x_0}{t_1 - t_0}, \\ \lambda(t; t_0, x_0, t_1, x_1) &= \frac{x_0 - x_1}{t_1 - t_0}. \end{aligned} \tag{17}$$

This is the unique solution of the control problem because it is the only solution of the necessary and sufficient conditions.

Now consider the structurally identical but truncated control problem

$$V(s, x_s, t_1, x_1) \stackrel{\text{def}}{=} \min_{u(\cdot)} \int_s^{t_1} \frac{1}{2}[u(t)]^2 \, dt$$
$$\text{s.t.} \quad \dot{x}(t) = u(t), x(s) = x_s, x(t_1) = x_1,$$

where $s \in (t_0, t_1)$ and x_s is an admissible value of the state variable. Because the truncated optimal control problem is identical in every way to the original optimal control problem, except for the fact that the truncated problem begins at time $t = s$ in state $x(s) = x_s$, the solution *functions* (but not necessarily their values) are identical too, a point we made earlier, as you may recall. The solution of the truncated control problem is therefore found by replacing t_0 with s and x_0 with x_s to get

$$\begin{aligned} z(t; s, x_s, t_1, x_1) &= \left[\frac{t_1 x_s - s x_1}{t_1 - s}\right] - \left[\frac{x_s - x_1}{t_1 - s}\right] t, \\ v(t; s, x_s, t_1, x_1) &= \frac{x_1 - x_s}{t_1 - s}, \\ \lambda(t; s, x_s, t_1, x_1) &= \frac{x_s - x_1}{t_1 - s}. \end{aligned} \tag{18}$$

As above, this is the unique solution of the truncated control problem because it is the only solution of the necessary and sufficient conditions.

The principle of optimality asserts that the solution triplet in Eq. (17) is identically equal to the solution triplet in Eq. (18) for all $t \in [s, t_1]$ when, of course, the latter triplet is evaluated at $x_s = z(s; t_0, x_0, t_1, x_1)$. Let's verify that this is true for the optimal path of the state variable:

$$
\begin{aligned}
& z(t; s, x_s, t_1, x_1)|_{x_s = z(s;t_0,x_0,t_1,x_1)} \\
&= \left[\frac{t_1\left[\frac{t_1x_0 - t_0x_1}{t_1-t_0}\right] - t_1\left[\frac{x_0-x_1}{t_1-t_0}\right]s - sx_1}{t_1 - s}\right] - \left[\frac{\left[\frac{t_1x_0-t_0x_1}{t_1-t_0}\right] - \left[\frac{x_0-x_1}{t_1-t_0}\right]s - x_1}{t_1 - s}\right]t \\
&= \left[\frac{t_1[t_1x_0 - t_0x_1] - st_1x_0 + st_0x_1}{[t_1 - s][t_1 - t_0]}\right] - \left[\frac{t_1x_0 - s[x_0 - x_1] - t_1x_1}{[t_1 - s][t_1 - t_0]}\right]t \\
&= \left[\frac{[t_1 - s][t_1x_0 - t_0x_1]}{[t_1 - s][t_1 - t_0]}\right] - \left[\frac{[t_1 - s][x_0 - x_1]}{[t_1 - s][t_1 - t_0]}\right]t \\
&= \left[\frac{t_1x_0 - t_0x_1}{t_1 - t_0}\right] - \left[\frac{x_0 - x_1}{t_1 - t_0}\right]t = z(t; t_0, x_0, t_1, x_1).
\end{aligned}
$$

The proof that the optimal control and costate paths satisfy the principle of optimality is left for a mental exercise.

Let's now turn to the problem of formally establishing the claim that $\lambda_j(s; \boldsymbol{\beta})$ is the marginal contribution of $x_{sj} = z_j(s; \boldsymbol{\beta})$ to the value of $V(\boldsymbol{\beta})$, which is the maximum value of the objective functional over the entire horizon $[t_0, t_1]$. That is, we wish to rigorously prove that the *j*th costate variable at any time *t* in the planning horizon of the original optimal control problem (OC) is the shadow value of the *j*th state variable at time *t*. To this end, redefine the state equation as

$$\dot{\mathbf{x}}(t) = \mathbf{g}(t, \mathbf{x}(t), \mathbf{u}(t); \boldsymbol{\alpha}) + \mathbf{h}(a), \tag{19}$$

where $\mathbf{h}(a) \in \Re^N$ is a vector of zeros save for the *j*th component, the latter of which is defined by

$$h^j(a) \stackrel{\text{def}}{=} \begin{cases} 0 & t \in [t_0, s), \\ a\varepsilon^{-1} & t \in [s, s + \varepsilon), \\ 0 & t \in [s + \varepsilon, t_1). \end{cases} \tag{20}$$

The number ε is an arbitrarily small and positive number that we will eventually allow to shrink to zero in the limit, whereas $a \in \Re$ is a parameter. The injection to the *j*th state variable takes place during the "short" interval $[s, s + \varepsilon)$, where the smaller is ε, the more abrupt the injection. When $\varepsilon \to 0^+$, this mimics the addition of a units to the jth state variable at time $t = s$, since

$$\lim_{\varepsilon\to 0^+}\int_s^{s+\varepsilon} h^j(a)\,dt = \lim_{\varepsilon\to 0^+}\int_s^{s+\varepsilon} a\varepsilon^{-1}\,dt = \lim_{\varepsilon\to 0^+} a\varepsilon^{-1}[s+\varepsilon-s] = \lim_{\varepsilon\to 0^+} a\varepsilon^{-1}\varepsilon = a.$$

Alternatively, we can see that when $\varepsilon \to 0^+$, this mimics the addition of a units to the jth state variable at time $t = s$ by the following sequence of mathematical operations. First, note that the jth state equation can be written as

$$\int_s^{s+\varepsilon} \dot{x}_j(t)\,dt = \int_s^{s+\varepsilon} [g^j(t,\mathbf{x}(t),\mathbf{u}(t);\boldsymbol{\alpha}) + a\varepsilon^{-1}]\,dt = \int_s^{s+\varepsilon} g^j(t,\mathbf{x}(t),\mathbf{u}(t);\boldsymbol{\alpha})\,dt + a \tag{21}$$

upon using the previous integration result. Because $dx_j = \dot{x}_j(t)dt$, it then follows that

$$\int_s^{s+\varepsilon} \dot{x}_j(t)\,dt = \int_{x_j(s)}^{x_j(s+\varepsilon)} dx_j = x_j(s+\varepsilon) - x_j(s).$$

Thus, Eq. (21) reduces to

$$x_j(s+\varepsilon) = x_j(s) + \int_s^{s+\varepsilon} g^j(t,\mathbf{x}(t),\mathbf{u}(t);\boldsymbol{\alpha})\,dt + a.$$

Now let $\varepsilon \to 0^+$ in the last equation to get

$$\begin{aligned}\lim_{\varepsilon\to 0^+} x_j(s+\varepsilon) &= \lim_{\varepsilon\to 0^+}\left[x_j(s) + \int_s^{s+\varepsilon} g^j(t,\mathbf{x}(t),\mathbf{u}(t);\boldsymbol{\alpha})\,dt + a\right] \\ &= \lim_{\varepsilon\to 0^+} x_j(s) + \lim_{\varepsilon\to 0^+}\int_s^{s+\varepsilon} g^j(t,\mathbf{x}(t),\mathbf{u}(t);\boldsymbol{\alpha})\,dt + \lim_{\varepsilon\to 0^+} a \\ &= x_j(s) + 0 + a \neq x_j(s),\end{aligned}$$

since the limit of a sum is the sum of the limits, provided each of the individual limits exists, which they clearly do here. The last equation asserts that the value of the jth state variable at the instant of time "just after" $t = s$ differs from the value of the jth state variable at time $t = s$ by the amount a. Therefore, a represents the injection of a units to the jth state variable at time $t = s$. Figure 9.2 gives the geometry of this construction.

The Hamiltonian for the optimal control problem formed with the state equation given by Eq. (19), which we define as the *perturbed* control problem, is defined as

$$\hat{H}(t,\mathbf{x},\mathbf{u},\boldsymbol{\mu};\boldsymbol{\alpha},a) \overset{\text{def}}{=} f(t,\mathbf{x},\mathbf{u};\boldsymbol{\alpha}) + \boldsymbol{\mu}'[\mathbf{g}(t,\mathbf{x},\mathbf{u};\boldsymbol{\alpha}) + \mathbf{h}(a)].$$

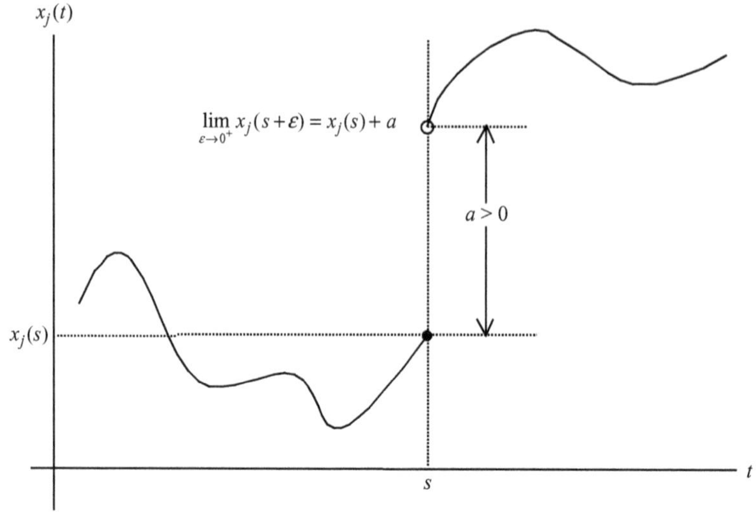

Figure 9.2

The optimal pair for the perturbed control problem, which is assumed to exist, is denoted by $(\hat{\mathbf{x}}(t;\boldsymbol{\beta},a), \hat{\mathbf{u}}(t;\boldsymbol{\beta},a))$, with corresponding costate vector $\boldsymbol{\mu}(t;\boldsymbol{\beta},a)$. Also define the optimal value function for the perturbed control problem constructively as

$$\hat{V}(\boldsymbol{\beta},a) \equiv \int_{t_0}^{t_1} f(t,\hat{\mathbf{x}}(t;\boldsymbol{\beta},a),\hat{\mathbf{u}}(t;\boldsymbol{\beta},a);\boldsymbol{\alpha})\,dt.$$

Note that when $a = 0$, $(\hat{\mathbf{x}}(t;\boldsymbol{\beta},0), \hat{\mathbf{u}}(t;\boldsymbol{\beta},0), \boldsymbol{\mu}(t;\boldsymbol{\beta},0)) \equiv (\mathbf{z}(t;\boldsymbol{\beta}), \mathbf{v}(t;\boldsymbol{\beta}), \boldsymbol{\lambda}(t;\boldsymbol{\beta}))$, that is, the perturbed control problem's solution is identically equal to the original control problem's solution. This, in turn, implies that the optimal value functions of the perturbed and original optimal control problems are also identically equal in value when $a = 0$, that is, $\hat{V}(\boldsymbol{\beta},0) \equiv V(\boldsymbol{\beta})$.

Our goal is to compute the derivative of $\hat{V}(\cdot)$ with respect to a evaluated at $a = 0$, that is, to compute $\hat{V}_a(\boldsymbol{\beta},a)\big|_{a=0}$. For sufficiently small ε, this will indicate the correct marginal value of the jth state variable at any time $s \in (t_0, t_1)$ along the *original* optimal path. We ultimately will show that $\hat{V}_a(\boldsymbol{\beta},a)\big|_{a=0} = \lambda_j(s;\boldsymbol{\beta})$ for any $s \in (t_0, t_1)$. This result will therefore permit us to rigorously interpret $\lambda_j(s;\boldsymbol{\beta})$ as the shadow value of the jth state variable at any time $s \in (t_0, t_1)$ along the optimal path of the *original* optimal control problem (OC), which is how we'd like to interpret it.

To derive $\hat{V}_a(\boldsymbol{\beta},a)$, apply part (i) of the dynamic envelope theorem to $\hat{V}(\cdot)$ to get

$$\hat{V}_a(\boldsymbol{\beta},a) = \int_{t_0}^{t_1} \frac{\partial \hat{H}}{\partial a}\bigg|_{\substack{\text{optimal}\\ \text{path}}} dt = \int_{t_0}^{t_1} \hat{\mu}_j(t;\boldsymbol{\beta},a)\frac{d}{da}h^j(a)\,dt = \int_{s}^{s+\varepsilon} \hat{\mu}_j(t;\boldsymbol{\beta},a)\varepsilon^{-1}\,dt, \tag{22}$$

because $\frac{d}{da}h^j(a) = 0\,\forall\, t \notin [s, s+\varepsilon)$ and $\frac{d}{da}h^j(a) = \varepsilon^{-1}\,\forall\, t \in [s, s+\varepsilon)$ from Eq. (20). Now evaluate Eq. (22) at $a = 0$ and recall that $\boldsymbol{\lambda}(t; \boldsymbol{\beta}) \equiv \boldsymbol{\mu}(t; \boldsymbol{\beta}, 0)$ to get

$$\hat{V}_a(\boldsymbol{\beta}, a)\Big|_{a=0} = \int_s^{s+\varepsilon} \lambda_j(t; \boldsymbol{\beta})\varepsilon^{-1}\, dt. \tag{23}$$

As previously demonstrated, we can approximate an instantaneous injection to the jth state variable at time s by letting ε get arbitrarily small in Eq. (23). More formally,

$$\lim_{\varepsilon \to 0^+} \hat{V}_a(\boldsymbol{\beta}, a)\Big|_{a=0} = \lim_{\varepsilon \to 0^+} \int_s^{s+\varepsilon} \lambda_j(t; \boldsymbol{\beta})\varepsilon^{-1}\, dt. \tag{24}$$

Define $\Lambda_j(t) \overset{\text{def}}{=} \int_{t_0}^{t} \lambda_j(\tau; \boldsymbol{\beta})\, d\tau$, so that by Leibniz's rule, $\dot{\Lambda}_j(t) = \lambda_j(t; \boldsymbol{\beta})$. Using this definition, Eq. (24) becomes

$$\begin{aligned}\lim_{\varepsilon \to 0^+} \hat{V}_a(\boldsymbol{\beta}, a)\Big|_{a=0} &= \lim_{\varepsilon \to 0^+} \int_s^{s+\varepsilon} \dot{\Lambda}_j(t)\varepsilon^{-1}\, dt \\ &= \lim_{\varepsilon \to 0^+} \frac{\Lambda_j(s+\varepsilon) - \Lambda_j(s)}{\varepsilon} = \dot{\Lambda}_j(s) = \lambda_j(s; \boldsymbol{\beta}) \end{aligned} \tag{25}$$

by the definition of the right-hand derivative. Seeing as $\hat{V}(\boldsymbol{\beta}, 0) \equiv V(\boldsymbol{\beta})$ is the optimal value function over the entire horizon, we have therefore shown that the rate of change of the optimal value function with respect to an injection in the jth state variable at any time $s \in (t_0, t_1)$ is the value of the jth costate variable at time s for the *original* optimal control problem (OC). Our proof is now complete.

To see the significance of Eq. (25), apply part (iii) of the dynamic envelope theorem to the truncated optimal control problem (OC′) and evaluate the result at $\mathbf{x}_s = \mathbf{z}(s; \boldsymbol{\beta})$ to get

$$\begin{aligned} V_{x_{sj}}(\boldsymbol{\alpha}, s, \mathbf{z}(s; \boldsymbol{\beta}), t_1, \mathbf{x}_1) &= \lambda_j(s; \boldsymbol{\alpha}, s, \mathbf{z}(s; \boldsymbol{\beta}), t_1, \mathbf{x}_1) \\ &\equiv \lambda_j(s; \boldsymbol{\beta}), \quad j = 1, 2, \ldots, N, \end{aligned} \tag{26}$$

where we have used the identity $\boldsymbol{\lambda}(t; \boldsymbol{\beta}) \equiv \boldsymbol{\lambda}(t; \boldsymbol{\alpha}, s, \mathbf{z}(s; \boldsymbol{\beta}), t_1, \mathbf{x}_1)$ from the principle of optimality (Theorem 9.2). The dynamic envelope results in Eqs. (25) and (26) are the same, but that in Eq. (25) applies to the original control problem (OC) and thus the entire planning horizon $[t_0, t_1]$, whereas that in Eq. (26) applies to the truncated control problem (OC′) and thus the truncated planning horizon $[s, t_1]$. This therefore means that the marginal gain from an increase in the jth stock at any time $s \in (t_0, t_1)$ is the same over the truncated planning horizon $[s, t_1]$ as it is over the entire planning horizon $[t_0, t_1]$.

So far, we have established the dynamic envelope theorem for a class of optimal control problems with many state and control variables, but without any constraints.

For the sake of completeness, we now present and discuss the dynamic envelope theorem for the general class of constrained control problems studied in Chapter 6, namely,

$$V(\boldsymbol{\beta}) \stackrel{\text{def}}{=} \max_{\mathbf{u}(\cdot)} \int_{t_0}^{t_1} f(t, \mathbf{x}(t), \mathbf{u}(t); \boldsymbol{\alpha})\, dt$$

$$\begin{aligned} \text{s.t.} \quad \dot{\mathbf{x}}(t) &= \mathbf{g}(t, \mathbf{x}(t), \mathbf{u}(t); \boldsymbol{\alpha}),\ \mathbf{x}(t_0) = \mathbf{x}_0,\ \mathbf{x}(t_1) = \mathbf{x}_1, \\ h^k(t, \mathbf{x}(t), \mathbf{u}(t); \boldsymbol{\alpha}) &\geq 0, \quad k = 1, 2, \ldots, K', \\ h^k(t, \mathbf{x}(t), \mathbf{u}(t); \boldsymbol{\alpha}) &= 0, \quad k = K'+1, K'+2, \ldots, K, \end{aligned} \tag{27}$$

where $\mathbf{x}(t) \stackrel{\text{def}}{=} (x_1(t), x_2(t), \ldots, x_N(t)) \in \Re^N$ is the state vector; $\mathbf{u}(t) \stackrel{\text{def}}{=} (u_1(t), u_2(t), \ldots, u_M(t)) \in \Re^M$ is the control vector; $\boldsymbol{\alpha} \stackrel{\text{def}}{=} (\alpha_1, \alpha_2, \ldots, \alpha_A) \in \Re^A$ is a vector of time-independent parameters that affect the state equation, integrand, and constraint functions; $\mathbf{g}(\cdot) \stackrel{\text{def}}{=} (g^1(\cdot), g^2(\cdot), \ldots, g^N(\cdot))$ is the transition function; $\dot{\mathbf{x}}(\cdot) \stackrel{\text{def}}{=} (\dot{x}_1(\cdot), \dot{x}_2(\cdot), \ldots, \dot{x}_N(\cdot))$, $\mathbf{h}(\cdot) \stackrel{\text{def}}{=} (h^1(\cdot), h^2(\cdot), \ldots, h^K(\cdot))$ is the vector of constraint functions; and $\boldsymbol{\beta} \stackrel{\text{def}}{=} (\boldsymbol{\alpha}, t_0, \mathbf{x}_0, t_1, \mathbf{x}_1) \in \Re^{2+2N+A}$ is the vector of parameters of the problem.

With the introduction of the constraints, we must now impose a few more assumptions on problem (27), in addition to assumptions (A.1) and (A.2) noted earlier. First of all, we assume that the rank constraint qualification of Chapter 6 holds for problem (27). Second, we impose the following assumption on the constraint functions:

(A.3) $\mathbf{h}(\cdot) \in C^{(1)}$ with respect to the $1 + N + M$ variables $(t, \mathbf{x}, \mathbf{u})$ and the A parameters $\boldsymbol{\alpha}$.

For the general class of control problems defined in Eq. (27), the dynamic envelope theorem takes on the following form.

Theorem 9.3 (Dynamic Envelope Theorem, Constraints): *Let* $(\mathbf{z}(t; \boldsymbol{\beta}), \mathbf{v}(t; \boldsymbol{\beta}))$ *be the optimal pair for problem (27),* $\boldsymbol{\lambda}(t; \boldsymbol{\beta})$ *be the corresponding time path of the costate vector, and* $\boldsymbol{\mu}(t; \boldsymbol{\beta})$ *be the corresponding time path of the Lagrange multiplier vector. Define the Hamiltonian as*

$$H(t, \mathbf{x}, \mathbf{u}, \boldsymbol{\lambda}; \boldsymbol{\alpha}) \stackrel{\text{def}}{=} f(t, \mathbf{x}, \mathbf{u}; \boldsymbol{\alpha}) + \sum_{\ell=1}^{N} \lambda_\ell g^\ell(t, \mathbf{x}, \mathbf{u}; \boldsymbol{\alpha}),$$

and the Lagrangian as

$$L(t, \mathbf{x}, \mathbf{u}, \boldsymbol{\lambda}, \boldsymbol{\mu}; \boldsymbol{\alpha}) \stackrel{\text{def}}{=} f(t, \mathbf{x}, \mathbf{u}; \boldsymbol{\alpha}) + \sum_{\ell=1}^{N} \lambda_\ell g^\ell(t, \mathbf{x}, \mathbf{u}; \boldsymbol{\alpha}) + \sum_{k=1}^{K} \mu_k h^k(t, \mathbf{x}, \mathbf{u}; \boldsymbol{\alpha}).$$

If $\mathbf{z}(\cdot) \in C^{(1)}$, $\mathbf{v}(\cdot) \in C^{(1)}$, *and* $\mu_k(\cdot) \in C^{(1)}$, $k = K'+1, K'+2, \ldots, K$, *in* $(t;\boldsymbol{\beta})\ \forall\ (t;\boldsymbol{\beta}) \in [t_0^\circ, t_1^\circ]B(\boldsymbol{\beta}^\circ;\delta)$, *then* $V(\cdot) \in C^{(1)}\ \forall\ \boldsymbol{\beta} \in B(\boldsymbol{\beta}^\circ;\delta)$, *and furthermore*, $\forall\ \boldsymbol{\beta} \in B(\boldsymbol{\beta}^\circ;\delta)$:

$$V_{\alpha_i}(\boldsymbol{\beta}) \stackrel{\text{def}}{=} \frac{\partial V(\boldsymbol{\beta})}{\partial \alpha_i}$$

$$\equiv \int_{t_0}^{t_1} L_{\alpha_i}(t, \mathbf{z}(t;\boldsymbol{\beta}), \mathbf{v}(t;\boldsymbol{\beta}), \boldsymbol{\lambda}(t;\boldsymbol{\beta}), \boldsymbol{\mu}(t;\boldsymbol{\beta}); \boldsymbol{\alpha})\, dt, \quad i = 1, 2, \ldots, A, \text{(i)}$$

$$V_{t_0}(\boldsymbol{\beta}) \equiv -H(t_0, \mathbf{x}_0, \mathbf{v}(t_0;\boldsymbol{\beta}), \boldsymbol{\lambda}(t_0;\boldsymbol{\beta}); \boldsymbol{\alpha}), \quad \text{(ii)}$$

$$V_{x_{0j}}(\boldsymbol{\beta}) \equiv \lambda_j(t_0;\boldsymbol{\beta}), \quad j = 1, 2, \ldots, N, \quad \text{(iii)}$$

$$V_{t_1}(\boldsymbol{\beta}) \equiv H(t_1, \mathbf{x}_1, \mathbf{v}(t_1;\boldsymbol{\beta}), \boldsymbol{\lambda}(t_1;\boldsymbol{\beta}); \boldsymbol{\alpha}), \quad \text{(iv)}$$

$$V_{x_{1j}}(\boldsymbol{\beta}) \equiv -\lambda_j(t_1;\boldsymbol{\beta}), \quad j = 1, 2, \ldots, N. \quad \text{(v)}$$

The proof of this theorem is rather technical for the following reasons. Recall from Chapter 6 that the presence of inequality constraints means that we can expect there to be intervals in the planning horizon when some of them are binding and some are not. As a result, there exists the possibility that the set of binding inequality constraints changes over the course of the planning horizon. That is, there exist times, referred to as *switching times*, when the set of binding inequality constraints change. We also know from Chapter 6 that at such switching times, the optimal control may not be differentiable with respect to a parameter. For these reasons, the proof of Theorem 9.3 is a bit technical and involved. We do, however, present a mental exercise in which you are asked to demonstrate some of the above assertions. A mental exercise also asks you to provide a proof of Theorem 9.3 when there are only equality constraints present, as the above features that cause the technical difficulties are not present in this instance.

In comparing Theorem 9.3 with Theorem 9.1, notice that there is actually very little difference in their conclusions. In particular, conclusions (ii) through (v) of both theorems are identical, except for the important fact that the solutions of the two different control problems are not, in general, equal. This is not surprising, for results (ii) through (v) are just the shadow values of time and the stocks and, as such, should not have fundamentally different expressions for them. It is important to recognize, though, that their values generally differ in the two types of control problems. The real difference between Theorem 9.3 and Theorem 9.1, therefore, pertains to result (i). This is not surprising either, for Theorem 9.3 deals with a constrained control problem whereas Theorem 9.1 does not, and the parameter under consideration is a general one. Hence, by analogy with the static envelope theorem, one would not expect the resulting dynamic envelope expressions to be identical, because they are not in the analogous static circumstance.

Before closing out this chapter, let's examine an intertemporal consumption problem in order to see the dynamic envelope theorem in action once again, and to help improve our understanding of it and its relation to the archetype static envelope theorem.

Example 9.4: Consider an individual who expects to live $T > 0$ years and who is contemplating a lifetime utility maximizing consumption plan. Preferences over the rates of consumption of the M goods $\mathbf{c}(t) \in \Re^M_+$ are given by the $C^{(2)}$ instantaneous utility function $U(\cdot)$, where $U_{c_m}(\mathbf{c}(t)) > 0$ and $U_{c_m c_m}(\mathbf{c}(t)) < 0$ for $m = 1, 2, \ldots, M$. The time-invariant price vector of the goods is given by $\mathbf{p} \in \Re^M_{++}$, whereas the individual's present value of lifetime wealth is $w_0 > 0$. Assuming the person has an intertemporal rate of discount given by $\rho > 0$, the isoperimetric problem faced by the individual is given by

$$V(\boldsymbol{\beta}) \stackrel{\text{def}}{=} \max_{\mathbf{c}(\cdot)} \int_0^T U(\mathbf{c}(t))\, e^{-\rho t}\, dt$$

$$\text{s.t.} \quad \int_0^T \mathbf{p}'\mathbf{c}(t)\, e^{-rt}\, dt = w_0,$$

where $r > 0$ is the discount rate on expenditures, say, the rate of interest earned on a money market account, and $\boldsymbol{\beta} \stackrel{\text{def}}{=} (\mathbf{p}, r, \rho, w_0, T)$. The intertemporal budget constraint states that the present discounted value of expenditures on the goods is equal to the individual's present discounted value of wealth, the intertemporal equivalent of the budget constraint from static consumer theory when the capital markets are perfect. The dynamic analogue of the indirect utility function from static consumer theory is the optimal value function $V(\cdot)$. It may be interpreted as the individual's discounted lifetime indirect utility function in the present setting.

As stated, the above intertemporal utility maximization problem is not in standard form. In order to transform it into standard form, define a state variable as follows:

$$E(t) \stackrel{\text{def}}{=} \int_0^t \mathbf{p}'\mathbf{c}(s)\, e^{-rs}\, ds.$$

This new state variable has the interpretation of the present discounted value of expenditures up to time t, or the present value of cumulative expenditures at time t. By Leibniz's rule, we have that $\dot{E}(t) = \mathbf{p}'\mathbf{c}(t)e^{-rt}$, with boundary conditions $E(0) = 0$ and $E(T) = w_0$. We may therefore restate the above isoperimetric problem in the ensuing equivalent standard form:

$$V(\boldsymbol{\beta}) \stackrel{\text{def}}{=} \max_{\mathbf{c}(\cdot)} \int_0^T U(\mathbf{c}(t))\, e^{-\rho t}\, dt$$

$$\text{s.t.} \quad \dot{E}(t) = \mathbf{p}'\mathbf{c}(t)e^{-rt},\ E(0) = 0,\ E(T) = w_0.$$

This is the form of the problem we shall work on with the dynamic envelope theorem. We assume that the consumption rate of each of the M goods is positive in every period of the individual's lifetime.

To begin the analysis, let's first establish that the costate variable is a negative constant in an optimal consumption plan (assuming that one actually exists). To see this, first define the Hamiltonian as $H(t, E, \mathbf{c}, \lambda; \mathbf{p}, r, \rho) \stackrel{\text{def}}{=} U(\mathbf{c})e^{-\rho t} + \lambda e^{-rt}\sum_{m=1}^{M} p_m c_m$, and note that the state variable E does not appear explicitly in it. As a result of this observation, the costate equation becomes $\dot{\lambda} = -H_E(t, E, \mathbf{c}, \lambda; \mathbf{p}, r, \rho) = 0$, thereby implying that λ is a constant and thus only a function of the parameter vector $\boldsymbol{\beta} \stackrel{\text{def}}{=} (\mathbf{p}, r, \rho, w_0, T)$ and not t, say, $\lambda(\boldsymbol{\beta})$. Moreover, the necessary condition $H_{c_j}(t, E, \mathbf{c}, \lambda; \mathbf{p}, r, \rho) = 0$ implies that $U_{c_j}(\mathbf{c})e^{-\rho t} = -\lambda p_j e^{-rt}$, $j = 1, 2, \ldots, M$. Because $U_{c_j}(\mathbf{c}) > 0$ and $p_j > 0$, $j = 1, 2, \ldots, M$, and $e^{-\rho t} > 0$ and $e^{-rt} > 0$, this necessary condition implies that $\lambda(\boldsymbol{\beta}) < 0$, as was to be established. This makes economic sense too, for the state variable $E(t)$ is the present value of cumulative expenditures at time t and thus is a "bad," in that the higher is $E(t)$ at any t, the lower is the remaining wealth of the individual for spending on future consumption. With this result established, we now turn to the implications of the dynamic envelope theorem for the intertemporal consumption problem. Let us denote the optimal pair by $(E^*(t; \boldsymbol{\beta}), \mathbf{c}^*(t; \boldsymbol{\beta}))$ in what follows.

By Theorem 9.1, we have the following dynamic envelope results:

$$\frac{\partial V}{\partial p_j}(\boldsymbol{\beta}) = \int_0^T \frac{\partial H}{\partial p_j}(t, E, \mathbf{c}, \lambda; \mathbf{p}, r, \rho)\bigg|_{\substack{\text{optimal}\\ \text{path}}} dt$$

$$= \lambda(\boldsymbol{\beta}) \int_0^T c_j^*(t; \boldsymbol{\beta})e^{-rt}\, dt < 0, \quad j = 1, 2, \ldots, M, \tag{28}$$

$$\frac{\partial V}{\partial r}(\boldsymbol{\beta}) = -\lambda(\boldsymbol{\beta}) \int_0^T t\mathbf{p}'\mathbf{c}^*(t; \boldsymbol{\beta})e^{-rt}\, dt > 0, \tag{29}$$

$$\frac{\partial V}{\partial \rho}(\boldsymbol{\beta}) = -\int_0^T tU(\mathbf{c}^*(t; \boldsymbol{\beta}))e^{-\rho t}\, dt \gtrless 0, \tag{30}$$

$$\frac{\partial V}{\partial w_0}(\beta) = -\lambda(\beta) > 0, \tag{31}$$

$$\frac{\partial V}{\partial T}(\beta) = H(T, E^*(T;\beta), \mathbf{c}^*(T;\beta), \lambda(\beta); \mathbf{p}, r, \rho)$$
$$= U(\mathbf{c}^*(T;\beta))e^{-\rho T} + \lambda(\beta)\mathbf{p}'\mathbf{c}^*(T;\beta)e^{-rT} \gtrless 0. \tag{32}$$

Equation (28) asserts that an increase in the price of any good makes the individual worse off, a completely analogous result to that in static consumer theory. This qualitative result is just as one would expect, for a price increase in effect lowers the purchasing power of the individual's wealth, which, in turn, lowers discounted lifetime utility. Similarly, Eq. (29) shows that an increase in the interest rate r lowers the present value of consumption expenditures, and thus effectively increases the purchasing power of the individual's wealth, thereby increasing lifetime discounted utility. These economic interpretations follow rigorously from Eq. (31), which demonstrates that an increase in the individual's present discounted value of wealth makes the individual better off, just as one would expect. In other words, $\lambda(\beta) < 0$ is behind these qualitative results, and as shown above, this fact is a result of our assumption that $U_{c_m}(\mathbf{c}(t)) > 0, m = 1, 2, \ldots, M$.

To finish up this example, we derive the intertemporal equivalent of the Antonelli-Roy lemma. In order to do so, simply divide the negative of Eq. (28) by Eq. (31) to get

$$\frac{-\partial V(\beta)/\partial p_j}{\partial V(\beta)/\partial w_0} = \frac{-\lambda(\beta)\int_0^T c_j^*(t;\beta)\, e^{-rt}\, dt}{-\lambda(\beta)}$$
$$= \int_0^T c_j^*(t;\beta)\, e^{-rt}\, dt > 0, \quad j = 1, 2, \ldots, M.$$

In the intertemporal theory of the consumer, therefore, the equivalent of the Antonelli-Roy lemma recovers the cumulative discounted demand function for a good. Referring back to Example 9.1, this is consistent with the results of the dynamic envelope theorem applied to the adjustment cost model of the firm, in which case, the dynamic envelope theorem also recovered the cumulative discounted demand functions.

In the next chapter, we use the dynamic envelope theorem to derive the necessary transversality conditions for a class of optimal control problems that are more or less ubiquitous in intertemporal economics. The dynamic envelope theorem permits this to be done in a simple and palatable manner. In the process, we will further hone our economic intuition about optimal control problems and their necessary conditions, as well as our understanding of the dynamic envelope theorem.

MENTAL EXERCISES

9.1 Starting at the bottom of page 169 through the top of page 172, Kamien and Schwartz (1991, 2nd Edition, *first* printing only) prove the dynamic envelope theorem for a parameter r entering the integrand function only. Find the error in their proof and explain it clearly. This error was corrected in the second printing of the 2nd edition.

9.2 Prove part (iii) of Theorem 9.1.

9.3 Prove part (iv) of Theorem 9.1.

9.4 Prove part (v) of Theorem 9.1.

9.5 Prove that $V(\cdot) \in C^{(1)} \, \forall \, \beta \in B(\beta^{\circ}; \delta)$ in Theorem 9.1.

9.6 In our economic interpretation of parts (ii) and (iv) of Theorem 9.1, we assumed that the value of the Hamiltonian was positive at the initial and terminal dates in the optimal plan.
   (a) Given this assumption, if you had the choice, would you prefer to start your planning sooner or later? Why?
   (b) Given this assumption, if you had the choice, would you prefer to end your planning sooner or later? Why?

9.7 For Example 9.1, derive the dynamic envelope results for the parameters (c, g, r, δ) by invoking Theorem 9.1, and then provide an economic interpretation of each. Also provide a thorough economic interpretation of the dynamic envelope result for the parameter K_T.

9.8 Consider the optimal control problem

$$V(\alpha, t_0, x_0, t_1) \stackrel{\text{def}}{=} \max_{u(\cdot), x_1} \int_{t_0}^{t_1} \alpha x(t) u(t) \, dt$$

$$\text{s.t.} \quad \dot{x}(t) = 0, \, x(t_0) = x_0, \, x(t_1) = x_1,$$

$$0 \le u(t) \le 1,$$

where $\alpha > 0$ is a time-independent parameter. Note that this is a generalization of the control problem in Example 9.2.
   (a) Determine the pair $(z(t; \alpha, t_0 x_0, t_1), v(t; \alpha, t_0 x_0, t_1))$ that solves the necessary conditions. Consider the cases $x_0 > 0$ and $x_0 < 0$ separately.
   (b) Prove that $(z(t; \alpha, t_0, x_0, t_1), v(t; \alpha, t_0, x_0, t_1))$ is a solution of the control problem for each case ($x_0 > 0$ and $x_0 < 0$) separately.
   (c) Prove that $V(\cdot)$ is not differentiable with respect to x_0 for all $x_0 \in \Re$, but that it is differentiable with respect to x_0 in any neighborhood of $x_0 \neq 0$ not containing the value $x_0 = 0$.

(d) Prove, however, that $V(\cdot)$ is differentiable with respect to (α, t_0, t_1) for all $x_0 \in \Re$.

9.9 For Example 9.3, show that
(a) $v(t; s, x_s, t_1, x_1)|_{x_s=z(s;t_0,x_0,t_1,x_1)} = v(t; t_0, x_0, t_1, x_1)\,\forall t \in [s, t_1]$,
(b) $\lambda(t; s, x_s, t_1, x_1)|_{x_s=z(s;t_0,x_0,t_1,x_1)} = \lambda(t; t_0, x_0, t_1, x_1)\,\forall t \in [s, t_1]$.
(c) Why does one need the restriction $t \in [s, t_1]$?

9.10 Recall our prototype inventory accumulation problem:

$$V(\boldsymbol{\beta}) \stackrel{\text{def}}{=} \min_{u(\cdot)} \int_0^T \left[c_1[u(t)]^2 + c_2 x(t)\right] dt$$

$$\text{s.t.} \quad \dot{x}(t) = u(t), x(0) = 0, x(T) = x_T,$$

where $\boldsymbol{\beta} \stackrel{\text{def}}{=} (c_1, c_2, T, x_T)$. Recall that in Example 4.5, we found the optimal solution to be given by the curves $z(t; \boldsymbol{\beta}) = \frac{1}{4}c_2c_1^{-1}t[t - T] + x_T T^{-1}t$, $v(t; \boldsymbol{\beta}) = \frac{1}{4}c_2c_1^{-1}[2t - T] + x_T T^{-1}$, and $\lambda(t; \boldsymbol{\beta}) = \frac{1}{2}c_2[T - 2t] - 2c_1 x_T T^{-1}$. Do not use these explicit formulas in answering this question unless asked. You may *invoke* Theorem 9.1 in what follows, unless specifically asked not to.

(a) Prove that $z(t; \boldsymbol{\beta})$ and $v(t; \boldsymbol{\beta})$ are positively homogeneous of degree zero in (c_1, c_2), Provide an economic interpretation of these results.
(b) Give an alternative definition of $V(\boldsymbol{\beta})$, and prove that $V(\boldsymbol{\beta})$ is positively homogeneous of degree one in (c_1, c_2). Do not derive an explicit expression for $V(\boldsymbol{\beta})$.
(c) Find the partial derivative $V_{c_1}(\boldsymbol{\beta})$, determine its sign, and provide an economic interpretation of it.
(d) Find the partial derivative $V_{c_2}(\boldsymbol{\beta})$, determine its sign, and provide an economic interpretation of it.
(e) Find the partial derivative $V_T(\boldsymbol{\beta})$, determine its sign, and provide an economic interpretation of it.
(f) Find the partial derivative $V_{x_T}(\boldsymbol{\beta})$, determine its sign, and provide an economic interpretation of it.
(g) Now derive an explicit formula for $V(\boldsymbol{\beta})$.
(h) Verify that parts (c) and (d) hold by using the explicit formulas for $V(\boldsymbol{\beta})$, $z(t; \boldsymbol{\beta})$, and $v(t; \boldsymbol{\beta})$.

9.11 Let $(z(t), v(t))$ be the optimal pair for the following control problem:

$$V(t_0, x_0, t_1, x_1) \stackrel{\text{def}}{=} \max_{u(\cdot)} \int_{t_0}^{t_1} f(t, x(t), u(t))\, dt$$

$$\text{s.t. } \dot{x}(t) = g(t, x(t), u(t)), x(t_0) = x_0, x(t_1) = x_1.$$

Explain clearly why the dynamic envelope theorem and principle of optimality *cannot* be used to interpret the costate variable $\lambda(t)$ corresponding to

$(z(t), v(t))$ as the shadow value of the state variable at any time $t \in [t_0, t_1]$ for the above optimal control problem.

9.12 Prove Theorem 9.3 when there are only *equality* constraints present.

9.13 In order to demonstrate some of the assertions made after Theorem 9.3, consider the following inequality constrained optimal control problem:

$$V(\alpha) \stackrel{\text{def}}{=} \max_{u(\cdot),x_2} \int_0^2 \left[\alpha x(t) + tu(t) - \frac{1}{2}(u(t))^2\right] dt$$

$$\text{s.t.} \quad \dot{x}(t) = u(t),\, x(0) = 0,\, x(2) = x_2,$$

$$u(t) \leq 1,$$

where $\alpha \in (-\infty, \frac{1}{2})$.

(a) Prove that a solution of the necessary conditions is a solution of the optimal control problem.

(b) Derive the necessary and sufficient conditions.

(c) Find $\lambda(t; \alpha)$, the solution of the costate equation and transversality condition.

(d) Notice that the integrand is an increasing function of the control variable for $t \in [0, 1]$ if $u(t) < t$, and for all $t \in (1, 2]$, since $u(t) \leq 1$ must hold. Hence it is natural to conjecture the existence of a unique switching time that is a function of $\alpha \in (-\infty, \frac{1}{2})$, say, $s(\alpha)$. Conjecture, therefore, that for $t \in [0, s(\alpha))$, the constraint on the control is not binding, whereas for $t \in (s(\alpha), 2]$ it is, so that $u(t) = 1$. Find the solution to the control problem using this conjecture, including the switching time.

(e) Show that the optimal control, Lagrange multiplier, and time derivative of the state variable are *not* differentiable in α at the switching time $s(\alpha)$, but that all three are $C^{(1)}$ in α for $t \in [0, 2] \sim s(\alpha)$.

(f) Show, however, that the optimal state and costate variables are $C^{(1)}$ in α for $t \in [0, 2]$.

(g) Find the value of $V(\cdot)$.

(h) Confirm the veracity of Theorem 9.1 part (i).

FURTHER READING

A superb (and, arguably, the best) reference on the static envelope theorem and comparative statics is Silberberg and Suen (2001). Besides the seminal paper by Eisner and Strotz (1963) on the adjustment cost model of the firm, Treadway (1970) is another excellent reference. Example 9.2 is culled from Seierstad and Sydsæter (1987). The rigorous proof that the *j*th costate variable at any time *t* in the planning horizon of the original optimal control problem (OC) is the shadow value of the *j*th state variable at time *t* is a result of Léonard (1987). A proof of Theorem 9.3 (under assumptions that are stronger than those employed here) can be found in

LaFrance and Barney (1991), which is also the source for Example 9.4 and Mental Exercise 9.13. Seierstad (1982) provides a thorough analysis of the differentiability of the optimal value function. Dual proofs of the static and dynamic envelope theorems can be found in Silberberg (1974) and Caputo (1990a, 1990b), respectively. In Chapter 11, we will explore the modern envelope approach to the dynamic envelope theorem and the concomitant implications it has for the comparative dynamics properties of optimal control problems.

REFERENCES

Caputo, M.R. (1990a), "Comparative Dynamics via Envelope Methods in Variational Calculus," *Review of Economics Studies*, 57, 689–697.

Caputo, M.R. (1990b), "How to Do Comparative Dynamics on the Back of an Envelope in Optimal Control Theory," *Journal of Economic Dynamics and Control*, 14, 655–683.

Eisner, R. and Strotz, R.H. (1963), "Determinants of Business Investment," Research Study Two in *Impacts of Monetary Policy* (Englewood Cliffs, N.J.: Prentice-Hall).

Kamien, M.I. and Schwartz, N.L. (1991, 2nd Ed.), *Dynamic Optimization: The Calculus of Variations and Optimal Control in Economics and Management* (New York: Elsevier Science Publishing Co., Inc.).

LaFrance, J.T. and Barney, L.D. (1991), "The Envelope Theorem in Dynamic Optimization," *Journal of Economic Dynamics and Control*, 15, 355–385.

Léonard, D. (1987), "Costate Variables Correctly Value Stocks at Each Instant: A Proof," *Journal of Economic Dynamics and Control*, 11, 117–122.

Seierstad, A. (1982), "Differentiability Properties of the Optimal Value Function in Control Theory," *Journal of Economic Dynamics and Control*, 4, 303–310.

Seierstad, A. and Sydsæter, K. (1987), *Optimal Control Theory with Economic Applications* (New York: Elsevier Science Publishing Co., Inc.).

Silberberg, E. (1974), "A Revision of Comparative Statics Methodology in Economics, or, How to Do Comparative Statics on the Back of an Envelope," *Journal of Economic Theory*, 7, 159–172.

Silberberg, E. and Suen, W. (2001, 3rd Ed.), *The Structure of Economics: A Mathematical Analysis* (New York: Irwin McGraw-Hill).

Treadway, A.B. (1970), "Adjustment Costs and Variable Inputs in the Theory of the Competitive Firm," *Journal of Economic Theory*, 2, 329–347.

TEN

The Dynamic Envelope Theorem and Transversality Conditions

We now exploit some benefits of the dynamic envelope theorem established in Chapter 9 by deriving the necessary transversality conditions corresponding to various endpoint conditions that are relatively common in economic applications of optimal control theory. The use of the dynamic envelope theorem renders this a relatively simple and economically revealing process. That is to say, the conclusions established will help build additional economic intuition about optimal control problems and their solutions, as well as the dynamic envelope theorem itself. Furthermore, we provide a rather general sufficiency theorem that is of value in solving optimal control problems.

To begin, consider the *variable endpoint* and *variable time* optimal control problem

$$V^*(\boldsymbol{\alpha}) \stackrel{\text{def}}{=} \max_{\mathbf{u}(\cdot), t_0, \mathbf{x}_0, t_1, \mathbf{x}_1} \int_{t_0}^{t_1} f(t, \mathbf{x}(t), \mathbf{u}(t); \boldsymbol{\alpha})\, dt \tag{1}$$

$$\text{s.t.} \quad \dot{\mathbf{x}}(t) = \mathbf{g}(t, \mathbf{x}(t), \mathbf{u}(t); \boldsymbol{\alpha}), \ \ \mathbf{x}(t_0) = \mathbf{x}_0, \ \ \mathbf{x}(t_1) = \mathbf{x}_1,$$

$$h^k(t, \mathbf{x}(t), \mathbf{u}(t); \boldsymbol{\alpha}) \geq 0, \quad k = 1, 2, \ldots, K',$$

$$h^k(t, \mathbf{x}(t), \mathbf{u}(t); \boldsymbol{\alpha}) = 0, \quad k = K'+1, K'+2, \ldots, K,$$

where $\mathbf{x}(t) \stackrel{\text{def}}{=} (x_1(t), x_2(t), \ldots, x_N(t)) \in \Re^N$ is the state vector; $\mathbf{u}(t) \stackrel{\text{def}}{=} (u_1(t), u_2(t), \ldots, u_M(t)) \in \Re^M$ is the control vector; $\dot{\mathbf{x}}(\cdot) \stackrel{\text{def}}{=} (\dot{x}_1(\cdot), \dot{x}_2(\cdot), \ldots, \dot{x}_N(\cdot))$, $\mathbf{g}(\cdot) \stackrel{\text{def}}{=} (g^1(\cdot), g^2(\cdot), \ldots, g^N(\cdot))$ is the vector of transition functions; $\mathbf{h}(\cdot) \stackrel{\text{def}}{=} (h^1(\cdot), h^2(\cdot), \ldots, h^K(\cdot))$ is the vector of constraint functions, both inequality and equality; and $\boldsymbol{\alpha} \stackrel{\text{def}}{=} (\alpha_1, \alpha_2, \ldots, \alpha_A) \in \Re^A$ is a vector of time-independent parameters that affect the state equations, integrand, and constraint functions. Assume that an optimal solution $(\mathbf{z}^*(t; \boldsymbol{\alpha}), \mathbf{v}^*(t; \boldsymbol{\alpha}))$ exists to problem (1) for all $\boldsymbol{\alpha} \in B(\boldsymbol{\alpha}^\circ; \delta_1)$, with corresponding costate vector $\boldsymbol{\lambda}^*(t; \boldsymbol{\alpha})$ and Lagrange multiplier vector $\boldsymbol{\mu}^*(t; \boldsymbol{\alpha})$, and let $\boldsymbol{\gamma}^*(\boldsymbol{\alpha}) \stackrel{\text{def}}{=} (t_0^*(\boldsymbol{\alpha}), \mathbf{x}_0^*(\boldsymbol{\alpha}), t_1^*(\boldsymbol{\alpha}), \mathbf{x}_1^*(\boldsymbol{\alpha}))$ be the optimal solution for the initial and terminal values of the horizon and state vector, where $B(\boldsymbol{\alpha}^\circ;\delta_1)$ is an open A – ball centered at the given value of the parameter vector $\boldsymbol{\alpha}^\circ$ of radius $\delta_1 > 0$. Given that the initial and terminal dates and states are decision variables, the optimal value function and solution functions for problem (1) depend only on the parameter vector $\boldsymbol{\alpha}$. Given the above definitions, it should be apparent that the identities $\mathbf{x}_0^*(\boldsymbol{\alpha}) \equiv \mathbf{z}^*(t_0^*(\boldsymbol{\alpha});\boldsymbol{\alpha})$ and $\mathbf{x}_1^*(\boldsymbol{\alpha}) \equiv \mathbf{z}^*(t_1^*(\boldsymbol{\alpha});\boldsymbol{\alpha})$ hold for the optimal initial and terminal values of the state vector.

Now recall our canonical *fixed endpoint* and *fixed-time* optimal control problem

$$\hat{V}(\boldsymbol{\alpha},\boldsymbol{\gamma}) \stackrel{\text{def}}{=} \max_{\mathbf{u}(\cdot)} \int_{t_0}^{t_1} f(t,\mathbf{x}(t),\mathbf{u}(t);\boldsymbol{\alpha})\,dt \tag{2}$$

$$\text{s.t.}\quad \dot{\mathbf{x}}(t) = \mathbf{g}(t,\mathbf{x}(t),\mathbf{u}(t);\boldsymbol{\alpha}),\ \ \mathbf{x}(t_0)=\mathbf{x}_0,\ \ \mathbf{x}(t_1)=\mathbf{x}_1,$$

$$h^k(t,\mathbf{x}(t),\mathbf{u}(t);\boldsymbol{\alpha}) \geq 0,\quad k=1,2,\ldots,K',$$

$$h^k(t,\mathbf{x}(t),\mathbf{u}(t);\boldsymbol{\alpha}) = 0,\quad k=K'+1,K'+2,\ldots,K,$$

where $\boldsymbol{\gamma} \stackrel{\text{def}}{=} (t_0,\mathbf{x}_0,t_1,\mathbf{x}_1) \in \Re^{2+2N}$ and $\boldsymbol{\beta} \stackrel{\text{def}}{=} (\boldsymbol{\alpha},t_0,\mathbf{x}_0,t_1,\mathbf{x}_1) \in \Re^{2+2N+A}$. Assume that an optimal solution $(\hat{\mathbf{z}}(t;\boldsymbol{\beta}),\hat{\mathbf{v}}(t;\boldsymbol{\beta}))$ exists to problem (2) for all $\boldsymbol{\beta} \in B(\boldsymbol{\beta}^\circ;\delta_2)$, with corresponding costate vector $\hat{\boldsymbol{\lambda}}(t;\boldsymbol{\beta})$ and Lagrange multiplier vector $\hat{\boldsymbol{\mu}}(t;\boldsymbol{\beta})$, where $B(\boldsymbol{\beta}^\circ;\delta_2)$ is an open $2+2N+A$ – ball centered at the given value of the parameter $\boldsymbol{\beta}^\circ$ of radius $\delta_2 > 0$. In view of the fact that $\boldsymbol{\gamma} \stackrel{\text{def}}{=} (t_0,\mathbf{x}_0,t_1,\mathbf{x}_1)$ is parametrically given in problem (2), the optimal value function and solution functions depend on these parameters in addition to $\boldsymbol{\alpha}$.

Because problems (1) and (2) depend on exogenous parameters, and because we intend to make use of the dynamic envelope theorem, we take it that assumptions (A.1) through (A.3) in Chapter 9 are in force throughout this chapter as well. Moreover, because of the presence of constraints in problems (1) and (2), we assume that the rank constraint qualification given in Chapter 6 holds throughout this chapter too. Given these preliminaries, we have the following set of necessary conditions for selecting the initial and terminal values of the planning horizon and state vector in problem (1).

Theorem 10.1 (Free Transversality Conditions): *If $\hat{V}(\cdot) \in C^{(1)}\ \forall\, \boldsymbol{\beta} \in B(\boldsymbol{\beta}^\circ;\delta_2)$, then in addition to the necessary conditions of Theorem 6.1, the following transversality conditions are necessary for the variable endpoint and variable time optimal control problem (1):*

$$H(t_0^*(\boldsymbol{\alpha}),\mathbf{z}^*(t_0^*(\boldsymbol{\alpha});\boldsymbol{\alpha}),\mathbf{v}^*(t_0^*(\boldsymbol{\alpha});\boldsymbol{\alpha}),\boldsymbol{\lambda}^*(t_0^*(\boldsymbol{\alpha});\boldsymbol{\alpha});\boldsymbol{\alpha}) = 0\,[t_0\,\text{free}], \tag{3}$$

$$\lambda_j^*(t_0^*(\boldsymbol{\alpha});\boldsymbol{\alpha}) = 0,\quad j=1,2,\ldots,N\ [\mathbf{x}_0\ \text{free}], \tag{4}$$

$$H(t_1^*(\boldsymbol{\alpha}),\mathbf{z}^*(t_1^*(\boldsymbol{\alpha});\boldsymbol{\alpha}),\mathbf{v}^*(t_1^*(\boldsymbol{\alpha});\boldsymbol{\alpha}),\boldsymbol{\lambda}^*(t_1^*(\boldsymbol{\alpha});\boldsymbol{\alpha});\boldsymbol{\alpha}) = 0\ [t_1\,\text{free}], \tag{5}$$

$$\lambda_j^*(t_1^*(\boldsymbol{\alpha});\boldsymbol{\alpha}) = 0,\quad j=1,2,\ldots,N\ [\mathbf{x}_1\,\text{free}]. \tag{6}$$

Proof: Given that $V^*(\boldsymbol{\alpha})$ is the value of the optimal value function for problem (1), in which no constraints are placed on the horizon or endpoints, it must be at least as large as the value of the optimal value function $\hat{V}(\boldsymbol{\alpha}, \boldsymbol{\gamma})$ for problem (2), in which the endpoints and horizon are constrained to be fixed. This observation follows directly from the very definition of an optimization problem. More formally, we have that $V^*(\boldsymbol{\alpha}) \geq \hat{V}(\boldsymbol{\alpha}, \boldsymbol{\gamma}) \forall \boldsymbol{\gamma} \stackrel{\text{def}}{=} (t_0, \mathbf{x}_0, t_1, \mathbf{x}_1)$ in a neighborhood of $\boldsymbol{\gamma}^*(\boldsymbol{\alpha}) \stackrel{\text{def}}{=} (t_0^*(\boldsymbol{\alpha}), \mathbf{x}_0^*(\boldsymbol{\alpha}), t_1^*(\boldsymbol{\alpha}), \mathbf{x}_1^*(\boldsymbol{\alpha}))$ for each $\boldsymbol{\alpha} \in B(\boldsymbol{\alpha}^\circ; \delta_1)$. The identity $V^*(\boldsymbol{\alpha}) \equiv \hat{V}(\boldsymbol{\alpha}, \boldsymbol{\gamma})$ therefore holds by definition when $\boldsymbol{\gamma} = \boldsymbol{\gamma}^*(\boldsymbol{\alpha})$, that is, $V^*(\boldsymbol{\alpha}) \equiv \hat{V}(\boldsymbol{\alpha}, \boldsymbol{\gamma}^*(\boldsymbol{\alpha})) \forall \boldsymbol{\alpha} \in B(\boldsymbol{\alpha}^\circ; \delta_1)$. In other words, $V^*(\boldsymbol{\alpha}) \stackrel{\text{def}}{=} \max_{\boldsymbol{\gamma}} \hat{V}(\boldsymbol{\alpha}, \boldsymbol{\gamma})$ and $\boldsymbol{\gamma}^*(\boldsymbol{\alpha}) \stackrel{\text{def}}{=} \arg\max_{\boldsymbol{\gamma}} \hat{V}(\boldsymbol{\alpha}, \boldsymbol{\gamma})$. Because $\hat{V}(\cdot) \in C^{(1)} \forall \boldsymbol{\beta} \in B(\boldsymbol{\beta}^\circ; \delta_2)$ by assumption and no constraints are placed on the choice of $\boldsymbol{\gamma}$ in the unconstrained optimization problem $V^*(\boldsymbol{\alpha}) \stackrel{\text{def}}{=} \max_{\boldsymbol{\gamma}} \hat{V}(\boldsymbol{\alpha}, \boldsymbol{\gamma})$, it follows from static optimization theory that the ensuing conditions are necessary:

$$\hat{V}_{t_0}(\boldsymbol{\alpha}, \boldsymbol{\gamma})\big|_{\boldsymbol{\gamma}=\boldsymbol{\gamma}^*(\boldsymbol{\alpha})} = 0, \quad \hat{V}_{\mathbf{x}_0}(\boldsymbol{\alpha}, \boldsymbol{\gamma})\big|_{\boldsymbol{\gamma}=\boldsymbol{\gamma}^*(\boldsymbol{\alpha})} = \mathbf{0}'_N,$$

$$\hat{V}_{t_1}(\boldsymbol{\alpha}, \boldsymbol{\gamma})\big|_{\boldsymbol{\gamma}=\boldsymbol{\gamma}^*(\boldsymbol{\alpha})} = 0, \quad \hat{V}_{\mathbf{x}_1}(\boldsymbol{\alpha}, \boldsymbol{\gamma})\big|_{\boldsymbol{\gamma}=\boldsymbol{\gamma}^*(\boldsymbol{\alpha})} = \mathbf{0}'_N.$$

By Theorem 9.3, the dynamic envelope theorem, these derivatives are given by

$$\begin{aligned}
\hat{V}_{t_0}(\boldsymbol{\alpha}, \boldsymbol{\gamma})\big|_{\boldsymbol{\gamma}=\boldsymbol{\gamma}^*(\boldsymbol{\alpha})} &= -H(t_0^*(\boldsymbol{\alpha}), \hat{\mathbf{z}}(t_0^*(\boldsymbol{\alpha}); \boldsymbol{\alpha}, \boldsymbol{\gamma}^*(\boldsymbol{\alpha})), \hat{\mathbf{v}}(t_0^*(\boldsymbol{\alpha}); \boldsymbol{\alpha}, \boldsymbol{\gamma}^*(\boldsymbol{\alpha})), \\
&\qquad \hat{\boldsymbol{\lambda}}(t_0^*(\boldsymbol{\alpha}); \boldsymbol{\alpha}, \boldsymbol{\gamma}^*(\boldsymbol{\alpha})); \boldsymbol{\alpha}) = 0, \\
\hat{V}_{x_{0j}}(\boldsymbol{\alpha}, \boldsymbol{\gamma})\big|_{\boldsymbol{\gamma}=\boldsymbol{\gamma}^*(\boldsymbol{\alpha})} &= \hat{\lambda}_j(t_0^*(\boldsymbol{\alpha}); \boldsymbol{\alpha}, \boldsymbol{\gamma}^*(\boldsymbol{\alpha})) = 0, \quad j = 1, 2, \ldots, N, \\
\hat{V}_{t_1}(\boldsymbol{\alpha}, \boldsymbol{\gamma})\big|_{\boldsymbol{\gamma}=\boldsymbol{\gamma}^*(\boldsymbol{\alpha})} &= H(t_1^*(\boldsymbol{\alpha}), \hat{\mathbf{z}}(t_1^*(\boldsymbol{\alpha}); \boldsymbol{\alpha}, \boldsymbol{\gamma}^*(\boldsymbol{\alpha})), \hat{\mathbf{v}}(t_1^*(\boldsymbol{\alpha}); \boldsymbol{\alpha}, \boldsymbol{\gamma}^*(\boldsymbol{\alpha})), \\
&\qquad \hat{\boldsymbol{\lambda}}(t_1^*(\boldsymbol{\alpha}); \boldsymbol{\alpha}, \boldsymbol{\gamma}^*(\boldsymbol{\alpha})); \boldsymbol{\alpha}) = 0, \\
\hat{V}_{x_{1j}}(\boldsymbol{\alpha}, \boldsymbol{\gamma})\big|_{\boldsymbol{\gamma}=\boldsymbol{\gamma}^*(\boldsymbol{\alpha})} &= -\hat{\lambda}_j(t_1^*(\boldsymbol{\alpha}); \boldsymbol{\alpha}, \boldsymbol{\gamma}^*(\boldsymbol{\alpha})) = 0, \quad j = 1, 2, \ldots, N.
\end{aligned}$$

Notice that the above derivatives are evaluated along the triplet $(\hat{\mathbf{z}}(t; \boldsymbol{\alpha}, \boldsymbol{\gamma}), \hat{\mathbf{v}}(t; \boldsymbol{\alpha}, \boldsymbol{\gamma}), \hat{\boldsymbol{\lambda}}(t; \boldsymbol{\alpha}, \boldsymbol{\gamma}))$, since it corresponds to the optimal value function $\hat{V}(\cdot)$ being differentiated. This means that we have not yet established the transversality conditions of Theorem 10.1, which apply to problem (1) and its solution. In order to do so, we must establish that the solutions to problems (1) and (2) are identical when $\boldsymbol{\gamma} = \boldsymbol{\gamma}^*(\boldsymbol{\alpha})$. If we therefore set $\boldsymbol{\gamma} = \boldsymbol{\gamma}^*(\boldsymbol{\alpha})$ in the fixed endpoint and fixed-time optimal control problem (2), then the horizon and endpoints in problem (2) are held fixed at the values that are optimal in the variable endpoint and variable time optimal control problem (1). In other words, if $\boldsymbol{\gamma} = \boldsymbol{\gamma}^*(\boldsymbol{\alpha})$ in problem (2), then the optimal pair that solves problem (2) passes through the same endpoints over the same time interval as the optimal pair that solves problem (1), and vice versa. Hence, seeing as problems (1) and (2) are otherwise identical, their solutions must be identical too when $\boldsymbol{\gamma} = \boldsymbol{\gamma}^*(\boldsymbol{\alpha})$, which in turn implies that the costate and Lagrange multiplier vectors are identical as well. This reasoning thus establishes the following identities for all $t \in [t_0^*(\alpha), t_1^*(\alpha)]$:

$$(\mathbf{z}^*(t;\alpha), \mathbf{v}^*(t;\alpha), \boldsymbol{\lambda}^*(t;\alpha), \boldsymbol{\mu}^*(t;\alpha))$$
$$\equiv (\hat{\mathbf{z}}(t;\alpha,\gamma^*(\alpha)), \hat{\mathbf{v}}(t;\alpha,\gamma^*(\alpha)), \hat{\boldsymbol{\lambda}}(t;\alpha,\gamma^*(\alpha)), \hat{\boldsymbol{\mu}}(t;\alpha,\gamma^*(\alpha))).$$

Substituting these identities into the four dynamic envelope derivatives above completes the proof of the necessity of the transversality conditions.

To complete the proof of Theorem 10.1, we must demonstrate that the quadruplet $(\mathbf{z}^*(t;\alpha), \mathbf{v}^*(t;\alpha), \boldsymbol{\lambda}^*(t;\alpha), \boldsymbol{\mu}^*(t;\alpha))$ satisfies the necessary conditions of Theorem 6.1, which pertain to the fixed endpoint and fixed-time optimal control problem (2). This conclusion follows immediately from the above identities, as we now intend to show. Because the quadruplet $(\hat{\mathbf{z}}(t;\alpha,\gamma^*(\alpha)), \hat{\mathbf{v}}(t;\alpha,\gamma^*(\alpha)), \hat{\boldsymbol{\lambda}}(t;\alpha,\gamma^*(\alpha)), \hat{\boldsymbol{\mu}}(t;\alpha,\gamma^*(\alpha)))$ is the solution of the fixed endpoint and fixed-time optimal control problem (2) when $\gamma = \gamma^*(\alpha)$, it satisfies the necessary conditions of Theorem 6.1. By the above identities, the quadruplet $(\mathbf{z}^*(t;\alpha), \mathbf{v}^*(t;\alpha), \boldsymbol{\lambda}^*(t;\alpha), \boldsymbol{\mu}^*(t;\alpha))$ is identically equal to the quadruplet $(\hat{\mathbf{z}}(t;\alpha,\gamma^*(\alpha)), \hat{\mathbf{v}}(t;\alpha,\gamma^*(\alpha)), \hat{\boldsymbol{\lambda}}(t;\alpha,\gamma^*(\alpha)), \hat{\boldsymbol{\mu}}(t;\alpha,\gamma^*(\alpha)))$. As a result, $(\mathbf{z}^*(t;\alpha), \mathbf{v}^*(t;\alpha), \boldsymbol{\lambda}^*(t;\alpha), \boldsymbol{\mu}^*(t;\alpha))$ also satisfies the necessary conditions of Theorem 6.1. Q.E.D.

The economic interpretation of these transversality conditions is straightforward and reinforces the economic intuition developed in the last chapter about the dynamic envelope theorem. This is not really surprising as the transversality conditions rely heavily on the dynamic envelope theorem. For example, Eq. (3) of Theorem 10.1 asserts that the optimal starting date for an intertemporal plan should be chosen such that all instantaneous profit opportunities are exhausted at the margin, both *current* through the integrand $f(t,\mathbf{x}(t),\mathbf{u}(t);\alpha)$, and *indirect* through the total shadow value of investment $\sum_{\ell=1}^{N} \lambda_\ell g^\ell(t,\mathbf{x}(t),\mathbf{u}(t);\alpha)$. Otherwise, there would be a gain to either delaying the start of the program or beginning it earlier. Equation (4) says that the optimal initial state vector should be chosen such that, at the margin, a unit of capital has no value in an optimal program. In other words, the firm should start with a capital stock such that it would not be willing to pay anything for an additional unit. In general, therefore, the transversality conditions reflect nothing other than the marginal principle that the optimal amount of an activity occurs when the net marginal value of it is zero. The economic interpretation of Eqs. (5) and (6) is left for a mental exercise.

Consider now the following *inequality constrained variable endpoint* and *variable time* optimal control problem:

$$\bar{V}(\boldsymbol{\theta}) \stackrel{\text{def}}{=} \max_{\mathbf{u}(\cdot),t_1,\mathbf{x}_1} \int_{t_0}^{t_1} f(t,\mathbf{x}(t),\mathbf{u}(t);\alpha)\,dt \tag{7}$$

$$\text{s.t.} \quad \dot{\mathbf{x}}(t) = \mathbf{g}(t,\mathbf{x}(t),\mathbf{u}(t);\alpha),\ \mathbf{x}(t_0) = \mathbf{x}_0,\ \mathbf{x}(t_1) = \mathbf{x}_1 \geq \mathbf{x}_T,\ t_1 \leq T,$$
$$h^k(t,\mathbf{x}(t),\mathbf{u}(t);\alpha) \geq 0, \quad k = 1,2,\ldots,K',$$
$$h^k(t,\mathbf{x}(t),\mathbf{u}(t);\alpha) = 0, \quad k = K'+1, K'+2,\ldots,K,$$

where $(\alpha, t_0, \mathbf{x}_0)$ are fixed (or given) parameters, but $(t_1, \mathbf{x}_1)$ are chosen subject to the stated inequality constraints, and $\boldsymbol{\theta} \stackrel{\text{def}}{=} (\alpha, t_0, \mathbf{x}_0, T, \mathbf{x}_T)$. As we did above, assume that an optimal solution $(\bar{\mathbf{z}}(t;\boldsymbol{\theta}), \bar{\mathbf{v}}(t;\boldsymbol{\theta}))$ exists to problem (7) for all $\boldsymbol{\theta} \in B(\boldsymbol{\theta}^\circ; \delta_3)$, with corresponding costate vector $\bar{\boldsymbol{\lambda}}(t;\boldsymbol{\theta})$ and Lagrange multiplier vector $\bar{\mu}(t;\boldsymbol{\theta})$, and let $\omega(\boldsymbol{\theta}) \stackrel{\text{def}}{=} (\bar{t}_1(\boldsymbol{\theta}), \bar{\mathbf{x}}_1(\boldsymbol{\theta}))$ be the optimal solution for the terminal values of the time horizon and the state vector, where $B(\boldsymbol{\theta}^\circ; \delta_3)$ is an open $2 + 2N + A$ – ball centered at the given value of the parameter vector $\boldsymbol{\theta}^\circ$ of radius $\delta_3 > 0$.

Problem (7) is a common form for optimal control problems to take in economics. It turns out to be relatively rare for the initial date or the initial state vector to be decision variables. We have therefore stuck with one of the principles enunciated in the preface, namely, that the theorems presented in the book will typically be those that are the most useful in economic applications of optimal control theory.

As demonstrated in the proof of Theorem 10.1, it is not only correct, but it is also very useful, to think of problem (7) as being solved in three distinct stages:

Stage 1: Treat $(t_1, \mathbf{x}_1)$ as fixed parameters in problem (7) and solve it as if it were a fixed endpoint and fixed-time control problem. Then construct its corresponding optimal value function. That is, literally solve problem (2) to find the vector $(\hat{\mathbf{z}}(t;\alpha,\gamma), \hat{\mathbf{v}}(t;\alpha,\gamma), \hat{\boldsymbol{\lambda}}(t;\alpha,\gamma), \hat{\mu}(t;\alpha,\gamma))$, and then derive the associated value of the optimal value function $\hat{V}(\alpha,\gamma)$.

Stage 2: Find $(t_1, \mathbf{x}_1)$ by solving the ensuing *static* constrained optimization problem:

$$\bar{V}(\boldsymbol{\theta}) \stackrel{\text{def}}{=} \max_{t_1,\mathbf{x}_1}\{\hat{V}(\alpha,\gamma) \text{ s.t. } t_1 \leq T, \mathbf{x}_1 \geq \mathbf{x}_T\}. \tag{8}$$

This yields the solution $\bar{\omega}(\boldsymbol{\theta}) \stackrel{\text{def}}{=} (\bar{t}_1(\boldsymbol{\theta}), \bar{\mathbf{x}}_1(\boldsymbol{\theta}))$ and value of the optimal value function $\bar{V}(\boldsymbol{\theta})$. In principle, $\bar{V}(\boldsymbol{\theta})$ is found by substituting the solution $\bar{\omega}(\boldsymbol{\theta}) \stackrel{\text{def}}{=} (\bar{t}_1(\boldsymbol{\theta}), \bar{\mathbf{x}}_1(\boldsymbol{\theta}))$ into $\hat{V}(\alpha,\gamma)$, that is, by employing the identity $\bar{V}(\boldsymbol{\theta}) \equiv \hat{V}(\alpha, t_0, \mathbf{x}_0, \bar{t}_1(\boldsymbol{\theta}), \bar{\mathbf{x}}_1(\boldsymbol{\theta}))$.

Stage 3: Derive the solution to problem (7) by substituting $\bar{\omega}(\boldsymbol{\theta}) \stackrel{\text{def}}{=} (\bar{t}_1(\boldsymbol{\theta}), \bar{\mathbf{x}}_1(\boldsymbol{\theta}))$ into the quadruplet $(\hat{\mathbf{z}}(t;\alpha,\gamma), \hat{\mathbf{v}}(t;\alpha,\gamma), \hat{\boldsymbol{\lambda}}(t;\alpha,\gamma), \hat{\mu}(t;\alpha,\gamma))$ from Stage 1, that is, use the identities

$$(\bar{\mathbf{z}}(t;\boldsymbol{\theta}), \bar{\mathbf{v}}(t;\boldsymbol{\theta})) \equiv (\hat{\mathbf{z}}(t;\alpha,t_0,\mathbf{x}_0,\bar{\omega}(\boldsymbol{\theta})), \hat{\mathbf{v}}(t;\alpha,t_0,\mathbf{x}_0,\bar{\omega}(\boldsymbol{\theta}))),$$
$$(\bar{\boldsymbol{\lambda}}(t;\boldsymbol{\theta}), \bar{\mu}(t;\boldsymbol{\theta})) \equiv (\hat{\boldsymbol{\lambda}}(t;\alpha,t_0,\mathbf{x}_0,\bar{\omega}(\boldsymbol{\theta})), \hat{\mu}(t;\alpha,t_0,\mathbf{x}_0,\bar{\omega}(\boldsymbol{\theta}))),$$

which hold for all $t \in [t_0, \bar{t}_1(\boldsymbol{\theta})]$. To see why the above identities must hold, we reason as follows. If the constraints in problem (8) [and thus problem (7)] are not binding, so that $\bar{t}_1(\boldsymbol{\theta}) < T$ and $\bar{\mathbf{x}}_1(\boldsymbol{\theta}) > \mathbf{x}_T$, then the solution to problem (2) when t_1 is held fixed at the value $\bar{t}_1(\boldsymbol{\theta})$ and $\mathbf{x}_1$ is held fixed at the value $\bar{\mathbf{x}}_1(\boldsymbol{\theta})$ is identical to the solution to problem (7), for in this instance, problems (2) and (7) are identical. On the other hand, if the constraints in problem (8) [and thus problem (7)] are binding, so that $\bar{t}_1(\boldsymbol{\theta}) = T$ and $\bar{\mathbf{x}}_1(\boldsymbol{\theta}) = \mathbf{x}_T$, then the solution to problem (2) when t_1 is held fixed at the value T and $\mathbf{x}_1$ is held fixed at the value $\mathbf{x}_T$ is identical to the solution to problem (7), for in this instance, problems (2) and (7) are again identical. Hence, the above identities hold whether the constraints in problem (7) bind or not.

Note that the identities in Stage 3 prove that the solution to problem (7) must satisfy the necessary conditions of Theorem 6.1, which as you may recall, apply to a fixed endpoint and fixed-time optimal control problem. To see this, recall that the quadruplet

$$(\hat{\mathbf{z}}(t;\boldsymbol{\alpha},t_0,\mathbf{x}_0,\bar{\boldsymbol{\omega}}(\boldsymbol{\theta})),\hat{\mathbf{v}}(t;\boldsymbol{\alpha},t_0,\mathbf{x}_0,\bar{\boldsymbol{\omega}}(\boldsymbol{\theta})),\hat{\boldsymbol{\lambda}}(t;\boldsymbol{\alpha},t_0,\mathbf{x}_0,\bar{\boldsymbol{\omega}}(\boldsymbol{\theta})),\hat{\boldsymbol{\mu}}(t;\boldsymbol{\alpha},t_0,\mathbf{x}_0,\bar{\boldsymbol{\omega}}(\boldsymbol{\theta})))$$

satisfies the necessary conditions of Theorem 6.1 because it solves the fixed endpoint and fixed-time problem (2) when $(t_1,\mathbf{x}_1) = (\bar{t}_1(\boldsymbol{\theta}),\bar{\mathbf{x}}_1(\boldsymbol{\theta}))$. Since the quadruplet $(\bar{\mathbf{z}}(t;\boldsymbol{\theta}),\bar{\mathbf{v}}(t;\boldsymbol{\theta}),\bar{\boldsymbol{\lambda}}(t;\boldsymbol{\theta}),\bar{\boldsymbol{\mu}}(t;\boldsymbol{\theta}))$ is identically equal to $(\hat{\mathbf{z}}(t;\boldsymbol{\alpha},t_0,\mathbf{x}_0,\bar{\boldsymbol{\omega}}(\boldsymbol{\theta}))$, $\hat{\mathbf{v}}(t;\boldsymbol{\alpha},t_0,\mathbf{x}_0,\bar{\boldsymbol{\omega}}(\boldsymbol{\theta}))$, $\hat{\boldsymbol{\lambda}}(t;\boldsymbol{\alpha},t_0,\mathbf{x}_0,\bar{\boldsymbol{\omega}}(\boldsymbol{\theta}))$, $\hat{\boldsymbol{\mu}}(t;\boldsymbol{\alpha},t_0,\mathbf{x}_0,\bar{\boldsymbol{\omega}}(\boldsymbol{\theta})))$, the quadruplet $(\bar{\mathbf{z}}(t;\boldsymbol{\theta}),\bar{\mathbf{v}}(t;\boldsymbol{\theta}),\bar{\boldsymbol{\lambda}}(t;\boldsymbol{\theta}),\bar{\boldsymbol{\mu}}(t;\boldsymbol{\theta}))$ must also satisfy the necessary conditions of Theorem 6.1. We are now in a position to state and prove the following theorem.

Theorem 10.2 (Inequality Constrained Transversality Conditions): *If $\hat{V}(\cdot) \in C^{(1)}\ \forall\, \boldsymbol{\beta} \in B(\boldsymbol{\beta}^\circ;\delta_2)$, then in addition to the necessary conditions of Theorem 6.1, the following transversality conditions are necessary for the inequality-constrained variable endpoint and variable time optimal control problem (7):*

$$\left.\begin{array}{l} H(\bar{t}_1(\boldsymbol{\theta}),\bar{\mathbf{z}}(\bar{t}_1(\boldsymbol{\theta});\boldsymbol{\theta}),\bar{\mathbf{v}}(\bar{t}_1(\boldsymbol{\theta});\boldsymbol{\theta}),\bar{\boldsymbol{\lambda}}(\bar{t}_1(\boldsymbol{\theta});\boldsymbol{\theta});\boldsymbol{\alpha}) \ge 0 \\ T - \bar{t}_1(\boldsymbol{\theta}) \ge 0 \\ H(\bar{t}_1(\boldsymbol{\theta}),\bar{\mathbf{z}}(\bar{t}_1(\boldsymbol{\theta});\boldsymbol{\theta}),\bar{\mathbf{v}}(\bar{t}_1(\boldsymbol{\theta});\boldsymbol{\theta}),\bar{\boldsymbol{\lambda}}(\bar{t}_1(\boldsymbol{\theta});\boldsymbol{\theta});\boldsymbol{\alpha})\,[T - \bar{t}_1(\boldsymbol{\theta})] = 0 \end{array}\right\}[t_1 \le T], \tag{9}$$

$$\left.\begin{array}{l} \bar{\lambda}_j(\bar{t}_1(\boldsymbol{\theta});\boldsymbol{\theta}) \ge 0, \quad j = 1,2,\ldots,N \\ \bar{z}_j(\bar{t}_1(\boldsymbol{\theta});\boldsymbol{\theta}) \ge x_{Tj}, \quad j = 1,2,\ldots,N \\ \bar{\lambda}_j(\bar{t}_1(\boldsymbol{\theta});\boldsymbol{\theta})\,[\bar{z}_j(\bar{t}_1(\boldsymbol{\theta});\boldsymbol{\theta}) - x_{Tj}] = 0, \quad j = 1,2,\ldots,N \end{array}\right\}[\mathbf{x}_1 \ge \mathbf{x}_T]. \tag{10}$$

Proof: Recall the static constrained optimization problem defined in Stage 2 above, namely,

$$\bar{V}(\boldsymbol{\theta}) \stackrel{\text{def}}{=} \max_{t_1,\mathbf{x}_1}\{\hat{V}(\boldsymbol{\alpha},\boldsymbol{\gamma}) \text{ s.t. } t_1 \le T, \mathbf{x}_1 \ge \mathbf{x}_T\},$$

and form the Lagrangian function associated with it:

$$L(t_1,\mathbf{x}_1,\chi,\boldsymbol{\varphi}) \stackrel{\text{def}}{=} \hat{V}(\boldsymbol{\alpha},t_0,\mathbf{x}_0,t_1,\mathbf{x}_1) + \chi[T - t_1] + \sum_{n=1}^{N}\varphi_n[x_{1n} - x_{Tn}],$$

where $(\chi,\boldsymbol{\varphi})$ are the Lagrange multipliers for the $N+1$ inequality constraints of the problem. The necessary conditions for the optimal choice of $(t_1,\mathbf{x}_1)$ are given by Theorem 18.4 of Simon and Blume (1994):

$$L_{t_1}(t_1, \mathbf{x}_1, \chi, \boldsymbol{\varphi}) = \hat{V}_{t_1}(\boldsymbol{\alpha}, t_0, \mathbf{x}_0, t_1, \mathbf{x}_1) - \chi = 0, \tag{11}$$

$$L_{x_{1j}}(t_1, \mathbf{x}_1, \chi, \boldsymbol{\varphi}) = \hat{V}_{x_{1j}}(\boldsymbol{\alpha}, t_0, \mathbf{x}_0, t_1, \mathbf{x}_1) + \varphi_j = 0, \quad j = 1, 2, \ldots, N, \tag{12}$$

$$L_{\chi}(t_1, \mathbf{x}_1, \chi, \boldsymbol{\varphi}) = T - t_1 \geq 0, \chi \geq 0, [T - t_1]\chi = 0, \tag{13}$$

$$L_{\varphi_j}(t_1, \mathbf{x}_1, \chi, \boldsymbol{\varphi}) = x_{1j} - x_{Tj} \geq 0, \varphi_j \geq 0, [x_{1j} - x_{Tj}]\varphi_j = 0, \quad j = 1, 2, \ldots, N. \tag{14}$$

These necessary conditions hold at $(t_1, \mathbf{x}_1) = (\bar{t}_1(\boldsymbol{\theta}), \bar{\mathbf{x}}_1(\boldsymbol{\theta}))$ by assumption. Now use part (iv) of Theorem 9.3 (the dynamic envelope theorem) and combine Eqs. (11) and (13) to derive

$$H(\bar{t}_1(\boldsymbol{\theta}), \hat{\mathbf{z}}(\bar{t}_1(\boldsymbol{\theta}); \boldsymbol{\alpha}, t_0, \mathbf{x}_0, \bar{\boldsymbol{\omega}}(\boldsymbol{\theta})), \hat{\mathbf{v}}(\bar{t}_1(\boldsymbol{\theta}); \boldsymbol{\alpha}, t_0, \mathbf{x}_0, \bar{\boldsymbol{\omega}}(\boldsymbol{\theta})),$$
$$\hat{\boldsymbol{\lambda}}(\bar{t}_1(\boldsymbol{\theta}); \boldsymbol{\alpha}, t_0, \mathbf{x}_0, \bar{\boldsymbol{\omega}}(\boldsymbol{\theta})); \boldsymbol{\alpha}) \geq 0, T - \bar{t}_1(\boldsymbol{\theta}) \geq 0,$$
$$H(\bar{t}_1(\boldsymbol{\theta}), \hat{\mathbf{z}}(\bar{t}_1(\boldsymbol{\theta}); \boldsymbol{\alpha}, t_0, \mathbf{x}_0, \bar{\boldsymbol{\omega}}(\boldsymbol{\theta})), \hat{\mathbf{v}}(\bar{t}_1(\boldsymbol{\theta}); \boldsymbol{\alpha}, t_0, \mathbf{x}_0, \bar{\boldsymbol{\omega}}(\boldsymbol{\theta})),$$
$$\hat{\boldsymbol{\lambda}}(\bar{t}_1(\boldsymbol{\theta}); \boldsymbol{\alpha}, t_0, \mathbf{x}_0, \bar{\boldsymbol{\omega}}(\boldsymbol{\theta})); \boldsymbol{\alpha})\,[T - \bar{t}_1(\boldsymbol{\theta})] = 0.$$

Note that the above derivatives are evaluated along the triplet $(\hat{\mathbf{z}}(t; \boldsymbol{\alpha}, \boldsymbol{\gamma}), \hat{\mathbf{v}}(t; \boldsymbol{\alpha}, \boldsymbol{\gamma}), \hat{\boldsymbol{\lambda}}(t; \boldsymbol{\alpha}, \boldsymbol{\gamma}))$, seeing as it corresponds to the optimal value function $\hat{V}(\cdot)$ being differentiated. Next, use part (v) of Theorem 9.3 and combine Eqs. (12) and (14) to derive

$$\hat{\lambda}_j(\bar{t}_1(\boldsymbol{\theta}); \boldsymbol{\alpha}, t_0, \mathbf{x}_0, \bar{\boldsymbol{\omega}}(\boldsymbol{\theta})) \geq 0, \bar{x}_{1j}(\boldsymbol{\theta}) - x_{Tj} \geq 0,$$
$$\hat{\lambda}_j(\bar{t}_1(\boldsymbol{\theta}); \boldsymbol{\alpha}, t_0, \mathbf{x}_0, \bar{\boldsymbol{\omega}}(\boldsymbol{\theta}))\,[\bar{x}_{1j}(\boldsymbol{\theta}) - x_{Tj}] = 0,$$

for $j = 1, 2, \ldots, N$. Using the identities of Stage 3 completes the proof. Q.E.D.

It should be clear that Theorem 10.2 is a generalization of Theorem 10.1. For example, if $\bar{t}_1(\boldsymbol{\theta}) < T$, implying that the terminal time constraint is not binding in problem (7), then Eq. (9) of Theorem 10.2 implies that value of the Hamiltonian vanishes at the terminal time, which is Eq. (5) of Theorem 10.1. Likewise, if $\bar{\mathbf{x}}_1(\boldsymbol{\theta}) > \mathbf{x}_T$, so that the terminal state constraint is not binding in problem (7), then Eq. (10) of Theorem 10.2 implies that the value of the costate vector is zero at the terminal time, which is Eq. (6) of Theorem 10.1. In other words, if the constraint is not binding, we are in the variable endpoint and variable time world, so Theorem 10.1 applies.

Conversely, if the value of the Hamiltonian is positive at the terminal date, then Eq. (9) of Theorem 10.2 implies that the terminal time constraint is binding in an optimal plan. Similarly, if the value of the costate vector is positive at the terminal date, then Eq. (10) of Theorem 10.2 implies that the terminal state constraint is binding in an optimal plan. Hence, Theorem 10.2 is just a *complementary slackness* theorem for inequality-constrained variable endpoints and variable time control problems, not unlike that encountered in linear and nonlinear programming.

In passing, observe that if a subset of the elements of the vector $\boldsymbol{\gamma} \stackrel{\text{def}}{=} (t_0, \mathbf{x}_0, t_1, \mathbf{x}_1)$ are decision variables in problem (1), say, $(t_1, \mathbf{x}_1)$, so that we are dealing with a variable terminal endpoint and terminal time optimal control problem, then only a subset of the necessary conditions of Theorem 10.1 apply, videlicet, Eqs. (5) and (6) in this instance. The veracity of this claim follows from the fact that the first-order necessary conditions are identical for the choice of $(t_1, \mathbf{x}_1)$ regardless of whether $(t_0, \mathbf{x}_0)$ are held parametrically fixed or are decision variables. The values of $(t_1, \mathbf{x}_1)$, however, differ, in general, depending on whether $(t_0, \mathbf{x}_0)$ are held parametrically fixed or are decision variables. This observation obviously carries over for any subset of the elements of the vector $\gamma \overset{\text{def}}{=} (t_0, \mathbf{x}_0, t_1, \mathbf{x}_1)$ that are choice or decision variables.

We now pause to illustrate how Theorem 10.2 is often used in economics. Note that we will provide an economic interpretation of the resulting necessary conditions, but will not actually solve them for an explicit solution.

Example 10.1: Let's reconsider the Hotelling model of a resource extracting firm, but now allow the firm to choose how much of the natural resource to leave in the ground when it decides to terminate its mining operation. Assume that the mining firm is a price taker in both the input and output markets. The firm is asserted to solve the static cost minimization problem

$$C(x, q; w) \overset{\text{def}}{=} \min_L \{w\, L \text{ s.t. } q = f(x, L)\}$$

at each point in the planning horizon, where $L > 0$ is the variable input used in extracting the resource from the ground, $w > 0$ is the unit price of the variable input, q is the extraction rate of the resource from the ground (or the output from the mine), x is the stock of the natural resource in the ground, $C(\cdot)$ is the minimum cost function, and $f(\cdot) \in C^{(2)}$ is the production function, assumed to have the typical properties, scilicet,

$$f_x(x, L) > 0,\ f_L(x, L) > 0,\ f_{xL}(x, L) \geq 0,$$

$$f_{xx}(x, L) < 0,\ f_{LL}(x, L) < 0,\ f_{xx}(x, L) f_{LL}(x, L) - [f_{xL}(x, L)]^2 > 0.$$

Given these properties for $f(\cdot)$, you will show in a mental exercise that $C(\cdot)$ satisfies

$$C \in C^{(2)},\ C_x(x, q; w) < 0,\ C_q(x, q; w) > 0,\ C_{qx}(x, q; w) < 0,$$

$$C_{xx}(x, q; w) > 0,\ C_{qq}(x, q; w) > 0,\ C_{xx}(x, q; w) C_{qq}(x, q; w) - [C_{qx}(x, q; w)]^2 > 0.$$

The optimal control problem can therefore be stated as

$$V(p, r, w, x_0) \overset{\text{def}}{=} \max_{q(\cdot), T, x_T} \int_0^T [p q(t) - C(x(t), q(t); w)]\, e^{-rt}\, dt$$

$$\text{s.t. } \dot{x}(t) = -q(t),\ x(0) = x_0,\ x(T) = x_T \geq 0,$$

$$q(t) \in U \overset{\text{def}}{=} \{q(\cdot) : q(t) \geq 0\},$$

where $p > 0$ is the constant output price and $r > 0$ is the discount rate. Note that we are implicitly assuming that the firm wants to be in the extraction business, in that we are presuming that the optimal T satisfies $T > 0$. This allows us to ignore the natural inequality constraint $T \geq 0$. You are asked to investigate the consequences of this constraint in a mental exercise. Notice that the optimal value function $V(\cdot)$ does not depend on (T, x_T), because they are decision variables in the present formulation of the mining problem.

To solve this problem, first form the Hamiltonian $H(t, x, q, \lambda) \stackrel{\text{def}}{=} [pq - C(x, q; w)]\, e^{-rt} - \lambda q$. Applying Theorem 10.2 yields the necessary conditions

$$H_q(t, x, q, \lambda) = [p - C_q(x, q; w)]\, e^{-rt} - \lambda \leq 0,\ q \geq 0,$$

$$\big[[p - C_q(x, q; w)]\, e^{-rt} - \lambda\big] q = 0,$$

$$\dot{x} = H_\lambda(t, x, q, \lambda) = -q,\ x(0) = x_0,$$

$$\dot{\lambda} = -H_x(t, x, q, \lambda) = C_x(x, q; w)\, e^{-rt},$$

$$H(T, x(T), q(T), \lambda(T)) \stackrel{\text{def}}{=} [pq(T) - C(x(T), q(T); w)]\, e^{-rt} - \lambda(T)q(T) = 0,$$

$$\lambda(T) \geq 0,\ x(T) \geq 0,\ \lambda(T)x(T) = 0.$$

Recall that the necessary conditions of Theorem 6.1 are part of those from Theorem 10.2. Let's now turn to an economic interpretation of these necessary conditions.

To begin, first note that $\lambda(t)$ is the *present value* shadow price of the unextracted resource at time t, since the optimal value function of the mining firm represents the maximum value of profits from its optimal mining plan discounted to time zero, the initial period of the planning horizon. If $q(t) > 0$ at any moment $t \in [0, T]$, then the necessary condition $H_q q = 0$ implies that $H_q = 0$, or equivalently, that $p - C_q(x, q; w) = \lambda e^{rt} \stackrel{\text{def}}{=} \mu$, where μ is the *current value* shadow price of the unextracted natural resource. This equation asserts that if at any moment in time it is optimal to extract the resource at a positive rate, then marginal profit must equal the current value shadow price of a unit of the resource in situ, that is, the resource in its natural environment. Thus the current value shadow price μ of the unextracted natural resource represents the amount by which the price of the extracted nonrenewable resource exceeds its marginal cost of extraction. That μ is positive follows intuitively from the observation that the stock of the unextracted natural resource is a good to the mining firm. In a mental exercise, you are asked to show that this intuition can be confirmed mathematically.

Turning to the costate equation $\dot{\lambda} = C_x(x, q; w)\, e^{-rt}$ and recalling that $C_x(x, q; w) < 0$, we see that the present value shadow price of the unextracted resource falls over the planning horizon. This, however, does not imply that the current value shadow price μ falls over the planning horizon. To see this, recall that $\mu \stackrel{\text{def}}{=} \lambda e^{rt}$, so that upon using the costate equation, we find that $\dot{\mu} = r\lambda e^{rt} + \dot{\lambda} e^{rt} = r\mu +$

$C_x(x, q; w)$. Because $C_x(x, q; w) < 0$ and $\mu > 0$, it is clear that the current value shadow price μ may be rising or falling over the planning horizon. The state equation implies that the rate of change of the stock can't be positive, since $\dot{x} = -q$ and $q \geq 0$. This is intuitive too, in view of the fact that without discovery of new resource deposits (which we have implicitly assumed to be zero), the stock of the resource in the ground cannot increase over time.

Now consider the transversality condition for the terminal stock of the resource. If the firm finds it optimal to leave some of the resource stock in the ground as the horizon comes to a close, that is, if $x(T) = x_T > 0$, then $\lambda(T)x(T) = 0$ implies that the present value shadow price of the stock in situ is zero at the terminal date of the planning horizon, that is, $\lambda(T) = 0$. Intuitively, this result says that if the firm decides to leave some of the resource in the ground as the planning horizon comes to a close, then they must not place any value on having another unit in situ, because they didn't find it optimal to extract all of what was there to begin with. Given that $C_x(x, q; w) < 0$ and $C_{qx}(x, q; w) < 0$, that is, because extraction costs and marginal extraction costs rise as the stock is depleted, this is likely to be the outcome in the model. Conversely, if the firm places a positive present value shadow price on the stock in situ at the terminal date, that is, if $\lambda(T) > 0$, then $\lambda(T)x(T) = 0$ implies that the entire stock of the resource will be extracted from the ground as the horizon comes to a close, that is, $x(T) = 0$. This makes economic sense too, for if the firm finds it optimal to extract all of the resource from its environment by the end of the planning period, then it would surely place a positive shadow value on another unit of the resource in situ.

Finally, turn to the transversality condition for the choice of the planning horizon, namely, $[pq(T) - C(x(T), q(T); w)]\, e^{-rt} - \lambda(T)q(T) = 0$. If we continue to assume that $x(T) = x_T > 0$ in an optimal plan, then $\lambda(T) = 0$, as noted above. In this instance, the transversality condition reduces to the simpler form

$$pq(T) - C(x(T), q(T); w) = 0.$$

This necessary condition asserts that if the firm finds it optimal to leave some of the resource stock in the ground at the terminal date of the planning horizon, then the optimal terminal date should be chosen such that total revenue equals total cost, or equivalently, such that profit is zero. Furthermore, if in addition, the firm finds it optimal to extract in the final period, that is, $q(T) > 0$, then $H_q(T, x(T), q(T), \lambda(T)) = 0$, as noted above. Upon combining the previous simplified transversality condition with this latter one, we have

$$p = C_q(x(T), q(T); w),$$

$$p = \frac{C(x(T), q(T); w)}{q(T)},$$

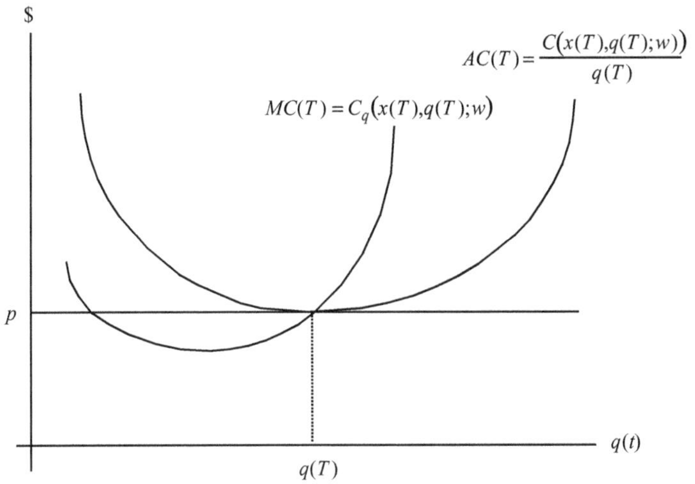

Figure 10.1

as the form of the two transversality conditions under the stated assumptions. Equating the previous two transversality conditions yields

$$MC(T) \stackrel{\text{def}}{=} C_q(x(T), q(T); w) = \frac{C(x(T), q(T); w)}{q(T)} \stackrel{\text{def}}{=} AC(T).$$

To sum up, we have shown that if $x(T) = x_T > 0$ and $q(T) > 0$ in an optimal plan, then at the optimal terminal date of the firm's planning horizon, its profit is zero and its marginal cost of production equals its average cost of production. Therefore, in the final period of its planning horizon under the given assumptions, the mining firm acts just like a prototypical static profit maximizing price-taking firm in long-run competitive industry equilibrium. Figure 10.1 presents a graphical representation of these conclusions.

Notice that because $MC(T) = AC(T)$, the mining firm must be at the minimum of $AC(T)$. Moreover, for the minimum of $AC(T)$ to occur at some $q(T) > 0$, the $AC(T)$ curve must be U-shaped, which can only occur if the mining firm faces some fixed cost of extraction. Finally, note that there are other configurations for the values of the resource stock, the extraction rate, and the current value shadow price of the stock that may occur in the terminal period of the planning horizon. You are asked to explore some of these in a mental exercise.

Before considering a more general set of transversality conditions, let's examine another economic problem and actually use the transversality conditions to find the explicit solution of the necessary conditions. The ubiquitous inventory accumulation problem turns out to be an excellent problem to which to apply

Theorem 10.1 for the reason that we can solve the necessary conditions for an explicit solution.

Example 10.2: A simple but rich variant of the workhorse inventory accumulation problem has the delivery date as a decision variable:

$$C(c_1, c_2, x_T) \stackrel{\text{def}}{=} \min_{u(\cdot),T} \int_0^T \left[c_1[u(t)]^2 + c_2 x(t)\right] dt$$

$$\text{s.t.} \quad \dot{x}(t) = u(t),\ x(0) = 0,\ x(T) = x_T.$$

Let's ignore the nonnegativity constraint on the production rate to begin with. If it turns out that the production rate is negative for some interval of time, we will then go back and explicitly include it in the control problem. Note that because T is a choice variable in this version of the problem, it does not appear as an argument of the minimum cost function $C(\cdot)$.

The Hamiltonian is given by $H(x, u, \lambda) \stackrel{\text{def}}{=} c_1 u^2 + c_2 x + \lambda u$, so that by Theorem 10.1, the necessary conditions are

$$H_u(x, u, \lambda) = 2c_1 u + \lambda = 0,$$

$$\dot{\lambda} = -H_x(x, u, \lambda) = -c_2,$$

$$\dot{x} = H_\lambda(x, u, \lambda) = u,\ x(0) = 0,\ x(T) = x_T,$$

$$H(x(T), u(T), \lambda(T)) = c_1[u(T)]^2 + c_2 x(T) + \lambda(T)u(T) = 0.$$

Solving $H_u(x, u, \lambda) = 2c_1 u + \lambda = 0$ for the control gives $u = -\lambda/2c_1$. The solution to the costate equation is easily found to be $\lambda(t) = -c_2 t + k_1$, where k_1 is a constant of integration. The general solution for the production rate is then given by $v(t) = c_2 t/2c_1 - k_1/2c_1$. Substituting this into the state equation yields $\dot{x} = c_2 t/2c_1 - k_1/2c_1$, which, upon separating the variables and integrating, gives the general solution $z(t) = c_2 t^2/4c_1 - k_1 t/2c_1 + k_2$, where k_2 is another constant of integration. Notice our strategy: we solve the necessary conditions, treating T as if it was a known constant, after which we solve for the constants of integration and the delivery date T.

The three equations we will use to find the three unknowns (k_1, k_2, T) are the initial condition $x(0) = 0$, the terminal endpoint condition $x(T) = x_T$, and the free terminal-time transversality condition $H(z(T), v(T), \lambda(T)) = 0$. First of all, it is easy to see that the initial condition $x(0) = 0$ implies that $k_2 = 0$. Next, substitute the general solution of the necessary conditions into the free terminal-time transversality condition $H(z(T), v(T), \lambda(T)) = 0$, and then simplify the result to get the equation

$$-\frac{1}{4c_1}k_1^2 + k_2 = 0.$$

Given that $k_2 = 0$, it follows from the above equation that $k_1 = 0$ too. Finally, apply the (fixed) terminal endpoint condition $x(T) = x_T$ to the general solution $z(t) = c_2 t^2/4c_1 - k_1 t/2c_1 + k_2$ of the state equation to arrive at

$$\frac{c_2 T^2}{4c_1} - \frac{k_1 T}{2c_1} + k_2 = x_T.$$

Because $k_1 = 0$ and $k_2 = 0$, this equation simplifies to $T^2 = 4c_1 x_T/c_2$. Clearly, there are two values of T that satisfy this equation, namely, $T = \pm 2\sqrt{c_1 x_T/c_2}$. For the control problem to make economic sense, we take the positive square root; thus $T^*(c_1, c_2, x_T) = 2\sqrt{c_1 x_T/c_2} > 0$. Recalling that $k_1 = 0$ and $k_2 = 0$, the specific solution of the necessary conditions is given by

$$T^*(c_1, c_2, x_T) = 2\sqrt{c_1 x_T/c_2} > 0,$$

$$z^*(t; c_1, c_2) = \frac{1}{4}c_1^{-1} c_2 t^2 \geq 0 \,\forall\, t \in [0, T^*(c_1, c_2, x_T)],$$

$$v^*(t; c_1, c_2) = \frac{1}{2}c_1^{-1} c_2 t \geq 0 \,\forall\, t \in [0, T^*(c_1, c_2, x_T)],$$

$$\lambda^*(t; c_2) = -c_2 t \leq 0 \,\forall\, t \in [0, T^*(c_1, c_2, x_T)].$$

Take note of the fact that the shadow cost of the inventory stock $\lambda^*(t; c_2) = -c_2 t$ is less than or equal to zero for the entire planning horizon. You are asked in a mental exercise to provide the economic intuition for this result. Also observe that the production rate is nonnegative throughout the planning horizon, so our strategy of ignoring the nonnegativity constraint on the production rate was without problems.

Let's now investigate the comparative dynamic properties of the solution to the necessary conditions of the above inventory accumulation problem, and compare them with those derived from the fixed time horizon version of the model given in Example 4.5 and Mental Exercise 4.15. To this end, differentiate the above solution of the necessary conditions with respect to the size of the order x_T to get

$$\frac{\partial T^*}{\partial x_T}(c_1, c_2, x_T) = \left[c_1 c_2^{-1} x_T\right]^{-\frac{1}{2}} c_1 c_2^{-1} > 0,$$

$$\frac{\partial z^*}{\partial x_T}(t; c_1, c_2) = \frac{\partial v^*}{\partial x_T}(t; c_1, c_2) = \frac{\partial \lambda^*}{\partial x_T}(t; c_2) \equiv 0.$$

The second set of equations implies that an increase in the size of the order doesn't affect the inventory level, the production rate, or the shadow value of the inventory. Hence the way the firm elects to meet the larger order is to produce over a longer period. This result contrasts sharply with that when the delivery date is fixed (see Mental Exercise 4.15), in which case, all the adjustments in the plan come from increasing the production rate. Moreover, by the dynamic envelope theorem,

$$\frac{\partial C}{\partial x_T}(c_1, c_2, x_T) = -\lambda^*(T^*(c_1, c_2, x_T); c_2) > 0.$$

Thus, not surprisingly, an increase in the size of the order drives up minimum production costs. This is true whether the horizon is fixed or a choice variable.

Now differentiate the solution of the necessary conditions with respect to the unit cost of holding inventory c_2:

$$\frac{\partial T^*}{\partial c_2}(c_1, c_2, x_T) = -\left[c_1 c_2^{-1} x_T\right]^{-\frac{1}{2}} c_1 c_2^{-2} x_T < 0,$$

$$\frac{\partial z^*}{\partial c_2}(t; c_1, c_2) = \frac{1}{4} c_1^{-1} t^2 \geq 0 \, \forall \, t \in [0, T^*(c_1, c_2, x_T)],$$

$$\frac{\partial v^*}{\partial c_2}(t; c_1, c_2) = \frac{1}{2} c_1^{-1} t \geq 0 \, \forall \, t \in [0, T^*(c_1, c_2, x_T)],$$

$$\frac{\partial \lambda^*}{\partial c_2}(t; c_2) = -t \leq 0 \, \forall \, t \in [0, T^*(c_1, c_2, x_T)].$$

The economic interpretation here is that an increase in the unit holding cost of inventory results in the firm shortening the delivery date, as holding the goods in inventory now costs more. Given the shorter planning period and the fact that the same amount of the good is still required to be produced, the higher unit holding cost results in a higher production rate and thus a higher inventory level at each moment in the planning horizon, except for the initial date, when neither is affected. In addition, the shadow value of the inventory falls. In contrast, when the planning horizon is fixed, Example 4.5 showed that the increase in the unit holding cost of inventory caused the production rate to decrease and the shadow value of the inventory to increase in the first half of the planning horizon, and the production rate to increase and the shadow value of the inventory to decrease in the second half of the planning horizon, such that total production was unchanged. Moreover, by the dynamic envelope theorem

$$\frac{\partial C}{\partial c_2}(c_1, c_2, x_T) = \int_0^T \frac{\partial H}{\partial c_2}(x, u, \lambda)\bigg|_{\substack{\text{optimal} \\ \text{solution}}} dt = \int_0^{T^*(c_1, c_2, x_T)} z^*(t; c_1, c_2)\, dt > 0.$$

This calculation confirms the intuitive conclusion that the higher holding cost of inventory also drives up the firm's minimum cost of production.

Finally, differentiate the solution of the necessary conditions with respect to the production cost coefficient c_1:

$$\frac{\partial T^*}{\partial c_1}(c_1, c_2, x_T) = \left[c_1 c_2^{-1} x_T\right]^{-\frac{1}{2}} c_2^{-1} x_T > 0,$$

$$\frac{\partial z^*}{\partial c_1}(t; c_1, c_2) = -\frac{1}{4} c_2 c_1^{-2} t^2 \leq 0 \,\forall\, t \in [0, T^*(c_1, c_2, x_T)],$$

$$\frac{\partial v^*}{\partial c_1}(t; c_1, c_2) = -\frac{1}{2} c_2 c_1^{-2} t \leq 0 \,\forall\, t \in [0, T^*(c_1, c_2, x_T)],$$

$$\frac{\partial \lambda^*}{\partial c_1}(t; c_2) \equiv 0.$$

These comparative dynamic results also have a straightforward economic interpretation. With higher production costs, the firm spreads them out over a longer period. Given the longer production period and the fact that the same number of units are required to be produced, the firm will produce them at a slower rate and carry less inventory at each moment of the planning horizon, thereby resulting in no effect on the shadow value of the inventory. In contrast, with the planning horizon fixed, Mental Exercise 4.15 showed that an increase in the production cost coefficient increased the production rate in the first half of the planning horizon and decreased it in the second half of the planning horizon, with the shadow value of the inventory being lower throughout. Regardless of whether T is fixed or a decision variable, however, the firm's minimum cost of production will increase, since

$$\frac{\partial C}{\partial c_1}(c_1, c_2, x_T) = \int_0^T \frac{\partial H}{\partial c_1}(x, u, \lambda)\bigg|_{\substack{\text{optimal}\\ \text{solution}}} dt = \int_0^{T^*(c_1, c_2, x_T)} [v^*(t; c_1, c_2)]^2 \, dt > 0$$

by the dynamic envelope theorem.

In Example 10.2, we applied the dynamic envelope theorem, that is, Theorem 9.1, to it to discern the effects of various parameters on the firm's minimum cost of production. Recall that the dynamic envelope theorems proven in Chapter 9 were established for a fixed-time and fixed endpoints optimal control problem. In the production planning problem of Example 10.2, however, the terminal time was a decision variable. Is it correct, therefore, to apply Theorem 9.1 to an optimal control problem that is not, strictly speaking, covered by it? The answer is yes, as we now proceed to demonstrate. More generally, we will show that the pertinent formulas of Theorems 9.1 and 9.3 remain valid when any subset of the $2n + 2$ element vector $(t_0, \mathbf{x}_0, t_1, \mathbf{x}_1)$ are decision variables. This claim follows directly from the Stage 2 argument underlying the proof of the transversality condition and the prototype static envelope theorem.

To see this, consider, for example, a control problem that has $(t_1, \mathbf{x}_1)$ as decision variables. Then the Stage 2 problem to find the relevant transversality conditions is given by

$$\breve{V}(\alpha, t_0, \mathbf{x}_0) \stackrel{\text{def}}{=} \max_{t_1, \mathbf{x}_1} \hat{V}(\alpha, t_0, \mathbf{x}_0, t_1, \mathbf{x}_1),$$

where $\breve{V}(\cdot)$ is the optimal value function for the control problem with $(t_1, \mathbf{x}_1)$ as decision variables and $\hat{V}(\cdot)$ is the optimal value function for control problem (2), where $(t_0, \mathbf{x}_0, t_1, \mathbf{x}_1)$ are fixed. An application of the prototype envelope theorem to the above unconstrained static optimization problem relating $\breve{V}(\cdot)$ to $\hat{V}(\cdot)$ yields

$$\breve{V}_{\alpha}(\alpha, t_0, \mathbf{x}_0) = \hat{V}_{\alpha}(\alpha, t_0, \mathbf{x}_0, t_1, \mathbf{x}_1)\Big|_{\substack{\text{optimal}\\ \text{solution}}},$$

$$\breve{V}_{t_0}(\alpha, t_0, \mathbf{x}_0) = \hat{V}_{t_0}(\alpha, t_0, \mathbf{x}_0, t_1, \mathbf{x}_1)\Big|_{\substack{\text{optimal}\\ \text{solution}}},$$

$$\breve{V}_{\mathbf{x}_0}(\alpha, t_0, \mathbf{x}_0) = \hat{V}_{\mathbf{x}_0}(\alpha, t_0, \mathbf{x}_0, t_1, \mathbf{x}_1)\Big|_{\substack{\text{optimal}\\ \text{solution}}}.$$

This proves that the envelope results for the parameters $(\alpha, t_0, \mathbf{x}_0)$ of the optimal control problem with $(t_1, \mathbf{x}_1)$ as decision variables are *identical* to the envelope results for the fixed-time and fixed endpoints optimal control problems of Theorems 9.1 and 9.3, as claimed.

Before turning to sufficient conditions, let's examine the transversality conditions for one more economically important class of optimal control problems. Specifically, the last generalization of importance for economic problems is the variable endpoint and variable time *salvage value* or *scrap value* class of control problems that we encountered earlier. This class of control problems is given by

$$\tilde{V}(\alpha) \stackrel{\text{def}}{=} \max_{\mathbf{u}(\cdot), t_0, \mathbf{x}_0, t_1, \mathbf{x}_1} \left\{ \int_{t_0}^{t_1} f(t, \mathbf{x}(t), \mathbf{u}(t); \alpha)\, dt + S(t_0, \mathbf{x}_0, t_1, \mathbf{x}_1; \alpha) \right\} \tag{15}$$

$$\text{s.t.} \quad \dot{\mathbf{x}}(t) = \mathbf{g}(t, \mathbf{x}(t), \mathbf{u}(t); \alpha), \;\; \mathbf{x}(t_0) = \mathbf{x}_0, \;\; \mathbf{x}(t_1) = \mathbf{x}_1,$$

$$h^k(t, \mathbf{x}(t), \mathbf{u}(t); \alpha) \geq 0, \quad k = 1, 2, \ldots, K',$$

$$h^k(t, \mathbf{x}(t), \mathbf{u}(t); \alpha) = 0, \quad k = K'+1, K'+2, \ldots, K,$$

where $S(\cdot) \in C^{(1)}$ is the salvage value function. Assume that an optimal solution $(\tilde{\mathbf{z}}(t;\alpha), \tilde{\mathbf{v}}(t;\alpha))$ exists to problem (15) for all $\alpha \in B(\alpha^{\circ}; \delta_4)$, with corresponding costate vector $\tilde{\boldsymbol{\lambda}}(t;\alpha)$ and Lagrange multiplier vector $\tilde{\boldsymbol{\mu}}(t;\alpha)$, and let $\tilde{\gamma}(\alpha) \stackrel{\text{def}}{=} (\tilde{t}_0(\alpha), \tilde{\mathbf{x}}_0(\alpha), \tilde{t}_1(\alpha), \tilde{\mathbf{x}}_1(\alpha))$ be the optimal solution for the initial and terminal values of the horizon and state vector, where $B(\alpha^{\circ}; \delta_4)$ is an open A – ball centered at the given value of the parameter vector $\boldsymbol{\alpha}^{\circ}$ of radius $\delta_4 > 0$. Because the initial and terminal dates and states are optimally chosen, the optimal value function and solution functions for problem (15) depend only on the parameter vector $\boldsymbol{\alpha}$. Given the above definitions, it should be clear that we have the identities $\tilde{\mathbf{x}}_0(\boldsymbol{\alpha}) \equiv \tilde{\mathbf{z}}(\tilde{t}_0(\boldsymbol{\alpha}); \boldsymbol{\alpha})$ and $\tilde{\mathbf{x}}_1(\boldsymbol{\alpha}) \equiv \tilde{\mathbf{z}}(\tilde{t}_1(\boldsymbol{\alpha}); \boldsymbol{\alpha})$.

The ensuing theorem is not unexpected at this point if you have been following and understanding the prior development of the transversality conditions. Consequently, its proof is left for a mental exercise.

Theorem 10.3 (Scrap Value Transversality Conditions): *If* $\hat{V}(\cdot) \in C^{(1)}\,\forall\,\boldsymbol{\beta} \in B(\boldsymbol{\beta}^{\circ}; \delta_2)$, *then in addition to the necessary conditions of Theorem 6.1, the following transversality conditions are necessary for the variable endpoint and variable time scrap value optimal control problem (15):*

$$H(\tilde{t}_0(\boldsymbol{\alpha}), \tilde{\mathbf{z}}(\tilde{t}_0(\boldsymbol{\alpha}); \boldsymbol{\alpha}), \tilde{\mathbf{v}}(\tilde{t}_0(\boldsymbol{\alpha}); \boldsymbol{\alpha}), \tilde{\boldsymbol{\lambda}}(\tilde{t}_0(\boldsymbol{\alpha}); \boldsymbol{\alpha}); \boldsymbol{\alpha})$$
$$= \frac{\partial S}{\partial t_0}(\tilde{t}_0(\boldsymbol{\alpha}), \tilde{\mathbf{x}}_0(\boldsymbol{\alpha}), \tilde{t}_1(\boldsymbol{\alpha}), \tilde{\mathbf{x}}_1(\boldsymbol{\alpha}); \boldsymbol{\alpha}) \; [t_0 \text{ free}], \tag{16}$$

$$\tilde{\lambda}_j(\tilde{t}_0(\boldsymbol{\alpha}); \boldsymbol{\alpha}) = -\frac{\partial S}{\partial x_{0j}}(\tilde{t}_0(\boldsymbol{\alpha}), \tilde{\mathbf{x}}_0(\boldsymbol{\alpha}), \tilde{t}_1(\boldsymbol{\alpha}), \tilde{\mathbf{x}}_1(\boldsymbol{\alpha})), \quad j = 1, 2, \ldots, N \; [\mathbf{x}_0 \text{ free}], \tag{17}$$

$$H(\tilde{t}_1(\boldsymbol{\alpha}), \tilde{\mathbf{z}}(\tilde{t}_1(\boldsymbol{\alpha}); \boldsymbol{\alpha}), \tilde{\mathbf{v}}(\tilde{t}_1(\boldsymbol{\alpha}); \boldsymbol{\alpha}), \tilde{\boldsymbol{\lambda}}(\tilde{t}_1(\boldsymbol{\alpha}); \boldsymbol{\alpha}); \boldsymbol{\alpha})$$
$$= -\frac{\partial S}{\partial t_1}(\tilde{t}_0(\boldsymbol{\alpha}), \tilde{\mathbf{x}}_0(\boldsymbol{\alpha}), \tilde{t}_1(\boldsymbol{\alpha}), \tilde{\mathbf{x}}_1(\boldsymbol{\alpha}); \boldsymbol{\alpha}) \; [t_1 \text{ free}], \tag{18}$$

$$\tilde{\lambda}_j(\tilde{t}_1(\boldsymbol{\alpha}); \boldsymbol{\alpha}) = \frac{\partial S}{\partial x_{1j}}(\tilde{t}_0(\boldsymbol{\alpha}), \tilde{\mathbf{x}}_0(\boldsymbol{\alpha}), \tilde{t}_1(\boldsymbol{\alpha}), \tilde{\mathbf{x}}_1(\boldsymbol{\alpha})), \quad j = 1, 2, \ldots, N \; [\mathbf{x}_1 \text{free}]. \tag{19}$$

The final issue in this chapter concerns sufficiency conditions for the free endpoint version of the salvage value control problem (15). It turns out that it is difficult to find sufficient conditions of any practical value for control problems in which the starting and/or ending dates of the planning horizon are choice variables because of an inherent lack of convexity properties in such problems. We will therefore not present such a theorem, but instead refer you to Seierstad and Sydsæter (1987, Chapter 2, Section 9) for a promising sufficiency theorem.

The final theorem of the chapter contains what should not be an unexpected result for the following *variable endpoint* version of the scrap value optimal control problem (15):

$$\widehat{V}(\boldsymbol{\varphi}) \stackrel{\text{def}}{=} \max_{\mathbf{u}(\cdot), \mathbf{x}_0, \mathbf{x}_1} \left\{ \int_{t_0}^{t_1} f(t, \mathbf{x}(t), \mathbf{u}(t); \boldsymbol{\alpha})\, dt + S(t_0, \mathbf{x}_0, t_1, \mathbf{x}_1; \boldsymbol{\alpha}) \right\}$$
$$\text{s.t.} \quad \dot{\mathbf{x}}(t) = \mathbf{g}(t, \mathbf{x}(t), \mathbf{u}(t); \boldsymbol{\alpha}), \; \mathbf{x}(t_0) = \mathbf{x}_0, \; \mathbf{x}(t_1) = \mathbf{x}_1, \tag{20}$$

$$h^k(t, \mathbf{x}(t), \mathbf{u}(t); \alpha) \geq 0, \; k = 1, 2, \ldots, K',$$

$$h^k(t, \mathbf{x}(t), \mathbf{u}(t); \alpha) = 0, \; k = K'+1, K'+2, \ldots, K,$$

where $\varphi \stackrel{\text{def}}{=} (\alpha, t_0, t_1)$ are fixed (or given) parameters but $(\mathbf{x}_0, \mathbf{x}_1)$ are now decision variables. Assume that an optimal solution $(\hat{\mathbf{z}}(t;\varphi), \hat{\mathbf{v}}(t;\varphi))$ exists to problem (20) for all $\varphi \in B(\varphi^\circ; \delta_5)$, with corresponding costate vector $\hat{\boldsymbol{\lambda}}(t;\varphi)$ and Lagrange multiplier vector $\hat{\boldsymbol{\mu}}(t;\varphi)$, and furthermore let $\hat{\boldsymbol{\Psi}}(\varphi) \stackrel{\text{def}}{=} (\hat{\mathbf{x}}_0(\varphi), \hat{\mathbf{x}}_1(\varphi))$ be the optimal solution for the initial and terminal values of the state vector, where $B(\varphi^\circ; \delta_5)$ is an open $2 + A$ – ball centered at the given value of the parameter vector φ° of radius $\delta_5 > 0$. Given the above definitions, it should again be clear that we have the identities $\hat{\mathbf{x}}_0(\varphi) \equiv \hat{\mathbf{z}}(t_0;\varphi)$ and $\hat{\mathbf{x}}_1(\varphi) \equiv \hat{\mathbf{z}}(t_1;\varphi)$.

The following sufficiency theorem can be proven following the approach given in Chapter 6, and so is left for a mental exercise.

Theorem 10.4 (Mangasarian Sufficient Conditions, Scrap Value): *Let $(\hat{\mathbf{z}}(t;\varphi)$, $\hat{\mathbf{v}}(t;\varphi))$ be an admissible pair for problem* (20). *Suppose that $(\hat{\mathbf{z}}(t;\varphi), \hat{\mathbf{v}}(t;\varphi))$ satisfies the appropriate subset of the necessary conditions of Theorem 10.3 with corresponding costate vector $\hat{\boldsymbol{\lambda}}(t;\varphi)$ and Lagrange multiplier vector $\hat{\boldsymbol{\mu}}(t;\varphi)$, and let $L(t, \mathbf{x}, \mathbf{u}, \boldsymbol{\lambda}, \boldsymbol{\mu}) \stackrel{\text{def}}{=} f(t, \mathbf{x}, \mathbf{u}) + \boldsymbol{\lambda}'\mathbf{g}(t, \mathbf{x}, \mathbf{u}) + \boldsymbol{\mu}'\mathbf{h}(t, \mathbf{x}, \mathbf{u})$ be the value of the Lagrangian function. If $L(\cdot)$ is a concave function of $(\mathbf{x}, \mathbf{u}) \, \forall \, t \in [t_0, t_1]$ over an open convex set containing all the admissible values of $(\mathbf{x}(\cdot), \mathbf{u}(\cdot))$ when the costate vector is $\hat{\boldsymbol{\lambda}}(t;\varphi)$ and Lagrange multiplier vector is $\hat{\boldsymbol{\mu}}(t;\varphi)$, and $S(\cdot)$ is a concave function of $(\mathbf{x}_0, \mathbf{x}_1)$ over an open convex set containing all the admissible values of $\mathbf{x}(\cdot)$, then $\hat{\mathbf{v}}(t;\varphi)$ is an optimal control and $(\hat{\mathbf{z}}(t;\varphi), \hat{\mathbf{v}}(t;\varphi))$ yields the absolute maximum of problem* (20). *If $L(\cdot)$ and $S(\cdot)$ are strictly concave functions under the same conditions, then $(\hat{\mathbf{z}}(t;\varphi), \hat{\mathbf{v}}(t;\varphi))$ yields the unique absolute maximum of problem* (20).

It is worthwhile to remember that the theorems developed in this chapter do not exhaust the possibilities for transversality conditions, yet they do cover those classes of optimal control problems that rear their head most often in economics. Note, however, that by following the strategy of proof established herein, one can establish the necessary transversality conditions for virtually any type of finite horizon optimal control problem of interest in economics.

In closing out this chapter, it is important to observe that the transversality conditions presented here are really just first-order necessary conditions corresponding to a Stage 2 static optimization problem. Naturally, this observation leads one to conjecture that there must exist a set of companion second-order necessary and second-order sufficient conditions of the Stage 2 static optimization problem. Moreover, by further analogy with static optimization theory, one would also conjecture that there exist comparative statics results for the endpoints that are decision variables. These conjectures are correct and constitute the subject matter of the article by Caputo and Wilen (1995), which you are now prepared to study.

MENTAL EXERCISES

10.1 Provide an economic interpretation of parts (iii) and (iv) of Theorem 10.1.

10.2 In Example 10.1, show that

$$C(x, q; w) \stackrel{\text{def}}{=} \min_{L}\{wL \text{ s.t. } q = f(x, L)\}$$

has the properties asserted, given those assumed about $f(\cdot)$.

10.3 In Example 10.1, show that if $x(T) = x_T > 0$ in an optimal plan, then $\mu(t) > 0\ \forall\, t \in [0, T)$. Provide an economic interpretation of this result.

10.4 Provide an economic interpretation of the necessary conditions of Example 10.1 under the assumptions that $\lambda(T) > 0$ and $q(T) > 0$ in an optimal plan.

10.5 Impose the inequality constraint $T \geq 0$ on the mining problem of Example 10.1. Under what condition will the firm choose to set $T = 0$? Provide an economic interpretation of this result.

10.6 What does it mean to say that the Maximum Principle, canonical differential equations, and appropriate transversality conditions are necessary conditions? Be precise.

10.7 What does it mean to say that concavity of the Lagrangian with respect to the state and control variables for all t, plus the appropriate necessary conditions, are sufficient conditions? Be precise.

10.8 What is the role played by transversality conditions in optimal control problems? How do they arise?

10.9 Consider the autonomous optimal control problem

$$\max_{\mathbf{u}(\cdot),T} \int_0^T f(\mathbf{x}(t), \mathbf{u}(t))\, dt$$

$$\text{s.t.} \quad \dot{\mathbf{x}}(t) = g(\mathbf{x}(t), \mathbf{u}(t)),\ \ \mathbf{x}(0) = \mathbf{x}_0,\ \ \mathbf{x}(T) = \mathbf{x}_T.$$

(a) Prove that the Hamiltonian for this control problem is constant at zero $\forall\, t \in [0, T]$ along an optimal solution path.

(b) Would the result in part (a) change if either or both of the endpoints for the state vector were freely chosen? Why or why not?

(c) Verify part (a) using Example 10.2.

10.10 Find the solution of the necessary conditions for the following free terminal time optimal control problem:

$$\max_{u(\cdot),T} \int_0^T -[t^2 + [u(t)]^2]\, dt$$

$$\text{s.t. } \dot{x}(t) = u(t),\ x(0) = 4,\ x(T) = 5.$$

Only consider solutions where $T > 0$.

10.11 Provide the economic intuition for why the shadow cost of the inventory is less than or equal to zero for the entire planning horizon in Example 10.2. In addition, provide an economic interpretation of the comparative dynamics for the shadow cost of the inventory.

10.12 Consider the *time-optimal* control problem

$$\max_{u(\cdot),T} J[x(\cdot), u(\cdot)] \stackrel{\text{def}}{=} \int_0^T -1\, dt$$

$$\text{s.t. } \dot{x}(t) = x(t) + u(t),\ x(0) = 5,\ x(T) = 11,$$

$$u(t) \in U \stackrel{\text{def}}{=} \{u(t) : 0 \leq u(t) \leq 1\}.$$

The objective of such optimal control problems is to reach the given terminal value of the state in the least amount of time. This can be seen more clearly by integrating the objective functional to get

$$J[x(\cdot), u(\cdot)] \stackrel{\text{def}}{=} \int_0^T -1 dt = -t\big|_{t=0}^{t=T} = -T.$$

Thus in order to *maximize* $J[x(\cdot), u(\cdot)]$, we want to *minimize* the time T required to reach the given terminal value of the state variable.

(a) Derive the necessary conditions for the time-optimal control problem.

(b) Find the general solution of the costate variable, letting c_1 be the constant of integration. Can you determine the sign of the costate variable at this juncture in the problem? Explain what it depends on.

(c) Assuming that $c_1 \neq 0$, describe qualitatively the nature of the optimal solution for the control variable.

(d) Use the transversality condition and terminal endpoint condition to determine the *sign* of c_1. What, therefore, is the optimal path of the control variable?

(e) Find the specific solution of the state equation.

(f) Return to the transversality condition to find the value of c_1, and thus the specific solution of the costate equation.

(g) Use the terminal endpoint condition to find the value of the planning horizon.

(h) Prove that you have found the unique optimal solution to the time-optimal control problem.

10.13 Prove Theorem 10.3.

10.14 Prove Theorem 10.4.

10.15 In Example 10.1, we examined the nonrenewable resource–extracting model of the firm when $x(t)$ was defined as the stock of the asset remaining in the ground at time t and the amount of the stock left in the ground at time T was a choice variable, as was the terminal date of the planning horizon T. In this exercise, we define $x(t)$ differently and only let the terminal date of the planning horizon T be a choice. To this end, let $x_0 > 0$ be the total quantity of a nonrenewable resource stock controlled by a monopolist who discounts continuously at the rate $r > 0$. The monopolist is asserted to maximize the present discounted value of revenue, defined as $R(q(t)) \stackrel{\text{def}}{=} p(q(t))q(t)$, where $q(t)$ is the extraction rate of the resource at time t, and $p(\cdot) \in C^{(2)}$ is the inverse demand function with $p'(q) < 0$ (the law of demand) and $p(0)$ finite. Cumulative extraction at time t, namely, $x(t)$, is defined as the "sum" of all the extraction rates up to and including time t, that is to say,

$$x(t) \stackrel{\text{def}}{=} \int_0^t q(s)\,ds.$$

By Leibniz's rule, $\dot{x}(t) = q(t)$ is the differential equation governing the rate of change of cumulative extraction, and hence the state equation. We assume that the stock is completely exhausted at the endogenously chosen terminal time T, thereby implying that

$$x(T) \stackrel{\text{def}}{=} \int_0^T q(s)\,ds = x_0$$

and $x(0) = 0$ are the boundary conditions. Thus, the optimal control problem to be solved by the monopolist is given by

$$\max_{q(\cdot),T} J[x(\cdot), q(\cdot)] \stackrel{\text{def}}{=} \int_0^T e^{-rt} p(q(t))q(t)\,dt$$

$$\text{s.t.} \quad \dot{x}(t) = q(t), \; x(0) = 0, x(T) = x_0.$$

Explicitly show, in the order given, that:

(a) $e^{-rt} R'(q(t)) = c$, a constant.

(b) $R''(q(t)) \le 0$ necessarily, along an optimal extraction path.

(c) $q(T) = 0$.

(d) At $t = T$, marginal revenue equals average revenue (per unit of extraction).

(e) $c = e^{-rt} p(0)$.

(f) $R'(q(t)) = e^{-r(T-t)}p(0)$ along an optimal extraction path.
(g) Assuming that $R''(q(t)) < 0$, the optimal rate of extraction declines over the planning horizon.
(h) The price of the extracted good rises over time.
(i) Assume that $p(q) \stackrel{\text{def}}{=} [1 - e^{-kq}]/q$ is the inverse demand curve, where $k > 0$ is a parameter. Find an explicit solution to the necessary conditions with the given inverse demand curve. Let $T^*(x_0, r)$ be the value of the terminal time.
(j) Show that $\partial T^*(x_0, r)/\partial x_0 > 0$ and that $\partial T^*(x_0, r)/\partial r < 0$. Provide an economic interpretation.
(k) Now suppose price depends on the cumulative amount of the resource extracted as well as on the current extraction rate, say, $p(x, q) \stackrel{\text{def}}{=} a - bx - cq$, where $a > 0, b > 0$, and $c > 0$ are parameters. Find an explicit solution to the necessary conditions with the new inverse demand curve. State the constants of integration and T implicitly as the solution of a simultaneous system of equations.

10.16 This mental exercise asks you to compare and contrast the comparative dynamics properties of the inventory accumulation problem under the assumptions of a fixed delivery date and an optimally chosen delivery date in some more detail.
(a) Set up identities linking the solution functions $(z^*(\cdot), v^*(\cdot), \lambda^*(\cdot))$ of Example 10.2 to the solution functions $(z(\cdot), v(\cdot), \lambda(\cdot))$ of its fixed horizon counterpart in Example 4.5. Do this symbolically first, and then with the explicit solutions to verify that you have the correct identities.
(b) Provide an economic interpretation of both identities.
(c) Differentiate both symbolic identities with respect to x_T to derive a Slutsky-like equation. Provide an economic interpretation of the results.
(d) Plug in the specific functions to verify the comparative dynamic results of Example 10.2.
(e) Repeat parts (c) and (d) for the production cost parameter c_1.
(f) Repeat parts (c) and (d) for the inventory-holding cost parameter c_2.

10.17 This question asks you to further explore the comparative dynamics properties of the inventory accumulation problem, but this time, *without* the aid of the transversality condition for a salvage function, that is, Theorem 10.3. To begin, define $\beta \stackrel{\text{def}}{=} (c_1, c_2, T, x_T)$ and recall that the fixed endpoints version of the model is given by the optimal control problem

$$C(\beta) \stackrel{\text{def}}{=} \min_{u(\cdot)} \int_0^T [c_1[u(t)]^2 + c_2 x(t)]\, dt$$

$$\text{s.t.} \quad \dot{x}(t) = u(t),\ x(0) = 0,\ x(T) = x_T,$$

where $z(t;\beta) = \frac{1}{4}c_2c_1^{-1}t[t-T] + x_T T^{-1}t$ and $v(t;\beta) = \frac{1}{4}c_2c_1^{-1}[2t-T] + x_T T^{-1}$. A more realistic version of this fixed endpoints problem, as you may recall from Example 2.4, is one in which the firm has control over the terminal stock of the good in inventory x_T that it is able to sell in a competitive market at price $p > 0$. This version of the inventory accumulation problem can thus be stated as the following scrap (or salvage) value optimal control problem:

$$\Pi(\gamma) \overset{\text{def}}{=} \max_{u(\cdot),x_T} \left\{ px_T - \int_0^T \left[c_1[u(t)]^2 + c_2x(t)\right] dt \right\}$$

$$\text{s.t.} \quad \dot{x}(t) = u(t),\ x(0) = 0,\ x(T) = x_T,$$

where $\gamma \overset{\text{def}}{=} (c_1, c_2, p, T)$. Let $(\hat{z}(t;\gamma), \hat{v}(t;\gamma))$ be the optimal pair of curves to the salvage value problem. Do *not* use the specific functional form given for the pair $(z(t;\beta), v(t;\beta))$ in what follows unless the question specifically asks you to. Note that even though we have a theorem that allows us to handle salvage value control problems, we will solve the above salvage value problem via a different and arguably more economically insightful route.

(a) One way to solve the salvage value problem is to first solve the fixed endpoints problem for its optimal pair, scilicet, $(z(t;\beta), v(t;\beta))$, which we have done already, and derive the optimal value function $C(\beta)$, and then solve a *static* maximization problem to find the optimal value of x_T. Write down the second-stage static maximization problem used to find x_T.

(b) Derive the first-order necessary and second-order sufficient conditions for this static optimization problem, and provide an economic interpretation of each.

(c) Let the solution to the first-order necessary condition be $\hat{x}_T(\gamma)$, and find an explicit formula for it. Provide an economic interpretation of the necessary and sufficient condition for $\hat{x}_T(\gamma) > 0$ to hold. **Hint:** You will find the dynamic envelope theorem useful here, as well as the explicit functional form of $z(t;\beta)$.

(d) Find $\partial\hat{x}_T(\gamma)/\partial c_2$ and provide an economic interpretation.

(e) Write down an identity that defines $\hat{v}(t;\gamma)$ in terms of $v(t;\beta)$ and $\hat{x}_T(\gamma)$ without using the explicit functions. In other words, write down the identity in general terms.

(f) Prove that

$$\frac{\partial\hat{v}}{\partial c_2}(t;\gamma) \equiv \frac{\partial v}{\partial c_2}(t;c_1,c_2,T,x_T^*(\gamma)) + \frac{\partial v}{\partial x_T}(t;c_1,c_2,T,x_T^*(\gamma))\frac{\partial\hat{x}_T}{\partial c_2}(\gamma)\,\forall\, t\in[0,T],$$

and provide an economic interpretation. Do *not* use the explicit functional forms for $v(t;\beta)$ and $\hat{x}_T(\gamma)$.

(g) Prove that

$$\frac{\partial \hat{v}}{\partial c_2}(t;\gamma) \le 0 \, \forall \, t \in [0, T].$$

Explain why this result differs from that obtained for $\partial v(t;\beta)/\partial c_2$. You should make use of the explicit functional forms for $v(t;\beta)$ and $\hat{x}_T(\gamma)$.

(h) Prove that

$$\frac{\partial \hat{v}}{\partial p}(t;\gamma) \equiv \frac{\partial v}{\partial x_T}(t; c_1, c_2, T, x_T^*(\gamma))\frac{\partial \hat{x}_T}{\partial p}(\gamma) > 0 \, \forall \, t \in [0, T],$$

and provide an economic interpretation. You should again make use of the explicit functional forms for $v(t;\beta)$ and $\hat{x}_T(\gamma)$.

10.18 This question asks you to explore the comparative dynamics properties of the adjustment cost model of the firm when it faces a known cyclical fluctuation in the market price of the good it produces. To begin, let the market-determined time varying output price be given by $P(t) \stackrel{\text{def}}{=} p + \alpha_1 \sin(\alpha_2 t)$, where $p > 0$ is the time-invariant portion of the output price, $\alpha_1 > 0$ is a parameter that determines the amplitude of the periodic motion of the output price, and $\alpha_2 > 0$ is a parameter that determines the period of the output price time path. The production function is assumed to be a linear function of the capital stock $k(t)$, say, $f(k(t)) \stackrel{\text{def}}{=} k(t)$, and the capital stock is assumed *not* to depreciate. The purchase price per unit of investment $I(t)$ is given by the constant $q > 0$, which is set by the market. Adjustment costs are taken to be a quadratic function of the investment rate, say, $C(I(t)) \stackrel{\text{def}}{=} \frac{1}{2}c[I(t)]^2$, where $c > 0$ is the adjustment cost parameter. The initial stock of capital $k_0 > 0$ is given to the firm, but the terminal stock of capital k_T is to be optimally chosen by the firm. The firm lives over the fixed and finite interval $[0, T]$ and does not discount its cash flow. The optimal control problem facing the firm can therefore be stated as

$$\Pi(\gamma) \stackrel{\text{def}}{=} \max_{I(\cdot),k_T} \int_0^T \left[[p + \alpha_1 \sin(\alpha_2 t)]k(t) - qI(t) - \frac{1}{2}c[I(t)]^2 \right] dt$$

$$\text{s.t.} \quad \dot{k}(t) = I(t), \; k(0) = k_0, \; k(T) = k_T,$$

where $\gamma \stackrel{\text{def}}{=} (\alpha_1, \alpha_2, c, p, q, k_0, T)$ is the parameter vector. Assume that the nonnegativity restriction on the capital stock, namely, $k(t) \ge 0 \, \forall \, t \in [0, T]$, is not binding.

(a) Determine the pair of curves $(k^*(t;\gamma), I^*(t;\gamma))$ and corresponding time path of the shadow value of the capital stock $\lambda(t;\gamma)$ that satisfy the necessary conditions.

(b) Prove that the pair of curves $(k^*(t;\gamma), I^*(t;\gamma))$ is the unique optimal solution of the control problem.

(c) Clearly explain how the optimal investment path of the firm is forward looking with respect to the output price path, or equivalently, how it anticipates the changes in direction of the output price path.

(d) Prove that

$$\Pi(\theta\alpha_1, \alpha_2, \theta c, \theta p, \theta q, k_0, T) = \theta\Pi(\alpha_1, \alpha_2, c, p, q, k_0, T)\,\forall\theta > 0$$

and provide an economic interpretation.

(e) Prove that

$$I^*(t; \theta\alpha_1, \alpha_2, \theta c, \theta p, \theta q, k_0, T) = I^*(t; \alpha_1, \alpha_2, c, p, q, k_0, T)\forall\,\theta > 0$$

and provide an economic interpretation.

(f) Prove that

$$\frac{\partial I^*(t;\gamma)}{\partial p} \geq 0\,\forall\, t \in [0, T],$$

and provide an economic interpretation. Is the firm better off facing a higher value of p? Show your work and explain.

(g) Prove that

$$\frac{\partial I^*(t;\gamma)}{\partial q} < 0\,\forall\, t \in [0, T],$$

and provide an economic interpretation. Is the firm better off facing a higher value of q? Show your work and explain.

(h) Prove that

$$\left.\frac{\partial I^*(t;\gamma)}{\partial \alpha_1}\right|_{t=0} \geq 0,$$

and provide an economic interpretation. Is the firm better off facing a higher value of α_1? Show your work and explain.

FURTHER READING

Léonard and Van Long (1992, Chapter 7) and Seierstad and Sydsæter (1987) present additional theorems giving necessary transversality conditions for other classes of optimal control problems. Caputo and Wilen (1995) establish second-order necessary and sufficient conditions for choosing the horizon and state endpoints for a general class of control problems, as well as prove some general comparative statics theorems about such choices using both primal and dual methods of comparative statics.

REFERENCES

Caputo, M.R. and Wilen, J.E. (1995), "Optimality Conditions and Comparative Statics for Horizon and Endpoint Choices in Optimal Control Theory," *Journal of Economic Dynamics and Control*, 19, 351–369.

Léonard, D. and Van Long, N. (1992), *Optimal Control Theory and Static Optimization in Economics* (New York: Cambridge University Press).

Seierstad, A. and Sydsaeter, K. (1987), *Optimal Control Theory with Economic Applications* (New York: Elsevier Science Publishing Co., Inc.).

Simon. C.P. and Blume, L. (1994), *Mathematics for Economics* (New York: W.W. Norton & Company, Inc).

ELEVEN

Comparative Dynamics via Envelope Methods

We continue our development of the dynamic envelope theorem in this chapter, but do so with a different purpose in mind as well as from a different point of view. The purpose herewith is the development of a general method of comparative dynamics, applicable to any sufficiently smooth optimal control problem. The point of view we take is that the parameters of the optimal control problem, rather than the control variables themselves, are viewed as the choice or decision variables. This *dual* point of view is fundamental to our development of a general method of comparative dynamics, in that without it, we would not be able to achieve our goal. We will see that by adopting a dual view of an optimal control problem, we can succeed in providing a one-line proof of the dynamic envelope theorem and, at the same time, more simply reveal the envelope nature of the result. More importantly, however, we will show that the comparative dynamics properties of *all* sufficiently smooth optimal control problems are contained in a symmetric and semidefinite matrix, typically subject to constraint. This matrix, in effect, is a generalized Slutsky-type matrix in integral form, and is shown to characterize the effects that parameter perturbations have on the entire time path of the optimal trajectories. We will also provide sufficient conditions for the optimal value function to be convex in the parameters. Let us now turn to the detailed development of these important results.

The primal form of the fixed endpoint and fixed-time optimal control problem under consideration is given by

$$V(\boldsymbol{\beta}) \stackrel{\text{def}}{=} \max_{\mathbf{u}(\cdot)} \int_{t_0}^{t_1} f(t, \mathbf{x}(t), \mathbf{u}(t); \boldsymbol{\alpha})\, dt \tag{P}$$

$$\text{s.t.} \quad \dot{\mathbf{x}}(t) = \mathbf{g}(t, \mathbf{x}(t), \mathbf{u}(t); \boldsymbol{\alpha}),\ \mathbf{x}(t_0) = \mathbf{x}_0,\ \mathbf{x}(t_1) = \mathbf{x}_1,$$

where $\mathbf{x}(t) \stackrel{\text{def}}{=} (x_1(t), x_2(t), \ldots, x_N(t)) \in \Re^N$ is the state vector, $\mathbf{u}(t) \stackrel{\text{def}}{=} (u_1(t), u_2(t), \ldots, u_M(t)) \in \Re^M$ is the control vector, $\dot{\mathbf{x}}(\cdot) \stackrel{\text{def}}{=} (\dot{x}_1(\cdot), \dot{x}_2(\cdot), \ldots, \dot{x}_N(\cdot))$, $\mathbf{g}(\cdot) \stackrel{\text{def}}{=} (g^1(\cdot), g^2(\cdot), \ldots, g^N(\cdot))$ is the vector of transition functions, $\boldsymbol{\alpha} \stackrel{\text{def}}{=} (\alpha_1,$

$\alpha_2, \ldots, \alpha_A) \in \Re^A$ is a vector of time-independent parameters that affect the state equations and integrand, and $\boldsymbol{\beta} \stackrel{\text{def}}{=} (\boldsymbol{\alpha}, t_0, \mathbf{x}_0, t_1, \mathbf{x}_1) \in \Re^{2+2N+A}$. With pedagogical considerations at the forefront, we thus impose the following assumptions on problem (P).

(A.1) $f(\cdot) \in C^{(2)}$ and $g^n(\cdot) \in C^{(2)}$, $n = 1, 2, \ldots, N$, on their respective domains.
(A.2) There exists a unique optimal solution to problem (P) for each $\boldsymbol{\beta} \in B(\boldsymbol{\beta}^\circ; \delta)$, which we denote by the triplet $(\mathbf{z}(t; \boldsymbol{\beta}), \mathbf{v}(t; \boldsymbol{\beta}), \boldsymbol{\lambda}(t; \boldsymbol{\beta}))$, where $B(\boldsymbol{\beta}^\circ; \delta)$ is an open $2 + 2N + A$ – ball centered at the given value of the parameter $\boldsymbol{\beta}^\circ$ of radius $\delta > 0$.
(A.3) The vector-valued functions $(\mathbf{z}(\cdot), \mathbf{v}(\cdot), \boldsymbol{\lambda}(\cdot))$ are $C^{(1)}$ in $(t; \boldsymbol{\beta})$ for all $(t; \boldsymbol{\beta}) \in [t_0^\circ, t_1^\circ] \times B(\boldsymbol{\beta}^\circ; \delta)$.
(A.4) $V(\cdot) \in C^{(2)}$ in $\boldsymbol{\beta}$ for all $\boldsymbol{\beta} \in B(\boldsymbol{\beta}^\circ; \delta)$.

Some comments on these assumptions are required before the necessary and sufficient conditions for problem (P) are discussed.

Assumption (A.1) is required because we plan to use the differential calculus in our qualitative characterization of problem (P) and, furthermore, because we intend to use second-order necessary conditions as part of our analysis, thereby necessitating the use of second-order partial derivatives. Assumption (A.2) guarantees that a unique optimal solution exists to problem (P) when the parameter vector takes on values in some open set, a rather mild assumption given the generic nature of problem (P). Assumptions (A.3) and (A.4) are similarly required in view of the fact that we are aiming for a differential characterization of the comparative dynamics properties of the generic problem (P). Note that we are not imposing any other assumptions on problem (P) and its solution, such as concavity, separability, linearity, and the like, and consequently, the results derived henceforth are truly fundamental or intrinsic to problem (P). In passing, observe that $\dot{\mathbf{z}}(\cdot) \in C^{(1)}$ in $(t; \boldsymbol{\beta})$ for all $(t; \boldsymbol{\beta}) \in [t_0^\circ, t_1^\circ] \times B(\boldsymbol{\beta}^\circ; \delta)$, a result that will be used in this chapter, and which you are asked to prove in a mental exercise.

The Hamiltonian for problem (P) is defined as

$$H(t, \mathbf{x}, \mathbf{u}, \boldsymbol{\lambda}; \boldsymbol{\alpha}) \stackrel{\text{def}}{=} f(t, \mathbf{x}, \mathbf{u}; \boldsymbol{\alpha}) + \boldsymbol{\lambda}'\mathbf{g}(t, \mathbf{x}, \mathbf{u}; \boldsymbol{\alpha}). \tag{1}$$

By Corollary 4.2, the necessary conditions are given by

$$H_{\mathbf{u}}(t, \mathbf{x}, \mathbf{u}, \boldsymbol{\lambda}; \boldsymbol{\alpha}) = \mathbf{0}'_M, \tag{2}$$

$$\mathbf{h}'H_{\mathbf{uu}}(t, \mathbf{x}, \mathbf{u}, \boldsymbol{\lambda}; \boldsymbol{\alpha})\mathbf{h} \leq 0 \,\forall\, \mathbf{h} \in \Re^M, \tag{3}$$

$$\dot{\boldsymbol{\lambda}}' = -H_{\mathbf{x}}(t, \mathbf{x}, \mathbf{u}, \boldsymbol{\lambda}; \boldsymbol{\alpha}), \tag{4}$$

$$\dot{\mathbf{x}}' = H_{\boldsymbol{\lambda}}(t, \mathbf{x}, \mathbf{u}, \boldsymbol{\lambda}; \boldsymbol{\alpha}), \tag{5}$$

$$\mathbf{x}(t_0) = \mathbf{x}_0, \;\; \mathbf{x}(t_1) = \mathbf{x}_1. \tag{6}$$

By Theorem 4.3, we know that if $H(\cdot)$ is a concave function of $(\mathbf{x}, \mathbf{u})$ for all $t \in [t_0, t_1]$ when the costate vector is $\boldsymbol{\lambda}(t; \boldsymbol{\beta})$, then a solution of Eqs. (2) through (6) is a solution of problem (P). With these fundamentals set out, we now turn to the dual view of problem (P) and its qualitative properties.

The so-called *dynamic primal-dual problem* corresponding to the primal problem (P) is defined as

$$\max_{\beta} D(\beta) \stackrel{\text{def}}{=} \int_{t_0}^{t_1} f(t, \mathbf{z}(t;\bar{\beta}), \mathbf{v}(t;\bar{\beta}); \alpha)\, dt - V(\beta)$$

$$\text{s.t.} \quad \mathbf{g}(t, \mathbf{z}(t;\bar{\beta}), \mathbf{v}(t;\bar{\beta}); \alpha) - \dot{\mathbf{z}}(t;\bar{\beta}) = 0, \qquad \text{(P-D)}$$

$$\mathbf{z}(t_0;\bar{\beta}) = \mathbf{x}_0, \;\; \mathbf{z}(t_1;\bar{\beta}) = \mathbf{x}_1,$$

where

$$V(\beta) \stackrel{\text{def}}{=} \int_{t_0}^{t_1} f(t, \mathbf{z}(t;\beta), \mathbf{v}(t;\beta); \alpha)\, dt \tag{7}$$

is the constructive, and equivalent, definition of the optimal value function for problem (P), for any $\beta \in B(\beta^\circ;\delta)$, and $(\mathbf{z}(t;\bar{\beta}), \mathbf{v}(t;\bar{\beta}))$ is the optimal pair of curves given that the parameter vector β is fixed at the *arbitrary* value $\bar{\beta} \in B(\beta^\circ;\delta)$. It is important to recognize that in problem (P-D), the pair of curves $(\mathbf{z}(t;\bar{\beta}), \mathbf{v}(t;\bar{\beta}))$ is fixed because the parameter vector β is fixed at the arbitrary value $\bar{\beta} \in B(\beta^\circ;\delta)$, whereas the parameter vector $\beta \stackrel{\text{def}}{=} (\alpha, t_0, \mathbf{x}_0, t_1, \mathbf{x}_1) \in \Re^{2+2N+A}$, not $\bar{\beta}$, can be freely chosen because it is not held fixed, as signified by the lack of an over bar. Therefore, by construction, or equivalently, by definition of problems (P) and (P-D), $D(\beta) \leq 0 \,\forall\, \beta \in B(\beta^\circ;\delta)$ seeing as $f(\cdot)$ is evaluated along the pair of curves $(\mathbf{z}(t;\bar{\beta}), \mathbf{v}(t;\bar{\beta}))$, which is optimal only when $\beta = \bar{\beta}$. Furthermore, when $\beta = \bar{\beta}$ in problem (P-D), $f(\cdot)$ is then evaluated along $(t, \mathbf{z}(t;\bar{\beta}), \mathbf{v}(t;\bar{\beta}), \bar{\alpha})$, thereby implying that $D(\bar{\beta}) = 0$. That is to say,

$$D(\bar{\beta}) = \int_{\bar{t}_0}^{\bar{t}_1} f(t, \mathbf{z}(t;\bar{\beta}), \mathbf{v}(t;\bar{\beta}); \bar{\alpha})\, dt - V(\bar{\beta}) = \max_{\beta} D(\beta) = 0$$

by assumption (A.2), the definition of the optimal value function $V(\cdot)$ in problem (P), and the definition of the dynamic primal-dual problem (P-D).

The above development demonstrates that the dynamic primal-dual problem (P-D) has a known solution by its very construction. Notice that we are treating the parameter vector β as the decision vector in the dynamic primal-dual problem (P-D), whereas the pair of curves $(\mathbf{z}(t;\bar{\beta}), \mathbf{v}(t;\bar{\beta}))$ are held fixed or parametric, an *exact inversion* of their roles in the primal (or usual) form of the control problem (P). It is precisely this dual view of the primal optimal control problem (P), that is, the inversion of the roles of the parameters and control variables, that leads to the powerful results derived herein. Simply put, the dynamic primal-dual problem

(P-D) treats the *explicit* appearance of the parameter vector $\boldsymbol{\beta} \stackrel{\text{def}}{=} (\boldsymbol{\alpha}, t_0, \mathbf{x}_0, t_1, \mathbf{x}_1) \in \Re^{2+2N+A}$ as the decision vector, but treats the *implicit* appearance of the parameter vector, that is, the occurrence of $\boldsymbol{\beta}$ as an argument of the state, control, and costate vectors, as fixed.

In passing, we should remark on the appellation *primal-dual* employed when defining problem (P-D). The *primal* portion of the name comes from the fact that if we adopt the perspective that the parameter vector $\boldsymbol{\beta}$ is fixed and the control vector is the decision vector in problem (P-D), just as we do in the primal problem (P), then problem (P-D) is identical to problem (P). On the other hand, if we adopt the perspective that the time paths of the state and control variables are fixed while the parameter vector $\boldsymbol{\beta}$ is the decision vector in problem (P-D), then we have a dual optimization problem (P-D). Dual, in this instance, simply means that we have two related optimization problems that can be generated from a single underlying optimization problem, and the decision vectors in each lie in different spaces. This usage of the word *dual* is in accord with that when one contemplates dual pairs of linear programming problems, for example. In sum, therefore, problem (P-D) contains the primal (or original) *and* dual optimization problems in a single problem statement. Let us now continue with the development of the dynamic primal-dual problem (P-D).

Observe that by Eqs. (1) and (7), and Eq. (5) expressed in identity form, we may obtain the revealing result that

$$
\begin{aligned}
V(\boldsymbol{\beta}) &\stackrel{\text{def}}{=} \int_{t_0}^{t_1} f(t, \mathbf{z}(t;\boldsymbol{\beta}), \mathbf{v}(t;\boldsymbol{\beta}); \boldsymbol{\alpha})\, dt \\
&= \int_{t_0}^{t_1} [H(t, \mathbf{z}(t;\boldsymbol{\beta}), \mathbf{v}(t;\boldsymbol{\beta}), \boldsymbol{\lambda}(t;\boldsymbol{\beta}); \boldsymbol{\alpha}) - \boldsymbol{\lambda}(t;\boldsymbol{\beta})'\mathbf{g}(t, \mathbf{z}(t;\boldsymbol{\beta}), \mathbf{v}(t;\boldsymbol{\beta}); \boldsymbol{\alpha})]\, dt \\
&= \int_{t_0}^{t_1} [H(t, \mathbf{z}(t;\boldsymbol{\beta}), \mathbf{v}(t;\boldsymbol{\beta}), \boldsymbol{\lambda}(t;\boldsymbol{\beta}); \boldsymbol{\alpha}) - \boldsymbol{\lambda}(t;\boldsymbol{\beta})'\dot{\mathbf{z}}(t;\boldsymbol{\beta})]\, dt \\
&\neq \int_{t_0}^{t_1} H(t, \mathbf{z}(t;\boldsymbol{\beta}), \mathbf{v}(t;\boldsymbol{\beta}), \boldsymbol{\lambda}(t;\boldsymbol{\beta}); \boldsymbol{\alpha})\, dt. \qquad (8)
\end{aligned}
$$

Equation (8) shows that the optimal value function $V(\cdot)$ is *not* defined as the integral of the Hamiltonian function $H(\cdot)$ evaluated along the optimal solution, but is instead defined as the integral of the Hamiltonian function $H(\cdot)$, minus the inner product of the costate vector and time derivative of the state vector, $\boldsymbol{\lambda}'\dot{\mathbf{x}}$, evaluated along the optimal solution. Therefore, even though the standard method of optimal control theory may be applied to problem (P) along with the static envelope theorem and static primal-dual methodology of Silberberg (1974) to derive the curvature properties of the Hamiltonian function $H(\cdot)$, Eq. (8) makes it clear that knowing the curvature properties of $H(\cdot)$ is not, in general, sufficient to demonstrate any curvature properties of $V(\cdot)$. Consequently, it is thus essential that the integral form of the solution to the optimal control problem be studied in order to ascertain the curvature properties of $V(\cdot)$. This provides the necessary motivation for studying the primal-dual problem (P-D) corresponding to the primal problem (P).

Because the parameter vector $\boldsymbol{\beta}$ is time independent, *static* Lagrangian optimization methods may be applied to the dynamic primal-dual problem (P-D) to study the comparative dynamics properties of the corresponding primal control problem (P). In order to form the proper Lagrangian function corresponding to problem (P-D), we begin with a few important observations. First, because the state equation constraint $\mathbf{g}(t, \mathbf{z}(t; \bar{\boldsymbol{\beta}}), \mathbf{v}(t; \bar{\boldsymbol{\beta}}); \boldsymbol{\alpha}) - \dot{\mathbf{z}}(t; \bar{\boldsymbol{\beta}}) = \mathbf{0}$ of problem (P-D) must hold for all $t \in [t_0, t_1]$, it must be integrated over the planning horizon $[t_0, t_1]$, just like the integrand function $f(\cdot)$, after it is taken with the inner product of the proper multiplier vector. Second, the correct multiplier vector for this operation is the time path of the costate vector when $\boldsymbol{\beta} = \bar{\boldsymbol{\beta}}$, scilicet, $\boldsymbol{\lambda}(t; \bar{\boldsymbol{\beta}})$, which is optimal when $\boldsymbol{\beta} = \bar{\boldsymbol{\beta}}$. To see that $\boldsymbol{\lambda}(t; \bar{\boldsymbol{\beta}})$ is the correct multiplier vector for the state equation constraint $\mathbf{g}(t, \mathbf{z}(t; \bar{\boldsymbol{\beta}}), \mathbf{v}(t; \bar{\boldsymbol{\beta}}); \boldsymbol{\alpha}) - \dot{\mathbf{z}}(t; \bar{\boldsymbol{\beta}}) = \mathbf{0}$ of problem (P-D), one need only recognize that $\boldsymbol{\lambda}(t; \bar{\boldsymbol{\beta}})$ is precisely the costate vector that corresponds to the pair of curves $(\mathbf{z}(t; \bar{\boldsymbol{\beta}}), \mathbf{v}(t; \bar{\boldsymbol{\beta}}))$, which is itself optimal when $\boldsymbol{\beta} = \bar{\boldsymbol{\beta}}$. Third, it is not necessary to adopt this procedure for the initial and terminal condition constraints in view of the fact that they hold only at one point in time in the planning horizon rather than over an interval. Finally, take note that the present development is wholly analogous to that employed in the proof of the necessary conditions in Chapter 2.

With the above observations in mind, the Lagrangian function $L(\cdot)$ corresponding to the dynamic primal-dual problem (P-D) is defined as

$$L(\boldsymbol{\beta}) \stackrel{\text{def}}{=} \int_{t_0}^{t_1} [f(t, \mathbf{z}(t; \bar{\boldsymbol{\beta}}), \mathbf{v}(t; \bar{\boldsymbol{\beta}}); \boldsymbol{\alpha}) + \boldsymbol{\lambda}(t; \bar{\boldsymbol{\beta}})'[\mathbf{g}(t, \mathbf{z}(t; \bar{\boldsymbol{\beta}}), \mathbf{v}(t; \bar{\boldsymbol{\beta}}); \boldsymbol{\alpha}) - \dot{\mathbf{z}}(t; \bar{\boldsymbol{\beta}})]]\, dt - V(\boldsymbol{\beta}) \tag{9}$$

$$= \int_{t_0}^{t_1} [H(t, \mathbf{z}(t; \bar{\boldsymbol{\beta}}), \mathbf{v}(t; \bar{\boldsymbol{\beta}}), \boldsymbol{\lambda}(t; \bar{\boldsymbol{\beta}}); \boldsymbol{\alpha}) - \boldsymbol{\lambda}(t; \bar{\boldsymbol{\beta}})'\dot{\mathbf{z}}(t; \bar{\boldsymbol{\beta}})]\, dt - V(\boldsymbol{\beta}),$$

which certainly smacks of, but is not identical to, Eq. (8). Integration of Eq. (9) by parts in what should now be a familiar manner, and use of the initial and terminal condition constraints on the state vector, to wit, $\mathbf{z}(t_0; \bar{\boldsymbol{\beta}}) = \mathbf{x}_0$ and $\mathbf{z}(t_1; \bar{\boldsymbol{\beta}}) = \mathbf{x}_1$, respectively, yields an alternative but equivalent form of the Lagrangian function for problem (P-D), namely,

$$L(\beta) \stackrel{\text{def}}{=} \int_{t_0}^{t_1} [H(t, \mathbf{z}(t; \bar{\beta}), \mathbf{v}(t; \bar{\beta}), \boldsymbol{\lambda}(t; \bar{\beta}); \boldsymbol{\alpha}) + \dot{\boldsymbol{\lambda}}(t; \bar{\beta})' \mathbf{z}(t; \bar{\beta})]\, dt$$

$$- \boldsymbol{\lambda}(t_1; \bar{\beta})' \mathbf{x}_1 + \boldsymbol{\lambda}(t_0; \bar{\beta})' \mathbf{x}_0 - V(\beta). \tag{10}$$

This is the form of the Lagrangian we intend to work with.

Alternatively, one could arrive at Eq. (10) by integrating Eq. (9) by parts, just as we did above. But rather than substitute $\mathbf{z}(t_0; \bar{\beta}) = \mathbf{x}_0$ and $\mathbf{z}(t_1; \bar{\beta}) = \mathbf{x}_1$ into that result, we could add the two inner product terms $\boldsymbol{\lambda}(t_0; \bar{\beta})'[\mathbf{x}_0 - \mathbf{z}(t_0; \bar{\beta})]$ and $\boldsymbol{\lambda}(t_1; \bar{\beta})'[\mathbf{z}(t_1; \bar{\beta}) - \mathbf{x}_1]$ into the integration-by-parts Lagrangian expression to account for the endpoint constraints on the state vector, and then cancel four of the terms in the resulting expression to arrive at Eq. (10). Accordingly, there are two different, but equivalent, ways to incorporate the two endpoint constraints on the state vector into the Lagrangian function corresponding to problem (P-D).

As remarked above, problem (P-D) is a static optimization problem. Using Eq. (10), we therefore have the following first-order necessary conditions for problem (P-D):

$$L_{\boldsymbol{\alpha}}(\beta) = \int_{t_0}^{t_1} H_{\boldsymbol{\alpha}}(t, \mathbf{z}(t; \bar{\beta}), \mathbf{v}(t; \bar{\beta}), \boldsymbol{\lambda}(t; \bar{\beta}); \boldsymbol{\alpha})\, dt - V_{\boldsymbol{\alpha}}(\beta) = \mathbf{0}'_A, \tag{11}$$

$$L_{t_0}(\beta) = -H(t_0, \mathbf{z}(t_0; \bar{\beta}), \mathbf{v}(t_0; \bar{\beta}), \boldsymbol{\lambda}(t_0; \bar{\beta}); \boldsymbol{\alpha})$$
$$- \dot{\boldsymbol{\lambda}}(t_0; \bar{\beta})' \mathbf{z}(t_0; \bar{\beta}) + \dot{\boldsymbol{\lambda}}(t_0; \bar{\beta})' \mathbf{x}_0 - V_{t_0}(\beta) = 0, \tag{12}$$

$$L_{\mathbf{x}_0}(\beta) = \boldsymbol{\lambda}(t_0; \bar{\beta})' - V_{\mathbf{x}_0}(\beta) = \mathbf{0}'_N, \tag{13}$$

$$L_{t_1}(\beta) = H(t_1, \mathbf{z}(t_1; \bar{\beta}), \mathbf{v}(t_1; \bar{\beta}), \boldsymbol{\lambda}(t_1; \bar{\beta}); \boldsymbol{\alpha})$$
$$+ \dot{\boldsymbol{\lambda}}(t_1; \bar{\beta})' \mathbf{z}(t_1; \bar{\beta}) - \dot{\boldsymbol{\lambda}}(t_1; \bar{\beta})' \mathbf{x}_1 - V_{t_1}(\beta) = 0, \tag{14}$$

$$L_{\mathbf{x}_1}(\beta) = -\boldsymbol{\lambda}(t_1; \bar{\beta})' - V_{\mathbf{x}_1}(\beta) = \mathbf{0}'_N, \tag{15}$$

$$\mathbf{g}(t, \mathbf{z}(t; \bar{\beta}), \mathbf{v}(t; \bar{\beta}); \boldsymbol{\alpha}) - \dot{\mathbf{z}}(t; \bar{\beta}) = 0, \tag{16}$$

$$\mathbf{x}_0 - \mathbf{z}(t_0; \bar{\beta}) = \mathbf{0}_N, \tag{17}$$

$$\mathbf{z}(t_1; \bar{\beta}) - \mathbf{x}_1 = \mathbf{0}_N, \tag{18}$$

which all hold at $\beta = \bar{\beta}$ by construction. In fact, because $(\mathbf{z}(t; \beta), \mathbf{v}(t; \beta))$ is an optimal pair and $\boldsymbol{\lambda}(t; \beta)$ is the corresponding costate vector for all $\beta \in B(\beta^\circ; \delta)$, and because $\bar{\beta} \in B(\beta^\circ; \delta)$ is an *arbitrary* value of β, the fact that Eqs. (11) through (18) hold for $\beta = \bar{\beta}$ implies that Eqs. (11) through (18) also hold for *any* $\beta \in B(\beta^\circ; \delta)$ as long as the domain of all the functions are evaluated at the same value of $\beta \in$

$B(\boldsymbol{\beta}^\circ;\delta)$. Moreover, seeing as $\mathbf{z}(t_0;\boldsymbol{\beta}) \equiv \mathbf{x}_0$ and $\mathbf{z}(t_1;\boldsymbol{\beta}) \equiv \mathbf{x}_1$ for all $\boldsymbol{\beta} \in B(\boldsymbol{\beta}^\circ;\delta)$ from Eqs. (17) and (18), respectively, the two inner product terms in Eqs. (12) and (14) cancel, thereby leaving a simplified expression for these equations and resulting in an alternative proof of Theorem 9.1, the dynamic envelope theorem for the optimal control problem (P).

Theorem 11.1 (Dynamic Envelope Theorem): *For optimal control problem (P), with assumptions (A.1) through (A.4) holding, the following envelope results exist and are $C^{(1)}$ for all $\boldsymbol{\beta} \in B(\boldsymbol{\beta}^\circ;\delta)$:*

$$V_{\boldsymbol{\alpha}}(\boldsymbol{\beta}) \equiv \int_{t_0}^{t_1} H_{\boldsymbol{\alpha}}(t,\mathbf{z}(t;\boldsymbol{\beta}),\mathbf{v}(t;\boldsymbol{\beta}),\boldsymbol{\lambda}(t;\boldsymbol{\beta});\boldsymbol{\alpha})\,dt,$$

$$V_{t_0}(\boldsymbol{\beta}) \equiv -H(t_0,\mathbf{z}(t_0;\boldsymbol{\beta}),\mathbf{v}(t_0;\boldsymbol{\beta}),\boldsymbol{\lambda}(t_0;\boldsymbol{\beta});\boldsymbol{\alpha}),$$

$$V_{\mathbf{x}_0}(\boldsymbol{\beta}) \equiv \boldsymbol{\lambda}(t_0;\boldsymbol{\beta})',$$

$$V_{t_1}(\boldsymbol{\beta}) \equiv H(t_1,\mathbf{z}(t_1;\boldsymbol{\beta}),\mathbf{v}(t_1;\boldsymbol{\beta}),\boldsymbol{\lambda}(t_1;\boldsymbol{\beta});\boldsymbol{\alpha}),$$

$$V_{\mathbf{x}_1}(\boldsymbol{\beta}) \equiv -\boldsymbol{\lambda}(t_1;\boldsymbol{\beta})'.$$

Recall that in Chapter 9, we proved the dynamic envelope theorem, that is, Theorem 9.1, by differentiating the constructive definition of the optimal value function, given by Eq. (7) in the present chapter, applying the integration-by-parts formula, and making use of the necessary condition of Corollary 4.2. That proof, therefore, may be considered the dynamic equivalent of the proof of the prototype static envelope theorem by Silberberg and Suen (2001, pp. 160–161). In contrast, the above proof of the dynamic envelope theorem may be considered the dynamic equivalent of the primal-dual proof of the static envelope theorem by Silberberg (1974).

Experience with static optimization theory strongly suggests that in searching for the qualitative properties of any mathematical model, the second-order or curvature properties of the model must be investigated. That is, although first-order properties such as the above dynamic envelope theorem do provide useful qualitative information about a particular problem, it is the second-order necessary conditions that provide the vast majority of qualitative information about an optimization problem, constrained or not.

Remembering that problem (P-D) is a static optimization problem, its second-order necessary conditions, which hold at $\boldsymbol{\beta} = \bar{\boldsymbol{\beta}}$ by construction, are given by

$$\mathbf{a}'L_{\boldsymbol{\beta}\boldsymbol{\beta}}(\boldsymbol{\beta})\mathbf{a} \le 0\,\forall\,\mathbf{a} \in \Re^{2+2N+A} \ni G_{\boldsymbol{\beta}}(\boldsymbol{\beta})\mathbf{a} = \mathbf{0}_{3N}, \tag{19}$$

where

$$\underset{1\times(2+2N+A)}{\mathbf{a}'} \overset{\text{def}}{=} \left(\underset{1\times A}{\mathbf{a}^{1\prime}}\quad \underset{1\times 1}{a^{2\prime}}\quad \underset{1\times N}{\mathbf{a}^{3\prime}}\quad \underset{1\times 1}{a^{4\prime}}\quad \underset{1\times N}{\mathbf{a}^{5\prime}}\right), \tag{20}$$

$$\underset{(2+2N+A)\times(2+2N+A)}{L_{\beta\beta}(\beta)} = \begin{bmatrix} \underset{A\times A}{L_{\alpha\alpha}(\beta)} & \underset{A\times 1}{L_{\alpha t_0}(\beta)} & \underset{A\times N}{L_{\alpha \mathbf{x}_0}(\beta)} & \underset{A\times 1}{L_{\alpha t_1}(\beta)} & \underset{A\times N}{L_{\alpha \mathbf{x}_1}(\beta)} \\ \underset{1\times A}{L_{t_0\alpha}(\beta)} & \underset{1\times 1}{L_{t_0 t_0}(\beta)} & \underset{1\times N}{L_{t_0 \mathbf{x}_0}(\beta)} & \underset{1\times 1}{L_{t_0 t_1}(\beta)} & \underset{1\times N}{L_{t_0 \mathbf{x}_1}(\beta)} \\ \underset{N\times A}{L_{\mathbf{x}_0\alpha}(\beta)} & \underset{N\times 1}{L_{\mathbf{x}_0 t_0}(\beta)} & \underset{N\times N}{L_{\mathbf{x}_0 \mathbf{x}_0}(\beta)} & \underset{N\times 1}{L_{\mathbf{x}_0 t_1}(\beta)} & \underset{N\times N}{L_{\mathbf{x}_0 \mathbf{x}_1}(\beta)} \\ \underset{1\times A}{L_{t_1\alpha}(\beta)} & \underset{1\times 1}{L_{t_1 t_0}(\beta)} & \underset{1\times N}{L_{t_1 \mathbf{x}_0}(\beta)} & \underset{1\times 1}{L_{t_1 t_1}(\beta)} & \underset{1\times N}{L_{t_1 \mathbf{x}_1}(\beta)} \\ \underset{N\times A}{L_{\mathbf{x}_1\alpha}(\beta)} & \underset{N\times 1}{L_{\mathbf{x}_1 t_0}(\beta)} & \underset{N\times N}{L_{\mathbf{x}_1 \mathbf{x}_0}(\beta)} & \underset{N\times 1}{L_{\mathbf{x}_1 t_1}(\beta)} & \underset{N\times N}{L_{\mathbf{x}_1 \mathbf{x}_1}(\beta)} \end{bmatrix}, \tag{21}$$

$$\underset{1\times 3N}{G(\beta)'} \overset{\text{def}}{=} \Big[\underset{1\times N}{\mathbf{g}(t,\mathbf{z}(t;\bar{\beta}),\mathbf{v}(t;\bar{\beta});\alpha)' - \dot{\mathbf{z}}(t;\bar{\beta})'} \quad \underset{1\times N}{\mathbf{x}_0' - \mathbf{z}(t_0;\bar{\beta})'} \quad \underset{1\times N}{\mathbf{z}(t_1;\bar{\beta})' - \mathbf{x}_1'}\Big], \tag{22}$$

and therefore

$$\underset{3N\times(2+2N+A)}{G_{\beta}(\beta)} = \begin{bmatrix} \underset{N\times A}{\mathbf{g}_{\alpha}(t,\mathbf{z}(t;\bar{\beta}),\mathbf{v}(t;\bar{\beta});\alpha)} & \underset{N\times 1}{\mathbf{0}} & \underset{N\times N}{\mathbf{0}} & \underset{N\times 1}{\mathbf{0}} & \underset{N\times N}{\mathbf{0}} \\ \underset{N\times A}{\mathbf{0}} & \underset{N\times 1}{-\dot{\mathbf{z}}(t_0;\bar{\beta})} & \underset{N\times N}{\mathbf{I}} & \underset{N\times 1}{\mathbf{0}} & \underset{N\times N}{\mathbf{0}} \\ \underset{N\times A}{\mathbf{0}} & \underset{N\times 1}{\mathbf{0}} & \underset{N\times N}{\mathbf{0}} & \underset{N\times 1}{\dot{\mathbf{z}}(t_1;\bar{\beta})} & \underset{N\times N}{-\mathbf{I}} \end{bmatrix}. \tag{23}$$

It is these conditions that reveal the qualitative properties of problem (P). The results achieved may be summed up as follows: the qualitative restrictions implied by the dynamic maximization assertion and the mathematical structure of problem (P), as revealed by the dynamic primal-dual methodology, are contained in a symmetric negative semidefinite matrix subject to constraint. Symmetry follows from the $C^{(2)}$ nature of $f(\cdot)$ and $\mathbf{g}(\cdot)$ from assumption (A.1), the local $C^{(1)}$ nature of the functions $(\mathbf{z}(\cdot), \mathbf{v}(\cdot), \boldsymbol{\lambda}(\cdot))$ from assumption (A.3), and the local $C^{(2)}$ nature of $V(\cdot)$ from assumption (A.4). This can be seen by the ensuing development and from inspection of the details of the appendix to this chapter, which constitutes the bulk of the proof of Theorem 11.2.

In order to turn the curvature condition in Eq. (19) into a meaningful comparative dynamics statement, we must express the elements of the matrix $L_{\beta\beta}(\beta)$ in terms of linear combinations of partial derivatives of the state, control, and costate functions with respect to the parameter vector β. Because $\beta \overset{\text{def}}{=} (\alpha, t_0, \mathbf{x}_0, t_1, \mathbf{x}_1) \in \Re^{2+2N+A}$, this derivation is rather involved. Therefore, instead of presenting all the details in the chapter proper, we relegate most of the computations to the appendix of this chapter. We thus present a detailed development of the terms only in the submatrix $L_{\alpha\alpha}(\beta)$, which for economic applications, is usually the matrix of interest.

To begin this process, first differentiate Eq. (11) with respect to α and evaluate the result at $\beta = \bar{\beta}$ to get

$$\underset{A\times A}{L_{\alpha\alpha}(\bar{\beta})} = \int_{\bar{t}_0}^{\bar{t}_1} \underset{A\times A}{H_{\alpha\alpha}(t, \mathbf{z}(t;\bar{\beta}), \mathbf{v}(t;\bar{\beta}), \boldsymbol{\lambda}(t;\bar{\beta}); \bar{\alpha})}\, dt - \underset{A\times A}{V_{\alpha\alpha}(\bar{\beta})}. \tag{24}$$

Next, use Theorem 11.1 to calculate the matrix $V_{\alpha\alpha}(\beta)$ and evaluate the result at $\beta = \bar{\beta}$:

$$\begin{aligned}\underset{A\times A}{V_{\alpha\alpha}(\bar{\beta})} \equiv \int_{\bar{t}_0}^{\bar{t}_1} \Bigg\{ & \underset{A\times N}{H_{\alpha\mathbf{x}}(t, \mathbf{z}(t;\bar{\beta}), \mathbf{v}(t;\bar{\beta}), \boldsymbol{\lambda}(t;\bar{\beta}); \bar{\alpha})} \underset{N\times A}{\frac{\partial \mathbf{z}(t;\bar{\beta})}{\partial \alpha}} \\ & + \underset{A\times M}{H_{\alpha\mathbf{u}}(t, \mathbf{z}(t;\bar{\beta}), \mathbf{v}(t;\bar{\beta}), \boldsymbol{\lambda}(t;\bar{\beta}); \bar{\alpha})} \underset{M\times A}{\frac{\partial \mathbf{v}(t;\bar{\beta})}{\partial \alpha}} \\ & + \underset{A\times N}{H_{\alpha\boldsymbol{\lambda}}(t, \mathbf{z}(t;\bar{\beta}), \mathbf{v}(t;\bar{\beta}), \boldsymbol{\lambda}(t;\bar{\beta}); \bar{\alpha})} \underset{N\times A}{\frac{\partial \boldsymbol{\lambda}(t;\bar{\beta})}{\partial \alpha}} \\ & + \underset{A\times A}{H_{\alpha\alpha}(t, \mathbf{z}(t;\bar{\beta}), \mathbf{v}(t;\bar{\beta}), \boldsymbol{\lambda}(t;\bar{\beta}); \bar{\alpha})} \Bigg\}\, dt \end{aligned} \tag{25}$$

Recall, however, that the point $\beta = \bar{\beta} \in B(\beta^\circ; \delta)$ at which Eqs. (24) and (25) are evaluated is arbitrary; thus they hold for all $\beta \in B(\beta^\circ; \delta)$. Noting this and then substituting Eq. (25) into Eq. (24) yields the result we are aiming for, videlicet, the elements of the submatrix $L_{\alpha\alpha}(\beta)$ are now expressed as linear combinations of the partial derivatives of the state, control, and costate functions with respect to the parameter vector α:

$$\begin{aligned}&\underset{A\times A}{L_{\alpha\alpha}(\beta)} \\ &= -\int_{t_0}^{t_1} \left[\underset{A\times N}{H_{\alpha\mathbf{x}}(t;\beta)} \underset{N\times A}{\frac{\partial \mathbf{z}(t;\beta)}{\partial \alpha}} + \underset{A\times M}{H_{\alpha\mathbf{u}}(t;\beta)} \underset{M\times A}{\frac{\partial \mathbf{v}(t;\beta)}{\partial \alpha}} + \underset{A\times N}{H_{\alpha\boldsymbol{\lambda}}(t;\beta)} \underset{N\times A}{\frac{\partial \boldsymbol{\lambda}(t;\beta)}{\partial \alpha}} \right] dt,\end{aligned} \tag{26}$$

where $H_{\alpha\mathbf{x}}(t;\beta) \overset{\text{def}}{=} H_{\alpha\mathbf{x}}(t, \mathbf{z}(t;\beta), \mathbf{v}(t;\beta), \boldsymbol{\lambda}(t;\beta); \alpha)$, $H_{\alpha\mathbf{u}}(t;\beta) \overset{\text{def}}{=} H_{\alpha\mathbf{u}}(t, \mathbf{z}(t;\beta), \mathbf{v}(t;\beta), \boldsymbol{\lambda}(t;\beta); \alpha)$, and $H_{\alpha\boldsymbol{\lambda}}(t;\beta) \overset{\text{def}}{=} H_{\alpha\boldsymbol{\lambda}}(t, \mathbf{z}(t;\beta), \mathbf{v}(t;\beta), \boldsymbol{\lambda}(t;\beta); \alpha) = \mathbf{g}_\alpha(t, \mathbf{z}(t;\beta), \mathbf{v}(t;\beta); \alpha)'$. This proves the formula for the (1,1) block element of the matrix $L_{\beta\beta}(\beta)$. The appendix derives the formulas for the remaining 24 blocks of $L_{\beta\beta}(\beta)$ in the same exact manner. We have therefore proven the following fundamental comparative dynamics result for problem (P).

Theorem 11.2 (Comparative Dynamics): *For control problem (P), with assumptions (A.1) through (A.4) holding, the matrix $L_{\beta\beta}(\beta)$ is negative semidefinite subject to the constraint that $G_{\beta}(\beta)\mathbf{a} = \mathbf{0}_{3N}$ for all $\beta \in B(\beta^{\circ};\delta)$, where*

$$\underset{(2+2N+A)\times(2+2N+A)}{L_{\beta\beta}(\beta)} = \begin{bmatrix} \underset{A\times A}{L_{\alpha\alpha}(\beta)} & \underset{A\times 1}{L_{\alpha t_0}(\beta)} & \underset{A\times N}{L_{\alpha\mathbf{x}_0}(\beta)} & \underset{A\times 1}{L_{\alpha t_1}(\beta)} & \underset{A\times N}{L_{\alpha\mathbf{x}_1}(\beta)} \\ \underset{1\times A}{L_{t_0\alpha}(\beta)} & \underset{1\times 1}{L_{t_0t_0}(\beta)} & \underset{1\times N}{L_{t_0\mathbf{x}_0}(\beta)} & \underset{1\times 1}{L_{t_0t_1}(\beta)} & \underset{1\times N}{L_{t_0\mathbf{x}_1}(\beta)} \\ \underset{N\times A}{L_{\mathbf{x}_0\alpha}(\beta)} & \underset{N\times 1}{L_{\mathbf{x}_0t_0}(\beta)} & \underset{N\times N}{L_{\mathbf{x}_0\mathbf{x}_0}(\beta)} & \underset{N\times 1}{L_{\mathbf{x}_0t_1}(\beta)} & \underset{N\times N}{L_{\mathbf{x}_0\mathbf{x}_1}(\beta)} \\ \underset{1\times A}{L_{t_1\alpha}(\beta)} & \underset{1\times 1}{L_{t_1t_0}(\beta)} & \underset{1\times N}{L_{t_1\mathbf{x}_0}(\beta)} & \underset{1\times 1}{L_{t_1t_1}(\beta)} & \underset{1\times N}{L_{t_1\mathbf{x}_1}(\beta)} \\ \underset{N\times A}{L_{\mathbf{x}_1\alpha}(\beta)} & \underset{N\times 1}{L_{\mathbf{x}_1t_0}(\beta)} & \underset{N\times N}{L_{\mathbf{x}_1\mathbf{x}_0}(\beta)} & \underset{N\times 1}{L_{\mathbf{x}_1t_1}(\beta)} & \underset{N\times N}{L_{\mathbf{x}_1\mathbf{x}_1}(\beta)} \end{bmatrix},$$

$$\underset{1\times(2+2N+A)}{\mathbf{a}'} \stackrel{\text{def}}{=} \left(\underset{1\times A}{\mathbf{a}^{1\prime}} \;\; \underset{1\times 1}{a^{2\prime}} \;\; \underset{1\times N}{\mathbf{a}^{3\prime}} \;\; \underset{1\times 1}{a^{4\prime}} \;\; \underset{1\times N}{\mathbf{a}^{5\prime}} \right),$$

$$\underset{1\times 3N}{G(\beta)'} \stackrel{\text{def}}{=} \Big[\underset{1\times N}{\mathbf{g}(t,\mathbf{z}(t;\bar{\beta}),\mathbf{v}(t;\bar{\beta});\alpha)' - \dot{\mathbf{z}}(t;\bar{\beta})'} \quad \underset{1\times N}{\mathbf{x}_0' - \mathbf{z}(t_0;\bar{\beta})'} \quad \underset{1\times N}{\mathbf{z}(t_1;\bar{\beta})' - \mathbf{x}_1'} \Big],$$

$$\underset{3N\times(2+2N+A)}{G_{\beta}(\beta)} = \begin{bmatrix} \underset{N\times A}{\mathbf{g}_{\alpha}(t,\mathbf{z}(t;\bar{\beta}),\mathbf{v}(t;\bar{\beta});\alpha)} & \underset{N\times 1}{\mathbf{0}} & \underset{N\times N}{\mathbf{0}} & \underset{N\times 1}{\mathbf{0}} & \underset{N\times N}{\mathbf{0}} \\ \underset{N\times A}{\mathbf{0}} & \underset{N\times 1}{-\dot{\mathbf{z}}(t_0;\bar{\beta})} & \underset{N\times N}{\mathbf{I}} & \underset{N\times 1}{\mathbf{0}} & \underset{N\times N}{\mathbf{0}} \\ \underset{N\times A}{\mathbf{0}} & \underset{N\times 1}{\mathbf{0}} & \underset{N\times N}{\mathbf{0}} & \underset{N\times 1}{\dot{\mathbf{z}}(t_1;\bar{\beta})} & \underset{N\times N}{-\mathbf{I}} \end{bmatrix},$$

$$\underset{A\times A}{L_{\alpha\alpha}(\beta)} = -\int_{t_0}^{t_1} \left[\underset{A\times N}{H_{\alpha\mathbf{x}}(t;\beta)} \underset{N\times A}{\frac{\partial \mathbf{z}(t;\beta)}{\partial \alpha}} + \underset{A\times M}{H_{\alpha\mathbf{u}}(t;\beta)} \underset{M\times A}{\frac{\partial \mathbf{v}(t;\beta)}{\partial \alpha}} + \underset{A\times N}{H_{\alpha\boldsymbol{\lambda}}(t;\beta)} \underset{N\times A}{\frac{\partial \boldsymbol{\lambda}(t;\beta)}{\partial \alpha}} \right] dt,$$

and where the remaining 24 blocks of $L_{\beta\beta}(\beta)$ are given by Eqs. (91) through (114) in the appendix.

The dynamic primal-dual methodology reveals that all dynamic optimization problems for which assumptions (A.1) through (A.4) are met possess a negative semidefinite matrix, subject to constraint, which captures the fundamental or intrinsic comparative dynamics properties of the model. It is important to understand that this theorem has relied only on the maximization assertion and assumptions (A.1) through (A.4), pointing to its truly basic nature. No assumptions relating to the concavity of the integrand or transitions functions, their functional forms, separability assumptions, and the like were imposed on problem (P) to derive Theorem 11.2.

Assumptions (A.1) through (A.4) are not that strong either, at least from an economic point of view, as nearly all applied modeling in economics adopts a set of assumptions similar to (A.1) through (A.4). Let's now consider a special case of the general result in Theorem 11.2 that arises frequently in intertemporal economic problems.

Consider the assumption $\mathbf{g}_{\boldsymbol{\alpha}}(t, \mathbf{x}, \mathbf{u}; \boldsymbol{\alpha}) \equiv \mathbf{0}_{N\times A}$, which implies that the parameter vector $\boldsymbol{\alpha}$ does not appear in the transitions functions. Moreover, because $\boldsymbol{\alpha}$ does not appear explicitly in the endpoint constraints on the state vector in problem (P-D), the choice of $\boldsymbol{\alpha}$ in problem (P-D) is unconstrained in this instance. Said equivalently, the first column block of the matrix $G_{\boldsymbol{\beta}}(\boldsymbol{\beta})$ is null, in which case, $G_{\boldsymbol{\beta}}(\boldsymbol{\beta})\mathbf{a} = \mathbf{0}_{3N}$ implies that the subvector $\mathbf{a}^1$ is arbitrary, that is, not subject to constraint. Hence the matrix $L_{\boldsymbol{\alpha\alpha}}(\boldsymbol{\beta})$ is negative semidefinite for all $\boldsymbol{\beta} \in B(\boldsymbol{\beta}^\circ; \delta)$ free of constraint. Seeing as $\mathbf{g}_{\boldsymbol{\alpha}}(t, \mathbf{x}, \mathbf{u}; \boldsymbol{\alpha}) \equiv \mathbf{0}_{N\times A}$ in the present case, Eq. (24) and the negative semidefiniteness of $L_{\boldsymbol{\alpha\alpha}}(\boldsymbol{\beta})$ imply

$$\mathbf{a}^{1\prime} \underset{A\times A}{L_{\boldsymbol{\alpha\alpha}}(\boldsymbol{\beta})} \mathbf{a}^1 = \mathbf{a}^{1\prime} \left[\int_{t_0}^{t_1} \underset{A\times A}{f_{\boldsymbol{\alpha\alpha}}(t, \mathbf{z}(t;\boldsymbol{\beta}), \mathbf{v}(t;\boldsymbol{\beta}); \boldsymbol{\alpha})}\, dt \right] \mathbf{a}^1 - \mathbf{a}^{1\prime} \underset{A\times A}{V_{\boldsymbol{\alpha\alpha}}(\boldsymbol{\beta})} \mathbf{a}^1 \le 0. \tag{27}$$

Thus if $f(\cdot)$ is convex in $\boldsymbol{\alpha}$ for all $\boldsymbol{\beta} \in B(\boldsymbol{\beta}^\circ; \delta)$, then it follows from Eq. (27) and Theorem 21.5 of Simon and Blume (1994) that $V(\cdot)$ is convex in $\boldsymbol{\alpha}$ for all $\boldsymbol{\beta} \in B(\boldsymbol{\beta}^\circ; \delta)$, because then

$$\mathbf{a}^{1\prime} \underset{A\times A}{V_{\boldsymbol{\alpha\alpha}}(\boldsymbol{\beta})} \mathbf{a}^1 \ge \mathbf{a}^{1\prime} \left[\int_{t_0}^{t_1} \underset{A\times A}{f_{\boldsymbol{\alpha\alpha}}(t, \mathbf{z}(t;\boldsymbol{\beta}), \mathbf{v}(t;\boldsymbol{\beta}); \boldsymbol{\alpha})}\, dt \right] \mathbf{a}^1 \ge 0. \tag{28}$$

This inequality also demonstrates that under the postulated assumptions, $V(\cdot)$ is *more* convex in $\boldsymbol{\alpha}$ than is $f(\cdot)$. We have therefore proven the following corollary to Theorem 11.2.

Corollary 11.2 (Convexity of the Optimal Value Function): *For control problem (P), with assumptions (A.1) through (A.4) holding, if (i)* $\mathbf{g}_{\boldsymbol{\alpha}}(t, \mathbf{x}, \mathbf{u}; \boldsymbol{\alpha}) \equiv \mathbf{0}_{N\times A}$ *and (ii)* $f(\cdot)$ *is convex in* $\boldsymbol{\alpha}$ *for all* $\boldsymbol{\beta} \in B(\boldsymbol{\beta}^\circ; \delta)$*, then* $V(\cdot)$ *is convex in* $\boldsymbol{\alpha}$ *for all* $\boldsymbol{\beta} \in B(\boldsymbol{\beta}^\circ; \delta)$.

An analogous result holds in the static profit maximizing model of the firm. The objective function contains all the model's parameters (output price and input prices) and is linear and thus convex in these parameters, and the constraint (the production function) is independent of the model's parameters. The static primal-dual methodology of Silberberg (1974) immediately reveals that the indirect profit function is convex in input prices and output price. This is simply a special case of a more general result derivable from the static primal-dual methodology, which states: if the objective function of a constrained static maximization problem is convex in the parameters of the problem and the constraints are independent of the parameters, then the indirect objective function is locally convex in the parameters. In passing, note that Corollary 11.2 holds for problem (P) for any subset of the parameters in α that do not appear in the transition functions.

We finish up the chapter with an extended application of Theorem 11.1 and Corollary 11.2.

Example 11.1: The adjustment cost model of the firm with two capital stocks is given by

$$V(\alpha) \stackrel{\text{def}}{=} \max_{u_1(\cdot),u_2(\cdot)} \int_0^T [pf(x_1(t), x_2(t), u_1(t), u_2(t))$$

$$- w_1x_1(t) - w_2x_2(t) - g_1u_1(t) - g_2u_2(t)]\, e^{-rt}\, dt$$

$$\text{s.t.} \quad \dot{x}_1(t) = u_1(t), \dot{x}_2(t) = u_2(t),$$

$$x_1(0) = x_{10},\ x_2(0) = x_{20},\ x_1(T) = x_{1T},\ x_2(T) = x_{2T},$$

where $\alpha \stackrel{\text{def}}{=} (p, w_1, w_2, g_1, g_2, r)$ is the vector of time-independent parameters. For notational simplicity, let $\mathbf{z}(t;\alpha) \stackrel{\text{def}}{=} (z_1(t;\alpha), z_2(t;\alpha))$ and $\mathbf{v}(t;\alpha) \stackrel{\text{def}}{=} (v_1(t;\alpha), v_2(t;\alpha))$ be the optimal paths of the capital stocks and investment rates. We have chosen to set $N = 2$ to sharpen the exposition and have assumed that the capital stocks do not depreciate. Moreover, as the notation conveys, we will focus solely on the vector $\alpha \stackrel{\text{def}}{=} (p, w_1, w_2, g_1, g_2, r)$ of parameters, which are those of more immediate economic interest.

Theorem 11.1, the dynamic envelope theorem, asserts that the partial derivative of the optimal value function with respect to a parameter may be obtained by (i) differentiating the Hamiltonian of the control problem directly with respect to the parameter of interest, that is, *prior to* substituting in the optimal paths, (ii) evaluating the derivative along the optimal paths, and (iii) integrating the result over the planning horizon. Defining $y(t;\alpha) \stackrel{\text{def}}{=} f(\mathbf{z}(t;\alpha), \mathbf{v}(t;\alpha))$ as the value of the supply function of the firm, and then applying this recipe to the model, yields

$$V_p(\alpha) \equiv \int_0^T y(t;\alpha)\, e^{-rt}\, dt > 0, \tag{29}$$

$$V_{w_n}(\alpha) \equiv -\int_0^T z_n(t;\alpha)\, e^{-rt}\, dt < 0, \quad n = 1, 2, \tag{30}$$

$$V_{g_n}(\alpha) \equiv -\int_0^T v_n(t;\alpha)\, e^{-rt}\, dt \gtrless 0, \quad n = 1, 2, \tag{31}$$

$$V_r(\alpha) \equiv -\int_0^T t\pi(t;\alpha)\, e^{-rt}\, dt \gtrless 0, \tag{32}$$

where $\pi(t;\boldsymbol{\alpha}) \stackrel{\text{def}}{=} pf(\mathbf{z}(t;\boldsymbol{\alpha}), \mathbf{v}(t;\boldsymbol{\alpha})) - \mathbf{w}'\mathbf{z}(t;\boldsymbol{\alpha}) - \mathbf{g}'\mathbf{v}(t;\boldsymbol{\alpha})$ is instantaneous profits along the optimal path. Rather than recovering the instantaneous demand and supply functions, as does the static envelope theorem, the dynamic envelope theorem recovers the *cumulative discounted demand and supply functions*, a feature of the dynamic envelope theorem we noted earlier in Chapter 9, when the theorem was first introduced. Notice that Eqs. (29) and (30) are unambiguously signed, for the firm must have some capital on hand to produce output if it is to be profitable. These two properties of the optimal value function are analogous to those static indirect profit function, namely, that it is increasing in the output price and decreasing in the input prices.

In contrast, Eqs. (31) and (32) are not unambiguously signed. Given that no nonnegativity restriction is imposed on the investment rates in the above version of the adjustment cost model, the firm may find it optimal to invest ($\mathbf{v}(t;\boldsymbol{\alpha}) > \mathbf{0}_2$) or disinvest ($\mathbf{v}(t;\boldsymbol{\alpha}) < \mathbf{0}_2$) in the capital stock at various points in the planning horizon, thereby yielding the ambiguous sign in Eq. (31). The ambiguity in the sign of Eq. (32) follows from the fact that although $V(\boldsymbol{\alpha}) > 0$ must hold for the firm to be in business, instantaneous profits along the optimal path may be positive or negative at any given point in the planning horizon. Naturally, if one is willing to assume that instantaneous profit is nonnegative at each point in time of the planning horizon along the optimal path, then $V_r(\boldsymbol{\alpha}) < 0$.

Because the integrand function of the adjustment cost model is linear in $\boldsymbol{\gamma} \stackrel{\text{def}}{=} (p, w_1, w_2, g_1, g_2)$, the model satisfies the conditions of Corollary 11.2, thereby implying that the optimal value function $V(\cdot)$ is locally convex in $\boldsymbol{\gamma}$. Thus, upon differentiating Eqs. (29) through (31) with respect to $\boldsymbol{\gamma}$ and using the convexity of $V(\cdot)$, we arrive at the own-price effects

$$V_{pp}(\boldsymbol{\alpha}) \equiv \frac{\partial}{\partial p}\int_0^T y(t;\boldsymbol{\alpha})\,e^{-rt}\,dt = \int_0^T \frac{\partial y}{\partial p}(t;\boldsymbol{\alpha})\,e^{-rt}\,dt \geq 0, \tag{33}$$

$$V_{w_n w_n}(\boldsymbol{\alpha}) \equiv -\frac{\partial}{\partial w_n}\int_0^T z_n(t;\boldsymbol{\alpha})\,e^{-rt}\,dt = -\int_0^T \frac{\partial z_n}{\partial w_n}(t;\boldsymbol{\alpha})\,e^{-rt}\,dt \geq 0, \quad n = 1, 2, \tag{34}$$

$$V_{g_n g_n}(\boldsymbol{\alpha}) \equiv -\frac{\partial}{\partial g_n}\int_0^T v_n(t;\boldsymbol{\alpha})\,e^{-rt}\,dt = -\int_0^T \frac{\partial v_n}{\partial g_n}(t;\boldsymbol{\alpha})\,e^{-rt}\,dt \geq 0, \quad n = 1, 2. \tag{35}$$

These equations have important economic interpretations and implications. For example, Eq. (33) demonstrates that cumulative discounted production (or supply) will not fall when the output price increases, that is, the cumulative discounted supply function is nondecreasing in the output price. Equivalently, it asserts that the discounted supply function slope, when integrated over the planning horizon, is nonnegative. In contrast, static profit maximization theory implies the slope of the supply function is nonnegative at each point in time. Although this implies the inequality in Eq. (33), the converse is certainly not true. In other words, one may find the firm behaving irrationally over some finite period of time according to static profit maximization theory, but when viewed over its entire planning horizon, its behavior may be quite rational from an intertemporal point of view, that is to say, Eq. (33) may nonetheless be satisfied. Similarly, Eq. (35) establishes that the cumulative discounted investment demand function is a nonincreasing function of its own price. In other words, the law of demand holds for cumulative discounted investment. Alternatively, the discounted own-price effect on investment, when integrated over the planning horizon, is nonpositive. Thus, at various points in the planning horizon, or even over some finite period of time in the planning horizon, $\partial v_n(t;\boldsymbol{\alpha})/\partial g_n > 0$ is possible, and in fact, it is perfectly consistent with Eq. (35). Analogous comments and interpretation apply to Eq. (34). Note that the results in Eqs. (33) through (35) may be just as easily derived from Theorem 11.2 directly, as you are asked to show in a mental exercise.

In the preceding paragraph, you may have noticed that we didn't derive or discuss the comparative dynamics of the discount rate r. This is a result of our use of Corollary 11.2 to derive the aforementioned comparative dynamics. Simply put, Corollary 11.2 can't be used to derive the comparative dynamics of the discount rate because the integrand function $F(\cdot)$ of the adjustment cost model, defined by

$$F(t,\mathbf{x},\mathbf{u};\boldsymbol{\alpha}) \stackrel{\text{def}}{=} [pf(x_1,x_2,u_1,u_2) - w_1x_1 - w_2x_2 - g_1u_1 - g_2u_2]\,e^{-rt},$$

is not, in general, convex in the discount rate r. Thus, in general, we must rely on Theorem 11.2 to determine the comparative dynamics of the discount rate. Note, in passing, that a mental exercise asks you to contemplate the case in which $F(\cdot)$ is locally convex in r.

Recalling that $\boldsymbol{\alpha} \stackrel{\text{def}}{=} (p, w_1, w_2, g_1, g_2, r)$, so that the sixth element of the parameter vector $\boldsymbol{\alpha}$ is the discount rate r, it follows from Theorem 11.2 that

$$L_{rr}(\boldsymbol{\beta}) = -\int_0^T \sum_{n=1}^{2}\Bigg[F_{rx_n}(t,\mathbf{z}(t;\boldsymbol{\alpha}),\mathbf{v}(t;\boldsymbol{\alpha});\boldsymbol{\alpha})\frac{\partial z_n}{\partial r}(t;\boldsymbol{\alpha}) + F_{ru_n}(t,\mathbf{z}(t;\boldsymbol{\alpha}),\mathbf{v}(t;\boldsymbol{\alpha});\boldsymbol{\alpha})\frac{\partial v_n}{\partial r}(t;\boldsymbol{\alpha})\Bigg]\,dt \le 0.$$

Using the definition of $F(\cdot)$ given above, this last equation can be rewritten as

$$\int_0^T \sum_{n=1}^{2}\Bigg[[pf_{x_n}(\mathbf{z}(t;\boldsymbol{\alpha}),\mathbf{v}(t;\boldsymbol{\alpha})) - w_n]\frac{\partial z_n}{\partial r}(t;\boldsymbol{\alpha}) + [pf_{u_n}(\mathbf{z}(t;\boldsymbol{\alpha}),\mathbf{v}(t;\boldsymbol{\alpha})) - g_n]\frac{\partial v_n}{\partial r}(t;\boldsymbol{\alpha})\Bigg]\,te^{-rt}\,dt \le 0. \tag{36}$$

This expression is less amenable to a clean and simple economic interpretation than are Eqs. (33) through (35) . Nevertheless, it represents the comparative dynamics of the discount rate in the adjustment cost model of the firm. We are therefore led to conclude that the comparative dynamics of the discount rate are more complicated than they are for the prices $\gamma \overset{\text{def}}{=} (p, w_1, w_2, g_1, g_2)$.

To finish up this example, let's consider a few of the symmetry or reciprocity relations revealed by the dynamic primal-dual method. Because $V(\cdot) \in C^{(2)}$, it thus follows by differentiating Eqs. (29) through (31) that

$$\begin{aligned} V_{pw_n}(\boldsymbol{\alpha}) &\equiv \frac{\partial}{\partial w_n} \int_0^T y(t;\boldsymbol{\alpha})\, e^{-rt}\, dt = -\frac{\partial}{\partial p} \int_0^T z_n(t;\boldsymbol{\alpha})\, e^{-rt}\, dt \\ &\equiv V_{w_n p}(\boldsymbol{\alpha}), \quad n = 1, 2, \end{aligned} \tag{37}$$

$$\begin{aligned} V_{w_n w_\ell}(\boldsymbol{\alpha}) &\equiv -\frac{\partial}{\partial w_\ell} \int_0^T z_n(t;\boldsymbol{\alpha})\, e^{-rt}\, dt = -\frac{\partial}{\partial w_n} \int_0^T z_\ell(t;\boldsymbol{\alpha})\, e^{-rt}\, dt \\ &\equiv V_{w_\ell w_n}(\boldsymbol{\alpha}), \quad n \neq \ell = 1, 2. \end{aligned} \tag{38}$$

Equations (37) and (38) may be compared with their static profit maximizing counterparts, to wit,

$$\pi^*_{pw_n}(p, \mathbf{w}) \equiv \frac{\partial y^*}{\partial w_n}(p, \mathbf{w}) = -\frac{\partial x_n^*}{\partial p}(p, \mathbf{w}) \equiv \pi^*_{w_n p}(p, \mathbf{w}), \quad n = 1, 2,$$

$$\pi^*_{w_n w_\ell}(p, \mathbf{w}) \equiv -\frac{\partial x_n^*}{\partial w_\ell}(p, \mathbf{w}) = -\frac{\partial x_\ell^*}{\partial w_n}(p, \mathbf{w}) \equiv \pi^*_{w_\ell w_n}(p, \mathbf{w}), \quad n \neq \ell = 1, 2,$$

where $\pi^*(p, \mathbf{w}) \overset{\text{def}}{=} \max_{\mathbf{x} \in \Re^2_{++}} \{pf(x_1, x_2) - w_1 x_1 - w_2 x_2\}$ is the value of the indirect profit function, $x_n^*(p, \mathbf{w})$, $n = 1, 2$, are the optimal values of the factor demand functions, and $y^*(p, \mathbf{w})$ is the optimal value of the supply function. The simplicity of all of the above reciprocity relations is a result of the conjugate and linear nature in which the parameters and decision variables appear in the adjustment cost model and the profit maximization model. Equations (37) and (38) show that it is the cumulative discounted demand and supply functions that possess the symmetry properties in the adjustment cost model, not unlike the comparative dynamics results in Eqs. (33) through (35). Thus, unlike static models, the symmetry does not have to hold at each point in time, but only over the entire planning horizon. Again, what appears to be irrational behavior from a static perspective may be perfectly consistent with rational dynamic behavior. Finally, note that the results in Eqs. (37) and (38) may also be derived directly from Theorem 11.2. A mental exercise asks you to complete the derivation of the comparative dynamics of the adjustment cost model.

We have shown that all optimal control problems of the class defined by problem (P) that meet assumptions (A.1) through (A.4) possess rich qualitative properties.

The dynamic primal-dual approach developed herein was used to determine the qualitative properties of such models, and in the process, an alternative proof of the dynamic envelope theorem was exhibited. The qualitative properties revealed by the dynamic primal-dual approach are contained in a symmetric negative semidefinite matrix subject to constraint. This matrix may be thought of as an intertemporal generalization of the Slutsky matrix. It places qualitative restrictions on the demand and supply functions over the entire planning horizon, rather than at each point in time. That is, the qualitative comparative dynamics properties are in terms of the cumulative discounted demand and supply functions, not to their instantaneous forms. Symmetry was shown to be a fundamental qualitative property of any optimal control problem that meets the stated assumptions. Finally, sufficient conditions for the optimal value function to be convex in the parameters were provided.

The power of the dual view is clearly revealed by the methods established herein, for it would be difficult, if not impossible, to derive Theorem 11.2, the central result of this chapter, from a strictly primal view of the optimal control problem (P). Moreover, it is not clear why anyone would even calculate such complicated expressions from a primal vista, nor is it clear why anyone would expect them to represent the intrinsic comparative dynamics properties of an optimal control problem. A dual view of problem (P), on the other hand, has led to refutable comparative dynamics results in a rather simple and elegant way.

APPENDIX

In the chapter proper, we derived the diagonal block matrix $L_{\alpha\alpha}(\boldsymbol{\beta})$ of the full comparative dynamics matrix $L_{\boldsymbol{\beta}\boldsymbol{\beta}}(\boldsymbol{\beta})$ in Theorem 11.2. The purpose of the appendix is to derive the remaining 24 blocks of the matrix $L_{\boldsymbol{\beta}\boldsymbol{\beta}}(\boldsymbol{\beta})$ in Theorem 11.2.

As a first step, differentiate Eqs. (11) through (15) with respect to the vector of parameters $\boldsymbol{\beta} \stackrel{\text{def}}{=} (\boldsymbol{\alpha}, t_0, \mathbf{x}_0, t_1, \mathbf{x}_1) \in \Re^{2+2N+A}$ and evaluate the results at $\boldsymbol{\beta} = \bar{\boldsymbol{\beta}}$ to get

$$L_{\alpha t_0}(\bar{\boldsymbol{\beta}}) = -H_{\alpha}(\bar{t}_0; \bar{\boldsymbol{\beta}}) - V_{\alpha t_0}(\bar{\boldsymbol{\beta}}), \tag{39}$$

$$L_{\alpha \mathbf{x}_0}(\bar{\boldsymbol{\beta}}) = -V_{\alpha \mathbf{x}_0}(\bar{\boldsymbol{\beta}}), \tag{40}$$

$$L_{\alpha t_1}(\bar{\boldsymbol{\beta}}) = H_{\alpha}(\bar{t}_1; \bar{\boldsymbol{\beta}}) - V_{\alpha t_1}(\bar{\boldsymbol{\beta}}), \tag{41}$$

$$L_{\alpha \mathbf{x}_1}(\bar{\boldsymbol{\beta}}) = -V_{\alpha \mathbf{x}_1}(\bar{\boldsymbol{\beta}}), \tag{42}$$

$$L_{t_0 \alpha}(\bar{\boldsymbol{\beta}}) = -H_{\alpha}(\bar{t}_0; \bar{\boldsymbol{\beta}}) - V_{t_0 \alpha}(\bar{\boldsymbol{\beta}}), \tag{43}$$

$$\begin{aligned} L_{t_0 t_0}(\bar{\boldsymbol{\beta}}) &= -H_t(\bar{t}_0; \bar{\boldsymbol{\beta}}) - H_{\mathbf{x}}(\bar{t}_0; \bar{\boldsymbol{\beta}})\,\dot{\mathbf{z}}(\bar{t}_0; \bar{\boldsymbol{\beta}}) - H_{\mathbf{u}}(\bar{t}_0; \bar{\boldsymbol{\beta}})\,\dot{\mathbf{v}}(\bar{t}_0; \bar{\boldsymbol{\beta}}) - H_{\boldsymbol{\lambda}}(\bar{t}_0; \bar{\boldsymbol{\beta}})\,\dot{\boldsymbol{\lambda}}(\bar{t}_0; \bar{\boldsymbol{\beta}}) \\ &\quad - \dot{\boldsymbol{\lambda}}(\bar{t}_0; \bar{\boldsymbol{\beta}})'\dot{\mathbf{z}}(\bar{t}_0; \bar{\boldsymbol{\beta}}) - \ddot{\boldsymbol{\lambda}}(\bar{t}_0; \bar{\boldsymbol{\beta}})'\mathbf{z}(\bar{t}_0; \bar{\boldsymbol{\beta}}) + \ddot{\boldsymbol{\lambda}}(\bar{t}_0; \bar{\boldsymbol{\beta}})'\bar{\mathbf{x}}_0 - V_{t_0 t_0}(\bar{\boldsymbol{\beta}}) \\ &= -H_t(\bar{t}_0; \bar{\boldsymbol{\beta}}) - \dot{\boldsymbol{\lambda}}(\bar{t}_0; \bar{\boldsymbol{\beta}})'\dot{\mathbf{z}}(\bar{t}_0; \bar{\boldsymbol{\beta}}) - V_{t_0 t_0}(\bar{\boldsymbol{\beta}}), \end{aligned} \tag{44}$$

$$L_{t_0 \mathbf{x}_0}(\bar{\boldsymbol{\beta}}) = \dot{\boldsymbol{\lambda}}(\bar{t}_0; \bar{\boldsymbol{\beta}})' - V_{t_0 \mathbf{x}_0}(\bar{\boldsymbol{\beta}}), \tag{45}$$

$$L_{t_0t_1}(\bar{\beta}) = -V_{t_0t_1}(\bar{\beta}), \tag{46}$$

$$L_{t_0\mathbf{x}_1}(\bar{\beta}) = -V_{t_0\mathbf{x}_1}(\bar{\beta}), \tag{47}$$

$$L_{\mathbf{x}_0\alpha}(\bar{\beta}) = -V_{\mathbf{x}_0\alpha}(\bar{\beta}), \tag{48}$$

$$L_{\mathbf{x}_0t_0}(\bar{\beta}) = \dot{\boldsymbol{\lambda}}(\bar{t}_0; \bar{\beta}) - V_{\mathbf{x}_0t_0}(\bar{\beta}), \tag{49}$$

$$L_{\mathbf{x}_0\mathbf{x}_0}(\bar{\beta}) = -V_{\mathbf{x}_0\mathbf{x}_0}(\bar{\beta}), \tag{50}$$

$$L_{\mathbf{x}_0t_1}(\bar{\beta}) = -V_{\mathbf{x}_0t_1}(\bar{\beta}), \tag{51}$$

$$L_{\mathbf{x}_0\mathbf{x}_1}(\bar{\beta}) = -V_{\mathbf{x}_0\mathbf{x}_1}(\bar{\beta}), \tag{52}$$

$$L_{t_1\alpha}(\bar{\beta}) = H_\alpha(\bar{t}_1; \bar{\beta}) - V_{t_1\alpha}(\bar{\beta}), \tag{53}$$

$$L_{t_1t_0}(\bar{\beta}) = -V_{t_1t_0}(\bar{\beta}), \tag{54}$$

$$L_{t_1\mathbf{x}_0}(\bar{\beta}) = -V_{t_1\mathbf{x}_0}(\bar{\beta}), \tag{55}$$

$$\begin{aligned} L_{t_1t_1}(\bar{\beta}) &= H_t(\bar{t}_1; \bar{\beta}) + H_{\mathbf{x}}(\bar{t}_1; \bar{\beta})\,\dot{\mathbf{z}}(\bar{t}_1; \bar{\beta}) + H_{\mathbf{u}}(\bar{t}_1; \bar{\beta})\,\dot{\mathbf{v}}(\bar{t}_1; \bar{\beta}) + H_{\boldsymbol{\lambda}}(\bar{t}_1; \bar{\beta})\,\dot{\boldsymbol{\lambda}}(\bar{t}_1; \bar{\beta}) \\ &\quad + \dot{\boldsymbol{\lambda}}(\bar{t}_1; \bar{\beta})'\dot{\mathbf{z}}(\bar{t}_1; \bar{\beta}) + \ddot{\boldsymbol{\lambda}}(\bar{t}_1; \bar{\beta})'\mathbf{z}(\bar{t}_1; \bar{\beta}) - \ddot{\boldsymbol{\lambda}}(\bar{t}_1; \bar{\beta})'\bar{\mathbf{x}}_1 - V_{t_1t_1}(\bar{\beta}) \qquad (56) \\ &= H_t(\bar{t}_1; \bar{\beta}) + \dot{\boldsymbol{\lambda}}(\bar{t}_1; \bar{\beta})'\dot{\mathbf{z}}(\bar{t}_1; \bar{\beta}) - V_{t_1t_1}(\bar{\beta}), \end{aligned}$$

$$L_{t_1\mathbf{x}_1}(\bar{\beta}) = -\dot{\boldsymbol{\lambda}}(\bar{t}_1; \bar{\beta})' - V_{t_1\mathbf{x}_1}(\bar{\beta}), \tag{57}$$

$$L_{\mathbf{x}_1\alpha}(\bar{\beta}) = -V_{\mathbf{x}_1\alpha}(\bar{\beta}), \tag{58}$$

$$L_{\mathbf{x}_1t_0}(\bar{\beta}) = -V_{\mathbf{x}_1t_0}(\bar{\beta}), \tag{59}$$

$$L_{\mathbf{x}_1\mathbf{x}_0}(\bar{\beta}) = -V_{\mathbf{x}_1\mathbf{x}_0}(\bar{\beta}), \tag{60}$$

$$L_{\mathbf{x}_1t_1}(\bar{\beta}) = -\dot{\boldsymbol{\lambda}}(\bar{t}_1; \bar{\beta}) - V_{\mathbf{x}_1t_1}(\bar{\beta}), \tag{61}$$

$$L_{\mathbf{x}_1\mathbf{x}_1}(\bar{\beta}) = -V_{\mathbf{x}_1\mathbf{x}_1}(\bar{\beta}). \tag{62}$$

Note that in simplifying Eqs. (44) and (56), we used the necessary conditions of Corollary 4.2 in identity form, to wit,

$$H_{\mathbf{u}}(t, \mathbf{z}(t; \beta), \mathbf{v}(t; \beta), \boldsymbol{\lambda}(t; \beta); \alpha) \equiv \mathbf{0}_M', \tag{63}$$

$$\dot{\boldsymbol{\lambda}}(t; \beta)' \equiv -H_{\mathbf{x}}(t, \mathbf{z}(t; \beta), \mathbf{v}(t; \beta), \boldsymbol{\lambda}(t; \beta); \alpha), \tag{64}$$

$$\dot{\mathbf{z}}(t; \beta)' \equiv H_{\boldsymbol{\lambda}}(t, \mathbf{z}(t; \beta), \mathbf{v}(t; \beta), \boldsymbol{\lambda}(t; \beta); \alpha), \tag{65}$$

$$\mathbf{z}(t_0; \beta) \equiv \mathbf{x}_0,\ \ \mathbf{z}(t_1; \beta) \equiv \mathbf{x}_1, \tag{66}$$

which hold for all $\beta \in B(\beta^\circ; \delta)$.

The next step is to differentiate the envelope results of Theorem 11.1 with respect to the parameter vector $\beta \stackrel{\text{def}}{=} (\alpha, t_0, \mathbf{x}_0, t_1, \mathbf{x}_1)$ and evaluate the results at $\beta = \bar{\beta}$ to get

$$V_{\alpha t_0}(\bar{\beta}) \equiv -H_\alpha(\bar{t}_0; \bar{\beta}) + \int_{\bar{t}_0}^{\bar{t}_1} \left[H_{\alpha\mathbf{x}}(t; \bar{\beta}) \frac{\partial \mathbf{z}(t; \bar{\beta})}{\partial t_0} + H_{\alpha\mathbf{u}}(t; \bar{\beta}) \frac{\partial \mathbf{v}(t; \bar{\beta})}{\partial t_0} + H_{\alpha\boldsymbol{\lambda}}(t; \bar{\beta}) \frac{\partial \boldsymbol{\lambda}(t; \bar{\beta})}{\partial t_0} \right] dt, \tag{67}$$

$$V_{\alpha\mathbf{x}_0}(\bar{\beta}) \equiv \int_{\bar{t}_0}^{\bar{t}_1} \left[H_{\alpha\mathbf{x}}(t; \bar{\beta}) \frac{\partial \mathbf{z}(t; \bar{\beta})}{\partial \mathbf{x}_0} + H_{\alpha\mathbf{u}}(t; \bar{\beta}) \frac{\partial \mathbf{v}(t; \bar{\beta})}{\partial \mathbf{x}_0} + H_{\alpha\boldsymbol{\lambda}}(t; \bar{\beta}) \frac{\partial \boldsymbol{\lambda}(t; \bar{\beta})}{\partial \mathbf{x}_0} \right] dt, \tag{68}$$

$$V_{\alpha t_1}(\bar{\beta}) \equiv H_\alpha(\bar{t}_1; \bar{\beta}) + \int_{\bar{t}_0}^{\bar{t}_1} \left[H_{\alpha\mathbf{x}}(t; \bar{\beta}) \frac{\partial \mathbf{z}(t; \bar{\beta})}{\partial t_1} + H_{\alpha\mathbf{u}}(t; \bar{\beta}) \frac{\partial \mathbf{v}(t; \bar{\beta})}{\partial t_1} + H_{\alpha\boldsymbol{\lambda}}(t; \bar{\beta}) \frac{\partial \boldsymbol{\lambda}(t; \bar{\beta})}{\partial t_1} \right] dt, \tag{69}$$

$$V_{\alpha\mathbf{x}_1}(\bar{\beta}) \equiv \int_{\bar{t}_0}^{\bar{t}_1} \left[H_{\alpha\mathbf{x}}(t; \bar{\beta}) \frac{\partial \mathbf{z}(t; \bar{\beta})}{\partial \mathbf{x}_1} + H_{\alpha\mathbf{u}}(t; \bar{\beta}) \frac{\partial \mathbf{v}(t; \bar{\beta})}{\partial \mathbf{x}_1} + H_{\alpha\boldsymbol{\lambda}}(t; \bar{\beta}) \frac{\partial \boldsymbol{\lambda}(t; \bar{\beta})}{\partial \mathbf{x}_1} \right] dt, \tag{70}$$

$$\begin{aligned} V_{t_0\alpha}(\bar{\beta}) &\equiv -H_{\mathbf{x}}(\bar{t}_0; \bar{\beta}) \frac{\partial \mathbf{z}(\bar{t}_0; \bar{\beta})}{\partial \alpha} - H_{\mathbf{u}}(\bar{t}_0; \bar{\beta}) \frac{\partial \mathbf{v}(\bar{t}_0; \bar{\beta})}{\partial \alpha} - H_{\boldsymbol{\lambda}}(\bar{t}_0; \bar{\beta}) \frac{\partial \boldsymbol{\lambda}(\bar{t}_0; \bar{\beta})}{\partial \alpha} \\ &\quad - H_\alpha(\bar{t}_0; \bar{\beta}) = -H_{\boldsymbol{\lambda}}(\bar{t}_0; \bar{\beta}) \frac{\partial \boldsymbol{\lambda}(\bar{t}_0; \bar{\beta})}{\partial \alpha} - H_\alpha(\bar{t}_0; \bar{\beta}), \end{aligned} \tag{71}$$

$$\begin{aligned} V_{t_0 t_0}(\bar{\beta}) &\equiv -H_t(\bar{t}_0; \bar{\beta}) - H_{\mathbf{x}}(\bar{t}_0; \bar{\beta}) \left[\dot{\mathbf{z}}(\bar{t}_0; \bar{\beta}) + \frac{\partial \mathbf{z}(\bar{t}_0; \bar{\beta})}{\partial t_0} \right] \\ &\quad - H_{\mathbf{u}}(\bar{t}_0; \bar{\beta}) \left[\dot{\mathbf{v}}(\bar{t}_0; \bar{\beta}) + \frac{\partial \mathbf{v}(\bar{t}_0; \bar{\beta})}{\partial t_0} \right] - H_{\boldsymbol{\lambda}}(\bar{t}_0; \bar{\beta}) \left[\dot{\boldsymbol{\lambda}}(\bar{t}_0; \bar{\beta}) + \frac{\partial \boldsymbol{\lambda}(\bar{t}_0; \bar{\beta})}{\partial t_0} \right] \\ &= -H_t(\bar{t}_0; \bar{\beta}) - H_{\boldsymbol{\lambda}}(\bar{t}_0; \bar{\beta}) \left[\dot{\boldsymbol{\lambda}}(\bar{t}_0; \bar{\beta}) + \frac{\partial \boldsymbol{\lambda}(\bar{t}_0; \bar{\beta})}{\partial t_0} \right], \end{aligned} \tag{72}$$

$$\begin{aligned} V_{t_0\mathbf{x}_0}(\bar{\beta}) &\equiv -H_{\mathbf{x}}(\bar{t}_0; \bar{\beta}) \frac{\partial \mathbf{z}(\bar{t}_0; \bar{\beta})}{\partial \mathbf{x}_0} - H_{\mathbf{u}}(\bar{t}_0; \bar{\beta}) \frac{\partial \mathbf{v}(\bar{t}_0; \bar{\beta})}{\partial \mathbf{x}_0} - H_{\boldsymbol{\lambda}}(\bar{t}_0; \bar{\beta}) \frac{\partial \boldsymbol{\lambda}(\bar{t}_0; \bar{\beta})}{\partial \mathbf{x}_0} \\ &= -H_{\mathbf{x}}(\bar{t}_0; \bar{\beta}) - H_{\boldsymbol{\lambda}}(\bar{t}_0; \bar{\beta}) \frac{\partial \boldsymbol{\lambda}(\bar{t}_0; \bar{\beta})}{\partial \mathbf{x}_0}, \end{aligned} \tag{73}$$

$$V_{t_0t_1}(\bar{\beta}) \equiv -H_{\mathbf{x}}(\bar{t}_0;\bar{\beta})\frac{\partial \mathbf{z}(\bar{t}_0;\bar{\beta})}{\partial t_1} - H_{\mathbf{u}}(\bar{t}_0;\bar{\beta})\frac{\partial \mathbf{v}(\bar{t}_0;\bar{\beta})}{\partial t_1} - H_{\boldsymbol{\lambda}}(\bar{t}_0;\bar{\beta})\frac{\partial \boldsymbol{\lambda}(\bar{t}_0;\bar{\beta})}{\partial t_1}$$

$$= -H_{\boldsymbol{\lambda}}(\bar{t}_0;\bar{\beta})\frac{\partial \boldsymbol{\lambda}(\bar{t}_0;\bar{\beta})}{\partial t_1}, \tag{74}$$

$$V_{t_0\mathbf{x}_1}(\bar{\beta}) \equiv -H_{\mathbf{x}}(\bar{t}_0;\bar{\beta})\frac{\partial \mathbf{z}(\bar{t}_0;\bar{\beta})}{\partial \mathbf{x}_1} - H_{\mathbf{u}}(\bar{t}_0;\bar{\beta})\frac{\partial \mathbf{v}(\bar{t}_0;\bar{\beta})}{\partial \mathbf{x}_1} - H_{\boldsymbol{\lambda}}(\bar{t}_0;\bar{\beta})\frac{\partial \boldsymbol{\lambda}(\bar{t}_0;\bar{\beta})}{\partial \mathbf{x}_1}$$

$$= -H_{\boldsymbol{\lambda}}(\bar{t}_0;\bar{\beta})\frac{\partial \boldsymbol{\lambda}(\bar{t}_0;\bar{\beta})}{\partial \mathbf{x}_1}, \tag{75}$$

$$V_{\mathbf{x}_0\boldsymbol{\alpha}}(\bar{\beta}) \equiv \frac{\partial \boldsymbol{\lambda}(\bar{t}_0;\bar{\beta})}{\partial \boldsymbol{\alpha}}, \tag{76}$$

$$V_{\mathbf{x}_0t_0}(\bar{\beta}) \equiv \dot{\boldsymbol{\lambda}}(\bar{t}_0;\bar{\beta}) + \frac{\partial \boldsymbol{\lambda}(\bar{t}_0;\bar{\beta})}{\partial t_0}, \tag{77}$$

$$V_{\mathbf{x}_0\mathbf{x}_0}(\bar{\beta}) \equiv \frac{\partial \boldsymbol{\lambda}(\bar{t}_0;\bar{\beta})}{\partial \mathbf{x}_0}, \tag{78}$$

$$V_{\mathbf{x}_0t_1}(\bar{\beta}) \equiv \frac{\partial \boldsymbol{\lambda}(\bar{t}_0;\bar{\beta})}{\partial t_1}, \tag{79}$$

$$V_{\mathbf{x}_0\mathbf{x}_1}(\bar{\beta}) \equiv \frac{\partial \boldsymbol{\lambda}(\bar{t}_0;\bar{\beta})}{\partial \mathbf{x}_1}, \tag{80}$$

$$V_{t_1\boldsymbol{\alpha}}(\bar{\beta}) \equiv H_{\mathbf{x}}(\bar{t}_1;\bar{\beta})\frac{\partial \mathbf{z}(\bar{t}_1;\bar{\beta})}{\partial \boldsymbol{\alpha}} + H_{\mathbf{u}}(\bar{t}_1;\bar{\beta})\frac{\partial \mathbf{v}(\bar{t}_1;\bar{\beta})}{\partial \boldsymbol{\alpha}}$$

$$+ H_{\boldsymbol{\lambda}}(\bar{t}_1;\bar{\beta})\frac{\partial \boldsymbol{\lambda}(\bar{t}_1;\bar{\beta})}{\partial \boldsymbol{\alpha}} + H_{\boldsymbol{\alpha}}(\bar{t}_1;\bar{\beta})$$

$$= H_{\boldsymbol{\lambda}}(\bar{t}_1;\bar{\beta})\frac{\partial \boldsymbol{\lambda}(\bar{t}_1;\bar{\beta})}{\partial \boldsymbol{\alpha}} + H_{\boldsymbol{\alpha}}(\bar{t}_1;\bar{\beta}), \tag{81}$$

$$V_{t_1t_0}(\bar{\beta}) \equiv H_{\mathbf{x}}(\bar{t}_1;\bar{\beta})\frac{\partial \mathbf{z}(\bar{t}_1;\bar{\beta})}{\partial t_0} + H_{\mathbf{u}}(\bar{t}_1;\bar{\beta})\frac{\partial \mathbf{v}(\bar{t}_1;\bar{\beta})}{\partial t_0} + H_{\boldsymbol{\lambda}}(\bar{t}_1;\bar{\beta})\frac{\partial \boldsymbol{\lambda}(\bar{t}_1;\bar{\beta})}{\partial t_0}$$

$$= H_{\boldsymbol{\lambda}}(\bar{t}_1;\bar{\beta})\frac{\partial \boldsymbol{\lambda}(\bar{t}_1;\bar{\beta})}{\partial t_0}, \tag{82}$$

$$V_{t_1\mathbf{x}_0}(\bar{\beta}) \equiv H_{\mathbf{x}}(\bar{t}_1;\bar{\beta})\frac{\partial \mathbf{z}(\bar{t}_1;\bar{\beta})}{\partial \mathbf{x}_0} + H_{\mathbf{u}}(\bar{t}_1;\bar{\beta})\frac{\partial \mathbf{v}(\bar{t}_1;\bar{\beta})}{\partial \mathbf{x}_0} + H_{\boldsymbol{\lambda}}(\bar{t}_1;\bar{\beta})\frac{\partial \boldsymbol{\lambda}(\bar{t}_1;\bar{\beta})}{\partial \mathbf{x}_0}$$

$$= H_{\boldsymbol{\lambda}}(\bar{t}_1;\bar{\beta})\frac{\partial \boldsymbol{\lambda}(\bar{t}_1;\bar{\beta})}{\partial \mathbf{x}_0}, \tag{83}$$

$$V_{t_1t_1}(\bar{\beta}) \equiv H_t(\bar{t}_1;\bar{\beta}) + H_{\mathbf{x}}(\bar{t}_1;\bar{\beta})\left[\dot{\mathbf{z}}(\bar{t}_1;\bar{\beta}) + \frac{\partial \mathbf{z}(\bar{t}_1;\bar{\beta})}{\partial t_1}\right]$$

$$+ H_{\mathbf{u}}(\bar{t}_1;\bar{\beta})\left[\dot{\mathbf{v}}(\bar{t}_1;\bar{\beta}) + \frac{\partial \mathbf{v}(\bar{t}_1;\bar{\beta})}{\partial t_1}\right] + H_{\boldsymbol{\lambda}}(\bar{t}_1;\bar{\beta})\left[\dot{\boldsymbol{\lambda}}(\bar{t}_1;\bar{\beta}) + \frac{\partial \boldsymbol{\lambda}(\bar{t}_1;\bar{\beta})}{\partial t_1}\right]$$

$$= H_t(\bar{t}_1;\bar{\beta}) + H_{\boldsymbol{\lambda}}(\bar{t}_1;\bar{\beta})\left[\dot{\boldsymbol{\lambda}}(\bar{t}_1;\bar{\beta}) + \frac{\partial \boldsymbol{\lambda}(\bar{t}_1;\bar{\beta})}{\partial t_1}\right], \tag{84}$$

$$V_{t_1\mathbf{x}_1}(\bar{\beta}) \equiv H_{\mathbf{x}}(\bar{t}_1;\bar{\beta})\frac{\partial \mathbf{z}(\bar{t}_1;\bar{\beta})}{\partial \mathbf{x}_1} + H_{\mathbf{u}}(\bar{t}_1;\bar{\beta})\frac{\partial \mathbf{v}(\bar{t}_1;\bar{\beta})}{\partial \mathbf{x}_1} + H_{\lambda}(\bar{t}_1;\bar{\beta})\frac{\partial \boldsymbol{\lambda}(\bar{t}_1;\bar{\beta})}{\partial \mathbf{x}_1}$$

$$= H_{\mathbf{x}}(\bar{t}_1;\bar{\beta}) + H_{\lambda}(\bar{t}_1;\bar{\beta})\frac{\partial \boldsymbol{\lambda}(\bar{t}_1;\bar{\beta})}{\partial \mathbf{x}_1}, \tag{85}$$

$$V_{\mathbf{x}_1\alpha}(\bar{\beta}) \equiv -\frac{\partial \boldsymbol{\lambda}(\bar{t}_1;\bar{\beta})}{\partial \alpha}, \tag{86}$$

$$V_{\mathbf{x}_1 t_0}(\bar{\beta}) \equiv -\frac{\partial \boldsymbol{\lambda}(\bar{t}_1;\bar{\beta})}{\partial t_0}, \tag{87}$$

$$V_{\mathbf{x}_1\mathbf{x}_0}(\bar{\beta}) \equiv -\frac{\partial \boldsymbol{\lambda}(\bar{t}_1;\bar{\beta})}{\partial \mathbf{x}_0}, \tag{88}$$

$$V_{\mathbf{x}_1 t_1}(\bar{\beta}) \equiv -\dot{\boldsymbol{\lambda}}(\bar{t}_1;\bar{\beta}) - \frac{\partial \boldsymbol{\lambda}(\bar{t}_1;\bar{\beta})}{\partial t_1}, \tag{89}$$

$$V_{\mathbf{x}_1\mathbf{x}_1}(\bar{\beta}) \equiv -\frac{\partial \boldsymbol{\lambda}(\bar{t}_1;\bar{\beta})}{\partial \mathbf{x}_1}. \tag{90}$$

In addition to the necessary conditions of Corollary 4.2 given in Eqs. (63) through (66), we also made use of the following implications of the fixed endpoints on the state vector:

$$\mathbf{z}(t_0;\beta) \equiv \mathbf{x}_0 \Rightarrow \begin{cases} \dfrac{\partial \mathbf{z}(t_0;\beta)}{\partial \alpha} \equiv \mathbf{0}_{N\times A}, \\ \dot{\mathbf{z}}(t_0;\beta) + \dfrac{\partial \mathbf{z}(t_0;\beta)}{\partial t_0} \equiv \mathbf{0}_N, \\ \dfrac{\partial \mathbf{z}(t_0;\beta)}{\partial \mathbf{x}_0} \equiv \mathbf{I}_N, \\ \dfrac{\partial \mathbf{z}(t_0;\beta)}{\partial t_1} \equiv \mathbf{0}_N, \\ \dfrac{\partial \mathbf{z}(t_0;\beta)}{\partial \mathbf{x}_1} \equiv \mathbf{0}_{N\times N}, \end{cases}$$

$$\mathbf{z}(t_1;\beta) \equiv \mathbf{x}_1 \Rightarrow \begin{cases} \dfrac{\partial \mathbf{z}(t_1;\beta)}{\partial \alpha} \equiv \mathbf{0}_{N\times A}, \\ \dfrac{\partial \mathbf{z}(t_1;\beta)}{\partial t_0} \equiv \mathbf{0}_N, \\ \dfrac{\partial \mathbf{z}(t_1;\beta)}{\partial \mathbf{x}_0} \equiv \mathbf{0}_{N\times N}, \\ \dot{\mathbf{z}}(t_1;\beta) + \dfrac{\partial \mathbf{z}(t_1;\beta)}{\partial t_1} \equiv \mathbf{0}_N, \\ \dfrac{\partial \mathbf{z}(t_1;\beta)}{\partial \mathbf{x}_1} \equiv \mathbf{I}_N, \end{cases}$$

in simplifying Eqs. (67) through (90).

Now recall that Eqs. (39) through (90) hold for all $\beta \in B(\beta^{\circ};\delta)$, as established in the chapter proper. As a result, we may drop the over bar on the parameters. Doing just that, substituting Eqs. (67) through (90) into Eqs. (39) through (62) respectively, and then canceling terms yields the results we seek, namely,

$$L_{\alpha t_0}(\boldsymbol{\beta}) = -\int_{t_0}^{t_1}\left[H_{\alpha\mathbf{x}}(t;\boldsymbol{\beta})\frac{\partial\mathbf{z}(t;\boldsymbol{\beta})}{\partial t_0} + H_{\alpha\mathbf{u}}(t;\boldsymbol{\beta})\frac{\partial\mathbf{v}(t;\boldsymbol{\beta})}{\partial t_0} + H_{\alpha\boldsymbol{\lambda}}(t;\boldsymbol{\beta})\frac{\partial\boldsymbol{\lambda}(t;\boldsymbol{\beta})}{\partial t_0}\right]dt, \quad (91)$$

$$L_{\alpha\mathbf{x}_0}(\boldsymbol{\beta}) = -\int_{t_0}^{t_1}\left[H_{\alpha\mathbf{x}}(t;\boldsymbol{\beta})\frac{\partial\mathbf{z}(t;\boldsymbol{\beta})}{\partial\mathbf{x}_0} + H_{\alpha\mathbf{u}}(t;\boldsymbol{\beta})\frac{\partial\mathbf{v}(t;\boldsymbol{\beta})}{\partial\mathbf{x}_0} + H_{\alpha\boldsymbol{\lambda}}(t;\boldsymbol{\beta})\frac{\partial\boldsymbol{\lambda}(t;\boldsymbol{\beta})}{\partial\mathbf{x}_0}\right]dt, \quad (92)$$

$$L_{\alpha t_1}(\boldsymbol{\beta}) = -\int_{t_0}^{t_1}\left[H_{\alpha\mathbf{x}}(t;\boldsymbol{\beta})\frac{\partial\mathbf{z}(t;\boldsymbol{\beta})}{\partial t_1} + H_{\alpha\mathbf{u}}(t;\boldsymbol{\beta})\frac{\partial\mathbf{v}(t;\boldsymbol{\beta})}{\partial t_1} + H_{\alpha\boldsymbol{\lambda}}(t;\boldsymbol{\beta})\frac{\partial\boldsymbol{\lambda}(t;\boldsymbol{\beta})}{\partial t_1}\right]dt, \quad (93)$$

$$L_{\alpha\mathbf{x}_1}(\boldsymbol{\beta}) = -\int_{t_0}^{t_1}\left[H_{\alpha\mathbf{x}}(t;\boldsymbol{\beta})\frac{\partial\mathbf{z}(t;\boldsymbol{\beta})}{\partial\mathbf{x}_1} + H_{\alpha\mathbf{u}}(t;\boldsymbol{\beta})\frac{\partial\mathbf{v}(t;\boldsymbol{\beta})}{\partial\mathbf{x}_1} + H_{\alpha\boldsymbol{\lambda}}(t;\boldsymbol{\beta})\frac{\partial\boldsymbol{\lambda}(t;\boldsymbol{\beta})}{\partial\mathbf{x}_1}\right]dt, \quad (94)$$

$$L_{t_0\alpha}(\boldsymbol{\beta}) = H_{\boldsymbol{\lambda}}(t_0;\boldsymbol{\beta})\frac{\partial\boldsymbol{\lambda}(t_0;\boldsymbol{\beta})}{\partial\boldsymbol{\alpha}}, \quad (95)$$

$$L_{t_0t_0}(\boldsymbol{\beta}) = H_{\boldsymbol{\lambda}}(t_0;\boldsymbol{\beta})\frac{\partial\boldsymbol{\lambda}(t_0;\boldsymbol{\beta})}{\partial t_0}, \quad (96)$$

$$L_{t_0\mathbf{x}_0}(\boldsymbol{\beta}) = H_{\boldsymbol{\lambda}}(t_0;\boldsymbol{\beta})\frac{\partial\boldsymbol{\lambda}(t_0;\boldsymbol{\beta})}{\partial\mathbf{x}_0}, \quad (97)$$

$$L_{t_0t_1}(\boldsymbol{\beta}) = H_{\boldsymbol{\lambda}}(t_0;\boldsymbol{\beta})\frac{\partial\boldsymbol{\lambda}(t_0;\boldsymbol{\beta})}{\partial t_1}, \quad (98)$$

$$L_{t_0\mathbf{x}_1}(\boldsymbol{\beta}) = H_{\boldsymbol{\lambda}}(t_0;\boldsymbol{\beta})\frac{\partial\boldsymbol{\lambda}(t_0;\boldsymbol{\beta})}{\partial\mathbf{x}_1}, \quad (99)$$

$$L_{\mathbf{x}_0\alpha}(\boldsymbol{\beta}) = -\frac{\partial\boldsymbol{\lambda}(t_0;\boldsymbol{\beta})}{\partial\boldsymbol{\alpha}}, \quad (100)$$

$$L_{\mathbf{x}_0t_0}(\boldsymbol{\beta}) = -\frac{\partial\boldsymbol{\lambda}(t_0;\boldsymbol{\beta})}{\partial t_0}, \quad (101)$$

$$L_{\mathbf{x}_0\mathbf{x}_0}(\boldsymbol{\beta}) = -\frac{\partial\boldsymbol{\lambda}(t_0;\boldsymbol{\beta})}{\partial\mathbf{x}_0}, \quad (102)$$

$$L_{\mathbf{x}_0t_1}(\boldsymbol{\beta}) = -\frac{\partial\boldsymbol{\lambda}(t_0;\boldsymbol{\beta})}{\partial t_1}, \quad (103)$$

$$L_{\mathbf{x}_0\mathbf{x}_1}(\boldsymbol{\beta}) = -\frac{\partial \boldsymbol{\lambda}(t_0;\boldsymbol{\beta})}{\partial \mathbf{x}_1}, \tag{104}$$

$$L_{t_1\boldsymbol{\alpha}}(\boldsymbol{\beta}) = -H_{\boldsymbol{\lambda}}(t_1;\boldsymbol{\beta})\frac{\partial \boldsymbol{\lambda}(t_1;\boldsymbol{\beta})}{\partial \boldsymbol{\alpha}}, \tag{105}$$

$$L_{t_1t_0}(\boldsymbol{\beta}) = -H_{\boldsymbol{\lambda}}(t_1;\boldsymbol{\beta})\frac{\partial \boldsymbol{\lambda}(t_1;\boldsymbol{\beta})}{\partial t_0}, \tag{106}$$

$$L_{t_1\mathbf{x}_0}(\boldsymbol{\beta}) = -H_{\boldsymbol{\lambda}}(t_1;\boldsymbol{\beta})\frac{\partial \boldsymbol{\lambda}(t_1;\boldsymbol{\beta})}{\partial \mathbf{x}_0}, \tag{107}$$

$$L_{t_1t_1}(\boldsymbol{\beta}) = -H_{\boldsymbol{\lambda}}(t_1;\boldsymbol{\beta})\frac{\partial \boldsymbol{\lambda}(t_1;\boldsymbol{\beta})}{\partial t_1}, \tag{108}$$

$$L_{t_1\mathbf{x}_1}(\boldsymbol{\beta}) = -H_{\boldsymbol{\lambda}}(t_1;\boldsymbol{\beta})\frac{\partial \boldsymbol{\lambda}(t_1;\boldsymbol{\beta})}{\partial \mathbf{x}_1}, \tag{109}$$

$$L_{\mathbf{x}_1\boldsymbol{\alpha}}(\boldsymbol{\beta}) = \frac{\partial \boldsymbol{\lambda}(t_1;\boldsymbol{\beta})}{\partial \boldsymbol{\alpha}}, \tag{110}$$

$$L_{\mathbf{x}_1t_0}(\boldsymbol{\beta}) = \frac{\partial \boldsymbol{\lambda}(t_1;\boldsymbol{\beta})}{\partial t_0}, \tag{111}$$

$$L_{\mathbf{x}_1\mathbf{x}_0}(\boldsymbol{\beta}) = \frac{\partial \boldsymbol{\lambda}(t_1;\boldsymbol{\beta})}{\partial \mathbf{x}_0}, \tag{112}$$

$$L_{\mathbf{x}_1t_1}(\boldsymbol{\beta}) = \frac{\partial \boldsymbol{\lambda}(t_1;\boldsymbol{\beta})}{\partial t_1}, \tag{113}$$

$$L_{\mathbf{x}_1\mathbf{x}_1}(\boldsymbol{\beta}) = \frac{\partial \boldsymbol{\lambda}(t_1;\boldsymbol{\beta})}{\partial \mathbf{x}_1}. \tag{114}$$

MENTAL EXERCISES

11.1 Prove that $\dot{\mathbf{z}}(\cdot) \in C^{(1)}$ in $(t;\boldsymbol{\beta})$ for all $(t;\boldsymbol{\beta}) \in [t_0^\circ, t_1^\circ] \times B(\boldsymbol{\beta}^\circ;\delta)$.

11.2 Explain why Eq. (8) is not identical to Eq. (9).

11.3 Prove that Eq. (10) can be derived from Eq. (9) by integration by parts.

11.4 Verify the assertion in the paragraph after Eq. (10).

11.5 Consider the unconstrained static optimization problem

$$\phi(\boldsymbol{\alpha}) \stackrel{\text{def}}{=} \max_{\mathbf{x}\in\Re^N} f(\mathbf{x};\boldsymbol{\alpha}),$$

where $\boldsymbol{\alpha} \in \Re^A$ and $\mathbf{x}^*(\boldsymbol{\alpha})$ is the optimal value of the decision vector for all $\boldsymbol{\alpha} \in B(\boldsymbol{\alpha}^\circ;\delta)$.

(a) Prove that the $A \times A$ matrix $f_{\boldsymbol{\alpha}\boldsymbol{\alpha}}(\mathbf{x}^*(\boldsymbol{\alpha});\boldsymbol{\alpha}) - \phi_{\boldsymbol{\alpha}\boldsymbol{\alpha}}(\boldsymbol{\alpha})$ is symmetric and negative semidefinite.

(b) Prove that the matrix $\mathbf{Q}(\boldsymbol{\alpha})$, the typical term of which is defined by

$$\mathbf{Q}_{ij}(\boldsymbol{\alpha}) \stackrel{\text{def}}{=} \sum_{n=1}^{N} f_{\alpha_i x_n}(\mathbf{x}^*(\boldsymbol{\alpha}); \boldsymbol{\alpha}) \frac{\partial x_n^*}{\partial \alpha_j}(\boldsymbol{\alpha}), \quad i, j = 1, 2, \ldots, A,$$

is symmetric and positive semidefinite.

(c) Prove that if $f(\cdot)$ is convex in $\boldsymbol{\alpha} \in \Re^A$, then $\phi(\cdot)$ is convex in $\boldsymbol{\alpha} \in \Re^A$.

11.6 Consider the constrained static optimization problem

$$\phi(\boldsymbol{\alpha}) \stackrel{\text{def}}{=} \max_{\mathbf{x} \in \Re^N} \{ f(\mathbf{x}; \boldsymbol{\alpha}) \text{ s.t. } g^k(\mathbf{x}) = 0, \quad k = 1, 2, \ldots, K < N \},$$

where $\boldsymbol{\alpha} \in \Re^A$ and $\mathbf{x}^*(\boldsymbol{\alpha})$ is the optimal value of the decision vector for all $\boldsymbol{\alpha} \in B(\boldsymbol{\alpha}^\circ; \delta)$.

(a) Prove that the $A \times A$ matrix $f_{\boldsymbol{\alpha}\boldsymbol{\alpha}}(\mathbf{x}^*(\boldsymbol{\alpha}); \boldsymbol{\alpha}) - \phi_{\boldsymbol{\alpha}\boldsymbol{\alpha}}(\boldsymbol{\alpha})$ is symmetric and negative semidefinite.

(b) Prove that the matrix $\mathbf{Q}(\boldsymbol{\alpha})$, the typical term of which is defined by

$$\mathbf{Q}_{ij}(\boldsymbol{\alpha}) \stackrel{\text{def}}{=} \sum_{n=1}^{N} f_{\alpha_i x_n}(\mathbf{x}^*(\boldsymbol{\alpha}); \boldsymbol{\alpha}) \frac{\partial x_n^*}{\partial \alpha_j}(\boldsymbol{\alpha}), \quad i, j = 1, 2, \ldots, A,$$

is symmetric and positive semidefinite.

(c) Prove that if $f(\cdot)$ is convex in $\boldsymbol{\alpha} \in \Re^A$, then $\phi(\cdot)$ is convex in $\boldsymbol{\alpha} \in \Re^A$. This establishes that if the objective function of a constrained static maximization problem is convex in the parameters of the problem and the constraints are independent of the parameters, then the indirect objective function is locally convex in the parameters.

11.7 Derive Eqs. (33) through (35) directly from Theorem 11.2.

11.8 Give a simple necessary and sufficient condition for the integrand function $F(\cdot)$ of the adjustment cost model to be locally convex in the discount rate r, where

$$F(t, \mathbf{x}, \mathbf{u}; \boldsymbol{\alpha}) \stackrel{\text{def}}{=} [pf(x_1, x_2, u_1, u_2) - w_1 x_1 - w_2 x_2 - g_1 u_1 - g_2 u_2] e^{-rt}.$$

Then derive the comparative dynamics of the discount rate using Corollary 11.1. Compare your result with that in Eq. (36).

11.9 Derive the 6×6 matrix $L_{\boldsymbol{\alpha}\boldsymbol{\alpha}}(\boldsymbol{\beta})$ for the adjustment cost model of the firm. Note that this has already been started for you in Eqs. (33) through (38). You have 24 more terms to derive.

11.10 This question asks you to explore the comparative dynamics properties of the inventory accumulation problem from a dual point of view. Recall that the model under investigation is given by the optimal control problem

$$C(\boldsymbol{\beta}) \stackrel{\text{def}}{=} \min_{u(\cdot)} \int_0^T \left[c_1 [u(t)]^2 + c_2 x(t) \right] dt$$

$$\text{s.t.} \quad \dot{x}(t) = u(t), x(0) = 0, x(T) = x_T,$$

where $z(t;\beta) = \frac{1}{4}c_2c_1^{-1}t[t-T] + x_T T^{-1}t$ and $v(t;\beta) = \frac{1}{4}c_2c_1^{-1}[2t-T] + x_T T^{-1}$ are the optimal time paths of the inventory stock and production rate, respectively, and $\beta \overset{\text{def}}{=} (c_1, c_2, T, x_T)$. Do *not* use the specific functional form given for $z(t;\beta)$ in what follows unless specifically asked to do so. Assume that $x_T \geq \frac{1}{4}c_2c_1^{-1}T^2$, so that $v(t;\beta) \geq 0$ for all $t \in [0, T]$.

(a) Carefully and rigorously set up the dynamic primal-dual problem corresponding to the primal optimal control problem. Treat (T, x_T) as fixed parameters in the primal-dual problem, that is, never make them objects of choice.

(b) Derive the first-order and second-order *necessary* conditions for the dynamic primal-dual problem.

(c) Prove that

$$\frac{\partial C}{\partial c_1}(\beta) \equiv \int_0^T [v(t;\beta)]^2\, dt > 0 \quad \text{and} \quad \frac{\partial C}{\partial c_2}(\beta) \equiv \int_0^T z(t;\beta)\, dt > 0,$$

and provide an economic interpretation of each.

(d) Use the envelope results in part (c) to rewrite the second-order necessary conditions, and in the process, prove that the matrix

$$\begin{bmatrix} \displaystyle\int_0^T 2v(t;\beta)\frac{\partial v(t;\beta)}{\partial c_1}\, dt & \displaystyle\int_0^T 2v(t;\beta)\frac{\partial v(t;\beta)}{\partial c_2}\, dt \\ \displaystyle\int_0^T \frac{\partial z(t;\beta)}{\partial c_1}\, dt & \displaystyle\int_0^T \frac{\partial z(t;\beta)}{\partial c_2}\, dt \end{bmatrix}$$

is symmetric and negative semidefinite.

(e) Prove that the minimum cost function $C(\cdot)$ is positively homogeneous of degree one in (c_1, c_2).

(f) Prove that the minimum cost function $C(\cdot)$ is concave in (c_1, c_2).

(g) Prove that the vector (c_1, c_2) lies in the null space of the Hessian matrix of the minimum cost function $C(\cdot)$ with respect to (c_1, c_2). What does this tell you about one of the eigenvalues of the Hessian matrix of the minimum cost function $C(\cdot)$ with respect to (c_1, c_2)? What, in turn, does this tell you about the rank of the Hessian matrix of the minimum cost function $C(\cdot)$ with respect to (c_1, c_2), and thus about whether the said matrix is singular?

(h) Verify that

$$\int_0^T \frac{\partial z(t;\beta)}{\partial c_2}\, dt < 0$$

using the specific functional form for $z(t;\beta)$. Provide an economic interpretation of this result.

FURTHER READING

The dynamic primal-dual methodology developed in this chapter is a continuous-time intertemporal equivalent of the static primal-dual methodology of Silberberg (1974) and is based upon the work of Caputo (1990a, 1990b), in which the dynamic primal-dual formalism was developed. The results of this chapter have been extended by Caputo (1992a) to the case in which the parameter vector α is a function of time. The dynamic primal-dual method has been fruitfully applied to study the comparative dynamics properties of the nonrenewable resource–extracting model of the firm [Caputo (1990c)], the adjustment cost model of the firm [Caputo (1992b)], the labor-managed model of the firm [Caputo (1992c)], and an intertemporal model of the consumer [Caputo (1994)].

REFERENCES

Caputo, M.R. (1990a), "Comparative Dynamics via Envelope Methods in Variational Calculus," *Review of Economics Studies*, 57, 689–697.

Caputo, M.R. (1990b), "How to Do Comparative Dynamics on the Back of an Envelope in Optimal Control Theory," *Journal of Economic Dynamics and Control*, 14, 655–683.

Caputo, M.R. (1990c), "New Qualitative Properties in the Competitive Nonrenewable Resource Extracting Model of the Firm," *International Economic Review*, 31, 829–839.

Caputo, M.R. (1992a), "A Primal-Dual Approach to Comparative Dynamics with Time-Dependent Parameters in Variational Calculus," *Optimal Control Applications and Methods*, 13, 73–86.

Caputo, M.R. (1992b), "Fundamental Symmetries and Qualitative Properties in the Adjustment Cost Model of the Firm," *Journal of Mathematical Economics*, 21, 99–112.

Caputo, M.R. (1992c), "Comparative Dynamics in the Labor-Managed Model of the Firm," *Journal of Comparative Economics*, 16, 272–286.

Caputo, M.R. (1994), "The Slutsky Matrix and Homogeneity in Intertemporal Consumer Theory," *Journal of Economics*, 60, 255–279.

Silberberg, E. (1974), "A Revision of Comparative Statics Methodology in Economics, or How to Do Comparative Statics on the Back of an Envelope," *Journal of Economic Theory*, 7, 159–172.

Silberberg, E. and Suen, W. (2001, 3rd Ed.), *The Structure of Economics: A Mathematical Analysis* (New York: Irwin/McGraw-Hill).

Simon, C.P. and Blume, L. (1994), *Mathematics for Economists* (New York: W.W. Norton & Company).

TWELVE

Discounting, Current Values, and Time Consistency

The majority of optimal control problems of interest to economists have the future values of the integrand, whether it is profit, cost, or utility, discounted at some positive constant rate, say, $r > 0$, which is often referred to as the *discount rate*. Because we are dealing with continuous-time optimization problems, the corresponding *discount factor* takes the exponential form e^{-rt}. The purpose of this chapter is to examine the implications this modification of the archetypal optimal control problem has on the economic interpretation of the optimal value function and costate vector, as well as the form that the necessary and sufficient conditions take. In addition, we will provide the logical and rigorous justification for the ubiquitous nature of the exponential form of the discount factor.

In light of the opening remarks, we must consider the following general class of optimal control problems in this chapter:

$$V(\boldsymbol{\alpha}, r, t_0, \mathbf{x}_0, t_1) \stackrel{\text{def}}{=} \max_{\mathbf{u}(\cdot),\mathbf{x}_1} \int_{t_0}^{t_1} f(t, \mathbf{x}(t), \mathbf{u}(t); \boldsymbol{\alpha})\, e^{-rt}\, dt$$

$$\text{s.t.} \quad \dot{\mathbf{x}}(t) = \mathbf{g}(t, \mathbf{x}(t), \mathbf{u}(t); \boldsymbol{\alpha}),\ \mathbf{x}(t_0) = \mathbf{x}_0,\ \mathbf{x}(t_1) = \mathbf{x}_1, \tag{1}$$

$$h^k(t, \mathbf{x}(t), \mathbf{u}(t); \boldsymbol{\alpha}) \geq 0, \quad k = 1, 2, \ldots, K',$$

$$h^k(t, \mathbf{x}(t), \mathbf{u}(t); \boldsymbol{\alpha}) = 0, \quad k = K'+1, K'+2, \ldots, K,$$

where $\mathbf{x}(t) \stackrel{\text{def}}{=} (x_1(t), x_2(t), \ldots, x_N(t)) \in \Re^N$ is the state vector, $\mathbf{u}(t) \stackrel{\text{def}}{=} (u_1(t), u_2(t), \ldots, u_M(t)) \in \Re^M$ is the control vector, $\dot{\mathbf{x}}(\cdot) \stackrel{\text{def}}{=} (\dot{x}_1(\cdot), \dot{x}_2(\cdot), \ldots, \dot{x}_N(\cdot))$, $\mathbf{g}(\cdot) \stackrel{\text{def}}{=} (g^1(\cdot), g^2(\cdot), \ldots, g^N(\cdot))$ is the vector of transition functions, $\mathbf{h}(\cdot) \stackrel{\text{def}}{=} (h^1(\cdot), h^2(\cdot), \ldots, h^K(\cdot))$ is the vector of constraint functions, both inequality and equality, and $\boldsymbol{\alpha} \stackrel{\text{def}}{=} (\alpha_1, \alpha_2, \ldots, \alpha_A) \in \Re^A$ is a vector of time-independent parameters that affect the state equation, integrand, and constraint functions. Let $(\mathbf{z}(t; \boldsymbol{\alpha}, r, t_0, \mathbf{x}_0, t_1), \mathbf{v}(t; \boldsymbol{\alpha}, r, t_0, \mathbf{x}_0, t_1))$ be the optimal pair with corresponding costate vector $\boldsymbol{\lambda}(t; \boldsymbol{\alpha}, r, t_0, \mathbf{x}_0, t_1) \in \Re^N$ and Lagrange multiplier vector $\boldsymbol{\mu}(t; \boldsymbol{\alpha}, r, t_0, \mathbf{x}_0, t_1) \in \Re^K$.

Let us first tackle the issue of the proper economic interpretation of the optimal value function and costate vector for problem (1).

Because of the discount factor e^{-rt} in the integrand, we must be careful to interpret the optimal value function $V(\cdot)$ suitably. In the case of problem (1), $V(\cdot)$ is referred to as the *present value optimal value function*. This is because $V(\cdot)$ has its value discounted back to time $t = 0$ rather than the initial date of the planning horizon, videlicet, $t = t_0$. To see this, first observe that at the initial date of the planning horizon, namely, $t = t_0$, the discount factor e^{-rt_0} is applied to the value $f(t_0, \mathbf{x}(t_0), \mathbf{u}(t_0); \boldsymbol{\alpha})$, thereby discounting it to some time *before* the initial date $t = t_0$. Second, note that at time $t = 0$, we have that $e^{-r0} = 1$, thereby implying that at time $t = 0$, no discounting takes place. Consequently, from these two facts, we may infer that the period to which the value $f(t_0, \mathbf{x}(t_0), \mathbf{u}(t_0); \boldsymbol{\alpha})\, e^{-rt_0}$ is discounted to is $t = 0$. In view of the fact that the same is true in any period of the planning horizon, $f(t, \mathbf{x}(t), \mathbf{u}(t); \boldsymbol{\alpha})\, e^{-rt}$ is discounted to period $t = 0$ for all $t \in [t_0, t_1]$ as well. Accordingly, the value of $V(\cdot)$ is also discounted to period $t = 0$, just as we asserted above.

Now recall that by the dynamic envelope theorem applied to problem (1), we have that $\partial V(\boldsymbol{\alpha}, r, t_0, \mathbf{x}_0, t_1)/\partial x_{0n} = \lambda_n(t_0; \boldsymbol{\alpha}, r, t_0, \mathbf{x}_0, t_1)$, $n = 1, 2, \ldots, N$, thereby implying that $\lambda_n(t_0; \boldsymbol{\alpha}, r, t_0, \mathbf{x}_0, t_1)$ is the *present value* shadow price of a unit of the nth stock at time $t = t_0$ in an optimal plan. In other words, $\lambda_n(t_0; \boldsymbol{\alpha}, r, t_0, \mathbf{x}_0, t_1)$ is the shadow value of a unit of the nth stock at time $t = t_0$ discounted back to time $t = 0$, since $V(\boldsymbol{\alpha}, r, t_0, \mathbf{x}_0, t_1)$ is the total value of the stock at time $t = t_0$ discounted back to period $t = 0$. Alternatively, $\lambda_n(t_0; \boldsymbol{\alpha}, r, t_0, \mathbf{x}_0, t_1)$ is what the owner of a firm who solves problem (1) would pay for a marginal increase in his capital stock at the initial time $t = t_0$ but discounted to period $t = 0$, since the period $t = 0$ is that which the present value optimal value function $V(\cdot)$ is discounted to, as noted above. Moreover, by the development in Chapter 9 in which we rigorously established the economic interpretation of the costate vector and the reasoning just applied to interpret $\lambda_n(t_0; \boldsymbol{\alpha}, r, t_0, \mathbf{x}_0, t_1)$, we may therefore conclude that for any time $t \in [t_0, t_1]$ in problem (1), $\lambda_n(t; \boldsymbol{\alpha}, r, t_0, \mathbf{x}_0, t_1)$ is the shadow value of the nth state variable at time $t \in [t_0, t_1]$ discounted to period $t = 0$. That is to say, $\lambda_n(t; \boldsymbol{\alpha}, r, t_0, \mathbf{x}_0, t_1)$ is the present value shadow price of the nth state variable at any time $t \in [t_0, t_1]$ in an optimal plan.

Let's now take this economic interpretation one step further by considering the following perturbation of problem (1):

$$\tilde{V}(\boldsymbol{\alpha}, r, t_0, \mathbf{x}_0, t_1) \stackrel{\text{def}}{=} \max_{\mathbf{u}(\cdot), \mathbf{x}_1} \int_{t_0}^{t_1} f(t, \mathbf{x}(t), \mathbf{u}(t); \boldsymbol{\alpha})\, e^{-r(t-t_0)}\, dt$$

$$\text{s.t.}\quad \dot{\mathbf{x}}(t) = \mathbf{g}(t, \mathbf{x}(t), \mathbf{u}(t); \boldsymbol{\alpha}),\ \ \mathbf{x}(t_0) = \mathbf{x}_0,\ \ \mathbf{x}(t_1) = \mathbf{x}_1, \tag{2}$$

$$h^k(t, \mathbf{x}(t), \mathbf{u}(t); \boldsymbol{\alpha}) \geq 0, \quad k = 1, 2, \ldots, K',$$

$$h^k(t, \mathbf{x}(t), \mathbf{u}(t); \boldsymbol{\alpha}) = 0, \quad k = K' + 1, K' + 2, \ldots, K.$$

The only difference between problems (1) and (2) is that problem (2) has its objective functional multiplied by e^{rt_0}. This observation yields the identity relating the optimal value functions in problems (1) and (2), to wit, $\tilde{V}(\boldsymbol{\alpha}, r, t_0, \mathbf{x}_0, t_1) \equiv e^{rt_0} V(\boldsymbol{\alpha}, r, t_0, \mathbf{x}_0, t_1)$. Given the interpretation of $V(\cdot)$, we may therefore interpret $\tilde{V}(\cdot)$ as the *current value optimal value function*, for its value is discounted to the initial date $t = t_0$ of the planning horizon. Consequently, by the dynamic envelope theorem, we have that $\partial \tilde{V}(\boldsymbol{\alpha}, r, t_0, \mathbf{x}_0, t_1)/\partial x_{0n} = \tilde{\lambda}_n(t_0; \boldsymbol{\alpha}, r, t_0, \mathbf{x}_0, t_1)$, $n = 1, 2, \ldots, N$, thereby implying that $\tilde{\lambda}_n(t_0; \boldsymbol{\alpha}, r, t_0, \mathbf{x}_0, t_1)$ is the *current value shadow price* of a unit of the nth stock at time $t = t_0$ in an optimal plan. That is, $\tilde{\lambda}_n(t_0; \boldsymbol{\alpha}, r, t_0, \mathbf{x}_0, t_1)$ is what the owner of a firm who solves problem (2) would pay for a marginal increase in her capital stock at time $t = t_0$ in period $t = t_0$, because the period $t = t_0$ is the one to which the current value optimal value function $\tilde{V}(\cdot)$ is discounted. Moreover, by the reasoning just applied to interpret $\tilde{\lambda}_n(t_0; \boldsymbol{\alpha}, r, t_0, \mathbf{x}_0, t_1)$ and the development in Chapter 9 in which we rigorously established the economic interpretation of the costate vector, we may conclude that for any time $t \in [t_0, t_1]$ of problem (2), $\tilde{\lambda}_n(t; \boldsymbol{\alpha}, r, t_0, \mathbf{x}_0, t_1)$ is the shadow value of the nth state variable at time $t \in [t_0, t_1]$ discounted to period $t = t_0$. That is to say, $\tilde{\lambda}_n(t; \boldsymbol{\alpha}, r, t_0, \mathbf{x}_0, t_1)$ is the current value shadow price of the nth state variable at any time $t \in [t_0, t_1]$ in an optimal plan. Thus the identity linking the current value and present value shadow values is given by $\tilde{\boldsymbol{\lambda}}(t; \boldsymbol{\alpha}, r, t_0, \mathbf{x}_0, t_1) \equiv e^{rt} \boldsymbol{\lambda}(t; \boldsymbol{\alpha}, r, t_0, \mathbf{x}_0, t_1)$ for all $t \in [t_0, t_1]$. In passing, observe that because $e^{rt_0} > 0$ and is independent of the state and control variables, the optimal values of the state and control vectors to problems (1) and (2) are identical.

In wrapping up the distinction between current values and present values, an important feature in our interpretation should be emphasized. In particular, we defined $\tilde{V}(\cdot)$ as the current value optimal value function *because* its value is discounted to the initial date $t = t_0$ of the planning horizon in problem (2). We are thus treating the initial date of the planning horizon as the current period. This should not be too surprising, inasmuch as when solving an optimal control problem, we take the point of view that we are placed at the initial date of the planning horizon when we select our optimal plan. That is, at the initial date $t = t_0$ of the planning horizon, we select the optimal time path of the control vector for the entire planning horizon, and therefore view the initial date $t = t_0$ of the planning horizon as the current period from which we plan.

With the interpretation of the optimal value function and costate vector of problem (1) finished, we now seek to express the necessary conditions of problem (1) in their current value form, that is, without explicit representation of the discount factor but still accounting for its presence in the optimal control problem. Recall that in order to find the necessary conditions of problem (1), we first form the present value Hamiltonian

$$H(t, \mathbf{x}, \mathbf{u}, \boldsymbol{\lambda}; \boldsymbol{\alpha}, r) \stackrel{\text{def}}{=} f(t, \mathbf{x}, \mathbf{u}; \boldsymbol{\alpha}) e^{-rt} + \sum_{n=1}^{N} \lambda_n g^n(t, \mathbf{x}, \mathbf{u}; \boldsymbol{\alpha}),$$

and then the present value Lagrangian

$$L(t, \mathbf{x}, \mathbf{u}, \boldsymbol{\lambda}, \boldsymbol{\mu}; \boldsymbol{\alpha}, r) \overset{\text{def}}{=} f(t, \mathbf{x}, \mathbf{u}; \boldsymbol{\alpha}) e^{-rt} + \sum_{n=1}^{N} \lambda_n g^n(t, \mathbf{x}, \mathbf{u}; \boldsymbol{\alpha})$$
$$+ \sum_{k=1}^{K} \mu_k h^k(t, \mathbf{x}, \mathbf{u}; \boldsymbol{\alpha}). \tag{3}$$

The necessary conditions are then given by Theorem 10.1:

$$L_{u_m}(t, \mathbf{x}, \mathbf{u}, \boldsymbol{\lambda}, \boldsymbol{\mu}; \boldsymbol{\alpha}, r) = 0, \quad m = 1, 2, \ldots, M, \tag{4}$$

$$L_{\mu_\ell}(t, \mathbf{x}, \mathbf{u}, \boldsymbol{\lambda}, \boldsymbol{\mu}; \boldsymbol{\alpha}, r) \geq 0,\ \mu_\ell \geq 0,\ \mu_\ell L_{\mu_\ell}(t, \mathbf{x}, \mathbf{u}, \boldsymbol{\lambda}, \boldsymbol{\mu}; \boldsymbol{\alpha}, r) = 0,$$
$$\ell = 1, 2, \ldots, K', \tag{5}$$

$$L_{\mu_\ell}(t, \mathbf{x}, \mathbf{u}, \boldsymbol{\lambda}, \boldsymbol{\mu}; \boldsymbol{\alpha}, r) = 0, \quad \ell = K' + 1, K' + 2, \ldots, K, \tag{6}$$

$$\dot{\lambda}_i = -L_{x_i}(t, \mathbf{x}, \mathbf{u}, \boldsymbol{\lambda}, \boldsymbol{\mu}; \boldsymbol{\alpha}, r),\ \lambda_i(t_1) = 0, \quad i = 1, 2, \ldots, N, \tag{7}$$

$$\dot{x}_i = L_{\lambda_i}(t, \mathbf{x}, \mathbf{u}, \boldsymbol{\lambda}, \boldsymbol{\mu}; \boldsymbol{\alpha}, r),\ x_i(t_0) = x_{0i}, \quad i = 1, 2, \ldots, N. \tag{8}$$

In many economic problems, it is often more natural and convenient to conduct the analysis, as well as the discussion of the problem and its economic interpretation, in terms of current values, that is, in terms of the values of $V(\cdot)$ and $\boldsymbol{\lambda}(\cdot)$ discounted to the initial (or current) period $t = t_0$ rather than in terms of their values discounted back to time $t = 0$. Another advantage from a mathematical point of view is that if the integrand function $f(\cdot)$, transition function $\mathbf{g}(\cdot)$, and constraint function $\mathbf{h}(\cdot)$ do not depend explicitly on t, then the canonical differential equations will be autonomous if the costate vector $\boldsymbol{\lambda}$ is transformed to its current value form. Let's first tackle the form of the necessary conditions in the current value format and then establish the latter result.

In order to express the necessary conditions for problem (1) in their current value form, we begin by rewriting the Lagrangian defined in Eq. (3) as

$$L(t, \mathbf{x}, \mathbf{u}, \boldsymbol{\lambda}, \boldsymbol{\mu}; \boldsymbol{\alpha}, r)$$
$$\overset{\text{def}}{=} e^{-rt}\left[f(t, \mathbf{x}, \mathbf{u}; \boldsymbol{\alpha}) + \sum_{n=1}^{N} e^{rt}\lambda_n g^n(t, \mathbf{x}, \mathbf{u}; \boldsymbol{\alpha}) + \sum_{k=1}^{K} e^{rt}\mu_k h^k(t, \mathbf{x}, \mathbf{u}; \boldsymbol{\alpha}) \right], \tag{9}$$

and then define

$$\tilde{\boldsymbol{\lambda}}(t) \overset{\text{def}}{=} e^{rt}\boldsymbol{\lambda}(t) \tag{10}$$

as the current value costate vector and

$$\tilde{\boldsymbol{\mu}}(t) \overset{\text{def}}{=} e^{rt}\boldsymbol{\mu}(t) \tag{11}$$

as the current value Lagrange multiplier vector. Recall that $\boldsymbol{\lambda}(t)$ gives the shadow value of the state vector at time t discounted to time zero, that is, it is the present value shadow price vector. Therefore, $\tilde{\boldsymbol{\lambda}}(t)$ gives the shadow value of the state vector at time t discounted to the initial date of the planning horizon, that is, it is the current value shadow price vector.

Using Eqs. (9), (10), and (11), define the *current value Lagrangian* by

$$\begin{aligned}\tilde{L}(t, \mathbf{x}, \mathbf{u}, \tilde{\boldsymbol{\lambda}}, \tilde{\boldsymbol{\mu}}; \boldsymbol{\alpha}) &\stackrel{\text{def}}{=} e^{rt} L(t, \mathbf{x}, \mathbf{u}, \boldsymbol{\lambda}, \boldsymbol{\mu}; \boldsymbol{\alpha}, r) \\ &= f(t, \mathbf{x}, \mathbf{u}; \boldsymbol{\alpha}) + \sum_{n=1}^{N} \tilde{\lambda}_n g^n(t, \mathbf{x}, \mathbf{u}; \boldsymbol{\alpha}) + \sum_{k=1}^{K} \tilde{\mu}_k h^k(t, \mathbf{x}, \mathbf{u}; \boldsymbol{\alpha}).\end{aligned} \tag{12}$$

Differentiating Eq. (10) with respect to t and using necessary condition (7) and Eq. (10) gives

$$\frac{d}{dt}\tilde{\lambda}_i(t) = e^{rt}\dot{\lambda}_i(t) + re^{rt}\lambda_i(t) = r\tilde{\lambda}_i - e^{rt} L_{x_i}(t, \mathbf{x}, \mathbf{u}, \boldsymbol{\lambda}, \boldsymbol{\mu}; \boldsymbol{\alpha}, r), \tag{13}$$

for $i = 1, 2, \ldots, N$. From Eq. (12), it follows that $\tilde{L}_{x_i}(t, \mathbf{x}, \mathbf{u}, \tilde{\boldsymbol{\lambda}}, \tilde{\boldsymbol{\mu}}; \boldsymbol{\alpha}) = e^{rt} L_{x_i}$ $(t, \mathbf{x}, \mathbf{u}, \boldsymbol{\lambda}, \boldsymbol{\mu}; \boldsymbol{\alpha}, r)$, thus implying that Eq. (13) can be written as

$$\dot{\tilde{\lambda}}_i = r\tilde{\lambda}_i - \tilde{L}_{x_i}(t, \mathbf{x}, \mathbf{u}, \tilde{\boldsymbol{\lambda}}, \tilde{\boldsymbol{\mu}}; \boldsymbol{\alpha}), \quad i = 1, 2, \ldots, N.$$

This is the costate equation in current value form. Using Eq. (10), the free boundary transversality condition $\boldsymbol{\lambda}(t_1) = \mathbf{0}_N$ implies that $\boldsymbol{\lambda}(t_1) = e^{-rt_1}\tilde{\boldsymbol{\lambda}}(t_1) = \mathbf{0}_N$. Moreover, seeing as $e^{-rt_1} \neq 0$, $\boldsymbol{\lambda}(t_1) = \mathbf{0}_N$ is equivalent to $\tilde{\boldsymbol{\lambda}}(T) = \mathbf{0}_N$. We are therefore finished with the conversion of necessary condition (7) to its current value form.

Turning to the necessary condition (8), that is, the state equation and initial condition, it follows easily from Eq. (12) that

$$\dot{x}_i = \tilde{L}_{\tilde{\lambda}_i}(t, \mathbf{x}, \mathbf{u}, \tilde{\boldsymbol{\lambda}}, \tilde{\boldsymbol{\mu}}; \boldsymbol{\alpha}) = g^i(t, \mathbf{x}, \mathbf{u}; \boldsymbol{\alpha}), \quad i = 1, 2, \ldots, N.$$

As far as the initial condition $\mathbf{x}(t_0) = \mathbf{x}_0$ is concerned, it clearly still holds in current value form, for the transformation to current values leaves the initial value of the state vector unaffected.

By employing Eq. (12), necessary condition (4) can be written as

$$L_{u_m}(t, \mathbf{x}, \mathbf{u}, \boldsymbol{\lambda}, \boldsymbol{\mu}; \boldsymbol{\alpha}, r) = \frac{\partial}{\partial u_m}[e^{-rt}\tilde{L}(t, \mathbf{x}, \mathbf{u}, \tilde{\boldsymbol{\lambda}}, \tilde{\boldsymbol{\mu}}; \boldsymbol{\alpha})] = 0, \quad m = 1, 2, \ldots, M.$$

Because $e^{-rt} \neq 0$ and is independent of the control vector, necessary condition (4) can be written equivalently in terms of the current value Lagrangian as

$$\tilde{L}_{u_m}(t, \mathbf{x}, \mathbf{u}, \tilde{\boldsymbol{\lambda}}, \tilde{\boldsymbol{\mu}}; \boldsymbol{\alpha}) = 0, \quad m = 1, 2, \ldots, M.$$

All that remains is to transform the necessary conditions (5) and (6) to current value form.

By employing Eq. (12) again, necessary condition (6) can be written as

$$L_{\mu_\ell}(t, \mathbf{x}, \mathbf{u}, \boldsymbol{\lambda}, \boldsymbol{\mu}; \boldsymbol{\alpha}, r) = \frac{\partial}{\partial \mu_\ell}[e^{-rt}\tilde{L}(t, \mathbf{x}, \mathbf{u}, \tilde{\boldsymbol{\lambda}}, \tilde{\boldsymbol{\mu}}; \boldsymbol{\alpha})] = 0,$$

$$\ell = K' + 1, K' + 2, \ldots, K.$$

Because $e^{-rt} \neq 0$ and is independent of the Lagrange multiplier vector, necessary condition (6) can be written equivalently in terms of the current value Lagrangian as

$$\tilde{L}_{\mu_\ell}(t, \mathbf{x}, \mathbf{u}, \tilde{\boldsymbol{\lambda}}, \tilde{\boldsymbol{\mu}}; \boldsymbol{\alpha}) = 0, \quad \ell = K' + 1, K' + 2, \ldots, K.$$

Let's finish up with necessary condition (5).

With respect to necessary condition (5), notice that we have to develop three equivalent current value expressions. By employing Eq. (12) again, the first necessary condition of Eq. (5) can be written as

$$L_{\mu_\ell}(t, \mathbf{x}, \mathbf{u}, \boldsymbol{\lambda}, \boldsymbol{\mu}; \boldsymbol{\alpha}, r) = \frac{\partial}{\partial \mu_\ell}[e^{-rt}\tilde{L}(t, \mathbf{x}, \mathbf{u}, \tilde{\boldsymbol{\lambda}}, \tilde{\boldsymbol{\mu}}; \boldsymbol{\alpha})] \geq 0, \quad \ell = 1, 2, \ldots, K'.$$

Because $e^{-rt} > 0$ and is independent of the Lagrange multiplier vector, the first necessary condition of Eq. (5) can be written equivalently in terms of the current value Lagrangian as

$$\tilde{L}_{\mu_\ell}(t, \mathbf{x}, \mathbf{u}, \tilde{\boldsymbol{\lambda}}, \tilde{\boldsymbol{\mu}}; \boldsymbol{\alpha}) \geq 0, \quad \ell = 1, 2, \ldots, K'.$$

Using Eq. (11) and the second necessary condition of Eq. (5), it follows that $\boldsymbol{\mu}(t) = e^{-rt}\tilde{\boldsymbol{\mu}}(t) \geq \mathbf{0}$. In view of the fact that $e^{-rt} > 0$, $\boldsymbol{\mu}(t) \geq \mathbf{0}$ is equivalent to $\tilde{\boldsymbol{\mu}}(t) \geq \mathbf{0}$. Finally, employing Eqs. (11) and (12) another time, the third necessary condition of Eq. (5) can be written as

$$\mu_\ell L_{\mu_\ell}(t, \mathbf{x}, \mathbf{u}, \boldsymbol{\lambda}, \boldsymbol{\mu}; \boldsymbol{\alpha}, r) = e^{-rt}\tilde{\mu}_\ell \frac{\partial}{\partial \mu_\ell}[e^{-rt}\tilde{L}(t, \mathbf{x}, \mathbf{u}, \tilde{\boldsymbol{\lambda}}, \tilde{\boldsymbol{\mu}}; \boldsymbol{\alpha})] = 0,$$

$$\ell = 1, 2, \ldots, K'.$$

Because $e^{-rt} \neq 0$ and is independent of the Lagrange multiplier vector, the third necessary condition of Eq. (5) can be written equivalently in terms of the current value Lagrangian and the current value Lagrange multiplier as

$$\tilde{\mu}_\ell \tilde{L}_{\mu_\ell}(t, \mathbf{x}, \mathbf{u}, \tilde{\boldsymbol{\lambda}}, \tilde{\boldsymbol{\mu}}; \boldsymbol{\alpha}) = 0, \quad \ell = 1, 2, \ldots, K'.$$

The above results have established the following theorem, which we will use quite often in our application of optimal control theory to economic problems.

Theorem 12.1: *In optimal control problem (1), the necessary conditions in Eqs. (4) through (8) from Theorem 10.1 can be written equivalently in current value form as*

$$\tilde{L}_{u_m}(t, \mathbf{x}, \mathbf{u}, \tilde{\boldsymbol{\lambda}}, \tilde{\boldsymbol{\mu}}; \boldsymbol{\alpha}) = 0, \quad m = 1, 2, \ldots, M, \tag{14}$$

$$\tilde{L}_{\mu_\ell}(t, \mathbf{x}, \mathbf{u}, \tilde{\boldsymbol{\lambda}}, \tilde{\boldsymbol{\mu}}; \boldsymbol{\alpha}) \geq 0, \ \tilde{\mu}_\ell \geq 0, \ \tilde{\mu}_\ell \tilde{L}_{\mu_\ell}(t, \mathbf{x}, \mathbf{u}, \tilde{\boldsymbol{\lambda}}, \tilde{\boldsymbol{\mu}}; \boldsymbol{\alpha}) = 0,$$
$$\ell = 1, 2, \ldots, K', \tag{15}$$

$$\tilde{L}_{\mu_\ell}(t, \mathbf{x}, \mathbf{u}, \tilde{\boldsymbol{\lambda}}, \tilde{\boldsymbol{\mu}}; \boldsymbol{\alpha}) = 0, \quad \ell = K' + 1, K' + 2, \ldots, K, \tag{16}$$

$$\dot{\tilde{\lambda}}_i = r\tilde{\lambda}_i - \tilde{L}_{x_i}(t, \mathbf{x}, \mathbf{u}, \tilde{\boldsymbol{\lambda}}, \tilde{\boldsymbol{\mu}}; \boldsymbol{\alpha}), \ \tilde{\lambda}_i(t_1) = 0, \quad i = 1, 2, \ldots, N, \tag{17}$$

$$\dot{x}_i = \tilde{L}_{\tilde{\lambda}_i}(t, \mathbf{x}, \mathbf{u}, \tilde{\boldsymbol{\lambda}}, \tilde{\boldsymbol{\mu}}; \boldsymbol{\alpha}), \ x_i(t_0) = x_{0i}, \quad i = 1, 2, \ldots, N. \tag{18}$$

Take note of the remarkable similarity between the necessary conditions in their present value and current value forms. The essential difference lies in the costate equation. The effect of the transformation to current values on the sufficiency theorems of Chapter 6 is in effect trivial. This is because the concavity of the present value Lagrangian $L(\cdot)$ in the state and control vectors is equivalent to the concavity of the current value Lagrangian $\tilde{L}(\cdot)$ in the state and control vectors, since $\tilde{L}(\cdot) \stackrel{\text{def}}{=} e^{rt}L(\cdot)$, $e^{rt} > 0$, and e^{rt} is independent of the state and control vectors. This is all that really needs to be said about sufficiency results when the current value formulation of an optimal control problem is analyzed.

Let's now turn to an analytical advantage of the current value formulation alluded to earlier. We formulate the advantage in the following theorem.

Theorem 12.2: *In optimal control problem (1), if the integrand function $f(\cdot)$, transition function $\mathbf{g}(\cdot)$, and constraint function $\mathbf{h}(\cdot)$ are not explicit functions of the independent variable t, that is, if $f_t(\cdot) \equiv 0$, $\mathbf{g}_t(\cdot) \equiv \mathbf{0}_N$, and $\mathbf{h}_t(\cdot) \equiv \mathbf{0}_K$, and furthermore, if the necessary conditions (14) through (16) of Theorem 12.1 determine the control vector and current value Lagrange multiplier vector as functions of the state vector, current value costate vector, and parameters, then the canonical differential equations in current value form are autonomous, that is, they do not depend explicitly on the independent variable t.*

Proof: First, observe that the current value Lagrangian for problem (1) under the assumptions $f_t(\cdot) \equiv 0$, $\mathbf{g}_t(\cdot) \equiv \mathbf{0}_N$, and $\mathbf{h}_t(\cdot) \equiv \mathbf{0}_K$ does not depend explicitly on the independent variable t. The necessary conditions of Theorem 12.1 thus reduce to

$$\tilde{L}_{u_m}(\mathbf{x}, \mathbf{u}, \tilde{\boldsymbol{\lambda}}, \tilde{\boldsymbol{\mu}}; \boldsymbol{\alpha}) = 0, \quad m = 1, 2, \ldots, M, \tag{19}$$

$$\tilde{L}_{\mu_\ell}(\mathbf{x}, \mathbf{u}, \tilde{\boldsymbol{\lambda}}, \tilde{\boldsymbol{\mu}}; \boldsymbol{\alpha}) \geq 0, \ \tilde{\mu}_\ell \geq 0, \ \tilde{\mu}_\ell \tilde{L}_{\mu_\ell}(\mathbf{x}, \mathbf{u}, \tilde{\boldsymbol{\lambda}}, \tilde{\boldsymbol{\mu}}; \boldsymbol{\alpha}) = 0,$$
$$\ell = 1, 2, \ldots, K', \tag{20}$$

$$\tilde{L}_{\mu_\ell}(\mathbf{x}, \mathbf{u}, \tilde{\boldsymbol{\lambda}}, \tilde{\boldsymbol{\mu}}; \boldsymbol{\alpha}) = 0, \quad \ell = K' + 1, K' + 2, \ldots, K, \tag{21}$$

$$\dot{\tilde{\lambda}}_i = r\tilde{\lambda}_i - \tilde{L}_{x_i}(\mathbf{x}, \mathbf{u}, \tilde{\boldsymbol{\lambda}}, \tilde{\boldsymbol{\mu}}; \boldsymbol{\alpha}), \ \tilde{\lambda}_i(t_1) = 0, \quad i = 1, 2, \ldots, N, \tag{22}$$

$$\dot{x}_i = \tilde{L}_{\tilde{\lambda}_i}(\mathbf{x}, \mathbf{u}, \tilde{\boldsymbol{\lambda}}, \tilde{\boldsymbol{\mu}}; \boldsymbol{\alpha}), \ x_i(t_0) = x_{0i}, \quad i = 1, 2, \ldots, N. \tag{23}$$

By assumption, necessary conditions (19) through (21) can in principle be solved for the control vector and Lagrange multiplier vector as functions of the state vector, current value costate vector, and parameters, say $\mathbf{u} = \mathbf{u}^*(\mathbf{x}, \tilde{\boldsymbol{\lambda}}; \boldsymbol{\alpha})$ and $\tilde{\boldsymbol{\mu}} = \tilde{\boldsymbol{\mu}}^*(\mathbf{x}, \tilde{\boldsymbol{\lambda}}; \boldsymbol{\alpha})$. Therefore, by substituting $\mathbf{u} = \mathbf{u}^*(\mathbf{x}, \tilde{\boldsymbol{\lambda}}; \boldsymbol{\alpha})$ and $\tilde{\boldsymbol{\mu}} = \tilde{\boldsymbol{\mu}}^*(\mathbf{x}, \tilde{\boldsymbol{\lambda}}; \boldsymbol{\alpha})$ into the canonical differential equations (22) and (23), they can be expressed as

$$\dot{\tilde{\lambda}}_i = r\tilde{\lambda}_i - \tilde{L}_{x_i}(\mathbf{x}, \mathbf{u}^*(\mathbf{x}, \tilde{\boldsymbol{\lambda}}; \boldsymbol{\alpha}), \tilde{\boldsymbol{\lambda}}, \tilde{\boldsymbol{\mu}}^*(\mathbf{x}, \tilde{\boldsymbol{\lambda}}; \boldsymbol{\alpha}); \boldsymbol{\alpha}),\ \tilde{\lambda}_i(t_1) = 0, \quad i = 1, 2, \ldots, N,$$

$$\dot{x}_i = \tilde{L}_{\tilde{\lambda}_i}(\mathbf{x}, \mathbf{u}^*(\mathbf{x}, \tilde{\boldsymbol{\lambda}}; \boldsymbol{\alpha}), \tilde{\boldsymbol{\lambda}}, \tilde{\boldsymbol{\mu}}^*(\mathbf{x}, \tilde{\boldsymbol{\lambda}}; \boldsymbol{\alpha}); \boldsymbol{\alpha}),\ x_i(t_0) = x_{0i}, \quad i = 1, 2, \ldots, N.$$

Because t does not appear explicitly in this pair of ordinary differential equations, they are, by definition, autonomous. Q.E.D.

In general, autonomous differential equations are easier to solve than nonautonomous differential equations. Even if an explicit solution is not possible, one can use a phase diagram to qualitatively analyze the solution of an autonomous differential equation system. We will demonstrate this feature of autonomous systems of differential equations in several of the ensuing chapters, in which we will also delve more deeply into this issue.

The next issue we wish to explore in this chapter is the form of the discount factor exhibited here and in virtually every optimal control problem in economics, to wit, e^{-rt}, where the discount rate $r > 0$ is constant, that is, it is not a function of the independent variable t. One generalization is a time varying discount rate, say, $\rho(t) > 0$, in which case the discount factor is of the form $\exp[-\int_0^t \rho(\tau)d\tau]$. Note that if $\rho(t) = r > 0$ is constant, then the time varying discount factor reduces to the familiar form, because then $\exp[-\int_0^t \rho(\tau)d\tau] = \exp[-\int_0^t r\,d\tau] = e^{-rt}$. In a mental exercise, you are asked to prove that optimal control problem (1) with the discount factor $\exp[-\int_0^t \rho(\tau)d\tau]$ can be reduced to current value form, but that the resulting canonical differential equations are not autonomous even when the integrand function $f(\cdot)$, transition function $\mathbf{g}(\cdot)$, and constraint function $\mathbf{h}(\cdot)$ do not depend explicitly on the independent variable t. This means that the current value approach is relatively less useful for an optimal control problem with a time varying discount rate than it is for one in which the discount rate is a positive constant. This, however, is not a good reason to avoid the use of a time varying discount rate. A sound and logically consistent reason is provided by the principle of *time consistency* or *dynamic consistency*, to which we now turn.

Consider, therefore, the ensuing optimal control problem without the presence of inequality or equality constraints:

$$\max_{\mathbf{u}(\cdot), \mathbf{x}_T} J_0[\mathbf{x}(\cdot), \mathbf{u}(\cdot)] \stackrel{\text{def}}{=} \int_0^T f(t, \mathbf{x}(t), \mathbf{u}(t); \boldsymbol{\alpha})\, \delta(t)\, dt \tag{24}$$

$$\text{s.t.} \quad \dot{\mathbf{x}}(t) = \mathbf{g}(t, \mathbf{x}(t), \mathbf{u}(t); \boldsymbol{\alpha}),\ \mathbf{x}(0) = \mathbf{x}_0, \mathbf{x}(T) = \mathbf{x}_T,$$

where $\delta(t)$ is a *time varying discount factor* that we normalize (without loss of generality) by setting $\delta(0) = 1$. Let $(\mathbf{z}(t;\boldsymbol{\alpha},\mathbf{x}_0,T), \mathbf{v}(t;\boldsymbol{\alpha},\mathbf{x}_0,T))$ be the optimal pair, which is assumed to exist. The subscript on the functional $J[\cdot]$ is there to indicate planning begins in period $t = 0$. Though the change from the discount factor e^{-rt} to the time varying one $\delta(t)$ may appear innocuous, it may lead to a problem of internal inconsistency of sorts. Let's now proceed to precisely define the internal consistency, demonstrate why the internal inconsistency exists and the crucial role played by the discount factor, and determine a necessary and sufficient condition to render the individual's plan internally consistent.

Suppose that the decision maker who solves problem (24) is allowed to recalculate her optimal plan starting at a later date, say, $s \in (0, T)$. Let's also suppose that the decision maker uses the discount factor $\delta(t - s)$ in the truncated problem and starts the planning given the state that was optimal at time $t = s$ in problem (24). All other functions and parameters, however, remained unchanged. She would use the discount factor $\delta(t - s)$ if it reflected the weight attached to the value of the integrand (which could be instantaneous utility) at time t because of its distance from the starting date of the planning horizon, *not* by virtue of its calendar date. The truncated control problem to be solved by the decision maker is therefore given by

$$\begin{aligned} &\max_{\mathbf{u}(\cdot),\mathbf{x}_T} J_s[\mathbf{x}(\cdot),\mathbf{u}(\cdot)] \stackrel{\text{def}}{=} \int_s^T f(t,\mathbf{x}(t),\mathbf{u}(t);\boldsymbol{\alpha})\,\delta(t-s)\,dt \\ &\text{s.t.}\quad \dot{\mathbf{x}}(t) = \mathbf{g}(t,\mathbf{x}(t),\mathbf{u}(t);\boldsymbol{\alpha}),\ \mathbf{x}(s) = \mathbf{x}_s,\ \mathbf{x}(T) = \mathbf{x}_T, \end{aligned} \tag{25}$$

where $\mathbf{x}_s = \mathbf{z}(s;\boldsymbol{\alpha},\mathbf{x}_0,T)$ is the optimal value of the state vector at time $t = s$ from problem (24) and $s \in (0, T)$ is any given initial or starting date at which the planning begins. Because the discount factor has been linearly shifted, the optimal pair for problem (25) is in general different from the optimal pair for problem (24). In concrete terms, this observation implies that if I plan optimally on Monday for consumption on Monday, Tuesday, and Wednesday [problem (24)], then when Tuesday rolls around and I reconsider my optimal consumption plan for Tuesday and Wednesday [problem (25)], I will generally find that my initial (i.e., from Monday's perspective) consumption plans for Tuesday and Wednesday are no longer optimal now that Tuesday has arrived! More generally, this observation means that it is not rational to obey a plan that was optimal when viewed from an earlier date [problem (24)] if it is not the optimal one at the present date [problem (25)]. Said differently, the optimal plan will in general change with a change in the initial date $s \in (0, T)$ from which one plans. Stated in this last manner, it is not at all surprising that the optimal pair for problem (24) is not, in general, the same as the optimal pair for problem (25), as comparative dynamics has taught us that, in general, a change in any parameter in an optimal control problem, including the starting date, affects the optimal solution pair.

At this point, it is important to make note of the fact that the relative weight a person may assign to the value of a future action or decision, that is, the manner of discounting, may depend on either or both of the following two things: (i) the *time distance* of the future date from the present date, or (ii) the *calendar date* of the future decision. For example, the weight I assign to the pleasure of drinking my favorite bottle of Petite Sirah on June 12, 2004, may depend on the fact that this date is a certain length of time away from the present date, or the fact that it is my birthday. To the extent that time-distance is important, I will likely assign a higher weight to June 12, 2004, as it draws near. If only the calendar date matters, then the weight will not change as June 12, 2004, approaches. Both bases for discounting a future date are included in the objective functional $J_s[\mathbf{x}(\cdot), \mathbf{u}(\cdot)]$. The importance of the calendar date enters through the explicit appearance of t in the integrand function $f(\cdot)$, whereas the importance of time-distance is given by the discount factor $\delta(t - s)$.

Let's provide a geometric view of the aforementioned divergence concerning the optimal solution pairs for problems (24) and (25) before moving on to the more formal aspects of the issue. Consider, therefore, an individual who reevaluates his optimal plan periodically, say, at times $s = s_1$, $s = s_2$, and $s = s_3$, where $0 < s_1 < s_2 < s_3 < T$, and set $M = 1$ for the purpose of graphing. Let $v_0(\cdot)$ be the optimal control function for this individual given $s = 0$, that is, it is the optimal control function for problem (24). Similarly, let $v_i(\cdot)$, $i = 1, 2, 3$, be the optimal control functions for $s = s_1$, $s = s_2$, and $s = s_3$, respectively, that is, they are the respective optimal control functions for problem (25) for initial dates $s = s_1$, $s = s_2$, and $s = s_3$.

Let's now consider Figure 12.1. If the individual does not reconsider his original optimal plan during the period $0 \leq t < s_1$, then he abides by it and follows the thicker curve $v_0(t)$ for this period of time. At s_1, however, he reconsiders his plan and chooses $v_1(\cdot)$ as the optimal control function and thus follows the curve $v_1(t)$ over the period $s_1 \leq t < s_2$. Therefore, at time s_1, the value of the individual's optimal control jumps from the thicker curve $v_0(t)$ to the thinner curve $v_1(t)$. The same argument applies when the next time comes for reevaluation of the optimal plan, and so on. This process of reevaluation of the original optimal plan at discrete intervals of the planning horizon thus leads to the optimal control path taking on the sawtooth pattern displayed in Figure 12.1. If the original plan is continuously reevaluated, then any single plan is optimal only at an instant $t = s$. In this case, actual behavior is given by the locus of the optimal control for $t = s$ as determined by the necessary conditions for the truncated control problem as s proceeds from 0 to T. We would say in this case that the individual's original optimal plan is *time inconsistent* or *dynamically inconsistent*, since the original plan would not be followed through if the individual reevaluated it at a later date in the planning horizon. A *time consistent* or *dynamically consistent* plan, therefore, is one in which the individual would stick to the original plan even when it was reevaluated at a later date in the planning horizon.

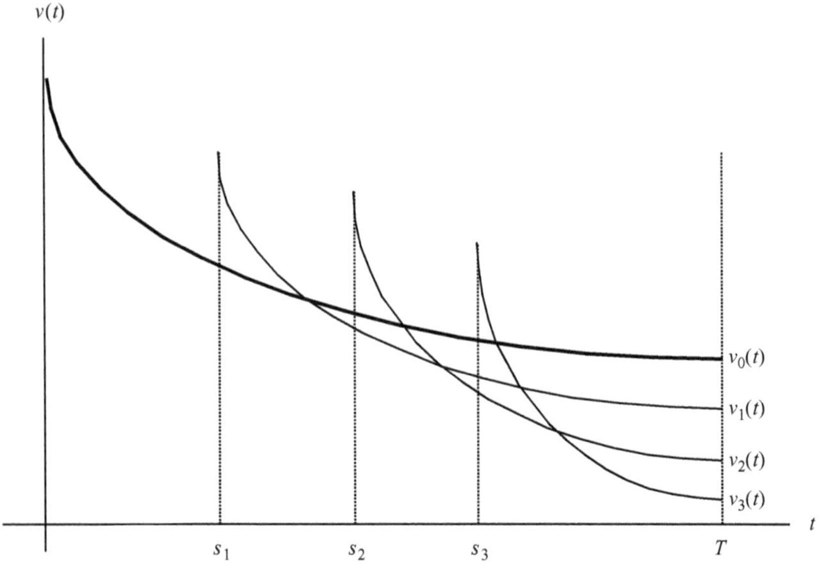

Figure 12.1

It is important to note that what we have been discussing here is the actual dynamics of intertemporal maximization, as opposed to the plan for the future that is made at a given moment. It is also equally important to remember that when the individual reconsiders his optimal plan at a later date, the only thing in the optimal control problem that has changed is the discount factor that weights the values of the integrand function. The parameters and functions are identical to those when the initial plan was set down. Moreover, there is no uncertainty in the problem, so that is not the source of time inconsistency. The time inconsistency is a result of the form of the discount factor. This is an extremely important observation to keep in mind when trying to gain intuition about time consistency.

To summarize, the question raised in the above discussion may be stated as follows: Is the optimal path for the control variables in problem (24) the same as that in problem (25)? Our answer has been *no* in general.

The following important theorem gives a simple but powerful necessary and sufficient condition for a plan to be time consistent or dynamically consistent. In other words, the theorem gives a precise condition under which an individual who continuously reevaluates his planned course of action will in fact confirm his earlier choices, and therefore carry out the plan of action originally selected. You will be asked to prove the sufficiency part of it in a mental exercise. The necessity part of the proof is given below.

Theorem 12.3 (Time Consistency): *The optimal pair* $(\mathbf{z}(t;\alpha,\mathbf{x}_0,T), \mathbf{v}(t;\alpha,\mathbf{x}_0,T))$ *for problem (24) is also the optimal pair for problem (25) over the planning horizon* $[s,T]$, $s \in [0,T)$, *if and only if* $\delta(t) = e^{-rt}$ *for some constant r.*

Proof: For expository purposes, we prove necessity under the assumptions $M = N = 1$, so that we are dealing with one control variable and one state variable. We seek to prove that if the solution to control problems (24) and (25) is the same over the planning horizon $[s, T]$, then the discount factor function $\delta(\cdot)$ takes the form $\delta(t) = e^{-rt}$ for some constant r. This implies that the necessary conditions for control problems (24) and (25) must be the same over the planning horizon $[s, T]$ for the answers to be identical. This equivalence will imply a differential equation that the discount factor must satisfy. Solution of this differential equation will yield the desired conclusion.

To begin, form the present value Hamiltonian function for problem (24), namely,

$$H(t, x, u, \lambda; \boldsymbol{\alpha}) \stackrel{\text{def}}{=} \delta(t) f(t, x, u; \boldsymbol{\alpha}) + \lambda g(t, x, u; \boldsymbol{\alpha}),$$

and compute the necessary conditions

$$H_u(t, x, u, \lambda; \boldsymbol{\alpha}) = \delta(t) f_u(t, x, u; \boldsymbol{\alpha}) + \lambda g_u(t, x, u; \boldsymbol{\alpha}) = 0, \tag{26}$$

$$\dot{\lambda} = -H_x(t, x, u, \lambda; \boldsymbol{\alpha}) = -\delta(t) f_x(t, x, u; \boldsymbol{\alpha}) - \lambda g_x(t, x, u; \boldsymbol{\alpha}),\ \lambda(T) = 0, \tag{27}$$

$$\dot{x} = H_\lambda(t, x, u, \lambda; \boldsymbol{\alpha}) = g(t, x, u; \boldsymbol{\alpha}),\ x(0) = x_0, \tag{28}$$

which hold over the planning horizon $[0, T]$. Given that the optimal pair must satisfy Eq. (26) identically for each value of t in the planning horizon $[0, T]$, it is valid to differentiate Eq. (26) with respect to t and the resulting differential equation will still be equal to zero. Doing just that yields

$$\frac{d}{dt} H_u(t, x, u, \lambda; \boldsymbol{\alpha}) = \delta(t) \dot{f}_u(t) + \dot{\delta}(t) f_u(t) + \lambda \dot{g}_u(t) + \dot{\lambda} g_u(t) = 0, \forall\, t \in [0, T], \tag{29}$$

where, for example, $\dot{f}_u(t) \stackrel{\text{def}}{=} \frac{d}{dt} f_u(t, x, u; \boldsymbol{\alpha}) = f_{ut}(t, x, u; \boldsymbol{\alpha}) + f_{ux}(t, x, u; \boldsymbol{\alpha})\dot{x} + f_{uu}(t, x, u; \boldsymbol{\alpha})\dot{u}$. Upon substituting for λ from Eq. (26) and $\dot{\lambda}$ from Eq. (27), we arrive at the following differential equation:

$$f_u(t)\left[\frac{\dot{\delta}(t)}{\delta(t)}\right] = -\dot{f}_u(t) + \frac{f_u(t)\dot{g}_u(t)}{g_u(t)} + g_u(t) f_x(t) - f_u(t) g_x(t), \forall\, t \in [0, T], \tag{30}$$

which you will be asked to verify in a mental exercise.

Because control problem (25) is identical to (24) except for the fact that $\delta(t - s)$ replaces $\delta(t)$ in the integrand and the planning horizon is $[s, T]$, it immediately follows that the recipe used in deriving Eq. (30), when applied to problem (25), gives

$$f_u(t)\left[\frac{\dot{\delta}(t - s)}{\delta(t - s)}\right] = -\dot{f}_u(t) + \frac{f_u(t)\dot{g}_u(t)}{g_u(t)} + g_u(t) f_x(t) - f_u(t) g_x(t), \forall\, t \in [s, T]. \tag{31}$$

Because the right-hand sides of Eqs. (30) and (31) are equal, so must be the left-hand sides. Equating the left-hand sides of Eqs. (30) and (31) and canceling the term $f_u(t)$ gives the differential equation that must be obeyed by the discount function, assuming that the solutions to control problems (24) and (25) are identical over the planning horizon $[s, T]$, videlicet,

$$\frac{\dot{\delta}(t)}{\delta(t)} = \frac{\dot{\delta}(t-s)}{\delta(t-s)}, \ \forall t \in [s, T]. \tag{32}$$

This must hold for *every* $s \in [0, T)$ seeing as s was arbitrary but fixed in the foregoing derivation. But the requirement that Eq. (32) hold for every $s \in [0, T)$ means that Eq. (32) must be constant, because the left-hand side of Eq. (32) is independent of s. Thus for $s = 0$, the differential equation obeyed by the discount factor in the time consistent case is

$$\frac{\dot{\delta}(t)}{\delta(t)} = c_1, \ \forall t \in [0, T],$$

where c_1 is a constant. This says the logarithmic rate of change of the discount factor must be a constant in a time consistent plan. Integrating this ordinary differential equation, either by separating the variables or by use of the integrating factor $e^{-c_1 t}$, gives the general solution of the differential equation, scilicet, $\delta(t) = c_2 e^{c_1 t}$, where c_2 is a constant of integration. Using the normalization condition $\delta(0) = 1$ implies that $c_2 = 1$. Thus the specific form of the discount factor is $\delta(t) = e^{c_1 t}$, where c_1 is a constant, which was what we wished to demonstrate. Q.E.D.

This theorem asserts that a decision maker who solves problem (24), if given an opportunity to reconsider her original optimal plan at a later date, as reflected by the truncated control problem (25), will find the continuation of the original optimal plan to be optimal in the truncated control problem if and only if the discount factor is of the form $\delta(t) = e^{-rt}$, the constant exponential variety. More concretely, a discount function of the form given by Theorem 12.3 implies that the relative importance of 2004 and 2005 is the same in 2004 as it is in 2003. Consequently, when one decides in 2003 how to apportion one's wealth between 2004 and 2005, this is the same decision one would make in 2004. Thus, in 2004, the plan laid down in 2003 is confirmed.

Note that the functions and parameters are identical in problems (24) and (25), and that the initial value of the state vector in the truncated control problem (25) is the optimal value of the state vector from the control problem (24). At first glance, therefore, one might *mistakenly* think that the principle of optimality can be applied to problem (25) to conclude that the optimal pairs for problems (24) and (25) are identical over $[s, T]$. The problem here is that the discount factor in problems (24) and (25) differ in how they weigh the integrand at common dates in the planning horizon; hence one cannot appeal to the principle of optimality to claim that the optimal pair for problems (24) and (25) are identical over $[s, T]$. For example, at time $t = s$, the value of the integrand in problem (24) is given by $f(\mathbf{x}(s), \mathbf{u}(s); \boldsymbol{\alpha})\,\delta(s)$, whereas that in problem (25) is given by $f(\mathbf{x}(s), \mathbf{u}(s); \boldsymbol{\alpha})\, \delta(0)$, which are not, in general, equal. Note that even if $\delta(t) = e^{-rt}$, the values of the integrands are not equal, as they differ by the constant $\delta(s) = e^{rs}$, since t is the dummy variable of integration. Note that this observation is the key to establishing the sufficiency part of Theorem 12.3.

To sum up, an original plan is time consistent if and only if the discount factor function $\delta(\cdot)$ is of the form $\delta(t) = e^{-rt}$ for some constant r. Any other form of the discount factor would render the original optimal plan time inconsistent. Thus one formal and economically valid justification for constant exponential discounting in dynamic economic theory is the principle of time consistency. This principle, therefore, is in large part responsible for the prevalence of $\delta(t) = e^{-rt}$ as a discount factor in continuous-time optimal control problems in economics. It also has the added advantage that if the integrand function $f(\cdot)$ and the transition function $\mathbf{g}(\cdot)$ do not depend explicitly on the independent variable t, then we may conclude from Theorem 12.2 that the canonical equations are autonomous. This simplification yields a nontrivial advantage for determining the qualitative properties of the solution of a control problem via a phase diagram.

In closing out this chapter, let's place a little more structure on problem (1) by assuming that the integrand function $f(\cdot)$ and the transition function $\mathbf{g}(\cdot)$ do not depend explicitly on the independent variable t, there are no inequality or equality constraints, the planner uses the time-consistent discount factor $\delta(t) = e^{-rt}$, $t_0 = 0$, and $t_1 = T$. That is, we are now interested in the following class of control problems:

$$\tilde{V}(\boldsymbol{\alpha}, r, \mathbf{x}_0, T) \stackrel{\text{def}}{=} \max_{\mathbf{u}(\cdot), \mathbf{x}_T} \int_0^T f(\mathbf{x}(t), \mathbf{u}(t); \boldsymbol{\alpha})\, e^{-rt}\, dt \tag{33}$$

$$\text{s.t.} \quad \dot{\mathbf{x}}(t) = \mathbf{g}(\mathbf{x}(t), \mathbf{u}(t); \boldsymbol{\alpha}),\ \mathbf{x}(0) = \mathbf{x}_0,\ \mathbf{x}(T) = \mathbf{x}_T.$$

Let $(\mathbf{z}(t; \boldsymbol{\alpha}, r, \mathbf{x}_0, T), \mathbf{v}(t; \boldsymbol{\alpha}, r, \mathbf{x}_0, T))$ be the optimal pair with corresponding current value costate vector $\tilde{\boldsymbol{\lambda}}(t; \boldsymbol{\alpha}, r, \mathbf{x}_0, T)$. Define the current value Hamiltonian as

$$\tilde{H}(\mathbf{x}, \mathbf{u}, \tilde{\boldsymbol{\lambda}}; \boldsymbol{\alpha}) \stackrel{\text{def}}{=} f(\mathbf{x}, \mathbf{u}; \boldsymbol{\alpha}) + \sum_{n=1}^{N} \tilde{\lambda}_n g^n(\mathbf{x}, \mathbf{u}; \boldsymbol{\alpha}),$$

which, by Theorem 12.1, produces the necessary conditions

$$\tilde{H}_{u_m}(\mathbf{x}, \mathbf{u}, \tilde{\boldsymbol{\lambda}}; \boldsymbol{\alpha}) = 0, \quad m = 1, 2, \ldots, M,$$

$$\dot{\tilde{\lambda}}_i = r\tilde{\lambda}_i - \tilde{H}_{x_i}(\mathbf{x}, \mathbf{u}, \tilde{\boldsymbol{\lambda}}; \boldsymbol{\alpha}),\ \tilde{\lambda}(T) = 0, \quad i = 1, 2, \ldots, N,$$

$$\dot{x}_i = \tilde{H}_{\tilde{\lambda}_i}(\mathbf{x}, \mathbf{u}, \tilde{\boldsymbol{\lambda}}; \boldsymbol{\alpha}),\ x_i(0) = x_{0i}, \quad i = 1, 2, \ldots, N.$$

Letting $\hat{\mathbf{u}}(\mathbf{x}, \tilde{\boldsymbol{\lambda}}; \boldsymbol{\alpha})$ be the solution to the necessary conditions $\tilde{H}_{u_m}(\mathbf{x}, \mathbf{u}, \tilde{\boldsymbol{\lambda}}; \boldsymbol{\alpha}) = 0$, $m = 1, 2, \ldots, M$, the canonical equations can be written as

$$\dot{\tilde{\lambda}}_i = r\tilde{\lambda}_i - \tilde{H}_{x_i}(\mathbf{x}, \hat{\mathbf{u}}(\mathbf{x}, \tilde{\boldsymbol{\lambda}}; \boldsymbol{\alpha}), \tilde{\boldsymbol{\lambda}}; \boldsymbol{\alpha}),\ \tilde{\lambda}(T) = 0, \quad i = 1, 2, \ldots, N, \tag{34}$$

$$\dot{x}_i = \tilde{H}_{\tilde{\lambda}_i}(\mathbf{x}, \hat{\mathbf{u}}(\mathbf{x}, \tilde{\boldsymbol{\lambda}}; \boldsymbol{\alpha}), \tilde{\boldsymbol{\lambda}}; \boldsymbol{\alpha}),\ x_i(0) = x_{0i}, \quad i = 1, 2, \ldots, N. \tag{35}$$

Now define the maximized current value Hamiltonian function $\tilde{M}(\cdot)$ by

$$\tilde{M}(\mathbf{x}, \tilde{\boldsymbol{\lambda}}; \boldsymbol{\alpha}) \stackrel{\text{def}}{=} \max_{\mathbf{u}} \tilde{H}(\mathbf{x}, \mathbf{u}, \tilde{\boldsymbol{\lambda}}; \boldsymbol{\alpha}).$$

By the prototype envelope theorem applied to this static optimization problem defining $\tilde{M}(\cdot)$, it follows that Eqs. (34) and (35) may be rewritten equivalently as

$$\dot{\tilde{\lambda}}_i = r\tilde{\lambda}_i - \tilde{M}_{x_i}(\mathbf{x}, \tilde{\boldsymbol{\lambda}}; \boldsymbol{\alpha}),\ \tilde{\lambda}(T) = 0, \quad i = 1, 2, \ldots, N, \tag{36}$$

$$\dot{x}_i = \tilde{M}_{\tilde{\lambda}_i}(\mathbf{x}, \tilde{\boldsymbol{\lambda}}; \boldsymbol{\alpha}),\ x_i(0) = x_{0i}, \quad i = 1, 2, \ldots, N, \tag{37}$$

a result you are asked to confirm in a mental exercise. We are now in a position to establish an important result that relates the value of the current value optimal value function $\tilde{V}(\boldsymbol{\alpha}, r, \mathbf{x}_0, T)$ in problem (33) to the value of the maximized current value Hamiltonian $\tilde{M}(\mathbf{x}, \tilde{\boldsymbol{\lambda}}; \boldsymbol{\alpha})$ evaluated at the optimal solution $(\mathbf{z}(t; \boldsymbol{\alpha}, r, \mathbf{x}_0, T), \tilde{\boldsymbol{\lambda}}(t; \boldsymbol{\alpha}, r, \mathbf{x}_0, T))$.

Theorem 12.4: *In problem (33), the value of the current value optimal value function* $\tilde{V}(\boldsymbol{\alpha}, r, \mathbf{x}_0, T)$ *is related to the value of the maximized current value Hamiltonian* $\tilde{M}(\mathbf{x}, \tilde{\boldsymbol{\lambda}}; \boldsymbol{\alpha})$ *evaluated at the optimal solution* $(\mathbf{z}(t; \boldsymbol{\alpha}, r, \mathbf{x}_0, T), \tilde{\boldsymbol{\lambda}}(t; \boldsymbol{\alpha}, r, \mathbf{x}_0, T))$ *by the formula*

$$\begin{aligned}\tilde{V}(\boldsymbol{\alpha}, r, \mathbf{x}_0, T) = \frac{1}{r}\,&[\tilde{M}(\mathbf{x}_0, \tilde{\boldsymbol{\lambda}}(0; \boldsymbol{\alpha}, r, \mathbf{x}_0, T); \boldsymbol{\alpha}) \\ &- e^{-rT}\tilde{M}(\mathbf{z}(T; \boldsymbol{\alpha}, r, \mathbf{x}_0, T), \tilde{\boldsymbol{\lambda}}(T; \boldsymbol{\alpha}, r, \mathbf{x}_0, T); \boldsymbol{\alpha})].\end{aligned}$$

Proof: For notational ease, define $\boldsymbol{\beta} \stackrel{\text{def}}{=} (\boldsymbol{\alpha}, r, \mathbf{x}_0, T)$ as the vector of parameters. Begin the proof by observing that

$$\begin{aligned}&-\frac{1}{r}\int_0^T \frac{d}{dt}[e^{-rt}\tilde{M}(\mathbf{z}(t; \boldsymbol{\beta}), \tilde{\boldsymbol{\lambda}}(t; \boldsymbol{\beta}); \boldsymbol{\alpha})]\,dt \\ &\quad = \frac{1}{r}[\tilde{M}(\mathbf{z}(0; \boldsymbol{\beta}), \tilde{\boldsymbol{\lambda}}(0; \boldsymbol{\beta}); \boldsymbol{\alpha}) - e^{-rT}\tilde{M}(\mathbf{z}(T; \boldsymbol{\beta}), \tilde{\boldsymbol{\lambda}}(T; \boldsymbol{\beta}); \boldsymbol{\alpha})]\end{aligned}$$

is a result of the inverse operations of integration and differentiation, whereas

$$\begin{aligned}-\frac{1}{r}\int_0^T \frac{d}{dt}[e^{-rt}\tilde{M}(\mathbf{z}(t; \boldsymbol{\beta}), \tilde{\boldsymbol{\lambda}}(t; \boldsymbol{\beta}); \boldsymbol{\alpha})]\,dt &= \int_0^T e^{-rt}\tilde{M}(\mathbf{z}(t; \boldsymbol{\beta}), \tilde{\boldsymbol{\lambda}}(t; \boldsymbol{\beta}); \boldsymbol{\alpha})\,dt \\ -\frac{1}{r}\int_0^T e^{-rt}\sum_{i=1}^{N}[\tilde{M}_{x_i}&(\mathbf{z}(t; \boldsymbol{\beta}), \tilde{\boldsymbol{\lambda}}(t; \boldsymbol{\beta}); \boldsymbol{\alpha})\dot{z}_i(t; \boldsymbol{\beta}) \\ &+ \tilde{M}_{\tilde{\lambda}_i}(\mathbf{z}(t; \boldsymbol{\beta}), \tilde{\boldsymbol{\lambda}}(t; \boldsymbol{\beta}); \boldsymbol{\alpha})\dot{\tilde{\lambda}}_i(t; \boldsymbol{\beta})]\,dt,\end{aligned}$$

is a result of carrying out the differentiation. In view of the fact that the left-hand sides of the last two equations are identical, so are the right-hand sides. Upon equating the right-hand sides and using Eqs. (36) and (37), we arrive at

$$\int_0^T e^{-rt}\tilde{M}(\mathbf{z}(t;\boldsymbol{\beta}),\tilde{\boldsymbol{\lambda}}(t;\boldsymbol{\beta});\boldsymbol{\alpha})\,dt$$

$$-\frac{1}{r}\int_0^T e^{-rt}\sum_{i=1}^{N}[r\tilde{M}_{\tilde{\lambda}_i}(\mathbf{z}(t;\boldsymbol{\beta}),\tilde{\boldsymbol{\lambda}}(t;\boldsymbol{\beta});\boldsymbol{\alpha})\tilde{\lambda}_i(t;\boldsymbol{\beta})]\,dt$$

$$=\frac{1}{r}[\tilde{M}(\mathbf{z}(0;\boldsymbol{\beta}),\tilde{\boldsymbol{\lambda}}(0;\boldsymbol{\beta});\boldsymbol{\alpha})-e^{-rT}\tilde{M}(\mathbf{z}(T;\boldsymbol{\beta}),\tilde{\boldsymbol{\lambda}}(T;\boldsymbol{\beta});\boldsymbol{\alpha})]. \quad (38)$$

Recall that the optimal path of the control vector is given by $\mathbf{v}(t;\boldsymbol{\beta})\overset{\text{def}}{=}\hat{\mathbf{u}}(\mathbf{z}(t;\boldsymbol{\beta}),\tilde{\boldsymbol{\lambda}}(t;\boldsymbol{\beta});\boldsymbol{\alpha})$. Using this observation and the definition of the maximized current value Hamiltonian, we have

$$\begin{aligned}\tilde{M}(\mathbf{z}(t;\boldsymbol{\beta}),\tilde{\boldsymbol{\lambda}}(t;\boldsymbol{\beta});\boldsymbol{\alpha}) &= \tilde{H}(\mathbf{z}(t;\boldsymbol{\beta}),\mathbf{v}(t;\boldsymbol{\beta}),\tilde{\boldsymbol{\lambda}}(t;\boldsymbol{\beta});\boldsymbol{\alpha})\\ &= f(\mathbf{z}(t;\boldsymbol{\beta}),\mathbf{v}(t;\boldsymbol{\beta});\boldsymbol{\alpha})\\ &\quad+\sum_{n=1}^{N}\tilde{\lambda}_n(t;\boldsymbol{\beta})g^n(\mathbf{z}(t;\boldsymbol{\beta}),\mathbf{v}(t;\boldsymbol{\beta});\boldsymbol{\alpha}). \quad (39)\end{aligned}$$

The archetype static envelope theorem applied to the definition of the maximized current value Hamiltonian $\tilde{M}(\cdot)$, along with the definition of the current value Hamiltonian $\tilde{H}(\cdot)$, yields

$$\begin{aligned}\tilde{M}_{\tilde{\lambda}_i}(\mathbf{z}(t;\boldsymbol{\beta}),\tilde{\boldsymbol{\lambda}}(t;\boldsymbol{\beta});\boldsymbol{\alpha}) &= \tilde{H}_{\tilde{\lambda}_i}(\mathbf{z}(t;\boldsymbol{\beta}),\mathbf{v}(t;\boldsymbol{\beta}),\tilde{\boldsymbol{\lambda}}(t;\boldsymbol{\beta});\boldsymbol{\alpha})\\ &= g^i(\mathbf{z}(t;\boldsymbol{\beta}),\mathbf{v}(t;\boldsymbol{\beta});\boldsymbol{\alpha}), \quad i=1,2,\ldots,N. \quad (40)\end{aligned}$$

Substituting Eqs. (39) and (40) into Eq. (38) therefore yields

$$\int_0^T e^{-rt}f(\mathbf{z}(t;\boldsymbol{\beta}),\mathbf{v}(t;\boldsymbol{\beta});\boldsymbol{\alpha})\,dt$$

$$=\frac{1}{r}[\tilde{M}(\mathbf{z}(0;\boldsymbol{\beta}),\tilde{\boldsymbol{\lambda}}(0;\boldsymbol{\beta});\boldsymbol{\alpha})-e^{-rT}\tilde{M}(\mathbf{z}(T;\boldsymbol{\beta}),\tilde{\boldsymbol{\lambda}}(T;\boldsymbol{\beta});\boldsymbol{\alpha})].$$

Noting that the current value optimal value function $\tilde{V}(\cdot)$ can be defined constructively as

$$\tilde{V}(\boldsymbol{\beta})\equiv\int_0^T e^{-rt}f(\mathbf{z}(t;\boldsymbol{\beta}),\mathbf{v}(t;\boldsymbol{\beta});\boldsymbol{\alpha})\,dt,$$

and that $\mathbf{z}(0;\boldsymbol{\beta})\equiv\mathbf{x}_0$, completes the proof. Q.E.D.

This is an important result for two reasons. First, the result of Theorem 12.4 turns out to be useful in determining which of several admissible paths are optimal for the adjustment cost model of the firm in the presence of certain types of nonconvexities [see, e.g., Davidson and Harris (1981)]. Second, it relates, in a very simple manner, the optimal value of the objective functional, which in general is difficult to explicitly compute, to the value of the maximized Hamiltonian at the initial and terminal dates of the planning horizon. Consequently, if T is a decision variable in problem (33), then we have the even simpler result given in the ensuing theorem, which you are asked to prove in a mental exercise. Observe that in this instance, T does not appear as an argument of the optimal pair or the current value optimal value function seeing as it is a choice variable and not a parameter.

Theorem 12.5: *In problem (33) with T a decision variable, the value of the current value optimal value function $\tilde{V}(\boldsymbol{\alpha}, r, \mathbf{x}_0)$ is related to the value of the maximized current value Hamiltonian $\tilde{M}(\mathbf{x}, \tilde{\boldsymbol{\lambda}}; \boldsymbol{\alpha})$ evaluated at the optimal solution $(\mathbf{z}(t; \boldsymbol{\alpha}, r, \mathbf{x}_0), \tilde{\boldsymbol{\lambda}}(t; \boldsymbol{\alpha}, r, \mathbf{x}_0))$ by the formula*

$$V(\boldsymbol{\alpha}, r, \mathbf{x}_0) = \frac{1}{r}[\tilde{M}(\mathbf{x}_0, \tilde{\boldsymbol{\lambda}}(0; \boldsymbol{\alpha}, r, \mathbf{x}_0); \boldsymbol{\alpha})].$$

We will return to an important variant of Theorem 12.5 two chapters hence, when infinite horizon problems, arguably the largest class of optimal control problems of interest in economic theory, are presented in some detail. In fact, we will encounter essentially the same theorem again in several other chapters in which we study intertemporal duality theory, pointing to its fundamental nature. Though it may not be readily apparent at present, this theorem permits empirical implementation of intertemporal economic models, an important feature that will be expanded upon in some detail in a later chapter as well.

MENTAL EXERCISES

12.1 Consider the standard model of the competitive nonrenewable resource–extracting firm without stock effects:

$$\max_{q(\cdot),T,x_T} \int_0^T [p(t)q(t) - C(q(t))]\, e^{-rt}\, dt$$

$$\text{s.t.} \quad \dot{x}(t) = -q(t),\ x(0) = x_0, x(T) = x_T \geq 0,\ q(t) \geq 0,$$

where $q(t)$ is the extraction rate, $x(t)$ is the stock of the resource in the ground, and $p(t)$ is the time-varying output price. Note the nonnegativity restriction on the terminal stock and extraction rate.

(a) Write down the necessary conditions for this problem in current value form.
(b) Show that if $x(T) > 0$, then $\lambda(t) \equiv 0 \,\forall\, t \in [0, T]$, where $\lambda(t)$ is the *current value* costate variable. Assuming that $q(t) > 0 \,\forall\, t \in [0, T]$, provide an economic interpretation of the result $\lambda(t) \equiv 0 \,\forall\, t \in [0, T]$.
(c) Show that if $C(0) = 0$, then $q(T) > 0$ is optimal regardless of whether $x(T) = 0$ or $x(T) > 0$. Provide an economic interpretation of this result and draw a graph of the situation at $t = T$.
(d) Show that if $q(T) = 0$, then $C(0) = 0$ regardless of whether $x(T) > 0$ or $x(T) = 0$. Provide an economic interpretation of this result.
(e) Show that if $\lambda(T) > 0$, then $x(T) = 0$. Provide an economic interpretation of this result.

12.2 Let's reconsider the prototype control problem studied in this chapter, but with the added twist that the discount rate is time dependent, say $\rho(t) > 0$, rather than a constant $r > 0$. That is, consider the optimal control problem

$$V(\boldsymbol{\alpha}, \mathbf{x}_0, T) \stackrel{\text{def}}{=} \max_{\mathbf{u}(\cdot),\mathbf{x}_T} \int_0^T f(t, \mathbf{x}(t), \mathbf{u}(t); \boldsymbol{\alpha})\, \delta(t)\, dt$$

$$\text{s.t.} \quad \dot{\mathbf{x}}(t) = \mathbf{g}(t, \mathbf{x}(t), \mathbf{u}(t); \boldsymbol{\alpha}), \;\; \mathbf{x}(t_0) = \mathbf{x}_0, \;\; \mathbf{x}(T) = \mathbf{x}_T,$$

where $\delta(t) \stackrel{\text{def}}{=} \exp[-\int_0^t \rho(\tau)\, d\tau]$ is the discount factor and $\rho(t) > 0$ is the time-varying discount rate.
(a) Write down the necessary conditions for the problem in present value form.
(b) Define the current value Hamiltonian and current value costate vector for the control problem.
(c) Write down the necessary conditions for the problem in current value form. Show all of your work.
(d) Show that even if the integrand function $f(\cdot)$ and state function $\mathbf{g}(\cdot)$ do not depend explicitly on the independent variable t, that is, even if $f_t(\cdot) \equiv 0$ and $\mathbf{g}_t(\cdot) \equiv \mathbf{0}_N$, the canonical differential equations in current value form are *not* autonomous.

12.3 Prove the sufficiency part of Theorem 12.3.

12.4 Consider the control problem

$$\max_{\mathbf{u}(\cdot),\mathbf{x}_T} \int_0^T f(\mathbf{x}(t), \mathbf{u}(t))\, e^{-rt}\, dt$$

$$\text{s.t.} \quad \dot{\mathbf{x}}(t) = \mathbf{g}(\mathbf{x}(t), \mathbf{u}(t)), \;\; \mathbf{x}(t_0) = \mathbf{x}_0, \;\; \mathbf{x}(T) = \mathbf{x}_T.$$

Let $(\mathbf{z}(t), \mathbf{v}(t))$ be the optimal pair with corresponding present value costate vector $\boldsymbol{\lambda}(t)$. Define the present value Hamiltonian by

$$H(t, \mathbf{x}, \mathbf{u}, \boldsymbol{\lambda}) \stackrel{\text{def}}{=} f(\mathbf{x}, \mathbf{u})e^{-rt} + \sum_{n=1}^{N} \lambda_n g^n(\mathbf{x}, \mathbf{u}).$$

Note that even though the functions $f(\cdot)$ and $\mathbf{g}(\cdot)$ do not depend explicitly on the independent variable t, the present value Hamiltonian does because of the appearance of the discount factor.

(a) Write down the necessary conditions for the control problem.

(b) Prove that

$$\frac{d}{dt} H(t, \mathbf{z}(t), \mathbf{v}(t), \boldsymbol{\lambda}(t)) = -rf(\mathbf{z}(t), \mathbf{v}(t))\, e^{-rt}.$$

This is very similar to the envelope result established in Mental Exercises 2.31, 4.13, and 6.11. In fact, the above result is a special case of Mental Exercises 4.13 and 6.11. Why?

(c) Define the current value Hamiltonian $\tilde{H}(\cdot)$ and current value costate vector $\tilde{\boldsymbol{\lambda}}(\cdot)$.

(d) Prove that

$$\frac{d}{dt} \tilde{H}(\mathbf{z}(t), \mathbf{v}(t), \tilde{\boldsymbol{\lambda}}(t)) = r \sum_{n=1}^{N} \tilde{\lambda}_n(t) g^n(\mathbf{z}(t), \mathbf{v}(t)).$$

This proves that even if the functions $f(\cdot)$ and $\mathbf{g}(\cdot)$ do not depend explicitly on the independent variable t, but a discount factor of the form e^{-rt} multiplies $f(\cdot)$, the current value Hamiltonian is not constant along the optimal path, in contrast to assertions made in the literature [see, e.g., Chiang (1992, p. 212)]. Note also that this result was used in the proof of Theorem 12.4.

(e) To ease the notation, define $\Omega(t) \stackrel{\text{def}}{=} \tilde{H}(\mathbf{z}(t), \mathbf{v}(t), \tilde{\boldsymbol{\lambda}}(t))$, which is simply the value of the current value Hamiltonian along the optimal path. Show that the result in part (d) can be written equivalently as $\dot{\Omega}(t) = r\Omega(t) - rf(\mathbf{z}(t), \mathbf{v}(t))$.

(f) Find the general solution of the differential equation $\dot{\Omega}(t) = r\Omega(t) - rf(\mathbf{z}(t), \mathbf{v}(t))$. Assuming that T is a decision variable, find the specific solution. Use $t = 0$ as the lower limit of integration.

(g) Prove that Theorem 12.5 is a special case of the specific solution you derived in part (f).

12.5 Derive Eq. (30).

12.6 Prove that Eqs. (34) and (35) can be written equivalently as Eqs. (36) and (37), respectively.

12.7 Prove Theorem 12.5.

12.8 *Optimal Consumption of a Stock of Wine by an Impatient Drunk.* You are told by your physician that you have $T > 0$ years to live at time $t = 0$, the present, and you know this to be true. Over the course of your life, you have been an avid collector of wine for the purpose of consuming it rather than using it as an investment. Given the news from your physician, you would like to develop a consumption plan that maximizes the utility of consumption of your stock of wine over your remaining lifetime. At present, you have $w(0) = w_0 > 0$ bottles of wine in your cellar, and because you cannot take the wine with you when you die, you've decided that you will consume it all by the time you die; hence $w(T) = 0$. The instantaneous utility that you derive from the consumption of wine is given by $U(c; \alpha_1) \stackrel{\text{def}}{=} \alpha_1 c$, where $\alpha_1 > 0$ is the marginal utility of wine consumption. This set of preferences implies that you only get utility from the consumption of wine, not from the mere presence of the stock of wine in your cellar, that is, in contrast to Mental Exercise 5.6, you do not like to brag about the quantity and quality of wine in your cellar because you get no enjoyment from that. The stock of wine in your cellar at any moment $t \in [0, T]$ is given by the archetype depletion equation in integral form, namely,

$$w(t) = w_0 - \int_0^t c(s)\, ds,$$

so that by Leibniz's rule,

$$\dot{w}(t) = -c(t),\ w(0) = w_0, w(T) = 0$$

are the state equation and boundary conditions for the optimal control problem that you will solve in order to determine your optimal time path of wine consumption. Given that your preferences are linear in the consumption rate, one must place lower and upper bounds on your consumption rate, say, $0 \le c(t) \le \bar{c}$, where $\bar{c} > w_0/T > 0$. Also in contrast to Mental Exercise 5.6, you *do* discount your instantaneous utility at the rate $r > 0$. Defining $\beta \stackrel{\text{def}}{=} (\alpha_1, \bar{c}, r, w_0, T) \in \Re^5_{++}$ as the vector of time-independent parameters, the optimal control problem that defines the optimal consumption rate of your stock of wine is therefore given by

$$V(\beta) \stackrel{\text{def}}{=} \max_{c(\cdot)} \int_0^T \alpha_1 c(t) e^{-rt}\, dt$$

$$\text{s.t.} \quad \dot{w}(t) = -c(t),\ w(0) = w_0,\ w(T) = 0,$$

$$c(t) \in U \stackrel{\text{def}}{=} \left\{c(\cdot) : 0 \le c(t) \le \bar{c}\, \forall\, t \in [0, T],\ \bar{c} > w_0 T^{-1} > 0\right\}.$$

(a) Provide an *economic* interpretation of the inequality $\bar{c} > w_0/T$. What would result if the inequality ran in the other direction?

(b) Write down the current value Hamiltonian for the optimal control problem, say $H(\cdot)$, letting λ be the current value costate variable. What is the economic interpretation of λ? Is it positive or negative? How do you know?

(c) Assuming that an optimal solution to the control problem exists, find the decision rule governing the selection of the optimal rate of wine consumption in terms of (α_1, λ). Provide an economic interpretation of the decision rule.

(d) Prove that $c(t) = 0 \, \forall \, t \in [0, T]$ is not an admissible solution. Explain why it therefore cannot be an optimal solution.

(e) Prove that $c(t) = \bar{c} \, \forall \, t \in [0, T]$ is not an admissible solution.

(f) Find the general solution for current value costate $\lambda(t)$, letting a_1 be the constant of integration. Prove that $\lambda(t) < \alpha_1 \, \forall \, t \in [0, T]$ and $\lambda(t) > \alpha_1 \, \forall \, t \in [0, T]$ cannot hold for $\lambda(t)$ in an optimal program.

(g) Based on your answer to the earlier parts of the question, what, therefore, is the nature of the solution for the optimal consumption rate? Justify your answer fully.

(h) Show that

$$c(t) = \begin{cases} \bar{c} \, \forall \, t \in [0, \tau] \\ 0 \, \forall \, t \in (\tau, T], \end{cases} \quad w(t) = \begin{cases} w_0 - \bar{c}t \, \forall \, t \in [0, \tau] \\ 0 \qquad \forall \, t \in (\tau, T], \end{cases}$$

$$\lambda(t) = \alpha_1 e^{-r(\tau - t)}, \quad \tau = \frac{w_0}{\bar{c}} < T,$$

where τ is the switch time, is a solution to the necessary conditions. Note that you must *derive* this solution, not just simply verify it satisfies the necessary conditions. Explain all the steps and reasoning clearly in your derivation.

(i) Provide an economic interpretation of the solution to the necessary conditions.

12.9 *The Baby Boomer Problem.* You are told by your physician that you have $T > 0$ years to live at time $t = 0$, the present, and you know this to be true. At present, you have an initial stock of assets $a(0) = a_0 > 0$, which may be thought of as a stock of money in some interest-bearing account, where $r > 0$ is the interest rate for the account. You also have a constant income of $y > 0$ for each $t \in [0, T]$. Letting $c(t)$ be your consumption expenditures (i.e., the rate at which you spend your money on consumption) at time $t \in [0, T]$, the dynamics of your asset are given by the first-order ordinary differential equation

$$\dot{a}(t) = y + ra(t) - c(t),$$

where $a(t)$ is your stock of the asset in the interest-bearing account at time $t \in [0, T]$. Note that we are allowing $a(t)$ to be negative, zero, or positive. The instantaneous utility that you derive from consumption is given by $U(c;\alpha_1) \stackrel{\text{def}}{=} \alpha_1 c$, where $\alpha_1 > 0$ is the marginal utility of consumption. This set of preferences implies that you only get utility from consumption, not from the mere presence of the stock of the asset you own, that is, you do not get enjoyment from bragging about how wealthy you are. Given that your preferences are linear in the consumption rate, one must place lower and upper bounds on your consumption rate, say, $0 \le c(t) \le \bar{c}$, where $\bar{c} > 0$. You discount your instantaneous utility at the rate $\rho > 0$, that is, your intertemporal rate of time preference is $\rho > 0$. In addition, you can choose how much of the asset to leave your spouse and/or children when you die, that is, you are free to choose the value $a(T) = a_T$, which, because it may be negative, zero, or positive, is *not* subject to any constraint. The utility that you receive from such a bequest is given by the instantaneous utility function $B(a_T;\alpha_2) \stackrel{\text{def}}{=} \alpha_2 a_T$, where $\alpha_2 > 0$ is a preference shift parameter. Defining $\boldsymbol{\beta} \stackrel{\text{def}}{=} (a_0, T, \alpha_1, \alpha_2, \bar{c}, \rho, r) \in \Re^7_{++}$ as the vector of time-independent parameters, the optimal control problem that defines the optimal consumption rate is therefore given by

$$V(\boldsymbol{\beta}) \stackrel{\text{def}}{=} \max_{c(\cdot),a_T} \left\{ \int_0^T \alpha_1 c(t) e^{-\rho t}\, dt + \alpha_2 a_T e^{-\rho T} \right\}$$

$$\text{s.t.} \quad \dot{a}(t) = y + ra(t) - c(t),\ a(0) = a_0,\ a(T) = a_T,$$

$$c(t) \in U \stackrel{\text{def}}{=} \{c(\cdot) : 0 \le c(t) \le \bar{c}\, \forall\, t \in [0, T],\ \bar{c} > 0\}.$$

Assume that $\rho > r$, and note that $\rho > 0$ is the discount factor in the integrand, *not* $r > 0$.

(a) Provide an economic interpretation of the inequality $\rho > r$.

(b) What is the economic implication of the inequality $a(t) < 0$? Moreover, what is the economic implication of having $r > 0$ be the same regardless of whether $a(t) > 0$ or $a(t) < 0$?

(c) Write down the *current value* Hamiltonian for the optimal control problem, say, $H(\cdot)$, letting λ be the *current value* costate variable. What is the economic interpretation of λ? Is it positive or negative? How do you know?

(d) Assuming that an optimal solution to the control problem exists, say, $c^*(t)$, find the decision rule governing the selection of the optimal consumption rate in terms of (α_1, λ). Provide an economic interpretation of the decision rule.

(e) Find the general *and* specific solution of the costate differential equation.

(f) Prove that if $\alpha_2 < \alpha_1$, then $c^*(t) = \bar{c}\, \forall\, t \in [0, T]$ is the solution to the necessary conditions for the consumption rate. Provide an economic interpretation of this solution.

(g) Find the general *and* specific solution of the state equation given that $c^*(t) = \bar{c}\ \forall t \in [0, T]$.

(h) Prove that if $\frac{1}{r}[\bar{c} - y][e^{rT} - 1] > a_0 e^{rT}$, then $a(T) = a_T < 0$ given that $c^*(t) = \bar{c}\ \forall t \in [0, T]$. Provide an economic interpretation of this circumstance. This is the "baby boomer" result alluded to in the problem.

(i) Derive sufficient conditions for the following bang-bang consumption plan to be a solution to the necessary conditions:

$$c^*(t) = \begin{cases} \bar{c}\ \forall t \in [0, \tau] \\ 0\ \forall t \in (\tau, T], \end{cases}$$

where τ is the switching time. You are *not* required to solve for the corresponding time paths of the state and costate variables.

12.10 *Optimal Waste Cleanup with Residual Consequences.* A spill of a toxic substance has occurred at time $t = 0$ (the present) in the known amount of $x(0) = x_0 > 0$, where $x(t)$ is the stock of the toxic substance left in the environment at time t. The federal government has a contract with your company for a fixed interval of time, say, $[0, T]$, to reduce the size of the toxic waste stock from its initial size of x_0. Compared with the previous version of this problem examined in Example 5.3, there are two significant changes. First, the firm is given the choice of how much to clean up, that is, $x(T) = x_T$ is a choice variable for the firm. Second, after the cleanup period comes to an end ($t > T$), the firm must pay a penalty for any of the stock they failed to clean up by time T, say, to the tune of $P(x_T; \beta, r, T) \stackrel{\text{def}}{=} \beta x_T e^{-rt}$ dollars, where $\beta > 0$ is a given parameter. As head economist of the company, you are charged with determining the cleanup rate path $u(t)$ that minimizes the present discounted cost of cleaning up a variable amount of the toxic waste over the fixed horizon, including any penalty associated with the stock you failed to clean up by time T. The cleanup technology is linear in the cleanup rate, say, $cu(t)$, where $c > 0$, and the discount rate is $r > 0$. The cleanup rate is bounded below by zero and bounded above by some fixed finite rate $\bar{u} > 0$, where $\bar{u} \leq x_0/T$. Because $x(t)$ is defined as the toxic stock left in the environment at time t, it follows that

$$x(t) \stackrel{\text{def}}{=} x_0 - \int_0^t u(s)\, ds.$$

Hence, by Leibniz's rule,

$$\dot{x}(t) = -u(t),\ x(0) = x_0,\ x(T) = x_T$$

are the state equation and boundary conditions for the problem. In full, the optimal control problem is

$$C(\beta, c, r, \bar{u}, x_0, T) \stackrel{\text{def}}{=} \min_{u(\cdot), x_T} \int_0^T cu(t)e^{-rt}\, dt + \beta x_T e^{-rT}$$

$$\text{s.t.} \quad \dot{x}(t) = -u(t), x(0) = x_0, \; x(T) = x_T,$$

$$u(t) \in U \stackrel{\text{def}}{=} \{u(\cdot) : 0 \leq u(t) \leq \bar{u}, \bar{u} \leq x_0/T\}.$$

Assume that $r^{-1} \ln c\beta^{-1} + T > 0$. The relevance of this assumption will become clear in the course of solving the problem.

(a) Write down the necessary conditions for this problem in current value form, letting λ be the current value costate variable. What is the economic interpretation of λ?

(b) Assuming that an optimal solution to the control problem exists, find the decision rule governing selection of the optimal control in terms of (c, λ).

(c) Find the specific solution for $\lambda(t)$. Prove that $\lambda(t) > 0 \, \forall \, t \in [0, T]$ and that $\dot{\lambda}(t) > 0 \, \forall \, t \in [0, T]$.

(d) Prove that if $\beta < c$, then $u(t) = 0 \, \forall \, t \in [0, T]$ is the solution to the necessary conditions. Provide an economic interpretation of this scenario.

(e) Prove that if $\beta e^{-rt} > c$, then $u(t) = \bar{u} \, \forall \, t \in [0, T]$ is the solution to the necessary conditions. Provide an economic interpretation of this scenario.

(f) Under what conditions is

$$u(t) = \begin{cases} 0 \; \forall \, t \in [0, s] \\ \bar{u} \; \forall \, t \in (s, \mathrm{T}], \end{cases}$$

where s is the switching time, a solution to the necessary conditions? Find the switching time s in this case. Provide an economic interpretation of this scenario.

(g) Prove that a solution to the necessary conditions is a solution to the control problem.

(h) What is the effect of an increase in β on the optimal cleanup policy, assuming that the bang-bang policy is optimal? Your economic interpretation must be backed up with formal mathematical calculations.

FURTHER READING

The seminal article by Strotz (1956) is the source for the material on time consistency. A brief discussion of time consistency appears in Léonard and Von Long (1992). Theorem 12.4 originates with Davidson and Harris (1981), who also provide an application of the infinite horizon version of Theorem 12.5 in the context of the adjustment cost model of the firm with nonconvexities.

REFERENCES

Chiang, A.C. (1992), *Elements of Dynamic Optimization* (New York: McGraw-Hill, Inc.).

Davidson, R. and Harris, R. (1981), "Non-Convexities in Continuous-Time Investment Theory," *Review of Economic Studies*, 48, 235–253.

Léonard, D. and Van Long, N. (1992), *Optimal Control Theory and Static Optimization in Economics* (New York: Cambridge University Press).

Strotz, R. (1956), "Myopia and Inconsistency in Dynamic Utility Maximization," *Review of Economic Studies*, 23, 165–180.

THIRTEEN

Local Stability and Phase Portraits of Autonomous Differential Equations

We temporarily break from the study of optimal control theory in this chapter in order to present some essential results from the theory of autonomous ordinary differential equations. These results form the foundation upon which we will build our understanding and the construction of phase portraits, and consequently, a qualitative understanding of the solution of such a class of differential equations. This is important in dynamic economic theory, for phase portraits are ubiquitous owing to the fact that economists characteristically specify only the qualitative properties of the integrand and transition functions in an optimal control problem, rather than their functional forms. Accordingly, one cannot usually derive an explicit solution of an optimal control problem. Hence all that one can typically expect is a qualitative characterization of the solution in such instances. This is where the phase portrait comes in, for this is what it provides.

To begin, consider the following system of N autonomous first-order nonlinear ordinary differential equations:

$$
\begin{aligned}
\dot{x}_1 &= f^1(x_1, x_2, \ldots, x_N),\\
\dot{x}_2 &= f^2(x_1, x_2, \ldots, x_N),\\
&\vdots\\
\dot{x}_N &= f^N(x_1, x_2, \ldots, x_N),
\end{aligned} \tag{1}
$$

or in vector notation, $\dot{\mathbf{x}} = \mathbf{f}(\mathbf{x})$, where $\mathbf{x} \in \Re^N$. We assume throughout this chapter that $f^n(\cdot) \in C^{(1)}$, $n = 1, 2, \ldots, N$, in some domain D. Then by the fundamental existence and uniqueness theorem, if $\mathbf{x}_0 \in D$, there exists a unique solution $\mathbf{x} = \phi(t; t_0, \mathbf{x}_0)$ of Eq. (1) satisfying the initial conditions

$$\mathbf{x}(t_0) = \mathbf{x}_0. \tag{2}$$

The solution is defined in some interval $\alpha < t < \beta$ that contains the point t_0. The system of ordinary differential equations in Eq. (1) is *autonomous* because the independent variable t does not appear explicitly in the functions $f^n(\cdot), n = 1, 2, \ldots, N$.

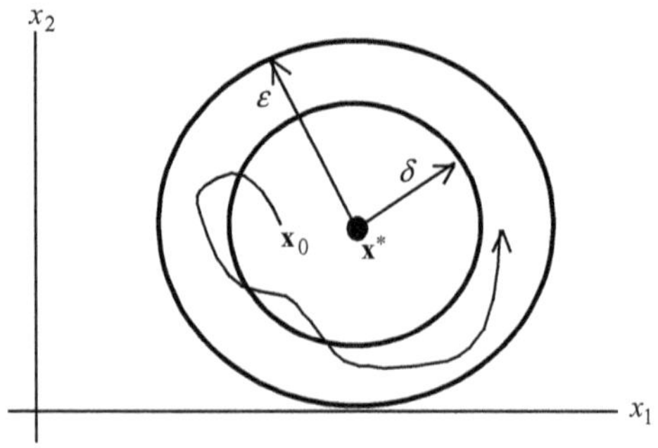

Figure 13.1

In economics, an autonomous system of differential equations is one in which the parameters of the system are *not* time dependent, nor is there exogenous technical change present in the system. Note that in what follows, we often elect to suppress the dependence of the solution on the parameters t_0 and $\mathbf{x}_0$ when they are not germane to the discussion, in which case, we write the solution of the Eq. (1) as $\mathbf{x} = \boldsymbol{\phi}(t)$.

The first definition of this chapter introduces an important type of solution that will play a central role in our investigation of the qualitative properties of the solution to optimal control problems.

Definition 13.1: A constant value of $\mathbf{x}$, say, $\mathbf{x}^*$, is called a *fixed point* or *steady state* of the nonlinear differential equation system $\dot{\mathbf{x}} = \mathbf{f}(\mathbf{x})$ if $\mathbf{f}(\mathbf{x}^*) = 0$. Moreover, if there exists a neighborhood about a fixed point $\mathbf{x}^*$ in which there are no other fixed points, then $\mathbf{x}^*$ is called an *isolated* fixed point or steady state.

Definition 13.1 asserts that a fixed point or steady state $\mathbf{x}^*$ is a constant solution of the differential equation system $\dot{\mathbf{x}} = \mathbf{f}(\mathbf{x})$, since $\mathbf{f}(\mathbf{x}^*) = 0$ and thus $\dot{\mathbf{x}} = 0$ at such a point. Isolated fixed points are just that, since no other fixed points lie "close" to them. By way of a reminder, let us note that the Euclidean norm of a vector $\mathbf{z} \in \Re^N$ is defined as $\|\mathbf{z}\| \overset{\text{def}}{=} \sqrt{z_1^2 + z_2^2 + \cdots + z_N^2}$. With this in mind, we can now introduce the three notions of stability of fixed points that will prove most useful to us when we examine the qualitative properties of a solution to an optimal control problem.

Definition 13.2: An isolated fixed point $\mathbf{x}^*$ of the autonomous differential equation system $\dot{\mathbf{x}} = \mathbf{f}(\mathbf{x})$ is said to be *stable* if, given any $\varepsilon > 0$, there exists a $\delta > 0$ such that every solution $\boldsymbol{\phi}(t; t_0, \mathbf{x}_0)$ of $\dot{\mathbf{x}} = \mathbf{f}(\mathbf{x})$, which at $t = t_0$ satisfies $\|\boldsymbol{\phi}(t_0; t_0, \mathbf{x}_0) - \mathbf{x}^*\| = \|\mathbf{x}_0 - \mathbf{x}^*\| < \delta$, implies that $\|\boldsymbol{\phi}(t; t_0, \mathbf{x}_0) - \mathbf{x}^*\| < \varepsilon$ for all $t \geq t_0$.

This definition states that all solutions of the autonomous differential equation system $\dot{\mathbf{x}} = \mathbf{f}(\mathbf{x})$ that start "sufficiently close" to an isolated fixed point $\mathbf{x}^*$ stay "close" to $\mathbf{x}^*$. Note, however, that this definition of stability does not require that the solution approach the fixed point. Figure 13.1 gives an illustration of this definition in the plane, that is, for $N = 2$. Notice that the trajectory in Figure 13.1 starts

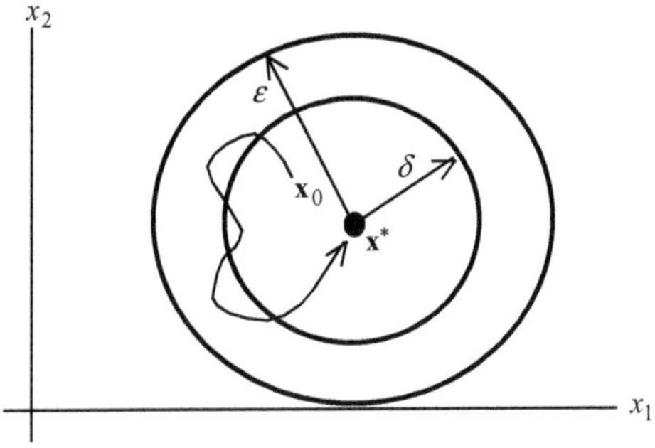

Figure 13.2

within the circle $(x_1 - x_1^*)^2 + (x_2 - x_2^*)^2 = \delta^2$ at $t = t_0$, and although it eventually passes outside this circle, it remains within the larger radius circle $(x_1 - x_1^*)^2 + (x_2 - x_2^*)^2 = \varepsilon^2$ for all $t \geq t_0$.

The next definition of stability builds upon that given in Definition 13.2. It turns out to be the type of stability that will be most prominent in the next five chapters.

Definition 13.3: An isolated fixed point $\mathbf{x}^*$ of the autonomous differential equation system $\dot{\mathbf{x}} = \mathbf{f}(\mathbf{x})$ is said to be *locally asymptotically stable* if it is stable and if there exists a δ_0, $0 < \delta_0 < \delta$, such that if a solution $\phi(t; t_0, \mathbf{x}_0)$ satisfies $\|\phi(t_0; t_0, \mathbf{x}_0) - \mathbf{x}^*\| = \|\mathbf{x}_0 - \mathbf{x}^*\| < \delta_0$, then $\lim_{t\to+\infty} \phi(t; t_0, \mathbf{x}_0) = \mathbf{x}^*$.

Definition 13.3 asserts that solutions of the autonomous differential equation system $\dot{\mathbf{x}} = \mathbf{f}(\mathbf{x})$ that start "sufficiently close" to an isolated fixed point $\mathbf{x}^*$ not only stay "close" to $\mathbf{x}^*$, but must eventually approach the fixed point $\mathbf{x}^*$ as t approaches infinity. Note that local asymptotic stability is a stronger requirement than is stability, in view of the fact that a fixed point must be stable before one can even talk about whether or not it is locally asymptotically stable. On the other hand, the convergence requirement of local asymptotic stability does not, in and of itself, imply stability. This concept of stability is illustrated in Figure 13.2.

The third, and for our purposes the final, definition of stability is not one that we will make as much use of as Definition 13.3, but is nonetheless important given its prominence in dynamic economic theory.

Definition 13.4: An isolated fixed point $\mathbf{x}^*$ of the autonomous differential equation system $\dot{\mathbf{x}} = \mathbf{f}(\mathbf{x})$ is said to be *globally asymptotically stable* if it is stable and if the solution $\phi(t; t_0, \mathbf{x}_0)$ satisfies $\lim_{t\to+\infty} \phi(t; t_0, \mathbf{x}_0) = \mathbf{x}^*$ for *any* initial point $\mathbf{x}_0$.

This definition says that regardless of how close to or far from the initial point $\mathbf{x}_0$ is the fixed point $\mathbf{x}^*$, solutions of the autonomous differential equation system $\dot{\mathbf{x}} = \mathbf{f}(\mathbf{x})$ approach the fixed point $\mathbf{x}^*$ as t approaches infinity. It should be clear, therefore, that if the fixed point $\mathbf{x}^*$ is globally asymptotically stable, then it is locally asymptotically stable, but not vice versa. Moreover, because all solutions of the differential equation converge at the fixed point $\mathbf{x}^*$ regardless of their initial value $\mathbf{x}_0$, a globally asymptotically stable fixed point is unique. Finally, we note that a fixed point that is not stable is said to be *unstable*.

With these basic definitions behind us, let's now turn to the task of establishing several fundamental properties of systems of autonomous differential equations in a deliberate and clear fashion. Before getting into the details of this undertaking, however, we first present some definitions of terms and concepts that are essential to our purpose, and then illustrate them with uncomplicated examples.

Our next definition is central to developing a qualitative understanding of the solution to a system of autonomous differential equations. That is to say, it is an essential ingredient in constructing the phase portrait of a nonlinear and autonomous system of differential equations, in that it gives the direction of motion, or forces acting on a point, in the phase portrait.

Definition 13.5: The *vector field* of the autonomous differential equation system (1) is defined as follows. Imagine the vector

$$\mathbf{f}(\mathbf{x}) = \begin{bmatrix} f^1(x_1, x_2, \ldots, x_N) \\ f^2(x_1, x_2, \ldots, x_N) \\ \vdots \\ f^N(x_1, x_2, \ldots, x_N) \end{bmatrix}$$

drawn at every point $\mathbf{x} = (x_1, x_2, \ldots, x_N) \in D$. This vector determines the tangent vector to the solution $\phi(t) = (\phi_1(t), \phi_2(t), \ldots, \phi_N(t))$ at every point.

The vector field of an autonomous system of differential equations is best visualized in the case $N = 2$, for then we can rather easily graph the vectors in the plane. The next example shows how this is done for a simple autonomous and nonlinear system of differential equations in the plane.

Example 13.1: Consider the autonomous and nonlinear system of differential equations

$$\dot{x}_1 = x_2^2,$$
$$\dot{x}_2 = x_1,$$

where $D = \Re^2$ in this case. In order to draw the vector field of this system of differential equations, Definition 13.5 directs us to plot the vector

$$\mathbf{f}(\mathbf{x}) = \begin{bmatrix} f^1(x_1, x_2) \\ f^2(x_1, x_2) \end{bmatrix} = \begin{bmatrix} x_2^2 \\ x_1 \end{bmatrix}$$

TABLE 13.1.

(x_1, x_2)	$\mathbf{f}(\mathbf{x})' = (x_2^2, x_1)$
$(0, 0)$	$(0, 0)$
$(1, 0)$	$(0, 1)$
$(0, 1)$	$(1, 0)$
$(-1, 0)$	$(0, -1)$
$(0, -1)$	$(1, 0)$
$(2, 1)$	$(1, 2)$
$(1, 1)$	$(1, 1)$
$(-1, 1)$	$(1, -1)$
$(-2, 1)$	$(1, -2)$
$(1, -2)$	$(4, 1)$

in the x_1x_2-plane for each $\mathbf{x} = (x_1, x_2) \in D = \Re^2$. To facilitate this, it is quite often convenient to make up a table with the values of the point (x_1, x_2) in one column, and the values of the vector $\mathbf{f}(\mathbf{x})' = (x_2^2, x_1)$ in the other. Doing just that for ten different points in the x_1x_2-plane yields Table 13.1.

In order to use the information contained in Table 13.1 to draw the vector field corresponding to the above system of differential equations, note that the vector given in column 2 has its tail at the position in the x_1x_2-plane given by the corresponding point in column 1. A sketch of the resulting vector field is given in Figure 13.3. Observe that we have been careful to draw the length and direction of the vectors reasonably accurately so as to impart a better feel to the vector field.

By filling in the vector field at each point (x_1, x_2) in the x_1x_2-plane, it would be possible, in principle, to construct the phase portrait of the above system. This, however, is not generally the best way to construct the phase portrait of a nonlinear

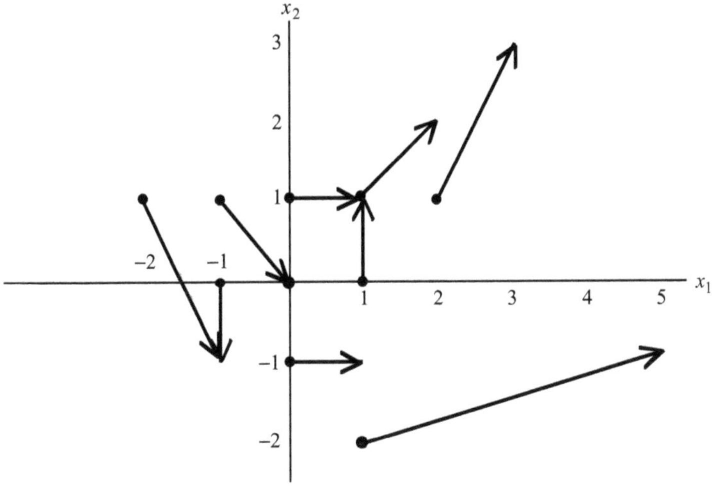

Figure 13.3

and autonomous system of differential equations, as we shall see. Doing so would not only be time consuming without the aid of a computer, but it would hopelessly clutter up the picture. Because we have chosen only ten points at which to compute the vector field, we have essentially presented only a partial picture of it.

Now consider the following two definitions.

Definition 13.6: A *trajectory* of an autonomous system of differential equations is the curve $\{(\phi_1(t), \phi_2(t), \ldots, \phi_N(t)) : \alpha < t < \beta\}$, where $\phi(t) = (\phi_1(t), \phi_2(t), \ldots, \phi_N(t))$ is the solution of the autonomous system of differential equations.

Definition 13.7: A *phase portrait* or *phase diagram* is the collection of all trajectories.

With these two definitions, we are now in a position to construct the phase portrait of an autonomous system of differential equations. Let's therefore return to the autonomous system of differential equations in Example 13.1 and draw its phase portrait. In the process of constructing the phase diagram, we will see how the vector field aids in this endeavor, as remarked above.

Example 13.2: Recall the autonomous and nonlinear system of differential equations

$$\dot{x}_1 = x_2^2,$$
$$\dot{x}_2 = x_1$$

from Example 13.1. Also recall that a partial sketch of the vector field is given in Figure 13.3. From it, we get some indication of the trajectories of this system, and thus a hint at the nature of the phase portrait. To complete the phase portrait, however, we must add to the information contained in the vector field. This is accomplished by dividing $\dot{x}_2 = x_1$ by $\dot{x}_1 = x_2^2$ to get the first-order differential equation for $x_2 = g(x_1)$:

$$\frac{\dot{x}_2}{\dot{x}_1} = \frac{dx_2/dt}{dx_1/dt} = \frac{dx_2}{dx_1} = \frac{x_1}{x_2^2}.$$

The procedure just used to get a first-order differential equation for $x_2 = g(x_1)$ is quite useful for sketching the trajectories of autonomous systems. We will discuss it more generally and more rigorously shortly.

Separating the variables of the above first-order differential equation gives $x_2^2 dx_2 = x_1 dx_1$, and integrating yields $\frac{1}{3}x_2^3 = \frac{1}{2}x_1^2 + c_1$, where c_1 is an arbitrary constant. We can equivalently rewrite the general solution as $x_2 = [\frac{3}{2}x_1^2 + c]^{\frac{1}{3}}$, where $c \stackrel{\text{def}}{=} 3c_1$. Hence, every trajectory of the above system of autonomous differential equations must lie on the graph of the function $x_2 = [\frac{3}{2}x_1^2 + c]^{\frac{1}{3}}$, because

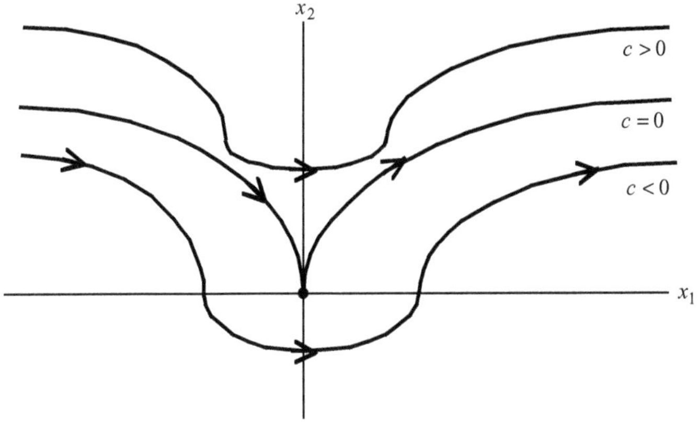

Figure 13.4

every point $(x_1, x_2) = (\phi_1(t), \phi_2(t))$ such that $(\phi_1(t), \phi_2(t))$ is a solution of the system of differential equations must satisfy this equation. The general solution $x_2 = [\frac{3}{2}x_1^2 + c]^{\frac{1}{3}}$ therefore permits us to rather easily construct the phase portrait of the system of differential equations, which we have done in Figure 13.4. Note that it is consistent with the vector field in Figure 13.3.

A question of some interest in this case is this: When does the solution escape to $+\infty$? The answer is almost always, as inspection of Figure 13.4 reveals. More precisely, the solution of the above system escapes to $+\infty$ except when the initial condition satisfies the equation $x_2 = [\frac{3}{2}x_1^2]^{\frac{1}{3}}$ for $x_1 \leq 0$, as this is the only trajectory that approaches the origin.

Before presenting the five fundamental results for autonomous systems of differential equations, let's consider one more example and derive its phase portrait.

Example 13.3: Consider the linear and autonomous system of differential equations

$$\dot{x}_1 = x_2,$$
$$\dot{x}_2 = -x_1.$$

In order to derive its phase portrait, first note that the origin is the only fixed point of this system. Proceeding as we did in Example 13.2, form the quotient

$$\frac{\dot{x}_2}{\dot{x}_1} = \frac{dx_2/dt}{dx_1/dt} = \frac{dx_2}{dx_1} = \frac{-x_1}{x_2}.$$

Separating the variables gives $x_2 dx_2 = -x_1 dx_1$, and integrating yields $\frac{1}{2}x_2^2 = -\frac{1}{2}x_1^2 + c_1$, where c_1 is an arbitrary constant. Alternatively, we can rewrite the general solution equivalently as $x_1^2 + x_2^2 = c$, where $c \stackrel{\text{def}}{=} 2c_1$. This is the equation of a circle, which any trajectory other than the fixed point $(0, 0)$ must lie on for $c \neq 0$.

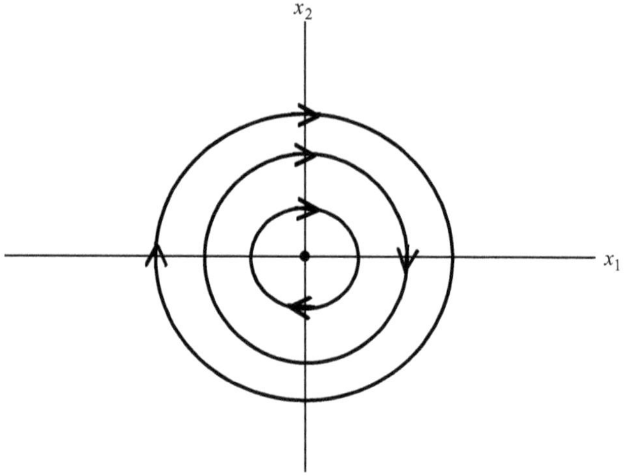

Figure 13.5

The fixed point of the above linear system is therefore called a *center*, and its phase portrait is given in Figure 13.5.

To determine whether the motion on the trajectories is clockwise or counter-clockwise, all we need to do is compute the vector field along one of the axes. For example, at the point $(x_1, x_2) = (1, 0)$, the vector field is given by $(\dot{x}_1, \dot{x}_2) = (x_2, -x_1) = (0, -1)$, hence the arrow pointing vertically downward along the positive part of the x_1-axis. Similarly, at the point $(x_1, x_2) = (0, 1)$, the vector field is given by $(\dot{x}_1, \dot{x}_2) = (x_2, -x_1) = (1, 0)$, hence the arrow pointing horizontally rightward along the positive part of the x_2-axis. We therefore conclude that the motion is clockwise on the trajectories.

Let's now turn to our first result for system (1). Geometrically, it says that we get another solution to an autonomous system of differential equations by translating the solution curve in the t-direction.

Theorem 13.1: *If $\phi(t)$ is a solution to the autonomous system of differential equations (1) for $t \in (\alpha, \beta)$, then so is $\phi(t + c)$ for $t \in (\alpha - c, \beta - c)$, where c is a constant.*

Proof: Differentiating $\phi(t + c)$ with respect to the independent variable t, using the chain rule and the fact that c is a constant, gives

$$\frac{\partial}{\partial t}\phi(t+c) = \frac{d}{d(t+c)}\phi(t+c)\frac{\partial}{\partial t}(t+c) = \frac{d}{d(t+c)}\phi(t+c) = \dot{\phi}(t+c),$$

where we have used the definition $\dot{\phi}(\tau) \stackrel{\text{def}}{=} \frac{d}{d\tau}\phi(\tau)$. This equation asserts that increments to the independent variable t have the same effect on $\phi(t + c)$ as do increments in the variable $t + c$. Because $\dot{\phi}(t) \equiv \mathbf{f}(\phi(t))$ for all $t \in (\alpha, \beta)$ by its

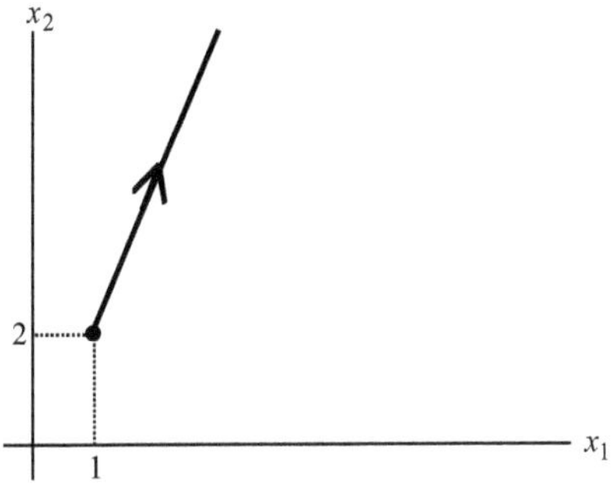

Figure 13.6

definition as a solution of system (1), it follows that $\dot{\phi}(t+c) \equiv \mathbf{f}(\phi(t+c))$ for all $t \in (\alpha - c, \beta - c)$, therefore proving that $\phi(t+c)$ is a solution to system (1), for all $t \in (\alpha - c, \beta - c)$. Q.E.D.

This property of autonomous systems of differential equations is of such fundamental importance that we pause for a moment and examine it in more detail by way of the following example. The example is intended to help build intuition about autonomous systems, whether linear or nonlinear.

Example 13.4: Suppose that particles are being continuously emitted at the point $x_1 = 1$ and $x_2 = 2$, and then move in the x_1x_2-phase according to the law

$$\dot{x}_1 = x_1, \quad \dot{x}_2 = x_2. \tag{3}$$

The particle emitted at the time $t = s$ is specified by the initial conditions $x_1(s) = 1$ and $x_2(s) = 2$. Separating the variables of the differential equations in Eq. (3), integrating, and then applying the initial conditions yields the solution

$$x_1 = \phi_1(t; s) = e^{t-s}, \quad x_2 = \phi_2(t; s) = 2e^{t-s}, \quad t \geq s. \tag{4}$$

The trajectories or paths followed by the particles emitted at different times s can be best visualized by eliminating t from Eq. (4). Doing just that yields the straight line

$$x_2 = 2x_1. \tag{5}$$

It should be clear from Eq. (4) that $x_1 \geq 1$ and $x_2 \geq 2$ for all $t \geq s$. The portion of the straight line determined by Eq. (5) corresponding to Eq. (4), with the direction of motion indicated by an arrow, is given in Figure 13.6.

By far the most important feature of Eq. (5) is that the initial time s does not appear in it. This means that no matter when a particle is emitted from the point $(x_1, x_2) = (1, 2)$, it *always* moves along the same curve, videlicet, the straight line given by Eq. (5).

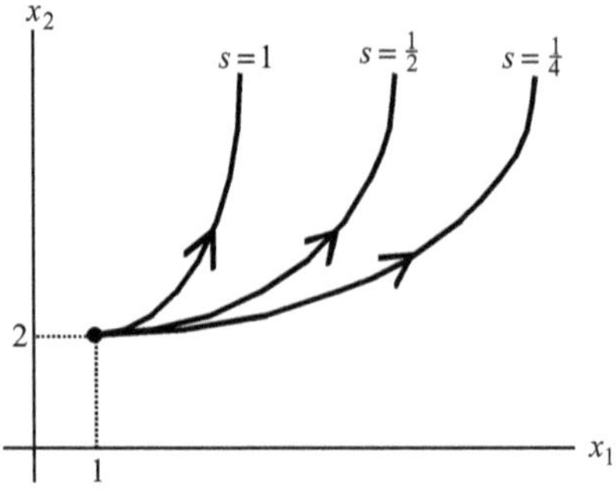

Figure 13.7

Now consider a similar pair of differential equations, namely,

$$\dot{x}_1 = t^{-1}x_1, \ \ \dot{x}_2 = x_2. \tag{6}$$

In contrast to Eq. (3), Eq. (6) is a pair of *nonautonomous* differential equations because of the explicit appearance of the independent variable t on the right-hand side. Separating the variables of the differential equations in Eq. (6), integrating, and then applying the initial conditions $x_1(s) = 1$ and $x_2(s) = 2$ yields the solution

$$x_1 = \phi_1(t; s) = s^{-1}t, \ \ x_2 = \phi_2(t; s) = 2e^{t-s}, \ t \geq s. \tag{7}$$

Solving the first of these equations for t yields $t = sx_1$. Substituting this into the second equation yields a result analogous to Eq. (5), namely,

$$x_2 = 2e^{s(x_1-1)}. \tag{8}$$

It should be clear from Eq. (7) that $x_1 \geq 1$ and $x_2 \geq 2$ for all $t \geq s$. Because the initial time s appears in Eq. (8), the path that a particle follows depends on the time at which it is emitted, that is, the time at which the initial condition is applied. Figure 13.7 highlights this feature of nonautonomous differential equations by showing the paths followed by particles emitted at several different initial times.

We are now in a position to compare our results for the differential equation systems given in Eqs. (3) and (6). In the case of the autonomous system (3), when we eliminated the independent variable t in deriving Eq. (5), we automatically eliminated the initial time s. This is a result of the fact that t and s appear only in the form $t - s$ in Eq. (4). For the nonautonomous system (6), on the other hand, when we eliminated the independent variable t in deriving Eq. (8), we were not able to eliminate the initial time s.

This example illustrates the essence of Theorem 13.4. In particular, it shows that autonomous systems of differential equations exhibit a special property not shared by nonautonomous systems of differential equations, to wit, that all particles passing through a given point follow the same trajectory in the phase plane. In other words, the same trajectory in the phase plane is represented parametrically by many different solutions differing from one another by a translation of the independent variable t.

In determining the trajectories of an autonomous system of differential equations in the plane, that is, the case of $N = 2$ for system (1), it is often quite useful to eliminate the independent variable t from the solution $x_n = \phi_n(t)$, $n = 1, 2$. Doing so results in a relation (and sometimes a function) between x_1 and x_2 describing the trajectory in the phase plane. We essentially did this when we derived Eq. (5) from the autonomous system (3) in Example 13.4. Another way to eliminate the independent variable t from the solution in Example 13.4 is to write down the ratio of $\dot{x}_2$ to $\dot{x}_1$ using system (3). This yields

$$\frac{\dot{x}_2}{\dot{x}_1} = \frac{dx_2/dt}{dx_1/dt} = \frac{dx_2}{dx_1} = \frac{x_2}{x_1}, \tag{9}$$

which is a first-order differential equation for $x_2 = g(x_1)$. Separating the variables in Eq. (9) and integrating using the initial conditions $x_1(s) = 1$ and $x_2(s) = 2$ yields Eq. (5), just as anticipated. Note that in order to form Eq. (9), it must be that $x_1 \neq 0$, which, as noted in Example 13.4, holds in this instance.

More generally, for a pair of autonomous differential equations $\dot{x}_n = f^n(x_1, x_2)$, $n = 1, 2$, we can proceed to eliminate the independent variable t from the solution $x_n = \phi_n(t)$, $n = 1, 2$, as follows. In a region where $f^1(x_1, x_2) \neq 0$, we can form the ratio

$$\frac{\dot{x}_2}{\dot{x}_1} = \frac{dx_2/dt}{dx_1/dt} = \frac{dx_2}{dt}\frac{dt}{dx_1} = \frac{dx_2}{dx_1} = \frac{f^2(x_1, x_2)}{f^1(x_1, x_2)}, \tag{10}$$

which is a first-order differential equation for $x_2 = g(x_1)$. The requirement that $f^1(x_1, x_2) \neq 0$ is needed so that we can divide by $f^1(x_1, x_2)$ to form Eq. (10). Moreover, because $\dot{x}_1 = f^1(x_1, x_2)$, the condition $f^1(x_1, x_2) \neq 0$ is equivalent to $\dot{x}_1 = dx_1/dt \neq 0$. By the implicit function theorem, this then implies that the solution $x_1 = \phi_1(t)$ can be solved for t as a function of x_1. This, in turn, implies that x_2 becomes a function of x_1, as in, for example, Eq. (5). The one-parameter family of solutions of Eq. (10) is the set of trajectories of the system $\dot{x}_n = f^n(x_1, x_2), n = 1, 2$. Equation (10) is especially convenient for determining the slope of a trajectory at a point in the phase plane, since it is an explicit representation of it. In a region where $f^2(x_1, x_2) \neq 0$, one can alternatively form the analogous differential equation to Eq. (10), that is to say,

$$\frac{\dot{x}_1}{\dot{x}_2} = \frac{dx_1/dt}{dx_2/dt} = \frac{dx_1}{dx_2} = \frac{f^1(x_1, x_2)}{f^2(x_1, x_2)}. \tag{11}$$

If both $f^1(x_1, x_2) \neq 0$ and $f^2(x_1, x_2) \neq 0$, then one can form either Eq. (10) or Eq. (11) to determine the trajectories of the system of autonomous differential equations.

If, however, there is a point such that $f^1(x_1, x_2) = 0$ *and* $f^2(x_1, x_2) = 0$, then we cannot solve for either dx_2/dx_1 or dx_1/dx_2. Recall that a point such that $f^1(x_1, x_2) = 0$ and $f^2(x_1, x_2) = 0$ is defined as a fixed point or steady state. Thus we see that fixed points have special significance in the study of differential equations. Also recall that if $\mathbf{x}^*$ is a fixed point of system (1), then $\mathbf{x} = \mathbf{x}^*$ is a solution of system (1), albeit a constant one. Moreover, it follows from the existence and uniqueness theorem that the only solution of system (1) passing through the fixed point $\mathbf{x}^*$ is the constant solution $\mathbf{x} = \mathbf{x}^*$ itself. The trajectory of this solution is just the fixed point $\mathbf{x}^*$. A particle at the point $\mathbf{x}^*$ is thus often said to be at rest, or in equilibrium. Let us also remark that a trajectory of system (1), which is represented by the solution $\mathbf{x} = \phi(t)$, $t \geq \alpha$, is said to approach the fixed point $\mathbf{x}^*$ as $t \to +\infty$ if $\phi(t) \to \mathbf{x}^*$ as $t \to +\infty$.

The importance of fixed points in the analysis of autonomous systems of differential equations is a result of the fact that (a) they are constant solutions of the system, and (b) the qualitative behavior of all trajectories in the phase plane is determined to a considerable degree by the location of the fixed points and the behavior of the trajectories near them.

Let us now turn to the four remaining fundamental properties of autonomous systems. Seeing as their proofs are relatively simple and direct, we provide them. After presenting and proving these results, we provide a summary of their implications for the study of autonomous systems of differential equations.

Theorem 13.2: *The trajectories of autonomous systems of differential equations do not intersect.*

Proof: Assume that there are two solutions of system (1), say $\phi^1(t)$ and $\phi^2(t)$, that is,

$$\dot{\phi}^1(t) = \mathbf{f}(\phi^1(t)),$$
$$\dot{\phi}^2(t) = \mathbf{f}(\phi^2(t)).$$

For the trajectories to intersect, there must exist a point $\mathbf{x}_0$ such that

$$\phi^1(0) = \mathbf{x}_0,$$
$$\phi^2(t_0) = \mathbf{x}_0.$$

By Theorem 13.1, we know that $\mathbf{y}(t) \stackrel{\text{def}}{=} \phi^2(t + t_0)$ is also a solution. Hence, we may conclude that $\phi^1(0) = \mathbf{x}_0$ and $\mathbf{y}(0) \stackrel{\text{def}}{=} \mathbf{x}_0$. By uniqueness, $\phi^1(t) = \mathbf{y}(t)$ for every t, which, by the definition of $\mathbf{y}(\cdot)$, is equivalent to $\phi^1(t) = \phi^2(t + t_0)$ for every t. Thus the trajectory determined by $\phi^1(\cdot)$ is the same as the trajectory determined by $\phi^2(\cdot)$. Q.E.D.

This theorem is essentially a corollary to the fundamental existence and uniqueness theorem. Its content is beautifully straightforward: *different trajectories never intersect*. If two trajectories did intersect, then there would be two solutions starting from the same point, scilicet, the point at which the two trajectories cross. This, however, violates the uniqueness part of the fundamental existence and uniqueness theorem. This argument, in essence, constitutes the proof of Theorem 13.2. Said in a more geometrical manner, Theorem 13.2 asserts that a trajectory can't move in two directions at once. Because trajectories for autonomous systems can't intersect, the associated phase portraits always have a neat and tidy appearance. Otherwise, they might degenerate into an entanglement of curves. The fundamental existence and uniqueness theorem prevents such a mess from happening.

Let's return to our task of laying out the fundamental properties of systems of autonomous differential equations. The next two theorems are especially important in dynamic economic theory, as we shall see in the next five chapters.

Theorem 13.3: *Let $\phi(t)$ be a solution to system (1). If $\lim_{t\to+\infty}\phi(t) = \mathbf{x}^*$, then $\mathbf{f}(\mathbf{x}^*) = \mathbf{0}_N$, so that $\mathbf{x}^*$ is a fixed point or steady state of system (1).*

Proof: Given that $\lim_{t\to+\infty}\phi(t) = \mathbf{x}^*$, it follows that

$$\lim_{t\to+\infty}[\phi(t+1) - \phi(t)] = \mathbf{0}_n. \tag{12}$$

On the other hand,

$$\lim_{t\to+\infty}[\phi(t+1) - \phi(t)] = \lim_{t\to+\infty}\left[\int_0^1 \dot{\phi}(t+\tau)d\tau\right] = \lim_{t\to+\infty}\left[\int_0^1 \mathbf{f}(\phi(t+\tau))\,d\tau\right]. \tag{13}$$

Using Eq. (13) and the facts that $t+\tau \to +\infty$ as $t \to +\infty$ and $\phi(t+\tau) \to \mathbf{x}^*$ as $t \to +\infty$ permits us to reach the conclusion that

$$\lim_{t\to+\infty}[\phi(t+1) - \phi(t)] = \mathbf{f}(\mathbf{x}^*). \tag{14}$$

Equations (12) and (14) then imply that $\mathbf{f}(\mathbf{x}^*) = \mathbf{0}_N$, so that $\mathbf{x}^*$ is a fixed point. Q.E.D.

Theorem 13.3 is actually more general than it may appear at first glance. The reason is that uniqueness of the solution is not a prerequisite to its conclusion, as is evident from the statement of the theorem ($\phi(t)$ is *a* solution, not *the* solution) and the proof (it was not used in it). This theorem simply asserts that if a solution of system (1) converges to a constant value in the limit as $t \to +\infty$, then that constant value is a fixed point of system (1). The next theorem is of a similar character, but relies on uniqueness of the solution, and therefore is less general, but often more useful, in intertemporal economic problems.

Theorem 13.4: *If the unique solution $\phi(t)$ of system (1) begins at a point $\mathbf{x}_0$ that is not a fixed point of the system, then it cannot reach a fixed point $\mathbf{x}^*$ in a finite length of time.*

Proof: We employ a contrapositive proof. To that end, assume that the unique solution $\phi(t)$ has reached the fixed point $\mathbf{x}^*$ in a finite length of time, say $\phi(\tau) = \mathbf{x}^*$ for some finite τ. Now recall that the fixed point $\mathbf{x}^*$ is a (constant) solution of system (1) satisfying the initial condition $\mathbf{x}(\tau) = \mathbf{x}^*$. By uniqueness $\phi(t) = \mathbf{x}^*$ for all t is the only solution of system (1) satisfying the initial condition $\mathbf{x}(\tau) = \mathbf{x}^*$. Thus the initial value of the solution $\phi(t)$ is the fixed point $\mathbf{x}^*$, contradicting the hypothesis of the theorem, and thereby completing its proof. Q.E.D.

Simply put, this theorem asserts that if $\mathbf{x}^*$ is a fixed point of an autonomous system and a solution of the system approaches $\mathbf{x}^*$, then necessarily $t \to +\infty$. The final fundamental result about autonomous systems concerns periodic solutions.

Theorem 13.5: *Let $\phi(t)$ be the solution to system (1). If $\phi(0) = \phi(T)$, then $\phi(t) = \phi(t + T)$ for every t, and thus the solution is periodic with period T.*

Proof: By Theorem 13.1, $\mathbf{y}(t) \stackrel{\text{def}}{=} \phi(t + T)$ is a solution to system (1). Because $\phi(0) = \mathbf{y}(0)$, by uniqueness it then follows that $\phi(t) = \mathbf{y}(t)$, or $\phi(t) = \phi(t + T)$, for every t. Q.E.D.

The implications of Theorems 13.1 through 13.5 are of fundamental importance in the study of autonomous systems of differential equations. They essentially say that if a solution starts at a point that is not a fixed point, then it moves on the same trajectory no matter at what time it starts, it can never come back to its initial point unless the motion is periodic, it can never cross another trajectory, and it can only "reach" a fixed point or steady state in the limit as $t \to +\infty$. These theorems thus suggest that a solution of an autonomous system of differential equations either approaches a fixed point, moves on a closed trajectory or approaches a closed trajectory as $t \to +\infty$, or else goes off to infinity. Moreover, they demonstrate that for autonomous systems of differential equations, the study of the fixed points and periodic solutions is of fundamental importance. Actually, other much less common behaviors may occur as well, but this is not something we are equipped to explore.

Let us now turn to the analytical determination of the stability of fixed points for systems of nonlinear and autonomous ordinary differential equations. In doing so, we will also extend our understanding of phase portraits by making use of our knowledge about the fundamental properties of autonomous differential equations exposited in Theorems 13.1 through 13.5.

As is typical when one studies nonlinear functions, the calculus is often initially employed to glean information about the nonlinear function at a given point. This information is then used to deduce properties of the nonlinear function in a neighborhood of the given point. It is no different with nonlinear differential equations. The basic idea is to replace the rather complicated system of nonlinear differential equations with a linear system of differential equations, with the hope that the linear system is a good enough approximation so that we can infer the behavior of the nonlinear system from that of its linear approximation. We will see that in most instances, the study of the simpler linear system corresponding to the nonlinear one is of value in deducing the local properties of the nonlinear system. Thus we begin with the so-called method of linearization at a fixed point, a central method of local stability analysis of nonlinear differential equation systems.

The basic idea behind the linearization method is really quite simple: replace the nonlinear differential equation system with a linear approximation to it at a fixed point of the nonlinear system. Then essentially use theorems about linear systems to deduce the phase portrait of the nonlinear system in a neighborhood of the fixed point. If there is more than one fixed point of the nonlinear system, which is not at all unusual, then one applies the method of linearization at each of the fixed points. Because the idea of approximation is important in what follows, it is advisable at this juncture to review the multivariate version of Taylor's theorem. We will concentrate on the case $N = 2$ seeing as this is the most common case encountered in dynamic economic theory, at least initially, and the case in which the geometry is best developed. The definitions and theorems, however, may be stated for the general system (1) when such generality creates no additional burden over the case $N = 2$.

Let $(x_1^*, x_2^*) \in D$ be a fixed point of system (1) when $N = 2$. Given that $f^n(\cdot) \in C^{(1)}$ for all $(x_1, x_2) \in D$, $n = 1, 2$, we can apply Taylor's theorem to these functions at the fixed point (x_1^*, x_2^*) to get

$$\begin{aligned} f^n(x_1, x_2) = f^n(x_1^*, x_2^*) &+ \frac{\partial f^n}{\partial x_1}(x_1^*, x_2^*)[x_1 - x_1^*] + \frac{\partial f^n}{\partial x_2}(x_1^*, x_2^*)[x_2 - x_2^*] \\ &+ R^n(x_1, x_2), \quad n = 1, 2. \end{aligned} \tag{15}$$

Recall that under our assumptions, the so-called remainder functions $R^n(\cdot)$ satisfy

$$\lim_{r \to 0} \frac{R^n(x_1, x_2)}{r} = 0, \quad n = 1, 2, \tag{16}$$

where $r \stackrel{\text{def}}{=} \sqrt{(x_1 - x_1^*)^2 + (x_2 - x_2^*)^2}$ is the Euclidean distance of the point $(x_1, x_2) \in D$ from the fixed point $(x_1^*, x_2^*) \in D$. Essentially, the functions $R^n(\cdot)$ are expressions containing the quadratic or higher-order terms $(x_1 - x_1^*)^2$, $(x_2 - x_2^*)^2$, and $(x_1 - x_1^*)(x_2 - x_2^*)$; hence that is why they go to zero faster than does $r \stackrel{\text{def}}{=} \sqrt{(x_1 - x_1^*)^2 + (x_2 - x_2^*)^2}$. Note that if $(x_1 - x_1^*)$ and $(x_2 - x_2^*)$ are small, then the quadratic terms are extremely small.

Because (x_1^*, x_2^*) is a fixed point of system (1), it follows from the very definition of a fixed point that $f^n(x_1^*, x_2^*) = 0$, $n = 1, 2$. Using this conclusion in Eq. (15), and then substituting Eq. (15) into system (1) yields the equivalent system

$$\dot{x}_1 = \frac{\partial f^1}{\partial x_1}(x_1^*, x_2^*)[x_1 - x_1^*] + \frac{\partial f^1}{\partial x_2}(x_1^*, x_2^*)[x_2 - x_2^*] + R^1(x_1, x_2),$$

$$\dot{x}_2 = \frac{\partial f^2}{\partial x_1}(x_1^*, x_2^*)[x_1 - x_1^*] + \frac{\partial f^2}{\partial x_2}(x_1^*, x_2^*)[x_2 - x_2^*] + R^2(x_1, x_2). \tag{17}$$

Note that because the partial derivatives of the functions $f^n(\cdot)$, $n = 1, 2$, are evaluated at the fixed point (x_1^*, x_2^*), they are numbers in Eqs. (17), not functions. In going from system (1) to system (17), we have replaced the nonlinear functions $f^n(\cdot)$, $n = 1, 2$, with the sum of a linear expression, given by the first two terms on the right-hand side of system (17), and a residual nonlinear term that is extremely small compared with the linear part of the system.

By defining the new variables $y_n \stackrel{\text{def}}{=} x_n - x_n^*$, $n = 1, 2$, we move the fixed point from (x_1^*, x_2^*) to the origin, as is straightforward to verify. Moreover, as $\dot{y}_n = \dot{x}_n$, $n = 1, 2$, we can rewrite system (17) in terms of the new coordinates as follows:

$$\dot{y}_1 = \frac{\partial f^1}{\partial x_1}(x_1^*, x_2^*)y_1 + \frac{\partial f^1}{\partial x_2}(x_1^*, x_2^*)y_2 + R^1(y_1 + x_1^*, y_2 + x_2^*),$$

$$\dot{y}_2 = \frac{\partial f^2}{\partial x_1}(x_1^*, x_2^*)y_1 + \frac{\partial f^2}{\partial x_2}(x_1^*, x_2^*)y_2 + R^2(y_1 + x_1^*, y_2 + x_2^*). \tag{18}$$

This is just system (17) with the fixed point moved to the origin.

Next, define the *Jacobian matrix* $\mathbf{J}(x_1^*, x_2^*)$ of the functions $f^n(\cdot)$, $n = 1, 2$, evaluated at the fixed point (x_1^*, x_2^*) by

$$\mathbf{J}(x_1^*, x_2^*) \stackrel{\text{def}}{=} \begin{bmatrix} \frac{\partial f^1}{\partial x_1}(x_1^*, x_2^*) & \frac{\partial f^1}{\partial x_2}(x_1^*, x_2^*) \\ \frac{\partial f^2}{\partial x_1}(x_1^*, x_2^*) & \frac{\partial f^2}{\partial x_2}(x_1^*, x_2^*) \end{bmatrix}. \tag{19}$$

The Jacobian matrix $\mathbf{J}(x_1^*, x_2^*)$ is just the multivariate analog of the derivative $f'(x^*)$ corresponding to the single nonlinear ordinary differential equation $\dot{x} = f(x)$. In view of the fact that one may use the derivative $f'(x^*)$ to determine the stability of a fixed point x^* in the scalar case, it is natural to conjecture that the Jacobian matrix $\mathbf{J}(x_1^*, x_2^*)$ may be similarly used to deduce the stability of a nonlinear system of differential equations. This conjecture is correct for the most part, as we shall shortly see.

Because the higher-order terms $R^n(x_1, x_2)$, $n = 1, 2$, are small, it would appear to be rather appealing to neglect them altogether. If in fact we do so, then we obtain the *linearized system* corresponding to the original nonlinear system (1), to wit,

$$\begin{bmatrix} \dot{y}_1 \\ \dot{y}_2 \end{bmatrix} = \begin{bmatrix} \dfrac{\partial f^1}{\partial x_1}(x_1^*, x_2^*) & \dfrac{\partial f^1}{\partial x_2}(x_1^*, x_2^*) \\ \dfrac{\partial f^2}{\partial x_1}(x_1^*, x_2^*) & \dfrac{\partial f^2}{\partial x_2}(x_1^*, x_2^*) \end{bmatrix} \begin{bmatrix} y_1 \\ y_2 \end{bmatrix}. \tag{20}$$

The goal at this juncture is to use our prior understanding of the behavior of the linearized system to come to some understanding about the behavior of the original nonlinear system in a neighborhood of a fixed point. Before presenting the first theorem on using the linearized system to study the qualitative properties of the original nonlinear system, however, we require a few definitions. We begin with one that should be somewhat familiar to you from your prior study of linear systems of ordinary differential equations.

Definition 13.8: A fixed point $\mathbf{x}^*$ of a nonlinear system $\dot{\mathbf{x}} = \mathbf{f}(\mathbf{x})$, $\mathbf{x} \in D \subseteq \Re^N$, is said to be *simple* if the $N \times N$ Jacobian matrix $\mathbf{J}(\mathbf{x}^*)$ of its linearized system has no zero eigenvalues, where

$$\mathbf{J}(\mathbf{x}^*) \stackrel{\text{def}}{=} \frac{\partial \mathbf{f}}{\partial \mathbf{x}}(\mathbf{x}^*) = \begin{bmatrix} \dfrac{\partial f^1}{\partial x_1}(\mathbf{x}^*) & \dfrac{\partial f^1}{\partial x_2}(\mathbf{x}^*) & \cdots & \dfrac{\partial f^1}{\partial x_N}(\mathbf{x}^*) \\ \dfrac{\partial f^2}{\partial x_1}(\mathbf{x}^*) & \dfrac{\partial f^2}{\partial x_2}(\mathbf{x}^*) & \cdots & \dfrac{\partial f^2}{\partial x_N}(\mathbf{x}^*) \\ \vdots & \vdots & \ddots & \vdots \\ \dfrac{\partial f^N}{\partial x_1}(\mathbf{x}^*) & \dfrac{\partial f^N}{\partial x_2}(\mathbf{x}^*) & \cdots & \dfrac{\partial f^N}{\partial x_N}(\mathbf{x}^*) \end{bmatrix}.$$

This definition extends the idea of simplicity for linear systems, which requires that the coefficient matrix be nonsingular, to the fixed points of a nonlinear system. An equivalent statement of simplicity for nonlinear systems is that $|\mathbf{J}(\mathbf{x}^*)| \neq 0$, or equivalently, that $\mathbf{J}(\mathbf{x}^*)$ is nonsingular, seeing as $\prod_{n=1}^{N} \lambda_n = |\mathbf{J}(\mathbf{x}^*)|$, where λ_n, $n = 1, 2, \ldots, N$, are the eigenvalues of $\mathbf{J}(\mathbf{x}^*)$.

Because a great deal is known about the trajectories of the linearized system (20), it would be outstanding to find out that by using the linearized system instead of the original nonlinear system, we could come to some understanding of the behavior of the trajectories of the nonlinear system in a neighborhood of the fixed point. That is, how safe is it to ignore the higher-order terms $R^n(x_1, x_2)$, $n = 1, 2$, in the system (18)? In other words, does the linearized system give a qualitatively correct depiction of the phase portrait of the nonlinear system near the fixed point? The following theorem, whose proof we omit, provides an affirmative answer to these questions, but with some important qualifications that we will subsequently explore.

Theorem 13.6: *Let* $(x_1^*, x_2^*) \in D$ *be an isolated and simple fixed point of the nonlinear system* $\dot{x}_n = f^n(x_1, x_2)$, $n = 1, 2$, *where* $f^n(\cdot) \in C^{(1)}$ *for all* $(x_1, x_2) \in D$, $n = 1, 2$, *and let* λ_n, $n = 1, 2$, *be the eigenvalues of the Jacobian matrix* $\mathbf{J}(x_1^*, x_2^*)$ *of the corresponding linearized system. If* λ_n, $n = 1, 2$, *are real and unequal, or complex conjugates with nonzero real parts, then the type of the fixed point is correctly predicted by the linearized system and so is its stability in a neighborhood of* (x_1^*, x_2^*).

To fully grasp this theorem, let us begin by recalling what it means for the type and stability of a fixed point in a linear system when the eigenvalues are structured as in Theorem 13.6. If the eigenvalues are real, negative, and unequal, then the fixed point is a globally asymptotically stable node of the linearized system, whereas if the eigenvalues are real, positive, and unequal, then the fixed point is an unstable node of the linearized system. If, however, the eigenvalues are complex conjugates with negative real parts, then the fixed point is a globally asymptotically stable spiral node of the linearized system, whereas if the eigenvalues are complex conjugates with positive real parts, then the fixed point is an unstable spiral node of the linearized system. Finally, if the eigenvalues are real and of the opposite sign, then the fixed point is an unstable saddle point of the linearized system. Thus Theorem 13.6 states that if the linearized system determines that a fixed point of the nonlinear system is a globally asymptotically stable or unstable node or spiral node, or an unstable saddle point, then the fixed point *really is* of the type so determined by the linearized system, and its stability is accurately predicted in a neighborhood of the fixed point. The reason we cannot claim that the stability property carries over globally is that there may be more than one fixed point of the nonlinear system. In this case, it is entirely possible that the linearized system predicts that one of the fixed points is a globally asymptotically stable node of the linearized system, but the type and stability of another fixed point in effect forces this node to be only locally asymptotically stable. We will in fact see this in the next example.

Let us now turn to the limitations of Theorem 13.6. Essentially, Theorem 13.6 asserts that near the fixed point (x_1^*, x_2^*) the higher-order terms $R^n(x_1, x_2)$, $n = 1, 2$, of system (18) are very small and do not affect the type and stability of the fixed point as determined by the linearized system *except* in two sensitive cases, scilicet, λ_1 and λ_2 pure imaginary (a center for the linearized system), and λ_1 and λ_2 real and equal (an improper node or star node for the linearized system). This should not be too surprising given that it is well known that small perturbations in the coefficients of a linear system, and thus in the eigenvalues λ_1 and λ_2, can alter the type and stability of a fixed point only in these two borderline cases. In particular, when λ_1 and λ_2 are pure imaginary, a small perturbation in the coefficients of a linear system can change the stable center into a globally asymptotically stable or an unstable spiral node, or even leave it as a center. When λ_1 and λ_2 are real and equal, a small

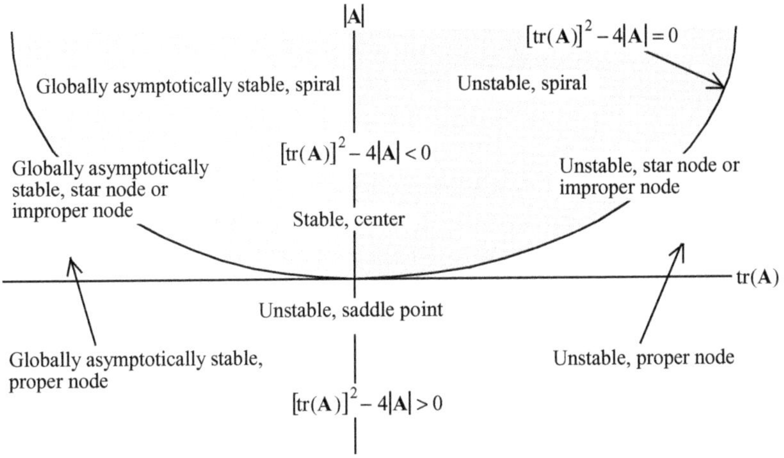

Figure 13.8

perturbation in the coefficients of the linear system do not affect the stability of the fixed point, but may change the star node or improper node into a spiral node. Thus, given these observations about linear systems in the two sensitive cases, it is not at all surprising that Theorem 13.6 asserts that the small nonlinear terms $R^n(x_1, x_2)$, $n = 1, 2$, of system (18) exhibit similar effects in the two sensitive cases.

That Theorem 13.6 is not that unexpected may also be seen from Figure 13.8. This figure, which you should be familiar with from a prior introductory course in differential equations, summarizes what is known about linear systems of autonomous ordinary differential equations with constant coefficients in the plane, in terms of the trace [tr(**A**)] and determinant [|**A**|] of the 2×2 coefficient matrix **A** of the linear system. Figure 13.8 shows that improper nodes, star nodes, and centers all "live" on curves in (as opposed to regions of) the trace-determinant plane, and as such, any slight perturbation of them will in general move them off the curve on which they once lived and thus change their type. The main significance of Theorem 13.6, however, is that in *all other cases*, the small nonlinear terms $R^n(x_1, x_2)$, $n = 1, 2$, do not alter the type of the fixed point or its local stability.

Let's turn to an example to see how one would use Theorem 13.6 to classify the fixed points and draw the phase portrait of a nonlinear and autonomous system.

Example 13.5: Consider the following nonlinear system:

$$\dot{x}_1 = -x_1 + x_1^3,$$

$$\dot{x}_2 = -2x_2.$$

Our first step is to determine the fixed points. Recall that fixed points are the solution to the above system when $\dot{x}_1 = 0$ and $\dot{x}_2 = 0$, that is, they are the solution to the algebraic equations

$$-x_1 + x_1^3 = 0,$$
$$-2x_2 = 0.$$

It should not be too hard to see that we have three fixed points in this nonlinear system, namely, (0, 0), (1, 0), and (−1, 0). Notice that unlike simple linear systems, simple nonlinear systems may have multiple isolated fixed points. At a general point (x_1, x_2), the Jacobian matrix of the linearized system is given by

$$\mathbf{J}(x_1, x_2) \stackrel{\text{def}}{=} \begin{bmatrix} \dfrac{\partial \dot{x}_1}{\partial x_1} & \dfrac{\partial \dot{x}_1}{\partial x_2} \\ \dfrac{\partial \dot{x}_2}{\partial x_1} & \dfrac{\partial \dot{x}_2}{\partial x_2} \end{bmatrix} = \begin{bmatrix} -1 + 3x_1^2 & 0 \\ 0 & -2 \end{bmatrix}.$$

Now recall that the eigenvalues of a diagonal matrix are the diagonal elements themselves. With this in mind, we therefore find that

$$\mathbf{J}(0, 0) = \begin{bmatrix} -1 & 0 \\ 0 & -2 \end{bmatrix}, (\lambda_1, \lambda_2) = (-1, -2),$$

$$\mathbf{J}(1, 0) = \begin{bmatrix} 2 & 0 \\ 0 & -2 \end{bmatrix}, (\lambda_1, \lambda_2) = (2, -2),$$

$$\mathbf{J}(-1, 0) = \begin{bmatrix} 2 & 0 \\ 0 & -2 \end{bmatrix}, (\lambda_1, \lambda_2) = (2, -2).$$

Thus the linearized system shows that the fixed point (0, 0) is a globally asymptotically stable node, and that the fixed points (1, 0) and (−1, 0) are unstable saddle points.

Inasmuch as nodes and saddle points are not borderlines cases, that is to say, they are covered by Theorem 13.6, we are certain that the type of the three fixed points is predicted correctly for the nonlinear system, and that the stability property holds in a neighborhood of the fixed point. We will see shortly that the fixed point (0, 0) is actually locally asymptotically stable for the nonlinear system. This shows that fixed points that are predicted as globally asymptotically stable by the linearized system may be only locally asymptotically stable for the nonlinear system when more than one isolated fixed point exists, just as Theorem 13.6 allows.

The above conclusions based on the linearized system and Theorem 13.6 can be readily verified for the above nonlinear system because the two differential equations are *uncoupled*, that is, the differential equation for x_1 is only a function of x_1 and the differential equation for x_2 is only a function of x_2. Hence the nonlinear system is essentially two independent equations at right angles to each other. This permits us

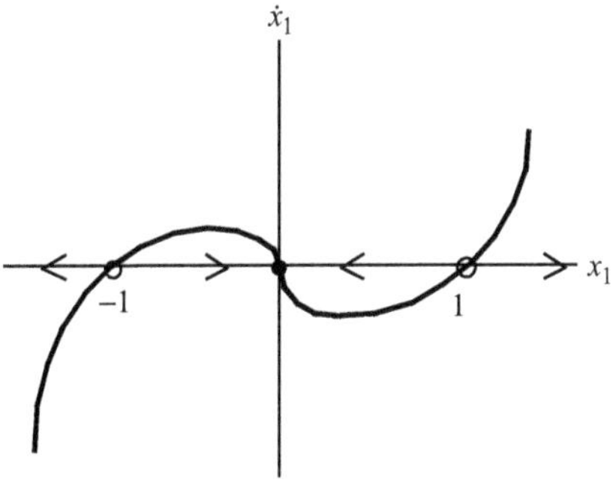

Figure 13.9

to draw the phase portrait for the nonlinear system quite easily. Let us now proceed to do just that.

First, observe that because $\dot{x}_2 = -2x_2$, $\dot{x}_2 < 0$ when $x_2 > 0$ and $\dot{x}_2 > 0$ when $x_2 < 0$. This implies that in the x_2-direction, all trajectories decay exponentially to $x_2 = 0$. Next, we plot the one-dimensional phase portrait for $\dot{x}_1 = -x_1 + x_1^3$, as in Figure 13.9. From this phase portrait, we see that the fixed points $x_1 = \pm 1$ are unstable whereas the origin is locally asymptotically stable. It is important to observe that the origin is *not* globally asymptotically stable, because if the initial condition for x_1 places it at a value greater than 1 or a value less than -1, then the trajectory will not converge to the origin, as is evident from Figure 13.9.

Next, observe that the vertical lines $x_1 = 0$ and $x_1 = \pm 1$ are *invariant* because $\dot{x}_1 = 0$ on them. This implies that any trajectory that starts on these lines can never leave them. Similarly, the line $x_2 = 0$ is an invariant horizontal line seeing as $\dot{x}_2 = 0$ when $x_2 = 0$, thus implying that any trajectory that starts on this line stays on it forever.

Finally, note that the phase portrait of the nonlinear system must be symmetric with respect to the x_1-axis and x_2-axis because the nonlinear system is invariant under the linear transformations $x_1 \to -x_1$ and $x_2 \to -x_2$. By bringing all of the information we have gathered about the nonlinear system together, we therefore arrive at its phase portrait, which we have depicted in Figure 13.10.

The phase portrait confirms that the fixed point $(0, 0)$ is a locally asymptotically stable node, whereas the fixed points $(1, 0)$ and $(-1, 0)$ are unstable saddle points, just as we anticipated based on the linearized system.

The next example, a classical one, shows that small nonlinear terms can change a center into a spiral node. A mental exercise asks you to consider another case in which the nonlinear terms can change a center into a spiral node.

Example 13.6: Consider the nonlinear system

$$\dot{x}_1 = -x_2 + ax_1\left(x_1^2 + x_2^2\right),$$

$$\dot{x}_2 = x_1 + ax_2\left(x_1^2 + x_2^2\right)$$

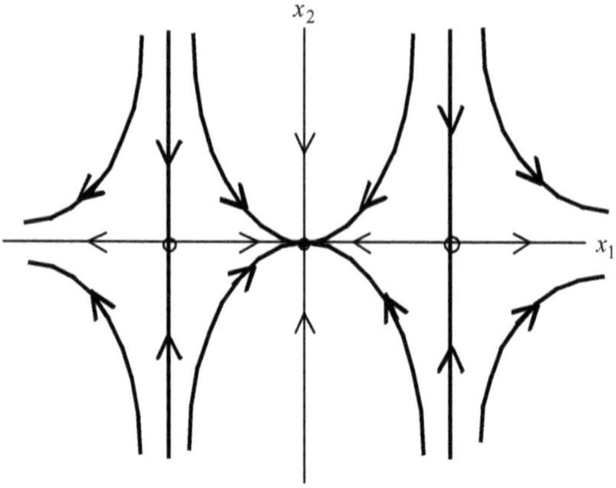

Figure 13.10

where a is a parameter. The point of this example is to show that the linearized system *incorrectly* predicts that the origin, the fixed point of the system, is a center for all values of the parameter a, whereas the origin is in fact a globally asymptotically stable spiral node for $a < 0$ and an unstable spiral node for $a > 0$. We begin by analyzing the linearized system.

The Jacobian matrix of the linearized system evaluated at the origin is given by

$$\mathbf{J}(0,0) \stackrel{\text{def}}{=} \begin{bmatrix} \dfrac{\partial \dot{x}_1}{\partial x_1} & \dfrac{\partial \dot{x}_1}{\partial x_2} \\ \dfrac{\partial \dot{x}_2}{\partial x_1} & \dfrac{\partial \dot{x}_2}{\partial x_2} \end{bmatrix}\Bigg|_{(x_1,x_2)=(0,0)} = \begin{bmatrix} 3ax_1^2 + ax_2^2 & -1 + 2ax_1x_2 \\ 1 + 2ax_1x_2 & ax_1^2 + 3ax_2^2 \end{bmatrix}\Bigg|_{(x_1,x_2)=(0,0)}$$

$$= \begin{bmatrix} 0 & -1 \\ 1 & 0 \end{bmatrix}.$$

Because $\operatorname{tr}(\mathbf{J}(0,0)) = 0$ and $|\mathbf{J}(0,0)| = 1 > 0$, the origin is always a center, at least according to linearization. Equivalently, the eigenvalues of $\mathbf{J}(0,0)$ are readily found to be $\lambda = \pm i$, thus confirming that the origin is a center for the linearized system.

To analyze the original nonlinear system, we make a change of variables to *polar coordinates*. That is, let $x_1 = r\cos\theta$ and $x_2 = r\sin\theta$, where r is the radius and θ is the angle. Using the trigonometric identity $\cos^2\theta + \sin^2\theta \equiv 1$, we have the corresponding identity $x_1^2 + x_2^2 \equiv r^2$. Differentiating this latter identity with respect to the independent variable t, we thus arrive at the differential equation $2x_1\dot{x}_1 + 2x_2\dot{x}_2 = 2r\dot{r}$. Substituting in for $\dot{x}_1$ and $\dot{x}_2$ yields

$$\begin{aligned} r\dot{r} &= x_1\left[-x_2 + ax_1\left(x_1^2 + x_2^2\right)\right] + x_2\left[x_1 + ax_2\left(x_1^2 + x_2^2\right)\right] \\ &= ax_1^2\left(x_1^2 + x_2^2\right) + ax_2^2\left(x_1^2 + x_2^2\right) = a\left(x_1^2 + x_2^2\right)^2 \\ &= ar^4. \end{aligned}$$

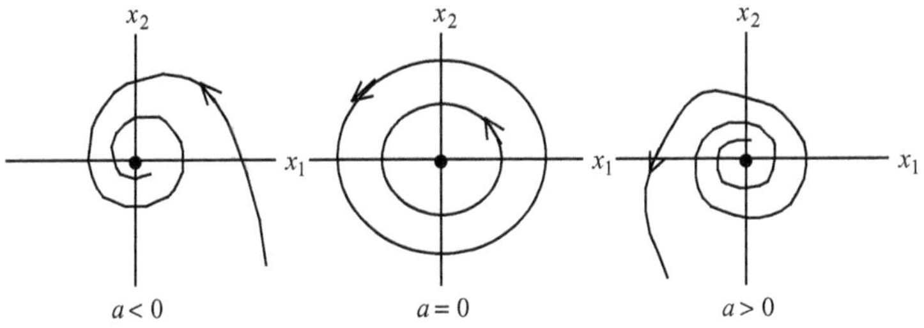

Figure 13.11

Therefore the differential equation for r is $\dot{r} = ar^3$. We now turn to the derivation of the differential equation for θ.

Given that $\tan\theta \stackrel{\text{def}}{=} \sin\theta/\cos\theta$, it follows from $x_1 = r\cos\theta$ and $x_2 = r\sin\theta$ that $\tan\theta = x_2/x_1$. Differentiating this latter equation with respect to the independent variable t and using the identity $x_1^2 + x_2^2 \equiv r^2$ gives

$$\frac{1}{\cos^2\theta}\dot{\theta} = \frac{x_1\dot{x}_2 - x_2\dot{x}_1}{x_1^2} = \frac{x_1^2 + ax_1x_2r^2 + x_2^2 - ax_1x_2r^2}{r^2\cos^2\theta}$$

$$= \frac{x_1^2 + x_2^2}{r^2\cos^2\theta} = \frac{r^2}{r^2\cos^2\theta} = \frac{1}{\cos^2\theta}.$$

Thus the differential equation for θ is simply $\dot{\theta} = 1$.

Summing up our results so far, we have shown that the original nonlinear differential equation system can be replaced by the following decoupled pair of differential equations in polar coordinates:

$$\dot{r} = ar^3, \ \dot{\theta} = 1. \tag{21}$$

This form of the nonlinear system is easy to analyze because the radial and angular motions are independent. As is plainly evident from inspection of these two differential equations, all the trajectories rotate about the origin with constant angular velocity $\dot{\theta} = 1$. The radial motion obviously depends on the sign of the parameter a. Figure 13.11 presents the phase diagram of the above system for the three qualitative values of the parameter a.

If $a < 0$, then Eq. (21) shows that $\dot{r} < 0$ for all $r > 0$, which implies that $r(t) \to 0$ monotonically as $t \to +\infty$, that is, the trajectories spiral inward toward the origin in view of the fact that the radius is shrinking. In this case, the origin is a globally asymptotically stable spiral node. This conclusion can also be verified by drawing the one-dimensional phase portrait for $\dot{r} = ar^3$ when $a < 0$. If $a = 0$, then $r(t) = r_0$ for all t and the origin is a stable center as the radius is constant on any given trajectory. Finally, if $a > 0$, then Eq. (21) shows that $\dot{r} > 0$ for all $r > 0$, thereby implying that $r(t) \to +\infty$ monotonically as $t \to +\infty$, that is, the trajectories spiral outward from the origin because the radius is growing without bound. Hence the origin is an unstable spiral node in this instance. As remarked above, this conclusion can be verified by drawing the one-dimensional phase portrait for $\dot{r} = ar^3$ when $a > 0$.

This example also clearly demonstrates why centers are so delicate: all trajectories must close *perfectly* after one cycle for a center, since even the slightest miss converts the center into a spiral node.

Just as centers can be altered by the small nonlinearities (recall Example 13.6 just discussed), so too can star nodes and improper nodes. There is, however, one significant difference between centers on the one hand and star nodes and improper nodes on the other, videlicet, the stability of star nodes and improper nodes isn't affected by small nonlinearities. A mental exercise asks you to consider an example in which the nonlinear terms change a locally asymptotically stable star node into a locally asymptotically stable spiral node, but not into an unstable spiral node. That the *stability* of star nodes and improper nodes cannot be changed by small nonlinearities is not too surprising given Figure 13.8. Notice that star nodes and improper nodes live squarely in the asymptotically stable or unstable regions. Hence any small perturbation of them leaves them firmly in the same region as far as stability is concerned. The same is not true for centers because they live on the boundary between the asymptotically stable and unstable regions. Thus, in general, a small perturbation of a center will affect both its type and stability. The observations of this paragraph, and more, are the content of the famous Hartman-Grobman theorem, also known as the linearization theorem, which we will shortly state as Theorem 13.7. Before doing so, however, we require one more definition.

Definition 13.9: A simple fixed point $\mathbf{x}^*$ of a nonlinear system $\dot{\mathbf{x}} = \mathbf{f}(\mathbf{x})$, $\mathbf{x} \in D \subseteq \Re^n$, is called *hyperbolic* if every eigenvalue of $\mathbf{J}(\mathbf{x}^*)$ has a nonzero real part, that is, if $\text{Re}(\lambda_n) \neq 0$, $n = 1, 2, \ldots, N$.

In other words, a simple fixed point is hyperbolic if none of the eigenvalues of its Jacobian matrix evaluated at the fixed point is pure imaginary. Hyperbolic fixed points are also called *generic*, because their occurrence is the rule rather than the exception. This may be seen from Figure 13.8, for it shows that pure imaginary eigenvalues occur very infrequently, since a dart thrown at the figure would almost never land exactly on the positive part of the determinant axis. In the case of the scalar nonlinear differential equation $\dot{x} = f(x)$, a hyperbolic fixed point x^* is one in which $f'(x^*) \neq 0$. Note, in passing, that the origin in Example 13.6 is not a hyperbolic fixed point because the eigenvalues of the Jacobian have zero real parts. With this definition in hand, we may state the Hartman-Grobman or linearization theorem, the proof of which we omit.

Theorem 13.7: *Let $(x_1^*, x_2^*) \in D$ be an isolated and hyperbolic fixed point of the nonlinear system $\dot{x}_i = f^i(x_1, x_2)$, $i = 1, 2$, where $f^i(\cdot) \in C^{(1)}$ for all $(x_1, x_2) \in D$, $i = 1, 2$. Then in a small enough neighborhood of (x_1^*, x_2^*), the nonlinear system and its corresponding linearized system have qualitatively equivalent phase* *portraits. Moreover, any trajectory of the nonlinear system that approaches* (x_1^*, x_2^*) *as* $t \to \pm\infty$ *is tangent to a trajectory of its corresponding linearized system that approaches* (x_1^*, x_2^*) *as* $t \to \pm\infty$.

Let's now pause to discuss and clarify certain aspects of this important theorem. To begin, first note that you probably have already seen this result in the case of a scalar nonlinear differential equation. In that case, you may recall that the stability of an isolated fixed point x^* of the scalar nonlinear differential equation $\dot{x} = f(x)$ was correctly predicted by its linearized equation as long as $f'(x^*) \neq 0$. The condition $f'(x^*) \neq 0$ is the exact analogue of $\text{Re}(\lambda_n) \neq 0$, $n = 1, 2, \ldots, N$, in the case of a system of nonlinear differential equations, that is, hyperbolicity of a fixed point, as we noted above. Theorem 13.7 therefore simply extends this result to the case of a system of nonlinear differential equations. It asserts that the stability of an isolated and hyperbolic fixed point of a system of nonlinear differential equations is determined by its corresponding linearized system, that is to say, the eigenvalues of the Jacobian of $\mathbf{f}(\mathbf{x})$ evaluated at the fixed point, videlicet, $\mathbf{J}(\mathbf{x}^*)$. In other words, if our interest centers on stability rather than on the detailed geometry of the trajectories, which is almost always the case in dynamic economic theory, then the marginal cases are only those in which at least one eigenvalue of $\mathbf{J}(\mathbf{x}^*)$ has a zero real part.

Second, let's turn to the meaning of the phrase "qualitatively equivalent phase portraits." A more precise and technically sophisticated way to state the relevant portion of the Hartman-Grobman theorem is this: the local phase portrait of a nonlinear system near a hyperbolic fixed point is topologically equivalent to the phase portrait of its linearized system. Here, *topologically equivalent* means that there is a continuous deformation with a continuous inverse (that is, a homeomorphism) that maps one local phase portrait onto the other, such that trajectories map onto trajectories and the sense of time (i.e., the direction of the arrows) is preserved. In other words, two phase portraits are topologically equivalent if one is a distorted version of the other. Distortions such as bending and warping are permitted, but distortions such as ripping are not because ripping involves discontinuities. Said in simple terms, therefore, Theorem 13.7 asserts that the trajectories of a nonlinear system and its linearization look similar in a neighborhood of a hyperbolic fixed point.

Let's now examine a simple example to drive home the essence of the linearization theorem. We will finish up the chapter with an example of how Theorems 13.6 and 13.7 are typically used in optimal control problems.

Example 13.7: Consider the nonlinear and autonomous system

$$\dot{x}_1 = e^{x_1+x_2} - x_2,$$
$$\dot{x}_2 = -x_1 + x_1x_2.$$

Our goal here is to determine all the fixed points of this system, classify their type and stability, and determine the local phase diagram at each of them.

The fixed points of this system are the solutions to the following simultaneous nonlinear equations:

$$e^{x_1+x_2} - x_2 = 0,$$
$$x_1(x_2 - 1) = 0.$$

The second of these equations is satisfied only by $x_1 = 0$ or $x_2 = 1$. If $x_1 = 0$, then the first equation reduces to $e^{x_2} = x_2$, which has no real solutions because $e^{x_2} > x_2$ for all $x_2 \in \Re$. We may thus conclude that there is no fixed point with $x_1 = 0$. If $x_2 = 1$, then the first equation reduces to $e^{x_1+1} = 1$, which has but one real solution, scilicet, $x_1 = -1$. Thus $(x_1, x_2) = (-1, 1)$ is the only fixed point, and is thus isolated.

Next we compute the Jacobian matrix of the nonlinear system and evaluate it at the fixed point. Doing just that yields

$$\mathbf{J}(-1,1) \overset{\text{def}}{=} \begin{bmatrix} \dfrac{\partial \dot{x}_1}{\partial x_1} & \dfrac{\partial \dot{x}_1}{\partial x_2} \\ \dfrac{\partial \dot{x}_2}{\partial x_1} & \dfrac{\partial \dot{x}_2}{\partial x_2} \end{bmatrix}\Bigg|_{(x_1,x_2)=(-1,1)} = \begin{bmatrix} e^{x_1+x_2} & e^{x_1+x_2} - 1 \\ x_2 - 1 & x_1 \end{bmatrix}\Bigg|_{(x_1,x_2)=(-1,1)}$$
$$= \begin{bmatrix} 1 & 0 \\ 0 & -1 \end{bmatrix}.$$

Given that $\mathbf{J}(-1, 1)$ is a diagonal matrix, the eigenvalues are simply the elements on the main diagonal; hence $\lambda_1 = 1$ and $\lambda_2 = -1$. Thus the linearization predicts the fixed point is an unstable saddle point, and by Theorem 13.7 (or Theorem 13.6 for that matter), the original nonlinear system is similarly an unstable saddle point in a neighborhood of its only fixed point $(x_1, x_2) = (-1, 1)$. It is simple to verify that the unstable manifold is the line spanned by the eigenvector $\mathbf{v}^1 = (1, 0)$ corresponding to the eigenvalue $\lambda_1 = 1$, whereas the stable manifold is the line spanned by the eigenvector $\mathbf{v}^2 = (0, 1)$ corresponding to the eigenvalue $\lambda_2 = -1$.

With the above information in hand, the local phase portrait of the nonlinear system can be constructed. It is given in Figure 13.12.

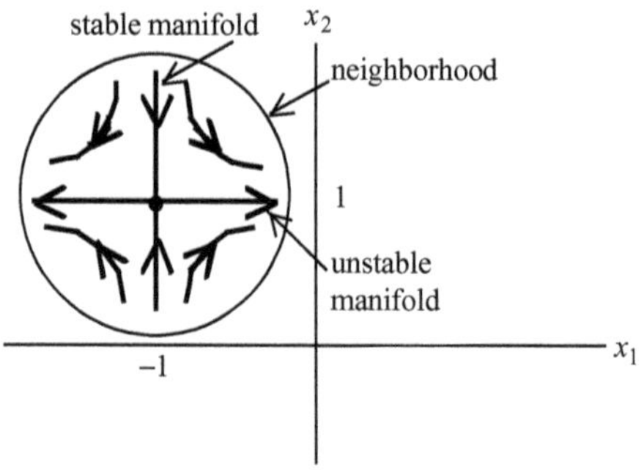

Figure 13.12

It is important to remember that the linearization theorem permits us only to infer the phase portrait of the original nonlinear system in a neighborhood of its unique fixed point $(x_1, x_2) = (-1, 1)$.

Before embarking on the final example of the chapter, we require one more definition.

Definition 13.10: Given a pair of autonomous nonlinear differential equations $\dot{x}_1 = f^1(x_1, x_2)$ and $\dot{x}_2 = f^2(x_1, x_2)$, the *nullclines* are curves such that $f^1(x_1, x_2) = 0$ or $f^2(x_1, x_2) = 0$.

Nullclines are implicit equations in general. The x_1 nullcline, or as it is often referred to, the $f^1(x_1, x_2) = 0$ or $\dot{x}_1 = 0$ *isocline*, is a curve in the x_1x_2-phase plane such that the flow is purely vertical, since $\dot{x}_1 = f^1(x_1, x_2) = 0$ along this nullcline, that is, x_1 is not changing with the passage of time. Similarly, the x_2 nullcline or $\dot{x}_2 = 0$ isocline is a curve in the x_1x_2-phase plane where the flow is purely horizontal, since $\dot{x}_2 = f^2(x_1, x_2) = 0$ along this nullcline, that is, x_2 is not changing with the passage of time. The exception to these two observations is where the two nullclines intersect, which is the fixed point of the system. The nullclines of the system partition the phase plane into regions, sometimes called *isosectors*, where $\dot{x}_1$ and $\dot{x}_2$ have various signs. In each isosector, the trajectories of the system are monotonic, in the sense that $\dot{x}_1$ and $\dot{x}_2$ have the same sign throughout the isosector. Nullclines are therefore especially useful for drawing the phase portraits of autonomous and nonlinear systems when no explicit functional form for the vector field is specified. We will see just how important they are in the next example. Let us note, in passing, that in some instances, nullclines do not exist, as is the case when $f^1(x_1, x_2) \stackrel{\text{def}}{=} x_1^2 + x_2^2 + 1$, for example.

Now that the fundamental properties of systems of autonomous and nonlinear differential equations have been laid out, as well as the basic ideas behind the construction of a phase diagram, we turn to an examination of how phase diagrams may be used in optimal control problems to provide a qualitative characterization of the solution to the necessary conditions. As will be made clear in the ensuing example, the phase portrait approach to studying the qualitative properties of optimal control problems is especially useful when the functional forms of the integrand and transition functions are not specified enough so as to yield an explicit solution of the necessary conditions, the typical case in economic applications of optimal control theory. For example, all one may know about the integrand function are some of its qualitative properties, such as monotonicity, curvature, and homogeneity.

Example 13.8: Consider the fixed endpoints and finite horizon optimal control problem

$$\max_{u(\cdot)} J[x(\cdot), u(\cdot)] \stackrel{\text{def}}{=} \int_0^T f(x(t), u(t))\, e^{-rt}\, dt$$
$$\text{s.t.} \quad \dot{x}(t) = g(x(t), u(t)), \; x(0) = x_0, \; x(T) = x_T, \tag{22}$$

where $r > 0$ is the discount rate. We assume that $f(\cdot) \in C^{(2)}$ and $g(\cdot) \in C^{(1)}$ on their domains, and furthermore that

$$f_{xx}(x, u) < 0, \;\; f_{uu}(x, u) < 0, \;\; f_{ux}(x, u) \equiv 0,$$

$$g_{xx}(x, u) < 0, \;\; g_{uu}(x, u) < 0, \;\; g_{ux}(x, u) \equiv 0.$$

We will not specify any further properties of $f(\cdot)$ and $g(\cdot)$, however, but you may be surprised at how much qualitative information will be forthcoming about the solution of the necessary conditions from these assumptions alone. It is worthwhile to note that because of the assumption of additive separability of $f(\cdot)$ and $g(\cdot)$ in x and u, we may simplify the notation a bit by writing the partial derivatives of $f(\cdot)$ and $g(\cdot)$ with respect to u as $f_u(u)$ and $g_u(u)$, respectively, and similarly for the partial derivatives with respect to x.

Define the current value Hamiltonian as $H(x, u, \lambda) \stackrel{\text{def}}{=} f(x, u) + \lambda g(x, u)$. By Theorem 12.1, the necessary conditions are given by

$$H_u(x, u, \lambda) = f_u(u) + \lambda g_u(u) = 0, \tag{23}$$

$$\dot{\lambda} = r\lambda - H_x(x, u, \lambda) = [r - g_x(x)]\lambda - f_x(x), \tag{24}$$

$$\dot{x} = H_\lambda(x, u, \lambda) = g(x, u), \;\; x(0) = x_0, \;\; x(T) = x_T, \tag{25}$$

and of course $H_{uu}(x, u, \lambda) = f_{uu}(u) + \lambda g_{uu}(u) \leq 0$. Observe that if the current value costate variable $\lambda(t)$ corresponding to the solution of the necessary conditions is nonnegative for the entire planning horizon, then the Hamiltonian is a strictly concave function of $(x, u)\, \forall\, t \in [0, T]$. Therefore, if a solution to the necessary conditions exists and $\lambda(t) \geq 0\, \forall\, t \in [0, T]$, the solution of the necessary conditions will be the unique maximizing solution to the posed optimal control problem by Theorem 4.3. Henceforth, we will accordingly assume that $\lambda(t) > 0\, \forall\, t \in [0, T]$. This, in conjunction with Eq. (23), implies that $f_u(u)g_u(u) < 0$, or equivalently, that $f_u(u)$ and $g_u(u)$ have opposite signs along the optimal path, that is, $\text{sign}\,[f_u(u)] = -\text{sign}\,[g_u(u)]$ along the optimal path. Finally, in agreement with the above assumption that the state variable is a good, that is to say, $\lambda(t) > 0\, \forall\, t \in [0, T]$, we also assume that $x(t) > 0\, \forall\, t \in [0, T]$ in an optimal plan. This assumption also has the added benefit of yielding a phase portrait that is more reminiscent of that typically encountered in intertemporal economic models, namely, the variables under consideration are nonnegative.

To begin the construction of the phase portrait corresponding to the necessary conditions of the optimal control problem, we must first reduce the necessary conditions down to two ordinary differential equations in order to draw it. We may proceed to do so in one of two ways. The approach we shall take is to reduce Eqs. (23) through (25) down to a pair of autonomous differential equations for (x, λ). The alternative approach is to reduce Eqs. (23) through (25) down to a pair of autonomous differential equations for (x, u). This is left for a mental exercise. Both approaches yield the same information about the solution, for they both begin by using the information contained in the necessary conditions (23) through (25). For optimal control problems with one state variable and one control variable, therefore, the choice of approach typically comes down to which pair of variables, namely, (x, λ) or (x, u), lend themselves to a more meaningful economic interpretation.

Seeing as $H_{uu}(x, u, \lambda) = f_{uu}(u) + \lambda g_{uu}(u) < 0$ under our assumptions, the implicit function theorem may be applied to Eq. (23) to solve it, in principle, for the control variable in terms of the current value costate variables, say, $u = \hat{u}(\lambda)$. The comparative statics properties of this solution are given by differentiating the identity $f_u(\hat{u}(\lambda)) + \lambda g_u(\hat{u}(\lambda)) \equiv 0$ with respect to λ, or equivalently, by applying the implicit function theorem to Eq. (23), to get

$$\hat{u}'(\lambda) \equiv \frac{-g_u(\hat{u}(\lambda))}{f_{uu}(\hat{u}(\lambda)) + \lambda g_{uu}(\hat{u}(\lambda))} \gtrless 0. \tag{26}$$

Because we have not made an assumption about the sign of $g_u(u)$, we cannot sign Eq. (26). Note, however, that because $f_{uu}(u) + \lambda g_{uu}(u) < 0$, we know that $\text{sign}[\hat{u}'(\lambda)] = \text{sign}[g_u(\hat{u}(\lambda))]$.

Substituting $u = \hat{u}(\lambda)$ into the canonical equations (24) and (25) yields the autonomous differential equations of interest:

$$\dot{\lambda} = [r - g_x(x)]\lambda - f_x(x), \tag{27}$$

$$\dot{x} = g(x, \hat{u}(\lambda)). \tag{28}$$

Because of the lack of functional form assumptions on $f(\cdot)$ and $g(\cdot)$, Eqs. (27) and (28) can't be solved for an explicit solution.

The last piece of information we require is the Jacobian matrix of Eqs. (27) and (28) evaluated at the fixed point. In accord with our prior observation concerning uniqueness of the solution of the control problem, we assume that there exists a unique fixed point of Eqs. (27) and (28), say, (x^*, λ^*). As you will recall, (x^*, λ^*) are found by setting $\dot{\lambda} = 0$ and $\dot{x} = 0$ in Eqs. (27) and (28), respectively, and solving the resulting simultaneous nonlinear algebraic equations. We now assume that $g_x(x^*) < 0$, so as to place just a bit more qualitative structure on the control problem. The Jacobian matrix of Eqs. (27) and (28) is therefore given by

$$\mathbf{J}(x^*, \lambda^*) = \begin{bmatrix} \frac{\partial \dot{\lambda}}{\partial \lambda} & \frac{\partial \dot{\lambda}}{\partial x} \\ \frac{\partial \dot{x}}{\partial \lambda} & \frac{\partial \dot{x}}{\partial x} \end{bmatrix}\Bigg|_{(x,\lambda)=(x^*,\lambda^*)} = \begin{bmatrix} \underset{(+)}{r - g_x(x^*)} & \underset{(+)}{-\lambda^* g_{xx}(x^*) - f_{xx}(x^*)} \\ \underset{(+)}{g_u(\hat{u}(\lambda^*))\, \hat{u}'(\lambda^*)} & \underset{(-)}{g_x(x^*)} \end{bmatrix}. \tag{29}$$

Note that we have indicated the sign of each element of $\mathbf{J}(x^*, \lambda^*)$ in Eq. (29). Inspection of Eq. (29) reveals that $\text{tr}[\mathbf{J}(x^*, \lambda^*)] = r > 0$. Because the sum of the

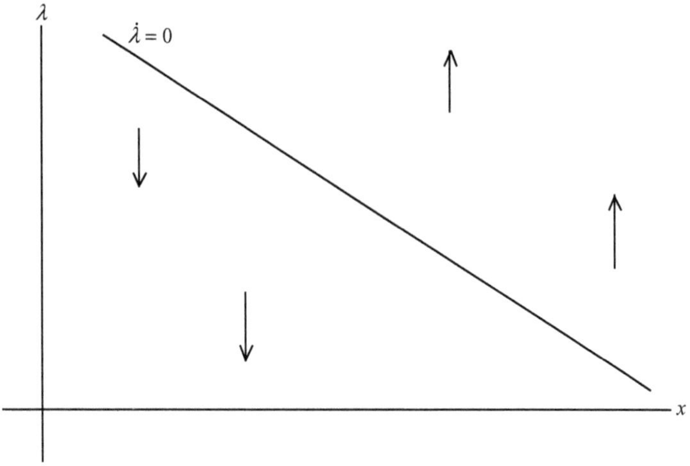

Figure 13.13

eigenvalues of $\mathbf{J}(x^*, \lambda^*)$ equals its trace, as you will prove in a mental exercise, this implies that at least one eigenvalue of $\mathbf{J}(x^*, \lambda^*)$ is positive. This, in turn, implies that the fixed point is not locally asymptotically stable. This conclusion is in fact true in general for discounted optimal control problems when the integrand and transition functions do not depend explicitly on the independent variable t, as we shall see in Chapter 18. Continuing on, inspection of the signs of the elements of $\mathbf{J}(x^*, \lambda^*)$ shows that $|\mathbf{J}(x^*, \lambda^*)| < 0$. Because the product of the eigenvalues of $\mathbf{J}(x^*, \lambda^*)$ equals its determinant, as you will also prove in a mental exercise, this implies that one eigenvalue of $\mathbf{J}(x^*, \lambda^*)$ is positive and one is negative. This structure of the eigenvalues of $\mathbf{J}(x^*, \lambda^*)$ is the defining property of a fixed point that is a *saddle point*. We may therefore conclude by Theorem 13.6 or Theorem 13.7 that the steady state (x^*, λ^*) is an unstable saddle point of the original nonlinear system of differential equations given by Eqs. (27) and (28). This is the final piece of information we require in order to construct the phase portrait corresponding to Eqs. (27) and (28).

We now describe, in detail, the construction of the phase portrait corresponding to Eqs. (27) and (28). We will do this in five distinct steps. What follows will be used repeatedly in several of the ensuing chapters.

Step 1: Let's determine the slope of the λ nullcline, or equivalently, the $\dot{\lambda} = 0$ isocline, first. To begin, draw a graph with λ plotted vertically and x plotted horizontally, as in Figure 13.13. In order to determine the λ nullcline, set $\dot{\lambda} = 0$ in Eq. (27) to get the algebraic equation $[r - g_x(x)]\lambda - f_x(x) = 0$. Given that λ appears linearly in this equation, we may solve it explicitly for λ to get the alternative form of the λ nullcline, to wit,

$$\lambda = \frac{f_x(x)}{[r - g_x(x)]}. \tag{30}$$

Because Theorems 13.6 and 13.7 permit us to reach conclusions regarding the steady state only locally, it suffices to consider the slope of the λ nullcline evaluated at the steady state. Hence, differentiating Eq. (30) with respect to x and evaluating at the steady state gives

$$\left.\frac{\partial\lambda}{\partial x}\right|_{(x,\lambda)=(x^*,\lambda^*)} = \frac{[r - g_x(x^*)]f_{xx}(x^*) + f_x(x^*)g_{xx}(x^*)}{[r - g_x(x^*)]^2} < 0, \tag{31}$$

where we have used the assumptions $f_{xx}(x^*) < 0$, $g_{xx}(x^*) < 0$, and $g_x(x^*) < 0$, the latter of which, when used in conjunction with the assumption $\lambda^* > 0$ and Eq. (30), implies that $f_x(x^*) > 0$. Equation (31) demonstrates that the slope of the $\dot{\lambda} = 0$ isocline is negative in a neighborhood of the steady state. Moreover, it is important to recognize that the λ nullcline divides the $x\lambda$-phase plane into two regions, one in which $\dot{\lambda} > 0$ and thus λ is increasing over time, and one in which $\dot{\lambda} < 0$ and thus λ is decreasing over time. The next step in the construction of the phase portrait seeks to determine precisely these two regions. Figure 13.13 displays the $\dot{\lambda} = 0$ isocline. Note that at this juncture, the arrows in the figure should be ignored.

The student well versed in implicit function theory should recognize that the slope of the $\dot{\lambda} = 0$ isocline may also be determined from the Jacobian matrix in Eq. (29). In particular, observe that the negative of the ratio of the (1,2) element to the (1,1) element of $\mathbf{J}(x^*, \lambda^*)$ gives

$$-\left.\frac{\partial\dot{\lambda}/\partial x}{\partial\dot{\lambda}/\partial\lambda}\right|_{(x,\lambda)=(x^*,\lambda^*)} = \frac{[r - g_x(x^*)]f_{xx}(x^*) + f_x(x^*)g_{xx}(x^*)}{[r - g_x(x^*)]^2} < 0,$$

which is identical to Eq. (31). This is as it should be by the implicit function theorem. Note that in arriving at the above result, we made use of Eq. (30).

Step 2: To determine the vector field associated with the $\dot{\lambda} = 0$ isocline in a neighborhood of the steady state, that is to say, the movement of, or forces acting on, a point *not* located on the λ nullcline but near the fixed point, we proceed as follows. To begin, let $(x, \lambda) = (x^*, \lambda^*)$, so that the point under consideration, namely, the fixed point, lies on the $\dot{\lambda} = 0$ isocline, thereby implying that $[r - g_x(x^*)]\lambda^* - f_x(x^*) = 0$. Then consider what happens to $\dot{\lambda}$ if we change x or λ by a small amount. This change results in a new point, say, $(x, \lambda) = (x^* + k_1, \lambda^*)$, $k_1 \neq 0$ and small, or $(x, \lambda) = (x^*, \lambda^* + k_2)$, $k_2 \neq 0$ and small. Neither of these new coordinates lies on the $\dot{\lambda} = 0$ isocline but they are still in a neighborhood of the steady state, that is, $[r - g_x(x^* + k_1)]\lambda^* - f_x(x^* + k_1) \neq 0$ and $[r - g_x(x^*)][\lambda^* + k_2] - f_x(x^*) \neq 0$. We can determine the effect of this perturbation on $\dot{\lambda}$ quite easily by recognizing that the effect of a change in x or λ on $\dot{\lambda}$ in a neighborhood of the fixed point is found by differentiating the conjugate differential equation (27) with respect to x or λ and evaluating the result at the steady state. The beauty of this observation is that we have already made this computation in deriving the Jacobian matrix $\mathbf{J}(x^*, \lambda^*)$ in Eq. (29).

In the case in which we move horizontally off the $\dot{\lambda} = 0$ isocline in a neighborhood of the steady state in the $x\lambda$-phase plane, we see from the (1,2) element of $\mathbf{J}(x^*, \lambda^*)$ that

$$\left.\frac{\partial \dot{\lambda}}{\partial x}\right|_{(x,\lambda)=(x^*,\lambda^*)} = -\lambda^* g_{xx}(x^*) - f_{xx}(x^*) > 0, \tag{32}$$

the sign of which follows from $f_{xx}(x^*) < 0$, $g_{xx}(x^*) < 0$, and $\lambda^* > 0$. Equation (32) shows that a small horizontal movement from the steady state to the right of the $\dot{\lambda} = 0$ isocline causes $\dot{\lambda}$ to increase from zero. That is, $\dot{\lambda} > 0$ as we move to the right of the λ nullcline in a neighborhood of the steady state, since $\dot{\lambda} = 0$ at the steady state. Symmetrically, Eq. (32) asserts that $\dot{\lambda} < 0$ as we move to the left of the λ nullcline in a neighborhood of the fixed point, since $\dot{\lambda} = 0$ at the steady state. Consequently, in Figure 13.13, we have drawn vertical arrows showing that λ is increasing to the right of the $\dot{\lambda} = 0$ isocline and vertical arrows showing that λ is decreasing to the left of the $\dot{\lambda} = 0$ isocline. Remember that because we are dealing with the λ nullcline, the vector field pertaining to points not on it points vertically because that is the direction in which λ is plotted in the phase portrait.

The analysis is essentially the same, and the qualitative conclusions are identical, if we consider the case in which we move vertically off the $\dot{\lambda} = 0$ isocline in a neighborhood of the steady state in the $x\lambda$-phase plane. This perturbation is exactly what is captured by the (1,1) element of $\mathbf{J}(x^*, \lambda^*)$, videlicet,

$$\left.\frac{\partial \dot{\lambda}}{\partial \lambda}\right|_{(x,\lambda)=(x^*,\lambda^*)} = r - g_x(x^*) > 0, \tag{33}$$

since $g_x(x^*) < 0$. Equation (33) demonstrates that a small vertical movement from the fixed point above the $\dot{\lambda} = 0$ isocline causes $\dot{\lambda}$ to increase from zero, exactly the same information conveyed by Eq. (32). This was to be expected, however, because a small positive horizontal or vertical movement from the steady state places the new point on the same side of the λ nullcline, as it is downward sloping in a neighborhood of the fixed point. In sum, therefore, λ is increasing to the right or above the $\dot{\lambda} = 0$ isocline, whereas λ is decreasing to the left or below the $\dot{\lambda} = 0$ isocline, in a neighborhood of the steady state. The latter result follows from the fact that we are free to interpret the derivatives in Eqs. (32) and (33) as a decrease in x or λ. Finally, note that even though we know that the $\dot{\lambda} = 0$ isocline is negatively sloped in a neighborhood of the steady state, we do not know any curvature properties of it. Nevertheless, we have drawn it as a straight line seeing as our analysis pertains only to the steady state and its surrounding neighborhood.

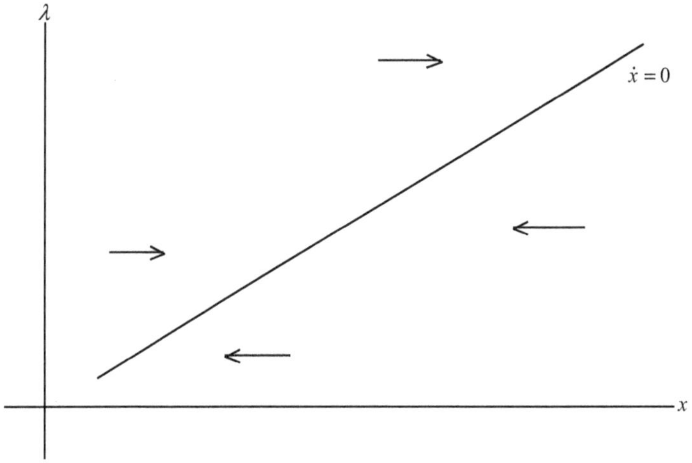

Figure 13.14

Step 3: Now we seek to determine the slope of the x nullcline. The $\dot{x} = 0$ isocline is found by setting $\dot{x} = 0$ in Eq. (28), thereby yielding the implicit relation

$$g(x, \hat{u}(\lambda)) = 0 \tag{34}$$

between x and λ. The Jacobian of Eq. (34) with respect to λ evaluated at the steady state is given by $g_u(\hat{u}(\lambda^*))\,\hat{u}'(\lambda^*) > 0$, the sign of which follows from an aforementioned result that $\text{sign}[\hat{u}(\lambda)] = \text{sign}[g_u(\hat{u}(\lambda))]$. Hence, by the implicit function theorem, Eq. (34) defines λ as a locally $C^{(1)}$ function of x in a neighborhood of the steady state, say, $\lambda = \Lambda(x)$. Consequently, the slope of the $\dot{x} = 0$ isocline in a neighborhood of the steady state is given by differentiating the identity $g(x, \hat{u}(\Lambda(x))) = 0$ with respect to x, or equivalently, by applying the implicit function theorem to Eq. (34), to arrive at

$$\left.\frac{\partial \lambda}{\partial x}\right|_{(x,\lambda)=(x^*,\lambda^*)} = \Lambda'(x^*) \equiv \frac{-g_x(x^*)}{g_u(\hat{u}(\Lambda(x^*)))\,\hat{u}'(\Lambda(x^*))} > 0, \tag{35}$$

since $\text{sign}[\hat{u}'(\lambda)] = \text{sign}[g_u(\hat{u}(\lambda))]$ and $g_x(x^*) < 0$. Equation (35) therefore establishes that the slope of the $\dot{x} = 0$ isocline is positive in the $x\lambda$-phase plane in a neighborhood of the steady state. The x nullcline thus divides the $x\lambda$-phase plane into two regions, one in which $\dot{x} > 0$ and thus x is increasing over time, and one in which $\dot{x} < 0$ and thus x is decreasing over time. This division of the $x\lambda$-phase plane into two regions by the x nullcline is analogous to the splitting of the $x\lambda$-phase plane into two regions by the λ nullcline, but with one important difference: the $\dot{x} = 0$ isocline splits the $x\lambda$-phase plane into two regions and governs the movement of x over time, whereas the $\dot{\lambda} = 0$ isocline splits the $x\lambda$-phase plane into two regions and governs the movement of λ over time. We have depicted the positive slope of the x nullcline in Figure 13.14.

As noted in Step 1, the student well versed in implicit function theory should recognize that the slope of the $\dot{x} = 0$ isocline may also be determined from the Jacobian matrix in Eq. (29). In this instance, the negative of the ratio of the (2,2) element to the (2,1) element of $\mathbf{J}(x^*, \lambda^*)$ gives

$$-\left.\frac{\partial \dot{x}/\partial x}{\partial \dot{x}/\partial \lambda}\right|_{(x,\lambda)=(x^*,\lambda^*)} = \frac{-g_x(x^*)}{g_u(\hat{u}(\lambda^*))\hat{u}'(\lambda^*)} > 0,$$

which is identical to Eq. (35) once one recognizes that $\lambda^* = \Lambda(x^*)$.

Step 4: To determine the vector field associated with the $\dot{x} = 0$ isocline in a neighborhood of the steady state, we proceed as we did in Step 2. As a result, we will be much more brief in the present derivation. If we move horizontally off the $\dot{x} = 0$ isocline in a neighborhood of the steady state in the $x\lambda$-phase plane, then we see from the (2,2) element of $\mathbf{J}(x^*, \lambda^*)$ that

$$\left.\frac{\partial \dot{x}}{\partial x}\right|_{(x,\lambda)=(x^*,\lambda^*)} = g_x(x^*) < 0. \tag{36}$$

Equation (36) shows that a small horizontal movement from the steady state to the right of the $\dot{x} = 0$ isocline causes $\dot{x}$ to decrease from zero. That is, $\dot{x} < 0$ as we move to the right of the x nullcline in a neighborhood of the fixed point, since $\dot{x} = 0$ at the fixed point, whereas $\dot{x} > 0$ as we move to the left of the x nullcline in a neighborhood of the fixed point. As a result, in Figure 13.14, we have drawn horizontal arrows showing that x is decreasing to the right of the $\dot{x} = 0$ isocline and horizontal arrows showing that x is increasing to the left of the $\dot{x} = 0$ isocline. Recall that because we are dealing with the x nullcline, the vector field pertaining to points not on it points horizontally, as that is the direction in which x is plotted in the phase portrait.

If we consider the case in which we move vertically off the $\dot{x} = 0$ isocline in a neighborhood of the steady state in the $x\lambda$-phase plane, then this perturbation is exactly captured by the (2,1) element of $\mathbf{J}(x^*, \lambda^*)$, namely,

$$\left.\frac{\partial \dot{x}}{\partial \lambda}\right|_{(x,\lambda)=(x^*,\lambda^*)} = g_u(\hat{u}(\lambda^*))\, \hat{u}'(\lambda^*) > 0. \tag{37}$$

Equation (37) demonstrates that a small vertical movement from the fixed point above the $\dot{x} = 0$ isocline causes $\dot{x}$ to increase from zero, exactly the same information conveyed by Eq. (36). This is not unexpected, however, because a small positive horizontal movement from the steady state places the new point on the opposite side of the x nullcline as does a small positive vertical movement, for the x nullcline is upward sloping in a neighborhood of the fixed point. All told, x is decreasing to the right or below the $\dot{x} = 0$ isocline, whereas x is increasing to the left or above the $\dot{x} = 0$ isocline, in a neighborhood of the steady state. These facts are depicted by the arrows in Figure 13.14.

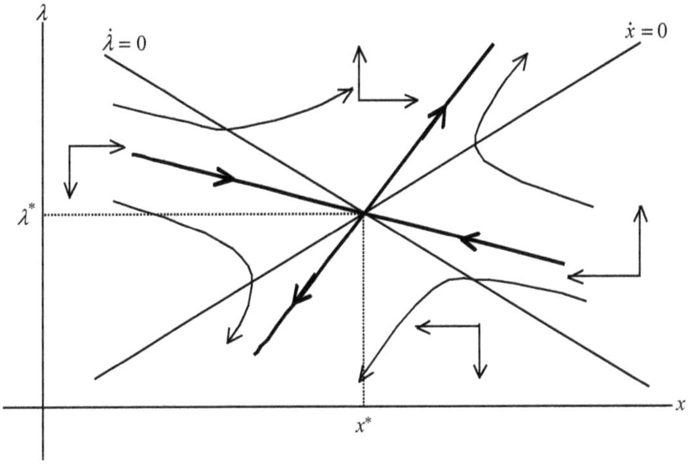

Figure 13.15

Step 5: By bringing Figures 13.13 and 13.14 together into one graph, we get the complete phase portrait corresponding to the canonical differential equations (27) and (28). This is shown in Figure 13.15. A point on any of the curves in Figure 13.15 indicates a value of (x, λ) that might be realized at a moment $t \in [0, T]$, which is consistent with the canonical differential equations. The direction arrows indicate how (x, λ) change with the passage of time. Given that we have used the canonical differential equations to construct Figure 13.15, it is simply a plot of all the possible solutions to them. In other words, Figure 13.15 is a graphical representation of the *general solution* to the canonical differential equations.

The heavy trajectories in Figure 13.15 are the stable and unstable manifolds of the saddle point. It turns out that this phase portrait, which depicts a fixed point or steady state that is an unstable saddle point, is typical of that encountered in dynamic economic models in which one state variable is present in the control problem, as we shall see repeatedly in several of the ensuing chapters.

With the construction of the phase diagram complete, our goal now is to incorporate the boundary conditions of the control problem into the phase diagram. To this end, remember that each trajectory in the phase diagram is a unique solution to the canonical differential equations for some given boundary conditions. In other words, for a given set of boundary conditions, there is a unique trajectory among the infinitely many present in the phase portrait that satisfies them. This trajectory thus represents a specific solution of the canonical differential equations. We will consider three cases for the boundary conditions in what follows.

Case 1: T finite and given, $x(0) = x_0$ given, and $x(T) = x_T$ given.

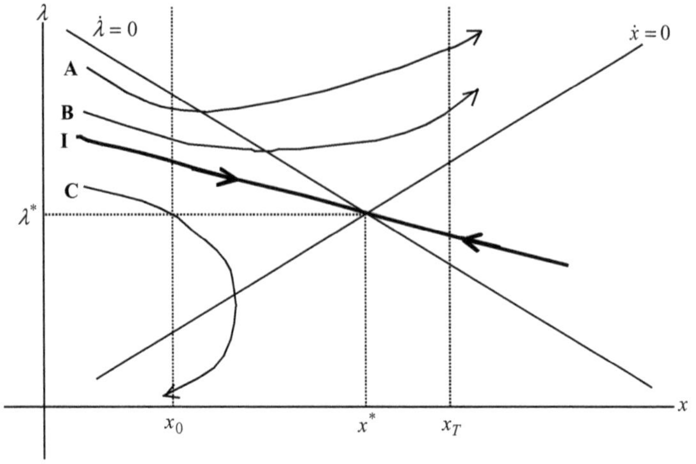

Figure 13.16

The optimal solution in this finite-horizon fixed–endpoints case is the trajectory that begins on the vertical line $x(0) = x_0$ and ends on the vertical line $x(T) = x_T$, in an elapsed time of T. Note that in this case, the initial stock may be greater than, less than, or equal to the terminal stock. In most economic problems, the initial and terminal states are positive, that is, $x_0 > 0$ and $x_T > 0$. Even so, it is often not known how large $x_0 > 0$ is relative to $x_T > 0$. Figure 13.16 depicts the situation in Case 1 assuming that $x_T > x_0 > 0$.

Given that $x_T > x_0$, trajectories **A** and **B** are both solutions to the canonical differential equations (27) and (28) and the boundary conditions. That is, they are both specific solutions to the canonical differential equations, but each takes a different amount of time to traverse the distance from $x_0 > 0$ to $x_T > 0$. Hence, say for some finite $T = T_B$, trajectory **B** is optimal, whereas for some other finite $T = T_A \neq T_B$, trajectory **A** is optimal. Trajectory **I**, on the other hand, is the stable manifold of the saddle point steady state, and thus takes an infinite amount of time to reach the steady state solution (x^*, λ^*) of the canonical differential equations by Theorem 13.4. Hence it cannot be a solution for Case 1 because of this feature. Consequently, trajectory **B** takes a longer time to travel from x_0 to x_T than does trajectory **A** in view of the fact that it is "closer" to trajectory **I**. More rigorously, trajectory **B** has a smaller value of $\dot{x}$ for a given value of x than does trajectory **A**, as inspection of Eq. (37) confirms, and therefore a smaller rate of change of the state variable. As a result, trajectory **B** takes longer to go from x_0 to x_T than does trajectory **A**. In other words, trajectory **B** is optimal for some finite planning horizon $T = T_B$ that is larger than the finite planning horizon $T = T_A$ that is optimal for trajectory **A**. Trajectory **C**, however, is not a solution to the canonical differential equations and boundary conditions as it violates the terminal boundary condition $x(T) = x_T$, as the vector field does not permit it to reach $x(T) = x_T$. More generally, any trajectory that begins

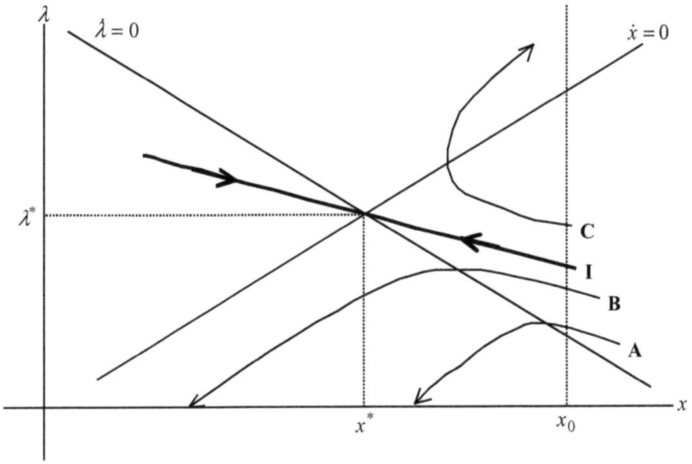

Figure 13.17

along the line $x(0) = x_0$ and lies below trajectory **I** is not a solution to the optimal control problem in Case 1 because it fails to satisfy the terminal boundary condition $x(T) = x_T$.

Case 2: T fixed and finite, $x(0) = x_0$ given, and $x(T) = x_T$ a decision variable.

Because $x(T) = x_T$ is a decision variable in this instance, we know from Theorem 12.1 that the necessary transversality condition is $\lambda(T) = 0$. The optimal solution is therefore given by the trajectory that begins on the vertical line $x(0) = x_0$ and reaches the horizontal line $\lambda(T) = 0$ in a total elapsed time of T. With reference to Figure 13.17, trajectories **A** and **B** are optimal solutions, but trajectory **A** is optimal for a shorter planning horizon than is trajectory **B** because $|\dot{x}|$ is larger for a given value of x for trajectory **A** than it is for trajectory **B**, as inspection of Eq. (37) confirms. Any trajectory that begins along the vertical line $x(0) = x_0$ at or above trajectory **I**, such as trajectory **C**, is not optimal, for it cannot meet the transversality condition $\lambda(T) = 0$ because of the vector field.

Case 3: $T = +\infty$, $x(0) = x_0$ given, and no conditions placed on $\lim_{t \to +\infty} x(t)$.

This is the prototypical infinite horizon case, in which we don't impose any limiting requirement on the time path of the state variable. Nonetheless, at this juncture, we assume that the optimal solution of the state variable converges to its steady state value as $t \to +\infty$, since we have not yet dealt with the necessary and sufficient conditions for this case. Geometrically, the steady state solution to the canonical differential equations is found at the intersection of the $\dot{x} = 0$ and $\dot{\lambda} = 0$ isoclines in the $x\lambda$-phase plane, as this is the only value of (x, λ) for which $\dot{x} = 0$

and $\dot{\lambda} = 0$, both conditions that define the steady state. Thus the optimal trajectory in this case is trajectory **I** in Figures 13.16 and 13.17, as it is the stable manifold of the saddle point steady state and thus takes an infinite amount of time to reach the steady state by Theorem 13.4.

In the next chapter, we return to the study of optimal control theory. In particular, we establish necessary and sufficient conditions for the important class of infinite horizon optimal control problems, arguably the most important class in all of dynamic economic theory. We will see that there are a few technical issues that must be addressed because of the presence of an infinite planning horizon. Moreover, we will see that some finite horizon results do not carry over in the expected fashion to the infinite horizon case, in contrast to what one may have anticipated.

MENTAL EXERCISES

13.1 Consider the linear system $\dot{x}_1 = ax_1, \dot{x}_2 = -x_2$, where $a \neq 0$ is a parameter.
   (a) Find the solution of this linear system satisfying the initial conditions $x_1(0) = x_{10}$ and $x_2(0) = x_{20}$.
   (b) Graph the phase portrait when $a < -1$. By considering the slope $dx_2/dx_1 = \dot{x}_2/\dot{x}_1$ along the trajectories, show that for $x_{20} \neq 0$, all the trajectories become parallel to the x_2-direction as $t \to +\infty$. Similarly, show that for $x_{10} \neq 0$, all the trajectories become parallel to the x_1-direction as $t \to -\infty$. What type of fixed point is it? Be sure to sketch in the slow and fast eigendirections.
   (c) Graph the phase portrait when $a = -1$. Show that all trajectories are straight lines through the origin. What type of fixed point is it?
   (d) Graph the phase portrait when $-1 < a < 0$. Show that for $x_{10} \neq 0$, all the trajectories become parallel to the x_1-direction as $t \to +\infty$. Similarly, show that for $x_{20} \neq 0$, all the trajectories become parallel to the x_2-direction as $t \to -\infty$. What type of fixed point is it? Be sure to sketch in the slow and fast eigendirections.
   (e) Graph the phase portrait when $a > 0$. Find the stable and unstable manifolds, and draw them in the phase portrait. What type of fixed point is it?

13.2 This exercise is designed to show how small changes in the coefficients of a linear system can affect a fixed point that is a center. Consider the linear system

$$\dot{x}_1 = 0x_1 + x_2,$$
$$\dot{x}_2 = -x_1 + 0x_2.$$

   (a) Find the eigenvalues of the coefficient matrix, classify the fixed point (which is the origin), and determine its stability.

Now consider the linear system

$$\dot{x}_1 = \varepsilon x_1 + x_2,$$
$$\dot{x}_2 = -x_1 + \varepsilon x_2,$$

where $|\varepsilon|$ is arbitrarily small.

(b) Find the eigenvalues of the coefficient matrix. Show that no matter how small $|\varepsilon| \neq 0$ is, the center has been changed into a different type of fixed point. What type of fixed point is it?

(c) Determine the stability of the fixed point for $\varepsilon < 0$ and $\varepsilon > 0$.

13.3 This exercise is designed to show how small changes in the coefficients of a linear system can affect the nature of a fixed point when the eigenvalues of the coefficient matrix are equal. Consider the linear system

$$\dot{x}_1 = -x_1 + x_2,$$
$$\dot{x}_2 = 0x_1 - x_2.$$

(a) Find the eigenvalues of the coefficient matrix, classify the fixed point (which is the origin), and determine its stability.

Now consider the linear system

$$\dot{x}_1 = -x_1 + x_2,$$
$$\dot{x}_2 = -\varepsilon x_1 - x_2,$$

where $|\varepsilon|$ is arbitrarily small.

(b) Find the eigenvalues of the coefficient matrix.

(c) Classify the fixed point and determine its stability if $\varepsilon > 0$.

(d) Classify the fixed point and determine its stability if $\varepsilon < 0$ but $\varepsilon \neq -1$.

13.4 Consider the linear autonomous system

$$\begin{aligned}\dot{x}_1 &= a_{11}x_1 + a_{12}x_2 \\ \dot{x}_2 &= a_{21}x_1 + a_{22}x_2\end{aligned}, \quad \mathbf{A} \overset{\text{def}}{=} \begin{bmatrix} a_{11} & a_{12} \\ a_{21} & a_{22} \end{bmatrix}.$$

This exercise represents part of the justification for Figure 13.8. We first ask you to establish a preliminary result.

(a) Prove that the sum of the eigenvalues of $\mathbf{A}$ equals tr($\mathbf{A}$), and that the product of the eigenvalues equals $|\mathbf{A}|$.

Given the results in part (a), show that the fixed point (0, 0) is a

(b) star node or improper node if $|\mathbf{A}| > 0$ and $[\text{tr}(\mathbf{A})]^2 - 4|\mathbf{A}| = 0$;

(c) proper node if $|\mathbf{A}| > 0$ and $[\text{tr}(\mathbf{A})]^2 - 4|\mathbf{A}| > 0$;

(d) saddle point if and only if $|\mathbf{A}| < 0$;

(e) spiral if $\text{tr}(\mathbf{A}) \neq 0$ and $[\text{tr}(\mathbf{A})]^2 - 4|\mathbf{A}| < 0$;

(f) center if $\text{tr}(\mathbf{A}) = 0$ and $|\mathbf{A}| > 0$.

13.5 Consider the linear autonomous system

$$\dot{x}_1 = a_{11}x_1 + a_{12}x_2,\ \dot{x}_2 = a_{21}x_1 + a_{22}x_2,$$

where the a_{ij}, $i, j = 1, 2$, are real constants.

(a) Show that if $|\mathbf{A}| = a_{11}a_{22} - a_{12}a_{21} \neq 0$, then the only fixed point is $(0, 0)$.

(b) Show that if $|\mathbf{A}| = a_{11}a_{22} - a_{12}a_{21} = 0$, then in addition to the fixed point $(0, 0)$, there is a line through the origin for which every point is a fixed point of the system. In this instance, the fixed point $(0, 0)$ is not isolated from the other fixed points of the system.

13.6 Show by direct integration that even though the right-hand side of the system

$$\dot{x}_1 = \frac{x_1}{1+t},\ \dot{x}_2 = \frac{x_2}{1+t}$$

depends on t, the paths followed by particles emitted at (x_{10}, x_{20}) at $t = s$ are the same regardless of the value of s. Why is this so? **Hint**: Consider Eq. (10).

13.7 Consider the system

$$\dot{x}_1 = f^1(t, x_1, x_2),$$
$$\dot{x}_2 = f^2(t, x_1, x_2).$$

Show that if the functions $f^1(\cdot)/[[f^1(\cdot)]^2 + [f^2(\cdot)]^2]^{\frac{1}{2}}$ and $f^2(\cdot)/[[f^1(\cdot)]^2 + [f^2(\cdot)]^2]^{\frac{1}{2}}$ are independent of t, then the solutions corresponding to the initial conditions $x_1(s) = x_{10}$ and $x_2(s) = x_{20}$ give the same trajectories regardless of the value of s.

13.8 A particle travels on the half-line $x \geq 0$ with a velocity given by $\dot{x} = -x^c$, where c is real and constant.

(a) Find all values of c such that the origin is a globally asymptotically stable fixed point.

(b) Define $f(x) \stackrel{\text{def}}{=} -x^c$. Draw a graph of $f(\cdot)$ for $c \in (0, 1)$, $c = 1$, and for $c > 1$.

(c) Show that for $c = 1$, $\lim_{t\to+\infty} \phi(t) = 0$, where $\phi(t)$ is the solution of the differential equation. You must find the formula for $\phi(\cdot)$ in this case.

(d) Show that for $c > 1$, $\lim_{t\to+\infty} \phi(t) = 0$. Do not compute $\phi(\cdot)$ in this case.

(e) Find an implicit form of the solution $\phi(t)$ when $c \in (0, 1)$, given the initial condition $x(0) = 1$.

(f) How long does it take the particle to travel from $x = 1$ to $x = 0$ as a function of the parameter c? How is this possible given Theorem 13.4? Explain.

13.9 For each of the ensuing systems, (i) find the fixed points, (ii) classify their type and stability, (iii) then sketch the nullclines, the vector field, and a plausible phase portrait.

(a) $\dot{x}_1 = x_1 - x_2$, $\dot{x}_2 = 1 - e^{x_1}$.

(b) $\dot{x}_1 = x_1 - x_1^3$, $\dot{x}_2 = -x_2$.

(c) $\dot{x}_1 = x_1[x_1 - x_2]$, $\dot{x}_2 = x_2[2x_1 - x_2]$.

(d) $\dot{x}_1 = x_2, \dot{x}_2 = x_1[1 + x_2] - 1$.
(e) $\dot{x}_1 = x_1[2 - x_1 - x_2], \dot{x}_2 = x_1 - x_2$.
(f) $\dot{x}_1 = x_1^2 - x_2, \dot{x}_2 = x_1 - x_2$.

13.10 For each of the ensuing systems, (i) find the fixed points, (ii) classify their type and stability, (iii) then sketch the nullclines, the vector field, and a plausible phase portrait.
(a) $\dot{x}_1 = x_1 - x_2, \dot{x}_2 = x_1^2 - 4$.
(b) $\dot{x}_1 = \sin x_2, \dot{x}_2 = x_1 - x_1^3$.
(c) $\dot{x}_1 = 1 + x_2 - e^{x_1}, \dot{x}_2 = x_1^3 - x_2$.
(d) $\dot{x}_1 = x_2 + x_1 - x_1^3, \dot{x}_2 = -x_2$.
(e) $\dot{x}_1 = \sin x_2, \dot{x}_2 = \cos x_1$.
(f) $\dot{x}_1 = x_1 x_2 - 1, \dot{x}_2 = x_1 - x_2^3$.

13.11 In Theorem 13.2, we established that different trajectories of autonomous systems can never intersect. In many phase portraits, however, different trajectories *appear* to intersect at a fixed point. Is there a contradiction here? Explain.

13.12 The purpose of this exercise is to demonstrate that the nonlinear terms can change a star node into a spiral node, but not change its stability, just as predicted by Theorem 13.6. Consider a system in polar coordinates given by $\dot{r} = -r, \dot{\theta} = 1/\ln r$.
(a) Find an explicit solution of this nonlinear system satisfying the initial condition $(r(0), \theta(0)) = (r_0, \theta_0)$, say, $(r(t; r_0, \theta_0), \theta(t; r_0, \theta_0))$.
(b) Show that $r(t; r_0, \theta_0) \to 0$ and $|\theta(t; r_0, \theta_0)| \to +\infty$ as $t \to +\infty$. Classify the type and stability of the origin given this information.
(c) Write the system in (x_1, x_2) coordinates.
(d) Show that the linearized system about the origin corresponding to the nonlinear one derived in part (c) is given by $\dot{x}_1 = -x_1, \dot{x}_2 = -x_2$. Classify the type and stability of the origin of the linearized system.

13.13 Here is another example in which the origin is a globally asymptotically stable spiral node for the original nonlinear system, but linearization predicts the origin is a center. Consider the nonlinear system $\dot{x}_1 = -x_2 - x_1^3, \dot{x}_2 = x_1$.
(a) By changing to polar coordinates, show that the origin is a globally asymptotically stable spiral node.
(b) Show that the corresponding linearized system predicts that the origin is a center.

13.14 Determine the type and stability of the fixed point at the origin for the nonlinear system $\dot{x}_1 = -x_2 + ax_1^3, \dot{x}_2 = x_1 + ax_2^3$, for all real values of the parameter a.

13.15 For each of the following nonlinear systems, show that the origin is a fixed point and classify its type and stability, if possible.
(a) $\dot{x}_1 = x_1 - x_2 + x_1 x_2, \dot{x}_2 = 3x_1 - 2x_2 - x_1 x_2$.
(b) $\dot{x}_1 = x_1 + x_1^2 + x_2^2, \dot{x}_2 = x_2 - x_1 x_2$.

(c) $\dot{x}_1 = -2x_1 - x_2 - x_1[x_1^2 + x_2^2]$, $\dot{x}_2 = x_1 - x_2 + x_2[x_1^2 + x_2^2]$.
(d) $\dot{x}_1 = x_2 + x_1[1 - x_1^2 - x_2^2]$, $\dot{x}_2 = -x_1 + x_2[1 - x_1^2 - x_2^2]$.
(e) $\dot{x}_1 = 2x_1 + x_2 + x_1 x_2^3$, $\dot{x}_2 = x_1 - 2x_2 - x_1 x_2$.
(f) $\dot{x}_1 = x_1 + 2x_1^2 - x_2^2$, $\dot{x}_2 = x_1 - 2x_2 + x_1^3$.
(g) $\dot{x}_1 = x_2$, $\dot{x}_2 = -x_1 + \mu x_2[1 - x_1^2]$, $\mu > 0$.
(h) $\dot{x}_1 = 1 + x_2 - e^{-x_1}$, $\dot{x}_2 = x_2 - \sin x_1$.
(i) $\dot{x}_1 = [1 + x_1]\sin x_2$, $\dot{x}_2 = 1 - x_1 - \cos x_2$.
(j) $\dot{x}_1 = e^{-x_1 + x_2} - \cos x_1$, $\dot{x}_2 = \sin[x_1 - 3x_2]$.

13.16 Find all of the real fixed points of the following systems of nonlinear differential equations, and then classify them and determine their stability.
(a) $\dot{x}_1 = x_1 + x_2^2$, $\dot{x}_2 = x_1 + x_2$.
(b) $\dot{x}_1 = 1 - x_1 x_2$, $\dot{x}_2 = x_1 - x_2^3$.
(c) $\dot{x}_1 = x_1 - x_1^2 - x_1 x_2$, $\dot{x}_2 = 3x_2 - x_1 x_2 - 2x_2^2$.
(d) $\dot{x}_1 = 1 - x_2$, $\dot{x}_2 = x_1^2 - x_2^2$.

13.17 This problem demonstrates a remark made in this chapter, videlicet, that even if the fixed point of a nonlinear system and its corresponding linear system are of the same type, the trajectories of the nonlinear system may be considerably different in appearance from those of the corresponding linear system. To this end, consider the ensuing nonlinear autonomous system:

$$\dot{x}_1 = x_2, \ \ \dot{x}_2 = x_1 + 2x_1^3.$$

(a) Show that the fixed point (0, 0) is a saddle point.
(b) Derive the corresponding linear system about the origin, and then sketch the trajectories of the linear system by integrating the differential equation for dx_2/dx_1.
(c) Show that the only trajectory on which $\lim_{t\to+\infty} x_1(t) = 0$ and $\lim_{t\to+\infty} x_2(t) = 0$ is the line $x_2 = -x_1$.
(d) Determine the trajectories of the nonlinear system by integrating the differential equation for dx_2/dx_1.
(e) Sketch the trajectories of the nonlinear system that correspond to $x_2 = -x_1$ and $x_2 = x_1$ for the linear system.

13.18 This problem also demonstrates a remark made in this chapter, to wit, that even if the fixed point of a nonlinear system and its corresponding linear system are of the same type, the trajectories of the nonlinear system may be considerably different in appearance from those of the corresponding linear system. To this end, consider the ensuing nonlinear autonomous system:

$$\dot{x}_1 = x_1, \ \ \dot{x}_2 = -2x_2 + x_1^3.$$

(a) Show that the fixed point (0, 0) is a saddle point.
(b) Derive the corresponding linear system about the origin, and then sketch the trajectories of the linear system.

(c) Show that the trajectory for which $\lim_{t\to+\infty} x_1(t) = 0$ and $\lim_{t\to+\infty} x_2(t) = 0$ is the line $x_1 = 0$.
(d) Determine the trajectories of the nonlinear system for $x_1 \neq 0$ by integrating the differential equation for dx_2/dx_1.
(e) Show that the trajectory corresponding to $x_1 = 0$ for the linear system is unaltered, but that the one corresponding to $x_2 = 0$ is $x_2 = x_1^5/5$. Also sketch the trajectories of the nonlinear system.

13.19 Reconsider Case 1 under the assumptions:
(a) $0 < x_0 < x_T < x^*$,
(b) $0 < x^* < x_0 < x_T$,
(c) $0 < x_T < x^* < x_0$.
Explain the resulting phase portrait carefully in each case.

13.20 Reconsider Case 2 under the assumption $0 < x_0 < x^*$. Explain the resulting phase portrait carefully.

FURTHER READING

As remarked in the Preface, this chapter was written under the assumption that readers have taken a standard introductory course in ordinary differential equations. This background material, including the fundamental existence and uniqueness theorem, may be found in the excellent textbook by Boyce and DiPrima (1977, 3rd Ed., Chapters 1–7). Simon and Blume (1994, Chapters 24 and 25) and Tu (1994, 2nd Ed., Chapters 2 and 5) also present this background material, albeit more compactly. The books by Arrowsmith and Place (1992) and Strogatz (1994) cover more advanced material such as that presented in this chapter. This chapter benefited from the lecture notes of Gravner (1996). The classic reference by Clark (1976) contains applications of the results developed in the present chapter to renewable and nonrenewable resource models. The article by Smith (1968) is an excellent paper with which to hone one's understanding of the material developed herewith.

REFERENCES

Arrowsmith, D.K. and Place, C.M. (1992), *Dynamical Systems* (London: Chapman and Hall).

Boyce, W.E. and DiPrima, R.C. (1977, 3rd Ed.), *Elementary Differential Equations and Boundary Value Problems* (New York: John Wiley and Sons, Inc.).

Clark, C.W. (1976), *Mathematical Bioeconomics* (New York: John Wiley and Sons, Inc.).

Gravner, J. (1996), Lecture Notes for Mathematics 119A, *Ordinary Differential Equations*, University of California, Davis.

Simon, C.P. and Blume, L. (1994), *Mathematics for Economists* (New York: W.W. Norton & Company, Inc.).

Smith, V.L. (1968), "Economics of Production from Natural Resources," *American Economic Review*, vol. 58, no. 3, pp. 409–431.

Strogatz, S.E. (1994), *Nonlinear Dynamics and Chaos* (Reading, Mass.: Addison-Wesley Publishing Co.).

Tu, P.N.V. (1994, 2nd Ed.), *Dynamical Systems* (Berlin: Springer-Verlag).

FOURTEEN

Necessary and Sufficient Conditions for Infinite Horizon Control Problems

In many optimal control problems in economics, the planning horizon is assumed to be of infinite length. This means that the person who solves such an optimal control problem is choosing the time path of the control variables for eternity at the initial date of the planning horizon. At first glance, the infinite horizon assumption may seem to be an arbitrary and extreme one, but in fact it is often less extreme than it first appears. For example, it is often just as arbitrary and extreme to assume that a firm would stop planning at some finite date in the future. This issue is especially pertinent if one takes the view of a planner making decisions for an entire economy. Thus the infinite horizon assumption is no more or less extreme, in general, than the assumption of a finite planning horizon. In the end, the choice of the horizon length should be made based on the appropriateness of the assumption for the economic question under consideration as well as the qualitative implications it implies, and their consistency with observed behavior. It is also important to point out that infinite horizon control problems have certain properties that help to considerably simplify the analysis of them that can render an otherwise intractable problem tractable, as this chapter and several others will demonstrate. On the other hand, infinite horizon control problems present two bodacious difficulties of their own.

One difficulty that rears its head for infinite planning horizon problems is whether the objective functional even exists, since it is now an improper integral rather than a proper one. That is, we now have to be more concerned with whether the improper integral converges for all admissible pairs, since our basic assumptions on the functions $f(\cdot)$, $\mathbf{g}(\cdot)$, and $\mathbf{h}(\cdot)$ are no longer sufficient to guarantee that it does. For example, what should our optimality criterion be when the objective functional diverges for some of the admissible pairs? Said differently, how do we select the optimal pair when one or several of the admissible pairs lead to the improper integral diverging to $+\infty$? Probing the convergence issue of the objective functional and thus the choice of optimality criteria will take us into somewhat deep mathematical territory, which we wish to avoid. Our adversity to probing this issue is a result of our focus on the most common and important classes of optimal control problems for economists. That said, we will therefore restrict the domain of the objective functional to those admissible pairs, if any, for which the objective functional converges, thereby completely sidestepping the convergence issue. As a practical matter, it is highly recommended to proceed by solving infinite horizon control problems under the assumption that the objective functional converges for all admissible pairs. Moreover, in seeing this material for the first time, it is of considerable pedagogical value to make this assumption. If, however, convergence fails to occur, then one would look for weaker optimality criteria for which an optimum may exist.

The other difficulty that arises when studying infinite horizon control problems is the appropriate set of *necessary* transversality conditions. A famous example given by Halkin (1974) shows that, in general, the natural transversality conditions for the finite horizon case do not carry over in the expected fashion to the infinite horizon case. A bit of time will be spent on this issue seeing as it is central to many problems in economics. It is important to note, however, that the sufficient transversality conditions for the finite horizon case do in fact carry over to the infinite horizon case in the expected manner.

The general class of optimal control problems of interest in this chapter is of the form

$$J[\mathbf{x}(\cdot), \mathbf{u}(\cdot)] \stackrel{\text{def}}{=} \int_0^{+\infty} f(t, \mathbf{x}(t), \mathbf{u}(t); \boldsymbol{\alpha})\, dt$$

$$\text{s.t.} \quad \dot{\mathbf{x}}(t) = \mathbf{g}(t, \mathbf{x}(t), \mathbf{u}(t); \boldsymbol{\alpha}), \;\; \mathbf{x}(0) = \mathbf{x}_0, \tag{1}$$

$$\lim_{t \to +\infty} x_n(t) = x_n^s, \quad n = 1, 2, \ldots, n_1,$$

$$\lim_{t \to +\infty} x_n(t) \geq x_n^s, \quad n = n_1 + 1, n_1 + 2, \ldots, n_2,$$

$$\text{no conditions on } x_n(t) \text{ as } t \to +\infty, n = n_2 + 1, n_2 + 2, \ldots, N,$$

$$h^k(t, \mathbf{x}(t), \mathbf{u}(t); \boldsymbol{\alpha}) \geq 0, \quad k = 1, 2, \ldots, K',$$

$$h^k(t, \mathbf{x}(t), \mathbf{u}(t); \boldsymbol{\alpha}) = 0, \quad k = K' + 1, K' + 2, \ldots, K,$$

in which we seek to optimize the objective functional $J[\mathbf{x}(\cdot), \mathbf{u}(\cdot)]$ in an as yet unspecified manner, where, just as in previous chapters, $\mathbf{x}(t) \stackrel{\text{def}}{=} (x_1(t), x_2(t), \ldots, x_N(t)) \in \Re^N$ is the state vector, $\mathbf{u}(t) \stackrel{\text{def}}{=} (u_1(t), u_2(t), \ldots, u_M(t)) \in \Re^M$ is the control vector, $\mathbf{g}(\cdot) \stackrel{\text{def}}{=} (g^1(\cdot), g^2(\cdot), \ldots, g^N(\cdot))$ is the vector of transition functions, $\dot{\mathbf{x}}(\cdot) \stackrel{\text{def}}{=} (\dot{x}_1(\cdot), \dot{x}_2(\cdot), \ldots, \dot{x}_N(\cdot))$, $\mathbf{h}(\cdot) \stackrel{\text{def}}{=} (h^1(\cdot), h^2(\cdot), \ldots, h^K(\cdot))$ is the vector of constraint functions, x_n^s, $n = 1, 2, \ldots, n_2$, are fixed values of the terminal value of the state vector, and $\boldsymbol{\alpha} \stackrel{\text{def}}{=} (\alpha_1, \alpha_2, \ldots, \alpha_A) \in \Re^A$ is a vector of time-independent parameters that affect the state equation, integrand, and constraint functions. Let $(\mathbf{z}(t; \boldsymbol{\alpha}, \mathbf{x}_0), \mathbf{v}(t; \boldsymbol{\alpha}, \mathbf{x}_0))$ be the optimal pair with corresponding costate vector $\boldsymbol{\lambda}(t; \boldsymbol{\alpha}, \mathbf{x}_0)$ and Lagrange multiplier vector $\boldsymbol{\mu}(t; \boldsymbol{\alpha}, \mathbf{x}_0)$. Note that we have yet to specify the precise optimality criterion and have simply written down the objective functional $J[\mathbf{x}(\cdot), \mathbf{u}(\cdot)]$. As in the finite horizon case, we have imposed various terminal conditions on the state vector as $t \to +\infty$. Those listed above are the most common forms encountered in dynamic economic theory when an infinite planning horizon is postulated, and are chosen for that reason. Before moving on to the necessary and sufficient conditions for this class of optimal control problems, let's first be precise about what we mean by admissibility for infinite horizon control problems.

Definition 14.1: We call $(\mathbf{x}(t), \mathbf{u}(t))$ an *admissible pair* if $\mathbf{u}(\cdot)$ is any piecewise continuous control vector function such that $\mathbf{u}(t) \in U(t, \mathbf{x}(t)) \forall\, t \in [0, +\infty)$ and $\mathbf{x}(\cdot)$ is a piecewise smooth state vector function such that $\dot{\mathbf{x}}(t) = \mathbf{g}(t, \mathbf{x}(t), \mathbf{u}(t))$, $\mathbf{x}(t_0) = \mathbf{x}_0$, and in addition, if the terminal boundary conditions in control problem (1) are satisfied, where the control set $U(t, \mathbf{x}(t))$ is defined as

$$U(t, \mathbf{x}(t)) \stackrel{\text{def}}{=} \{\, \mathbf{u}(\cdot) : h^k(t, \mathbf{x}(t), \mathbf{u}(t)) \geq 0,\ k = 1, \ldots, K',$$
$$h^k(t, \mathbf{x}(t), \mathbf{u}(t)) = 0, \quad k = K' + 1, \ldots, K\}.$$

For the terminal endpoint conditions $\lim_{t\to+\infty} x_n(t) = x_n^s$, $n = 1, 2, \ldots, n_1$, the requirement for admissibility is that the $\lim_{t\to+\infty} x_n(t)$ exists and equals x_n^s, $n = 1, 2, \ldots, n_1$. The requirement for admissibility for the terminal conditions $\lim_{t\to+\infty} x_n(t) \geq x_n^s$, $n = n_1 + 1, n_1 + 2, \ldots, n_2$, is that the $\lim_{t\to+\infty} x_n(t)$ exists and that it must be at least as large as x_n^s, $n = n_1 + 1, n_1 + 2, \ldots, n_2$. This terminal condition implies that paths of the state vector with some components tending to $+\infty$ or with some components exhibiting undamped cyclical movements are not admissible, since the appropriate limits do not exist in such circumstances. The last terminal condition, namely, that no conditions are placed on $x_n(t)$ as $t \to +\infty$ for $n = n_2 + 1, n_2 + 2, \ldots, N$, is analogous to the case in which $\mathbf{x}_T$ is a choice variable in finite horizon optimal control problems. In general, this terminal condition allows for the *nonexistence* of $\lim_{t\to+\infty} x_n(t)$ for $n = n_2 + 1, n_2 + 2, \ldots, N$. This may occur if $x(t) = \sin t$ or $x(t) = e^t$, for example.

As we noted above, one concern in connection with infinite horizon problems is the choice of the optimality criterion, especially when the objective functional does not converge for all admissible pairs. We will consider only one possibility here, but refer the reader to Seierstad and Sydsæter (1987, Chapter 3, sections 7, 8, 9) for four other optimality criteria that apply when the objective functional does not converge for all admissible pairs in the infinite horizon case.

The case we are interested in is a direct generalization of the finite horizon case, to wit, we look for an admissible pair of functions $(\mathbf{x}(\cdot), \mathbf{u}(\cdot))$ that *maximizes* the improper integral $J[\mathbf{x}(\cdot), \mathbf{u}(\cdot)]$. In other words, our objective is to

$$\max_{\mathbf{u}(\cdot)} J[\mathbf{x}(\cdot), \mathbf{u}(\cdot)] \stackrel{\text{def}}{=} \int_0^{+\infty} f(t, \mathbf{x}(t), \mathbf{u}(t); \alpha)\, dt, \tag{2}$$

subject to the constraints listed in problem (1). Because our objective functional is an improper integral, for the maximization to make sense, the integral in Eq. (2) must converge for all admissible pairs. We *assume* this to be the case. Although this may seem like a reasonable and possibly innocuous assumption, do not be misled, for this is a reasonable assumption in most economic models, but it is certainly not innocuous, as Seierstad and Sydsæter (1987, Chapter 3) show.

Given that we are assuming that the objective functional $J[\mathbf{x}(\cdot), \mathbf{u}(\cdot)]$ exists for all admissible pairs, that is, the improper integral converges, we begin the technical discussion by examining sufficient conditions for convergence of $J[\mathbf{x}(\cdot), \mathbf{u}(\cdot)]$. We do this by presenting two theorems that are simple to understand and use. The second theorem is the most relevant for the kinds of infinite horizon optimal control models that economists study. The proof of the first theorem is straightforward and is therefore left as a mental exercise, whereas the proof of the second is provided.

Theorem 14.1: *Given the improper integral*

$$J[\mathbf{x}(\cdot), \mathbf{u}(\cdot)] \stackrel{\text{def}}{=} \int_0^{+\infty} f(t, \mathbf{x}(t), \mathbf{u}(t); \boldsymbol{\alpha})\, dt,$$

if the integrand function $f(\cdot)$ *is finite* $\forall\, t \in [0, +\infty)$, *and if* $f(t, \mathbf{x}(t), \mathbf{u}(t); \boldsymbol{\alpha}) = 0\, \forall\, t \geq \tau$, *where* $\tau \in [0, +\infty)$, *then the improper integral will converge.*

In words, this theorem says that if the integrand function of an improper integral is finite and takes on a value of zero at some finite point in time and remains at zero thereafter, then the improper integral will converge. In effect, under the conditions of Theorem 14.1, the improper integral has a finite upper limit of integration of τ, and is therefore really a proper integral whose value is finite. This is a sufficient condition for convergence of the improper integral.

The next sufficient condition for convergence of an improper integral is an extremely useful one in dynamic economic theory. We will make use of it in later chapters.

Theorem 14.2: *Given the improper integral*

$$J[\mathbf{x}(\cdot), \mathbf{u}(\cdot)] \stackrel{\text{def}}{=} \int_0^{+\infty} f(t, \mathbf{x}(t), \mathbf{u}(t); \boldsymbol{\alpha})\, dt,$$

if $f(t, \mathbf{x}(t), \mathbf{u}(t); \boldsymbol{\alpha}) \stackrel{\text{def}}{=} \phi(t, \mathbf{x}(t), \mathbf{u}(t); \boldsymbol{\alpha})\, e^{-rt}$, *where* $r > 0$, *and if the function* $\phi(\cdot)$ *is bounded, say,* $|\phi(t, \mathbf{x}(t), \mathbf{u}(t); \boldsymbol{\alpha})| \leq B \in \Re_{++}$, *then the improper integral will converge and not exceed* $\frac{B}{r}$.

Proof: The proof is a straightforward application of some elementary properties of the absolute value operator, which yield a string of equalities and inequalities, the explanations of which are below the ensuing equation:

$$\left| \int_0^{+\infty} f(t, \mathbf{x}(t), \mathbf{u}(t); \alpha)\, dt \right|$$

$$= \left| \int_0^{+\infty} \phi(t, \mathbf{x}(t), \mathbf{u}(t); \alpha) e^{-rt}\, dt \right| \le \int_0^{+\infty} \left| \phi(t, \mathbf{x}(t), \mathbf{u}(t); \alpha) e^{-rt} \right| dt$$

$$= \int_0^{+\infty} |\phi(t, \mathbf{x}(t), \mathbf{u}(t); \alpha)| \left| e^{-rt} \right| dt \le B \int_0^{+\infty} e^{-rt}\, dt = \frac{B}{r}.$$

The first equality follows from the definition of the function $f(\cdot)$; the first weak inequality follows from the theorem that asserts that the absolute value of the integral of a function is less than or equal to the integral of the absolute value of that function; the next equality follows from the fact that the absolute value of a product of functions is equal to the product of their absolute values; the last inequality follows from the assumed boundedness of the function $\phi(\cdot)$. Q.E.D.

The bodacious feature of Theorem 14.2 is the form of the integrand function, which we have denoted by $f(t, \mathbf{x}(t), \mathbf{u}(t); \alpha) \stackrel{\text{def}}{=} \phi(t, \mathbf{x}(t), \mathbf{u}(t); \alpha)\, e^{-rt}$, $r > 0$ and constant. In particular, it is the presence of the exponential discount factor e^{-rt} that is the most noteworthy. This is because the function $\phi(\cdot)$ is bounded and the exponential discount factor e^{-rt} goes to zero sufficiently fast as $t \to +\infty$, thereby providing the driving force behind the convergence of the improper integral. Moreover, the appearance of the exponential discount factor e^{-rt} is common to nearly every dynamic optimization problem in economics, whether it is a firm discounting its profits in computing its present value, or an individual discounting her instantaneous utility to arrive at her wealth maximizing consumption plan. Furthermore, after Chapter 12, we now understand precisely why this is so, videlicet, the principle of time consistency or dynamic consistency. Thus, Theorem 14.2 is very useful in that it gives a simple sufficient condition for convergence of an improper integral for a class of optimal control problems that are central to, and ubiquitous in, dynamic economic theory.

We are now in a position to state and prove the necessary conditions for optimal control problem (1). First, we note that if $(\mathbf{z}(t; \alpha, \mathbf{x}_0), \mathbf{v}(t; \alpha, \mathbf{x}_0))$ is an optimal pair for problem (1) under our assumption of convergence of the objective functional for all admissible pairs, then for any $T < +\infty$, it follows from the principle of optimality that it must also be an optimal pair for the truncated control problem

$$\max_{\mathbf{u}(\cdot)} J[\mathbf{x}(\cdot), \mathbf{u}(\cdot)] \stackrel{\text{def}}{=} \int_0^T f(t, \mathbf{x}(t), \mathbf{u}(t); \boldsymbol{\alpha})\, dt$$

$$\text{s.t.} \quad \dot{\mathbf{x}}(t) = \mathbf{g}(t, \mathbf{x}(t), \mathbf{u}(t)), \ \mathbf{x}(0) = \mathbf{x}_0, \ \mathbf{x}(T) = \mathbf{z}(T; \boldsymbol{\alpha}, \mathbf{x}_0), \tag{3}$$

$$h^k(t, \mathbf{x}(t), \mathbf{u}(t); \boldsymbol{\alpha}) \geq 0, \quad k = 1, 2, \ldots, K',$$

$$h^k(t, \mathbf{x}(t), \mathbf{u}(t); \boldsymbol{\alpha}) = 0, \quad k = K' + 1, K' + 2, \ldots, K.$$

But this is the prototype finite-horizon fixed–endpoint optimal control problem, whose necessary conditions are given by Theorem 6.1. Thus the pair $(\mathbf{z}(t; \boldsymbol{\alpha}, \mathbf{x}_0), \mathbf{v}(t; \boldsymbol{\alpha}, \mathbf{x}_0))$ must satisfy all the necessary conditions of Theorem 6.1, *except for the transversality conditions that go with it,* since problem (3) does not have the same endpoint conditions as problem (1). That is, all the necessary conditions for finite horizon problems must also hold for infinite horizon problems with the exception of the transversality conditions. For notational clarity, we suppress the dependence of the optimal pair and associated costate and Lagrange multiplier vectors on the parameters $(\boldsymbol{\alpha}, \mathbf{x}_0)$, as well as suppress the dependence of the functions $f(\cdot)$, $\mathbf{g}(\cdot)$, $\mathbf{h}(\cdot)$, $H(\cdot)$, and $L(\cdot)$ on $\boldsymbol{\alpha}$. With this in mind, we have established the following theorem.

Theorem 14.3 (Necessary Conditions, Infinite Horizon): *Let* $(\mathbf{z}(t), \mathbf{v}(t))$ *be an admissible pair for problem (1), and assume that the rank constraint qualification is satisfied. Then if* $(\mathbf{z}(t), \mathbf{v}(t))$ *yields the absolute maximum of* $J[\cdot]$, *it is necessary that there exist a piecewise smooth vector-valued function* $\boldsymbol{\lambda}(\cdot) \stackrel{\text{def}}{=} (\lambda_1(\cdot), \lambda_2(\cdot), \ldots, \lambda_N(\cdot))$ *and a piecewise continuous vector-valued Lagrange multiplier function* $\boldsymbol{\mu}(\cdot) \stackrel{\text{def}}{=} (\mu_1(\cdot), \mu_2(\cdot), \ldots, \mu_K(\cdot))$, *such that for all* $t \in [0, +\infty)$,

$$\mathbf{v}(t) = \arg\max_{\mathbf{u}} \{H(t, \mathbf{z}(t), \mathbf{u}, \boldsymbol{\lambda}(t)) \text{ s.t. } \mathbf{u} \in U(t, \mathbf{z}(t))\},$$

that is, if

$$M(t, \mathbf{z}(t), \boldsymbol{\lambda}(t)) \stackrel{\text{def}}{=} \max_{\mathbf{u}} \{H(t, \mathbf{z}(t), \mathbf{u}, \boldsymbol{\lambda}(t)) \text{ s.t. } \mathbf{u} \in U(t, \mathbf{z}(t))\},$$

then

$$M(t, \mathbf{z}(t), \boldsymbol{\lambda}(t)) \equiv H(t, \mathbf{z}(t), \mathbf{v}(t), \boldsymbol{\lambda}(t)),$$

or equivalently

$$H(t, \mathbf{z}(t), \mathbf{v}(t), \boldsymbol{\lambda}(t)) \geq H(t, \mathbf{z}(t), \mathbf{u}, \boldsymbol{\lambda}(t)) \, \forall \, \mathbf{u} \in U(t, \mathbf{z}(t)),$$

where $U(t, \mathbf{x}(t)) \stackrel{\text{def}}{=} \{\mathbf{u}(\cdot) : h^k(t, \mathbf{x}(t)\mathbf{u}(t)) \geq 0, \ k = 1, \ldots, K', h^k(t, \mathbf{x}(t), \mathbf{u}(t)) = 0, \ k = K' + 1, \ldots, K\}$. *Because the rank constraint qualification is assumed to hold, the above necessary condition implies that*

$$\frac{\partial L}{\partial u_m}(t, \mathbf{z}(t), \mathbf{v}(t), \boldsymbol{\lambda}(t), \boldsymbol{\mu}(t)) = 0, \quad m = 1, 2, \ldots, M,$$

$$\frac{\partial L}{\partial \mu_\ell}(t, \mathbf{z}(t), \mathbf{v}(t), \boldsymbol{\lambda}(t), \boldsymbol{\mu}(t)) \geq 0, \quad \mu_\ell(t) \geq 0,$$

$$\mu_\ell(t)\frac{\partial L}{\partial \mu_\ell}(t, \mathbf{z}(t), \mathbf{v}(t), \boldsymbol{\lambda}(t), \boldsymbol{\mu}(t)) = 0, \quad \ell = 1, 2, \ldots, K',$$

$$\frac{\partial L}{\partial \mu_\ell}(t, \mathbf{z}(t), \mathbf{v}(t), \boldsymbol{\lambda}(t), \boldsymbol{\mu}(t)) = 0, \quad \ell = K'+1, K'+2, \ldots, K,$$

where

$$\begin{aligned} L(t, \mathbf{x}, \mathbf{u}, \boldsymbol{\lambda}, \boldsymbol{\mu}) &\stackrel{\text{def}}{=} H(t, \mathbf{x}, \mathbf{u}, \boldsymbol{\lambda}) + \boldsymbol{\mu}'\mathbf{h}(t, \mathbf{x}, \mathbf{u}) \\ &= f(t, \mathbf{x}, \mathbf{u}) + \sum_{n=1}^{N} \lambda_n g^n(t, \mathbf{x}, \mathbf{u}) + \sum_{k=1}^{K} \mu_k h^k(t, \mathbf{x}, \mathbf{u}) \end{aligned}$$

is the Lagrangian. Furthermore, except for the points of discontinuities of $\mathbf{v}(t)$*,*

$$\dot{z}_i(t) = \frac{\partial L}{\partial \lambda_i}(t, \mathbf{z}(t), \mathbf{v}(t), \boldsymbol{\lambda}(t), \boldsymbol{\mu}(t)) = g^i(t, \mathbf{z}(t), \mathbf{v}(t)), \quad i = 1, 2, \ldots, N,$$

$$\dot{\lambda}_i(t) = -\frac{\partial L}{\partial x_i}(t, \mathbf{z}(t), \mathbf{v}(t), \boldsymbol{\lambda}(t), \boldsymbol{\mu}(t)), \quad i = 1, 2, \ldots, N,$$

where the above notation means that the functions are first differentiated with respect to the particular variable and then evaluated at $(t, \mathbf{z}(t), \mathbf{v}(t), \boldsymbol{\lambda}(t), \boldsymbol{\mu}(t))$.

It is important to note that this theorem is valid for *any* type of terminal boundary condition. In fact, if the three terminal boundary conditions in problem (1) were replaced with $\lim_{t\to+\infty} x_n(t) = x_n^s$, $n = 1, 2, \ldots, N$, so that problem (1) becomes a fixed–endpoint infinite-horizon control problem, then Theorem 14.3 contains enough information to single out one or a few candidates for optimality. To see why, simply observe that in this case, the canonical equations generate $2N$ constants of integration when solved, which can in principle be found by using the $2N$ boundary conditions $\mathbf{x}(t_0) = \mathbf{x}_0$ and $\lim_{t\to+\infty} x_n(t) = x_n^s$, $n = 1, 2, \ldots, N$.

If the terminal boundary conditions are as given in problem (1), however, then Theorem 14.3 does not contain enough information to single out one or a few candidates for optimality. This is because the $2N$ constants of integration generated when solving the canonical equations cannot be completely determined because there are only $N + n_1$ endpoint conditions given in problem (1), namely, $\mathbf{x}(t_0) = \mathbf{x}_0$ and $\lim_{t\to+\infty} x_n(t) = x_n^s$, $n = 1, 2, \ldots, n_1$, and no transversality conditions are provided by Theorem 14.3 to determine the remaining $N - n_1$ constants of integration. For this reason, some infinite horizon optimal control problems in economics simply assume that the terminal endpoint condition is $\lim_{t\to+\infty} x_n(t) = x_n^s$

for all $n = 1, 2, \ldots, N$, thereby permitting Theorem 14.3 to single out one or a few candidates for optimality, as noted in the prior paragraph. In this case, the terminal endpoints of the state variables are typically assumed to be their steady state values.

As far as the transversality conditions for problem (1) are concerned, let us state again that there are *none in general.* Given the three types of terminal endpoint conditions in problem (1), videlicet,

$$\lim_{t\to+\infty} x_n(t) = x_n^s, \quad n = 1, 2, \ldots, n_1,$$

$$\lim_{t\to+\infty} x_n(t) \geq x_n^s, \quad n = n_1 + 1, n_1 + 2, \ldots, n_2,$$

$$\text{no conditions on } x_n(t) \text{ as } t \to +\infty, \quad n = n_2 + 1, n_2 + 2, \ldots, N,$$

one might be tempted to infer by analogy with the finite horizon case that the corresponding transversality conditions are

$$\text{no conditions on } \lambda_n(t) \text{ as } t \to +\infty, \quad n = 1, 2, \ldots, n_1,$$

$$\lim_{t\to+\infty} \lambda_n(t) \geq 0, \quad n = n_1 + 1,\ n_1 + 2, \ldots, n_2,$$

$$\lim_{t\to+\infty} \lambda_n(t) = 0, \quad n = n_2 + 1,\ n_2 + 2, \ldots, N,$$

respectively. Unfortunately, this is not true in general, as we have repeatedly emphasized. Only by imposing additional and somewhat strong restrictions on the functions $f(\cdot)$, $\mathbf{g}(\cdot)$, and $\mathbf{h}(\cdot)$, does one obtain transversality conditions similar to these. The interested reader is referred to Benveniste and Scheinkman (1982), Michel (1982), Araujo and Scheinkman (1983), and of course, Seierstad and Sydsæter (1987, Chapter 3) for such matters. We will, however, present and prove the necessary transversality condition in Michel (1982), for it is useful in analyzing a large class of infinite horizon optimal control models in economics under mild assumptions that are typically encountered in dynamic economic theory. But first, we consider two sufficiency theorems and a necessary one.

The first sufficiency theorem extends the Mangasarian sufficiency theorem to infinite horizon problems, whereas the second extends the Arrow sufficiency theorem to infinite horizon problems. We prove the first and leave the proof of the second for a mental exercise. We again elect to suppress the dependence of the functions on the parameters for notational clarity.

Theorem 14.4 (Mangasarian Sufficient Conditions, Infinite Horizon): *Let* $(\mathbf{z}(t), \mathbf{v}(t))$ *be an admissible pair for problem (1). Suppose that* $(\mathbf{z}(t), \mathbf{v}(t))$ *satisfies the necessary conditions of Theorem 14.3 for problem* (1) *with costate vector* $\boldsymbol{\lambda}(t)$ *and Lagrange multiplier vector* $\boldsymbol{\lambda}(t)$, *and let* $L(t, \mathbf{x}, \mathbf{u}, \boldsymbol{\lambda}, \boldsymbol{\mu}) \stackrel{\text{def}}{=} f(t, \mathbf{x}, \mathbf{u}) + \boldsymbol{\lambda}'\mathbf{g}(t, \mathbf{x}, \mathbf{u}) + \boldsymbol{\mu}'\mathbf{h}(t, \mathbf{x}, \mathbf{u})$ *be the value of the Lagrangian function. If* $L(\cdot)$ *is a concave function of* $(\mathbf{x}, \mathbf{u})\,\forall\, t \in [0, +\infty)$ *over an open convex set containing all the* *admissible values of* $(\mathbf{x}(\cdot), \mathbf{u}(\cdot))$ *when the costate vector is* $\boldsymbol{\lambda}(t)$ *and Lagrange multiplier vector is* $\boldsymbol{\mu}(t)$*, and if for every admissible control path* $\mathbf{u}(t)$, $\lim_{t\to+\infty} \boldsymbol{\lambda}(t)'[\mathbf{z}(t) - \mathbf{x}(t)] \le 0$*, where* $\mathbf{x}(t)$ *is the time path of the state variable corresponding to* $\mathbf{u}(t)$*, then* $\mathbf{v}(t)$ *is an optimal control and* $(\mathbf{z}(t), \mathbf{v}(t))$ *yields the global maximum of* $J[\cdot]$*. If* $L(\cdot)$ *is a strictly concave function under the same conditions, then* $(\mathbf{z}(t), \mathbf{v}(t))$ *yields the unique global maximum of* $J[\cdot]$*.*

Proof: Let $(\mathbf{x}(t), \mathbf{u}(t))$ be any admissible pair. By hypothesis, $L(\cdot)$ is a $C^{(1)}$ concave function of $(\mathbf{x}, \mathbf{u})\,\forall\, t \in [0, +\infty)$. It therefore follows from Theorem 21.3 of Simon and Blume (1994) that

$$\begin{aligned} L(t, \mathbf{x}(t), \mathbf{u}(t), \boldsymbol{\lambda}(t), \boldsymbol{\mu}(t)) &\le L(t, \mathbf{z}(t), \mathbf{v}(t), \boldsymbol{\lambda}(t), \boldsymbol{\mu}(t)) \\ &\quad + L_{\mathbf{x}}(t, \mathbf{z}(t), \mathbf{v}(t), \boldsymbol{\lambda}(t), \boldsymbol{\mu}(t))\,[\mathbf{x}(t) - \mathbf{z}(t)] \\ &\quad + L_{\mathbf{u}}(t, \mathbf{z}(t), \mathbf{v}(t), \boldsymbol{\lambda}(t), \boldsymbol{\mu}(t))\,[\mathbf{u}(t) - \mathbf{v}(t)], \end{aligned} \tag{4}$$

for every $t \in [0, +\infty)$. Using the fact that $L_{\mathbf{u}}(t, \mathbf{z}(t), \mathbf{v}(t), \boldsymbol{\mu}(t), \boldsymbol{\mu}(t)) \equiv \mathbf{0}'_M$ by Theorem 14.3 in Eq. (4), and then integrating both sides of the resulting reduced inequality over the interval $[0, +\infty)$ using the definitions of $L(\cdot)$ and $J[\cdot]$, yields

$$\begin{aligned} J[\mathbf{x}(\cdot), \mathbf{u}(\cdot)] \le J[\mathbf{z}(\cdot), \mathbf{v}(\cdot)] &+ \int_0^{+\infty} \boldsymbol{\lambda}(t)'\,[\mathbf{g}(t, \mathbf{z}(t), \mathbf{v}(t)) - \mathbf{g}(t, \mathbf{x}(t), \mathbf{u}(t))]\,dt \\ &+ \int_0^{+\infty} \boldsymbol{\mu}(t)'\,[\mathbf{h}(t, \mathbf{z}(t), \mathbf{v}(t)) - \mathbf{h}(t, \mathbf{x}(t), \mathbf{u}(t))]\,dt \\ &+ \int_0^{+\infty} L_{\mathbf{x}}(t, \mathbf{z}(t), \mathbf{v}(t), \boldsymbol{\lambda}(t), \boldsymbol{\mu}(t))\,[\mathbf{x}(t) - \mathbf{z}(t)]\,dt. \end{aligned} \tag{5}$$

By admissibility, $\dot{\mathbf{z}}(t) \equiv \mathbf{g}(t, \mathbf{z}(t), \mathbf{v}(t))$ and $\dot{\mathbf{x}}(t) \equiv \mathbf{g}(t, \mathbf{x}(t), \mathbf{u}(t))$ for every $t \in [0, +\infty)$, whereas Theorem 14.3 implies that $\dot{\boldsymbol{\lambda}}(t)' \equiv -L_{\mathbf{x}}(t, \mathbf{z}(t), \mathbf{v}(t), \boldsymbol{\lambda}(t), \boldsymbol{\mu}(t))$ for every $t \in [0, +\infty)$. Substituting these three results in Eq. (5) gives

$$\begin{aligned} J[\mathbf{x}(\cdot), \mathbf{u}(\cdot)] \le J[\mathbf{z}(\cdot), \mathbf{v}(\cdot)] &+ \int_0^{+\infty} [\boldsymbol{\lambda}(t)'[\dot{\mathbf{z}}(t) - \dot{\mathbf{x}}(t)] + \dot{\boldsymbol{\lambda}}(t)'[\mathbf{z}(t) - \mathbf{x}(t)]]\,dt \\ &+ \int_0^{+\infty} \boldsymbol{\mu}(t)'\,[\mathbf{h}(t, \mathbf{z}(t), \mathbf{v}(t)) - \mathbf{h}(t, \mathbf{x}(t), \mathbf{u}(t))]\,dt. \end{aligned} \tag{6}$$

Moreover, Theorem 14.3 also implies that (i) $\mu_k(t)h^k(t, \mathbf{z}(t), \mathbf{v}(t)) \equiv 0$ for $k = 1, 2, \ldots, K$ because $\mu_k(t)h^k(t, \mathbf{z}(t), \mathbf{v}(t)) \equiv 0$ for $k = 1, 2, \ldots, K'$ and

$h^k(t, \mathbf{z}(t), \mathbf{v}(t)) \equiv 0$ for $k = K'+1, K'+2, \ldots, K$, (ii) $\mu_k(t)h^k(t, \mathbf{x}(t), \mathbf{u}(t)) \geq 0$ for $k = 1, 2, \ldots, K'$ by virtue of $\mu_k(t) \geq 0$ and $h^k(t, \mathbf{x}(t), \mathbf{u}(t)) \geq 0$ for $k = 1, 2, \ldots, K'$, and (iii) $\mu_k(t)h^k(t, \mathbf{x}(t), \mathbf{u}(t)) \equiv 0$ for $k = K'+1, K'+2, \ldots, K$ on account of $h^k(t, \mathbf{x}(t), \mathbf{u}(t)) \equiv 0$ for $k = K'+1, K'+2, \ldots, K$. These three implications of Theorem 14.3 therefore imply that

$$\int_0^{+\infty} \boldsymbol{\mu}(t)' \left[\mathbf{h}(t, \mathbf{z}(t), \mathbf{v}(t)) - \mathbf{h}(t, \mathbf{x}(t), \mathbf{u}(t))\right] dt \leq 0. \tag{7}$$

Using the inequality in Eq. (7) permits Eq. (6) to be rewritten in the reduced form

$$J[\mathbf{x}(\cdot), \mathbf{u}(\cdot)] \leq J[\mathbf{z}(\cdot), \mathbf{v}(\cdot)] + \int_0^{+\infty} [\boldsymbol{\lambda}(t)'[\dot{\mathbf{z}}(t) - \dot{\mathbf{x}}(t)] + \dot{\boldsymbol{\lambda}}(t)'[\mathbf{z}(t) - \mathbf{x}(t)]]\, dt. \tag{8}$$

To wrap up the proof, simply note that

$$\frac{d}{dt}[\boldsymbol{\lambda}(t)'[\mathbf{z}(t) - \mathbf{x}(t)]] = \boldsymbol{\lambda}(t)'[\dot{\mathbf{z}}(t) - \dot{\mathbf{x}}(t)] + \dot{\boldsymbol{\lambda}}(t)'[\mathbf{z}(t) - \mathbf{x}(t)],$$

and substitute this result into Eq. (8) to get

$$\begin{aligned} J[\mathbf{x}(\cdot), \mathbf{u}(\cdot)] &\leq J[\mathbf{z}(\cdot), \mathbf{v}(\cdot)] + \int_0^{+\infty} \frac{d}{dt}[\boldsymbol{\lambda}(t)'[\mathbf{z}(t) - \mathbf{x}(t)]]\, dt \\ &= J[\mathbf{z}(\cdot), \mathbf{v}(\cdot)] + \lim_{t\to+\infty} \boldsymbol{\lambda}(t)'\,[\mathbf{z}(t) - \mathbf{x}(t)] - \boldsymbol{\lambda}(0)'\,[\mathbf{z}(0) - \mathbf{x}(0)] \\ &= J[\mathbf{z}(\cdot), \mathbf{v}(\cdot)] + \lim_{t\to+\infty} \boldsymbol{\lambda}(t)'\,[\mathbf{z}(t) - \mathbf{x}(t)], \end{aligned}$$

since by admissibility we have $\mathbf{x}(0) = \mathbf{x}_0$ and $\mathbf{z}(0) = \mathbf{x}_0$. Now if for every admissible control path $\mathbf{u}(t)$, $\lim_{t\to+\infty} \boldsymbol{\lambda}(t)'[\mathbf{z}(t) - \mathbf{x}(t)] \leq 0$, where $\mathbf{x}(t)$ is the time path of the state variable corresponding to $\mathbf{u}(t)$, then it follows that $J[\mathbf{x}(\cdot), \mathbf{u}(\cdot)] \leq J[\mathbf{z}(\cdot), \mathbf{v}(\cdot)]$ for all admissible functions $(\mathbf{x}(\cdot), \mathbf{u}(\cdot))$, just as we wished to show. If $L(\cdot)$ is a strictly concave function of $(\mathbf{x}, \mathbf{u})\, \forall\, t \in [0, +\infty)$, then the inequality in Eq. (4) becomes strict if either $\mathbf{x}(t) \neq \mathbf{z}(t)$ or $\mathbf{u}(t) \neq \mathbf{v}(t)$ for some $t \in [0, +\infty)$. In this instance, $J[\mathbf{x}(\cdot), \mathbf{u}(\cdot)] < J[\mathbf{z}(\cdot), \mathbf{v}(\cdot)]$ follows. This shows that any admissible pair of functions $(\mathbf{x}(\cdot), \mathbf{u}(\cdot))$ that is not identically equal to $(\mathbf{z}(\cdot), \mathbf{v}(\cdot))$ is suboptimal. Q.E.D.

It is important to emphasize that the transversality condition

$$\lim_{t\to+\infty} \boldsymbol{\lambda}(t)'[\mathbf{z}(t) - \mathbf{x}(t)] \leq 0$$

is an inner product expression. As a result, it can be written equivalently as

$$\lim_{t\to+\infty} \boldsymbol{\lambda}(t)'[\mathbf{z}(t) - \mathbf{x}(t)] = \lim_{t\to+\infty} \sum_{n=1}^{N} \lambda_n(t)[z_n(t) - x_n(t)] \leq 0,$$

using index notation. This form may often be useful in checking whether it is satisfied in particular control problems.

Let's determine sufficient conditions under which $\lim_{t\to+\infty} \boldsymbol{\lambda}(t)'[\mathbf{z}(t) - \mathbf{x}(t)] \leq 0$ is satisfied for the fixed endpoints version of problem (1), that is, the case in which $\lim_{t\to+\infty} x_n(t) = x_n^s$, $n = 1, 2, \ldots, N$, is the terminal endpoint condition. In this case, for the pairs of curves $(\mathbf{x}(t), \mathbf{u}(t))$ and $(\mathbf{z}(t), \mathbf{v}(t))$ to be admissible, $\lim_{t\to+\infty} x_n(t) = x_n^s$ and $\lim_{t\to+\infty} z_n(t) = x_n^s$, $n = 1, 2, \ldots, N$, must hold, respectively. This implies that $\lim_{t\to+\infty}[z_n(t) - x_n(t)] = x_n^s - x_n^s = 0$, $n = 1, 2, \ldots, N$. Therefore, if $\lambda_n(t)$, $n = 1, 2, \ldots, N$ is bounded, or if $\lim_{t\to+\infty} \lambda_n(t)$ exists for $n = 1, 2, \ldots, N$, then it follows that $\lim_{t\to+\infty} \boldsymbol{\lambda}(t)'[\mathbf{z}(t) - \mathbf{x}(t)] = 0$. Hence the transversality conditions of the Mangasarian sufficiency theorem are satisfied for the fixed endpoints version of problem (1) if either $\lambda_n(t)$ is bounded, $n = 1, 2, \ldots, N$, or if $\lim_{t\to+\infty} \lambda_n(t)$ exists for $n = 1, 2, \ldots, N$.

Obviously, there are many sufficient conditions that ensure that the transversality condition $\lim_{t\to+\infty} \boldsymbol{\lambda}(t)'[\mathbf{z}(t) - \mathbf{x}(t)] \leq 0$ holds in problem (1). These sufficient conditions are often of great value in checking the sufficient transversality condition in infinite horizon problems of interest to economists. The following is one such set of sufficient conditions.

Lemma 14.1: *In problem (1), if the following conditions hold for all admissible* $\mathbf{x}(t)$

(i) *for* $n = 1, 2, \ldots, n_1$, *either* $|\lambda_n(t)| < P$ *for some number P, or* $\lim_{t\to+\infty} \lambda_n(t)$ *exists, or* $\lim_{t\to+\infty} \lambda_n(t)[z_n(t) - x_n(t)] \leq 0$, *and*

(ii) $\lim_{t\to+\infty} \lambda_n(t) \geq 0$ *for* $n = n_1 + 1, n_1 + 2, \ldots, N$, *and*

(iii) $\lim_{t\to+\infty} \lambda_n(t) z_n(t) = 0$ *for* $n = n_1 + 1, n_1 + 2, \ldots, N$, *and*

(iv) $0 \leq x_n(t) < Q$ *for some number* $Q \in \Re_{++}$ *for* $n = n_1 + 1, n_1 + 2, \ldots, N$,

then $\lim_{t\to+\infty} \boldsymbol{\lambda}(t)'[\mathbf{z}(t) - \mathbf{x}(t)] \leq 0$ *for all admissible* $\mathbf{x}(t)$.

Theorem 14.4 is the Mangasarian sufficiency theorem for unbounded time horizons. Following our discussion in Chapter 6, we now present the necessary conditions for problem (1) using the maximized Hamiltonian, and then the Arrow sufficiency theorem. The proofs of both theorems are by now straightforward and thus will be left as mental exercises.

Theorem 14.5 (Necessary Conditions, Infinite Horizon): *Let* $(\mathbf{z}(t), \mathbf{v}(t))$ *be an admissible pair for problem (1), and assume that the rank constraint qualification is satisfied. Then if* $(\mathbf{z}(t), \mathbf{v}(t))$ *yields the absolute maximum of* $J[\cdot]$, *it is necessary that there exist a piecewise smooth vector-valued function* $\boldsymbol{\lambda}(\cdot) \stackrel{\text{def}}{=} (\lambda_1(\cdot), \lambda_2(\cdot), \ldots, \lambda_N(\cdot))$ *and a piecewise continuous vector-valued Lagrange multiplier function* $\boldsymbol{\mu}(\cdot) \stackrel{\text{def}}{=} (\mu_1(\cdot), \mu_2(\cdot), \ldots, \mu_K(\cdot))$, *such that for all* $t \in [0, +\infty)$,

$$\mathbf{v}(t) = \arg\max_{\mathbf{u}}\{H(t, \mathbf{z}(t), \mathbf{u}, \boldsymbol{\lambda}(t)) \text{ s.t. } \mathbf{u} \in U(t, \mathbf{z}(t))\},$$

that is, if

$$M(t, \mathbf{z}(t), \boldsymbol{\lambda}(t)) \stackrel{\text{def}}{=} \max_{\mathbf{u}}\{H(t, \mathbf{z}(t), \mathbf{u}, \boldsymbol{\lambda}(t)) \text{ s.t. } \mathbf{u} \in U(t, \mathbf{z}(t))\},$$

then

$$M(t, \mathbf{z}(t), \boldsymbol{\lambda}(t)) \equiv H(t, \mathbf{z}(t), \mathbf{v}(t), \boldsymbol{\lambda}(t)),$$

or equivalently

$$H(t, \mathbf{z}(t), \mathbf{v}(t), \boldsymbol{\lambda}(t)) \geq H(t, \mathbf{z}(t), \mathbf{u}, \boldsymbol{\lambda}(t)) \ \forall \ \mathbf{u} \in U(t, \mathbf{z}(t)),$$

where $U(t, \mathbf{x}(t)) \stackrel{\text{def}}{=} \{\mathbf{u}(\cdot) : h^k(t, \mathbf{x}(t)\mathbf{u}(t)) \geq 0,\ k = 1, \ldots, K',\ h^k(t, \mathbf{x}(t), \mathbf{u}(t)) = 0,$ $k = K' + 1, \ldots, K\}$ *and* $\mathbf{v}(t) \stackrel{\text{def}}{=} \hat{\mathbf{u}}(t, \mathbf{z}(t), \boldsymbol{\lambda}(t))$. *Because the rank constraint qualification is assumed to hold, the above necessary condition implies that*

$$\frac{\partial L}{\partial u_m}(t, \mathbf{z}(t), \mathbf{v}(t), \boldsymbol{\lambda}(t), \boldsymbol{\mu}(t)) = 0, \quad m = 1, 2, \ldots, M,$$

$$\frac{\partial L}{\partial \mu_\ell}(t, \mathbf{z}(t), \mathbf{v}(t), \boldsymbol{\lambda}(t), \boldsymbol{\mu}(t)) \geq 0, \quad \mu_\ell(t) \geq 0,$$

$$\mu_\ell(t)\frac{\partial L}{\partial \mu_\ell}(t, \mathbf{z}(t), \mathbf{v}(t), \boldsymbol{\lambda}(t), \boldsymbol{\mu}(t)) = 0, \quad \ell = 1, 2, \ldots, K',$$

$$\frac{\partial L}{\partial \mu_\ell}(t, \mathbf{z}(t), \mathbf{v}(t), \boldsymbol{\lambda}(t), \boldsymbol{\mu}(t)) = 0, \quad \ell = K' + 1, K' + 2, \ldots, K,$$

where

$$\begin{aligned} L(t, \mathbf{x}, \mathbf{u}, \boldsymbol{\lambda}, \boldsymbol{\mu}) \stackrel{\text{def}}{=} H(t, \mathbf{x}, \mathbf{u}, \boldsymbol{\lambda}) + \boldsymbol{\mu}'\mathbf{h}(t, \mathbf{x}, \mathbf{u}) &= f(t, \mathbf{x}, \mathbf{u}) \\ &+ \sum_{n=1}^{N} \lambda_n g^n(t, \mathbf{x}, \mathbf{u}) + \sum_{k=1}^{K} \mu_k h^k(t, \mathbf{x}, \mathbf{u}) \end{aligned}$$

is the Lagrangian. Furthermore, except for the points of discontinuities of $\mathbf{v}(t)$,

$$\dot{z}_i(t) = \frac{\partial M}{\partial \lambda_i}(t, \mathbf{z}(t), \boldsymbol{\lambda}(t)) = g^i(t, \mathbf{z}(t), \mathbf{v}(t)), \quad i = 1, 2, \ldots, N,$$

$$\dot{\lambda}_i(t) = -\frac{\partial M}{\partial x_i}(t, \mathbf{z}(t), \boldsymbol{\lambda}(t)), \quad i = 1, 2, \ldots, N,$$

where the above notation means that the functions are first differentiated with respect to the particular variable and then evaluated at $(t, \mathbf{z}(t), \boldsymbol{\lambda}(t))$.

Theorem 14.6 (Arrow Sufficiency Theorem, Infinite Horizon): *Let* $(\mathbf{z}(t), \mathbf{v}(t))$ *be an admissible pair for problem (1). Suppose that* $(\mathbf{z}(t), \mathbf{v}(t))$ *satisfies the necessary conditions of Theorem 14.5 for problem (1) with costate vector* $\boldsymbol{\lambda}(t)$ *and Lagrange multiplier vector* $\boldsymbol{\mu}(t)$, *and let* $M(t, \mathbf{x}, \boldsymbol{\lambda}) \stackrel{\text{def}}{=} \max_{\mathbf{u}}\{H(t, \mathbf{x}, \mathbf{u}, \boldsymbol{\lambda}) \text{ s.t. } \mathbf{u} \in U(t, \mathbf{x})\}$ *be the value of the maximized Hamiltonian function. If* $M(\cdot)$ *is a concave function* *of* $\mathbf{x}\,\forall\, t \in [0, +\infty)$ *over an open convex set containing all the admissible values of* $\mathbf{x}(\cdot)$ *when the costate vector is* $\boldsymbol{\lambda}(t)$, *and if for every admissible control path* $\mathbf{u}(t)$, $\lim_{t\to+\infty} \boldsymbol{\lambda}(t)'[\mathbf{z}(t) - \mathbf{x}(t)] \leq 0$, *where* $\mathbf{x}(t)$ *is the time path of the state vector corresponding to* $\mathbf{u}(t)$, *then* $\mathbf{v}(t)$ *is an optimal control and* $(\mathbf{z}(t), \mathbf{v}(t))$ *yields the global maximum of* $J[\cdot]$. *If* $M(\cdot)$ *is a strictly concave function of* $\mathbf{x}\,\forall\, t \in [0, +\infty)$ *under the same conditions, then* $(\mathbf{z}(t), \mathbf{v}(t))$ *yields the unique global maximum of* $J[\cdot]$ *and* $\mathbf{z}(t)$ *is unique, but* $\mathbf{v}(t)$ *is not necessarily unique.*

Let's now turn to a detailed examination of the famous Halkin (1974) counterexample, which demonstrates that *in general*, there are no necessary transversality conditions for infinite horizon optimal control problems. It is important to note that initially in this example we will *not* assume that the objective functional converges for all admissible pairs, thereby breaking with a basic maintained assumption of this chapter. We then reexamine the example under the assumption that the objective functional converges for all admissible pairs. Even under this stronger assumption, we will still conclude that the Halkin (1974) counterexample is a valid counterexample for demonstrating that the intuitive transversality condition $\lim_{t+\infty} \lambda(t) = 0$ is not necessary, contrary to the claim of Chiang (1992, Chapter 9).

Example 14.1: The Halkin (1974) counterexample is given by the optimal control problem

$$\max_{u(\cdot)} J[x(\cdot), u(\cdot)] \stackrel{\text{def}}{=} \int_0^{+\infty} u(t)[1 - x(t)]\, dt$$

$$\text{s.t.} \quad \dot{x}(t) = u(t)[1 - x(t)], \; x(0) = 0,$$

$$u(t) \in U \stackrel{\text{def}}{=} \{u(\cdot) : 0 \leq u(t) \leq 1\}.$$

It is worthwhile to emphasize that we are not imposing any conditions on $\lim_{t\to+\infty} x(t)$, so this limit may not even exist. Also recall that at least initially, we are not assuming that $J[x(\cdot), u(\cdot)]$ exists for all admissible function pairs $(x(\cdot), u(\cdot))$.

Given that the constraints on the control variable are independent of the state variable and do not vary with *t*, we do not have to introduce a Lagrangian function in order to compute the necessary conditions. Consequently, we may simply define the Hamiltonian for this problem as $H(x, u, \lambda) \stackrel{\text{def}}{=} u[1 - x] + \lambda\, u[1 - x] = [1 - x][1 + \lambda]\, u$, and then appeal to Theorem 14.3 to compute the necessary conditions:

$$\max_{u\in[0,1]} [1 - x][1 + \lambda]\, u,$$

$$\dot{\lambda} = -H_x(x, u, \lambda) = [1 + \lambda]\, u,$$

$$\dot{x} = H_\lambda(x, u, \lambda) = u\,[1 - x], \; x(0) = 0.$$

Inspection of the objective functional, the state equation, and the initial condition reveals that the objective functional can be expressed as

$$J[x(\cdot), u(\cdot)] \stackrel{\text{def}}{=} \int_0^{+\infty} u(t)[1 - x(t)]\,dt = \int_0^{+\infty} \dot{x}(t)\,dt = \lim_{t\to+\infty} x(t).$$

To get a handle on the value of the objective functional $J[x(\cdot), u(\cdot)]$, therefore, we will first solve the first-order differential equation $\dot{x} = [1 - x]\,u(t)$.

As a first step in this process, separate the variables and rewrite the state equation in differential form as

$$\frac{dx}{1 - x} = u(t)\,dt,$$

which readily integrates to yield

$$-\ln[1 - x] = \int_0^t u(s)\,ds + k,$$

where k is a constant of integration. Note that we have chosen the lower limit of integration to be zero because that is where our initial condition applies. A little bit of straightforward algebra then gives the general solution to the state equation

$$x(t) = 1 - e^{-k} e^{-\int_0^t u(s)\,ds}.$$

The specific solution is found by applying the initial condition $x(0) = 0$ to the above general solution, which implies that $k = 0$. Hence the specific solution of the state equation that satisfies the initial condition is

$$x(t) = 1 - e^{-\omega(t)},$$

where $\omega(t) \stackrel{\text{def}}{=} \int_0^t u(s)\,ds$. This specific solution is admissible for all values of $u(t)$ that satisfy the control constraint, that is, for all $u(t) \in [0, 1]$. Note that $J[x(\cdot), u(\cdot)] = \lim_{t\to+\infty} x(t)$ does not necessarily exist for all admissible pairs, since one could select an admissible control that smoothly oscillates between zero and unity but does not have a limit as $t \to +\infty$. This is consistent with our initial assumption for this example, to wit, that $J[x(\cdot), u(\cdot)]$ does not necessarily exist for all admissible pairs. Also note that because $u(t) \in [0, 1]$ for all $t \in [0, +\infty)$, $x(t) = 1 - e^{-\omega(t)} \in [0, 1)$ for all $t \in [0, +\infty)$.

Given that $J[x(\cdot), u(\cdot)] = \lim_{t\to+\infty} x(t)$ and $u(t) \in [0, 1]\,\forall\, t \in [0, +\infty)$, it follows from the specific solution of the state equation, to wit, $x(t) = 1 - e^{-\omega(t)}$, that *any* admissible control path such that $\omega(t) \stackrel{\text{def}}{=} \int_0^t u(s)\,ds \to +\infty$ as $t \to +\infty$ is optimal, since this implies that $x(t) \to 1$ as $t \to +\infty$, which is its least upper bound, that is, supremum. This observation implies that there are infinitely many optimal controls for this problem. We intend to pick a particularly simple one that will aid in the solution to this problem, namely,

$$v(t) = \frac{1}{2} \; \forall \, t \in [0, +\infty].$$

This optimal control has two nice features: (i) it is constant, and (ii) it is interior to the control region [0, 1]. Given this optimal control, the corresponding state trajectory is therefore given by $z(t) = 1 - e^{-\frac{1}{2}t}$. You are asked to verify the optimality of the pair $(z(t), v(t))$ in a mental exercise. Note that we have yet to find the corresponding time path of the costate variable.

To find $\lambda(t)$, observe that because $v(t) = \frac{1}{2}$ is an optimal control and is in the interior of the control region, it is necessarily a solution to $H_u(z(t), u, \lambda) = [1 - z(t)][1 + \lambda] = 0$. But seeing as $z(t) = 1 - e^{-\frac{1}{2}t} \in [0, 1)$ for all $t \in [0, +\infty]$, it follows that $H_u(z(t), u, \lambda) = [1 - z(t)][1 + \lambda] = 0$ if and only if $1 + \lambda = 0$, thereby implying that $\lambda(t) = -1 \; \forall \, t \in [0, +\infty]$ is the corresponding time path of the costate variable. We conclude, therefore, that $\lim_{t \to +\infty} \lambda(t) = -1$. Recalling that no conditions are placed on $x(t)$ as $t \to +\infty$, we see that the costate function does not satisfy the transversality condition $\lim_{t \to +\infty} \lambda(t) = 0$ that one might expect to hold based on analogy with the finite-horizon case. This example has thus shown that *in general*, there are no necessary transversality conditions. It is important to remember that we have *not* assumed that the objective functional converges for all admissible pairs in reaching this conclusion, and this is what has allowed us to claim the generality of the conclusion concerning the lack of a necessary transversality condition in infinite horizon optimal control problems.

To get some additional qualitative insight into this problem, let's construct the phase portrait corresponding to the canonical differential equations in the $x\lambda$-phase space. Recalling that $v(t) = \frac{1}{2}$ is an optimal control, the canonical differential equations are given by $\dot{\lambda} = \frac{1}{2}[1 + \lambda]$ and $\dot{x} = \frac{1}{2}[1 - x]$. Hence the nullclines are given by

$$\dot{x} = 0 \quad \Leftrightarrow \quad x = 1,$$

$$\dot{\lambda} = 0 \quad \Leftrightarrow \quad \lambda = -1.$$

Because $\dot{\lambda} = \frac{1}{2}[1 + \lambda]$, it follows that $\dot{\lambda} > 0$ if and only if $\lambda > -1$. Similarly, because $\dot{x} = \frac{1}{2}[1 - x]$, it follows that $\dot{x} > 0$ if and only if $x < 1$. These observations yield the vector field for the canonical equations, and Figure 14.1 depicts the completed phase diagram.

The steady state or fixed point of the canonical equations is $(x^s, \lambda^s) = (1, -1)$, as is easily verified. Notice that two paths converge to the fixed point and that both occur along the $\dot{\lambda} = 0$ isocline, whereas all other paths diverge from the steady state. The phase diagram therefore suggests that the fixed point is a saddle point, with the stable manifold given by the λ nullcline and the unstable manifold given

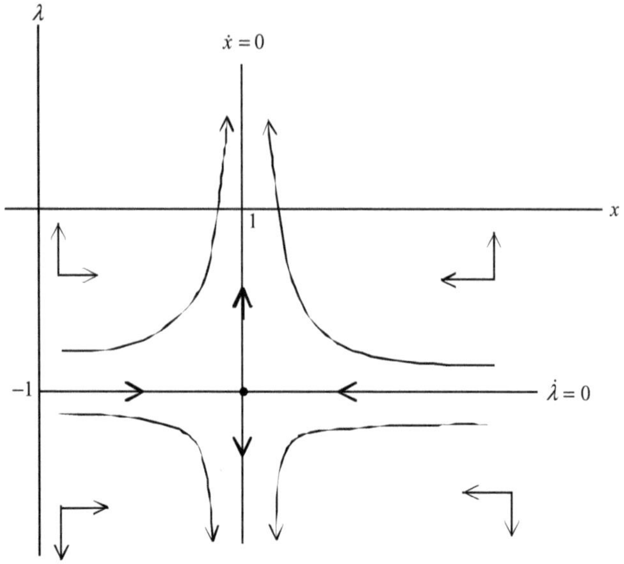

Figure 14.1

by the x nullcline. You are asked to prove that this is in fact the case in a mental exercise. Given that $x(0) = 0$, the optimal path is the one that at $t = 0$ has the value $(x, \lambda) = (0, -1)$, and goes to $(x^s, \lambda^s) = (1, -1)$ as $t \to +\infty$. Any path that does not begin at $(x, \lambda) = (0, -1)$ is not optimal because such paths have $\lambda(t) \to \pm\infty$ as $t \to +\infty$, and we know that $\lambda(t) = -1$ corresponds to the optimal pair.

Let us reconsider our conclusions under the assumption that $J[x(\cdot), u(\cdot)]$ exists for all admissible pairs of functions $(x(\cdot), u(\cdot))$, a basic assumption we have maintained throughout this chapter. As derived earlier, $x(t) = 1 - e^{-\omega(t)}$, where $\omega(t) \stackrel{\text{def}}{=} \int_0^t u(s)\,ds$, is the specific solution of the state equation. It therefore represents all the admissible time paths of the state variable when $u(t) \in [0, 1]$ for all $t \in [0, +\infty]$. Because $J[x(\cdot), u(\cdot)] = \lim_{t\to+\infty} x(t)$, the additional assumption that $J[x(\cdot), u(\cdot)]$ exists for all admissible pairs of functions $(x(\cdot), u(\cdot))$ furthermore requires that $\lim_{t\to+\infty} x(t)$ exist for all admissible pairs, thereby ruling out, for example, control paths that smoothly oscillate between zero and unity but do not have a limit as $t \to +\infty$. Thus the piecewise continuous infinite family of control functions $u(\cdot)$ defined by

$$u(t) \stackrel{\text{def}}{=} \begin{cases} k \in [0, 1] \ \forall t \in [0, \tau], \ \tau < +\infty \\ 0 \qquad\qquad \forall t \in (\tau, +\infty) \end{cases}$$

is admissible and generates a corresponding infinite family of admissible state variable time paths given by $x(t) = 1 - e^{-\omega(t)}$, where $\omega(t) \stackrel{\text{def}}{=} \int_0^t u(s)\,ds$. Moreover, for each member of this family of control functions, $\lim_{t\to+\infty} x(t)$ exists and equals a *different* value depending on the value of the constant k. In other words, the admissible time paths of the state variable do not converge to the same limiting value, thereby implying that the Halkin counterexample does *not* have a fixed terminal endpoint under the assumption that the objective functional exists for all admissible pairs, contrary to the claims of Chiang (1992, p. 246). Thus the Halkin counterexample remains a true counterexample to the necessity of the transversality condition $\lim_{t+\infty} \lambda(t) = 0$. This observation finishes up our examination of the Halkin counterexample.

Let's now contemplate the slightly less general class of infinite horizon optimal control problems defined by

$$V(\boldsymbol{\alpha}, r, 0, \mathbf{x}_0) \stackrel{\text{def}}{=} \max_{\mathbf{u}(\cdot)} \int_0^{+\infty} f(\mathbf{x}(t), \mathbf{u}(t); \boldsymbol{\alpha})\, e^{-rt}\, dt$$

$$\text{s.t.} \quad \dot{\mathbf{x}}(t) = \mathbf{g}(\mathbf{x}(t), \mathbf{u}(t); \boldsymbol{\alpha}), \;\; \mathbf{x}(0) = \mathbf{x}_0, \tag{9}$$

$$\lim_{t \to +\infty} x_n(t) = x_n^s, \quad n = 1, 2, \ldots, n_1,$$

$$\lim_{t \to +\infty} x_n(t) \geq x_n^s, \quad n = n_1 + 1, n_1 + 2, \ldots, n_2,$$

$$\text{no conditions on } x_n(t) \text{ as } t \to +\infty, \quad n = n_2 + 1, n_2 + 2, \ldots, N,$$

$$h^k(\mathbf{x}(t), \mathbf{u}(t); \boldsymbol{\alpha}) \geq 0, \quad k = 1, 2, \ldots, K',$$

$$h^k(\mathbf{x}(t), \mathbf{u}(t); \boldsymbol{\alpha}) = 0, \quad k = K' + 1, K' + 2, \ldots, K.$$

It is important to observe that for this class of optimal control problems, the functions $f(\cdot)$, $\mathbf{g}(\cdot)$, and $\mathbf{h}(\cdot)$ do not depend explicitly on the independent variable t. The zero appearing as the third argument of the *current value* optimal value function $V(\cdot)$ is placed there explicitly to reflect the fact that the initial time or starting date is $t = 0$ in problem (9). It is imperative that you understand why $V(\cdot)$ is the current value (as opposed to present value) optimal value function. As you may recall from Chapter 12, one simple way to understand why is to recognize that at the initial date of the planning horizon ($t = 0$), the value of the discount factor is unity, thereby implying that no discounting takes place in the initial period, the time period in which the decisions are made. This means that all future values of the integrand are discounted back to the initial date of the planning horizon ($t = 0$). This class of optimal control problems is known as the *infinite-horizon current-value autonomous* variety, because when put in current value form, the canonical equations do not depend explicitly on the independent variable t, a fact we established in Theorem 12.2. Without a doubt, this is the most prevalent class of optimal control problems in dynamic economic theory. Note that we continue to assume that the objective functional converges for all admissible pairs.

In order to establish several important results about this class of control problems, we introduce the following *family of control problems*, parameterized by the starting date $t_0 \in [0, +\infty)$:

$$V(\boldsymbol{\alpha}, r, t_0, \mathbf{x}_0) \stackrel{\text{def}}{=} \max_{\mathbf{u}(\cdot)} \int_{t_0}^{+\infty} f(\mathbf{x}(t-t_0), \mathbf{u}(t-t_0); \boldsymbol{\alpha})\, e^{-r(t-t_0)}\, dt$$

$$\text{s.t.}\quad \dot{\mathbf{x}}(t-t_0) = \mathbf{g}(\mathbf{x}(t-t_0), \mathbf{u}(t-t_0); \boldsymbol{\alpha}),\quad \mathbf{x}(t-t_0)|_{t=t_0} = \mathbf{x}_0, \tag{10}$$

$$\lim_{t\to+\infty} x_n(t-t_0) = x_n^s, \quad n = 1, 2, \ldots, n_1,$$

$$\lim_{t\to+\infty} x_n(t-t_0) \geq x_n^s, \quad n = n_1+1, n_1+2, \ldots, n_2,$$

$$\text{no conditions on } x_n(t-t_0) \text{ as } t \to +\infty, \quad n = n_2+1, n_2+2, \ldots, N,$$

$$h^k(\mathbf{x}(t-t_0), \mathbf{u}(t-t_0); \boldsymbol{\alpha}) \geq 0, \quad k = 1, 2, \ldots, K',$$

$$h^k(\mathbf{x}(t-t_0), \mathbf{u}(t-t_0); \boldsymbol{\alpha}) = 0, \quad k = K'+1, K'+2, \ldots, K.$$

Notice that in advancing the starting date from 0 in problem (9) to t_0 in problem (10), we have correspondingly subtracted t_0 from the independent variable t wherever the latter occurs in the problem, whether that be explicitly in the exponential discount factor or implicitly as the argument of the state and control variables. Such an operation implies that the value of the current value optimal value functions in problems (9) and (10) are identically equal. This follows from the facts that both problems (i) begin in state $\mathbf{x}_0$, (ii) last indefinitely, (iii) have identical integrand and transition functions, and (iv) the delay prompted by starting problem (10) at time t_0 is exactly compensated for by a forward translation of t_0 units in the time dimension of every state and control variable and the discount function. In passing, note that problem (9) can be generated from problem (10) by setting $t_0 = 0$ in the latter.

To prove that $V(\boldsymbol{\alpha}, r, t_0, \mathbf{x}_0) \equiv V(\boldsymbol{\alpha}, r, 0, \mathbf{x}_0)\, \forall\, t_0 \in [0, +\infty)$ in a formal manner, first define a new variable $s \stackrel{\text{def}}{=} t - t_0$, which is precisely the forward translation of t_0 units in the time dimension noted above. It then follows that $t = t_0 \Leftrightarrow s = 0$, $t \to +\infty \Leftrightarrow s \to +\infty$, and that $ds = dt$, since t_0 is a given parameter. Substituting these results in problem (10) gives an *equivalent* representation of it, scilicet,

$$V(\boldsymbol{\alpha}, r, t_0, \mathbf{x}_0) \stackrel{\text{def}}{=} \max_{\mathbf{u}(\cdot)} \int_{0}^{+\infty} f(\mathbf{x}(s), \mathbf{u}(s); \boldsymbol{\alpha})\, e^{-rs}\, ds$$

$$\text{s.t.}\quad \dot{\mathbf{x}}(s) = \mathbf{g}(\mathbf{x}(s), \mathbf{u}(s); \boldsymbol{\alpha}),\quad \mathbf{x}(s)|_{s=0} = \mathbf{x}_0, \tag{11}$$

$$\lim_{s\to+\infty} x_n(s) = x_n^s, \quad n = 1, 2, \ldots, n_1,$$

$$\lim_{s\to+\infty} x_n(s) \geq x_n^s, \quad n = n_1+1, n_1+2, \ldots, n_2,$$

$$\text{no conditions on } x_n(s) \text{ as } s \to +\infty, \quad n = n_2+1, n_2+2, \ldots, N,$$

$$h^k(\mathbf{x}(s), \mathbf{u}(s); \boldsymbol{\alpha}) \geq 0, \quad k = 1, 2, \ldots, K',$$

$$h^k(\mathbf{x}(s), \mathbf{u}(s); \boldsymbol{\alpha}) = 0, \quad k = K'+1, K'+2, \ldots, K.$$

Observing that the independent variables t in problem (9) and s in problem (11) are dummy variables of integration and hence arbitrary, it follows that optimal control problems (9) and (11) are identical. This, in turn, implies that the value of their respective current value optimal value functions are identical too, thereby yielding the identity $V(\alpha, r, t_0, \mathbf{x}_0) \equiv V(\alpha, r, 0, \mathbf{x}_0) \forall t_0 \in [0, +\infty)$, just as we wished to show. Given that the identity holds *for all* $t_0 \in [0, +\infty)$, this implies that the current value optimal value function $V(\cdot)$ *does not depend explicitly* on the initial date or starting time t_0. To see this in perhaps a more transparent way, recall that $\mathbf{x}(t_0) = \mathbf{x}_0$ and substitute it into the identity $V(\alpha, r, t_0, \mathbf{x}_0) \equiv V(\alpha, r, 0, \mathbf{x}_0) \forall t_0 \in [0, +\infty)$ to arrive at the alternative, but equivalent, identity $V(\alpha, r, t_0, \mathbf{x}(t_0)) \equiv V(\alpha, r, 0, \mathbf{x}(t_0)) \forall t_0 \in [0, +\infty)$. This latter form of the identity should make it clear that $V(\cdot)$ does not vary with direct or explicit changes in t_0, since the third argument of the right-hand-side of the identity is zero. The change in the value of $V(\cdot)$ that comes about by changing the initial time t_0 is thus solely a result of $\mathbf{x}(t_0) = \mathbf{x}_0$ changing with the initial time t_0. As a result, we are justified in dropping the explicit argument t_0 of $V(\cdot)$, and therefore may write its value as $V(\alpha, r, \mathbf{x}_0)$, a practice we shall adhere to from now on. This is a crucial property of the *current value* optimal value function because it paves the way for dynamic duality theory in an ensuing chapter. In sum, therefore, the value of the current value optimal value function depends on the initial value of the state vector, the discount rate, and the parameter vector, but *not* explicitly on the initial date or starting time.

Using problem (10) as a benchmark, we may now define the *present value* optimal value function $\hat{V}(\cdot)$ by the following problem:

$$\hat{V}(\alpha, r, t_0, \mathbf{x}_0) \stackrel{\text{def}}{=} \max_{\mathbf{u}(\cdot)} e^{-rt_0} \int_{t_0}^{+\infty} f(\mathbf{x}(t - t_0), \mathbf{u}(t - t_0); \alpha)\, e^{-r(t-t_0)}\, dt$$

$$\text{s.t.} \quad \dot{\mathbf{x}}(t - t_0) = \mathbf{g}(\mathbf{x}(t - t_0), \mathbf{u}(t - t_0); \alpha), \quad \mathbf{x}(t - t_0)|_{t=t_0} = \mathbf{x}_0, \tag{12}$$

$$\lim_{t \to +\infty} x_n(t - t_0) = x_n^s, \quad n = 1, 2, \ldots, n_1,$$

$$\lim_{t \to +\infty} x_n(t - t_0) \geq x_n^s, \quad n = n_1 + 1, n_1 + 2, \ldots, n_2,$$

$$\text{no conditions on } x_n(t - t_0) \text{ as } t \to +\infty, \quad n = n_2 + 1, n_2 + 2, \ldots, N,$$

$$h^k(\mathbf{x}(t - t_0), \mathbf{u}(t - t_0); \alpha) \geq 0, \quad k = 1, 2, \ldots, K',$$

$$h^k(\mathbf{x}(t - t_0), \mathbf{u}(t - t_0); \alpha) = 0, \quad k = K' + 1, K' + 2, \ldots, K.$$

It should be evident from inspection of problem (12) that the value of the integral is discounted to time t_0, whereas the presence of the discount factor e^{-rt_0} in front of the integral further discounts these values back to time $t = 0$. It is this observation that justifies the use of the adjective present value in describing the function $\hat{V}(\cdot)$. That is, although the initial period in problem (12) is t_0, the values of the objective functional are discounted back to time $t = 0$, hence making $\hat{V}(\cdot)$ the present value optimal value function. Defining $s \stackrel{\text{def}}{=} t - t_0$, just as we did above, we may rewrite problem (12) in an *equivalent* manner, namely,

$$
\begin{aligned}
\hat{V}(\boldsymbol{\alpha}, r, t_0, \mathbf{x}_0) &\stackrel{\text{def}}{=} e^{-rt_0} \max_{\mathbf{u}(\cdot)} \int_0^{+\infty} f(\mathbf{x}(s), \mathbf{u}(s); \boldsymbol{\alpha})\, e^{-rs}\, ds \\
\text{s.t. } & \dot{\mathbf{x}}(s) = \mathbf{g}(\mathbf{x}(s), \mathbf{u}(s); \boldsymbol{\alpha}), \ \ \mathbf{x}(s)|_{s=0} = \mathbf{x}_0, \\
& \lim_{s \to +\infty} x_n(s) = x_n^s, \quad n = 1, 2, \ldots, n_1, \\
& \lim_{s \to +\infty} x_n(s) \geq x_n^s, \quad n = n_1 + 1, n_1 + 2, \ldots, n_2, \\
& \text{no conditions on } x_n(s) \text{ as } s \to +\infty, \quad n = n_2 + 1, n_2 + 2, \ldots, N, \\
& h^k(\mathbf{x}(s), \mathbf{u}(s); \boldsymbol{\alpha}) \geq 0, \quad k = 1, 2, \ldots, K', \\
& h^k(\mathbf{x}(s), \mathbf{u}(s); \boldsymbol{\alpha}) = 0, \quad k = K' + 1, K' + 2, \ldots, K.
\end{aligned} \tag{13}
$$

Because of the presence of the discount factor e^{-rt_0} in problem (13), it follows that in general, the present value optimal value function $\hat{V}(\cdot)$ depends explicitly on the initial date or starting time t_0, in sharp contrast with the current value optimal value function $V(\cdot)$. Upon inspecting problems (11) and (13), and recalling the fact that $V(\cdot)$ does not depend explicitly on t_0, it should be clear that the identity $\hat{V}(\boldsymbol{\alpha}, r, t_0, \mathbf{x}_0) \equiv e^{-rt_0} V(\boldsymbol{\alpha}, r, \mathbf{x}_0)\, \forall\, t_0 \in [0, +\infty)$ also holds. This is an intuitive result, for it asserts that the value of the present value optimal value function is identically equal to the value of the current value optimal value function discounted back to time $t = 0$. Hence when $t_0 = 0$, the values of the present value and current value optimal value functions are one and the same. We pause momentarily and summarize the two results thus far established for this class of control problems.

Theorem 14.7: *Let $V(\cdot)$ be defined as in problem (10) and let $\hat{V}(\cdot)$ be defined as in problem (12). Then (i) the current value optimal value function $V(\cdot)$ does not depend explicitly on the initial time t_0, $\forall\, t_0 \in [0, +\infty)$, and (ii) $\hat{V}(\boldsymbol{\alpha}, r, t_0, \mathbf{x}_0) \equiv e^{-rt_0} V(\boldsymbol{\alpha}, r, \mathbf{x}_0)\, \forall\, t_0 \in [0, +\infty)$.*

The ensuing result is an implication of part (i) of Theorem 14.7. Its proof, which you are asked to provide in a mental exercise, will test if you have fully internalized the results of Theorem 14.7 and the necessary conditions for problems (9) and (10).

Corollary 14.1: *In optimal control problems (9) and (10), the optimal values of the current value costate function, the optimal control function, and the Lagrange multiplier function at any time t can be expressed solely as functions of the corresponding value of the state vector at time t and the parameters $(\boldsymbol{\alpha}, r)$.*

It is worthwhile to emphasize that Theorem 14.7(i), and consequently Corollary 14.1, do not hold for the finite-horizon version of optimal control problems (9) and

(10), nor do they hold if any of the functions $f(\cdot)$, $\mathbf{g}(\cdot)$, or $\mathbf{h}(\cdot)$ are explicit functions of the independent variable t and time consistency of the optimal plan is assumed. A mental exercise probes these aspects more deeply.

In wrapping up this chapter, let us consider a further simplification of the general optimal control problem (1), namely,

$$V(\alpha, r, \mathbf{x}_0) \stackrel{\text{def}}{=} \max_{\mathbf{u}(\cdot)} \int_0^{+\infty} f(\mathbf{x}(t), \mathbf{u}(t); \alpha)\, e^{-rt}\, dt \tag{14}$$

$$\text{s.t.} \quad \dot{\mathbf{x}}(t) = \mathbf{g}(\mathbf{x}(t), \mathbf{u}(t); \alpha), \ \ \mathbf{x}(0) = \mathbf{x}_0,$$

where *no conditions* are imposed on $x_n(t)$ as $t \to +\infty$, $n = 1, 2, \ldots, N$. We continue to assume that the objective functional converges for all admissible pairs. Our goals in the remainder of this chapter are to (i) derive a fundamental equation for problem (14) linking the value of the current value optimal value function to the value of the current value maximized Hamiltonian, (ii) derive a general transversality condition that is necessary for the class of optimal control problems defined by problem (14), and (iii) revisit the dynamic envelope theorem.

To begin, let $(\mathbf{z}(t;\beta), \mathbf{v}(t;\beta))$ be the optimal pair for problem (14), and let $\boldsymbol{\lambda}(t;\beta)$ be the corresponding current value costate vector, where $\beta \stackrel{\text{def}}{=} (\alpha, r, \mathbf{x}_0)$. Then for *any* $\tau \in [0, +\infty)$, it follows from the definition of $V(\cdot)$ in Eq. (14), the fact that an integral is additive with respect to the limits of integration, and the principle of optimality that

$$V(\alpha, r, \mathbf{x}_0) = \int_0^{\tau} f(\mathbf{z}(t;\beta), \mathbf{v}(t;\beta); \alpha)\, e^{-rt}\, dt + e^{-r\tau} V(\alpha, r, \mathbf{z}(\tau;\beta)). \tag{15}$$

Because Eq. (15) holds for all $\tau \in [0, +\infty)$, that is, it is an *identity* in τ, we may differentiate it with respect to τ and it still holds identically. Doing just that, we obtain

$$\begin{aligned} 0 = {} & f(\mathbf{z}(\tau;\beta), \mathbf{v}(\tau;\beta); \alpha)\, e^{-r\tau} - re^{-r\tau} V(\alpha, r, \mathbf{z}(\tau;\beta)) \\ & + e^{-r\tau} V_{\mathbf{x}}(\alpha, r, \mathbf{z}(\tau;\beta))\, \dot{\mathbf{z}}(\tau;\beta). \end{aligned}$$

Upon multiplying through by $e^{r\tau}$ and using the necessary condition $\dot{\mathbf{z}}(\tau;\beta) \equiv \mathbf{g}(\mathbf{z}(\tau;\beta), \mathbf{v}(\tau;\beta); \alpha)$, the above equation simplifies to

$$\begin{aligned} rV(\alpha, r, \mathbf{z}(\tau;\beta)) = {} & f(\mathbf{z}(\tau;\beta), \mathbf{v}(\tau;\beta); \alpha) \\ & + V_{\mathbf{x}}(\alpha, r, \mathbf{z}(\tau;\beta))\, \mathbf{g}(\mathbf{z}(\tau;\beta), \mathbf{v}(\tau;\beta); \alpha). \end{aligned} \tag{16}$$

Now recall that $V_{\mathbf{x}}(\alpha, r, \mathbf{z}(\tau;\beta))$ is the current value costate vector $\boldsymbol{\lambda}(\tau;\beta)'$ by the dynamic envelope theorem and the principle of optimality, and that the maximized current value Hamiltonian for problem (14) is defined as

$$M(\mathbf{x}, \boldsymbol{\lambda}; \alpha) \stackrel{\text{def}}{=} \max_{\mathbf{u}} H(\mathbf{x}, \mathbf{u}, \boldsymbol{\lambda}; \alpha),$$

where $H(\mathbf{x}, \mathbf{u}, \boldsymbol{\lambda}; \boldsymbol{\alpha}) \stackrel{\text{def}}{=} f(\mathbf{x}, \mathbf{u}; \boldsymbol{\alpha}) + \boldsymbol{\lambda}'\mathbf{g}(\mathbf{x}, \mathbf{u}; \boldsymbol{\alpha})$ is the current value Hamiltonian for problem (14). These two observations therefore permit Eq. (16) to be rewritten as

$$rV(\boldsymbol{\alpha}, r, \mathbf{z}(\tau; \boldsymbol{\beta})) = M(\mathbf{z}(\tau; \boldsymbol{\beta}), \boldsymbol{\lambda}(\tau; \boldsymbol{\beta}); \boldsymbol{\alpha}), \tag{17}$$

or equivalently as

$$rV(\boldsymbol{\alpha}, r, \mathbf{z}(\tau; \boldsymbol{\beta})) = H(\mathbf{z}(\tau; \boldsymbol{\beta}), \mathbf{v}(\tau; \boldsymbol{\beta}), \boldsymbol{\lambda}(\tau; \boldsymbol{\beta}); \boldsymbol{\alpha}), \tag{18}$$

both of which hold for all $\tau \in [0, +\infty)$. We have therefore established an important relationship between the value of the current value optimal value function and the value of the maximized current value Hamiltonian evaluated at the optimal solution. Equations (17) and (18) are known as the *Hamilton-Jacobi-Bellman* equation. You may recall that we derived another, more general form of the Hamilton-Jacobi-Bellman equation in our rigorous proof of the Maximum Principle in Chapter 4. As alluded to earlier, this equation plays a fundamental role in dynamic duality theory, as we shall see in two ensuing chapters. We summarize this fundamental result in the following theorem.

Theorem 14.8 (Hamilton-Jacobi-Bellman Equation): *Let $(\mathbf{z}(t; \boldsymbol{\beta}), \mathbf{v}(t; \boldsymbol{\beta}))$ be the optimal pair for problem (14), and let $\boldsymbol{\lambda}(t; \boldsymbol{\beta})$ be the corresponding current value costate vector, where $\boldsymbol{\beta} \stackrel{\text{def}}{=} (\boldsymbol{\alpha}, r, \mathbf{x}_0)$. Define $V(\cdot)$ by problem (14), assume that $V_{\mathbf{x}}(\cdot) \in C^{(0)}$, and let $M(\cdot)$ be the corresponding maximized current value Hamiltonian function. Then for all $\tau \in [0, +\infty)$,*

$$rV(\boldsymbol{\alpha}, r, \mathbf{z}(\tau; \boldsymbol{\beta})) = M(\mathbf{z}(\tau; \boldsymbol{\beta}), \boldsymbol{\lambda}(\tau; \boldsymbol{\beta}); \boldsymbol{\alpha}),$$

or equivalently,

$$rV(\boldsymbol{\alpha}, r, \mathbf{z}(\tau; \boldsymbol{\beta})) = H(\mathbf{z}(\tau; \boldsymbol{\beta}), \mathbf{v}(\tau; \boldsymbol{\beta}), \boldsymbol{\lambda}(\tau; \boldsymbol{\beta}); \boldsymbol{\alpha}).$$

Let's now turn to the derivation of a general transversality condition that is necessary for the class of problems defined by Eq. (14). To that end, first recall the result of Theorem 14.7(ii), namely, the identity $\hat{V}(\boldsymbol{\alpha}, r, t_0, \mathbf{x}_0) \equiv e^{-rt_0} V(\boldsymbol{\alpha}, r, \mathbf{x}_0)\, \forall\, t_0 \in [0, +\infty)$, which clearly applies to problem (14) as it is a special case of problem (10). Substituting $\mathbf{x}(t_0) = \mathbf{x}_0$ in the identity and then letting $t_0 \to +\infty$ gives

$$\lim_{t_0 \to +\infty} \hat{V}(\boldsymbol{\alpha}, r, t_0, \mathbf{x}(t_0)) \equiv \lim_{t_0 \to +\infty} e^{-rt_0} V(\boldsymbol{\alpha}, r, \mathbf{x}(t_0)) = 0,$$

since $V(\cdot)$ exists for all admissible pairs. Replacing t_0 with τ and applying this result to Theorem 14.8 gives

$$\lim_{\tau \to +\infty} e^{-r\tau} M(\mathbf{z}(\tau; \boldsymbol{\beta}), \boldsymbol{\lambda}(\tau; \boldsymbol{\beta}); \boldsymbol{\alpha}) = \lim_{\tau \to +\infty} re^{-r\tau} V(\boldsymbol{\alpha}, r, \mathbf{z}(\tau; \boldsymbol{\beta})) = 0, \tag{19}$$

which is the necessary transversality condition we were after for the class of optimal control problems defined by problem (14). Equation (19) asserts that along the optimal path of problem (14), the *present value* of the maximized Hamiltonian goes to zero as time goes to infinity. Note that because we used Theorem 14.8 in the proof of this transversality condition, we have therefore assumed that $V_{\mathbf{x}}(\cdot) \in C^{(0)}$.

An alternative, and possibly more intuitive, proof follows from Eq. (15). Given that the value $V(\alpha, r, \mathbf{x}_0)$ is independent of τ, take the limit of Eq. (15) as $\tau \to +\infty$ to get

$$\begin{aligned}
V(\alpha, r, \mathbf{x}_0) &= \lim_{\tau\to+\infty}\left[\int_0^\tau f(\mathbf{z}(t;\beta), \mathbf{v}(t;\beta);\alpha)\, e^{-rt}\,dt + e^{-r\tau}V(\alpha, r, \mathbf{z}(\tau;\beta))\right]\\
&= \lim_{\tau\to+\infty}\int_0^\tau f(\mathbf{z}(t;\beta), \mathbf{v}(t;\beta);\alpha)\, e^{-rt}\,dt + \lim_{\tau\to+\infty} e^{-r\tau}V(\alpha, r, \mathbf{z}(\tau;\beta))\\
&= \int_0^{+\infty} f(\mathbf{z}(t;\beta), \mathbf{v}(t;\beta);\alpha)\, e^{-rt}\,dt + \lim_{\tau\to+\infty} e^{-r\tau}V(\alpha, r, \mathbf{z}(\tau;\beta))\\
&= V(\alpha, r, \mathbf{x}_0) + \lim_{\tau\to+\infty} e^{-r\tau}V(\alpha, r, \mathbf{z}(\tau;\beta)).
\end{aligned}$$

Note that we have used the definition of $V(\cdot)$ from Eq. (14) and the fact that $V(\cdot)$ is assumed to exist for all admissible pairs. Upon canceling $V(\alpha, r, \mathbf{x}_0)$ from both sides of the above equation, we arrive at the result $\lim_{\tau\to+\infty} e^{-r\tau}V(\alpha, r, \mathbf{z}(\tau;\beta)) = 0$. Applying this result to Theorem 14.8 yields the transversality condition $\lim_{\tau\to+\infty} e^{-r\tau}M(\mathbf{z}(\tau;\beta), \boldsymbol{\lambda}(\tau;\beta);\alpha) = 0$, just as in the previous proof. We summarize this important result in the following theorem.

Theorem 14.9 (Transversality Condition): *Let $(\mathbf{z}(t;\beta), \mathbf{v}(t;\beta))$ be the optimal pair for problem (14), and let $\boldsymbol{\lambda}(t;\beta)$ be the corresponding current value costate vector, where $\beta \stackrel{\text{def}}{=} (\alpha, r, \mathbf{x}_0)$. Let $M(\cdot)$ be the maximized current value Hamiltonian function for problem (14). Then*

$$\lim_{\tau\to+\infty} e^{-r\tau}M(\mathbf{z}(\tau;\beta), \boldsymbol{\lambda}(\tau;\beta);\alpha) = 0,$$

or equivalently,

$$\lim_{\tau\to+\infty} e^{-r\tau}H(\mathbf{z}(\tau;\beta), \mathbf{v}(\tau;\beta), \boldsymbol{\lambda}(\tau;\beta);\alpha) = 0,$$

is a necessary condition for problem (14).

Rather than present an example that uses Theorem 14.9 here, we prefer to use it in the following three chapters when we study several fundamental dynamic economics models.

For the final theorem of this chapter, we return to the dynamic envelope theorem. We reexamine this central theorem for the class of optimal control problems defined by problem (14) and its associated assumptions, a ubiquitous class of control problems in dynamic economic theory. As a result, we now impose the ensuing assumptions on the functions $f(\cdot)$ and $\mathbf{g}(\cdot)$:

(A.1) $f(\cdot) \in C^{(1)}$ with respect to the $N + M$ variables $(\mathbf{x}, \mathbf{u})$ and the A parameters $\boldsymbol{\alpha}$.

(A.2) $\mathbf{g}(\cdot) \in C^{(1)}$ with respect to the $N + M$ variables $(\mathbf{x}, \mathbf{u})$ and the A parameters $\boldsymbol{\alpha}$.

Given these additional assumptions, we are now in a position to state the dynamic envelope theorem for the discounted infinite horizon class of optimal control problems defined by problem (14). The proof of the theorem is left for a mental exercise.

Theorem 14.10 (Dynamic Envelope Theorem): *Let* $(\mathbf{z}(t;\boldsymbol{\beta}), \mathbf{v}(t;\boldsymbol{\beta}))$, $\boldsymbol{\beta} \stackrel{\text{def}}{=} (\boldsymbol{\alpha}, r, \mathbf{x}_0)$, *be the optimal pair for problem (14), with the property that as* $t \to +\infty$, $(\mathbf{z}(t;\boldsymbol{\beta}), \mathbf{v}(t;\boldsymbol{\beta})) \to (\mathbf{x}^s(\boldsymbol{\alpha}, r), \mathbf{u}^s(\boldsymbol{\alpha}, r))$, *where* $(\mathbf{x}^s(\boldsymbol{\alpha}, r), \mathbf{u}^s(\boldsymbol{\alpha}, r))$ *is the locally* $C^{(1)}$ *steady state solution of the necessary conditions, and let* $\boldsymbol{\lambda}^{pv}(t;\boldsymbol{\beta}) \stackrel{\text{def}}{=} \boldsymbol{\lambda}(t;\boldsymbol{\beta})e^{-rt}$ *be the corresponding time path of the present value costate vector. Define the present value Hamiltonian as* $H^{pv}(t, \mathbf{x}, \mathbf{u}, \boldsymbol{\lambda}^{pv}; \boldsymbol{\alpha}) \stackrel{\text{def}}{=} f(\mathbf{x}, \mathbf{u}; \boldsymbol{\alpha})e^{-rt} + \sum_{\ell=1}^{N} \lambda_\ell^{pv} g^\ell(\mathbf{x}, \mathbf{u}; \boldsymbol{\alpha})$. *If* $\mathbf{z}(\cdot) \in C^{(1)}$ *and* $\mathbf{v}(\cdot) \in C^{(1)}$ *in* $(t;\boldsymbol{\beta})\,\forall\,(t;\boldsymbol{\beta}) \in [0, +\infty) \times B(\boldsymbol{\beta}^\circ;\delta)$, *then* $V(\cdot) \in C^{(1)}\,\forall\,\boldsymbol{\beta} \in B(\boldsymbol{\beta}^\circ;\delta)$. *Furthermore, if* $\partial\mathbf{z}(t;\boldsymbol{\beta})/\partial\boldsymbol{\beta} \to \partial\mathbf{x}^s(\boldsymbol{\alpha}, r)/\partial\boldsymbol{\beta}$ *as* $t \to +\infty$, *then for all* $\boldsymbol{\beta} \in B(\boldsymbol{\beta}^\circ;\delta)$:

$$V_{\alpha_i}(\boldsymbol{\beta}) \stackrel{\text{def}}{=} \frac{\partial V(\boldsymbol{\beta})}{\partial \alpha_i} \equiv \int_0^{+\infty} H^{pv}_{\alpha_i}(\mathbf{z}(t;\boldsymbol{\beta}), \mathbf{v}(t;\boldsymbol{\beta}), \boldsymbol{\lambda}^{pv}(t;\boldsymbol{\beta}); \boldsymbol{\alpha})\, dt, \quad i = 1, 2, \ldots, A, \tag{i}$$

$$V_r(\boldsymbol{\beta}) \equiv \int_0^{+\infty} -tf(\mathbf{z}(t;\boldsymbol{\beta}), \mathbf{v}(t;\boldsymbol{\beta}); \boldsymbol{\alpha})\, e^{-rt}\, dt, \tag{ii}$$

$$V_{x_{0j}}(\boldsymbol{\beta}) \equiv \lambda_j^{pv}(0;\boldsymbol{\beta}) = \lambda_j(0;\boldsymbol{\beta}), \quad j = 1, 2, \ldots, N. \tag{iii}$$

Several remarks concerning the proof of Theorem 14.10 are in order. First, inasmuch as $V(\cdot)$ is defined by an improper integral, which we have assumed to exist for all admissible pairs of functions, an alternative version of Leibniz's rule must be used in the proof. This version of Leibniz's rule, appropriate for improper integrals, is given in the appendix to this chapter as Theorem A.14.1. Second, as part of the proof, one must establish that the current value costate vector $\boldsymbol{\lambda}(t;\boldsymbol{\beta})$ converges to its steady state solution $\boldsymbol{\lambda}^s(\boldsymbol{\alpha}, r)$ in the limit of the planning horizon. This result, in conjunction with the assumption that as $t \to +\infty$, $\partial\mathbf{z}(t;\boldsymbol{\beta})/\partial\boldsymbol{\beta} \to \partial\mathbf{x}^s(\boldsymbol{\alpha}, r)/\partial\boldsymbol{\beta}$, is crucial in eliminating an inner product expression resulting from the integration-by-parts operation. Finally, note that one may easily rewrite Theorem 14.10 using the current value Hamiltonian.

One purpose of this chapter has been to introduce necessary and sufficient conditions for a general optimal control problem with an infinite planning horizon. For the most part, these theorems are very similar to their finite horizon counterparts, the necessary transversality conditions being the exception. We demonstrated via the Halkin (1974) counterexample that *in general*, there are no necessary transversality conditions in infinite-horizon optimal control problems. The sufficiency theorems, however, make use of a transversality condition, and there is no controversy surrounding its veracity. We also studied a slightly less general class of infinite-horizon optimal control problems, namely, those in which the integrand, transition, and constraint functions do not depend explicitly on time, and the integrand is exponentially discounted. For this class of problems, we derived some fundamental properties of the current value optimal value function that we will return to in a later chapter. Finally, for another less general, but quite common, class of infinite-horizon control problems, we derived a general necessary transversality condition and established the dynamic envelope theorem.

In the next three chapters, we employ the theorems developed herein to study several infinite-horizon current-value autonomous optimal control problems of fundamental importance in intertemporal economic theory. In particular, we examine in great detail the local stability, steady state comparative statics, and local comparative dynamics properties of these models.

APPENDIX

In order to be in a position to extend Leibniz's rule to integrals with infinite intervals of integration, we first require a definition. To prepare for the definition, let $F(\cdot): S \to \Re$ be continuous on the infinite strip $S \stackrel{\text{def}}{=} \{(t, y) : c \leq t < +\infty, a \leq y \leq b\}$, and suppose that

$$\lim_{t \to +\infty} F(t, y)$$

exists for each $y \in I \stackrel{\text{def}}{=} \{y : a \leq y \leq b\}$. We denote the above limit by $\phi(y)$.

Definition A.14.1: The function $F(\cdot)$ *tends to (or converges to)* $\phi(\cdot)$ *uniformly* on $I \stackrel{\text{def}}{=} \{y : a \leq y \leq b\}$ as $t \to +\infty$ if and only if for every $\varepsilon > 0$, there is a number T depending on ε such that

$$|F(t, y) - \phi(y)| < \varepsilon$$

holds for all $t > T$ and all $y \in I$. The number T depends on ε but not on y.

Theorem A.14.1 (Leibniz's Rule for Infinite Intervals of Integration): *Suppose that* $f(\cdot): S \to \Re$ *is continuous on* $S \stackrel{\text{def}}{=} \{(t, y) : c \leq t < +\infty,\ a \leq y \leq b\}$. *Define*

$$F(t, y) \stackrel{\text{def}}{=} \int_c^t f(\tau, y)\, d\tau.$$

Also suppose that the improper integral

$$\phi(y) \overset{\text{def}}{=} \int_c^{+\infty} f(\tau, y)\, d\tau$$

exists for all $y \in I \overset{\text{def}}{=} \{y : a \leq y \leq b\}$, *that* $\lim_{t\to+\infty} F(t, y) = \phi(y)$ *exists uniformly for* $y \in I$, *and that* $f_y(\cdot)$ *is continuous on S. If* $F_y(\cdot)$ *converges to* $\psi(\cdot)$ *as* $t \to +\infty$ *uniformly in y, then*

$$\psi(y) = \phi'(y) = \int_c^{+\infty} f_y(\tau, y)\, d\tau.$$

Example A.14.1: Define the function $\phi(\cdot)$ by the integral

$$\phi(r) \overset{\text{def}}{=} \int_0^{+\infty} e^{-rt}\, dt,$$

where $r > 0$, and the function $F(\cdot)$ by the integral

$$F(t, r) \overset{\text{def}}{=} \int_0^{t} e^{-rs}\, ds = \frac{1 - e^{-rt}}{r}.$$

It therefore follows that

$$F_r(t, r) = \frac{r(te^{-rt}) - (1 - e^{-rt})}{r^2} = -\frac{1 - e^{-rt} - rte^{-rt}}{r^2}.$$

We thus have the following limits:

$$\lim_{t\to+\infty} F(t, r) = \lim_{t\to+\infty} \frac{1 - e^{-rt}}{r} = \frac{1}{r},$$

$$\lim_{t\to+\infty} F_r(t, r) = -\lim_{t\to+\infty} \frac{1 - e^{-rt} - rte^{-rt}}{r^2} = -\frac{1}{r^2}.$$

To show that the convergence is uniform, observe that for $h > 0$,

$$\left| F(t, r) - \frac{1}{r} \right| = \frac{e^{-rt}}{r} \leq \frac{e^{-ht}}{h} \text{ for all } r \geq h,$$

$$\left| F_r(t, r) - \left(-\frac{1}{r^2}\right) \right| = \frac{e^{-rt}(1 + rt)}{r^2} \leq \frac{e^{-ht}(1 + ht)}{h^2} \text{ for all } r \geq h.$$

Therefore the convergence is uniform on any interval $r \geq h$ for $h > 0$. Now define $f(s, r) \overset{\text{def}}{=} e^{-rs}$ so that $f_r(s, r) = -se^{-rs}$, both of which are continuous on an infinite strip. Thus, all the hypotheses of Theorem A.14.1 are met. We may therefore apply

Theorem A.14.1 to the function $\phi(\cdot)$ to compute its derivative with respect to r, namely,

$$\phi'(r) = \int_0^{+\infty} -te^{-rt}\,dt,$$

which is what we were after to begin with.

MENTAL EXERCISES

14.1 Prove Theorem 14.1.

14.2 Prove Lemma 14.1.

14.3 Prove Theorem 14.5.

14.4 Prove the infinite horizon version of the Arrow sufficiency theorem, Theorem 14.6.

14.5 In the Halkin counterexample, is $u(t) = 0\,\forall\, t \in [0, +\infty)$ an optimal control? Explain clearly why or why not. Is it possible for the optimal control to be equal to zero for some *finite* period of time? Explain clearly why or why not.

14.6 Recall Example 14.1, the Halkin counterexample.

(a) Prove that the Hamiltonian $H(\cdot)$ for the Halkin counterexample is *not* concave in (x, u), and thus that the Mangasarian sufficiency theorem cannot be applied to this problem to deduce optimality of the pair $(z(t), v(t)) = (1 - e^{-\frac{1}{2}t}, \frac{1}{2})$.

(b) Prove that $(z(t), v(t)) = (1 - e^{-\frac{1}{2}t}, \frac{1}{2})$ is an optimal pair by using the infinite-horizon Arrow sufficiency theorem.

14.7 Prove that the fixed point of the canonical equations of the Halkin counterexample is a saddle point.

14.8 Let $\lambda(t) = -e^{-t}, x(t) = e^t$, and $z(t) = 1$. Prove that the following implication is incorrect:

$$\lim_{t\to+\infty} \lambda(t) \geq 0,\ \lim_{t\to+\infty} \lambda(t)z(t) = 0,\ \text{and}$$
$$x(t) \geq 0\,\forall\, t \in [t_0, +\infty) \Rightarrow \lim_{t\to+\infty} \lambda(t)[x(t) - z(t)] \geq 0.$$

This is thought to be true by some authors; see, for example, Arrow and Kurz (1970, p. 46).

14.9 Prove Corollary 14.1.

14.10 This exercise asks you to show that Theorem 14.7(i), and consequently Corollary 14.1, do not hold for the finite horizon version of problem (10), nor do they hold if any of the functions $f(\cdot)$, $\mathbf{g}(\cdot)$, or $\mathbf{h}(\cdot)$ are explicit functions of the independent variable t and time consistency of the optimal plan is assumed.

(a) Determine which step of the proof of Theorem 14.7(i) breaks down if problem (10) has a finite horizon. That is, prove that $V(\cdot)$ depends on the initial date or starting time if problem (10) has a finite planning horizon. Show your work and explain your reasoning.

Now assume that $f(\cdot)$, $\mathbf{g}(\cdot)$, and $\mathbf{h}(\cdot)$ are explicit functions of the independent variable t in problem (10), and that the planning horizon is infinite.

(b) Argue that if the *explicit* appearance of t in the functions $f(\cdot)$, $\mathbf{g}(\cdot)$, and $\mathbf{h}(\cdot)$ undergoes the linear shift to $t - t_0$ in problem (10) (in addition to the variables and discount function), then the resulting optimal plan is *not* time consistent.

(c) Assume that the optimal solution to problem (10) is time consistent. Prove that $V(\cdot)$ depends on the initial date or starting time in this case.

14.11 *Professor Halkin and his Counterexample Redux.* The famous Halkin counterexample in Example 14.1 shows that the "natural" or intuitive transversality condition, videlicet, $\lim_{t\to+\infty} \lambda(t) = 0$, is *not*, in general, a necessary condition for infinite-horizon optimal control problems when no conditions are placed on $\lim_{t\to+\infty} x(t)$ and when convergence of the objective functional for all admissible pairs is not assumed. This question asks you to reexamine this famous problem, incorporating a small but significant change in its mathematical structure.

Consider, therefore, the following perturbation of the Halkin counterexample:

$$\max_{u(\cdot)} J[x(\cdot), u(\cdot)] \stackrel{\text{def}}{=} \int_0^{+\infty} u(t)[1 - x(t)]\, e^{-rt}\, dt$$

$$\text{s.t.} \quad \dot{x}(t) = u(t)[1 - x(t)], x(0) = 0,$$

$$u(t) \in U \stackrel{\text{def}}{=} \{u(\cdot) : 0 \le u(t) \le 1 \,\forall\, t \in [0, +\infty)\},$$

where no conditions are placed on $\lim_{t\to+\infty} x(t)$ and $r > 0$ is the discount rate. Compared with the Halkin counterexample, this problem differs from it only by the inclusion of the discount factor e^{-rt} in the integrand.

(a) Prove that $J[\cdot]$ exists for all admissible function pairs $(x(\cdot), u(\cdot))$.

(b) Show that the admissible path of the state variable satisfies

$$x(t) = 1 - e^{-\int_0^t u(s)\, ds},$$

just as in the Halkin counterexample.

(c) Verify that the triplet

$$v(t) = 1, z(t) = 1 - e^{-t}, \lambda(t) = \frac{-1}{1 + r} e^{-rt}$$

is a solution to the necessary conditions of the perturbation of the Halkin counterexample. Do *not* use the current value formulation of the problem; this means that $\lambda(t)$ represents the present value shadow price of the state.

(d) Can you use the Mangasarian sufficiency theorem to prove the optimality of the above triplet? Show your work and explain carefully.
(e) Can you use the Arrow sufficiency theorem to prove the optimality of the above triplet? Show your work and explain carefully.
(f) Does the solution to the perturbation of the Halkin counterexample represent a counterexample to the necessity of the "natural" or intuitive transversality condition $\lim_{t\to+\infty}\lambda(t) = 0$? Explain.

14.12 *A Seemingly Standard Optimal Control Problem.* This question shows that a seemingly standard optimal control problem, that is, one with a quadratic integrand, linear dynamics, and a positive discount rate, has only one finite steady state and it is an *unstable proper node*. Without further ado, the optimal control problem under consideration is given by

$$\max_{u(\cdot)} J[x(\cdot), u(\cdot)] \stackrel{\text{def}}{=} \int_0^{+\infty} \left[-\frac{1}{2}(u(t))^2 + x(t)u(t) - \frac{1}{2}(x(t))^2 \right] e^{-rt}\, dt$$

$$\text{s.t.} \quad \dot{x}(t) = u(t),\ x(0) = x_0 > 0.$$

Assume that $1 < r < 2$.

(a) Write down the necessary conditions for this problem in *current value* form.
(b) Prove that the current value Hamiltonian is a concave function of the state and control variables. Is it a strictly concave function of the state and control? Why or why not? Note that this condition alone is not sufficient to claim that the solution of the necessary conditions is a solution of the optimal control problem, since the planning horizon is infinite.
(c) Reduce the necessary conditions down to a pair of linear differential equations involving only (x, λ).
(d) Prove that the origin is the *only* fixed point of the ordinary differential equations (ODEs) in part (c).
(e) Prove that the origin is an unstable proper node.
(f) Find the general solution of the linear system of ODEs in part (c).
(g) Draw the phase portrait for the linear system of ODEs in part (c).
(h) Prove that

$$x^*(t; x_0) = x_0 e^t,\ u^*(t; x_0) = x_0 e^t,\ \lambda(t; x_0) = 0,\ J[x^*(\cdot), u^*(\cdot)] = 0$$

is the optimal solution of the control problem.

14.13 This question probes your understanding of infinite-horizon optimal control problems by asking you to compare them to their finite-horizon counterparts. Even though you are not asked to prove anything in this question, it may behoove you to write down a few equations in answering the question.

(a) What two features or aspects of finite horizon problems do not, in general, carry over to infinite-horizon problems? Explain precisely.
(b) Explain carefully how economists typically deal with these two complications posed by infinite-horizon problems.

14.14 Consider the following class of infinite-horizon optimal control problems:

$$\max_{u(\cdot)} J[x(\cdot), u(\cdot)] \stackrel{\text{def}}{=} \int_0^{+\infty} f(x(t), u(t))\, e^{-rt}\, dt$$

$$\text{s.t.} \quad \dot{x}(t) = u(t),\, x(0) = x_0,$$

where $f(\cdot) \in C^{(2)}$, $r > 0$ is the discount rate, and no conditions are placed on $\lim_{t\to+\infty} x(t)$. Assume that $(z(t; r, x_0), v(t; r, x_0))$ are the optimal pair of curves to this problem, with corresponding current value costate curve $\lambda(t; r, x_0)$. Furthermore, let $(x^*(r), u^*(r))$ be the simple steady state of the control problem, with $\lambda^*(r)$ being the corresponding steady state value of the costate. Assume that the objective functional exists for all admissible pairs of curves and that $f_{uu}(z(t; r, x_0), v(t; r, x_0)) < 0\, \forall\, t \in [0, +\infty)$.

(a) Derive the necessary conditions for this control problem in current value form.

(b) Transform the necessary conditions into a pair of autonomous ordinary differential equations in (x, u). **Hint:** Differentiate $H_u(x(t), u(t), \lambda(t)) = 0$ with respect to t, and use the necessary conditions to derive a differential equation for $u(t)$.

(c) Prove that $\text{tr}(\mathbf{J}(x^*(r), u^*(r))) = r$ and $|\mathbf{J}(x^*(r), u^*(r))| \neq 0$, where $\mathbf{J}(x^*(r), u^*(r))$ is the Jacobian of the system of ordinary differential equations in part (b) evaluated at the fixed point. Is the steady state locally stable? Explain.

(d) In principle, how do you find the steady state values $(x^*(r), u^*(r))$? What condition must hold for $(x^*(r), u^*(r))$ to be well defined by the implicit function theorem? Does this condition hold? Explain.

(e) Prove that if $\lim_{t\to+\infty} z(t; r, x_0) = x^*(r)$, then $|\mathbf{J}(x^*(r), u^*(r))| < 0$. Interpret this result in words.

(f) Now assume that $f_{xu}(x^*(r), u^*(r)) = 0$ and that $f_{xx}(x^*(r), u^*(r)) < 0$. Prove that $|\mathbf{J}(x^*(r), u^*(r))| < 0$. Interpret this result in words.

(g) Assume that the steady state is a local saddle point. Prove that

$$\text{sign}\left[\frac{\partial x^*(r)}{\partial r}\right] = -\text{sign}[\lambda^*(r)].$$

Provide an interpretation of this steady state comparative statics result.

14.15 Prove Theorem 14.10.

FURTHER READING

Lemma 14.1 is nearly identical to that given in Léonard and Van Long (1992, Chapter 9, Corollary 9.3.2). Other sufficient conditions for $\lim_{t\to+\infty} \boldsymbol{\lambda}(t)'[\mathbf{z}(t) - \mathbf{x}(t)] = 0$ to hold in problem (1) can be found in Seierstad and Sydsæter (1987, Chapter 3, note 16). Michel (1982) has shown that Theorem 14.9 holds without assuming that $V_{\mathbf{x}}(\cdot) \in$

$C^{(0)}$. This relaxation is unimportant for understanding the transversality condition, and, more often than not, its application to dynamic economic problems. Benveniste and Scheinkman (1982) and Araujo and Scheinkman (1983) study concave infinite-horizon control problems using advanced mathematical tools from convex analysis, and establish necessary transversality conditions. Kamihigashi (2001) generalizes and unifies much of the existing work on the necessary transversality conditions. Makris (2001) derives necessary conditions for discounted infinite-horizon control problems in which the time to switch between alternative and consecutive regimes is a decision variable, the so-called two-stage optimal control problem. Romer (1986) establishes an existence theorem for a class of infinite-horizon control problems. The material in the appendix is drawn from Protter and Morrey (1991).

REFERENCES

Araujo, A. and Scheinkman, J.A. (1983), "Maximum Principle and Transversality Condition for Concave Infinite Horizon Economic Models," *Journal of Economic Theory*, 30, 1–16.

Arrow, K.J. and Kurz, M. (1970), *Public Investment, the Rate of Return, and Optimal Fiscal Policy* (Baltimore: Johns Hopkins University Press).

Benveniste, L.M. and Scheinkman, J.A. (1982), "Duality Theory for Dynamic Optimization Models of Economics: The Continuous Time Case," *Journal of Economic Theory*, 27, 1–19.

Chiang, A.C. (1992), *Elements of Dynamic Optimization* (New York: McGraw-Hill, Inc.).

Halkin, H. (1974), "Necessary Conditions for Optimal Control Problems with Infinite Horizons," *Econometrica*, 42, 267–272.

Kamihigashi, T. (2001), "Necessity of Transversality Conditions for Infinite Horizon Problems," *Econometrica*, 69, 995–1012.

Léonard, D. and Van Long, N. (1992), *Optimal Control Theory and Static Optimization in Economics* (New York: Cambridge University Press).

Makris, M. (2001), "Necessary Conditions for Infinite-Horizon Discounted Two-Stage Optimal Control Problems." *Journal of Economic Dynamics and Control*, 25, 1935–1950.

Michel, P. (1982), "On the Transversality Condition in Infinite Horizon Optimal Problems," *Econometrica*, 50, 975–985.

Protter, M.H. and Morrey, C.B. (1991, 2nd Ed.), *A First Course in Real Analysis* (New York: Springer-Verlag, Inc.).

Romer, P. (1986), "Cake Eating, Chattering, and Jumps: Existence Results for Variational Problems," *Econometrica*, 54, 897–908.

Seierstad, A. and Sydsæter, K. (1987), *Optimal Control Theory with Economic Applications* (New York: Elsevier Science Publishing Co., Inc.).

Simon, C.P. and Blume, L. (1994), *Mathematics for Economists* (New York: W.W. Norton & Company, Inc.).

FIFTEEN

The Neoclassical Optimal Economic Growth Model

This chapter is the first in a series of three to use the theorems developed in Chapter 14 to study the qualitative properties of a classical intertemporal economic model. The focus of this chapter is on the neoclassical model of optimal economic growth. As is typical in most economic applications of optimal control theory, we provide a thorough economic interpretation of the necessary and sufficient conditions of the optimal economic growth model. More important, however, is the fact that we rather exhaustively study the local stability, steady state comparative statics, and local comparative dynamics properties of the model as well. This later feature is oftentimes neglected in economic research, which is a shame, for such a qualitative analysis really lies at the core of economic policy discussions.

The model we now proceed to develop is neoclassical because its analytical framework revolves around a neoclassical production function, say, $K, L \mapsto F(K, L)$, where $K > 0$ is the capital stock and $L > 0$ is the labor force, the latter of which we assume to be equal to the population of the economy under consideration. The single output of the economy Y is produced using this production function, thereby implying that $Y = F(K, L)$. It is assumed that $F(\cdot) \in C^{(2)}$ and has the following neoclassical properties:

$$F_K(K, L) > 0, \;\; F_L(K, L) > 0, \;\; F_{KK}(K, L) < 0, \tag{1}$$

$$F(\mu K, \mu L) \equiv \mu F(K, L) \, \forall \, \mu > 0. \tag{2}$$

Because the production function $F(\cdot)$ is assumed to be positively homogeneous of degree unity in capital and labor, and $L > 0$, we can let $\mu = L^{-1}$. This and Eq. (2) allow us to rewrite the production function $F(\cdot)$ as $F(L^{-1}K, 1) \equiv L^{-1}F(K, L)$. Note that the expression on the right-hand side of this identity is the average product of labor. Defining $k \stackrel{\text{def}}{=} K/L$ as the capital-labor ratio and letting $f(k) \stackrel{\text{def}}{=} F(L^{-1}K, 1)$, we can rewrite $F(L^{-1}K, 1) \equiv L^{-1}F(K, L)$ so as to express the average product of labor as

$$f(k) \equiv L^{-1}F(K, L). \tag{3}$$

Using the identity $F(K, L) \equiv Lf(k)$, you are asked to establish the ensuing technical result in a mental exercise. It plays an important role in the development of the optimal growth model, as we will see.

Lemma 15.1: *Under the assumptions in Eqs. (1) and (2), it follows that*

(a) $f'(k) > 0$ *if and only if* $F_K(K, L) > 0$.
(b) $f(k) - kf'(k) > 0$ *if and only if* $F_L(K, L) > 0$.
(c) $f''(k) < 0$ *if and only if* $F_{KK}(K, L) < 0$.
(d) $f''(k) < 0$ *if and only if* $F_{LL}(K, L) < 0$.
(e) $F_{KK}(K, L) < 0$ *if and only if* $F_{KL}(K, L) > 0$ *if and only if* $F_{LL}(K, L) < 0$.

An interesting feature of this lemma is that we need only assume that the marginal product of capital is declining, *or* the marginal product of labor is declining, *or* that labor and capital are complements in production, in order to have the average product of labor increase at a decreasing rate with respect to the capital-to-labor ratio. The positive homogeneity of degree one of $F(\cdot)$ is the crucial assumption behind all of these results.

In addition to the assumptions in Eqs. (1) and (2), we also assume that

$$f(0) = 0, \lim_{k \to 0} f'(k) = +\infty, \lim_{k \to +\infty} f'(k) = 0. \tag{4}$$

The first assumption means that capital is essential for production because without it, no output can be produced. The second implies that the marginal product of capital gets infinitely large as the capital stock shrinks to zero, whereas the third assumption asserts that the marginal product of capital goes to zero as the capital stock becomes arbitrarily large.

Total output Y is allocated between gross investment I and consumption C. Assuming the goods market is in equilibrium therefore implies the market clearing condition $Y = C + I$. Gross investment consists of net investment $\dot{K}$ and replacement investment δK, which is a result of depreciation at the constant exponential rate $\delta > 0$. Hence the goods market equilibrium condition can be rewritten as $F(K, L) = C + \dot{K} + \delta K$, since $Y = F(K, L)$ and $I = \dot{K} + \delta K$. Dividing this differential equation by $L > 0$, defining $c \stackrel{\text{def}}{=} C/L$ as per-capita consumption, using Eq. (3), and rearranging yields

$$\frac{\dot{K}}{L} = f(k) - \delta k - c. \tag{5}$$

Observe that the right-hand side of this differential equation is in per-capita terms, but that the left-hand side is not. To reconcile this, first note that $\dot{K} \stackrel{\text{def}}{=} \frac{d}{dt}[kL] = k\dot{L} + L\dot{k}$. Now assume that the labor force (or equivalently, the population) is growing at the constant exponential $\eta > 0$, that is, $\dot{L}/L = \eta$. This assumption permits us to rewrite the differential equation $\dot{K} = k\dot{L} + L\dot{k}$ as $\dot{K} = k\eta L + L\dot{k}$, or

$$\frac{\dot{K}}{L} = \eta k + \dot{k}. \tag{6}$$

Equating Eq. (5) and Eq. (6) reduces the differential equation to per-capita terms, that is,

$$\dot{k} = f(k) - [\delta + \eta]k - c. \tag{7}$$

Equation (7) is the fundamental differential equation of neoclassical growth theory, and describes how the capital-labor ratio k varies over time. It is the state equation in the neoclassical optimal growth model. The value of the capital-labor ratio is given to the economy at the initial date of the planning horizon $t = 0$, say, from the past actions of the planner, and is denoted by $k(0) = k_0$. It represents the initial condition for the state equation.

The welfare of the society at each instant of the planning horizon is assumed to depend exclusively on society's per-capita consumption c of the single good via the instantaneous utility function $U(\cdot)$, which is assumed to be $C^{(2)}$ on $(0, +\infty)$ and to have the following properties:

$$U'(c) > 0 \,\forall\, c > 0,\;\; U''(c) < 0 \,\forall\, c > 0,\;\; \lim_{c\to 0} U'(c) = +\infty,\;\; \lim_{c\to +\infty} U'(c) = 0. \tag{8}$$

In words, we assume that the social instantaneous utility function has positive and declining marginal utility of per-capita consumption, that the marginal utility of the first unit of consumption is arbitrarily large, and that the marginal utility of consumption goes to zero as per-capita consumption gets arbitrarily large. These are known as the Inada conditions. In a mental exercise, you are asked to show that the function $c \mapsto \ln c$ exhibits such properties. The social utility function is an *instantaneous utility function*, that is, it measures the social value at a point in time of a given per-capita rate of consumption. Consequently, it must be integrated over the entire future in order to obtain the correct social welfare index, that is, the social utility functional. At the end of this chapter, we return to a more technical discussion of the *utility functional* we use, and examine some of its properties.

Recall that we have assumed that the population (or equivalently, the labor force) is growing at the constant exponential $\eta > 0$, that is to say, $\dot{L}/L = \eta$, thereby implying that $L(t) = L_0 e^{\eta t}$, where $L(0) = L_0$ is the size of the population at time $t = 0$. As a result of this assumption, we weight the instantaneous utility function by the population size before integrating it over the planning horizon. Assuming a positive social discount rate $\rho > 0$ and an infinite planning horizon, the utility functional is given by the integral

$$\int_0^{+\infty} U(c(t))L(t)\,e^{-\rho t}\,dt = \int_0^{+\infty} U(c(t))L_0 e^{\eta t} e^{-\rho t}\,dt = L_0 \int_0^{+\infty} U(c(t))\,e^{-[\rho-\eta]t}\,dt.$$

Because of the assumed infinite planning horizon, we furthermore assume that $r \stackrel{\text{def}}{=} \rho - \eta > 0$. If we also assume that $U(\cdot)$ is bounded, then by Theorem 14.2, the utility functional converges for all admissible pairs and our control problem is in principle solvable by the theorems we've developed in Chapter 14. What's more, if we let $L_0 = 1$ by an appropriate choice of units, then our utility functional can be written as

$$\Psi[c(\cdot)] \stackrel{\text{def}}{=} \int_0^{+\infty} U(c(t))\, e^{-rt}\, dt.$$

Notice that upon comparing the previous two utility functionals, we see that weighting instantaneous utility by an exponentially growing population size and simultaneously requiring that the social discount rate exceed the growth rate of the population is mathematically equivalent to *not* weighting social utility by the exponentially growing population size but adopting a new positive social discount rate $r > 0$.

It is natural to include some constraints on the state and control variables. There are the rather obvious economic ones that constrain the values of per-capita consumption $c(t)$ and the capital-labor ratio $k(t)$ to be nonnegative at every instant in the planning horizon. We will explicitly take into account the control restriction $c(t) \geq 0\, \forall\, t \in [0, +\infty)$, and in the course of the analysis show that an optimal path of per-capita consumption, assuming one exists, always involves positive consumption at each instant of the planning horizon. In contrast, we will initially ignore the state variable restriction $k(t) \geq 0\, \forall\, t \in [0, +\infty)$, yet by the end of the analysis, we will similarly conclude that the optimal path of the capital-labor ratio is positive at every instant of the planning horizon. In addition, we could also place an upper bound on per-capita consumption at each instant of the planning horizon, namely, per-capita output, resulting in the inequality constraint $c(t) \leq f(k(t))\, \forall\, t \in [0, +\infty)$. This constraint means that all consumption $c(t)$ must come out of current production $f(k(t))$, thereby implying that the capital stock $k(t)$ cannot be eaten up. For the sake of exposition and economic insight into this model, however, we ignore this constraint.

The complete statement of the optimal growth problem is therefore to find a per-capita consumption function $c(\cdot)$ that solves the infinite-horizon optimal control problem

$$\max_{c(\cdot)} \Psi[c(\cdot)] \stackrel{\text{def}}{=} \int_0^{+\infty} U(c(t))\, e^{-rt}\, dt$$

$$\text{s.t.} \quad \dot{k}(t) = f(k(t)) - [\delta + \eta]k(t) - c(t),\; k(0) = k_0, \tag{9}$$

$$c(t) \geq 0\, \forall\, t \in [0, +\infty).$$

Notice that we have not imposed any conditions on $\lim_{t\to+\infty} k(t)$. Given the rather general nature of problem (9), we assume that a solution exists to the necessary conditions and denote it by the pair $(k^*(t; \delta, \eta, r), c^*(t; \delta, \eta, r))$, with corresponding current value costate variable $\lambda(t; \delta, \eta, r)$. Because we are interested in a qualitative characterization of the optimal solution, which is all we can hope for given the lack of specific functional forms for the instantaneous utility function and the production function, we assume that the solution $(k^*(t; \delta, \eta, r), c^*(t; \delta, \eta, r))$ of the necessary conditions converges to a simple, finite, and positive steady state solution of the necessary conditions, that is, $k^*(t; \delta, \eta, r) \to k^s(\delta, \eta, r) > 0$ and $c^*(t; \delta, \eta, r) \to c^s(\delta, \eta, r) > 0$ as $t \to +\infty$, where the superscript s indicates that it is the steady state solution. This implies the same is true for the current value shadow price of the per-capita capital stock, that is, $\lambda(t; \delta, \eta, r) \to \lambda^s(\delta, \eta, r) > 0$ as $t \to +\infty$. Notice that we have *not* assumed that the pair $(k^*(t; \delta, \eta, r), c^*(t; \delta, \eta, r))$ is the solution of the optimal control problem, however. We now proceed to the analysis of the model.

The current value Hamiltonian for this problem is defined as

$$H(k, c, \lambda) \stackrel{\text{def}}{=} U(c) + \lambda[f(k) - c - [\delta + \eta]k],$$

whereas the current value Lagrangian is defined as

$$L(k, c, \lambda, \mu) \stackrel{\text{def}}{=} U(c) + \lambda[f(k) - c - [\delta + \eta]k] + \mu c,$$

where μ is the Lagrange multiplier associated with the nonnegativity constraint on per-capita consumption. Note that the rank constraint qualification is satisfied because the constraint is linear in the control variable. Given that we have used a current value formulation, the necessary conditions of Theorems 14.3 take the form

$$L_c(k, c, \lambda, \mu) = U'(c) - \lambda + \mu = 0, \tag{10}$$

$$L_\mu(k, c, \lambda, \mu) = c \geq 0,\ \ \mu \geq 0,\ \ L_\mu(k, c, \lambda, \mu) \cdot \mu = c\mu = 0, \tag{11}$$

$$\dot{\lambda} = r\lambda - L_k(k, c, \lambda, \mu) = \lambda[\delta + \eta + r - f'(k)], \tag{12}$$

$$\dot{k} = L_\lambda(k, c, \lambda, \mu) = f(k) - [\delta + \eta]k - c,\ \ k(0) = k_0. \tag{13}$$

We now proceed to analyze these necessary conditions.

To begin, it should be obvious that $c = 0$, whether for an instant, a finite interval of time, or the entire planning period, satisfies the necessary conditions (11). But as we now show, $c = 0$ does not satisfy the necessary condition (10) under our assumptions, and thus cannot be optimal even for an instant. To see this, first recall that we assumed the instantaneous utility function satisfied the Inada condition $\lim_{c \to 0} U'(c) = +\infty$. Next observe that if $c = 0$ at any finite point of time in the planning horizon or over any finite period of time in the planning horizon, then the necessary condition (10) would imply that $\lambda(t) = \mu + \infty$. This, however, cannot hold because $\lambda(\cdot)$ is a continuous function of time by Theorem 14.3 and thus can only take on finite values at finite points of time in the planning horizon, or over any finite period of time in the planning horizon. Moreover, as $t \to +\infty$, it cannot be the case that $c \to 0$ as we have assumed that the per-capita capital stock, and thus per-capita consumption, converge to finite and positive steady state values. Hence $c(t) > 0\, \forall\, t \in [0, +\infty)$ in an optimal plan. By Eq. (10), this implies that $\mu(t) = 0\, \forall\, t \in [0, +\infty)$ in an optimal plan, and therefore that $U'(c(t)) = \lambda(t)\, \forall\, t \in [0, +\infty)$ in an optimal plan as well. That is, the marginal utility of per-capita consumption should be equated with the current value shadow price of the per-capita capital stock in an optimal plan. What's more, because $U'(c) > 0\,\forall c > 0$ from Eq. (8), it follows from the necessary condition $U'(c(t)) = \lambda(t)\,\forall t \in [0, +\infty)$ that $\lambda(t) > 0\,\forall t \in [0, +\infty)$ in an optimal plan. In other words, the capital stock is viewed as a good by society in an optimal plan.

The sufficiency conditions of Theorem 14.4 can be checked in a straightforward fashion. This is done by examining the principle minors of the Hessian matrix of the Lagrangian with respect to the state and control variables, and recalling that $U''(c) < 0$, $f''(k) < 0$, and that $\lambda(t) > 0\,\forall t \in [0, +\infty)$:

$$L_{cc}(k, c, \lambda, \mu) = U''(c) < 0,$$

$$L_{KK}(k, c, \lambda, \mu) = \lambda f''(k) < 0,$$

$$L_{cc}(k, c, \lambda, \mu)L_{KK}(k, c, \lambda, \mu) - [L_{ck}(k, c, \lambda, \mu)]^2 = \lambda f''(k)U''(c) > 0.$$

These calculations demonstrate that the current value Lagrangian is a strictly concave function of the state and control variables. Note that although we are dealing with the current value Lagrangian, Theorem 14.4 is instead stated in terms of the present value Lagrangian. This is of no consequence for the above conclusion, however, as the two Lagrangians differ only by the positive constant e^{-rt}.

The last condition to check in Theorem 14.4 is the limiting transversality condition that is part of the sufficient conditions, scilicet, $\lim_{t\to+\infty} e^{-rt}\lambda(t; \delta, \eta, r)[k(t) - k^*(t; \delta, \eta, r)] \geq 0$ for all admissible curves $k(t)$. If this transversality condition holds, then we may conclude from Theorem 14.4 that $(k^*(t; \delta, \eta, r), c^*(t; \delta, \eta, r))$ is the unique solution to the optimal growth problem. Observe that we have multiplied $\lambda(t; \delta, \eta, r)$ by e^{-rt} in the statement of the limiting transversality condition in order to convert $\lambda(t; \delta, \eta, r)$ to a present value costate variable, as is required by Theorem 14.4. Now recall that the assumptions $k^*(t; \delta, \eta, r) \to k^s(\delta, \eta, r)$ and $c^*(t; \delta, \eta, r) \to c^s(\delta, \eta, r)$ as $t \to +\infty$ imply that $\lambda(t; \delta, \eta, r) \to \lambda^s(\delta, \eta, r)$ as $t \to +\infty$. Therefore, given that $\lim_{t\to+\infty} e^{-rt} = 0$, it follows that $\lim_{t\to+\infty} e^{-rt}\lambda(t; \delta, \eta, r) = \lim_{t\to+\infty} e^{-rt} \lim_{t\to+\infty} \lambda(t; \delta, \eta, r) = 0$, where we have used the fact that the limit of a product is equal to the product of the limits when the individual limits exist, as they do here. Consequently, if all the admissible paths of the per-capita capital stock $k(t)$ are bounded, or if $\lim_{t\to+\infty} k(t)$ exists for all admissible paths, then the limiting transversality condition holds with an equality. Note, however, that under the assumptions adopted herein, all the admissible paths of the per-capita capital stock are indeed bounded, as you will be asked to demonstrate in a mental exercise. Accordingly, we may conclude that the solution of the necessary conditions that converges to the fixed point of the necessary conditions is the unique solution to the optimal growth problem. We now turn to a discussion of the stability of the steady state solution of the necessary and sufficient conditions.

To begin, first recall that because $\mu(t) = 0\,\forall t \in [0, +\infty)$ in an optimal plan, the current value Lagrangian and current value Hamiltonian functions are identical in an optimal plan. Because $H_{cc}(k, c, \lambda) = U''(c) < 0$ and $U(\cdot) \in C^{(2)}\,\forall c > 0$, we may use the implicit function theorem to solve the equation $H_c(k, c, \lambda) = U'(c) - \lambda = 0$, in principle, for c as a locally $C^{(1)}$ function of λ, say $c = \hat{c}(\lambda)$. We may also use the implicit function theorem to find the derivative of $\hat{c}(\lambda)$ with respect to λ, that is to say,

$$\hat{c}'(\lambda) = \left.\frac{-H_{c\lambda}}{H_{cc}}\right|_{c=\hat{c}(\lambda)} = \frac{1}{U''(\hat{c}(\lambda))} < 0. \tag{14}$$

This comparative statics result says that an increase in the current value shadow price of the per-capita capital stock reduces per-capita consumption, ceteris paribus. Note that this inverse relationship between the per-capita consumption rate and the current value shadow price of the per-capita capital stock is entirely a result of the assumption of declining marginal utility.

The next step is to eliminate c from the canonical differential equations (12) and (13) using the expression $c = \hat{c}(\lambda)$:

$$\dot{\lambda} = \lambda[\delta + \eta + r - f'(k)], \tag{15}$$
$$\dot{k} = f(k) - [\delta + \eta]k - \hat{c}(\lambda). \tag{16}$$

Observe that this dynamical system is a function of only (λ, k) and their time derivatives, as c has been substituted out of the system via the Maximum Principle and the implicit function theorem. By definition, the steady state solution $(k^s(\delta, \eta, r), \lambda^s(\delta, \eta, r))$ of the necessary and sufficient conditions (15) and (16) is found by setting $\dot{\lambda} = 0$ and $\dot{k} = 0$ in Eqs. (15) and (16) to get

$$\dot{\lambda} = 0 \Leftrightarrow \lambda[\delta + \eta + r - f'(k)] = 0, \tag{17}$$
$$\dot{k} = 0 \Leftrightarrow f(k) - [\delta + \eta]k - \hat{c}(\lambda) = 0, \tag{18}$$

and then, in principle, simultaneously solving these two equations for k and λ in terms of the parameters (δ, η, r). Because $\lambda(t) > 0\,\forall\, t \in [0, +\infty)$ in an optimal plan, as discussed above, one could simplify the expression in Eq. (17) to read $\delta + \eta + r - f'(k) = 0$, but this results in a loss of symmetry in the exposition, something we wish to avoid.

To determine the local stability of the fixed point $(k^s(\delta, \eta, r), \lambda^s(\delta, \eta, r))$, we compute the Jacobian matrix of the dynamical system (15) and (16) with respect to (λ, k) and evaluate it at the fixed point $(k^s(\delta, \eta, r), \lambda^s(\delta, \eta, r))$, resulting in

$$\mathbf{J}(k^s(\delta, \eta, r), \lambda^s(\delta, \eta, r))$$
$$\stackrel{\text{def}}{=} \left.\begin{bmatrix} \dfrac{\partial \dot{\lambda}}{\partial \lambda} & \dfrac{\partial \dot{\lambda}}{\partial k} \\ \dfrac{\partial \dot{k}}{\partial \lambda} & \dfrac{\partial \dot{k}}{\partial k} \end{bmatrix}\right|_{\substack{\dot{\lambda}=0\\ \dot{k}=0}} = \left.\begin{bmatrix} \delta + \eta + r - f'(k) & -\lambda f''(k) \\ -\hat{c}'(\lambda) & f'(k) - [\delta + \eta] \end{bmatrix}\right|_{\substack{\dot{\lambda}=0\\ \dot{k}=0}}$$
$$= \begin{bmatrix} 0 & -\lambda^s(\delta, \eta, r) f''(k^s(\delta, \eta, r)) \\ -\hat{c}'(\lambda^s(\delta, \eta, r)) & r \end{bmatrix}, \tag{19}$$

where we have used Eq. (17) to simplify the (2, 2) element. Because $\hat{c}'(\lambda^s(\delta, \eta, r)) < 0$ from Eq. (14), $\lambda^s(\delta, \eta, r) > 0$, and $f''(k^s(\delta, \eta, r)) < 0$, it follows from Eq. (19) that

$$\mathrm{tr}\mathbf{J}(k^s(\delta, \eta, r),\ \lambda^s(\delta, \eta, r)) = r > 0, \tag{20}$$

$$\left|\mathbf{J}(k^s(\delta, \eta, r), \lambda^s(\delta, \eta, r))\right| = -\lambda^s(\delta, \eta, r)\hat{c}'(\lambda^s(\delta, \eta, r))f''(k^s(\delta, \eta, r)) < 0. \tag{21}$$

Now recall that by Mental Exercise 13.4, or equivalently, by Theorem 23.9 of Simon and Blume (1994), the product of the eigenvalues of $\mathbf{J}(k^s(\delta, \eta, r), \lambda^s(\delta, \eta, r))$ equals its determinant. As a result, because $|\mathbf{J}(k^s(\delta, \eta, r), \lambda^s(\delta, \eta, r))| < 0$, one eigenvalue is real and positive and the other is real and negative, thereby implying that the steady state is hyperbolic. Thus by Theorem 13.6 or Theorem 13.7, the steady state $(k^s(\delta, \eta, r), \lambda^s(\delta, \eta, r))$ of the nonlinear system of differential equation composed of Eqs. (15) and (16) is an unstable saddle point, with two trajectories in the $k\lambda$ phase plane converging to it as $t \to +\infty$.

With the local stability of the steady state settled, let's now proceed to show that the steady state functions $(k^s(\cdot), \lambda^s(\cdot))$ are well defined and locally $C^{(1)}$ in the parameters (δ, η, r). This conclusion is a straightforward application of the implicit function theorem and the fact that the steady state is a saddle point. To see this, first observe that the Jacobian determinant of the steady state equations (17) and (18) with respect to (k, λ) evaluated at the steady state solution $(k^s(\delta, \eta, r), \lambda^s(\delta, \eta, r))$ is identical to $\mathbf{J}(k^s(\delta, \eta, r), \lambda^s(\delta, \eta, r))$ given in Eq. (19), as is easily verified. This result implies that the Jacobian determinant of the steady state equations (17) and (18) with respect to (k, λ) evaluated at the steady state is not zero, that is, $|\mathbf{J}(k^s(\delta, \eta, r), \lambda^s(\delta, \eta, r))| \neq 0$. Hence, by the implicit function theorem, we can in principle solve Eqs. (17) and (18) simultaneously for the per-capita capital stock and the current value shadow price of the per-capita capital stock as functions of the parameters (δ, η, r), say, $(k^s(\delta, \eta, r), \lambda^s(\delta, \eta, r))$, just as we assumed. Furthermore, the implicit function theorem guarantees that the functions $(k^s(\cdot), \lambda^s(\cdot))$ are locally $C^{(1)}$ in the parameters seeing as the implicit equations (17) and (18) defining the steady state are at least locally $C^{(1)}$ functions of (k, λ) and (δ, η, r), thus ensuring that we can conduct a comparative statics analysis of the steady state. It is worthwhile to emphasize that $(k^s(\delta, \eta, r), \lambda^s(\delta, \eta, r))$ are the values that the optimal paths of the per-capita capital stock and the current value shadow price of the per-capita capital stock converge to as $t \to +\infty$. With these matters behind us, we turn to the construction of the phase portrait corresponding to the canonical equations (15) and (16).

To construct the phase diagram, first consider the $\dot{\lambda} = 0$ isocline, which is defined by

$$\dot{\lambda} = 0 \Leftrightarrow \lambda[\delta + \eta + r - f'(k)] = 0. \tag{22}$$

Because $\lambda > 0$, the $\dot{\lambda} = 0$ isocline can be equivalently written as $\delta + \eta + r - f'(k) = 0$. This form of the $\dot{\lambda} = 0$ isocline shows that it is independent of λ, thereby

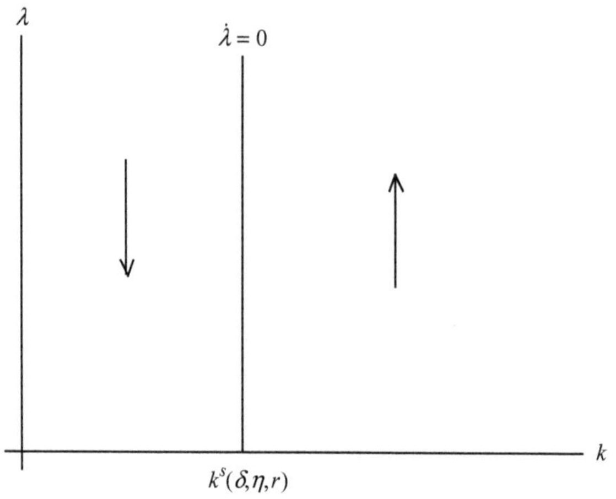

Figure 15.1

implying that the solution to Eq. (22) is the steady state solution for the per-capita capital stock, that is, $k = k^s(\delta, \eta, r) > 0$. This same fact also implies that the $\dot{\lambda} = 0$ isocline is a vertical line positioned at the steady state per-capita capital stock level in the $k\lambda$-phase space, just as Figure 15.1 depicts. Because the Jacobian determinant of Eq. (22) with respect to k is nonzero at $k = k^s(\delta, \eta, r)$, the implicit function theorem implies that we can in principle solve it for k in terms of the parameters (δ, η, r), and furthermore, that $k^s(\cdot) \in C^{(1)}$ locally, since $f'(\cdot) \in C^{(1)}$. This is a redundant observation in light of the above remark that the steady state functions $(k^s(\cdot), \lambda^s(\cdot))$ are at least locally $C^{(1)}$ functions of the parameters. A similar remark will not prove to be redundant when we study the $\dot{k} = 0$ isocline.

To find the vector field acting on λ just off the $\dot{\lambda} = 0$ isocline in a neighborhood of the steady state, differentiate Eq. (15) with respect to λ or k and evaluate the result at the steady state solution $(k^s(\delta, \eta, r), \lambda^s(\delta, \eta, r))$ to get

$$\left.\frac{\partial \dot{\lambda}}{\partial \lambda}\right|_{\substack{\dot{\lambda}=0 \\ \dot{k}=0}} = \delta + \eta + r - f'(k)\big|_{\dot{\lambda}=\dot{k}=0} = \delta + \eta + r - f'(k^s(\delta, \eta, r)) \equiv 0, \quad (23)$$

$$\left.\frac{\partial \dot{\lambda}}{\partial k}\right|_{\substack{\dot{\lambda}=0 \\ \dot{k}=0}} = -\lambda f''(k)\big|_{\dot{\lambda}=\dot{k}=0} = -\lambda^s(\delta, \eta, r) f''(k^s(\delta, \eta, r)) > 0. \quad (24)$$

These derivatives are the elements of the first row of the Jacobian matrix $\mathbf{J}(k^s(\delta, \eta, r), \lambda^s(\delta, \eta, r))$. Hence, once we compute the Jacobian matrix of the canonical differential equations (15) and (16) and evaluate it at the steady state solution $(k^s(\delta, \eta, r), \lambda^s(\delta, \eta, r))$, the vector field of the canonical differential equations is known in a neighborhood of the steady state.

Equation (23) asserts that in a neighborhood of the steady state, an increase in λ does not change $\dot{\lambda}$ from zero, exactly what the vertical $\dot{\lambda} = 0$ isocline shows geometrically. In contrast, Eq. (24) shows that in a neighborhood of the steady state, an increase in k increases $\dot{\lambda}$ from zero to a positive number, thereby implying that points to the right of the $\dot{\lambda} = 0$ isocline in a neighborhood of the steady state have $\dot{\lambda} > 0$. Symmetric reasoning applies to points to the left of the $\dot{\lambda} = 0$ isocline in a neighborhood of the steady state, resulting in $\dot{\lambda} < 0$ for such points. This is how the vector field in Figure 15.1 is derived.

Now turn to the $\dot{k} = 0$ isocline, which is defined by

$$\dot{k} = 0 \Leftrightarrow f(k) - [\delta + \eta]k - \hat{c}(\lambda) = 0. \tag{25}$$

Let $\lambda = \Lambda(k; \delta, \eta)$ be the solution to Eq. (25). Now observe that the Jacobian determinant of Eq. (25) evaluated at the solution $\lambda = \Lambda(k; \delta, \eta)$ is $-\hat{c}'(\Lambda(k; \delta, \eta)) > 0$. Thus the implicit function theorem guarantees that if a solution to the $\dot{k} = 0$ isocline exists, then it can in principle be expressed in the form $\lambda = \Lambda(k; \delta, \eta)$ as claimed, and furthermore, that $\Lambda(\cdot) \in C^{(1)}$ locally, since the implicit equation (25) defining $\lambda = \Lambda(k; \delta, \eta)$ is at least a locally $C^{(1)}$ function. Note, however, that $\lambda = \Lambda(k; \delta, \eta)$ is not the steady state value of λ, in contrast to the solution of Eq. (22) (the $\dot{\lambda} = 0$ isocline), for both k and λ appear in Eq. (25). Moreover, $\lambda = \Lambda(k; \delta, \eta)$ is not the simultaneous solution of both isoclines, as is required for it to be a steady state solution. Hence $\lambda = \Lambda(k; \delta, \eta)$ is the solution to the $\dot{k} = 0$ isocline and not the steady state value of λ.

By the implicit function theorem, the slope of the $\dot{k} = 0$ isocline in a neighborhood of the steady state solution is given by

$$\left.\frac{\partial \lambda}{\partial k}\right|_{\substack{\dot{\lambda}=0\\ \dot{k}=0}} = \Lambda_k(k; \delta, \eta)|_{\dot{\lambda}=0, \dot{k}=0} = \left.\frac{-\partial \dot{k}/\partial k}{\partial \dot{k}/\partial \lambda}\right|_{\substack{\dot{\lambda}=0\\ \dot{k}=0}}$$

$$= \frac{f'(k^s(\delta, \eta, r)) - [\delta + \eta]}{\hat{c}'(\lambda^s(\delta, \eta, r))} = \frac{r}{\hat{c}'(\lambda^s(\delta, \eta, r))} < 0,$$

where use has been made of Eq. (17), or equivalently, Eq. (22), in arriving at the last equality. This calculation shows that in a neighborhood of the steady state, the $\dot{k} = 0$ isocline is negatively sloped in the $k\lambda$-phase space. Although it is possible to get a relatively global picture of the $\dot{k} = 0$ isocline for this model, we do not do so here, for the theorems we have invoked concerning stability are local in nature, as is the implicit function theorem, the tool we shall employ to conduct the steady state comparative statics. Therefore, in order to be consistent, we characterize the dynamics only locally via the phase diagram. The qualitative information about the $\dot{k} = 0$ isocline is displayed in Figure 15.2.

We note, in passing, that there is a unique value of k for which the slope of the $\dot{k} = 0$ isocline is zero, namely, that which is the solution to

$$\left.\frac{\partial \lambda}{\partial k}\right|_{\dot{k}=0} = \Lambda_k(k; \delta, \eta)|_{\dot{k}=0} = \left.\frac{f'(k) - [\delta + \eta]}{\hat{c}'(\lambda)}\right|_{\dot{k}=0} = \frac{f'(k) - [\delta + \eta]}{\hat{c}'(\Lambda(k; \delta, \eta))}$$

$$= 0 \Leftrightarrow f'(k) - [\delta + \eta] = 0. \tag{26}$$

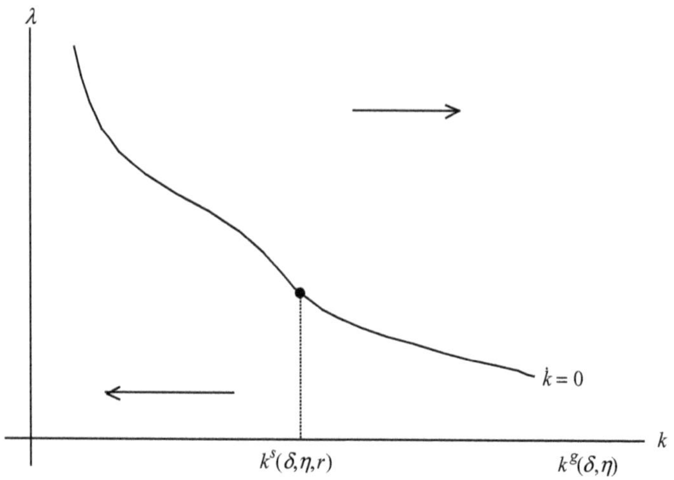

Figure 15.2

We denote the unique solution to this equation by $k = k^g(\delta, \eta)$, the superscript g standing for the "golden-rule" level of the per-capita capital stock. In a mental exercise, you are asked to establish an important relationship between the steady state level of the per-capita capital stock $k = k^s(\delta, \eta, r)$ and the golden-rule level of the per-capita capital stock $k = k^g(\delta, \eta)$, videlicet, that $k^s(\delta, \eta, r) < k^g(\delta, \eta)$, along with a few other properties concerning the shape of the $\dot{k} = 0$ isocline.

To determine the vector field for the $\dot{k} = 0$ isocline in a neighborhood of the steady state, we compute the following derivatives from Eq. (16):

$$\left.\frac{\partial \dot{k}}{\partial \lambda}\right|_{\substack{\dot{\lambda}=0 \\ \dot{k}=0}} = -\hat{c}'(\lambda)\big|_{\dot{\lambda}=\dot{k}=0} = -\hat{c}'(\lambda^s(\delta, \eta, r)) > 0, \tag{27}$$

$$\left.\frac{\partial \dot{k}}{\partial k}\right|_{\substack{\dot{\lambda}=0 \\ \dot{k}=0}} = f'(k) - [\delta + \eta]\big|_{\dot{\lambda}=\dot{k}=0} = f'(k^s(\delta, \eta, r)) - [\delta + \eta] = r > 0. \tag{28}$$

As expected, these are just the elements in the second row of the Jacobian $\mathbf{J}(k^s(\delta, \eta, r), \lambda^s(\delta, \eta, r))$. Equation (27) asserts that in a neighborhood of the steady state, an increase in λ increases $\dot{k}$ from zero to a positive value, thereby implying that all points above the $\dot{k} = 0$ isocline in a neighborhood of the steady state have k increasing over time. Symmetric reasoning applies for points below the $\dot{k} = 0$ isocline. Similarly, Eq. (28) demonstrates that in a neighborhood of the steady state, an increase in k increases $\dot{k}$ from zero to a positive value. Hence all points to the right of the $\dot{k} = 0$ isocline in a neighborhood of the steady state have k increasing over time, which is identical to the conclusion drawn from Eq. (27). This is just as it should be, since the $\dot{k} = 0$ isocline has a negative slope in a neighborhood of the steady state.

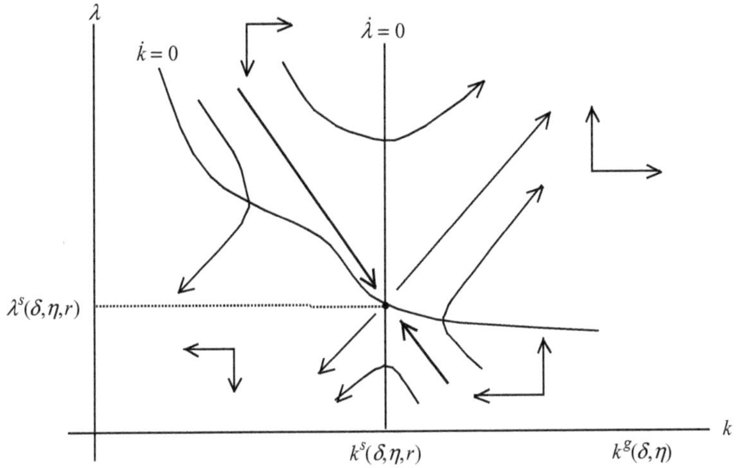

Figure 15.3

Bringing Figures 15.1 and 15.2 together, we arrive at Figure 15.3, the phase diagram for the neoclassical optimal growth problem. The phase paths consistent with the vector field in Figure 15.3 indicate that the steady state $(k^s(\delta, \eta, r), \lambda^s(\delta, \eta, r))$ is a saddle point with two paths approaching it as $t \to +\infty$, just as we found when we studied the Jacobian of the canonical equations (15) and (16). In passing, note that the steady state values of (k, λ) are found at the intersection of the $\dot{k} = 0$ and $\dot{\lambda} = 0$ isoclines.

The optimal phase paths to the neoclassical optimal growth problem are the pair of trajectories that converge to the steady state. Which of these is the unique optimal path depends on the initial condition $k(0) = k_0 > 0$ relative to the steady state value $k^s(\delta, \eta, r)$. For example, if $k_0 < k^s(\delta, \eta, r)$, then the optimal trajectory is the one in which λ falls over time and k increases over time until their steady state values are reached asymptotically. Because the optimal time path of per-capita consumption is defined by $c^*(t; \delta, \eta, r) \stackrel{\text{def}}{=} \hat{c}(\lambda(t; \delta, \eta, r))$, it follows from the chain rule that $\dot{c}^*(t; \delta, \eta, r) = \hat{c}'(\lambda(t; \delta, \eta, r))\dot{\lambda}(t; \delta, \eta, r) > 0$ when $k_0 < k^s(\delta, \eta, r)$. Thus, in this case, per-capita consumption rises over time until its steady state value, defined by $c^s(\delta, \eta, r) \stackrel{\text{def}}{=} \hat{c}(\lambda^s(\delta, \eta, r))$, is attained asymptotically. A symmetric conclusion is obtained if $k_0 > k^s(\delta, \eta, r)$, as you are asked to show in a mental exercise. Note that in the steady state, (k, c, λ) are constant at their steady state values, as is per-capita output, since it is defined as $y^s(\delta, \eta, r) \stackrel{\text{def}}{=} f(k^s(\delta, \eta, r))$. Furthermore, because (k, c, λ) are per-capita variables and the labor force (or population) is growing at the constant rate $\eta > 0$, the consumption rate, capital stock, and output rate must all be growing at the rate η in the steady state too if their per-capita values are constant.

Let's return to a remark made earlier concerning the nonnegativity constraint on the per-capita capital stock, that is, $k(t) \geq 0 \,\forall\, t \in [0, +\infty)$. It should be clear from Figure 15.3 that this constraint never binds in an optimal solution as long as $k(0) = k_0 > 0$. To see this, simply recall that the two trajectories that converge to the steady state are the only optimal ones, and that if $k(0) = k_0 > 0$, then all along these two paths, we have that $k(t) > 0 \; \forall \, t \in [0, +\infty)$. Hence the nonnegativity constraint on the per-capita capital stock is not binding in the optimal plan as long as $k(0) = k_0 > 0$.

At this point, one might be tempted to come to the conclusion that this is all the information that can be gleaned from the neoclassical optimal growth model without specifying the functional forms of the instantaneous utility function $U(\cdot)$ and the per-capita production function $f(\cdot)$. But you should know by now that this is false, for the steady state comparative statics and the local comparative dynamics have yet to be investigated. It is in this direction that we now turn. First we will investigate the steady state comparative statics of an increase in the discount rate r, and then turn to the corresponding local comparative dynamics, leaving the remaining parameters for you to contemplate in a mental exercise.

In identity form, the steady state necessary and sufficient conditions (17) and (18) are given by

$$\lambda^s(\delta, \eta, r)[\delta + \eta + r - f'(k^s(\delta, \eta, r))] \equiv 0, \tag{29}$$

$$f(k^s(\delta, \eta, r)) - [\delta + \eta]k^s(\delta, \eta, r) - \hat{c}(\lambda^s(\delta, \eta, r)) \equiv 0. \tag{30}$$

Differentiating these identities with respect to r yields

$$\begin{bmatrix} 0 & -\lambda^s(\delta, \eta, r) f''(k^s(\delta, \eta, r)) \\ -\hat{c}'(\lambda^s(\delta, \eta, r)) & r \end{bmatrix} \begin{bmatrix} \partial \lambda^s(\delta, \eta, r)/\partial r \\ \partial k^s(\delta, \eta, r)/\partial r \end{bmatrix} \equiv \begin{bmatrix} -\lambda^s(\delta, \eta, r) \\ 0 \end{bmatrix},$$

where we have used Eq. (29) to simplify the (2, 2) element of the Jacobian. Observe that the Jacobian matrix of the above system of comparative statics equations is identical to the Jacobian matrix $\mathbf{J}(k^s(\delta, \eta, r), \lambda^s(\delta, \eta, r))$ of the canonical equations (15) and (16) given in Eq. (19), just as it should be. Solving the above linear equations via Cramer's rule yields the steady state comparative statics

$$\frac{\partial \lambda^s}{\partial r} \equiv \frac{-r\lambda^s(\delta, \eta, r)}{|\mathbf{J}(k^s(\delta, \eta, r), \lambda^s(\delta, \eta, r))|} > 0,$$

$$\frac{\partial k^s}{\partial r} \equiv \frac{-\lambda^s(\delta, \eta, r)\hat{c}'(\lambda^s(\delta, \eta, r))}{|\mathbf{J}(k^s(\delta, \eta, r), \lambda^s(\delta, \eta, r))|} < 0,$$

which you should verify before reading on. Using the definitions $c^s(\delta, \eta, r) \overset{\text{def}}{=} \hat{c}(\lambda^s(\delta, \eta, r))$ and $y^s(\delta, \eta, r) \overset{\text{def}}{=} f(k^s(\delta, \eta, r))$, we can compute the steady state comparative statics of an increase in the social discount rate on the per-capita consumption rate and the per-capita output rate:

$$\frac{\partial c^s}{\partial r} = \hat{c}'(\lambda^s(\delta, \eta, r))\frac{\partial \lambda^s}{\partial r} = \frac{-r\hat{c}'(\lambda^s(\delta, \eta, r))\lambda^s(\delta, \eta, r)}{|\mathbf{J}(k^s(\delta, \eta, r), \lambda^s(\delta, \eta, r))|} < 0,$$

$$\frac{\partial y^s}{\partial r} = f'(k^s(\delta, \eta, r))\frac{\partial k^s}{\partial r} = \frac{-f'(k^s(\delta, \eta, r))\lambda^s(\delta, \eta, r)\hat{c}'(\lambda^s(\delta, \eta, r))}{|\mathbf{J}(k^s(\delta, \eta, r), \lambda^s(\delta, \eta, r))|} < 0.$$

Observe that in each of the above four steady state comparative statics expressions, the Jacobian determinant of the canonical equations (15) and (16) appears in the denominator. This is an elemental feature of the steady state comparative statics of an optimal control problem. That is to say, it is not specific to the optimal economic growth model, as we shall see in the next three chapters. This conclusion therefore implies two noteworthy facts: (i) one must determine the local stability of a steady state before the steady state comparative statics are derived, and (ii) the local stability of a steady state plays an analogous role in the signing of the steady state comparative statics as does the second-order sufficient condition of static optimization problems. Let's now turn to the economic interpretation of these steady state comparative statics results.

An increase in the social discount rate $r > 0$ lowers the steady state stock of per-capita capital, and consequently, steady state per-capita output falls as well. With a smaller per-capita capital stock, society values it more at the margin, and hence the steady state current value shadow price of the per-capita capital stock rises. This all seems intuitively plausible, since an increase in the social discount rate implies that society prefers to receive benefits sooner rather than later, since future benefits are valued lower in present value terms. What may seem a bit odd is that both the per-capita capital stock and the per-capita consumption rate are lowered by an increase in the social discount rate. That is, how can the per-capita capital stock be lower when per-capita consumption is also lower? This apparent puzzle is resolved once we investigate the local comparative dynamics of the model. More generally, a complete economic interpretation of an optimal control model can only be achieved by a thorough examination of its steady state comparative statics and comparative dynamics properties.

To find the local comparative dynamics of an increase in the social discount rate, we make use of Figure 15.3 and the above steady state comparative statics. The first thing to notice is that the solution to the $\dot{k} = 0$ isocline, namely, $\lambda = \Lambda(k; \delta, \eta)$, is independent of the social discount rate r in view of the fact that the $\dot{k} = 0$ isocline defined by Eq. (25) is independent of the social discount rate. Hence, any change in the social discount rate does not affect the $\dot{k} = 0$ isocline. This means that the $\dot{\lambda} = 0$ isocline must be the one that shifts when the social discount rate r increases, since we know from the steady state comparative statics that all of the model's variables do indeed change when the social discount rate r increases. This is consistent with the observation that the $\dot{\lambda} = 0$ isocline, defined by Eq. (22), depends explicitly

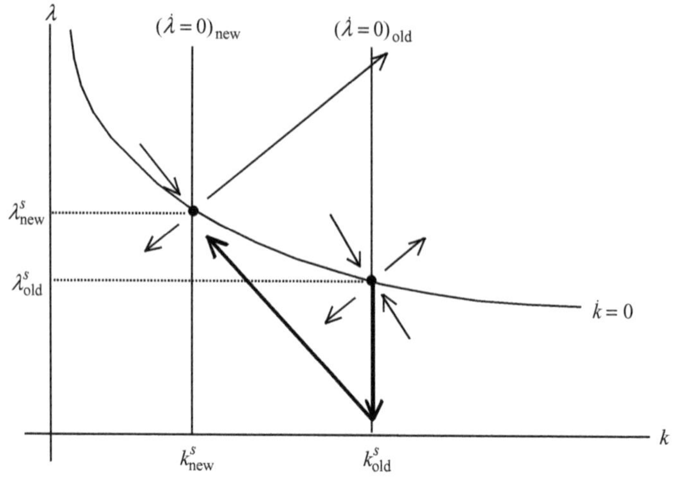

Figure 15.4

on the social discount rate. Specifically, because $\partial k^s/\partial r < 0$ and $\partial \lambda^s/\partial r > 0$, an increase in the social discount rate must shift the $\dot{\lambda} = 0$ isocline to the left in order for the steady state comparative statics to be verified in the phase diagram. The local comparative dynamics phase diagram must therefore appear as in Figure 15.4. Note that only the most relevant portion of the phase diagram is drawn, namely, the part of it in a neighborhood of the old and new steady states.

In drawing the comparative dynamics phase diagram, three important factors must be kept in mind. The first is that the local dynamics depicted in Figure 15.3 apply to *both* of the steady states depicted in Figure 15.4. In other words, the local dynamics around the old and the new steady states are qualitatively identical and are therefore of the saddle point variety. As a result, there is no need to fully draw in the vector field around each steady state in Figure 15.4 (which would clutter up the diagram severely), since the complete vector field for Figure 15.4 can be inferred from that in Figure 15.3. Second, before the increase in the social discount rate occurs, the economy is assumed to be at rest at the old steady state. Third, the economy is assumed to come to rest at the new steady state as a result of the increase in the social discount rate. That is, the old steady state value of per-capita capital is taken as the initial condition in the local comparative dynamics exercise, whereas the new steady state value of per-capita capital is taken as the terminal condition. The comparative dynamics phase diagram therefore depicts the optimal transition path from the old steady state to the new steady state that results from the increase in the social discount rate.

To begin a more detailed look at the construction of the local comparative dynamics phase portrait, first recall that in general, at any given moment in the planning horizon, the state variable is given and thus does not change when a parameter of the optimal control model initially changes. After the initial change in the parameter, however, the state variable does indeed generally change. This observation means that when the social discount rate initially increases, the per-capita capital stock is unaffected. Hence the only variable in the phase diagram that can move initially is the current value shadow price of per-capita capital. This implies that the initial movement in Figure 15.4 has to be vertical. Because the local dynamics of the new steady state are operative as soon as the social discount rate increases, a vertical upward movement in Figure 15.4 cannot lead to the new steady state, for it results in a subsequent trajectory pointing northeast and thus away from the new steady state. Consequently, a downward vertical movement must occur initially, as Figure 15.4 shows. In this case, the economy asymptotically reaches the new steady state using the stable manifold. The heavy lines in Figure 15.4 therefore depict the local comparative dynamics of the increase in the social discount rate in the neoclassical optimal growth model.

With the local comparative dynamics settled, a comprehensive economic interpretation of an increase in the social discount rate can now be given. Figure 15.4 shows that the initial effect of the social discount rate increase is to decrease the current value shadow price of per-capita capital. By differentiating the definition $c^*(t;\delta,\eta,r) \stackrel{\text{def}}{=} \hat{c}(\lambda(t;\delta,\eta,r))$ of the optimal path of per-capita consumption with respect to r and evaluating the result at $t = 0$, we find that

$$\left.\frac{\partial c^*(t;\delta,\eta,r)}{\partial r}\right|_{t=0} = \underbrace{\hat{c}'(\lambda(t;\delta,\eta,r))\big|_{t=0}}_{(-)} \underbrace{\left.\frac{\partial \lambda(t;\delta,\eta,r)}{\partial r}\right|_{t=0}}_{(-)} > 0.$$

This shows that the initial effect of the increase in the social discount rate is to increase the per-capita consumption rate. This makes economic sense too, for the higher social discount rate means that current consumption is favored over future consumption. Inasmuch as the per-capita consumption rate is inversely related to the current value shadow price of per-capita capital by Eq. (14), this is exactly what we see in Figure 15.4. After this initial effect, the per-capita capital stock begins its monotonic decline toward its new steady state level. The current value shadow price of per-capita capital, however, begins to rise but remains below its old steady state value for some finite period of time. This implies that the per-capita consumption rate begins to fall but still remains above its old steady state rate for some finite period of time. After enough time has passed since the initial increase in the social discount rate, the current value shadow price of per-capita capital increases above its old steady state value and asymptotically converges to its new higher steady state value. This implies that the per-capita consumption rate eventually falls below its old steady state rate and asymptotically converges to its new lower steady state rate. Because the per-capita capital stock declines monotonically from its old to its new steady state level, so too does the per-capita output rate of the economy. This can be seen by differentiating the definition $y^*(t;\delta,\eta,r) \stackrel{\text{def}}{=} f(k^*(t;\delta,\eta,r))$ of the optimal time path of per-capita output with respect to r, thereby yielding $\partial y^*(t;\delta,\eta,r)/\partial r = f'(k^*(t;\delta,\eta,r))\partial k^*(t;\delta,\eta,r)/\partial r < 0$. The local comparative dynamics computations clearly show that the reason for the lower per-capita output rate and per-capita capital stock in the steady state is the higher initial rate of per-capita consumption. Without examining the local comparative dynamics, therefore, it would not have been clear as to why the higher social discount rate leads to a lower per-capita stock of capital and a lower per-capita consumption rate in the steady state. A mental exercise asks you to derive and interpret the steady state comparative statics and local comparative dynamics of the depreciation rate and the growth rate of the labor force.

We close out this chapter by returning to the *utility functional* we used for the analysis of the neoclassical optimal growth model, videlicet, $\Psi[\cdot]$, which is a real-valued functional defined on some function space of consumption functions $c(\cdot)$ (we no longer need to think in per-capita terms). The utility functional provides a numerical measure of merit or worth for a given time path of consumption $c(t)$ over a given time interval τ, $\tau \overset{\text{def}}{=} \{t : t_0 \leq t \leq t_1 \text{ (or } +\infty)\}$, or over the union of several such intervals. In particular, the utility functional we used was a special case of

$$\Psi[c(\cdot)] \overset{\text{def}}{=} \int_{t_0}^{t_1} U(c(t))\, e^{-rt}\, dt, \tag{31}$$

where $U(\cdot)$ is a real-valued function, referred to as an instantaneous utility function, and $r > 0$ is the social discount rate. Our intention here is to examine some properties of the utility functional and relate them to what we know about the archetype utility function from neoclassical consumer theory. To begin, we provide a general definition of time additivity for utility functionals.

Let $c_1(\cdot)$ be a consumption function, the domain of which is the time interval τ_1, and let $c_2(\cdot)$ be a consumption function, the domain of which is the time interval τ_2. Suppose the time intervals do not overlap, so that $\tau_1 \cap \tau_2 = \emptyset$. Furthermore, define a consumption function $c_3(\cdot)$ on the set of time values $\tau_1 \cup \tau_2$ by

$$c_3(t) \overset{\text{def}}{=} \begin{cases} c_1(t), & t \in \tau_1 \\ c_2(t), & t \in \tau_2. \end{cases} \tag{32}$$

We therefore have the following definition of time additivity.

Definition 15.1: The utility functional $\Psi[\cdot]$ is *time additive* if

$$\Psi[c_3(\cdot)] = \Psi[c_1(\cdot)] + \Psi[c_2(\cdot)] \tag{33}$$

for all τ_1 and τ_2 and all functions $c_1(\cdot)$ and $c_2(\cdot)$.

Essentially, this definition asserts that the contributions to the measure of utility from consumption in different time intervals are additive. For example, the particular type of utility functional adopted in Eq. (31) has the property

$$\begin{aligned}\Psi[c_3(\cdot)] &\overset{\text{def}}{=} \int_{\tau_1 \cup \tau_2} U(c_3(t))\, e^{-rt}\, dt = \int_{\tau_1} U(c_1(t))\, e^{-rt}\, dt + \int_{\tau_2} U(c_2(t))\, e^{-rt}\, dt \\ &= \Psi[c_1(\cdot)] + \Psi[c_2(\cdot)],\end{aligned} \tag{34}$$

and is therefore time additive, since the integral is additive with respect to its interval of integration.

We now establish the following fundamental theorem.

Theorem 15.1: *Let $\Psi[\cdot]$ be a time additive utility functional.*

(i) If $\Psi^*[c(\cdot)] \stackrel{\text{def}}{=} h(\Psi[c(\cdot)])$ is a time additive utility functional, where $h(\cdot) : \Re \to \Re$ and $h(\cdot) \in C^{(2)}$, then $\Psi^*[\cdot] = a\Psi[\cdot] + b,\ a > 0$.

(ii) Any functional $\Psi^*[\cdot]$ defined by $\Psi^*[\cdot] = a\Psi[\cdot] + b,\ a > 0$, is a time additive utility functional.

(iii) Define the utility functionals $\Psi[\cdot]$ and $\Psi^*[\cdot]$ by

$$\Psi[c(\cdot)] \stackrel{\text{def}}{=} \int_{t_0}^{t_1} U(c(t))\, e^{-rt}\, dt \quad \text{and} \quad \Psi^*[c(\cdot)] \stackrel{\text{def}}{=} \int_{t_0}^{t_1} U^*(c(t))\, e^{-rt}\, dt.$$

Then $U^*(\cdot) = aU(\cdot),\ a > 0$.

Proof: Start with part (i). Let $c_1(\cdot)$ be any consumption function not identically zero and defined over the time interval τ_1, and let $c_2(\cdot)$ be any consumption function not identically zero and defined over the time interval τ_2, $\tau_1 \cap \tau_2 = \emptyset$. Define the modified consumption functions $c_i^*(\cdot) \stackrel{\text{def}}{=} \xi_i c_i(\cdot)$, where $\xi_i > 0$, $i = 1, 2$, and also define $c_3^*(\cdot)$ in a manner analogous to Eq. (32):

$$c_3^*(t) \stackrel{\text{def}}{=} \begin{cases} c_1^*(t),\ t \in \tau_1 \\ c_2^*(t),\ t \in \tau_2. \end{cases}$$

This construction implies that $\Psi[c_i^*(\cdot)]$ is a *function* of the parameter $\xi_i > 0$, say, $\Lambda_i(\xi_i)$, $i = 1, 2$, an observation that is analogous to our framework for deriving the necessary conditions for a simplified class of optimal control problems in Chapter 2. Given that $\Psi[\cdot]$ is time additive, $\Psi[c_3^*(\cdot)]$ is a function of both parameters, say, $\Omega(\xi_1, \xi_2) \stackrel{\text{def}}{=} \Lambda_1(\xi_1) + \Lambda_2(\xi_2)$. Assume that the functions $\Lambda_i(\cdot) \in C^{(1)}$, $i = 1, 2$. Similarly, if $\Psi^*[\cdot]$ is time additive, then $\Psi^*[c_3^*(\cdot)]$ is also a function of both parameters, say, $\Xi(\xi_1, \xi_2) \stackrel{\text{def}}{=} \Delta_1(\xi_1) + \Delta_2(\xi_2)$. Thus, since $\Psi^*[c(\cdot)] \stackrel{\text{def}}{=} h(\Psi[c(\cdot)])$, it follows that

$$\Xi(\xi_1, \xi_2) = h(\Omega(\xi_1, \xi_2)) = h(\Lambda_1(\xi_1) + \Lambda_2(\xi_2)) = \Delta_1(\xi_1) + \Delta_2(\xi_2).$$

Taking the cross-partial derivative of this equation yields

$$\Xi_{\xi_1\xi_2}(\xi_1, \xi_2) = h''(\Omega(\xi_1, \xi_2))\Lambda_1'(\xi_1)\Lambda_1'(\xi_2) \equiv 0, \tag{35}$$

since $\Omega_{\xi_1\xi_2}(\xi_1, \xi_2) \equiv 0$ and $\Xi_{\xi_1\xi_2}(\xi_1, \xi_2) \equiv 0$ by construction. Furthermore, because $c_1(\cdot)$ and $c_2(\cdot)$ are not identically zero, $\Lambda_1'(\xi_1) \neq 0$ and $\Lambda_2'(\xi_2) \neq 0$. Because Eq. (35) holds for every $c_1(\cdot)$ and $c_2(\cdot)$, and on account of $\Lambda_1'(\xi_1) \neq 0$ and $\Lambda_2'(\xi_2) \neq 0$, Eq. (35) implies that $h''(\cdot) \equiv 0$ over the range of the functional $\Psi[\cdot]$, which is the differential equation of interest. The solution to the differential equation $h''(\cdot) \equiv 0$ is the linear function $h(x) = ax + b$, where a and b are constants of integration. This observation leads to the conclusion that $\Psi^*[\cdot] = a\Psi[\cdot] + b$ if $\Psi[\cdot]$ and $\Psi^*[\cdot]$ are time additive. To complete the proof of part (i), we must show that $a > 0$. But this is straightforward, since if $\Psi^*[\cdot]$ is a utility functional, then when $\Psi[c_\ell(\cdot)] > \Psi[c_m(\cdot)]$, it must also be true that $\Psi^*[c_\ell(\cdot)] > \Psi^*[c_m(\cdot)]$, thereby yielding the conclusion that $a > 0$.

To prove part (ii), let $\Psi^*[\cdot] = a\Psi[\cdot] + b$, $a > 0$. Then $\Psi^*[\cdot]$ is time additive if $\Psi[\cdot]$ is time additive, and the same ordering of consumption paths is provided by $\Psi[\cdot]$ and $\Psi^*[\cdot]$, since $a > 0$. Thus $\Psi[\cdot]$ and $\Psi^*[\cdot]$ are equivalent as utility functionals.

Finally, to prove part (iii), simply note that

$$\Psi^*[c(\cdot)] \stackrel{\text{def}}{=} \int_{t_0}^{t_1} U^*(c(t))\, e^{-rt}\, dt = a\Psi[c(\cdot)] + b$$

$$= a \int_{t_0}^{t_1} U(c(t))\, e^{-rt}\, dt + b, \ a > 0.$$

This means that $U^*(\cdot) = aU(\cdot)$, $a > 0$. Q.E.D.

Parts (i) and (ii) of Theorem 15.1 assert that every time additive utility functional is a positive affine transformation of a time additive utility functional. In other words, a time additive utility functional is uniquely determined to the same extent that a thermometer scale is determined, namely, only the zero point and the unit of measurement can be arbitrarily chosen. This conclusion, as you may recall, is exactly analogous to that obtained in expected utility theory, scilicet, the expected utility function is unique up to a positive affine transformation. This is not all that surprising when you consider that the operation of expectation is performed by integration for continuous random variables.

Part (iii) of the theorem asserts that the instantaneous utility function corresponding to a time additive utility functional is a positive linear transformation of an instantaneous utility function corresponding to any other time additive utility functional. That is, the instantaneous utility function corresponding to a time additive utility functional is unique up to a positive scalar multiple, or equivalently, is unique up to the unit of measure adopted.

In the next chapter, we examine a seminal dynamic model from industrial organization theory, that of the limit pricing firm. The analysis again focuses on the local stability of the steady state, the steady state comparative statics, and the local comparative dynamics of the model. Rather than conduct the analysis in the state-costate phase plane, we elect to conduct the analysis of this model in the state-control phase plane. The choice of the phase space in which to conduct the investigation is a matter of taste when only one state variable and one control variable are present in an optimal control model.

MENTAL EXERCISES

15.1 Prove Lemma 15.1.

15.2 Show that the function $c \mapsto \ln c$ satisfies

$$U'(c) > 0 \,\forall\, c > 0,\; U''(c) < 0 \,\forall\, c > 0,\; \lim_{c \to 0} U'(c) = +\infty,\; \lim_{c \to +\infty} U'(c) = 0.$$

15.3 This question asks you to prove some global properties concerning the shape of the $\dot{k} = 0$ isocline.

(a) Prove that $k^s(\delta, \eta, r) < k^g(\delta, \eta)$. Draw a simple graph that provides the geometric support for your proof.

(b) Prove that

$$\left.\frac{\partial \lambda}{\partial k}\right|_{\dot{k}=0} = \Lambda_k(k; \delta, \eta)|_{\dot{k}=0} \begin{cases} < 0 \;\forall\; k < k^g(\delta, \eta) \\ > 0 \;\forall\; k > k^g(\delta, \eta) \end{cases}.$$

Note that this result is not evaluated at the steady state, but only along the $\dot{k} = 0$ isocline.

(c) Prove that the $\dot{k} = 0$ isocline is convex in a neighborhood of $k = k^g(\delta, \eta)$.

15.4 Define the optimal path of the per-capita output rate in the neoclassical optimal growth model. For $k_0 < k^s(\delta, \eta, r)$, is the optimal path of the per-capita output rate rising or falling on its approach to the steady state? Explain.

15.5 For the case $k_0 > k^s(\delta, \eta, r)$, determine the rates of change of the per-capita output rate, per-capita consumption rate, and the per-capita capital stock on their approach to the steady state in the neoclassical optimal growth model. Show your work.

15.6 For the neoclassical optimal growth model:

(a) Derive the steady state comparative statics of an increase in the growth rate of the population (or labor force) η on $(k^s(\delta, \eta, r), c^s(\delta, \eta, r), y^s(\delta, \eta, r), \lambda^s(\delta, \eta, r))$. Provide an economic interpretation of your results.

(b) Determine the local comparative dynamics of an increase in the growth rate of the population (or labor force) η on $(k^*(t; \delta, \eta, r), c^*(t; \delta, \eta, r), y^*(t; \delta, \eta, r), \lambda(t; \delta, \eta, r))$ using a phase diagram. Provide an economic interpretation of your results.

(c) Explain clearly why you do not have to recompute parts (a) and (b) for an increase in the depreciation rate of the capital stock δ.

15.7 Recall the neoclassical optimal growth model discussed in this chapter.

(a) Define the optimal value function, say, $V(\cdot)$, in two ways, being careful to denote the parameters on which it depends.

(b) Is the economy better off or worse off with a higher growth rate of the labor force (or population)? Show your work and provide an economic explanation.

(c) Is the economy better off or worse off with a higher depreciation rate of the capital stock? Show your work and provide an economic explanation.

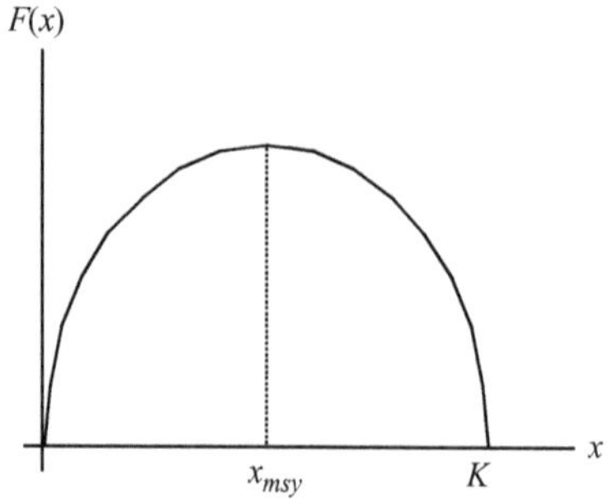

Figure 15.5

15.8 Consider a lake in which edible fish live, and denote the stock of fish at time t by $x(t)$. If undisturbed by humans, the fish grow according to the ordinary differential equation

$$\dot{x}(t) = F(x(t)),$$

where $F(\cdot)$, the growth function of the fish, has the following properties:

$$F(\cdot) \in C^{(2)},\ F(0) = 0,\ F(K) = 0,\ F'(x_{msy}) = 0,\ F''(x) < 0.$$

A prototypical graph of $F(x)$ is given by Figure 15.5, where x_{msy} is known as the maximum sustainable yield level of the stock. A local community situated by the lake can catch and consume the fish at rate c, yielding instantaneous utility $u(c;\alpha)$, where α is a parameter representing the community's taste for the fish. It is assumed that

$$u(\cdot) \in C^{(2)},\ u_c(c;\alpha) > 0,\ u_{cc}(c;\alpha) < 0,$$
$$u_{c\alpha}(c;\alpha) < 0,\ |u(c;\alpha)| \leq u_{\max} < +\infty.$$

Thus an increase in α lowers the community's enjoyment from catching and consuming fish at the margin; otherwise, the instantaneous utility function has the expected positive but declining marginal utility of consumption. Given the consumption of the fish, the rate of change of the stock is now given by the differential equation

$$\dot{x}(t) = F(x(t)) - c(t).$$

The community wishes to choose its consumption rate function $c(\cdot)$ so as to maximize their present discounted utility of consumption, that is, the community solves the problem

$$\max_{c(\cdot)} \int_0^{+\infty} u(c(t);\alpha)\, e^{-rt}\, dt$$

$$\text{s.t.}\quad \dot{x}(t) = F(x(t)) - c(t),\ x(0) = x_0,$$
$$c(t) \geq 0\, \forall\, t \in [0, +\infty),$$

where $r > 0$ is the community's discount rate, $x_0 > 0$ is the initial stock of fish in the lake, and no conditions are imposed on $\lim_{t\to+\infty} x(t)$. Assume that the nonnegativity constraint $x(t) \geq 0 \,\forall\, t \in [0, +\infty)$ is not binding, and that there exists a simple, finite, and positive steady state solution of the necessary conditions, say, $(x^s(\alpha, r), c^s(\alpha, r))$, with corresponding current value costate variable $\lambda^s(\alpha, r)$.

(a) Write down the current value Hamiltonian and Lagrangian. Does the objective functional converge for all admissible pairs? Show your work. Derive the necessary conditions for this problem. Provide an economic interpretation of the costate variable.

(b) Assume that an admissible solution exists to the community's planning problem that satisfies the necessary conditions and for which $\lim_{t\to+\infty} x(t) = x^s(\alpha, r) > 0$. Prove, under suitable additional assumptions to be identified by you, that this solution is the unique optimal solution of the planning problem. Show your work and explain clearly.

(c) Assume that in an optimal plan $c(t) > 0 \,\forall\, t \in [0, +\infty)$. Show that the necessary conditions can be reduced to the following pair of ordinary differential equations:

$$\dot{c} = \frac{u_c(c; \alpha)[r - F'(x)]}{u_{cc}(c; \alpha)},$$

$$\dot{x} = F(x) - c.$$

Hint: Differentiate the necessary condition $H_c = 0$ with respect to t, and use the other necessary conditions to get a differential equation for c.

(d) Prove that the steady state solution of the necessary conditions in part (c), namely, $(x^s(\alpha, r), c^s(\alpha, r))$, is a local saddle point.

(e) Derive the phase diagram corresponding to the system of ordinary differential equations in part (c). Show your work and label the diagram carefully, indicating the optimal trajectory.

(f) Write down the steady state version of the necessary conditions in part (c). Explain how you would derive, in principle of course, the steady state solution $(x^s(\alpha, r), c^s(\alpha, r))$ of these necessary conditions. Explain carefully and rigorously how you know that such functions are locally $C^{(1)}$.

(g) Interpret an increase in α as an increase in the community's awareness about the negative effects of eating fish from this now polluted lake. The sign $u_{c\alpha}(c; \alpha) < 0$ reflects this kind of interpretation. *Without any mathematics*, provide an economic explanation for the signs of the steady state comparative statics, to wit,

$$\frac{\partial x^s}{\partial \alpha}, \frac{\partial c^s}{\partial \alpha}, \quad \text{and} \quad \frac{\partial \lambda^s}{\partial \alpha},$$

that you expect *a priori*. Now show that your so-called economic intuition was wrong for $\partial x^s(\alpha, r)/\partial \alpha$ and $\partial c^s(\alpha, r)/\partial \alpha$! Also compute $\partial \lambda^s(\alpha, r)/\partial \alpha$.

(h) Derive the steady state comparative statics for an increase in r.

(i) Derive the local comparative dynamics phase portrait for an increase in the discount rate. Label the diagram carefully and provide an economic interpretation.

15.9 Environmental resources provide services that range from essential life support, such as air and water, to unadulterated amenities, such as a field of wild mustard in the Napa Valley. Using a simple optimal control model, this question examines the inherent trade-off between consumption, which depletes the environmental resource stock and thus reduces its amenity value, and preservation of the resource stock, which maintains its amenity value. We assume, therefore, that society has preferences over both its rate of consumption $c(t)$ and the stock of the amenity value $a(t)$, which are represented by the $C^{(2)}$ instantaneous utility function $U(\cdot)$ with values $U(a, c)$. Assume that $U(\cdot)$ has the following properties:

$$U_a(a, c) > 0,\ U_c(a, c) > 0,\ U_{aa}(a, c) < 0,\ U_{cc}(a, c) < 0,\ U_{ac}(a, c) \equiv 0.$$

The differential equation governing the dynamics of the amenity value of the resource stock is given by $\dot{a}(t) = \gamma[\bar{a} - a(t)] - c(t)$, where $\gamma > 0$ is a constant parameter that indicates the natural vigor of the environment, and $\bar{a} > 0$ is the globally asymptotically stable fixed point of the differential equation in the absence of consumption, as is easily verified via a phase portrait. Define $a(0) = a_0 > 0$ as the initial stock of the amenity. Then the optimal control problem under consideration can be stated as

$$V(\beta) \stackrel{\text{def}}{=} \max_{c(\cdot)} \int_0^{+\infty} U(a(t), c(t))\, e^{-rt}\, dt$$

$$\text{s.t.}\quad \dot{a}(t) = \gamma[\bar{a} - a(t)] - c(t),\ a(0) = a_0 > 0,$$

where $\beta \stackrel{\text{def}}{=} (\bar{a}, \gamma, r, a_0) \in \Re^4_{++}$. Assume that the pair $(a^*(t; \beta), c^*(t; \beta))$ is an admissible solution of the necessary conditions of the optimal control problem, with corresponding current value costate variable $\lambda^*(t; \beta)$, such that $(a^*(t; \beta), c^*(t; \beta)) \to (a^s(\alpha), c^s(\alpha))$ as $t \to +\infty$, where $(a^s(\alpha), c^s(\alpha))$ are the simple steady state values of the amenity value and consumption rate, and $\alpha \stackrel{\text{def}}{=} (\bar{a}, \gamma, r) \in \Re^3_{++}$. Finally, assume that $a^*(t; \beta) > 0$ and that $c^*(t; \beta) > 0$ for all $t \in [0, +\infty)$.

(a) Write down the necessary conditions for this problem in *current value* form.

(b) Make an assumption so as to guarantee that the solution $(a^*(t; \beta), c^*(t; \beta))$ to the necessary conditions is the unique solution of the control problem. Make sure you verify that your assumption does indeed yield the desired conclusion and show your work.

(c) Reduce the necessary conditions down to a pair of differential equations involving only (a, c).

(d) Prove that the steady state $(a^s(\alpha), c^s(\alpha))$ is a local saddle point.

(e) Draw the phase portrait for the system of ordinary differential equations in part (c). Show your work and label the diagram carefully.

(f) Derive the steady state comparative statics for the discount rate r, that is, find

$$\frac{\partial a^s(\alpha)}{\partial r}, \quad \frac{\partial c^s(\alpha)}{\partial r}, \quad \frac{\partial \lambda^s(\alpha)}{\partial r}.$$

(g) Derive the local comparative dynamics phase diagram for the discount rate. Provide an economic interpretation of your results, taking into account the steady state comparative statics from part (f).

(h) Derive the steady state comparative statics for the natural vigor of the environment γ, that is to say, find

$$\frac{\partial a^s(\alpha)}{\partial \gamma}, \quad \frac{\partial c^s(\alpha)}{\partial \gamma}, \quad \frac{\partial \lambda^s(\alpha)}{\partial \gamma}.$$

(i) Derive the local comparative dynamics phase diagrams for the natural vigor of the environment. Provide an economic interpretation of your results, taking into account the steady state comparative statics from part (h).

15.10 Prove that all the admissible paths of the per-capita capital stock $k(t)$ are bounded in the neoclassical optimal economic growth model. **Hints:** In order to do so, you should employ Eqs. (4) and (7), the fact that $\delta + \eta > 0$, and the nonnegativity constraints on $c(t)$ and $k(t)$. Set $c(t) \equiv 0 \, \forall \, t \in [0, +\infty)$ so Eq. (7) reduces to $\dot{k} + [\delta + \eta]k = f(k)$. Use an appropriate integrating factor for the left-hand side of $\dot{k} + [\delta + \eta]k = f(k)$ and then integrate it using the initial condition to arrive at an implicit solution. Use this implicit solution to prove the result.

FURTHER READING

The neoclassical model of optimal economic growth has a rather long and important history in intertemporal economic theory. The seminal paper on the subject is the classic by Ramsey (1928), published when he was only 25 years old. Takayama (1985, Chapter 5, Section D) and Takayama (1993, Chapter 9) contain numerous references to much of the ensuing literature that sought to generalize the basic Ramsey (1928) model, one of the most important of which is Cass (1965). The more recent works of Romer (1986, 1990) examining increasing returns and growth, and endogenous technical change, are arguably the most important of the recent extensions of the basic model. Mental Exercise 15.8 is drawn from Plourde (1970), whereas Mental Exercise 15.9 is based on an exercise in Neher (1990). More recent work on the renewable resource–extracting model of the firm includes Caputo (1989), who presents a rather complete qualitative analysis of the model akin to that of this chapter, and Levhari and Withagen (1992), who study the model when the growth rate of the resource can be influenced directly by the actions of the exploiting firm. The material on the properties of the utility functional is drawn from Hadley and Kemp (1971).

REFERENCES

Caputo, M.R. (1989), "The Qualitative Content of Renewable Resource Models," *Natural Resource Modeling*, 3, 241–259.

Cass, D. (1965), "Optimum Growth in an Aggregate Model of Capital Accumulation," *Review of Economic Studies*, 32, 233–240.

Hadley, G. and Kemp, M.C. (1971), *Variational Methods in Economics* (Amsterdam: North-Holland Publishing Co.).

Levhari, D. and Withagen, C. (1992), "Optimal Management of the Growth Potential of Renewable Resources," *Journal of Economics*, 56, 297–309.

Neher, P.A. (1990), *Natural Resource Economics: Conservation and Exploitation* (New York: Cambridge University Press).

Plourde, C.G. (1970), "A Simple Model of Replenishable Natural Resource Exploitation," *American Economic Review*, 60, 518–523.

Ramsey, F.P. (1928), "A Mathematical Theory of Saving," *Economic Journal*, 38, 543–559.

Romer, P.M. (1986), "Increasing Returns and Long-Run Growth," *Journal of Political Economy*, 94, 1002–1037.

Romer, P.M. (1990), "Endogenous Technical Change," *Journal of Political Economy*, 98, S71–S102.

Simon, C.P. and Blume, L. (1994), *Mathematics for Economists* (New York: W.W. Norton & Company, Inc.).

Takayama, A. (1985, 2nd Ed.), *Mathematical Economics* (New York: Cambridge University Press).

Takayama, A. (1993), *Analytical Methods in Economics* (Ann Arbor: University of Michigan Press).

SIXTEEN

A Dynamic Limit Pricing Model of the Firm

The limit pricing model developed in this chapter is an attempt to gain some insight into the optimal pricing strategy for a dominant firm or group of joint profit-maximizing oligopolists facing potential entry into the product market. Early research on this subject was from a static perspective, and, for the most part, concluded that the dominant firm will maximize its present value by either (i) charging the short-run profit-maximizing price and allowing its market share to decline, or (ii) setting price at the limit price thereby precluding all entry. A firm practicing short-run profit maximization would have to continually ignore the reality of entry by other firms induced by its pricing strategy. On the other hand, a firm charging the limit price has to think that its current market share is in fact its long-run optimal market share. Economic intuition suggests that the optimal pricing strategy entails a balancing of current profits and long-run market share. For example, a dominant firm currently charging a high price and earning high current profits is likely sacrificing some future profits through the erosion of its current market share. It is this dependence of the dominant firm's future market share, and thus its profits, on its current pricing strategy that makes this model inherently dynamic.

We assert that the optimal pricing strategy of the dominant firm will maximize the present discounted value of its profits, as given by the functional

$$\max_{p(\cdot)} J[x(\cdot), p(\cdot)] \stackrel{\text{def}}{=} \int_{0}^{+\infty} [p(t) - c]\, q(p(t), x(t))\, e^{-rt}\, dt, \tag{1}$$

where $p(t)$ is the price charged by the dominant firm at time t for its good, $c > 0$ is the constant average (and marginal) cost of production of the dominant firm, $x(t)$ is the level of competitive fringe (or rival) firms' sales at time t, $q(\cdot)$ is the residual demand function facing the dominant firm, and $r > 0$ is the constant discount rate of the dominant firm. Note that we may also interpret $x(t)$ as the number of fringe firms in the market at time t as long as we assume that each fringe firm sells just one unit of the good.

We assume that the residual demand curve $q(p(t), x(t))$ facing the dominant firm is given by the total market demand curve for the product $f(p(t))$, less the level of rival firms' sales $x(t)$, that is to say,

$$q(p(t), x(t)) \stackrel{\text{def}}{=} f(p(t)) - x(t). \tag{2}$$

In other words, the residual demand curve at any given point in time can be found by subtracting the output of the competitive fringe from the total market demand for the product. Equation (2) therefore indicates that the net effect of rival entry into the product market is to shift the dominant firm's residual demand curve laterally.

We assume that the fringe firms are rational actors in the sense that their rate of entry, or the rate of change of fringe sales, $\dot{x}(t)$, is determined by their expected rate of return from entering the market. If potential entrants view the current product price as a proxy for the future price, then the rate of entry can be approximated by a monotonically increasing function of the current product price. We assume that such a relationship can be represented by the linear state equation and initial condition

$$\dot{x}(t) = k[p(t) - \bar{p}],\ x(0) = x_0, \tag{3}$$

where $k > 0$ is the time invariant fringe response coefficient, $\bar{p} > 0$ is the time invariant limit price, and $x_0 > 0$ is the initial level of fringe sales. The limit price $\bar{p}$ is defined as that price for which net entry is zero, that is, $\dot{x}(t) = 0 \Leftrightarrow p(t) = \bar{p}$. As Eq. (3) makes clear, any price below the limit price $\bar{p}$ causes exit from the market by fringe firms ($\dot{x}(t) < 0$), and any price above the limit price $\bar{p}$ attracts new entrants to the market ($\dot{x}(t) > 0$). Alternatively, we have that sign $\dot{x}(t) = \text{sign}[p(t) - \bar{p}]$.

The following assumptions are also imposed on the dynamic limit pricing model:

$$f(\cdot) \in C^{(2)}\,\forall\, p > 0,\ f'(p) < 0\,\forall\, p \geq 0,$$

$$p(t) > 0\,\forall\, t \in [0, +\infty) \quad \text{and} \quad x(t) > 0\,\forall\, t \in [0, +\infty),$$

$$\bar{p} \geq c.$$

The first two assumptions say that the market demand function has two continuous derivatives for all positive prices and is downward sloping for nonnegative product prices. The next two state that the dominant firm will never give the product away, even for an instant, and that there are always some fringe sales of the product. These two assumptions are made so we can more readily focus on the basic economic content of the problem. Finally, the last assumption says the dominant firm's average cost of production is never greater than the limit price. The difference between the limit price and the dominant firm's average cost of production is a measure of the cost advantage enjoyed by the dominant firm.

Bringing all this information together, the complete statement of the dynamic limit pricing model is

$$V(c,k,\bar{p},r,x_0) \overset{\text{def}}{=} \max_{p(\cdot)} \int_0^{+\infty} [p(t)-c]\,[f(p(t))-x(t)]\,e^{-rt}\,dt \tag{4}$$

$$\text{s.t.} \quad \dot{x}(t) = k[p(t)-\bar{p}],\ x(0)=x_0.$$

Note that we have not imposed any assumptions on $\lim_{t\to+\infty} x(t)$, nor do we intend to. As you will show in a mental exercise, without imposing any other assumptions on control problem (4), we cannot invoke a sufficiency theorem to solve it. Consequently, we assume that an optimal solution exists to this limit pricing problem and denote it by $(x^*(t;\beta), p^*(t;\beta))$, with corresponding current value costate variable $\lambda(t;\beta)$, where $\beta \overset{\text{def}}{=} (c,k,\bar{p},r,x_0)$ is the parameter vector of problem (4).

The current value Hamiltonian for problem (4) is defined as

$$H(x,p,\lambda;c,k,\bar{p}) \overset{\text{def}}{=} [p-c][f(p)-x] + \lambda k[p-\bar{p}]. \tag{5}$$

Given the assumptions made so far on problem (4), and furthermore assuming that the objective functional exists for all admissible pairs of curves $(x(t), p(t))$, Theorems 14.3 and 14.9 imply the following necessary conditions:

$$H_p(x,p,\lambda;c,k,\bar{p}) = [p-c]f'(p) + f(p) - x + \lambda k = 0, \tag{6}$$

$$H_{pp}(x,p,\lambda;c,k,\bar{p}) = [p-c]f''(p) + 2f'(p) \le 0, \tag{7}$$

$$\dot{\lambda} = r\lambda - H_x(x,p,\lambda;c,k,\bar{p}) = r\lambda + p - c, \tag{8}$$

$$\dot{x} = H_\lambda(x,p,\lambda;c,k,\bar{p}) = k[p-\bar{p}],\ x(0)=x_0, \tag{9}$$

$$\lim_{t\to+\infty} e^{-rt} H(x,p,\lambda;c,k,\bar{p}) = 0. \tag{10}$$

Equation (6) says the present value profit-maximizing price charged by the dominant firm results in the marginal profit being proportional to the negative of the current value shadow price of rival sales, the constant of proportionality being the fringe response coefficient. Because fringe firms' sales are a bad (rather than a good), that is, more fringe firms' sales means less dominant firm sales, ceteris paribus, the current value shadow price of rival sales is negative in an optimal plan, that is, $\lambda(t;\beta) < 0\ \forall\, t \in [0,+\infty)$. The transversality condition in Eq. (10) asserts that the present value of the Hamiltonian along the optimal path is zero in the limit of the planning horizon. It helps to place more structure on the optimal pair $(x^*(t;\beta), p^*(t;\beta))$ than we would otherwise be able to detect without it, as we now proceed to show.

To this end, assume that a simple steady state solution to the limit pricing problem exists, say, $(x^s(\alpha), p^s(\alpha))$, with corresponding steady state current value shadow price of fringe sales $\lambda^s(\alpha)$, where $\alpha \overset{\text{def}}{=} (c,k,\bar{p},r)$. Now if $(x^*(t;\beta), p^*(t;\beta)) \to (x^s(\alpha), p^s(\alpha))$ as $t \to +\infty$, thereby implying that $\lambda(t;\beta) \to \lambda^s(\alpha)$ as $t \to +\infty$ by

Eq. (6), then such an optimal solution does indeed satisfy the limiting transversality condition in Eq. (10). To see this, observe that $e^{-rt} \to 0$ as $t \to +\infty$ and that the value of the current value Hamiltonian along such a converging path goes to a finite value as $t \to +\infty$, since $H(\cdot) \in C^{(2)}$. These two facts imply that Eq. (10) is satisfied for an optimal solution that converges to its steady state solution. Accordingly, we assume that the optimal solution to the limit pricing model converges to its simple steady state solution in the limit of the planning horizon, since such a solution satisfies the necessary limiting transversality condition given in Eq. (10).

We also assume that the local second-order sufficient condition $H_{pp}(x, p, \lambda; c, k, \bar{p}) < 0$ for maximizing the current value Hamiltonian holds along the optimal path. This implies that in a neighborhood of the optimal solution, marginal profit is downward sloping in the product price, since $H_{pp}(x, p, \lambda; c, k, \bar{p}) = \pi_{pp}(x, p; c)$. Given Eq. (6), the fact that $\lambda(t; \beta) < 0 \,\forall\, t \in [0, +\infty)$, and the assumption that $H_{pp}(x, p, \lambda; c, k, \bar{p}) = \pi_{pp}(x, p; c) < 0$ in a neighborhood of the optimal solution, we can prove the following preliminary result.

Proposition 16.1: *If $H_{pp}(x, p, \lambda; c, k, \bar{p}) < 0$ along the optimal solution, then the optimal dynamic price $p^*(t; \beta)$ will always be less than the short-run profit-maximizing price p_m all along the optimal path.*

Proof: If the dominant firm has been moving along the optimal path, then its instantaneous profit at any given moment in the planning horizon is given by

$$\pi(x, p; c) \stackrel{\text{def}}{=} [p - c][f(p) - x].$$

The short-run profit-maximizing price p_m therefore necessarily satisfies

$$\pi_p(x, p; c) = [p - c]f'(p) + f(p) - x = 0, \tag{11}$$

where x is evaluated at its optimal value for the given point in time under consideration. From Eq. (6), it follows that the optimal dynamic price path $p^*(t; \beta)$ necessarily satisfies

$$\pi_p(x, p; c) = [p - c]f'(p) + f(p) - x = -\lambda k > 0, \tag{12}$$

where the strict inequality follows from the fact that $\lambda(t; \beta) < 0 \,\forall\, t \in [0, +\infty)$ and the assumption that $k > 0$. Because $H_{pp}(x, p, \lambda; c, k, \bar{p}) = \pi_{pp}(x, p; c) < 0$ along the optimal solution by assumption, the curve $\pi_p(x, p; c)$, plotted as a function of p, is downward sloping. Hence the optimal dynamic price $p^*(t; \beta)$, which satisfies Eq. (12), must necessarily be less than the short-run profit-maximizing price p_m, which satisfies Eq. (11). Q.E.D.

Proposition 16.1 establishes that, ceteris paribus, the dynamic limit pricing firm sets its optimal price below that of a myopic monopolistic firm. The most important

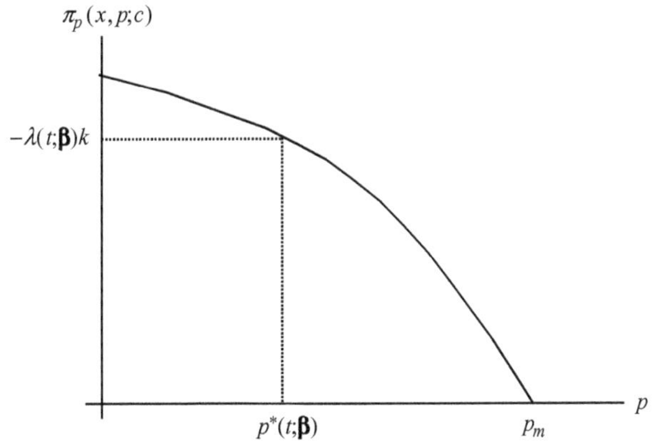

Figure 16.1

features of the model in reaching this conclusion are the presence of the current value costate variable in Eq. (6) and the fact that it is negative. This proposition therefore shows that one of the conclusions derived from a static investigation of the limit pricing model is incorrect, namely, that the dominant firm will maximize its present value by charging the short-run profit-maximizing price and allowing its market share to decline. Figure 16.1 provides a graphical representation of the proposition.

Our task now is to determine the local stability of the steady state, which the optimal solution converges to in the limit of the planning horizon. In order to do so, we must reduce the three necessary conditions (6), (8), and (9), down to two differential equations involving just two of the three variables (x, p, λ). The two variables of primary interest are the price set by the dominant firm and the level of fringe sales. As a result, we must eliminate λ from the necessary conditions. To do this, the following recipe, which is used often in the literature, is employed.

The first step is to differentiate the necessary condition $H_p(x, p, \lambda; c, k, \bar{p}) = 0$ with respect to t to get

$$\frac{d}{dt}H_p(x, p, \lambda; c, k, \bar{p}) = [[p - c]f''(p) + 2f'(p)]\dot{p} - \dot{x} + \dot{\lambda}k = 0. \tag{13}$$

This is a valid operation because the optimal solution must necessarily satisfy $H_p(x, p, \lambda; c, k, \bar{p}) = 0$ identically for all $t \in [0, +\infty)$, and thus must satisfy $\frac{d}{dt}H_p(x, p, \lambda; c, k, \bar{p}) = 0$ as well. Heuristically, if a solution satisfies an equation for all values of t, then it must also satisfy that same equation when t is perturbed slightly.

The second step is to solve Eq. (6) for λ to get

$$\lambda = k^{-1}[x - f(p) - [p - c]f'(p)]. \tag{14}$$

This step is required seeing as we want to eliminate λ from the necessary conditions.

The final step is to substitute Eqs. (8), (9), and (14) into Eq. (13) to eliminate $\dot{\lambda}$, $\dot{x}$, and λ from Eq. (13), thereby yielding

$$[[p-c]f''(p)+2f'(p)]\dot{p}-k[p-\bar{p}]$$
$$+k[rk^{-1}[x-f(p)-[p-c]f'(p)]+p-c]=0. \tag{15}$$

Solving Eq. (15) for $\dot{p}$ and combining the resulting differential equation with the state equation gives the pair of necessary conditions of economic interest

$$\dot{p}=\frac{r[[p-c]f'(p)+f(p)-x]+k[c-\bar{p}]}{[p-c]f''(p)+2f'(p)}, \tag{16}$$

$$\dot{x}=k[p-\bar{p}]. \tag{17}$$

Note that because we have assumed that $H_{pp}(x, p, \lambda; c, k, \bar{p}) < 0$ along the optimal path, the denominator of Eq. (16) is nonzero and thus the differential equation is well defined. With the reduction of the necessary conditions to a pair of simultaneous differential equations now complete, we may now turn to the determination of the local stability of the steady state.

We begin by finding the steady state solution of necessary conditions (16) and (17). Inasmuch as $\dot{p}=0$ and $\dot{x}=0$ by definition of a steady state, the steady state versions of Eqs. (16) and (17) take the form

$$\dot{p}=0 \Leftrightarrow r[[p-c]f'(p)+f(p)-x]+k[c-\bar{p}]=0, \tag{18}$$

$$\dot{x}=0 \Leftrightarrow p-\bar{p}=0. \tag{19}$$

From Eq. (19), it is clear that the steady state solution for the dominant firm's price exists and is given by

$$p=p^s(\alpha) \stackrel{\text{def}}{=} \bar{p}>0. \tag{20}$$

Upon substituting Eq. (20) into Eq. (18) and solving for x, we find that the steady state solution for fringe sales exists and is given by

$$x=x^s(\alpha) \stackrel{\text{def}}{=} f(\bar{p})-[\bar{p}-c]\,[r^{-1}k-f'(\bar{p})]. \tag{21}$$

Using Eq. (21), we may then define the steady state market share of the dominant firm as

$$m^s(\alpha) \stackrel{\text{def}}{=} \frac{f(\bar{p})-x^s(\alpha)}{f(\bar{p})}=\frac{[\bar{p}-c][r^{-1}k-f'(\bar{p})]}{f(\bar{p})} \geq 0. \tag{22}$$

In passing, note that there is no need to discuss or compute the Jacobian matrix of Eqs. (18) and (19), as explicit steady state solutions for the dominant firm's price and fringe sales have been obtained. Before examining the local stability of the steady state solution, we pause and present a few observations about this solution.

The first is that if the dominant firm does not enjoy a cost advantage over the fringe firms, that is, if $\bar{p}=c$, then from Eqs. (21) and (22) it follows that the fringe firms supply the entire market and the market share of the dominant firm is zero in the steady state, that is to say, $x^s(\alpha)|_{\bar{p}=c} = f(c)$ and $m^s(\alpha)|_{\bar{p}=c} = 0$. Therefore, if the dominant firm does not enjoy a cost advantage over the fringe firms, then the optimal pricing strategy of the dominant firm results in it pricing itself out of the market in the long run. Because this is the optimal policy given $\bar{p} = c$, any other pricing strategy is inferior.

Second, the steady state market share of the dominant firm and fringe sales are positive in the steady state for all $\bar{p} > c$ and $\bar{p}$ sufficiently close to c. To see this, differentiate Eq. (21) with respect to $\bar{p}$ and evaluate the result at $\bar{p} = c$ to get

$$\left.\frac{\partial x^s(\alpha)}{\partial \bar{p}}\right|_{\bar{p}=c} = [f'(\bar{p}) + [\bar{p} - c]f''(\bar{p}) - [r^{-1}k - f'(\bar{p})]]\big|_{\bar{p}=c}$$
$$= 2f'(c) - r^{-1}k < 0. \tag{23}$$

Given that $x^s(\alpha)|_{\bar{p}=c} = f(c)$ and $\partial x^s(\alpha)/\partial \bar{p}$ is continuous, it follows from Eq. (23) that $x^s(\alpha) < f(\bar{p})$ for all $\bar{p} > c$ and $\bar{p}$ sufficiently close to c. This, in turn, implies that $m^s(\alpha) > 0$ for all $\bar{p} > c$ and $\bar{p}$ sufficiently close to c using Eq. (22). Thus our assumption of an interior solution can be justified under the assumptions that $\bar{p} > c$ and that $\bar{p}$ is sufficiently close to c.

The local stability of the steady state is determined by finding the eigenvalues of the Jacobian matrix corresponding to Eqs. (16) and (17) evaluated at the steady state, namely,

$$\mathbf{J}(p^s(\alpha), x^s(\alpha)) \overset{\text{def}}{=} \begin{bmatrix} \dfrac{\partial \dot{p}}{\partial p} & \dfrac{\partial \dot{p}}{\partial x} \\[2ex] \dfrac{\partial \dot{x}}{\partial p} & \dfrac{\partial \dot{x}}{\partial x} \end{bmatrix}_{\substack{\dot{p}=0\\ \dot{x}=0}} = \begin{bmatrix} r & \dfrac{-r}{H_{pp}(\bar{p}; c)} \\ k & 0 \end{bmatrix}, \tag{24}$$

where $H_{pp}(p; c) = [p - c]f''(p) + 2f'(p) < 0$. Note that in the notation for $H_{pp}(\cdot)$, we have made explicit only those variables on which it depends. Now recall that by Mental Exercise 13.4, or equivalently, by Theorem 23.9 of Simon and Blume (1994), the product of the eigenvalues of $\mathbf{J}(p^s(\alpha), x^s(\alpha))$ equals its determinant. As a result, because $|\mathbf{J}(p^s(\alpha), x^s(\alpha))| = rk/H_{pp}(\bar{p}; c) < 0$, one eigenvalue is real and positive and the other is real and negative, thereby implying that the steady state is hyperbolic. Therefore, by Theorem 13.6 or Theorem 13.7, the steady state $(p^s(\alpha), x^s(\alpha))$ of the nonlinear system of differential equations comprising Eqs. (16) and (17) is an unstable saddle point, with two trajectories in the xp-phase plane converging to it as $t \to +\infty$. With the local stability of the steady state determined, we turn to the derivation of the phase diagram for the limit pricing model.

First we examine the $\dot{p} = 0$ isocline, defined as

$$\dot{p} = 0 \Leftrightarrow r[[p - c]f'(p) + f(p) - x] + k[c - \bar{p}] = 0. \tag{25}$$

Because the Jacobian of the $\dot{p} = 0$ isocline with respect to p evaluated at the steady state is $rH_{pp}(\bar{p}; c) = r[[\bar{p} - c]f''(\bar{p}) + 2f'(\bar{p})] < 0$, the implicit function theorem implies that we can, in principle, express p as a function of $(x;\alpha)$ along the $\dot{p}=0$ isocline in a neighborhood of the steady state, say, $p=P(x;\alpha)$. Hence, by the implicit function theorem, the slope of the $\dot{p}=0$ isocline in a neighborhood of the steady state is given by

$$\left.\frac{\partial p}{\partial x}\right|_{\substack{\dot{p}=0\\ \dot{x}=0}} = P_x(x^s(\alpha);\alpha) = \left.\frac{-\partial\dot{p}/\partial x}{\partial\dot{p}/\partial p}\right|_{\substack{\dot{p}=0\\ \dot{x}=0}} = \frac{1}{H_{pp}(\bar{p};c)} < 0. \tag{26}$$

This means that the $\dot{p}=0$ isocline is downward sloping in a neighborhood of the steady state in the xp-phase space.

To find the vector field associated with the $\dot{p}=0$ isocline, differentiate Eq. (16) with respect to p or x, and then evaluate the result at the steady state to get

$$\left.\frac{\partial\dot{p}}{\partial p}\right|_{\substack{\dot{p}=0\\ \dot{x}=0}} = r > 0, \tag{27}$$

$$\left.\frac{\partial\dot{p}}{\partial x}\right|_{\substack{\dot{p}=0\\ \dot{x}=0}} = \frac{-r}{H_{pp}(\bar{p};c)} > 0. \tag{28}$$

Thus, in a neighborhood of the steady state, a movement in the direction of p or x increases $\dot{p}$ from zero to a positive number. Because the $\dot{p}=0$ isocline is negatively sloped in a neighborhood of the steady state, it follows that $\dot{p}>0$ above the $\dot{p}=0$ isocline and $\dot{p}<0$ below the $\dot{p}=0$ isocline, in a neighborhood of the steady state. Observe that the derivatives in Eqs. (27) and (28) are the elements of the first row of $\mathbf{J}(p^s(\alpha), x^s(\alpha))$, and that the negative of the ratio of the $(1,2)$ to $(1,1)$ elements of $\mathbf{J}(p^s(\alpha), x^s(\alpha))$ gives the slope of the $\dot{p}=0$ isocline in a neighborhood of the steady state. Thus, as remarked in Chapter 15, once the Jacobian matrix of the dynamical system is calculated, the slopes of the nullclines and the vector field are known in a neighborhood of the steady state.

Note that in computing Eqs. (24), (27), and (28), use was made of the following insight, which you are asked to prove in a mental exercise. This is a useful trick that should be filed away in your memory for future use.

Lemma 16.1: *Consider a differential equation of the form*

$$\dot{y} = \frac{F(x,y)}{G(x,y)},$$

where $F(\cdot)\in C^{(1)}$ and $G(\cdot)\in C^{(1)}$. The derivative of $\dot{y}$ with respect to x or y evaluated where $\dot{y}=0$, or where $\dot{x}=0$ and $\dot{y}=0$, is found by differentiating only the numerator function $F(\cdot)$ with respect to x or y.

The $\dot{x}=0$ isocline is easy to determine because of its simple linear structure and its independence from the state variable:

$$\dot{x}=0 \Leftrightarrow p-\bar{p}=0. \tag{29}$$

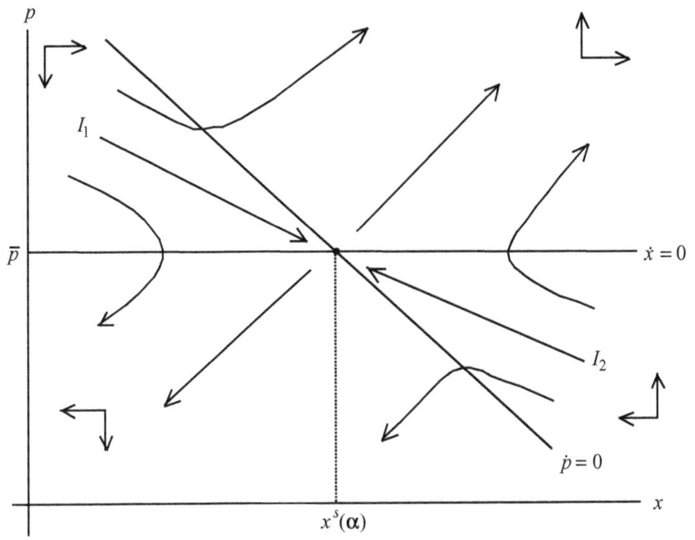

Figure 16.2

Equation (29) demonstrates that the $\dot{x} = 0$ isocline is a horizontal line at the value $p = \bar{p}$ in the xp-phase plane, and that its solution is the steady state value of the dominant firm's price. By inspection of Eq. (17), it is easy to see that if $p > \bar{p}$, then $\dot{x} > 0$, whereas if $p < \bar{p}$, then $\dot{x} < 0$. Note that these properties hold globally, not just in a neighborhood of the steady state. Figure 16.2 brings all the qualitative information gathered so far together in a phase portrait.

Inspection of Figure 16.2 reveals that the steady state, which occurs at the intersection of the $\dot{p} = 0$ and $\dot{x} = 0$ isoclines, is a local saddle point, confirming our earlier conclusion when we examined the eigenvalues of $\mathbf{J}(p^s(\alpha), x^s(\alpha))$. Note that only the trajectories I_1 and I_2 asymptotically approach the steady state, that is to say, as $t \to +\infty$. Because we assumed that the optimal solution to the limit pricing model converges to its steady state solution in the limit of the planning horizon, these trajectories are indeed the optimal ones. Moreover, as demonstrated earlier, they meet all the necessary conditions, including the necessary transversality condition. None of the other trajectories reach the steady state and so cannot be optimal.

Referring to Figure 16.2, we see that if $x_0 < x^s(\alpha)$, then the optimal pricing policy for the dominant firm is to set its initial price above the limit price and gradually lower it over time until the limit price is reached asymptotically. Because the dominant firm's price is above the limit price for the entire planning horizon, this optimal policy induces rival entry and thus erodes the dominant firm's market share over time. In contrast, when $x_0 > x^s(\alpha)$, the dominant firm sets its initial price below the limit price and gradually raises it over time until the limit price is reached asymptotically. Given that the dominant firm's price is below the limit price for the entire planning horizon in this instance, this policy drives rival firms from the market and thus increases the dominant firm's market share over time. With the local stability of the model determined and the basic qualitative nature of the optimal pricing policy laid out, we now turn toward the steady state comparative statics of the model.

Instead of considering changes in all of the parameters $(c, k, \bar{p}, r)$, we will instead focus on the parameters (c, k), and leave the remaining two for a mental exercise. Observe that since the steady state price is equal to the limit price, changes in (c, k) leave it unchanged. Differentiating Eqs. (20), (21), and (22) with respect to (c, k) yields the following steady state comparative statics:

$$\frac{\partial x^s(\alpha)}{\partial c} = -f'(\bar{p}) + \frac{k}{r} > 0, \quad \frac{\partial p^s(\alpha)}{\partial c} = 0,$$

$$\frac{\partial m^s(\alpha)}{\partial c} = -\frac{\partial x^s(\alpha)/\partial c}{f(\bar{p})} = \frac{f'(\bar{p}) - r^{-1}k}{f(\bar{p})} < 0, \tag{30}$$

$$\frac{\partial x^s(\alpha)}{\partial k} = r^{-1}[c - \bar{p}] \leq 0, \quad \frac{\partial p^s(\alpha)}{\partial k} = 0,$$

$$\frac{\partial m^s(\alpha)}{\partial k} = -\frac{\partial x^s(\alpha)/\partial k}{f(\bar{p})} = \frac{r^{-1}[\bar{p} - c]}{f(\bar{p})} \geq 0. \tag{31}$$

The economic interpretation of Eq. (30) is seemingly straightforward. For example, an increase in the dominant firm's average cost of production reduces its cost advantage over the fringe firms. Consequently, the dominant firm will not change its price, but sales to the fringe firms increase (or more fringe firms enter the market) and the dominant firm's market share falls. Thus the falling cost advantage of the dominant firm induces substitution by consumers toward the fringe firms' product. What is less than clear about this interpretation is why the dominant firm loses market share when its steady state price is unchanged. To fully understand the economics of this steady state comparative statics result, we must therefore determine the corresponding local comparative dynamics of an increase in the dominant firm's average cost of production.

Similarly, the economic story is not entirely clear for Eq. (31) either, the steady state comparative statics of the fringe response coefficient. An increase in k means that the fringe firms respond more quickly (or efficiently) to the price signals sent out by the dominant firm. As a result of this increased responsiveness on the part of the fringe firms, Eq. (31) shows they lose sales (assuming $\bar{p} > c$) in the steady state to the dominant firm while the steady state market share of the dominant firm rises, even though it didn't change its steady state price. As in the previous case of an increase in the dominant firm's average cost of production, the economics of these steady state comparative statics results are less than satisfactory. Therefore, let's now turn to an examination of the corresponding local comparative dynamics results so as to more fully understand the qualitative effects of increasing c and k on the dominant firm's optimal pricing policy.

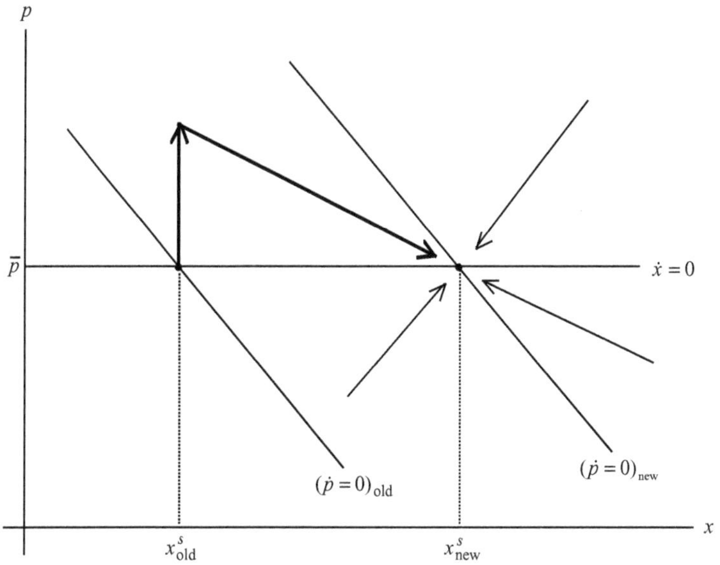

Figure 16.3

Consider an increase in the dominant firm's average cost of production c first. From Eq. (29), we know that the $\dot{x} = 0$ isocline is independent of c and therefore doesn't shift when c increases. We also know from Eq. (30) that steady state rival sales increase, whereas the steady state price of the dominant firm doesn't change, when c increases. Combining these three observations, we therefore conclude that the only way for this to occur in the phase diagram is for the $\dot{p} = 0$ isocline to shift up. This conclusion may be verified analytically by finding $\partial p/\partial c$ along the $\dot{p} = 0$ isocline and evaluating the result at the steady state. By Eq. (25) and the implicit function theorem, we find that

$$\left.\frac{\partial p}{\partial c}\right|_{\substack{\dot{p}=0\\ \dot{x}=0}} = P_c(x^s(\alpha); \alpha) = \left.\frac{-\partial \dot{p}/\partial c}{\partial \dot{p}/\partial p}\right|_{\substack{\dot{p}=0\\ \dot{x}=0}} = \frac{rf'(\bar{p}) - k}{r H_{pp}(\bar{p}; c)} > 0.$$

This means that along the $\dot{p} = 0$ isocline, an increase in c holding $(x, k, \bar{p}, r)$ constant causes p to increase in a neighborhood of the steady state. That is, for the same value of x, p is larger because of the larger value of c. This implies that the $\dot{p} = 0$ isocline shifts up when c increases, just as we deduced above. Figure 16.3 depicts this shift of the $\dot{p} = 0$ isocline in the phase plane.

It is worthwhile at this juncture to pause and repeat three remarks made in Chapter 15 concerning the construction of a local comparative dynamics phase diagram. The first remark is that the local dynamics depicted in Figure 16.2 apply to *both* of the steady states depicted in Figure 16.3. In other words, the local dynamics around the old and the new steady states are qualitatively identical, and are therefore of the saddle point variety. As a result, there is no need to fully draw in the vector field around each steady state in Figure 16.3 because the complete vector field for it can be inferred from that in Figure 16.2. Second, before the increase in the average cost of production occurs, the dominant firm is assumed to be at rest at the old steady state. Third, the dominant firm is assumed to eventually come to rest at the new steady state as a result of the increase in the average cost of production. That is, the old steady state value of rival sales is taken as the initial condition in the local comparative dynamics exercise, whereas the new steady state value of rival sales is taken as the terminal condition. The local comparative dynamics phase diagram therefore depicts the optimal transition path from the old to the new steady state that results from the increase in the average cost of production of the dominant firm.

The economic story that emanates from Figure 16.3 is not only relatively straightforward but, more importantly, is sound. The instant the dominant firm's average cost of production increases, it responds by increasing its price above the limit price. The initial increase in the dominant firm's price is such that it jumps to the stable manifold corresponding to the new steady state. Seeing as rival sales are fixed at its old steady state value initially, they do not initially respond to the higher price charged by the dominant firm, hence the initial vertical upward jump in Figure 16.3. The instant after the dominant firm raises its price to cover its higher average production costs, fringe firms enter the market, or equivalently, fringe sales increase, for the dominant firm's price is now above the limit price. Fringe firms continue to enter the market until the new steady state is reached and the dominant firm's price returns to the limit price, at which point entry of new fringe firms ceases. We therefore see that even though the dominant firm's steady state price is not affected by an increase in its average production costs, the price it charges is higher during the transition from the old to the new steady state, and this is what accounts for the larger fringe sales in the new steady state. In other words, even though there are no long-run effects on the dominant firm's price because of its higher average cost of production, there are transitory effects.

To wrap up the qualitative characterization of the effects of an increase in the dominant firm's average cost of production, let's apply Theorem 14.10, the dynamic envelope theorem for discounted autonomous infinite-horizon control problems, to the limit pricing model. In order to do so, first recall that Theorem 14.10 part (i) is stated in terms of the present value Hamiltonian, whereas we have been working with the current value Hamiltonian $H(\cdot)$, as defined in Eq. (5). Thus, we must first multiply $H(\cdot)$ by e^{-rt} to convert it into the present value Hamiltonian. Then we may differentiate $e^{-rt}H(\cdot)$ with respect to c, evaluate the resulting derivative along the optimal path, and finally, integrate the expression over the planning horizon in order to get the correct envelope expression. Doing just that yields

$$V_c(\beta) \equiv -\int_0^{+\infty} [f(p^*(t;\beta)) - x^*(t;\beta)]\, e^{-rt}\, dt < 0.$$

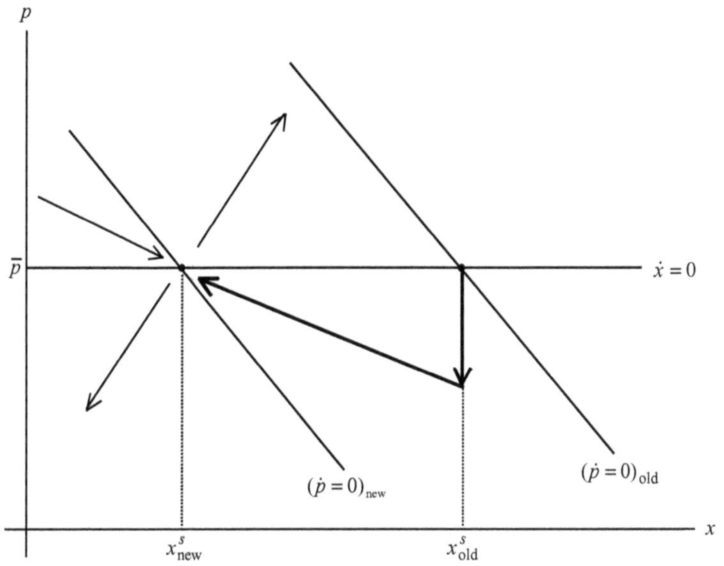

Figure 16.4

Hence, an increase in the dominant firm's average cost of production reduces its present discounted value of profits, even though the dominant firm temporarily raised its price above the limit price in an attempt to cover its higher average costs of production.

Finally, we consider the local comparative dynamics of an increase in the fringe response coefficient k. From Eq. (29), we know that the $\dot{x} = 0$ isocline is independent of k and therefore doesn't shift when k increases. In the case in which $\bar{p} > c$, we see from Eq. (31) that steady state fringe sales fall with the increase in k while the steady state price of the dominant firm is unaffected. These facts imply that the $\dot{p} = 0$ isocline shifts downward in the xp-phase plane. As before, this can be verified analytically by computing $\partial p/\partial k$ along the $\dot{p} = 0$ isocline and evaluating the result at the steady state. By Eq. (25) and the implicit function theorem, we find that

$$\left.\frac{\partial p}{\partial k}\right|_{\substack{\dot{p}=0\\ \dot{x}=0}} = P_k(x^s(\alpha); \alpha) = \left.\frac{-\partial \dot{p}/\partial k}{\partial \dot{p}/\partial p}\right|_{\substack{\dot{p}=0\\ \dot{x}=0}} = \frac{\bar{p} - c}{r H_{pp}(\bar{p}; c)} < 0.$$

This calculation shows that along the $\dot{p} = 0$ isocline, an increase in k holding $(x, c, \bar{p}, r)$ constant causes p to decrease in a neighborhood of the steady state. That is, for the same value of x, p is smaller because of the larger value of k. This implies that the $\dot{p} = 0$ isocline shifts down in the phase plane. The local comparative dynamics phase diagram for an increase in k is depicted in Figure 16.4.

The local comparative dynamics phase diagram provides the additional information required to fully understand the qualitative effects of an increase in k. The moment k increases, the dominant firm responds by lowering its price below the limit price so as to jump to the stable manifold corresponding to the new steady state. Because the dominant firm's price is now below the limit price, this action drives fringe firms out of the market, thereby increasing the dominant firm's market share. Over time, the dominant firm gradually increases its price back toward the limit price, all the while continuing to drive fringe firms from the market and increasing its market share. The local comparative dynamics thus reveal why the fringe sales are smaller in the new steady state even though the dominant firm's steady state price is unchanged: in the transition from the old steady state to the new steady state, the dominant firm lowers its price below the limit price, thereby driving fringe firms from the market. The effects of a perturbation in k thus clearly spell out the need for a local comparative dynamic analysis in addition to a steady state comparative static analysis in order to get a complete and sound qualitative understanding of a dynamic economic model.

Note that our analysis of the dynamic limit pricing model has focused on the qualitative properties of the state and control variables, not the state and costate variables. You may recall that in the previous chapter, we studied the optimal economic growth model and focused instead on the state and costate variables. Because both pairs of the ordinary differential equations used for the analysis, namely, the state/costate and state/control pairs, are derived from the same set of necessary conditions, the information contained in either pair of differential equations is identical, and thus yields identical qualitative conclusions. It is thus the economic question of interest that dictates which pair of differential equations to analyze, not some fundamental mathematical property or logical reason. Note, however, that when there is more than one control variable but still a single state variable, there is a mathematical advantage to using the state and costate differential equations for analysis, scilicet, there is only a pair of them to analyze. This means that a phase portrait may be used for the qualitative analysis, a real advantage indeed.

We undertake a systematic qualitative investigation of the adjustment cost model of the firm in the next chapter. In addition to employing a phase diagram for studying the local comparative dynamics properties of the model, we will augment our approach by introducing some analytical material.

MENTAL EXERCISES

16.1 Prove Lemma 16.1.

16.2 This exercise asks you to complete the qualitative analysis of the limit pricing model studied in this chapter by considering the remaining two parameters $(\bar{p}, r)$. Answer the questions below for the dominant firm's price, fringe sales, and market share.

(a) Derive the steady state comparative statics for the limit price $\bar{p}$.

(b) Derive the local comparative dynamics for the limit price $\bar{p}$ using a phase diagram.
(c) Provide an economic interpretation of the above two qualitative results.
(d) Derive the steady state comparative statics for the discount rate r.
(e) Derive the local comparative dynamics phase diagram for the discount rate r.
(f) Provide an economic interpretation of the above two qualitative results.

16.3 We did not analyze any of the qualitative properties of the current value shadow price of fringe sales in this chapter. You are asked to do so in this exercise. Note that you may use any of the results or equations established in the chapter in your answer.
(a) Define the steady state current value shadow price of fringe sales.
(b) Derive the steady state comparative statics for the current value shadow price of fringe sales for the parameters $(c, k, \bar{p}, r)$.
(c) Provide an economic interpretation of the results.

16.4 This exercise asks you to reconsider the qualitative analysis of the dynamic limit pricing model presented in the chapter by deriving the phase diagram in the λx-phase plane.
(a) Reduce the three necessary conditions (6), (8), and (9) down to two differential equations involving just the two variables (x, λ).
(b) Write down the steady state version of the canonical equations from part (a). Find the steady state values of x and λ, say $x^s(\alpha)$ and $\lambda^s(\alpha)$, respectively. Is there any need to compute the Jacobian matrix of the steady state equations? Explain.
(c) Derive the steady state comparative statics $\partial x^s(\alpha)/\partial c$ and $\partial \lambda^s(\alpha)/\partial c$.
(d) Derive the steady state comparative statics $\partial x^s(\alpha)/\partial k$ and $\partial \lambda^s(\alpha)/\partial k$.
(e) Derive the local comparative dynamics phase diagram for the parameter c. Show all your work and label the diagram carefully.
(f) Derive the local comparative dynamics phase diagram for the parameter k. Show all your work and label the diagram carefully.

16.5 Apply Theorem 14.10 to derive the dynamic envelope results for the parameters k and $\bar{p}$ of the limit pricing model. Provide an economic interpretation of the results.

16.6 Consider a farmer who is concerned about the effects of production on the soil quality of her farm. It is assumed that the soil characteristic of interest can be represented by a single state variable x, say, for example, soil depth. The output of the farm is given by the production relationship $y = f(x, v)$, $f(\cdot) \in C^{(2)}$, where y is the output of the farm and v is the variable input used. The farmer is asserted to solve the static cost minimization problem given by

$$C(x, y; w) \stackrel{\text{def}}{=} \min_{v}\{w \cdot v \text{ s.t. } y = f(x, v)\},$$

at each moment in time of the planning horizon, where w is the unit cost of the variable input. The restricted minimum cost function $C(\cdot)$ has the following properties:

$$C_x(x, y; w) < 0, C_y(x, y; w) > 0, C_{yx}(x, y; w) < 0, C_{xx}(x, y; w) > 0,$$

$$C_{yy}(x, y; w) > 0, C_{xx}(x, y; w)C_{yy}(x, y; w) - [C_{yx}(x, y; w)]^2 > 0, C \in C^{(2)}.$$

The time rate of change of the soil characteristic $\dot{x}(t)$ is assumed to be negatively affected by the output of the farm via the differential equation

$$\dot{x}(t) = B - \alpha y(t),$$

where $B > 0$ is the constant rate of soil improvement and $\alpha > 0$ measures the marginal impact output has on the rate of change of soil quality. Bringing all the information together, the control problem the farmer is asserted to solve is

$$V(\boldsymbol{\beta}) \stackrel{\text{def}}{=} \max_{y(\cdot)} \int_0^{+\infty} [py(t) - C(x(t), y(t); w)]\, e^{-rt}\, dt$$

$$\text{s.t.} \quad \dot{x}(t) = B - \alpha y(t),\ x(0) = x_0,$$

where $\boldsymbol{\beta} \stackrel{\text{def}}{=} (\boldsymbol{\gamma}, x_0) \stackrel{\text{def}}{=} (\alpha, B, p, r, w, x_0)$, $x_0 > 0$ is the initial soil quality, $r > 0$ is the farmer's discount rate, and $p > 0$ is the constant price of the output. It is assumed that the inequality constraints $x(t) \geq 0$ and $y(t) \geq 0$ are not binding $\forall\, t \in [0, +\infty)$ in an optimal plan, that there exists a solution $(x^*(t; \boldsymbol{\beta}), y^*(t; \boldsymbol{\beta}))$ of the necessary conditions that converges to the simple steady state solution of the necessary conditions $(x^s(\boldsymbol{\gamma}), y^s(\boldsymbol{\gamma}))$ as $t \to +\infty$, and that the objective functional exists for all admissible pairs of functions. Let $\lambda(t; \boldsymbol{\beta})$ be the corresponding time path of the current value costate variable, and note that no conditions are placed on $\lim_{t \to +\infty} x(t)$.

(a) Write down the necessary conditions for the problem in current value form. Provide an economic interpretation to the Maximum Principle equation.

(b) Prove that under suitable additional assumptions to be determined by you, the solution $(x^*(t; \boldsymbol{\beta}), y^*(t; \boldsymbol{\beta}))$ to the necessary conditions is the unique solution of the control problem.

(c) Reduce the necessary conditions down to two differential equations in the variables (x, y). Prove that the fixed point $(x^s(\boldsymbol{\gamma}), y^s(\boldsymbol{\gamma}))$ is a local saddle point.

(d) Find the steady state comparative statics $\partial x^s(\boldsymbol{\gamma})/\partial p$ and $\partial y^s(\boldsymbol{\gamma})/\partial p$. Provide an economic interpretation of the results.

(e) Draw a phase diagram in the xy-phase space, and label it carefully. Plot x on the horizontal axis and y on the vertical axis.

(f) Draw the local comparative dynamics phase diagram for the change in p. Label your diagram carefully, showing the optimal path from one steady state to another. Provide an economic interpretation. Is the firm better off facing a higher value of p? Show your work and explain.

(g) Find the steady state comparative statics $\partial x^s(\gamma)/\partial B$ and $\partial y^s(\gamma)/\partial B$. Provide an economic interpretation of the results.

(h) Draw the local comparative dynamics phase diagram for the change in B. Label your diagram carefully, showing the optimal path from one steady state to another. Provide an economic interpretation. Is the firm better off facing a higher value of B? Show your work and explain.

16.7 A society is concerned about the negative externalities associated with its consumption rate $C(t)$, namely, the accumulation of a stock of pollution $P(t)$. The instantaneous utility of the society depends on both the rate of consumption of a homogeneous good and the resulting stock of pollution generated by the consumption, say,

$$U(C, P; \alpha_1, \alpha_2) \stackrel{\text{def}}{=} U^1(C; \alpha_1) + U^2(P; \alpha_2),$$

where $U^i(\cdot) : \Re^2_{++} \to \Re$, $U^i(\cdot) \in C^{(2)}$, $i = 1, 2$, and

$$U^1_C(C; \alpha_1) > 0,\ U^1_{CC}(C; \alpha_1) < 0,\ U^1_{C\alpha_1}(C; \alpha_1) > 0,$$
$$U^2_P(P; \alpha_2) < 0,\ U^2_{PP}(P; \alpha_2) < 0,\ U^2_{P\alpha_2}(P; \alpha_2) < 0.$$

In addition, it is assumed that

$$\lim_{C\to 0^+} U^1_C(C; \alpha_1) = +\infty\,\forall\,\alpha_1 > 0,\ \lim_{P\to 0^+} U^2_P(P; \alpha_2) = 0\,\forall\,\alpha_2 > 0.$$

A constant rate of output $Y > 0$ is to be divided between consumption $C(t)$ and pollution control (or pollution elimination) $E(t)$, so that $Y = C(t) + E(t)$ must hold for all t. The stock of pollution is assumed to increase with consumption at an increasing rate as given by the twice continuously differentiable function $g(\cdot)$, that is,

$$g(\cdot) \in C^{(2)}\,\forall\,C > 0,\ g(0) = 0,\ g'(C) > 0, \text{ and } g''(C) > 0\,\forall\,C > 0.$$

Society can slow the accumulation or hasten the decline of pollution by devoting some output to pollution control. The amount of pollution cleaned up is given by the function $h(\cdot) \in C^{(2)}\,\forall\,E > 0$, where

$$h(0) = 0,\ h'(E) > 0 \text{ and } h''(E) < 0\,\forall\,E > 0,\ \lim_{h\to 0^+} h'(E) = +\infty.$$

Thus society's net contribution to the flow of pollution is given by $g(C) - h(E)$. However, given the assumption of a fixed level of output, the choice of consumption completely determines pollution control expenditure via

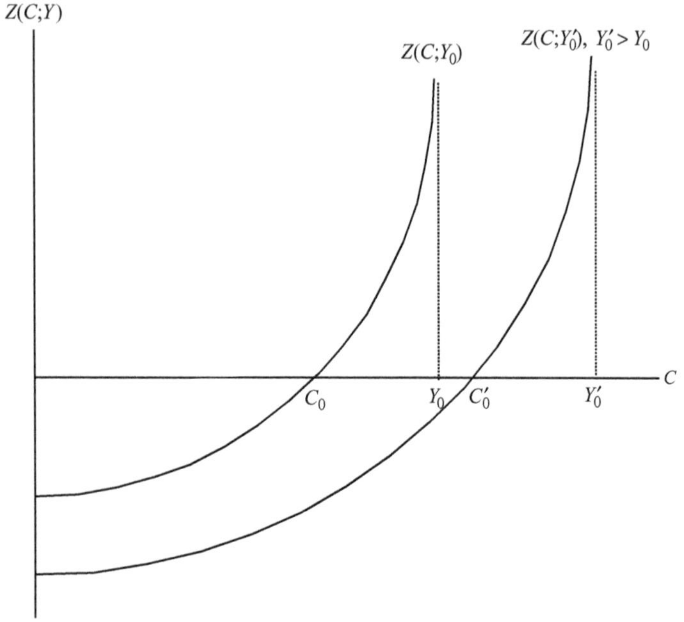

Figure 16.5

$E(t) = Y - C(t)$. Therefore the net contribution to the flow of pollution is given by $Z(C; Y) \stackrel{\text{def}}{=} g(C) - h(Y - C)$, where

$$Z_C(C; Y) = g'(C) + h'(Y - C) > 0,$$
$$Z_{CC}(C; Y) = g''(C) - h''(Y - C) > 0,$$
$$Z_Y(C; Y) = -h'(Y - C) < 0, \;\; Z_{CY}(C; Y) = h''(Y - C) < 0.$$

Hence the flow of pollution increases with consumption at an increasing rate, and an increase in the output of society reduces pollution in total and at the marginal. Finally, let $C = C_0$ be the consumption rate such that the net flow of pollution is zero, that is, $Z(C_0; Y) = 0$. Given that $Z_C(C; Y) > 0$, it follows that

$$Z(C; Y) \begin{cases} < 0 \, \forall C \in [0, C_0) \\ = 0 \text{ at } C = C_0 \\ > 0 \, \forall C \in (C_0, +\infty). \end{cases}$$

Thus for all $C \in [0, C_0)$, society is net abating, whereas for all $C \in (C_0, +\infty)$, it is net polluting. Figure 16.5 summarizes the qualitative information about the function $Z(\cdot)$.

The function $Z(\cdot)$ may be thought of as the pollution control function for a given Y. By selecting the consumption rate, society uniquely determines the amount of pollution it generates in net terms, since Y is constant. The pollution control function therefore has two components: (i) an *active* control given by $h(E)$, where society cleans up pollution directly by devoting part of its output to cleanup activities, and (ii) a *passive* control given by $g(C)$, where society can reduce the rate of pollution accumulation by lowering its consumption rate. It is also assumed that pollution decays at the rate $\delta > 0$. Putting all the above information together, the optimal control problem facing the planning authority is given by

$$V(\beta) \stackrel{\text{def}}{=} \max_{C(\cdot)} \int_0^{+\infty} [U^1(C(t);\alpha_1) + U^2(P(t);\alpha_2)]e^{-rt}\,dt$$

$$\text{s.t.} \quad \dot{P}(t) = Z(C(t);Y) - \delta P(t), \;\; P(0) = P_0,$$

where $\beta \stackrel{\text{def}}{=} (\alpha, P_0) \stackrel{\text{def}}{=} (\alpha_1, \alpha_2, \delta, r, Y, P_0)$ is the vector of time invariant parameters of the control problem, $r > 0$ is the social rate of discount, $P_0 > 0$ is the initial stock of pollution, and no conditions are placed on $\lim_{t\to+\infty} P(t)$. Assume that there exists a solution $(P^*(t;\beta), C^*(t;\beta))$ of the necessary conditions that converges to the simple steady state solution of the necessary conditions $(P^s(\alpha), C^s(\alpha))$ as $t \to +\infty$, and that the objective functional exists for all admissible pairs of functions. Let $\lambda(t;\beta)$ be the corresponding time path of the current value costate variable.

(a) Provide an economic interpretation of the assumptions made on the instantaneous utility function.
(b) Derive the necessary conditions in current value form.
(c) What is the economic interpretation of the current value costate variable? Is it positive or negative in an optimal plan? Show your work.
(d) Prove that under suitable additional assumptions to be determined by you, the solution $(P^*(t;\beta), C^*(t;\beta))$ to the necessary conditions is the unique solution of the control problem.
(e) Reduce the necessary conditions down to a pair of ordinary differential equations in the variables (P, C). Prove that the fixed point $(P^s(\alpha), C^s(\alpha))$ is a local saddle point, and that $(P^s(\cdot), C^s(\cdot))$ are locally $C^{(1)}$ in α.
(f) Carefully draw the phase diagram for the system of ordinary differential equations in part (e). Label the optimal trajectories. Plot P on the horizontal axis and C on the vertical axis.
(g) Derive the steady state comparative statics $\partial P^s(\alpha)/\partial r$ and $\partial C^s(\alpha)/\partial r$. Draw the corresponding local comparative dynamics phase diagram. Provide an economic interpretation.
(h) Derive the steady state comparative statics $\partial P^s(\alpha)/\partial \alpha_1$ and $\partial C^s(\alpha)/\partial \alpha_1$. Draw the corresponding local comparative dynamics phase diagram. Is

society better off or worse off facing a higher value of α_1? Provide an economic interpretation.

(i) Derive the steady state comparative statics $\partial P^s(\boldsymbol{\alpha})/\partial \alpha_2$ and $\partial C^s(\boldsymbol{\alpha})/\partial \alpha_2$. Draw the corresponding local comparative dynamics phase diagram. Is society better off or worse off facing a higher value of α_2? Provide an economic interpretation.

(j) Derive the steady state comparative statics $\partial P^s(\boldsymbol{\alpha})/\partial Y$ and $\partial C^s(\boldsymbol{\alpha})/\partial Y$. Draw the corresponding local comparative dynamics phase diagram. Is society better off or worse off facing a higher value of Y? Provide an economic interpretation.

16.8 A local planning council has been charged with managing a community's lake. The community has well-defined preferences over both the stock of water in the lake $w(t)$ and the consumption rate $c(t)$ of the water, say, $U(c, w; \alpha)$, where $U(\cdot) \in C^{(2)}$ and α is a taste shift parameter. The community has locally nonsatiated preferences over both the consumption rate and stock of water in the lake, thereby implying that $U_c(c, w; \alpha) > 0$ and $U_w(c, w; \alpha) > 0$. In addition, both marginal utilities are declining; hence $U_{cc}(c, w; \alpha) < 0$ and $U_{ww}(c, w; \alpha) < 0$. Assume, for simplicity, that $U_{cw}(c, w; \alpha) \equiv 0$ and that the natural nonnegativity constraints $c(t) \geq 0$ and $w(t) \geq 0$ are not binding in the optimal plan. The planning council discounts future instantaneous utility at the rate $r > 0$, and plans over the indefinite future for the community. The lake recharges at the constant rate $R > 0$, whereas consumption $c(t)$ reduces the rate of recharge, so that on net, the rate of change of the stock of water in the lake is given by $\dot{w}(t) = R - c(t)$. The initial stock of water is given as $w(0) = w_0 > 0$, and no assumptions are placed on $\lim_{t \to +\infty} w(t)$. The planning council wants to choose the consumption function $c(\cdot)$ to maximize the present discounted utility of the community over the infinite planning horizon. Assume that the objective functional exists for all admissible function pairs. For notational clarity, define $\boldsymbol{\beta} \stackrel{\text{def}}{=} (\boldsymbol{\theta}, w_0) \stackrel{\text{def}}{=} (\alpha, r, R, w_0)$.

(a) Set up the planning council's optimal control problem.

(b) Find the necessary conditions for an optimal plan using the current value Hamiltonian. Provide an economic interpretation of the current value costate variable.

(c) Assume that $(w^*(t; \boldsymbol{\beta}), c^*(t; \boldsymbol{\beta}))$ is a solution to the necessary conditions with the property that as $t \to +\infty$, $(w^*(t; \boldsymbol{\beta}), c^*(t; \boldsymbol{\beta})) \to (w^s(\boldsymbol{\theta}), c^s(\boldsymbol{\theta}))$, where $(w^s(\boldsymbol{\theta}), c^s(\boldsymbol{\theta}))$ is the simple steady state solution of the necessary conditions, and $\lambda(t; \boldsymbol{\beta})$ is the corresponding time path of the current value costate. Prove that $(w^*(t; \boldsymbol{\beta}), c^*(t; \boldsymbol{\beta}))$ is the unique optimal solution of the control problem under suitable additional assumptions to be identified by you.

(d) Reduce the necessary conditions down to a pair of ordinary differential equations in the variables (w, c). Prove that the fixed point $(w^s(\boldsymbol{\theta}), c^s(\boldsymbol{\theta}))$ is a local saddle point, and that $(w^s(\cdot), c^s(\cdot))$ are locally $C^{(1)}$ in $\boldsymbol{\theta}$.

(e) Draw the phase diagram corresponding to the system of ordinary differential equations in part (d). Show all your work and label your phase diagram carefully. Identify the optimal trajectories in the phase diagram. Plot w on the horizontal axis and c on the vertical axis.

(f) Assume that $U_{c\alpha}(c, w; \alpha) \equiv 0$ and that $U_{w\alpha}(c, w; \alpha) > 0$. What is the economic interpretation of these assumptions?

(g) Prove that $\partial w^s(\boldsymbol{\theta})/\partial\alpha > 0$, $\partial c^s(\boldsymbol{\theta})/\partial\alpha \equiv 0$, and $\partial \mu^s(\boldsymbol{\theta})/\partial\alpha \equiv 0$ under the assumptions in part (f). Provide an economic interpretation.

(h) Draw the local comparative dynamics phase diagram for an increase in α under the assumptions in part (f). Provide an economic interpretation and carefully justify your answer. Is the community better off with a higher value of α? Explain.

16.9 This question is concerned with the adjustment cost model of the capital accumulating firm. Let $f(\cdot): \Re_+ \to \Re_+$ be the $C^{(2)}$ production function, where $f(0) = 0$, $f'(K) > 0$ for all $K \in \Re_{++}$, $\lim_{K\to+\infty} f'(K) = 0$, and $f''(K) < 0$ for all $K \in \Re_{++}$, where K is the capital stock of the firm. The output of the firm is sold at the constant price of $p > 0$ per unit of output, the capital stock has maintenance costs of $w > 0$ per unit of capital, and $g > 0$ is the constant cost per unit of purchased capital, that is, the purchase price of investment I. In addition, let $C(\cdot): \Re \to \Re_+$ be the $C^{(2)}$ cost of adjustment function (in dollars), where $C(0) = 0$, $C'(0) = 0$, $\text{sign}(C'(I)) = \text{sign}(I)$, and $C''(I) > 0$ for all $\forall\, I \in \Re$. The firm is asserted to operate over the indefinite future and discounts its instantaneous profits at the constant rate $r > 0$. The state equation is the prototype capital accumulation equation with a constant rate of decay of $\delta > 0$, to wit, $\dot{K} = I - \delta K$. Finally, the firm begins its planning at time $t = 0$ with the given stock of capital $K(0) = K_0 > 0$, but no restrictions are placed on $\lim_{t\to+\infty} K(t)$. The optimal control problem the firm must solve in order to determine its optimal investment plan is therefore given by

$$V(\boldsymbol{\beta}) \stackrel{\text{def}}{=} \max_{I(\cdot)} \int_0^{+\infty} [pf(K(t)) - wK(t) - gI(t) - C(I(t))]\, e^{-rt}\, dt$$

$$\text{s.t.} \quad \dot{K}(t) = I(t) - \delta K(t),\ K(0) = K_0,$$

$$I(t) \in U \stackrel{\text{def}}{=} \{I(\cdot) : I(t) \geq 0\},$$

where $\boldsymbol{\beta} \stackrel{\text{def}}{=} (K_0, \boldsymbol{\alpha}) \stackrel{\text{def}}{=} (K_0, p, w, g, r, \delta) \in \Re^6_{++}$ are the time invariant parameters of the problem. Assume that the objective functional exists for all admissible pairs of functions, and that there exists a solution $(K^*(t; \boldsymbol{\beta}), I^*(t; \boldsymbol{\beta}))$ of the necessary conditions that converges to the simple steady state solution of the necessary conditions $(K^s(\boldsymbol{\alpha}), I^s(\boldsymbol{\alpha}))$ as $t \to +\infty$, where $\lambda(t; \boldsymbol{\beta})$ is the corresponding time path of the costate variable.

(a) Write down the current value Hamiltonian with costate variable λ. What is the economic interpretation of λ?

(b) Write down the necessary conditions for this problem. Provide an economic interpretation of the Maximum Principle equation. In particular, if $I(t) > 0$ holds at some $t \in [0, +\infty)$ along the optimal path, then interpret the necessary condition. Similarly, provide an economic interpretation of the sufficient condition for $I(t) = 0$ to hold for some $t \in [0, +\infty)$ along the optimal path.

(c) Assume that $I(t) > 0$ holds for all $t \in [0, +\infty)$ in an optimal program. Prove that under suitable additional assumptions to be determined by you, that the solution $(K^*(t; \beta), I^*(t; \beta))$ to the necessary conditions is the unique solution of the control problem.

(d) Assuming that $I(t) > 0$ holds for all $t \in [0, +\infty)$ in an optimal program, show that the necessary and sufficient conditions can be reduced to a pair of autonomous ordinary differential equations in the variables (K, I). Prove that the fixed point $(K^s(\alpha), I^s(\alpha))$ is a local saddle point, and that $(K^s(\cdot), I^s(\cdot))$ are locally $C^{(1)}$ in α.

(e) Derive the phase portrait corresponding to the ordinary differential equations in part (d). Show your work. Plot K on the horizontal axis and I on the vertical axis.

(f) Find the steady state comparative statics $\partial K^s(\alpha)/\partial p$ and $\partial I^s(\alpha)/\partial p$. Provide an economic interpretation.

(g) Draw the local comparative dynamics phase portrait for the output price p, and identify the optimal path from the old steady state to the new steady state. Provide an economic interpretation of the comparative dynamics result. Is the firm better off facing a higher output price? Show your work and explain.

(h) Find the steady state comparative statics $\partial K^s(\alpha)/\partial w$ and $\partial I^s(\alpha)/\partial w$. Provide an economic interpretation.

(i) Draw the comparative dynamics phase portrait for the maintenance cost w, and identify the optimal path from the old steady state to the new steady state. Provide an economic interpretation of the comparative dynamics result. Is the firm better off facing a higher maintenance cost? Show your work and explain.

FURTHER READING

The material in this chapter is based on the seminal paper by Gaskins (1971). Numerous extensions of the basic model have appeared in the literature over the past three decades. An important one is that by Kamien and Schwartz (1971), in which the entry and exit of the rival firms are stochastic from the point of view of the dominant firm. Leung (1991) presents a thorough discussion of the transversality conditions associated with the Kamien and Schwartz (1971) model. The dissertation of Ardila Vasquez (1991) is the source for the model of soil depletion in Mental Exercise 16.6. The papers by Barrett (1991) and LaFrance (1992) are closely related to this mental exercise too. Mental Exercise 16.7 is based on the work of Forster (1973). Neher (1990) is a good reference for optimal control theory applied to natural resource economics models, and is the reference that spurred Mental Exercise 16.8. Brown and Deacon (1972) is an early application of optimal control theory to groundwater use. For references on the adjustment cost model of the firm, please see the references in Chapter 17.

REFERENCES

Ardila Vasquez, S. (1991), "An Analytical Treatment of the Economics of Soil Depletion," Dissertation, Department of Agricultural and Resource Economics, University of California, Davis.

Barrett, S. (1991), "Optimal Soil Conservation and the Reform of Agricultural Pricing Policies," *Journal of Development Economics*, 36, 167–187.

Brown Jr., G. and Deacon, R. (1972), "Economic Optimization of a Single-Cell Aquifer," *Water Resources Research*, 8, 557–564.

Forster, B.A. (1973), "Optimal Consumption Planning in a Polluted Environment," *Economic Record*, 49, 534–545.

Gaskins, D.W. (1971), "Dynamic Limit Pricing: Optimal Pricing Under Threat of Entry," *Journal of Economic Theory*, 3, 306–322.

Kamien, M.I. and Schwartz, N.L. (1971), "Limit Pricing with Uncertain Entry," *Econometrica*, 39, 441–454.

LaFrance, J.T. (1992), "Do Increased Commodity Prices Lead to More or Less Soil Degradation?" *Australian Journal of Agricultural Economics*, 36, 57–82.

Leung, S.F. (1991), "Transversality Conditions and Optimality in a Class of Infinite Horizon Continuous Time Economic Models," *Journal of Economic Theory*, 54, 224–233.

Neher, P.A. (1990), *Natural Resource Economics: Conservation and Exploitation* (New York: Cambridge University Press).

Simon, C.P. and Blume, L. (1994), Mathematics for Economists (New York: W.W. Norton & Company, Inc.).

SEVENTEEN

The Adjustment Cost Model of the Firm

We continue with the theme of the previous two chapters by examining the local stability, steady state comparative statics, and local comparative dynamics properties of the adjustment cost model of the firm. The analysis is carried one step further in the present chapter, however, in that we augment the local comparative dynamics phase diagram with some analytical calculations. To help hone our economic intuition, the qualitative results derived herewith will be compared and contrasted with those of the static price-taking profit-maximizing model of the firm. Because we have already spent considerable time in formulating the adjustment cost model of the firm in Examples 1.2 and 9.1, we will be a bit more succinct this time around.

To begin, the mathematical statement of the adjustment cost model of the firm, extended to the case of an infinite planning horizon, is given by

$$V(\beta) \stackrel{\text{def}}{=} \max_{I(\cdot)} \int_0^{+\infty} [pf(K(t), I(t)) - cK(t) - gI(t)]\, e^{-rt}\, dt$$

$$\text{s.t.} \quad \dot{K}(t) = I(t) - \delta K(t), \;\; K(0) = K_0. \tag{1}$$

The function $f(\cdot) : \Re^2_+ \to \Re_+$ is the $C^{(2)}$ *generalized* production function of the firm, for it depends not only on the capital stock of the firm $K(t)$ at time t, but also on the gross rate of change of the capital stock, or the gross investment rate $I(t)$ at time t. It is assumed that $f_K(K, I) > 0$, $\text{sign}[f_I(K, I)] = -\text{sign}[I]$, and furthermore, that $f(\cdot)$ is concave in (K, I). The assumption that $\text{sign}[f_I(K, I)] = -\text{sign}[I]$ is equivalent to the requirement that $f_I(K, I) \lesseqgtr 0$ as $-I \lesseqgtr 0$, and asserts that output decreases as investment $(I > 0)$ *or* disinvestment $(I < 0)$ in the capital stock takes place. The intuition behind the negative effect of investment on the output of the firm is that when capital is purchased, it must be installed for it to become a productive asset. The process of installation, however, takes resources away from production, thereby resulting in the fall in output. Similarly, when disinvestment takes place, the process of uninstalling the capital also takes resources away from production, thereby resulting in the decrease in output as well. The assumption that $\text{sign}[f_I(K, I)] = -\text{sign}[I]$ is therefore the backbone of the adjustment cost model. The concavity of $f(\cdot)$ in (K, I) implies that the capital stock and the investment rate display diminishing marginal productivity. These assumptions are not that strong, and moreover, they are consistent with assumptions we are familiar with from the static theory of the profit-maximizing firm. What is more, they will help sharpen our qualitative results and thus allow us to focus on the economic content of the model rather than on some of its tangential mathematical details.

The single good the firm produces via its production function is sold at the constant price of $p > 0$, $c > 0$ is the constant holding cost per unit of the capital stock, and $g > 0$ is the constant price paid per unit of investment or disinvestment in the capital stock. The firm discounts its cash flow at the constant rate $r > 0$ and begins its planning with a given capital stock $K_0 > 0$, but no assumptions are placed on $\lim_{t\to+\infty} K(t)$ at this juncture. We assume that the natural nonnegativity constraint on the capital stock $K(t) \geq 0$ is not binding for all $t \in [0, +\infty)$. We do not, however, assume that $I(t) \geq 0$ for all $t \in [0, +\infty)$. In other words, we permit the firm to disinvest, that is to say, $I(t) \leq 0$ is permitted. Note that $\dot{K}(t)$ is net investment, since depreciation, assumed proportional to the existing stock of capital with depreciation rate $\delta > 0$, is subtracted from gross investment $I(t)$ to arrive at $\dot{K}(t)$. For notational clarity, define $\boldsymbol{\beta} \stackrel{\text{def}}{=} (\boldsymbol{\alpha}, K_0) \stackrel{\text{def}}{=} (c, g, p, r, \delta, K_0) \in \Re^6_{++}$ as the vector of time-independent parameters. Finally, assume that there exists a solution of the necessary conditions of Theorem 14.3, which we denote by the pair $(K^*(t; \boldsymbol{\beta}), I^*(t; \boldsymbol{\beta}))$, with the property that $(K^*(t; \boldsymbol{\beta}), I^*(t; \boldsymbol{\beta})) \to (K^s(\boldsymbol{\alpha}), I^s(\boldsymbol{\alpha}))$ as $t \to +\infty$, where $\lambda(t; \boldsymbol{\beta})$ is the corresponding time path of the current value costate variable and $(K^s(\boldsymbol{\alpha}), I^s(\boldsymbol{\alpha}))$ is the simple steady state solution of the necessary conditions.

To begin the analysis, define the current value Hamiltonian by

$$H(K, I, \lambda; \boldsymbol{\alpha}) \stackrel{\text{def}}{=} pf(K, I) - cK - gI + \lambda[I - \delta K]. \tag{2}$$

Assuming that the objective functional exists for all admissible pairs of functions, Theorems 14.3 and 14.9 imply the following necessary conditions:

$$H_I(K, I, \lambda; \boldsymbol{\alpha}) = pf_I(K, I) - g + \lambda = 0, \tag{3}$$

$$H_{II}(K, I, \lambda; \boldsymbol{\alpha}) = pf_{II}(K, I) \leq 0, \tag{4}$$

$$\dot{\lambda} = r\lambda - H_K(K, I, \lambda; \boldsymbol{\alpha}) = [r + \delta]\lambda - pf_K(K, I) + c, \tag{5}$$

$$\dot{K} = H_\lambda(K, I, \lambda; \boldsymbol{\alpha}) = I - \delta K, \ K(0) = K_0, \tag{6}$$

$$\lim_{t\to+\infty} e^{-rt} H(K(t), I(t), \lambda(t); \boldsymbol{\alpha}) = 0. \tag{7}$$

Just like the two previous chapters, we have not assumed much specific mathematical structure on the problem, and as a result, we cannot get a closed-form solution of the necessary conditions. Nonetheless, we will be able to characterize the solution qualitatively. Before doing so, however, we deal with three preliminary features of the solution $(K^*(t;\beta), I^*(t;\beta))$ to the necessary conditions of Theorem 14.3.

Let us first verify that the necessary transversality condition (7) from Theorem 14.9 is satisfied by the solution $(K^*(t;\beta), I^*(t;\beta))$. From Eq. (3), we have $\lambda = g - pf_I(K, I)$. Because we have assumed that $(K^*(t;\beta), I^*(t;\beta)) \to (K^s(\alpha), I^s(\alpha))$ as $t \to +\infty$, it then follows from $\lambda = g - pf_I(K, I)$ that $\lambda(t;\beta) \to \lambda^s(\alpha)$ as $t \to +\infty$, where $\lambda^s(\alpha)$ is the corresponding steady state solution of the current value costate variable. Consequently, $\lim_{t\to+\infty} H(K^*(t;\beta), I^*(t;\beta), \lambda(t;\beta); \alpha)$ exists, and seeing as $\lim_{t\to+\infty} e^{-rt} = 0$, the necessary transversality condition (7) of Theorem 14.9 is satisfied by the solution $(K^*(t;\beta), I^*(t;\beta))$ and $\lambda(t;\beta)$.

Second, even though one may believe that the capital stock is a good in this model, and therefore that $\lambda(t;\beta) > 0$ for all $t \in [0, +\infty)$, this is not necessarily the case. To see this, we again use the necessary condition $\lambda = g - pf_I(K, I)$, the assumption that $\text{sign}[f_I(K, I)] = -\text{sign}[I]$, and the fact that $g > 0$. Clearly, if $I^*(t;\beta) > 0$, then $f_I(K^*(t;\beta), I^*(t;\beta)) < 0$, and thus $\lambda(t;\beta) > 0$. If, however, $I^*(t;\beta) < 0$, then $f_I(K^*(t;\beta), I^*(t;\beta)) > 0$, and it is possible that $\lambda(t;\beta) < 0$. These conclusions are intuitive, too, for if the firm is investing in the capital stock, then it obviously considers the capital stock a good, since it wants more of it rather than less, thus implying that current value shadow price of capital is positive. On the other hand, if the firm is disinvesting in the capital stock, then it wants less of it rather than more, in which case, if the firm wants to disinvest at a sufficiently high rate, as indicated by a "large" positive value of $f_I(K^*(t;\beta), I^*(t;\beta))$, then it views the capital stock as a bad, thereby implying that current value shadow price of capital is negative. Note that necessary condition (4) holds globally due to our assumption that $f(\cdot)$ is concave in (K, I). In fact, in order to rule out division by zero when we derive a differential equation for the investment rate, given in Eq. (11) below, we will assume that the second-order sufficient condition for I to maximize $H(\cdot)$ holds, that is, $H_{II}(K, I, \lambda; \alpha) = pf_{II}(K, I) < 0$ holds when evaluated along the curves $(K^*(t;\beta), I^*(t;\beta))$.

Lastly, let's establish that the solution $(K^*(t;\beta), I^*(t;\beta))$ of the necessary conditions is a solution of the adjustment cost model under suitable additional assumptions. By Theorem 14.4, if we can verify that $\lim_{t\to+\infty} e^{-rt}\lambda(t;\beta)[K^*(t;\beta) - K(t)] \le 0$ for all admissible paths $K(t)$ of the capital stock, then we may conclude that $(K^*(t;\beta), I^*(t;\beta))$ is a solution of the adjustment cost model. Since $\lim_{t\to+\infty} e^{-rt} = 0$, and $K^*(t;\beta) \to K^s(\alpha)$ and $\lambda(t;\beta) \to \lambda^s(\alpha)$ as $t \to +\infty$, if all admissible paths $K(t)$ are bounded, or $\lim_{t\to+\infty} K(t)$ exists for all admissible paths, then it follows that $\lim_{t\to+\infty} e^{-rt}\lambda(t;\beta)[K^*(t;\beta) - K(t)] = 0$ and the limiting transversality condition is satisfied. In this case, therefore, the solution $(K^*(t;\beta), I^*(t;\beta))$ of the necessary conditions is a solution of the adjustment cost model. Let's now turn to the qualitative characterization of the model.

To begin, we reduce the necessary conditions given in Eqs. (3), (5), and (6) down to two ordinary differential equations in the variables (K, I). First, differentiate

Eq. (3) with respect to t to get

$$pf_{IK}(K, I)\dot{K} + pf_{II}(K, I)\dot{I} + \dot{\lambda} = 0. \tag{8}$$

Next, substitute $\dot{\lambda} = [r + \delta]\lambda - pf_K(K, I) + c$ from Eq. (5) and $\dot{K} = I - \delta K$ from Eq. (6) into Eq. (8) to eliminate $\dot{\lambda}$ and $\dot{K}$, respectively. This process yields the ordinary differential equation

$$pf_{IK}(K, I)[I - \delta K] + pf_{II}(K, I)\dot{I} + [r + \delta]\lambda - pf_K(K, I) + c = 0. \tag{9}$$

Finally, substitute $\lambda = g - pf_I(K, I)$ from Eq. (3) into Eq. (9) and solve for $\dot{I}$, which, in conjunction with Eq. (6) yields

$$\dot{K} = I - \delta K, \tag{10}$$

$$\dot{I} = \frac{pf_K(K, I) + [r + \delta][pf_I(K, I) - g] - c - pf_{IK}(K, I)[I - \delta K]}{pf_{II}(K, I)} \tag{11}$$

as the system of ordinary differential equations of interest. Note that $(K^*(t; \boldsymbol{\beta}), I^*(t; \boldsymbol{\beta}))$ necessarily satisfy Eqs. (10) and (11). Given this solution, we may then define the dynamic supply function $y^*(\cdot)$ by $y^*(t; \boldsymbol{\beta}) \stackrel{\text{def}}{=} f(K^*(t; \boldsymbol{\beta}), I^*(t; \boldsymbol{\beta}))$, completely analogous to the way the supply function of a profit-maximizing firm is defined.

Now recall that $(K^s(\boldsymbol{\alpha}), I^s(\boldsymbol{\alpha}))$ is the simple steady state solution of the necessary conditions. Therefore, by definition, $(K^s(\boldsymbol{\alpha}), I^s(\boldsymbol{\alpha}))$ is the simultaneous solution of the necessary conditions (10) and (11) when $\dot{K} = 0$ and $\dot{I} = 0$. That is to say, $(K^s(\boldsymbol{\alpha}), I^s(\boldsymbol{\alpha}))$ is the solution of the following pair of algebraic equations:

$$I - \delta K = 0, \tag{12}$$

$$pf_K(K, I) + [r + \delta][pf_I(K, I) - g] - c = 0. \tag{13}$$

Note that we used the fact that $\dot{I} = 0$ if and only if the numerator of Eq. (11) is equal to zero, along with Eq. (12), to arrive at the final form of Eq. (13). Given the steady state solution $(K^s(\boldsymbol{\alpha}), I^s(\boldsymbol{\alpha}))$, we may define the steady state supply function $y^s(\cdot)$ by $y^s(\boldsymbol{\alpha}) \stackrel{\text{def}}{=} f(K^s(\boldsymbol{\alpha}), I^s(\boldsymbol{\alpha}))$.

The first qualitative result for the adjustment cost model is contained in the following proposition. Its proof is left for a mental exercise.

Proposition 14.1 (Homogeneity): *The functions* $(K^*(\cdot), I^*(\cdot), y^*(\cdot))$ *and* $(K^s(\cdot), I^s(\cdot), y^s(\cdot))$ *are positively homogeneous of degree zero in the parameters* (c, g, p).

This homogeneity property is the exact intertemporal analogue of the homogeneity of the static profit-maximizing demand and supply functions with respect to input and output prices. Let's now turn to the examination of the local stability of the steady state.

As usual, we begin this endeavor by calculating the Jacobian matrix of Eqs. (10) and (11) and evaluating the result at the simple steady state solution $(K^s(\alpha), I^s(\alpha))$:

$$\mathbf{J}_d(K^s(\alpha), I^s(\alpha)) \stackrel{\text{def}}{=} \left[\begin{array}{cc} \dfrac{\partial \dot{K}}{\partial K} & \dfrac{\partial \dot{K}}{\partial I} \\ \dfrac{\partial \dot{I}}{\partial K} & \dfrac{\partial \dot{I}}{\partial I} \end{array}\right]\Bigg|_{\substack{\dot{K}=0 \\ \dot{I}=0}}$$

$$= \left[\begin{array}{cc} -\delta & 1 \\ \dfrac{f_{KK}(K^s(\alpha), I^s(\alpha)) + [r+2\delta] f_{IK}(K^s(\alpha), I^s(\alpha))}{f_{II}(K^s(\alpha), I^s(\alpha))} & r+\delta \end{array}\right]. \tag{14}$$

Because $\text{tr}[\mathbf{J}_d(K^s(\alpha), I^s(\alpha))] = r > 0$, the eigenvalues of $\mathbf{J}_d(K^s(\alpha), I^s(\alpha))$ sum to the discount rate and therefore cannot both have negative real parts, thereby ruling out local asymptotic stability of the steady state. But we have already established that the optimal solution of the adjustment cost model converges to the steady state in the limit of the planning horizon. Therefore, there must exist at least one trajectory in the *KI*-phase plane that asymptotically approaches the steady state. This means that it *cannot* be the case that $|\mathbf{J}_d(K^s(\alpha), I^s(\alpha))| > 0$, for then both eigenvalues would have positive real parts and thus *no* trajectories would approach the steady state as $t \to +\infty$. Moreover, the assumed simplicity of the steady state implies that $|\mathbf{J}_d(K^s(\alpha), I^s(\alpha))| \neq 0$ by definition. Consequently, $|\mathbf{J}_d(K^s(\alpha), I^s(\alpha))| < 0$, or equivalently, the eigenvalues are real and of the opposite sign, since their product equals $|\mathbf{J}_d(K^s(\alpha), I^s(\alpha))|$. That is to say, the steady state is a local saddle point, with two trajectories approaching the steady state. These trajectories represent the stable manifold of the saddle point steady state. In sum, therefore, because we were able to establish that (i) the optimal solution of the adjustment cost model converges to the simple steady state solution of the necessary conditions, and (ii) $\text{tr}[\mathbf{J}_d(K^s(\alpha), I^s(\alpha))] = r > 0$, we were led to the conclusion that the simple steady state is a local saddle point.

With the local stability of the steady state resolved, we turn to the construction of the phase portrait. First consider the $\dot{K} = 0$ isocline, which by definition is given by $I - \delta K = 0$. In the *KI*-phase plane, the $\dot{K} = 0$ isocline is thus a straight line emanating from the origin with slope $\delta > 0$. For points above the $\dot{K} = 0$ isocline, $\dot{I} > 0$, whereas for points below the $\dot{K} = 0$ isocline, $\dot{I} < 0$. These observations are a straightforward consequence of the simple structure of the state equation.

The $\dot{I} = 0$ isocline is much more complicated, however. Using Eq. (11), the $\dot{I} = 0$ isocline is by definition given implicitly by

$$\dot{I} = 0 \Leftrightarrow pf_K(K, I) + [r+\delta][pf_I(K, I) - g] - c - pf_{IK}(K, I)[I - \delta K] = 0. \tag{15}$$

By the implicit function theorem, we may use $\mathbf{J}_d(K^s(\alpha), I^s(\alpha))$ given in Eq. (14) to derive the slope of the $\dot{I} = 0$ isocline in a neighborhood of the steady state:

$$\left.\frac{\partial I}{\partial K}\right|_{\substack{\dot{K}=0\\ \dot{I}=0}} = \left.\frac{-\partial \dot{I}/\partial K}{\partial \dot{I}/\partial I}\right|_{\substack{\dot{K}=0\\ \dot{I}=0}}$$
$$= \frac{-f_{KK}(K^s(\alpha), I^s(\alpha)) - [r+2\delta] f_{IK}(K^s(\alpha), I^s(\alpha))}{[r+\delta] f_{II}(K^s(\alpha), I^s(\alpha))} \gtrless 0. \quad (16)$$

Because we have not specified a sign for $f_{IK}(K, I)$, we cannot unequivocally determine the sign of $\partial \dot{I}/\partial K|_{\dot{K}=\dot{I}=0}$ and consequently the slope of the $\dot{I} = 0$ isocline in a neighborhood of the steady state. If, however, we assume that $f_{IK}(K^s(\alpha), I^s(\alpha)) \leq 0$, then $\partial \dot{I}/\partial K|_{\dot{K}=\dot{I}=0} > 0$ and the slope of the $\dot{I} = 0$ isocline is negative in a neighborhood of the steady state. Even without making this assumption, we may glean useful information about the slope of the $\dot{I} = 0$ isocline in a neighborhood of the steady state by examining the condition $|\mathbf{J}_d(K^s(\alpha), I^s(\alpha))| < 0$.

Using Eq. (14) and the fact that $|\mathbf{J}_d(K^s(\alpha), I^s(\alpha))| < 0$, we have

$$|\mathbf{J}_d(K^s(\alpha), I^s(\alpha))| = \left|\begin{matrix} \frac{\partial \dot{K}}{\partial K} & \frac{\partial \dot{K}}{\partial I} \\ \frac{\partial \dot{I}}{\partial K} & \frac{\partial \dot{I}}{\partial I} \end{matrix}\right|_{\substack{\dot{K}=0\\ \dot{I}=0}} = \left.\left[\underbrace{\frac{\partial \dot{K}}{\partial K}}_{-}\underbrace{\frac{\partial \dot{I}}{\partial I}}_{+} - \underbrace{\frac{\partial \dot{K}}{\partial I}}_{+}\underbrace{\frac{\partial \dot{I}}{\partial K}}_{?}\right]\right|_{\substack{\dot{K}=0\\ \dot{I}=0}} < 0.$$

Noting the signs below each term of the above determinant, we have that

$$\left.\left[\underbrace{\frac{\partial \dot{K}}{\partial K}}_{-}\underbrace{\frac{\partial \dot{I}}{\partial I}}_{+} - \underbrace{\frac{\partial \dot{K}}{\partial I}}_{+}\underbrace{\frac{\partial \dot{I}}{\partial K}}_{?}\right]\right|_{\substack{\dot{K}=0\\ \dot{I}=0}} < 0 \Leftrightarrow \left.\frac{-\partial \dot{K}/\partial K}{\partial \dot{K}/\partial I}\right|_{\substack{\dot{K}=0\\ \dot{I}=0}} > \left.\frac{-\partial \dot{I}/\partial K}{\partial \dot{I}/\partial I}\right|_{\substack{\dot{K}=0\\ \dot{I}=0}}. \quad (17)$$

Invoking the implicit function theorem, Eq. (17) asserts that the slope of the $\dot{K} = 0$ isocline is greater than the slope of the $\dot{I} = 0$ isocline in a neighborhood of the steady state if and only if the steady state is a local saddle point. Thus even though the $\dot{I} = 0$ isocline may slope upward or downward in a neighborhood of the steady state, its slope must be less than that of the $\dot{K} = 0$ isocline. That is, the saddle point nature of the steady state rules out the $\dot{I} = 0$ isocline having a greater slope than the $\dot{K} = 0$ isocline in a neighborhood of the steady state.

The vector field associated with the differential equation for the investment rate in Eq. (11) is determined by the elements of the second row of the Jacobian matrix $\mathbf{J}_d(K^s(\alpha), I^s(\alpha))$ defined in Eq. (14). Given that

$$\left.\frac{\partial \dot{I}}{\partial I}\right|_{\substack{\dot{K}=0\\ \dot{I}=0}} = r + \delta > 0, \quad (18)$$

points above the $\dot{I} = 0$ isocline in a neighborhood of the steady state have $\dot{I} > 0$, whereas points below the $\dot{I} = 0$ isocline in a neighborhood of the steady state have $\dot{I} < 0$. This is true regardless of the slope of the $\dot{I} = 0$ isocline because the above element of $\mathbf{J}_d(K^s(\alpha), I^s(\alpha))$ is unambiguously signed. At first glance, this conclusion seems to be at odds with the fact that

$$\left.\frac{\partial \dot{I}}{\partial K}\right|_{\substack{\dot{K}=0\\ \dot{I}=0}} = \frac{f_{KK}(K^s(\alpha), I^s(\alpha)) + [r + 2\delta] f_{IK}(K^s(\alpha), I^s(\alpha))}{f_{II}(K^s(\alpha), I^s(\alpha))} \gtrless 0.$$

That is to say, it may appear to be a contradiction that the vector field associated with the investment rate differential equation is fully determined in a neighborhood of the steady state, but at the same time the slope of the $\dot{I} = 0$ isocline is not unequivocally known. This is not the case, however, as we now proceed to show.

Because the slope of the $\dot{I} = 0$ isocline in a neighborhood of the steady state is given by Eq. (16) and $\partial \dot{I}/\partial I|_{\dot{K}=\dot{I}=0} = r + \delta > 0$, it follows that knowing the sign of $\partial \dot{I}/\partial K|_{\dot{K}=\dot{I}=0}$ is equivalent to knowing the slope of the $\dot{I} = 0$ isocline in a neighborhood of the steady state. For example, if the slope of the $\dot{I} = 0$ isocline is negative in a neighborhood of the steady state, then this is equivalent to $\partial \dot{I}/\partial K|_{\dot{K}=\dot{I}=0} > 0$. In this instance, $\partial \dot{I}/\partial K|_{\dot{K}=\dot{I}=0} > 0$ implies that points to the right of the $\dot{I} = 0$ isocline in a neighborhood of the steady state have $\dot{I} > 0$, which is perfectly consistent with the vector field calculation based on Eq. (18). Of course, this is not too surprising in view of the fact that with a downward sloping isocline, points to the right of it lie on the same side of it, as do points above it. If, however, the slope of the $\dot{I} = 0$ isocline is positive in a neighborhood of the steady state (but less than that of the $\dot{K} = 0$ isocline), then this is equivalent to $\partial \dot{I}/\partial K|_{\dot{K}=\dot{I}=0} < 0$. In this case, $\partial \dot{I}/\partial K|_{\dot{K}=\dot{I}=0} < 0$ implies that points to the right of the $\dot{I} = 0$ isocline in a neighborhood of the steady state have $\dot{I} < 0$. This is also perfectly consistent with the vector field calculation based on Eq. (18) because with an upward sloping isocline, points to the right of it lie on the opposite side of it, as do points above it. In sum, therefore, it is not a contradiction that the vector field associated with the investment rate differential equation is fully determined in a neighborhood of the steady state, but at the same time, the slope of the $\dot{I} = 0$ isocline is not unequivocally known.

At this juncture, we have completely determined the type and local stability of the steady state solution of the differential equations given by Eqs. (10) and (11). The information we've gathered so far is displayed in Figure 17.1 under the assumption that the slope of the $\dot{I} = 0$ isocline is negative in a neighborhood of the steady state. As should be evident by inspection of Figure 17.1, the optimal solution to the adjustment cost model is represented by trajectory **A** or **B**, as these are the only trajectories that reach the simple steady state as $t \to +\infty$. None of the other trajectories in the phase plane have this property and therefore are not optimal.

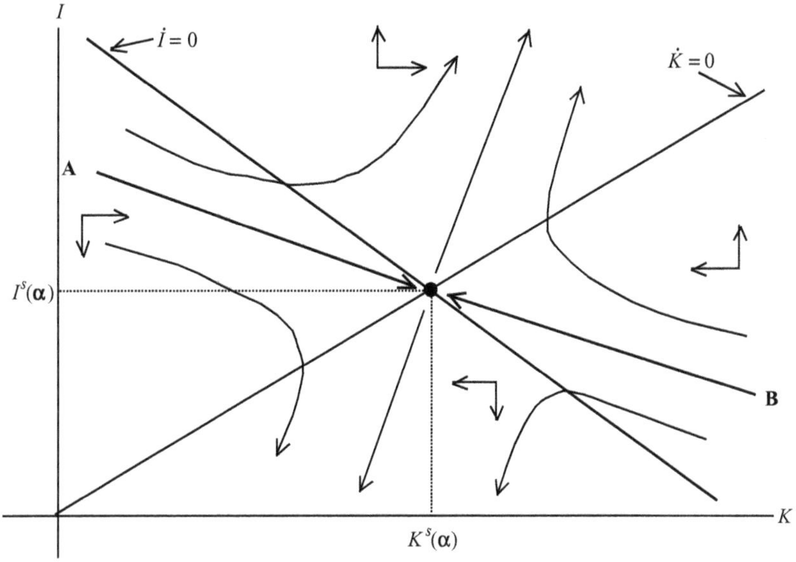

Figure 17.1

If $K_0 > K^s(\alpha)$, that is, if the initial stock of capital exceeds its steady state value, then path **B** is optimal and net disinvestment in the capital stock continually takes place until it is driven down to its steady state value $K^s(\alpha)$, that is, $\dot{K}^*(t;\beta) < 0\,\forall\, t \in [0, +\infty)$. In this case, the stock of capital declines monotonically over time until the smaller steady state stock of capital is reached. If, however, $K_0 < K^s(\alpha)$, that is, if the initial stock of capital is less than its steady state value, then path **A** is optimal and net investment in the capital stock continually takes place until it is driven up to its steady state value $K^s(\alpha)$, that is, $\dot{K}^*(t;\beta) > 0\,\forall\, t \in [0, +\infty)$. In this case, the stock of capital rises monotonically over time until the larger steady state stock of capital is reached.

As of this point, we have graphically found the solution to the adjustment cost model of the firm under the given assumptions, and have determined a few of its qualitative properties by constructing the phase diagram corresponding to the necessary conditions. It would be unfortunate, however, to stop here in the characterization of the solution of the adjustment cost model seeing as the real economic questions of interest are those that ask how the solution changes when some parameter of the model changes. In static economic theory, these questions are answered by a comparative statics analysis. In dynamic economic theory, there are two such analyses for infinite horizon problems:

(a) *steady state comparative statics*: these determine the effect of a parameter change on the steady state values of the choice variables.
(b) *comparative dynamics*: these determine the effect of a parameter change on the time path of the decision variables.

We now turn to an examination of these matters in the adjustment cost model of the firm.

To begin, by the implicit function theorem, a sufficient condition for the steady state solution $(K^s(\alpha), I^s(\alpha))$ to be locally well defined is that the Jacobian determinant of Eqs. (12) and (13) with respect to (K, I) be nonzero when evaluated at the steady state, that is,

$$\left|\mathbf{J}_s(K^s(\alpha), I^s(\alpha))\right| = \begin{vmatrix} -\delta & 1 \\ pf_{KK}(K^s(\alpha), I^s(\alpha)) & pf_{KI}(K^s(\alpha), I^s(\alpha)) \\ +[r+\delta]pf_{IK}(K^s(\alpha), I^s(\alpha)) & +[r+\delta]pf_{II}(K^s(\alpha), I^s(\alpha)) \end{vmatrix} \neq 0. \quad (19)$$

This nonzero Jacobian determinant condition holds by virtue of the assumption that $H_{II}(K, I, \lambda; \alpha) = pf_{II}(K, I) < 0$ when evaluated along the optimal curves $(K^*(t; \beta), I^*(t; \beta))$, and the assumed simplicity of the steady state. In order to establish the veracity of the claim, you are asked in a mental exercise to prove that $|\mathbf{J}_s(K^s(\alpha), I^s(\alpha))| = pf_{II}(K^s(\alpha), I^s(\alpha))\,|\mathbf{J}_d(K^s(\alpha), I^s(\alpha))|$. Given this result, it follows from the aforementioned two assumptions that $|\mathbf{J}_s(K^s(\alpha), I^s(\alpha))| \neq 0$. Hence, by the implicit function theorem, the steady state necessary conditions given in Eqs. (12) and (13) can be solved, in principle, for K and I in terms of the parameters $\alpha \stackrel{\text{def}}{=} (c, g, p, r, \delta)$ locally. Moreover, because $f(\cdot) \in C^{(2)}$, thereby implying that $f_K(\cdot) \in C^{(1)}$ and $f_I(\cdot) \in C^{(1)}$, the functions $K^s(\cdot)$ and $I^s(\cdot)$ are locally $C^{(1)}$ in α by the implicit function theorem too. These conclusions rigorously justify the steady state comparative statics that follow. Finally, because $pf_{II}(K, I) < 0$ when evaluated along the curves $(K^*(t; \beta), I^*(t; \beta))$ and $|\mathbf{J}_d(K^s(\alpha), I^s(\alpha))| < 0$, it follows from $|\mathbf{J}_s(K^s(\alpha), I^s(\alpha))| = pf_{II}(K^s(\alpha), I^s(\alpha))\,|\mathbf{J}_d(K^s(\alpha), I^s(\alpha))|$ that $|\mathbf{J}_s(K^s(\alpha), I^s(\alpha))| > 0$. This is a crucial result, for $|\mathbf{J}_s(K^s(\alpha), I^s(\alpha))|$ appears in the denominator of all the steady state comparative statics expressions. In sum, therefore, the second-order sufficient condition for the investment rate to maximize the current value Hamiltonian and the local saddle point nature of the steady state play an analogous role to the second-order sufficient conditions of the static profit-maximization model in signing the comparative statics expressions.

The steady state comparative statics are found by first substituting $(K^s(\alpha), I^s(\alpha))$ into the steady state necessary conditions, Eqs. (12) and (13), thus creating the identities

$$I^s(\alpha) - \delta K^s(\alpha) \equiv 0, \quad (20)$$

$$pf_K(K^s(\alpha), I^s(\alpha)) + [r+\delta]\left[pf_I(K^s(\alpha), I^s(\alpha)) - g\right] - c \equiv 0, \quad (21)$$

and then differentiating these identities with respect to the parameter of interest using the multivariate chain rule. For example, differentiating identities (20) and

(21) with respect to the discount rate r gives

$$\begin{bmatrix} -\delta & 1 \\ pf_{KK}(K^s(\alpha), I^s(\alpha)) & pf_{KI}(K^s(\alpha), I^s(\alpha)) \\ +[r+\delta]pf_{IK}(K^s(\alpha), I^s(\alpha)) & +[r+\delta]pf_{II}(K^s(\alpha), I^s(\alpha)) \end{bmatrix} \begin{bmatrix} \dfrac{\partial K^s(\alpha)}{\partial r} \\ \dfrac{\partial I^s(\alpha)}{\partial r} \end{bmatrix}$$

$$\equiv \begin{bmatrix} 0 \\ g - pf_I(K^s(\alpha), I^s(\alpha)) \end{bmatrix}. \tag{22}$$

An application of Cramer's rule thus yields the solution

$$\frac{\partial K^s(\alpha)}{\partial r} \equiv \frac{pf_I(K^s(\alpha), I^s(\alpha)) - g}{|\mathbf{J}_s(K^s(\alpha), I^s(\alpha))|} < 0, \tag{23}$$

$$\frac{\partial I^s(\alpha)}{\partial r} \equiv \frac{\delta\left[pf_I(K^s(\alpha), I^s(\alpha)) - g\right]}{|\mathbf{J}_s(K^s(\alpha), I^s(\alpha))|} = \delta\frac{\partial K^s(\alpha)}{\partial r} < 0. \tag{24}$$

The inequalities in Eqs. (23) and (24) follow from $|\mathbf{J}_s(K^s(\alpha), I^s(\alpha))| > 0$, $g > 0$, $p > 0$, $\delta > 0$, and the adjustment cost assumption $\text{sign}[f_I(K, I)] = -\text{sign}[I]$ in conjunction with the fact that $I^s(\alpha) \equiv \delta K^s(\alpha) > 0$. These comparative statics results assert that an increase in the firm's discount rate leads to a decline in its steady state stock of capital and steady state investment rate. Because the increase in the discount rate makes the firm more impatient, it prefers to do beneficial things earlier rather than later. In the adjustment cost model, this leads the firm to have less capital around in the long run.

Turning to the steady state supply function $y^s(\cdot)$, its comparative statics are found by differentiating $y^s(\alpha) \stackrel{\text{def}}{=} f(K^s(\alpha), I^s(\alpha))$ with respect to the discount rate:

$$\frac{\partial y^s(\alpha)}{\partial r} = f_K(K^s(\alpha), I^s(\alpha))\frac{\partial K^s(\alpha)}{\partial r} + f_I(K^s(\alpha), I^s(\alpha))\frac{\partial I^s(\alpha)}{\partial r}.$$

Using Eq. (24), this may be simplified to read

$$\frac{\partial y^s(\alpha)}{\partial r} = \left[f_K(K^s(\alpha), I^s(\alpha)) + \delta f_I(K^s(\alpha), I^s(\alpha))\right]\frac{\partial K^s(\alpha)}{\partial r} < 0,$$

since $f_K(K^s(\alpha), I^s(\alpha)) + \delta f_I(K^s(\alpha), I^s(\alpha)) \equiv p^{-1}[c + g[r+\delta]] - rf_I(K^s(\alpha), I^s(\alpha)) > 0$ by Eq. (21). Thus the negative effect on output brought about by the lower capital stock outweighs the positive effect on output brought about by the lower investment rate and its concomitant lower adjustment costs. Consequently, output falls in the steady state when the discount rate rises.

Now consider an increase in the output price. Differentiating identities (20) and (21) with respect to p gives

$$\begin{bmatrix} -\delta & 1 \\ pf_{KK}(K^s(\alpha), I^s(\alpha)) & pf_{KI}(K^s(\alpha), I^s(\alpha)) \\ +[r+\delta]pf_{IK}(K^s(\alpha), I^s(\alpha)) & +[r+\delta]pf_{II}(K^s(\alpha), I^s(\alpha)) \end{bmatrix} \begin{bmatrix} \dfrac{\partial K^s(\alpha)}{\partial p} \\ \dfrac{\partial I^s(\alpha)}{\partial p} \end{bmatrix}$$

$$\equiv \begin{bmatrix} 0 \\ -f_K(K^s(\alpha), I^s(\alpha)) \\ -[r+\delta]f_I(K^s(\alpha), I^s(\alpha)) \end{bmatrix}.$$

Solving this linear system of equations via Cramer's rule yields

$$\frac{\partial K^s(\alpha)}{\partial p} \equiv \frac{f_K(K^s(\alpha), I^s(\alpha)) + [r+\delta]f_I(K^s(\alpha), I^s(\alpha))}{|\mathbf{J}_s(K^s(\alpha), I^s(\alpha))|}$$

$$= \frac{p^{-1}[c + [r+\delta]g]}{|\mathbf{J}_s(K^s(\alpha), I^s(\alpha))|} > 0, \tag{25}$$

$$\frac{\partial I^s(\alpha)}{\partial p} \equiv \frac{\delta f_K(K^s(\alpha), I^s(\alpha)) + \delta[r+\delta]f_I(K^s(\alpha), I^s(\alpha))}{|\mathbf{J}_s(K^s(\alpha), I^s(\alpha))|}$$

$$= \frac{\delta p^{-1}[c + [r+\delta]g]}{|\mathbf{J}_s(K^s(\alpha), I^s(\alpha))|} = \delta \frac{\partial K^s(\alpha)}{\partial p} > 0. \tag{26}$$

Note that we have employed Eq. (21) in arriving at the final form of Eqs. (25) and (26). Differentiating $y^s(\alpha) \overset{\text{def}}{=} f(K^s(\alpha), I^s(\alpha))$ with respect to p and using Eq. (26) gives the slope of the steady state supply function

$$\frac{\partial y^s(\alpha)}{\partial p} = \left[f_K(K^s(\alpha), I^s(\alpha)) + \delta f_I(K^s(\alpha), I^s(\alpha))\right] \frac{\partial K^s(\alpha)}{\partial p} > 0, \tag{27}$$

since $f_K(K^s(\alpha), I^s(\alpha)) + \delta f_I(K^s(\alpha), I^s(\alpha)) > 0$, as shown above. Equation (27) demonstrates that when the output price increases, the firm produces more of the now more valuable good in the steady state, a result that jibes with that from the static profit-maximizing model of the firm. In order to do so, Eq. (25) shows that the firm must increase its steady state capital stock (the only productive input the firm uses) in order to produce the larger rate of output in the steady state. Equation (26) then shows that this necessitates a higher investment rate in the steady state. The remaining steady state comparative statics and their economic interpretation are left for the mental exercises.

One limitation of a steady state comparative statics analysis is that it only explains where the position of new steady state is relative to the old steady state. In other words, it does not demonstrate how the approach path to the new steady state is affected by a change in a parameter. This is what a local comparative dynamics analysis, to which we now turn, tells us. Note that for the remainder of this chapter, our attention will be focused on the local comparative dynamics of an increase in the output price. Moreover, we will conduct the investigation under the assumption that the slope of the $\dot{I} = 0$ isocline is negative in a neighborhood of the steady state.

Let's first consider the local comparative dynamics from a graphical point of view, with the aid of the phase diagram in Figure 17.1 and a little bit of implicit function theorem work. We know from Figure 17.1 that the steady state is a local saddle point, with two paths converging to it as $t \to +\infty$ and all other paths diverging from it as $t \to +\infty$. Equations (25) and (26) show that the new steady state capital stock and investment rate are larger than their old steady state values because of the output price increase. Now we come to the important observation that the $\dot{K} = 0$ isocline is unaffected by a change in the output price. That this is true is a result of the fact that p does not appear in the $\dot{K} = 0$ isocline, as is plainly obvious because it is given by $I - \delta K = 0$. Hence, in order for the new steady state stock of capital and investment rate to be larger than their old steady values when the output price increases, the $\dot{I} = 0$ isocline must shift up.

We can verify the upward shift in the $\dot{I} = 0$ isocline by applying the implicit function theorem to the $\dot{I} = 0$ isocline defined in Eq. (15). Specifically, we wish to compute the partial derivative of I with respect to p along the $\dot{I} = 0$ isocline and evaluate the result at the steady state. Invoking the implicit function theorem, the result of this set of operations is

$$\left.\frac{\partial I}{\partial p}\right|_{\substack{\dot{K}=0\\ \dot{I}=0}} = \left.\frac{-\partial \dot{I}/\partial p}{\partial \dot{I}/\partial I}\right|_{\substack{\dot{K}=0\\ \dot{I}=0}} = \frac{-f_K(K^s(\alpha), I^s(\alpha)) - [r+\delta] f_I(K^s(\alpha), I^s(\alpha))}{p[r+\delta] f_{II}(K^s(\alpha), I^s(\alpha))} > 0,$$

since $f_K(K^s(\alpha), I^s(\alpha)) + [r+\delta] f_I(K^s(\alpha), I^s(\alpha)) \equiv p^{-1}[c + g[r+\delta]] > 0$ by Eq. (21). This result demonstrates that an increase in p along the $\dot{I} = 0$ isocline, holding K and (c, g, r, δ) constant, increases I in a neighborhood of the steady state. In other words, this implicit function theorem calculation shows that the $\dot{I} = 0$ isocline shifts up when the output price increases in a neighborhood of the steady state. This means that the new $\dot{I} = 0$ isocline associated with the higher output price must lie above the old $\dot{I} = 0$ isocline, just as we argued above. The local comparative dynamics phase diagram corresponding to an increase in the output price is given in Figure 17.2.

It is worthwhile at this juncture to pause and again repeat the three remarks made in Chapters 15 and 16 concerning the construction of a local comparative dynamics phase diagram. The first remark is that the local dynamics depicted in Figure 17.1 apply to *both* of the steady states depicted in Figure 17.2. In other words, the local dynamics around the old and the new steady states are qualitatively identical, and are therefore of the saddle point variety. As a result, there is no need to fully draw in the vector field around each steady state in Figure 17.2, since the complete vector field for it can be inferred from that in Figure 17.1. Second, before the increase in the output price occurs, the firm is assumed to be at rest at the old steady state. Third,

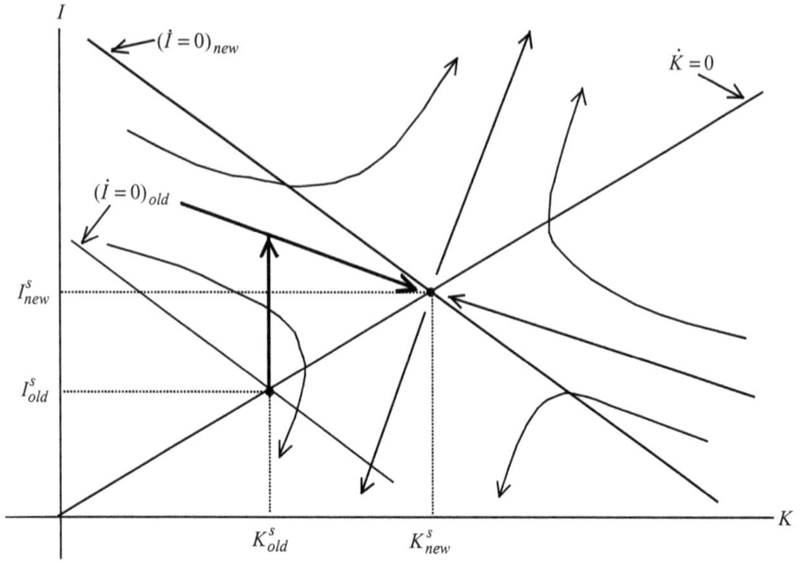

Figure 17.2

the firm is assumed to eventually come to rest at the new steady state as a result of the increase in the output price. That is, the old steady state value of the capital stock is taken as the initial condition in the local comparative dynamics exercise, whereas the new steady state value of the capital stock is taken as the terminal condition. The local comparative dynamics phase diagram therefore depicts the optimal transition path from the old to the new steady state that results from the increase in the output price.

The local comparative dynamics follow from this phase portrait. Initially, the firm is positioned at the old steady state (K^s_{old}, I^s_{old}). We know from the steady state comparative statics that when the output price increases, the steady state stock of capital and investment rate both increase. Because the capital stock is fixed at any given moment in time – in particular, the initial moment the output price increases – the capital stock cannot change the instant the output price increases. Hence, the only way the firm can get from the old steady state (K^s_{old}, I^s_{old}) to the new steady state (K^s_{new}, I^s_{new}) is for the firm to increase its initial rate of investment as soon as the output price increases. In this way, the firm can get on the trajectory in the phase plane that takes it to the new steady state. This trajectory is labeled with the thick lines in Figure 17.2. Note that this is achieved by increasing the investment rate by a *precise amount* the instant the output price increases. If when the output price increases, the initial investment rate is increased too much or too little, or if it is decreased, the firm will not be on the trajectory that allows it to reach the new steady state. Because the initial increase in the investment rate drives it above its new steady state value, the investment rate must fall over time as the new steady state is approached. All the while, the capital stock of the firm increases monotonically from its old to its new steady state value.

In order to gain some analytical insight into the aforementioned comparative dynamics results, as well as to rigorously justify the geometry, we return to the method of linearization exposited in Chapter 13 to study the local stability properties of a system of autonomous and nonlinear differential equations. Remember that the linearization approach involves using Taylor's theorem to linearly approximate a system of nonlinear ordinary differential equations in a neighborhood of the steady state. Because we already have computed the Jacobian matrix of the necessary conditions (10) and (11), we have essentially derived the corresponding linearized system of differential equations that we shall work with.

The linearized form of the necessary conditions (10) and (11) is therefore given by

$$\begin{bmatrix} \Delta\dot{K} \\ \Delta\dot{I} \end{bmatrix} = \begin{bmatrix} -\delta & 1 \\ j_{21}(\alpha) & r+\delta \end{bmatrix} \begin{bmatrix} \Delta K \\ \Delta I \end{bmatrix}, \tag{28}$$

where

$$j_{21}(\alpha) \stackrel{\text{def}}{=} \frac{f_{KK}(K^s(\alpha), I^s(\alpha)) + [r+2\delta] f_{IK}(K^s(\alpha), I^s(\alpha))}{f_{II}(K^s(\alpha), I^s(\alpha))} = \left.\frac{\partial \dot{I}}{\partial K}\right|_{\substack{\dot{K}=0 \\ \dot{I}=0}},$$

and $\Delta K \stackrel{\text{def}}{=} K - K^s(\alpha)$ and $\Delta I \stackrel{\text{def}}{=} I - I^s(\alpha)$, thereby implying that $\Delta\dot{K} \stackrel{\text{def}}{=} \dot{K}$ and $\Delta\dot{I} \stackrel{\text{def}}{=} \dot{I}$. Recall that because we are working under the assumption that the slope of the $\dot{I} = 0$ isocline is negative in a neighborhood of the steady state, $j_{21}(\alpha) > 0$. Also recall that Eq. (28) is the result of applying Taylor's theorem to Eqs. (10) and (11) and neglecting terms of order two or higher from the expansion.

Equation (28) is a linear and homogeneous system of ordinary differential equations with constant coefficients. As you may recollect from your prior coursework in elementary differential equations, because the eigenvalues (γ_1, γ_2) of the Jacobian matrix $\mathbf{J}_d(K^s(\alpha), I^s(\alpha))$ are real and unequal, a fact we have already established, the general solution of system (28) takes the form

$$\begin{bmatrix} \Delta K(t) \\ \Delta I(t) \end{bmatrix} = c_1 \mathbf{v}^1 e^{\gamma_1 t} + c_2 \mathbf{v}^2 e^{\gamma_2 t} \tag{29}$$

by Theorem 25.1 of Simon and Blume (1994), where c_1 and c_2 are constants of integration and $\mathbf{v}^i \in \Re^2$ is an eigenvector of $\mathbf{J}_d(K^s(\alpha), I^s(\alpha))$ corresponding to the eigenvalue $\gamma_i, i = 1, 2$. Given that $\Delta K \stackrel{\text{def}}{=} K - K^s(\alpha)$ and $\Delta I \stackrel{\text{def}}{=} I - I^s(\alpha)$, we may rewrite Eq. (29) equivalently as

$$\begin{bmatrix} K(t) \\ I(t) \end{bmatrix} = \begin{bmatrix} K^s(\alpha) \\ I^s(\alpha) \end{bmatrix} + c_1 \mathbf{v}^1 e^{\gamma_1 t} + c_2 \mathbf{v}^2 e^{\gamma_2 t}. \tag{30}$$

By definition, the eigenvector $\mathbf{v}^i \in \Re^2$, $i = 1, 2$, is the solution to the following homogeneous system of linear algebraic equations:

$$\begin{bmatrix} -\delta - \gamma_i & 1 \\ j_{21}(\alpha) & r+\delta-\gamma_i \end{bmatrix} \begin{bmatrix} v_1^i \\ v_2^i \end{bmatrix} = \begin{bmatrix} 0 \\ 0 \end{bmatrix}. \tag{31}$$

Without loss of generality, we may let $\gamma_1 < 0$ and $\gamma_2 > 0$. Because the above coefficient matrix is singular by the definition of an eigenvalue, we may use either row of it to find the corresponding eigenvector. Setting $i = 1$ and using the second row of Eq. (31), we find that

$$\mathbf{v}^1 = \begin{bmatrix} v_1^1 \\ v_2^1 \end{bmatrix} = \begin{bmatrix} 1 \\ \dfrac{j_{21}(\alpha)}{\gamma_1 - r - \delta} \end{bmatrix}, \tag{32}$$

whereas setting $i = 2$ and using the first row of Eq. (31), we find that

$$\mathbf{v}^2 = \begin{bmatrix} v_1^2 \\ v_2^2 \end{bmatrix} = \begin{bmatrix} 1 \\ \delta + \gamma_2 \end{bmatrix}. \tag{33}$$

Because $j_{21}(\alpha) > 0$ and $\gamma_1 < 0, v_2^1 < 0$, whereas $v_2^2 > 0$, since $\gamma_2 > 0$. Thus the stable manifold of the steady state, which is spanned by the eigenvector $\mathbf{v}^1$ corresponding to the eigenvalue $\gamma_1 < 0$, has a negative slope in the *KI*-phase plane, whereas the unstable manifold of the steady state, which is spanned by the eigenvector $\mathbf{v}^2$ corresponding to the eigenvalue $\gamma_2 > 0$, has a positive slope in the *KI*-phase plane. Inspection of Figure 17.1 shows that this conclusion is confirmed geometrically.

To determine the constants of integration and thus the specific solution to Eq. (28), first recall that the optimal time paths of the capital stock and investment rate satisfy the limiting properties $\lim_{t\to+\infty} K(t) = K^s(\alpha)$ and $\lim_{t\to+\infty} I(t) = I^s(\alpha)$. Using Eq. (30), this yields

$$\lim_{t\to+\infty} \begin{bmatrix} K(t) \\ I(t) \end{bmatrix} = \lim_{t\to+\infty} \left\{ \begin{bmatrix} K^s(\alpha) \\ I^s(\alpha) \end{bmatrix} + c_1\mathbf{v}^1 e^{\gamma_1 t} + c_2\mathbf{v}^2 e^{\gamma_2 t} \right\} = \begin{bmatrix} K^s(\alpha) \\ I^s(\alpha) \end{bmatrix}.$$

The last term in the curly bracketed expression, however, does not possess a limit if $c_2 \neq 0$ because $\gamma_2 > 0$, that is, $c_2\mathbf{v}^2 e^{\gamma_2 t} \to [\begin{smallmatrix}\pm\infty \\ \pm\infty\end{smallmatrix}]$ as $t \to +\infty$ if $c_2 \neq 0$, thereby violating the convergence property of the optimal solution curves. Hence, in order for $\lim_{t\to+\infty} K(t) = K^s(\alpha)$ and $\lim_{t\to+\infty} I(t) = I^s(\alpha)$ to hold, $c_2 = 0$. Equation (30) therefore reduces to

$$\begin{bmatrix} K(t) \\ I(t) \end{bmatrix} = \begin{bmatrix} K^s(\alpha) \\ I^s(\alpha) \end{bmatrix} + c_1\mathbf{v}^1 e^{\gamma_1 t}. \tag{34}$$

Applying the initial condition $K(0) = K_0$ to Eq. (34) and using Eq. (32) yields

$$K(0) = K^s(\alpha) + c_1 = K_0 \Rightarrow c_1 = K_0 - K^s(\alpha).$$

Thus the specific solution to the linearized system of differential equations given in Eq. (28) is

$$\begin{bmatrix} K^*(t;\beta) \\ I^*(t;\beta) \end{bmatrix} = \begin{bmatrix} K^s(\alpha) \\ I^s(\alpha) \end{bmatrix} + [K_0 - K^s(\alpha)] \begin{bmatrix} 1 \\ \dfrac{j_{21}(\alpha)}{\gamma_1 - r - \delta} \end{bmatrix} e^{\gamma_1 t}. \tag{35}$$

Equation (35) describes the optimal time path of the capital stock and investment rate in a neighborhood of the steady state.

The local comparative dynamics are derived from Eq. (35) by differentiating with respect to the parameter of interest and evaluating the resulting derivative at $K_0 = K^s(\boldsymbol{\alpha})$. Thus in the local comparative dynamics exercise, we take the initial capital stock to be the steady state value of the capital stock. This is exactly how we have conducted the local comparative dynamics via a phase diagram in this and the previous two chapters. As you will establish in a mental exercise, the eigenvalues (γ_1, γ_2) of the Jacobian matrix $\mathbf{J}_d(K^s(\boldsymbol{\alpha}), I^s(\boldsymbol{\alpha}))$ are functions of the parameter vector $\boldsymbol{\alpha} \stackrel{\text{def}}{=} (c, g, p, r, \delta)$. This is important to remember in the local comparative dynamics calculations.

To carry out the local comparative dynamics analysis, first differentiate Eq. (35) with respect to the output price p and recall that γ_1 is a function of $\boldsymbol{\alpha} \stackrel{\text{def}}{=} (c, g, p, r, \delta)$:

$$\frac{\partial K^*}{\partial p}(t;\boldsymbol{\beta}) = \frac{\partial K^s}{\partial p}(\boldsymbol{\alpha}) + [K_0 - K^s(\boldsymbol{\alpha})]\, e^{\gamma_1 t}\frac{\partial \gamma_1}{\partial p} t - e^{\gamma_1 t}\frac{\partial K^s}{\partial p}(\boldsymbol{\alpha}),$$

$$\frac{\partial I^*}{\partial p}(t;\boldsymbol{\beta}) = \frac{\partial I^s}{\partial p}(\boldsymbol{\alpha}) + [K_0 - K^s(\boldsymbol{\alpha})]$$
$$\times \left[\frac{j_{21}(\boldsymbol{\alpha})}{\gamma_1 - r - \delta} e^{\gamma_1 t}\frac{\partial \gamma_1}{\partial p} t + e^{\gamma_1 t}\frac{\partial}{\partial p}\left[\frac{j_{21}(\boldsymbol{\alpha})}{\gamma_1 - r - \delta}\right]\right] - e^{\gamma_1 t}\left[\frac{j_{21}(\boldsymbol{\alpha})}{\gamma_1 - r - \delta}\right]\frac{\partial K^s}{\partial p}(\boldsymbol{\alpha}).$$

Then evaluate the above derivatives at $K_0 = K^s(\boldsymbol{\alpha})$, and use Eq. (26) to derive the local comparative dynamics for an increase in the output price:

$$\left.\frac{\partial K^*}{\partial p}(t;\boldsymbol{\beta})\right|_{K_0=K^s(\boldsymbol{\alpha})} = [1 - e^{\gamma_1 t}]\frac{\partial K^s}{\partial p}(\boldsymbol{\alpha}) \geq 0\,\forall\, t \in [0, +\infty), \tag{36}$$

$$\left.\frac{\partial I^*}{\partial p}(t;\boldsymbol{\beta})\right|_{K_0=K^s(\boldsymbol{\alpha})} = \left[\delta - e^{\gamma_1 t}\left[\frac{j_{21}(\boldsymbol{\alpha})}{\gamma_1 - r - \delta}\right]\right]\frac{\partial K^s}{\partial p}(\boldsymbol{\alpha}) > 0\,\forall\, t \in [0, +\infty). \tag{37}$$

The inequalities are a result of the facts $\partial K^s(\boldsymbol{\alpha})/\partial p > 0$ from Eq. (25), $\gamma_1 < 0$, which implies that $e^{\gamma_1 t} \in (0, 1]\,\forall\, t \in [0, +\infty)$, and $j_{21}(\boldsymbol{\alpha}) > 0$. Furthermore, when $t = 0$, that is, at the moment p is increased, we have

$$\left.\frac{\partial K^*}{\partial p}(0;\boldsymbol{\beta})\right|_{K_0=K^s(\boldsymbol{\alpha})} = 0, \tag{38}$$

$$\left.\frac{\partial I^*}{\partial p}(0;\boldsymbol{\beta})\right|_{K_0=K^s(\boldsymbol{\alpha})} = \left[\delta - \left[\frac{j_{21}(\boldsymbol{\alpha})}{\gamma_1 - r - \delta}\right]\right]\frac{\partial K^s}{\partial p}(\boldsymbol{\alpha}) > 0. \tag{39}$$

Finally, letting $t \to +\infty$ in Eqs. (36) and (37) yields

$$\lim_{t\to+\infty} \frac{\partial K^*}{\partial p}(t;\beta)\bigg|_{K_0=K^s(\alpha)} = \lim_{t\to+\infty} \left[[1 - e^{\gamma_1 t}] \frac{\partial K^s}{\partial p}(\alpha) \right]$$

$$= \frac{\partial K^s}{\partial p}(\alpha) \lim_{t\to+\infty} [1 - e^{\gamma_1 t}] = \frac{\partial K^s}{\partial p}(\alpha), \tag{40}$$

$$\lim_{t\to+\infty} \frac{\partial I^*}{\partial p}(t;\beta)\bigg|_{K_0=K^s(\alpha)} = \lim_{t\to+\infty} \left[\left[\delta - e^{\gamma_1 t} \left[\frac{j_{21}(\alpha)}{\gamma_1 - r - \delta} \right] \right] \frac{\partial K^s}{\partial p}(\alpha) \right]$$

$$= \frac{\partial K^s}{\partial p}(\alpha) \lim_{t\to+\infty} \left[\left[\delta - e^{\gamma_1 t} \left[\frac{j_{21}(\alpha)}{\gamma_1 - r - \delta} \right] \right] \right]$$

$$= \delta \frac{\partial K^s}{\partial p}(\alpha) = \frac{\partial I^s}{\partial p}(\alpha). \tag{41}$$

Let us now turn to an economic interpretation of Eqs. (36) through (41). We will see that they confirm all of the qualitative implications we deduced via the local comparative dynamics phase portrait in Figure 17.2.

By Eq. (38), the moment the output price increases ($t = 0$), the capital stock remains at its old steady state level and is therefore unaffected, just as we claimed when we discussed the local comparative dynamics via the phase diagram in Figure 17.2. On the other hand, the instant the output price increases, the investment rate rises by the precise amount given in Eq. (39). In fact, because $\gamma_1 < 0$ and $j_{21}(\alpha) > 0$, it follows from Eq. (39) that

$$\frac{\partial I^*}{\partial p}(0;\beta)\bigg|_{K_0=K^s(\alpha)} = \left[\delta - \left[\frac{j_{21}(\alpha)}{\gamma_1 - r - \delta} \right] \right] \frac{\partial K^s}{\partial p}(\alpha) > \delta \frac{\partial K^s}{\partial p}(\alpha) = \frac{\partial I^s}{\partial p}(\alpha) > 0.$$

Thus the moment the output price increases, the investment rate increases so much that it exceeds its new steady state investment rate, a result that we were able to deduce with the aid of the local comparative dynamics phase diagram in Figure 17.2. After the initial increase in the output price, Eqs. (36) and (37) show that the capital stock and investment rate are both higher all along their approach to the new steady state. As $t \to +\infty$, Eqs. (40) and (41) show that the capital stock and investment rate approach their new steady state values, both of which exceed their old steady state values.

The last remark we wish to make about the local comparative dynamics of the adjustment cost model brings us back to Theorem 14.10, the dynamic envelope theorem for discounted infinite horizon optimal control models. As you may recall, in order to establish Theorem 14.10, we had to make an assumption that, in the context of the adjustment cost model, was of the form

$$\lim_{t\to+\infty} \frac{\partial K^*}{\partial p}(t;\beta) = \frac{\partial K^s}{\partial p}(\alpha).$$

By Eq. (40), if we take the initial stock of capital to be the steady state stock of capital, that is, $K_0 = K^s(\alpha)$, then this condition holds. The same conclusion applies to the optimal investment rate as well, as can be seen by inspection of Eq. (41).

In the next chapter, we undertake a systematic qualitative study of a general infinite horizon discounted autonomous control problem with one state variable and one control variable. The theorems developed will permit a more complete understanding of the basic mathematical structure responsible for many of the qualitative properties of numerous optimal control models used in dynamic economic theory.

MENTAL EXERCISES

17.1 Prove Proposition 17.1.

17.2 Prove that $|\mathbf{J}_s(K^s(\alpha), I^s(\alpha))| = pf_{II}(K^s(\alpha), I^s(\alpha))\,|\mathbf{J}_d(K^s(\alpha),\ I^s(\alpha))|$.

17.3 Prove that the steady state value of the current value shadow price of the capital stock is positive, that is, $\lambda^s(\alpha) > 0$. Is the capital stock a good or a bad in the steady state? Explain.

17.4 Assume, in contrast to the chapter proper, that the slope of the $\dot{I} = 0$ isocline is positive in a neighborhood of the steady state.
- (a) Draw the phase portrait in KI-phase space. Compare it to that in Figure 17.1.
- (b) Draw the local comparative dynamics phase portrait corresponding to an increase in the output price. Compare it to that in Figure 17.2.

17.5 This exercise asks you to prove that eigenvectors of $\mathbf{J}_d(K^s(\alpha), I^s(\alpha))$ are identical regardless of which row of Eq. (31) is used to find them.
- (a) Derive $\mathbf{v}^1$ using the first row of Eq. (31).
- (b) Derive $\mathbf{v}^2$ using the second row of Eq. (31).
- (c) Show that $\mathbf{v}^1$ and $\mathbf{v}^2$ derived in parts (a) and (b) are identical to $\mathbf{v}^1$ and $\mathbf{v}^2$ derived in Eqs. (32) and (33), respectively.

17.6 Prove that the eigenvalues (γ_1, γ_2) of the Jacobian matrix $\mathbf{J}_d(K^s(\alpha), I^s(\alpha))$ are functions of the parameter vector $\alpha \stackrel{\text{def}}{=} (c, g, p, r, \delta)$.

17.7 Derive the local comparative dynamics associated with an increase in the discount rate r for the adjustment cost model of the firm. Your derivation of the qualitative properties should be as complete and exhaustive as that given in the text. Draw the comparative dynamics phase portraits, and provide an economic explanation of the results.

17.8 Derive the steady state comparative statics and local comparative dynamics associated with an increase in the holding cost of capital c for the adjustment cost model of the firm. Your derivation of the qualitative properties should be as complete and exhaustive as that given in the text. Draw the comparative dynamics phase portraits, and provide an economic explanation of the results.

17.9 Derive the steady state comparative statics and local comparative dynamics associated with an increase in the purchase price of capital g for the adjustment cost model of the firm. Your derivation of the qualitative properties should be as complete and exhaustive as that given in the text. Draw the comparative dynamics phase portraits, and provide an economic explanation of the results.

17.10 Derive the steady state comparative statics and local comparative dynamics associated with an increase in the initial stock of capital K_o for the adjustment cost model of the firm. Your derivation of the qualitative properties should be as complete and exhaustive as that given in the text. Draw the comparative dynamics phase portraits, and provide an economic explanation of the results.

17.11 *Dynamics of the Adjustment Cost Model of the Firm in State-Costate Phase Space*. This question reexamines the adjustment cost model of the capital-accumulating firm assuming that the generalized production function is additively separable in the capital stock and investment rate. This has the effect of sharpening and simplifying some of the analysis. Let $f(\cdot) : \Re_+ \to \Re_+$ be the $C^{(2)}$ production function, where $f(0) = 0$, $f'(K) > 0$ and $f''(K) < 0 \,\forall\, K \in \Re_{++}$, $\lim_{K\to 0^+} f'(K) = +\infty$, and $\lim_{K\to+\infty} f'(K) = 0$, where $K(t)$ is the capital stock of the firm at time t. The output of the firm is sold at the constant price $p > 0$, the capital stock has unit maintenance costs of $c > 0$, and $g > 0$ is the constant cost per unit of purchased capital, that is, the purchase price of investment $I(t)$. In addition, let $C(\cdot) : \Re \to \Re_+$ be the $C^{(2)}$ cost of adjustment function (in dollars), with $C(0) = 0$, $C'(0) = 0$, $\text{sign}(C'(I)) = \text{sign}(I)$, and $C''(I) > 0 \,\forall\, I \in \Re_+$. The firm is asserted to operate over the indefinite future and discounts its instantaneous profits at the constant rate $r > 0$. The state equation is the prototype capital accumulation equation with a constant rate of decay $\delta > 0$. Finally, the firm begins its planning at time $t = 0$ with the given stock of capital $K(0) = K_0 > 0$. The optimal control problem the firm must solve in order to determine its optimal investment plan is therefore given by

$$V(\beta) \stackrel{\text{def}}{=} \max_{I(\cdot)} \int_0^{+\infty} [pf(K(t)) - cK(t) - gI(t) - C(I(t))]\, e^{-rt}\, dt$$

$$\text{s.t.} \quad \dot{K}(t) = I(t) - \delta K(t), \; K(0) = K_0,$$

where $\beta \stackrel{\text{def}}{=} (\alpha, K_0) \stackrel{\text{def}}{=} (c, g, p, r, \delta, K_0) \in \Re^6_{++}$ are the time invariant parameters of the problem. Notice that we are not imposing a nonnegativity constraint on the investment rate. This means that the firm can buy capital $(I(t) > 0)$ or sell capital $(I(t) < 0)$ at the market price of $g > 0$. We are therefore not considering the case of irreversible investment in this question. Assume that there exists a solution of the necessary conditions of Theorem 14.3, say, $(K^*(t;\beta), I^*(t;\beta))$, with the property that $(K^*(t;\beta), I^*(t;\beta)) \to (K^s(\alpha), I^s(\alpha))$ as $t \to +\infty$, where $\lambda(t;\beta)$ is the corresponding time path of the current value costate variable and $(K^s(\alpha), I^s(\alpha))$ is the simple steady state solution of the necessary conditions. Finally, assume that the objective functional exists for all admissible pairs of functions.

(a) Write down the necessary conditions for this problem in current value form. Provide an economic interpretation of the Maximum Principle equation.
(b) Prove that the solution $(K^*(t;\beta), I^*(t;\beta))$ of the necessary conditions is the unique optimal solution to the adjustment cost model of the firm under a suitable additional assumption to be determined by you.
(c) Show that the necessary and sufficient conditions can be reduced to a pair of autonomous ordinary differential equations in (K, λ).
(d) Prove that the steady state is a saddle point.
(e) Prove that the steady state defines (K, λ) as locally $C^{(1)}$ functions of the parameter vector α, say, $K^s(\alpha)$ and $\lambda^s(\alpha)$.
(f) Derive the phase portrait for the ordinary differential equations you derived in part (c). Be sure to include your derivations of the slopes of the $\dot{K} = 0$ and $\dot{\lambda} = 0$ isoclines, as well as the vector field in the $K\lambda$-phase plane.
(g) Derive the steady state comparative statics for the output price p. Provide an economic interpretation of the comparative statics result.
(h) Draw the local comparative dynamics phase portrait for the output price p, making sure to label the optimal path from the old to the new steady state clearly. Provide an economic interpretation of the comparative dynamics result.
(i) Find the steady state comparative statics for the purchase price of the investment good g. Provide an economic interpretation of the comparative statics result.
(j) Draw the local comparative dynamics phase portrait for the purchase price of the investment good g. Provide an economic interpretation of the comparative dynamics result.
(k) Find the steady state comparative statics for the unit maintenance cost c. Provide an economic interpretation of the comparative statics result.
(l) Draw the local comparative dynamics phase portrait for the unit maintenance cost c. Provide an economic interpretation of the comparative dynamics result.

FURTHER READING

The seminal paper on the adjustment cost model of the firm is by Eisner and Strotz (1963). Treadway (1970) provides a qualitative analysis of the model akin to that developed in this chapter. Treadway (1971) and Mortensen (1974) analyze some of the qualitative properties of a multivariate extension of the adjustment cost model. Epstein (1982) and Caputo (1992) provide rather extensive comparative dynamics characterizations of the model. See the references in Chapter 20 for the fundamental papers that develop an intertemporal duality theory for the adjustment cost model and for those that attempt to empirically test it and use it for policy purposes.

REFERENCES

Caputo, M.R. (1992), "Fundamental Symmetries and Qualitative Properties in the Adjustment Cost Model of the Firm," *Journal of Mathematical Economics*, 21, 99–112.

Eisner, R. and Strotz, R.H. (1963), "Determinants of Business Investment," Research Study Two in *Impacts of Monetary Policy* (Englewood Cliffs, N.J.: Prentice-Hall).

Epstein, L.G. (1982), "Comparative Dynamics in the Adjustment Cost Model of the Firm," *Journal of Economic Theory*, 27, 77–100.

Mortensen, D.T. (1974), "Generalized Costs of Adjustment and Dynamic Factor Demand Theory," *Econometrica*, 41, 657–665.

Simon, C.P. and Blume, L. (1994), *Mathematics for Economists* (New York: W.W. Norton & Company, Inc.).

Treadway, A.B. (1970), "Adjustment Costs and Variable Inputs in the Theory of the Competitive Firm," *Journal of Economic Theory*, 2, 329–347.

Treadway, A.B. (1971), "The Rational Multivariate Flexible Accelerator," *Econometrica*, 39, 845–855.

EIGHTEEN

Qualitative Properties of Infinite Horizon Optimal Control Problems with One State Variable and One Control Variable

Since the publication of Samuelson's *Foundations of Economic Analysis* (1947), economists have been aware of the importance of developing theories that are, at least in principle, refutable. As you may recall, refutable theories are those that lead to well-defined predictions about potentially observable variables in response to perturbations in parameters, as well as curvature properties, homogeneity restrictions, and reciprocity or symmetry results. Such empirically interesting models are the standard fare in the static theory of the consumer and firm, and via duality theory, these models have been subjected to numerous tests of their veracity.

In contrast, the economics literature using dynamic optimization models contains many analyses that are deficient in testable implications. For example, many authors usually state the problem under consideration, derive and economically interpret the necessary conditions, make some reference to sufficient conditions, discuss the existence and multiplicity of steady state equilibria, and finally, analyze the stability of the steady state equilibria. Although all these aspects are important, they do not represent a complete picture of an optimal control model, for the qualitative properties of the model are not examined.

The purpose of this chapter is to examine a ubiquitous class of optimal control models for its particular mathematical structure that leads to steady state comparative statics and local comparative dynamics refutable propositions. The class of optimal control problems under consideration is one with an infinite time horizon, time entering explicitly only through the exponential discount factor, a single state variable, a single control variable, a time-independent vector of parameters influencing the integrand and state equation, a given initial state, and an optimal solution that converges to the steady state solution as an indefinite amount of time passes. Arguably, this class of optimal control problems comprises the largest class of applied dynamic optimization models in economic theory.

We take a systematic approach to uncovering the qualitative properties of one-dimensional optimal control problems. First, the local stability of the steady state is investigated. Next, using the local stability result, a comparative statics analysis of the steady state is carried out. Finally, using the local stability property of the steady state and the steady state comparative statics, a local comparative dynamics analysis is performed. The theorems are applied to the adjustment cost model of the firm to demonstrate their usefulness in deriving qualitative results in optimal control problems, as well as to elucidate the underlying mathematical structure responsible for such qualitative results. We refer the reader to Caputo (1997), on which this chapter is based, for a more complete literature review and further technical details.

The optimal control problem under consideration is to find a control function $u(\cdot)$ and its associated response function $x(\cdot)$ that solve

$$\max_{u(\cdot)} \int_0^{+\infty} f(x(t), u(t); \boldsymbol{\alpha})\, e^{-rt}\, dt$$

$$\text{s.t.} \quad \dot{x}(t) = g(x(t),\ u(t); \boldsymbol{\beta}),\ x(0) = x_0, \tag{1}$$

$$(x(t), u(t)) \in X \times U.$$

The following assumptions are imposed on problem (1) and explained subsequently:

(A.1) $f(\cdot) : X \times U \times A \to \Re$ and $f(\cdot) \in C^{(2)}$ for all $(x, u; \boldsymbol{\alpha}) \in X \times U \times A$, where $X \subset \Re$, $U \subset \Re$, and $A \subset \Re^{K_1}$ are convex and compact sets, and $\boldsymbol{\alpha}$ is a time-independent vector of parameters.

(A.2) $g(\cdot) : X \times U \times B \to \Re$ and $g(\cdot) \in C^{(2)}$ for all $(x, u; \boldsymbol{\beta}) \in X \times U \times B$, where $B \subset \Re^{K_2}$ is a compact and convex set, $\boldsymbol{\beta}$ is a time-independent vector of parameters, and $g_u(x(t), u(t); \boldsymbol{\beta}) \neq 0$ along the optimal path.

(A.3) There exists a unique optimal solution pair to the optimal control problem (1) for all $(\boldsymbol{\alpha}, \boldsymbol{\beta}, r, x_0) \in \text{int}(A \times B \times D \times X)$, denoted by $(z(t; \boldsymbol{\theta}, x_0), v(t; \boldsymbol{\theta}, x_0))$ with corresponding current value costate variable $\lambda(t; \boldsymbol{\theta}, x_0)$, where $\boldsymbol{\theta} \stackrel{\text{def}}{=} (\boldsymbol{\alpha}, \boldsymbol{\beta}, r)$, $D \subset \Re_+$ is a compact and convex set, and r is the time-independent discount rate.

(A.4) The optimal pair $(z(t; \boldsymbol{\theta}, x_0), v(t; \boldsymbol{\theta}, x_0)) \in \text{int}(X \times U)$ for all $(\boldsymbol{\theta}, x_0) \in \text{int}(A \times B \times D \times X)$ and for all $t \in [0, +\infty)$.

(A.5) $H_{uu}(x(t), u(t), \lambda(t); \boldsymbol{\alpha}, \boldsymbol{\beta}) \neq 0$ along the optimal path, where $H(\cdot)$ is the current value Hamiltonian function associated with problem (1).

(A.6) There exists a unique, interior, and simple steady state solution to problem (1) for all $\boldsymbol{\theta} \in \text{int}(A \times B \times D)$, denoted by $(x^*(\boldsymbol{\theta}), u^*(\boldsymbol{\theta})) \in \text{int}(X \times U)$, which is the unique solution to the steady state version of the necessary conditions.

(A.7) $\lim_{t\to+\infty}(z(t; \boldsymbol{\theta}, x_0), v(t; \boldsymbol{\theta}, x_0)) = (x^*(\boldsymbol{\theta}), u^*(\boldsymbol{\theta}))$ for all $(\boldsymbol{\theta}, x_0) \in \text{int}(A \times B \times D \times X)$.

Consider assumptions (A.1) and (A.2) first. The assumed differentiability of the functions $f(\cdot)$ and $g(\cdot)$ is common to virtually all applied papers in economics that use optimal control theory. It allows the use of the differential calculus in computing the local comparative dynamics and steady state comparative statics of the model. Furthermore, by Theorem 6.29 of Protter and Morrey (1991), $f(\cdot)$ and $g(\cdot)$ and their first-and second-order partial derivatives are bounded because their domains are compact and $f(\cdot)$ and $g(\cdot)$ are $C^{(2)}$. Moreover, the bounded nature of $f(\cdot)$ along with the exponential discounting implies the objective functional of problem (1) converges for all admissible pairs. The assumption that $g_u(x(t), u(t); \boldsymbol{\beta}) \neq 0$ along the optimal path means that the control variable affects the evolution of the state variable in an optimal plan, and in conjunction with Eq. (3), it implies that $\lambda(t)$ is well defined in an optimal plan. Additionally, $g_u(x(t), u(t); \boldsymbol{\beta}) \neq 0$, Eq. (3), and the boundedness of the first partial derivatives of $f(\cdot)$ and $g(\cdot)$ imply that $\lambda(\cdot)$ is bounded in an optimal plan. Hence the present value costate variable has a value of zero in the limit of the planning horizon, that is, $\lim_{t\to+\infty} e^{-rt}\lambda(t) = 0$.

Assumption (A.3) is important in that without it, one cannot guarantee that a solution to problem (1) exists unless some other assumptions are employed. Given that the focus of this chapter is on the qualitative properties of problem (1), this assumption is innocuous from an economic (but not a mathematical) point of view. The restriction that the parameters lie in the interior of their convex and compact sets rules out the mathematical complications that arise when the optimal solution functions are differentiated with respect to a parameter that is at the boundary of its set. Furthermore, note that the parameter vector $\boldsymbol{\theta}$ is constant over time, implying that the agent that solves problem (1) has static expectations.

Assumption (A.4) allows the analysis to ignore the mathematical complications necessitated when the optimal paths are at the boundary of the feasible region. In practice, this assumption implies that, say, nonnegativity restrictions on the state and control variables are not binding for optimal paths. Furthermore, the compact nature of X and U rules out unbounded $(x(t), u(t))$ pairs as optimal.

Assumption (A.5) implies that the second-order sufficient condition for maximizing the current value Hamiltonian holds along the optimal path. Moreover, it allows the necessary conditions to be reduced to a pair of differential equations in $(x(t), u(t))$.

Assumption (A.6) asserts the existence of a unique and simple steady state solution to problem (1). Recall that a simple fixed point, that is, steady state, is one in which both of the eigenvalues associated with the Jacobian matrix of the linearization of the differential equations evaluated at the fixed point are nonzero, or equivalently, that the determinant of the said Jacobian matrix is not zero. It will be shown below that the assumed simplicity of the steady state and the mathematical structure of problem (1) imply that the steady state is hyperbolic. A hyperbolic fixed point, as you may recall, is one in which the real part of the eigenvalues associated with the Jacobian matrix of the linearization of the differential equations evaluated at the fixed point is nonzero. This means that the classical linearization theorem of ordinary differential equations, scilicet, Theorem 13.7, can be applied to study the local stability properties of the fixed point. Moreover, it implies that the phase portraits of the original nonlinear system and its linearization at the fixed point are qualitatively equivalent in a neighborhood of the fixed point.

Finally, assumption (A.7) asserts that the optimal paths of the state and control variables converge to their steady state values as $t \to +\infty$. In other words, problem (1) is a class of discounted infinite-horizon optimal control problems in which it turns out that the free terminal endpoint optimal solutions converge to their steady state values as $t \to +\infty$. It will be shown that assumptions (A.6) and (A.7) imply that the steady state is a local saddle point.

In order to derive the necessary conditions for problem (1), first define the current value Hamiltonian by

$$H(x, u, \lambda; \alpha, \beta) \stackrel{\text{def}}{=} f(x, u; \alpha) + \lambda g(x, u; \beta). \tag{2}$$

By Theorems 14.3 and 14.9, the necessary conditions that must hold along the optimal path are

$$H_u(x, u, \lambda; \alpha, \beta) = f_u(x, u; \alpha) + \lambda g_u(x, u; \beta) = 0, \tag{3}$$

$$H_{uu}(x, u, \lambda; \alpha, \beta) = f_{uu}(x, u; \alpha) + \lambda g_{uu}(x, u; \beta) \leq 0, \tag{4}$$

$$\dot{\lambda} = r\lambda - H_x(x, u, \lambda; \alpha, \beta) = [r - g_x(x, u; \beta)]\lambda - f_x(x, u; \alpha), \tag{5}$$

$$\dot{x} = H_\lambda(x, u, \lambda; \alpha, \beta) = g(x, u; \beta), \ x(0) = x_0, \tag{6}$$

$$\lim_{t \to +\infty} e^{-rt} H(x, u, \lambda; \alpha, \beta) = \lim_{t \to +\infty} e^{-rt} [f(x, u; \alpha) + \lambda g(x, u; \beta)] = 0. \tag{7}$$

Because $f(\cdot)$ and $g(\cdot)$ are bounded and $\lambda(\cdot)$ is bounded in an optimal plan, as noted above, the limiting transversality condition (7) does indeed hold in an optimal plan. In light of the ensuing analysis, it will prove convenient to reduce the necessary conditions (3), (5), and (6) to a pair of nonlinear first-order ordinary differential equations in (x, u).

To this end, first note that $H_{uu}(x, u, \lambda; \alpha, \beta) < 0$ along the optimal path by Eq. (4) and assumption (A.5), which in turn permits us to differentiate Eq. (3) with respect to t to get

$$\begin{aligned} f_{uu}(x, u; \alpha)\dot{u} + f_{ux}(x, u; \alpha)\dot{x} + \lambda[g_{uu}(x, u; \beta)\dot{u} \\ + g_{ux}(x, u; \beta)\dot{x}] + g_u(x, u; \beta)\dot{\lambda} = 0. \end{aligned} \tag{8}$$

In view of the fact that $g_u(x(t), u(t); \beta) \neq 0$ along the optimal path by assumption (A.2), we can solve Eq. (3) for the current value costate variable, namely, $\lambda = -f_u(x, u; \alpha)/g_u(x, u; \beta)$, and substitute it along with Eqs. (5) and (6) into Eq. (8) to get

$$\begin{aligned} \dot{u} = & \frac{f_u(x, u; \alpha)[r - g_x(x, u; \beta)] + g_u(x, u; \beta) f_x(x, u; \alpha)}{f_{uu}(x, u; \alpha) - f_u(x, u; \alpha)[g_u(x, u; \beta)]^{-1} g_{uu}(x, u; \beta)} \\ & + \frac{g(x, u; \beta) \left[\dfrac{f_u(x, u; \alpha)}{g_u(x, u; \beta)} g_{ux}(x, u; \beta) - f_{ux}(x, u; \alpha) \right]}{f_{uu}(x, u; \alpha) - f_u(x, u; \alpha)[g_u(x, u; \beta)]^{-1} g_{uu}(x, u; \beta)} \end{aligned} \tag{9}$$

$$\dot{x} = g(x, u; \beta) \tag{10}$$

as the pair of necessary conditions for problem (1). Because the denominator of Eq. (9) is equal to $H_{uu}(x, u, \lambda; \boldsymbol{\alpha}, \boldsymbol{\beta})$, as can be seen by solving Eq. (3) for $\lambda = -f_u(x, u; \boldsymbol{\alpha})/g_u(x, u; \boldsymbol{\beta})$ and substituting into Eq. (4), and $H_{uu}(x, u, \lambda; \boldsymbol{\alpha}, \boldsymbol{\beta}) < 0$ along the optimal path as noted above, Eq. (9) is well defined. For future reference, define $h(x, u; \boldsymbol{\theta})$ as the right-hand side of Eq. (9). This definition is of value when we discuss the local stability of the steady state solution of Eqs. (9) and (10).

Note that we could have reduced the necessary conditions (3), (5), and (6) to a pair of nonlinear first-order ordinary differential equations in (λ, x) as follows. By assumption (A.5), we can apply the implicit function theorem to Eq. (3) to express u locally as a function of $(x, \lambda; \boldsymbol{\alpha}, \boldsymbol{\beta})$, say, $u = \hat{u}(x, \lambda; \boldsymbol{\alpha}, \boldsymbol{\beta})$. Then by substituting $u = \hat{u}(x, \lambda; \boldsymbol{\alpha}, \boldsymbol{\beta})$ into Eqs. (5) and (6), we would have the desired result. Seeing as the information in the (λ, x) dynamical system is the same as that in Eqs. (9) and (10), there is no need to pursue the alternative approach as well.

The steady state of problem (1) is defined as the solution to Eqs. (9) and (10) when $\dot{x} = \dot{u} = 0$, in which case they reduce to

$$f_u(x, u; \boldsymbol{\alpha})[r - g_x(x, u; \boldsymbol{\beta})] + g_u(x, u; \boldsymbol{\beta}) f_x(x, u; \boldsymbol{\alpha}) = 0, \tag{11}$$

$$g(x, u; \boldsymbol{\beta}) = 0. \tag{12}$$

Given any value of $\boldsymbol{\theta} \in \operatorname{int}(A \times B \times D)$, say, $\boldsymbol{\theta} = \boldsymbol{\theta}^\circ$, assumption (A.6) asserts the existence of a unique point $(x^\circ, u^\circ) = (x^*(\boldsymbol{\theta}^\circ), u^*(\boldsymbol{\theta}^\circ)) \in \operatorname{int}(X \times U)$ that satisfies Eqs. (11) and (12). Thus, by assumptions (A.1), (A.2), and (A.6), and the implicit function theorem,

$$u = u^*(\boldsymbol{\theta}), \tag{13}$$

$$x = x^*(\boldsymbol{\theta}), \tag{14}$$

$$\lambda = \lambda^*(\boldsymbol{\theta}) = \frac{-f_u\,(x^*(\boldsymbol{\theta}), u^*(\boldsymbol{\theta}); \boldsymbol{\alpha})}{g_u\,(x^*(\boldsymbol{\theta}), u^*(\boldsymbol{\theta}); \boldsymbol{\beta})} \tag{15}$$

are the unique $C^{(1)}$ solutions to Eqs. (11) and (12) for all $\boldsymbol{\theta} \in B(\boldsymbol{\theta}^\circ; \varepsilon)$, since the steady state Jacobian determinant of Eqs. (11) and (12), scilicet,

$$\begin{aligned} |J_s| \overset{\text{def}}{=} \; & g_x^*[[r - g_x^*] f_{uu}^* + f_x^* g_{uu}^*] - g_{ux}^*[g_u^* f_x^* + f_u^* g_x^*] - [g_u^*]^2 f_{xx}^* \\ & + g_u^*[f_u^* g_{xx}^* - [r - 2g_x^*] f_{ux}^*], \end{aligned} \tag{16}$$

is nonzero at $(x^\circ, u^\circ, \boldsymbol{\theta}^\circ)$ by assumption (A.6) and Eq. (23), where $g_x^* \overset{\text{def}}{=} g_x(x^*(\boldsymbol{\theta}), u^*(\boldsymbol{\theta}); \boldsymbol{\beta})$ and so on signify the evaluation of the derivatives at the steady state.

Given the existence of the simple steady state of problem (1), attention is now turned to the local stability properties of the steady state. To this end, apply Taylor's theorem to Eqs. (9) and (10), and recall the definition of $h(x, u; \boldsymbol{\theta})$ given after Eq. (10) in order to derive the linearized system of differential equations evaluated at the steady state:

$$\begin{bmatrix} \Delta\dot{u} \\ \Delta\dot{x} \end{bmatrix} = \begin{bmatrix} h_u^* & h_x^* \\ g_u^* & g_x^* \end{bmatrix} \begin{bmatrix} \Delta u \\ \Delta x \end{bmatrix}, \tag{17}$$

where

$$h_u^* \stackrel{\text{def}}{=} \frac{[r - g_x^*]f_{uu}^* + f_x^* g_{uu}^*}{f_{uu}^* - f_u^*[g_u^*]^{-1}g_{uu}^*}, \tag{18}$$

$$h_x^* \stackrel{\text{def}}{=} \frac{[r - 2g_x^*]f_{ux}^* - f_u^* g_{xx}^* + g_u^* f_{xx}^* + g_{ux}^*\left[f_u^*[g_u^*]^{-1}g_x^* + f_x^*\right]}{f_{uu}^* - f_u^*[g_u^*]^{-1}g_{uu}^*}, \tag{19}$$

$$J_d \stackrel{\text{def}}{=} \begin{bmatrix} h_u^* & h_x^* \\ g_u^* & g_x^* \end{bmatrix}, \tag{20}$$

and $\Delta u \stackrel{\text{def}}{=} u - u^*(\boldsymbol{\theta})$, $\Delta x \stackrel{\text{def}}{=} x - x^*(\boldsymbol{\theta})$, $\Delta\dot{u} \stackrel{\text{def}}{=} \dot{u}$, and $\Delta\dot{x} \stackrel{\text{def}}{=} \dot{x}$. You are asked to verify these calculations in a mental exercise.

The local stability of the simple steady state is determined by finding the eigenvalues of the coefficient matrix of Eq. (17), the dynamic Jacobian J_d defined in Eq. (20). Because the steady state is assumed to be simple by assumption (A.6), it follows from the definition of simplicity that $|J_d| \neq 0$. The eigenvalues δ_ℓ, $\ell = 1, 2$, of J_d are found by solving the characteristic equation associated with J_d, which is given by

$$\begin{aligned} |J_d - \delta I| &= \begin{vmatrix} h_u^* - \delta & h_x^* \\ g_u^* & g_x^* - \delta \end{vmatrix} = [h_u^* - \delta][g_x^* - \delta] - h_x^* g_u^* \\ &= \delta^2 - [\text{tr}J_d]\delta + |J_d| = 0. \end{aligned} \tag{21}$$

Equating the identity $(\delta - \delta_1)(\delta - \delta_2) \equiv \delta^2 - (\delta_1 + \delta_2)\delta + \delta_1\delta_2$ to zero and comparing it to characteristic polynomial in Eq. (21) implies that

$$\delta_1 + \delta_2 = \text{tr}J_d = h_u^* + g_x^* = r > 0, \tag{22}$$

$$\delta_1\delta_2 = |J_d| = h_u^* g_x^* - h_x^* g_u^* = |J_s|\left[f_{uu}^* - f_u^*[g_u^*]^{-1}g_{uu}^*\right]^{-1} \neq 0, \tag{23}$$

where the result in Eq. (22) was obtained by solving Eq. (11) for $f_x^* = -f_u^*[g_u^*]^{-1}[r - g_x^*]$ and using this expression to substitute out f_x^* in h_u^*. Recalling that $|J_d| \neq 0$ by assumption (A.6), as noted above, Eq. (23) implies that $|J_s|\,[f_{uu}^* - f_u^*[g_u^*]^{-1}g_{uu}^*]^1 \neq 0$. Because $H_{uu}^* = f_{uu}^* - f_u^*[g_u^*]^{-1}g_{uu}^* < 0$ by assumption (A.5) and Eqs. (4) and (15), as also remarked above, it follows that $|J_s| \neq 0$. Note that the conclusion $|J_s| \neq 0$ was alluded to in the discussion of Eq. (16) when the implicit function theorem was applied to Eqs. (11) and (12) to arrive at the steady state solution in Eqs. (13) through (15).

From Eq. (22), the sum of the eigenvalues is positive, so that if they are complex conjugates, their real part is nonzero, which implies that the steady state is hyperbolic. Given that the sum of the eigenvalues is positive, at least one eigenvalue is positive, thus ruling out the possibility that the steady state is locally asymptotically stable. Now if both eigenvalues are positive or have positive real parts, then the steady state is an unstable node or an unstable spiral, respectively, and any trajectory that does not begin at the steady state cannot reach it, as all trajectories diverge from the steady state with the passage of time. Thus both eigenvalues cannot be positive or have positive real parts, as this violates the convergence requirement of assumption (A.7). Because the steady state is hyperbolic and must be reached as $t \to +\infty$ by assumption (A.7), the only possibility left for the eigenvalues of J_d is that one is negative, say, $\delta_1 < 0$, and the other is positive, say $\delta_2 > 0$, thereby implying that the steady state is a local saddle point and $|J_d| = \delta_1\delta_2 < 0$. From Eq. (22), it follows that $\delta_2 > r > 0$ and $\delta_2 > |\delta_1|$, and that both eigenvalues are real. Thus the steady state can be reached by following one of the two trajectories that approach it as $t \to +\infty$. The discussion of this paragraph is summarized by

Theorem 18.1 (Local Stability): *Under assumptions (A.1) through (A.7), the steady state of problem (1) is a local saddle point. Moreover, J_d has real eigenvalues $\delta_1 < 0, \delta_2 > r > 0, \delta_2 > |\delta_1|$, and $|J_d| < 0$.*

In one sense, this is quite a surprising result. The surprise is that the rather general and ubiquitous class of optimal control problems defined by problem (1) and assumptions (A.1) through (A.7) has an unstable steady state. That is to say, it is not possible for this class of control problems to have a locally asymptotically stable steady state. Inasmuch as many intertemporal economic models fit within this class of control problems, they too have unstable steady states. Thus the "best" one may expect, as far as local stability is concerned, is that the steady state is a saddle point, as this type of fixed point at least has a stable manifold that asymptotically reaches the steady state. Even so, there is a practical difficulty when a steady state is a local saddle point. To see this, observe that in the context of problem (1), the stable manifold of the saddle point steady state is a line in the two-dimensional phase space, and hence of one dimension less than the space itself. Consequently, if one were to imagine the phase portrait overlaid on a dart board, and one had to throw darts at it to establish the initial value of the control variable for a given initial value of the state variable, then the probability is zero that a dart would land on the stable manifold. This implies that for all practical purposes, it is impossible to select the initial value of the control variable to lie on the stable manifold, thereby ruling out reaching the steady state asymptotically.

On the other hand, the above conclusion is not a limitation from a theoretical point of view. To comprehend this claim, simply observe that one can always set the constant of integration associated with the positive eigenvalue of J_d equal to zero, just as we did in arriving at Eq. (35) in Chapter 17 or in Eq. (37) below. The resulting time paths of the state and control variables would therefore lie on the stable manifold of the saddle point steady state. Furthermore, the fact that the stable manifold is of dimension one for a local saddle point steady state leads to the uniqueness of an optimal solution. Moreover, the uniqueness of the optimal solution is generally considered to be a much "nicer" property than the nonuniqueness that would result if the steady state was locally asymptotically stable, that is, if both eigenvalues of J_d were negative. Because the steady state has been shown to be a local saddle point and thus can, in principle, be reached starting from a point $x_0 \neq x^*(\boldsymbol{\theta})$, attention is now turned to the steady state comparative statics of problem (1).

The saddle point nature of the steady state will now be used to provide some steady state comparative statics information about problem (1). First, recall from Eq. (23) and Theorem 18.1 that $|J_d| = |J_s|\,[f_{uu}^* - f_u^*[g_u^*]^{-1}g_{uu}^*]^{-1} < 0$. Next, recall that from assumption (A.5) and Eqs. (4) and (15), $H_{uu}^* = f_{uu}^* - f_u^*[g_u^*]^{-1}g_{uu}^* < 0$. Putting the last two conclusions together, we see that $|J_s| > 0$, that is, the saddle point nature of the steady state and satisfaction of the second-order sufficient condition for the control to maximize the current value Hamiltonian imply that the steady state Jacobian determinant is positive. This implies that a steady state comparative static analysis of problem (1) can be carried out via the implicit function theorem. The discussion of this paragraph is summarized by the following corollary.

Corollary 18.1 (Steady State Jacobian): *Under assumptions (A.1) through (A.7) on problem (1), the steady state Jacobian determinant is positive, that is,* $|J_s| > 0$.

This is an important result, for $|J_s|$ appears in *all* the steady state comparative statics expressions. Analogously, recall that it is the second-order sufficient conditions of static optimization problems that imply the Jacobian determinant of the first-order necessary conditions is nonzero, thereby allowing a comparative statics analysis of the problem to be carried out via the implicit function theorem.

The steady state comparative statics for problem (1) are found by substituting the steady state solution of the necessary conditions $(x^*(\boldsymbol{\theta}), u^*(\boldsymbol{\theta}))$ back into Eqs. (11) and (12), the equations from which they were derived by the implicit function theorem, thereby creating local identities in the parameter vector $\boldsymbol{\theta}$:

$$f_u(x^*(\boldsymbol{\theta}), u^*(\boldsymbol{\theta}); \boldsymbol{\alpha})[r - g_x(x^*(\boldsymbol{\theta}), u^*(\boldsymbol{\theta}); \boldsymbol{\beta})] + g_u(x^*(\boldsymbol{\theta}), u^*(\boldsymbol{\theta}); \boldsymbol{\beta}) f_x(x^*(\boldsymbol{\theta}), u^*(\boldsymbol{\theta}); \boldsymbol{\alpha}) \equiv 0, \tag{24}$$

$$g(x^*(\boldsymbol{\theta}), u^*(\boldsymbol{\theta}); \boldsymbol{\theta}) \equiv 0. \tag{25}$$

Differentiating Eqs. (24) and (25) with respect to the parameter of interest using the multivariate chain rule, and solving the resulting linear system with Cramer's rule yields the steady state comparative statics. For example, differentiation of Eqs. (24) and (25) with respect to the parameter α_i, $i = 1, 2, \ldots, K_1$, yields the system of linear equations

$$\begin{bmatrix} f_{uu}^*[r-g_x^*]-f_u^*g_{xu}^* & f_{ux}^*[r-g_x^*]-f_u^*g_{xx}^* \\ +g_u^*f_{xu}^*+f_x^*g_{uu}^* & +g_u^*f_{xx}^*+f_x^*g_{ux}^* \\ g_u^* & g_x^* \end{bmatrix} \begin{bmatrix} \dfrac{\partial u^*}{\partial \alpha_i} \\ \dfrac{\partial x^*}{\partial \alpha_i} \end{bmatrix}$$

$$\equiv \begin{bmatrix} -f_{u\alpha_i}^*[r-g_x^*]-g_u^*f_{x\alpha_i}^* \\ 0 \end{bmatrix}. \tag{26}$$

Applying Cramer's rule to this linear system of equations yields Eqs. (27) and (28) of Theorem 18.2. Using the same recipe for the parameters $(\boldsymbol{\beta}, r)$ yields the proof of the remaining parts of the theorem, which you are asked to provide in a mental exercise.

Theorem 18.2 (Steady State Comparative Statics): *In problem (1), with assumptions (A.1) through (A.7) holding, the steady state comparative statics are given by*

$$\frac{\partial x^*(\boldsymbol{\theta})}{\partial \alpha_i} \equiv \frac{f_{u\alpha_i}^*[r-g_x^*]g_u^*+[g_u^*]^2 f_{x\alpha_i}^*}{|J_s|}, \quad i=1,\ldots,K_1, \tag{27}$$

$$\frac{\partial u^*(\boldsymbol{\theta})}{\partial \alpha_i} \equiv \frac{-f_{u\alpha_i}^*[r-g_x^*]g_x^*-g_u^*g_x^*f_{x\alpha_i}^*}{|J_s|}, \quad i=1,\ldots,K_1, \tag{28}$$

$$\frac{\partial x^*(\boldsymbol{\theta})}{\partial \beta_j} \equiv \frac{g_{\beta_j}^*[f_u^*g_{xu}^*-[r-g_x^*]f_{uu}^*-g_u^*f_{xu}^*-f_x^*g_{uu}^*]+g_u^*[f_x^*g_{u\beta_j}^*-f_u^*g_{x\beta_j}^*]}{|J_s|},$$
$$j=1,\ldots,K_2, \tag{29}$$

$$\frac{\partial u^*(\boldsymbol{\theta})}{\partial \beta_j} \equiv \frac{g_{\beta_j}^*[-f_u^*g_{xx}^*+[r-g_x^*]f_{ux}^*+g_u^*f_{xx}^*+f_x^*g_{ux}^*]+g_x^*[f_u^*g_{x\beta_j}^*-f_x^*g_{u\beta_j}^*]}{|J_s|},$$
$$j=1,\ldots,K_2, \tag{30}$$

$$\frac{\partial x^*(\boldsymbol{\theta})}{\partial r} \equiv \frac{f_u^*g_u^*}{|J_s|}, \tag{31}$$

$$\frac{\partial u^*(\boldsymbol{\theta})}{\partial r} \equiv \frac{-f_u^*g_x^*}{|J_s|}. \tag{32}$$

At this level of generality, no signs are implied for any of the steady state comparative statics, just as one would suspect. The denominator of these expressions, however, is positive as noted in Corollary 18.1. Given this observation, the following corollary is a direct consequence of Theorem 18.2, as can be seen by inspection.

Corollary 18.2.1 (Steady State Comparative Statics): *In problem (1), with assumptions (A.1) through (A.7) holding,*

(A) If a perturbation in the discount rate r occurs in the steady state, then

$$\operatorname{sign}\left[\frac{\partial x^*(\boldsymbol{\theta})}{\partial r}\right] = \operatorname{sign}[f_u^* g_u^*],$$

$$\operatorname{sign}\left[\frac{\partial u^*(\boldsymbol{\theta})}{\partial r}\right] = -\operatorname{sign}[f_u^* g_x^*].$$

(B) If $f_{u\alpha_i}^* = 0,\ i = 1, \ldots, K_1$, *then*

$$\operatorname{sign}\left[\frac{\partial x^*(\boldsymbol{\theta})}{\partial \alpha_i}\right] = \operatorname{sign}[f_{x\alpha_i}^*], \quad i = 1, \ldots, K_1,$$

$$\operatorname{sign}\left[\frac{\partial u^*(\boldsymbol{\theta})}{\partial \alpha_i}\right] = -\operatorname{sign}[g_u^* g_x^* f_{x\alpha_i}^*], \quad i = 1, \ldots, K_1.$$

(C) If $f_{x\alpha_i}^* = 0,\ i = 1, \ldots, K_1$, *then*

$$\operatorname{sign}\left[\frac{\partial x^*(\boldsymbol{\theta})}{\partial \alpha_i}\right] = \operatorname{sign}[f_{u\alpha_i}^*[r - g_x^*]g_u^*], \quad i = 1, \ldots, K_1,$$

$$\operatorname{sign}\left[\frac{\partial u^*(\boldsymbol{\theta})}{\partial \alpha_i}\right] = -\operatorname{sign}[f_{u\alpha_i}^*[r - g_x^*]g_x^*], \quad i = 1, \ldots, K_1.$$

The results of Corollary 18.2.1 are important enough to be given an economic interpretation. The first part of (A) asserts that the effect of an increase in the discount rate on the steady state value of the state variable is qualitatively the same as the product of the marginal impact of the control variable on the integrand and the marginal impact of the control variable on the state variable's rate of change, evaluated at the steady state. In economic problems, if the state variable is a good, say, capital or fish, then ordinarily $\lambda^*(\boldsymbol{\theta}) = -f_u^*/g_u^* > 0$, or equivalently $f_u^* g_u^* < 0$, thereby implying that $\partial x^*/\partial r < 0$. On the other hand, if the state variable is a bad, say, toxic waste, then typically $\lambda^*(\boldsymbol{\theta}) = -f_u^*/g_u^* < 0$, or equivalently $f_u^* g_u^* > 0$, thereby implying that $\partial x^*/\partial r > 0$. In other words, if the stock is a good, then an increase in the discount rate usually decreases the stock in the steady state, whereas if the stock is a bad, then an increase in the discount rate normally increases the stock in the steady state.

The second assertion of part (A) says that if the discount rate increases, then its impact on the steady state value of the control variable is the opposite qualitatively of the product of the marginal impact of the control variable on the integrand and the marginal product of the state variable, evaluated at the steady state. If the stock is a good, then typically $f_u^* g_x^* > 0$, so that an increase in the discount rate decreases the steady state value of the control variable. Similarly, if the stock is a bad, then usually $f_u^* g_x^* < 0$, so that an increase in the discount rate increases the steady state value of the control variable. In light of the above steady state comparative statics for the state and control variables, it is usually the case that the state and control variables have the same qualitative steady state response to an increase in the discount rate.

Part (B) of the corollary is a conjugate pairs result. It asserts that if a parameter α_i is additively separable from the control variable at the steady state, then the effect of an increase in α_i on the steady state value of the state variable is the same qualitatively as the effect the increase in α_i has on the marginal impact the state variable has on the integrand, evaluated at the steady state. This means that if a parameter α_i enters problem (1) in such a manner, then all one has to do to compute the sign of $\partial x^*/\partial \alpha_i$ is to find the sign of $f_{x\alpha_i}^*$. Clearly, this represents a vast simplification over using Theorem 18.2 in computing the steady state comparative statics. The corresponding result for the control variable is slightly more complicated (but just as easy to use) because of the presence of the product $g_u^* g_x^*$. The conjugate pairs structure of part (B) is common to many papers in economics that use optimal control theory, and is therefore responsible for many of the refutable steady state comparative statics of such papers.

Finally, part (C) is also a conjugate pairs result, but in this case, α_i and the state variable must be additively separable at the steady state. In this instance, the sign of the steady state comparative statics depends not only on the sign of the partials g_u^*, g_x^*, and $f_{u\alpha_i}^*$, but also on the size of g_x^* relative to r. Thus although this part of the corollary is no more difficult to use than any of the other parts, it requires more information in that the magnitude of g_x^* is required. It should again be noted that the conjugate pairs structure of part (C) is common to many papers in economics that use optimal control theory, and is therefore responsible for many of the refutable steady state comparative statics in such papers.

Notice that in Theorem 18.2, g_x^* appears in every term of the numerator of $\partial u^*/\partial \alpha_i$ and $\partial u^*/\partial r$. Hence if $g_x^* = 0$, then the steady state value of the control variable is independent of any parameter that appears in the integrand of problem (1). This observation yields

Corollary 18.2.2 (Steady State Comparative Statics): *In problem (1), with assumptions (A.1) through (A.7) holding, if* $g_x^* = 0$, *then* $\partial u^*/\partial r \equiv 0$ *and* $\partial u^*/\partial \alpha_i \equiv 0, i = 1, \ldots, K_1$.

The economic interpretation of this result is that if the marginal product of the state variable is zero at the steady state, then the steady state value of the control variable is unaffected by changes in any parameter that enters the integrand of problem (1). An immediate application of Corollary 18.2.2 is in the dynamic limit pricing model of Gaskins (1971) examined in Chapter 16, where the state equation is independent of the state variable (rival sales), thereby implying that the dominant firm's price (the control variable) is unaffected by changes in the discount rate or average cost of production. This corollary is also applicable to the model of soil conservation examined in Mental Exercise 16.6, since soil quality (the state variable) does not enter the state equation, and therefore a rise in the output price, input price, or discount rate leaves steady state output (the control variable) unaffected. It is important to note, however, that just because the steady state value of the control variable is independent of (α, r), this *does not* mean that the control variable's optimal trajectory is independent of these same parameters. This will be spelled out carefully in what follows.

Notice that the expressions in Theorem 18.2 for perturbations in (α, r) are relatively simple compared with those that involve perturbations in β. This is straightforward to explain. Seeing as (α, r) appear *explicitly* in only one of the steady state necessary conditions, scilicet, Eq. (24), differentiating Eqs. (24) and (25) with respect to (α, r) and writing in matrix notation, as in Eq. (26) for example, reveals that the right-hand side column vector has only one nonzero element. When Cramer's rule is used to solve for the steady state comparative statics, the zero element in the right-hand side vector will reduce the number of terms in the numerator of the resulting comparative statics expressions. If one follows the same recipe for perturbations in β, however, both elements of the right-hand side vector will be nonzero, for β appears explicitly in both steady state necessary conditions. When Cramer's rule is applied to this system, terms in the numerator will not drop out as they did for perturbations in (α, r). The important point is that when a parameter enters the state equation explicitly, it is in general more difficult to derive refutable steady state comparative statics of the form $\partial x^*/\partial\beta_j$ and $\partial u^*/\partial\beta_j$. This is important, for if the steady state comparative statics for some parameter are ambiguous, then so too will be the corresponding local comparative dynamics, as will be demonstrated later.

It is important also to keep in mind that the steady state comparative statics of Theorem 18.2 have been simplified by allowing a parameter to enter only the integrand function $f(\cdot)$ or the transition function $g(\cdot)$. If a parameter entered both of these functions, then the resulting steady state comparative statics would be more complicated, as is straightforward to show. In this case, there are no simple sufficient conditions like Corollaries 18.2.1 and 18.2.2 available to render the results more user-friendly. In passing, note that there appear to be relatively few problems in the economic literature where a parameter appears in both $f(\cdot)$ and $g(\cdot)$.

Before moving on to the local comparative dynamics, it is worthwhile to remember that the conjugacy conditions of parts (B) and (C) of Corollary 18.2.1 and the sufficient condition of Corollary 18.2.2 are local conditions, that is, they need only hold in some neighborhood of the steady state for one to use the corollaries. Now if $f_{u\alpha_i} \equiv 0$, $f_{x\alpha_i} \equiv 0$, or $g_x \equiv 0$, or in other words, if the conjugacy conditions hold over the entire domain of the integrand or the marginal product of the state variable is identically zero, then the corollaries can also be used. Naturally, the global requirements on the functions are stronger than the local requirements needed for the use of the corollaries, but in practice, the global conditions are easier to verify, since this can be done simply by inspection of the control problem under consideration.

Finally, note that the steady state comparative statics for the current value shadow price follow from Eq. (15) and use of Theorem 18.2.

The local comparative dynamics properties of problem (1) are determined by solving the linearized pair of ordinary differential equations given in Eq. (17). Since the eigenvalues of J_d are real and unequal by Theorem 18.1, Theorem 25.1 of Simon and Blume (1994) asserts that the general solution of Eq. (17) is given by

$$\begin{bmatrix} \Delta u(t) \\ \Delta x(t) \end{bmatrix} = c_1 \mathbf{Q}^1 e^{\delta_1 t} + c_2 \mathbf{Q}^2 e^{\delta_2 t}, \tag{33}$$

where c_1 and c_2 are arbitrary constants of integration and $\mathbf{Q}^\ell \in \Re^2$ is an eigenvector of the coefficient matrix J_d corresponding to the eigenvalue δ_ℓ, $\ell = 1, 2$. The eigenvalues $\delta_1 < 0$ and $\delta_2 > r > 0$ were derived earlier; hence only the eigenvectors need to be determined. The eigenvectors (Q_1^ℓ, Q_2^ℓ) corresponding to the eigenvalues δ_ℓ, $\ell = 1, 2$, are by definition the solution to the following homogeneous system of linear algebraic equations:

$$\begin{bmatrix} h_u^* - \delta_\ell & h_x^* \\ g_u^* & g_x^* - \delta_\ell \end{bmatrix} \begin{bmatrix} Q_1^\ell \\ Q_2^\ell \end{bmatrix} = \begin{bmatrix} 0 \\ 0 \end{bmatrix}, \quad \ell = 1, 2. \tag{34}$$

The rows of Eq. (34) are linearly dependent because the eigenvalues of J_d were chosen such that $|J_d - \delta_\ell I| = 0$, $\ell = 1, 2$, and this is the determinant of the coefficient matrix in Eq. (34). This means that the eigenvectors (Q_1^ℓ, Q_2^ℓ) corresponding to the eigenvalues δ_ℓ, $\ell = 1, 2$, are unique only up to a scalar multiple. Taking $Q_2^\ell = 1$, $\ell = 1, 2$, as the normalization, the eigenvectors are

$$(Q_1^\ell, Q_2^\ell) = \left(\frac{-h_x^*}{h_u^* - \delta_\ell}, 1 \right) \equiv \left(\frac{\delta_\ell - g_x^*}{g_u^*}, 1 \right), \quad \ell = 1, 2. \tag{35}$$

The two formulas for the Q_1^ℓ component of the eigenvectors given in Eq. (35) are identical because of the way the eigenvalues were chosen, as you are asked to demonstrate in a mental exercise.

Given that the eigenvalues and eigenvectors of J_d are now known, let us rewrite the general solution of the homogeneous first-order differential equation system (17) as

$$\begin{bmatrix} v(t; \boldsymbol{\theta}, x_0) \\ z(t; \boldsymbol{\theta}, x_0) \end{bmatrix} = \begin{bmatrix} u^*(\boldsymbol{\theta}) \\ x^*(\boldsymbol{\theta}) \end{bmatrix} + c_1 \begin{bmatrix} Q_1^1 \\ 1 \end{bmatrix} e^{\delta_1 t} + c_2 \begin{bmatrix} Q_1^2 \\ 1 \end{bmatrix} e^{\delta_2 t}, \tag{36}$$

rather than as we did in Eq. (33). The arbitrary constants of integration are determined from the initial condition $x(0) = x_0$ and the convergence requirement on the optimal path of the state variable from assumption (A.7), namely, $\lim_{t \to +\infty} z(t; \boldsymbol{\theta}, x_0) = x^*(\boldsymbol{\theta})$. Taking the latter condition first yields

$$\lim_{t \to +\infty} z(t; \boldsymbol{\theta}, x_0) = \lim_{t \to +\infty} \left[x^*(\boldsymbol{\theta}) + c_1 e^{\delta_1 t} + c_2 e^{\delta_2 t} \right] = x^*(\boldsymbol{\theta}).$$

Seeing as $\delta_1 < 0$, $c_1 e^{\delta_1 t} \to 0$ as $t \to +\infty$, but because $\delta_2 > 0$, $c_2 e^{\delta_2 t} \to \pm\infty$ as $t \to +\infty$ if $c_2 \neq 0$, in which case the limit of the entire bracketed term does not exist, thus violating the convergence condition. Hence $c_2 = 0$ for convergence to the steady state to be met. Note that the conclusion $c_2 = 0$ may also be obtained from the convergence requirement on the optimal path of the control variable from assumption (A.7). Now apply the initial condition to find c_1:

$$z(0; \boldsymbol{\theta}, x_0) = x^*(\boldsymbol{\theta}) + c_1 = x_0 \Rightarrow c_1 = x_0 - x^*(\boldsymbol{\theta}).$$

Thus the specific solution to Eq. (17) that satisfies the initial condition and convergence requirement is given by

$$\begin{bmatrix} v(t; \boldsymbol{\theta}, x_0) \\ z(t; \boldsymbol{\theta}, x_0) \end{bmatrix} = \begin{bmatrix} u^*(\boldsymbol{\theta}) \\ x^*(\boldsymbol{\theta}) \end{bmatrix} + [x_0 - x^*(\boldsymbol{\theta})] \begin{bmatrix} Q_1^1 \\ 1 \end{bmatrix} e^{\delta_1 t}, \tag{37}$$

along with its time derivative

$$\begin{bmatrix} \dot{v}(t; \boldsymbol{\theta}, x_0) \\ \dot{z}(t; \boldsymbol{\theta}, x_0) \end{bmatrix} = \delta_1 [x_0 - x^*(\boldsymbol{\theta})] \begin{bmatrix} Q_1^1 \\ 1 \end{bmatrix} e^{\delta_1 t}. \tag{38}$$

The local comparative dynamics of problem (1) follow from differentiating Eqs. (37) and (38) with respect to $(\boldsymbol{\theta}, x_0)$ and evaluating the resulting derivatives at $x_0 = x^*(\boldsymbol{\theta})$. They are summarized by the following theorem, whose proof is left for the mental exercises.

Theorem 18.3 (Local Comparative Dynamics): *In problem (1), under assumptions (A.1) through (A.7), the effects of parameter perturbations for all $t \in [0, +\infty)$ on the time path of the optimal solution in a neighborhood of an optimal steady state are given by*

$$\left.\frac{\partial v(t; \boldsymbol{\theta}, x_0)}{\partial x_0}\right|_{x_0 = x^*(\boldsymbol{\theta})} = Q_1^1 e^{\delta_1 t}, \tag{39}$$

$$\left.\frac{\partial z(t; \boldsymbol{\theta}, x_0)}{\partial x_0}\right|_{x_0 = x^*(\boldsymbol{\theta})} = e^{\delta_1 t} \geq 0, \tag{40}$$

$$\left.\frac{\partial \dot{v}(t; \boldsymbol{\theta}, x_0)}{\partial x_0}\right|_{x_0 = x^*(\boldsymbol{\theta})} = \delta_1 Q_1^1 e^{\delta_1 t}, \tag{41}$$

$$\left.\frac{\partial \dot{z}(t; \boldsymbol{\theta}, x_0)}{\partial x_0}\right|_{x_0 = x^*(\boldsymbol{\theta})} = \delta_1 e^{\delta_1 t} \leq 0, \tag{42}$$

$$\left.\frac{\partial v(t; \boldsymbol{\theta}, x_0)}{\partial \theta_k}\right|_{x_0 = x^*(\boldsymbol{\theta})} = \frac{\partial u^*(\boldsymbol{\theta})}{\partial \theta_k} - Q_1^1 e^{\delta_1 t} \frac{\partial x^*(\boldsymbol{\theta})}{\partial \theta_k}, \quad k = 1, \ldots, K_1 + K_2 + 1, \tag{43}$$

$$\left.\frac{\partial z(t; \boldsymbol{\theta}, x_0)}{\partial \theta_k}\right|_{x_0 = x^*(\boldsymbol{\theta})} = \frac{\partial x^*(\boldsymbol{\theta})}{\partial \theta_k} [1 - e^{\delta_1 t}], \quad k = 1, \ldots, K_1 + K_2 + 1, \tag{44}$$

$$\left.\frac{\partial \dot{v}(t;\boldsymbol{\theta},x_0)}{\partial \theta_k}\right|_{x_0=x^*(\boldsymbol{\theta})} = -\delta_1 Q_1^1 e^{\delta_1 t}\frac{\partial x^*(\boldsymbol{\theta})}{\partial \theta_k}, \quad k=1,\ldots,K_1+K_2+1, \tag{45}$$

$$\left.\frac{\partial \dot{z}(t;\boldsymbol{\theta},x_0)}{\partial \theta_k}\right|_{x_0=x^*(\boldsymbol{\theta})} = -\delta_1 e^{\delta_1 t}\frac{\partial x^*(\boldsymbol{\theta})}{\partial \theta_k}, \quad k=1,\ldots,K_1+K_2+1. \tag{46}$$

By definition, the *impact effects* of parameter perturbations follow from Theorem 18.3 by evaluating the derivatives at $t=0$. Because $\delta_1<0$, the following corollary is evident upon inspection of Theorem 18.3.

Corollary 18.3 (Local Comparative Dynamics): *In problem (1), under assumptions (A.1) through (A.7), the following local comparative dynamics results hold for all $t\in[0,+\infty)$:*

$$\operatorname{sign}\left[\left.\frac{\partial v(t;\boldsymbol{\theta},x_0)}{\partial x_0}\right|_{x_0=x^*(\boldsymbol{\theta})}\right] = \operatorname{sign}\left[Q_1^1\right], \tag{47}$$

$$\operatorname{sign}\left[\left.\frac{\partial \dot{v}(t;\boldsymbol{\theta},x_0)}{\partial x_0}\right|_{x_0=x^*(\boldsymbol{\theta})}\right] = -\operatorname{sign}\left[Q_1^1\right], \tag{48}$$

$$\operatorname{sign}\left[\left.\frac{\partial z(t;\boldsymbol{\theta},x_0)}{\partial \theta_k}\right|_{x_0=x^*(\boldsymbol{\theta})}\right] = \operatorname{sign}\left[\frac{\partial x^*(\boldsymbol{\theta})}{\partial \theta_k}\right], \quad k=1,\ldots,K_1+K_2+1, \tag{49}$$

$$\operatorname{sign}\left[\left.\frac{\partial \dot{v}(t;\boldsymbol{\theta},x_0)}{\partial \theta_k}\right|_{x_0=x^*(\boldsymbol{\theta})}\right] = \operatorname{sign}\left[Q_1^1\frac{\partial x^*(\boldsymbol{\theta})}{\partial \theta_k}\right], \quad k=1,\ldots,K_1+K_2+1, \tag{50}$$

$$\operatorname{sign}\left[\left.\frac{\partial \dot{z}(t;\boldsymbol{\theta},x_0)}{\partial \theta_k}\right|_{x_0=x^*(\boldsymbol{\theta})}\right] = \operatorname{sign}\left[\frac{\partial x^*(\boldsymbol{\theta})}{\partial \theta_k}\right], \quad k=1,\ldots,K_1+K_2+1. \tag{51}$$

Theorem 18.3 and Corollary 18.3 point out four important facts about the qualitative properties of discounted infinite-horizon optimal control models with one state and one control variable. The first point is that one must know the steady state comparative statics for the control *and* state variables before any refutable local comparative dynamics will emerge for the level of the control variable. This follows from Eq. (43), for it shows that the steady state comparative statics for the state and control variables appear in the local comparative dynamics for the level of the control variable. Simply put, one must know where one's exact destination is before the best path to take there can be determined.

Second, the local comparative dynamics of the state variable and its time derivative depend only on the steady state comparative statics of the state variable, as shown by Eqs. (49) and (51). Thus the impact of a parameter perturbation on the optimal path of the control variable is, in general, more difficult to pin down than that on the state variable and its time derivative.

Third, it is, in general, easier to determine the impact that a parameter perturbation has on the time derivative of the control variable than on the level of the control variable. This follows from Eq. (50), and is a result of the fact that only the steady state comparative statics for the state variable and the eigenvector corresponding to the negative eigenvalue are required for computing the effects of parameter perturbations on the time derivative of the control variable. The steady state comparative statics of the control variable do not play a role here.

The fourth and final point is that even if the steady state value of the control variable is independent of some parameter, this does *not* mean that the time path of the control variable is independent of this parameter. This is readily seen from Eq. (43), for if $\partial u^*/\partial \theta_k = 0$, then as long as $\partial x^*/\partial \theta_k \neq 0$ and $Q_1^1 \neq 0$, the time path of the control variable will still be affected by a perturbation in θ_k, even though its steady state position does not change. The idea is that as long as the terminal position of the state variable is affected, the control variable must change, at least temporarily, for it to drive the state to its new destination.

Recall that Theorems 18.2 and 18.3 and their associated corollaries apply to the optimal control problem (1). Therefore, in order to find the corresponding result in a prototypical calculus of variations problem, simply set $g(x, u; \boldsymbol{\beta}) \stackrel{\text{def}}{=} u$ and note that $Q_1^1 = \delta_1 < 0$ from Eq. (35). It then follows from inspection of Theorem 18.3 that the steady state comparative statics for the state variable *completely* determine the local comparative dynamics of a prototypical calculus of variations problem.

Before presenting an example, one final remark on Theorem 18.3 is in order, as it relates to Theorem 14.10, the dynamic envelope theorem for discounted infinite-horizon optimal control models. As you may recall, in order to establish Theorem 14.10, we had to make an assumption that, in the notation of this chapter, was of the form

$$\lim_{t\to+\infty} \frac{\partial z}{\partial \theta_k}(t; \boldsymbol{\theta}, x_0) = \frac{\partial x^*}{\partial \theta_k}(\boldsymbol{\theta}), \quad k = 1, \ldots, K_1 + K_2 + 1.$$

If we take the initial value of the state variable to be the steady state value of the state variable, that is to say, $x_0 = x^*(\boldsymbol{\theta})$, then the above condition holds. This can be confirmed by letting $t \to +\infty$ in Eq. (44). Note that the same conclusion applies to the optimal control variable as well, as can be confirmed by letting $t \to +\infty$ in Eq. (43).

Let's pause briefly in order to present an example of some of the points just made. In it, we contemplate the classical model of a dynamic limit pricing dominant firm introduced into the literature by Gaskins (1971) and studied rather extensively in Chapter 16.

Example 18.1: The dynamic limit pricing model of Gaskins (1971) can be stated in the notation of the present chapter as follows: $f(x, u; \alpha) \stackrel{\text{def}}{=} [u - c][D(u) - x]$, $g(x, u; \beta) \stackrel{\text{def}}{=} k[u - \bar{u}]$, $\bar{u} > 0$ is the limit price, u is the dominant firm's product price, x is fringe or rival sales, $c > 0$ is the dominant firm's constant average cost of production, $k > 0$ is the response coefficient, and $D(u)$ is the total demand for the product. Because $g_x(\cdot) \equiv 0$, the dominant firm's steady state price is independent of its discount rate and average production cost by Corollary 18.2.2, as noted earlier. By Eq. (30), the dominant firm's steady state price is also independent of the fringe's response coefficient k, whereas by Eq. (29), steady state rival sales fall as k increases, which may seem odd without considering the local comparative dynamics of the problem. Given that $Q_1^1 = \delta_1 k^{-1} < 0$ from Eq. (35), Eq. (43) shows that as k increases, the dominant firm responds by lowering the price of its product below the limit price, which in turn drives some of its rivals from the market. As time passes, Eq. (45) shows that the dominant firm gradually raises its price above the level it fell the moment k first increased but below the limit price, all the while driving more rivals from the market. Eventually, when a long enough period of time passes, that is, as $t \to +\infty$, the dominant firm's price increases back to its original level (the limit price), and rival sales are smaller in the new steady state.

This brief example should convince you that an examination of only the steady state comparative statics of an optimal control problem may not give a sound economic understanding of its qualitative properties. Investigating the local comparative dynamics of the parameter perturbation may, in many cases, lead to a sound economic interpretation of the steady state comparative statics, which if taken in isolation, may seem counterintuitive. Furthermore, the local comparative dynamics may often yield qualitative results that show that the steady state policy implications may differ quite substantially from their impact effects. These observations will be further reinforced in the next, more extended, example.

In this final example of the chapter, we examine a classical dynamic economic problem in some detail in order to show how the theorems and corollaries of this chapter can be used to (i) simplify the derivation of its qualitative properties, and (ii) uncover the mathematical structure of the model responsible for its qualitative properties.

Example 18.2: Consider the following simplified version of the adjustment cost model of the price-taking firm we studied in Chapter 17:

$$\max_{I(\cdot)} \int_0^{+\infty} [pF(K(t)) - cK(t) - gI(t) - C(I(t); \gamma)]\, e^{-rt}\, dt$$

$$\text{s.t.} \quad \dot{K}(t) = I(t) - \delta K(t), \;\; K(0) = K_0,$$

where $K(t)$ is the capital stock, $I(t)$ is the investment rate, $F(\cdot)$ is the production function with $F'(K) > 0$ and $F''(K) < 0$, $C(\cdot)$ is the cost of adjustment function with

$C(0;\gamma) = 0$, $C_I(I;\gamma) > 0$ for $I > 0$, $C_I(I;\gamma) < 0$ for $I < 0$, $C_I(0;\gamma) = 0$, and $C_{II}(I;\gamma) > 0$, $p > 0$ is the unit price of output, $c > 0$ is the holding or maintenance cost per unit of capital, $g > 0$ is the purchase price per unit of investment, $\gamma > 0$ is a cost of adjustment shift parameter with $C_{I\gamma}(I;\gamma) > 0$ for $I > 0$, $C_{I\gamma}(I;\gamma) < 0$ for $I < 0$, $C_{I\gamma}(0;\gamma) = 0$, $r > 0$ is the discount rate on cash flows, $\delta > 0$ is the depreciation rate of the capital stock, $K_0 > 0$ is the given initial stock of capital, $\boldsymbol{\alpha} \overset{\text{def}}{=} (c, g, p, \gamma)$, $\beta \overset{\text{def}}{=} \delta$, and $\boldsymbol{\theta} \overset{\text{def}}{=} (\boldsymbol{\alpha}, \beta, r) = (c, g, p, \gamma, \delta, r)$. It is assumed that assumptions (A.1) through (A.7) hold for the adjustment cost model. Denote the optimal pair by $(K(t;\boldsymbol{\theta}, K_0), I(t;\boldsymbol{\theta}, K_0))$.

We begin the analysis by investigating the steady state comparative statics of an increase in the purchase price of investment $g > 0$. Upon defining $f(K, I;\boldsymbol{\alpha}) \overset{\text{def}}{=} pF(K) - cK - gI - C(I;\gamma)$ as the integrand of the problem and $g(K, I;\beta) \overset{\text{def}}{=} I - \delta K$ as the transition equation, Theorem 18.2, Eqs. (27) and (28), yield

$$\frac{\partial K^*(\boldsymbol{\theta})}{\partial g} \equiv \frac{-[r+\delta]}{|J_s|} < 0, \tag{52}$$

$$\frac{\partial I^*(\boldsymbol{\theta})}{\partial g} \equiv \frac{-\delta[r+\delta]}{|J_s|} \equiv \delta \frac{\partial K^*(\boldsymbol{\theta})}{\partial g} < 0. \tag{53}$$

These results demonstrate that an increase in the purchase price of the investment good leads to a decrease in the steady state capital stock and investment rate. Because the price of the investment good and the investment rate form a conjugate pair, that is, $f_{Kg}(\cdot) \equiv 0$, the sufficient condition of part (C) of Corollary 18.2.1 may be used to reach the same qualitative conclusion. Moreover, it follows from the definition of the steady state level of output $y^*(\boldsymbol{\theta}) \overset{\text{def}}{=} F(K^*(\boldsymbol{\theta}))$ and Eq. (52) that $\partial y^*(\boldsymbol{\theta})/\partial g = F'(K^*(\boldsymbol{\theta}))\partial K^*(\boldsymbol{\theta})/\partial g < 0$. In other words, the steady state level of output decreases with an increase in the purchase price of the investment good.

Before moving on to the local comparative dynamics, let's pause and construct the phase portrait in the *KI*-phase plane. This will be beneficial when we go to characterize the local comparative dynamics graphically. In order to do so efficiently, we simply employ Eqs. (9) and (10) to derive

$$\dot{I} = \frac{pF'(K) - w - [g + C_I(I;\gamma)][r+\delta]}{-C_{II}(I;\gamma)}, \tag{54}$$

$$\dot{K} = I - \delta K. \tag{55}$$

By definition, the nullclines are given by

$$\dot{I} = 0 \Leftrightarrow pF'(K) - w - [g + C_I(I;\gamma)][r+\delta] = 0, \tag{56}$$

$$\dot{K} = 0 \Leftrightarrow I - \delta K = 0. \tag{57}$$

The slopes of the nullclines in a neighborhood of the steady state $(K^*(\boldsymbol{\theta}), I^*(\boldsymbol{\theta}))$ are given by the implicit function theorem as

$$\left.\frac{\partial I}{\partial K}\right|_{\substack{\dot{I}=0 \\ (K^*(\boldsymbol{\theta}),\, I^*(\boldsymbol{\theta}))}} = \frac{pF''(K^*(\boldsymbol{\theta}))}{[r+\delta]C_{II}(I^*(\boldsymbol{\theta});\gamma)} < 0, \tag{58}$$

$$\left.\frac{\partial I}{\partial K}\right|_{\substack{\dot{K}=0 \\ (K^*(\boldsymbol{\theta}),\, I^*(\boldsymbol{\theta}))}} = \delta > 0. \tag{59}$$

Because the $\dot{K} = 0$ isocline is given by the linear equation $I - \delta K = 0$, it is a simple matter to determine its global properties. But seeing as we are deriving the steady state comparative statics and local comparative dynamics in a neighborhood of the steady state, all we require for the geometry to support our qualitative results is the slope of the isoclines in a neighborhood of the steady state. The same is true for the vector field associated with the differential equations (54) and (55), to which we now turn.

The vector field associated with Eqs. (54) and (55) is determined from the dynamic Jacobian matrix of these differential equations, as you should recall. We can either calculate the vector field directly from Eqs. (54) and (55) or use Eqs. (18) and (19) to aid us in this endeavor. Either way, we find the vector field to be given by

$$h_u^* = \left.\frac{\partial \dot{I}}{\partial I}\right|_{\dot{K}=\dot{I}=0} = [r+\delta] > 0,\ \ h_x^* = \left.\frac{\partial \dot{I}}{\partial K}\right|_{\dot{K}=\dot{I}=0} = \frac{pF''(K^*(\boldsymbol{\theta}))}{-C_{II}(I^*(\boldsymbol{\theta});\gamma)} > 0, \tag{60}$$

$$g_u^* = \left.\frac{\partial \dot{K}}{\partial I}\right|_{\dot{K}=\dot{I}=0} = 1 > 0,\ \ g_x^* = \left.\frac{\partial \dot{K}}{\partial K}\right|_{\dot{K}=\dot{I}=0} = -\delta < 0. \tag{61}$$

Upon comparing Eqs. (58) and (59) to Eqs. (60) and (61), the following conclusions should be evident: (i) the slope of the I nullcline in a neighborhood of the steady state is equal to the negative of the ratio of the second column entry to the first column entry of row one of the dynamic Jacobian matrix J_d associated with the differential equations (54) and (55), and (ii) the slope of the K nullcline in a neighborhood of the steady state is equal to the negative of the ratio of the second column entry to the first column entry of row two of the dynamic Jacobian matrix J_d associated with the differential equations (54) and (55). That this is true more generally for any two-dimensional system of ordinary differential equations is the subject of a mental exercise. Note that in establishing the general result, we take it that the control variable is represented on the so-called y-axis and the state variable is represented on the so-called x-axis. This convention implies that the slope of a nullcline is thus found by taking the derivative of the control variable with respect to the state variable along the said nullcline via the implicit function theorem, and then evaluating the

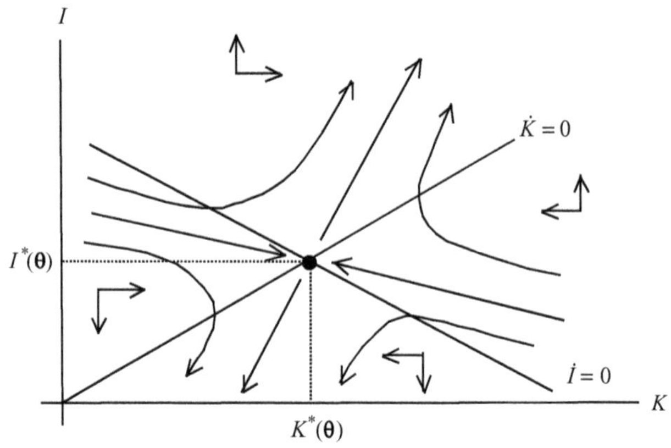

Figure 18.1

result at the steady state solution. Let's now return to the matter at hand, to wit, the derivation of the local phase portrait corresponding to the system of differential equations comprising Eqs. (54) and (55).

Using Eqs. (60) and (61), we find that $|J_d| = h_u^* g_x^* - h_x^* g_u^* < 0$. Moreover, because $\delta_1\delta_2 = |J_d|$ by Eq. (23), one eigenvalue is negative and the other is positive, thereby implying that the steady state is a local saddle point. The local phase portrait corresponding to differential equations (54) and (55) can now be constructed using the qualitative information in Eqs. (58) through (61) and the fact that the steady state is a local saddle point. Figure 18.1 gives the local phase portrait.

Before we calculate the local comparative dynamics for g, observe that by using both forms of Eq. (35) and the aforementioned properties of the production function and adjustment cost function, that $Q_1^1 = \frac{pF''(K^*(\theta))/C_{II}(I^*(\theta);\gamma)}{r+\delta-\delta_1} \equiv \delta_1 + \delta < 0$. Then by Eq. (43) of Theorem 18.3, it follows that

$$\left.\frac{\partial I(t;\theta, K_0)}{\partial g}\right|_{K_0=K^*(\theta)} = \frac{\partial I^*(\theta)}{\partial g} - [\delta_1 + \delta]e^{\delta_1 t}\frac{\partial K^*(\theta)}{\partial g} < \frac{\partial I^*(\theta)}{\partial g} < 0 \tag{62}$$

for all $t \in [0, +\infty)$, the inequalities being a result of Eqs. (52) and (53). Moreover, by Eq. (45) of Theorem 18.3, it also follows that

$$\left.\frac{\partial \dot{I}(t;\theta, K_0)}{\partial g}\right|_{K_0=K^*(\theta)} = -\delta_1[\delta_1 + \delta]e^{\delta_1 t}\frac{\partial K^*(\theta)}{\partial g} > 0 \tag{63}$$

for all $t \in [0, +\infty)$. Equations (62) and (63) demonstrate that the moment g increases, the investment rate falls by its largest amount, which is more than what is dictated by the steady state comparative statics. This impact effect is gradually reversed over time, as Eq. (63) shows, until the new (but lower) steady state investment rate is reached. All the while, the capital stock displays its typical monotonic

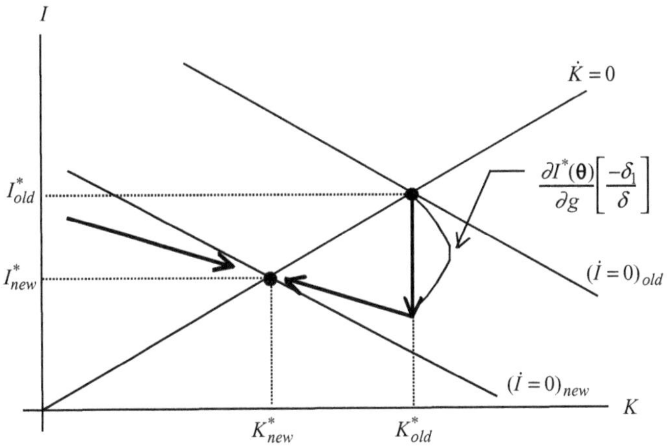

Figure 18.2

decline from its old to its new steady state level, for

$$\left.\frac{\partial K(t;\boldsymbol{\theta}, K_0)}{\partial g}\right|_{K_0=K^*(\boldsymbol{\theta})} = \frac{\partial K^*(\boldsymbol{\theta})}{\partial g}[1-e^{\delta_1 t}] \leq 0 \,\forall t \in [0,+\infty), \tag{64}$$

$$\left.\frac{\partial \dot{K}(t;\boldsymbol{\theta}, K_0)}{\partial g}\right|_{K_0=K^*(\boldsymbol{\theta})} = -\delta_1 e^{\delta_1 t}\frac{\partial K^*(\boldsymbol{\theta})}{\partial g} < 0 \,\forall t \in [0,+\infty) \tag{65}$$

using Eqs. (44) and (46) of Theorem 18.3

Figure 18.2 presents the local comparative dynamics phase diagram for an increase in the purchase price of the investment good. In passing, observe that in Figure 18.2, we have indicated the precise amount by which the investment rate must fall the instant the purchase price of investment increases in order for the trajectory to asymptotically reach the new steady state. The precise amount is given by the impact effect

$$\left.\frac{\partial I(t;\boldsymbol{\theta}, K_0)}{\partial g}\right|_{\substack{K_0=K^*(\boldsymbol{\theta})\\ t=0}} = \frac{\partial I^*(\boldsymbol{\theta})}{\partial g}\left[\frac{-\delta_1}{\delta}\right] < \frac{\partial I^*(\boldsymbol{\theta})}{\partial g} < 0,$$

which you are asked to verify in a mental exercise.

In order to make sure that you understand the derivation of the comparative dynamics phase portrait given in Figure 18.2, several remarks are in order. First, recognize that Eqs. (52) and (53) imply that the new steady state lies to the southwest of the old steady state in the *KI*-phase plane. Second, observe that the $\dot{K}=0$ isocline given in Eq. (57) does not depend on the purchase price g of the investment good, but that the $\dot{I}=0$ isocline given in Eq. (56) does. Given these two facts, it then follows that the $\dot{I}=0$ isocline shifts down when g increases, as this is the only way for the new steady state to lie to the southwest of the old steady state. This conclusion can also be confirmed by application of the implicit function theorem to the $\dot{I} = 0$ isocline given in Eq. (56). This calculation is left as a mental exercise. Third, the local dynamics are qualitatively identical around the old and the new steady states. Fourth, the initial value of the capital stock for the local comparative dynamics exercise is taken as the old steady state value of the capital stock, and thus is fixed or given to the firm when the purchase price of the investment good first increases. This, in turn, implies that the capital stock (the state variable) does not *immediately* change when g increases, as this is the meaning of a state variable. This is easily verified by evaluating Eq. (64) at $t = 0$. As a result of this latter point, it follows that the investment rate (the control variable) must immediately respond to the increase in g if the new steady state is to be reached asymptotically. In order to find out which direction the investment rate must initially move in response to the increase in g, we simply note the two stable trajectories corresponding to the new steady state and seek to determine whether an increase or decrease in the investment rate is required to reach one of these trajectories. Using Figure 18.2 as a guide, we see that the investment rate must decrease initially when g increases, a fact we have already deduced from Eq. (62). The precise amount by which the investment rate decreases is given by the vertical distance from the old steady state to the stable arm to the right of the new steady state, and is determined by the impact effect of g on the investment rate as indicated in the Figure 18.2.

Finally, let us point out another important feature of the theorems and corollaries of this chapter as highlighted by the adjustment cost model. In particular, the steady state comparative statics for the parameters (c, γ, r) need not be discussed in detail, for Corollary 18.2.1 shows that their steady state comparative statics are qualitatively identical to that of g just discussed, and therefore by Theorem 18.3, so are their local comparative dynamics. The same conclusion does *not* hold for the depreciation rate of the capital stock, as inspection of Eq. (30) of Theorem 18.2 reveals. Furthermore, note that it is the conjugacy between g and I that is responsible for the refutable qualitative properties we uncovered in the adjustment cost model. Such a conjugacy is in fact the driving force behind many of the refutable qualitative results in the intertemporal economics literature.

For optimal control problems of the form of problem (1), which arguably comprise the largest class of models in dynamic economic theory, this chapter has provided an exhaustive qualitative characterization of their steady state comparative statics and local comparative dynamics properties. This was achieved by studying, in order, (i) the local stability of the steady state, (ii) the steady state comparative statics, and (iii) the local comparative dynamics of the problem.

The limitations of the linearization method presented in this chapter for studying the qualitative properties of optimal control problems are significant enough to be spelled out. For control problems with more than one state variable, but that otherwise meet the assumptions of the chapter, the linearization method may be applied, but as pointed out by Nagatani (1976), the qualitative results derivable by the method are few. If the control problem has a finite horizon but is otherwise consistent with the assumptions adopted in this chapter, then the linearization method cannot generally be used, for the steady state is not the focus in such problems. The variational differential equation approach of Oniki (1973) and the dynamic primal-dual formalism of Caputo (1990a, 1990b, 1992) exposited in Chapter 11, however, may be applied to such problems. Even if there are more than two states, the latter two methods may still be applied, but Oniki's (1973) approach is very difficult to extract qualitative information from, whereas Caputo's (1990a, 1990b, 1992) method is just as easy to use as when only one state is present, and in fact yields a richer set of qualitative properties because of symmetry. Finally, the method presented herein is not applicable when the control problem is nonautonomous, regardless of the dimension of the state, whereas Oniki's (1973) and Caputo's (1990a, 1990b, 1992) methods are perfectly at home in such instances.

In the next two chapters, we shift attention to the dynamic programming approach for solving optimal control problems. This will permit us to delve into intertemporal duality results that form the basis for empirical work that is based on optimal control formulations of intertemporal economic models.

MENTAL EXERCISES

18.1 Show that the necessary conditions for problem (1) can be reduced to a pair of differential equations in (λ, x).

18.2 Derive the steady state Jacobian matrix of Eqs. (11) and (12), and show that its determinant is given by Eq. (16).

18.3 Verify the expressions given in Eqs. (17) through (20).

18.4 Prove that $|J_d| = |J_s|\,[f_{uu}^* - f_u^*[g_u^*]^{-1}g_{uu}^*]^{-1}$ in Eq. (23).

18.5 Prove the remaining parts of Theorem 18.2.

18.6 Derive the steady state comparative statics of the current value shadow price.

18.7 Show that the two formulas for the Q_1^ℓ component of the eigenvectors given in Eq. (35) are identical.

18.8 Prove Theorem 18.3.

18.9 Consider the pair of autonomous ordinary differential equations

$$\dot{x}_1 = F^1(x_1, x_2),$$

$$\dot{x}_2 = F^2(x_1, x_2).$$

Imagine that x_1 is plotted horizontally and x_2 is plotted vertically in the x_1x_2-phase plane. Prove that the slope of the x_1 nullcline in a neighborhood of the steady state is equal to the negative of the ratio of the first column entry to the second column entry of row one of the Jacobian matrix associated with the differential equations evaluated at the steady state solution. Also prove the corresponding result for the x_2 nullcline.

18.10 With reference to Example 18.2:

(a) Prove that the impact effect of g on the investment rate is given by the formula in Figure 18.2.

(b) Prove that the $\dot{I} = 0$ isocline shifts down when g increases by using the implicit function theorem.

18.11 The neoclassical optimal growth model may be stated as

$$\max_{c(\cdot)} \int_0^{+\infty} U(c(t); \alpha) e^{-rt} \, dt$$

$$\text{s.t.} \quad \dot{k}(t) = \phi(k(t); \gamma) - c(t) - [\eta + \delta]k(t), \; k(0) = k_0,$$

where $c(t)$ is per-capita consumption, $k(t)$ is the capital-to-labor ratio, $U(\cdot)$ is the social instantaneous utility function with $U_c(c; \alpha) > 0$ and $U_{cc}(c; \alpha) < 0$, $\phi(\cdot)$ is the average product of labor function with $\phi_k(k; \gamma) > 0$ and $\phi_{kk}(k; \gamma) < 0$, $r > 0$ is the social discount rate, α is a taste change parameter such that $U_{c\alpha}(c; \alpha) > 0$, γ is a technology parameter such that $\phi_\gamma(k; \gamma) > 0$ and $\phi_{k\gamma}(k; \gamma) > 0$, $\eta > 0$ is the exogenous growth rate of the labor force, $\delta > 0$ is the depreciation rate of capital, $k_0 > 0$ is the initial capital-to-labor ratio, $\boldsymbol{\beta} \overset{\text{def}}{=} (\gamma, \delta, \eta)$, and $\boldsymbol{\theta} \overset{\text{def}}{=} (\alpha, \gamma, \delta, \eta, r)$. It is assumed that assumptions (A.1) through (A.7) hold for this model.

(a) Show that the steady state comparative statics of the social discount rate are

$$\frac{\partial k^*(\boldsymbol{\theta})}{\partial r} \equiv \frac{-U_c^*}{|J_s|} < 0, \quad \frac{\partial c^*(\boldsymbol{\theta})}{\partial r} \equiv \frac{-rU_c^*}{|J_s|} < 0.$$

(b) Show that the qualitative conclusions in part (a) could have just as easily been reached using Corollary 18.2.1.

These steady state comparative statics assert that an increase in the social discount rate reduces the steady state capital-to-labor ratio and per-capita consumption, which at first glance seems incongruous. For example, how can the capital-to-labor ratio fall if per-capita consumption has also fallen? The answer and intuition become clear only when the local comparative dynamics are investigated.

(c) In order to make complete sense of these steady state comparative statics, therefore, show that the impact effect of an increase in r is given by

$$\left. \frac{\partial c(t; \boldsymbol{\theta}, k_0)}{\partial r} \right|_{\substack{k_0 = k^*(\boldsymbol{\theta}) \\ t=0}} = \delta_1 \frac{\partial k^*(\boldsymbol{\theta})}{\partial r} > 0,$$

where $\delta_1 < 0$ is the negative eigenvalue associated with the linearized system of differential equations.

(d) Now provide a complete economic interpretation of the effect of an increase in the discount rate. Be sure to draw the corresponding local comparative dynamics phase portrait.

(e) Show that $\partial k^*(\boldsymbol{\theta})/\partial\alpha = \partial c^*(\boldsymbol{\theta})/\partial\alpha \equiv 0$. Provide an economic interpretation.

(f) Show that a change in tastes has no effect on the time paths of the capital-to-labor ratio and per-capita consumption in a neighborhood of the steady state.

One's intuition may suggest that a rise in the marginal utility of per-capita consumption should affect the steady state of the system or the approach to it, but the mathematics show that such intuition is faulty in the neoclassical growth model.

(g) Show that the steady state comparative statics of the technology parameter are

$$\frac{\partial k^*(\boldsymbol{\theta})}{\partial\gamma} \equiv \frac{U_c^*\phi_{k\gamma}^*}{|J_s|} > 0,$$

$$\frac{\partial c^*(\boldsymbol{\theta})}{\partial\gamma} \equiv \frac{-\phi_\gamma^* U_c^* \phi_{kk}^* + \phi_k^* U_c^* \phi_{k\gamma}^*}{|J_s|} > 0.$$

Provide an economic interpretation of these results.

(h) Show that the impact effect of a change in γ is given by

$$\left.\frac{\partial c(t;\boldsymbol{\theta},k_0)}{\partial\gamma}\right|_{\substack{k_0=k^*(\boldsymbol{\theta})\\ t=0}} = \frac{\partial c^*(\boldsymbol{\theta})}{\partial\gamma} - [r-\delta_1]\frac{\partial k^*(\boldsymbol{\theta})}{\partial\gamma}.$$

In contrast to the case of an increase in the social discount rate, the sign of this expression cannot be determined in general. Thus the moment the increase in γ occurs, it is not possible, in general, to determine if per-capita consumption rises or falls. If the increase in steady state per-capita consumption is large relative to the increase in the steady state capital-to-labor ratio, then per-capita consumption jumps up when γ increases in order to reach its relatively larger steady state value. If, however, the increase in steady state per-capita consumption is small relative to the increase in the steady state capital-to-labor ratio, then per-capita consumption jumps down when γ increases, as there is no need to have per-capita consumption rise initially to meet the relatively smaller increase in its steady state value.

18.12 *Optimal Advertising by a Monopolist.* The basic idea of the model is that a monopolistic firm has a stock of advertising goodwill, $A(t)$, that summarizes the effects of current and past advertising expenditures by the monopolist on the demand for its products. The advertising goodwill (or capital) changes over time according to the ordinary differential equation $\dot{A}(t) = g(u(t);\alpha_2) - \delta A(t)$, where $u(t)$ is the current advertising rate in dollars, $\delta > 0$ is the constant depreciation rate of advertising goodwill, $\alpha_2 > 0$ is a shift parameter, and $A_0 > 0$ is the initial stock of goodwill. Let $g(\cdot) : \Re_+ \times \Re_{++} \to \Re_+$ be the $C^{(2)}$ function that maps advertising expenditures into advertising goodwill, that is, $g(\cdot)$ is the goodwill production function. Assume that $g(0;\alpha_2)=0$, which means that if the monopolist decides not to spend any money on advertising, then the stock of advertising goodwill does not change. In addition, assume that for all $(u,\alpha_2)\in\Re_{++}\times\Re_{++}$, $g_u(u;\alpha_2)>0$, $g_{u\alpha_2}(u;\alpha_2)>0$, and $g_{uu}(u;\alpha_2)<0$, and $\lim_{u\to+\infty} g_u(u;\alpha_2)=0$ and $\lim_{u\to 0^+} g_u(u;\alpha_2)=+\infty$. The monopolist is asserted to operate over the indefinite future and discount its instantaneous profits $\pi(A;\alpha_1)$ at the constant rate $r>0$. It is assumed that the $C^{(2)}$ profit function $\pi(\cdot):\Re_+\times\Re_{++}\to\Re_+$ satisfies $\pi_A(A;\alpha_1)>0$, $\pi_{A\alpha_1}(A;\alpha_1)>0$, and $\pi_{AA}(A;\alpha_1)<0$ for all $(A,\alpha_1)\in\Re_{++}\times\Re_{++}$. The monopolist begins its planning at time $t=0$ with a given stock of advertising goodwill, namely, $A(0)=A_0>0$. The optimal control problem the firm must solve in order to determine its optimal advertising expenditure plan is thus given by

$$V(\boldsymbol{\beta}) \stackrel{\text{def}}{=} \max_{u(\cdot)} \int_0^{+\infty} [\pi(A(t);\alpha_1)-u(t)]\,e^{-rt}\,dt$$

$$\text{s.t.}\quad \dot{A}(t)=g(u(t);\alpha_2)-\delta A(t),\ A(0)=A_0,$$

$$A(t)\geq 0,\ u(t)\geq 0\ \forall\, t\in[0,+\infty),$$

where $(\boldsymbol{\theta},A_0)\stackrel{\text{def}}{=}(\alpha_1,\alpha_2,r,\delta,A_0)\in\Re^5_{++}$ are the time invariant parameters of the problem. Assume that assumptions (A.1) through (A.7) hold for this model. Note that the problem statement explicitly includes nonnegativity restrictions on the paths of the control and state variables.

(a) Prove that if $u(t)\geq 0\ \forall\, t\in[0,+\infty)$, then the nonnegativity constraint on the state variable is not binding $\forall\, t\in[0,+\infty)$. This means that you can ignore the state variable inequality constraint.

(b) Write down the current value Hamiltonian $H(\cdot)$ with current value costate variable λ, and derive the necessary conditions for this problem. Prove that $u(t)>0\ \forall\, t\in[0,+\infty)$ in an optimal plan.

(c) Prove that the necessary conditions are also sufficient for determining the uniquely optimal solution to the monopolist's advertising problem under suitable additional assumptions to be determined by you.

(d) Show that the necessary (and sufficient) conditions reduce to the following pair of autonomous ordinary differential equations in (u,A):

$$\dot{u}=\frac{g_u(u;\alpha_2)[g_u(u;\alpha_2)\pi_A(A;\alpha_1)-(r+\delta)]}{g_{uu}(u;\alpha_2)}$$

$$\dot{A}=g(u;\alpha_2)-\delta A.$$

(e) Derive the phase portrait for the ordinary differential equations derived in part (d). Be sure to include your derivations of the slopes of the $\dot{u}=0$ and $\dot{A}=0$ isoclines, as well as the vector field in the (u,A) phase plane. What type of steady state equilibrium does the model have?

(f) Let $(u^s(\boldsymbol{\alpha}), A^s(\boldsymbol{\alpha}))$ be the solution to the steady state version of the necessary and sufficient conditions in part (d). Prove that the functions $(u^s(\cdot), A^s(\cdot))$ are locally $C^{(1)}$ in $\boldsymbol{\alpha}$. Present your argument carefully using the correct theorem.

(g) Find the steady state comparative statics for the discount rate. Provide an economic interpretation.

(h) Draw the local comparative dynamics phase portrait for the discount rate, making sure to label the optimal path from the old to the new steady state clearly. Provide an economic interpretation of the comparative dynamics result.

(i) Find the steady state comparative statics for the parameter α_1. Provide an economic interpretation.

(j) Draw the local comparative dynamics phase portrait for the parameter α_1, making sure to label the optimal path from the old to the new steady state clearly. Provide an economic interpretation of the comparative dynamics result.

18.13 *The Consumer's Lifetime Allocation Process.* This question extends Mental Exercise 12.9 by considering a consumer with a nonlinear utility function and an infinite planning horizon. You should review the aforementioned mental exercise if you did not attempt it or have forgotten much of its setup. As a result, only those parts of the problem that differ from the previous version will be exposited here. In particular, we now consider the case in which the preferences of the consumer are represented by a nonlinear and additively separable function of the consumption rate and the stock of the asset, to wit, $W(a(t), c(t); \alpha_1, \alpha_2) \stackrel{\text{def}}{=} U(c(t); \alpha_1) + V(a(t); \alpha_2)$, where $U(\cdot) \in C^{(2)}$, $U_c(c; \alpha_1) > 0$, $U_{cc}(c; \alpha_1) < 0$, and $U_{c\alpha_1}(c; \alpha_1) > 0 \; \forall \; (c; \alpha_1) \in \Re^2_{++}$, $\lim_{c \to 0} U_c(c; \alpha_1) = +\infty \; \forall \; \alpha_1 \in \Re_{++}$, and $V(\cdot) \in C^{(2)}$, $V_a(a; \alpha_2) > 0$, $V_{aa}(a; \alpha_2) < 0$, and $V_{a\alpha_2}(a; \alpha_2) > 0 \; \forall \; (c; \alpha_1) \in \Re^2_{++}$. It is still assumed that $a(t) \gtrless 0$ is possible, so there is no constraint on the stock of the asset, but the consumption rate is required to be nonnegative. In sum then, the optimal control problem to be solved for the optimal consumption plan is given by

$$\max_{c(\cdot)} \int_0^{+\infty} [U(c(t); \alpha_1) + V(a(t); \alpha_2)] \, e^{-\rho t} \, dt$$

$$\text{s.t.} \quad \dot{a}(t) = y + ra(t) - c(t), \; a(0) = a_0,$$

$$c(t) \geq 0 \; \forall \, t \in [0, +\infty),$$

where $(\boldsymbol{\theta}, a_0) \stackrel{\text{def}}{=} (\alpha_1, \alpha_2, \rho, r, y, a_0) \in \Re^6_{++}$ are the time-invariant parameters of the problem. Assume that assumptions (A.1) through (A.7) hold for this model. As in the previous version of this model, also assume that $\rho > r$.

(a) Write down the current value Hamiltonian $H(\cdot)$ with current value costate variable λ, and derive the necessary conditions for this problem. Prove that $c(t) > 0\,\forall\, t \in [0, +\infty)$ in an optimal plan.

(b) Prove that the necessary conditions are also sufficient for determining the uniquely optimal solution to the consumption planning problem under suitable additional assumptions to be determined by you.

(c) Reduce the three necessary and sufficient conditions to a pair of autonomous ordinary differential equations involving only (a, c).

(d) Derive the phase portrait for the autonomous ordinary differential equations derived in part (c). Be sure to include your derivations of the slopes of the $\dot{a} = 0$ and $\dot{c} = 0$ nullclines, as well as the vector field in the ac-phase plane.

You will discover that two phase diagrams are possible based on the vector field. It is therefore your task to decide which phase portrait is the one that describes the optimal solution to the control problem. Moreover, you must justify your answer carefully and rigorously.

(e) Let $(a^s(\boldsymbol{\alpha}), c^s(\boldsymbol{\alpha}))$ be the solution to the steady state version of the necessary and sufficient conditions in part (c). Find the steady state comparative statics for an increase in income. Provide an economic interpretation.

(f) Draw the local comparative dynamics phase portrait for income, making sure to label the optimal path from the old steady state to the new steady state clearly. Provide an economic interpretation of the comparative dynamics result.

(g) Find the steady state comparative statics for an increase in the parameter α_2. Provide an economic interpretation.

(h) Draw the local comparative dynamics phase portrait for the parameter α_2, making sure to label the optimal path from the old steady state to the new steady state clearly. Provide an economic interpretation of the comparative dynamics result.

FURTHER READING

Samuelson (1947) was the first to systematically use the implicit function theorem to investigate the comparative statics properties of economic models. The method of comparative dynamics put forth by Oniki (1973) is essentially a generalization of the classical method of variational differential equations. His method and the dynamic primal-dual formalism of Caputo (1990a, 1990b, 1992) are approaches to conducting a comparative dynamics analysis of an optimal control problem that are *complementary* to the linearization approach of this chapter. Caputo (1989) provides a detailed account of the linearization approach given here in the context of the nonrenewable resource–extracting model of the firm, whereas Caputo and Ostrom (1996) provide another application in the context of drug policy. This chapter is based on the work of Caputo (1997). Otani (1982) derives comparative dynamics formulas for the multiple state class of symmetric calculus of variations problems. Mental Exercise 18.12 is motivated by the research of Nerlove and Arrow (1962). See Sethi (1977) and Feichtinger et al. (1994) for survey articles dealing with optimal control models in advertising. Dockner (1985) presents a detailed analysis of the local stability of steady states in optimal control problems with two state variables akin to that of this chapter. Tahvonen (1991) provides an extension of one of Dockner's (1985) stability theorems.

REFERENCES

Caputo, M.R. (1989), "The Qualitative Content of Renewable Resource Models," *Natural Resource Modeling*, 3, 241–259.

Caputo, M.R. (1990a), "Comparative Dynamics via Envelope Methods in Variational Calculus," *Review of Economic Studies*, 57, 689–697.

Caputo, M.R. (1990b), "How to Do Comparative Dynamics on the Back of an Envelope in Optimal Control Theory," *Journal of Economic Dynamics and Control*, 14, 655–683.

Caputo, M.R. (1992), "A Primal-Dual Approach to Comparative Dynamics with Time Dependent Parameters in Variational Calculus," *Optimal Control Applications and Methods*, 13, 73–86.

Caputo, M.R. (1997), "The Qualitative Structure of a Class of Infinite Horizon Optimal Control Problems," *Optimal Control Applications and Methods* 18, 195–215.

Caputo, M.R. and Ostrom, B.J. (1996), "Optimal Government Policy Regarding a Previously Illegal Commodity," *Southern Economic Journal*, 62, 690–709.

Dockner, E. (1985), "Local Stability Analysis in Optimal Control Problems with Two State Variables," in Feichtinger, G. (ed.), *Optimal Control Theory and Economic Analysis*, Vol 2 (Amsterdam: North-Holland).

Feichtinger, G., Hartl, R.F., and Sethi, S.P. (1994), "Dynamic Optimal Control Models in Advertising: Recent Developments," *Management Science*, 40, 195–226.

Gaskins, D.W. (1971), "Dynamic Limit Pricing: Optimal Pricing under Threat of Entry," *Journal of Economic Theory*, 3, 306–322.

Nagatani, K. (1976), "On the Comparative Statics of Temporary Equilibrium," Discussion paper, University of British Columbia, No. 76–30.

Nerlove, M. and Arrow, K.J. (1962), "Optimal Advertising Policy under Dynamic Conditions," *Economica*, 29, 129–142.

Oniki, H. (1973), "Comparative Dynamics (Sensitivity Analysis) in Optimal Control Theory," *Journal of Economic Theory*, 6, 265–283.

Otani, K. (1982), "Explicit Formulae of Comparative Dynamics," *International Economic Review*, 23, 411–419.

Protter, M.H. and Morrey, C.B. (1991, 2nd Ed.), *A First Course in Real Analysis* (New York: Springer-Verlag, Inc.).

Samuelson, P.A. (1947), *Foundations of Economic Analysis* (Cambridge, Mass.: Harvard University Press).

Sethi, S.P. (1977), "Dynamic Optimal Control Models in Advertising: A Survey," *SIAM Review*, 19, 685–725.

Simon, C.P. and Blume, L. (1994), *Mathematics for Economists* (New York: W.W. Norton & Company, Inc.).

Tahvonen, O. (1991), "On the Dynamics of Renewable Resource Harvesting and Pollution Control," *Environmental and Resource Economics* 1, 97–117.

NINETEEN

Dynamic Programming and the Hamilton-Jacobi-Bellman Equation

In this chapter, we turn our attention away from the derivation of necessary and sufficient conditions that can be used to find the optimal time paths of the state, costate, and control variables, and focus on the optimal value function more closely. In particular, we will derive the fundamental first-order partial differential equation obeyed by the optimal value function, known as the *Hamilton-Jacobi-Bellman* equation. This shift in our attention, moreover, will lead us to a different *form* for the optimal value of the control vector, namely, the *feedback* or *closed-loop* form of the control. This form of the optimal control typically gives the optimal value of the control vector as a function of the current date, the current state, and the parameters of the control problem. In contrast, the form of the optimal control vector derived via the necessary conditions of optimal control theory is termed *open-loop*, and in general gives the optimal value of the control vector as a function of the independent variable time, the parameters, and the initial and/or terminal values of the planning horizon and the state vector. Essentially, the feedback form of the optimal control is a decision rule, for it gives the optimal value of the control for *any* current period and *any* admissible state in the current period that may arise. In contrast, the open-loop form of the optimal control is a curve, for it gives the optimal values of the control as the independent variable time varies over the planning horizon. We will see, however, that even though the closed-loop and open-loop controls differ in form, they yield identical values for the optimal control at each date of the planning horizon.

The approach we take in this chapter is known as *dynamic programming*. The main logic used to derive the Hamilton-Jacobi-Bellman (H-J-B) equation is the *principle of optimality*. To quote Bellman (1957, page 83):

> An optimal policy has the property that whatever the initial state and initial decision are, the remaining decisions must constitute an optimal policy with regard to the state resulting from the first decision.

Recall that we've already given two different proofs of the principle of optimality, one in Theorem 4.1 and another in Theorem 9.2. As a result, there is no need to provide another one here. Now would be an appropriate time to look back at these proofs if your memory of them is a bit vague or you skipped over them, however.

The optimal control problem under consideration is given by

$$\max_{\mathbf{u}(\cdot),\mathbf{x}_T} \int_0^T f(s,\mathbf{x}(s),\mathbf{u}(s);\boldsymbol{\alpha})\,ds + \phi(\mathbf{x}(T),T)$$
$$\text{s.t.}\quad \dot{\mathbf{x}}(s) = \mathbf{g}(s,\mathbf{x}(s),\mathbf{u}(s);\boldsymbol{\alpha}),\ \ \mathbf{x}(0)=\mathbf{x}_0,\ \ \mathbf{x}(T)=\mathbf{x}_T, \tag{1}$$

where $\mathbf{u}(\cdot):\Re\to\Re^M$ is the control function, $\mathbf{x}(\cdot):\Re\to\Re^N$ is the state function, $\boldsymbol{\alpha}\in\Re^A$ is a vector of exogenous and constant parameters, $\mathbf{x}_0\in\Re^N$ is the initial state, $\phi(\cdot):\Re^{N+1}\to\Re$ is the salvage value or scrap value function, $\mathbf{g}(\cdot):\Re\times\Re^N\times\Re^M\times\Re^A\to\Re^N$ is the vector-valued transition function, $f(\cdot):\Re\times\Re^N\times\Re^M\times\Re^A\to\Re$ is the integrand function, and s is the dummy variable of integration rather than t. As we shall see, this change in the dummy variable of integration serves an important pedagogical device, for it frees us up to use t as an arbitrary initial date of the optimal control problem. Let $(\mathbf{z}(s;\boldsymbol{\alpha},\mathbf{x}_0,T), \mathbf{v}(s;\boldsymbol{\alpha},\mathbf{x}_0,T))$ be the optimal open-loop pair for problem (1), and let $\boldsymbol{\lambda}(s;\boldsymbol{\alpha},\mathbf{x}_0,T)$ be the corresponding open-loop costate vector. Note that we are now emphasizing the open-loop nature of the above solution triplet, since we intend to contrast it with its closed-loop or feedback counterpart.

Define the *optimal value function* $V(\cdot)$ as the maximum value of the objective functional that can be obtained starting at *any* time $t\in[0,T]$ and in *any* admissible state $\mathbf{x}_t$, given the parameter vector $\boldsymbol{\alpha}$. The optimal value function $V(\cdot)$ is therefore defined $\forall\, t\in[0,T]$ and for any admissible state $\mathbf{x}_t$ that may occur given the assumptions we have adopted. More formally, we have the following definition of $V(\cdot)$:

$$V(\boldsymbol{\alpha},t,\mathbf{x}_t,T) \stackrel{\text{def}}{=} \max_{\mathbf{u}(\cdot),\mathbf{x}_T} \int_t^T f(s,\mathbf{x}(s),\mathbf{u}(s);\boldsymbol{\alpha})\,ds + \phi(\mathbf{x}(T),T)$$
$$\text{s.t.}\quad \dot{\mathbf{x}}(s) = \mathbf{g}(s,\mathbf{x}(s),\mathbf{u}(s);\boldsymbol{\alpha}),\ \ \mathbf{x}(t)=\mathbf{x}_t,\ \ \mathbf{x}(T)=\mathbf{x}_T. \tag{2}$$

Note that we will often suppress the dependence of $V(\cdot)$ on T for notational clarity in problem (2). The present development should be familiar up to this point; however, now the optimal value function $V(\cdot)$ is defined as starting at any date $t\in[0,T]$ and for any admissible state $\mathbf{x}_t$, given the parameter vector $\boldsymbol{\alpha}$. Given the above optimal solution to problem (1), it should be clear that $(\mathbf{z}(s;\boldsymbol{\alpha},t,\mathbf{x}_t,T), \mathbf{v}(s;\boldsymbol{\alpha},t,\mathbf{x}_t,T))$ is the optimal open-loop pair for problem (2) and $\boldsymbol{\lambda}(s;\boldsymbol{\alpha},t,\mathbf{x}_t,T)$ is the corresponding open-loop costate vector, for the *only* difference between problems (1) and (2) is the initial time and initial state. That is, the solution functions must be the same for problems (1) and (2) in view of the fact that they are structurally identical, but the values of the solution functions will in general differ because of the difference in the initial time and initial state. You should recall, however, that if we set

$\mathbf{x}_t = \mathbf{z}(t; \boldsymbol{\alpha}, \mathbf{x}_0, T, \mathbf{x}_T)$ in problem (2), then the solutions to the optimal control problems (1) and (2) are identical on the closed interval $[t, T]$ by the principle of optimality. The initial (or starting) date t in problem (2) is often referred to as the *base period*. Notice that from the definition of $V(\cdot)$ in Eq. (2),

$$V(\boldsymbol{\alpha}, T, \mathbf{x}(T)) = \phi(\mathbf{x}(T), T). \tag{3}$$

This is a boundary condition for the H-J-B partial differential equation given in Theorem 19.1 below. Let us now turn to the development of the H-J-B equation.

Theorem 19.1(H-J-B equation): *If $V(\cdot) \in C^{(1)}$, then the first-order nonlinear partial differential equation obeyed by the optimal value function $V(\cdot)$ defined in Eq. (2) is given by*

$$-V_t(\boldsymbol{\alpha}, t, \mathbf{x}_t) = \max_{\mathbf{u}}[f(t, \mathbf{x}_t, \mathbf{u}; \boldsymbol{\alpha}) + V_{\mathbf{x}}(\boldsymbol{\alpha}, t, \mathbf{x}_t)\mathbf{g}(t, \mathbf{x}_t, \mathbf{u}; \boldsymbol{\alpha})] \tag{4}$$

in vector notation, or equivalently by

$$-V_t(\boldsymbol{\alpha}, t, \mathbf{x}_t) = \max_{\mathbf{u}} \left[f(t, \mathbf{x}_t, \mathbf{u}; \boldsymbol{\alpha}) + \sum_{n=1}^{N} V_{x_n}(\boldsymbol{\alpha}, t, \mathbf{x}_t) g^n(t, \mathbf{x}_t, \mathbf{u}; \boldsymbol{\alpha}) \right]$$

in index notation, where $t \in [0, T]$ is any base period, $\mathbf{x}_t$ is any admissible state, and $\boldsymbol{\alpha}$ is a vector of constant parameters.

Proof: For any $\Delta t > 0$ and small, Eq. (2) can be rewritten as

$$\begin{aligned} V(\boldsymbol{\alpha}, t, \mathbf{x}_t) = \max_{\substack{\mathbf{u}(\cdot),\, \mathbf{x}_T \\ s \in [t, T]}} & \left[\int_t^{t+\Delta t} f(s, \mathbf{x}(s), \mathbf{u}(s); \boldsymbol{\alpha})\, ds \right. \\ & \left. + \int_{t+\Delta t}^{T} f(s, \mathbf{x}(s), \mathbf{u}(s); \boldsymbol{\alpha})\, ds + \phi(\mathbf{x}(T), T) \right] \end{aligned} \tag{5}$$

$$\text{s.t.} \quad \dot{\mathbf{x}}(s) = \mathbf{g}(s, \mathbf{x}(s), \mathbf{u}(s); \boldsymbol{\alpha}), \;\; \mathbf{x}(t) = \mathbf{x}_t, \;\; \mathbf{x}(T) = \mathbf{x}_T.$$

In arriving at Eq. (5), notice that we have broken up the interval $[t, T]$ in Eq. (2) into the subintervals $[t, t + \Delta t]$ and $(t + \Delta t, T]$. This is a basic property of integrable functions [see, e.g., Apostol (1974), Theorem 7.4]. It is simply an assertion that the integral is additive with respect to the interval of integration. Now, by the principle of optimality, the control function $\mathbf{u}(\cdot)$, $s \in (t + \Delta t, T]$ must be optimal, that is, it must maximize the objective functional for the control problem beginning at time $s = t + \Delta t$ in the state $\mathbf{x}(t + \Delta t)$; otherwise $V(\boldsymbol{\alpha}, t, \mathbf{x}_t)$ could not be the maximum value of the objective functional as defined by Eq. (2). Note that the state at time $s = t + \Delta t$, namely, $\mathbf{x}(t + \Delta t)$, depends on the state $\mathbf{x}_t$ prevailing at time $s = t$ and on the control function chosen over the first subinterval $\mathbf{u}(\cdot)$, $s \in [t, t + \Delta t]$. By the principle of optimality, Eq. (5) can therefore be rewritten as

$$V(\boldsymbol{\alpha}, t, \mathbf{x}_t) = \max_{\substack{\mathbf{u}(\cdot) \\ s\in[t,\, t+\Delta t]}} \left[\int_t^{t+\Delta t} f(s, \mathbf{x}(s), \mathbf{u}(s); \boldsymbol{\alpha})\, ds \right.$$

$$\left. + \max_{\substack{\mathbf{u}(\cdot),\, \mathbf{x}_T \\ s\in(t+\Delta t,\, T]}} \left[\int_{t+\Delta t}^{T} f(s, \mathbf{x}(s), \mathbf{u}(s); \boldsymbol{\alpha})\, ds + \phi(\mathbf{x}(T), T) \right] \right] \tag{6}$$

$$\text{s.t.} \quad \dot{\mathbf{x}}(s) = \begin{cases} \mathbf{g}(s, \mathbf{x}(s), \mathbf{u}(s); \boldsymbol{\alpha}),\ \mathbf{x}(t) = \mathbf{x}_t, & s \in [t, t+\Delta t] \\ \mathbf{g}(s, \mathbf{x}(s), \mathbf{u}(s); \boldsymbol{\alpha}),\ \mathbf{x}(t+\Delta t) \text{ given},\ \mathbf{x}(T) = \mathbf{x}_T, & s \in (t+\Delta t, T]. \end{cases}$$

Using the definition of the optimal value function $V(\cdot)$ in Eq. (2) applied to the subinterval $(t + \Delta t, T]$ and the given value of the state vector $\mathbf{x}(t + \Delta t)$, Eq. (6) can be rewritten as

$$V(\boldsymbol{\alpha}, t, \mathbf{x}_t) = \max_{\substack{\mathbf{u}(\cdot) \\ s\in[t,\, t+\Delta t]}} \left[\int_t^{t+\Delta t} f(s, \mathbf{x}(s), \mathbf{u}(s); \boldsymbol{\alpha})\, ds + V(\boldsymbol{\alpha}, t+\Delta t, \mathbf{x}(t+\Delta t)) \right]$$

$$\text{s.t.} \quad \dot{\mathbf{x}}(s) = \mathbf{g}(s, \mathbf{x}(s), \mathbf{u}(s); \boldsymbol{\alpha}),\ \mathbf{x}(t) = \mathbf{x}_t. \tag{7}$$

Equation (7) asserts that the maximum value of the optimal control problem defined in Eq. (2), which is given by the value $V(\boldsymbol{\alpha}, t, \mathbf{x}_t)$, can be broken up into the sum of the optimal return over the initial subinterval $[t, t + \Delta t]$, plus the return by continuing optimally from the terminal position $(t + \Delta t, \mathbf{x}(t + \Delta t))$ of the first subinterval. Note that the immediate return over the initial subinterval $[t, t + \Delta t]$ and the future return over the second subinterval $(t + \Delta t, T]$ are affected by the choice of the optimal control over the initial subinterval $[t, t + \Delta t]$ because of the state equation.

Equation (7) can now be put into the more useful form asserted by the theorem. First, define the function $F(\cdot)$ by

$$F(t + \Delta t) \stackrel{\text{def}}{=} V(\boldsymbol{\alpha}, t + \Delta t, \mathbf{x}(t + \Delta t)). \tag{8}$$

Given that $V(\cdot) \in C^{(1)}$ by hypothesis, use Taylor's theorem and the chain rule to expand $F(t + \Delta t)$ about the point t to get

$$\begin{aligned} F(t + \Delta t) &= F(t) + F'(t)\Delta t + o(\Delta t) \\ &= V(\boldsymbol{\alpha}, t, \mathbf{x}(t)) + [V_t(\boldsymbol{\alpha}, t, \mathbf{x}(t)) + V_{\mathbf{x}}(\boldsymbol{\alpha}, t, \mathbf{x}(t))\dot{\mathbf{x}}(t)]\, \Delta t + o(\Delta t) \\ &= V(\boldsymbol{\alpha}, t, \mathbf{x}_t) + [V_t(\boldsymbol{\alpha}, t, \mathbf{x}_t) + V_{\mathbf{x}}(\boldsymbol{\alpha}, t, \mathbf{x}_t)\mathbf{g}(t, \mathbf{x}_t, \mathbf{u}(t); \boldsymbol{\alpha})]\, \Delta t + o(\Delta t), \end{aligned} \tag{9}$$

where $o(\Delta t)$ denotes the terms in the Taylor expansion of higher order than one, that is, the remainder, with the property that $\lim_{\Delta t \to 0} [o(\Delta t)/\Delta t] = 0$. Observe that we also used the state equation evaluated at $s = t$, namely, $\dot{\mathbf{x}}(t) = \mathbf{g}(t, \mathbf{x}(t), \mathbf{u}(t); \boldsymbol{\alpha})$, and the initial condition $\mathbf{x}(t) = \mathbf{x}_t$ of problem (2) in arriving at the final form of Eq. (9). Inspection of Eqs. (8) and (9) shows that we have established that

$$\begin{aligned} V(\alpha, t + \Delta t, \mathbf{x}(t + \Delta t)) &= V(\alpha, t, \mathbf{x}_t) \\ &+ [V_t(\alpha, t, \mathbf{x}_t) + V_{\mathbf{x}}(\alpha, t, \mathbf{x}_t)\,\mathbf{g}(t, \mathbf{x}_t, \mathbf{u}(t); \alpha)]\,\Delta t + o(\Delta t). \end{aligned} \tag{10}$$

We will return to this equation shortly.

In a similar vein, we can use Taylor's theorem to rewrite the integral on the right-hand side of Eq. (7) as follows. To this end, define the function $G(\cdot)$ by

$$G(t + \Delta t) \stackrel{\text{def}}{=} \int_t^{t+\Delta t} f(s, \mathbf{x}(s), \mathbf{u}(s); \alpha)\, ds. \tag{11}$$

Then use Taylor's theorem and Leibniz's rule to expand $G(t + \Delta t)$ about the point t to get

$$\begin{aligned} G(t + \Delta t) &= G(t) + G'(t)\Delta t + o(t) \\ &= 0 + f(t, \mathbf{x}(t), \mathbf{u}(t); \alpha)\Delta t + o(t) \\ &= 0 + f(t, \mathbf{x}_t, \mathbf{u}(t); \alpha)\Delta t + o(t), \end{aligned} \tag{12}$$

where we have again used the initial condition $\mathbf{x}(t) = \mathbf{x}_t$ of problem (2). Inspection of Eqs. (11) and (12) shows that

$$\int_t^{t+\Delta t} f(s, \mathbf{x}(s), \mathbf{u}(s); \alpha)\, ds = f(t, \mathbf{x}_t, \mathbf{u}(t); \alpha)\Delta t + o(t). \tag{13}$$

We are now in a position to simplify Eq. (7).

Substituting Eqs. (10) and (13) into Eq. (7) yields

$$\begin{aligned} V(\alpha, t, \mathbf{x}_t) = \max_{\substack{\mathbf{u}(\cdot) \\ s\in[t,\, t+\Delta t]}} & [f(t, \mathbf{x}_t, \mathbf{u}(t); \alpha)\Delta t + V(\alpha, t, \mathbf{x}_t) \\ & + [V_t(\alpha, t, \mathbf{x}_t) + V_{\mathbf{x}}(\alpha, t, \mathbf{x}_t)\mathbf{g}(t, \mathbf{x}_t, \mathbf{u}(t); \alpha)]\Delta t + o(\Delta t)] \\ \text{s.t.} \quad & \dot{\mathbf{x}}(s) = \mathbf{g}(s, \mathbf{x}(s), \mathbf{u}(s); \alpha),\ \mathbf{x}(t) = \mathbf{x}_t. \end{aligned} \tag{14}$$

By the definition of $V(\cdot)$ given in Eq. (2), $V(\cdot)$ is not a function of the control vector because it has been maximized out of problem (2). As a result, the term $V(\alpha, t, \mathbf{x}_t)$ can be canceled from both sides of Eq. (14). Furthermore, upon dividing Eq. (14) by Δt, we have that

$$\begin{aligned} 0 = \max_{\substack{\mathbf{u}(\cdot) \\ s\in[t,\, t+\Delta t]}} & \Bigg[f(t, \mathbf{x}_t, \mathbf{u}(t); \alpha) + V_t(\alpha, t, \mathbf{x}_t) \\ & + V_{\mathbf{x}}(\alpha, t, \mathbf{x}_t)\mathbf{g}(t, \mathbf{x}_t, \mathbf{u}(t); \alpha) + \frac{o(\Delta t)}{\Delta t} \Bigg] \\ \text{s.t.} \quad & \dot{\mathbf{x}}(s) = \mathbf{g}(s, \mathbf{x}(s), \mathbf{u}(s); \alpha),\ \mathbf{x}(t) = \mathbf{x}_t. \end{aligned} \tag{15}$$

Now let $\Delta t \to 0$ in Eq. (15). Recalling that $\lim_{\Delta t \to 0}[o(\Delta t)/\Delta t] = 0$ and that $V_t(\cdot)$ is not a function of the control vector, Eq. (15) therefore reduces to

$$-V_t(\boldsymbol{\alpha}, t, \mathbf{x}_t) = \max_{\mathbf{u}(t)}[f(t, \mathbf{x}_t, \mathbf{u}(t); \boldsymbol{\alpha}) + V_{\mathbf{x}}(\boldsymbol{\alpha}, t, \mathbf{x}_t)\mathbf{g}(t, \mathbf{x}_t, \mathbf{u}(t); \boldsymbol{\alpha})], \tag{16}$$

upon bringing $V_t(\boldsymbol{\alpha}, t, \mathbf{x}_t)$ to the left-hand side.

It is important to note that because we have let $\Delta t \to 0$ in Eq. (15) in arriving at Eq. (16), the maximization with respect to the *control function* in Eq. (15) reduces to choosing the *value* of the control function at a single point in time in Eq. (16). That is, we are choosing the *control function* $\mathbf{u}(\cdot)\, \forall\, s \in [t, t + \Delta t]$ in Eq. (15), which is equivalent to choosing a curve, whereas in Eq. (16), we are choosing the *value* of the control function $\mathbf{u}(\cdot)$ at the point $s = t$, which is equivalent to choosing a point on the curve. The latter observation means that in Eq. (16), we are solving a *static* maximization problem.

Finally, we can put Eq. (16) in the form of the theorem by letting $\mathbf{u}$ represent the *value* of the control function $\mathbf{u}(\cdot)$ at the point $s = t$, thereby yielding

$$-V_t(\boldsymbol{\alpha}, t, \mathbf{x}_t) = \max_{\mathbf{u}}[f(t, \mathbf{x}_t, \mathbf{u}; \boldsymbol{\alpha}) + V_{\mathbf{x}}(\boldsymbol{\alpha}, t, \mathbf{x}_t)\mathbf{g}(t, \mathbf{x}_t, \mathbf{u}; \boldsymbol{\alpha})].$$

This completes the proof. Q.E.D.

Theorem 19.1 gives the fundamental nonlinear first-order partial differential equation obeyed by the optimal value function $V(\cdot)$. In principle, one solves the *static* maximization problem on the right-hand side of Eq. (4) and expresses $\mathbf{u}$ as a function of $(\boldsymbol{\alpha}, t, \mathbf{x}_t)$ and the unknown function $V_{\mathbf{x}}(\cdot)$, say, $\mathbf{u} = \bar{\mathbf{u}}(\boldsymbol{\alpha}, t, \mathbf{x}_t, V_{\mathbf{x}}(\cdot))$. Then this solution for $\mathbf{u}$ is substituted back into the H-J-B equation to get the nonlinear first-order partial differential equation

$$-V_t = f(t, \mathbf{x}_t, \bar{\mathbf{u}}(\boldsymbol{\alpha}, t, \mathbf{x}_t, V_{\mathbf{x}}); \boldsymbol{\alpha}) + V_{\mathbf{x}}\, \mathbf{g}(t, \mathbf{x}_t, \bar{\mathbf{u}}(\boldsymbol{\alpha}, t, \mathbf{x}_t, V_{\mathbf{x}}); \boldsymbol{\alpha}),$$

which is to be solved for $V(\boldsymbol{\alpha}, t, \mathbf{x}_t, T)$ using the boundary condition given in Eq. (3). Finally, to determine the optimizing value of $\mathbf{u}$, say, $\mathbf{u}^c(\boldsymbol{\alpha}, t, \mathbf{x}_t, T)$, differentiate $V(\boldsymbol{\alpha}, t, \mathbf{x}_t, T)$ with respect to the state to get $V_{\mathbf{x}}(\boldsymbol{\alpha}, t, \mathbf{x}_t, T)$, and then substitute $V_{\mathbf{x}}(\boldsymbol{\alpha}, t, \mathbf{x}_t, T)$ into $\mathbf{u} = \bar{\mathbf{u}}(\boldsymbol{\alpha}, t, \mathbf{x}_t, V_{\mathbf{x}}(\cdot))$, that is to say, $\mathbf{u}^c(\boldsymbol{\alpha}, t, \mathbf{x}_t, T)$ is given by the identity $\mathbf{u}^c(\boldsymbol{\alpha}, t, \mathbf{x}_t, T) \equiv \bar{\mathbf{u}}(\boldsymbol{\alpha}, t, \mathbf{x}_t, V_{\mathbf{x}}(\boldsymbol{\alpha}, t, \mathbf{x}_t, T))$. Example 19.1 demonstrates how this is done for a simple control problem.

As one might surmise, the superscript c in the expression $\mathbf{u}^c(\boldsymbol{\alpha}, t, \mathbf{x}_t, T)$ is used to signify that $\mathbf{u}^c(\boldsymbol{\alpha}, t, \mathbf{x}_t, T)$ is the value of the optimal closed-loop (or feedback) control. Consequently, it is beneficial at this juncture to have a precise and formal definition of an optimal closed-loop control function. The ensuing definition provides one.

Definition 19.1: If, given an admissible initial state $\mathbf{x}_t$ in problem (2), there exists a unique optimal control path $\mathbf{v}(s; \boldsymbol{\alpha}, t, \mathbf{x}_t, T)$, $s \in [t, T]$, then the *optimal value of the closed-loop control function* is given by $\mathbf{v}(t; \boldsymbol{\alpha}, t, \mathbf{x}_t, T) \stackrel{\text{def}}{=} \mathbf{v}(s; \boldsymbol{\alpha}, t, \mathbf{x}_t, T)|_{s=t}$.

Definition 19.1 says that if the optimal open-loop control is unique, then the optimal value of the closed-loop control is found by evaluating the optimal open-loop control at the base period. It is important to observe that in the paragraph just before Definition 19.1, we asserted, but did not establish, that $\mathbf{u}^c(\alpha, t, \mathbf{x}_t, T)$, derived by solving the H-J-B equation, is in fact the optimal value of the closed-loop control as given in Definition 19.1. We will address this deficiency shortly. As you may recall, most of the examples we have encountered in this book have had a unique optimal control path; consequently, Definition 19.1 may be applied to such control problems to derive the optimal closed-loop control. We will see that this is the case in Example 19.1 as well.

Theorem 19.1 may be used to derive the necessary conditions of optimal control theory, as we will now show. First observe that the expression on the right-hand side of Eq. (4) that is to be maximized with respect to $\mathbf{u}$ looks strikingly similar to the Hamiltonian. In fact, the two expressions are identical. To see this, recall that by the dynamic envelope theorem and the principle of optimality, $\boldsymbol{\lambda}(t; \alpha) = V_{\mathbf{x}}(\alpha, t, \mathbf{x}(t))'$, since $\mathbf{x}(t) = \mathbf{x}_t$. Hence the right-hand side of Eq. (4) instructs us to maximize the Hamiltonian with respect to the control vector $\mathbf{u}$, which is precisely the Maximum Principle of Pontryagin. In passing, observe that Eq. (4) is *identical* to that part of the dynamic envelope theorem that pertains to the effect of an increase in the initial time on the optimal value function, a result you should verify by looking back at the dynamic envelope theorem.

The state equation was also used to derive Theorem 19.1 and is also part of the admissibility criteria and therefore part of the necessary conditions of optimal control theory. So that matches up exactly too.

Finally, we want to show that the ordinary differential equation for the costate variable $\boldsymbol{\lambda}(t)$ follows from Eq. (4). First recall that $\mathbf{u} = \bar{\mathbf{u}}(\alpha, t, \mathbf{x}_t, V_{\mathbf{x}})$ solves the maximization problem in Eq. (4). Next, assume that we have substituted this solution back into the H-J-B equation, that is, Eq. (4), resulting in the partial differential equation

$$-V_t = f(t, \mathbf{x}_t, \bar{\mathbf{u}}(\alpha, t, \mathbf{x}_t, V_{\mathbf{x}}); \alpha) + \sum_{n=1}^{N} V_{x_n} g^n(t, \mathbf{x}_t, \bar{\mathbf{u}}(\alpha, t, \mathbf{x}_t, V_{\mathbf{x}}); \alpha).$$

Now assume that we have solved this partial differential equation for $V(\alpha, t, \mathbf{x}_t)$ and that $V(\cdot) \in C^{(2)}$. Upon substituting $V(\alpha, t, \mathbf{x}_t)$ back into the above form of the H-J-B equation, we get the identity

$$-V_t(\alpha, t, \mathbf{x}(t)) \equiv f(t, \mathbf{x}(t), \bar{\mathbf{u}}(\alpha, t, \mathbf{x}(t), V_{\mathbf{x}}(\alpha, t, \mathbf{x}(t))); \alpha)$$
$$+ \sum_{n=1}^{N} V_{x_n}(\alpha, t, \mathbf{x}(t)) g^n(t, \mathbf{x}(t), \bar{\mathbf{u}}(\alpha, t, \mathbf{x}(t), V_{\mathbf{x}}(\alpha, t, \mathbf{x}(t))); \alpha), \tag{17}$$

since $\mathbf{x}(t) = \mathbf{x}_t$. Because Eq. (4) is a static optimization problem, we can invoke the prototype static envelope theorem and differentiate Eq. (17) with respect to x_i using the chain rule and the assumption that $V(\cdot) \in C^{(2)}$ to get

$$-V_{tx_i} = f_{x_i} + \sum_{n=1}^{N} V_{x_n} g_{x_i}^n + \sum_{n=1}^{N} g^n V_{x_i x_n}, \quad i = 1, 2, \ldots, N. \tag{18}$$

Note that we have suppressed the arguments of the functions in Eq. (18) seeing as they are easily recoverable from Eq. (17). Now because $\lambda_i(t;\boldsymbol{\alpha}) = V_{x_i}(\boldsymbol{\alpha}, t, \mathbf{x}(t))$, $i = 1, 2, \ldots, N$, it therefore follows from the chain rule that

$$\begin{aligned}\dot{\lambda}_i(t;\boldsymbol{\alpha}) &\stackrel{\text{def}}{=} \frac{d}{dt}\lambda_i(t;\boldsymbol{\alpha}) = \frac{d}{dt}V_{x_i}(\boldsymbol{\alpha}, t, \mathbf{x}(t)) = V_{x_i t} + \sum_{n=1}^{N} V_{x_i x_n}\dot{x}_n(t) \\ &= V_{x_i t} + \sum_{n=1}^{N} V_{x_i x_n} g^n, \quad i = 1, 2, \ldots, N,\end{aligned} \tag{19}$$

upon using the state equation. Solving Eq. (18) for V_{tx_i}, recalling the assumption that $V(\cdot) \in C^{(2)}$, and substituting the expression into Eq. (19) yields

$$\begin{aligned}\dot{\lambda}_i(t;\boldsymbol{\alpha}) &= -f_{x_i} - \sum_{n=1}^{N} V_{x_n} g_{x_i}^n - \sum_{n=1}^{N} g^n V_{x_i x_n} + \sum_{n=1}^{N} V_{x_i x_n} g^n \\ &= -f_{x_i} - \sum_{n=1}^{N} V_{x_n} g_{x_i}^n, \quad i = 1, 2, \ldots, N.\end{aligned}$$

Again using the fact that $\lambda_n = V_{x_n}$, $n = 1, 2, \ldots, N$, as well as the definition of the Hamiltonian $H(t, \mathbf{x}, \mathbf{u}, \boldsymbol{\lambda}; \boldsymbol{\alpha}) \stackrel{\text{def}}{=} f(t, \mathbf{x}, \mathbf{u}; \boldsymbol{\alpha}) + \sum_{n=1}^{N} \lambda_n g^n(t, \mathbf{x}, \mathbf{u}; \boldsymbol{\alpha})$, gives the costate equation

$$\dot{\lambda}_i = -f_{x_i} - \sum_{n=1}^{N} \lambda_n g_{x_i}^n = -H_{x_i}, \quad i = 1, 2, \ldots, N.$$

Thus, under the assumptions that $V(\cdot) \in C^{(2)}$, the H-J-B equation can be used to prove the necessary conditions of optimal control theory, just as we intended to demonstrate.

Before turning to an example, let's establish the aforementioned claim that $\mathbf{u}^c(\boldsymbol{\alpha}, t, \mathbf{x}_t, T)$, derived by solving the H-J-B equation, is in fact the optimal closed-loop control as defined in Definition 19.1. In order to prove this assertion, we must show that the value of the closed-loop control $\mathbf{u}^c(\boldsymbol{\alpha}, t, \mathbf{x}_t, T)$ is identical to the value of the open-loop control in the base period t for problem (2), namely, $\mathbf{v}(t;\boldsymbol{\alpha}, t, \mathbf{x}_t, T)$. First, in order to use Definition 19.1, we assume that the optimal control path $\mathbf{v}(s;\boldsymbol{\alpha}, t, \mathbf{x}_t, T)$, $s \in [t, T]$, is unique. It then follows from the unique optimality of the control path $\mathbf{v}(s;\boldsymbol{\alpha}, t, \mathbf{x}_t, T)$, $s \in [t, T]$, that $\mathbf{v}(t;\boldsymbol{\alpha}, t, \mathbf{x}_t, T)$ is the only solution to $\max_{\mathbf{u}}[f(t, \mathbf{x}_t, \mathbf{u}; \boldsymbol{\alpha}) + V_{\mathbf{x}}(\boldsymbol{\alpha}, t, \mathbf{x}_t)\mathbf{g}(t, \mathbf{x}_t, \mathbf{u}; \boldsymbol{\alpha})]$, the maximization problem on the right-hand side of the H-J-B equation in the base period t. This follows from the heretofore established fact that $f(t, \mathbf{x}_t, \mathbf{u}; \alpha) + V_{\mathbf{x}}(\alpha, t, \mathbf{x}_t)\mathbf{g}(t, \mathbf{x}_t, \mathbf{u}; \alpha)$ is nothing other than the Hamiltonian in a different guise. Moreover, because $\mathbf{u}^c(\alpha, t, \mathbf{x}_t, T)$ is also the solution to $\max_{\mathbf{u}}[f(t, \mathbf{x}_t, \mathbf{u}; \alpha) + V_{\mathbf{x}}(\alpha, t, \mathbf{x}_t)\mathbf{g}(t, \mathbf{x}_t, \mathbf{u}; \alpha)]$, as we established above, it follows from uniqueness that $\mathbf{u}^c(\alpha, t, \mathbf{x}_t, T) \equiv \mathbf{v}(t; \alpha, t, \mathbf{x}_t, T)$, which is what we wished to show. In sum, therefore, we have established if the optimal control path of problem (2) is unique, then the value of the control that maximizes the right-hand side of the H-J-B equation *is* the value of the optimal closed-loop control.

Let's now turn to a simple mathematical example to see how this all works.

Example 19.1: Consider the following purely mathematical optimal control problem:

$$V(t, x_t) \stackrel{\text{def}}{=} \min_{u(\cdot), x_T} \left[\int_t^T (u(s))^2 \, ds + (x(T))^2 \right]$$

$$\text{s.t.} \quad \dot{x}(s) = x(s) + u(s), \;\; x(t) = x_t, \;\; x(T) = x_T.$$

This problem is devoid of economic content in order to demonstrate the steps involved in solving the H-J-B equation and in constructing the optimal closed-loop control. Note that we initially suppress the dependence of $V(\cdot)$ on T so as to keep the notation relatively uncluttered.

By Theorem 19.1, the H-J-B equation is given by

$$-V_t = \min_u \left\{u^2 + V_x[x + u]\right\}.$$

Observe that we have also dropped the subscript t on the state variable because we know the base period is t from the problem statement, and for notational clarity. In view of the fact that the Hamiltonian, which as you know is the right-hand-side expression to be minimized, is a convex function of the state and control variables, a solution of the necessary conditions is a solution of the optimal control problem. Thus the necessary and sufficient condition for the above minimization problem in the H-J-B equation is given by $2u + V_x = 0$, which is easily solved to get $u = \bar{u}(V_x) \stackrel{\text{def}}{=} -\frac{1}{2}V_x$. Substituting this solution for the control variable into the H-J-B equation yields the partial differential equation to be solved for the optimal value function $V(\cdot)$, namely,

$$-V_t = xV_x - \frac{1}{4}V_x^2. \tag{20}$$

This happens to be a partial differential equation that can be solved for the unknown optimal value function $V(\cdot)$; this is why the example was chosen. To solve this partial differential equation, we propose a general functional form for $V(\cdot)$, and then seek to determine a set of parameter values for it so that the proposed function satisfies Eq. (20).

To that end, we guess that a solution to the H-J-B partial differential equation is a polynomial in x. This guess is motivated by the fact that the integrand, transition, and salvage functions of the optimal control problem under consideration are quadratic or linear functions of the state variable. For a polynomial of order k in x, the left-hand side of Eq. (20) is a polynomial of order k, whereas the right-hand side is a polynomial of order $2(k-1)$ because of the term V_x^2. In order for the left-hand and right-hand sides to be of the same order, that is, for $k = 2(k-1)$ to hold, it follows that $k = 2$. Thus we conclude that a quadratic function of x will suffice. In contrast, we leave our guess about the functional form with respect to t in general terms. Hence our guess is that the optimal value function is of the form

$$V(t, x) = A(t)x^2,$$

where $A(\cdot)$ is an unknown function of t that we wish to ascertain. Next we seek to determine if our proposed guess is in fact a solution of the H-J-B equation.

To that end, compute the first-order partial derivatives of $V(t, x) = A(t)x^2$:

$$V_t(t, x) = \dot{A}(t)x^2 \quad \text{and} \quad V_x(t, x) = 2A(t)x.$$

Substituting these derivatives into Eq. (20) gives $-\dot{A}(t)x^2 = 2A(t)x^2 - [A(t)]^2x^2$, or

$$[\dot{A}(t) + 2A(t) - [A(t)]^2]\,x^2 = 0. \tag{21}$$

Equation (21) must hold for all admissible values of x in order for $V(t, x) = A(t)x^2$ to be a solution to Eq. (20), which is true if and only if the function $A(\cdot)$ is a solution to the nonlinear ordinary differential equation $\dot{A}(t) + 2A(t) = [A(t)]^2$. This looks to be a formidable differential equation to solve explicitly, since it is nonlinear. Recall that we want an explicit solution of the differential equation $\dot{A}(t) + 2A(t) = [A(t)]^2$ because we want an explicit expression for the optimal value function and the feedback solution for the control variable.

As you may recall from an elementary differential equation course, $\dot{A}(t) + 2A(t) = [A(t)]^2$ is a Bernoulli differential equation with $n = 2$. A standard solution procedure for this class of differential equations begins by defining a new variable $y \overset{\text{def}}{=} A^{1-n} = A^{-1}$, which implies that $\dot{y} = -A^{-2}\dot{A}$. Multiplying the Bernoulli equation through by $-A^{-2}$ gives $-A^{-2}\dot{A} - 2A^{-1} = -1$. This latter form of the differential equation can be rewritten in terms of the variable y as

$$\dot{y} - 2y = -1, \tag{22}$$

which is a linear first-order constant coefficient ordinary differential equation whose integrating factor is $\exp[2t]$. The general solution of Eq. (22) is thus

$$y(t) = \frac{1}{2} + ce^{2t}, \tag{23}$$

where c is a constant of integration. Recall that the boundary condition for the H-J-B equation (20) is given by $V(T, x_T) = x_T^2$. Because we've assumed that

$V(t, x) = A(t)x^2$, this implies that the boundary condition takes the simple form $A(T) = 1$. But seeing as $y \stackrel{\text{def}}{=} A^{1-n} = A^{-1}$, this translates into the boundary condition $y(T) = 1$ for Eq. (23). Using this boundary condition implies that $c = \frac{1}{2}e^{-2T}$. Hence the specific solution of Eq. (22) takes the form $y(t) = \frac{1}{2}[1 + e^{2(t-T)}]$, which in turn implies the specific solution

$$A(t) = \frac{2}{1 + e^{2(t-T)}} \tag{24}$$

for the unknown function $A(\cdot)$. Note that it satisfies the boundary condition $A(T) = 1$.

With the function $A(\cdot)$ given by Eq. (24), we now have the information to construct the optimal value function $V(\cdot)$. Because we guessed that $V(t, x) = A(t)x^2$, Eq. (24) implies that the optimal value function is of the form

$$V(t, x, T) = \frac{2x^2}{1 + e^{2(t-T)}}. \tag{25}$$

Note that we have now included T as an argument of $V(\cdot)$. Given that $A(T) = 1$, it follows that $V(T, x, T) = A(T)x^2 = x^2$; hence the boundary condition is satisfied. We leave it as a mental exercise to verify that Eq. (25) satisfies the H-J-B equation (20).

Turning to the *feedback* or *closed-loop* form of the solution for the control variable, we see that because $u = \bar{u}(V_x) \stackrel{\text{def}}{=} -\frac{1}{2}V_x$, use of Eq. (25) gives

$$u = u^c(t, x, T) \stackrel{\text{def}}{=} \frac{-2x}{1 + e^{2(t-T)}}. \tag{26}$$

Recall that the adjectives *feedback* and *closed-loop* refer to the fact that the optimal control in Eq. (26) is expressed as a function of the base period t, the value of the state variable in the base period, and the parameter T. This contrasts with the open-loop form of an optimal control that we derived in all the previous chapters dealing with optimal control theory. You should also recall that the open-loop form of the optimal control is typically expressed as a function of the independent variable time (denoted by s in the present chapter), the parameters of the problem, and the initial and/or terminal values of the planning horizon and state variables, the latter two sets of variables depending on whether they are decision variables or parametrically given.

To find the corresponding open-loop solution for the control variable, one could substitute the closed-loop solution for the control from Eq. (26) into the state equation $\dot{x} = x + u$ to get the ordinary differential equation $\dot{x} = x - [2x/(1 + e^{2(t-T)})]$. Rather than attempt to solve this differential equation, we leave it as a mental exercise to show that

$$u = u^o(s; t, x_t, T) \stackrel{\text{def}}{=} \frac{-2x_t e^{(T-t)} e^{(T-s)}}{1 + e^{2(T-t)}}, \tag{27}$$

$$\lambda = \lambda^o(s; t, x_t, T) \stackrel{\text{def}}{=} \frac{4x_t e^{(T-t)} e^{(T-s)}}{1 + e^{2(T-t)}}, \tag{28}$$

$$x = x^o(s; t, x_t, T) \stackrel{\text{def}}{=} \left[\frac{x_t e^{(T-t)}}{1 + e^{2(T-t)}}\right] [e^{(T-s)} - e^{(T+s-2t)}] + x_t e^{(s-t)}, \tag{29}$$

$$x_T = x_T^o(t, x_t, T) \stackrel{\text{def}}{=} \frac{2x_t e^{(T-t)}}{1 + e^{2(T-t)}} \tag{30}$$

is the unique optimal open-loop solution to the control problem. It is obtained using the appropriate necessary conditions of optimal control theory.

Prior to this example, we proved that if the optimal control path is unique, then the value of the control that maximizes the right-hand side of the H-J-B equation is the value of the optimal closed-loop control. That is, we have the following identity linking the value of the open-loop and closed-loop solutions for the control variable:

$$u^o(t; t, x_t, T) \equiv u^c(t, x_t, T).$$

This identity is straightforward to verify using the explicit formulas for the open-loop and closed-loop forms of the control variable given in Eqs. (30) and (26), respectively. It asserts that the value of the open-loop control in the base period, that is, the value of the closed-loop control, is identically equal to the value of the control that solves the H-J-B equation. This is as it should be, because the limiting process used to establish the H-J-B equation shows that it applies to any base period of the underlying optimal control problem.

Another noteworthy observation, akin to that just mentioned, is that when the open-loop costate is evaluated at the base period $s = t$, then its value is identical to that of the closed-loop costate. In symbols, we are asserting that

$$\lambda^o(t; t, x_t, T) \equiv V_x(t, x_t, T).$$

You are asked to verify the above two identities in a mental exercise. These identities turn out to be important results in a general sense because they help solidify one's understanding of the relationship between the open-loop and closed-loop forms of the solution. As a result, we will return to them, as well as related ones, at a later point in the chapter, when we study another class of optimal control problems.

Most economic applications of optimal control theory involve discounting, an infinite planning horizon, and functions $f(\cdot)$ and $\mathbf{g}(\cdot)$ that do not depend explicitly on time, the independent variable, as we have noted in several earlier chapters. With this mathematical structure, the H-J-B equation reduces to a simpler form, namely, an ordinary differential equation. This simplification is of great value for the dynamic duality theory to be expounded upon in the next chapter. Let us therefore proceed to establish this and other, related results.

In light of the aforementioned remarks, let us now consider the following class of discounted autonomous infinite-horizon optimal control problems:

$$\max_{\mathbf{u}(\cdot)} \int_{0}^{+\infty} f(\mathbf{x}(s), \mathbf{u}(s); \boldsymbol{\alpha})\, e^{-rs}\, ds$$
$$\text{s.t.} \quad \dot{\mathbf{x}}(s) = \mathbf{g}(\mathbf{x}(s), \mathbf{u}(s); \boldsymbol{\alpha}),\ \mathbf{x}(0) = \mathbf{x}_0, \tag{31}$$

where $r > 0$ is the discount rate. Note that we have not placed any condition on the limiting value of the state variables, that is, no conditions are placed on $\lim_{t\to+\infty} \mathbf{x}(t)$. For any initial time or base period $t \in [0, +\infty)$, and any admissible value of the state vector in the base period $\mathbf{x}(t) = \mathbf{x}_t$, define the *present value optimal value function* $V^{pv}(\cdot)$ by

$$V^{pv}(\boldsymbol{\alpha}, r, t, \mathbf{x}_t) \stackrel{\text{def}}{=} \max_{\mathbf{u}(\cdot)} \int_{t}^{+\infty} f(\mathbf{x}(s), \mathbf{u}(s); \boldsymbol{\alpha})\, e^{-rs}\, ds$$
$$\text{s.t.} \quad \dot{\mathbf{x}}(s) = \mathbf{g}(\mathbf{x}(s), \mathbf{u}(s); \boldsymbol{\alpha}),\ \mathbf{x}(t) = \mathbf{x}_t. \tag{32}$$

Thus, $V^{pv}(\boldsymbol{\alpha}, r, t, \mathbf{x}_t)$ is the maximum present value of the optimal control problem (31) that begins in the admissible state $\mathbf{x}(t) = \mathbf{x}_t$ in any base period $t \in [0, +\infty)$, given the parameter vector $(\boldsymbol{\alpha}, r)$. The adjective *present value* is required because the values of the integrand function are discounted back to time zero rather than the base period t in Eq. (32), and it is the base period t that is the current period from which planning begins. To see this, simply evaluate the integrand at time $s = t$ and observe that the value of $f(\cdot)$ is multiplied by e^{-rt}, thereby implying it is discounted back to time zero rather than the base period t. Consequently, if we take the base period to be time zero, that is, we set $t = 0$ in Eq. (32), then the values of the integrand are discounted to the base period $t = 0$, which is the same as the current period in this case. This means that if we set $t = 0$ in Eq. (32), then $V^{pv}(\cdot)$ is equal to the current value optimal value function.

Now multiply Eq. (32) by the identity $e^{-rt}e^{rt} \equiv 1$, and note that this term is independent of the dummy variable of integration s. This yields an alternative but equivalent expression for the present value optimal value function, videlicet,

$$V^{pv}(\boldsymbol{\alpha}, r, t, \mathbf{x}_t) \stackrel{\text{def}}{=} e^{-rt} \max_{\mathbf{u}(\cdot)} \int_{t}^{+\infty} f(\mathbf{x}(s), \mathbf{u}(s); \boldsymbol{\alpha})\, e^{-r(s-t)}\, ds$$
$$\text{s.t.} \quad \dot{\mathbf{x}}(s) = \mathbf{g}(\mathbf{x}(s), \mathbf{u}(s); \boldsymbol{\alpha}),\ \mathbf{x}(t) = \mathbf{x}_t. \tag{33}$$

This is an equation we will make use of below. Given Eq. (33), the *current value optimal value function* $V^{cv}(\cdot)$ can be defined by

$$V^{cv}(\alpha, r, t, \mathbf{x}_t) \stackrel{\text{def}}{=} \max_{\mathbf{u}(\cdot)} \int_t^{+\infty} f(\mathbf{x}(s), \mathbf{u}(s); \alpha)\, e^{-r(s-t)}\, ds$$

$$\text{s.t.} \quad \dot{\mathbf{x}}(s) = \mathbf{g}(\mathbf{x}(s), \mathbf{u}(s); \alpha),\ \mathbf{x}(t) = \mathbf{x}_t. \tag{34}$$

Consequently, $V^{cv}(\alpha, r, t, \mathbf{x}_t)$ is the maximum current value of the optimal control problem (31) that begins in the admissible state $\mathbf{x}(t) = \mathbf{x}_t$ in any base period $t \in [0, +\infty)$, given the parameter vector (α, r).

By examining Eqs. (33) and (34) carefully, it should be apparent that the following relationship holds between the present value and current value optimal value functions for infinite-horizon current value autonomous optimal control problems:

$$V^{pv}(\alpha, r, t, \mathbf{x}_t) \equiv e^{-rt} V^{cv}(\alpha, r, t, \mathbf{x}_t)\, \forall\, t \in [0, +\infty). \tag{35}$$

This says that the present value optimal value function has the same value as the current value optimal value function once we discount the latter's value back to time $s = 0$ of the control problem, which is a quite intuitive and natural result. The most important feature of the current value optimal value function $V^{cv}(\cdot)$ is that it is independent of the initial date or base period t, one of several properties presented in the ensuing theorem.

Theorem 19.2: *The ensuing properties hold for the present value optimal value function $V^{pv}(\cdot)$ and the current value optimal value function $V^{cv}(\cdot)$ for the class of discounted autonomous infinite-horizon optimal control problems defined in Eq. (31):*

(a) $V^{cv}(\alpha, r, t, \mathbf{x}_t) \equiv V^{cv}(\alpha, r, 0, \mathbf{x}_t)\, \forall\, t \in [0, +\infty)$,
(b) $V^{pv}(\alpha, r, 0, \mathbf{x}_t) \equiv V^{cv}(\alpha, r, 0, \mathbf{x}_t)$, and
(c) $V^{pv}(\alpha, r, t, \mathbf{x}_t) \equiv e^{-rt} V^{pv}(\alpha, r, 0, \mathbf{x}_t)\, \forall\, t \in [0, +\infty)$.

Proof: We begin by proving part (a). First, use Eq. (34), the equation defining the current value optimal value function $V^{cv}(\cdot)$, to write down the definition of $V^{cv}(\alpha, r, 0, \mathbf{x}_t)$:

$$V^{cv}(\alpha, r, 0, \mathbf{x}_t) \stackrel{\text{def}}{=} \max_{\mathbf{u}(\cdot)} \int_0^{+\infty} f(\mathbf{x}(s), \mathbf{u}(s); \alpha)\, e^{-rs}\, ds$$

$$\text{s.t.} \quad \dot{\mathbf{x}}(s) = \mathbf{g}(\mathbf{x}(s), \mathbf{u}(s); \alpha),\ \mathbf{x}(s)|_{s=0} = \mathbf{x}_t. \tag{36}$$

Second, employ Eq. (36) to write down the definition of $V^{cv}(\alpha, r, t, \mathbf{x}_t)$. We want to be extra careful in writing down the definition of $V^{cv}(\alpha, r, t, \mathbf{x}_t)$ by keeping in mind what we intend to prove, scilicet, $V^{cv}(\alpha, r, t, \mathbf{x}_t) \equiv V^{cv}(\alpha, r, 0, \mathbf{x}_t)\,\forall\, t \in [0, +\infty)$. Thus, in writing down the definition of $V^{cv}(\alpha, r, t, \mathbf{x}_t)$, we want only the third argument of it to be different from that in $V^{cv}(\alpha, r, 0, \mathbf{x}_t)$. To accomplish this, when we advance the base period from zero to t in Eq. (36), we at the same time subtract t from the dummy variable of integration s wherever it appears in the state and control functions. Doing just that gives

$$V^{cv}(\alpha, r, t, \mathbf{x}_t) \stackrel{\text{def}}{=} \max_{\mathbf{u}(\cdot)} \int_t^{+\infty} f(\mathbf{x}(s-t), \mathbf{u}(s-t); \alpha)\, e^{-r(s-t)}\, ds$$
$$\text{s.t.} \quad \dot{\mathbf{x}}(s-t) = \mathbf{g}(\mathbf{x}(s-t), \mathbf{u}(s-t); \alpha),\ \mathbf{x}(s-t)|_{s=t} = \mathbf{x}_t,$$

which holds for any $t \in [0, +\infty)$. Now let's change the dummy variable of integration from s to $\tau \stackrel{\text{def}}{=} s - t$, which implies that $d\tau = ds$. Moreover, this change of variables also implies that if $s = t$, then $\tau = 0$, whereas if $s \to +\infty$, then $\tau \to +\infty$. Using these results allows us to rewrite the previous definition of $V^{cv}(\alpha, r, t, \mathbf{x}_t)$ equivalently as

$$V^{cv}(\alpha, r, t, \mathbf{x}_t) \stackrel{\text{def}}{=} \max_{\mathbf{u}(\cdot)} \int_0^{+\infty} f(\mathbf{x}(\tau), \mathbf{u}(\tau); \alpha) e^{-r\tau}\, d\tau$$
$$\text{s.t.} \quad \dot{\mathbf{x}}(\tau) = \mathbf{g}(\mathbf{x}(\tau), \mathbf{u}(\tau); \alpha),\ \mathbf{x}(\tau)|_{\tau=0} = \mathbf{x}_t. \tag{37}$$

Now observe that the right-hand side of Eq. (37) is identical to the right-hand side of Eq. (36), since they differ only with respect to their dummy variables of integration, which is immaterial. Hence the left-hand sides of Eqs. (36) and (37) are identical too, that is,

$$V^{cv}(\alpha, r, t, \mathbf{x}_t) \equiv V^{cv}(\alpha, r, 0, \mathbf{x}_t)\,\forall\, t \in [0, +\infty),$$

which is what we set out to prove.

To prove part (b), that is, $V^{pv}(\alpha, r, 0, \mathbf{x}_t) \equiv V^{cv}(\alpha, r, 0, \mathbf{x}_t)$, simply set $t = 0$ in the definitions in Eqs. (33) and (34) and note that identical expressions result. This result also follows immediately by evaluating Eq. (35) at $t = 0$.

To prove part (c), namely, $V^{pv}(\alpha, r, t, \mathbf{x}_t) \equiv e^{-rt} V^{pv}(\alpha, r, 0, \mathbf{x}_t)\,\forall\, t \in [0, +\infty)$, note that by parts (a) and (b), $V^{cv}(\alpha, r, t, \mathbf{x}_t) \equiv V^{pv}(\alpha, r, 0, \mathbf{x}_t)\,\forall\, t \in [0, +\infty)$. Substituting this result into Eq. (35) then produces the desired result. Q.E.D.

Part (a) of Theorem 19.2, scilicet, $V^{cv}(\alpha, r, t, \mathbf{x}_t) \equiv V^{cv}(\alpha, r, 0, \mathbf{x}_t) \forall\, t \in [0, +\infty)$, asserts that for a given value of the state variable in the base period

$\mathbf{x}_t$, a given vector of parameters $\boldsymbol{\alpha}$, and a given discount rate r, the base period has no effect on the value of the current value optimal value function in discounted autonomous infinite-horizon optimal control problems. This is intuitive in that no matter when you start in the future, you still have an infinite amount of time left in the optimal control problem (31). Thus the only things that determine the value of $V^{cv}(\cdot)$ are the parameter vector $\boldsymbol{\alpha}$, the discount rate r, and the value of state variable $\mathbf{x}_t$ in the base period. As a result of this part of Theorem 19.2, we are permitted to write the value of the current value optimal value function $V^{cv}(\cdot)$ as $V^{cv}(\boldsymbol{\alpha}, r, \mathbf{x}_t)$, in which we completely suppress the appearance of the base period. We will adopt this simplified notation for $V^{cv}(\cdot)$ from this point forward when discussing such a class of control problems. Finally, it is worthwhile to recognize that an *equivalent* way to write part (a) is $\partial V^{cv}(\boldsymbol{\alpha}, r, \mathbf{x}_t)/\partial t \equiv 0$, since this says that $V^{cv}(\cdot)$ is independent of the base period t.

Part (b) of Theorem 19.2, which we may now write as $V^{pv}(\boldsymbol{\alpha}, r, 0, \mathbf{x}_t) \equiv V^{cv}(\boldsymbol{\alpha}, r, \mathbf{x}_t)$ in light of the notational convention adopted in the previous paragraph, asserts that the present value and current value optimal value functions have identical values if we take as the base period the first instant of the planning horizon $t = 0$. Recall that we made a remark to this effect after Eq. (32). This result is also intuitive, for if the date we are discounting to is the current date we are starting our planning from, then there is no difference between the present value and current value of our optimal plan. In passing, note that because part (c) of Theorem 19.2 is equivalent to Eq. (35), as the proof revealed, there is no need to provide an economic interpretation of it here, for that was done when Eq. (35) was introduced.

Before establishing that the H-J-B equation of Theorem 19.1 reduces to an ordinary differential equation for the class of discounted autonomous infinite-horizon optimal control problems defined by Eq. (31), let's pause and demonstrate the results of Theorem 19.2 with an nonrenewable resource–extraction model. We leave some of the more tedious calculations for a mental exercise so as to emphasize the content of Theorem 19.2.

Example 19.2: Consider the following discounted autonomous infinite-horizon model of a nonrenewable resource–extracting firm:

$$V^{pv}(\alpha, r, t, x_t) \overset{\text{def}}{=} \max_{q(\cdot)} \left\{ \int_t^{+\infty} [\alpha \ln q(s)]\, e^{-rs}\, ds \right\}$$

$$\text{s.t.} \quad \dot{x}(s) = -q(s),\, x(t) = x_t, \quad \lim_{s\to+\infty} x(s) = 0.$$

By this point in the text, the economic interpretation of this model should be completely clear: $x(s)$ is the stock of the nonrenewable resource in the ground at time s, $q(s)$ is the extraction rate of the nonrenewable resource at time s, and the instantaneous profit from extracting at the rate $q(s)$ is $\alpha \ln q(s)$, where $\alpha > 0$ is a parameter of the profit function. Two features of some significance in this model are (i) the infinite planning horizon, and (ii) the limiting terminal condition on the resource stock. The latter requires that the resource stock be exhausted only in the limit of the planning horizon.

In order to solve this optimal control problem, we begin, as usual, by writing down the current value Hamiltonian, scilicet, $H(x, q, \lambda; \alpha) \stackrel{\text{def}}{=} \alpha \ln q - \lambda q$. At this point in the book, you shouldn't have any problem deriving the solution to the control problem, so that will be left for a mental exercise. Consequently, we simply state the solution here for future reference:

$$q^o(s-t; r, x_t) = r x_t e^{-r(s-t)},$$

$$x^o(s-t; r, x_t) = x_t e^{-r(s-t)},$$

$$\lambda(s-t; \alpha, r, x_t) = \alpha r^{-1} x_t^{-1} e^{r(s-t)}.$$

Before we delve into verifying Theorem 19.2, let's pause to make two remarks. First, notice that the independent variable s and the base period t always enter the solution in the form $s-t$, and we have indicated this in the notation. This was to be expected if you followed the proof of Theorem 19.2 carefully. Second, the above solution is the open-loop form, since it was derived using the methods of optimal control theory.

To find the present value optimal value function, substitute the optimal path of the control variable into the objective functional and integrate by substitution and by parts to get

$$V^{pv}(\alpha, r, t, x_t) = \frac{\alpha}{r}[\ln r x_t - 1]e^{-rt}.$$

You will be asked to verify this in a mental exercise. Given that $V^{pv}(\alpha, r, 0, x_t) = \frac{\alpha}{r}[\ln r x_t - 1]$, it is immediate that $V^{pv}(\alpha, r, t, x_t) \equiv e^{-rt} V^{pv}(\alpha, r, 0, x_t) \forall t \in [0, +\infty)$, which is part (c) of Theorem 19.2. Moreover, because the current value optimal value function is, by definition, e^{rt} times the present value optimal value function, we have that $V^{cv}(\alpha, r, x_t) = \frac{\alpha}{r}[\ln r x_t - 1] = V^{pv}(\alpha, r, 0, x_t)$, which is part (b) of Theorem 19.2. Moreover, because $V^{cv}(\alpha, r, x_t) = \frac{\alpha}{r}[\ln r x_t - 1]$ is independent of the base period t, this verifies part (a) of Theorem 19.2.

Let's return to the basic identity linking the present value and current value optimal value functions, either Eq. (35) or a combination of parts (b) and (c) of Theorem 19.2, namely,

$$V^{pv}(\boldsymbol{\alpha}, r, t, \mathbf{x}) \equiv e^{-rt} V^{cv}(\boldsymbol{\alpha}, r, \mathbf{x}) \forall t \in [0, +\infty), \tag{38}$$

for the class of problems under consideration, that is, the discounted autonomous infinite-horizon variety defined by Eq. (31). Note that we have dropped the subscript on the initial value of the state variable since by now the base period is clear. Partially differentiating identity (38) with respect to the initial date and the corresponding state gives

$$V_t^{pv}(\alpha, r, t, \mathbf{x}) \equiv -re^{-rt}V^{cv}(\alpha, r, \mathbf{x})\,\forall\, t \in [0, +\infty), \tag{39}$$

$$V_{x_n}^{pv}(\alpha, r, t, \mathbf{x}) \equiv e^{-rt}V_{x_n}^{cv}(\alpha, r, \mathbf{x})\,\forall\, t \in [0, +\infty], \quad n = 1, 2, \ldots, N. \tag{40}$$

For the current value autonomous infinite-horizon class of control problems given by Eq. (31), the H-J-B equation given by Theorem 19.1 takes the form

$$-V_t^{pv}(\alpha, r, t, \mathbf{x}) = \max_{\mathbf{u}}\left[f(\mathbf{x}, \mathbf{u}; \alpha)e^{-rt} + \sum_{n=1}^{N} V_{x_n}^{pv}(\alpha, r, t, \mathbf{x})g^n(\mathbf{x}, \mathbf{u}; \alpha)\right]. \tag{41}$$

Substituting Eqs. (39) and (40) into the H-J-B equation (41), and then multiplying through by e^{rt} yields

$$rV^{cv}(\alpha, r, \mathbf{x}) = \max_{\mathbf{u}}\left[f(\mathbf{x}, \mathbf{u}; \alpha) + \sum_{n=1}^{N} V_{x_n}^{cv}(\alpha, r, \mathbf{x})g^n(\mathbf{x}, \mathbf{u}; \alpha)\right], \tag{42}$$

which is an ordinary differential equation obeyed by the current value optimal value function. It is important to remember that this result holds only for the current value optimal value function for current value autonomous, infinite-horizon optimal control problems defined by Eq. (31). In other words, if the independent variable s appears explicitly in the integrand function $f(\cdot)$ or vector-valued transition function $\mathbf{g}(\cdot)$, or if the time horizon is finite, then Eq. (42) does not hold. This is a very important result because of the ubiquitous nature of current value autonomous infinite horizon optimal control problems in intertemporal economic theory. We therefore record this result in the ensuing theorem.

Theorem 19.3: *If $V^{cv}(\cdot) \in C^{(1)}$, then the current value optimal value function for the class of discounted autonomous infinite-horizon optimal control problems defined by Eq. (31) obeys the ordinary differential equation*

$$rV^{cv}(\alpha, r, \mathbf{x}_t) = \max_{\mathbf{u}}\left[f(\mathbf{x}_t, \mathbf{u}; \alpha) + \sum_{n=1}^{N} V_{x_n}^{cv}(\alpha, r, \mathbf{x}_t)g^n(\mathbf{x}_t, \mathbf{u}; \alpha)\right]$$

in index notation, or equivalently

$$rV^{cv}(\alpha, r, \mathbf{x}_t) = \max_{\mathbf{u}}\left[f(\mathbf{x}_t, \mathbf{u}; \alpha) + V_{\mathbf{x}}^{cv}(\alpha, r, \mathbf{x}_t)\mathbf{g}(\mathbf{x}_t, \mathbf{u}; \alpha)\right]$$

in vector notation. This holds for any base period $t \in [0, +\infty)$ and any state $\mathbf{x}_t$ that is admissible.

Let's further examine Example 19.2 in light of Theorem 19.3.

Example 19.3: Recall that we derived an explicit expression for the current value optimal value function in Example 19.2, to wit, $V^{cv}(\alpha, r, x_t) = \frac{\alpha}{r}[\ln rx_t - 1]$. The current value shadow price of the stock is therefore found by partially differentiating $V^{cv}(\alpha, r, x_t) = \frac{\alpha}{r}[\ln rx_t - 1]$ with respect to the stock, thereby yielding $V^{cv}_{x_t}(\alpha, r, x_t) = \frac{\alpha}{rx_t}$. Having an explicit expression for the current value shadow price of the stock means that in this example at least, we can derive an explicit expression for the right-hand side of the H-J-B equation given in Theorem 19.3. This, in turn, allows us to derive an explicit expression for the value of the control that maximizes the right-hand side of the H-J-B equation, which we now know to be the closed-loop form of the optimal extraction rate.

To this end, Theorem 19.3 directs us to solve the static maximization problem

$$rV^{cv}(\alpha, r, x_t) = \max_q \left\{\alpha \ln q - V^{cv}_{x_t}(\alpha, r, x_t)q\right\} = \max_q \left\{\alpha \ln q - \frac{\alpha}{rx_t}q\right\}$$

in order to find the optimal control. Given that the function to be maximized is strictly concave in q, the first-order necessary condition $\frac{\alpha}{q} - \frac{\alpha}{rx_t} = 0$ is also sufficient for determining the unique global maximum of the problem. Solving $\frac{\alpha}{q} - \frac{\alpha}{rx_t} = 0$ gives the optimal control $q^c(r, x_t) = rx_t$. Substituting $q^c(r, x_t) = rx_t$ back into the H-J-B equation above gives

$$rV^{cv}(\alpha, r, x_t) = \alpha \ln q^c(r, x_t) - \frac{\alpha}{rx_t}q^c(r, x_t) = \alpha[\ln rx_t - 1],$$

from which it follows that $V^{cv}(\alpha, r, x_t) = \frac{\alpha}{r}[\ln rx_t - 1]$, as expected.

In comparing the optimal extraction rate derived by way of the H-J-B equation, to wit, $q^c(r, x_t) = rx_t$, with the open-loop form of the optimal extraction rate given in Example 19.2 and derived via the necessary conditions of optimal control theory, scilicet, $q^o(s - t; r, x_t) = rx_t e^{-r(s-t)}$, two important relationships between the solutions emerge. First, the values of the two forms of the extraction rates are identical when one substitutes the open-loop solution of the resource stock $x^o(s - t; r, x_t) = x_t e^{-r(s-t)}$ for the base period stock x_t in the optimal extraction rate derived by way of the H-J-B equation, as is easily verified:

$$q^c(r, x^o(s - t; r, x_t)) = rx^o(s - t; r, x_t) = rx_t e^{-r(s-t)} = q^o(s - t; r, x_t). \quad (43)$$

This is as it should be, since (i) the planning horizon is infinite, thereby implying that no matter what date one takes as the base period, there is always an infinite amount of time left in the planning horizon, and (ii) the integrand function $f(\cdot)$ and the transition function $g(\cdot)$ do not depend explicitly on the independent time variable s (though $f(\cdot)$ is multiplied by the discount factor e^{-rs}). If either one of these conditions does not hold, then the relationship between the two solutions given in Eq. (43) will not, in general, hold either. A mental exercise asks you to verify this by using the two forms of the solution for the control variable of the autonomous finite-horizon control problem in Example 19.1.

One way to better understand Eq. (43) is as follows. Because the optimal control $q^c(r, x_t) = rx_t$ depends only on the value of the state variable in the base period and the discount rate, the base period has no effect on it. This is a result of properties

(i) and (ii) noted in the previous paragraph. Consequently, no matter what base period one adopts, when the base period stock is set equal to the value of the stock that corresponds to the optimal open-loop extraction rate, the optimal extraction rate determined by way of the H-J-B equation must be the same as the value of the extraction rate determined by the open-loop control at the date in the planning horizon that corresponds to the value of the resource stock used in the calculation. Another way to understand Eq. (43) is to observe that because all the parameters are known with certainty in any base period, one can either solve for the entire time path of the extraction rate in the base period and thus derive the open-loop solution or, equivalently, solve for the optimal control by repeatedly solving the H-J-B equation by varying the base period continuously over the interval $[0, +\infty)$, taking the base period stock of each static optimization problem to be the value determined by the preceding optimal extraction rate. Either way, one would have determined the identical optimal extraction rate over the planning horizon.

In passing, it should not be too surprising that the analogue to Eq. (43) holds between the open-loop $\lambda(s-t;\alpha,r,x_t)$ and current value shadow price of the stock derived by way of the H-J-B equation, namely, $V_{x_t}^{cv}(\alpha,r,x_t)$, that is to say,

$$V_{x_t}^{cv}(\alpha,r,x^o(s-t;r,x_t)) = \frac{\alpha}{rx^o(s-t;r,x_t)} = \frac{\alpha}{rx_t e^{-r(s-t)}}$$
$$= \alpha r^{-1} x_t^{-1} e^{r(s-t)} = \lambda(s-t;\alpha,r,x_t),$$

and for exactly the same reason.

The second important relationship between the closed-loop and open-loop extraction rates was noted in Example 9.1, and can similarly be determined from inspection of the two forms of the solutions, namely, $q^c(r,x_t) = rx_t$ and $q^o(s-t;r,x_t) = rx_t e^{-r(s-t)}$. In particular, evaluating the open-loop extraction rate at the base period $s=t$ yields the extraction rate determined via the H-J-B equation, that is,

$$q^o(s-t;r,x_t)\big|_{s=t} = rx_t e^{-r(s-t)}\big|_{s=t} = rx_t = q^c(r,x_t), \tag{44}$$

with the same property holding for the current value shadow price of the stock:

$$\lambda(s-t;\alpha,r,x_t)|_{s=t} = \alpha r^{-1} x_t^{-1} e^{r(s-t)}\big|_{s=t} = \frac{\alpha}{rx_t} = V_{x_t}^{cv}(\alpha,r,x_t).$$

This relationship between the two forms of the solution means that we can, in principle, avoid solving the H-J-B equation to determine the closed-loop solution. This is of limited practical value, however, for as you know, it is a formidable task to solve for the open-loop solution of a control problem for all but the most simple, and often economically uninteresting, functional forms of the integrand and transition functions. In any case, Definition 19.1 shows that one can derive the closed-loop solution by employing the necessary and sufficient conditions of optimal control theory to find the open-loop solution, and then simply evaluate the open-loop solution at the base period to arrive at the closed-loop form of the solution.

We will make use of this fact in the next chapter, when we study the qualitative and intertemporal duality properties of the adjustment cost model of the firm.

The final observation in this example concerns the closed-loop form of the optimal extraction rate. In view of the fact that $q^c(r, x_t) = rx_t$, the optimal extraction rate in the base period is expressed solely in terms of the state variable in the base period and the parameters of the problem, which in this example is the discount rate. The important observation is that the base period is not an argument of the closed-loop form of the optimal extraction rate. This feature is typical of *all* discounted autonomous infinite-horizon optimal control problems, that is, control problems of the form given by Eq. (31), as we shall shortly see. Note, however, that this property does not hold in general for autonomous finite-horizon optimal control problems, as is readily seen from the closed-loop control of Example 19.1 given in Eq. (26), namely, $u = u^c(t, x, T) \stackrel{\text{def}}{=} -2x/1 + e^{2(t-T)}$. Observe that the solution depends explicitly on the base period t.

The stationary property noted in Example 19.3, scilicet, that the closed-loop form of the optimal control is independent of the base period, is a result of the fact that the optimal value function is independent of the base period for the class of discounted autonomous infinite-horizon optimal control problems. This observation is the key to proving the following general result, the details of which we leave as a mental exercise.

Theorem 19.4: *For the class of discounted autonomous infinite-horizon optimal control problems defined by Eq. (31), the optimal values of the closed-loop control vector and the current value costate vector are a function of the value of the state variable in the base period* $\mathbf{x}_t$*, the discount rate* r*, and the parameter vector* $\boldsymbol{\alpha}$*, but not the base period* t*, that is to say,* $\mathbf{u} = \mathbf{u}^c(\boldsymbol{\alpha}, r, \mathbf{x}_t)$ *and* $\boldsymbol{\lambda} = \boldsymbol{\lambda}^c(\boldsymbol{\alpha}, r, \mathbf{x}_t)$.

Theorem 19.4 asserts that the closed-loop solution of the control vector and the current value costate vector do not vary with the base period, ceteris paribus. This is not really surprising upon reflection, since (i) no matter when one begins planning in a discounted autonomous infinite-horizon control problem, that is, no matter what base period is adopted, there is still an infinite amount of time left in the planning horizon, and (ii) the integrand and transition functions do not vary with a change in the base period, that is to say, they are stationary. Hence, the control problem looks identical from the perspective of *any* base period under these circumstances, thus resulting in the same value of the control regardless of the starting date one plans from, that is, the base period, ceteris paribus. It is worthwhile to reiterate that Theorem 19.4 does not, in general, hold for nonautonomous control problems nor for autonomous control problems with a finite-planning horizon, pointing out just how special the discounted autonomous infinite-horizon variety is.

This chapter has laid the groundwork for the ensuing one on intertemporal duality theory. Because we will rely heavily on this material, especially Theorem 19.3, it is critically important that you fully understand the contents of this chapter before pressing on. Note that even though we have solved for the closed-loop controls and optimal value functions of various optimal control problems in the examples presented herewith, this is not how we intend to use the results of this chapter. In contrast, what we intend to do in the next chapter is akin to how one goes about developing the generic comparative statics and duality properties of the prototype profit maximization and cost minimization models of the firm, albeit for a dynamic economic model. In passing, also note that we could have presented the H-J-B equation as a sufficient condition for optimality, but have chosen not to do so because we do not intend to make use of it in that form.

MENTAL EXERCISES

19.1 Recall the optimal control problem of Example 19.1:

$$V(t, x_t) \stackrel{\text{def}}{=} \min_{u(\cdot), x_T} \left[\int_t^T (u(s))^2 \, ds + (x(T))^2 \right]$$

$$\text{s.t.} \quad \dot{x}(s) = x(s) + u(s), \; x(t) = x_t, \; x(T) = x_T.$$

(a) Verify that the optimal value function given in Eq. (25) satisfies the H-J-B equation (20).

(b) Show that

$$u = u^o(s; t, x_t, T) \stackrel{\text{def}}{=} \frac{-2x_t e^{(T-t)} e^{(T-s)}}{1 + e^{2(T-t)}},$$

$$\lambda = \lambda^o(s; t, x_t, T) \stackrel{\text{def}}{=} \frac{4x_t e^{(T-t)} e^{(T-s)}}{1 + e^{2(T-t)}},$$

$$x = x^o(s; t, x_t, T) \stackrel{\text{def}}{=} \left[\frac{x_t e^{(T-t)}}{1 + e^{2(T-t)}} \right] [e^{(T-s)} - e^{(T+s-2t)}] + x_t e^{(s-t)},$$

$$x_T = x_T^o(t, x_t, T) \stackrel{\text{def}}{=} \frac{2x_t e^{(T-t)}}{1 + e^{2(T-t)}}$$

is the unique optimal open-loop solution to the control problem.

(c) Verify the identity $u^o(t; t, x_t, T) \equiv u^c(t, x_t, T)$ using the explicit expressions for the open-loop and closed-loop controls.

(d) Show that $u^o(s; t, x_t, T) \neq u^c(t, x^o(s; t, x_t, T), T)$ using the explicit expressions for the open-loop and closed-loop controls. Explain.

(e) Verify the identity $\lambda^o(t; t, x_t, T) \equiv V_x(t, x_t, T)$ using the explicit expressions for the open-loop and closed-loop costates.

(f) Show that $\lambda^o(s; t, x_t, T) \neq V_x(t, x^o(s; t, x_t, T), T)$ using the explicit expressions for the open-loop and closed-loop costates. Explain.

19.2 Recall the optimal control problem of Examples 19.2 and 19.3:

$$V^{pv}(\alpha, r, t, x_t) \stackrel{\text{def}}{=} \max_{q(\cdot)} \left\{ \int_t^{+\infty} [\alpha \ln q(s)]\, e^{-rs}\, ds \right\}$$

$$\text{s.t.} \quad \dot{x}(s) = -q(s),\ x(t) = x_t,\ \lim_{s\to+\infty} x(s) = 0.$$

(a) Prove that the optimal open-loop solution to this problem is given by

$$q^o(s-t; r, x_t) = r x_t e^{-r(s-t)},$$

$$x^o(s-t; r, x_t) = x_t e^{-r(s-t)},$$

$$\lambda(s-t; \alpha, r, x_t) = \alpha r^{-1} x_t^{-1} e^{r(s-t)}.$$

(b) Verify that the present value optimal value function is given by

$$V^{pv}(\alpha, r, t, x_t) = \frac{\alpha}{r}[\ln r x_t - 1]\, e^{-rt}.$$

19.3 Consider the following discounted autonomous infinite-horizon optimal control problem:

$$\min_{u(\cdot)} \int_0^{+\infty} [a[x(s)]^2 + b[u(s)]^2]\, e^{-rs}\, ds$$

$$\text{s.t.} \quad \dot{x}(s) = u(s),\ x(0) = x_0 > 0,$$

where $a > 0$ and $b > 0$ are given parameters and $r > 0$ is the discount rate. You will use Theorem 19.3 to solve this optimal control problem.

(a) For a given base period $t \in [0, +\infty)$, define the current value optimal value function $V(\cdot)$. Also write down the H-J-B equation obeyed by $V(\cdot)$ for any admissible state in the base period x_t.

(b) Determine the unique and globally optimal solution to the minimization problem dictated by the H-J-B equation, say, $u = \bar{u}(b, V_x)$.

(c) Derive the ordinary differential equation satisfied by the current value optimal value function $V(\cdot)$.

Guess that the current value optimal value function $V(\cdot)$ is of the form $V(x) = Ax^2$, where A is a constant to be determined. Note that this guess is motivated by the facts that the ordinary differential equation in part (c) is quadratic in x, that V_x is squared, and that $V(\cdot)$ is independent of the base period by Theorem 19.2.

(d) Determine the value of the constant A and thus find the precise form of the optimal value function.

(e) Find the closed-loop form of the control, say, $u = u^c(a, b, r, x)$.

(f) Using $u = u^c(a, b, r, x)$ in the state equation, find the open-loop form of the solution for the control, say, $u = u^o(s - t; a, b, r, x_t)$, using the initial condition $x(t) = x_t$ in the base period $s = t$. Take note of the fact that this solution depends on the difference between the time index dummy s and the base period t.

(g) Verify that the following two identities hold for the control problem:

$$u^o(s-t; a, b, r, x_t) \equiv u^c(a, b, r, x^o(s-t; a, b, r, x_t)),$$

$$u^o(s-t; a, b, r, x_t)|_{s=t} \equiv u^c(a, b, r, x_t).$$

19.4 Consider the following optimal control problem:

$$\max_{u(\cdot)} \int_0^T \ln u(s)\, ds$$

$$\text{s.t.} \quad \dot{x}(s) = \delta x(s) - u(s), \; x(0) = x_0, \; x(T) = x_T.$$

(a) Define the optimal value function $V(\cdot)$ and write down the H-J-B equation for the control problem for a given base period $t \in [0, +\infty)$ and any admissible state in the base period x_t.

(b) Derive the value of the control that maximizes the right-hand side of the H-J-B equation, say, $u = \bar{u}(V_x)$.

(c) Show that the optimal value function

$$V(\delta, t, x_t, T, x_T) \overset{\text{def}}{=} [T-t] \ln\left[\frac{x_t e^{-\delta t} - x_T e^{-\delta T}}{T-t}\right] + \frac{\delta}{2}[T^2 - t^2]$$

satisfies the H-J-B equation.

(d) Derive the optimal value function in part (c) using the necessary (and sufficient) conditions of optimal control theory.

19.5 Consider the optimal control problem

$$\max_{u(\cdot)} \int_0^T \ln u(s) e^{-rs}\, ds$$

$$\text{s.t.} \quad \dot{x}(s) = \delta x(s) - u(s), \; x(0) = x_0, \; x(T) = x_T,$$

where $r > 0$.

(a) Define the optimal value function $V(\cdot)$ and write down the H-J-B equation for the control problem for a given base period $t \in [0, +\infty)$ and any admissible state in the base period x_t.

(b) Derive the value of the control that maximizes the right-hand side of the H-J-B equation, say, $u = \bar{u}(V_x)$.

(c) Show that the optimal value function

$$V(\delta, r, t, x_t, T, x_T) \overset{\text{def}}{=} \frac{e^{-rt} - e^{-rT}}{r} \ln\left[\frac{re^{-\delta(t+T)}[x_T e^{\delta t} - x_t e^{\delta T}]}{e^{-rT} - e^{-rt}}\right]$$

$$+ \frac{\delta - r}{r}[te^{-rt} - Te^{-rt}] + r^2[\delta - r][e^{-rt} - e^{-rt}]$$

satisfies the H-J-B equation.

19.6 Prove Theorem 19.4.

19.7 Consider the following discounted infinite-horizon optimal control problem:

$$\max_{u(\cdot)} \int_0^{+\infty} e^{-s} \sqrt{u(s)}\, ds$$

$$\text{s.t.} \quad \dot{x}(s) = x(s) - u(s), \; x(0) = x_0 > 0.$$

(a) Define the current value optimal value function $V(\cdot)$ and write down the H-J-B equation for the control problem for a given base period $t \in [0, +\infty)$ and any admissible state in the base period x_t.

(b) Derive the value of the control that maximizes the right-hand side of the H-J-B equation, say, $u = \bar{u}(V_x)$.

(c) Show that the current value optimal value function

$$V(\alpha, t, x_t) \overset{\text{def}}{=} \alpha x_t + \frac{1}{4\alpha}$$

satisfies the H-J-B equation for $\alpha \in \Re_{++}$.

(d) Derive the optimal value of the closed-loop control.

(e) Derive the current value optimal value function $V(\cdot)$ by examining the H-J-B equation and making an educated guess about its functional form. Show that your guess leads you to the same function as in part (c).

FURTHER READING

Bellman (1957) is the seminal reference on dynamic programming, and may still be consulted with positive net benefits. The basic approach followed in this chapter in deriving the H-J-B equation of Theorem 19.1 may be found in various guises in Nemhauser (1966), Barnett (1975), Bryson and Ho (1975), Kamien and Schwartz (1991), and Léonard and Van Long (1992). Dockner et al. (2000) present the H-J-B equation as a sufficient condition of optimality. Hadley and Kemp (1971, Chapter 4) and Leitmann (1981, Chapter 16) present excellent discussions of the so-called synthesis of an optimal feedback control, that is, the problem of converting an optimal open-loop control into an optimal closed-loop (or feedback) control.

REFERENCES

Apostol, T.M. (1974, 2nd Ed.), *Mathematical Analysis* (Reading, Mass: Addison-Wesley Publishing Co.).

Barnett, S. (1975), *Introduction to Mathematical Control Theory* (London: Oxford University Press).

Bellman, R. (1957), *Dynamic Programming* (Princeton, N.J.: Princeton University Press).

Bryson Jr., A.E. and Ho, Y.C. (1975, Revised Printing), *Applied Optimal Control: Optimization, Estimation, and Control* (New York: John Wiley & Sons).

Dockner, E., Jϕrgensen, S., Van Long, N., and Sorger, G. (2000), *Differential Games in Economics and Management Science* (Cambridge, U.K.: Cambridge University Press).

Hadley, G. and Kemp, M.C. (1971), *Variational Methods in Economics* (Amsterdam: North-Holland Publishing Co.).

Kamien, M.I. and Schwartz, N.L. (1991, 2nd Ed.), *Dynamic Optimization: The Calculus of Variations and Optimal Control in Economics and Management* (New York: Elsevier Science Publishing Co., Inc.).

Leitmann, G. (1981), *The Calculus of Variations and Optimal Control* (New York: Plenum Press).

Léonard, D. and Van Long, N. (1992), *Optimal Control Theory and Static Optimization in Economics* (New York: Cambridge University Press).

Nemhauser, G.L. (1966), *Introduction to Dynamic Programming* (New York: John Wiley & Sons).

TWENTY

Intertemporal Duality in the Adjustment Cost Model of the Firm

This chapter builds directly on the last in developing a duality for the adjustment cost model of the firm. In particular, the current value form of the H-J-B equation given in Theorem 19.3 will be exploited to develop a method to derive the duality properties of the adjustment cost model of the firm. Moreover, we will establish envelope results that will allow the *explicit* construction of the *feedback* or *closed-loop* forms of the investment demand, variable input demand, and output supply functions, given a functional form for the current value optimal value function with known properties. The importance of such a development is monumental in dynamic economic theory for the reasons well summarized by Epstein (1981, page 82):

> In static models, duality is a convenience. Demand functions cannot generally be determined explicitly from the technology but they are defined implicitly by first order conditions which can serve as the basis for estimation, though perhaps requiring complicated simultaneous equations techniques. Explicit solutions for calculus of variations problems are even rarer and the implicit representation of solutions generally involves a second order nonlinear differential equation (system) and non-trivial boundary conditions. The differential equation system can serve as the basis for estimation only if the generally unrealistic assumption is made that the firm does not revise its plans for several periods and continues along the same optimal path. Thus duality is indispensable for empirical work based on functional forms that are too complicated to be derived directly from the technology as explicit solutions of a problem of intertemporal optimization.

The basic assertion that will be used throughout the chapter is that at any point in time $t \in [0, +\infty)$, called a *base period* (or starting date), the firm solves the following discounted autonomous infinite-horizon optimal control problem:

$$V(\mathbf{K}_t, \mathbf{c}, \mathbf{w}) \stackrel{\text{def}}{=} \max_{\mathbf{L}(\cdot),\mathbf{I}(\cdot)} \int_t^{+\infty} [F(\mathbf{L}(s), \mathbf{K}(s), \mathbf{I}(s)) - \mathbf{w}'\mathbf{L}(s) - \mathbf{c}'\mathbf{K}(s)]\, e^{-r(s-t)}\, ds$$
$$\text{s.t.}\quad \dot{\mathbf{K}}(s) = \mathbf{I}(s) - \delta\mathbf{K}(s),\ \mathbf{K}(t) = \mathbf{K}_t > 0, \tag{1}$$
$$(\mathbf{K}(s), \mathbf{c}, \mathbf{w}) \in \Theta\ \forall\, s \in [t, +\infty),$$

where $F(\cdot)$ is a production function giving the maximum amount of the scalar output y that can be produced from the variable input $\mathbf{L}(s) \in \Re_{+}^{M}$ and the quasi-fixed factor $\mathbf{K}(s) \in \Re_{++}^{N}$, the N capital stocks, given that the gross investment rate is $\mathbf{I}(s) \in \Re_{+}^{N}$. The vector $\mathbf{w} \in \Re_{++}^{M}$ is the normalized rental price of the variable input vector $\mathbf{L}(s) \in \Re_{+}^{M}$, whereas the vector $\mathbf{c} \in \Re_{++}^{N}$ is the normalized rental price of the capital stock vector $\mathbf{K}(s) \in \Re_{++}^{N}$. The normalization is implicit in the statement of the adjustment cost problem (1), since we have set the scalar output price equal to unity for the entire planning period. The prices denote actual market prices at time $s = t$, which are expected to persist indefinitely. This is the static expectations assumption often made in the literature, whereby current prices are expected to remain constant for the foreseeable future. As the base period changes and new market prices are observed, the firm revises its expectations and its previous plans, thus only the $s = t$ part of the solution to the control problem (1) is in general carried out. This is a crucial assumption that will be maintained throughout this chapter. The discount rate is $r > 0$, and $\boldsymbol{\delta}$ is a diagonal $N \times N$ matrix of depreciation rates $\delta_n > 0$ for the nth capital stock, $n = 1, 2, \ldots, N$, whereas $\mathbf{K}_t \in \Re_{++}^{N}$ is the initial vector of capital stocks. Note that $V(\cdot)$ is the *current value* optimal value function for problem (1), and as such, by Theorem 19.3, does not depend explicitly on the base period $t \in [0, +\infty)$ in which the optimization problem begins (or starts). Hence one could set $t = 0$ in problem (1) without loss of generality, as is often done in the literature. The set $\Theta \subset \Re_{++}^{2N+M}$ is assumed to be bounded and open, and will be taken to be the domain of the current value optimal value function $V(\cdot)$. By way of a reminder, recall that all vectors are taken to be column vectors, the superscript symbol $'$ denotes transposition, and we adopt the convention that the derivative of a scalar valued function with respect to a column vector is a row vector that has the dimension of the vector variable the derivative was taken with respect to.

Two additional assumptions are maintained for the remainder of the chapter. First, the same real rate of discount and same depreciation matrix are used by the firm in all base periods to discount future profits and depreciate the capital stocks. Hence the discount rate r and the depreciation matrix $\boldsymbol{\delta}$ are constants and therefore may be suppressed as arguments of $V(\cdot)$, a simplification we have already employed. Second, the domain of definition of $F(\cdot)$ is restricted to a bounded open set $\Phi \subset \Re_{++}^{2N+M}$, and thus defines an implicit constraint in problem (1). In particular, because $\Phi \subset \Re_{++}^{2N+M}$, we are assuming that the natural nonnegativity constraints on $(\mathbf{L}(s), \mathbf{K}(s), \mathbf{I}(s))$ are not binding at any point in time in the planning horizon. Such an assumption is typically not restrictive for empirical work based on aggregate data.

Now define the following two sets:

$$\Phi(\mathbf{K}) \stackrel{\text{def}}{=} \{(\mathbf{L}, \mathbf{I}) : (\mathbf{L}, \mathbf{K}, \mathbf{I}) \in \Phi\},$$

$$\Theta(\mathbf{K}) \stackrel{\text{def}}{=} \{(\mathbf{c}, \mathbf{w}) : (\mathbf{K}, \mathbf{c}, \mathbf{w}) \in \Theta\}.$$

These sets will be the domains of the primal and dual optimization problems given in Eqs. (2) and (3), respectively. For each $\mathbf{K} \in \Re_{++}^{N}$, it is assumed that $\Phi(\mathbf{K})$ is empty if and only if $\Theta(\mathbf{K})$ is empty. Denote the empirically relevant decisions corresponding to problem (1) by $\dot{\mathbf{K}}^*(\mathbf{K}_t, \mathbf{c}, \mathbf{w})$, $\mathbf{L}^*(\mathbf{K}_t, \mathbf{c}, \mathbf{w})$, and $y^*(\mathbf{K}_t, \mathbf{c}, \mathbf{w})$. That is, $\dot{\mathbf{K}}^*(\mathbf{K}_t, \mathbf{c}, \mathbf{w})$, $\mathbf{L}^*(\mathbf{K}_t, \mathbf{c}, \mathbf{w})$, and $y^*(\mathbf{K}_t, \mathbf{c}, \mathbf{w})$ are the optimal solution to problem (1) at $s = t$. The functions $(\dot{\mathbf{K}}^*(\cdot), \mathbf{L}^*(\cdot), y^*(\cdot))$ are called the *policy functions*. We will also refer to them as the net investment demand function, the variable input demand function, and the output supply function, respectively. Given that policy functions are expressed solely as functions of the capital stock in the base period and the parameters of the problem, or because they are optimal in the base period $s = t$, you should immediately recognize them as the closed-loop or feedback form of the solution. Finally, let $\boldsymbol{\lambda}^*(\mathbf{K}_t, \mathbf{c}, \mathbf{w})$ denote the corresponding current value shadow price at time $s = t$ in problem (1).

Our main goal in this chapter is to establish a duality between the production function $F(\cdot)$ and the current value optimal value function $V(\cdot)$. The dynamic duality results of Epstein (1981) to be expounded upon below are local. This, however, normally suffices for empirical purposes, for our interest is usually focused on a neighborhood of prices and quantities defined by the data we have at hand. This is the reason that the solution of problem (1) is restricted to an open and bounded set.

The following regularity conditions, valid throughout Φ, are imposed on the production function $F(\cdot)$:

(T.1) $F(\cdot) : \Phi \to \Re_+$, $F(\cdot) \in C^{(1)}$, $F_{\mathbf{L}}(\cdot) \in C^{(1)}$, and $F_{\mathbf{I}}(\cdot) \in C^{(1)}$.

(T.2) $F_{\mathbf{L}}(\mathbf{L}, \mathbf{K}, \mathbf{I}) > \mathbf{0}'_M$, $F_{\mathbf{K}}(\mathbf{L}, \mathbf{K}, \mathbf{I}) > \mathbf{0}'_N$, and $F_{\mathbf{I}}(\mathbf{L}, \mathbf{K}, \mathbf{I}) < \mathbf{0}'_N$.

(T.3) $F(\cdot)$ is strongly concave in $(\mathbf{L}, \mathbf{I})$.

(T.4) For each $(\mathbf{K}_t, \mathbf{c}, \mathbf{w}) \in \Theta$, a unique solution exists for problem (1) in the sense of convergent integrals; the policy functions $(\dot{\mathbf{K}}^*(\cdot), \mathbf{L}^*(\cdot), y^*(\cdot))$ are $C^{(1)}$ on Θ, and the current value shadow price function $\boldsymbol{\lambda}^*(\cdot) \in C^{(2)}$ on Θ.

(T.5) $\boldsymbol{\lambda}^*_{\mathbf{c}}(\mathbf{K}, \mathbf{c}, \mathbf{w})$ is nonsingular for each $(\mathbf{K}, \mathbf{c}, \mathbf{w}) \in \Theta$.

(T.6) For each $(\mathbf{L}^\circ, \mathbf{K}_t, \mathbf{I}^\circ) \in \Phi$, there exists $(\mathbf{K}_t, \mathbf{c}^\circ, \mathbf{w}^\circ) \in \Theta$ such that $(\mathbf{L}^\circ, \mathbf{I}^\circ)$ is optimal in problem (1) at $s = t$ given the initial capital stock $\mathbf{K}_t$ and prices $(\mathbf{c}^\circ, \mathbf{w}^\circ)$.

(T.7) For each $(\mathbf{K}_t, \mathbf{c}, \mathbf{w}) \in \Theta$, problem (1) has a unique steady state capital stock $\mathbf{K}^s(\mathbf{c}, \mathbf{w}) \in \Theta$ that is globally asymptotically stable, that is, optimal paths converge to $\mathbf{K}^s(\mathbf{c}, \mathbf{w})$ regardless of the initial stock $\mathbf{K}_t$.

Generalizations of assumptions (T.1) through (T.7) are possible and consistent with a theory of duality. They were chosen by Epstein (1981) so as to simplify the exposition without doing undue violence to potential empirical applications.

Assumptions (T.1) through (T.3) are more or less standard. In particular, because we intend to use the differential calculus to characterize the duality between $F(\cdot)$ and $V(\cdot)$, some smoothness assumptions are required. Assumption (T.2) means that the marginal product of every variable input and every capital stock is positive whereas the marginal product of every investment rate is negative. In particular, the assumption $F_{\mathbf{I}}(\mathbf{L}, \mathbf{K}, \mathbf{I}) < \mathbf{0}'_N$, where $\mathbf{0}_N$ is the null column N-vector, implies that each component of the vector is negative, and thus reflects the internal adjustment costs associated with gross investment. The results given here would not be materially altered if adjustment costs were external and/or depended on net investment. Condition (T.3) holds if the Hessian matrix of $F(\cdot)$ with respect to $(\mathbf{L}, \mathbf{I})$ is negative definite throughout Φ. Note that we must be careful in interpreting the curvature properties of $F(\cdot)$ with respect to $(\mathbf{L}, \mathbf{I})$ because $\Phi(\mathbf{K})$ may not be a convex set. Thus, $F(\cdot)$ concave in $(\mathbf{L}, \mathbf{I})$ for each $\mathbf{K}$ should be taken to mean that the appropriate Hessian matrix is negative semidefinite throughout $\Phi(\mathbf{K})$ for each $\mathbf{K}$. An analogous interpretation applies to the convexity of $V(\cdot)$ in $(\mathbf{c}, \mathbf{w})$ because $\Theta(\mathbf{K})$ need not be a convex set. Condition (T.4) asserts the existence of well-defined and differentiable solutions associated with problem (1), and that $V(\mathbf{K}_t, \mathbf{c}, \mathbf{w})$ is finite for each $(\mathbf{K}_t, \mathbf{c}, \mathbf{w}) \in \Theta$. The nonsingularity of $\boldsymbol{\lambda}_{\mathbf{c}}^*(\cdot)$ asserted in (T.5) could be dispensed with, but at the cost of considerable additional complexity in the exposition. Moreover, the nonsingularity of $\boldsymbol{\lambda}_{\mathbf{c}}^*(\cdot)$ could not be refuted empirically, and it is a sufficient condition for the functional relationship $\boldsymbol{\lambda} = \boldsymbol{\lambda}^*(\mathbf{K}, \mathbf{c}, \mathbf{w})$ to be locally invertible in $\mathbf{c}$ for given $(\mathbf{K}, \mathbf{w})$ by the implicit function theorem. Points $(\mathbf{L}^\circ, \mathbf{K}_t, \mathbf{I}^\circ) \in \Phi$ that violated (T.6) would never be observed, and so there is no loss in ruling them out. Condition (T.7) could be weakened to require only that any given capital stock profile that is optimal in problem (1) lie in a compact subset of $\{\mathbf{K} : (\mathbf{K}, \mathbf{c}, \mathbf{w}) \in \Theta\}$. We are now in a position to derive the main results of Epstein (1981).

Assume that the production function $F(\cdot)$ satisfies assumptions (T.1) through (T.7), and let the current value optimal value function $V(\cdot)$ be defined by problem (1). Then by Theorem 19.3, $V(\cdot)$ satisfies the H-J-B equation

$$rV(\mathbf{K}, \mathbf{c}, \mathbf{w}) = \max_{(\mathbf{L},\mathbf{I})\in\Phi(\mathbf{K})} \{F(\mathbf{L}, \mathbf{K}, \mathbf{I}) - \mathbf{w}'\mathbf{L} - \mathbf{c}'\mathbf{K} + V_{\mathbf{K}}(\mathbf{K}, \mathbf{c}, \mathbf{w})[\mathbf{I} - \delta\mathbf{K}]\},$$
$$(\mathbf{K}, \mathbf{c}, \mathbf{w}) \in \Theta, \tag{2}$$

where $t \in [0, +\infty)$ is *any* base period and $\mathbf{K}$ is *any admissible* vector of capital in the base period. It is important to understand that the maximizing values of $\mathbf{L}$ and $\mathbf{I}$ in problem (2) when $\mathbf{K} = \mathbf{K}_t$ and $(\mathbf{K}_t, \mathbf{c}^\circ, \mathbf{w}^\circ) \in \Theta$ are precisely the demands that are optimal in problem (1) at $s = t$ by assumption (T.6). More generally, for each $(\mathbf{K}, \mathbf{c}, \mathbf{w}) \in \Theta$, the maximizing values of $\mathbf{L}$ and $\mathbf{I}$ in problem (2) are given by the values of the policy functions $(\mathbf{L}^*(\mathbf{K}, \mathbf{c}, \mathbf{w}), \mathbf{I}^*(\mathbf{K}, \mathbf{c}, \mathbf{w}))$, which are the optimal values of the control variables in the optimal control problem (1) in any base period $t \in [0, +\infty)$, given that the corresponding value of the capital stock in the base period is $\mathbf{K}$. This is precisely what we observed in the last chapter: the value of the open-loop form of the control vector in the base period is identical to the value of the feedback form of the control vector.

The most important aspect of the H-J-B equation (2) is that it is a static optimization problem relating the functions $F(\cdot)$ and $V(\cdot)$. Therefore, the duality theory of Silberberg (1974) for static optimization problems may be applied to establish a duality between the functions $F(\cdot)$ and $V(\cdot)$. This is the intertemporal duality we seek to establish below.

The *dual* (or inverse) problem of Eq. (2) defines a production function $F^*(\cdot)$, given a function $V(\cdot)$ that satisfies an appropriate set of regularity conditions, and is given by

$$F^*(\mathbf{L}, \mathbf{K}, \mathbf{I}) = \min_{(\mathbf{c},\mathbf{w})\in\Theta(\mathbf{K})} \{rV(\mathbf{K}, \mathbf{c}, \mathbf{w}) + \mathbf{w}'\mathbf{L} + \mathbf{c}'\mathbf{K} - V_{\mathbf{K}}(\mathbf{K}, \mathbf{c}, \mathbf{w})[\mathbf{I} - \delta\mathbf{K}]\},$$
$$(\mathbf{L}, \mathbf{K}, \mathbf{I}) \in \Phi. \tag{3}$$

If problem (3) seems unnatural or otherwise strange, simply rewrite problem (2) as a primal-dual optimization problem, maximizing with respect to $(\mathbf{c}, \mathbf{w}) \in \Theta(\mathbf{K})$. By doing so, problem (3) immediately follows with $F^*(\cdot)$ replaced by $F(\cdot)$. We will see such details below when we prove Theorems 20.1 and 20.2.

Before presenting the regularity conditions that will be shown to characterize the current value optimal value function $V(\cdot)$, we first present the following formulas:

$$\tilde{\mathbf{I}}(\mathbf{K}, \mathbf{c}, \mathbf{w}) \overset{\text{def}}{=} V_{\mathbf{cK}}^{-1}(\mathbf{K}, \mathbf{c}, \mathbf{w})[rV_{\mathbf{c}}'(\mathbf{K}, \mathbf{c}, \mathbf{w}) + \mathbf{K}] + \delta\mathbf{K}, \tag{4}$$

$$\tilde{\mathbf{L}}(\mathbf{K}, \mathbf{c}, \mathbf{w}) \overset{\text{def}}{=} -rV_{\mathbf{w}}'(\mathbf{K}, \mathbf{c}, \mathbf{w}) + V_{\mathbf{wK}}(\mathbf{K}, \mathbf{c}, \mathbf{w})V_{\mathbf{cK}}^{-1}(\mathbf{K}, \mathbf{c}, \mathbf{w})[rV_{\mathbf{c}}'(\mathbf{K}, \mathbf{c}, \mathbf{w}) + \mathbf{K}], \tag{5}$$

$$\begin{aligned}\tilde{y}(\mathbf{K}, \mathbf{c}, \mathbf{w}) &\overset{\text{def}}{=} rV(\mathbf{K}, \mathbf{c}, \mathbf{w}) + \mathbf{w}'\tilde{\mathbf{L}}(\mathbf{K}, \mathbf{c}, \mathbf{w}) + \mathbf{c}'\mathbf{K} \\ &\quad - V_{\mathbf{K}}(\mathbf{K}, \mathbf{c}, \mathbf{w})[\tilde{\mathbf{I}}(\mathbf{K}, \mathbf{c}, \mathbf{w}) - \delta\mathbf{K}] \\ &= r[V(\mathbf{K}, \mathbf{c}, \mathbf{w}) - V_{\mathbf{w}}(\mathbf{K}, \mathbf{c}, \mathbf{w})\mathbf{w} \\ &\quad - V_{\mathbf{c}}(\mathbf{K}, \mathbf{c}, \mathbf{w})\mathbf{c}] - [V_{\mathbf{K}}(\mathbf{K}, \mathbf{c}, \mathbf{w}) - \mathbf{w}'V_{\mathbf{wK}}(\mathbf{K}, \mathbf{c}, \mathbf{w}) \\ &\quad - \mathbf{c}'V_{\mathbf{cK}}(\mathbf{K}, \mathbf{c}, \mathbf{w})\mathbf{c}]\left[V_{\mathbf{cK}}^{-1}(\mathbf{K}, \mathbf{c}, \mathbf{w})[rV_{\mathbf{c}}'(\mathbf{K}, \mathbf{c}, \mathbf{w}) + \mathbf{K}]\right].\end{aligned} \tag{6}$$

Note that these are simply definitions of the left-hand-side functions and hence hold for all $(\mathbf{K}, \mathbf{c}, \mathbf{w}) \in \Theta$. What we intend to show is that they describe optimal behavior in problem (1), that is, the policy or closed-loop solution functions for problem (1) are equal to them. One way to get some intuition on them is to recognize that they are simply the envelope results for the primal H-J-B problem (2).

Given these definitions, the following conditions will be shown to characterize the current value optimal value function $V(\cdot)$ for problem (1):

(V.1) $V(\cdot)$ is a real-valued, bound-from-below function defined on Θ; $V(\cdot) \in C^{(2)}$ and $V_{\mathbf{K}}(\cdot) \in C^{(2)}$.

(V.2) (i) $(r\mathrm{I}_N + \delta)V_{\mathbf{K}}'(\mathbf{K}, \mathbf{c}, \mathbf{w}) + \mathbf{c} - V_{\mathbf{KK}}(\mathbf{K}, \mathbf{c}, \mathbf{w})[\tilde{\mathbf{I}}(\mathbf{K}, \mathbf{c}, \mathbf{w}) - \delta\mathbf{K}] > \mathbf{0}_N$, and (ii) $V_{\mathbf{K}}'(\mathbf{K}, \mathbf{c}, \mathbf{w}) > \mathbf{0}_N$.

(V.3) For each $(\mathbf{K}, \mathbf{c}, \mathbf{w}) \in \Theta$, $\tilde{y}(\mathbf{K}, \mathbf{c}, \mathbf{w}) \geq 0$; for each $\mathbf{K}$ such that $\Theta(\mathbf{K})$ is nonempty, $(\tilde{\mathbf{L}}(\mathbf{K}, \cdot, \cdot), \mathbf{K}, \tilde{\mathbf{I}}(\mathbf{K}, \cdot, \cdot))$ maps $\Theta(\mathbf{K})$ onto $\Phi(\mathbf{K})$.

(V.4) The dynamical system $\dot{\mathbf{K}} = \tilde{\mathbf{I}}(\mathbf{K}, \mathbf{c}, \mathbf{w}) - \delta\mathbf{K}$, $\mathbf{K}(t) = \mathbf{K}_t$, $(\mathbf{K}_t, \mathbf{c}, \mathbf{w}) \in \Theta$, defines a curve $\mathbf{K}(s)$ such that $(\mathbf{K}(s), \mathbf{c}, \mathbf{w}) \in \Theta\, \forall\, s \in [t, +\infty)$, and $\mathbf{K}(s) \to \mathbf{K}^s(\mathbf{c}, \mathbf{w}) \in \Theta$ as $s \to +\infty$, a globally asymptotically stable steady state.

(V.5) $V_{\mathbf{cK}}(\mathbf{K}, \mathbf{c}, \mathbf{w})$ is nonsingular for each $(\mathbf{K}, \mathbf{c}, \mathbf{w}) \in \Theta$.

(V.6) For $(\mathbf{K}, \mathbf{c}^{\circ}, \mathbf{w}^{\circ}) \in \Theta$, the minimum in problem (3) is attained at $(\mathbf{c}^{\circ}, \mathbf{w}^{\circ})$ if $(\mathbf{I}, \mathbf{L}) = (\tilde{\mathbf{I}}(\mathbf{K}, \mathbf{c}^{\circ}, \mathbf{w}^{\circ}), \tilde{\mathbf{L}}(\mathbf{K}, \mathbf{c}^{\circ}, \mathbf{w}^{\circ}))$.

(V.7) The $(M + N) \times (M + N)$ matrix

$$\underbrace{\begin{bmatrix} \underbrace{\frac{\partial \tilde{\mathbf{L}}}{\partial \mathbf{w}}(\mathbf{K}, \mathbf{c}, \mathbf{w})}_{M\times M} & \underbrace{\frac{\partial \tilde{\mathbf{L}}}{\partial \mathbf{c}}(\mathbf{K}, \mathbf{c}\mathbf{w})}_{M\times N} \\ \underbrace{\frac{\partial \tilde{\mathbf{I}}}{\partial \mathbf{w}}(\mathbf{K}, \mathbf{c}, \mathbf{w})}_{N\times M} & \underbrace{\frac{\partial \tilde{\mathbf{I}}}{\partial \mathbf{c}}(\mathbf{K}, \mathbf{c}, \mathbf{w})}_{N\times N} \end{bmatrix}}_{(M+N)\times(M+N)}$$

is nonsingular for $(\mathbf{K}, \mathbf{c}, \mathbf{w}) \in \Theta$.

Let us remark that the "onto" property in (V.3) simply means that the range of the functions is the target space of the functions and that I_N is the $N \times N$ identity matrix.

The following two theorems are the main results of Epstein (1981). They establish a formal intertemporal duality between the production function $F(\cdot)$ and the current value optimal value function $V(\cdot)$, as well as give specific formulas for the empirically relevant policy functions, that is, the feedback or closed-loop form of the optimal control functions.

Theorem 20.1 (Intertemporal Duality):

(a) Let $F(\cdot)$ satisfy (T.1) through (T.7) and define $V(\cdot)$ by Eq. (1). Then $V(\cdot)$ satisfies (V.1) through (V.7). If further $V(\cdot)$ is used to define $F^*(\cdot)$ by Eq. (3), then $F^*(\cdot) \equiv F(\cdot)$.

(b) Let $V(\cdot)$ satisfy (V.1) through (V.7) and define $F(\cdot)$ by Eq. (3). Then $F(\cdot)$ satisfies (T.1) through (T.7). If further $F(\cdot)$ is used to define $V^*(\cdot)$ by Eq. (1), then $V^*(\cdot) \equiv V(\cdot)$.

Theorem 20.2 (Policy Function Formulae): *Let $F(\cdot)$ satisfy (T.1) through (T.7) and let $V(\cdot)$ be the current value optimal value function defined by Eq. (1). Then the policy functions are given by*

$$\dot{\mathbf{K}}^*(\mathbf{K}, \mathbf{c}, \mathbf{w}) = \tilde{\mathbf{I}}(\mathbf{K}, \mathbf{c}, \mathbf{w}) - \delta\mathbf{K},$$

$$\mathbf{L}^*(\mathbf{K}, \mathbf{c}, \mathbf{w}) = \tilde{\mathbf{L}}(\mathbf{K}, \mathbf{c}, \mathbf{w}),$$

$$y^*(\mathbf{K}, \mathbf{c}, \mathbf{w}) = \tilde{y}(\mathbf{K}, \mathbf{c}, \mathbf{w}),$$

for all $(\mathbf{K}, \mathbf{c}, \mathbf{w}) \in \Theta$, where the functions $\tilde{\mathbf{I}}(\cdot)$, $\tilde{\mathbf{L}}(\cdot)$, and $\tilde{y}(\cdot)$ are defined by Eqs. (4), (5), and (6), respectively.

Before we embark on the proof of these theorems, we pause and make several remarks. First, the ensuing proof is long and detailed, so don't expect to be able to breeze through it and fully understand it on the first reading. Second, in the course of proving Theorem 20.1, we will also prove Theorem 20.2. Third, there are at least two different ways of proving several parts of the theorems. We offer one proof in the text and leave the alternative methods of proof for the mental exercises.

Proof of both theorems: We begin by proving part (a) of Theorem 20.1, and in the process prove Theorem 20.2. To this end, assume that $F(\cdot)$ satisfies assumptions (T.1) through (T.7) and define $V(\cdot)$ by Eq. (1).

(V.1) The current value optimal value function $V(\cdot)$ is real-valued on Θ because for each $(\mathbf{K}_t, \mathbf{c}, \mathbf{w}) \in \Theta$, a unique solution exists for problem (1) in the sense of convergent integrals by assumption (T.4). The assumed boundedness of the sets Φ and Θ implies that $V(\cdot)$ is bounded below over Θ. By the dynamic envelope theorem and the principle of optimality, we know that $V_{\mathbf{K}}'(\mathbf{K}, \mathbf{c}, \mathbf{w}) \equiv \boldsymbol{\lambda}^*(\mathbf{K}, \mathbf{c}, \mathbf{w})$. Moreover, given that $\boldsymbol{\lambda}^*(\cdot) \in C^{(2)}$ on Θ by assumption (T.4), it follows that $V_{\mathbf{K}}(\cdot) \in C^{(2)}$ on Θ too. To finish this part, we must show that $V(\cdot) \in C^{(2)}$. Actually, all we have to show is that the second-order partial derivatives of $V(\cdot)$ with respect to the prices $(\mathbf{c}, \mathbf{w})$ are continuous, because we already know that $V_{\mathbf{K}}(\cdot) \in C^{(2)}$ on Θ. Thus, applying the static envelope theorem to problem (2) yields

$$r V_{c_i}(\mathbf{K}, \mathbf{c}, \mathbf{w}) \equiv -K_i + \sum_{n=1}^{N} V_{K_n c_i}(\mathbf{K}, \mathbf{c}, \mathbf{w})[I_n^*(\mathbf{K}, \mathbf{c}, \mathbf{w}) - \delta_n K_n], \ i = 1, 2, \ldots, N,$$

$$r V_{w_j}(\mathbf{K}, \mathbf{c}, \mathbf{w}) \equiv -L_j^*(\mathbf{K}, \mathbf{c}, \mathbf{w}) + \sum_{n=1}^{N} V_{K_n w_j}(\mathbf{K}, \mathbf{c}, \mathbf{w})[I_n^*(\mathbf{K}, \mathbf{c}, \mathbf{w}) - \delta_n K_n],$$

$$j = 1, 2, \ldots, M.$$

The right-hand sides of these two equations are a $C^{(1)}$ function of $(\mathbf{K}, \mathbf{c}, \mathbf{w}) \in \Theta$ seeing as $V_{\mathbf{K}}(\cdot) \in C^{(2)}$ on Θ by assumption (T.1) and the policy functions $(\mathbf{L}^*(\cdot), \mathbf{I}^*(\cdot)) = (\mathbf{L}^*(\cdot), \dot{\mathbf{K}}^*(\cdot) + \boldsymbol{\delta}\mathbf{K})$ are $C^{(1)}$ on Θ by assumption (T.4). It therefore follows that the second-order partial derivatives of $V(\cdot)$ with respect to the prices $(\mathbf{c}, \mathbf{w})$ are continuous functions on Θ, thereby implying that $V(\cdot) \in C^{(2)}$ on Θ. You will be asked to compute these second-order partial derivatives in a mental exercise to further enhance your understanding of this part of the proof.

(V.5) By the dynamic envelope theorem and the principle of optimality, we know that $V_{\mathbf{K}}'(\mathbf{K}, \mathbf{c}, \mathbf{w}) \equiv \boldsymbol{\lambda}^*(\mathbf{K}, \mathbf{c}, \mathbf{w})$. Differentiating this identity with respect to $\mathbf{c}$ results in the identity $V_{\mathbf{Kc}}(\mathbf{K}, \mathbf{c}, \mathbf{w}) \equiv \boldsymbol{\lambda}_{\mathbf{c}}^*(\mathbf{K}, \mathbf{c}, \mathbf{w})$. Because $\boldsymbol{\lambda}_{\mathbf{c}}^*(\mathbf{K}, \mathbf{c}, \mathbf{w})$ is nonsingular for each $(\mathbf{K}, \mathbf{c}, \mathbf{w}) \in \Theta$ by assumption (T.5), it follows from the last identity that the same is true for $V_{\mathbf{Kc}}(\mathbf{K}, \mathbf{c}, \mathbf{w})$. But because $V_{\mathbf{Kc}}(\mathbf{K}, \mathbf{c}, \mathbf{w}) \equiv V_{\mathbf{cK}}'(\mathbf{K}, \mathbf{c}, \mathbf{w})$, as you will show in a mental exercise, $V_{\mathbf{cK}}'(\mathbf{K}, \mathbf{c}, \mathbf{w})$ is nonsingular for each $(\mathbf{K}, \mathbf{c}, \mathbf{w}) \in \Theta$. Finally, you should recall a basic theorem of linear algebra that states that a matrix is invertible, that is, nonsingular, if and only if its transpose is invertible. Applying this theorem yields the desired conclusion that $V_{\mathbf{cK}}(\mathbf{K}, \mathbf{c}, \mathbf{w})$ is nonsingular for each $(\mathbf{K}, \mathbf{c}, \mathbf{w}) \in \Theta$.

(V.6) and Theorem 20.2 Let $(\mathbf{K}, \mathbf{c}^\circ, \mathbf{w}^\circ) \in \Theta$. By assumption (T.6), $\mathbf{I}^\circ = \mathbf{I}^*(\mathbf{K}, \mathbf{c}^\circ, \mathbf{w}^\circ)$ and $\mathbf{L}^\circ = \mathbf{L}^*(\mathbf{K}, \mathbf{c}^\circ, \mathbf{w}^\circ)$ solve the primal H-J-B problem (2) when $(\mathbf{c}, \mathbf{w}) = (\mathbf{c}^\circ, \mathbf{w}^\circ)$. Given this fact, the primal-dual problem corresponding to problem (2) is

$$0 = \max_{(\mathbf{c},\mathbf{w})\in\Theta(\mathbf{K})} \{F(\mathbf{L}^\circ, \mathbf{K}, \mathbf{I}^\circ) - \mathbf{w}'\mathbf{L}^\circ - \mathbf{c}'\mathbf{K} + V_{\mathbf{K}}(\mathbf{K}, \mathbf{c}, \mathbf{w})[\mathbf{I}^\circ - \delta\mathbf{K}]$$
$$- rV(\mathbf{K}, \mathbf{c}, \mathbf{w})\}, (\mathbf{L}^\circ, \mathbf{K}, \mathbf{I}^\circ) \in \Phi, \tag{7}$$

where, by construction, the price vector $(\mathbf{c}^\circ, \mathbf{w}^\circ)$ is optimal in problem (7) given that we have set $(\mathbf{I}, \mathbf{L}) = (\mathbf{I}^\circ, \mathbf{L}^\circ) = (\mathbf{I}^*(\mathbf{K}, \mathbf{c}^\circ, \mathbf{w}^\circ), \mathbf{L}^*(\mathbf{K}, \mathbf{c}^\circ, \mathbf{w}^\circ))$. Because $F(\mathbf{L}^\circ, \mathbf{K}, \mathbf{I}^\circ)$ is independent of the decision variables $(\mathbf{c}, \mathbf{w})$ for the primal-dual optimization problem (7), we can subtract $F(\mathbf{L}^\circ, \mathbf{K}, \mathbf{I}^\circ)$ from both sides to get

$$-F(\mathbf{L}^\circ, \mathbf{K}, \mathbf{I}^\circ) = \max_{(\mathbf{c},\mathbf{w})\in\Theta(\mathbf{K})} \{-\mathbf{w}'\mathbf{L}^\circ - \mathbf{c}'\mathbf{K} + V_{\mathbf{K}}(\mathbf{K}, \mathbf{c}, \mathbf{w})[\mathbf{I}^\circ - \delta\mathbf{K}]$$
$$- rV(\mathbf{K}, \mathbf{c}, \mathbf{w})\}, (\mathbf{L}^\circ, \mathbf{K}, \mathbf{I}^\circ) \in \Phi.$$

Now we can use the fact that $-\min_{\mathbf{x}} f(\mathbf{x}) = \max_{\mathbf{x}}[-f(\mathbf{x})]$ and multiply the preceding equation on both sides by minus unity to get

$$F(\mathbf{L}^\circ, \mathbf{K}, \mathbf{I}^\circ) = \min_{(\mathbf{c},\mathbf{w})\in\Theta(\mathbf{K})} \{rV(\mathbf{K}, \mathbf{c}, \mathbf{w}) + \mathbf{w}'\mathbf{L}^\circ + \mathbf{c}'\mathbf{K} - V_{\mathbf{K}}(\mathbf{K}, \mathbf{c}, \mathbf{w})[\mathbf{I}^\circ - \delta\mathbf{K}]\},$$
$$(\mathbf{L}^\circ, \mathbf{K}, \mathbf{I}^\circ) \in \Phi. \tag{8}$$

Finally, note that our choice of the point $(\mathbf{K}, \mathbf{c}^\circ, \mathbf{w}^\circ) \in \Theta$ was arbitrary, hence making problem (8) equivalent to problem (3), thereby proving that $F(\mathbf{L}, \mathbf{K}, \mathbf{I}) \equiv F^*(\mathbf{L}, \mathbf{K}, \mathbf{I})\,\forall\,(\mathbf{L}, \mathbf{K}, \mathbf{I}) \in \Phi$ and establishing property (V.6).

We can say more at this juncture. In particular, the first-order necessary conditions for an optimum in problem (3), or equivalently, problem (8), are given by

$$rV_{\mathbf{c}}'(\mathbf{K}, \mathbf{c}, \mathbf{w}) + \mathbf{K} - V_{\mathbf{Kc}}'(\mathbf{K}, \mathbf{c}, \mathbf{w})[\mathbf{I}^\circ - \delta\mathbf{K}] = \mathbf{0}_N, \tag{9}$$
$$rV_{\mathbf{w}}'(\mathbf{K}, \mathbf{c}, \mathbf{w}) + \mathbf{L}^\circ - V_{\mathbf{Kw}}'(\mathbf{K}, \mathbf{c}, \mathbf{w})[\mathbf{I}^\circ - \delta\mathbf{K}] = \mathbf{0}_M, \tag{10}$$

which hold at $(\mathbf{K}, \mathbf{c}^\circ, \mathbf{w}^\circ) \in \Theta$ by construction. Because $V_{\mathbf{Kc}}(\mathbf{K}, \mathbf{c}, \mathbf{w}) \equiv V_{\mathbf{cK}}'(\mathbf{K}, \mathbf{c}, \mathbf{w})$, as noted in the proof of property (V.5), the first-order necessary condition (9) can be solved for $\mathbf{I}^\circ = \mathbf{I}^*(\mathbf{K}, \mathbf{c}^\circ, \mathbf{w}^\circ)$ upon setting $(\mathbf{c}, \mathbf{w}) = (\mathbf{c}^\circ, \mathbf{w}^\circ)$ and recalling that $V_{\mathbf{cK}}^{-1}(\mathbf{K}, \mathbf{c}, \mathbf{w})$ exists for each $(\mathbf{K}, \mathbf{c}, \mathbf{w}) \in \Theta$ by property (V.5), that is,

$$\mathbf{I}^*(\mathbf{K}, \mathbf{c}^\circ, \mathbf{w}^\circ) = V_{\mathbf{cK}}^{-1}(\mathbf{K}, \mathbf{c}^\circ, \mathbf{w}^\circ)[rV_{\mathbf{c}}'(\mathbf{K}, \mathbf{c}^\circ, \mathbf{w}^\circ) + \mathbf{K}] + \delta\mathbf{K}. \tag{11}$$

Inspection of Eqs. (4) and (11) reveals that $\tilde{\mathbf{I}}(\mathbf{K}, \mathbf{c}^\circ, \mathbf{w}^\circ) = \mathbf{I}^*(\mathbf{K}, \mathbf{c}^\circ, \mathbf{w}^\circ)$. Inasmuch as our choice of the point $(\mathbf{K}, \mathbf{c}^\circ, \mathbf{w}^\circ) \in \Theta$ was arbitrary, however, we have established that

$$\mathbf{I}^*(\mathbf{K}, \mathbf{c}, \mathbf{w}) \equiv \tilde{\mathbf{I}}(\mathbf{K}, \mathbf{c}, \mathbf{w})\,\forall\,(\mathbf{K}, \mathbf{c}, \mathbf{w}) \in \Theta,$$

which proves the first formula of Theorem 20.2, upon recalling that $\mathbf{I}^*(\mathbf{K}, \mathbf{c}, \mathbf{w}) \equiv \dot{\mathbf{K}}^*(\mathbf{K}, \mathbf{c}, \mathbf{w}) + \delta\mathbf{K}$.

Similarly, in view of the fact that $V_{\mathbf{Kw}}(\mathbf{K}, \mathbf{c}, \mathbf{w}) \equiv V'_{\mathbf{wK}}(\mathbf{K}, \mathbf{c}, \mathbf{w})$, the first-order necessary condition (10) can be solved for $\mathbf{L}^\circ = \mathbf{L}^*(\mathbf{K}, \mathbf{c}^\circ, \mathbf{w}^\circ)$ upon setting $(\mathbf{c}, \mathbf{w}) = (\mathbf{c}^\circ, \mathbf{w}^\circ)$, that is,

$$\begin{aligned}\mathbf{L}^*(\mathbf{K}, \mathbf{c}^\circ, \mathbf{w}^\circ) &= -rV'_{\mathbf{w}}(\mathbf{K}, \mathbf{c}^\circ, \mathbf{w}^\circ) + V_{\mathbf{wK}}(\mathbf{K}, \mathbf{c}^\circ, \mathbf{w}^\circ)[\mathbf{I}^\circ - \delta\mathbf{K}] \\ &= -rV'_{\mathbf{w}}(\mathbf{K}, \mathbf{c}^\circ, \mathbf{w}^\circ) + V_{\mathbf{wK}}(\mathbf{K}, \mathbf{c}^\circ, \mathbf{w}^\circ)V_{\mathbf{cK}}^{-1}(\mathbf{K}, \mathbf{c}^\circ, \mathbf{w}^\circ) \\ &\quad \times [rV'_{\mathbf{c}}(\mathbf{K}, \mathbf{c}^\circ, \mathbf{w}^\circ) + \mathbf{K}],\end{aligned}$$

where we used the fact that $\mathbf{I}^\circ = \mathbf{I}^*(\mathbf{K}, \mathbf{c}^\circ, \mathbf{w}^\circ)$ and Eq. (11). Inspection of Eq. (5) reveals that $\tilde{\mathbf{L}}(\mathbf{K}, \mathbf{c}^\circ, \mathbf{w}^\circ) = \mathbf{L}^*(\mathbf{K}, \mathbf{c}^\circ, \mathbf{w}^\circ)$. However, because our choice of the point $(\mathbf{K}, \mathbf{c}^\circ, \mathbf{w}^\circ) \in \Theta$ was arbitrary, we have actually shown that

$$\mathbf{L}^*(\mathbf{K}, \mathbf{c}, \mathbf{w}) \equiv \tilde{\mathbf{L}}(\mathbf{K}, \mathbf{c}, \mathbf{w}) \,\forall\, (\mathbf{K}, \mathbf{c}, \mathbf{w}) \in \Theta,$$

which proves the second formula of Theorem 20.2. Consequently, there is no need to distinguish between the functions $(\mathbf{I}^*(\cdot), \mathbf{L}^*(\cdot))$ and $(\tilde{\mathbf{I}}(\cdot), \tilde{\mathbf{L}}(\cdot))$, for they are identical for all $(\mathbf{K}, \mathbf{c}, \mathbf{w}) \in \Theta$. As remarked earlier, these are intertemporal envelope results for the adjustment cost model.

Finally, to complete the proof of Theorem 20.2, first note that the supply function $y^*(\cdot)$ is defined as $y^*(\mathbf{K}, \mathbf{c}, \mathbf{w}) \overset{\text{def}}{=} F(\mathbf{L}^*(\mathbf{K}, \mathbf{c}, \mathbf{w}), \mathbf{K}, \mathbf{I}^*(\mathbf{K}, \mathbf{c}, \mathbf{w}))$, and $F(\mathbf{L}, \mathbf{K}, \mathbf{I}) \equiv F^*(\mathbf{L}, \mathbf{K}, \mathbf{I}) \,\forall\, (\mathbf{L}, \mathbf{K}, \mathbf{I}) \in \Phi$, as shown above. The latter identity means that we can find the supply function in identity form from problem (2) or problem (3), that is,

$$\begin{aligned}y^*(\mathbf{K}, \mathbf{c}, \mathbf{w}) \equiv\ & rV(\mathbf{K}, \mathbf{c}, \mathbf{w}) + \mathbf{w}'\mathbf{L}^*(\mathbf{K}, \mathbf{c}, \mathbf{w}) \\ & + \mathbf{c}'\mathbf{K} - V_{\mathbf{K}}(\mathbf{K}, \mathbf{c}, \mathbf{w})[\mathbf{I}^*(\mathbf{K}, \mathbf{c}, \mathbf{w}) - \delta\mathbf{K}].\end{aligned} \tag{12}$$

This is the first expression for the supply function in Theorem 20.2. Recalling the preceding two proofs regarding the policy functions $(\mathbf{I}^*(\cdot), \mathbf{L}^*(\cdot))$ and then substituting in their formulas from Eqs. (4) and (5) allows us to rewrite Eq. (12) as

$$\begin{aligned}y^*(\mathbf{K}, \mathbf{c}, \mathbf{w}) \equiv\ & rV(\mathbf{K}, \mathbf{c}, \mathbf{w}) + \mathbf{w}' \big[-rV'_{\mathbf{w}}(\mathbf{K}, \mathbf{c}, \mathbf{w}) \\ & + V_{\mathbf{wK}}(\mathbf{K}, \mathbf{c}, \mathbf{w})V_{\mathbf{cK}}^{-1}(\mathbf{K}, \mathbf{c}, \mathbf{w})[rV'_{\mathbf{c}}(\mathbf{K}, \mathbf{c}, \mathbf{w}) + \mathbf{K}]\big] \\ & + \mathbf{c}'\mathbf{K} - V_{\mathbf{K}}(\mathbf{K}, \mathbf{c}, \mathbf{w})V_{\mathbf{cK}}^{-1}(\mathbf{K}, \mathbf{c}, \mathbf{w})[rV'_{\mathbf{c}}(\mathbf{K}, \mathbf{c}, \mathbf{w}) + \mathbf{K}].\end{aligned} \tag{13}$$

From the first formula of Theorem 20.2, to wit, $\mathbf{I}^*(\mathbf{K}, \mathbf{c}, \mathbf{w}) \equiv V_{\mathbf{cK}}^{-1}(\mathbf{K}, \mathbf{c}, \mathbf{w}) \times [rV'_{\mathbf{c}}(\mathbf{K}, \mathbf{c}, \mathbf{w}) + \mathbf{K}] + \delta\mathbf{K}$, we can derive the identity

$$\mathbf{c}'\mathbf{K} \equiv -r\mathbf{c}'V'_{\mathbf{c}}(\mathbf{K}, \mathbf{c}, \mathbf{w}) + \mathbf{c}'V_{\mathbf{cK}}(\mathbf{K}, \mathbf{c}, \mathbf{w})V_{\mathbf{cK}}^{-1}(\mathbf{K}, \mathbf{c}, \mathbf{w})[rV'_{\mathbf{c}}(\mathbf{K}, \mathbf{c}, \mathbf{w}) + \mathbf{K}], \tag{14}$$

which you are asked to show in a mental exercise. Upon substituting Eq. (14) into Eq. (13), and using the fact that, for example, $\mathbf{c}'V'_{\mathbf{c}}(\mathbf{K}, \mathbf{c}, \mathbf{w}) = V_{\mathbf{c}}(\mathbf{K}, \mathbf{c}, \mathbf{w})\mathbf{c}$ as it is a scalar, we get

$$\begin{aligned} y^*(\mathbf{K},\mathbf{c},\mathbf{w}) \equiv\ & r[V(\mathbf{K},\mathbf{c},\mathbf{w}) - V_{\mathbf{c}}(\mathbf{K},\mathbf{c},\mathbf{w})\mathbf{c} - V_{\mathbf{w}}(\mathbf{K},\mathbf{c},\mathbf{w})\mathbf{w}] \\ & - [V_{\mathbf{K}}(\mathbf{K},\mathbf{c},\mathbf{w}) - \mathbf{c}' V_{\mathbf{cK}}(\mathbf{K},\mathbf{c},\mathbf{w}) \\ & - \mathbf{w}' V_{\mathbf{wK}}(\mathbf{K},\mathbf{c},\mathbf{w})] V_{\mathbf{cK}}^{-1}(\mathbf{K},\mathbf{c},\mathbf{w})[rV_{\mathbf{c}}'(\mathbf{K},\mathbf{c},\mathbf{w}) + \mathbf{K}]. \end{aligned}$$

This equation is the second formula for the supply function $y^*(\cdot)$ and therefore completes the proof of Theorem 20.2 on the formulas for the policy functions.

(V.2) Differentiate problem (2) with respect to $\mathbf{K}$ and apply the static envelope theorem to get

$$\begin{aligned} rV_{\mathbf{K}}(\mathbf{K},\mathbf{c},\mathbf{w}) \equiv\ & F_{\mathbf{K}}(\mathbf{L}^*(\mathbf{K},\mathbf{c},\mathbf{w}),\mathbf{K},\mathbf{I}^*(\mathbf{K},\mathbf{c},\mathbf{w})) - \mathbf{c}' - V_{\mathbf{K}}(\mathbf{K},\mathbf{c},\mathbf{w})\delta \\ & + [\mathbf{I}^*(\mathbf{K},\mathbf{c},\mathbf{w}) - \delta\mathbf{K}]' V_{\mathbf{KK}}(\mathbf{K},\mathbf{c},\mathbf{w}). \end{aligned}$$

Take the transpose of the preceding equation to get an $N \times 1$ column vector, observe that $rV_{\mathbf{K}}'(\mathbf{K},\mathbf{c},\mathbf{w}) = r\mathbf{I}_N V_{\mathbf{K}}'(\mathbf{K},\mathbf{c},\mathbf{w})$, and then rearrange it to arrive at

$$\begin{aligned} (r\mathbf{I}_N + \delta)V_{\mathbf{K}}'(\mathbf{K},\mathbf{c},\mathbf{w}) + \mathbf{c} - V_{\mathbf{KK}}(\mathbf{K},\mathbf{c},\mathbf{w})[\mathbf{I}^*(\mathbf{K},\mathbf{c},\mathbf{w}) - \delta\mathbf{K}] \\ \equiv F_{\mathbf{K}}'(\mathbf{L}^*(\mathbf{K},\mathbf{c},\mathbf{w}),\mathbf{K},\mathbf{I}^*(\mathbf{K},\mathbf{c},\mathbf{w})) > \mathbf{0}_N, \end{aligned}$$

where we have used the facts that δ and $V_{\mathbf{KK}}(\mathbf{K},\mathbf{c},\mathbf{w})$ are $N \times N$ symmetric matrices and that $F_{\mathbf{K}}'(\mathbf{L},\mathbf{K},\mathbf{I}) > \mathbf{0}_N$ throughout Φ by assumption (T.2). This equation thus proves part (i).

Given that we have assumed that the optimal solution is interior, the first-order necessary condition for $\mathbf{I}$ from problem (2) in identity form is given by

$$F_{\mathbf{I}}(\mathbf{L}^*(\mathbf{K},\mathbf{c},\mathbf{w}),\mathbf{K},\mathbf{I}^*(\mathbf{K},\mathbf{c},\mathbf{w})) + V_{\mathbf{K}}(\mathbf{K},\mathbf{c},\mathbf{w}) \equiv \mathbf{0}_N'.$$

This identity can be rearranged to read

$$V_{\mathbf{K}}(\mathbf{K},\mathbf{c},\mathbf{w}) \equiv -F_{\mathbf{I}}(\mathbf{L}^*(\mathbf{K},\mathbf{c},\mathbf{w}),\mathbf{K},\mathbf{I}^*(\mathbf{K},\mathbf{c},\mathbf{w})) > \mathbf{0}_N',$$

because $F_{\mathbf{I}}'(\mathbf{L},\mathbf{K},\mathbf{I}) < \mathbf{0}_N$ throughout Φ by assumption (T.2). This completes the proof of part (ii).

(V.3) Seeing as $F(\cdot): \Phi \to \Re_+$ by assumption (T.1), $F(\mathbf{L},\mathbf{K},\mathbf{I}) \geq 0$ throughout Φ, which implies that $y^*(\mathbf{K},\mathbf{c},\mathbf{w}) \geq 0$ for each $(\mathbf{K},\mathbf{c},\mathbf{w}) \in \Theta$ because $y^*(\mathbf{K},\mathbf{c},\mathbf{w}) \stackrel{\text{def}}{=} F(\mathbf{L}^*(\mathbf{K},\mathbf{c},\mathbf{w}),\mathbf{K},\mathbf{I}^*(\mathbf{K},\mathbf{c},\mathbf{w}))$. The rest of property (V.3) is implied by assumption (T.6).

(V.4) This is easy to prove because assumptions (T.4) and (T.7) imply property (V.4). In particular, assumption (T.4) asserts the existence of a unique solution to the optimal control problem (1) for each $(\mathbf{K}_t,\mathbf{c},\mathbf{w}) \in \Theta$, whereas assumption (T.7) asserts that the corresponding time path of the capital stock converges to the unique steady state value of the capital stock for any initial value of the capital stock, which is exactly what property (V.4) asserts.

(V.7) Because $\mathbf{L}^*(\mathbf{K},\mathbf{c},\mathbf{w}) > \mathbf{0}_M$ and $\mathbf{I}^*(\mathbf{K},\mathbf{c},\mathbf{w}) > \mathbf{0}_N$ are the optimal solution to the primal H-J-B problem (2) for all $(\mathbf{K},\mathbf{c},\mathbf{w}) \in \Theta$, they satisfy the following first-order necessary conditions identically:

$$F'_{\mathbf{L}}(\mathbf{L}^*(\mathbf{K},\mathbf{c},\mathbf{w}),\mathbf{K},\mathbf{I}^*(\mathbf{K},\mathbf{c},\mathbf{w})) - \mathbf{w} \equiv \mathbf{0}_M,$$
$$F'_{\mathbf{I}}(\mathbf{L}^*(\mathbf{K},\mathbf{c},\mathbf{w}),\mathbf{K},\mathbf{I}^*(\mathbf{K},\mathbf{c},\mathbf{w})) + V'_{\mathbf{K}}(\mathbf{K},\mathbf{c},\mathbf{w}) \equiv \mathbf{0}_N.$$

Differentiating these identities with respect to $\mathbf{w}$ yields

$$\begin{bmatrix} \underset{M\times M}{F_{\mathbf{LL}}(\mathbf{L}^*(\mathbf{K},\mathbf{c},\mathbf{w}),\mathbf{K},\mathbf{I}^*(\mathbf{K},\mathbf{c},\mathbf{w}))} & \underset{M\times N}{F_{\mathbf{LI}}(\mathbf{L}^*(\mathbf{K},\mathbf{c},\mathbf{w}),\mathbf{K},\mathbf{I}^*(\mathbf{K},\mathbf{c},\mathbf{w}))} \\ \underset{N\times M}{F_{\mathbf{IL}}(\mathbf{L}^*(\mathbf{K},\mathbf{c},\mathbf{w}),\mathbf{K},\mathbf{I}^*(\mathbf{K},\mathbf{c},\mathbf{w}))} & \underset{N\times N}{F_{\mathbf{II}}(\mathbf{L}^*(\mathbf{K},\mathbf{c},\mathbf{w}),\mathbf{K},\mathbf{I}^*(\mathbf{K},\mathbf{c},\mathbf{w}))} \end{bmatrix}$$

$$\times \begin{bmatrix} \underset{M\times M}{\dfrac{\partial \mathbf{L}^*}{\partial \mathbf{w}}(\mathbf{K},\mathbf{c},\mathbf{w})} \\ \underset{N\times M}{\dfrac{\partial \mathbf{I}^*}{\partial \mathbf{w}}(\mathbf{K},\mathbf{c},\mathbf{w})} \end{bmatrix} \equiv \begin{bmatrix} \mathrm{I}_M \\ \underset{N\times M}{-V_{\mathbf{Kw}}(\mathbf{K},\mathbf{c},\mathbf{w})} \end{bmatrix}.$$

Differentiating the above identity form of the first-order necessary conditions again, but now with respect to $\mathbf{c}$, yields

$$\begin{bmatrix} \underset{M\times M}{F_{\mathbf{LL}}(\mathbf{L}^*(\mathbf{K},\mathbf{c},\mathbf{w}),\mathbf{K},\mathbf{I}^*(\mathbf{K},\mathbf{c},\mathbf{w}))} & \underset{M\times N}{F_{\mathbf{LI}}(\mathbf{L}^*(\mathbf{K},\mathbf{c},\mathbf{w}),\mathbf{K},\mathbf{I}^*(\mathbf{K},\mathbf{c},\mathbf{w}))} \\ \underset{N\times M}{F_{\mathbf{IL}}(\mathbf{L}^*(\mathbf{K},\mathbf{c},\mathbf{w}),\mathbf{K},\mathbf{I}^*(\mathbf{K},\mathbf{c},\mathbf{w}))} & \underset{N\times N}{F_{\mathbf{II}}(\mathbf{L}^*(\mathbf{K},\mathbf{c},\mathbf{w}),\mathbf{K},\mathbf{I}^*(\mathbf{K},\mathbf{c},\mathbf{w}))} \end{bmatrix}$$

$$\times \begin{bmatrix} \underset{M\times N}{\dfrac{\partial \mathbf{L}^*}{\partial \mathbf{c}}(\mathbf{K},\mathbf{c},\mathbf{w})} \\ \underset{N\times N}{\dfrac{\partial \mathbf{I}^*}{\partial \mathbf{c}}(\mathbf{K},\mathbf{c},\mathbf{w})} \end{bmatrix} \equiv \begin{bmatrix} \mathbf{0}_{M\times N} \\ \underset{N\times N}{-V_{\mathbf{Kc}}(\mathbf{K},\mathbf{c},\mathbf{w})} \end{bmatrix},$$

where $\mathbf{0}_{M\times N}$ is an $M \times N$ null matrix. We can combine the previous two matrix equations into one expression to get

$$\begin{bmatrix} \underset{M\times M}{F^*_{\mathbf{LL}}} & \underset{M\times N}{F^*_{\mathbf{LI}}} \\ \underset{N\times M}{F^*_{\mathbf{IL}}} & \underset{N\times N}{F^*_{\mathbf{II}}} \end{bmatrix} \begin{bmatrix} \underset{M\times M}{\dfrac{\partial \mathbf{L}^*}{\partial \mathbf{w}}(\mathbf{K},\mathbf{c},\mathbf{w})} & \underset{M\times N}{\dfrac{\partial \mathbf{L}^*}{\partial \mathbf{c}}(\mathbf{K},\mathbf{c},\mathbf{w})} \\ \underset{N\times M}{\dfrac{\partial \mathbf{I}^*}{\partial \mathbf{w}}(\mathbf{K},\mathbf{c},\mathbf{w})} & \underset{N\times N}{\dfrac{\partial \mathbf{I}^*}{\partial \mathbf{c}}(\mathbf{K},\mathbf{c},\mathbf{w})} \end{bmatrix}$$

$$\equiv \begin{bmatrix} \mathrm{I}_M & \mathbf{0}_{M\times N} \\ \underset{N\times M}{-V_{\mathbf{Kw}}(\mathbf{K},\mathbf{c},\mathbf{w})} & \underset{N\times N}{-V_{\mathbf{Kc}}(\mathbf{K},\mathbf{c},\mathbf{w})} \end{bmatrix},$$

where $F^*_{\mathbf{LL}} \overset{\text{def}}{=} F_{\mathbf{LL}}(\mathbf{L}^*(\mathbf{K},\mathbf{c},\mathbf{w}),\mathbf{K},\mathbf{I}^*(\mathbf{K},\mathbf{c},\mathbf{w}))$, and similarly for the other terms. Because $F(\cdot)$ is strongly concave in $(\mathbf{L},\mathbf{I})$ by assumption (T.3), or equivalently, the

Hessian matrix of $F(\cdot)$ with respect to $(\mathbf{L}, \mathbf{I})$ is negative definite, the Hessian matrix of $F(\cdot)$ with respect to $(\mathbf{L}, \mathbf{I})$ is invertible. As a result, the above matrix equation can be rewritten as

$$\begin{bmatrix} \underset{M\times M}{\frac{\partial \mathbf{L}^*}{\partial \mathbf{w}}(\mathbf{K}, \mathbf{c}, \mathbf{w})} & \underset{M\times N}{\frac{\partial \mathbf{L}^*}{\partial \mathbf{c}}(\mathbf{K}, \mathbf{c}, \mathbf{w})} \\ \underset{N\times M}{\frac{\partial \mathbf{I}^*}{\partial \mathbf{w}}(\mathbf{K}, \mathbf{c}, \mathbf{w})} & \underset{N\times N}{\frac{\partial \mathbf{I}^*}{\partial \mathbf{c}}(\mathbf{K}, \mathbf{c}, \mathbf{w})} \end{bmatrix} \equiv \begin{bmatrix} \underset{M\times M}{F^*_{\mathbf{LL}}} & \underset{M\times N}{F^*_{\mathbf{LI}}} \\ \underset{N\times M}{F^*_{\mathbf{IL}}} & \underset{N\times N}{F^*_{\mathbf{II}}} \end{bmatrix}^{-1} \begin{bmatrix} \mathbf{I}_M & \mathbf{0}_{M\times N} \\ -\underset{N\times M}{V_{\mathbf{Kw}}(\mathbf{K}, \mathbf{c}, \mathbf{w})} & -\underset{N\times N}{V_{\mathbf{Kc}}(\mathbf{K}, \mathbf{c}, \mathbf{w})} \end{bmatrix}. \tag{15}$$

Now recall that in proving property (V.5), we showed that $V_{\mathbf{Kc}}(\mathbf{K}, \mathbf{c}, \mathbf{w}) \equiv \boldsymbol{\lambda}^*_{\mathbf{c}}(\mathbf{K}, \mathbf{c}, \mathbf{w})$, which, because of assumption (T.5), implies that $V_{\mathbf{Kc}}(\mathbf{K}, \mathbf{c}, \mathbf{w})$ is nonsingular. The second matrix on the right-hand side in Eq. (15) is thus nonsingular seeing as its determinant equals $(-1)^N |V_{\mathbf{Kc}}(\mathbf{K}, \mathbf{c}, \mathbf{w})|$, which is nonzero because $V_{\mathbf{Kc}}(\mathbf{K}, \mathbf{c}, \mathbf{w})$ is nonsingular. Therefore, each of the matrices on the right-hand side of Eq. (15) is nonsingular. But the product of nonsingular matrices is nonsingular, and thus the matrix

$$\begin{bmatrix} \underset{M\times M}{\frac{\partial \mathbf{L}^*}{\partial \mathbf{w}}(\mathbf{K}, \mathbf{c}, \mathbf{w})} & \underset{M\times N}{\frac{\partial \mathbf{L}^*}{\partial \mathbf{c}}(\mathbf{K}, \mathbf{c}, \mathbf{w})} \\ \underset{N\times M}{\frac{\partial \mathbf{I}^*}{\partial \mathbf{w}}(\mathbf{K}, \mathbf{c}, \mathbf{w})} & \underset{N\times N}{\frac{\partial \mathbf{I}^*}{\partial \mathbf{c}}(\mathbf{K}, \mathbf{c}, \mathbf{w})} \end{bmatrix}$$

is nonsingular for $(\mathbf{K}, \mathbf{c}, \mathbf{w}) \in \Theta$. Hence the proof of part (a) of Theorem 20.1 is complete.

Let us now turn to the proof of part (b) of Theorem 20.1. To that end, assume that $V(\cdot)$ satisfies assumptions (V.1) through (V.7) and define $F(\cdot)$ by Eq. (3). We intend to show that $F(\cdot)$ satisfies properties (T.1) through (T.7). First observe that because of assumptions (V.3) and (V.6), the function $F(\cdot)$ is well defined.

(T.4) Let $(\mathbf{K}_t, \mathbf{c}^\circ, \mathbf{w}^\circ) \in \Theta$. By the definition of $F(\cdot)$, that is to say, Eq. (3), we have that

$$\begin{aligned} F(\mathbf{L}, \mathbf{K}, \mathbf{I}) - \mathbf{w}^{\circ\prime}\mathbf{L} - \mathbf{c}^{\circ\prime}\mathbf{K} &\le rV(\mathbf{K}, \mathbf{c}^\circ, \mathbf{w}^\circ) \\ &\quad - V_{\mathbf{K}}(\mathbf{K}, \mathbf{c}^\circ, \mathbf{w}^\circ)[\mathbf{I} - \delta\mathbf{K}], \; (\mathbf{L}, \mathbf{I}) \in \Phi(\mathbf{K}). \end{aligned} \tag{16}$$

Equation (16) holds with equality if and only if $(\mathbf{L}, \mathbf{I}) = (\mathbf{L}^*(\mathbf{K}, \mathbf{c}^\circ, \mathbf{w}^\circ), \mathbf{I}^*(\mathbf{K}, \mathbf{c}^\circ, \mathbf{w}^\circ))$, in which case, $(\mathbf{c}^\circ, \mathbf{w}^\circ)$ is the optimal solution to problem (3) by assumption (V.6). Therefore, for any finite $T > t$ and any admissible pair, it follows from the inequality in Eq. (16) that

$$\int_t^T [F(\mathbf{L}(s), \mathbf{K}(s), \mathbf{I}(s)) - \mathbf{w}^{\circ\prime}\mathbf{L}(s) - \mathbf{c}^{\circ\prime}\mathbf{K}(s)]\, e^{-r(s-t)}\, ds$$

$$\leq \int_t^T [rV(\mathbf{K}(s), \mathbf{c}^\circ, \mathbf{w}^\circ) - V_{\mathbf{K}}(\mathbf{K}(s), \mathbf{c}^\circ, \mathbf{w}^\circ)\dot{\mathbf{K}}(s)]\, e^{-r(s-t)}\, ds$$

$$= -\int_t^T \frac{d}{ds}[e^{-r(s-t)} V(\mathbf{K}(s), \mathbf{c}^\circ, \mathbf{w}^\circ)]\, ds$$

$$= V(\mathbf{K}_t, \mathbf{c}^\circ, \mathbf{w}^\circ) - e^{-r(T-t)} V(\mathbf{K}(T), \mathbf{c}^\circ, \mathbf{w}^\circ),$$

where we have used the fact that the state equation $\dot{\mathbf{K}}(s) = \mathbf{I}(s) - \delta\mathbf{K}(s)$ holds for all admissible pairs. The above inequality shows that the value of all admissible pairs is bounded above by $V(\mathbf{K}_t, \mathbf{c}^\circ, \mathbf{w}^\circ) - e^{-r(T-t)} V(\mathbf{K}(T), \mathbf{c}^\circ, \mathbf{w}^\circ)$. By assumption (V.6), this upper bound is uniquely obtained by setting $(\mathbf{L}, \mathbf{I}) = (\mathbf{L}^*(\mathbf{K}, \mathbf{c}^\circ, \mathbf{w}^\circ), \mathbf{I}^*(\mathbf{K}, \mathbf{c}^\circ, \mathbf{w}^\circ))$, in which case, the above inequality becomes the equality

$$\int_t^T [F(\mathbf{L}^*(\mathbf{K}^*(s), \mathbf{c}^\circ, \mathbf{w}^\circ), \mathbf{K}^*(s), \mathbf{I}^*(\mathbf{K}^*(s), \mathbf{c}^\circ, \mathbf{w}^\circ))$$

$$- \mathbf{w}^{\circ\prime}\mathbf{L}^*(\mathbf{K}^*(s), \mathbf{c}^\circ, \mathbf{w}^\circ) - \mathbf{c}^{\circ\prime}\mathbf{K}^*(s)]\, e^{-r(s-t)}\, ds$$

$$= V(\mathbf{K}_t, \mathbf{c}^\circ, \mathbf{w}^\circ) - e^{-r(T-t)} V(\mathbf{K}^*(T), \mathbf{c}^\circ, \mathbf{w}^\circ), \qquad (17)$$

where $\mathbf{K}^*(s)$ is the time path of the capital stock determined by solving the state equation and initial condition using the optimal value of the investment rate, that is, it is the solution to $\dot{\mathbf{K}} = \mathbf{I}^*(\mathbf{K}, \mathbf{c}^\circ, \mathbf{w}^\circ) - \delta\mathbf{K}$, $\mathbf{K}(t) = \mathbf{K}_t$. By assumption (V.4), we have $\lim_{T\to+\infty} \mathbf{K}^*(T) = \mathbf{K}^s(\mathbf{c}^\circ, \mathbf{w}^\circ)$, which implies that $\lim_{T\to+\infty} V(\mathbf{K}^*(T), \mathbf{c}^\circ, \mathbf{w}^\circ) = V(\mathbf{K}^s(\mathbf{c}^\circ, \mathbf{w}^\circ), \mathbf{c}^\circ, \mathbf{w}^\circ)$ as $V(\cdot) \in C^{(2)}$ by assumption (V.1). Moreover, $\lim_{T\to+\infty} e^{-r(T-t)} = 0$ because $r > 0$. Using these two results and the fact that the limit of a product of functions is the product of their individual limits when such limits exist, it follows that $\lim_{T\to+\infty} e^{-r(T-t)} V(\mathbf{K}^*(T), \mathbf{c}^\circ, \mathbf{w}^\circ) = 0$. Letting $T \to +\infty$ in Eq. (17) and using this latter result therefore yields

$$\int_t^{+\infty} [F(\mathbf{L}^*(\mathbf{K}^*(s), \mathbf{c}^\circ, \mathbf{w}^\circ), \mathbf{K}^*(s), \mathbf{I}^*(\mathbf{K}^*(s), \mathbf{c}^\circ, \mathbf{w}^\circ))$$

$$- \mathbf{w}^{\circ\prime}\mathbf{L}^*(\mathbf{K}^*(s), \mathbf{c}^\circ, \mathbf{w}^\circ) - \mathbf{c}^{\circ\prime}\mathbf{K}^*(s)]\, e^{-r(s-t)}\, ds = V(\mathbf{K}_t, \mathbf{c}^\circ, \mathbf{w}^\circ).$$

This demonstrates that $V(\mathbf{K}_t, \mathbf{c}^\circ, \mathbf{w}^\circ)$ is the value of the optimal plan corresponding to the production function $F(\cdot)$. This proves the first part of property (T.4).

To prove the differentiability of the policy functions, recall that by Eqs. (4) through (6) and Theorem 20.2,

$$\begin{aligned}
\mathbf{I}^*(\mathbf{K}, \mathbf{c}, \mathbf{w}) &= V_{\mathbf{cK}}^{-1}(\mathbf{K}, \mathbf{c}, \mathbf{w})[rV_{\mathbf{c}}'(\mathbf{K}, \mathbf{c}, \mathbf{w}) + \mathbf{K}] + \delta\mathbf{K}, \\
\mathbf{L}^*(\mathbf{K}, \mathbf{c}, \mathbf{w}) &= -rV_{\mathbf{w}}'(\mathbf{K}, \mathbf{c}, \mathbf{w}) + V_{\mathbf{wK}}(\mathbf{K}, \mathbf{c}, \mathbf{w})V_{\mathbf{cK}}^{-1}(\mathbf{K}, \mathbf{c}, \mathbf{w})[rV_{\mathbf{c}}'(\mathbf{K}, \mathbf{c}, \mathbf{w}) + \mathbf{K}], \\
y^*(\mathbf{K}, \mathbf{c}, \mathbf{w}) &= rV(\mathbf{K}, \mathbf{c}, \mathbf{w}) + \mathbf{w}'\tilde{\mathbf{L}}(\mathbf{K}, \mathbf{c}, \mathbf{w}) + \mathbf{c}'\mathbf{K} - V_{\mathbf{K}}(\mathbf{K}, \mathbf{c}, \mathbf{w})[\tilde{\mathbf{I}}(\mathbf{K}, \mathbf{c}, \mathbf{w}) - \delta\mathbf{K}] \\
&= r[V(\mathbf{K}, \mathbf{c}, \mathbf{w}) - V_{\mathbf{w}}(\mathbf{K}, \mathbf{c}, \mathbf{w})\mathbf{w} - V_{\mathbf{c}}(\mathbf{K}, \mathbf{c}, \mathbf{w})\mathbf{c}] \\
&\quad - [V_{\mathbf{K}}(\mathbf{K}, \mathbf{c}, \mathbf{w}) - \mathbf{w}'V_{\mathbf{wK}}(\mathbf{K}, \mathbf{c}, \mathbf{w}) - \mathbf{c}'V_{\mathbf{cK}}(\mathbf{K}, \mathbf{c}, \mathbf{w})] \\
&\quad \times \left[V_{\mathbf{cK}}^{-1}(\mathbf{K}, \mathbf{c}, \mathbf{w})[rV_{\mathbf{c}}'(\mathbf{K}, \mathbf{c}, \mathbf{w}) + \mathbf{K}]\right].
\end{aligned}$$

Because $V(\cdot) \in C^{(2)}$ and $V_{\mathbf{K}}(\cdot) \in C^{(2)}$ on Θ by assumption (V.1), and $\dot{\mathbf{K}}^*(\mathbf{K}, \mathbf{c}, \mathbf{w}) = \mathbf{I}(\mathbf{K}, \mathbf{c}, \mathbf{w}) - \delta\mathbf{K}$, inspection of the above formulae shows that $(\dot{\mathbf{K}}^*(\cdot), \mathbf{L}^*(\cdot), y^*(\cdot)) \in C^{(1)}$ on Θ. To prove the differentiability of the current value shadow price function, first recall that $V_{\mathbf{K}}'(\mathbf{K}, \mathbf{c}, \mathbf{w}) \equiv \boldsymbol{\lambda}^*(\mathbf{K}, \mathbf{c}, \mathbf{w})$ by the principle of optimality and the dynamic envelope theorem. Then, because $V_{\mathbf{K}}(\cdot) \in C^{(2)}$ on Θ by assumption (V.1), it immediately follows that $\boldsymbol{\lambda}(\cdot) \in C^{(2)}$ on Θ.

(T.5) By assumption (V.5), $V_{\mathbf{cK}}(\mathbf{K}, \mathbf{c}, \mathbf{w})$ is nonsingular for each $(\mathbf{K}, \mathbf{c}, \mathbf{w}) \in \Theta$, thus so is its transpose $V_{\mathbf{cK}}'(\mathbf{K}, \mathbf{c}, \mathbf{w})$. Given that $V_{\mathbf{Kc}}(\mathbf{K}, \mathbf{c}, \mathbf{w}) \equiv \boldsymbol{\lambda}_{\mathbf{c}}^*(\mathbf{K}, \mathbf{c}, \mathbf{w})$ and $V_{\mathbf{Kc}}(\mathbf{K}, \mathbf{c}, \mathbf{w}) \equiv V_{\mathbf{cK}}'(\mathbf{K}, \mathbf{c}, \mathbf{w})$, as we showed in the proof of property (V.5), it therefore follows that $\boldsymbol{\lambda}_{\mathbf{c}}^*(\mathbf{K}, \mathbf{c}, \mathbf{w})$ is nonsingular for each $(\mathbf{K}, \mathbf{c}, \mathbf{w}) \in \Theta$.

(T.6) Let $(\mathbf{L}^\circ, \mathbf{K}_t, \mathbf{I}^\circ) \in \Phi$, and let $(\mathbf{c}^\circ, \mathbf{w}^\circ) \in \Theta(\mathbf{K}_t)$ be optimal in problem (3). In the proof of property (T.4), we showed that given $(\mathbf{c}^\circ, \mathbf{w}^\circ) \in \Theta(\mathbf{K}_t)$, $(\mathbf{L}^\circ, \mathbf{I}^\circ) = (\mathbf{L}^*(\mathbf{K}, \mathbf{c}^\circ, \mathbf{w}^\circ), \mathbf{I}^*(\mathbf{K}, \mathbf{c}^\circ, \mathbf{w}^\circ))$, where $\mathbf{K} = \mathbf{K}^*(s)$ is the solution to $\dot{\mathbf{K}} = \mathbf{I}^*(\mathbf{K}, \mathbf{c}^\circ, \mathbf{w}^\circ) - \delta\mathbf{K}$, $\mathbf{K}(t) = \mathbf{K}_t$, is the solution to optimal control problem (1). It is therefore optimal in problem (1) in the base period $s = t$, which is what we wished to demonstrate.

(T.7) Property (T.7) is simply a restatement of assumption (V.4), for they are both asserting the global asymptotic stability of the steady state capital stock.

(T.1) and (T.2) We have yet to prove the differentiability of $F(\cdot)$, though we did note that it is well defined prior to starting the proof of property (T.4). Consider, therefore, the following system of $M + N$ equations:

$$\mathbf{L} = \mathbf{L}^*(\mathbf{K}, \mathbf{c}, \mathbf{w}), \tag{18}$$

$$\mathbf{I} = \mathbf{I}^*(\mathbf{K}, \mathbf{c}, \mathbf{w}). \tag{19}$$

The Jacobian of Eqs. (18) and (19) is given by the $(M + N) \times (M + N)$ matrix

$$\begin{bmatrix} \dfrac{\partial \mathbf{L}^*}{\partial \mathbf{w}}(\mathbf{K}, \mathbf{c}, \mathbf{w}) & \dfrac{\partial \mathbf{L}^*}{\partial \mathbf{c}}(\mathbf{K}, \mathbf{c}, \mathbf{w}) \\[2ex] \dfrac{\partial \mathbf{I}^*}{\partial \mathbf{w}}(\mathbf{K}, \mathbf{c}, \mathbf{w}) & \dfrac{\partial \mathbf{I}^*}{\partial \mathbf{c}}(\mathbf{K}, \mathbf{c}, \mathbf{w}) \end{bmatrix}.$$

By assumption (V.7), this matrix is nonsingular for $(\mathbf{K}, \mathbf{c}, \mathbf{w}) \in \Theta$. Thus, by the implicit function theorem and the fact that $(\mathbf{I}^*(\cdot), \mathbf{L}^*(\cdot)) \in C^{(1)}$ on Θ, the solution $(\mathbf{c}, \mathbf{w}) = (\mathbf{c}^*(\mathbf{L}, \mathbf{K}, \mathbf{I}), \mathbf{w}^*(\mathbf{L}, \mathbf{K}, \mathbf{I}))$ to Eqs. (18) and (19) is locally well defined and $C^{(1)}$ on Φ. Moreover, by assumption (V.6), for $(\mathbf{K}, \mathbf{c}, \mathbf{w}) \in \Theta$, the minimum of problem (3) is attained at $(\mathbf{c}, \mathbf{w}) = (\mathbf{c}^*(\mathbf{L}, \mathbf{K}, \mathbf{I}), \mathbf{w}^*(\mathbf{L}, \mathbf{K}, \mathbf{I}))$ when $(\mathbf{L}, \mathbf{I}) = (\mathbf{L}^*(\mathbf{K}, \mathbf{c}, \mathbf{w}), \mathbf{I}^*(\mathbf{K}, \mathbf{c}, \mathbf{w}))$.

Given that $F(\cdot)$ is defined by problem (3), the above facts applied to problem (3) imply that $F(\cdot) \in C^{(1)}$ on Φ. To see this, apply the static envelope theorem to problem (3) to get

$$F'_{\mathbf{L}}(\mathbf{L}, \mathbf{K}, \mathbf{I}) = \mathbf{w}^*(\mathbf{L}, \mathbf{K}, \mathbf{I}) > \mathbf{0}_M, \tag{20}$$

$$\begin{aligned} F'_{\mathbf{K}}(\mathbf{L}, \mathbf{K}, \mathbf{I}) &= (r\mathbf{I}_N + \delta)V'_{\mathbf{K}}(\mathbf{K}, \mathbf{c}^*(\mathbf{L}, \mathbf{K}, \mathbf{I}), \mathbf{w}^*(\mathbf{L}, \mathbf{K}, \mathbf{I})) + \mathbf{c}^*(\mathbf{L}, \mathbf{K}, \mathbf{I}) \\ &\quad - V_{\mathbf{KK}}(\mathbf{K}, \mathbf{c}^*(\mathbf{L}, \mathbf{K}, \mathbf{I}), \mathbf{w}^*(\mathbf{L}, \mathbf{K}, \mathbf{I}))[\mathbf{I} - \delta\mathbf{K}] > \mathbf{0}_N, \end{aligned} \tag{21}$$

$$F'_{\mathbf{I}}(\mathbf{L}, \mathbf{K}, \mathbf{I}) = -V'_{\mathbf{K}}(\mathbf{K}, \mathbf{c}^*(\mathbf{L}, \mathbf{K}, \mathbf{I}), \mathbf{w}^*(\mathbf{L}, \mathbf{K}, \mathbf{I})) < \mathbf{0}_N, \tag{22}$$

where we have used assumption (V.2) and the basic assumption that $\mathbf{w}^*(\mathbf{L}, \mathbf{K}, \mathbf{I}) \in \Re^M_{++}$ in order to sign the gradients. The inequalities in Eqs. (20) through (22) prove property (T.2). Because $(\mathbf{c}^*(\cdot), \mathbf{w}^*(\cdot)) \in C^{(1)}$ on Φ, as established above, and $V_{\mathbf{K}}(\cdot) \in C^{(2)}$ by assumption (V.1), inspection of Eqs. (20) through (22) implies that $F(\cdot) \in C^{(1)}$, $F_{\mathbf{L}}(\cdot) \in C^{(1)}$, and $F_{\mathbf{I}}(\cdot) \in C^{(1)}$ on Φ. This completes the proof of property (T.1).

(T.3) Application of the primal-dual method to problem (3) readily establishes that $F(\cdot)$ is concave in $(\mathbf{L}, \mathbf{I})$, the details of which you are asked to provide in a mental exercise. To prove the strong concavity of $F(\cdot)$ with respect to $(\mathbf{L}, \mathbf{I})$, we will show that its Hessian matrix with respect to $(\mathbf{L}, \mathbf{I})$ is nonsingular. To this end, differentiate Eqs. (20) and (22) with respect to $\mathbf{L}$ to get

$$F_{\mathbf{LL}}(\mathbf{L}, \mathbf{K}, \mathbf{I}) = \frac{\partial \mathbf{w}^*}{\partial \mathbf{L}},$$

$$\begin{aligned} F_{\mathbf{IL}}(\mathbf{L}, \mathbf{K}, \mathbf{I}) &= -V_{\mathbf{Kc}}(\mathbf{K}, \mathbf{c}^*(\mathbf{L}, \mathbf{K}, \mathbf{I}), \mathbf{w}^*(\mathbf{L}, \mathbf{K}, \mathbf{I}))\frac{\partial \mathbf{c}^*}{\partial \mathbf{L}} \\ &\quad - V_{\mathbf{Kw}}(\mathbf{K}, \mathbf{c}^*(\mathbf{L}, \mathbf{K}, \mathbf{I}), \mathbf{w}^*(\mathbf{L}, \mathbf{K}, \mathbf{I}))\frac{\partial \mathbf{w}^*}{\partial \mathbf{L}}. \end{aligned}$$

Differentiating Eqs. (20) and (22) with respect to $\mathbf{I}$ this time yields

$$F_{\mathbf{LI}}(\mathbf{L}, \mathbf{K}, \mathbf{I}) = \frac{\partial \mathbf{w}^*}{\partial \mathbf{I}},$$

$$\begin{aligned} F_{\mathbf{II}}(\mathbf{L}, \mathbf{K}, \mathbf{I}) &= -V_{\mathbf{Kc}}(\mathbf{K}, \mathbf{c}^*(\mathbf{L}, \mathbf{K}, \mathbf{I}), \mathbf{w}^*(\mathbf{L}, \mathbf{K}, \mathbf{I}))\frac{\partial \mathbf{c}^*}{\partial \mathbf{I}} \\ &\quad - V_{\mathbf{Kw}}(\mathbf{K}, \mathbf{c}^*(\mathbf{L}, \mathbf{K}, \mathbf{I}), \mathbf{w}^*(\mathbf{L}, \mathbf{K}, \mathbf{I}))\frac{\partial \mathbf{w}^*}{\partial \mathbf{I}}. \end{aligned}$$

The previous four matrix equations may be combined to form one matrix equation, namely,

$$\begin{bmatrix} F_{\mathbf{LL}}(\mathbf{L},\mathbf{K},\mathbf{I}) & F_{\mathbf{LI}}(\mathbf{L},\mathbf{K},\mathbf{I}) \\ F_{\mathbf{IL}}(\mathbf{L},\mathbf{K},\mathbf{I}) & F_{\mathbf{II}}(\mathbf{L},\mathbf{K},\mathbf{I}) \end{bmatrix} = \begin{bmatrix} \mathbf{I}_M & \mathbf{0}_{M\times N} \\ -V^*_{\mathbf{Kw}} & -V^*_{\mathbf{Kc}} \end{bmatrix} \begin{bmatrix} \dfrac{\partial \mathbf{w}^*}{\partial \mathbf{L}} & \dfrac{\partial \mathbf{w}^*}{\partial \mathbf{I}} \\ \dfrac{\partial \mathbf{c}^*}{\partial \mathbf{L}} & \dfrac{\partial \mathbf{c}^*}{\partial \mathbf{I}} \end{bmatrix}, \tag{23}$$

where $V^*_{\mathbf{Kw}} \stackrel{\text{def}}{=} V_{\mathbf{Kw}}(\mathbf{K},\mathbf{c}^*(\mathbf{L},\mathbf{K},\mathbf{I}),\mathbf{w}^*(\mathbf{L},\mathbf{K},\mathbf{I}))$ and similarly for the other term. Next, differentiate the identity form of Eqs. (18) and (19) with respect to $\mathbf{L}$ and $\mathbf{I}$, and then similarly combine them into a single matrix equation. This process yields the matrix equation

$$\begin{bmatrix} \mathbf{I}_M & \mathbf{0}_{M\times N} \\ \mathbf{0}_{N\times M} & \mathbf{I}_N \end{bmatrix} = \begin{bmatrix} \dfrac{\partial \mathbf{L}^*}{\partial \mathbf{w}} & \dfrac{\partial \mathbf{L}^*}{\partial \mathbf{c}} \\ \dfrac{\partial \mathbf{I}^*}{\partial \mathbf{w}} & \dfrac{\partial \mathbf{I}^*}{\partial \mathbf{c}} \end{bmatrix} \begin{bmatrix} \dfrac{\partial \mathbf{w}^*}{\partial \mathbf{L}} & \dfrac{\partial \mathbf{w}^*}{\partial \mathbf{I}} \\ \dfrac{\partial \mathbf{c}^*}{\partial \mathbf{L}} & \dfrac{\partial \mathbf{c}^*}{\partial \mathbf{I}} \end{bmatrix}, \tag{24}$$

a result you are asked to prove in a mental exercise. Seeing as the $(M+N)\times(M+N)$ identity matrix on the left-hand side of Eq. (24) is nonsingular, both of the matrices on the right-hand side of Eq. (24) are nonsingular too. As $V_{\mathbf{cK}}(\mathbf{K},\mathbf{c},\mathbf{w})$ is nonsingular for each $(\mathbf{K},\mathbf{c},\mathbf{w}) \in \Theta$ by assumption (V.5), and $V_{\mathbf{Kc}}(\mathbf{K},\mathbf{c},\mathbf{w}) \equiv V'_{\mathbf{cK}}(\mathbf{K},\mathbf{c},\mathbf{w})$ as shown in the proof of property (V.5), $V_{\mathbf{Kc}}(\mathbf{K},\mathbf{c},\mathbf{w})$ is nonsingular for each $(\mathbf{K},\mathbf{c},\mathbf{w}) \in \Theta$ as well because the transpose of a nonsingular matrix is nonsingular. Thus *both* matrices on the right-hand side of Eq. (23) are nonsingular, thereby implying that the Hessian matrix of $F(\cdot)$ with respect to $(\mathbf{L},\mathbf{I})$ on the left-hand side of Eq. (23) is nonsingular too.

To complete the proof of part (b), use $F(\cdot)$ to define $V^*(\cdot)$ by way of Eq. (1). We showed in the proof of property (T.4) above that $V^*(\cdot) \equiv V(\cdot)$. Hence the proofs of Theorems 20.1 and 20.2 are complete. Q.E.D.

Condition (V.6) is central in the above development of intertemporal duality in that it asserts the existence of a solution to the dual problem (3). To get a better feel for it, note that it could have been expressed in the following equivalent manner:

(V.6′) Given $(\mathbf{K},\mathbf{c}^\circ,\mathbf{w}^\circ) \in \Theta$, there exists $(\mathbf{I}^\circ,\mathbf{L}^\circ) \in \Phi(\mathbf{K})$ such that $(\mathbf{c}^\circ,\mathbf{w}^\circ)$ is optimal in problem (3) given $(\mathbf{L}^\circ,\mathbf{K},\mathbf{I}^\circ)$.

Stated in this form, it should be apparent that property (V.6) is dual to property (T.6), for the two are worded in essentially symmetrical ways. Another interpretation of property (V.6) is that it requires that the first-order necessary conditions be sufficient for a global minimum in problem (3) over $\Theta(\mathbf{K})$. This is clearly a curvature restriction in the sense that the attainment of a global minimum implies that second-order necessary conditions hold at the optimum, and as you know from your prior work in microeconomic theory, such second-order necessary conditions are equivalent to the local convexity of the objective function.

Note, in passing, that an alternative derivation of the policy function formulas in Theorem 20.2 is given by differentiating the identity form of problem (2) and invoking the static envelope theorem, since problem (2) is a static optimization problem. The derivation of the policy function formulae via this route is left for a mental exercise.

We close our theoretical discussion of intertemporal duality by looking more closely at the monotonicity and curvature properties of the current value optimal value function $V(\cdot)$ defined in problem (1).

Theorem 20.3: *Let $V(\cdot)$ be defined by problem* (1) *and let $F(\cdot)$ satisfy conditions (T.1) through (T.7). Then $V(\cdot)$ is*

(a) increasing in $\mathbf{K}_t$,
(b) decreasing in $\mathbf{c}$,
(c) decreasing in $\mathbf{w}$,
(d) convex in $(\mathbf{c}, \mathbf{w}) \in \Theta(\mathbf{K})$,
(e) concave in $\mathbf{K}_t$ if $F(\cdot)$ is concave in $(\mathbf{L}, \mathbf{K}, \mathbf{I}) \in \Phi$.
(f) For any $(\mathbf{K}, \mathbf{c}^\circ, \mathbf{w}^\circ) \in \Theta$, the function $Z(\cdot)$ defined by

$$Z(\mathbf{c}, \mathbf{w}) \stackrel{\text{def}}{=} rV(\mathbf{K}, \mathbf{c}, \mathbf{w}) - V_{\mathbf{K}}(\mathbf{K}, \mathbf{c}, \mathbf{w})[\mathbf{I}^*(\mathbf{K}, \mathbf{c}^\circ, \mathbf{w}^\circ) - \delta\mathbf{K}]$$

is convex in $(\mathbf{c}, \mathbf{w})$ locally around $(\mathbf{c}^\circ, \mathbf{w}^\circ)$.

Proof: There are a few ways to go about proving some of the parts of this theorem. We will adopt one strategy here and ask you to provide an alternative proof of some parts of the theorem in a mental exercise.

(a) We already proved this property of $V(\cdot)$ in proving property (V.2) part (ii) of Theorem 20.1(a). You are asked to prove it by way of the dynamic envelope theorem and the Maximum Principle applied to problem (1) in a mental exercise.

(b) Let $\mathbf{c}^1 \leq \mathbf{c}^2$, where the inequality $\leq$ for vectors $\mathbf{a}, \mathbf{b} \in \Re^n$ is defined as follows: $\mathbf{a} \leq \mathbf{b}$ if and only if $a_\ell \leq b_\ell$, $\ell = 1, 2, \ldots, n$, and $a_k < b_k$ for at least one index $k \in \{1, 2, \ldots, n\}$. Let the triplet $(\mathbf{L}^i(s), \mathbf{K}^i(s), \mathbf{I}^i(s))$ be optimal for $\mathbf{c} = \mathbf{c}^i$ and $\mathbf{K}^i(t) = \mathbf{K}_t$, $i = 1, 2$. Then we have the following string of identities and inequalities, the explanation of each being given below each step in the proof:

$$V(\mathbf{K}_t, \mathbf{c}^2, \mathbf{w}) \equiv \int_t^{+\infty} [F(\mathbf{L}^2(s), \mathbf{K}^2(s), \mathbf{I}^2(s)) - \mathbf{w}'\mathbf{L}^2(s) - \mathbf{c}^{2\prime}\mathbf{K}^2(s)]\, e^{-r(s-t)}\, ds$$

by the definition of the optimal value function $V(\cdot)$ in problem (1)

$$< \int_t^{+\infty} [F(\mathbf{L}^2(s), \mathbf{K}^2(s), \mathbf{I}^2(s)) - \mathbf{w}'\mathbf{L}^2(s) - \mathbf{c}^{1\prime}\mathbf{K}^2(s)]\, e^{-r(s-t)}\, ds$$

the integrand is a strictly decreasing function of $\mathbf{c}$, since the optimal triplet is interior and $\mathbf{c}^1 \leq \mathbf{c}^2$

$$\leq \int_t^{+\infty} [F(\mathbf{L}^1(s), \mathbf{K}^1(s), \mathbf{I}^1(s)) - \mathbf{w}'\mathbf{L}^1(s) - \mathbf{c}^{1\prime}\mathbf{K}^1(s)]\, e^{-r(s-t)}\, ds$$

$(\mathbf{L}^2(s),\mathbf{K}^2(s),\mathbf{I}^2(s))$ is not necessarily optimal for $\mathbf{c}=\mathbf{c}^1$, but $(\mathbf{L}^1(s),\mathbf{K}^1(s),\mathbf{I}^1(s))$ is

$$\equiv \quad V(\mathbf{K}_t, \mathbf{c}^1, \mathbf{w}).$$

definition of $V(\cdot)$ in Eq. (1)

That is, $V(\mathbf{K}_t, \mathbf{c}^1, \mathbf{w}) > V(\mathbf{K}_t, \mathbf{c}^2, \mathbf{w})$ for $\mathbf{c}^1 \leq \mathbf{c}^2$, which is what we set out to prove. You are asked to provide another proof of this result via the dynamic envelope theorem in a mental exercise.

(c) The proof of this part of Theorem 20.3 is left for a mental exercise in which you are asked to prove it in two different ways, one as in the proof of part (b), and the other via the dynamic envelope theorem.

(d) Consider price vectors $(\mathbf{c}^i, \mathbf{w}^i)$, $i = 1, 2$, and $(\mathbf{c}^\omega, \mathbf{w}^\omega) \overset{\text{def}}{=} \omega(\mathbf{c}^1, \mathbf{w}^1) + [1 - \omega](\mathbf{c}^2, \mathbf{w}^2)$, where $\omega \in [0, 1]$. As you should recall, the vector $(\mathbf{c}^\omega, \mathbf{w}^\omega)$ is called a *convex combination* of the vectors $(\mathbf{c}^1, \mathbf{w}^1)$ and $(\mathbf{c}^2, \mathbf{w}^2)$. Let the optimal time paths corresponding to these three price vectors be given by $(\mathbf{L}^j(s), \mathbf{K}^j(s), \mathbf{I}^j(s))$ for $\mathbf{K}^j(t) = \mathbf{K}_t$ and $j = 1, 2, \omega$. Then we have the following string of identities and inequalities, the explanation of each again being given below each step in the proof:

$$V(\mathbf{K}_t, \mathbf{c}^\omega, \mathbf{w}^\omega)$$

$$\equiv \int_t^{+\infty} [F(\mathbf{L}^\omega(s), \mathbf{K}^\omega(s), \mathbf{I}^\omega(s)) - \mathbf{w}^{\omega\prime}\mathbf{L}^\omega(s) - \mathbf{c}^{\omega\prime}\mathbf{K}^\omega(s)]\, e^{-r(s-t)}\, ds$$

by the definition of the optimal value function $V(\cdot)$ in problem (1)

$$\equiv \omega \int_t^{+\infty} [F(\mathbf{L}^\omega(s), \mathbf{K}^\omega(s), \mathbf{I}^\omega(s)) - \mathbf{w}^{1\prime}\mathbf{L}^\omega(s) - \mathbf{c}^{1\prime}\mathbf{K}^\omega(s)]\, e^{-r(s-t)}\, ds$$

$$+ [1-\omega] \int_t^{+\infty} [F(\mathbf{L}^\omega(s), \mathbf{K}^\omega(s), \mathbf{I}^\omega(s)) - \mathbf{w}^{2\prime}\mathbf{L}^\omega(s) - \mathbf{c}^{2\prime}\mathbf{K}^\omega(s)]\, e^{-r(s-t)}\, ds$$

the definition $(\mathbf{c}^\omega,\mathbf{w}^\omega) \overset{\text{def}}{=} \omega(\mathbf{c}^1,\mathbf{w}^1)+[1-\omega](\mathbf{c}^2,\mathbf{w}^2), \omega\in[0,1]$, was used to rewrite the integrand

$$\leq \omega \int_t^{+\infty} [F(\mathbf{L}^1(s), \mathbf{K}^1(s), \mathbf{I}^1(s)) - \mathbf{w}^{1\prime}\mathbf{L}^1(s) - \mathbf{c}^{1\prime}\mathbf{K}^1(s)]\, e^{-r(s-t)}\, ds$$

$$+ [1-\omega] \int_t^{+\infty} [F(\mathbf{L}^2(s), \mathbf{K}^2(s), \mathbf{I}^2(s)) - \mathbf{w}^{2\prime}\mathbf{L}^2(s) - \mathbf{c}^{2\prime}\mathbf{K}^2(s)]\, e^{-r(s-t)}\, ds$$

$(\mathbf{L}^\omega(s),\mathbf{K}^\omega(s),\mathbf{I}^\omega(s))$ is not necessarily optimal for $(\mathbf{c}^i,\mathbf{w}^i)$, $i=1,2$, but $(\mathbf{L}^i(s),\mathbf{K}^i(s),\mathbf{I}^i(s))$, $i=1,2$, is

$$\equiv \omega V(\mathbf{K}_t, \mathbf{c}^1, \mathbf{w}^1) + [1-\omega] V(\mathbf{K}_t, \mathbf{c}^2, \mathbf{w}^2).$$

by definition of the optimal value function $V(\cdot)$ in Eq. (1)

In other words, we have shown that

$$V(\mathbf{K}_t, \omega \mathbf{c}^1 + [1-\omega]\mathbf{c}^2, \omega \mathbf{w}^1 + [1-\omega]\mathbf{w}^2) \le \omega V(\mathbf{K}_t, \mathbf{c}^1, \mathbf{w}^1) + [1-\omega] V(\mathbf{K}_t, \mathbf{c}^2, \mathbf{w}^2),$$

which is the definition for $V(\cdot)$ to be convex in $(\mathbf{c}, \mathbf{w}) \in \Theta(\mathbf{K})$. Note that this result can also be established by applying the dynamic primal-dual formalism to problem (1), as you are asked to show in a mental exercise. Note that this proof does not rely on the fact that $V(\cdot) \in C^{(2)}$ on Θ, whereas the proof by way of the dynamic envelope theorem does.

(e) Let $(\mathbf{L}^i(s), \mathbf{K}^i(s), \mathbf{I}^i(s))$ be the optimal triplet for $\mathbf{K}^i(t) = \mathbf{K}_t^i$, $i = 1, 2$. Define the vector $\mathbf{K}_t^{\omega} \overset{\text{def}}{=} \omega \mathbf{K}_t^1 + [1-\omega]\mathbf{K}_t^2$, where $\omega \in [0, 1]$, and let $(\mathbf{L}^{\omega}(s), \mathbf{K}^{\omega}(s), \mathbf{I}^{\omega}(s))$ be the optimal triplet for $\mathbf{K}^{\omega}(t) = \mathbf{K}_t^{\omega}$. To begin, we must first establish that the triplet

$$\omega(\mathbf{L}^1(s), \mathbf{K}^1(s), \mathbf{I}^1(s)) + [1-\omega](\mathbf{L}^2(s), \mathbf{K}^2(s), \mathbf{I}^2(s)), \ \omega \in [0, 1]$$

is an admissible solution when the initial capital stock is $\mathbf{K}_t^{\omega} \overset{\text{def}}{=} \omega \mathbf{K}_t^1 + [1-\omega]\mathbf{K}_t^2$. Recall that in order to demonstrate admissibility, we must verify that the proposed control vector satisfies any constraints placed on it and that the proposed state and control curves satisfy the state equation and given initial condition. The only constraint on the values of the state and control variables, which is implicit, is that they are positive. This constraint is satisfied by the above triplet because it is a convex combination of optimal curves. Next, recall that $(\mathbf{K}^i(s), \mathbf{I}^i(s))$, $i = 1, 2$, satisfy the state equation by their virtue of being optimal for $\mathbf{K}^i(t) = \mathbf{K}_t^i$, $i = 1, 2$. Using this observation, we therefore have that

$$\begin{aligned}
&\frac{d}{ds}[\omega \mathbf{K}^1(s) + [1-\omega]\mathbf{K}^2(s)] \\
&\quad = \omega \dot{\mathbf{K}}^1(s) + [1-\omega]\dot{\mathbf{K}}^2(s) = \omega[\mathbf{I}^1(s) - \delta \mathbf{K}^1(s)] + [1-\omega][\mathbf{I}^2(s) - \delta \mathbf{K}^2(s)] \\
&\quad = [\omega \mathbf{I}^1(s) + [1-\omega]\mathbf{I}^2(s)] - \delta[\omega \mathbf{K}^1(s) + [1-\omega]\mathbf{K}^2(s)],
\end{aligned}$$

which demonstrates that the above triplet satisfies the state equation. Finally, we have that

$$\omega \mathbf{K}^1(t) + [1-\omega]\mathbf{K}^2(t) = \omega \mathbf{K}_t^1 + [1-\omega]\mathbf{K}_t^2 \overset{\text{def}}{=} \mathbf{K}_t^{\omega}$$

in view of the fact that $\mathbf{K}^i(t) = \mathbf{K}_t^i$, $i = 1, 2$. This shows that the initial condition is also satisfied by the above triplet and thus completes the proof of admissibility. Note, in passing, that we did not have to perform the verification of admissibility in the proof of part (d) because the state equation and initial condition are independent of the price vectors $\mathbf{c}$ and $\mathbf{w}$.

To complete the proof, we have the following string of identities and inequalities, the explanation of each being given below each step in the proof:

$$V(\mathbf{K}_t^{\omega}, \mathbf{c}, \mathbf{w})$$

$$\equiv \int_t^{+\infty} [F(\mathbf{L}^{\omega}(s), \mathbf{K}^{\omega}(s), \mathbf{I}^{\omega}(s)) - \mathbf{w}'\mathbf{L}^{\omega}(s) - \mathbf{c}'\mathbf{K}^{\omega}(s)]\, e^{-r(s-t)}\, ds$$

by the definition of the optimal value function $V(\cdot)$ in problem (1)

$$\geq \int_t^{+\infty} [F(\omega(\mathbf{L}^1(s), \mathbf{K}^1(s), \mathbf{I}^1(s)) + [1-\omega](\mathbf{L}^2(s), \mathbf{K}^2(s), \mathbf{I}^2(s)))]\, e^{-r(s-t)}\, ds$$

$$- \int_t^{+\infty} [\mathbf{w}'(\omega\mathbf{L}^1(s) + [1-\omega]\mathbf{L}^2(s)) + \mathbf{c}'(\omega\mathbf{K}^1(s) + [1-\omega]\mathbf{K}^2(s))]\, e^{-r(s-t)}\, ds$$

$\omega(\mathbf{L}^1(s),\mathbf{K}^1(s),\mathbf{I}^1(s))+[1-\omega](\mathbf{L}^2(s),\mathbf{K}^2(s),\mathbf{I}^2(s))$ is admissible but not necessarily optimal for $\mathbf{K}_t^{\omega} \stackrel{\text{def}}{=} \omega\mathbf{K}_t^1+[1-\omega]\mathbf{K}_t^2$

$$\geq \omega \int_t^{+\infty} [F(\mathbf{L}^1(s), \mathbf{K}^1(s), \mathbf{I}^1(s)) - \mathbf{w}'\mathbf{L}^1(s) - \mathbf{c}'\mathbf{K}^1(s)]\, e^{-r(s-t)}\, ds$$

$$+ [1-\omega] \int_t^{+\infty} [F(\mathbf{L}^2(s), \mathbf{K}^2(s), \mathbf{I}^2(s)) - \mathbf{w}'\mathbf{L}^2(s) - \mathbf{c}'\mathbf{K}^2(s)]\, e^{-r(s-t)}\, ds$$

follows from the assumed concavity of $F(\cdot)$ in $(\mathbf{L},\mathbf{K},\mathbf{I})$

$$\equiv \omega V\left(\mathbf{K}_t^1, \mathbf{c}, \mathbf{w}\right) + [1-\omega] V\left(\mathbf{K}_t^2, \mathbf{c}, \mathbf{w}\right).$$

by definition of the optimal value function $V(\cdot)$ in Eq. (1)

In other words, we have shown that

$$V\left(\omega\mathbf{K}_t^1 + [1-\omega]\mathbf{K}_t^2, \mathbf{c}, \mathbf{w}\right) \geq \omega V\left(\mathbf{K}_t^1, \mathbf{c}, \mathbf{w}\right) + [1-\omega] V\left(\mathbf{K}_t^2, \mathbf{c}, \mathbf{w}\right),$$

which is the definition for $V(\cdot)$ to be concave in $\mathbf{K}_t$.

(f) First recall the dual optimization problem (3), that is,

$$F(\mathbf{L}, \mathbf{K}, \mathbf{I}) = \min_{(\mathbf{c},\mathbf{w})\in\Theta(\mathbf{K})} \{rV(\mathbf{K}, \mathbf{c}, \mathbf{w}) + \mathbf{w}'\mathbf{L} + \mathbf{c}'\mathbf{K} - V_{\mathbf{K}}(\mathbf{K}, \mathbf{c}, \mathbf{w})[\mathbf{I} - \delta\mathbf{K}]\},$$

$$(\mathbf{L}, \mathbf{K}, \mathbf{I}) \in \Phi.$$

The function on the right-hand side that is to be minimized, namely, the Hamiltonian, is a $C^{(2)}$ function of $(\mathbf{c}, \mathbf{w}) \in \Theta(\mathbf{K})$ by Theorem 20.1. If we set

$$(\mathbf{L}, \mathbf{I}) = (\mathbf{L}^{\circ}, \mathbf{I}^{\circ}) = (\mathbf{L}^*(\mathbf{K}, \mathbf{c}^{\circ}, \mathbf{w}^{\circ}), \mathbf{I}^*(\mathbf{K}, \mathbf{c}^{\circ}, \mathbf{w}^{\circ})), (\mathbf{c}^{\circ}, \mathbf{w}^{\circ}) \in \Theta(\mathbf{K}),$$

in problem (3), then by Theorem 20.1, it follows that the solution of problem (3) occurs at $(\mathbf{c}^{\circ}, \mathbf{w}^{\circ})$. Because $Z(\mathbf{c}, \mathbf{w}) \stackrel{\text{def}}{=} rV(\mathbf{K}, \mathbf{c}, \mathbf{w}) - V_{\mathbf{K}}(\mathbf{K}, \mathbf{c}, \mathbf{w})[\mathbf{I}^*(\mathbf{K}, \mathbf{c}^{\circ}, \mathbf{w}^{\circ}) - \delta\mathbf{K}]$, we can rewrite problem (3) in the form

$$F(\mathbf{L}^{\circ}, \mathbf{K}, \mathbf{I}^{\circ}) = \min_{(\mathbf{c},\mathbf{w})\in\Theta(\mathbf{K})} \{Z(\mathbf{c}, \mathbf{w}) + \mathbf{w}'\mathbf{L}^{\circ} + \mathbf{c}'\mathbf{K}^{\circ}\},\ (\mathbf{L}^{\circ}, \mathbf{K}, \mathbf{I}^{\circ}) \in \Phi.$$

Inasmuch as this problem is an unconstrained static minimization problem that attains a global and hence a local minimum at $(\mathbf{c}, \mathbf{w}) = (\mathbf{c}^\circ, \mathbf{w}^\circ)$, the second-order necessary conditions for this problem immediately imply that the Hessian matrix of $Z(\mathbf{c}, \mathbf{w})$ with respect to $(\mathbf{c}, \mathbf{w})$ is negative semidefinite at $(\mathbf{c}^\circ, \mathbf{w}^\circ)$. Because the choice of the point $(\mathbf{c}^\circ, \mathbf{w}^\circ) \in \Theta(\mathbf{K})$ that we used to fix the values of $(\mathbf{L}, \mathbf{I})$ in problem (3) was arbitrary, $Z(\cdot)$ is convex in $(\mathbf{c}, \mathbf{w})$ for all $(\mathbf{c}, \mathbf{w}) \in \Theta(\mathbf{K})$, and the proof is complete. Q.E.D.

Part (f) is an important result, in that unlike the static profit-maximizing model of the firm, convexity of $V(\cdot)$ in the prices $(\mathbf{c}, \mathbf{w})$ is *not* sufficient to completely characterize the optimal value function in the adjustment cost model of the firm. In particular, third-order properties of $V(\cdot)$, that is, third-order partial derivatives of $V(\cdot)$, are required to obtain a complete characterization of it. This follows because convexity of

$$Z(\mathbf{c}, \mathbf{w}) \stackrel{\text{def}}{=} rV(\mathbf{K}, \mathbf{c}, \mathbf{w}) - V_{\mathbf{K}}(\mathbf{K}, \mathbf{c}, \mathbf{w})[\mathbf{I}^*(\mathbf{K}, \mathbf{c}^\circ, \mathbf{w}^\circ) - \delta\mathbf{K}]$$

in $(\mathbf{c}, \mathbf{w})$ requires computation of its Hessian matrix with respect to $(\mathbf{c}, \mathbf{w})$, and thus will involve third-order partial derivatives of the value function $V(\cdot)$. This is an unusual result from the perspective of static optimization theory, in which second-order properties always suffice in characterizing indirect objective functions.

The significance of Theorems 20.1 and 20.2 is that they provide a straightforward, though possibly tedious, way to derive systems of factor demand and output supply equations fully consistent with the intertemporal optimization problem (1). The recipe is simple: hypothesize a functional from for $V(\cdot)$ and then use Theorem 20.2 to derive the closed-loop factor demand and supply functions, that is, the policy functions. The resulting policy functions are then estimated with data on $(\mathbf{L}, \mathbf{I}, \mathbf{K}, \mathbf{c}, \mathbf{w})$. The resulting parameter estimates can then be used to determine if $V(\cdot)$ satisfies properties (V.1) through (V.7), and thus if the data are consistent with the adjustment cost model of the firm.

From the viewpoint of the practitioner, the ease with which properties (V.1) through (V.7) may be verified for a particular functional form of $V(\cdot)$ is of some importance because it can determine which functional forms for $V(\cdot)$ are practical to work with. The set Θ, which is the domain of $V(\cdot)$, is determined by the capital stock and normalized price data one has at hand. The verification of properties (V.1) through (V.5) and (V.7) is a relatively straightforward matter, as we will see in an ensuing example. Recall from the proof of Theorem 20.1 that property (V.7) was necessary only to show that $F(\cdot)$ was sufficiently smooth and strongly concave in $(\mathbf{L}, \mathbf{I})$. As a result, in the example to follow, we will ignore this property.

Before presenting the example, however, a few more remarks concerning the crucial property (V.6) are warranted. Assume that $\Theta(\mathbf{K})$ is a convex set. Then a sufficient condition for property (V.6) to hold is that $Z(\mathbf{c}, \mathbf{w}) \stackrel{\text{def}}{=} rV(\mathbf{K}, \mathbf{c}, \mathbf{w})$

$- V_{\mathbf{K}}(\mathbf{K}, \mathbf{c}, \mathbf{w})[\mathbf{I}^*(\mathbf{K}, \mathbf{c}^\circ, \mathbf{w}^\circ) - \delta\mathbf{K}]$ is convex in $(\mathbf{c}, \mathbf{w})$ over $\Theta(\mathbf{K})$. Thus if $V_K(\cdot)$ is linear in $(\mathbf{c}, \mathbf{w})$, then property (V.6) is equivalent to the convexity of $V(\cdot)$ in $(\mathbf{c}, \mathbf{w})$, an observation of great practical importance. In either of these instances, only the convexity of a function need be checked, which requires the examination of an appropriate Hessian matrix. We will rely on the linearity of $V_{\mathbf{K}}(\cdot)$ in $(\mathbf{c}, \mathbf{w})$ in the ensuing example, as well as assume that $\Theta(\mathbf{K})$ is a convex set for each $\mathbf{K}$.

In the static theory of duality, the so-called flexible functional forms take center stage in empirical applications of the theory. In this context, a flexible functional form is one that may provide a second-order approximation to an arbitrary function. For example, the quadratic or translog functional forms are flexible, since for suitable parameter values, they may assume any given theoretically consistent set of values for zero-, first-, and second-order partial derivatives at a point. In the dynamic theory of duality presented in this chapter, flexibility must be defined in a slightly different manner.

Let's now examine the issue of flexibility of the optimal value function $V(\cdot)$ in the context of the adjustment cost model of the firm defined in Eq. (1). Because the objective of most intertemporal empirical work is the estimation of demand, supply, and shadow price elasticities, we adopt the following definition of flexibility.

Definition 20.1: A functional form for a value function is said to be *flexible* if the derived policy and shadow price functions can provide a first-order approximation at a point to a corresponding set of functions generated by an arbitrary value function that satisfies properties (V.1) through (V.7).

To render this definition in specific terms, recall Theorem 20.2, the formulae for the policy functions $(\mathbf{I}^*(\cdot), \mathbf{L}^*(\cdot), y^*(\cdot))$ given in Eqs. (4) through (6), respectively, and the fact that $\boldsymbol{\lambda}^*(\cdot) = V'_{\mathbf{K}}(\cdot)$. It then follows that a functional form is flexible if and only if it can assume, at a point, any given set of theoretically consistent values for $V(\cdot)$, all first- and second-order partial derivatives for $V(\cdot)$, and all first-order partial derivatives of $V_{\mathbf{cK}}(\cdot)$ and $V_{\mathbf{wK}}(\cdot)$. This observation again highlights the importance of the third-order properties of the optimal value function in achieving a complete qualitative characterization of the adjustment cost model.

In order to achieve the required flexibility for $V(\cdot)$, therefore, one must typically estimate a large number of parameters because of the importance of third-order properties. For example, if $M = 2$ and $N = 1$, then one must estimate 24 parameters in a flexible functional form for $V(\cdot)$, whereas if $M = 1$ and $N = 2$, then one must estimate 42 parameters, numbers you are asked to verify in a mental exercise. Thus, even with rather low dimensions for the control and state spaces, numerous parameters must be estimated when employing flexible functional forms for $V(\cdot)$. The example that follows does not use a flexible functional form for $V(\cdot)$, but it is nonetheless useful in applied work.

Example 20.1: Let $M = 1$ and $N = 1$ for clarity of exposition, and consider the following candidate for an optimal value function:

$$V(K, c, w) = a_0 + a_1 K + a_2 c + a_3 w + \frac{1}{2}A_{11}K^2 + A_{12}Kc + A_{13}Kw$$
$$+ \frac{1}{2}A_{22}c^2 + A_{23}cw + \frac{1}{2}A_{33}w^2, \tag{25}$$

where a_0, a_i, and A_{ij}, $i, j = 1, 2, 3$, are the parameters to be estimated. Using Theorem 20.2, Eqs. (4) through (6), and the state equation, we can derive the policy functions

$$\dot{K}^*(K, c, w) = \left(\frac{a_2 r}{A_{12}}\right) + \left(\frac{A_{22} r}{A_{12}}\right) c + \left(\frac{A_{23} r}{A_{12}}\right) w + \left(\frac{1 + rA_{12}}{A_{12}}\right) K, \tag{26}$$

$$L^*(K, c, w) = \left(\frac{(a_2 A_{13} - a_3 A_{12})r}{A_{12}}\right) + \left(\frac{(A_{13}A_{22} - A_{12}A_{23})r}{A_{12}}\right) c$$
$$+ \left(\frac{(A_{13}A_{23} - A_{12}A_{33})r}{A_{12}}\right) w + \left(\frac{A_{13}}{A_{12}}\right) K, \tag{27}$$

$$y^*(K, c, w) = a_0 r + a_1 r K - \frac{1}{2}A_{22} r c^2 - \frac{1}{2}A_{33} r w^2 - A_{23} r c w$$
$$+ \frac{1}{2}A_{11} r K^2 - a_1 \dot{K}^*(K, c, w) - A_{11} K \dot{K}^*(K, c, w) \tag{28}$$

using the optimal value function in Eq. (25). You are asked to verify these calculations in a mental exercise. In carrying out the estimation of the parameters of the optimal value function, one must jointly estimate all three policy functions, for this is the only way to get estimates of all the parameters of the optimal value function *and* carry out the statistical tests of properties (V.1) through (V.6). Furthermore, recall that the discount rate and the rate of depreciation are assumed to be given constants in the analysis. As a result, when carrying out the estimation of the parameters in Eqs. (26) through (28), the values of r and δ are inserted in the policy functions as constants and then the estimation is carried out. Thus r and δ are not variables in the way that (K, c, w) are, nor are they parameters to be estimated.

Let's now investigate the restrictions imposed on the policy functions by properties (V.1) through (V.6). To that end, first consider property (V.1). That $V(\cdot) \in C^{(2)}$ and $V_K(\cdot) \in C^{(2)}$ follows from the fact that the hypothesized optimal value function in Eq. (25) is a quadratic function of (K, c, w). The strict inequalities in property (V.2) require that

$$[r + \delta]V_K(K, c, w) + c - V_{KK}(K, c, w)\dot{K}^*(K, c, w)$$
$$= [r + \delta][a_1 + A_{11}K + A_{12}c + A_{13}w] + c - A_{11}\dot{K}^*(K, c, w) > 0,$$
$$V_K(K, c, w) = a_1 + A_{11}K + A_{12}c + A_{13}w > 0.$$

Notice that these restrictions involve the parameters we are trying to estimate and the data. As such, statistical testing of them is a nontrivial matter, for they are not inequality restrictions involving just the parameters to be estimated. The empirically relevant property in condition (V.3) is that $y^*(K, c, w) \geq 0$, which is certainly met in all the data one would encounter. Property (V.4) requires that the steady state is globally asymptotically stable. Because the policy function $\dot{K}^*(K, c, w)$ given in Eq. (26) is a constant coefficient linear differential equation in K, the steady state is globally asymptotically stable if its Jacobian is negative, that is, if $\partial \dot{K}^*(K, c, w)/\partial K < 0$. Using the policy function for the net investment rate in Eq. (26), this condition becomes

$$\left(\frac{1 + rA_{12}}{A_{12}}\right) = r + A_{12}^{-1} < 0.$$

Thus the steady state is globally asymptotically stable if and only if the reciprocal of the coefficient A_{12} is less than the negative of the firm's discount rate. Seeing as $V_{cK}(K, c, w) = A_{12}$, property (V.5) is met if $A_{12} \neq 0$, which it will be if the steady state is globally asymptotically stable. Finally, property (V.6), the generalized curvature condition derived from the dual H-J-B equation, turns out to be equivalent to the positive semidefiniteness of the coefficient matrix

$$\begin{bmatrix} A_{22} & A_{23} \\ A_{23} & A_{33} \end{bmatrix}.$$

To see this, first observe that $V_K(K, c, w)$ is a linear function of (c, w). Now recall our earlier observation that when such a condition holds, the curvature condition (V.6) is equivalent to the convexity of the optimal value function $V(\cdot)$ in (c, w). Because the Hessian matrix of $V(\cdot)$ with respect to (c, w) is given by the preceding matrix, we now see why its positive semidefiniteness is equivalent to property (V.6) when $V_K(K, c, w)$ is a linear function of (c, w).

The steady state value of the capital stock $K^s(c, w)$ is found by setting $\dot{K}^*(K, c, w) = 0$ in Eq. (26) and solving for K, that is,

$$K^s(c, w) = -r[1 + rA_{12}]^{-1}[a_2 + A_{22}c + A_{23}w]. \tag{29}$$

Using Eq. (29), Eq. (26) can be written in the so-called accelerator form, to wit,

$$\dot{K}^*(K, c, w) = \left[r + A_{12}^{-1}\right][K - K^s(c, w)], \tag{30}$$

a result you are asked to verify in a mental exercise. Now recall that $r + A_{12}^{-1} < 0$ for global asymptotic stability of the steady state. Hence, by differentiating Eq. (30) with respect to c and w, we find that

$$\frac{\partial \dot{K}^*(K, c, w)}{\partial c} = -\left[r + A_{12}^{-1}\right] \frac{\partial K^s(c, w)}{\partial c},$$

$$\frac{\partial \dot{K}^*(K, c, w)}{\partial w} = -\left[r + A_{12}^{-1}\right] \frac{\partial K^s(c, w)}{\partial w}.$$

These two equations demonstrate that the effect of an increase in c or w on the steady state capital stock is qualitatively the same as it is on the base period net investment rate. This is an implication of the particular functional form adopted for the optimal value function, and is not, in general, implied by the adjustment cost model, as we have previously seen in Chapter 17. This is one particular inflexibility exhibited by the optimal value function given in Eq. (25).

Following Epstein (1981), we have developed a dynamic duality theory in the context of the adjustment cost model of the firm. Numerous perturbations and generalizations of the basic theory presented here are possible. One perturbation of the theory is its extension to the nonrenewable resource–extracting model of the firm. A generalization of some importance would extend the intertemporal duality theory to cover the case of nonstatic price expectations. Complementary to a dynamic duality theory is the comparative dynamics properties of the feedback form of the optimal control vector. Consequently, you are asked to consider the comparative dynamics properties of the policy functions for a simplified version of the adjustment cost model in a mental exercise.

MENTAL EXERCISES

20.1 It is common for the adjustment cost model to include the cost of gross investment in the objective functional rather than the rental cost of the capital stock, that is, the optimal control problem often takes the alternative form

$$\max_{\mathbf{I}(\cdot),\mathbf{L}(\cdot)} \hat{J}[\mathbf{K}(\cdot),\mathbf{L}(\cdot),\mathbf{I}(\cdot)] \stackrel{\text{def}}{=} \int_t^{+\infty} [F(\mathbf{L}(s),\mathbf{K}(s),\mathbf{I}(s)) - \mathbf{w}'\mathbf{L}(s) - \mathbf{q}'\mathbf{I}(s)]\, e^{-r(s-t)}\, ds$$

$$\text{s.t.}\quad \dot{K}_n(s) = I_n(s) - \delta_n K_n(s),\ \ K_n(t) = K_{nt} > 0,\quad n = 1, 2, \ldots, N,$$

where $\mathbf{q} \in \Re^N_{++}$ is the normalized purchase price of the investment goods. Define the objective functional of problem (1) by $J[\mathbf{K}(\cdot),\mathbf{L}(\cdot),\mathbf{I}(\cdot)]$, and recall that problem (1) is stated in terms of the rental cost of capital. Assume that all admissible paths of the capital stocks are bounded.

(a) Using integration by parts, prove that $\hat{J}[\mathbf{K}(\cdot),\mathbf{L}(\cdot),\mathbf{I}(\cdot)] = J[\mathbf{K}(\cdot),\mathbf{L}(\cdot),\mathbf{I}(\cdot)] + \mathbf{q}'\mathbf{K}_t$, where $\mathbf{c} \stackrel{\text{def}}{=} (r\mathbf{I}_N + \boldsymbol{\delta})\mathbf{q}$.

(b) What does the result in part (a) imply about the solutions of the two optimal control problems? Explain clearly.

20.2 Does assumption (T.1) imply that $F(\cdot) \in C^{(2)}$? Does $F(\cdot) \in C^{(2)}$ imply the smoothness assumptions in (T.1)? Explain clearly.

20.3 Compute the second-order partial derivatives of the current value optimal value function $V(\cdot)$ by using the equations

$$rV_{c_i}(\mathbf{K}, \mathbf{c}, \mathbf{w}) \equiv -K_i + \sum_{n=1}^{N} V_{K_n c_i}(\mathbf{K}, \mathbf{c}, \mathbf{w})[I_n^*(\mathbf{K}, \mathbf{c}, \mathbf{w}) - \delta_n K_n],$$
$$i = 1, 2, \ldots, N,$$

$$rV_{w_j}(\mathbf{K}, \mathbf{c}, \mathbf{w}) \equiv -L_j^*(\mathbf{K}, \mathbf{c}, \mathbf{w}) + \sum_{n=1}^{N} V_{K_n w_j}(\mathbf{K}, \mathbf{c}, \mathbf{w})[I_n^*(\mathbf{K}, \mathbf{c}, \mathbf{w}) - \delta_n K_n],$$
$$j = 1, 2, \ldots, M.$$

Now prove that $V(\cdot) \in C^{(2)}$.

20.4 Prove that $V_{\mathbf{Kc}}(\mathbf{K}, \mathbf{c}, \mathbf{w}) \equiv V'_{\mathbf{cK}}(\mathbf{K}, \mathbf{c}, \mathbf{w})$ by differentiating with respect to the components of the vectors and writing out the associated matrix in detail. Note that this is the matrix form of Young's theorem.

20.5 Derive the identity $\mathbf{c}'\mathbf{K} \equiv -r\mathbf{c}'V'_{\mathbf{c}}(\mathbf{K}, \mathbf{c}, \mathbf{w}) + \mathbf{c}'V_{\mathbf{cK}}(\mathbf{K}, \mathbf{c}, \mathbf{w})V_{\mathbf{cK}}^{-1}(\mathbf{K}, \mathbf{c}, \mathbf{w})[rV'_{\mathbf{c}}(\mathbf{K}, \mathbf{c}, \mathbf{w}) + \mathbf{K}]$ in Eq. (14) by using the result that $\mathbf{I}^*(\mathbf{K}, \mathbf{c}, \mathbf{w}) \equiv V_{\mathbf{cK}}^{-1}(\mathbf{K}, \mathbf{c}, \mathbf{w})[rV'_{\mathbf{c}}(\mathbf{K}, \mathbf{c}, \mathbf{w}) + \mathbf{K}] + \delta\mathbf{K}$.

20.6 Prove that $F(\cdot)$ is concave in $(\mathbf{L}, \mathbf{I})$ by applying the primal-dual method to problem (3).

20.7 Show that by differentiating the identity form of Eqs. (18) and (19) with respect to $\mathbf{L}$ and $\mathbf{I}$, and then combining them into a single matrix equation, you arrive at Eq. (24), namely,

$$\begin{bmatrix} \mathbf{I}_M & \mathbf{0}_{M\times N} \\ \mathbf{0}_{N\times M} & \mathbf{I}_N \end{bmatrix} = \begin{bmatrix} \dfrac{\partial \mathbf{L}^*}{\partial \mathbf{w}} & \dfrac{\partial \mathbf{L}^*}{\partial \mathbf{c}} \\ \dfrac{\partial \mathbf{I}^*}{\partial \mathbf{w}} & \dfrac{\partial \mathbf{I}^*}{\partial \mathbf{c}} \end{bmatrix} \begin{bmatrix} \dfrac{\partial \mathbf{w}^*}{\partial \mathbf{L}} & \dfrac{\partial \mathbf{w}^*}{\partial \mathbf{I}} \\ \dfrac{\partial \mathbf{c}^*}{\partial \mathbf{L}} & \dfrac{\partial \mathbf{c}^*}{\partial \mathbf{I}} \end{bmatrix}.$$

20.8 Recall the primal H-J-B equation (2)

$$rV(\mathbf{K}, \mathbf{c}, \mathbf{w}) = \max_{(\mathbf{L},\mathbf{I})\in\Phi(\mathbf{K})} \{F(\mathbf{L}, \mathbf{K}, \mathbf{I}) - \mathbf{w}'\mathbf{L} - \mathbf{c}'\mathbf{K} + V_{\mathbf{K}}(\mathbf{K}, \mathbf{c}, \mathbf{w})[\mathbf{I} - \delta\mathbf{K}]\},$$
$$(\mathbf{K}, \mathbf{c}, \mathbf{w}) \in \Theta,$$

where $(\mathbf{L}, \mathbf{I}) = (\mathbf{L}^*(\mathbf{K}, \mathbf{c}, \mathbf{w}), \mathbf{I}^*(\mathbf{K}, \mathbf{c}, \mathbf{w}))$ are the optimal solutions to this optimization problem, known as the policy functions, feedback, or closed-loop controls. Use the static envelope theorem on the above H-J-B equation to prove that

(a) $\mathbf{I}^*(\mathbf{K}, \mathbf{c}, \mathbf{w}) \equiv V_{\mathbf{cK}}^{-1}(\mathbf{K}, \mathbf{c}, \mathbf{w})[rV'_{\mathbf{c}}(\mathbf{K}, \mathbf{c}, \mathbf{w}) + \mathbf{K}] + \delta\mathbf{K}$,

(b) $\mathbf{L}^*(\mathbf{K}, \mathbf{c}, \mathbf{w})$
$\equiv -rV'_{\mathbf{w}}(\mathbf{K}, \mathbf{c}, \mathbf{w}) + V_{\mathbf{wK}}(\mathbf{K}, \mathbf{c}, \mathbf{w})V_{\mathbf{cK}}^{-1}(\mathbf{K}, \mathbf{c}, \mathbf{w})[rV'_{\mathbf{c}}(\mathbf{K}, \mathbf{c}, \mathbf{w}) + \mathbf{K}]$.

For the next two parts of this question, you do not have to use the static envelope theorem to establish the result.

(c) $y^*(\mathbf{K}, \mathbf{c}, \mathbf{w}) \equiv rV(\mathbf{K}, \mathbf{c}, \mathbf{w}) + \mathbf{w}'\mathbf{L}^*(\mathbf{K}, \mathbf{c}, \mathbf{w}) + \mathbf{c}'\mathbf{K}$
$- V_{\mathbf{K}}(\mathbf{K}, \mathbf{c}, \mathbf{w})[\mathbf{I}^*(\mathbf{K}, \mathbf{c}, \mathbf{w}) - \delta\mathbf{K}]$.

(d) $y^*(\mathbf{K}, \mathbf{c}, \mathbf{w}) \equiv r[V(\mathbf{K}, \mathbf{c}, \mathbf{w}) - V_{\mathbf{w}}(\mathbf{K}, \mathbf{c}, \mathbf{w})\mathbf{w} - V_{\mathbf{c}}(\mathbf{K}, \mathbf{c}, \mathbf{w})\mathbf{c}]$
$- [V_{\mathbf{K}}(\mathbf{K}, \mathbf{c}, \mathbf{w}) - \mathbf{w}' V_{\mathbf{wK}}(\mathbf{K}, \mathbf{c}, \mathbf{w}) - \mathbf{c}' V_{\mathbf{cK}}(\mathbf{K}, \mathbf{c}, \mathbf{w})]$
$\times [V_{\mathbf{cK}}^{-1}(\mathbf{K}, \mathbf{c}, \mathbf{w})[rV_{\mathbf{c}}'(\mathbf{K}, \mathbf{c}, \mathbf{w}) + \mathbf{K}]]$.

20.9 In this exercise, you are asked to provide the alternative proofs of parts of Theorem 20.3. To this end, let $V(\cdot)$ be defined by problem (1) and let $F(\cdot)$ satisfy conditions (T.1) through (T.7).

(a) Prove that $V(\cdot)$ is increasing in $\mathbf{K}_t$ by way of the dynamic envelope theorem and the Maximum Principle applied to problem (1).

(b) Prove that $V(\cdot)$ is decreasing in $\mathbf{c}$ via the dynamic envelope theorem.

(c) Prove that $V(\cdot)$ is decreasing in $\mathbf{w}$ by mimicking the proof given for Theorem 20.3 part (b).

(d) Prove that $V(\cdot)$ is decreasing in $\mathbf{w}$ via the dynamic envelope theorem.

(e) Prove that $V(\cdot)$ is convex in $(\mathbf{c}, \mathbf{w}) \in \Theta(\mathbf{K})$ by applying the dynamic primal-dual formalism to problem (1).

20.10 As remarked in the chapter, in order to achieve the required flexibility for $V(\cdot)$, one must typically estimate a large number of parameters because of the importance of third-order properties. Show that if $M = 2$ and $N = 1$, then one must estimate 24 parameters in a flexible functional form for $V(\cdot)$, whereas if $M = 1$ and $N = 2$, then one must estimate 42 parameters. How many parameters must one estimate in a flexible functional form for $V(\cdot)$ if $M = 1$ and $N = 1$?

20.11 Verify that the three policy functions given in Eqs. (26) through (28) of Example 20.1 can be derived from the optimal value function given in Eq. (25). Also verify the accelerator form of the net investment rate policy function given in Eq. (30).

20.12 In this exercise, you will explore the comparative dynamics properties of the policy functions of the adjustment cost model. To this end, assume that $M = N = 1$ for simplicity. In this case, problem (1) takes the form

$$V(K_t, c, w) \stackrel{\text{def}}{=} \max_{L(\cdot), I(\cdot)} \int_t^{+\infty} [F(L(s), K(s), I(s)) - wL(s) - cK(s)]\, e^{-r(s-t)}\, ds$$

$$\text{s.t.} \quad \dot{K}(s) = I(s) - \delta K(s), \;\; K(t) = K_t > 0.$$

Assume that properties (T.1) through (T.7) hold on the production function $F(\cdot)$.

(a) Write down the primal form of the H-J-B equation corresponding to the above optimal control problem.

(b) Derive the first-order necessary and second-order sufficient conditions for the maximization problem in the H-J-B equation. How do you know that the second-order sufficient conditions hold for the maximization problem? Denote the optimal solutions of the H-J-B maximization problem by $(L^*(K,c,w), I^*(K,c,w))$. Recall that these are the values of the policy functions.

(c) Derive the comparative dynamics of the policy functions with respect to w. Can you sign either of the comparative dynamics results? Why? If adjustment costs are additively separable so that $F_{LI}(L,K,I) = F_{KI}(L,K,I) \equiv 0$, then show that

$$\frac{\partial L^*(K,c,w)}{\partial w} < 0 \text{ and } \operatorname{sign}\left[\frac{\partial I^*(K,c,w)}{\partial w}\right] = \operatorname{sign}[V_{Kw}(K,c,w)].$$

(d) Derive the comparative dynamics of the policy functions with respect to c. Can you sign either of the comparative dynamics results? Why? If adjustment costs are additively separable, then show that

$$\frac{\partial L^*(K,c,w)}{\partial c} \equiv 0 \text{ and } \operatorname{sign}\left[\frac{\partial I^*(K,c,w)}{\partial c}\right] = \operatorname{sign}[V_{Kc}(K,c,w)].$$

(e) Derive the comparative dynamics of the policy functions with respect to K. Can you sign either of the comparative dynamics results? Why? If adjustment costs are additively separable, then show that

$$\operatorname{sign}\left[\frac{\partial L^*(K,c,w)}{\partial K}\right] = \operatorname{sign}[F_{LK}(L^*(K,c,w), K, I^*(K,c,w))]$$

and that

$$\operatorname{sign}\left[\frac{\partial I^*(K,c,w)}{\partial K}\right] = \operatorname{sign}[V_{KK}(K,c,w)].$$

FURTHER READING

The subject matter of this chapter, videlicet, intertemporal or dynamic duality, is a relatively recent development, dating to the papers of Cooper and McLaren (1980), McLaren and Cooper (1980), and Epstein (1981). Cooper and McLaren (1993) survey the different approaches one may take in solving and characterizing the solution of an intertemporal model of the consumer. Lasserre and Ouellette (1999) present a rather general duality theory for an expected cost-minimizing firm facing costs of adjustment in discrete time. Though we have not discussed the details of the estimation of the policy functions in much detail in this chapter, an excellent place to begin such an inquiry is the paper by Epstein and Denny (1983), the first one to empirically implement and test the adjustment cost model via the duality laid down here. Galeotti (1996) provides a nice survey of dynamic production theory. Closely related to the duality theory presented here is the comparative dynamics properties of the policy functions or feedback controls. On this subject, one may consult the recent paper by Caputo (2003), which derives general comparative dynamics results for the feedback or closed-loop form of the optimal control vector for a ubiquitous class of optimal control problems, and then applies the theorems to the nonrenewable resource–extracting model of the firm.

REFERENCES

Caputo, M.R. (2003), "The Comparative Dynamics of Closed-Loop Controls for Discounted Infinite Horizon Optimal Control Problems," *Journal of Economic Dynamics and Control*, 27, 1335–1365.

Cooper, R.J. and McLaren, K.R. (1980), "Atemporal, Temporal and Intertemporal Duality in Consumer Theory," *International Economic Review*, 21, 599–609.

Cooper, R.J. and McLaren, K.R. (1993), "Approaches to the Solution of Intertemporal Consumer Demand Models," *Australian Economic Papers*, 32, 20–39.

Epstein, L.G. (1981), "Duality Theory and Functional Forms for Dynamic Factor Demands," *Review of Economic Studies*, 48, 81–96.

Epstein, L.G. and Denny, M. (1983), "The Multivariate Flexible Accelerator Model: Its Empirical Restrictions and an Application to U.S. Manufacturing," *Econometrica*, 51, 647–674.

Galeotti, M. (1996), "The Intertemporal Dimension of Neoclassical Production Theory," *Journal of Economic Surveys*, 10, 421–460.

Lasserre, P. and Ouellette, P. (1999), "Dynamic Factor Demands and Technology Measurement under Arbitrary Expectations," *Journal of Productivity Analysis*, 11, 219–241.

McLaren, K.R. and Cooper, R.J. (1980), "Intertemporal Duality: Application to the Theory of the Firm," *Econometrica*, 48, 1755–1762.

Silberberg, E. (1974), "A Revision of Comparative Statics Methodology in Economics, or How to Do Comparative Statics on the Back of an Envelope," *Journal of Economic Theory*, 7, 159–172.

Index

For EU product safety concerns, contact us at Calle de José Abascal, 56–1°, 28003 Madrid, Spain or eugpsr@cambridge.org.

www.ingramcontent.com/pod-product-compliance
Ingram Content Group UK Ltd.
Pitfield, Milton Keynes, MK11 3LW, UK
UKHW020250090825
461507UK00020B/911
* 9 7 8 0 5 2 1 6 0 3 6 8 3 *